Nineteenth-Century Literature Criticism

Guide to Thomson Gale Literary Criticism Series

For criticism on	Consult these Thomson Gale series
Authors now living or who died after December 31, 1999	*CONTEMPORARY LITERARY CRITICISM (CLC)*
Authors who died between 1900 and 1999	*TWENTIETH-CENTURY LITERARY CRITICISM (TCLC)*
Authors who died between 1800 and 1899	*NINETEENTH-CENTURY LITERATURE CRITICISM (NCLC)*
Authors who died between 1400 and 1799	*LITERATURE CRITICISM FROM 1400 TO 1800 (LC)* *SHAKESPEAREAN CRITICISM (SC)*
Authors who died before 1400	*CLASSICAL AND MEDIEVAL LITERATURE CRITICISM (CMLC)*
Authors of books for children and young adults	*CHILDREN'S LITERATURE REVIEW (CLR)*
Dramatists	*DRAMA CRITICISM (DC)*
Poets	*POETRY CRITICISM (PC)*
Short story writers	*SHORT STORY CRITICISM (SSC)*
Literary topics and movements	*HARLEM RENAISSANCE: A GALE CRITICAL COMPANION (HR)* *THE BEAT GENERATION: A GALE CRITICAL COMPANION (BG)* *FEMINISM IN LITERATURE: A GALE CRITICAL COMPANION (FL)* *GOTHIC LITERATURE: A GALE CRITICAL COMPANION (GL)*
Asian American writers of the last two hundred years	*ASIAN AMERICAN LITERATURE (AAL)*
Black writers of the past two hundred years	*BLACK LITERATURE CRITICISM (BLC)* *BLACK LITERATURE CRITICISM SUPPLEMENT (BLCS)*
Hispanic writers of the late nineteenth and twentieth centuries	*HISPANIC LITERATURE CRITICISM (HLC)* *HISPANIC LITERATURE CRITICISM SUPPLEMENT (HLCS)*
Native North American writers and orators of the eighteenth, nineteenth, and twentieth centuries	*NATIVE NORTH AMERICAN LITERATURE (NNAL)*
Major authors from the Renaissance to the present	*WORLD LITERATURE CRITICISM, 1500 TO THE PRESENT (WLC)* *WORLD LITERATURE CRITICISM SUPPLEMENT (WLCS)*

ISSN 0732-1864

Volume 181

Nineteenth-Century Literature Criticism

Criticism of the
Works of Novelists, Philosophers, and Other
Creative Writers Who Died between 1800
and 1899, from the First Published Critical
Appraisals to Current Evaluations

Kathy D. Darrow
Russel Whitaker
Project Editors

THOMSON

GALE

Detroit • New York • San Francisco • New Haven, Conn. • Waterville, Maine • London

Nineteenth-Century Literature Criticism, Vol. 181

Project Editors
Kathy Darrow and Russel Whitaker

Editorial
Jeffrey W. Hunter, Jelena O. Krstović, Michelle Lee, Thomas J. Schoenberg, Noah Schusterbauer, Lawrence J. Trudeau

Data Capture
Frances Monroe, Gwen Tucker

Indexing Services
Factiva, Inc.

Rights and Acquisitions
Emma Hull, Kelly Quin, Tracie Richardson

Composition and Electronic Capture
Tracey L. Matthews

Manufacturing
Rhonda Dover

Associate Product Manager
Marc Cormier

LIBRARY OF CONGRESS CATALOG CARD NUMBER 84-643008

ISBN-13: 978-0-7876-9852-2
ISBN-10: 0-7876-9852-0
ISSN 0732-1864

Printed in the United States of America
10 9 8 7 6 5 4 3 2 1

Contents

Preface vii

Acknowledgments xi

Literary Criticism Series Advisory Board xiii

Preface

Since its inception in 1981, *Nineteenth-Century Literature Criticism* (*NCLC*) has been a valuable resource for students and librarians seeking critical commentary on writers of this transitional period in world history. Designated an "Outstanding Reference Source" by the American Library Association with the publication of is first volume, *NCLC* has since been purchased by over 6,000 school, public, and university libraries. The series has covered more than 500 authors representing 38 nationalities and over 28,000 titles. No other reference source has surveyed the critical reaction to nineteenth-century authors and literature as thoroughly as *NCLC*.

Scope of the Series

NCLC is designed to introduce students and advanced readers to the authors of the nineteenth century and to the most significant interpretations of these authors' works. The great poets, novelists, short story writers, playwrights, and philosophers of this period are frequently studied in high school and college literature courses. By organizing and reprinting commentary written on these authors, *NCLC* helps students develop valuable insight into literary history, promotes a better understanding of the texts, and sparks ideas for papers and assignments. Each entry in *NCLC* presents a comprehensive survey of an author's career or an individual work of literature and provides the user with a multiplicity of interpretations and assessments. Such variety allows students to pursue their own interests; furthermore, it fosters an awareness that literature is dynamic and responsive to many different opinions.

Every fourth volume of *NCLC* is devoted to literary topics that cannot be covered under the author approach used in the rest of the series. Such topics include literary movements, prominent themes in nineteenth-century literature, literary reaction to political and historical events, significant eras in literary history, prominent literary anniversaries, and the literatures of cultures that are often overlooked by English-speaking readers.

NCLC continues the survey of criticism of world literature begun by Thomson Gale's *Contemporary Literary Criticism* (*CLC*) and *Twentieth-Century Literary Criticism* (*TCLC*).

Organization of the Book

An *NCLC* entry consists of the following elements:

- The **Author Heading** cites the name under which the author most commonly wrote, followed by birth and death dates. Also located here are any name variations under which an author wrote, including transliterated forms for authors whose native languages use nonroman alphabets. If the author wrote consistently under a pseudonym, the pseudonym will be listed in the author heading and the author's actual name given in parenthesis on the first line of the biographical and critical information. Uncertain birth or death dates are indicated by question marks. Single-work entries are preceded by a heading that consists of the most common form of the title in English translation (if applicable) and the original date of composition.

- The **Introduction** contains background information that introduces the reader to the author, work, or topic that is the subject of the entry.

- The list of **Principal Works** is ordered chronologically by date of first publication and lists the most important works by the author. The genre and publication date of each work is given. In the case of foreign authors whose works have been translated into English, the list will focus primarily on twentieth-century translations, selecting those works most commonly considered the best by critics. Unless otherwise indicated, dramas are dated by first performance, not first publication. Lists of **Representative Works** by different authors appear with topic entries.

- Reprinted **Criticism** is arranged chronologically in each entry to provide a useful perspective on changes in critical evaluation over time. The critic's name and the date of composition or publication of the critical work are given at the beginning of each piece of criticism. Unsigned criticism is preceded by the title of the source in which it appeared. All titles by the author featured in the text are printed in boldface type. Footnotes are reprinted at the end of each essay or excerpt. In the case of excerpted criticism, only those footnotes that pertain to the excerpted texts are included. Criticism in topic entries is arranged chronologically under a variety of subheadings to facilitate the study of different aspects of the topic.

- A complete **Bibliographical Citation** of the original essay or book precedes each piece of criticism.

- Critical essays are prefaced by brief **Annotations** explicating each piece.

- An annotated bibliography of **Further Reading** appears at the end of each entry and suggests resources for additional study. In some cases, significant essays for which the editors could not obtain reprint rights are included here. Boxed material following the further reading list provides references to other biographical and critical sources on the author in series published by Thomson Gale.

Indexes

Each volume of *NCLC* contains a **Cumulative Author Index** listing all authors who have appeared in a wide variety of reference sources published by Thomson Gale, including *NCLC*. A complete list of these sources is found facing the first page of the Author Index. The index also includes birth and death dates and cross references between pseudonyms and actual names.

A **Cumulative Nationality Index** lists all authors featured in *NCLC* by nationality, followed by the number of the *NCLC* volume in which their entry appears.

A **Cumulative Topic Index** lists the literary themes and topics treated in the series as well as in *Classical and Medieval Literature Criticism, Literature Criticism from 1400 to 1800, Twentieth-Century Literary Criticism,* and the *Contemporary Literary Criticism* Yearbook, which was discontinued in 1998.

An alphabetical **Title Index** accompanies each volume of *NCLC*, with the exception of the Topics volumes. Listings of titles by authors covered in the given volume are followed by the author's name and the corresponding page numbers where the titles are discussed. English translations of foreign titles and variations of titles are cross-referenced to the title under which a work was originally published. Titles of novels, dramas, nonfiction books, and poetry, short story, or essay collections are printed in italics, while individual poems, short stories, and essays are printed in roman type within quotation marks.

In response to numerous suggestions from librarians, Thomson Gale also produces an annual paperbound edition of the *NCLC* cumulative title index. This annual cumulation, which alphabetically lists all titles reviewed in the series, is available to all customers. Additional copies of this index are available upon request. Librarians and patrons will welcome this separate index; it saves shelf space, is easy to use, and is recyclable upon receipt of the next edition.

Citing *Nineteenth-Century Literature Criticism*

When citing criticism reprinted in the Literary Criticism Series, students should provide complete bibliographic information so that the cited essay can be located in the original print or electronic source. Students who quote directly from reprinted criticism may use any accepted bibliographic format, such as University of Chicago Press style or Modern Language Association style.

The examples below follow recommendations for preparing a bibliography set forth in *The Chicago Manual of Style,* 14th ed. (Chicago: The University of Chicago Press, 1993); the first example pertains to material drawn from periodicals, the second to material reprinted from books:

Franklin, J. Jeffrey. "The Victorian Discourse of Gambling: Speculations on *Middlemarch* and *The Duke's Children.*" *ELH* 61, no. 4 (winter 1994): 899-921. Reprinted in *Nineteenth-Century Literature Criticism.* Vol. 168, edited by Jessica Bomarito and Russel Whitaker, 39-51. Detroit: Thomson Gale, 2006.

Frank, Joseph. "*The Gambler*: A Study in Ethnopsychology." In *Freedom and Responsibility in Russian Literature: Essays in Honor of Robert Louis Jackson,* edited by Elizabeth Cheresh Allen and Gary Saul Morson, 69-85. Evanston, Ill.: Northwestern University Press, 1995. Reprinted in *Nineteenth-Century Literature Criticism.* Vol. 168, edited by Jessica Bomarito and Russel Whitaker, 75-84. Detroit: Thomson Gale, 2006.

The examples below follow recommendations for preparing a works cited list set forth in the *MLA Handbook for Writers of Research Papers,* 6th ed. (New York: The Modern Language Association of America, 2003); the first example pertains to material drawn from periodicals, the second to material reprinted from books:

Franklin, J. Jeffrey. "The Victorian Discourse of Gambling: Speculations on *Middlemarch* and *The Duke's Children.*" *ELH* 61.4 (Winter 1994): 899-921. Reprinted in *Nineteenth-Century Literature Criticism.* Eds. Jessica Bomarito and Russel Whitaker. Vol. 168. Detroit: Thomson Gale, 2006. 39-51.

Frank, Joseph. "*The Gambler*: A Study in Ethnopsychology." *Freedom and Responsibility in Russian Literature: Essays in Honor of Robert Louis Jackson.* Eds. Elizabeth Cheresh Allen and Gary Saul Morson. Evanston, Ill.: Northwestern University Press, 1995. 69-85. Reprinted in *Nineteenth-Century Literature Criticism.* Eds. Jessica Bomarito and Russel Whitaker. Vol. 168. Detroit: Thomson Gale, 2006. 75-84.

Suggestions are Welcome

Readers who wish to suggest new features, topics, or authors to appear in future volumes, or who have other suggestions or comments are cordially invited to call, write, or fax the Associate Product Manager:

Associate Product Manager, Literary Criticism Series
Thomson Gale
27500 Drake Road
Farmington Hills, MI 48331-3535
1-800-347-4253 (GALE)
Fax: 248-699-8054

Acknowledgments

The editors wish to thank the copyright holders of the criticism included in this volume and the permissions managers of many book and magazine publishing companies for assisting us in securing reproduction rights. Following is a list of the copyright holders who have granted us permission to reproduce material in this volume of *NCLC*. Every effort has been made to trace copyright, but if omissions have been made, please let us know.

COPYRIGHTED MATERIAL IN *NCLC*, VOLUME 181, WAS REPRODUCED FROM THE FOLLOWING PERIODICALS:

American Literature: A Journal of Literary History, Criticism, and Bibliography, v. 39, May, 1967; v. 47, May, 1975; v. 51, March, 1979; v. 59, December, 1987. Copyright © 1967, 1975, 1979, 1987. Duke University Press. All rights reserved. All used by permission of the publisher.—*American Quarterly,* v. 15, fall, 1963. Copyright © 1963 The Johns Hopkins University Press. Reproduced by permission.—*American Transcendental Quarterly,* v. 6, December, 1992; v. 8, June, 1994. Copyright © 1992, 1994 by The University of Rhode Island. Both reproduced by permission.—*Arizona Quarterly,* v. 24, summer, 1968 for "The Soundings of *Moby-Dick*" by Charles Child Walcutt; v. 46, autumn, 1990 for "Grammar and Etymology in *Moby-Dick*" by Mark Bauerlein; v. 59, spring, 2003 for "Cannibalism, Slavery, and Self-Consumption in *Moby-Dick*" by Homer B. Pettey. Copyright © 1968, 1990, 2003 by the Regents of the University of Arizona. All reproduced by permission of the publisher and the respective authors.—*CLIO: A Journal of Literature, History, and the Philosophy of History,* v. 20, winter, 1991 for "The Abandonment of Time and Place: History and Narrative, Metaphysics and Exposition in Melville's *Moby-Dick*" by Paul Lukacs. Copyright © 1991 by Henry Kozicki. Reproduced by permission of the author.—*ELH,* v. 32, March, 1965; v. 39, June, 1972; v. 71, winter, 2004. Copyright © 1965, 1972, 2004 The Johns Hopkins University Press. All reproduced by permission.—*ESQ: A Journal of the American Renaissance,* v. 31, 4th quarter, 1985 for "The Word and the Thing: *Moby-Dick* and the Limits of Language" by Gayle L. Smith. Copyright © 1985 by Gayle L. Smith. Reproduced by permission of the author./ v. 21, 3rd quarter, 1975 for "Melville's Apocalypse: American Millennialism and *Moby-Dick*" by Michael T. Gilmore. Copyright © 1975 by Emerson Society Quarterly. Reproduced by permission of the publisher.—*Georgia Review,* v. 23, spring, 1969. Copyright © 1969 by The University of Georgia. Reproduced by permission.—*Interpretation: A Journal of Political Philosophy,* v. 23, winter, 1996 for "*Moby-Dick* and Melville's Quarrel with America" by John Alvis. Copyright © 1996 *Interpretation.* Reproduced by permission of the publisher and the author.—*Massachusetts Review,* v. 35, spring, 1994; v. 40, spring, 1999. Copyright © 1994, 1999. Both reprinted by permission from the *Massachusetts Review.*—*Modern Language Studies,* v. 21, summer, 1991 for "*Moby-Dick*: Ishmael's Fiction of Ahab's Romantic Insurgency" by John W. Rathbun; v. 27, fall-winter, 1997 for "The Angel in the Envelope: The Letters of Jane Welsh Carlyle" by Jean Wasko. Copyright © 1991, 1997 by the Northeast Modern Language Association. Both reproduced by permission of the publisher and the authors.—*New Orleans Review,* v. 10, winter, 1983. Copyright © 1983 by Loyola University. Reproduced by permission.—*New Zealand Slavonic Journal,* 1974. Reproduced by permission.—*The Russian Review,* v. 50, January, 1991. Copyright © 1991 Basil Blackwell Ltd. Reproduced by permission of Blackwell Publishers.—*Slavic and East European Journal,* v. 32, summer, 1988. Copyright © 1988 by AATSEEL of the U.S., Inc. Reproduced by permission.—*Studies in the Novel,* v. 10, fall, 1978; v. 12, summer, 1980; v. 15, winter, 1983; v. 16, fall, 1984; v. 19, summer, 1987. Copyright © 1978, 1980, 1983, 1984, 1987 by North Texas State University. All reproduced by permission.

COPYRIGHTED MATERIAL IN *NCLC*, VOLUME 181, WAS REPRODUCED FROM THE FOLLOWING BOOKS:

Bayley, John. From an Introduction to *Russian Schoolboy* by Sergei Aksakov. Edited and translated by J. D. Duff. Oxford University Press, 1983. Introduction copyright © 1978 by John Bayley. Reproduced by permission of Oxford University Press.—Cecil, David. From an Introduction to *Years of Childhood* by Sergei Aksakov. Edited and translated by J. D. Duff. Oxford University Press, 1983. Introduction copyright © 1983 by Lord David Cecil. Reproduced by permission of Oxford University Press.—Chamberlain, Kathy. From "'A Creative Adventure': Jane Welsh Carlyle's 'Simple Story'" in *The Carlyles at Home and Abroad.* Edited by David R. Sorenson and Rodger L. Tarr. Ashgate Publishers Limited, 2004. Copyright © 2004 David R. Sorenson and Rodger L. Tarr. Reproduced by permission.—Christianson, Aileen. From "Jane Welsh Carlyle's Travel Narratives: 'Portable Perspectives'" in *The Carlyles at Home and Abroad.* Edited by David R. Sorenson and

Thomson Gale Literature Product Advisory Board

The members of the Thomson Gale Literature Product Advisory Board—reference librarians from public and academic library systems—represent a cross-section of our customer base and offer a variety of informed perspectives on both the presentation and content of our literature products. Advisory board members assess and define such quality issues as the relevance, currency, and usefulness of the author coverage, critical content, and literary topics included in our series; evaluate the layout, presentation, and general quality of our printed volumes; provide feedback on the criteria used for selecting authors and topics covered in our series; provide suggestions for potential enhancements to our series; identify any gaps in our coverage of authors or literary topics, recommending authors or topics for inclusion; analyze the appropriateness of our content and presentation for various user audiences, such as high school students, undergraduates, graduate students, librarians, and educators; and offer feedback on any proposed changes/enhancements to our series. We wish to thank the following advisors for their advice throughout the year.

Sergei Timofeevich Aksakov
1791-1859

Russian novelist, essayist, memoirist, short story writer, and poet.

The following entry presents an overview of Aksakov's life and works. For additional information on his career, see *NCLC,* Volume 2.

INTRODUCTION

At the height of his career, Sergei Timofeevich Aksakov was among the most popular writers in mid-nineteenth-century Russia. A key figure in the development of Russian literary realism, Aksakov wrote fiction that was firmly rooted in his own life, drawing from family history and personal experience to craft narratives that are distinguished by both their fidelity to verisimilitude and their plain, unadorned prose. In such works as *Semeinaia khronika* (1856; *The Family Chronicle*) and *Detskie gody Bagrova-vnuka* (1858; *Years of Childhood*), he creates a vivid portrait of country life in Tsarist Russia. These sagas blend historical detail with fictionalized characterizations to tell the story of Aksakov's family heritage, from his grandfather's settlement of a vast estate in the Southern Urals to the author's own coming of age. Aksakov's writing embodies a stark repudiation of the more worldly Romanticism of such writers as Nikolai Karamzin, espousing instead a classical, Slavophilic approach to storytelling. In spite of its reactionary aspects, Aksakov's work contributed vitally to the development of the modern novel form, notably in its straightforward prose style and its liberal intermingling of fact and fiction. While Aksakov's works are still widely read in Russia, they remain relatively unknown in the West, and only a handful of critical studies devoted to Aksakov's career have appeared in English. Still, his role as a central figure in nineteenth-century Russian literary culture remains indisputable; his works influenced such pioneers of Russian literature as Ivan Turgenev and Leo Tolstoy, among numerous others.

BIOGRAPHICAL INFORMATION

Sergei Timofeevich Aksakov was born in Ufa, Russia, on September 20, 1791, the son of Timofei Stepanovich Aksakov, a court official, and Maria Nikolaevna Zubova, a descendant of landed nobility. Aksakov's paternal grandfather, Stepan Aksakov, owned a vast estate, which he named Novo-Aksakovo, on the banks of the Buguruslan River. As a boy Aksakov spent much of his time exploring the forests and rivers of Novo-Aksakovo, where through his father's guidance he mastered the arts of hunting and fishing. These experiences would foster a deep-seated love of the natural world in Aksakov and would later form the basis for his best-known nonfiction works.

While Aksakov inherited his appreciation for nature from his father, his mother cultivated his passion for literature. Maria Nikolaevna was a cultured, intelligent woman, well-read in both Russian and Western European literature, and she taught her son to read and write when he was only four. In 1801 Aksakov enrolled in the Kazan gymnasium, a boarding school, although he soon became seriously ill with a nervous disorder and was forced to return home. He reentered the gymnasium a year later, where he embarked on a course of study that included literature, science, mathematics, and history; he also published poems and short stories in the student literary journal. His early writings were inspired by the sentimental school of Nikolai Karamzin, one of Russia's leading literary figures of the era. Aksakov played an active role in student theater and gained prestige among his classmates for his ability to memorize and act out entire plays by himself.

In 1804 Kazan gymnasium expanded to become Kazan University, and for the next three years Aksakov attended both high school and university classes, receiving a certificate of attendance in 1807. Although Aksakov later regarded his formal education as inadequate, his school experiences exerted a powerful influence on his mature writings. Shortly after leaving school, Aksakov's literary philosophy underwent a dramatic transformation. He repudiated Karamzin's cosmopolitan, Eurocentric attitude toward literature, espousing instead the conservative literary ideals of Admiral Aleksandr Shishkov, who advocated the nurturing of a nationalistic, Slavophile form of literature.

In 1807 Aksakov moved with his family to Moscow. A year later the family relocated to St. Petersburg, where Aksakov went to work for the civil service while continuing to write poetry. In St. Petersburg Aksakov became personally acquainted with Admiral Shishkov, who introduced him to the various writers, artists, and actors who frequented his salon. Although Aksakov's noble birth prohibited him from becoming an actor, at Shishkov's urging he staged a number of amateur plays for his friends and colleagues. Aksakov quit his civil service job in 1811 and moved to Moscow; following Napoleon's invasion a year later he returned to the family estate. For the next several years he traveled throughout the country, stopping regularly in Moscow and St. Petersburg to visit friends and see plays. Aksakov also produced translations of plays by Sophocles and Molière during these years, although these works were never published.

In 1816 Aksakov married Olga Semenovna Zaplatina, the daughter of a retired army officer. Little is known about Aksakov's married life, apart from the depictions that appear in his autobiographical novels and some brief descriptions in the writings of his son, Ivan Aksakov. By both accounts, Aksakov enjoyed a healthy relationship with Olga, as well as a happy and stable family life. Over the course of their marriage, Aksakov and his wife had fourteen children, although four died in infancy. Shortly after their marriage they settled in the countryside near Aksakov's paternal estate, where they remained for the next decade. During these years Aksakov dedicated himself to his duties as a landowner and father, while devoting his free time to hunting and fishing.

Aksakov's life underwent a dramatic change following the Decembrist Revolt of 1825. In addition to provoking harsh reprisals from Tsar Nicholas I, the uprising inspired a conservative backlash among Russia's leading intelligentsia, providing fertile ground for Admiral Shishkov's Slavophilic ideology. Shishkov himself was named minister of education in 1826. A year later, after accepting Shishkov's invitation to serve as government censor, Aksakov moved with his family to Moscow. He held the government position sporadically for the next several years. Throughout this period he published numerous articles and reviews in literary journals and befriended a number of influential writers, among them the historian and journalist Mikhail Pogodin, as well as the literary critic Nikolai Nadezhdin, with whom he collaborated in publishing the short-lived journal *Teleskop.* Aksakov also met the author Nikolai Gogol during these years, forming a friendship that would endure until Gogol's death in 1852.

In 1833 Aksakov published his first short story, "Buran" ("The Blizzard"), in the *Dennitsa* almanac. That same year he was named inspector of the Konstantin Geodetic School, a training academy for land surveyors. He eventually became director of the school, retiring from his post in 1839 after receiving substantial inheritances following the deaths of his parents. Free to pursue his literary interests full-time, and with Gogol's encouragement, Aksakov began to write prose in earnest. His home became a salon for the next generation of writers

and critics, among them Gogol, Pogodin, and Vissarion Belinsky. His first volume of essays, a collection of sketches on fishing entitled *Zapiski ob uzhen'e* (*Notes on Fishing*), appeared in 1847. In 1852 he published a book of hunting essays, *Zapiski ruzheĭnogo okhotnika Orenburgskoĭ gubernii* (*Notes of a Provincial Wildfowler*). During these years Aksakov also worked diligently on his chronicles of Russian pastoral life, publishing both *The Family Chronicle* and *Vospominaniia prezhnei zhizni* (*A Russian Schoolboy*) in 1856, followed in 1858 by *Years of Childhood.* In 1857 he had begun working on a novel, *Kopyt'ev,* although by this time he had become gravely ill, and the work remained unfinished at his death. In spite of his worsening health, Aksakov managed to maintain contact with Russia's literati in his last years, befriending younger authors like Leo Tolstoy and Ivan Turgenev. Aksakov died of kidney failure on April 30, 1859.

MAJOR WORKS

Aksakov's reputation rests primarily on his trilogy of autobiographical novels: *The Family Chronicle, A Russian Schoolboy,* and *Years of Childhood.* The first of these sagas, *The Family Chronicle,* focuses on Stepan Mikhailovich Bagrov, the fictional alter-ego of Aksakov's grandfather. In many respects, Bagrov is the quintessential patriarch, a strong-willed, larger-than-life figure whose determination and ambition enable him to carve a family empire out of the unsettled regions of central Russia. Into Bagrov's world Aksakov introduces the acutely different character Mikhailo Maksimovich Kurolesov, an opportunistic and unscrupulous young man who contrives to marry Bagrov's cousin. Eventually, Kurolesov's philandering and cruelty provoke Bagrov's wrath, and the patriarch has one of his serfs poison Kurolesov. The work concludes with an extended chronicle devoted to Bagrov's son, Alexei Stepanich, depicting the early days of his marriage and culminating with the birth of his son, Sergei. In *A Russian Schoolboy,* considered by the majority of scholars to be the most autobiographical of the three works, Aksakov recounts his personal experience of leaving home to attend Kazan gymnasium. The novel provides one of the few existing accounts of Aksakov's formative years, while serving as a valuable chronicle of Russian life during the Napoleonic years. *Years of Childhood* moves backward in time, recounting Aksakov's earliest years from the point of view of his childhood self. In each of the three narratives, Aksakov delivers a profound statement on the importance of family, suggesting that the individual is always subservient to the broader forces of history, society, and custom. The novels remain important examples of nineteenth-century fictional realism.

Aksakov was also an accomplished essayist. In such works as *Notes on Fishing* and *Notes of a Provincial Wildfowler,* he describes his life-long passion for fishing

and hunting. The books offer practical advice for anglers and hunters and include painstaking descriptions
of technique, gear, and habitats. On a deeper level,
however, the works reveal Aksakov's ideas concerning
the powerful relationship between human beings and
the natural world. The essays are also noteworthy for
their unpretentious, conversational style and are in
themselves important examples of the realistic mode. A
collection of essays and memoirs, *Rasskazy i vospominaniia okhotnika o raznykh okhotakh,* appeared in 1855,
and the memoir *Literaturnye i teatral'nye vospominaniia* (1856) followed a year later. Published posthumously, *Istoriia moego znakomstva s Gogolem* (1890)
chronicles Aksakov's friendship with Nikolai Gogol
and offers valuable insights into Gogol's personality,
his writing methods, and his impact on his contemporaries.

CRITICAL RECEPTION

Sergei Aksakov enjoyed widespread acclaim in Russia
during his lifetime. His earliest champions included Leo
Tolstoy, who praised the naturalness and realism of Aksakov's prose, and the radical critic N. A. Dobroliubov,
who was among the first to argue for the inherent political value of Aksakov's approach to fiction. Opponents of Dobroliubov, notably Pavel Annenkov, focused
on the objective aspects of Aksakov's work, insisting
that the contemplative qualities of his narratives di-
vorced them from any particular social context. By the
1890s, historian Pavel Milukov had singled out Aksakov's autobiographical novels as among the most enduring and influential works of the nineteenth century; indeed, Milukov argued that the average Russian's idea
of childhood had been shaped to a large degree by Aksakov's chronicles. Although Aksakov's works were
banned during much of the Soviet era, they remained of
interest to scholars in the West. Important twentieth-
century commentators included J. D. Duff, who was the
first to translate the trilogy into English, and D. S. Mirsky, who offered a valuable critique of Aksakov's works
in his *A History of Russian Literature from Its Beginnings to 1900* (1927). Writing in the 1960s, Ralph Matlaw examined the relationship between Aksakov's attitude toward nature and his realistic prose style. In the
late twentieth century, Aksakov's work began to attract
the attention of a new generation of scholars, among
them Andrew Durkin, whose 1983 publication *Sergei
Aksakov and Russian Pastoral* remains one of the only
book-length studies of the author's work in English;
and Richard Gregg, who has investigated questions of
genre as they relate to Aksakov's innovative fiction-
writing practices. In the late 1990s the Northwestern
University Press produced the first English translations
of Aksakov's essays: *Notes on Fishing* came out in
1997 and *Notes of a Provincial Wildfowler* in 1998.

PRINCIPAL WORKS

"Buran" ["The Blizzard"] (short story) 1833; published
in almanac *Dennitsa*

*Zapiski ob uzhen'e [Notes on Fishing] (essays) 1847;
also published as *Zapiski ob uzhen'e ryby,* 1854

*Zapiski ruzheĭnogo okhotnika Orenburgskoĭ gubernii
[Notes of a Provincial Wildfowler]* (essays) 1852

*Rasskazy i vospominaniia okhotnika o raznykh okho-
takh* (essays and memoirs) 1855

Literaturnye i teatral'nye vospominaniia (memoirs)
1856

*Semeinaia khronika [Memoirs of the Aksakov Family (A
Family Chronicle, Part I); A Russian Gentleman;
The Family Chronicle]* (novel) 1856

Vospominaniia prezhnei zhizni [A Russian Schoolboy]
(novel) 1856

Detskie gody Bagrova-vnuka [Years of Childhood]
(novel) 1858

Polnoe sobranie sochinenii S. T. Aksakova. 6 vols.
(prose) 1886

Istoriia moego znakomstva s Gogolem (memoirs) 1890

Sobranie sochinenii. 4 vols. (prose) 1955-56

Sobranie sochinenii. 5 vols. (prose) 1966

*Includes additional translations of selected essays and poems.

CRITICISM

Xenia Glowacki-Prus (essay date 1974)

SOURCE: Glowacki-Prus, Xenia. "Sergey Aksakov as
a Biographer of Childhood." *New Zealand Slavonic
Journal,* n.s. no. 2 (1974): 19-37.

[*In the following essay, Glowacki-Prus examines the
narrative strategies Aksakov uses in his 1858 autobiography* Years of Childhood.]

> *Mon âme est ce lac même où le soleil qui penche
> Par un beau soir d'automne envoie un feu mourant.*
>
> Sainte-Beuve

I

Aksakov wrote *Detskiye gody Bagrova vnuka*[1] in 1857
(at the age of sixty-five), and published it in the following year. It was the last of his important works and, as
far as the author was concerned, the most demanding
one. Aksakov told Pogodin: "I finished my book on 19
June. For a night and a day I was sad like a child. I do
not know if my work is good, but I have put a great
deal of my soul into it and feel a kind of emptiness."[2]

Detskiye gody [*Detskie gody Bagrova-vnuka*] has achieved considerable fame both in Russia and abroad.[3] It was the only book by Aksakov to be allowed publication after the Revolution, when most of his work was banned,[4] and it seems to have enjoyed the same popularity in post-revolutionary Russia as in Aksakov's own days. Very few critics were hostile to the book,[5] most saw it in a favourable light,[6] and a few considered it an idealisation.[7] Although many articles and reviews have been published about it there is no comprehensive critical analysis and appraisal of the work, for critics, when writing about *Detskiye gody,* have usually quoted from the book only to illustrate its chief protagonists and its treatment of nature and the peasants, and have drawn rather superficial conclusions. Some neglected problems are the influence of his surroundings on the little narrator, the role of the narrator himself, and finally the question as to why Aksakov found it necessary to disguise himself under a pseudonym in *Detskiye gody* and *Semeynaya khronika* whereas in *Vospominaniya* he did not use this device. Aksakov was annoyed when critics of the day linked *Vospominaniya* and *Semeynaya khronika* together, as can be seen in both his introductions to the latter work.[8]

Although Aksakov gave little Seryozha the name Bagrov, and otherwise tried to dissociate himself from the work, his book is nonetheless completely autobiographical. Unlike Tolstoy's *Detstvo,* where there is an intentional fictional element, Aksakov's work does recount the story of Sergey Timofeyevich's own childhood. It is enough to read Arkhangel'sky's article on this subject to be completely reassured about the authenticity of most of the happenings in *Detskiye gody,*[9] and Aksakov's own introduction to the book is most revealing. No one could have written this kind of introduction if he were recounting somebody else's childhood.[10] It would have been dishonest and unnecessary to write such an introduction had Aksakov been describing somebody else's childhood. Aksakov must have had his reasons for this masquerade and one may only attempt to guess at them.

In order to appreciate fully the role of the little narrator it is important to study first the environment in which he grew up and the various forces that converged on him. In particular we must assess these from Seryozha's point of view, and only later will it be possible to evaluate which elements played a part in the author's development and remained with him for over sixty years. Aksakov wrote a book about his childhood; the reading audience he had in mind was children. This in itself is a unique phenomenon in his day; another feature of this book is that there is a constant dialogue between Seryozha the little boy and the wise old man rediscovering and unveiling the past with all the sensitivity and dawning awareness of the child.[11] Yet the illusion that the child is telling the story is complete.

II

Sof'ya Nikolavna, Seryozha's mother (Aksakov spells several names phonetically in *Detskiye gody*), is considered an outstandingly brilliant and progressive woman, *krasavitsa ufimskogo bomonda*[12] and a 'Russian Cinderella'.[13] She is the character who, after Seryozha himself, has attracted most attention, yet she has always been appraised from what is known about Aksakov's own mother and from the descriptions of Sof'ya Nikolavna, before and after her marriage to Aleksey Stepanych Bagrov in *Semeynaya khronika.* There is no reason why Seryozha's mother should not be assessed simply in the light of how she appears and behaves throughout *Detskiye gody,* where she is one of the more interesting, if less charming, protagonists.

We learn very little from Seryozha about his mother's looks. He notices that sometimes she looks very beautiful, that in fact she is the most beautiful lady he knows,[14] but he also frequently points out how drawn and tired she seems, how jaundiced she looks when she is ill. He seems to notice his mother's ill health far more than her outward appearance. He hardly ever comments on her dresses, except that we can deduce that they were different from those of his grandmother and aunt in Bagrovo, for they seemed to dress like the servants.[15] He only once points out that his mother took great care in getting dressed, and that was when they were invited to see the rich landowner Durasov.[16] The same applies to his father. Aksakov, who always liked to describe in detail the physiognomy and clothing of his characters, gives us no clues as to the appearance of all those around him, whom he loved. What Sof'ya Nikolavna or her husband, his little sister Nadezha or his brother, Yevseich, his *dyad'ka,* or Parasha, looked like is completely irrelevant to the little boy; all that matters is that they love him, he feels at home with them and therefore he notices their spiritual qualities and none of their physical ones. It is only when the family travels to Churasovo that we find out that Seryozha's little sister is described as *zamukhryshka,* and his brother *chernushka,* by their grand-aunt, Praskov'ya Ivanovna.[17] On the other hand Seryozha notes in great detail all the ordinary and extraordinary people he meets and all the strange new sights.

Seryozha's portrayal of his family and Yevseich is chiefly a psychological one; even then a great deal remains unsaid and the reader must draw his own conclusions. It seems that in all autobiographies there is a 'cone of darkness at the centre, even in those outstanding psychological documents',[18] and *Detskiye gody* undoubtedly is a 'psychological document'.

The reader sees from the very beginning of the tale how different Seryozha's parents are from most of their relatives, who are on the whole ignorant, petty and jealous. Seryozha's grandfather, the formidable Stepan Mikhaylych, and his eldest daughter Aksin'ya Stepanovna are the only relatives of Aleksey Stepanych who have the same regard for truth and honesty as he and his wife; another characteristic Aleksey Stepanych shares with his father is his faith in tradition and the awareness of the responsibility which he carries towards his peasants as their landowner. Stepan Mikhaylych is an autocrat and rules his household in the old patriarchal way; he is occasionally violent[19] and has little time to waste on Seryozha who is afraid of him and cannot speak up for himself. His son, Aleksey Stepanych, is meek on the surface and never fights unnecessary battles with his wife. Most critics[20] are content to stop at this meekness, but in fact it conceals a great deal of determination. It is not the strong-willed Sof'ya Nikolavna who gets her own way with Praskov'ya Ivanovna,[21] another autocratic personality, but the meek Aleksey Stepanych. He also gets his own way with the peasants, not by using violence or force but by means of gentleness. Mironych does as he is told,[22] and even the spoilt and badly-trained Churasov servants behave with more courtesy towards the Bagrovs than towards anyone else,[23] while the peasants are genuinely devoted to him. Sof'ya Nikolavna, on the other hand, cannot stand any contact with servants or peasants. This is one of her most unpleasant characteristics. Seryozha reiterates many times how intelligent his mother is, and the aforementioned critics also stress her intellectual superiority over her husband.[24] Yet there is very little trace of any outstanding intelligence about her, especially in her behaviour towards the peasants, whom she always refuses to see (thereby making herself extremely unpopular with them),[25] and in her behaviour towards her relatives. She mocks her husband's favourite hobbies, such as fishing, hunting and collecting mushrooms,[26] and is inordinately possessive of Seryozha, although, by the end of the book, she has four children. Seryozha recounts her behaviour faithfully, together with his own astonishment at it, and, although she is by no means a stupid woman, she behaves in a most shortsighted and spoilt fashion towards many people, displaying trivial and vulgar class-conscious traits which her allegedly less intelligent husband does not possess.

Unlike his wife, Aleksey Stepanych and the little Seryozha remain unaware of class distinctions. They remain what they are, and are valued for what they are by the peasants; and they in turn treat both the peasants and their work with the deference due to any human being.[27] Sof'ya Nikolavna is incapable of this, just as she is incapable of forgiving and trying to understand her relatives, whom she simply despises, as she tells her sister-in-law Tat'yana Stepanovna.[28] She chooses the way of least resistance in certain situations. Instead of assuming her role as mistress of the house when her mother-in-law dies (she may be forgiven for not assuming this

role earlier) she simply asks Tat'yana Stepanovna, her husband's unmarried youngest sister, to carry on looking after the house. If she really had this fine intelligence which is attributed to her, if she were not such an intransigent egoist towards anyone except her own children (and at times her husband and particular friends), if she were more aware of other people's feelings, she would have been a far more endearing character. Her one great redeeming feature is her love for her children—and particularly for Seryozha whom she virtually saved from an untimely death when he was a very young child. Yet even her love for the child seems excessive, as her husband points out to her.[29] Time and again she limits little Seryozha's enjoyment of life by her cold and dispassionate attitude to his dearly beloved sports, but he faithfully recounts everything to her, and in the end she makes him feel so guilty that he does not love her enough[30] that the child stays with his mother almost all the time. It is fortunate for Seryozha that his love for nature proves a very serious rival for his mother's affection; had it not been for that and the extreme level-headedness of his father, Sof'ya Nikolavna might have caused a great deal of damage to Seryozha by her excessive, demanding love, which verges on hysteria.

Sof'ya Nikolavna is neither an outstandingly brilliant and intelligent woman nor a Russian Cinderella, even if it is in old Bagrov that (according to Pritchett) she finds her Prince Charming.[31] She is simply an honest, moderately intelligent woman, a town-dweller despising country-folk and life, who is bored with the country and, finding little companionship in her immediate circle, promotes her eldest son to the role of friend and confidant. She loves her husband, which is evident in the closing chapters when her mother-in-law dies and Aleksey Stepanych is overcome by grief,[32] but she does not have the loving heart which her husband, son and daughter possess. She has none of the qualities that Baring sees in Seryozha, when he writes that:

> One is spellbound by the charm, the dignity, the good-nature, the gentle easy accent of the speaker, in whom one feels convinced not only that there was nothing common or mean, but who was a gentleman by character as well as by lineage, one of God's as well as one of Russia's nobility.[33]

Moore maintained that it was not Seryozha but his father who was the chief character of ***Detskiye gody.***[34] As mentioned earlier, Aleksey Stepanych is usually considered as not particularly intelligent, and too weak compared to his wife. It is true that one may miss the resolution hidden underneath Aleksey Stepanych's meekness, but it is impossible not to appreciate his great spiritual qualities, and admire him for preserving them intact regardless of a milieu not very conducive to gentleness, sweetness of disposition or fairness. Seryozha's father is no more the 'principal character'[35] than Seryozha himself. Moore is wrong; ***Detskiye gody*** does not possess a principal character, and the little narrator, his father and mother are simply to be considered *primi inter pares*.

Yevseich, Seryozha's *dyad'ka* and constant companion, is another purely Russian type, cast in the same mould as old Bagrov. Parasha, Seryozha's sister Nadezha's nanny, likes her charge, but we get the feeling she is merely doing her work whereas Yevseich has a strong attachment to his work and to Seryozha. In many ways childlike, he enjoys fishing and collecting mushrooms as much as the little boy. He is a man with apparently no family ties (or at least they are never mentioned), who loves and protects little Seryozha, guarding him from such pitfalls as falling into a river or seeing the uncomely behaviour of the Churasov servants. He is in many ways a simpler version of Aleksey Stepanych, and it seems throughout *Detskiye gody* that Seryozha is happiest when in the company of his father or Yevseich. Yevseich as he is portrayed in *Detskiye gody* does not display any negative characteristics.

Seryozha frequently mentions his love for his little sister and his mother, less frequently does he analyse his feelings towards his father; he certainly never discusses his emotions with Aleksey Stepanych. But he never mentions his affection for Yevseich. It seems that the idea of loving or not loving his most faithful companion has never occurred to him. Unlike his mother, father and sister, Yevseich is always there to look after Seryozha, care for him, make his fishing rods and share the joys of catching fish, picking mushrooms and berries with him. The little boy tells Yevseich everything, just as he does with his little sister. It seems therefore that both for Seryozha, and for Aksakov writing the book sixty years later, it was unnecessary to uncover what Pascal calls the 'cone of darkness': Yevseich was Seryozha's friend, and Seryozha did not need to reassure himself that he loved him, he took it for granted that it was so.

Seryozha's little sister is portrayed only in glimpses. From what her brother recounts she must have been an extraordinarily patient child, for she always listens to the fairy tales and accounts of books that Seryozha has read, and all the new sights he has seen, shares wholeheartedly in his joys and grief and above all is not jealous of her mother's attention to her eldest son. Seryozha is aware of this, and points out that his sister did not like to stay in his mother's room, that she would leave at the earliest opportunity; and although at the time he thought she did not love her mother enough, she did in fact love her far more deeply than he himself.[36] Hardly anything is mentioned about the youngest brother, who is born during the tale, except that both children were delighted about this new arrival and were fully prepared to accept him and love him as much as they did one another. The children never quarrel; this

may be accounted for by the literary interests of the brother and the compliant character of his sister who listened to Seryozha for hours, and even put up with Seryozha's attempts to teach her how to read. The first attempts led to little success but, when the teacher reached the mature age of seven and his sister five, some results were achieved.

This is the small circle of people that counted for Seryozha. He learnt to like his grandfather and grandmother, after their death, and later his aunt Tat'yana Stepanovna. The grandmother, not a very likeable character, with a predilection for bad eggs and wormy mushrooms, scares little Seryozha by shouting and beating one of the servant girls.[37] After the death of her husband, Arina Vasil'yevna seems to age greatly and hardly takes any part in the life of Bagrovo, so that we learn little about her. Seryozha avoided her after the episode with the servant girl and possibly because he felt a hidden hostility towards himself and his mother. Arina Vasil'yevna's dislike of Sof'ya Nikolavna, whose position was made very difficult on this account, is clear from her dying words as reported by Aksin'ya Stepanovna asking for Sof'ya Nikolavna's forgiveness.[38] Tat'yana Stepanovna is faintly sketched by Seryozha except for her hoarding habits. She has a *zavetnyy ambar* where she has collected a rather overwhelming dowry which is guarded by Matryosha when all the things in it are taken out for an airing in spring. She does not seem to be a particularly intelligent woman, and is fully aware that she is a country bumpkin (*derevenshchina*).[39] For this reason she refuses to visit Praskov'ya Ivanovna in the more fashionable Churasovo and causes a great deal of amusement to Parasha and Yevseich by asking her brother to transport the contents of the *zavetnyy ambar* to her sister's estate, as she did not consider it safe to leave it unattended in Bagrovo.[40] She is basically kind—unlike her other sisters, particularly the *General'sha,* Yelizaveta Stepanovna.

Praskov'ya Ivanovna is portrayed in the book more as the older Bagrov, that is Sergey Timofeyevich, knew her, rather than through Seryozha. Her tale is told in *Semeynaya khronika.* As far as the little Seryozha is concerned he likes her and values her, for she too is straightforward, honest, and cannot stand any artificiality; but the child cannot appreciate or understand this extraordinary woman and therefore she remains a driving force in the background, somebody whose wish is everybody's command, whom nobody dares disobey.

III

Pearsall-Smith wrote in his review of Duff's translation of *Years of Childhood*:

> The fact that the boy is a Russian boy largely explains our interest, and this for several reasons. There is in the first place the charm of geography and local colour; for

if Aksakoff's experiences themselves are not unusual, their setting is quite strange and unfamiliar to us; we are transported to one of the remotest corners of Europe . . . into a half barbaric country full of Tartars and nomad tribes; and the life of this region is presented to us with extraordinary richness.[41]

However, Pearsall-Smith is wrong in thinking that only the English reading public would find these traits interesting. The Russian reading public in 1858 had found Seryozha's descriptions of nature, people and traditions just as fascinating, and so have many readers since. When describing 'geography and local colour' Aksakov reverts to his usual descriptive style, using every minute detail that he can recollect, in order to give the reader as clear a picture as possible. Some critics found the detail excessive and unnecessary; if Stankevich had had his way *Detskiye gody* would have been reduced by at least two thirds,[42] and Vengerov says that the descriptions of nature are very tedious.[43]

Detskiye gody is a treasure house of information, conveyed quite unconsciously by the author, about a way of life that survived until the Revolution. In Seryozha's tale, customs, traditions and people deserve some of our attention.

It is impossible to enumerate all the customs portrayed in the book, for one cannot dissociate them from the life of those days. Seryozha mentions many little points: his father blessing the children before they retire to bed,[44] the description of the peasants meeting the Bagrovs and being genuinely delighted at seeing them, although they did not personally know them;[45] the icon of Saint Nicholas that Seryozha spots in the stable;[46] the jam-making, when the children are given the sugary coating that forms on top of the jam boiling in huge brass cauldrons;[47] the wet-nurse, dressed in her 'finery' and full of her own importance;[48] and Yevseich telling the little boy that he was too late to see how *solnyshko igrayet* on Easter Day.[49]

These are just a few small details of traditional life with which the little narrator acquaints us. Two more important aspects are the relationship between landowner and peasant, and the attitude to death; for in *Detskiye gody* we witness three deaths, those of Seryozha's grandfather and grandmother, and the old miller Boltunyonok, who dies by misadventure on Easter Day.[50]

Seryozha's father takes the little boy with him when he is overseeing the work at Bagrovo or in some of the villages belonging to Praskov'ya Ivanovna. The child is struck by the rhythmic beauty of the work in the fields and notes that, although the work is hard, the peasants remain cheerful[51] except when either the weather, shortage of labour or illness amongst the cattle depress them; even as a very young child, during his first encounter with the peasants, Seryozha feels as sorry as his father

and the peasants that they will not have time to store the corn.[52] The usual greeting uttered by Seryozha's father was: *Bog na pomoshch'*; to which the peasants would answer: *Blagodarstvuyte, Aleksey Stepanych*; after which they would either carry on with their work, or the *starshina* would have a conversation with Bagrov. Once when there has been a particularly bad drought in Parashino one of the peasants points out the weeds growing in the fields. Aleksey Stepanych answers: *Kak byt', volya Bozh'ya . . .* to which the peasant replies gently: *Vestimo tak, batyushka.*[53] These words remained with Aksakov all his life; it was only later on, he notes, that he understood their true meaning.[54] Golovin's comment is particularly appropriate when he writes that the relationship between the people in Aksakov's book is based not on the letter of the law but on a tradition which has become part of the people,[55] and which they accept and honour.

Death is accepted in a matter of fact way. The household wail, as apparently was the custom in those days,[56] but no-one seems to lose his appetite after a death, be it of a father or mother, except for Sof'ya Nikolavna. The womenfolk in the family, although they wail, do not seem to be excessively cast down in spirits and even manage to get slightly tipsy during Stepan Mikhaylych's wake.[57] This does not necessarily show lack of affection or grief for the departed: after all, Tat'yana Stepanovna, who takes part in the wake, gives as one of her reasons for not going to Churasovo the fact that she has to go and visit her mother's grave and order *panikhidy* to be sung.[58]

All the traditional customs surrounding a death are strictly observed. Two *psalomshchiki* read in the room of the departed for nine days, day and night, and the little Seryozha goes and reads from the Book of Psalms on the ninth day,[59] when a Requiem is always sung in the Russian Orthodox Church. The relatives all congregate on the ninth day of Stepan Mikhaylych's death and on the fortieth day of Arina Vasil'yevna's for this again is traditional. The guests wail, cry and grieve, dutifully go to church although the road to the church is virtually impassable (Arina Vasil'yevna died in November) and, as Aksakov recalls for the fourth time, the guests ate, drank, cried, reminisced and then left.[60]

In *Detskiye gody,* as in all his other works, Aksakov remains a master portrait-painter. There is the pathetic figure of the *zasypka*, Vasiliy Terent'yev,[61] the shrewd Mironych with his extraordinary eyes,[62] descriptions of the Mordva,[63] the Bashkirs.[64] Aksakov shows people working, having a day off, or simply gazing at the river Belaya when the ice started breaking up, feeling sorry about a black cow that got stranded on a little island of ice, but laughing at the antics of a dog in a similar plight, since they thought, according to Seryozha, that the dog would save itself, whereas the cow would certainly drown.[65] Some figures stand out in this crowd of people. One is the Bashkir Mavlyutka, whose size alone makes him extraordinary; others are Miten'ka and his mother, the parvenu landowner Durasov, and the brilliant, blind peasant-lawyer Panteley Grigor'yich.[66]

Mavlyutka appears on the scene when the Bagrovs are visiting the half-built Sergeyevka, where he forecasts that there will be great difficulties in arguing about the boundaries of the estate as it seemed to be filled with the equivalent of squatters, whom it proved difficult to evict. Aksakov describes him as a *strannaya gromada* which suddenly appeared before their gates; his further progress is described as: *[gromada] vvalilas' k nam v dvor.* The *kantonyy starshina* Mavlyutka was apparently no less than twelve *vershki* in diameter and weighed all of twelve poods,[67] while his clothing was quite worthy of a Gogolian hero. The little Seryozha inevitably felt fear at such a sight and likened this gentleman to the evil Tissaphernes, leader of the Persian army who fought against Cyrus the Younger.[68]

Another very amusing sketch is that of a suitor for Tat'yana Stepanovna's hand. Miten'ka Rozhnov is probably slightly more slender than the huge Bashkir *starshina,* yet it takes the concerted efforts of six ablebodied men to extract him from his enormous carriage. Little Seryozha, with the tactlessness of all children, exclaimed *Akh, eto Mavlyutka!*[69] Yevseich, to whom this remark was directed, seemed to think that Miten'ka was even larger than Mavlyutka. Miten'ka's mother, a lady of less generous proportions (it took only two flunkeys to extract her out from her own separate carriage), complained all the time about her dear son's health, which was allegedly poor. Her son in the meanwhile consumed a great deal of food. Both mother and son, whom Seryozha likens to a Kalmyk *kibitka,*[70] eventually took their leave and the prospective bride declared her unwillingness to marry such a monstrosity. The question that worried little Seryozha most was that a wife is supposed to help her husband, and what would the thin Tat'yana Stepanovna do if Miten'ka were to fall, for she could not possibly help him to get up again? He was very relieved to hear her refusal to marry Miten'ka.[71]

Another comic character is Durasov, whose idiosyncrasy is a fondness for pigs. He had two shipped over from England, and their chief characteristic seems to be their size, particularly the dimension of their ears, which, according to their proud owner, are as large as stove shutters.[72] Seryozha, when visiting Durasov's manor, seeing the marble fountain and the sun-dial imagines himself in some knight's castle and then in Scheherazade's Palace. He notices the extraordinary clocks which were placed in the stomach of a lion and another pair in a man's head, and seems to think that the butler resembles the Governor in Ufa, for his dress is even more magnificent. When an orchestra suddenly starts playing during their lunch, Seryozha spills soup over himself and causes his mother acute embarrassment. He has the good taste at least to prefer the singing of the peasant girl Matryosha at Bagrovo to the two young ladies who sing for the guests' entertainment during the meal. Durasov's magnificent home, gardens, hothouses and conservatories make the little boy ask his parents a great deal of questions. His mother tells him off for behaving like a peasant's child who had never seen anything in his life except his *izba,* to which Seryozha artlessly replies that he truly has never seen anything similar, but noticing that his mother is annoyed has the sense to remain quiet.[73] Aksakov's description of Nikol'skoye (Durasov's estate) and Churasovo are wonderfully vivid and colourful; both houses are furnished in a way that their owners no doubt thought was beautiful, but Nikol'skoye can be awarded top marks for bad taste with Churasovo a close runner-up. No wonder Seryozha preferred the unpretentious Bagrovo his mother so hated.

Panteley Grigor'yich is a totally different figure from the *opéra comique* characters described above. He is an orphaned peasant, whom Mikhayla Maksimych Kurolesov, Praskov'ya Ivanovna's late husband, found and sent to Moscow (with Stepan Mikhaylych's permission) to study law. Pantyushka is eventually promoted to 'Panteley Grigor'yich' and becomes a lawyer. The nerves of his eyes are suddenly paralysed and he becomes blind when still a young man. His great skill in all things legal and his fantastic memory would have made it possible for him to carry on practising law in Moscow, but he preferred to return to Bagrovo where he deals with all legal matters and usually has a few boarders whom he teaches. Even as a well-known and universally respected lawyer, he would never sit in the presence of Aleksey Stepanych or the little Seryozha, which curtailed Seryozha's visits to his house as the little boy felt embarrassed that the old man should stand and absolutely refused to sit in his presence.[74]

Reading *Detskiye gody* one may fairly apply to it the term which Belinsky used to describe *Yevgeny Onegin*—an encyclopaedia of Russian life—for the wealth of characters and situations described, although they do not embrace high society or typical *kuptsy,* make this famous quotation far more appropriate to Aksakov's rather than to Pushkin's work.

IV

The Bagrov family as seen by Seryozha has already been discussed, but Seryozha the child and his development still remains to be studied. The little boy had been very ill and was saved from dying by the constant attention of his mother. Seryozha's illness is important for it was to affect his childhood profoundly, turning him into an introverted child, cowardly, afraid of strangers and much too dependent on his mother, who in return was too possessive and sheltered the child too much. Sensitive by nature, Seryozha remains very timid, easily upset, with hysterical tendencies and a much greater need for security than his little sister. The most striking characteristic of the very young Seryozha is his *zhalostlivost'*, his compassion towards all that suffer[75] and his abhorrence of all violence, an unusual trait in so young a child, for children cannot understand the concept of cruelty, just as they can seldom comprehend the idea of compassion. For some inexplicable reason, known only to true hunters, Seryozha does not feel this compassion towards the animals he hunts or earlier on sees caught. This puzzles him[76] and remains an unsolved question.

Seryozha's abhorrence of violence in everyday life is particularly well shown in his visit to the *narodnoye uchilische,* which lasted only one day but proved a traumatic experience for the child;[77] Seryozha recalls it each time he witnesses any violence. Just as he cannot stand violence around him—for it makes him physically ill—he cannot tolerate nature in turmoil: crossing the raging Volga on his way from Churasovo to Bagrovo is a nightmare for the little boy.[78] After Seryozha witnesses his grandmother flogging a servant girl, and hears his own mother shouting at Parasha,[79] he eventually adopts a course of not telling his mother the complete truth about what he has seen and heard as he wishes to protect others from any form of violence. He recounts the episode when Volkov and his uncles tease him by saying that Volkov will marry his five-year-old sister. They forge a document to the effect that Sergeyevka, Seryozha's own estate, would become Volkov's. This mystification and teasing does not involve any physical violence, but for the child the mental torture is intolerable. All he understands is that Volkov, whom he does not like, will take his sister away, as well as his beloved Sergeyevka, and in his tale this simple practical joke takes on the proportion of mental cruelty. Little Seryozha, never before driven to violence himself, takes a wooden hammer and throws it at Volkov. Later on he is told to beg forgiveness, and after standing in a corner in punishment for a whole day he is taken ill and develops a fever. It is only after his recovery that he suddenly wants to beg forgiveness from his uncles and Volkov and regains his equanimity.[80] This is the first collision which Seryozha has with the adult world, a world (as he says) incomprehensible for a child, for a child cannot tell the difference between a joke and the truth.[81]

Another characteristic of Seryozha is his extreme cowardice, resulting usually from the feeling of hostility which the child senses in other people, the fear of the unknown and particularly of death. Aksakov considered that a child's heart was naturally timid and it was his own experience which made him praise all those who protect a child from the awareness of his own coward-

ice.[82] Seryozha's father alone never comments on his son's lack of courage, and the little boy is well aware that his timidity makes him unpopular with his relatives, particularly Stepan Mikhaylych. The way in which Aksakov traces Seryozha's emotions when experiencing fear of any kind make *Detskiye gody* an outstanding document on child psychology just as valid nowadays as it was over a hundred years ago.

Seryozha's main interests in life are books when he is in town or in Churasovo, and nature when travelling at Sergeyevka or Bagrovo. He could read at the age of five, and would forget the whole world when plunged in his *Detskoye chteniye dlya serdtsa i razuma* or the tales of Scheherazade. He recounts all that he has read immediately to Yevseich, his sister or his mother, sometimes to his aunt, adding details from his own imagination. But his one great love was nature. He discovered nature by himself; when he was still very ill his parents stopped the carriage in order to break the journey and the child lay on the ground in a clearing in the forest, listening and feeling the peace around him and begging his parents to leave him where he was.[83] From this moment onwards a bond begins to exist between the little Seryozha and nature that was to last all his life. Later, Aksakov professed that only in close contact with nature can man find his true self and real values, namely simplicity and the absence of all artificiality.[84]

Aksakov's descriptions of nature are not only some of the most poetic in the Russian language, but they show the reader beauty in a country which Gogol described as flat and uninteresting; Gogol saw no miracles of nature,[85] but for Aksakov these miracles did exist, for he loved nature enough to find them and was possessed of that special poetic talent, and love, which alone can enable a writer to describe it. Turgenev's descriptions of nature are beautiful, but his nature is a relentless force, blind and cold. For Aksakov nature is a friend and Seryozha is in complete harmony with it, except for the trip on the Volga, which is not so much a description of nature as a description of the child's fear of the raging elements. Nature as we see it in *Detskiye gody,* or for that matter in all Aksakov's work, can be compared to the *sfumato* effect of Leonardo da Vinci's sketches,[86] though at times we find the more brilliant and joyful colours of van Gogh.[87] In these unassuming sketches of nature Aksakov repaid his greatest debt to Gogol, by doing what lay outside the scope of Gogol's own talent and vision.

Dudyshkin quite correctly points out that Aksakov's love for nature does not prove anything, he loves it for its own sake.[88] It is in this particular sense that Aksakov is different from other writers who described nature, with the exception possibly of Paustovsky whose approach is similar although not as poetic. In *Detskiye gody* nature participates in Seryozha's life just as much as his family and Yevseich; it leads a life of its own, not in the background but in the forefront of the work.

V

Critics writing about **Detskiye gody Bagrova vnuka** have failed to analyse the role of the narrator. They take it for granted that Seryozha is the narrator, and Mashinsky repeats the common theme that in the book life is seen with the eyes of a child.[89] He stresses later on in the same chapter that Aksakov's memory faithfully reproduced all the events of the past, which had lived side by side with the artistic fantasy of the writer.[90]

The problem of the narrator nevertheless still remains unsolved, as well as the question of why Aksakov endowed Seryozha with a different surname from his own and disclaimed that there was a link between **Vospominaniya** and **Detskiye gody.**

As a work **Vospominaniya** is much less intimate than **Detskiye gody,** and involves mainly Aksakov himself and hardly any other members of his family. In **Detskiye gody** on the other hand practically all the members of his family are involved and some were still alive at the time of writing. It is also possible that by changing the names Aksakov could find a better perspective between himself and his characters, disassociate himself just a little bit more from them, especially from Seryozha, for however old and wise a person may be, it is always difficult to portray oneself truthfully and, although Seryozha is a very good child, he is excessively cowardly and far too dependent on his mother. This Aksakov understood only later on, as he points out in his book. Nonetheless it must have been both difficult and painful for him to describe himself as faithfully as he does, therefore laying himself open to the kind of criticism which Stankevich hastened to provide. This is inevitably a risk any memoirist must take when writing his autobiography but it does help to have a mask, even if it is a very transparent one.

The narrator is an interesting phenomenon. Tolstoy and Gor'ky endowed their childhood reminiscences with a hero, the child himself. Aksakov does not have a hero; he portrays worlds which are independent of one another and overlap only at times; the world of the little Seryozha is by necessity dependent on the world of the adults around him, but that world could have existed just as well without Seryozha: the characters of Sof'ya Nikolavna and Aleksey Stepanych, old Bagrov and the peasants would have been unaffected. It is not Seryozha but Aksakov himself who directs our attention to the child. Pascal points this out:

> . . . With exemplary discretion Aksakoff directs us firmly to what the child knows or feels, so that all events become the substance of his awakening consciousness.[91]

Aksakov is there all the time in the background, adding his comments on the effect of roads on health,[92] exclaiming about the joys of hunting and fishing, sketching nature, reminiscing about Praskov'ya Ivanovna,[93] seeing himself as a child and analysing the feelings of the child as only an adult can, yet remaining one with the child. We know from the accounts of Aksakov's son that all his life he was addicted to fishing and hunting, and Sergey Timofeyevich repeats this on numerous occasions in his book; we also learn from Ivan Sergeyevich that his father always kept to the strict precepts of truth and honesty that he had been taught as a child by his mother and father, and that he never cured himself of excessive enthusiasm for anything that he liked.

Mashinsky's assumption, made by generations of critics before him, that **Detskiye gody** is life seen through the eyes of a child is incorrect. This would be impossible, just as a completely faithful reproduction is impossible. In any autobiography, however honest, there is bound to be an element of distortion. What little of it there is in Aksakov's work comes across in the form of the gentle nostalgia that pervades the whole book. Children seldom suffer from nostalgia, for they are usually unaware of the passing of time.

VI

In the history of literature and particularly memoir literature Aksakov's **Detskiye gody** is 'unsurpassed as a revelation of childhood',[94] while amongst the many other reminiscences of childhood it remains, as Hudson wrote, a 'notable exception'. Hudson pointed out:

> Another difficulty in the way of those who write of their childhood is that unconscious artistry will steal or sneak in to erase unseemly lines and blots. The poor, miserable autobiographer naturally desires to make his personality as interesting to the reader as it appears to himself. I feel this strongly in reading other men's recollections of their early years. There are however a few notable exceptions, the best one I know being Serge Aksakoff's **History of my childhood**; and in his case the picture was not falsified, simply because the temper, the tastes and passions of his early boyhood . . . endured unchanged to the end and kept him a boy in heart. . . .[95]

Alsakov's **Detskiye gody** is notable for one more exception: the all-pervading peace of the work. Not only has the author found internal peace, he is also at peace with the world. In literature this is a very rare phenomenon.

Notes

1. S. T. Aksakov, *Sobraniye sochineniy,* 4 vols, Moscow, 1956, I, pp. 285-582. Later in the notes this collection is referred to simply as 'Aksakov'.

2. N. Barsukov, *Zhizn' i trudy M. P. Pogodina,* 22 vols, St. Petersburg, 1888-1910, XV, p. 287.

3. For an English version see S. Aksakoff, *Years of Childhood,* trans. J. D. Duff, Oxford, 1951.

4. M. Friedberg, *Russian Classics in Soviet Jackets,* Columbia, 1962, pp. 70, 145.

5. The following critics have written unfavourable reviews of Aksakov's work, but have usually stressed its literary merit: N. A. Dobrolyubov, 'Raznyye sochineniya S. Aksakova', in *Polnoye sobraniye sochineniy,* 9 vols, Moscow & Leningrad, 1961-64, IV, pp. 16-178; N. P. Belkin, 'Problema polozhitel'nogo geroya v avtobiograficheskoy trilogii Gor'kogo', *Gor'kovskiye chteniya,* Moscow & Leningrad, 1949, pp. 89-90; S. Vengerov, *Kritiko-biograficheskiy slovar',* 6 vols, St Petersburg, 1889-1897, V, pp. 149-200; 'The Objective Russian', *The Nation,* London, 1916, Vol. XIX, p. 24; M. A. Protopopov, *Literaturno-kriticheskiye kharakteristiki,* St Petersburg, 1898, pp. 285-303; A. Stankevich, 'Detskiye gody Bagrova vnuka', *Ateney,* Moscow, 1858, No. xiv, pp. 337-356; T-L., 'Raznyye sochineniya S. T. Aksakova', *Otechestvennyye zapiski,* St Petersburg, 1859, No. ii, pp. 123-129.

6. The following critics have taken a very fair and reasonable stand towards *Detskiye gody*: A. M. Skabichevsky, *Istoriya noveyshey russkoy literatury,* St Petersburg, 1891, p. 203; V. F. Savodnik, *Istoriya russkoy literatury,* 2 vols, Moscow, 1909, pp. 332-341; S. Trubachov, *Russky biograficheskiy slovar',* St Petersburg [n.d.], Vol. 1, pp. 103-107; P. Milyukov, *Iz istorii russkoy intelligentsii,* St Petersburg, 1902, pp. 52-72; V. Shenrok, 'S. T. Aksakov i yego sem'ya', *Zhurnal Ministerstva Narodnogo Prosveshcheniya,* St Petersburg, 1904, Vol. CCCLV, pp. 355-418, Vol. CCCLVI, pp. 166, 229-290; A. Gornfel'd (ed.), *Detskiye gody Bagrova vnuka,* Moscow, 1941, pp. 5-18; V. Soloukhin (ed.), *Detskiye gody Bagrova vnuka,* Moscow, 1962, pp. 3-8; K. S. Nefelov, *Russkaya literatura v biografiyakh i obraztsakh,* Prague, 1946, pp. 117-119; V. S. Pritchett, *The Living Novel,* Dublin, 1960, pp. 244-250; R. Pascal, *Design and Truth in Autobiography,* London, 1960, pp. 86-89; E. Salaman, *The Great Confession,* London, 1973, pp. 7-29; A. I. Khomyakov, 'S. T. Aksakov. Osobennosti yego darovaniya—yego iskrennost', *Sobraniye sochineniy,* 2 vols, Moscow, 1878, I, pp. 717-723; 'A Child in Russia', *The Spectator,* London, 1916, Vol. CXVI, pp. 754-75; S. Waterlow, 'Serge Aksakoff', *The New Statesman,* London, 1916, Vol. VI, pp. 595-596; L. Pearsall-Smith, 'Aksakoff', *The New Statesman,* London, 1918, Vol. X, pp. 354-355; 'The Boyhood of Serge Aksakoff', *The Saturday Review,* London, 1916, Vol. CXXI, pp. 210-211; 'A Child of Russia', *Times Literary Supplement,* London, 1916, 24 February, p. 91; V. Desnitsky, 'Avtobiograficheskiye povesti M. Gor'kogo', in *M. Gor'ky,* Leningrad, 1959, pp. 316-348; F. D. Reeve, *The Russian Novel,* London, 1966, pp. 280-283.

7. The following critics think there is an element of idealisation in the book: E. lo Gatto, *Storia della letteratura russa,* 5 vols, Florence, 1935-1943, IV, pp. 183-192; K. Waliszewski, *A History of Russian Literature,* London, 1900, pp. 330-332; W. E. Harkins, *Dictionary of Russian Literature,* London, 1957, pp. 3-4.

8. See M. N. Longinov (intr.), S. T. Aksakov, *Semeynaya khronika,* Vienna, 1922, p. 3.

9. K. P. Arkhangel'sky, 'Sreda, gde ros Aksakov i kul'turnyye vliyaniya na nego v detstve', in *S. T. Aksakov—yego zhizn' i sochineniya,* ed. V. Pokrovsky, Moscow, 1905, pp. 5-41.

10. Aksakov, I, p. 287: "I do not know myself if it is possible to believe completely in everything which my memory has preserved. . . . Of course, I cannot remember things in a connected way, in uninterrupted sequence: but many events live on in my memory with all the bright colouring, all the liveliness of yesterday."

11. Professor Pascal points out: "If he [the author] treats childhood without reference to what he has become, it tends to be in many parts irrelevant to his story and to reflect perhaps a sentimental indulgence in his private memories. . . ." Because of the inner dialogue existing throughout the book Aksakov can be spared this criticism. (R. Pascal, *Design and Truth in Autobiography,* London, 1960, p. 95.)

12. P. Milyukov, op. cit., p. 57.

13. V. S. Pritchett, *The Living Novel,* Dublin, 1960, p. 244.

14. Aksakov, I, pp. 358, 536, passim.

15. Ibid., pp. 332-333.

16. Ibid., p. 536.

17. Ibid., p. 465.

18. R. Pascal, op. cit., p. 184.

19. Aksakov, I, p. 344.

20. See footnotes 6 & 7.

21. Aksakov, I, p. 487.

22. Ibid., p. 320.

23. Ibid., p. 580.

24. P. Milyukov, op. cit., p. 57.

25. Aksakov, I, p. 513.

26. Ibid., p. 528.

27. Ibid., p. 454.

28. Ibid., pp. 571-572.

29. Aleksey Stepanych finds both his wife and Seryozha sobbing hysterically, after Sof'ya Nikolavna had accused her son of forgetting that he had a mother (I, p. 505). Aleksey Stepanych, having listened to what had occurred as told to him by Seryozha, says:

> Охота вам мучить себя понапрасну из пустяков и растраивать свое здоровье. ты еще ребенок, а матери твоей грешно.

After which he empties a bucket of cold water over his son. (I, p. 506).

30. Ibid.

31. V. S. Pritchett, op. cit., p. 246.

32. Aksakov, I, pp. 559-563.

33. M. Baring, *An Outline of Russian Literature,* Oxford, 1945, p. 158.

34. G. Moore, *Avowals,* London, 1924, p. 56.

35. Gosse talking to Moore says: 'We had an interesting talk; . . . you maintaining that Serge Aksakoff was not the principal character, but Serge's father, whereas I looked upon the narrator as the chief character. But I can see now that I was wrong, for Serge does not attempt to narrate himself like Rousseau. . . .' (Ibid.)

36. Aksakov, I, p. 570.

37. Ibid., p. 451.

38. Ibid., p. 564.

39. Ibid., p. 569.

40. Ibid., p. 575.

41. L. Pearsall-Smith, 'Aksakoff', *The New Statesman,* London, 1918, Vol. X, p. 355.

42. A. Stankevich, 'Detskiye gody Bagrova vnuka', *Ateney,* Moscow, 1858, No. 14, pp. 343-344, 347, 353.

43. S. Vengerov, op. cit., Vol. V, p. 180.

44. Aksakov, I, p. 306.

45. Ibid., p. 314.

46. Ibid., p. 317.

47. Ibid., p. 398.

48. Ibid., p. 436.

49. Ibid., p. 498.

50. Ibid., p. 500.

51. Ibid., p. 322.

52. Ibid., p. 315.

53. Ibid., p. 441.

54. Aksakov writes:

> впоследствии понял я высокий смысл этих простых слов, которые успокаивают всякое волнение, усмиряют всякий человеческий ропот и под благодатною силою которых до сих пор живет православная русь. ясно и тихо становится на душе человека, с верою сказавшего и с верою услышавшего их.

> (Ibid.)

55. K. Golovin, *Russkiy roman i russkoye obshchestvo,* St Petersburg, 1897, p. 114.

56. Aksakov, I, p. 417.

57. The scene which Aksakov portrays is pathetic and at the same time very humorous:

> сели за стол и принялись так кушать (за исключением моей матери), что я с удивлением смотрел на всех. тетушка татьяна степановна разливала налимью уху из огромной кастрюли и, накладывая груды икры и печенок, приговаривала: 'Покушайте, матушка, братец, сестрица, икорки-то и печеночек-то ведь как батюшка-то любил их . . .' я сам видел как слезы у ней капали в тарелку. точно так же и другие плакали и ели с удивительным аппетитом.

> (Ibid., p. 418)

58. Ibid., p. 573.

59. Ibid., p. 425.

60. Ibid., p. 576.

61. Ibid., p. 320.

62. Ibid., pp. 316-327.

63. Ibid., pp. 308, 407.

64. Ibid., pp. 311-312.

65. Ibid., pp. 381-386.

66. Ibid., p. 376.

67. Ibid., p. 385. In English measurements this is equivalent to twenty-one inches and thirty stone. The meaning of the Russian is controversial. A more natural translation might be that the man was twelve *vershki* tall—in which case one would, however, need to assume that Aksakov did not know what a *vershok* was!

68. Ibid., p. 386.

69. Ibid., p. 489.

70. Ibid.

71. Ibid., pp. 488-491.

72. Ibid., p. 537.

73. Ibid., pp. 536-539.

74. Ibid., pp. 460-462.

75. Ibid., p. 292.

76. Ibid., p. 396.

77. Ibid., pp. 372-373.

78. Ibid., pp. 556-557.

79. Ibid., pp. 423-424.

80. Ibid., pp. 366-370.

81. Ibid., p. 363.

82. Ibid., p. 419.

83. Ibid., pp. 292-293.

84. Aksakov wrote:

> Деревня, не подмосковная,—далекая деревня, в ней только можно чувствовать полную, не оскорбленную людьми жизнь природы . . . туда бежать от праздности, пустоты и недостатка интересов . . . вместе с благовонным, свободным, освежительным воздухом вдохнете вы в себя безмятежность мысли, кротость чувства, снисхождение к другим и даже к самому себе . . .
>
> (IV, p. 11)

85. N. V. Gogol', *Myortvyye dushi*, 2 vols, Moscow, 1965, II, p. 461.

86. Aksakov, I, p. 331.

87. Ibid., pp. 503-504, passim.

88. S. Dudyshkin, 'Semeynaya khronika S. T. Aksakova', *Otechestvennyye zapiski*, Moscow, 1856, Vol. CV, p. 74.

89. S. Mashinsky, *S. T. Aksakov. Zhizn' i tvorchestvo*, Moscow, 1961, p. 427.

90. Ibid., p. 444.

91. R. Pascal, op. cit., p. 88.

92. Aksakov, I, p. 326.

93. Ibid., pp. 477-481.

94. R. Pascal, op. cit., p. 88.

95. W. H. Hudson, *Far Away and Long Ago*, London, 1954, p. 195.

John Bayley (essay date 1978)

SOURCE: Bayley, John. Introduction to *A Russian Schoolboy*, by Sergei Aksakov, translated by J. D. Duff, pp. vii-xi. Oxford: Oxford University Press, 1983.

[*In the following essay, which originally introduced the 1978 edition of* A Russian Schoolboy, *Bayley praises the subtle charm of Aksakov's autobiographical novel. Bayley suggests that the beauty and poignancy of Aksakov's descriptions of youth lie in their simplicity.*]

Aksakov, who was born in 1791, is one of the earliest of the great Russian writers, older than Pushkin, and already a mature man of thirty when Tolstoy was born. In terms of English literature, it is strange to think he was four years older than Keats. Strange, because Aksakov, like Keats, grew up at a time when literature was still dominated by the classical ideal, in which literary expression, both in poetry and prose, had to be squeezed into some appropriately conventional form. Keats's *Ode to A Nightingale* transforms that ideal while still depending on it: in its magical verses we can feel a real young man listening to a real bird singing under the trees in Hampstead. It conveys almost involuntarily the sense of being young, with all its joy and sorrow and romance. Aksakov was fifty when he began to write about his experience of being young, and he wrote in plain and simple prose, but his recollections had for his contemporaries something of the same revelation of freshness and charm that Keats's poems had for an English audience.

It seems so obvious to us that a masterpiece might be written by merely recalling the humdrum events and pleasures and anxieties of one's life as a schoolboy, but it was not at all obvious in 1840, either in England or in Russia. Nor, in all probability, would Aksakov have had the courage to attempt it, if it had not been for his friendship with Gogol, the most extraordinary and original genius in the history of Russian letters. Aksakov had become great friends with Gogol, had indeed set up a sort of cult of Gogol worship among his Moscow friends. Gogol's genius was not in the least like Aksakov's: it was fantastic and theatrical, full of pathos and peculiar humour. But in his first major work, *Evenings on a Farm at Dikanka*, Gogol had conveyed something of the homely charm of Russian rural life.

Ever since he grew up Aksakov had been attempting to write. But his enthusiasm for the stage, of which we hear a good deal in *A Russian Schoolboy*, proved to be something of a red herring. He translated French comedies, wrote a few poor things himself in the same vein, some essays and articles. He took the job of press censor in Moscow (though conservative, he must, one suspects, have been the most uncensorious man to have held that office) and then retired from the public service in 1839, still without having written anything. He had married and had two sons, one of whom, Constantin, was particularly devoted to his father and lived with him till his death.

Aksakov's life had been remarkably uneventful. But now suddenly, aged nearly fifty and inspired by Gogol, he began to write *A Family Chronicle*, a memoir of his parents and grandparents. Grandfather Aksakov, or Bagrov as he is called in the memoir, was a more than life-sized figure, a Russian patriarch who had removed with all his possessions, flocks, herds and serfs, to the distant province of Orenburg, near Siberia. There he built up a large estate, and there his grandson the writer was born.

Everyone who enjoys *A Russian Schoolboy* would also enjoy this remarkable portrait of a Homeric figure, obeyed unquestioningly by all his family and dependants, in general as kindly as he was dignified and independent, but given to sudden bursts of uncontrollable rage. He was especially fond of his daughter-in-law, the writer's mother, obviously a woman of great energy and character, as we learn from *A Russian Schoolboy.* The portrait in the earlier memoir is more detailed, and Aksakov analyses there with remarkable shrewdness and understanding the relations between his mother and father, which were by no means entirely happy ones. His father was an eminently good-hearted man, but with none of his mother's passionate and affectionate temperament. He had, his son observes, the 'gold' of love but none of 'the small change': he could not be tender and assiduous daily, and over trivial matters. And there was more than that. One passage is so revealing, both of the author's sympathy and understanding, and of how he may have come to have the sort of temperament he did, that it is worth quoting in full.

> Alexei Stepanich [the author's father] was a man singularly unable to appreciate excessive display of feeling, or to sympathize with it, from whatever cause it arose. Thus his wife's power of passionate devotion frightened him: he dreaded it, just as he used to dread his father's furious fits of anger. Excessive feeling always produces an unpleasant impression upon quiet, unemotional people: they cannot recognize such a state of mind to be natural, and regard it as a morbid condition to which some persons are liable at times. They disbelieve in the permanence of a mental composure which may break down at any moment; and they are afraid of people with such a temperament. And fear is fatal to love, even to a child's love for his parents. And in point of mutual sympathy and understanding I must say that the relations between Alexei Stepanich and his wife, instead of becoming closer, as might have been expected, grew gradually less intimate. This may seem strange, but it often happens thus in life.

The tone is of course quite different, but for perception and insight, that might be compared with one of Tolstoy's descriptions of domestic life, just as *A Russian Schoolboy* is in the same class of literary achievement as Tolstoy's *Childhood, Boyhood and Youth.* We may form the impression, too, of which we also get hints in *A Russian Schoolboy,* that though the young Aksakov passionately loved his mother, and was so miserable away from her that he had to be brought home from school, his temperament actually resembled much more

that of his father. Or rather, perhaps, that the two extremes were balanced in him, so that strong emotions were held in check by an instinctive placidity and repose. That may well be the clue to the charm of his literary personality, as it is to the secret of his style.

Something like this seems to me to be borne out by the delightful account in *A Russian Schoolboy* of his Aunt Tatyana's marriage to her elderly admirer, the retired Lieutenant-Colonel. Their establishment, neat as a new pin, with its ludicrous lap-dogs and pot-plants and cage-birds that sang 'louder and more gaily' than anyone else's, is just the kind of thing Aksakov most liked:

> I wondered whether this was not the true happiness for man—a life without passions and excitements, a life undisturbed by insoluble questions and unsatisfied desires. The peace and order of their life remained long with me; I felt a vague agitation and regret for the lack of something so near at hand and so easily procured; but, whenever I put to myself the question, 'Would you like to be what your uncle is?'—I was afraid to reply, and my feeling of agitation vanished instantly.

That is a subtle passage, of the kind not infrequent in Aksakov's writings. He is attracted by absolute contentment and calm, and the spectacle of it, but when it comes to the point he realizes he cannot live that way. 'Insoluble questions and unsatisfied desires' do remain to haunt him, and us; which is why Aksakov, even at his most idyllic and reposeful, never cloys us, or seems to be aiming at a picture of life which is too pleasant to be true.

The success of *A Family Chronicle,* which first appeared in magazines in the forties, was immediate. Encouraged by it, Aksakov brought out several books on shooting and fishing and sporting activities in his native country and childhood paradise in the province of Orenburg. Turgenev admired them, and Gogol wrote to Aksakov: 'Your birds and fishes are more real than my men and women'. In 1856 the memoirs were published in volume form and confirmed Aksakov's reputation. In the few years that remained to him he produced *Years of Childhood* and *A Russian Schoolboy,* becoming ever more 'himself' in terms of style and manner, giving up any pretence of a fictitional framework—he uses his own name and that of the estate, Aksakovo—and shedding even the kind of speculation that had caused him to invent, for instance, scenes between his parents and grandparents which he could not have known about at first-hand.

In many ways this is a further gain, for no one is more persuasive and convincing about plain facts than Aksakov. Do we want to know how a school for the gentry was run at the close of the eighteenth century; how people travelled in winter across the great rivers and snowbound steppes of eastern Russia; how butterflies were collected and mounted; how fish were caught, and what fish they were; where sporting guns were made and what they looked like; what subjects were studied in school and at what ages? Aksakov will tell us, and in the most congenial manner, never boring and never obtrusive. Younger readers in particular will respond to this effective simplicity and to all the detailed information about another country and age. But, more than that, they will become entirely absorbed, I think, in the progress of young Aksakov from childhood to young manhood. He is a hero with whom we identify so readily that we hardly know we are doing so. And he is full of quiet humour too, as when he tells us about the play they organized at college in which he played two parts—'an old hermit in the first two acts, and a robber chief, who got killed by a pistol shot, in the third. I distinguished myself chiefly as the hermit.'

There are comparatively few books about being young which can be read with equal pleasure by young and old alike. The probable reason is that most authors in this genre try too deliberately to catch the attention of the young, or to identify with them. One of Aksakov's secrets is that he seems to co-exist equally with himself when young and when old, and never to call attention—in the manner that can be so irritating in Dickens and Thackeray for instance—to the difference between them. In my category of books for both young and old would come Mark Twain's *Huckleberry Finn,* Kipling's Puck stories, Alain-Fournier's *Le Grand Meaulnes,* Stevenson's *Treasure Island* and *Kidnapped,* even such tales avowedly written for the young as Hardy's *Our Exploits at West Poley,* or Arthur Ransome's *Swallows and Amazons.* (Ransome, who knew Russia well, was incidentally a great admirer of Aksakov's work.) All these are masterpieces in a rare genre, and though it does not resemble them **A Russian Schoolboy** will be appreciated by the same readers and in the same sort of way.

David Cecil (essay date 1983)

SOURCE: Cecil, David. Introduction to *Years of Childhood,* by Sergei Aksakov, translated by J. D. Duff, pp. vii-xiii. Oxford: Oxford University Press, 1983.

[*In the following essay, Cecil discusses the relationship between memory and narrative in* Years of Childhood. *In Cecil's view, Aksakov's memoir represents a vital chronicle of rural life in Russia during the late eighteenth and early nineteenth centuries.*]

The first thing to be said about this book [*Years of Childhood*] is that it is one of the world's few literary masterpieces; for me unrivalled, the best book of childhood reminiscences I have ever read.

Its author's genius flowered late. Sergei Aksakov was born in 1791 in Ufa, a town 700 miles east of Moscow, the son of Alexei Aksakov, an official of the local law-courts, and his wife Sofya, the daughter of another local officer. Alexei's father, however, was a country proprietor: a man of outstanding personality, gifted and enterprising, who during the later part of the eighteenth century had sold his inherited land and purchased 1,200 acres several days' journey away in the rural district of Orenburg. Thither he moved his family and his serfs—for these were still the days of serfdom—to create a new and prosperous patriarchal settlement called in this book Bagrovo, complete with a manor-house, a mill, huts for the peasants and later a church.

In 1796 he died and Alexei his son decided to give up his work at Ufa and carry on his father's life and work at Bagrovo. He was ready to do this for he too was by nature a countryman, interested in farming, a keen sportsman and who liked a quiet rustic life. Not so his wife, brought up a townswoman, beautiful, sociable, intelligent and who had already made herself a centre of cultivated society at Ufa. Though a more powerful personality than her husband and often at odds with him, she loved him and agreed. The rest of her life was spent mainly at Bagrovo, her existence there made easier by the fact that Alexei was also the heir to a rich widowed cousin, Praskovya Ivanovna Kurolesova, a wilful, dominating and eccentric personality fond of conversation and social life, who filled her house with guests and liked her heir and his wife and family to spend some months of the year visiting her.

Meanwhile the children—there were to be five of them—were happy at Bagrovo. Sergei was more than happy. He discovered in himself what was to be a permanent and passionate love of the country and country life. Delightedly he observed trees and flowers, insects, birds and animals. It was his great pleasure to accompany his father when he was inspecting the peasants at their work on the land, and still more when he went fishing and shooting. Indeed, before little Sergei was six years old he had got his first chance to fish himself. From then on and for the rest of his life he was a dedicated and enthusiastic sportsman. At the same time, his mother saw to it that his education was not neglected. Mentally precocious, he had learned to read early: he enjoyed reading almost as much as he enjoyed fishing.

In **Years of Childhood** he tells his story up to the age of eight, when his parents thought he had come to an age when he needed a more thorough education and sent him to school at Kazan. He was to stay there—but for a year's interval—first at school then at college until he was eighteen years old. After he had got over an early acute attack of homesickness, he enjoyed those Kazan years, largely because he occupied his time there less in regular study than in reading poetry, collecting butterflies, taking part in theatricals, and talking to his friends.

His mature life was spent partly in town and partly at Bagrovo. Now and again he took a temporary job in the government service; but, since he was a man of independent means, he did this no longer than he wanted to. He married when he was twenty-four, happily, and had several children, including two intelligent sons with whom he had an affectionate relationship.

Aksakov from schooldays on had been taken with the idea of authorship. He wrote an occasional poem, play or translation, but till 1840 nothing he produced showed signs of any special literary gift. In that year, partly inspired by Gogol with whom he became friendly and who, it is said, made him realize the possibilities of Russian country life as a literary subject, he began writing sketches. Some were about sport and some recorded his own memories of the past. In these sketches, his particular genius first began to show itself. It revealed itself fully in 1856 with the publication of the book entitled in its English translation *A Russian Gentleman,* which described the life and character of his grandfather; it also recorded the earlier history of his parents and of Praskovya Ivanovna. The whole composes a vivid and authentic account of country life in late-eighteenth-century Russia.

Nothing like it had appeared in Russian literature before. It was a sensational success and set Aksakov in one bound in the first rank of living writers, praised to the skies by such younger men of genius as Turgenev and the twenty-eight-year-old Tolstoy. Aksakov followed it up in 1856 by *A Russian Schoolboy,* an account of his years at Kazan. *Years of Childhood,* which covered the intervening years, appeared in 1858, a few months before he died at the age of sixty-five.

The three books form a trilogy; but each is an independent work that composes itself into a unity and can be read without reference to the others. All three maintain the same high level; which one likes best is a question of taste. The first is the most dramatic, containing as it does the terrible story of Praskovya's first marriage and the ups and downs which characterized the courtship of Aksakov's parents, and the whole book centring on the formidable and lovable figure of his grandfather and set against the background of a society to us at least as strange and as picturesque as that of Elizabethan England. *Years of Childhood* is less sensational but has a more universal interest: for, though the society it portrays is primitive by Western standards in its structure and customs, we are shown them through the eyes of a child who seems a contemporary of our own; or rather, a child in any period, so real and recognizable are his feelings and thoughts and reactions. The other characters in his story too—his parents, his little sister, the dashing uncles who tease him, and Evseich the delightful devoted male serf whose job it is to look after little Sergei—strike us like contemporaries; odd, foreign contemporaries living in a world unlike our own, but not remote from us in the way that characters in English books written in the same period so often seem to be. As for Bagrovo, whether in springtime with its woods and deep clear streams and fresh smelling meadows all astir with the song and flight of birds, or frozen and snowbound in winter, it is so vividly realized to us that one can hardly believe one is not reading an account written by someone who has just spent a year there. The book stays in the memory less as a picture of a foreign country and a bygone age than as an evocation of child life seen from a child's outlook anywhere and at any time.

Paradoxically, this impression is due to its being a product of a genius peculiarly Russian. The great Russian writers of the nineteenth century are distinguished from other great writers in particular by their extreme, relentless truthfulness: the most characteristic Russian genius is primarily and strictly inspired by fact. Even in its novels the line between fact and fiction is thin: some of Turgenev's *Sportsman's Sketches* are almost pieces of autobiography. In contrast, Aksakov's trilogy sometimes seems like a piece of fiction. Especially in its first section, he recounts conversations that took place before his birth of which he must have been told the substance; but he has taken the liberty to retell them in such a way as to make them clear and coherent. All the same, there is no question of them being fictional. He is careful to be as vigilantly true to the facts that he has learnt from others as to those that have been part of his own experience.

Of course Aksakov's are never facts in the more limited and prosaic sense of the term; they are facts vitalized and illuminated by the author's continuous reaction to them, by his live and personal response to what in them fires his imagination and stirs his feelings. Moreover, these are always a child's feelings and reactions. Here it is that his are so different from most famous books of childhood reminiscence. These nearly always depict the past as seen through the eyes of a mature man or woman looking back on it and with their vision of it coloured and modified by the light of subsequent experience and the mood which this evokes in them. If the childhood has been happy, like that of Charles Lamb for instance, this mood is likely to be tender and nostalgic: if unhappy, like Maxim Gorky's, the mood is dark and embittered. But Aksakov's picture is not modified in this way. After describing an episode in his childhood he sometimes pauses to reflect on it from the point of view of a grown man; but his actual description is of his feelings at the time they occurred, freshly and accurately preserved in his memory. He can even recapture the physical sensations of early childhood; for example, the pleasure he felt when barely three years old at the resin on his nursery window-frames:

Then I begged successfully for little bits or drops of
the fir resin which was everywhere on the walls and
window-frames, melting and dropping and making little
streams, cooling and drying as it went, and hanging in
the air like icicles, with a shape exactly like the common icicles of winter. I was very fond of the smell of
resin, which was sometimes used to fumigate our nursery. I smelt the sweet transparent blobs of resin, admired them and played with them; they melted in my
hands and made my long thin fingers sticky . . .

With a similar and subtle accuracy Aksakov traces a
child's mental processes, in particular the way truth and
imagination can blend in his mind so that he scarcely
knows one from the other. Listen to his account of his
excitement after first reading *The Arabian Nights* at the
age of five:

With what avidity, with what insatiable interest I devoured these stories! Yet I knew all the time that they
were mere inventions, descriptions of what never was
and never can be in this world. What, then, is the secret of the spell they laid on me? I believe it is to be
found in that passion for the marvellous which is innate, more or less, in all children, and was less repressed by sober sense in my case than in most. While
reading the book I was carried away as usual by excitement and enthusiasm; but I was not content with reading it myself: I began to repeat the contents to my sister and aunt with such burning animation and what
may be called self-forgetfulness, that, without being
aware of it, I filled out the narratives of Scheherazade
with many details of my own invention; I spoke of all I
had read, exactly as if I had been on the spot and seen
it with my own eyes. When I had excited the attention
and curiosity of my two hearers, I began, complying
with their wishes, to read the book to them aloud; and
then my own additions were detected and pointed out
. . . I was much taken aback by such an accusation,
and forced to reflect. I was a very honest boy at that
age, and could not endure lying; but in this case I saw
myself that I had really put into Scheherazade's mouth
a great deal which she never said. I was surprised myself, not to find in the book what I believed I had read
there, and what was firmly fixed in my head. I became
more cautious, and kept myself in hand, until I got excited; when once excited, I forgot all precautions, and
my heated imagination usurped absolute power.

With equal truth Aksakov recalls his reactions as a child
to other people. He and his mother loved each other
with a lyrical intensity and he approved of such love as
least as much as did any Victorian writer celebrating
the sacredness of the domestic affections. This does not
prevent him from noting his mother's embarrassment at
the uncontrolled surprise and emotion he showed when
on a visit to a rich man's house he first heard an orchestra playing: she did not like her host to think that
someone as civilized as she wanted him to think her
was the mother of a child so naïf and rustic as never
before to have listened to an orchestra. The typical Victorian writer would have shrunk from admitting this
streak of snobbishness in a mother he loved. Not so Ak-

sakov. He did not hold it against his mother: it was
simply a fact he remembered about her and he saw no
reason not to mention it. That he does so makes it all
the easier for us to believe him when he expresses his
love for her with so extraordinary an intensity.

Children of necessity live and judge by feeling and
little Aksakov's feelings were unusually strong and uninhibited. Some were distressing: the acute panic he felt
when his parents left him and his sister behind alone
with his grandparents at Bagrovo; the chill horror that
struck him when the old miller was drowned so that for
the first time he realized the meaning of death. But Aksakov's was a happy childhood and the book records
pleasant feelings more often than unpleasant: his delight in playing with the little sister he loved so much,
his enraptured absorption in a fairy tale told him by a
peasant woman; the intoxicating thrill that went through
him the first time he went fishing. The English are a nation of sportsmen, but no English writer surely has
communicated the special delight felt by the sportsman
as vividly as does Aksakov. He is nearer to the original
primitive hunting animal in man; almost as near to the
hound as he is to the horseman. As so often and paradoxically, love of the chase goes in him with love of
animals, with his passionate affection for his dog Surka,
with the untiring pleasure he takes in bird watching.

Both join together to contribute to the unique joy roused
in him by his sense of the natural world. Once again
this is a Russian kind of joy, always and strictly related
to his sense of fact. There is nothing Wordsworthian or
mystical about it; Aksakov does not look on visible nature as the expression of some transcendental spirit. But
more than Wordsworth he feels himself part of it. At
the coming of spring he seems actually to identify with
the young trees bursting into bud, with the torrential
waters cracking the ice and flooding the fields, with the
returning migrant birds sweeping in exultant myriads
down from the sky. Because he is a child, he is able to
feel closer to trees and torrents and birds than a grown
man could do. But with a difference; unlike trees and
torrents and birds, children have souls. Though the child
Aksakov was not a mystic, he was far from being un-
spiritual. Indeed the most unforgettable pages in this
book are those in which, as it were involuntarily and by
implication rather than statement, he reveals this. For
example in his account of a night spent camping by
firelight on his first journey to Bagrovo:

Words cannot convey the pleasure I got from the kindling of this fire: I ran constantly from the big pile to
the small one, carrying shavings and sticks and dry
grass to keep the flame bright, till I got so hot that my
mother had to make me sit down beside her. We had
tea and then chicken broth, which was boiled for us by
our cook. It was then settled that my mother and the
children should pass the night in the carriage, and my
father in the covered cart. My mother soon lay down

and put my sister beside her; the child had long been asleep in her nurse's arms. But I had no wish to sleep: I sat up with my father, talking of our halt next day, to which I looked forward with joyful impatience; but in the middle of our talk we both, for some reason, became thoughtful and sat for a long time without saying a word. The sky glittered with stars; the fragrance of the drying grasses of the steppe filled the air; the streamlet babbled in the hollow beneath; the blazing fire threw a strong light on our servants, as they sat round a kettle and supped their smoking porridge, laughing and talking merrily; the horses too, as they munched their oats, reflected the firelight on one side. 'Time for you to go to bed, Serezha,' said my father, after a long silence. He kissed me and made the sign of the cross on me, and then put me in the carriage, taking care not to wake my mother. It was long before I went to sleep.

This single paragraph is enough surely to show that *Years of Childhood* is a masterpiece.

Andrew R. Durkin (essay date 1983)

SOURCE: Durkin, Andrew R. "The Strategy of the Hunter." In *Sergei Aksakov and Russian Pastoral*, pp. 66-88. New Brunswick, N.J.: Rutgers University Press, 1983.

[*In the following chapter, Durkin analyzes the role of the narrative persona in Aksakov's writings on hunting and fishing. According to Durkin, the natural world, as well as the act of describing it, provided Aksakov with a crucial release from the stifling, artificial atmosphere of Moscow society.*]

Aksakov's works during his real literary career, from the 1840s until his death in 1859, can be seen, from one point of view, as a series of attempts to enter literature, specifically, prose literature, through genres that were either nonliterary or on the edge of literature (**"The Blizzard"** was Aksakov's only earlier original prose work and derives in part from a fragment of poetry). The later 1840s and 1850s were of course a period of great ferment in Russian literature, of debuts and literary experimentation, primarily in realistic prose and often in forms that had previously been deemed peripheral or subliterary: sketches, notes, memoirs, in a certain sense even the novel itself. Aksakov was by far the oldest of these debutants, but as though to compensate for this fact, many of his works can be considered successive debuts, presenting themselves as new forms or as novel recombinations of existing forms.

Aksakov's first two lengthy prose works, *Notes on Fishing* (*Zapiski ob uzhen'e*), 1846, and *Notes of a Hunter of Orenburg Province* (*Zapiski ruzheinogo okhotnika orenburgskoi gubernii*), 1852, represent the initial stage, both chronologically and conceptually, in

Aksakov's campaign for literary stature. They are the furthest of all of Aksakov's works from the standard literary forms, for they are ostensibly handbooks for the angler or hunter, texts which seem to have a purely practical orientation and to lack obvious aesthetic value. However, they also aspire to interest the nonhunting audience and employ a stylistic and structural complexity beyond the requirements of the practical manual.

As a serious hunter and angler, Aksakov was familiar with earlier works on the subject, such as V. A. Levshin's *Book for Hunters of Beasts and Birds* (*Kniga dlia okhotnikov do zverinoi i ptichei lovli*), 1810-1812, which he mentions ironically in the second edition of *Notes on Fishing.*[1] Aksakov intended both his books to meet standards of accuracy and literacy lacking in previous books on the subject: "In Russian, insofar as I know, until the present there has not been printed even a single line about fishing in general or angling in particular that is written by a literate sportsman, intimately knowledgeable in his subject" (4:13). If Aksakov considered his books on fishing and hunting to be improvements on the practical level, their predecessors must have had even less value as literary models.[2] However, the literary potential of a work concerned primarily with nature may have been suggested to Aksakov not by hunting manuals, Russian or foreign, but by writings of naturalists, such as an article entitled "Scenes from the Life of a Naturalist" ("Stseny iz zhizni naturalista") that appeared in N. I. Nadezhdin's *Telescope* (*Teleskop*) in 1832. As Nadezhdin's unofficial associate in *Telescope* and *Rumor* (*Molva*), its supplement, Aksakov was presumably aware of the article; in addition, in his capacity as censor he passed the particular issue of *Telescope* in which the article appeared. "Scenes" consists of a translation of excerpts from J. J. Audubon's *Ornithological Biography* which were quoted at length in a review of the book in *Blackwood's Magazine* for July and August 1831. Although Audubon's brief appearance in *Telescope* can hardly be considered a major influence on Aksakov's hunting books, the precedent of an engaging, yet generally accurate and informative account of natural history in a remote area is worth nothing. In particular, Audubon's sometimes excessive willingness to enter his narrative in the first person and generally to employ his narrating self to validate the entire text is pertinent to the narrative strategy of Aksakov's own hunting books.

From the start, Aksakov intended his works on hunting and fishing to be simultaneously pragmatic and aesthetic and to be the reflection of a definite, if not overly specific, observing personality. The orientation of this personality toward nature was of crucial significance, as he indicated in a letter to Gogol: "I have undertaken to write a book about angling, not only in its technical aspect, but in relation to nature in general; my passionate angler likewise passionately loves the beauties of nature as well; in a word, I have fallen in love with my work and I hope that this book will be pleasant not only for the lover of fishing, but also for everyone whose heart is open to the impressions of early morning, late evening, luxuriant midday, etc."[3] Aksakov's mastery of the technical aspect of fishing can be judged by the frequent mention of fishing, alone or with Konstantin, in his letters. According to a record book dating from the early forties, some 1,500 fish were landed at Abramtsevo from June to October 1846, and like numbers in the summers of 1845 and 1847; fish caught are often tabulated by date and species. Despite this considerable experience, Aksakov distrusted his unaided memory in the description of each species, and strove, like a painter, for complete accuracy of depiction: "I am continuing the dictation of my little book on fishing nearly every morning; at present I'm writing about the fish, but I have forgotten some, and in general it is necessary to describe their appearance from nature; and so all this will be corrected later on."[4]

Having established technical exactness and reliability as the foundation on which the book rests and the source from which its deeper theme draws its validity, Aksakov remained apprehensive about the value of his *Notes* [*Notes on Fishing*] for the nonfisherman. Praise from Mikhail Pogodin after the book's appearance reassured him that a larger audience would accept his book and that critical opinion, which keenly interested Aksakov throughout his late-blooming career as a writer, would be favorable: "Particularly important for me is the fact that you are not a sportsman and even dislike this form of sport. Therefore, independent of fishing, my little book must have some interest. Reality, truth, sincerity can be sensed in it. I admit that I found all this in it, but I see little reason that others should find it."[5] The qualities of reality, truth, and sincerity that Aksakov considers his book's primary values for the nonfisherman depend on the establishment of the authenticity (as distinct from the accuracy) of the *Notes.* Aksakov sought to achieve this authenticity by emphasizing his identity with the narrator-observer, whose devotion to and experience in angling is such that he has become an expert. Thus the work is not merely an impersonal, informative book; it is "not a treatise on angling, not a natural history of fish. My little book is no more and no less than the simple notes of a passionate sportsman" (4:13).

The entire text, in both its technical and artistic aspects, becomes an expression of this unifying personality, which reveals itself primarily through its memories. Although restricted to one area of activity, *Notes on Fishing* represents an attempt to record a specific individual's experience, as Aksakov indicates in a letter to his son Ivan from the autumn of 1845: "My book is developing in an unexpected manner. With each day this labor becomes more pleasant for me. I have raised from the bottom much that was forgotten, decayed in the dim

repository of my memories. A good deal of myself, of my youthful impressions, will be in this book if I succeed in writing it the way I sometimes imagine it. For people close to me, and for all those who love me, it will have a double worth."[6] Thus Aksakov's first book, in addition to its characteristic blending of genres, also established another recurrent feature of Aksakov's prose: its intensely personal quality of memory. The process of composing each work becomes for Aksakov a means of revivifying the past; the completed work is a form of ordering and preserving a particular aspect of his past, endowing it with value perhaps not apparent in the evanescent moment of experience.

Following the successful appearance of *Notes on Fishing* in 1847, Aksakov undertook a more ambitious project employing the same basic form: a book on hunting. Once again he could draw on a lifetime of observation and expertise, as attested by records he maintained of migration dates in Orenburg province from 1811 to 1826,[7] daily entries of birds bagged, and yearly totals in the hundreds (898 birds in 1813). Aksakov was indeed the passionate hunter he claims to have been in his youth. Brief descriptions in Aksakov's hand of hare, snipe, ducks, and other game have been preserved;[8] Aksakov later employed these early notes in writing his serious work on the subject.

Notes of a Hunter required greater effort than *Notes on Fishing,* not only because of its greater length but also because of the greater significance Aksakov attached to it, both as a personal document and as a literary effort. In its initial concept, however, it was intended as a companion to *Notes on Fishing*: "If God fulfills my wish and I spend this winter in the country, then I will start to write another little book 'on hunting with a gun'; from the age of twelve to thirty-six [i.e., when Aksakov left for Moscow in 1826], I was absolutely madly devoted to this form of hunting. I have already written **'Arrival of Birds in the Spring'**; I think that even a nonhunter can read this fragment with pleasure."[9]

Like *Notes on Fishing,* which Aksakov also referred to as a little, minor book (*knizhka*), this book was to draw on his own past and was addressed to two audiences, the primary one consisting of hunters and the secondary and larger one composed of readers who were only tangentially concerned with the facts of hunting, if at all. Aksakov realized that the second audience must be captured by his style and rhetoric, and he displays considerable concern for the organization and tone: "I've written an enormous article of eight and a half printer's sheets on the grouse. . . . Konsta and Vera praise it highly; but I, while admitting its worth with regard to liveliness and veracity of the description, still see a multitude of shortcomings. . . . The main shortcoming consists in the fact that much is not in its proper place."[10]

Of even more concern to Aksakov than internal order was the problem of creating and maintaining a tone of narration that was in harmony with the subject. During the winter of 1849-1850, when Aksakov was working regularly on his *Notes of a Hunter,* his letters frequently allude to his efforts to avoid any too-apparent departure from the hunter's sensibility in the direction of a self-conscious perception of nature as intrinsically beautiful. Such direct reaction to nature figures more prominently in *Notes on Fishing,* where it suits the somewhat more meditative activity of angling, but even there it is never excessively indulged: "I constantly hold myself in check, lest I get carried away in describing nature and subjects extraneous to hunting. . . . I fear, like fire, senile prattle."[11] In another letter, Aksakov expresses even more clearly his fear of lapsing too readily into a facilely poetic stance: "I can't find the proper tone, can't establish boundaries for myself with accuracy; everything I've written till now displeases me. It's the account of a simple hunter with an unconscious poetic sensitivity, who in the simplicity of his heart isn't aware that he is describing nature poetically. It's a man of letters pretending to be a simple man."[12] To allow the narrator to turn into a naïve poet, or worse, a hackneyed littérateur, would undermine the claim to authenticity implicit throughout the text and call into question the general reliability of the narrator, whose knowledge and memory support the entire text.

Maintaining "a unified depiction, written in the same spirit"[13] was perhaps more difficult in *Notes of a Hunter* than in *Notes on Fishing,* if only because of the differences in stereotype between the somewhat reflective and even garrulous angler and the more taciturn and active hunter. That Aksakov was well aware of the narrator he was creating is further attested by his comments on Turgenev's sympathetic review of the book. While thanking Turgenev for the praise, doubly valuable because Turgenev himself was a serious hunter, and so a member both of the primary and secondary audiences Aksakov was addressing, he takes exception to Turgenev's mention of Shakespeare and Pushkin, for fear that they might "crush my insignificant persona with their enormous personalities."[14] Aksakov is of course hardly using *persona* in its modern sense, but he seems to be contrasting Shakespeare and Pushkin as creative individuals not so much with himself as with the hunter-narrator he has created for his work.

Following the completion of *Notes of a Hunter* and its publication in 1852, Aksakov turned to other subjects, primarily literary memoirs, but he did not completely abandon his interest in the subject of hunting. The second edition of *Notes on Fishing* (*Zapiski ob uzhen'e ryby*) appeared in 1853, with some additions, the most important being a section "On Fish in General" ("O rybakh voobshche"). Aksakov also planned to start an annual journal for hunters, but permission to begin a periodical was denied, and the articles he had intended for it eventually appeared in the *Muscovite* and in a separate volume entitled *Tales and Reminiscences of a Hunter on Various Types of Hunting* (*Rasskazy i vospominaniia okhotnika o raznykh okhotakh*), 1855. Limited to a discussion of various specialized types of hunting such as falconry and snaring with which Aksakov was familiar in his youth, the articles in *Tales and Reminiscences* tend to assume the form of a memoir more consistently than either of its two predecessors. The final interpenetration of memoir and hunt can be seen in the late **"Butterfly Collecting"** (**"Sobiranie babochek"**), 1858, which serves both as the conclusion of Aksakov's memoirs of the University of Kazan and as a discussion of butterfly collecting. While minor, these later texts are helpful in defining Aksakov's notion of the hunt and in elucidating the significance of hunting as a human activity, the major theme of *Notes on Fishing* and *Notes of a Hunter.*

Hunting (*okhota*) of one sort or another constitutes the sole human activity depicted in Aksakov's first three books. The narrator is a hunter, his memories are restricted to that one activity, and his style is partly determined by his being a hunter; his audience, at least the primary (if largely fictive) one, is composed of hunters. The Russian word *okhota* can signify not only the pursuit and capture of wild animals but also any partiality or desire, even a hobby.[15] Aksakov includes both of these meanings in his notion of *okhota,* as can be seen by considering the various activities he chooses to discuss as forms of *okhota*: angling, hunting of game proper, whether with gun, falcon, trap, or snare, collecting butterflies, and even gathering mushrooms. Keeping songbirds, pigeons, and small animals are also included as "hunts that are, so to speak, profitless, which are rewarded only by pleasure" (4:469), but such hobbies clearly skirt the edges of what Aksakov includes in the idea of *okhota.*

The hunt is not fully defined by object, but neither is it adequately determined by the instruments; rod and gun are merely the most generalized means, as is clear from his discussion of special techniques in *Tales and Reminiscences.* What, then, characterizes a valid object of hunting and what constitutes a valid method? In **"Comments and Observations of a Lover of Mushroom Gathering,"** written in 1856, Aksakov discusses the object of the hunt in some detail:

> Among the number of various types of *okhota,* the placid *okhota* of going for mushrooms, or gathering mushrooms, has its place. . . . I am even prepared to prefer gathering mushrooms, because it is necessary to seek them out, consequently it is also possible not to find them; there is here involved a certain skill, knowledge of the habitat of mushrooms, knowledge of the locale, and luck. . . . Here there is uncertainty, unexpectedness, there is success and failure, and all this

together arouses desire [*okhota*] in man and forms its particular interest.

(4:590)

The gathering of mushrooms shares an essential characteristic with other forms of the hunt and indeed its attraction seems to rest almost entirely in that characteristic: one may find mushrooms, but it is also possible not to find them. The element of risk, of probability but not total predictability, is essential. For a hunt to have value, this factor of uncertainty must be preserved even by conscious effort, and Aksakov dismisses the shooting of grouse, attracted by a decoy, from a comfortable blind, with the telling question: "But where then is the hunt?" (4:410). A relationship must be maintained in which "the superiority of the hunter over the hunted cannot be absolute."[16] Hunting involves the pursuit and attempted capture of an elusive being, by means which do not completely eliminate the prey's ability to escape.

A true hunt may involve a certain self-handicapping, in which the hunter's potential for technological advantage is consciously curbed in order to maintain the equilibrium of action. Thus mushroom gathering is oddly enough a perfect hunt; no instruments of any sort are needed and the outcome depends entirely on the hunter's keenness, knowledge, and skill, which alone provide a marginal advantage over the elusive, if sessile, prey. Hunting thus entails a certain ethical dimension: practice, training, and internal discipline outweigh instruments in the hunt and contribute significantly to the pleasure of the pursuit.

Hunting, in the context of the modern world at any rate, demands an acceptance of the terms suggested by nature and thereby a return to it. That the essence of the hunt does not lie in the means of hunting is suggested by a letter from Aksakov to Turgenev, in which he states that he tended to avoid descriptions of equipment in *Notes of a Hunter* because he was rather behind the times in this regard.[17]

In addition to the risk or gamble, hunting also touches another chord in man. As Aksakov says in the opening of *Notes on Fishing,* there is an irrational pull in hunting activities and he directs his text in the first instance to those "fishermen by inclination, *okhotniki* for whom the words 'fishing pole' and 'fishing' are magic words, acting powerfully on the soul. . . . Angling, like other forms of hunting [*okhoty,*] can be both a simple inclination and a powerful passion" (4:9).

Part of the power of hunting derives from its effect on the hunter, from the fact that, as a nonrational but not purposeless or unstructured activity, hunting liberates the hunter from his ordinary circumstances. It places him in a situation in which only his own choices and action determine the result and in which his skill alone

is capable of countering all attempts by the prey to avoid capture. Thus another disadvantage of technology in hunting may be overdetermination; simpler equipment permits the human being to stand independent in what Ortega y Gasset calls the venatic relationship.

The hunter, having chosen to limit the instruments that reason could provide, becomes an *okhotnik-artist,* a hunter-artist (4:44). The artist for Aksakov is the product not only of passion but also of practice, and he stresses the importance of skill or craft (*umen'e*) in hunting. At times, reversing his stylistic precepts for ironic effect, he resorts to a less technical vocabulary than a true hunter would use in order to point out the degree of competence required: "No, there is nothing simpler, it seems, than to take a fishing pole, put a worm or a bit of bread on the hook, toss it into the water, and when the bobber starts to sink, pull a fish out onto the bank. That's all true, but it's no less true that there exists great skill in fishing. To acquire this skill requires a great deal of experience" (4:44). *Umen'e,* which raises hunting to the level of an art, depends directly on the development of the two key virtues of the hunter, *opytnost'* ("experience") and *nabliudatel'nost'* ("power of observation"). The two qualities function reciprocally, with interdependent levels of development, but they are distinguishable at least in concept. In **"The Blizzard"** (1834), Aksakov had already established the centrality of experience, the attainment of or approach to perfection in interaction with the environment. Although the concept is dealt with more prosaically in the hunting books, it remains crucial to the ethic of the hunter, whose ability to locate and capture his prey depends on constantly selecting the one valid course of action.

Experience depends on observation, the second essential quality in the hunter, which transcends passive observation and involves an empathetic identification of the hunter with the quarry. In *Notes on Fishing* Aksakov declares: "For the real fisherman, the hunter-artist, study of the habits of fish is necessary, but this is a most difficult and obscure undertaking, although fish dwell in transparent chambers. Their habits must be guessed at; there are very little data and therefore it is essential to possess insight and imagination, as well as so much effort and worry!" (4:44). Like the old peasant in **"The Blizzard,"** the observer engages in a constant interpretation of and adjustment to his environment, although for the hunter the primary source of information is not nature as a whole so much as his prey within the context of nature. Thus the stark opposition and even antagonism of man and nature that underlies **"The Blizzard"** is attenuated or even effaced in the works on hunting, where the hunter elects his temporary position of integration with nature rather than being permanently subject to it and seeking only to survive. This mitigation of nature as an omnipotent force continues as Aksakov's works focus more and more on the world of human society, so that nature is rather peripheral in *Tales and Reminiscences* and becomes the benign environment of the butterflies in **"Butterfly Collecting,"** Aksakov's last lengthy work with a hunting theme.

One of the principal merits of Aksakov's works on hunting, viewed as works of literature, lies in their transposition of the pattern of the hunt itself into the structure and style of the text. In this regard *Notes on Fishing* and *Notes of a Hunter* are excellent examples of the fallacy of imitative action, since all the details and their ordering are relevant to the passion of hunting and derivative from the narrator's observation or experience. Furthermore, the manner of presenting these details is intended to engender in the reader attitudes similar to those of the hunter. That the two virtues of the hunter are central to his hunting books may be seen in the first paragraph of *Notes of a Hunter*: "I will speak as well about that which my long experience, passionate hunting, and powers of observation have noted" (4:147).

The reader is meant to become a hunter, however briefly, by reading a text that requires him to participate in verbally presented patterns of action and, more importantly, in the mode of being and perceiving that is characteristic of the hunter. The step to independent action (i.e., whether the text is to be didactic) is of course the reader's choice, but he is provided with a clear model of both the hunter and the hunt. The discussions of equipment and its use, of methods of stalking or fishing a given species, constitute a demonstration of experience; the descriptions of individual species and their behavior are a summation of the narrator's observation. The discussion of each species within the encyclopedic format of *Notes on Fishing* and *Notes of a Hunter* is organized as a brief hunt for that particular species. The pattern followed actually predates the start of serious work on *Notes on Fishing*; in a notebook entitled **"Description of Various Game in Our Parts,"** dating from Aksakov's period of residence in Orenburg province, the marginal headings indicate the kernels from which each description is generated and the basic sequence of such elements. Thus, for the great snipe:

> Shape and color of their feathers
> habitat
> food
> nests and young
> methods of capture
> shooting great snipe
> how and when to shoot great snipe
> flavor of their meat.[18]

In the early, unformed attempt at describing game, Aksakov often departs from the hunting order, such that other entries in the notebook display striking incongruities: "The flavor of their meat is first-rate and woodcock in general is considered prime game. They arrive early and disappear very late."[19] Aksakov observes the basic order much more consistently in both *Notes on Fishing* and *Notes of a Hunter,* and of course develops each element much more fully. In its later development the formulaic pattern of recording reveals its inner correlation with the pattern of the hunt itself and deepens the significance of each stage of the process.

First, the quarry must be positively identified. Aksakov regularly begins the discussion of a species with consideration of the names by which it is known, particularly their etymology:

> The folk don't know at all the word *forel'*; they call this handsome fish *pestriak*,[20] or in the collective, *pestrushka*—a most fitting name, for the entire fish is spotted with black, red, and white dots.
>
> (*Notes on Fishing*; 4:128)
>
> [The mallard] is also called *kriakva* and *kriakusha*. Obviously, all three names derive from the word *kriakat'* [to quack], fully expressing the voice, or cry, of the duck.
>
> (*Notes of a Hunter*; 4:266)

The name of the prey, however important, is preliminary to the physical description. The fullness of this description, that is, the degree of observation displayed by the narrator-hunter, derives directly from the hunt, and is roughly proportional to the desirability of the given species as a quarry. Species such as frogs, songbirds, or birds of prey are outside the hunter's goal-defined field of vision and are excluded from consideration. Other species may have only a temporary value; the diving ducks, who arrive before other birds, evoked in Aksakov a certain respect, which he expressed in true hunterly fashion by seeking to shoot them. "Fine gratitude and respect, nonhunters will say, but we have our own logic: the more a bird is respected, the more one tries to bag it" (4:292).

This hierarchy of respect and empathy is reflected in the etiquette of description observed by Aksakov. In *Notes on Fishing,* a small fish, the *golets* ("loach"), fairly insignificant as game, is described in one sentence that is really a nondescription, being organized in negative terms: "Its name, from *golyi* [naked, bare], derives from the character of the skin: it is bare, there are no scales at all on it; the fish is very slim and slippery, of some indefinite color, grayish-yellowish or whitish, with irregular, unclear spots, more or less dark" (4:76). In contrast, a larger species, the *okun'* ("perch"), whose game value is generally accepted—"almost all anglers like to fish for perch very much, and many prefer it to all other types of fishing" (4:112)—is anatomized into constituent parts, each of which is carefully described:[21]

> The perch is rather broad in figure, somewhat humpbacked, covered with scales of a greenish, somewhat golden color; on its back it has a crest with sharp spines

and between it and the tail, a swim fin; the tail and particularly the ventral fins are red, the stomach whitish,
the eyes yellowish with black pupils; across the whole
body lie five bands, which make the perch variegated
and in general very handsome.

(4:112)

Although identification remains the organizing principle, the amount of information exceeds the level necessary, particularly for a common species like the perch.
A certain aesthetic emerges, based on observation of
and empathy for a valued species, recording features
for their own sake (such as the perch's eyes). The relationship of value to detail appears with especial clarity
in the description of the woodcock in *Notes of a Hunter.*
The woodcock is easily defined as the only forest-
dwelling bird of a snipelike appearance, but its exceptional desirability as game, determined in part by its
comparative rarity and elusiveness, prompts a detailed
and appreciative description:

> The woodcock, incontrovertibly, is most excellent,
> prime game in all respects; it even takes pride of place
> in the noble snipe family, to which it belongs, by the
> excellent flavor of its meat, by its similarity to them in
> its mottled plumage, by the beauty of its large black
> eyes, by its speed and twisting in flight, by its manner
> of procuring food, and even by the difficulty in shoot-
> ing it. . . . The woodcock is very handsome. All the
> spots, or mottlings, of its feathers consist of dark, red-
> dish, gray-ashen shades, too subtle to describe, as with
> other snipe species. On the upper part of the wood-
> cock's head lie four transverse stripes, or elongated
> spots, of a dark color; there is more reddish color on
> the back and upper side of the wings, while the lower
> side, crop, and stomach are lighter and covered with
> regular transverse ash-gray bands; the tail is rather
> short, its underfeathers are somewhat longer than the
> uppers, very dark, even black, and each one ends with
> a small white spot on the underside, red-gray on the
> upper side.

(4:436)

The description of the woodcock illustrates well the relation between the fullness, even excess, of description
and the hunter's positive attitude toward his prey; not
only is the bird compared to its near relatives and defined in terms of its similarity to them, but the direct
description depends on approximations and comparisons of parts one with the other.

Following the identification of the prey (including its
name) and the preliminary assessment of its value, the
focus shifts to the next phase of the hunt, or rather, to
the beginning of the hunt proper, in which the observation and experience of the hunter operate synergetically
to force the prey to appear and then to effect its capture. Space and time of course function as the primary
coordinates of any search, and both *Notes on Fishing*
and *Notes of a Hunter* reflect the importance of these
factors in their organization. A special section in each

book deals with selecting a place ("O vybore mesta");
in *Notes on Fishing* mill-ponds are especially recommended, and four types of habitat (marsh, water, steppe,
and forest) are discussed in *Notes of a Hunter,* all game
being classified according to one of these four habitats.
For each species of fish or game, there is of course a
specific niche within this larger framework; the hunter
must know the place where a given quarry is most likely
to appear. In *Notes on Fishing,* the key term, introducing the discussion of niche, is the verb *vodit'sia,* implying not only presence, but also permanence, including
breeding: "Ruffs inhabit [vodiatsia] only pure waters
and, in great numbers, rivers with sandy or clay bottoms, as well as lakes flooded by high water in spring"
(4:88). In *Notes of a Hunter* such regularity is not observed, partly because general descriptions of habitat
open each major section of the text and partly because
habitat for birds is often also a function of season.

The factor of time is even more crucial than that of
place in gaining the appearance of the prey, and is usually specified to a greater degree in the discussion of
each species. The hunter must consider and allow for
such variables as time of day, time of year, and weather.
The presence, movements, habits, and location of his
quarry, as well as its value (a fish's or bird's flavor or
weight) may be affected by these variables. For example, the tench (*lin'*) in early spring will bite in most
locations, in the summer only in the weedy margins and
upper reaches of mill-ponds, never in an undammed
river (4:105). With birds, some of which are present in
a given region only during migration or are most abundant or easily found at this time, the migratory habits of
most species constitute the primary temporal restrictions on hunting. A special discussion of spring migration, "Passage and Arrival of Game" ("Prolet i prilet
dichi") (4:168ff.), in *Notes of a Hunter* complements
the information on the arrival of each species in the article devoted to it. "The first isolated appearance of
woodcock in the spring sometimes occurs very early, so
that there are no thawed areas anywhere. . . . Then,
with the onset of warm weather and mild spring (almost
always about April 12 in Orenburg province), there begins the mass passage of woodcock" (4:437). Departure
is also noted: "By and large, woodcock disappear
around the middle of October" (4:440).

Within these limits, movements and activities such as
courtship, nesting, and the raising of young are recorded; again the degree of inclusiveness is usually a
function of desirability. The descriptions of the daily
and annual patterns of behavior of each species of fish
and bird marks the fullest development of observation;
behavior is presented as a constantly self-modifying
system in continuous dynamic interaction with all aspects of the environment. At this point the hunter, having exerted all his effort to understand the quarry and
make it appear, now demonstrates his own power of in-

terpreting the environment by turning to the active employment of experience in order to effect a capture, to intervene in the environment and its processes in a manner that does not essentially violate the operation of the system and thereby affirms the human being's rightful place in it.

After thus exhaustively fixing the identity of the prey, the hunter's attention shifts to the means by which it is captured, the bait, hook, shot, and so on. This is frequently followed by the direct appearance of the hunter himself, the narrator in the role of reminiscer, recalling specific incidents from his past experience in hunting the particular species. By shifting from the general to the particular at this point, Aksakov established his narrator as the emblematic hunter, who demonstrates concretely the successful conclusion of the exercise of the hunter's observation and experience:

> Eighteen twenty-two is a particularly memorable year for me . . . all the woodcock, without exception, flocked to the low brush growing in damp and clammy places, stayed there until November 8 and grew incredibly plump! Abandoning all other forms of hunt, I tirelessly, daily went out after woodcock: November 6 I killed eight, on the seventh, twelve. . . . In the roots of unpassable brush around a small spring-fed marsh, my tireless dog flushed a woodcock, which I at once killed.

(4:339-340)

After the climax of the hunt there frequently follows, in both *Notes on Fishing* and *Notes of a Hunter,* a comment on the flavor of the particular fish or game bird and the recommended method of preparation. The highly respected snipe, along with the woodcock, are even accorded the honor of a page and a half in "On the Flavor of the Meat and the Preparation of Snipe Species" ("O vkuse miasa i prigotovlenii bekasinykh porod") (4:201-203). Although this feature at first glance may seem to serve only as practical advice, its persistent repetition suggests that the reference to eating also functions in the dynamic pattern of the segments of both volumes of Aksakov's *Notes* [*Notes on Fishing* and *Notes of a Hunter*]. Eating serves as a coda to the capture and celebrates the successful conclusion of the hunt by formalizing the hunter's mastery over the prey by the ritual of consumption. The correct decoding of the prey's message culminates in the total identification of hunter and prey; the communication of the hunt ends in a form of communion.

Aksakov's hunting works are of course to be distinguished from traditional literary or poetic pastoral (although that in itself is a rather amorphous and commodious category), first of all by their narrative authenticity and secondly by their emphasis on the hunt, the occasional brutality of which contrasts with the usual pastoral emphasis on ease and accommodation among all denizens of the pastoral region. It may be worth noting, however, that Aksakov begins with the most indolent and "harmless" form of the hunt, angling, and devotes little or no attention in the entirety of his hunting works to the pursuit of very large game such as wolves or bear; of the traditionally aristocratic forms of hunting, only falconry seems to have attracted Aksakov's attention to any degree.[22] Still, broad areas of affinity with the themes and some of the devices of literary pastoral can be discerned, particularly if we consider the origins of pastoral in Theocritus and disregard later accretions and embellishments.[23]

Of all widely accepted forms or modes, pastoral is perhaps the most diffuse, emphasizing "separation and dispersal, not unity" and presenting "a loose combination of independent elements."[24] Aksakov's two books of *Notes,* although hardly formless, consist of discrete, rather rigidly constructed units devoted to individual species. This paratactic, bead-like combination of units (also reflected in the disjunct elements in the first chapter of *Family Chronicle*) is predicated on the intrinsic worth of each species, which merits full and individual attention by the hunter and thus by the reader. The pastoral, like the epic, "refuses to prescribe an absolute hierarchy of values; each element or inhabitant of the pastoral world is savored as independently important."[25]

One of the most common devices of Theocritan pastoral is the catalogue, which also presents objects sequentially yet independently. Although Aksakov does not make extensive use of simple catalogues per se, his detailed inventories of equipment for hunting or fishing, as well as his elaborate descriptions of prized game, are in part motivated by a similar sense of fondness for things in themselves. More importantly, the detailed lists in later works (the menu at the wedding banquet in *Family Chronicle,* chapter 4, for example) can be compared to such pastoral catalogues. In addition, such enumeration of things could be described as the "nominal" form of the epic retardation of action which Aksakov so often employs in describing significant acts, in works ranging from his epistles to his brother, through his hunting works, to the major works of his last years.

Pastoral of course rests on the assumption of man's being part of nature, one element equal to others in a harmonious whole, and thus often involves a flight from the city and its concerns, at least on the part of the reader. The opposition of city and nature (or of the urban and the rustic) is an essential one for Aksakov. This can be noted in his verse epistles to Arkadii Timofeevich, but even earlier, in his St. Petersburg days, Aksakov develops the contrast at length in a letter to his sister Nadezhda Timofeevna:

> You, my dear friend, write that strolling in the country is dull. I am amazed at this; is it possible to prefer our stone and brick walks to the soft earth, clad with grass

and mottled with flowers; our dismal gardens, in which every little leaf is weighted down with dust and every tree, like a slave, is forcibly positioned in order, to your happy varied groves, in which freedom and joy reign and which beneficent nature and not art, our gardens' cold attendant, planted like a loving mother. . . . Wherever I direct my glances, everywhere there is bondage—there is no spot where cursed people have not distorted nature.[26]

Although the emotional depth of this letter, which, like many of Aksakov's early efforts in literature, suggests a rhetorical exercise, may be open to doubt, the attributes it assigns to city and country do remain constant for Aksakov and the preference for the country becomes an internalized and strongly held conviction, even as its expression becomes less and less strident. The city is frequently characterized by excessive rationality, force, imposed order, monotony, and illness, while the country is associated with freedom, variety, health, and natural order arising from the absence of boundaries. The world of urban society also provides its own characteristic form of release, namely theater, which is really a transcendence of convention rather than an escape from it. Thus the angler and the actor are paradoxically complementary, one free through the rejection of social artificiality, the other by total mastery of artifice; both are of course artists in the Aksakovian sense by virtue of their immersion in their chosen avocation.

In his later years, including the period during which he wrote his hunting books, Aksakov often expresses dissatisfaction in his letters with the vacuous vulgarity (*poshlost'*) of Moscow life, with its "banal round of daily conversation with guests and daily playing of whist-solitaire with Zagoskin."[27] The country remains the primary source of vital energy, its power if anything intensified from Aksakov's younger days:

> The country beneficently embraced me with its fresh scent of young leaves and flowering shrubs, with its space, its quiet and peace. I don't know how to explain it to you, such peace has flowed into my soul. Toward the end of my stay in Moscow I was on edge from morning till night.[28]

Nature's primary qualities are in fact negative ones, the absence of features typical of the city and its social relations; the country lacks boundaries, noise, and motion. "What a marvelous effect Bogorodskoe is having on me! It is infusing some sort of stillness, peace, calm (*tishinu, mir, spokoistvie*) into my embittered heart!"[29] The terms *tishina, mir,* and *spokoistvie,* as well as *chudo* ("marvel," "miracle"), form a constellation in Aksakov's letters and in his writings whenever he feels moved to express the effect of nature on himself or others.

The hunt provides the most reliable means of perceiving and truly assimilating these qualities of nature. In the introduction to **Notes on Fishing,** Aksakov, arguing

that *okhota* draws hunters closer to nature (4:10), explicitly states that fishing (and by implication all hunting) affords modern man an excellent means of overcoming the effects of urban, social existence and of regaining his primeval relationship with nature: "The sense of nature is born in us, from the rude savage to the most educated person. Unnatural upbringing, a forced, false direction, a false life—all this together tends to stifle the powerful voice of nature and often stifles or gives a distorted development to this sense" (4:10). The corrupted or distorted sense of nature perceives its environment only globally, maintaining its distance and relying on already canonized notions of the beautiful. In other words, it prevents true involvement in nature. Such is the city-dweller's reaction "to a beautiful locale, a picturesque distant view, a magnificent sunrise, to a bright moonlit night; but this is still not love of nature; this is love of landscape, scenery, of the prismatic refractions of light" (4:10). Nature cannot be adequately approached through the fallacious categories appropriate to such conventional areas of human activity as painting, theater, or science, none of which can ever surpass the limits of human rationality and society. People capable only of such perceptions are in essence dead; after a superficial glance at nature, they "are already thinking about their banal petty affairs and hurry home, into their filthy whirlpool, into the dusty, choking atmosphere of the city" (4:10-11).

Opposed to this dead world of the city and its sterile inhabitants is the true world of nature: country, peace, stillness, quiet (*derevnia, mir, tishina, spokoistvie*) (4:11). It is accessible through observation, the hunter's manner of looking at the world:

> Flee there from idleness, emptiness and lack of interests; flee there as well from restless, external activity. . . . On a green, flowering bank, above the dark depths of a river or lake, in the shade of bushes, under the canopy of a giant black poplar or leafy alder, silently shaking its leaves in the bright mirror of the water, on which your floats bob or lie motionlessly— seeming passions grow still, supposed tempests fall quiet, egotistic dreams dissolve, unrealizable hopes fly away! Nature enters into its eternal rights, you hear her voice, muffled temporarily by the vanity, bustle, laughter, shouts and all the banality of human speech.
>
> (4:11)

Aksakov's hunting works seek to impart a particular way of seeing the natural world, or rather to cleanse the reader's vision of the categories and accretions of "refined" or "civilized" modes of perception. Of course the underlying purpose of the pastoral mode as such is to bring the reader to see the things of nature whole and unique. Aksakov's fisherman or hunter, like Robert Frost, sees "both the subject of vision and its perspective; the mode of perception is embodied in the images themselves," so that "the unity between the thing observed and the way of seeing, between object and thought, between man's work . . . and his esthetic experience," reemerges with all its pristine force.[30] Pastoral vision is cleansed vision.

The fisherman or hunter, and by implication Aksakov's reader, escapes the constraints and restrictions of society and enters nature, perceiving it from within, himself a part of it; he conducts a constant dialogue with it as a free and equal denizen of the primeval world. The basic constituents of this newly perceived cosmos are earth, water, and vegetation, especially trees, all of them archaic loci of being and life, of the sacred; in combination they are the major features of traditional models of the world.[31] For Aksakov, "water is alive; it moves and imparts life," "forests are the conservers of water," and a tree "presents . . . the visible phenomena of organic life" (4:245, 377, 386). The world of stillness and freshness is not only beneficial to man and his psyche, but is in fact the source and wellspring of life. Aksakov pays appropriate and stylistically characteristic tribute to this in one of his most striking catalogues, unusual both for its length and for its extreme particularization of description, action, and sound:

> On the branches of trees, in thickets of green leaves and generally in the forest there live the motley, beautiful, various-voiced, infinitely varied species of birds: wood and black grouse boom their mating-call, hazel-hens shriek, woodcock whistle on their mating flights, each species of wild dove coos in its own manner, thrushes cheep and clack, sadly, melodiously, orioles chirp back and forth, variegated cuckoos moan, piebald woodpeckers trumpet, jays rattle; waxwings, wood larks, hawfinches and all the numerous tribe of tiny, winged singers fill the air with various voices and vivify the stillness of the forests; on the branches and in the hollows of trees birds build their nests, lay their eggs and raise their young.
>
> (4:381)

This catalogue of species and calls, its lexical diversity and precision pointing to Aksakov's Shishkovite antecedents, presents a stylistic analogue of the fullness of life, which the tree and its attendant species, arranged in a more or less ascending order from the ground to the treetops, represents.

Although Aksakov indirectly indicates his awareness of the symbolic power of water and trees, as well as of man's need to escape the city and time and reestablish his relations with the primitive realities that persist in the natural environment, direct statement of this theme in the hunting books is rare. Rather, as befits the persona of the simple hunter or fisherman unconcerned with the world of urban society or literary artifice, it is achieved through the oblique means of inclusion and repetition. The pastoral and even mythic perception of nature, central to Aksakov's general view of nature and

to his hunting books, appears explicitly in his **"Epistle to M. A. Dmitriev" ("Poslanie k M. A. Dmitrievu")**, a poem employing a verse form that is considerably less innovative than his prose. Aksakov intended to use the concluding lines of this poem, one of the few from his later years that are not concerned with family matters, as an epigraph for the second edition of *Notes of a Hunter* (1853), but because of objections by the censor to the word *freedom* (*svoboda*), the plan was dropped; the lines did appear, however inconsistently from the point of view of the censor, in the second edition of *Notes on Fishing.* In the **"Epistle,"** Aksakov opposes to the world of nature his unquiet old age.

> Net serdechnoi tishiny,
> Mir dushevnyi nevozmozhen
> Posredi mirskoi volny!
>
> (3:686)

> There is no quiet in the heart,
> Peace of spirit is impossible
> Midst the mundane wave.

Beset by the chaos of life in society and by the physical inroads of age, Aksakov finds in nature peace and renewal:

> Est' odnako primiritel',
> Vechno iunyi i zhivoi,
> Chudotvorets i tselitel',—
> Ukhozhu k nemu poroi.
> Ukhozhu ia v mir prirody,
> Mir spokoistviia, svobody,
> V tsarstvo ryb i kulikov,
> Na svoi rodnye vody,
> Na prostor stepnykh lugov,
> V ten' prokhladnuiu lesov,
> I—v svoi mladye gody!
>
> (3:686)

> There is however a reconciler,
> Eternally young and vital,
> A wonder-worker and healer—
> I escape to it at times.
> I escape to the world of nature,
> A world of peace and freedom,
> To the realm of fish and snipe,
> To my own native waters,
> To the expanse of the steppe meadows,
> Into the cool shade of the forests,
> And—into the years of my own youth!

Here in a limited space are all the essential characteristics of nature that pervade Aksakov's hunting books (and function in his other works as well); the microcosm of space, water, and trees overflows with life and is endowed with the characteristic features of peace, silence, and healing. However, Aksakov's separate realm of peace, freedom, life, and beauty clearly resides not only in nature but also in the representation of nature, the realm of fish and snipe which are the subjects of his first two books. Thus art and nature merge in their psychological significance; both reconcile humanity and its environment by affording people the opportunity of experiencing or re-creating a world in which the apparent contradictions of existence dissolve in a harmonious reintegration. The last line, adumbrating the theme of memory and the past that becomes central in his subsequent works, suggests the equal powers of memory, art, and nature as means of overcoming time. All of Aksakov's works are essentially unified attempts to escape his own condition.

Notes

1. Mashinskii, *S. T. Aksakov,* pp. 320-321 and p. 320 n2. Aksakov refers to Levshin's book in *Sobranie sochinenii,* vol. 4, p. 118 n2.

2. A. V. Chicherin, "Russkoe slovo Sergeia Aksakova," pp. 120-121, draws attention to earlier works on hunting, but the 1793 article he cites is exclusively practical.

3. S. T. Aksakov to N. V. Gogol, 22 November 1845, included in *Istoriia moego znakomstva s Gogolem,* in *Sobranie sochinenii,* 3:326. Of the times Aksakov mentions, midday is particularly common in traditional pastoral.

4. S. T. Aksakov to family, 25 November 1845. Ts-GALI [Central Government Archive of Literature and Art, Moscow (Tsentral'nyi gosudarstvennyi arkhiv literatury i iskusstva)], *fond* 10, inventory 3, storage unit 15, fol. 13.

5. S. T. Aksakov to M. P. Pogodin, 16 May 1847. LL [Manuscript Division of the Lenin Library, Moscow (Rukopisnyi otdel, Biblioteka imeni Lenina)], Pogodin, *fond* II, carton I, item 57, letter 5.

6. S. T. Aksakov to Ivan Aksakov. PD [Institute of Russian Literature and Art, Pushkin House, Leningrad (Institut russkoi literatury i iskusstva, Push-kinskii dom)], *fond* 3, inventory 3, item 13, fol. 103. The date of this letter is missing, but it was probably written in the autumn of 1845.

7. "Prilet dichi i nekotorykh drugikh ptits v oren-burgskoi gubernii," *Sobranie sochinenii,* 4:504-514.

8. "Opisanie raznoi dichi v nashikh mestakh" (12 folios), LL, *fond* 3, folder 5, item 2a.

9. S. T. Aksakov to N. V. Gogol, 21 June 1848, in *Sobranie sochinenii,* 3:364.

10. S. T. Aksakov to Ivan Aksakov, 24 November 1849, in A. A. Dunin, "Materialy po istorii russkoi literatury i kul'tury: I. S. Aksakov v Iaroslavle," p. 117.

11. S. T. Aksakov to Ivan Aksakov, 1 December 1849, ibid., p. 123.

12. S. T. Aksakov to Ivan Aksakov, 17 February 1850. LL, *fond* 3, folder 3, item 22g.

13. S. T. Aksakov to Ivan Aksakov, 3 February 1850. Ibid.

14. S. T. Aksakov to I. S. Turgenev, January 1853, in Maikov, ed., "Pis'ma Aksakovykh," no. 9, p. 11.

15. Etymologically the word *okhota* is related to the verb *khotet',* to want, and may have acquired the meaning "hunt" in East Slavic languages from use as a replacement for tabooed words dealing with hunting. Cf. M. Vasmer, *Russisches etymologisches Wörterbuch.*

16. Ortega y Gasset's phrase, in *Meditations on Hunting,* p. 57.

17. S. T. Aksakov to I. S. Turgenev, January 1853, in Maikov, ed., "Pis'ma Aksakovykh," no. 9, p. 10.

18. "Opisanie raznoi dichi v nashikh mestakh." LL, *fond* 3, folder 5, item 2a, fols. 4-7.

19. Ibid., fols. 8v-9.

20. *Forel',* "trout," from German *Forelle. Pestryi,* "variegated, motley." Such etymologizing might also be taken as an echo of Shishkovite interest in word origins.

21. Chicherin, "Russkoe slovo Sergeia Aksakova," p. 120, draws attention to the coloristic aspects of Aksakov's descriptions.

22. Only one brief article, "Okhota s iastrebom za perepelkami" [Hunting Quail with a Hawk], included in *Tales and Reminiscences of a Hunter,* and a prefatory note to an 1856 edition of Tsar Aleksei Mikhailovich's *Rules of Falconry,* a seventeenth century handbook, deal with this form of hunting. *Sobranie sochinenii,* 4: 480-503, 584-589.

23. Aksakov's hunting works could be strictly labeled as prose georgic because of their didactic element. However, the broader category seems more useful in light of Aksakov's other works.

24. Thomas G. Rosenmeyer, *The Green Cabinet: Theocritus and the European Pastoral Lyric,* p. 47.

25. Ibid., pp. 104, 53.

26. S. T. Aksakov to N. T. Aksakova, undated. PD, 1068/XVI, item 42, fol. 1-1v.

27. S. T. Aksakov to Ivan Aksakov, in Dunin, "Materialy," p. 123.

28. S. T. Aksakov to Ivan Aksakov, 26 May 1849. PD, *fond* 3, inventory 3, item 13, fol. 3.

29. To O. S. Aksakova, 15 June 1836. Ibid., inventory 15, item 26, fol. 30.

30. John F. Lynen, *The Pastoral Art of Robert Frost,* p. 22.

31. Mircea Eliade, *Patterns in Comparative Religion,* p. 269.

Bibliography

I. AKSAKOV'S WORKS

There is no complete edition of all of Aksakov's works. However, all of his major works appear in each of the following editions.

Aksakov, Sergei Timofeevich. *Polneo sobranie sochinenii S. T. Aksakova.* 6 vols. St. Petersburg: Martynov, 1886.

———. *Sobranie sochinenii.* 4 vols. Moscow: GIKhL, 1955-1956.

———. *Sobranie sochinenii.* 5 vols. Moscow: Pravda, 1966.

I have used the 1955-1956 edition for most references. Aksakov's three major works have been translated into English. The trilogy was translated by J. D. Duff, under the titles *A Russian Gentleman* (*Semeinaia khronika*) (London: E. Arnold; New York: Longmans, Green, 1917); *Years of Childhood* (*Detskie gody Bagrovavnuka*) (London: E. Arnold; New York: Longmans, Green, 1916); and *A Russian Schoolboy* (*Vospominaniia*), which also includes a translation of "Butterfly Collecting" (London: E. Arnold; New York: Longmans, Green, 1917). *Family Chronicle,* along with excerpts from *Years of Childhood* and *Reminiscences,* has also been translated by M. C. Beverley (London: Routledge; New York: E. P. Dutton, 1924), and *Years of Childhood* has been translated by Alec Brown (New York: Random House, 1960). The Duff translations were republished by Oxford University Press in 1923 (*Years of Childhood*) and 1924 (*A Russian Gentleman* and *A Russian Schoolboy*), with various subsequent editions. They have also been reissued in paperback by Hyperion Press of Westport, Conn. (1977). The Beverley translation of *Family Chronicle* was reissued in paperback by Dutton in 1961.

II. MANUSCRIPTS AND UNPUBLISHED LETTERS

Letters, manuscripts, and other archival material cited are preserved for the most part in the Aksakov *fondy* (files) and other *fondy* of the following archives in the Soviet Union:

Central Government Archives of Literature and Art, Moscow (Tsentral'nyi gosudarstvennyi arkhiv literatury i iskusstva). Abbreviation: TsGALI.

Institute of Russian Literature and Art, Pushkin House, Leningrad (Institut russkoi literatury i iskusstva, Pushkinskii dom). Abbreviation: PD.

Manuscript Division of the Lenin Library, Moscow (Biblioteka imeni Lenina, rukopisnyi otdel). Abbreviation: LL.

III. PUBLISHED SOURCES

Chicherin, A. V. "Russkoe slovo Sergeia Aksakova." *Russkaia literatura,* 1976, no. 2, pp. 120-126.

Dunin, A. A. "Materialy po istorii russkoi literatury i kul'tury: I. S. Aksakov v Iaroslavle." *Russkaia mysl',* 1915, no. 8, pp. 107-131.

Eliade, Mircea. *Patterns in Comparative Religion.* Translated by Rosemary Sheed. Cleveland: World Publishing Co., 1963.

Lynen, John F. *The Pastoral Art of Robert Frost.* Yale Studies in English, no. 147. New Haven: Yale University Press, 1960.

Maikov, L. N., ed. "Pis'ma S. T., K. S., i I. S. Aksakovykh k I. S. Turgenevu," *Russkoe obozrenie,* 1894, no. 8, pp. 460-484; no. 9, pp. 5-38; no. 10, pp. 478-501; no. 11, pp. 7-30; and no. 12, pp. 591-601.

Mashinskii, S. I. *S. T. Aksakov: Zhizn' i tvorchestvo.* Moscow: GIKhL, 1961.

———. *S. T. Aksakov: Zhizn' i tvorchestvo.* 2d, expanded ed. Moscow: Khudozhestvennaia literatura, 1973.

Ortega y Gasset, José. *Meditations on Hunting.* Translated by Howard B. Wescott. New York: Scribners, 1972.

Rosenmeyer, Thomas G. *The Green Cabinet: Theocritus and the European Pastoral Lyric.* Berkeley and Los Angeles: University of California Press, 1969; paperback ed. 1973.

Marcus C. Levitt (essay date summer 1988)

SOURCE: Levitt, Marcus C. "Aksakov's *Family Chronicle* and the Oral Tradition." *Slavic and East European Journal* 32, no. 2 (summer 1988): 198-212.

[*In the following essay, Levitt examines elements of Russian folk tradition in Aksakov's* Family Chronicle.]

> Farewell, my images, bright and dark . . . You were not great heroes, not imposing personalities; you trod the earth in silence and obscurity . . . By the mighty power of pen and print your descendants have now been made acquainted with you.
>
> —from the *envoi* to **Family Chronicle**

Ever since its appearance, critics have been at pains to define the genre of Aksakov's masterpiece *Family Chronicle* and its place within the Russian prose tradition. The unresolved question of *Family Chronicle*'s literary status has put all precise attempts at interpretation in doubt. Virtually all critics have noted a larger generic dualism in *Family Chronicle,* and have described it variously as that between documentary/imaginative literature, history/fiction, objective/subjective, or autobiography/novel. Andrew Durkin, in his recent literary biography of Aksakov, states the problem this way: "*Family Chronicle* resists identification as autobiography or history pure and simple, as indeed it defies complete categorization as fiction. Since these two forms differ radically in their existential import, the perceptive reader is forced to accept ambiguity and to recognize the unique status of the text in question" (*Aksakov,* 99). The problem here, it seems to me, hinges upon the profound distance separating the "perceptive *reader*"—immersed in, and in a very real sense blinkered by the limits imposed by the printed page—from the pre-literate world of oral culture and folk tradition depicted in *Family Chronicle,* a world to which modern literary scholars like Milman Parry, Albert Lord, Eric Havelock, and Walter Ong have been drawing our attention over the last decades (Ong; Foley). Critics have failed, I think, to appreciate *Family Chronicle* as an attempt to capture the vanishing world of oral culture in print. The oral world described in *Family Chronicle* has left a profound imprint on the work, and requires a different set of assumptions on the part of its audience, both about the nature of the artistic process and about the existential import of the world it portrays. Such a new "reading" (the word itself indicates our built-in bias against viewing the text as a story which is *told*) provides a key both to many of the text's formal peculiarities as well as to its "unique generic status."

Family Chronicle tells the story of the clash between the old way of life and the new, a clash of two cultures and two ways of apprehending the world. Aksakov sets out the parameters of this conflict in the first of the five "fragments" into which the work is divided. The first segment of fragment 1, which tells the story of Stepan Bagrov's emigration to Ufa Province, culminates in the building of a mill at the new settlement. As Durkin has argued in his book, which focuses specifically on the "pastoral" element in Aksakov, the subjugation of the wild Buguruslan River symbolizes the new Arcadian order Stepan Bagrov establishes at New Bagrovo: an image of a perfect, unchanging balance between man and nature. The clacking of the mill, "which goes on working and grinding to this day," Durkin suggests, creates a new order of time, an equilibrium fixed in mythic timelessness. However, almost immediately, Aksakov provides a negative analogue to this pastoral "foundation myth" in his story about the destruction of the old Bagrovo.

Following the idyllic image of the mill, the author sings a nostalgic hymn of praise to the former unspoiled natural wealth and beauty of Orenburg as it was in his youth, still "undeflowered by hordes of settlers from every quarter" (11/83)[1]—clearly suggesting that the the the "timeless" utopian harmony established by grandfather Bagrov and symbolized in the mill—like the natural unspoiled beauty of Ufa province—has already been destroyed at the time of writing, is already "no longer the same." Aksakov expands on the opposition in segment 3, which contrasts the beautiful and ugly sides of Bagrov's behavior (his righteousness and his rages) and the old and New Bagrovo. While New Bagrovo appears virginal, untrammelled, and of infinite possibility, the story of the old Bagrovo makes a grim counterpoint to the story of the mill: a story about modern man's destruction of the natural environment.

> You will wonder why I have described Troickoe [the old estate] as arid. Had my ancestors been so imprudent as to set up their dwelling in a barren country? Not so, for a different state of affairs existed formerly, and no reproach attaches to my forebears. Once [*nekogda*] Troickoe lay situated on the beautiful little stream of the Maina, that . . . took its rise in the wonderful Mossy Lakes, and moreover, beside the settlement stretched a narrow but long and clear lake, deep in the middle and whose bed was of white sand; out of this lake there even flowed a brook which used to be called the *White Spring*. That's how it was in the old days, a long time ago, it is true, a very long time ago [*Tak bylo v starinu, davno, pravda, očen' davno*]. According to the tradition [*po predaniju*], it is known that the Mossy Lakes once were deep round basins in the depths of the forest, filled with transparent icy water and surrounded by marshy banks, so that no one dared approach them at any time except in winter, because they feared that the quaking banks would instantly swallow up the impertinent intruder who transgressed upon the inviolable kingdom of water-sprites [*neprikosnovennogo carstva vodjanyx čertej*]. But man is an inveterate and triumphant alterer [*izmenitel'*] of the face of nature! They ceased to believe in ancient tradition [*starinnomu predaniju*], unconfirmed by new events, and little by little the Mossy Lakes grew foul through the soaking of flax and the watering of cattle on their shores, and they became shallow and even began to dry up as the surrounding forest was cut down. . . . Probably as a result of the dwindling of the Mossy Lakes, the Maina rivulet has shrunk and now only makes its appearance some versts beyond the settlement, and the long, deep, transparent lake has been turned into a stinking slough; its sandy bed is fathom-deep with slime and covered with all sorts of refuse from the peasants' barnyards; the last trace of the White Spring has long since vanished, and soon it will be altogether forgotten [*skoro ne budet o nem i pamjati*].

(17-18/86-87)

Where the mill represented a timeless equilibrium, the story of the Mossy Lakes' demise chronicles the destructive intrusion of History into a pre- or ahistorical setting. It is clearly a parable about the dangerous consequences of Modern Russia's break with the old ways. When people cease to believe in water-sprites and ancient taboos, a vital link with nature is not only lost but almost certainly doomed to oblivion ("soon it will be altogether forgotten . . ."). Tradition (*predanie*) is opposed to modernity, the ancient collective inherited folk wisdom to new "scientific" empiricism.[2] In contrast, Bagrov's mill stands for an ideal balance between man and his environment, an emblem of Russia's prehistorical harmony with nature, nature that is superstitiously feared, but also deeply respected. Aksakov's "pastoral" includes irrepressibly creative man as part of the landscape; that is, there is no necessary discord between man and nature. The intrusion of modernity—of History—into the old way of life constitutes the central conflict in *Family Chronicle.* History (change) represents the negation of pastoral (stasis, utopia), and, at the same time, paradoxically, an active element in its creation. This paradox or tension between the two models (the "pastoral" of the founding of the mill, and the "anti-utopia" of the Mossy Lakes) lies at the heart of *Family Chronicle* and its unique literary qualities.

In this passage, and in *Family Chronicle* in general, the narrator's goal is to preserve the near-forgotten family and folk memory. In what we may take as a key admission, the narrator at one point defines himself as "the impartial chronicler of oral traditions" (*bespristrastnyj peredavatel' izustnyx predanij* 247/177). Like the memory of the White Spring, the traditional world described in *Family Chronicle* is in danger of oblivion, and it falls to Aksakov to preserve its story by writing it down. It falls to him to record on paper his family's prehistorical, preliterate way of life—a fundamentally contradictory and ultimately impossible undertaking, as sensitive critics of oral culture like Walter Ong have made us aware (10-15). In trying to put into print the record of a culture to which the world of letters was totally alien, Aksakov stood on the threshold between the two spheres, both historically and as an artist.

Aksakov's task in *Family Chronicle* is not to present the *history* of a family, to present "the facts"; rather, it is to record the *family*'s history, its oral tradition, the *memory* of the past—not to reconstruct a "literal" record of the past itself (a concept which is absent in oral cultures). In this, the task Aksakov set himself seems strikingly similar to that of Herodotus, who also stood at the crossroads of oral and written cultures. In the first sentence of his *Histories,* Herodotus promised to tell not what happened in Greece's past but "to preserve the memory of the past." Significantly, in Russian, the term *xronika* sometimes denotes oral history in precisely the sense I am using it here.[3] Like Herodotus, Aksakov was working in what was still mostly a vacuum: creating a prose tradition where there was almost none before.

Both relied heavily upon oral culture, even as they were, by recording it on paper, both signalling, and in a sense contributing, to its demise.

1. FAMILY CHRONICLE'S GENERIC PECULIARITY: THE ART OF THE LOGOS

Critics have noted the fragmented, episodic nature of *Family Chronicle* and the "narrative and temporal inconsistencies" it entails. Mašinskij notes that the narration in *Family Chronicle* "is constructed like a living oral story [*živoj ustnyj rasskaz*] with innumerable repetitions" (352), and suggests that the work contains many separate "novellas" (*novelly*) which are more or less integrated into the work as a whole. As an alternative appellation, I suggest the ancient Greek "logos" as the basic generic unit of the *Family Chronicle.* The first ancient Greek historians (of whom Herodotus is the most famous example) were called "logographers" or storytellers. "Logos" (word) meant 'what was said': the historian wrote down and studied what people said (Thomson, chap. 1). The logos embodies the latent conflict between the oral source of historical material and the art of the logographer who systematizes it and gives it literary shape. A logos is not the oral performance itself, nor the illusion of oral performance in writing, as in a "skaz" (Rice, 412-14). In a logos, the narrator seeks to preserve and explain the oral world on paper for a literate audience. The early sections of *Family Chronicle* may be said to be a paratactical chain of logoi linked by a loose narrative frame rather than a homogeneous or unitary (continuous) narrative (characteristic of modern history writing and of the novel).

As Aksakov proceeds from the realm of Story into that of History (that is, from the author's "prehistory" into his own life), the narrative becomes more homogeneous and syntactical, and less digressive. There is no temporal gap or discontinuity between fragments 3, 4, and 5, as there are between fragments 1 and 2, 2 and 3. By the last fragment, an inserted romance—the story of Timašev and Sal'me—is sharply felt as a digression, something Tolstoj criticized in 1856 (Mašinskij, 353). By the last volume of the trilogy, things are called by their literal names, and all pretense of pseudonymity is dropped (e.g., Bagrovo becomes Aksakovo). Here we are already in the recognizable historical world of written records—the world of unmistakable autobiography.[4]

The story of the Mossy Lakes, quoted above, provides a good example of a logos. It is a self-contained unit, which may be lifted from the book (as I have done) without harm to its artistic integrity. As J. A. K. Thomson has shown in his study of Herodotus, the logos combines elements of history, legend, myth, and fairytale in a most often indistinguishable blend. While at first glance we might assume the Mossy Lakes logos to be historical, there is really very little identifiable in it as such. In oral cultures, time is not absolute and linear, but cyclical, repetitive, like the seasons, limited and colored by what memory alone can preserve. Each episode—like the Mossy Lakes logos—exists in and for itself, expressing a bit of typical, universal, parable-like truth, rather than as a fact in some larger chain of events; details are given to make the point of the story clearer rather than as documentary facts for their own sake. As with much of the early parts of *Family Chronicle,* the action takes place "nekogda," in some ill-defined once upon a time long, long ago ("tak bylo v starinu, davno, pravda, očen' davno"). We are not given a date or "historical framework" to which we can refer—something that is generally true for the work as a whole as well. As Mašinskij puts it, Aksakov "lacks the spirit of historicity [*dux istorizma*]"; major historical events, such as the Pugačev revolt, are only mentioned in passing and have no connection with the action (391). Fragment 1 gives no dates. Fragment 2 begins with a brief note that the Kurolesov story began "in the 1760s," beginning before the events related in the first fragment and ending after them. The third fragment—in which we more clearly enter historical time—begins with an epic-like invocation: "Many years flew quickly by, many events took place," making a clear break with the previous fragments. In this fragment we are given the only precisely dated event in *Family Chronicle*—Aleksej and Sof'ja's wedding day, 10 May 1788 (we later learn the day of Sergej's birth: 20 September—no year specified).

In the oral world of the *Family Chronicle,* time is marked by the cycle of birth and death, planting and harvest, and the Church feasts that celebrate them. Lacking specific corroborative evidence about what happened to the Mossy Lakes, we cannot determine the balance here between historical fact and legend. Taken as a whole, the logos suggests a typical fairy-tale pattern: retribution which follows the violation of a sacred taboo, the "transgression" of "the inviolable kingdom of the water-sprites."

2. The Problem of the Narrator

The problem of defining the logos as history/legend/ myth or fairy tale brings us directly to the question of the narrator's relation to the action, which is the key to our definition of the logos. Does Aksakov present the story to us as straight history or as fairy-tale; i.e., to what extent does Aksakov believe that the Mossy Lakes were spoiled due to retribution by water-sprites? The question might seem ludicrous at first, yet it strikes at the heart of the method and form of the logos. Despite the ethnographic and documentary illusion which much of Aksakov's prose conveys (and which has been much praised by critics), the narrator's attitude towards his material is complex, and not merely or consistently

"objective." In the logos, as in many examples of "skaz," we may distinguish between two voices: the *inner narrative* (the "skaz" itself), "told" by a narrator-teller, and the *outer frame* which creates an ironic distance between the narrator-writer and what he narrates.[5] This narrative dichotomy forms the central tension of the logos, a "threshold genre" which partakes not only of two genres (oral storytelling and written narrative) but of two mutually exclusive perceptions of the world. Like Herodotus, Aksakov the logographer procedes on these two levels, first as mere *recorder* of tales (as historian, or as "impartial chronicler of oral traditions") who stands apart from the tales he relates, and second, as *storyteller,* someone who is deeply enmeshed in the world to which he gives expression. As historian, the narrator frames the stories, and sometimes intercedes to explain their sources or the material evidence for them (e.g., when he tells us that he saw Kurolesov's seven-tailed whip himself before it was burned by his father); it is this narrative voice who sometimes states that he does not necessarily *believe* the stories he relates. This narrator, who is self-conscious of himself as recorder-chronicler, distances himself from the action and makes us aware of the story as an artificial literary and historical construct.

Aksakov frames the logos of the Mossy Lakes as an objective recorder, somewhat ironically motivating the tale as a defense of his ancestors, not against the charge of having been a party to the destruction of the old Bagrovo but against the implication that they were so stupid as to have settled in such a nasty spot! The storyteller, on the other hand, is always necessarily involved in the stories he relates and the world he re-creates. "The oral tradition is both the story and the author" (Scholes and Kellogg, 55). In traditional oral societies, the storyteller represents a primary repository of collective, inherited folk memory, and is, in that sense, deeply at one with his audience. Further, the storyteller's assertion of the truth of the events he is relating is a prime generic imperative of the logos's inner narrative; he uses all the means at his command to convince the audience of the veracity of his tale, no matter how far-fetched and impossible what he relates may seem. In the logos of the Mossy Lakes, for example, the narrator nowhere implies that the ancient traditions about water-sprites were false.

A more striking example of the storyteller's involvement with his tale occurs in the episode concerning Sof'ja's struggle with her evil stepmother Mme. Zudina, a story which V. S. Prichett has recognized as coming right out of the folk repertoire—a variant of the Cinderella story (Pritchett, 413-19).[6] Sof'ja, about to commit suicide due to the humiliations to which she has been subjected, changes her mind when, after fainting, she awakes to find a candle which she had extinguished now burning. The narrator's presentation of the "facts" of the story is unequivocal: Sof'ja "was saved from it [suicide] by a miracle" (*ona spaslas' ot nego čudom*; 70/141). Further, Mme. Zudina's subsequent death—we are told—was because "the measure of God's patience had brimmed over" (*ispolnilas' mera dolgoter-penija bož'ego*; 71/142).

3. CHARACTERIZATION

Critics of **Family Chronicle** have noted that the text is often internally inconsistent. From episode to episode there may be only tenuous connections. Within neighboring stories the same character may be given different, even contradictory, parts to play. When the logos's roots in the oral world are understood, however, this problem disappears. The interest of the storyteller focuses on each individual logos as it is told (rather than as it relates to any other stories or events). At the same time, it is very difficult for the audience, absorbed in the story's immediate performance and without the aid of a text, to keep track of inconsistencies or lacunae in the story. What is crucial, and what the good storyteller must do, is to give each story verisimilitude at the moment of the telling. Hence in the story of Sof'ja's miraculous salvation, the narrator embellishes upon her role as Cinderella—a role the audience can recognize and appreciate. The logos is populated by typical, "storybook" characters. In a culture where the sum of experience can only be preserved by human memory, people and events are seen as reflecting known stages in the ever-repeating cycle of life, rather than as individual phenomena with unique "histories" and absolute, independent value. Hence in one story Sof'ja may appear as beleaguered step-daughter, and in others as city slicker or persecuted sister-in-law, with no necessary linkage between them. Like Xerxes in book 7 of *The Histories,* who may be shown to be a bloodthirsty tyrant acting out of rage in one scene, and a philosopher-king meditating on the vanity of all human endeavor in the next, characters interest the storyteller in terms of the way they function in the given story rather than for any intrinsic "historical" features they may have. However, within each episode, as Durkin has aptly noted, characters remain true to their given "roles"; "at any given moment [they are] totally homogeneous" (*Aksakov*, 111). Characters from the world of the logos lack consciousness of themselves as historical, idiosyncratic individuals; they are simple and uncomplicated, and their problems are universally comprehensible (e.g., that of the persecuted step-daughter, the envied sister-in-law, and so on). They do not suffer from "modern psychology," resulting from man's alienation from the environment and characteristic of, for example, the protagonists of the realistic novel—or, for that matter, of autobiography—individuals who need to regain their "place" in the universe because they have lost their prehistoric symbiosis with the environment. (In both of these cases, the simpler, prehistoric paradise to be re-

gained is often that of childhood.) Elliot Cohen notes that "Identity for Aksakov [in contrast to identity for Tolstoj, and, we might add, for the modern hero in general] is a given rather than an undefined, an 'x' which must be sought, pondered or developed. . . . His sense of self is based on a firm sense of place in the world" (78). Because of their "flatness," their clear and unquestioned identity, characters in the oral world easily assume larger-than-life, epic dimensions when seen from the outside and looking back in time, as to a lost heroic world. (See Forster, 46-54, on the contrast between "flat" and "round" characters, and Ong, 151-55.)

4. LITERARY MODELS

According to the logic of the Mossy Lakes logos, literacy is a marker of the new, often destructive modern ways. In the oral world presented in fragments 1 and 2, unequivocally positive characters are mostly illiterate, while the villains and problematic ones are associated with the new literate, urban-oriented way of life. Virtually all of the people associated with Stepan Bagrov and his generation are nonliterate; "Of course, given the general ignorance [*nevežestvo*] of landowners of the time, he too [Stepan Bagrov] had had no real education, and could hardly read and write his native language [*russkuju gramotu znal ploxo*]" (4/76). The same phrase is repeated almost exactly for Bagrov's niece Praskov'ja Ivanovna (61-62/134), heroine of the second fragment. As a literary creation, Bagrov is inseparable from his oral world. He is on a close cultural par with his serfs, and speaks virtually the same language—the language of folktales, saturated with formulaic sayings and proverbs that represent the crystallization of age-old wisdom, preserved not in books but in the spoken language itself. Bagrov's first words in **Family Chronicle** come right out of the timeless world of the folk-tale, and proverbs and sayings not only play a major role in both characterization and in plot development, they also often form the basis for the narrative. (See for example the passage on pages 194-95/265-66, in which a proverb forms the basis for a substantial analysis of Sof'ja and Alexej's relationship.) On the other hand, Bagrov's nemesis, the villain Kurolesov, while he too had "no real education," has a glib tongue which is associated with his witty and smooth writing style and with his deceptively charming, subversively seductive modern ways; he is a distinctively, self-consciously "literary" character.

The traditional wisdom of the oral world which the logos aims to capture—as in the story of the Mossy Lakes—suggests that

> Old = Nonliterate ("absence of model") = Natural = Russian = Good

and that

> New = Literate (artificiality) = Unnatural = European = Bad.

The opposition between Bagrov and Kurolesov, at least initially, supports such a view. The story of Kurolesov's villainy, which as Durkin has shown, takes the shape of a Gothic horror tale, inverts and subverts Bagrov's world. Kurolesov's downfall, through the direct intervention of Praskov'ja and Bagrov, represents the moral bankruptcy of this modern cultural model. At the same time, Praskov'ja Ivanovna frustrates the expected outcome of the Gothic romance (true love) by her pious, nonjudgmental, "Russian" response to her husband's death, and thus transcends and debunks her prescribed role as Gothic heroine. In Durkin's words, the story's ending "neatly confounds a literary pattern at a point where it seems to have become dominant" (*Aksakov,* 126). Bagrov, unlike Kurolesov, is a character out of the oral world; even when Bagrov does write, he is fully within the oral context.[7] His literary mode of existence is perceived as neutral, unfelt, "natural" or non-literary, and from this perspective, Bagrov's "natural" world may be seen to have thwarted the false and artificial model Kurolesov represents.

However, in the logos, the oral is translated through the prism of the written, and Aksakov, a literary man who had thoroughly assimilated the norms of modern life, did not accept such an extreme anti-cultural stance, which would logically have led to a rejection of modernity and the world of letters (as, for example, it did later with Tolstoj). While the parable of the demise of the Mossy Lakes suggests that we live in a fallen, anti-utopian world of history, at the same time, the story of the establishment of the mill—an act requiring a high degree of technology and ingenuity—indicates that pastoral can be achieved in history via man's active efforts. Aksakov's "pastoral" ideal does not represent man in some sort of "pure" "state of nature," that is, without active influence on his environment. While fully conscious of the dangers of modernity, Aksakov did not reject either history or culture; indeed Aksakov's vision is one of balance and pluralism, and the mission of the logos is to preserve the wisdom of the past for the future.

As *Family Chronicle* advances further and further into historical time, the bipolar value schema of the oral world becomes less and less relevant. The need for, and indeed the inescapability of, literary models becomes more and more manifest as we enter the historical world, in which the writer must pick and choose from among a broad range of cultural and literary patterns. While stylization, as we have seen, may function within the context of the logos to enhance typicality, within the broader frame of the work as a whole, seen from the perspective of oral culture, the presence of self-consciously "literary" patterns signals the breakup of the oral world. What was felt as neutral appears more and more as stylized and literary. When Sof'ja the city slicker visits Bagrovo, and is classified as a witch by

the women-folk, it is clear that the oral paradigm has already become but one of many literary models. Both Bagrov and Zudin refer to Sof'ja as a witch. In fragment 4, the narrator explains that Sof'ja actually did have a "magical" influence on people, and he explains it by a sophisticated psychological analysis of her personality (155/226). Like the superstitions guarding the Mossy Lakes, the old ways have validity, and may be shown to have relevance when translated into modern, rational terms; both analytical models have validity. Although from the point of view of the self-contained oral world, "literary models" represent the anti-utopia of history and change, Aksakov the writer recognizes them as a necessary part of human communication and creativity, which, like the activity of mill-building, hold the potential for creating, or re-creating, a true and balanced picture of reality. "Literariness" is a function of a new cultural pluralism, yet does not necessarily doom all communication to failure.

In *Family Chronicle,* the central problems arise due to the inadequacy of given literary-cultural models. On the one hand, this is because modernization comes too fast, and is too mindless of the value of tradition (as in the Mossy Lakes logos).[8] On the other, the tried and true remedies of the past prove unable to cope with new challenges. Neither the "old" or the "new" provides a full solution. The second fragment is a case in point. Praskov'ja Ivanovna, while innocent and ignorant of her husband's wrongdoings, is nevertheless to some extent implicated in them. She had, we are told, the direct responsibility to look after the well-being of her serfs, and, if necessary, to restrain her husband's cruelty; her passivity, it is clearly suggested, may even have encouraged his excessive behavior. Significantly, her lack of action, and indeed, her resolution "never to listen to tales against her husband" had been taken on Bagrov's advice (58/130). "She knew that people like to meddle with what does not concern them, and like to trouble the water, that they may catch fish; and [so] she made up her mind at once and laid down an absolute rule, to listen to no tales against her husband" (48/119-20). The wisdom of the proverb, and the "absolute" traditional model of conduct which Bagrov represents, while ultimately vindicated, falters before the extremism and unpredictable quiddities of modern life.

The later sections of *Family Chronicle*—the story of the marriage between Aleksej Stepanyč and Sof'ja Nikolaevna—explore the further paradoxes and difficulties encountered when the old gives way to the new. The main crisis arises when these characters are forced to transcend their traditional story-book roles and are stricken with "psychology." In fragment 3, at first both Aleksej and Sof'ja play highly literary, stylized parts, which are later reversed. Aleksej models himself as a suitor upon second-rate Sentimental novels. It is through his histrionic threat of suicide that he challenges his father's objections to his betrothal and overcomes the traditional, patriarchal imperative. Aleksej's use of this literary strategem is comical, and even pathetic. Similarly, Sof'ja's initial appearance as a fairy-tale heroine is highly stylized and melodramatic. For both Sof'ja and Aleksej, their initial literary models contradict the "historical" roles of the two characters—Sof'ja a sophisticated modern woman, Aleksej a poorly educated country bumpkin. In Ufa, when Aleksej meets Sof'ja, she is the hostess of a salon who hobnobs and corresponds with modern writers, knows both Russian and French, and who, as manager of her ailing father's affairs, wields (and enjoys) significant power. Aleksej, no hero out of a Sentimental novel, is completely out of place in Sof'ja's urban world. In Durkin's words, the two are "products of, and even metonymns for, their respective geographic and social milieus" and representations of "mental paradigms of the two sides of Russian culture in the eighteenth century" (*Aksakov,* 139 and 157).

The problem of their relationship comes into sharp relief when, as they prepare to leave Bagrovo, the Old Testament patriarch Stepan Bagrov is at a loss to explain or even fully comprehend what is in store for them:

> For all his want of education and rough-and-ready [*potopornomu*] way of expressing himself, his natural sagacity and power of intuition revealed to him the whole difference of character between the two; and he found here matter for serious reflection. Their present love for one another was a pleasant sight to him and he felt happy when he saw Sof'ja Nikolaevna's eyes constantly fixed on her husband and her eager desire to please him; but his happiness had a shade of fear and disbelief in the solidity and permanence of a state of things in itself so charming. He would have liked to speak his mind on the subject, to give them some hints or some useful advice; but whenever he began, he could not find the right words for thoughts and feelings which he could not make clear even to himself; and he went no further than those trivial commonplaces [*pošlymi vyraženijami*] which, for all their triviality, have been bequeathed to us by the practical wisdom of past generations and are verified by our own experience. His failure troubled him, and he said so frankly to his daughter-in-law. She was a clever woman, yet she failed to understand the thoughts which were turning over in his brain, and the feeling hidden in his heart.
>
> (164-65/235-36)

Bagrov, man of "natural sagacity," who expresses the age old truth of Russian proverbs, realizes that these "commonplaces bequeathed to us by the practical wisdom of the past" and "verified by our own experience" are not enough to meet the challenges presented by the modern world. The modern world into which Bagrov sends his children represents a different kind of experience that will demand different truths and a different way of communicating. Bagrov correctly senses that this "hybrid" couple face a very uncertain future, and

Sof'ja's failure to understand him serves to corroborate his fears for the reader.

Sof'ja is "clever" with book smarts but completely fails—here, and throughout the book—to understand or sympathize with Bagrov's world and the old ways to which Aleksej is associated. Unlike Ufa with its "noble views,"

> this little village in a hollow, the time-stained and weather-beaten wooden house, the pond surrounded by swamps, and the unending clack of the mill—all this seemed to her actually repulsive. And the people were no better: from her husband's family to the peasants' children, she could love none of them.
>
> (130/200-201)

Sof'ja is repeatedly and specifically contrasted to Aleksej as having no feeling for Bagrovo and its way of life, or for the pastoral ideal symbolized in the mill. (The narrator, we should note, is solidly on Alexej's side, from his appreciation of Bagrovo's unassuming splendor to the passion for hunting he shares with him—a pleasure which he notes "was impossible to make intelligible to Sof'ja Nikolaevna" [193/264]).

When near the end of the book Sof'ja is forced from her sick father's house by a malicious servant, she cannot overcome this affront and suffers a breakdown. Roles are reversed, as Alexej with his simple, natural, old-fashioned common sense rises to the occasion:

> Though weaker in character and less far-sighted than she was, he never ran to extremes and never lost presence of mind and power of judgement in the trying hours of life. It may seem strange that Alexej Stepanyč could give moral support to Sof'ja Nikolaevna; but this exceptional woman, for all her exceptional intelligence and apparent strength of will, had the unfortunate characteristic to lose courage and become utterly bewildered due to unexpected moral blows. . . . Alexej Stepanyč had love and that sanity and simplicity of mind [*duševnaja prostota*] which was wanting in his wife to teach him. . . . The truth of his simple words and his plain way of looking at things—these breathed comfort and joy into her heart, and seemed to her new and wise.
>
> (177-78/247)

Family Chronicle ends with the birth of their son Sergej—the author. After this point the oral tradition—the art of the logos—will give way to unalloyed autobiography. The narrator tells us that he was "born under a happy star" as "the answer to prayers and the object of fond desires," as rightful heir to the world of Bagrovo. Yet at the same time he is product of the problematic union of Alexej and Sof'ja, of new and old ways, and it is he who in the two succeeding volumes will be fully initiated into the modern, historical world and receive a literary education.

Family Chronicle could be located within a variety of literary traditions—the hunting manual or travelogue, nature writing, the autobiographical trilogy, the Gothic, Sentimental or psychological novel, etc.[9] However, as an attempt to preserve the oral world in print, *Family Chronicle* represents a work which generates itself, the creation of "literature" where it did not exist before, ex nihilo—a kind of literary "big bang." Bagrov's pastoral world gives birth to a proliferation of new literary models, yet at the same time it provides a secure cosmological base from which they can draw inspiration, a strong sense of rootedness in the past.

Many other of the great Russian writers of the last century also hoped to find or return to some past Golden Age, some moment of genesis which was "beyond literature," most often with a sharp sense of the irretrievability or impossibility of the task. The faith that a compromise, a new equilibrium could be achieved between the old and the new came to seem increasingly distant. In the works of Turgenev, Gončarov, and Tolstoj the oral culture of the village is either an alien culture, an impossible dream of childhood, or an ideal to be emulated and a counterweight against corrupt modernity. By the time of Bunin's "Suxodol" (1911), the hopelessly decrepit Russian village seemed to have receded into the black depths of extinction, retrievable only by the imperfect, highly subjective power of memory. However, for many Russian writers of the next generation, Babel', Pil'njak, and others, the Revolution represented a clash between urban and country, literate and oral, perceptions of the world. The most recent attempts to evoke the oral world of old Russia may be seen in the works of the "village prose writers" of the last twenty-five years, writers who grew up during the 1930s, when the remnants of Russian village culture were being forcibly destroyed in the name of literacy and progress. Aksakov himself was already well aware that the "timeless" oral universe was facing oblivion. Indeed, his mission, to preserve oral culture by writing it down, to a greater or lesser extent, already signaled its imminent end. To borrow a phrase from Thomson: Aksakov, like Herodotus, purchased "one kind of immortality at the expense of another—the immortality of literature for the immortality of tradition."

Notes

An earlier version of this paper was presented at the annual meeting of AATSEEL, Chicago, December 1985.

1. Page citations in brackets refer to, first, Sergei Aksakov, *A Russian Gentleman* (an accepted, if misleading title given to *Semejnaja xronika*), in a few places modified for accuracy, and second, to the Russian text, found in Aksakov, *Sobranie sočinenij.*

2. In Russian, *predanie* means both 'orally-related history' and 'tradition', something handed over or handed down (from the verb *predat', peredat'*) (*Slovar'*, vol. 11, col. 95). The need to respect "predanie" was a key notion for those in the 1850s and 60s who tried to refute the radical literary critics, as for example, for those who defended Puškin. (Levitt, 100-101).

3. In Russian, *xronika* may signify (among other things) written history, history itself, or—what concerns us here—oral history (*Slovar'*, vol. 17, col. 483-86). Cf. [Gončarov,] *Oblomov,* where the narrator explains why Zaxar continues to wear his worn-out livery in the city: "Without these caprices, he somehow would not have felt that he had a master over him; without them nothing would have resurrected for him his youth, the country . . . , and the stories [*predanija*] of that ancient house, the sole chronicle [*xronika*] of which was preserved by the old servants, nannies and wet-nurses, and passed down from generation to generation. . . . Only the greying servants of the house preserved and passed on the true memory of the past, treasuring it like a sacred thing" (149; my translation—MCL).

Many critics have tried—not very convincingly—to define *Family Chronicle* as a *letopis'*. The question of *Family Chronicle*'s relation to the *letopis'*, and to such medieval Russian genres as *xronika, xronograf,* and *polixron* deserves research.

4. Aksakov denied that *Family Chronicle* was an autobiography, and got angry when critics referred to Bagrovo as Aksakovo. I do not think that this anger was only due to his desire to protect living relatives from embarrassment. One thinks here of Tolstoj, who was very displeased when Nekrasov published his *Childhood* as *My Childhood* in 1852.

5. A possible confusion arises here—as in "skaz"—when we speak of the "frame" and the "inner narrative." "Skaz" or "logos" may refer to the inner narrative alone (Rice speaks here of "pure" skaz [420]), or to the inner narrative plus frame. While we could conceive of "pure logos," in absolute terms no "pure" skaz or logos can exist, even without the frame, since they are both in the final analysis written genres, mere *representations* of the oral world. Logos as I am defining it refers to inner narrative plus frame; as I suggest below, the tension between the oral and written aspects forms the genre's narrative uniqueness.

The interrelations between the two narrative voices are complex, and may be related to other developing patterns seen in Russian prose. To borrow the expression Leon Stillman applied to *Eugene Onegin,* we have here "two realities": the reality of the created world and the reality of the creator (329). In specific ways, the structure of narrative intrusions here also recalls that of *Dead Souls* (which may itself have been adapted from Puškin, as Donald Fanger has suggested, 37). At one point near the start of *Family Chronicle*—just to cite one example—the narrator stops to "apologize" "for interrupting my narrative in order to meet an imaginary objection on the part of the reader" (20/92).

6. Pritchett probably got the idea from Duff's translation, in which he actually calls Sof'ja "a ragged and oppressed Cinderella," a reference not in the text of *Family Chronicle*.

7. For example, when Bagrov writes to Sof'ja when she is pregnant. The narrator tells us he has seen this letter and that "it is hard to believe that a man with so little refinement of manner [*grubyj celovek*] . . . could give verbal expression to such tender and delicate solicitude as breathed through the whole of this letter" (174-75/244-45). The few words the narrator recalls are: "if you were living in my house . . . I would not suffer the wind to blow on you or a grain of dust to settle on your skin [*ja by ne dal na tebja vertu venut' i porošinke sest'*]." These are the very same formulaic words which the Beast of the Forest in the *skazka* "Alen'kij cvetoček" (appended to *Detskie gody Bagrova-vnuka*) addresses to the heroine. Bagrov's literacy fully belongs to the "pre-literate" folk universe.

8. In this connection it is curious to follow up the fate of the mill at New Bagrovo later in Aksakov's trilogy. In the last volume, Alexej plans to build "a better mill." To this end he employs "a great talker" named Krasnov to do the work. Despite the warnings of the old miller and some of the peasants, Alexej has "blind belief" in him because, as he puts it, "He has made a plan of it all on paper." Almost predictably, when it is finally completed, "the [new] mill worked much worse than the old one" (*A Russian Schoolboy*, 72-75). Elsewhere Aksakov makes a similar point when he chastises the "contemptuous view" on the part of "enlightenment and science" which disregards the accumulated truths of traditional folk medicine out of hand as mere "superstition" (58).

9. These are perhaps only the most obvious. See also Durkin's comments, *Aksakov*, 243-47. We must beware the urge to read *Family Chronicle* backwards into the later tradition, that is, to see it in terms of what the Russian prose tradition later became, rather than what it meant for Aksakov. Kathryn B. Feuer's article on Aksakov, which argues that *Family Chronicle* "is closer to the Dos-

toevskian novel than any other work of nineteenth century literature" (88), suffers from such anachronism.

Works Cited

Aksakov, Sergei. *A Russian Gentleman* [*Semejnaja xronika*]. Trans. J. D. Duff. 1916. Reprinted. N. Y.: Oxford Univ. Press, 1982.

Aksakov, Sergei. *A Russian Schoolboy*. Trans. J. D. Duff. 1916. Reprinted. N. Y.: Oxford Univ. Press, 1983.

Aksakov, S. T. *Semejnaja xronika*. In *Sobranie sočinenij v četyrex tomax*, t. 1, 73-237. M.: Xudož. lit-ra, 1955.

Cohen, Elliott. "The Genre of the Autobiographical Account of Childhood—Three Test Cases: The Trilogies of Tolstoy, Aksakov, and Gorky." Ph.D. diss., Yale Univ., 1973.

Durkin, Andrew R. "Pastoral in Aksakov: The Transformation of Poetry." *Ulbandus Review* 2, no. 1 (1979):62-75.

Durkin, Andrew R. *Sergei Aksakov and Russian Pastoral*. New Brunswick: Rutgers Univ. Press, 1983.

Fanger, Donald. "Influence and Tradition in the Russian Novel." In *The Russian Novel From Pushkin to Pasternak*, ed. John Garrard, 29-50. New Haven: Yale Univ. Press, 1983.

Feuer, Kathryn B. "*Family Chronicle*: The Indoor Art of Sergei Aksakov." *Ulbandus Review* 2, no. 1 (1979):86-102.

Foley, John Miles. *Oral-Formulaic Theory and Research: An Introduction and Annotated Bibliography*. N. Y.: Garland, 1985.

Forster, E. M. *Aspects of the Novel and Related Writings*. London: Edward Arnold, 1974.

Gončarov, I. A. *Oblomov*. In *Izbrannye sočinenija*, 145-374. M.: GIXL, 1948.

Levitt, Marcus C. "The Pushkin Celebration of 1880 and the Politics of Literature in Russia." Ph.D. diss., Columbia Univ., 1984.

Mašinskij, S. *S. T. Aksakov, žizn' i tvorčestvo*. M.: Xudož. lit-ra, 1961.

Ong, Walter J. *Orality and Literacy*. N. Y.: Methuen, 1982.

Pritchett, V. S. *The Living Novel and Later Appreciations*. N. Y.: Vintage, 1967.

Rice, Martin P. "On 'Skaz.'" *Russian Literature Triquarterly*, no. 12 (1975):409-24.

Scholes, Robert and Robert Kellogg. "The Oral Heritage of Written Narrative." Chap. 2 in *The Nature of Narrative*. N. Y.: Oxford Univ. Press, 1966.

Slovar' sovremennogo russkogo literaturnogo jazyka. 17 vols. M.: AN SSSR, 1950-65.

Stilman, Leon, "Problemy literaturnyx žanrov i tradicii v 'Evgenii Onegine' Puškina." In *American Contributions to the Fourth International Congress of Slavists, Moscow, September, 1958,* 321-65. The Hague: Mouton, 1958.

Thomson, J. A. K. *The Art of the Logos.* London: George Allen and Unwin, 1935.

Richard Gregg (essay date January 1991)

SOURCE: Gregg, Richard. "The Decline of a Dynast: From Power to Love in Aksakov's *Family Chronicle.*" *The Russian Review* 50, no. 1 (January 1991): 35-47.

[*In the following essay, Gregg explores questions of genre as they relate to Aksakov's* Family Chronicle. *According to Gregg, the work explores two distinct literary forms: the "Homeric" epic, as embodied in the portrait of the patriarch, Stepan Mikhailovich Bagrov; and the more subtle, naturalistic chronicle of Bagrov's descendents. Gregg sees this shift in biblical terms as a movement from the Old Testament principle of masculine authority to the New Testament ideals of community and maternal love.*]

Although the generic peculiarities of *Family Chronicle* have been the main focus of its investigators,[1] thematics—to use the convenient neologism—has not been entirely neglected. Thus, commentators are likely to remind us that the larger-than-life proportions of old Bagrov enhance the central theme of the patriarch; that his voyage eastward rehearses the pioneering thrust which informs many narratives of exploration; or that the segments dominated by Aleksei and Sof'ia Nikolaevna embody the themes of urbanization and domesticity. Loosely tying up these (and other) strands is the comment of a recent scholar that the central conflict of the work as a whole is the "incursion of modernity . . . on the old way of life."[2]

To some these truths may seem like truisms. They lie, as it were, on the surface of the text. But this very stricture helps, I think, to define the nature of the narrative. For, with its clear, unhurried, expansive, and richly detailed evocation of an earlier age, *Family Chronicle* is an unusually pure example of that mimetic mode which Erich Auerbach, in his classic study, called "Homeric." Everything—or almost everything—in these pages is, in Auerbach's words, "direct," "visible," "leisurely," "copiously related," and "fully externalized"—a world, as it were, without shadows.[3] And it is precisely this manner of relation (applied to the blind Aksakov reciting the heroic exploits of bygone years, the word "Homeric" seems oddly apt) that, according to the critic, lacks polyvalence ("a multiplicity of meanings") and, as a consequence, defies, or at least discourages, "interpretations."[4]

"Clear" and "visible" as Aksakov's main themes are, they are suspended in—and colored by—an *ethical* medium which has yet to be defined. Present throughout the work, this medium changes as the narrative unfolds. To trace these changes and assess their significance is the main purpose of this article.

I

In the beginning was the trek. Feeling cramped in the confines of his native Simbirsk, and harassed by litigious neighbor-relatives bent on increasing their lands at the expense of his own, Stepan Mikhailovich Bagrov, patriarch and "grandfather,"[5] having bought some thirteen thousand acres of virgin soil in the Orenburg Province, sets out to the southeast with his family, serfs, and belongings, crosses the Volga, and proceeds to the Ural Piedmont, where, some four hundred versts from his ancestral home, he will build a farmstead, plough fresh lands, and start a new life. Such, in slightly simplified terms, is the narrative core of "The Migration" (*pereselenie*), the first part of the first segment of *Family Chronicle* entitled "Stepan Mikhailovich Bagrov."

Despite the unhappiness of the Bagrov serfs at this uprooting, despite the length and the slowness of the journey, executed by stages and in relays, the undertaking is completely successful, for what the pioneers find at the end of their journey is a rural Eden, whose beauties elicit that panegyric that constitutes "Orenburg Province" (Part 2). "My God," exclaims the narrator, "how good was then that wild, virginal, luxurious nature!";[6] "how picturesque and varied . . . the forests, steppes and hilly regions" (p. 85); "bright and transparent, like deep, enormous cups, thy lakes;" "marvelous were those . . . rivers" (p. 84), and so forth. Indeed, in the eyes of the eulogist (*pace* those who see in Aksakov an unfailingly sober realist), the only defect of this "blessed" land would seem to be its vulnerability to human exploitation. An ecologist *avant la lettre,* he laments:

> Marvelous and blessed land,
> Storehouse of terrestial riches,
> Forgotten one, thou shalt not serve eternally
> As grazing fields for shepherds.
> Enamored of thy free expanses,
> Throngs of men will hasten here
> And, sullied by their hands,
> No longer wilt thou know thyself!
> For they will trample down thy meadows, fell thy forests,
> And roil the heavenly azure of thy waters!
>
> (p. 81)

It is not through geographical space alone, however, that we move as we travel toward this "promised (*obetovannyi*) corner" of the earth (p. 80). For as the world of Old Bagrovo recedes into the past and the Bu-guruslan valley opens before us, it is the youth of the earth itself—"green," "fertile," "fresh," and "virginal" (the epithets recur repeatedly)—which we seem to find and, in so doing, observe in ourselves signs of juvenescence: "not only did [Bagrov's] spirits rise, but his body became stronger (*pozdorovel telom*")" (p. 86). Ignorant of the "petitions, complaints, [and] quarrels" (p. 86) bred by civilized life, the nomadic tribes, who graze their flocks in peace and lead "patriarchal" lives (p. 84), evoke the pastoral simplicities of an earlier age and provide a fitting background for the immemorial activities of ploughing, sowing, and reaping, which the settlers begin to pursue. Or, to put the pseudocontradiction of the folk tale ("in the olden days when the world was young") in a biographical framework: as the aging Aksakov—his frail condition is briefly evoked in these pages (p. 92)—recollects the idyllic places of his childhood, so the reader feels himself retreating in time toward that "antiquity of history," which in Bacon's well-known phrase "is the youth of the world."

If Parts 1 and 2 describe the pioneers' trek and the virgin wilderness which awaits them, the heterogeneous and digressive nature of the third part ("New Places") resists neat thematic labeling. Its basic narrative thrust is nonetheless clear: under the guidance of Stepan Mikhailovich, the settlers have consolidated their holdings, while the patriarch himself, by virtue of his honesty and Solomonic wisdom, has become a revered figure throughout the region. As for the fourth section, its basic nature is best understood in the perspective of its antecedents. Having traveled far, acquired much, built tirelessly, and governed well (Parts 1-3), it is natural that the master of New Bagrovo should pause to admire his own handiwork. And, in "Stepan Mikhailovich's Good Day," that is what he does: "It delighted him to look at his manor already equipped with all the necessary buildings" (p. 93); "viewing the healthy cattle as a sure sign . . . of his peasants' well-being, he was filled with admiration" (p. 93); "out in the fields he was satisfied with everything" (p. 96), and so forth.

II

Such are the main thematic components of the first chapter of *Family Chronicle.* Their affinity to certain literary archetypes which perennially recur in a variety of narrative genres is not hard to show. Thus, the long trek of Stepan Mikhailovich to the "promised" land of Orenburg rehearses on a small scale the voyage toward some cherished goal which has informed innumerable narratives from Homer to Tolkien. In Bagrov's excited discovery of a corner of the earth that is pristine and teeming with natural riches we recognize an analogue of the Edens and Arcadias of antiquity, the El Dorados and "brave new worlds" of the Renaissance, and (more recently) those unspoiled wildernesses which provide

the natural setting for any number of romantically colored fictions.[7] As for the culminating event, the building of New Bagrovo and the satisfaction that this achievement provides its builder, the secular cosmogony, describing how human resourcefulness can triumph over natural obstacles to create a viable new order, has since *Robinson Crusoe* proved to be a perennially popular fictional theme.[8]

Given the acumen, integrity, great physical strength, and the almost superhuman energy with which old Bagrov is endowed, it is not surprising that critics have been moved to use such epithets as "colossal," "stupendous," and "epic" to describe him.[9] Viewed in surroundings redolent of Biblical times—primitive, pastoral, patriarchal—this monolithic creator, ruler, and judge recalls in fact the anthropomorphic Jehovah of Genesis Himself.[10] Like that all-wise Father-Founder, Bagrov has created a world, given it a name, and peopled it with his people who till its fields and enjoy its bounty. All but infallible in his judgment of men and things—he is to his neighbors a veritable "oracle" (p. 89)—he assumes attitudes that imply omnipotence as well:

> Lord and master of not only his own lands but of others as well, he could graze his flocks, mow the grass, fell the timber—and no one would say a word.
>
> (p. 86)

Like the omnipotent Jehovah, however, Bagrov also has a darker side. For when his chosen people seek to deceive him or otherwise limit his power, his anger is terrible to behold: "He shook all over, convulsion twisted his face, and a furious fire welled from his eyes, which had grown dark and turbid with rage" (p. 90). And while the punishment which he metes out is invariably just, the forms which it takes can be shocking. Once the culprit has been duly punished, however, the reign of the "good, benign, even indulgent" (p. 90) autocrat returns. And in "Stepan Mikhailovich's Good Day" (the fourth and final section) we see him, purged as it were of his fury, going out in the early morning freshness (cf. the Biblical "cool of the day") to inspect with deep satisfaction the "garden" he has planted.[11]

Reinforcing the Old Testament aura which invests this figure is the small circle of inferior women who surround him. Though not unkind, Arisha, the wife, is a stupid and gullible creature, whose low status may be inferred from the fact that as a sign of special favor Stepan Mikhailovich allows her to kiss his hand. Qualitatively different from their mother, the daughters are depicted in even less attractive colors. Crafty, mendacious, and "without good qualities," these "granddaughters of Eve" (p. 95) come close to fulfilling the role of their Biblical ancestress. For with the connivance of the weak-willed Arisha they are responsible for letting a very substantial kind of evil into their small world.

III

The trek, the discovery, the creation, the celebration—such are the basic archetypes informing "Stepan Mikhailovich Bagrov." And the power, mental as well as physical, spiritual as well as mental, of him who launched that voyage, discovered the lands, and built upon them is such that—within the limits of this excerpt at least—any diminution of that power seems inconceivable. The chronological proviso is crucial. For, viewed as a whole, **Family Chronicle** records precisely such a decline. True, Bagrov's authority is never openly challenged: he remains to the last the nominal sovereign of his little world. But as the chronicle unfolds and the narrative focus shifts to include new scenes and faces, the aura of his omnipotence fades. And, by the end, the quondam mover-and-shaker has become a peripheral figure, a crochety and error-prone old man out of touch with events and powerless to control them.

Viewed in a literary context, this decline is by no means anomalous. Narratives that trace the fortunes of a family from generation to generation often have as their theme the erosion of the dynastic principle—witness Mann's Buddenbrooks, Galsworthy's Forsytes, Martin du Garde's Thibaults, and Saltykov-Shchedrin's Golovlevs. But in contrast to these stories of dispersal or decay, **Family Chronicle** possesses a kind of spiritual resiliency which its "happy ending" (the birth of the longed-for grandson) can only partly explain. For, as the patriarchal figure of old Bagrov recedes into the background, another personality, no less vivid for embodying a very different set of values, moves to the fore. It is this displacement that provides the basic dynamics of the work viewed as a whole.

It is in the logical—and chronological—order of things that the chapter which follows, "Mikhail Maksimovich Kurolesov," witnesses the first sign of Bagrov's decline.[12] Far from attenuating the Old Testament pattern, this chapter lends it an extra dimension. If the omnipotent father-creator of New Bagrovo evokes *toutes proportions gardées* the anthropomorphic Creator of Eden, the incursion of the satanic tempter, Kurolesov, on His domain cannot but recall—among other, more recent literary models[13]—the serpent of Genesis. Like the brightest of angels before his fall, Kurolesov is seductively attractive—dashing (*molodets soboi*), well-spoken, and handsome. (Indeed, not unlike the Antichrist of the Apocalypse, he resembles in certain respects the "Deity," that is, old Bagrov Himself.)[14] Beneath this suave and courtly veneer, however, lurks a *nechistaia sila* (cf. the demonic *nechistii dukh* of popular parlance, p. 112),[15] which uses flattery and guile to win over the "granddaughters of Eve," thwarting the will of their lord and master and introducing through his "forbidden" marriage discord into the Bagrov family. Fittingly, the perpetrator of these deeds bears a name which evokes his impious essence. For if in modern Russian *kurolesit'* means to "play tricks" or to "work mischief," etymologically that same verb derives from a sacrilegious distortion of the *Kyrie eleison* ("Lord have mercy on us") of the Orthodox liturgy.

On superficial inspection the image of old Bagrov in these pages might seem unchanged from the first segment. Alone among his entourage, Bagrov is strongly suspicious of Kurolesov, whose suit for the hand of his niece Praskov'ia Ivanovna he opposes. And when at the end he sallies forth to rescue his Praskov'ia from her husband, he inevitably recalls the archetypal *deus ex machina* of folklore and myth. These heroic manifestations notwithstanding, Bagrov's image in the second segment falls somewhat short of the God-like. Early outmaneuvered by Kurolesov, who takes advantage of Bagrov's ill-timed absence to compass his schemes, Bagrov is later guilty of less pardonable lapses. Impressed by Kurolesov's respectful demeanor and managerial skills, he disregards his own inner promptings, is reconciled with his "nephew," and even promises him—conditionally to be sure—his "love and friendship" (p. 114). On hearing reports of the latter's bloodthirsty excesses at Parashino, Bagrov is at first incredulous and, when offered irrefutable proof of their truth, he refuses to take any action at all, on the morally questionable grounds that these "filthy doings" are no concern of his (p. 130). It is only when his niece herself falls afoul of Kurolesov's fury that his connivance with lawlessness—for it amounts to that—comes to an end and he decides to act.

As the superhuman aura surrounding old Bagrov begins to fade, a new positive force, embodied in Praskov'ia Ivanovna, makes itself felt. True, Parasha's debut is not auspicious. A pampered and childish girl (on the eve of her wedding she is still playing with dolls), she is an easy mark for Kurolesov and her scheming cousins. "Miraculously," however, that marriage, which in the long run proves so disastrous, works immediate effects that are beneficial. Within a year's time, we are told, the flighty fiancée has grown into a woman of maturity, wisdom, and lasting affections. These changes notwithstanding, it will be more than a decade before Praskov'ia's mettle will be put to a serious test. Protected from the facts by her insularity (only on far-lying estates does Kurolesov give rein to his sadistic instincts) and a misplaced sense of conjugal loyalty, she remains unsuspecting—despite dark rumors and Kurolesov's prolonged absences. But finally, when she receives a circumstantial account of her husband's crimes from an unimpeachable source, she embarks on a course of action that, Aksakov tells us, even "the most daring of men" would hesitate to undertake (p. 125). Rounding up three servants, she sets out on a 250-mile journey to confront the accused. Catching him red-handed (an orgy is in full swing as she arrives), she demands that he surrender the powers of attorney once granted him. Infuriated, he beats her senseless, locks her up, and for five days tries in vain to force his battered and feverish prisoner to sign over the estates in question. "What might have happened next," Aksakov speculates, "God only knows" (p. 129). In fact, when old Bagrov finally arrives after six days, the woman whom he rescues has little in common with the languishing "damsel in distress" of fictional stereotypes. By dint of her bold initiatives, steadfast defiance under duress, and deep religious faith, Praskov'ia has proved herself to be an authentically *heroic* heroine, the moral equal of her deliverer.

IV

Many years had gone by, and many events had taken place [in the Orenburg region]; there had been famine; there had been epidemic diseases; there had been Pugachev's uprising.

(p. 138)

With this laconic recital of mass misfortunes the third segment begins. For the chronicler, however, these epic disturbances are incidental to the simple fact that "old" Bagrov, whose apparent noninvolvement in these events may be symptomatic, has grown truly old: this fact sets in motion a major shift in the narrative focus. Advancing now to the center of the stage are Aleksei Stepanovich (the son) and Sof'ia Nikolaevna Zubina (successively fiancée, wife and mother), whose romance and marriage constitute the subject of the last three segments: "The Marriage of Young Bagrov," "The Newlyweds at Bagrovo," and "Life at Ufa."

In itself this shift is hardly remarkable, the eclipse of the older generation by the younger being a constituent part of any "dynastic" narrative. But as the account of the young couple's betrothal unfolds, it becomes clear that another, quite different change has occurred, a change that—by the standards of the age at least—was anything but normal, namely, *the displacement of the male-oriented world which has heretofore obtained by a gynocentric one in the middle of which stands Sof'ia Nikolaevna herself.*

This change does not come entirely unheralded. Already, Praskov'ia Ivanovna had during the course of the Kurolesov chapter risen far above the ruck of feminine mediocrity embodied by Arisha and her daughters. But however courageous her conduct may have been, it posed no threat to the traditional principle that in marriage the husband should lead and the wife should follow. The example of Sof'ia Nikolaevna in the last three excerpts does exactly that.

The vast superiority of this beautiful and brilliant woman to her gauche and simple-minded suitor (later husband) is, arguably, the basic underlying fact of these chapters: compounded by parental opposition on both sides, it not only constitutes a major obstacle to their marital plans, it will later become a source of continuing tension between husband and wife. And precisely because this discrepancy looms so large, it tends to obscure a third fundamental change in the values that obtain in these chapters—a change related to, and yet quite different from the slow eclipse of the patriarch on one hand or the ascendancy of a strong female on the other: in short, *the emergence of love as the regnant moral principle.*

In the traditional sense, love is almost entirely absent from the first two segments—the fear, devotion, and awe that Sergei Mikhailovich variously inspires in his entourage having little to do with that affect as it is commonly understood.[16] We are therefore scarcely surprised to learn that Bagrov seems never to have experienced romantic love and has no understanding of it (p. 153). Symptomatic in this respect is the fact that the only relationship described in these pages where romantic love plays any role, namely, the courtship of Praskov'ia, is founded on deceit and ends in disaster.

To propose that the "love ethic" (to adapt the popular phrase) displaces that of power in the last three segments does not mean, however, that the former vanishes without a trace. Stepan Mikhailovich remains, after all, the head of the family and continues to exercise—though to a diminished degree—the prerogatives of that position. More surprisingly, on closer inspection, the character of Sof'ia Nikolaevna reveals a temperamental affinity to that of the autocrat himself. For, analyzing the reasons why the urbane and brilliant Sof'ia Nikolaevna responds to Aleksei's overtures more sympathetically than one might under the circumstances expect, Aksakov observes that in the depths of her nature lay a "love for power" (p. 167) which the prospect of a docile and pliable husband might well appease.

The persistence in muted (or transmuted) form of a power ethic qualifies but does not undermine the primacy of love in the last "half" of the chronicle, its most obvious manifestation being, of course, Aleksei's love for Sof'ia Nikolaevna, as related in "The Marriage of Young Bagrov." Replete with vicissitudes of various kinds—the most formidable being old Bagrov's resolute opposition to the match—Aleksei's courtship is crowned with success when Bagrov, acting under his despairing son's threat of suicide, relents. No star-crossed swain in the sentimental novels of which he is fond could have suffered more pathetically or triumphed more completely.[17] *Amor omnia vincit* or, as Sonia herself succinctly puts it, "*Vasha liubov' preodolela vse prepiatsviia*" (p. 180).

As if to orchestrate his main theme, Aksakov makes his heroine the object of love in a variety of nonromantic contexts. Thus, we are told that her weak and ailing father loves his daughter passionately (p. 140), that Katerina Alekseevna Cheprunova, a female relative, adores her endlessly (p. 251), and that Ufa high society was positively smitten by her beauty (p. 144). But easily the most important of Sof'ia's platonic admirers is, of course, Stepan Mikhailovich himself. For if, as the title denotes, the subject of the fourth segment is the newly-weds' visit to New Bagrovo, its underlying theme is the unusually close and touching relationship that develops between the bride and her father-in-law. True, there is a touch of calculation here: to consolidate her position in her new family, Sof'ia must, she knows, ingratiate herself with its strongest member. But the bond which spontaneously springs up between the young woman and the aging patriarch, replete with delicate attentions and chaste embraces, transcends selfish considerations and indeed results in a unique kind of emotional fulfillment for each. In Stepan Mikhailovich, Sof'ia finds that wise and resolute paterfamilias that her weak-willed father had so signally failed to be. In Sof'ia, Bagrov recognizes a woman who so far surpasses the members of his own immediate family in character and charm that she quickly assumes—to the dismay of her sisters-in-law—a privileged position within its confines. Precisely this shared spiritual superiority confers on this unlikely pair—so profoundly different in many respects—a dignity which the tense and agitated courtship of unequals (the brilliant Sof'ia wooed by the uncouth Aleksei) too often lacks.

Of all the feelings that human beings can feel, none, Aksakov assures us, is as deep or as powerful as maternal love (p. 274). It is therefore fitting that the culminating member of the "love triptych" (as the last three segments might be called) should exemplify this emotion. For Sof'ia Nikolaevna's love for her firstborn is of quite exceptional intensity. All her energies, all her thoughts are absorbed by her baby girl, the loving care for whom becomes a jealously preserved monopoly. Alas, this obsession (for it amounts to that) is as short-lived as it is intense. Four months after her birth, little Praskov'ia—sickly from the start—is dead. The grief of the bereaved mother is such that her family fears for her sanity, and—when she falls ill—for her life itself.

This harrowing ordeal emphasizes by way of contrast the joyous events that are to follow and that conclude the chronicle—the full recovery of Sof'ia Nikolaevna and the arrival of her second-born. Described far more circumstantially than its antecedent, this pregnancy is twice blessed. Not only does the baby live, but to the joy of old Bagrov it is a boy. That the mother will love her little son as passionately as she had her infant daughter can scarcely be doubted.[18]

One further dimension of this "love syndrome" remains to be noted, namely Sof'ia Nikolaevna's love of God. The absence of religious motifs in the earlier "epic"

sections of the work[19] is somewhat surprising, given its "slavophile" aura, and may well be rooted in the requirements of *Dichtung* as well as those of *Wahrheit*: If old Bagrov had regularly exhibited the reverential and obedient attitudes implicit in the man-God relationship, his own aura of absolute omnipotence would be somewhat diminished.

Such is not the case with Sof'ia Nikolaevna. Protected by the gender-related stereotype of the "naturally" pious female, she is, like Praskov'ia before her, both heroic and deeply religious. Among the repeated manifestations of these traits, the first is by far the most memorable. Daily tormented by the persecutions of her stepmother, the fifteen-year-old girl decides to put an end to her life. Having prayed long and fervently before the icon of the Virgin, she faints away, only to discover, on coming to her senses, that the taper that she had extinguished the night before is now burning brightly. Seeing in this small miracle (the only supernatural occurrence in the work) proof that her love for God is actively reciprocated, Sof'ia finds the strength to endure her martyrdom until the providential death of her tormentor.

V

In view of Aleksei's triumph over his father's explicit wishes, it is, in a sense, as victors that the newlyweds arrive at New Bagrovo (fourth segment), where it is now Sof'ia Nikolaevna's turn to play the role of the conqueror. For through her devoted attentions, manifold charms, and, even, small hypocrisies (her interest in New Bagrovo is wholly feigned: she detests the place) this "sorceress" (the word is Bagrov's) in a few short days completely captures the old man's heart: "*Ia bol'no poliubil tebia*," he confesses as they part (p. 236). But there is more to Sof'ia's conquest than this. By virtue of her charisma she has, in effect, uncovered a new person: a tender, generously affectionate old man (the word *laska* and its derivatives accompany the couple like a leitmotif) who contrasts strikingly with the stern autocrat of earlier years. Thus, when on one occasion the newlyweds fail to meet the time-hallowed dinner hour, Bagrov stuns the assembled company by—an unheard of concession—*delaying the meal for a few minutes.* Or again, accustomed to giving uninhibited vent to his anger when provoked, in the presence of Sof'ia Nikolaevna he quells an incipient outburst, and even feels "ashamed" of his impulse (p. 225). Or still again, in the bosom of his own family this pillar of male supremacy is obliged to witness—not, to be sure, without protest—Sof'ia Nikolaevna's cavalier treatment of her husband, that is, of *his* own son. Most modern readers will applaud these breaches of "chauvinist" etiquette. But it is precisely from such a code—redolent at times of the *domostroi*—that the icon of the earlier chapters was partly constructed. In his more human—and more humane—form Stepan Mikhailovich forfeits some of his larger-than-life dimensions.

The gradual disappearance of these dimensions leaves, it should be emphasized, an impressive human being intact. Less awe-inspiring than in the first excerpt, Bagrov remains during the "middle" chapters a person whose sound judgment and unimpeachable rectitude command the respect of all who know him. In the fifth and final segment, however, it is precisely his stature as a human being that suffers diminution.

One reason for this is the sharply altered narrative focus. Although in the second, third, and fourth segments Bagrov has ceased to be the monolithic presence that dominated "Stepan Mikhailovich Bagrov," crucial episodes in each, for example, the rescue of Praskov'ia Ivanovna, the marriage of Aleksei, the idyll with Sof'ia Nikolaevna, continue to hinge on his decisions, his acts. Without him the narrative structure of these chapters would collapse. This is hardly true of "Life in Ufa." Removed from the events taking place in the city (the young couple does not return to New Bagrovo; he never visits Ufa), Stepan Mikahilovich now stands at the periphery of things, his brief appearances in the narrative depending on events beyond his control.

Even passive, peripheral characters can sometimes influence the course of events by the sheer force of their personalities, but Bagrov of the fifth segment fails even in this. Age has impaired his powers of judgment; his opinions, ill-informed and rooted in prejudice, are ignored; his only "positive" act produces disastrous results. Specifically, the old man's absolute certainty that his daughter-in-law will present him with a grandson not only smacks of hubris (one thinks of some primitive potentate, who cannot believe that nature will disobey his will), it is patently silly. And when Sof'ia finally delivers a daughter, Bagrov's incredulity and bewilderment are such that he becomes what he has never been before—ridiculous (p. 256). More seriously, while his contempt for female offspring is, if judged by the "sexist" standards of that age, not unusual, his complete indifference to the death of Sof'ia's adored baby girl is more than "chauvinistic"—it is repellent. Or again, when, ignoring the facts of the case, he rebukes Sof'ia for "deserting" her sick father (it is in point of fact the spite of a scheming servant, coupled with Zubin's abject weakness, which drives her from the paternal home), he is both meddlesome and wrong. Similarly misguided are his petulant protests—fortunately unheeded—against the regimen (kumys and horseback riding) prescribed for his gravely ill daughter-in-law. Precisely these remedies, we are given to believe, speed her recovery.

Emblematic of this quasi-senile capriciousness is the way Bagrov chooses to celebrate the news of Sof'ia's first, ill-fated pregnancy. Acting on a whim, he forces a handsome young male serf to marry a spiteful and ugly maidservant ten years his senior. The result of this union is, not surprisingly, a calamity for both. And while it would be wrong to impute deliberate cruelty to Bagrov's motives (for mysterious reasons the old man is fond of the shrew in question), the moral obtuseness of his choice, underscored by his apparent indifference to the misery he has caused, is obvious. A decade earlier, one is permitted to think, such an act on his part would have been unthinkable.

In contrast to these dispiriting pictures of senescence is the image of Bagrov in the culminating scene. Apprised by a messenger that Sof'ia has given birth to a baby boy, the old man makes the sign of the cross, rises from his bed, takes down the family register, and enters the name of him who will ensure the survival of the Bagrov dynasty. On this triumphant note **Family Chronicle** comes to an end. And yet, while the picture just sketched is true in every detail, the same event may be viewed from a much less flattering angle: far removed from the festivities at Ufa, an enfeebled old man, barefoot and apparently alone, scrambles out of bed to record the name of the infant who will (vanitas vanitatum!) perpetuate his name. And in truth, this second, "subversive" portrait is the better likeness of the crotchety figure whom we sporadically glimpse in these pages. For Ufa, not New Bagrovo, is now the locus of events; the domestic life at Ufa—replete with the problems that typically beset young married couples (the ailing parent, the jealous spouse, the difficult pregnancy)—constitutes its subject. And at its center stands the spiritual heir (and temperamental opposite) of Stepan Mikhailovich, the brilliant, high-strung Sof'ia, who comes to embody the deepest of all human emotion (sic Aksakov)—maternal love.

The transformations which I have traced need no further elaboration. But one can gain a deeper insight into their significance if one compares the thematic substance of the first and final segments in terms of two synchronic images or icons. Thus, while individual responses will vary, certain iconic constants may be recognized in "Stepan Mikhailovich Bagrov." Specifically, against a backdrop of untamed wilderness are scattered the appurtenances of the Bagrov farmstead (ploughed fields, fences, buildings); in the middle distance are grouped its creatures (family, domestic animals, serfs), while in the foreground, proudly surveying his possessions, rises the monolithic figure of the founding father. And while the resemblance this fourfold configuration bears to the iconography of Genesis (wilderness, creatures, garden, Creator) has already been indicated, when juxtaposed to the ruling icon of the final segment it becomes sharper by way of contrast. For few would dispute the basic visual image which "Life at Ufa" evokes: standing before us is a young mother; in her arms her adored child, while in the background looms the figures of the half-forgotten husband. And that of course is an icon which recalls the Gospel account of the Nativity.

These Biblical analogues could, of course, be accidental. In describing the creation of New Bagrovo and the birth of Praskov'ia (and later Sergei), Aksakov may have had neither Eden nor the Nativity specifically in mind. What lends a more-than-adventitious character to these parallels is their affinity to that "transvaluation of values" which we have been tracing here. For if Power, Male Supremacy, and the Patriarchal Family are concepts central to "Stepan Mikhailovich Bagrov," then the congruence of imagery recalling the Old Testament, where these same ideas play such a crucial role, is obvious. At the opposite end of the spectrum: if the "Ufa chapters" mark the emergence of a gynocentric world, in which the "love ethic," the Christian religion, and the cult of motherhood figure prominently, is not an icon recalling the Holy Family an apt symbol of that world?

VI

"The old order changeth." And it may be appropriate by way of conclusion to ask how the modern reader is likely to respond to the fact. If ethics were our only guide, we would scarcely hesitate. However greatly we may admire the acumen, courage, and rectitude of Stepan Mikhailovich, his autocratic and sometimes savage exercise of power cannot be condoned. In comparison the "love ethic" embodied by Sof'ia Nikolaevna marks a step in the direction of comity and enlightenment.

Esthetic criteria, however, offer a more ambiguous perspective. As the larger-than-life figure of old Bagrov recedes into the background; as Buguruslan's primitive wilderness gives way to the smaller, more confined surroundings of Ufa; as the long-range, "wide-lens" view of man in nature yields to a more tightly knit urban society, perceived at closer quarters and in more intimate psychological detail; as, in sum, the "civilized" world, repudiated by Bagrov a generation earlier, begins to reassert itself (we have, in a sense, come full circle), the heroic dimension of the narrative inevitably suffers eclipse. More specifically, if, as we have seen, "Stepan Mikhailovich Bagrov" relates the creation of a new world, its analogue in the last segment is "merely" the birth of a baby boy. If, in the early parts, domestic strife sporadically erupts in the sudden, seismic rages of old Bagrov, later the same theme assumes the more prosaic form of the repeated squabbling of the newly-weds. Or again, whereas Kurolesov is a villain of truly satanic stature, who, pitted against an even more formidable adversary, is eventually overcome, his villainous counterpart in "Life in Ufa" is Zubin's scheming man-servant, a *melkii bes*, whose crafty manipulation of his weak master ultimately *succeeds*. Finally—and on a quite different level—if, as few would deny, low com-

edy tends to undermine the epic afflatus, then the introduction in the later segments of such buffoonish types as the drunken scandalmonger, Flena Ivanovna, the wildly mendacious Afrosin'ia Andreevna, and Klaus, Sof'ia Nikolaevna's yellow-wigged obstetrician, cannot but further reduce the epic scale of things.

It is, however, a revolution in literary taste, culminating in the early years of the author's own life, that provides the most suggestive generic framework for the changes we have been tracing. As late as the 1770s (the decade of old Bagrov's migration), educated Russians continued to exalt the epic above all genres.[20] And, as noted, the early parts of our chronicle offer a setting (the simple, spacious, primitive world of bygone days), characters (the all-powerful hero-leader, his diabolical adversary), and an array of themes (the long voyage, the discovery, the cosmogony—all accomplished by a single, sovereign will) that had unmistakable affinities with that genre. But with the advent in Russia of Sentimentalism (c. 1790), the epic yielded pride of place to a less lofty narrative type. Focused on the contemporary scene, eschewing larger-than-life people and events, depicting men and women in a societal context,[21] assigning central roles to female characters, and preferring the theme of love (licit or illicit, passionate or platonic) to that of the odyssey, the conquest, or the foundation, the sentimental novel offered its (predominantly female) readers a world with which they could more easily identify. This is the world and these are the values that, as we have seen, emerge in the Ufa chapters. And while the eclipse of the epic ambiance of Buguruslan cannot but evoke in us a sense of loss, entering the more "novelistic" surroundings of Ufa, the modern reader will find by way of compensation a more familiar world, more reassuringly ordinary, more imbued with values that are recognizably his own.

Notes

1. See S. I. Mashinskii, *S. T. Aksakov* (Moscow, 1961), pp. 361-85; Kathryn B. Feuer, "*Family Chronicle*: The Indoor Art of Sergei Aksakov," *Ulbandus Review,* vol. 1 (1979), pp. 86-102; Andrew Durkin, *Serge Aksakov and Russian Pastoral* (New Brunswick, NJ: Rutgers University Press, 1983), pp. 89-162; Marcus C. Levitt, "Aksakov's *Family Chronicle* and the Oral Tradition," *Slavic and East European Journal,* vol. 32 (1988), pp. 198-212.

2. Levitt, p. 200.

3. Erich Auerbach, *Mimesis: The Representation of Reality in Western Literature* (Princeton, NJ: Princeton University Press, 1953), pp. 3 and 6.

4. Auerbach, p. 23. Of course, *Family Chronicle* is not unique in this respect. A "Homeric" tendency, as defined by Auerbach, is characteristic of sev-

eral of the great exemplars of Russian realism, most notably Tolstoy (himself an admirer of *Family Chronicle*), whose copious, capacious, and transparent narrative style has obvious "Homeric" affinities. In this respect one recalls that Tolstoy himself claimed that he had *The Iliad* in mind when he was writing *War and Peace*.

5. In point of chronological fact, Stepan Mikhailovich is not yet a grandfather. But Aksakov's repeated use in the early chapters of the words *staryi* and *dedushka* confer a grandfatherly aura on him from the outset. *Dedushka* appears in fact in the very first sentence.

6. S. T. Aksakov, *Sobranie sochinenii* (Moscow, 1955). vol. 1, p. 83. All page references to the work are to this edition and are henceforth cited parenthetically in the text.

7. E.g., Bernardin de Saint-Pierre's *Paul et Virginie,* Chateaubriand's *Atala,* Cooper's frontier novels and Melville's *Typee.*

8. E.g., such diverse narratives as Wyss' *Swiss Family Robinson,* the introduction to *The Bronze Horseman,* Verne's *The Mysterious Island,* and any number of pioneering or colonizing sagas.

9. Respectively, Ralph E. Matlaw, in the introduction to *The Family Chronicle,* translated by M. C. Beverley (New York: E. F. Dutton, 1961), p. xix; Carl Van Doren, in the foreword to Aksakov's *A Russian Gentleman,* translated by J. D. Duff (New York, 1943), p. viii; Mashinskii, p. 324.

10. Without drawing any Biblical parallels Andrew Durkin has before me noted that Bagrov resembles a "chthonic deity, both beneficent and punitive" (Durkin, p. 119).

11. The sequence I trace here (the terrible rage followed by the satisfied tour of inspection) is to be found in the *siuzhet* not the *fabula.* There is no suggestion that, chronologically speaking, the latter occurred immediately after the former.

12. Actually the marriage of Praskov'ia and Kurolesov straddles the events recounted in "Stepan Mikhailovich Bagrov," the courtship and wedding occurring before the removal to New Bagrovo, the denouement occurring well after that event. The importance that the theme of declension had for Aksakov is suggested by the fact that he chose to describe the founding of New Bagrovo first, followed by the diabolical inroads of Kurolesov.

13. For a perceptive discussion of the similarities which Kurolesov shares with the hero-villain of the Gothic novel, see Durkin, pp. 121-25.

14. For a more detailed discussion of these resemblances see Feuer, pp. 89-91.

15. By using such expressions in connection with Kurolesov as "*on rassypalsia . . . melkim besom*" (p. 109) and "*chort emu ne brat*" (p. 104), Aksakov further reinforces Kurolesov's diabolical aura.

16. True, we are told that Bagrov's serfs "loved" (*liubili*) him (p. 89), but the Russian word is less emphatic than the English, and the respect and devotion which a serf can have for his master (*a fortiori,* a master who is capable of meting out brutal punishment when crossed) can scarcely be called *love* in the conventional sense.

17. Durkin (p. 133) connects the account of Aleksei's passionate courtship with the sentimental fiction of the age. Aksakov himself states that the desperate suitor's threat to commit suicide if the parental ban is not lifted was doubtless inspired by the novels he had read (p. 161).

18. This supposition is borne out by the passionate love that Sof'ia Nikolaevna bears little Sergei, described in "The Childhood Years of Bagrov Grandson" (pp. 288-94).

19. Bagrov's resolve to build a church on his newly acquired estate, fulfilled many years later by his son (p. 81), and his passing expression of gratitude to God for a good wheat crop (p. 96) do not, it seems to me, exceed conventional gestures of piety.

20. The most famous eighteenth-century Russian epic poem, Kheraskov's *Rossiada,* was published in 1779.

21. As Durkin notes (p. 142), the society of Ufa exemplifies *Gesellschaft,* as defined by German nineteenth-century sociologists, the world of New Bagrovo—*Gemeinschaft.*

Thomas P. Hodge (essay date 1997)

SOURCE: Hodge, Thomas P. "Aksakov's *Notes on Fishing,* in Russian Context." In *Notes on Fishing,* by Sergei Aksakov, translated by Thomas P. Hodge, pp. xi-xxxvi. Evanston, Ill.: Northwestern University Press, 1997.

[*In the following introduction to Aksakov's* Notes on Fishing, *Hodge examines the circumstances surrounding the book's publication, its critical reception, and its various antecedents in Russian and world literature. Praising the work's directness and quiet simplicity, Hodge argues that it rivals the writings of Ernest Hemingway, Izaak Walton, and Henry David Thoreau.*]

Angling or float fishing I can only compare to a stick and a string, with a worm at one end and a fool at the other.

Attributed to Samuel Johnson

Sergei Timofeevich Aksakov is revered outside Russia for his great autobiographical trilogy: *A Family Chronicle, Childhood Years of a Bagrov Grandson,* and *Memoirs.* When these works arrived on the literary scene in the middle of the nineteenth century, they caused a sensation, but this was neither Aksakov's first triumph as a writer nor his first trilogy. Those distinctions go to the cycle we may conveniently call his "sporting trilogy": *Notes on Fishing, Notes of an Orenburg-Province Hunter,* and *A Sportsman's Stories and Memoirs on Various Kinds of Sport.* These writings, little known in the West, appeared first, and they achieved a level of literary fame their author had scarcely dreamed possible.

As the first and most painstakingly revised part of the sporting trilogy, *Notes on Fishing* deserves pride of place. It was Aksakov's first book, and his first major success as a writer, but its significance transcends Aksakov's own oeuvre and the borders of his native Russia. *Notes on Fishing* is a literary achievement that merits mention alongside such works as Juliana Berners's *Treatise of Fishing with an Angle,* Walton's *The Compleat Angler,* Gilbert White's *Natural History of Selborne,* Thoreau's *Walden,* Hemingway's *The Old Man and the Sea,* and Norman Maclean's *A River Runs Through It.* In short, it belongs among the Western classics of fishing literature and nature writing.

Sergei Aksakov (1791-1859) probably began work on *Notes on Fishing* in 1845, some seven years after his retirement from government service, and just after he had started to go blind. Family letters written in the autumn of that year mention that he was occupied with "a little book on angling." This was the commencement of Aksakov's most ambitious literary project after the short piece of fictionalized family history he had written in 1840 (the seed that would eventually grow into *A Family Chronicle*). The most informative early description of *Notes on Fishing* dates from November 1845, when Aksakov himself told his friend, the renowned Nikolai Gogol, of his goals for the work:

> I undertook to write a little book about angling not only in relation to its technical side, but in relation to nature in general: my passionate fisherman loves natural beauty just as passionately. In a word, I fell in love with my work, and I hope this little book will prove pleasant not only to the angling sportsman, but also to anyone whose heart is open to the impressions of early morning, late evening, luxurious noontide, etc. The wondrous natural world of the Orenburg region, as I came to know it forty-five years ago, will play its part. This project has enlivened and reinvigorated me.[1]

Aksakov finished his book by the end of 1846. After receiving approval from the censorship on 5 February 1847, it was published in Moscow in 1847 under the title *Notes on Angling,* and ran to 163 pages. The dedi-

cation read, "To my brothers and friends, N. T. and A. T. A—." Encouraged by the success of *Notes on Angling,* Aksakov finally published the second component of the sporting trilogy, *Notes of an Orenburg-Province Hunter,* in 1852, less than a month after Gogol, who passionately championed that work, had died. Aksakov dedicated that book to his brothers as well.

Aksakov's "considerably enlarged" edition of his first book, now called *Notes on Fishing* (literally, notes on the angling of fish), came out in 1854. This edition passed the censor on 6 November 1853, and sported the verse epigraph from his "Epistle to M. A. Dmitriev" that Aksakov had unsuccessfully attempted to publish the previous year in the front matter of the second edition of *Orenburg-Province Hunter.* The Moscow censorship, nervous after foolishly allowing Turgenev to publish his supposedly subversive eulogy of Gogol in *Moscow Gazette,* had rejected Aksakov's proposed epigraph because the lines "I venture into nature's world, / The world of serenity and freedom" were deemed too libertarian. Fortunately, that opinion had softened enough a year later to allow the verse epigraph to appear, but only with the offending phrase "and freedom" ellided.

Now 274 pages long, the second edition of *Notes on Fishing* contained two entirely new chapters—"On Fish in General" and "Crayfish"—as well as a host of new material both inserted into the text and added in the form of footnotes. Aksakov's preface remained virtually unchanged, while "The Hook," "Bait," and "On Fishing Skill" were significantly supplemented; "Selecting a Swim" doubled in size, and "Boulters and Trimmers" tripled. To the chapters on individual fish species, Aksakov added short comments on spawning and biting habits, regional names, and favorable swims. "Gudgeon," "Ide," "Crucian Carp," "Perch," "Pike," "Taimen," "Trout," and "Grayling" were considerably expanded, usually with new paragraphs appended to chapter-ends.

In the early 1850s, Aksakov planned to publish a periodical he would call *The Sportsman's Miscellany,* but his proposal was rejected by the censorship. He gathered the material he had intended for that series and published it in book form. Aksakov's *A Sportsman's Stories and Memoirs on Various Kinds of Sport, with an Appended Article on Nightingales by I. S. Turgenev* thus became the third and final component of the sporting trilogy; its first edition appeared in 1855, the second in 1856. Turgenev, a literary sportsman even more famous than Aksakov, had befriended the aging nobleman in December 1850, and the two writers quickly developed a warm relationship based on mutual respect in matters both literary and sporting. Turgenev opened his contribution to Aksakov's *Sportsman's Stories and Memoirs* with a laudatory salutation: "I send you, dear and most esteemed S[ergei] T[imofeevich], a lover of and expert in all forms of sport, the following story about nightingales, their singing, their keeping, their capture, etc., transcribed by me from the words of an old and experienced hunter from among the house serfs."[2]

The third edition of **Notes on Fishing** (the last to appear in Aksakov's lifetime) passed the censor on 20 July 1856, with the scandalous word "freedom" at last restored to the verse epigraph. Aksakov added very little new material to this edition, as he noted at the end of his preface. The main change in this version of **Notes on Fishing** was the inclusion of illustrations and notes. Aksakov was now seeking to make his sporting books more scientifically rigorous and to open them further—in the spirit of the ill-fated **Sportsman's Miscellany**—to contributions by others. For these reasons he arranged a collaboration with the distinguished biologist Karl Frantsevich Rul'e (1814-58), a pioneer in evolutionary paleontology and zoology, who found engraved illustrations of the fish species, added taxonomic footnotes, and provided a concluding article entitled "The Fish's Upstream Journey." Unfortunately, Rul'e found it difficult to identify positively all the species Aksakov described, which resulted in some rather confusing footnotes and a dearth of illustrations: only eighteen of the twenty-five fish species had a portrait, and the engravings that did appear were of uneven quality and inconsistent provenance. Though Rul'e's scholarly afterword contained interesting generalized speculation on the origin of spawning-migration impulses in fish, its style and content were only tenuously linked to Aksakov's text.[3] Rul'e likewise added scientific footnotes to the third edition of **Orenburg-Province Hunter,** which was published in 1857, the last appearance of a component of the sporting trilogy before Aksakov's death in 1859.

The third edition of **Notes on Fishing** was reprinted, with Rul'e's material included, as a "fourth edition" in 1871, but it was not until 1886, with the publication of Aksakov's **Complete Works,** that the work received its first satisfactory annotation. Though the confusing Rul'e notes were reprinted, these were corrected and explained by ichthyologist N. A. Varpakhovskii, who also furnished new supplemental notes as well as an excellent scientific afterword, "A Short Description of the Fish Species Mentioned in S. T. Aksakov's **Notes on Fishing.**"[4] Here Varpakhovskii provided a classification key, detailed measurements of body parts, up-to-date scientific names, and even invited readers to send preserved specimens—postage paid—to the Academy of Sciences for identification: "If only one amateur fisherman sends fish from his locality to the museum—either as a gift to the museum or for classification—I will count myself rewarded in full for the effort I have expended in compiling the present article" (191). At last, Aksakov's *loshók* was properly identified as a minnow (Phoxinus phoxinus), though Varpakhovskii believed—mistakenly,

in my view—that Aksakov's *lokh* (*krasúlia*) was a form of trout rather than a taimen. Finally, Varpakhovskii initiated the tradition of replacing the unsatisfactory illustrations that had accompanied the third edition with engravings from Heckel and Kner's ichthyological classic, *Die Süsswasserfische der ostreichischen Monarchie* (Leipzig, 1858). These beautiful engravings, almost contemporaneous with the third edition of **Notes on Fishing,** were matched with all twenty-five of Aksakov's species, and have been reproduced in the best Aksakov editions ever since.

In the twentieth century, Aksakov's **Notes on Fishing** has been reprinted at least a dozen times, including many editions during the Soviet period. The finest modern edition appeared in volume 4 of Aksakov's **Collected Works** (Moscow, 1956), exactly a century after the definitive text of the third edition. S. I. Mashinskii, Aksakov's chief Russian exponent in the twentieth century, provided fine literary (as opposed to ichthyological) notes for that edition, drawing extensively on valuable archival material. Numerous mass-produced editions of **Notes on Fishing** continue to appear in Russia, and the affection that greeted "the little book on angling" Aksakov wrote a century and a half ago, as he went blind and old age ravaged his health, seems only to have grown deeper with the passage of time.

* * *

Though Aksakov clearly had serious literary intentions for **Notes on Fishing,** the book's enthusiastic reception in 1847 took him by surprise. When M. A. Dmitriev received a copy from Aksakov, he replied, "Your talent as a writer is such that even this subject becomes literary in your hands."[5] One of the first published notices appeared in Ivan Panaev and Nikolai Nekrasov's *The Contemporary,* the leading literary journal of mid-nineteenth-century Russia. "Lovers of 'quiet delight' will find in this brochure reliable instruction on the successful execution of their undertaking," wrote the anonymous reviewer. "The naturalist will glean from the author's descriptions fascinating details of our ordinary fishes' way of life."[6] *Notes of the Fatherland,* from which Nekrasov and Panaev had just defected, published a similarly laudatory review: "A sensible book which will be read with pleasure and utility by angling sportsmen. The author knows and passionately loves his subject."[7] The *Finnish Herald* made bolder claims for **Notes on Fishing,** calling it "a book that can be read, at leisure, with pleasure not only by sportsmen keen on angling, but also by any educated person."[8] The only negative review of the first edition appeared in *Library for Reading,* whose anonymous critic parodied what he or she perceived as Aksakov's snobbish approach: "There are people who sit down to angle only in order to catch fish; these people do not know how to fish. . . . Such fishermen only dishonor a noble profession whose proper goal is reflection, not a plate of fish. How sweet is the lofty, poetic dream of drowsy angling with a cast outfit in your hand, on a bankside rock. . . . These pleasures are accessible only to fishermen-philosophers. . . . The uninitiated mob does not understand them."[9]

The critical praise soon accorded *Notes of an Orenburg-Province Hunter* in 1852 helped earn redoubled critical enthusiasm for the second, enlarged edition of *Notes on Fishing* in 1854. "We now hasten to gladden our readers," wrote the *Moscow Gazette* in a review devoted mainly to *Orenburg-Province Hunter,* "with news of the imminent publication of the second edition of a previous work by the same author: *On Fishing* [*sic*]. This new edition is no mere repetition of the previous one; the small booklet has grown into quite a large one; its contents have increased by a whole third over the previous edition. Among new additions, the large chapter on fish in general is especially interesting."[10] Another reviewer wrote, "Five years before this one the first edition of this little book—useful and diverting in the highest degree—appeared, and indeed it is now so *enlarged* that . . . it is a superb manual—the only one in Russian—on the proper angling of fish, whose physiology the author has researched in the finest detail. . . . And all this is set forth as pleasantly and as captivatingly as is characteristic of the author of *Notes of an Orenburg-Province Hunter.*"[11] Still higher praise came from Panaev, who reviewed the second edition of *Notes on Fishing* for *The Contemporary*:

> There is so much simplicity and truth [in *Notes on Fishing*] that one could confidently trade it for dozens of the so-called novels, stories, and dramas that have enjoyed particularly noteworthy success in Russia of late. There is more poetry in this little booklet than you will find in whole volumes of the assorted poems and epics that have found favor and actually do possess certain poetic merits. *Notes on Fishing,* perhaps, has more significance for artists and *littérateurs* than it does for specialists, for sportfishermen.[12]

When the third edition of Aksakov's book came out, *Notes of the Fatherland* and *The Contemporary* published very favorable reviews yet again.[13]

The full acceptance of Aksakov's *Notes on Fishing*—and of his sporting trilogy in general—was also due in large part to the brilliant review of *Notes of an Orenburg-Province Hunter* that Ivan Turgenev published in *The Contemporary* in 1853. This essay is certainly one of the most insightful appraisals of Aksakov's art yet written. Turgenev had recently earned fame (and infamy) for his early masterpiece, *Notes of a Hunter,* a cycle of stories that had begun to appear in *The Contemporary* in 1847, and that were then gathered and published in book form in 1852. Turgenev's frank depiction of the pitiable lot of Russian serfs in *Notes of*

a Hunter made his book a cause célèbre for liberals, and, along with his Gogol eulogy, landed him first in jail and then in exile on his country estate of Spasskoe. The magnificent natural descriptions suffusing Turgenev's book both supported his abolitionist agenda and established him as one of nineteenth-century Russia's most gifted prosaists.

The details of hunting and the hunter's quarry yield to descriptive art and political suggestion in Turgenev's *Notes of a Hunter,* and this seems to have made him especially grateful to Aksakov for writing in concrete terms about the sport itself—for leaving Russia's social ills out of the picture:

> He looks upon nature (both animate and inanimate) not from some sort of exclusive point of view, but as one should look at her: clearly, simply, and with complete concern; he does not act the sage, use cunning or add extraneous motives and goals: he observes intelligently, conscientiously and keenly; he only wants to learn, to see. And before such scrutiny, nature opens up and allows him to "peep in" at her. You will laugh at this, but I assure you that when I read, for example, the chapter on the black grouse, it actually seemed to me that it would be impossible to live better than a black grouse. . . . I am extraordinarily fond of the style. This is real Russian speech: genial and direct, supple and deft. There is nothing precious and nothing extraneous, nothing strained and nothing sluggish—freedom and precision of expression are equally noteworthy.[14]

Turgenev was an avid hunter, but, as Aksakov himself declared in *A Sportsman's Stories and Memoirs on Various Kinds of Sport,* Turgenev detested fishing and therefore left no direct commentary on *Notes on Fishing.* His assessment of Aksakov's style in *Orenburg-Province Hunter,* however, is perfectly applicable to *Notes on Fishing,* in which Aksakov adopts precisely the same approach. Turgenev goes on to discuss over-observant, overrefined writers who seek to describe the hidden details of nature, and expresses relief that Aksakov is not one of them: "He does not act the sage, does not notice anything unusual, anything 'the few' strive for; but what he sees, he sees clearly, and, with a firm hand and forceful brushstrokes, paints a broad, well-balanced picture."[15] Then—in what might strike us today as outrageous hyperbole had it not been confirmed by subsequent generations of Russian critics—Turgenev likens Aksakov's style to that of Pushkin, Gogol, and even Shakespeare, at least in Edgar's description of the seacoast to blind Gloucester in *King Lear.* In late January 1853, Aksakov responded in a blushing letter that he "expected less praise,"[16] and inserted in the second edition of *Notes on Fishing* a subtle dig at Turgenev by including the phrase "slyly play the sage" dressed in italics.[17] It is clear in his review that Turgenev aims much of the critique at himself, suggesting that he lacks the Aksakovian virtue of shunning political subtexts.[18] Turgenev was the Westernizer par excellence, while Aksakov was patriarch of Russia's most illustrious Slavophile family. The two men, who were ideological foes, found common ground in their love of outdoor sport and literary art.

A few years later, however, Aleksei Khomiakov—the formidable Slavophile poet and theoretician—subtly claimed Sergei Aksakov for the Slavophile aesthetic camp. Khomiakov's obituary article on Aksakov offers a superb analysis of Aksakov's authorial heritage and strategy:

> The simplicity of Pushkin's forms in the stories, and especially those by his good friend Gogol, influenced him [Aksakov]; all this could have been the case, and all this was the case; but there is no doubt that it never entered his mind—it could not enter his mind—to choose fishing lessons, even serious ones, as the subject for a work of art. The concept of art was removed: he freed himself of it entirely. A passionate fisherman deprived of his accustomed enjoyment by the vagaries of life, he wanted to recall years gone by, former quiet joys, and, owing to a temperament that was sociable in the highest degree, he wanted to communicate them, explain them to others—and a book was written, a book the author never dreamed would earn him literary fame. And the reader took it just as good-naturedly, without the expectation of artistic enjoyment, but simply in hopes of learning something about the art of fishing . . . and then, as he got a grasp of the text, with a strange sense of astonishment he noticed that the subject became more and more absorbing, that the whims of the water's currents and the floods of lakes and ponds became more and more alluring and beautiful; the fish themselves, from the common gudgeon to the rare taimen, grew more lovable. There were some people who guessed that there was art concealed here— true art; but the majority of simple readers—lovers of fishing—felt only a deep sense of gratitude to the author for his useful information and especially for his love of the sport they had in common. Their letters of thanks breathed this sense of simple-hearted gratefulness; but S. T. Aksakov had already acquired his literary fame, which surprised even him. They listened to him, and they listened with pleasure, with animation; he himself gave rein to his reminiscences, he himself began to be animated by them more and more, feeling that he had before him, so to speak, not merely cold, unseen, unknown readers, but sympathetic friends. The relatively narrow circle of the fisherman's reminiscences gave way to the reminiscences of a hunter. In them, Russia's natural world was spread out in wondrous beauty, and the Russian written language took a step forward, even after Pushkin and Gogol. Sergei Timofeevich's reputation was ensured and confirmed for good. Afterward, other subjects drew his attention, but he never lost what he had acquired. This infinitely important acquisition was freedom from artistic premeditation.[19]

Khomiakov's Slavophile reading of Aksakov offers as much insight as Turgenev's appraisal, and, in at least one important way, it offers the *same* insight: that Aksakov achieved art by abandoning art. Turgenev's "not

acting the sage" and Khomiakov's "freedom from artistic premeditation" point to the same literary quality: the guilelessness of Aksakov's choice of a subject as "stupid" as fishing and the simplicity of its verbal description. "After the doctor's departure," wrote Lev Tolstoy of the most important intellectual in *Anna Karenina*, "Koznyshëv wished to ride to the river with his fishing gear. He loved angling and seemed proud that he could love such a stupid activity." Unlike Tolstoy's Koznyshëv, however, Aksakov is a master at concealing his "premeditation."

Khomiakov, like Turgenev, has a great deal to say about Aksakovian language:

> But what are the basic elements of Aksakov's art? The first is language, in which he scarcely has a rival for correctness and precision of expression and for turns of phrase that are entirely Russian and alive . . . it was unbearable for Sergei Timofeevich to use an incorrect word or an adjective inappropriate to the subject he was discussing and which failed to express it. He felt incorrectness of expression as a kind of insult to the subject itself, as a kind of untruth in relation to his own impression, and he would rest easy only when he found the right word. It stands to reason that he found it easily, because this very demand arose from clarity of feeling and awareness of linguistic wealth. This strictness toward his own language, and consequently toward his own thought, gave all his stories and all his descriptions matchless clarity and simplicity, while it imparted to the descriptions of nature a truthfulness of color and distinctness of outline that you will not find in anyone else. Gogol was nearly the first to recognize this quality and he admired it when he listened to Sergei Timofeevich's first, still unpublished sporting reminiscences.[20]

Khomiakov's tribute to Aksakov's language hinges on his faith in the intrinsic greatness of the Russian language—another opinion he shared with Turgenev the Westernizer—and once again the Slavophile program is subtly advanced.

Linguistic precision is a hallmark of Aksakov's style in both the autobiographical and sporting trilogies; the passion of his search for the *mot juste* is evident on virtually every page of his prose. In 1847, one of Aksakov's first reviewers had noted the attention he paid to provincial vocabulary in *Notes on Fishing*: "Comparative lexicography will be indebted to *Notes* for pointing out many of the folk terms used for the same fish in various regions of Russia."[21] Writing in the 1880s, the prodigious literary historian Semën Vengerov also called particular attention to Aksakov's precise use of rich, concrete language:

> The Academy of Sciences is at present undertaking the publication of dictionaries of the language of our classic writers, beginning with Lomonosov. We have no doubt that if some day Sergei Aksakov has his turn, the

dictionary of his language will be one of the fullest, one of the richest in subtle and various shades of meaning. And, of course, this dictionary will be rich and abundant not in abstract words, but in concrete terms necessary for the description of real qualities and traits. In a word, this will be the dictionary of a true artist who speaks not in allegories and tropes, but in images and pictures.[22]

This dictionary was never compiled, but **Notes on Fishing** is filled with specialized, local, technical, and folk terms that have indeed proved useful to general lexicographers: the Academy of Sciences *Dictionary of the Modern Russian Literary Language*—Russia's monumental equivalent of the *Oxford English Dictionary*—actually employs excerpts from **Notes on Fishing** as the first or only illustrative quotations for dozens of Russian terms.

Khomiakov's is correct in pointing out that Gogol, who in his later years was strongly influenced by Slavophilism, admired Aksakov's sporting works. "Regarding your little book," Aksakov's daughter wrote to him in 1848 of Gogol's reaction to **Notes on Fishing,** "he said that although he has no interest at all in the subject, he nonetheless read the whole thing from cover to cover with great pleasure."[23] In 1851, Gogol wrote to Aksakov that his only wish was that his own characters in volume 2 of *Dead Souls* "might be as alive as your birds" in **Notes of an Orenburg-Province Hunter.**[24] After "invention," Khomiakov gives the third "basic element of Aksakov's art" as his natural ability to inject himself into seemingly objective narratives—to animate the inanimate world: "S. T. Aksakov lives in his works: if he is discussing a sunny day, you feel his joyous smile in reply to the smiling natural world. . . . He was the first of our writers to look upon our life with a positive, rather than negative, point of view. This is true, but it could not have been otherwise."[25]

* * *

Sergei Aksakov was born on 20 September 1791 in Ufa, Orenburg Province, a town founded in the late sixteenth century in the steppe country at the confluence of the Belaia and Dëma rivers. Ufa, one thousand miles east of Moscow, was at the center of Bashkiria—since 1992 the Republic of Bashkortostan—homeland of the Bashkirs, a nomadic Muslim people who speak a Turkic language similar to Tatar. The Aksakovs were an old gentry family of modest means, and Sergei's paternal grandfather had been lured to Orenburg Province from the Simbirsk region by the prospect of inexpensive, fertile land where crops and livestock would thrive.

Aksakov spent his early childhood in Ufa and his boyhood in the wild country 160 miles southwest, at Novo-Aksakovo, the estate his grandfather had founded. The settlement was located on the banks of the Great Bugu-ruslanka River, some nineteen miles downstream from the headwaters and sixteen miles north of the town of Buguruslan. It was here that Sergei spent most of his time between the ages of five and ten, before entering the Kazan' Gymnasium in 1801.

Though it is somewhat fictionalized, Aksakov's autobiographical trilogy is generally thought to be accurate on the details of its author's early life and family relationships. In that trilogy, fishing is constantly mentioned,[26] and, significantly, "Bagrov"—the pseudonym that replaces "Aksakov"—is derived from *bagór,* the Russian word for "gaff." In **A Family Chronicle,** the account of Aksakov's father's generation, Sergei Aksakov writes that the Great Buguruslanka "seethed with all the species of fish that could bear its freezing water: pike, perch, chub, ide, even grayling and taimen were found there in abundance; there was an incredible multitude of every kind of beast in both forest and steppe; in a word, this was—and still is—a little piece of the Promised Land."[27] In this wilderness at the edge of European Russia, Aksakov spent so much time fishing and hunting with his father and his servant, Efrem Evseich, that it hampered his early studies. In **Childhood Years of a Bagrov Grandson,** Aksakov explains that the women of his father's family—most notably his Aunt Tat'iana—were also excellent anglers; in **Memoirs,** we learn that Tat'iana eventually marries a fellow angler and moves to an estate with fine trout-fishing. Aksakov's mother, however, openly hated fishing and could never understand her husband's appetite for the sport. According to **Childhood Years,** she felt jealous of the time he and Sergei spent outdoors, and often forbade the frail and excitable boy to go fishing. Young Aksakov therefore struggled constantly with the choice between the two loves of his boyhood—his mother and his fishing—and this tension made its way into **Notes on Fishing**: on the first page of his preface, Aksakov defended angling against precisely the imprecations he had constantly heard from his mother as he grew up.[28]

After leaving the Kazan' Gymnasium, Aksakov attended the just-opened Kazan' University from 1805 to 1807, but did not finish his degree. His schooling had left him as passionate about amateur theatricals as he was about outdoor pursuits, and in 1808 he moved to Saint Petersburg, where he worked as a translator in the civil service and plunged himself into the literary-theatrical whirl of the capital. There Aksakov became acquainted with the greatest poet of the time, Gavriil Derzhavin, and with the conservative arbiter of Russian language and literature, Admiral A. S. Shishkov, whom he later credited as an early pioneer of Slavophilism. Aksakov moved to Moscow in 1811, where he would become close to such renowned figures as the actors Ia. E. Shusherin and F. F. Kokoshkin, the novelist M. N. Zagoskin, the dramatists A. A. Shakhovskoi and A. I. Pisarev, and the composer A. N. Verstovskii. Even in this talented company, Aksakov gained a considerable reputation as a declaimer and storyteller. After enlisting in the Moscow militia to fight Napoleon's forces in 1812, Aksakov returned to Orenburg Province during the occupation of Moscow, then came back to Saint Petersburg in 1814.

In 1816, Aksakov married Ol'ga Semënovna Zaplatina, the daughter of a landowner in Kursk Province, and the young couple moved to Novo-Aksakovo, where their son Konstantin, the future Slavophile leader, was born in 1817. In 1821, Aksakov lived in Moscow, but in 1822 he moved the family to another family estate, Nadëzhdino (where his second son, Ivan, was born in 1823), but his attempts to succeed as a gentleman-farmer came to naught, and in 1826 he returned to Moscow and began working as a censor there in 1827. Aksakov was fired in 1832 for accidentally passing a veiled satire of the Moscow police; he then worked for the Konstantinovskii Surveying Institute until his retirement in 1838.

From the late 1820s through the 1840s, Aksakov and his wife hosted one of Moscow's most famous salons. It was at one of the Aksakovs' "Saturdays" in 1832 that Sergei met Gogol, who would become his close friend and literary hero. The Aksakov salon's regular visitors included some of the most important writers and thinkers of the day, and the chief topic of debate in their circle was the conflict between the liberal Westernizers, who felt Russia should turn to Europe for enlightenment, and the most conservative Slavophiles, who held that the native culture of Russia held all that was necessary. Among members of the former group who visited the Aksakovs were such luminaries as N. V. Stankevich, A. I. Gertsen (Herzen), M. A. Bakunin, V. G. Belinskii, T. N. Granovskii, and P. Ia. Chaadaev. In the Slavophile camp were Aksakov, his sons Ivan and Konstantin, M. P. Pogodin, S. P. Shevyrëv, Verstovskii, M. A. Dmitriev, Khomiakov, the Kireevskii brothers, and Iu. F. Samarin.

In 1843, Aksakov purchased Abramtsevo, a lovely estate northeast of Moscow with excellent fishing. As Aksakov's blindness and ill health grew worse toward the end of the 1840s, his late-blooming literary career gathered momentum. He wrote intensively at Abramtsevo, dictating his work to members of his family. The oral transmission of Aksakov's works resulted in a natural, clear, informal Russian liberally spiced with arcane, but precise and apposite vocabulary. In the 1850s, Aksakov continued his friendship with Gogol, cultivated his tie with Turgenev, and by 1856 was also receiving the young Lev Tolstoy. In the autumn of 1858, ill health prompted Aksakov to vacate his beloved Abramtsevo, and he died in Moscow on 30 April 1859.

Forced to give up hunting because of his failing eyesight, Aksakov had nonetheless gratefully continued to fish through the 1840s and 1850s, systematically re-cording and evaluating his own techniques, and comparing his angling experiences around Moscow with his halcyon days on the waters of Orenburg Province. The incredibly productive fishing of his boyhood and early manhood combined with the more scientific approach he adopted in his later suburban angling to produce a mixture of poignant nostalgia and clear-eyed technical expertise. That mastery—what Aksakov always referred to as "fishing skill"—is clearly evinced by his fishing success in later years; the author's fishing records for the summer of 1843 (17 June through 6 October), for example, tell us that he landed 375 perch, 733 crucian carp, 5 pike, 13 gudgeon, 53 roach, 55 dace, 7 ide, 1 chub, 48 bleak, and 11 tench, for a total of 1,301 fish.[29]

Aksakov wrote a good deal of poetry during the 1820s and 1830s, as well as numerous theater reviews. His only significant literary success prior to the creative explosion of his retirement, however, was **"The Snowstorm"** (1834), a critically acclaimed sketch depicting the effects of a blizzard near Orenburg; Pushkin drew on the story for a crucial snowstorm scene in his historical novel, *The Captain's Daughter.*[30] As we have seen, the popular sporting trilogy's components appeared from 1847 to 1855. *A Family Chronicle* and *Memoirs* were first published in 1856, followed by *Childhood Years of a Bagrov Grandson* in 1858. Throughout the 1850s, Aksakov also published important biographical, critical, and memoiristic sketches.

After Khomiakov, Aksakov's most perceptive nineteenth-century critic was Vengerov, who keenly understood the intermingling of Aksakov's personal experience and his art. Aksakov, Vengerov asserted, had two passions: "sport in all its forms—from collecting butterflies and catching fish to fox- and wolf-hunting—and the theater. . . . With regard to his passion for sport, one could say that it was this that made Aksakov a real writer."[31] Vengerov, who consistently contrasted the technique of Aksakov's sporting works with Turgenev's in *Notes of a Hunter,* had nothing but praise for Aksakov's disciplined artistic response to his literary success:

> Any other person in his position would probably have been carried away, would not have held firm within the humble boundaries of various technical instructions and suggestions on sport. But Sergei Timofeevich did not give in to temptation and, even though he knew, for example, that he had a masterly talent for writing natural descriptions, he did not abuse this talent and provided them in exactly the quantity required by the progress of his exposition. And that is why his second sporting book retained the chief attraction of the first: simplicity, directness, and freshness. . . . Any other writer in Aksakov's position, if he had wanted to interest the reader in sandpipers and gudgeon, would probably have resorted either to stories of some sort of unusual sporting occurrences, or to the comparison and similarity of the psychology of animals and people, as even very good writers do. . . . Sergei Timofeevich

did not lay out for the reader all the details known to him. As an artist of great merit, he took only details that were absolutely characteristic, only those details that delineated the individuality of each bird, fish, or beast he described, and because of this his characterizations are so vivid and clear, because of this his sporting notes are not a collection of remarks by an idle sportsman, but a truly splendid gallery of animal *portraits*.[32]

Eventually, Aksakov did indulge himself by relating "unusual sporting occurrences" in some of the fishing literature he wrote after completing *Notes on Fishing.* These more conventionally entertaining works, which offer rich material in the vein of traditional "fish stories," are gathered together in Appendix 1 of the present volume.

* * *

Vengerov also captured the excitement that readers of Aksakov's *Notes on Fishing* and *Notes of an Orenburg-Province Hunter* must have felt in the middle of the nineteenth century:

> The sporting "notes" of Aksakov must doubtless be recognized as wonderful literary works in which a great talent for painting vivid pictures with words brilliantly manifested itself. For the reader of those years [the late 1840s and early 1850s] who approached both of these books in hopes of learning something about gudgeon or sandpipers and suddenly stumbled on first-class descriptions of nature, on characterizations of representatives of the animal kingdom expounded in wondrous language and sketched vividly, distinctly—for such a reader Sergei Timofeevich's sporting books were a valuable literary acquisition and could afford a great deal of artistic pleasure.[33]

Notes on Fishing, as Ivan Aksakov told his father in 1854, also possessed enough scientific validity to enter an ichthyological debate at Khar'kov University: "Tomorrow a certain Master's student's thesis defense is scheduled on some sort of fish fry, and [botany professor V. M.] Cherniaev, with your book in hand, intends to refute him or demonstrate that this fish is identical to the toppie or bluelet you described."[34] But Vladimir Nabokov, who was a distinguished lepidopterist, hinted in his novel *The Gift* that Aksakov lacked scientific rigor; near the end of chapter 1, Godunov-Cherdyntsev tells Koncheev: "My father used to find all kinds of howlers in Turgenev's and Tolstoy's hunting scenes and descriptions of nature, and as for the wretched Aksakov, let's not even discuss his disgraceful blunders in that field." The context suggests that Nabokov himself might have agreed with this pronouncement, even though Aksakov made very few outright "mistakes" in *Notes on Fishing,* such as his belief that zander and grayling are kinds of trout, and his apparent acceptance of exaggerated longevity claims for carp. On the contrary, Aksakov only ventures opinions verified by his own obser-

vations, and is always suspicious of fishermen's exaggerations. Though he lacked formal training in ichthyology, Aksakov's general approach—that of a learned country gentleman—could be informally described as scientific.

Vengerov's point on the pleasant surprise that awaited readers of *Notes on Fishing* is certainly valid: before Aksakov, Russia's homegrown sporting works were few and of poor quality, for the most part consisting of anonymous, short, clumsily written or translated instructions on various aspects of fishing or hunting.[35] "As far as I know," Aksakov boldly asserted in his preface to *Notes on Fishing,* "not a single line has thus far been printed in Russian about fishing in general or angling in particular that was written by a literate sportsman who knew his subject intimately." This statement is a deliberate swipe at the only important Russian fishing writer who antedated Aksakov: Vasilii Alekseevich Lëvshin (1746-1826).[36] Though the prolific Lëvshin frequently dabbled in belles lettres, he is chiefly remembered today—if he is remembered at all—as an old-fashioned writer of agricultural handbooks. In *Eugene Onegin* (canto 7, stanza 4), Pushkin jocularly mentions Lëvshin as a mentor to "Priams of the countryside." In the first edition of *Notes on Fishing,* Aksakov alluded comically to Lëvshin's *The Perfect Huntsman* (1779), and, in the second edition, twice mocked the doubtful ichthyological assertions Lëvshin had made in *A Book for Sportsmen* (1819).

Nowhere, however, does Aksakov acknowledge the most significant Russian precursor of his *Notes on Fishing*: volume 4, chapters 5 and 6 of Lëvshin's *Universal and Complete Art of Housekeeping* (1795). Lëvshin translated and adapted most of his handbooks from French or German, and this hefty work—a Russian adaptation of Louis Liger's *La nouvelle maison rustique*—was no exception.[37] In it, Lëvshin offers 49 pages of advice on fish culture (chapter 5), and another 48 on fishing techniques and fish species (chapter 6).[38] This latter section resembles Aksakov's work in scope and structure, but sorely lacks the depth and literary quality of *Notes on Fishing.* In his preface, Aksakov alluded to his knowledge of foreign fishing treatises ("In French and English we find many whole books on the topic and even more small booklets strictly about angling"), but claimed they had never been translated into Russian, which suggests he simply had no knowledge of Lëvshin's 1795 translation. Nonetheless, with his series of anonymous, translated fishing articles in Nikolai Novikov's *Economic Magazine* in the 1780s, Lëvshin at least earned the honor of being the first Russian writer to publish serious piscatory works in Russian.[39]

After Aksakov, Leonid Pavlovich Sabaneev (1844-98) produced the next most popular Russian fishing works of the nineteenth century in his frequently reprinted

Fishes of Russia and *Fishing Calendar,* which first appeared in 1875 and 1885. These lengthy books were much closer to ichthyological and fisheries manuals than Aksakov's literary *Notes on Fishing,* but Sabaneev's writings too have become Russian classics. In his essay entitled "Clear Spring-water," the prominent "village prose" writer Vladimir Soloukhin (b. 1924) offers a modern appraisal of Aksakov and Sabaneev:

> In the cultural life of nineteenth-century Russia, two books have had an amazing and enviable fate: Sergei Timofeevich Aksakov's *Notes on Fishing* and Leonid Pavlovich Sabaneev's *Fishes of Russia.* Neither book is a novel, fascinating topical narrative, or even belles lettres, but both books are nonetheless read with keen interest by generation after generation of Russians; they do not grow old, do not lose their significance, and, I daresay, their charm.
>
> There are several reasons for this, it seems to me. Let's dwell on one of them.
>
> First of all (though this is not the most important thing for this kind of literary success), there is thorough grounding in and knowledge of the subject. . . .
>
> But not only by knowledge of the subject, or, to put it more forcefully, by the author's learning and the work's erudition, can the book's success be explained. It is perfectly evident that still another force is coming into play, that that force is love for the nature of one's native land.
>
> If we glance at the history of Russian literature, poetry, painting, music, we immediately come up with dozens of names to which our notion of, and love for, Russian nature are connected: Pushkin, Lermontov, Gogol, Tiutchev, Turgenev, Fet, A. K. Tolstoi, Nekrasov, Lev Tolstoy, Aksakov, Savrasov, Shishkin, Levitan . . .
>
> But in art—from poetry to landscape in a novel, from the art-song to the symphony, to say nothing of painting—this feeling expresses itself clearly and definitely. Meanwhile, love for the nature of one's native land and, generally, love as a spiritual and moral principle, can color and illuminate human activity not connected at all with the direct expression or display of love.
>
> Aksakov's book on fishing, mentioned above, and the present subject of discussion—Sabaneev's *Fishes of Russia*—both confirm this. Not once do the authors of these books cry out, sigh, or confess their love for nature. On the contrary, in a very businesslike tone they describe concrete, practical things—the structure of a fish's body, habitat, food, spawning, biological characteristics, floats and hooks, bait and longlines—and meanwhile the feeling of love for the nature of their native land involuntarily springs up within the reader and washes over him as a clear, warm wave, because this feeling is imperceptibly dissolved in a businesslike narrative, and it colors and illuminates him because it lived in the soul of the one who wrote the book and now communicates itself to readers.[40]

Sincere love for fishing links Aksakov not only with zoologist Sabaneev, but also with other prominent Russian writers of the nineteenth century who happened to be passionate anglers, most notably the poet Apollon Maikov, novelist Ivan Goncharov, and dramatists Aleksandr Ostrovskii and Anton Chekhov.[41] Serving as a soldier in Semipalatinsk, Siberia, after his release from prison camp, Dostoevsky is known to have spent happy hours during the summer of 1855 lying on the grassy banks of the Irtysh reading Aksakov's *Notes on Fishing* and *Orenburg-Province Hunter* as a young friend fished the great river.[42]

One of twentieth-century Russia's finest nature writers, Konstantin Paustovskii (1892-1968), another passionate fisherman-author, described his abiding love for Aksakov and his work. In the late 1940s and early 1950s, Paustovskii wrote a series of four essays he called "fishing notes" and gathered them under the title, "In Memory of Aksakov." He opens "A Few Words about Fishing" (1948) by referring to a famous nineteenth-century "brother of the angle": "Chekhov never got angry if he was reproached for literary errors, but took serious offense when anyone questioned his ability as a fisherman."[43] In "The Great Tribe of Fishermen" (1952), Paustovskii begins his essay with a tribute to Aksakov:

> The old Russian writer, grandfather Aksakov, was, as everyone knows, an experienced and passionate fisherman. He wrote a magnificent book about fishing. It's called *Notes on Fishing.* This book is attractive not only because it splendidly conveys the poetry of fishing, but also because it's written in language as clear as springwater.
>
> I called Aksakov "grandfather." Up to now, it was customary for Russians to use that name for Krylov, the writer of fables. For his good-heartedness, serenity and insight, Aksakov has as much right to that affectionate name as Krylov.
>
> Aksakov was the first in Russian literature to write about fishing—that astonishing activity that makes a person come to know the natural world, to love it, and to live as one with it.[44]

* * *

Determining the genre of *Notes on Fishing* is no easy task. In his preface, Aksakov disavowed "treatise" and "natural history" as labels for the work, calling it instead "neither more nor less than the simple notes of a passionate sportsman." "Notes" (*zapiski*) have constituted something of a catch-all genre in Russia; the definitive register of Russian literature lists more than 250 "notes"-titles published since 1801.[45] The genre was embraced by all the canonical Russian writers of the nineteenth century—Pushkin, Gogol, Turgenev, Dostoevsky, Tolstoy—and was employed for both fiction and nonfiction.

The structure of *Notes on Fishing* is simple and logical. Aksakov begins with a preface in which he defends angling and outlines his motives for writing such a book. This is followed by eleven short chapters on the various components of a good fishing outfit as well as on selecting a promising place to fish. Next come two long chapters on the skills necessary for successful angling, and on fish behavior. At the heart of the book are Aksakov's twenty-five chapters on important Russian fish species, each of which is carefully, lovingly described. Name origins, size, shape, color, spawning cycles, general habits, fishing strategies, and cooking advice are included in nearly all these chapters; occasionally, restrained fishing-stories are included. Crayfish, a favorite delicacy of Russians and of their piscine quarry as well, are accorded their own chapter before the concluding sections on set-lines and lures. Throughout *Notes on Fishing,* lyrical digressions—made all the more vivid by their pragmatic context—season the text with welcome modulations in tone and thematics. The result is an extraordinarily versatile book. ***Notes on Fishing*** is, among other things, an angling primer, a biological field guide, a culinary manual, a collection of literary nature-sketches, a memoir, and a philosophical case study.

As Russia's best-loved classic of fishing literature, Aksakov's book is often compared to Izaak Walton's masterpiece, *The Compleat Angler; or, The Contemplative Man's Recreation,* first published in 1653.[46] Readers familiar with *The Compleat Angler* will immediately sense the analogy to be made between ***Notes on Fishing*** and the Walton classic. Both works began as short booklets, then achieved immense popularity and went through numerous enlarged editions; both works were written by baitfishermen; both works open with defenses of angling before moving on to systematic discussions of important species of gamefish; both works enlist the aid of collaborators in late editions; both works subtly endorse ideological causes (Walton's "Great Tew" Christian communitarianism and Aksakov's Slavophilism); the language of both works has been especially praised; and both works generally strive for a tone of serenity, civility, and friendliness.

The differences, though, are numerous. There was already a long tradition of distinguished piscatory writing in England when Walton wrote his nonpareil of the genre; Aksakov, as we have seen, was really the founder of his nation's fishing literature. Walton frequently showed little regard for protection of the natural environment (consider the passages on slaughtering otters), while Aksakov's work boasts a more conscious and consistent sense of ecological propriety—almost an early Russian form of conservationism. Perhaps most significant, Aksakov's ***Notes on Fishing*** lacks the polyphonic structure of *The Compleat Angler.* The Russian writer has no Piscator, Venator, or Auceps, no comely milkmaids, no cheery inns, no dramatized dialogues, no stage directions, no interpolations of poetry, no flights of theological ecstasy.

Instead, ***Notes on Fishing*** is a monologue, erudite and inspired, by a single, confident intelligence who warmly invites the reader to view natural phenomena—and their skillful human manipulation—through the prism of Aksakov's systematic mind and congenial spirit. Literary and social comments, old friends, fishing companions, and fondly remembered places and times are all introduced into the text, but these refreshing asides appear quietly, as organic extensions of the author's unforced stream of expert commentary. All the qualities enumerated by Aksakov's Russian admirers—his authority, clarity, artlessness, eloquence, self-discipline, restraint, and love—are conveyed to the reader directly, intimately, often with a poignant sense of solitude. Aksakov, the gifted dramatic reader and lifelong devotee of the theater, shuns theatrical device in ***Notes on Fishing.*** The result is a fishing book without rival in Russia, and with few peers in Europe.

Notes

1. S. T. Aksakov's letter of 22 November 1845 to N. V. Gogol', *Istoriia moego znakomstva s Gogolem,* in *Sobranie sochinenii v chetyrëkh tomakh* (Moscow: Gosudarstvennoe izdatel'stvo khudozhestvennoi literatury, 1956), 3:326.

2. I. S. Turgenev, "O solov'iakh," *Polnoe sobranie sochinenii i pisem v dvadtsati vos'mi tomakh: Sochineniia* (Moscow: Izdatel'stvo Nauka, 1967), 14:172.

3. K. F. Rul'e, "Khod ryby protiv techeniia vody," in *Zapiski ob uzhen'e ryby,* 3d ed. (Moscow: V universitetskoi tipografii, 1856), 326-45.

4. S. T. Aksakov, *Polnoe sobranie sochinenii* (Saint Petersburg: 1886), 5:174-91; Varpakhovskii's notes appear on 192-95.

5. S. I. Mashinskii, *S. T. Aksakov: Zhizn' i tvorchestvo,* 2d ed. (Moscow: Khudozhestvennaia literatura, 1973), 314.

6. *Sovremennik* 6 (1847): 114.

7. *Otechestvennye zapiski* 52 (1847): 127.

8. *Finskii vestnik* 18 (June 1847); quoted from A. G. Gornfel'd, "Okhotnich'i sochineniia S. T. Aksakova," in *Sobranie sochinenii,* by S. T. Aksakov (Saint Petersburg: Tipolitografiia Tovarischestva Prosveshchenie, 1910), 5:4.

9. *Biblioteka dlia chteniia* 82 (May 1847); quoted from Gornfel'd, "Okhotnich'i sochineniia S. T. Aksakova," 5:4.

10. *Moskovskii vestnik,* no. 28 (1854); quoted from *Sergei Timofeevich Aksakov: Ego zhizn' i tvorchestvo,* ed. V. I. Pokrovskii, 2d ed. (Moscow: Sklad v knizhnom magazine V. Spiridonova i A. Mikhailova, 1912), 78.

11. *Trudy Imperatorskogo Vol'nogo Ekonomicheskogo Obshchestva* 2 (1854): 98-99.

12. *Sovremennik,* no. 8 (1854): 130-31; quoted from Mashinskii, *S. T. Aksakov,* 314.

13. *Otechestvennye zapiski* 110, no. 1 (1857): 50-51; *Sovremennik* 61 (1857): 43.

14. I. S. Turgenev, *Polnoe sobranie sochinenii,* 5:416, 418.

15. Ibid., 419.

16. Ibid., 644.

17. See note 25 in *Notes on Fishing.*

18. See S. A. Vengerov, "Sergei Timofeevich Aksakov," in *Kritikobiograficheskii slovar' russkikh pisatelei i uchënykh (ot nachala russkoi obrazovannosti do nashikh dnei)* (Saint Petersburg: Semënovskaia Tipolitografiia I. Efrona, 1889), 1, nos. 1-21:185.

19. A. S. Khomiakov, "Sergei Timofeevich Aksakov," first published in *Russkaia beseda,* no. 3 (1859): i-viii; quoted from A. S. Khomiakov, *O starom i o novom: Stat'i i ocherki,* Biblioteka "Liubiteliam rossiiskoi slovesnosti": Iz literaturnogo naslediia (Moscow: Sovremennik, 1988), 409-10.

20. Ibid., 411-12.

21. From the 1847 review in *Sovremennik;* quoted from Pokrovskii, *Sergei Timofeevich Aksakov,* 77.

22. Vengerov, "Sergei Timofeevich Aksakov," 188.

23. "Gogol' v neizdannoi perepiske sovremennikov," *Literaturnoe nasledstvo* [Moscow] 58 (1952): 706.

24. N. V. Gogol''s letter of 20 September 1851 to S. T. Aksakov, in *Polnoe sobranie sochinenii,* by N. V. Gogol' (Leningrad: Izdatel'stvo Akademii Nauk SSSR, 1952), 14:250.

25. Khomiakov, "Sergei Timofeevich Aksakov," 412-13.

26. For a useful survey of the fishing passages in Aksakov's autobiographical trilogy, see Arthur Ransome, "Aksakov on Fishing," in *Rod and Line,* The Travellers' Library (London: Jonathan Cape, 1935), 243-69.

27. "The Migration," in *A Family Chronicle* [Translated by M. C. Beverley. New York: Dutton, 1961].

28. See note 5 in *Notes on Fishing.*

29. Quoted from Gornfel'd, "Okhotnich'i sochineniia S. T. Aksakova," 5:5n.

30. See A. S. Pushkin, *Kapitanskaia dochka,* Literaturnye pamiatniki (Leningrad: Izdatel'stvo Nauka, Leningradskoe otdelenie, 1985), 284.

31. Vengerov, "Sergei Timofeevich Aksakov," 154.

32. Ibid., 181, 186.

33. Ibid., 181-82.

34. Quoted in S. T. Aksakov, *Sobranie sochinenii,* 4:632-33.

35. The best bibliography of these scattered and extremely rare pre-Aksakov angling works—just over a dozen in all—is L. P. Sabaneev, "Ukazatel' russkoi literatury po rybolovstvu i rybovodstvu," in his *Rybolovnyi kalendar',* Chelovek i priroda (Moscow: Terra, 1992), 416-17.

36. On Lëvshin, see Viktor Shklovskii, *Chulkov i Lëvshin* (Leningrad: Izdatel'stvo pisatelei v Leningrade, 1933), 137-51, 249-62.

37. Louis Liger, *La nouvelle maison rustique, ou Économie rurale, pratique et générale de tous les biens de campagne,* 11th ed., vol. 2 (Paris: Chez les Libraires Associés, 1790). Volume 4, chapters 5 and 6 of Lëvshin's *Universal and Complete Art of Housekeeping* were simply translations of Liger (1790), vol. 2, part 4, book 1, 449-504 ("Des Etangs . . . ," and "De la Pêche").

38. The contents of Lëvshin's Chapter 6: On Fishing; On the Eel; On Lampreys; On Loach; On the Viper; On River Carp; A Method of Catching Pike with Trimmers; A Method of Catching Pike on Rod and Line; On Carp; A Method of Catching Carp on Rod and Line; A Method of Catching Carp Among Roots Under Banks; Another Method; On Gudgeon, Ruff and Other Separate Fish; On Chub, Perch, and Roach; On Salmon and How to Catch Them; On Spottie, Anchovies, and Sardines, and a Secret for Catching Trout; On Several Fisherman's Secrets for Luring Fish and Catching Them by Hand or Other Methods; A Method for Catching Fish by Hand; A Trustworthy Trap; A Method of Angling; A Method of Gathering Fish Into One Place; A Method of Attracting Fish into Nets; A Method of Catching Fish With Fire; A Way of Keeping Large Fish from Jumping Over the Net; A Method of Catching Fish with a Hand-Net; An Artificial Pen for Gathering Fish, and How to Catch Them in It; A Method of Catching Fish With Gates; A Method of Catching Fish in Top-Traps; On Catching Fish With the Net Known as the "Hawk," and on the Fishing Technique Called "Chain"; On Crayfish and How to Catch Them; On Frogs and How to Catch Them; On Live Baits Used on Rod and Line and Trimmers.

39. Lëvshin, who frequently translated for Novikov's publications, is the most likely author (or adaptor) of these items, especially when we recall that Catherine II's Free Economic Society, of which

Lëvshin was a fellow, sponsored *Ekonomicheskii magazin* as well as Lëvshin's *Vseobshchee i polnoe domovodstvo*; see Lëvshin's comments on this in *Vseobshchee i polnoe domovodstvo* (Moscow: Universitetskoi tipografii, 1795), 1:vi. The articles can be found in *Ekonomicheskii magazin* 4 (1780): 330-32, 337-39; 12 (1782): 314-16, 337-51; 20 (1784): 241-302; 28 (1786): 289-94.

40. Vladimir Soloukhin, "Chistaia kliuchevaia voda," in his *Volshebnaia palochka* (Moscow: Moskovskii rabochii, 1983), 174, 176.

41. See N. Koval', "Pisateli-rybolovy: A. N. Maikov i ego druz'ia," *Rybovodstvo i rybolovstvo,* no. 3 (May-June 1961): 51-53. Chekhov admired Aksakov's nature writing; see Mashinskii, *S. T. Aksakov,* 314.

42. A. E. Vrangel', "Vospominaniia o F. M. Dostoevskom v Sibiri," in *F. M. Dostoevskii v vospominaniiakh sovremennikov,* ed. K. T'iunkin (Moscow: Khudozhestvennaia literatura, 1990), 1:361.

43. K. G. Paustovskii, *Sobranie sochinenii v shesti tomakh* (Moscow: Gosudarstvennoe izdatel'stvo khudozhestvennoi literatury, 1968), 6:596.

44. Ibid., 617. Soloukhin's title "Clear Springwater" (see note 40, above) is taken from Paustovskii's phrase in the first paragraph.

45. *Ukazatel' zaglavii proizvedenii khudozhestvennoi literatury, 1801-1975* (Moscow: Gosudarstvennaia biblioteka SSSR imeni V. I. Lenina, 1986), 2:173-77.

46. See, for example, Arthur Ransome's comments in Ransome, "Aksakov on Fishing," 270, 276.

Bibliography

Aksakov, Sergei Timofeevich. *A Family Chronicle.* Translated by M. C. Beverley. New York: Dutton, 1961.

———. *Istoriia moego znakomstva s Gogolem* [The story of my acquaintance with Gogol']. Literaturnye pamiatniki. Moscow: Izdatel'stvo Nauka, 1960.

———. *Rasskazy i vospominaniia okhotnika o raznykh okhotakh* [A sportsman's stories and memoirs on various kinds of sport]. Moscow: Tipografiia L. Stepanovoi, 1855.

———. *Rasskazy i vospominaniia okhotnika o raznykh okhotakh* [A sportsman's stories and memoirs on various kinds of sport]. 2d ed. Moscow: Tipografiia L. Stepanovoi, 1856.

———. *A Russian Gentleman* [translation of *Semeinaia khronika*]. Translated by J. D. Duff. The World's Classics. New York: Oxford University Press, 1982.

———. *A Russian Schoolboy* [translation of *Vospominaniia*]. Translated by J. D. Duff. The World's Classics. New York: Oxford University Press, 1983.

———. *Sobranie sochinenii v chetyrëkh tomakh* [Collected works in four volumes]. Edited by S. I. Mashinskii. Moscow: Gosudarstvennoe izdatel'stvo khudozhestvennoi literatury, 1955-56.

———. *Years of Childhood* [translation of *Detskie gody Bagrova-vnuka*]. Translated by J. D. Duff. New York: Longmans, Green, 1916.

———. *Years of Childhood* [translation of *Detskie gody Bagrova-vnuka*]. Translated by Alec Brown. New York: Vintage, 1960.

———. "Zamechaniia i nabliudeniia okhotnika brat' griby" [Remarks and observations of a mushroom-gatherer]. *Vestnik estestvennykh nauk* [Natural sciences herald], no. 6 (1856): 162-71.

———. *Zapiski ob uzhen'e* [Notes on angling]. Moscow: V Tipografii Nikolaia Stepanova, 1847.

———. *Zapiski ob uzhen'e ryby* [Notes on fishing]. 2d ed. Moscow: V Tipografii L. Stepanovoi, 1854.

———. *Zapiski ob uzhen'e ryby* [Notes on fishing]. With engravings, and an afterword by K. F. Rul'e. 3d ed. Moscow: V Universitetskoi Tipografii, 1856.

———. *Zapiski ob uzhen'e ryby* [Notes on fishing]. In *Polnoe sobranie sochinenii* [Complete works], vol. 5. With notes by K. F. Rul'e and N. A. Varpakhovskii, and engravings. Saint Petersburg, 1886.

———. *Zapiski ruzheinogo okhotnika Orenburgskoi gubernii* [Notes of an Orenburg-Province hunter]. Moscow: V Tipografii L. Stepanovoi, 1852.

Gogol', N. V. *Polnoe sobranie sochinenii* [Complete works]. 14 vols. Leningrad: Izdatel'stvo Akademii Nauk SSSR, 1938-52.

Gornfel'd, A. G. "Okhotnich'i sochineniia S. T. Aksakova" [Aksakov's sporting works]. In *Sobranie sochinenii* [Collected works], by S. T. Aksakov, 5:3-10. Saint Petersburg: Tipolitografiia Tovarishchestva Prosveshchenie, 1910.

Heckel, Johann Jakob, and Rudolf Kner. *Die Süsswasserfische der ostreichischen Monarchie mit Rücksicht auf die angrenzänder Länder.* Leipzig: W. Englmann, 1858.

Khomiakov, A. S. "Sergei Timofeevich Aksakov." First published in *Russkaia beseda* [Russian conversation], no. 3 (1859): i-viii. Quoted from A. S. Khomiakov, *O starom i o novom: Stat'i i ocherki* [On old and new: articles and essays]. Biblioteka "Liubiteliam rossiiskoi slovesnosti": Iz literaturnogo naslediia. Moscow: Sovremennik, 1988.

Koval', N. "Pisateli-rybolovy: A. N. Maikov i ego druz'ia" [Fishermen-writers: A. N. Maikov and his friends]. *Rybovodstvo i rybolovstvo* [Fish culture and fishing], no. 3 (May-June 1961): 51-53.

Lëvshin, V. A., trans. and adapter. *Kniga dlia okhotnikov do zverinoi i ptichei lovli, takzhe do ruzheinoi strel' by i soderzhaniia pevchikh ptits* [A book for sportsmen interested in animals and other game, as well as in shooting and the keeping of songbirds]. Vol. 4. Moscow: V Tipografii S. Selivanovskogo, 1819.

———. "O prudakh, sazhelkakh, rvakh, zavedenii ryby, torgovle ryboiu i proch" [On ponds, pens, ditches, raising fish, trading in fish, and so forth]. In *Vseobshchee i polnoe domovodstvo* [The universal and complete art of housekeeping]. Vol. 4. Moscow: V Universitetskoi Tipografii, 1795.

———. "O rybnoi lovle" [On fishing]. In *Vseobshchee i polnoe domovodstvo* [The universal and complete art of housekeeping]. Vol. 4. Moscow: V Universitetskoi Tipografii, 1795.

———. *Sovershennyi eger', ili Znanie o vsekh prinadlezhashchikh k ruzheinoi i prochei okhote* [The perfect huntsman, or knowledge of all the appurtenances of field sport with guns and other means]. Saint Petersburg, 1779.

Liger, Louis. *La nouvelle maison rustique, ou Économie rurale, pratique et générale de tous les biens de campagne.* 11th ed. Vol. 2. Paris: Chez les Libraires Associés, 1790.

Paustovskii, K. G. *Sobranie sochinenii v shesti tomakh* [Collected works in six volumes]. Vol. 6. Moscow: Gosudarstvennoe izdatel'stvo khudozhestvennoi literatury, 1968.

Pokrovskii, V. I., ed. *Sergei Timofeevich Aksakov: Ego zhizn' i tvorchestvo* [Sergei Timofeevich Aksakov: His life and work]. 2d ed. Moscow: Sklad v knizhnom magazine V. Spiridonova i A. Mikhailova, 1912.

Pushkin, A. S. *Kapitanskaia dochka* [The captain's daughter]. Literaturnye pamiatniki. Leningrad: Izdatel'stvo Nauka, Leningradskoe otdelenie, 1985.

Ransome, Arthur. "Aksakov on Fishing." In *Rod and Line.* London: Jonathan Cape, 1929.

Sabaneev, L. P. *Rybolovnyi kalendar', Trudy po rybolovstvu* [The fisherman's calendar, works on fishing]. Moscow: Terra, 1992.

———. *Ryby Rossii: Zhizn' i lovlia (uzhen'e) nashikh presnovodnykh ryb* [Fishes of Russia: the life and capture (angling) of our freshwater fishes]. 2 vols. Moscow: Terra, 1992.

Shklovskii, Viktor. *Chulkov i Lëvshin* [Chulkov and Lëvshin]. Leningrad: Izdatel'stvo pisatelei v Leningrade, 1933.

Soloukhin, Vladimir. "Chistaia kliuchevaia voda" [Clear springwater]. In *Volshebnaia palochka* [The magic wand]. Moscow: Moskovskii rabochii, 1983.

Turgenev. I. S. *Polnoe sobranie sochinenii i pisem v dvadtsati vos'mi tomakh: Sochineniia* [Complete works and letters in twenty-eight volumes: works]. 15 vols. Moscow: Izdatel'stvo Nauka, 1960-68.

Vengerov, S. A. "Sergei Timofeevich Aksakov." In *Kritiko-biograficheskii slovar' russkikh pisatelei i uchënykh (ot nachala russkoi obrazovannosti do nashikh dnei)* [Critical-biographical dictionary of Russian writers and scholars (from the beginning of education in Russia to the present)], vol. 1, nos. 1-21. Saint Petersburg: Semënovskaia Tipolitografiia I. Efrona, 1889.

Vinogradov, V. V. *Istoriia slov* [The history of words]. Moscow: Tolk, 1994.

Walton, Izaak. *The Complete Angler, or The Contemplative Man's Recreation.* Edited and with an Introduction by Jonquil Bevan. London: J. M. Dent, 1993.

Walton, Izaak, and Charles Cotton. *The Compleat Angler.* Edited by John Buxton. With an Introduction by John Buchan. The World's Classics. Oxford: Oxford University Press, 1982.

Kevin Windle (essay date 1998)

SOURCE: Windle, Kevin. Introduction to *Notes of a Provincial Wildfowler,* by Sergei Timofeevich Aksakov, translated by Kevin Windle, pp. xi-xvii. Evanston, Ill.: Northwestern University Press, 1998.

[*In the following introduction, Windle discusses* Notes of a Provincial Wildfowler *as an important early example of Russian nature writing. In Windle's view, the work exhibits Aksakov's rare talent for observation, as well as his passion and respect for the natural world.*]

In the history of nineteenth-century Russian literature Sergei Timofeevich Aksakov (1791-1859) is more important than is generally realized in the English-speaking world, where his reputation has been overshadowed by those of his great contemporaries. Although his best-known works came late in his career, he was close to the world of letters and the theater from his youth and made a substantial contribution as a drama critic and by his translations from the French of Molière and Boileau. Incongruously perhaps, he was able to enrich his store of literary knowledge during a period of service in the office of the censor, from 1827 until 1832, when he was dismissed. His most spectacular transgression was to permit publication of a satirical work that aroused the ire of the authorities, including Aksakov's master, the head of the Emperor's Third Section, Count Benckendorff.[1]

Sergei Aksakov was born in 1791 in Ufa, a provincial town to the west of the Urals, where his father was a court official in government service. Here and in the neighboring province of Orenburg he spent most of his early childhood until at nine he was sent to school in Kazan', where he later attended the university. After a period in Saint Petersburg and Moscow he spent the greater part of the years 1812 to 1826 managing the family estate in Orenburg province. He then moved with his family to Moscow and entered the office of the censor, which was then expanding its operations in the repressive years following the Decembrist uprising of 1825, and made only rare visits to his beloved Urals and the steppe regions of his youth.

In Moscow he became deeply involved in the world of literature and ideas, the theater and the arts. His acquaintance with other literary figures of the day led him to write his recollections of Gavriil Derzhavin, Aleksandr Shishkov, Nikolai Gogol, and others, providing an invaluable source of background information about these writers. Later his house became a center of Slavophile social thought, when his son Konstantin came to occupy a central position in this school.

In 1843 Aksakov purchased the estate known as Abramtsevo, thirty-five miles to the east of Moscow in beautiful rural surroundings. The estate is now preserved as a museum, partly in remembrance of Aksakov but also commemorating the colony of artists that flourished there in later times. Here he spent most of his remaining years and wrote the works for which he became famous. As his health and eyesight began to fail in the mid-1840s he was obliged to rely increasingly on dictation to produce them.

The first major work to attract a wide readership bore the seemingly unlikely title *Notes on Fishing,* first published in 1847. Readers were quick to notice that although the title was a faithful reflection of the content—Aksakov intended to write only a practical guide to a subject he knew well—there was more to the book than the title announced. His feeling for nature and extraordinary ability to describe it, together with his expert knowledge of botany and wildlife in all its forms, produced a work that had few if any precedents in Russian writing.

A similar if not even greater success attended his *Notes of a Provincial Wildfowler* and his more orthodox autobiographical fiction written in the 1850s, *The Childhood Years of Bagrov's Grandson* and *A Family Chronicle.* While the latter two have long been known in English translation, his shooting and fishing notes have not previously been translated, perhaps because they fall outside the familiar genres of nineteenth-century Russian literature. Yet the fictional and autobiographical writings, for all their charm and merit, produce a somewhat incomplete picture of the man and the writer, since so much of his time was spent in the wilds of his native province with only his shotgun and dog for company. He was a man of wide interests and talents, as much a drama critic as he was a hunter and naturalist, equally at home in the company of Saint Petersburg writers and intellectuals and in solitary reflection on the life of the wild.

In writing of his shooting days in Orenburg he is remembering his youth and reproducing the details he had faithfully recorded in his diaries at the time. His experience in the field reaches back to his childhood, to around the year 1800, and his interest in nature and wildlife endured long after the end of his Orenburg period in 1826. In his *Notes of a Provincial Wildfowler* he shows himself in the gentleman-sportsman tradition to a degree; unlike most of his contemporaries, however, he maintained an abiding interest in wildlife and made a close study of the birds that he shot—that is, most species larger than finches, exception being made for families such as the raptors and corvids. The result is far more than a shooting man's guide to game; rather it is an attempt at a comprehensive guide to local birdlife. His detailed descriptions have all the precision and immediacy of the later British ornithologist Thomas Coward, and his close personal observations on the behavior of various species invite comparison with those of an earlier writer, the English country vicar Gilbert White. White dealt with the natural history of a very small area, the little Hampshire village of Selborne.[2] Aksakov also maintains his focus on a particular area, a much bigger one: the forests, steppes, and marshland of the vast province of Orenburg. Modestly he claims little knowledge of the wildlife beyond its borders, although it is clear that his ornithological knowledge in fact extends far wider.

When first published in 1852, the work enjoyed popularity greatly exceeding the author's expectations, largely because it was the first such book to be written in Russian. It was highly praised by readers as varied but discerning as Turgenev, Nekrasov, Gogol, and Chernyshevsky, and later specialists in the field of ornithology also held it in high regard. It was Turgenev who made the famous comment, "If a black grouse could tell its own story, I am quite sure it would have nothing to add to what Mr Aksakov has told us."[3] On the basis of reviews and correspondence with knowledgeable readers, Aksakov was able to revise and improve the work in two later editions (1853 and 1857), correcting some of his earlier misconceptions—for example, about the roding of the woodcock—and offering different opinions on contentious matters such as the drumming of the snipe (a subject that had earlier exercised Gilbert White's skill as an observer).

It should not surprise us if faults can be found in Aksakov's taxonomy and if he occasionally fails to distinguish species. He was, after all, observing without any visual aids and did not necessarily collect specimens of both sexes of all birds that he saw. There is some confusion regarding the females of divers, grebes, and sawbills, and he does not separate the swans. An added difficulty here is the terminology of the period, which had not yet been standardized. Aksakov used the names then current in his wildfowling milieu. Most of these are in use today but some have been applied to different species. This is particularly true of the ducks, grebes, and divers (loons), as may be seen from a perusal of these terms in the dictionary of a slightly later period by Vladimir Dal'. The occasional gaps in Aksakov's knowledge do not detract from the work, which still provides a fascinating insight into the state of ornithological knowledge in Russia in the mid-nineteenth century.

As a naturalist, Aksakov was very much a man of his time. A love of the natural world meant to many a love of the chase in all its forms and of the meat thus procured for the table. The sense of Russian *dich'*; does not correspond exactly to the closest English equivalent "game." It is related to the adjective *dikii* (wild) and it is applied to all forms of wildlife deemed to be edible. It is thus broader than the concept of "game species" in English and few ethical constraints hampered the shooting of birds and animals. Likewise there was no such thing as a "closed season" in which the birds could breed in relative safety. As long as they were present the season was open and the peak of the season was the time when the birds were at their fattest. Apparently nothing in the sportsman's code of ethics proscribed the shooting of sitting birds. The bird was fair game whether in flight, on water, or on land. Aksakov himself describes with more than a tinge of regret the ravages wrought by his shooting confrères and himself on the breeding marshes of the black-tailed godwit.

The Anglo-Saxon reader may need to bear in mind the very different shooting traditions of Continental Europe. It is not only in Russia and not only in the nineteenth century that the indiscriminate shooting of wildlife, particularly migratory birds, reaches devastating proportions.

As Aksakov himself points out, the more respect a hunter has for a particular species of bird, the harder he tries to kill it. His own joy at finding his first little bustard's nest is the greater for being able to rob it of all its eggs. On finding a coot's nest with eggs he takes the nest home with him, while the parent bird pipes in alarm. He tells with pleasure how he shot every bird in the only family of partridges he encountered. The acquaintance whom he quotes at length gives advice on the surest way to hunt down every bird in a covey.

Aksakov is well aware of the paradoxes here and occasionally gives them some emphasis, while speaking of the destruction in which he himself so energetically participated. Only rarely does he recount how his affection for certain species that he has observed caused him to steal away without attempting to shoot them (see Category I, Chapter 17, on the little stint).

The modern reader needs to bear in mind that the concept of conservation had not yet been invented; shocking as Aksakov's attitudes may sometimes appear to naturalists and ecologists of a later age, they do not exclude a deep feeling for the life of the wild or a genuine interest in increasing the store of human knowledge. Aksakov is typically self-deprecating in disclaiming any pretensions to serious science: he repeatedly insists that this work and his fishing notes are not a natural history of all forms of game, "merely the notes of a passionate hunter and observer." It must be acknowledged, however, that his observations as a collector (to use a possibly outdated term) yield a fuller picture of many species than can be obtained by most modern bird-watchers with binoculars. The many hours spent by the dedicated wildfowler in pursuit of his prey, or in patient observation while waiting for the chance to make a kill, yield a wealth of knowledge of behavioral characteristics. We have only to read his account of the feeding habits of the black grouse or the nesting behavior of the black-tailed godwit to appreciate that the extent of his knowledge compares very favorably with that of many field ornithologists. His hunter's eye and his examination of freshly killed specimens yield much detail on seasonal variations in size and weight within species, and by dissecting the birds he obtains detailed information on their diet. But to many readers he will seem at his best in his loving descriptions, feather by feather, of the plumage and physical characteristics of these specimens, in his precision in conveying every tint and every curve of beak or wing.

Aksakov takes a highly individual view of the wildlife he knows so well. Of certain species he is very fond. These include the partridge, for its appearance and its flavor; the crane, whose courtship antics are so entertaining; the wood pigeon, whose conjugal devotion he finds most affecting; and several small sandpipers with endearing habits. (Aksakov's fondness for the wood pigeon would surprise many in western Europe, where the bird is regarded as a pest.) Others he holds in contempt for a variety of personal reasons: the oystercatcher has unattractive plumage, he says, and an unpleasant flavor, even when fat; the tufted duck is also an unappealing bird and one that merits no special attention as game. We learn that most fowlers have no time for the lapwing because it is found everywhere and is very tame. Some species, such as the common merganser (goosander) are practically inedible but still good sport because their habits make them elusive quarry.

Soviet editors and commentators on Aksakov's work were given to pointing out that he set much store by the views, myths, and sayings of the *narod,* the common people. While it is clear that ideological considerations played a role here, it is undoubtedly true that Aksakov had absorbed much peasant lore relating to wildlife and found in it a store of valuable knowledge. Who, after all, would be likely to have a closer knowledge of bird and animal life than the peasant working the land? While no doubt greatly appreciating the factual element, Aksakov is also fond of retailing the folklore attached to some species. His accounts of their lives and habits gain color from the mythology, such as the story of the mating of the black grouse: impregnation is supposedly achieved by the gray-hen consuming the saliva of the male; or of the turtledove: on losing its mate, the surviving member of the pair is so distraught that it commits suicide by plunging to earth from a height.

Humans, other than the author and unnamed drivers, trappers, and informants, do not figure prominently in a work that has as its heroes a large number of species of bird. We do, however, learn something of the class distinctions between types of fowlers and trappers. Though all classes eat their quarry, there are those who kill game for a livelihood, therefore taking as much as they can for sale or consumption, and those whose material need is less acute or nonexistent, for whom shooting is above all a sport. To the latter it is a question of prowess in overcoming, for example, the speed and zigzag flight of a snipe or the wariness of the capercaillie. Aksakov of course is firmly in the category of the sportsmen, though doubtless untypical in the extent and depth of his study of game.

* * *

With this work and the earlier ***Notes on Fishing,*** Aksakov established himself as a leading practitioner of the nascent art of nature writing, a genre that was to be developed in a later period by Mikhail Prishvin, Ivan Sokolov-Mikitov, and Vladimir Soloukhin, among others. It has been a less visible tradition in the turbulent twentieth century than the prose and poetry of massive social upheaval and has not caught the attention of translators to the same extent. Nevertheless it remains well known and well loved by Russian readers and repays serious attention. Aksakov, one of its earliest exponents, has proved the most enduring and abidingly popular.

Notes

1. Readers interested in learning more about Aksakov's life and work may refer to A. R. Durkin, *Sergej Aksakov and Russian Pastoral* (New Brunswick, N.J., 1983). In Russian the standard work is S. I. Mashinsky, *S. T. Aksakov: zhizn'i tvorchestvo* (Moscow, 1973).

2. A more detailed comparison of Aksakov and White as ornithologists may be found in Kevin

Windle, "Sergei Timofeevich Aksakov i Gil'bert Uait: zametki o dvukh literatorakh-ornitologakh," in *Problemy sovremennoi rusistiki,* ed. Antoni Markunas (Poznań, 1995).

3. The comment was made in a review published in *Sovremennik*; see I. S. Turgenev, *Polnoe sobranie sochinenii v 30-ti tomakh* (Moscow, 1980), 4:518.

Christine Rydel (essay date 2007)

SOURCE: Rydel, Christine. "'You Are Not Great Heroes': Sergei Aksakov and the Emergence of Russian Realism." In *Nineteenth-Century Literature Criticism,* Vol. 181, pp. 59-70. Farmington Hills, Mich.: Thomson Gale, 2007.

[In the following essay, Rydel analyzes Aksakov's writings within the context of nineteenth-century Russian realism. Rydel suggests that Aksakov's vivid, direct prose style emerged out of the tension between the traditional, Old Russian ideals of Aleksandr Shishkov and the more cosmopolitan, and modern, attitude of Nikolai Karamzin.]

Sergei Timofeevich Aksakov appeared on the Russian literary scene at exactly the right time—the middle of the nineteenth century. Although he had earlier contributed theatrical reviews and articles to popular journals, he began his writing career in earnest only during the last fifteen years of his life. Aksakov was mainly drawn to prose genres, but in his youth, like most aspiring authors, first wrote some poetry. His poems, though, could never compete with the works of the great names of Russia's Golden Age of poetry: Aleksandr Sergeevich Pushkin (1799-1837), Mikhail Iur'evich Lermontov (1814-1841), and Ivan Fedorovich Tiutchev (1803-1873), among others. However, the prose that he wrote mid-century set the standard for the great nineteenth century writers who followed, especially Lev Nikolaevich Tolstoy (1828-1910), Ivan Sergeevich Turgenev (1818-1883), Ivan Aleksandrovich Goncharov (1812-1891), and Anton Pavlovich Chekhov (1860-1904). With the appearance of his books on fishing and hunting in the late 1840s and early 1850s, followed by his autobiographical and biographical fiction and then his theatrical and literary reminiscences, Aksakov provided an early model of realistic prose in a pure Russian language that still delights and continues to influence modern Russian writers. Known to all literate Russians, Aksakov unfortunately does not enjoy a wide readership in the West; undeservedly, he remains largely unknown outside of Russia.

At the beginning of the nineteenth century, the Russian literary world was locked in debate over several issues, not the least important among them what kind of language was appropriate for specific genres. Two camps arose—the conservatives who rallied around Admiral Aleksandr Semenovich Shishkov (1754-1841) and the innovators who became disciples of Nikolai Mikhailovich Karamzin (1766-1826). A writer and statesman who upheld Old Russian values both in politics and in language, Shishkov fought an ultimately losing battle with his opponents. Author of a famous dictionary and of *Discourse on the Old and New Style of the Russian Language* (*Rassuzhdeniia o starom i novom sloge rossiiskogo iazyka*, 1803), Shishkov proposed that Old Church Slavonic provide the roots to form new words and expressions. He advocated an old, formal model of a stilted, three-tiered level of styles that would use ecclesiastical and colloquial language in degrees proportionate to a hierarchy of genres, with prose—especially fiction—occupying the lowest place. On the other hand, Shishkov saw real virtue in using the simple, informal language of the folk as a source for new words to enhance literary Russian.

Karamzin, Shishkov's linguistic opponent, began his literary career as a journalist, poet, and prose writer in the sentimental mold of late European Enlightenment. He bemoaned the convoluted rules and almost obscure language that the leading neoclassical writers championed. Karamzin wanted to reform, renew, and refresh Russian and turn it into a language worthy of the life of the salon, not unlike cultured French. In fact, Karamzin used French as the basis of forming calques and thus creating new words to enrich the Russian vocabulary. He created a language equally suited to all realms of discourse and to all genres, and most important, accessible to all levels of society. Karamzin's own prose works such as travel literature patterned after that of Laurence Sterne, *Letters of a Russian Traveler* (*Pis'ma russkogo puteshestvenika*, 1791); gothic stories such as "The Island of Bornholm" ("Ostrov Borngol'm," 1794); and the vaguely Rousseauesque and wildly popular story of star-crossed lovers, "Poor Liza" ("Bednaia Liza," 1792) made him the most influential Russian writer of the eighteenth century, one whose influence was so great that most critics acknowledge that Karamzin changed the course of Russian literature. Appointed Russia's official historiographer by Tsar Alexander I in 1803, Karamzin devoted the rest of his life to writing his *History of the Russian State* (*Istoriia gosudarstva Rossiiskago*, 1818-1826); this work influenced Russian writers to the same degree as did his short works of fiction.

Against this background young Sergei Aksakov attended school in the provincial city of Kazan'. During his tenure at the school (*gymnasium*) and at the newly opened university there, Aksakov was able to indulge in two areas that captivated his imagination and captured his heart to the end of his days: literature and the theater. His initial attempt at writing, a few poems, appeared in a handwritten high-school journal, *Arcadian Shepherds*

(*Arkadskie pastushki*) and attest to Aksakov's brief infatuation with Karamzin's sentimentalism. The very titles of the lyrics, **"To a Nightingale" ("K solov'iu")** and **"To an Unfaithful One" ("K nevernoi")** alert the reader to their melancholy nature and their sentimental theme: love. Exhilarated by seeing his poems in print, Aksakov founded, along with some school pals, a "more serious" literary enterprise, *Journal of Our Activities* (*Zhurnal nashikh zaniatii*). By this time (1806-1807) he had already emerged as one of Karamzin's adversaries and a follower of Shishkov, a source of Aksakov's own brand of moderate, non-ideological Slavophilism.

In his **Reminiscences** (**Vospominaniia**, 1856; translated as **A Russian Schoolboy**, 1917), Aksakov describes his attitude toward followers of Karamzin: "This [the new journal, *CAR*] was a more serious undertaking than *Shepherds of Arcadia*, and I did all I could to keep out of this magazine all mechanical imitation of Karamzin, and to discourage the predilections of my friend for pastoral writing. Against the former I was struggling with all my might, and I found support in a book by Shishkoff, *A Discussion of the Old and New Styles*, which carried me to the opposite extreme."[1] Later, when a new professor of Russian literature joins the faculty, he admits to being a passionate "Shishkovite"; much to Aksakov's delight, the professor becomes his ally. Of course the tables are turned and now Aksakov becomes the one left out of activities, and also the butt of student jokes. ". . . I could not escape from the banter of my companions, which went on until they grew tired of it. They laughed . . . at the similarity of taste between me and the professor. For several days running, a number of them greeted me with low bows and congratulated me on having found a kindred spirit, by which they meant a worshipper of Shishkoff and an opponent of Karamzin's innovations . . . Their mockery annoyed me, but quarrelling did no good, and patience was the only remedy."[2] Ultimately, though, Aksakov's clear, transparent, pleasant language resembles the so-called "middle-style" that Karamzin had advocated.

At school Aksakov also participated in play productions, often acting in the main roles. This experience later stood him in good stead, for he became a real master of the declamatory style of acting popular in Russian theater at the time. Later, when he met two of his literary idols, Admiral Shishkov and the great poet, Gavrila Romanovich Derzhavin (1743-1816), he first won his way into their affections, as well as their inner-circles, by declaiming from memory huge portions of their works, even entire plays. Aksakov later wrote charming accounts of his friendship with them in **Recollection of Aleksandr Semenovich Shishkov** (**Vospominanie ob Aleksandre Semenoviche Shishkove,** 1856) and **"My Acquaintance with Derzhavin"** (**"Znakomstvo s Derzhavinym,"** 1856). These memoirs, written many years after the events, also are an indirect result of his years in the theater, when Aksakov developed the wonderful memory that made him such a good memoirist and autobiographer.

Aksakov rarely makes any political statements or offers historical analyses of major events in either his prose or his poetry; rather, he dwells on personalities and the dynamics of social intercourse on personal levels. When he does refer to historical events, such as Napoleon's invasion of Moscow, he merely mentions them in passing. A rare exception is an 1814 poem, **"To A. I. Kaznacheev"** (**"A. I. Kaznacheevu"**), in which he chastises Russian society for allowing Gallomania to continue its powerful hold even after Napoleon's brutal assault. When Aksakov sees Moscow, the traditional Russian capital, lying in ruins and holy Russian Orthodox churches reduced to rubble and ashes, he cannot imagine how Muscovites can still seek out the favor and patronage of the very people who ravaged Russian maidens and killed their wives and children. He expected that the citizens of Moscow would return to Old Russian customs and would embrace their native language; rather, he finds the enemy in their midst, even in the homes of his friends: "And in our very celebrations I see our disgrace!" The poem clearly echoes the sentiments of Aksakov's friend, Admiral Shishkov. As Andrew Durkin notes, it "is his most thoroughly Shishkovian effort, not only in its rather archaic diction but also in its ascription of the lapses in public morality to thoughtless imitation of French customs and uncritical use of the French language."[3] We can see Shishkov's influence in another of Aksakov's poems, **"Epistle to Prince Viazemsky"** (**"Poslanie k kn. Viazemskomu,"** 1821), in which he advocates a "Classical," rationalistic, analytical approach to poetry over hazy Romantic style and tone.

The themes in Aksakov's verses of the 1820s parallel those that also informed his prose until his death: the lure of the beautiful countryside surrounding his ancestral home, the delights of hunting and fishing, nostalgia for the past, the preeminence of family life and love for those closest to him, and his preference for rural life over urban existence. Some of the best poems of this period include the following: **"Behold My Homeland"** (**"Vot rodina moia"**), **"About Hunting"** (**"Ob okhote"**), **"Autumn. To my brother Arkadii Timofeevich in St. Petersburg"** (**"Osen'. Bratu Arkadiiu Timofeevichu v Peterburg"**), and **"A Fisherman's Misfortune. A Russian Idyll"** (**"Rybach'e gore. Russkaia idilliia"**). After 1830 Aksakov limited his poetry writing to purely personal verses, often to celebrate personal milestones in his family, likes birthdays and weddings.

Although he was not a master of technique, Aksakov's poetry appeals to the reader because of its simplicity and sincerity. Sometimes he adopts a joking tone when he describes amusing incidents or relates tales of hunting and fishing. Just as in his prose, the autobiographical content of his poetry is probably the feature most important for the contemporary reader. A number of pieces are poetically rather strong, for example, **"Lament of a Birch Tree's Spirit"** (**"Plach dukha berezy,"** 1853) and **"October 17. For A[pollon] N[ikolaevich] Maikov"** (**"17 oktiabra [A. N. Maikovu],"** 1857). In the former poem, a birch tree's spirit addresses the person whose cruel hand has ruthlessly felled the tree thereby terminating thirty years of life and enjoyment of the companionship of other wonders of nature. The spirit admonishes the destroyer: "And so, tireless old man, / You will go mushroom hunting, / But you will no longer find in its accustomed place / The birch tree you love so much. / For now across your path / Lies its fresh corpse, / And quietly it moves its branches / As it conducts its own wake."[4] Those who destroy nature suffer; but those who love it in all of its guises, in all of its moods, reap the rewards and joys of sincere understanding and of grateful appreciation of all of its moods. In **"October 17"** the lyrical narrator can find communion with nature even in bad weather, even in the bleakest landscape: "Again the rains, again the fogs, / And falling leaves and naked woods, / And darkened fields, / And the low, grey firmament. / Again autumn weather! / But full of gentle moistness, / it fills my heart with joy: / I love this time of year."[5]

Aksakov's lyrical hero keenly understands nature and continually tries to unlock more and more of its mysteries. He may love to hunt and fish, but at times he may simply enjoy looking at the landscape without any purpose at all. Although Aksakov's poetry lacks technical distinction, it does exude a certain lyricism that testifies to its author's rich poetic understanding of life and the abundance of feeling he has for it. Even though Aksakov's poetry may not be great, it still hints at a lyrical sensibility that found its voice mainly in his prose works, and throughout his life he remained a poet at heart who never ceased reading poetry. Although he never really took his own verses seriously, his prose works devoted to hunting, fishing, and country life, and especially his nature descriptions, often burst forth with poetic expressions of incredible beauty.

Aksakov's first artistic prose piece, a short sketch called **"The Blizzard"** (**"Buran"**) appeared in 1833 in the almanac *Dennitsa* (*Day Star*). In the short introduction that Aksakov added to the second edition (1858), he informs the reader that the incident actually occurred, though many years in the past, and then emphasizes the role memory plays in his writing. The critic D. S. Mirsky labels **"The Blizzard"** as experimental and immature;[6] Durkin, however, sees it as a seminal work in which Aksakov has already defined the central theme of his entire body of work: man must develop his "ability to interpret nature through its signs and to set a course of action in harmony with it.'"[7] Almost a prose poem, but usually called a sketch, **"The Blizzard"** relates how a group of ten peasant drovers find themselves trapped on the open steppes of the Orenburg province by an unexpected blizzard. Stylistically more complex than it initially seems, the two linguistic levels underscore the central theme: practical language, full of regionalisms and colloquialisms, belongs to the prosaic peasants; lyrical style, with its elevated rhetoric, imbues the nature passages with beauty and power. Thus the linguistic dichotomy underlines the theme of man against nature. Here, as in all of Aksakov's works, the force of nature dominates man, who must seek and find his place in it and adapt to its whims. The peasants are divided: the young and inexperienced, led by a callow youth, versus an experienced old man who has lived long in nature and has subsequently learned some of its secrets and can interpret its code.

The first paragraph of **"The Blizzard"** with its detailed description of nature sets the scene for the entire sketch.

> Not one cloud appeared in the hazy, whitish sky; not even the slightest breeze [blew] over the snowy plain. A red, but vaguely outlined sun was moving over the rather low southern horizon on its way to its not-far-off setting in the western sky. A cruel, severe frost plunged all of nature into a frozen state; it gripped, scorched, and burned every living thing. No man can reconcile himself with the fury of the elements; but the Russian peasant does not fear the cold.[8]

The scene depicts a severe frost; to the untrained eye nature seems calm, even static, except for the slowly moving sun. As the caravan goes along, the men joke and chatter, but then catch sight of the havoc the weather has wreaked on the surrounding landscape. In the interminable steppe they see a small birch grove turned into a wasteland, with trees broken in two, debris lying about, and raggedy, naked stumps sticking up into the air. When one of the young peasants sees the grove, he exclaims: "What kind of devil's work do we have here? What wood goblin has ruined the little birch grove?" A wise old peasant, experienced in the ways of nature, explains that no wood goblin, but a severe frost after a thaw has mangled the trees. He tells the young men that this sign bodes well for an abundant harvest.

The old man then orders the others to stop their chatter, looks around in all directions, and decides the caravan should make haste to the distant way station. Though the others balk, they know that in order to survive they must obey "the stern voice of the old man, made wise by years of experience, whose penetrating gaze had foreseen a tempest in the light darkness, in the stillness."[9] The others step to it, gather the horses, and hop onto their carts, even though "[a]s before it seemed to be clear in the sky and quiet on the earth."[10] The sense of peace and stasis continues. "The sun was inclining toward the west and, slipping with its slanted rays over the immense mountains of the snows, it clothed them with a diamond crust, and the grove, distorted by clinging frost, presented from afar wondrous and variously shaped obelisks also bestrewn with a diamond glitter. All was magnificent."[11] Here Aksakov employs a technique that he will use over and again later in his biographical and autobiographical fiction: a scene remains the same but the motion of a journey changes perceptions. In this instance perspective gives beauty to something the men initially thought to be ugly. In *Years of Childhood* (*Detskie gody Bagrova-vnuka* [*Childhood Years of the Bagrov Grandson*], 1858), when young Sergei travels over the same route year after year, his perceptions of a constant scene change because he understands and sees more as he matures.

As the convoy continues its journey, the surrounding scenery still appears static and peaceful under a diamond crust of frost. Then, suddenly, nature has a surprise for the men, but not for the experienced old peasant. "Quickly a white clod rose up and was growing large in the east, and when the last pale rays of the setting sun disappeared behind a mountain, a huge snow cloud had already obscured the greater half of the sky and was sprinkling down a fine snowy powder; the steppes began to boil with snow; within the normal noise of the wind something rang out that sounded like the distant weeping of a child, but sometimes like the howl of a hungry wolf."[12] The wise old peasant decides to unharness the horses and proceed slowly on foot. As they go on the storm intensifies. "A snowy white storm cloud, as huge as the sky, cloaked the entire horizon and covered the last light of the red, burnt-out sunset with a thick shroud. Night suddenly descended . . . the blizzard came down with all of its fury, with all of its terrors. The wind of the wilderness rose up on the wide open spaces; it ploughed up the snowy steppes as if [they were made of] swan's down, and threw it up into the skies."[13]

Everything turns to chaos; everything is churned about in one furious upheaval of nature. The blood of the peasants runs cold, not from external chill but from inner fear. The old man tells everyone to stop, that they will now make camp for the night and huddle under the upturned carts: "We must give ourselves over to God's will; we must spend the night here."[14] The leader of the young men protests, says that the way station is close by, and adds that they still have their lives to live, not like the dried out old man; he says that they "do not want to croak." Five of the ten men follow the lead of the impetuous youth in a curious decision. Why do the young men reject the advice of the old man at the height of the storm, but willingly followed his advice when the weather was calm? Of course, they want to reach the way station and earlier followed his lead on their way toward safety; but now, they have no patience to wait out the storm. However, this action on the part of the youths also points to a future recurring theme in Aksakov's works: the need to be experienced when dealing with nature in all of its forms.

The blizzard rages for two whole nights, and then the storm halts as abruptly as it began. "The tempestuous wind became still, the snow settled down. The steppe took on the appearance of a stormy sea, instantly frozen unawares . . . The sun rose in the bright sky immediately over the horizon; its rays began to play on the wavy snow."[15] Predictably the old peasant and the three others survive, huddled together for warmth and buried under the snow. They are unconscious when passers-by dig them out of their snowy fortress, but they soon awake with no memory of their ordeal. The six inexperienced young men all perish, one right at the fence of the way station. The sketch has now come full circle and ends with calm, static scenery; but now the sun is shining. The nature descriptions all indicate a delicate balance in nature that teeters back and forth between life and death, calm and storm, stasis and motion, the beneficent and the dangerous (cf. the baby's cry vs. howling of a hungry wolf), and light and darkness. Within this world the experienced man who approaches nature with respect survives; the inexperienced man who views natures with unseeing eyes ultimately perishes.

In the 1840s when Aksakov moved to his country estate, Abramtsevo, the quiet, slow-paced, peaceful life there evoked in him happy memories of childhood: the joys of communing with nature, the first fish he caught, the first bear he shot. In 1840, even before he moved to the country, Aksakov had begun work on his memoirs; however, during his years at Abramtsevo, Aksakov turned back to nature after his busy life in Moscow. In the next few years he concentrated on writing his books on fishing and hunting.

Even as a child Aksakov had displayed a keen interest in fishing, which he later described in his fictional autobiography, *Childhood Years*; but as an adult he preferred hunting, a sport that became another passion in his life. In his later years when he was ill and blind and could no longer hunt, Aksakov again went out to fish, sitting for hours on the shores of the river Bor' in Abramtsevo. In 1845 Aksakov began work on *Notes on Fishing* (*Zapiski ob uzhen'e ryby,* 1847); in 1846 he finished the book, which came out the following year.

In *Notes on Fishing* Aksakov reveals not only his passion for the sport, but also his attitude toward nature, the essence of which lies not in aesthetic admiration of its beauties of nature but in man's search to understand the secrets of the world around him. Aksakov thought that simple admiration of the magnificence of nature constituted nothing more than some dilatory attraction to the landscape as an escape from people's tedious lives. Aksakov believed that all of man's base passions fall silent before the grandeur of nature.

Aksakov wanted to write a book on fishing that was practical but whose narrator was clearly literate and keenly observant. He wanted to convey the experienced narrator's own life in nature. Durkin quotes an excerpt from one of Aksakov's letters to his friend the writer Nikolai Vasil'evich Gogol (1809-1852) about his reasons for writing this book. "I have undertaken to write a book about angling, not only in its technical aspect, but in relation to nature in general; my passionate angler likewise passionately loves the beauties of nature as well; in a word, I have fallen in love with my work and I hope that this book will be pleasant not only for the lover of fishing, but also for everyone whose heart is open to the impressions of early morning, late evening, luxuriant midday, etc."[16] According to Ralph Matlaw, another appealing aspect of the work consists of Aksakov's method of concentrating neither on the pleasures of the sport nor on its idyllic qualities, but on the "loving detail and expert analyses of angling and of fishes."[17]

Even from his youngest years Aksakov kept meticulous notes on and records of the fish he caught. *Notes on Fishing* systematically discusses every aspect of angling, such as all manner of gear, bait, locations, various waters, strategies, types, diet, size, personalities, and even flavors of various fish along with recipes for cooking them. These data as well as his own observations of piscine behavior provide his readers with entertaining and enlightening pictures of fish life. Sometimes his asides on the nature of the Russian, himself included, can be amusing. In an early section in which he discusses the proper method of assembling a rod, he says: "all this must be done methodically and neatly—qualities opposed to the nature of the Russian: each time there's the disassembling, rubbing dry, inserting, screwing, unscrewing, tying and untying the line and float, sinker and hook, and then the line again needs to be wound onto something, put in to a case or little box and stores somewhere. . . . Isn't all this tedious and dreary"?[18] The conversational tone of the *Notes on Fishing* gives the book a charming, homely quality.

When Aksakov describes various families of fish, he often tells amusing anecdotes about their behavior. A particularly captivating section on the training of carp anticipates Ivan Petrovich Pavlov's experiments with conditioned responses. "Carpia raised in ponds are easily trained to take groundbait at an appointed hour and place. If one consistently rings a bell at feeding time, then they'll become so accustomed to it that they'll start to gather when they hear the bell's peal, even at a time other than the usual one. Other fish could probably be traind to do the same thing." He then provides a funny account of mass interaction between people and the carp at a public garden.

> Not very long ago in the Presnia ponds, there was a multitude of very large carpia, and people used to enjoy feeding them kalaches [a special kind of Russian bread, CAR]. This was an amusing spectacle indeed. As soon as a kalach had been thrown into the pond, several of the largest carpia (sometimes just one) would seize the kalach and plunge it into the water. Unable to bite bits off, the fish would soon release the booty from its mouth, and it would immediately float up to the water's surface. Other carpia, in larger numbers, would immediately appear behind it, and with greater greed and boldness seize the kalach from all sides, drag it, tug it, and dive with it. As soon as the bread became somewhat sodden, the fish would tear it into pieces and swallow the loaf in a minute. The people accompanied all these escapades with loud exclamations and hearty laughter.[19]

Such observations helped to establish the "authenticity (as distinct from the accuracy)" of his notes, a characteristic important to the author.

Aksakov hoped that his book would appeal to more than just fishermen; in this regard *Notes on Fishing* became wildly popular, something that surprised even Aksakov. Overwhelmingly positive critical reviews accompanied public admiration of the book. Aksakov took advantage of the situation, and with the publication of a second edition he expanded the existing chapters and added a new one. The sincere, personal, conversational tone of the text, with its reliance on memory to recall the narrator's past, undoubtedly contributed to the book's extraordinary reception and lasting appeal.

Aksakov finished writing a companion volume, *Notes of a Rifle Hunter of the Orenburg Province* (*Zapista ruzheinego okhotnika Orensburgskoi gubernii*) in 1851 and it appeared in print in 1852. Because of its popularity, a second edition appeared at the end of January 1853; it won even more critical acclaim than the first volume, and thus became established as a major work of Russian literature. Like *Notes on Fishing,* the book on hunting exudes authenticity. Aksakov kept a tally on the number of birds he had caught just as he had with his fish. For Aksakov hunting became an even greater passion than fishing and the sport that was closest to his heart. In his works about hunting he describes all of its aspects with loving detail, and *The Notes of a Rifle Hunter* is no exception. Even richer in detail than the volume on fishing Aksakov describes not only the plumage of the birds, but categorizes them according to their habitat, which he also describes accurately and poetically. He presents his readers with almost painterly visions of the marshland, the waters, the steppe and grasslands, and the forests. Especially beautiful is his description of the steppe, with the life teeming in it—both human and animal. But Aksakov is sad at the encroachment of modern life onto the steppe and fears for its future. "In time not a strip of untilled land will remain in the province of Orenburg. Whatever the surveyors' land registers may say, all this land is fertile, all will be populated, and everything I have said about this wonderful region will be no more than a story from the forgotten past."[20] Aksakov's comment about the unhappy future of the land may add conservationist to his as roles as botanist, hunter, ethnographer, naturalist, etymologist, and ornithologist.

When Aksakov leaves the land and talks about the birds, he discusses their molting habits, mating rituals, "family life," dietary preferences, seasonal habitats, their migratory patterns, and even the etymology of their common names among the people. On a more practical side, Aksakov advises the proper size of shot to use for each type of bird, methods of successfully hunting them, and even cooking them. One piquant example of culinary advice concerns preservation of two types of snipe. "I recently learned from the esteemed hunter P. V. B., that he keeps common and great snipe—as well as other game, no doubt—perfectly fresh until the spring, even when shot as early as July. The bird is placed in large mold of the type used for ice cream, turned and frozen hard. Then the mold is cut into ice, and since the ice will not melt in an icebox, the bird is kept as fresh as if it had only just been shot."[21] This helpful hint follows a discussion of whether it is better to cook snipe, and all wading birds, gutted or ungutted.

In his attitude toward the hunt, Aksakov follows a seemingly paradoxical principle: the more he respects a certain species, the more he needs to hunt it. Yet in many places he deplores the plundering of various species, and in some cases, even their habitat. For example, in his section on the black-tailed godwit (*bolotnyi kulik*) he says: "I recall with sadness the massacre of birds that I, like all other fowlers, was responsible for in the vast marshes of Orenburg, teeming with all manner of game, chiefly godwits, which stand out among waders by their unusual determination in the defense of their young. These ravages are all the more devastating when the birds are incubating. In this way whole generations are exterminated."[22] He then goes on to describe how the mature birds sacrifice themselves to protect their young, a trait common to many of the species he hunts. Without anthropomorphizing his birds, Aksakov tells of their own form of "home life," especially when he describes the various birds that mate for life, like the swan.

Not all of Aksakov's birds, though, lend themselves to romanticized portraits, especially ducks and geese. Here his matter-of-fact description of the mating habits of all ducks ends on a proverbial note.

> It will be apparent that, when copulation takes place at display grounds, at communal gatherings, neither the males nor the females can be joined by any special

feeling for each other. One day the male mates with one female, the next day with another, defending whom he happens to meet. The behavior of the female is exactly the same. From this it follows that they never form pairs and that the female alone, unaided by any mate, has to take responsibility for building a nest, incubating the eggs and rearing the young. Where there is no marriage there is no father.[23]

And any farmer who has ever suffered encounters with a domestic goose can appreciate the following lament: "Woe betide the farmer who belatedly discovers that geese are visiting his fields! They will eat all his grain, lay his standing crops flat, and trample them down as if a small herd of cattle had grazed on them."[24]

Always conscious of his style of narration, Aksakov wanted it to be "in harmony with its subject."[25] Vivid word pictures of the animals appear with pleasing regularity. Take, for example, this description of the plumage and habits of the moorhen (*bolotnaia kuritsa*):

> Its plumage is all dark green, shot with very beautiful steel-blue tints and with fine white speckling, especially on the lower neck, chest, and belly. The upper parts are much darker and the under parts lighter. The male is uncommonly handsome: while his plumage is exactly the same as the hen's, he has on his head a fleshy shield of bright red scarlet and bands of the same color on his legs, a finger wide, right at the bend of the knee; the rest of the leg is greenish. . . . In very small numbers this beautiful bird frequents the wettest of the marshland, preferably close to pools or lakes well grown with reeds, flags, and sedge, and covered in summer duckweed. Moorhens like running about on this green carpet when it is thick enough to support them. They run so lightly and so nimbly that they leave behind them only patterns of their feet on the soft surface; on water lilies, however, they skid as if on polished floor.[26]

This passage demonstrates that Aksakov's style has no literariness to spoil its conversational, spontaneous reality, even though the narrator is conscious of its composition. Ralph Matlaw notes that the book is "consciously wrought." He goes on to say that "it is the expression of something grounded in the native tradition, of a purity of vocabulary unequaled in Russian." Aksakov rarely uses foreign words and then only for effect. His aesthetic principles forbade him to depict nature without its connection to man. He believed that without a human presence in the works the reader would remain indifferent to descriptions of nature. Nevertheless, Matlaw says, Aksakov showed that nature existed "independent of man, sufficient unto itself, with life and movement and grandeur that endow it with a kind of active existence. To be sure, man moves and acts within it through ordinary necessity . . . [but] only as one of its lesser dependents." Most readers and critics of Aksakov, according to Matlaw, agree that nature plays the starring role in his prose. What man learns from nature

and how he reacts to it tell exactly who and what he is. For Aksakov nature teaches his characters "the richness and complexity of life, the limits of man's activity."[27]

In 1855 Aksakov published an expanded version of his *Notes of a Rifle Hunter of the Orenburg District* under the title *Tales and Reminiscences of a Hunter on Various Types of Hunting* (*Rasskazy i vospominaniia okhotnike o raznykh okhotakh*); it included short discourses on snaring, falconry, spear fishing, fox hunts, and wolf hunts as well as a collection of five *Little Hunting Stories* (*Melkie okhotnich'i rasskazy*). *Tales and Reminiscences of a Hunter on Various Types of Hunting* supplements the earlier tales of hunting and fishing. One of Aksakov's last works, **"Butterfly Collecting"** ("*Sobiranie babochek*," 1858), adds a treatise on butterfly collecting to reminiscences of his school days in Kazan.[28]

Aksakov tried many times to write a story of his own life and work on the trilogy that became the main focus of the last ten years of his life, *Memoirs of a Former Life* (*Vospominaniia prezhnei zhizni*), consisting of *Family Chronicle* (*Semeinaia khronika*), *Childhood Years of the Bagrov Grandson* (*Detskie gody Bagrova-vnuka*), and *Reminiscences* (*Vospominaniia*). The trilogy has proved to be fertile ground for literary critics who have grappled with the problem of genre. Marcus Levitt proposes that *Family Chronicle* continues the oral tradition of Russian story telling, while Kathryn B. Feuer sees it as a true novel. Esther Salaman puts the books in a category with Proust because of their meditations on memory. Andrew Baruch Wachtel makes a case that *Childhood Years of the Bagrov Grandson* is a pseudo autobiography. Andrew Durkin, on the other hand, sees all of Aksakov's works as a return to the age of the pastoral. Aksakov himself described his thoughts about the nature of the book in its epilogue.

> Farewell, my images, bright or dark, my people, good or bad—or should I rather say, images that have their bright and dark sides, people who have virtues and vices. You are not great heroes, not imposing personalities; you trod your path on earth in silence and in obscurity, and it is a long, a very long time since you left it. But you were people, and your inward and outward life was as full of poetry, as interesting and instructive to us as we and our life will be in turn interesting and instructive to our descendants. You were characters in that mighty spectacle which mankind has presented on this earth since time immemorial . . . May no harsh judgment and no heedless word offend your memory.[29]

Part of the originality of *Semeinaia khronika* lies in its relationship between fact and fiction in an atmosphere of historical accuracy counteracted by fictional bias. Reality finds its place within the constricting borders of the book. The narrator presents events and characters' personal lives as subordinate to history, to which he generally refers only in passing. Nevertheless, Aksakov follows his own impulses to provide an aesthetic representation of real life.

Within the form of a "historical memoir," Aksakov introduces his own versions of a variety of genres: historical chronicles, historical documents, Gothic novels, rogue literature (akin to the picaresque), sentimental romances and adventure novels, the Sketch, (*ocherk*), fairy tales, and even folktales (with grandfather Stepan Mikhailovich Bagrov akin to a *bogatyr'*, a folk hero of great physical and moral strength). Stepan Mikhailovich also resembles Homeric and biblical archetypes, especially an Old Testament patriarch.

Dealing with the last third of the eighteenth century, *Semeinaia khronika* gives a positive view of Russia, a land of wide-open spaces. Not unlike an American pioneer, Stepan Mikhailovich Bagrov, the narrator/author's grandfather, leaves a good estate because he felt constricted and settles his family in Bashkir territory across the Volga near Ufa, a city in the Urals. The first chapter of the book describes the move of the whole family along with their serfs to a new home. The narrator lovingly details all features of daily life to produce an idyllic, though not ideal, depiction of Russian life on the steppe. The first chapter, or fragment, introduces the nearly mythical figure of Stepan Mikhailovich, almost as a force of nature unto himself. He emerges as a character of great integrity, simplicity, wisdom, and morality. However, Stepan Mikhailovich can act arbitrarily and at times indulges in terrible rages that affect everyone in sight.

Mikhailo Maksimovich Kurolesov, whose name derives from the verb *kurolesit'* (to play tricks),[30] serves as Stepan Mikhailovich's antithesis in the second chapter. A fortune hunter poor in assets but rich in charm, Kurolesov secretly marries Stepan Mikhailovich's extremely young, childlike, rich cousin Praskovia. When Bagrov learns of the marriage, he is at first angry but eventually accepts the situation. On the surface Kurolesov seems to be a good manager and husband; in addition, Praskovia appears to be happy. However, he manages to lead a double life for fourteen years until someone sends Praskovia a letter that exposes her husband's depravity, which consists of wild orgies and sadistic behavior, such as whipping people for his pleasure. When Praskovia arrives at her distant estate, Parashino, she secretly witnesses his debauchery. Confused and horrified, she spends the night in prayer; then with newfound courage she confronts her husband. Kurolesov beats her and locks her up until Stepan Mikhailovich, like a *bogatyr* of old, comes to rescue her with an "army" of serfs. Ultimately, a vengeful retainer poisons Kurolesov.

The next three chapters describe the courtship and marriage of old Bagrov's son, Alexei Stepanich, who falls completely and sincerely in love with Sofia Nikolaevna Zubina, an educated woman who enjoys respect and admiration in the social circles of Ufa. After the death of her wicked stepmother, Sofia cares for her invalid father. Extremely popular in society for her beauty, intelligence, nobility and charm, she feels sorry for the shy, immature, socially inept Alexei and agrees to marry him—even though she does not love him. When Stepan Mikhailovich refuses to allow the marriage, Alexei threatens to commit suicide if his father does not grant him permission to wed. The wedding eventually takes place with old Bagrov's blessing, but he and his wife do not attend the ceremony. Though the love story is sentimental, the description of the wedding, strangely enough, seems rather objective. The third chapter ends with the couple's arrival at the family estate, Novoe Bagrovo, and in great detail describes the customs surrounding the introduction of the new couple to family, friends, and serfs.

The fourth chapter chronicles the couple's first days with the Bagrovs. Sofia does not like country life, but politely attends to her father-in-law's wishes. Gradually the two grow to love and respect each other. Sofia and Alexei set off on a round of visits to all of the neighboring relatives, mainly because Stepan Mikhailovich demands that they follow traditions and customs. The couple visits some truly wretched places. The worst of their visits occurs at the home of one of Alexei's sisters. Thoroughly upset at her brother's marriage, she treats Sofia badly, even to the extent of giving the couple a room infested with rats. Sofia becomes angry when her weak husband does not defend her. The final episode of the chapter—a ceremonial dinner back at Novoe Bagrovo—reveals how old Stepan has greatly changed his original opinion of his daughter-in-law, whom he now genuinely loves and even treats as his own daughter.

In the final chapter the newlyweds return to Ufa, where Sofia struggles to win back the affections of her own weak, dying father, whose servant, a Kalmuk, has gained absolute power over him. After the couple move to their own home, Alexei begins his work at the law courts. Sofia becomes pregnant, much to the joy of her father-in-law, who eagerly awaits the birth of a grandson. Stepan Mikhailovich becomes angry when a granddaughter is born instead and resorts to rash behavior that ruins the lives of two of his peasants. When the poor little girl dies shortly after her birth, Sofia nearly perishes. The death of Sofia's father compounds her grief at the loss of her child. But life does go on, and Sofia once again becomes pregnant. The book ends with a famous passage in which, after first crossing himself in thanksgiving at the birth of the long-awaited grandson, Stepan Mikhailovich gleefully inscribes the child's name in the family tree: Sergei. Thus the author announces his own birth at the end of his own "prehistory."

Aksakov always insisted that *Family Chronicle* was a work of art in spite of its biographical form. The self-conscious narrator reveals much about himself as he relates the story of his ancestors. He tries to be objective and impartial but does not always succeed; he creates no totally positive or negative types, but shows at least two sides of the people he describes in various degrees.

The omniscient narrator introduces the main characters first with a physical portrait that he follows with profiles of their psychology and character. His methods of characterization are calm, orderly, and straightforward; he relies neither on narrative tricks nor deep psychological analyses. He rarely uses interior monologue or psychological eavesdropping but simply informs his readers of what they need to know. The reader then must deduce the characters' thoughts by observing their actions. And though he employs the device of many contrasting pairs (old Bagrov and his wife, Sophia and Aleksei, Kurolesov and Praskovia, Aleksei and Kurolesov, Bagrov and Kurolesov, and the two daughters—Aleksandra the Sly and Tatiana the Simple), he never resorts to the schematic dualism of Gogol or the sophisticated juxtapositions of Tolstoy. Characters rarely change; subsequently they are generally one-sided, though at times they reveal conflicting traits. Of all the characters, Stepan Mikhailovich best exhibits this tension of opposing elements: his furious rages and arbitrary decisions temper his depiction as a heroic/patriarchal archetype and lend a realistic grounding to his character.

The structure of *Family Chronicle* also reinforces one of the basic themes of the book: contrasts and their ensuing tensions. The first chapter introduces a good man, albeit one who flies into terrible rages; the second one describes a man almost totally evil. The second chapter examines a false marriage based on the venal motives of a man of the world who enchants an immature girl; the third chapter focuses on the courtship between an unformed, shy young man genuinely in love with a sophisticated, adept young woman. Their marriage, though not without problems, turns out to be good—especially in contrast to Praskovia and Kurolesov's. The third chapter also shows Alexei alienated in the city, while the next chapter finds Sofia hostile to the country.

Chapters two and three set up one of the basic themes in Aksakov's works—country life versus city life. People's reactions to the countryside invariably provides clues to their inner being: estrangement from nature signals a negative character. The fourth chapter recounts Sofia's gradual transformation from mere daughter-in-law to Stepan Bagrov's genuine daughter. Perhaps the regard and affection Sofia receives from Stepan Mikhailovich strengthens her as she tries to regain the love of her own estranged father. When *Family Chronicle* ends with the new grandson's name, Aksakov completes the final contrast: a book that begins by looking back ends by looking forward.

Published along with *Family Chronicle, Reminiscences* is a real memoir in which Aksakov relates the experiences of his school days in Kazan'. Based on his life, this autobiographical work most closely adheres to historical fact. The book documents and portrays the daily lives of students and teachers, Aksakov's early interest in theater and literature, and various events from his young life, including some of great historical import. The opening of the Kazan' University coincided with the beginning of Russia's war against Napoleon. Aksakov tells how "electrifying" the events of the war seemed to him and his classmates. But ultimately the book focuses on memory and nostalgia for the golden age of youth, a time clearly important to the young (and old) Aksakov. *Reminiscences* treats Aksakov's past as a gradual integration of a young boy into the social world of adults. This memoir reveals Aksakov's first forays into two worlds that became lifelong passions: theater and literature. It also portrays his first experiences of two other lifelong passions: fishing and hunting.

Aksakov endows this genuine memoir with artistic touches, especially its structure, which Durkin describes as a "cyclical journey, with change and development in the self rendered tangible by the hero's recurrent visits to places that remain constant."[31] The young boy's response to life in the city and the country changes in proportion as time goes by and provides insights into Sergei's internal, emotional, and psychological evolution as he approaches manhood. The events that contribute to his process of maturation take place against the backdrop of the seasons; almost schematically, negative occurrences take place in the winter and positive ones in the spring.

The complex process of the creation of a child's personality told mainly from the child's point of view comprises the last part of the "autobiographical" trilogy, *Childhood Years of the Bagrov Grandson,* which Aksakov initially conceived as a book for children. It continues the saga of the Bagrovs as it concentrates on the earliest, preschool years in the life of Sergei, whose birth ended *Family Chronicle.* Along with a narrator, little Sergei tells his own story; the two narratives complement each other to form a single voice. The narrator must rely on his memory to relate the remembered events in the voice of the child, who tells his tale in the present tense. In the introduction to the book Aksakov even discusses the reliability of his memory.

Little Sergei's travels from one place to another form the basic structure of the memoir as his perceptions of people and places change during the course of various journals. The larger world around Sergei constantly invades his small universe when new, different sides of life present themselves to the youngster. He makes his greatest discovery—that not everything is perfect in his world. He observes the shortcomings yet never tries to confront them. Even this early, young Aksakov establishes himself as an objective observer of reality. Life, though, always presents new and complex problems to a child; they force him to make moral choices and ask questions about the nature of good and evil. In the narrative, Aksakov manages to sustain the feelings that a child would have as he confronts ethical questions.

At the end of **Reminiscences** the young Aksakov goes off with his family to St. Petersburg where for several years he took full advantage of the life in the capital. Most of his friends there were connected either with the theater or with literature; the most important of them were the famous tragic actor Iakov Emel'ianovich Shusherin, the poet Derzhavin, and Admiral Shishkov. He also renewed the acquaintance of an old family friend, Vasily Vasil'evich Romanovsky, a leading Martinist prominent in esoteric spiritualist circles. All of these later found their way into sketches such as **"Iakov Emel'ianovich Shusherin and Theatrical Celebrities of His Time"** (1854; **"Iakov Emel'ianovich Shisherin i sovremennye emu teatral'nye znamenitosti"**), **"Reminiscence of Aleksandr Semenovich Shishkov"** (1856; **"Vospominaniia ob Aleksandre Semenoviche Shusherine"**), **"My Acquaintance with Derzhavin"** (1852-56; **"Znakomstvo s Derzhavinym"**), and **"A Meeting with Martinists"** (1852; **"Vstrecha s Martinistami"**). Though these sketches are mainly praised because their subjects come alive, they are also delightful to read because of their style. Thanks to Aksakov's acclaimed powers of memory, he relates conversations almost verbatim and describes the scenes in minute detail. He enters into the life of the families and friends of his subjects and provides an inside view of their social and intellectual milieu.

Of all of his acquaintances, Aksakov's friendship was more lasting and complex and yielded the most critically acclaimed of his reminiscences, the posthumously published **History of My Acquaintance with Gogol** (1890; **Istoriia moego znakomstva s Gogolem**). In it he is as scrupulously honest as he tried to be in all of his works and describes both the high and low points of his relationship with the famous writer. In his discussion of Aksakov's works, D. S. Mirsky thus characterizes the writer:

> [He] was not as a rule a student of other people's minds. He took people as they came, as parts of his world, and gave them a sensual rather than a mental re-

ality. But in the case of Gogol the elusive and evasive personality of the great writer caused him such bitter disappointment and disillusionment that he was forced to make an exceptional effort to understand the workings of the strange man's mind, where genius and baseness were so strangely mingled. The effort was painful but extraordinarily successful, and Aksakov's memoir is to this day our principal approach to the problem of Gogol.[32]

Sergei Aksakov remains one of the best examples of Russian realist writing. Never a fan of the dreamy, hazy mists of Romanticism, he preferred the real world of his friends, family, fish and fowl. He comes as close to the ideal of being objective as any reliable narrator in the history of fiction. His talent allows his books to spur the interest of his readers even when the "issues" no longer seem relevant. Aksakov also has the uncanny ability of turning ordinary people into memorable characters. His language preserves the best of the so-called "middle style" of educated Russian. In an obituary article on Aksakov, the Slavophile poet and theoretician Aleksei Stepanovich Khomiakov (1804-60) describes his use of language.

> But what are the basic elements of Aksakov's art? The first is language, in which he scarcely has a rival for correctness and precision of expression and for turns of phrase that are entirely Russian and alive . . . it was unbearable for Sergei Timofeevich to use an incorrect word or an adjective inappropriate for the subject he was discussing and which failed to express it. He felt incorrectness of expression as a kind of insult to the subject itself, as a kind of untruth in relation to his own impression, and he could rest easy only when he found the right word. It stands to reason that he found it easily, because this very demand arose from clarity of feeling and awareness of linguistic wealth. This strictness toward his own language, and consequently toward his own thought, gave all his stories and all his descriptions matchless clarity and simplicity, while he imparted to the description of nature a truthfulness of color and distinctness of outline that you will not find in anyone else.[33]

Aksakov's beautiful language, vivid portrayals of Russian types—from child to grand *paterfamilias*—nostalgic recreation of the past, and grand descriptions of nature, high moral principles, and spiritual health all unite to keep him as popular today for the Russians as he was to his contemporary readers. By relying on his own prodigious memory he was able to preserve for them their own collective memory. For the contemporary Western reader, Aksakov offers a glimpse into the special world of what it meant to be a Russian in a more gracious and civil time.

Notes

1. Sergei Aksakov, *Memoirs of the Aksakov Family: A Russian Schoolboy.* Tr. J. D. Duff (Westport, Connecticut: Hyperion Press, Inc., 1977), p. 145.

2. Aksakov, *A Russian Schoolboy,* p. 156.

3. Andrew R. Durkin, *Sergei Aksakov and Russian Pastoral* (New Brunswick, New Jersey: Rutgers University Press, 1983), p. 56.

4. Aksakov, "Plach dukha berezy," in his *Sobranie sichinenii* [Collected Works], 4 vols. (Moscow: Gosudarstvennoe izdatel'stvo khudozhestvennoi literatury, 1956), volume 3, pp. 687-88.

5. Aksakov, *op. cit.,* pp. 692-94.

6. D. S. Mirsky, *A History of Russian Literature,* (ed.) Francis J. Whitfield (New York: Alfred A. Knopf, 1966), p. 177.

7. Durkin, p. 64.

8. Aksakov, *Sobranie sochinenii,* vol. 2, p. 406.

9. Durkin, p. 64.

10. Aksakov, *op. cit.,* p. 408.

11. Durkin, pp. 61-62.

12. Aksakov, vol. 2, p. 409.

13. *Ibid.*

14. Aksakov, vol. 2, p. 410.

15. Aksakov, vol. 2, pp. 410-411.

16. Durkin, pp. 67-68.

17. Ralph Matlaw, "Introduction," in S. T. Aksakov, *The Family Chronicle,* tr. M. C. Beverley (New York; E. P. Dutton & Co., Inc., 1961), p. xi.

18. Sergei Timofeevich Aksakov, *Notes on Fishing,* translated, introduced and annotated by Thomas P. Hodge (Evanston, Illinois: Northwestern University Press, 1997), p. 11.

19. Aksakov, *Notes on Fishing,* p. 108.

20. Sergei Timofeevich Aksakov, *Notes of a Provincial Wildfowler,* translated, introduced and annotated by Kevin Windle. (Evanston, Illinois: Northwestern University Press, 1998), p. 152.

21. Aksakov, *Notes of a Wildfowler,* p. 41.

22. Aksakov, *Notes of a Wildfowler,* p. 44.

23. Aksakov, *Notes of a Wildfowler,* p. 107.

24. Aksakov, *Notes of a Wildfowler,* p. 103.

25. Durkin, p. 70.

26. Aksakov, *Notes of a Wildfowler,* p. 75.

27. Matlaw, pp. xii-xvi.

28. An English translation of this sketch appears as an appendix to Aksakov, *A Russian Schoolboy* noted above.

29. Quoted in Durkin, p. 102.

30. Richard Gregg offers an etymology of the name Kurolesov that further strengthens his ties to evil: "[*kurolesit'*] derives from a sacrilegious distortion of the *Kyriw eleison* ('Lord have mercy on us') of the Orthodox liturgy." "The Decline of a Dynast: From Power to Love in Aksakov's *Family Chronicle,*" *Russian Review* 50 (January 1991): 35-47.

31. Durkin, p. 171.

32. D. S. Mirsky, p. 179.

33. *Notes on Fishing,* pp. xx-xxi

Primary Sources

Sergei Timofeevich Aksakov, *Sobranie sochinenii,* 4 volumes (Moscow: Goslitizdat, 1955-1956);

———, *Years of Childhood,* translated by J. D. Duff (London: Arnold, 1916; New York: Longmans, Green, 1916);

———, *A Russian Gentleman* (*Semeinaia khronika*), translated by Duff (London: Arnold, 1917; New York: Longmans, Green, 1917);

———, *A Russian Schoolboy,* translated by Duff (London: Arnold, 1917; New York: Longmans, Green, 1917)—comprises *Recollections and* "Butterfly Collecting"; reprinted (Westport, Conn.: Hyperion Press, Inc., 1971);

———, *Years of Childhood,* translated by Alex Brown (New York: Vintage, 1960);

———, *The Family Chronicle,* translated by M. C. Beverley (New York: E. P. Dutton & Co., Inc., 1961);

———, *Notes on Fishing,* translated, introduced, and annotated by Thomas P. Hodge (Evanston, Ill.: Northwestern University Press, 1997);

———, *Notes of a Provincial Wildfowler,* translated, introduced, and annotated by Kevin Windle (Evanston, Ill.: Northwestern University Press, 1998).

Secondary Sources

Nonna Hordowsky Carr, "S. T. Aksakov in Russian Literary Criticism Before 1917," dissertation, University of Colorado, 1976.

Andrew R. Durkin, "Pastoral in Aksakov: The Transformation of Poetry," *Ulbandus Review,* 2 (1979): 62-75.

———, *Sergei Aksakov and Russian Pastoral* (New Brunswick, N.J.: Rutgers University Press, 1983).

———, "Two Instances of Prose Pastoral: Nemcova and Aksakov," in *American Contributions to the Ninth*

International Congress of Slavists, Kiev, September, 1983, edited by Paul Debreczny, volume 2: *Literature, Poetics, History* (Columbus, Ohio: Slavica, 1983), pp. 125-133.

Pamela Evans, "The Portrayal of Childhood." dissertation, University of Toronto, 1980.

Kathryn B. Feuer, "*Family Chronicle*: The Indoor Art of Sergei Aksakov," *Ulbandus Review,* 2 (1979): 86-102.

Marsha Gayle Gauntt, "S. T. Aksakov's *The Family Chronicle*: An Exceptional Novel," dissertation, University of California, Los Angeles, 1975.

Xenia Glowacki-Prus, "The Biographical Sketches of S. T. Aksakov," *New Zealand Slavonic Journal,* 2 (1977): 1-12.

Glowacki-Prus, "Sergey Aksakov as a Biographer of Childhood," *New Zealand Slavonic Journal,* 2 (1974): 19-37.

Richard Gregg, "The Decline of a Dynasty: From Power to Love in Aksakov's *Family Chronicle,*" *Russian Review,* 50 (January 1991): 35-47.

Zenon Kuk, "*Detskie gody Bagrova-vnuka* by Sergei T. Aksakov: A Marvel of 'Pure' Russian," *Proceedings of the Kentucky Foreign Language Conference: Slavic Section,* 3, no. 1 (1985): 35-43.

Marcus C. Levitt, "Aksakov's *Family Chronicle* and the Oral Tradition," *Slavic and East European Journal,* 32 (summer 1988): 198-212.

S. I. Mashinskii, *S. T. Aksakov: Zhizn' i tvorchestvo* (Moscow: Khudozhestvennaia literatura, 1973; second expanded edition).

Ralph Matlaw, "Sergey Aksakov: The Genius of Ingenuousness," in *S. T. Aksakov, The Family Chronicle,* translated by M. C. Beverley (New York: Dutton, 1961), pp. vii-xxiv.

D. S. Mirsky, *A History of Russian Literature from Its Beginnings to 1900,* edited by Francis J. Whitfield (New York: Vintage, 1958).

Viktor Ostrogorskii, *Sergei Timofeevich Aksakov: Kritiko-biograficheskii ocherk* (St. Petersburg: Martynov, 1901).

Jerome Joseph Rinkus, "The World View of Sergei Aksakov," dissertation, Brown University, 1971.

Esther Salaman, *The Great Confession: From Aksakov and DeQuincey to Tolstoy and Proust* (London: Allen Lane The Penguin Press, 1973), pp. 1-29; 295-300.

Andrew Baruch Wachtel, *The Battle for Childhood: Creation of a Russian Myth* (Stanford: Stanford University Press, 1990), pp. 42ff.; 59-86; 91-97 *passim*; 148 ff.; 168-84 *passim*; 202-204.

Patrick Joseph Wreath, "A Critical Study of S. T. Aksakov," dissertation, Cornell University, 1969.

FURTHER READING

Criticism

Durkin, Andrew R. "Pastoral in Aksakov: The Transformation of Poetry." *Ulbandus Review: A Journal of Slavic Languages and Literatures* 2, no. 1 (fall 1979): 62-75.

    Examines the influence of pastoral verse on Aksakov's mature prose style.

———. *Sergei Aksakov and Russian Pastoral.* New Brunswick, N.J.: Rutgers University Press, 1983, 258 p.

    Provides a broad survey of Aksakov's major and minor works, focusing on his role in the emergence of Russian literary realism.

———. "Two Instances of Prose Pastoral: Nemcová and Aksakov." In *American Contributions to the Ninth International Congress of Slavists, Kiev, September, 1983, II: Literature, Poetics, History,* edited by Paul Debreczeny, pp. 125-33. Columbus, Ohio: Slavica, 1983.

    Offers a comparison between Aksakov's pastoral writings and those of nineteenth-century Czech author Bozena Nemcová.

Glowacki-Prus, Xenia. "A Brief Survey of Memoirs Written in Russian from Peter the Great to S. T. Aksakov." *New Zealand Slavonic Journal* 12 (summer 1973): 10-26.

    Examines Aksakov's contribution to the development of the Russian memoir form.

———. "The Biographical Sketches of S. T. Aksakov." *New Zealand Slavonic Journal* (1974): 1-12.

    Discusses the autobiographical elements in Aksakov's major works.

Kuk, Zenon M. "*Detskie gody Bagrova-vnuka* by Sergei T. Aksakov: A Marvel of 'Pure' Russian." *Proceedings of the Kentucky Foreign Language Conference: Slavic Section* 3, no. 1 (1985): 35-43.

Evaluates the novel's autobiographical qualities, analyzing Aksakov's style within the framework of Russian literary tradition.

Matlaw, Ralph. "Sergey Aksakov: The Genius of Ingenuousness." In *The Family Chronicle,* by S. T. Aksakov, translated by M. C. Beverley, pp. vii-xxiv. New York: Dutton, 1961.

Explores the relationship between Aksakov's life-long respect for nature and the development of his straightforward, realistic prose style.

Pritchett, V. S. "A Russian Cinderella." In *The Living Novel,* pp. 241-46. New York: Reynal & Hitchcock, 1947.

Examines Aksakov's depictions of Russian family life in his autobiographical writings.

Additional coverage of Aksakov's life and career is contained in the following sources published by Thomson Gale: *Dictionary of Literary Biography,* **Vol. 198;** *Literature Resource Center***; and** *Nineteenth-Century Literature Criticism,* **Vol. 2.**

Jane Welsh Carlyle
1801-1866

Scottish letter writer and diarist.

INTRODUCTION

Many modern scholars regard Jane Welsh Carlyle as one of the premiere letter writers of Victorian England. During her lifetime she was known primarily as the wife of British historian and author Thomas Carlyle, and their tumultuous marriage was a frequent subject of gossip among literary circles during the mid-nineteenth century. While she spent most of her married life living in the shadow of her more famous husband, Carlyle had her share of admirers, and for a time she presided over an elite social circle, playing hostess to such luminaries as Charles Dickens, Harriet Martineau, John Forster, and other popular writers and intellectuals of the Victorian era. In the decades following her death, critics were divided in their characterization of her work. Some early commentators, notably James Anthony Froude, characterized her as a victim—a brilliant woman whose talent was stifled by the demands of a self-absorbed husband. Others regarded her as a fraud, arguing that her writings contained little merit in their own right. Although few book-length studies of Carlyle's literary oeuvre have emerged, a number of biographies have shed light on her role in the literary culture of her times. In recent years several critical essays have devoted greater attention to Jane Carlyle's writings, finding them valuable for their fluid, lively prose and for their insights into the personality of a complex, fiercely intelligent woman.

BIOGRAPHICAL INFORMATION

Jane Baillie Welsh was born on July 14, 1801, in Haddington, a prosperous town on the outskirts of Edinburgh, Scotland. She was the only child of John Welsh, a physician, and Grace Baillie Welsh. A precocious and energetic girl, Jane began learning Latin at the age of five. She also proved a talented conversationalist, as at ease with adults as she was with her childhood friends. Throughout her childhood and early adolescence, she studied at local schools, as well as with private tutors—primarily with a popular local preacher named Edward Irving, with whom she would later have a brief flirtation. Adolescence proved difficult for Jane; her relationship with her mother became increasingly stormy, and

she began to suffer from the headaches that would plague her for the rest of her life. In her early teens she produced her first writings, including a novel and a play, and also discovered a passion for the piano. At sixteen she left home to attend boarding school in Edinburgh, where she remained for two years. In September 1819, shortly after she returned home, Jane's father died of typhus. His absence left a void in Jane's emotional life, one that she would attempt to fill through her marriage to Thomas Carlyle.

Jane first met Carlyle in May 1821, when they were introduced to each other by Edward Irving. Although Jane initially found Carlyle's awkwardness and rude manners distasteful, she was soon charmed by his intellectual and rhetorical talents, and she gradually became infatuated with the ambitious young author. Carlyle took it upon himself to further Jane's education, recommending books and teaching her German. Their romance emerged very slowly over the next several years, aided largely by their correspondence, which already demonstrated Jane's insight and sharp wit. Throughout their long courtship, Jane engaged in numerous flirtations, though none of them proved serious. In spite of her lingering ambivalence, she finally married Carlyle on October 17, 1826, and they settled in Edinburgh.

Jane's marriage to Carlyle exerted profound changes on her personality, and the vivacious young girl soon emerged as a serious and diligent wife. Confronted with a meager income, as well as with Carlyle's disorderly work habits and powerful desire for solitude, Jane devoted herself full-time to the management of the household. At the same time, she played an important role in cultivating a social life for herself and her husband, and she succeeded in developing friendships with a number of young Edinburgh writers and intellectuals with whom they socialized regularly. Jane also provided invaluable encouragement for Carlyle's career during a time when he found himself unable to earn a regular income from his writings.

In 1828 the Carlyles moved to Craigenputtoch, a remote farmhouse in the Scottish countryside on land owned by Jane's family. Although the isolation of Craigenputtoch invigorated Thomas Carlyle's imagination, Jane found the solitude and boredom of daily life there unbearable, and her already poor health worsened. Finally in 1834 the couple moved to London, where Jane immediately built a network of social acquaintances. During these years Jane developed a turbulent friendship with the novelist Geraldine Jewsbury, in whom she confided the intimate details of her personal life; Jewsbury's memoirs would later provide valuable information about Jane's childhood and adolescence. Although the social life of London proved more agreeable to Jane's temperament, financial concerns continued to demand most of her time, and she devoted a great deal of energy to managing their home, in addition to tending to her husband's dietary needs and his demands for privacy and silence. Jane chronicled these years in numerous letters, describing her married life, her social engagements, and the workings of her household with vivid, sometimes sardonic humor.

In 1836 Thomas Carlyle achieved his first success with the philosophical novel *Sartor Resartus*; a year later he published his landmark work, *The French Revolution: A History*. Most scholars agree that Jane played a pivotal role in the success of both books, as a champion of her husband's work and as his critical reader. Still, though the couple remained devoted to each other, they led largely separate lives, and they rarely traveled anywhere together. Their time apart created many occasions for letter writing, and Jane's notes to her husband reveal a deep affection and loyalty. Their relationship became strained in the 1840s, however, shortly after the death of Jane's mother in 1842. The source of their difficulties revolved around Lady Harriet Barrie, whom Jane befriended in 1843. Within a year Thomas Carlyle had become unusually close to Harriet, an intimacy they maintained even after Harriet married Lord Ashburton in 1848. Thomas Carlyle's relationship with Harriet proved agonizing to Jane, embittering her toward her husband. During this bleak period of her life, Jane fell into a debilitating depression, developed a host of physical illnesses, and burned many of her notebooks and journals.

In the early 1860s Jane's health problems became more severe, and she began to suffer from intense migraines and neuralgia. She visited various specialists, leaving home for several months at a time to seek treatment. In spite of her poor health, Jane Carlyle remained a vital part of her social group until her death. She died of heart failure on April 21, 1866, while riding in a carriage through London's Hyde Park. Her death proved devastating to her husband; Thomas Carlyle wrote little during the remainder of his life. In his final years he dedicated much of his energy to writing his autobiography, *Reminiscences by Thomas Carlyle* (1881), which contains a heartfelt memorial to his wife. Carlyle also played a key role in compiling and editing his wife's letters, collaborating with James Anthony Froude in the publication of *Letters and Memorials of Jane Welsh Carlyle* (1883), the first volume of her writings to appear in print.

MAJOR WORKS

Carlyle's literary reputation rests entirely on her letters and surviving journal writings, none of which appeared in print until many years after her death. Notable early editions of her work include *Letters and Memorials of Jane Welsh Carlyle* and *Early Letters of Jane Welsh Carlyle, Together with a Few of Later Years and Some of Thomas Carlyle* (1889). Written in a conversational style, the letters demonstrate a keen eye for detail, as well as a brutally honest sense of humor. While frequently ungrammatical, Jane's writing exhibits an easy grace that verges on poetry. The informal tone of the letters offers a personal glimpse into the everyday life of one of Victorian England's preeminent literary couples. At times Jane focused on mundane details concerning debts, shopping, and other household concerns; at others she revealed her deep devotion to her husband in sincere, unpretentious language. The letters also reveal a great deal about Jane Carlyle's cultural milieu and contain sharp, often catty depictions of various acquaintances and friends, including some devastating portraits of some of the era's most eminent writers. As Jane grew older, her letters revealed more and more about her various ailments, although even these writings contain her characteristically self-effacing wit and charm. In the twentieth century a number of new editions of Carlyle's letters were published, most notably the thirty-two volume *The Collected Letters of Thomas and Jane Welsh Carlyle* (1970-2005).

CRITICAL RECEPTION

Anonymous contemporary reviews of *Letters and Memorials of Jane Welsh Carlyle* attest to the caliber of Carlyle's intelligence and wit, as well as to the emotional power of her depictions of married life. Geraldine Jewsbury, a lifelong friend of Carlyle, offered insight into Carlyle's childhood in her own letters, included in the 1892 volume *A Selection of the Letters of Geraldine Jewsbury to Jane Welsh Carlyle*. James Anthony Froude, the original editor of Carlyle's letters, also revealed a number of intimate details of the Carlyle marriage in his biography *My Relations with Carlyle* (1903), which included the assertion that the marriage was never consummated, a charge that has since been disputed. Among the earliest champions of Jane's work was her husband, who elegized her at great length in his *Reminiscences by Thomas Carlyle,* praising her for her "spontaneous nobleness of mind and intellect," while asserting that her letters "equal and surpass whatever of best I know to exist in that kind." Virginia Woolf examined the relationship between Jane Carlyle and Geraldine Jewsbury in her 1932 essay "Geraldine and Jane." A number of valuable biographies have offered insightful analyses of Carlyle's role in the literary life of her age; among the most noteworthy are Elizabeth Drew's *Jane Welsh and Jane Carlyle* (1928) and Townsend Scudder's *Jane Welsh Carlyle* (1939). Lawrence and Elizabeth M. Hanson examined Carlyle's life through an analysis of her writings in *Necessary Evil: The Life of Jane Welsh Carlyle* (1952). Since the 1990s, critical essays investigating Carlyle's writings from a purely literary standpoint have begun to emerge. Jean Wasko has discussed the subversive qualities in Jane Carlyle's unique literary style, while Aileen Christianson has analyzed the satirical elements in Carlyle's prose.

PRINCIPAL WORKS

*Letters and Memorials of Jane Welsh Carlyle. 3 vols. (letters and diaries) 1883

†*Early Letters of Jane Welsh Carlyle, Together with a Few of Later Years and Some of Thomas Carlyle* (letters) 1889

New Letters and Memorials of Jane Welsh Carlyle. 2 vols. (letters and diaries) 1903

The Love Letters of Thomas Carlyle and Jane Welsh. 2 vols. (letters) 1909

Jane Welsh Carlyle: Letters to Her Family, 1839-1863 (letters) 1924

Letters of Jane Welsh Carlyle to Joseph Neuberg, 1848-1862 (letters) 1931

Jane Welsh Carlyle: A New Selection of Her Letters (letters) 1949

The Collected Letters of Thomas and Jane Welsh Carlyle. 32 vols. (letters) 1970-2005

*This work was prepared for publication by Thomas Carlyle and edited by James Anthony Froude.

†This work was annotated by Thomas Carlyle and edited by Alexander Carlyle.

CRITICISM

Jane Welsh Carlyle (letter date 12 February 1848)

SOURCE: Carlyle, Jane Welsh. "To Jeannie Welsh." In *Jane Welsh Carlyle: Letters to Her Family, 1839-1863*, edited by Leonard Huxley, pp. 306-07. Garden City, N.Y.: Doubleday, Page and Company, 1924.

[*In the following letter written to her cousin and confidante Jeannie Welsh, Carlyle describes her notion of an honest correspondence, one "written out of the heart."*]

This last is the only letter I have had from you for an age that I have felt a *besoin* to answer *at once*, I would have written yesterday had not my head been too bad for writing. Perhaps you wonder what was in *this* letter to make it particularly acceptable—but no—you cannot but have an inward sense that it was *the real transcript of your mind at the moment* which your letters have long ceased to be—I have had letters of many *sheets* from you—not "*stupid*" letters by any means—as *kindly phrased* too as I had any business to expect—which I have nevertheless thrown into the fire the minute after reading them, with a feeling of the most profound disappointment and chagrin—because they contained no one word that seemed to have come out of any deeper source than your ink bottle—were not in fact letters from *you* to *me,* but such as might stand labelled in the *Ready letter writer letter from a young Lady residing in the country to a female cousin in town*—letters written *not* to *communicate* your real thoughts but to *conceal* them. And yet who is there who can understand all that is in your heart—even the saddest of it, and what you may feel to be the least creditable to you—your discontents with yourself—your circumstances &c. so well as just I who have passed my whole existence in that sort of thing—and to whom there is no sorrow in life, no weakness in human nature that is not intelligible thro' my own experience! You may say my own letters are as little written out of the heart as yours—certainly! I am very sensitive—morbidly so—and I can only be confidential where I am met by confidence—besides *my* inward life is connected with outward *facts* on which I am bound to be silent—so that I could not always let you see into my heart without exposing myself to cruel misconstructions.

Thomas Carlyle (journal date 8 July 1866)

SOURCE: Carlyle, Thomas. "Jane Welsh Carlyle." In *Reminiscences by Thomas Carlyle*. Vol. 1, edited by Charles Eliot Norton, pp. 53-258. London: Macmillan and Co., 1887.

[*In the following excerpt of a journal entry, Thomas Carlyle reflects on the emotional power of his deceased wife's letters, describing her writing as "an electric shower of all-illuminating brilliancy." At the same time, Carlyle ponders the deeply personal nature of the letters, asserting that he is the only reader who can fully understand, and appreciate, their meaning.*]

The whole of yesterday I spent in reading and arranging the *letters* of 1857; such a day's *reading* as I perhaps never had in my life before. What a piercing radiancy of meaning to me in those dear records, hastily thrown off, full of misery, yet of bright eternal love; all as if on wings of lightning, tingling through one's very heart of hearts! Oh, I was blind not to see how *brittle* was that thread of noble celestial (almost more than terrestrial) life; how much it was all in all to me, and how impossible it should long be left with me. Her sufferings seem little short of those in an hospital fever-ward, as she painfully drags herself about; and yet constantly there is such an electric shower of all-illuminating brilliancy, penetration, recognition, wise discernment, just enthusiasm, humour, grace, patience, courage, love,—and in fine of spontaneous nobleness of mind and intellect,—as I know not where to parallel! I have asked myself, Ought all this to be lost, or kept for myself, and the brief time that now belongs to *me? Can nothing* of it be saved, then, for the worthy that still remain among these roaring myriads of profane unworthy? I really must consider it further; and already I feel it to have become uncertain to me whether at least this poor Notebook ought to be burnt ere my decease, or left to its chances among my survivors? As to "talent," epistolary and other, these *Letters,* I perceive, equal and surpass whatever of best I know to exist in that kind; for "talent," "genius," or whatever we may call it, what an evidence, if my little woman needed that to me! Not all the *Sands* and *Eliots* and babbling *cohue* of "celebrated scribbling women" that have strutted over the world, in my time, could, it seems to me, if all boiled down and distilled to essence, make one such woman. But it is difficult to make these Letters fairly legible; except myself there is nobody at all that can completely *read* them, as they now are. They abound in allusions, very full of meaning in this circle, but perfectly dark and void in all others: "*Coterie-sprache,*" as the Germans call it, "family-circle dialect," occurs every line or two; nobody ever so *rich* in that kind as she; ready to pick up every diamond-spark, out of the common floor-dust, and keep it brightly available; so that hardly, I think in any house, was there *more* of "Coterie-speech," shining innocently, with a perpetual expressiveness and twinkle generally of quiz and real humour about it, than in ours. She mainly was the creatress of all this; unmatchable for quickness (and trueness) in regard to it;—and in her letters it is continually recurring; shedding such a lambency of "own fireside" over everything, if you are in the secret.

Littell's Living Age (review date April 1883)

SOURCE: "Mrs. Carlyle," review of *Letters and Memorials of Jane Welsh Carlyle,* edited by James Anthony Froude. *Littell's Living Age* 42 (5th series), no. 2028 (5 May 1883): 290-95.

[*In the following review, originally published in the* Athenaeum *in April 1883 under the title "Mrs. Carlyle's Letters," the anonymous author evaluates Froude's edition of Jane Carlyle's letters. While lamenting certain aspects of Froude's editorship, notably his failure to suppress some of the more personal correspondence between Carlyle and her husband, Thomas Carlyle, as well as his misrepresentation of their married life in the work's preface, the reviewer nevertheless praises the work for providing an "extremely valuable" record of Jane Carlyle's literary talent.*]

Mr. Froude must not be blamed for publishing the collection of Mrs. Carlyle's letters [***Letters and Memorials of Jane Welsh Carlyle***], which, as he tells us, her husband, having "annotated" them in 1868 and 1869, entrusted to him in 1871. "Mr. Carlyle," he says in his preface, "did not order the publication of these letters, though he anxiously desired it;" and he adds:—

> Mr. Carlyle asked me, a few months before his end, what I meant to do. I told him that, when the *Reminiscences* had been published, I had decided that the Letters might and should be published also.

The inference to be drawn from these words is that Carlyle assented in 1880 to the carrying out of a project he had formed in 1871, and if Mr. Froude considers that in printing the letters he is honestly fulfilling the duties imposed upon him, the heaviest charge that can be brought against him as regards those letters is that he has erred through excess of zeal. We do not think he has thus erred.

In these volumes, however, there are other letters and papers which, on Mr. Froude's own showing, were not, as the title-page professes, "prepared for publication by Thomas Carlyle," and concerning the most important of his interpolations he admits that he has violated his trust. In his introduction to the passages quoted from Mrs. Carlyle's journal for 1855 and 1856, he says, "A part only of the following extracts was selected by Mr. Carlyle." By what right does he print, for the public to laugh at and misinterpret if it chooses, the private notes which Mrs. Carlyle made for her own morbid satisfaction at a time of great mental depression, and which her husband, when he read them after her death, discreetly wished to suppress, though he was not discreet enough to destroy them, or, at any rate, to prevent them from falling into the hands of a literary executor so rash as Mr. Froude has proved himself to be?

This is a far greater offence than Mr. Froude committed in publishing the *Reminiscences* within a few weeks of Carlyle's burial, and without such comments and explanations as, if it was allowable for them to be published at all, were required to make their real value apparent to the public. The *Reminiscences* were, at any rate, Carlyle's own property, and evidences of his own infirmities which he was not unwilling for the world to look at after his death. But his dead wife's diary was a sacred document of which even he had no right to make public any portions that she would herself have wished to conceal. If, as Mr. Froude says, the passages in the diary which Carlyle thought of publishing were "sufficient merely to leave a painful impression, without explaining the origin of his wife's discomfort," Mr. Froude would have had good excuse for leaving these out of his volumes. In printing along with them all the other passages that he thought "necessary in the way of elucidation," he has been guilty of conduct which cannot be excused on the score of misguided zeal.

As Mr. Froude must have foreseen, whether he desired it or not, his rude exposure of Mrs. Carlyle's secret lamentations during what was apparently the unhappiest year of her life has already caused great injustice to be done to her as well as to her husband. All that is really shown by her journal and by the letters written by her at the same time is that in 1855 a growing discontent at her husband's enjoyment of the society of Lady Ashburton and her fashionable friends, from which she herself obtained no pleasure, became so great that life itself seemed almost intolerable to her. "Much movement under the free sky," she wrote in one page,

> is needful for me to keep my heart from throbbing up into my head, and maddening it. They must be comfortable people who have leisure to think about going to heaven! My most constant and pressing anxiety is to keep out of Bedlam! that's all.

There are other pathetic passages, revealing grievous unhappiness, and bespeaking for the writer nothing but sympathy in her undeserved sufferings. The letters that she wrote to her intimate friends tell the same tale; and those she sent to her husband at this time, especially when he was visiting at Lord Ashburton's house, are by their coldness and shortness in notable contrast to the tender letters that she addressed to him afterwards, as well as during the previous five-and-twenty years of their married life. But in the fact that the coldness came to an end, and that the love-letter style was resumed, we have the best proof that Mrs. Carlyle had far less real cause for jealousy and offence than Mr. Froude is cruel enough to hint, and, intentionally or not, encourages his readers to suppose. That Carlyle treated his wife with less consideration than she deserved is well known and amply proved by many of the letters that Mr. Froude was quite justified in publishing. That, however, only makes the more inexcusable his action in printing the private reflections of an heroic woman who, always careful to hide her sorrows from the public, even if she was fond of confiding some of them to her dearest friends, evidently desired, when the worst of her trouble was over, to hide the recollection of it even from herself.

Biographies, of course, are useless and misleading unless they truthfully set forth the faults as well as the merits of the persons of whom they treat, and Mr.

Froude evidently regards it as his chief duty in publishing the Carlyle documents to show that Carlyle's remorse, after his wife's death, at his not having made her life in all respects as happy as it might have been, was well founded. But he has erred in these volumes, even more than he did in his *History of the First Forty Years of Carlyle's Life,* by exaggerating both Carlyle's faults and his wife's sufferings. A far truer view of both would have been presented had he, without suppressing anything that it was right to print, judiciously omitted so much as was of a strictly private nature, and allowed the letters to speak for themselves.

These volumes as they stand, however, are extremely valuable. If a few of the three hundred and thirty-three letters contained in them, and all Mr. Froude's comments, might have been kept back with advantage, they form altogether a pathetic and instructive record of the private history of a woman who will henceforth be remembered and honored, not only or chiefly because she was the wife of a man of genius, but on account of her own talents and virtues. They take up the story of Mrs. Carlyle's life from the point to which it was brought down in the *History of the First Forty Years,* when, at the age of thirty-three, she settled down with her husband in their Chelsea house; and they continue it step by step, with the addition of many autobiographical notes by her husband, until her last letter was written in April, 1866, a few hours before her sudden death.

Whatever troubles afterwards befell her, neither her husband's poverty nor his rough temper, both of which were well known to her before their marriage, and which had led to considerable discomfort at Craigenputtock and elsewhere, appears to have been a serious affliction during Mrs. Carlyle's early residence in Chelsea. In one of the many charming letters written to her mother-in-law she said:—

> I have just had a call from an old rejected lover, who has been in India these ten years: though he has come home with more thousands of pounds than we are ever likely to have hundreds, or even scores, the sight of him did not make me doubt the wisdom of my preference. Indeed, I continue quite content with my bargain; I could wish him a little *less yellow,* and a little more *peaceable*; but that is all.

Friends were not wanting, Mill, Sterling, and others being more congenial company than Mrs. Carlyle's nearest neighbors, Leigh Hunt and his wife; and, having a talent for housekeeping, she evidently found amusement in the hard work that her straitened means brought upon her. Her husband having gone on a visit to his kindred in October, 1835, while her own mother was in London with her, she thus made light of her difficulties in assisting the maid-of-all-work, whose cockney rendering of her name, Sarah Heather, caused her to be nicknamed Sereetha:

I have not been a day in bed since you went—have indeed been almost free of headache, and all other aches; and everybody says Mrs. Carlyle begins to look better—and what everybody says must be true. With this improved health everything becomes tolerable, even to the peesweep Sereetha (for we are still without other help). Now that I do not see you driven desperate with the chaos, I can take a quiet view of it, and even reduce it to some degree of order. Mother and I have fallen naturally into a fair division of labor, and we keep a very tidy house. Sereetha has attained the unhoped-for perfection of getting up at half after six of her own accord, lighting the parlor fire, and actually placing the breakfast things (*nil desperandum me duce!*). I get up at half after seven, and prepare the coffee and bacon-ham (which is the life of me, making me always hungrier the more I eat of it). Mother, in the interim, makes her bed, and sorts her room. After breakfast, mother descends to the inferno, where she jingles and scours, and from time to time scolds Sereetha till all is right and tight there. I, above stairs, sweep the parlor, blacken the grate—make the room look cleaner than it has been since the days of Grace Macdonald; then mount aloft to make my own bed (for I was resolved to enjoy the privilege of having a bed of my own); then clean myself (as the servants say), and sit down to the Italian lesson. A bit of meat roasted at the oven suffices two days cold, and does not plague us with cookery. Sereetha can fetch up tea-things, and the porridge is easily made on the parlor fire; the kitchen one being allowed to go out (for economy), when the Peesweep retires to bed at eight o'clock.

It was two years later, after her husband had returned from another short visit to Scotland, that she added this postscript to one of his letters to his mother:—

You know the saying, "It is not lost which a friend gets," and in the present case it must comfort you for losing him. Moreover, you have others behind, and I have only him, only him in the whole wide world to love me and take care of me, poor little wretch that I am. Not but that numbers of people love me after their fashion far better than I deserve; but then his fashion is so different from all these, and seems alone to suit the crotchety creature that I am. Thank you then for having, in the first place, been kind enough to produce him into this world, and for having, in the second place, made him scholar enough to recognize my various excellencies; and for having, in the last place, sent him back to me again to stand by me in this cruel east wind.

Mrs. Carlyle had given up much when she agreed to throw in her lot with the crabbed writer whose genius was then recognized by few besides herself; but she did it cheerfully, and was for some time, at any rate, well satisfied, as she said, with her bargain. Whenever her husband was away from home she took advantage of his absence to have more thorough house-cleanings than were possible while he was in the way, and if some of the difficulties she had to face were more distressing to her than to many cockneys, she found in them amusing material for her letters to him. Here is a sample:—

Only fancy, while I was brightening up the outside of the platter to find in Helen's bed a new colony of bugs! I tell you of it fearlessly this time, as past victory gives me a sense of superiority over the creatures. She said to me one morning in putting down my breakfast, "My! I was just standing this morning, looking up at the corner of my bed, ye ken, and there what should I see but two bogues! I hope there's na mair." "You hope?" said I immediately kindling into a fine phrenzy; "how could you live an instant without making sure? A pretty thing it will be if you have let your bed get full of bugs again!" The shadow of an accusation of remissness was enough of course to make her quite positive. "How was she ever to have thought of bogues, formerly? What a thing to think about! But since, she has been just most particular! To be sure, these two must have come off these Mudies' shawls!" I left her protesting and "appealing to posterity," and ran off myself to see into the business. She had not so much as taken off the curtains; I tore them off distractedly, pulled in pieces all of the bed that was pullable, and saw and killed two, and in one place which I could not get at without a bed-key, "beings" (as Mazzini would say) were clearly moving! Ah, mercy, mercy, my dismay was considerable! Still, it was not the acme of horror this time, as last time, for now I knew they could be annihilated root and branch. When I told her there were plenty, she went off to look herself, and came back and told me in a peremptory tone that "she had looked and there was not a single bogue there!" It was needless arguing with a wild animal. I had Pearson to take the bed down, and he soon gave me the pleasant assurance that "they were pretty strong!" Neither did he consider them a recent importation.

The thrifty couple had been living nine years in Chelsea before they could afford to buy a sofa, and then it was only by unusual cleverness that Mrs. Carlyle managed to achieve the luxury:—

Just when I seemed to be got pretty well through my sewing, I have rushed wildly into a new mess of it. I have realized an ideal, have actually acquired a small sofa, which needs to be covered, of course. I think I see your questioning look at this piece of news: "A sofa? Just now, above all, when there had been so much else done and to pay for! This little woman is falling away from her hitherto thrifty character, and become downright extravagant." Never fear! this little woman knows what she is about; the sofa costs you simply nothing at all! Neither have I sillily paid four or five pounds away for it out of my own private purse. It is a sofa which I have known about for the last year and a half. The man who had it asked 4*l.* 10*s.* for it; was willing to sell it without mattress or cushions for 2*l.* 10*s.* I had a spare mattress which I could make to fit it, and also pillows lying by of no use. But still, 2*l.* 10*s.* was more than I cared to lay out of my own money on the article, so I did a stroke of trade with him. The old green curtains of downstairs were become filthy; and, what was better, superfluous. No use could be made of them, unless first dyed at the rate of 7*d.* per yard; it was good to be rid of them, that they might not fill the house with moths, as those sort of woollen things lying by always do; so I sold them to the broker for thirty shillings; I do honestly think more than their value; but

I higgled a full hour with him, and the sofa had lain on his hands. So you perceive there remained only one pound to pay; and that I paid with Kitty Kirkpatrick's sovereign, which I had laid aside not to be appropriated to my own absolutely individual use. So there is a sofa created in a manner by the mere wish to have it.

It is open to prejudiced readers, and even to incompetent editors, to infer from such lively descriptions of domestic troubles as the above that Mrs. Carlyle found her domestic troubles great and unbearable,—that she was oppressed by her husband's meanness and selfishness, and was a melancholy martyr to his moral and physical infirmities. It would be about as fair to conclude from such passages as the following, which refers to the completion of the rewriting of part of the "French Revolution," that she was a drunkard and a Roman Catholic:—

> One chapter more brings him to the end of his second "first volume," and then we shall sing a *Te Deum* and get drunk—for which, by the way, we have unusual facilities at present, a friend (Mr. Wilson) having yesterday sent us a present of a hamper (some six or seven pounds' worth) of the finest old Madeira wine. These Wilsons are about the best people we know here; the lady, verging on old-maidenism, is distinctly the cleverest woman I know.

It is quite true that Mrs. Carlyle needed more tender sympathy and thoughtful kindness than it was in her husband's nature to give her; but that is the way with a good many husbands and wives who jog through the world very comfortably, and Mrs. Carlyle at any rate understood her husband's temperament and made allowances for it. Here is a characteristic extract from a letter written to a friend who made a special effort to console her soon after the death of her mother:—

> Only think of my husband, too, having given me a little present! he who never attends to such nonsenses as birthdays, and who dislikes nothing in the world so much as going into a shop to buy anything, even his own trowsers and coats; so that, to the consternation of cockney tailors, I am obliged to go about them. Well, he actually risked himself in a jeweller's shop, and bought me a very nice smelling-bottle! I cannot tell you how *wae* his little gift made me, as well as glad; it was the first thing of the kind he ever gave to me in his life. In great matters he is always kind and considerate; but these little attentions, which we women attach so much importance to, he was never in the habit of rendering to any one; his up-bringing, and the severe turn of mind he has from nature, had alike indisposed him towards them. And now the desire to replace to me the irreplaceable, makes him as good in little things as he used to be in great.

As Mr. Froude records in a foot-note, "Carlyle never forgot her birthday afterwards." Once in 1846, she thought he had forgotten her, and she told the story of her mistake and its correction thus:—

> Oh! my dear husband, fortune has played me such a cruel trick this day! and I do not even feel any resentment against fortune, for the suffocating misery of the last two hours. I know always, when I seem to you most exacting, that whatever happens to me is nothing like so bad as I deserve. But you shall hear how it was. Not a line from you on my birthday, the postmistress averred! I did not burst out crying, did not faint—did not do anything absurd, so far as I know; but I walked back again, without speaking a word; and with such a tumult of wretchedness in my heart as you, who know me, can conceive. And then I shut myself in my own room to fancy everything that was most tormenting. Were you, finally, so out of patience with me that you had resolved to write to me no more at all? Had you gone to Addiscombe, and found no leisure there to remember my existence? Were you taken ill, so ill that you could not write? That last idea made me mad to get off to the railway, and back to London. Oh, mercy! what a two hours I had of it! And just when I was at my wits' end, I heard Julia crying out through the house: "Mrs. Carlyle, Mrs. Carlyle! Are you there? Here is a letter for you." And so there was after all! The postmistress had overlooked it, and had given it to Robert, when he went afterwards, not knowing that we had been. I wonder what love-letter was ever received with such thankfulness! Oh, my dear! I am not fit for living in the world with this organization. I am as much broken to pieces by that little accident as if I had come through an attack of cholera or typhus fever. I cannot even steady my hand to write decently. But I felt an irresistible need of thanking you, by return of post. Yes, I have kissed the dear little card-case; and now I will lie down awhile, and try to get some sleep. At least, to quiet myself, I will try to believe—oh, why cannot I believe it once for all—that, with all my faults and follies, I am "dearer to you than any earthly creature."

Such letters are almost too sacred to be printed, but as Mr. Froude ignores their significance in his efforts to misrepresent the relations between Mr. and Mrs. Carlyle, it is right that they should be taken at their true value, as indications of the only too sympathetic nature of a wife who wrote and thought love-letters to the last. Here is one of the very latest, written nineteen days before her death, while her husband was delivering his rectorial address in Edinburgh:—

> Dearest,—By the time you get this you will be out of your trouble, better or worse, but out of it, please God. And if ever you let yourself be led or driven into such a horrid thing again, I will never forgive you—never! What I have been suffering, vicariously, of late days is not to be told. If you had been to be hanged I don't see that I could have taken it more to heart. This morning, after about two hours of off and on sleep, I awoke, long before daylight, to sleep no more. While drinking a glass of wine and eating a biscuit at five in the morning, it came into my mind, "What is *he* doing, I wonder, at this moment?" and then, instead of picturing you sitting smoking up the stranger chimney, or anything else that was likely to be, I found myself always dropping off into details of a regular execution! Now they will be telling him it is time! now they will be pinioning his arms and saying last words! Oh, mercy!

was I dreaming or waking? was I mad or sane? Upon my word, I hardly know now. Only that I have been having next to no sleep all the week, and that at the best of times I have a too "fertile imagination," like "oor David." When the thing is over I shall be content, however it have gone as to making a good "appearance" or a bad one. That you have made your "address," and are alive, that is what I long to hear, and, please God! shall hear in a few hours. My "imagination" has gone the length of representing you getting up to speak before an awful crowd of people, and, what with fuss, and "bad air," and confusion, dropping down dead. Why on earth did you ever get into this galley?

We have no space left in which to do justice to the humor and the pungent wit, the delicious *naïveté,* and the power of expressing spontaneous thoughts, grave and gay, in a choice language, which make at least a hundred of the letters contained in these volumes worth preserving as choice specimens of letter-writing, apart altogether from their personal interest as illustrations of Mrs. Carlyle's character and of her relations with her husband and her friends. Her records of her visits, after many years of absence, to her birthplace are intensely pathetic; and other letters, such as one describing her interview with Father Matthew, are no less interesting for other qualities. Here is part of an account of an evening spent in seeing the private theatricals got up by Dickens and Forster in 1845:—

Upon my honor, I do not feel as if I had penny-a-liner genius enough, this cold morning, to make much entertainment out of that. Enough to clasp one's hands, and exclaim, like Helen before the Virgin and Child, "Oh, how expensive!" But "how did the creatures get through it?" Too well; and not well enough! The public theatre, scenes painted by Stansfield, costumes "rather exquisite," together with the certain amount of proficiency in the amateurs, overlaid all idea of private theatricals; and, considering it as public theatricals, the acting was "most insipid," not one performer among them that could be called good, and none that could be called absolutely bad. Douglas Jerrold seemed to me the best, the oddity of his appearance greatly helping him; he played Stephen the Cull. Forster as Kitely and Dickens as Capt. Bobadil were much on a par; but Forster preserved his identity, even through his loftiest flights of Macreadyism; while poor little Dickens, all painted in black and red, and affecting the voice of a man of six feet, would have been unrecognizable for the mother that bore him! On the whole, to get up the smallest interest in the thing, one needed to be always reminding oneself: "all these actors were once men!" and will be men again to-morrow morning. The greatest wonder for me was how they had contrived to get together some six or seven hundred ladies and gentlemen (judging from the clothes) at this season of the year; and all utterly unknown to me, except some half-dozen. So long as I kept my seat in the dress circle I recognized only Mrs. Macready (in one of the four private boxes), and in my nearer neighborhood Sir Alexander and Lady Gordon. But in the interval betwixt the play and the farce I took a notion to make my way to

Mrs. Macready. John, of course, declared the thing "clearly impossible, no use trying it;" but a servant of the theatre, overhearing our debate, politely offered to escort me where I wished; and then John, having no longer any difficulties to surmount, followed, to have his share in what advantages might accrue from the change. Passing through a long dim passage, I came on a tall man leant to the wall, with his head touching the ceiling like a caryatid, to all appearance asleep, or resolutely trying it under most unfavorable circumstances. "Alfred Tennyson!" I exclaimed in joyful surprise. "Well!" said he, taking the hand I held out to him, and forgetting to let it go again. "I did not know you were in town," said I. "I should like to know who you are," said he; "I know that I know you, but I cannot tell your name." And I had actually to name myself to him. Then he woke up in good earnest, and said he had been meaning to come to Chelsea. "But Carlyle is in Scotland," I told him with due humility. "So I heard from Spedding already, but I asked Spedding, would he go with me to see Mrs. Carlyle? and he said he would." I told him if he really meant to come, he had better not wait for backing, under the present circumstances; and then pursued my way to the Macreadys' box; where I was received by William (whom I had not divined) with a "Gracious heavens!" and spontaneous dramatic start, which made me all but answer, "Gracious heavens!" and start dramatically in my turn. And then I was kissed all round by his women; and poor Nell Gwyn, Mrs. M—— G——, seemed almost pushed by the general enthusiasm on the distracted idea of kissing me also! They would not let me return to my stupid place, but put in a third chair for me in front of their box; "and the latter end of that woman was better than the beginning." Macready was in perfect ecstasies over the *Life of Schiller,* spoke of it with tears in his eyes. As "a sign of the times," I may mention that in the box opposite sat the Duke of Devonshire, with Payne Collier! Next to us were D'Orsay and "Milady"! Between eleven and twelve it was all over—and the practical result? Eight-and-sixpence for a fly, and a headache for twenty-four hours! I went to bed as wearied as a little woman could be, and dreamt that I was plunging through a quagmire seeking some herbs which were to save the life of Mrs. Maurice; and that Maurice was waiting at home for them in an agony of impatience, while I could not get out of the mud-water!

There is a painful sadness in many of the letters, especially those in the third volume. They show that the increased income that came from Carlyle's later popularity brought no relief to him, tortured by the labor of book-writing, or to his wife, as great though not so noisy a sufferer as he was from weak health and sleeplessness. When Mrs. Carlyle's jealousy of Lady Ashburton had spent itself, the strain of her husband's work on Frederick the Great, the writing of which both he and she regarded as a solemn duty, to which all personal comfort must be sacrificed, was nearly as irksome. Perhaps Carlyle, having married his charming wife, ought to have abandoned the calling of author, philosopher, and prophet, to which he had pledged himself, and to have made no effort to give play—which, as it turned out, was anything but play—to his genius.

But his wife married him for his genius, and there is nothing to show that he would have been a better husband or made his wife happier had he abandoned his calling.

Blackwood's Edinburgh Magazine (review date May 1883)

SOURCE: "Mrs. Carlyle's Letters," review of *Letters and Memorials of Jane Welsh Carlyle*, edited by James Anthony Froude. *Blackwood's Edinburgh Magazine* 133, no. 811 (May 1883): 614-27.

[*In the following excerpts, an anonymous reviewer expresses high praise for Jane Carlyle's letters, lauding their emotional sincerity, their intellectual breadth, and their wit.*]

There are occasions when the reader desires to ascertain not what the critic thinks, but what the writer says; and the remarkable letters of Mrs Carlyle, which Mr Froude has recently published [*Letters and Memorials of Jane Welsh Carlyle*], is certainly a case in point.

That they are remarkable letters, no one, we think, will venture to dispute,—the most remarkable, probably, that have been written by a woman—in our time at least. We do not know any letters, indeed, with which we would care to compare them—they are so idiomatic, so vivid, so altogether personal and uncommon. The story, moreover, which they disclose, is one of intense interest; but it is an interest which does not depend upon incident, which is often painful, and sometimes enigmatic and obscure. It requires not a little patience and discernment to find out what it exactly imports,— how far the husband, how far the wife, was to blame for what amounted during many years to virtual alienation. The narrative, though related with more than French vivacity, is thus essentially sombre. Into all these matters, when the evidence is complete, it may be proper to enter; in the meantime, we propose for once to revert to the earlier usage of our craft, and to lay before our readers such a summary of the contents of the volumes as may enable each for himself to form his own conclusions.

Without any considerable departure from the line marked out, however, one or two prefatory observations may be ventured upon, and, indeed, are almost indispensable. In the first place, the high literary quality of the letters is undeniable. Mr Froude, and even Mr Carlyle, may have doubted at times the propriety of making them public property; but the risk was well worth running. No such letters, so far as we can remember, are to be found in our literature. Instinct with life and passion, brilliantly direct, bitterly contemptuous, the scorn and the pathos alike are original and unborrowed. There is not an alien or artificial note in one of them,— every word comes straight from the heart. The woman who wrote them was indeed in one sense a great artist; but, as Polixenes says, "the art itself is nature." They are crowded with details of domestic misadventures, which a commonplace story-teller would have made insufferably dull and insipid: but Mrs Carlyle was not a commonplace story-teller; and the fine touch of the comic artist is everywhere manifest. The mean miseries and discomforts of a narrow and unlovely life are related in the true spirit of Comedy. The soft light of the humorous imagination plays about them. Helen the cook-maid, or Jane the maid-of-all-work, are such figures as one might find in a play by Congreve or Sheridan. The language is marvellously flexible—adapting itself with natural ease and rapidity to whatever mood, grave or gay, lively or severe, happens to be the mood of the moment. The nimble wit never flags. Its *unexpectedness* is perhaps its most noticeable characteristic,—the banter has alway a turn which no one else could have given it, and which constantly takes us by surprise. Ursa Major himself, and his "Immensities" and "Eternities" and "Upper Powers," is treated with a charming playfulness—a playfulness, however, which at length (for several unhappy years at least) assumes an almost sibylline air of severity and reticence. That Mrs Carlyle indulged in a freedom of speech which is rare in those days cannot be denied,—one fancies sometimes that she must have agreed with the old Scottish gentlewoman who held that swearing was a great ornament to conversation,—but it is never rude or vulgar, or inconsistent with the true refinement and natural delicacy of her character. Her keen and incisive intellect was impatient to intolerance of the vapid conventions of society; and this impatience is reflected in the language she uses. It cuts to the quick. But in her case, trenchant keenness of insight was closely united with true and tender sympathy; and it is hard to say which strikes us most in these letters—the fierce hostility to the unworthy, or the beautiful compassion for the unhappy. Her temperament was acutely sensitive, and this sensitiveness, easily wounded, gave vivacity to her mockery and bitterness to her reproach.

It is easy to understand the fascination which such a character must have exercised in the society to which she belonged. It may be said quite truly that there was no one who knew her who did not love her. The first and most famous men of the time were her devoted slaves. Hardly a woman then in the great London world was at once so strong and so lovable, so simple and sincere and yet so uncommon. She told William Forster once that her grandfather was a gipsy who had "suffered" for sheep-stealing at Lanark. *That*, he replied, explained the mystery,—she was a cross between the Gipsy and John Knox.[1] The weird brilliancy of her intellect had unquestionably, as Scotch people would say, something "uncanny," something elfin, about it. She was a woman who had no awe—who looked all things frankly and fearlessly in the face—to whom mental reserves and pious frauds were an abomination—who was as untamable as Meg Merrilies. Was she a woman or was she a witch? She was a very witch in her wilful humours, her irreverent mockery, her fitful gusts of passion,—a very woman in her tenderness, her purity, her compassion, her soft pitifulness. . . .

Mrs Carlyle's writings abound in epigram as well as in passages of really charming tenderness. Her epigrams, like the *Pensées* of Joubert, are the concentrated expression of sense and thought; but they have a sparkle of witty scorn besides, which we miss in Joubert's. If any collection of her "ana" is made hereafter, the only difficulty of the collector will be the abundance of material. . . .

The more tender passages have always a note, or undertone, of sadness; but for genuineness (and *that* is the touchstone) both the tenderness and the sadness have seldom been surpassed. Not a few of them read like passages from the Great Masters; even the style has a characteristic "distinction" of its own. There is, for instance, a little dialogue enclosed in a letter to John Sterling, entitled **"The Bird and the Watch,"** which is quite out of the common, as may be gathered from this extract:—

> Unhappy Chico! not in thy circumstances, but in thyself, lies the mean impediment over which thou canst not gain the mastery. The lot thou complainest of so petulantly is, with slight variation, the lot of all. Thou art not free? Tell me who is? Alas, my bird! Here sit prisoners; there also do prisoners sit. This world is all prison, the only difference for those who inhabit it being in the size and aspect of the cells; while some of these stand revealed in cold strong nakedness for what they really are, others are painted to look like sky overhead, and open country all around, but the bare and the painted walls are alike impassable, and fall away only at the coming of the Angel of Death.

There was an unusual wealth of affection in "Jeannie Welsh"'s nature, which, though habitually restrained, was all the more lavishly bestowed when it found an outlet. Sitting on her old nurse's knee (she goes round by Edinburgh merely "for a kiss of old Betty"), or moving among her early Haddington friends, she is as nearly as possible happy. "The hearts of these two old women are as fresh as gowans. It is like being pretty well up towards heaven, being here." "The people at Haddington seem all to grow so good and kind as they grow old. That isn't the way with us in the south." And what a homely but charming picture is this!—

> I went and drank tea with Mrs David Davidson, the worst-used woman I ever knew; and at seventy-eight years of age she hasn't a drop of gall in her whole

composition, and is as serene as if she had never had a sorrow. She has still the same servant, Mary Jeffrys, who was with her when I was a child; she has served her with the same relish for fifty years. 'Ye dinna find us as perfect as I could wuss,' she (Mary) said to me (the house was clean as a new pin); 'but I'm as wullin as ever to work, only no' just sae able.' At the door she called after me: 'Ye'll find us aye here while we're to the fore; but it's no' unco lang we can expect to get bided.' I don't think either mistress or maid could survive the other a month.

The habitual mood, however, is different. The hardness and the weariness of life in "this great big absurdity of a world," are constantly brought home to us, with an almost Swiftian scorn. "The triumphal-procession-air which, in our manners and customs, is given to marriage at the outset—that singing of *Te Deum* before the battle has begun—has, ever since I could reflect, struck me as somewhat senseless and somewhat impious. If ever one is to pray—if ever one is to feel grave and anxious—if ever one is to shrink from vain show and vain babble—surely it is just on the occasion of two human beings binding themselves to one another, for better and for worse, till death part them; just on that occasion which it is customary to celebrate only with rejoicings, and congratulations, and *trousseaux,* and white ribbon! Good God!" "I should not be at all afraid that after a few weeks my new maid would do well enough, if it weren't for Mr C.'s frightful impatience with any new servant untrained to his ways, which would drive a woman out of the house with her hair on end if allowed to act directly upon her! So that I have to stand between them, and imitate in a small, humble way, the Roman soldier who gathered his arms full of the enemy's spears, and received them all into his own breast. It is this which makes a change of servants, even when for the better, a terror to me in prospect, and an agony in realisation—for a time." The hard life told upon her health and spirits, and there were moments when even Death would have been welcome.

> I would not, if I might, be blest;
> I want no Paradise, but—rest,

she exclaims, in Byron's words; and she looks forward to the unknown future with strange composure:—

Yes, nobody out of Bedlam, even educated in Edinburgh, can contrive to doubt of death. One may go a far way in scepticism; may get to disbelieve in God and the devil, in virtue and in vice, in love, in one's own soul; never to speak of time and space, progress of the species, rights of women, greatest happiness of the greatest number, 'isms,' world without end; everything, in short, that the human mind ever believed in, or 'believed that it believed in;' only not in death. The most outrageous sceptic,—even I, after two nights without sleep,—cannot go ahead against that fact—a rather cheering one on the whole—that, let one's earthly difficulties be what they may, death will make them all smooth sooner or later, and either one shall have a trial as existing again under new conditions, or sleep soundly through all eternity. That last used to be a horrible thought for me, but it is not so any longer. I am weary, weary to such a point of moral exhaustion, that any anchorage were welcome, even the stillest, coldest, where the wicked should cease from troubling, and the weary be at rest,—understanding both by the wicked and the weary myself.

These last extracts bring us to what is not the least interesting part of the book—the view which it presents of Carlyle's own character. Her tone, when speaking of her husband, is at once playful and bitter. She freely recognises his great qualities; but her mockery plays about him like summer lightning. In the earlier years the ridicule is always sweet-tempered, and even tender—like Miss Brontë's ridicule of Paul Emmanuel; but it grows more and more bitter as the years pass on, and she feels herself passing more and more out of his life. . . .

The Scotch Ursa Major of our century, as he appears in these letters, bears a certain resemblance to the English Ursa Major of the last. Carlyle was certainly the last man to whom such a fine and delicate piece of mechanism as "Jeannie Welsh" should have been intrusted. Yet till her health broke down, her keenly humorous perception saved her from utter misery. Much of the Comedy in which her husband figures is just inimitable. . . .

The mixed nature of the man is revealed with surprising vivacity. His arbitrariness, his masterfulness, his wilfulness, the gloomy cloud which so seldom lifted, the awkward and ungainly tenderness, the gruff and whimsical humours, are grouped together into a living picture which a Rembrandt or a Millais could not surpass.

Note

1. "Next morning was bright as diamonds, and we walked all about the town and neighbouring heights; where, rendered unusually communicative by our isolated position, I informed William Edward that my maternal grandmother was 'descended from a gang of gipsies'; was, in fact, grand-niece to Matthew Baillie, who 'suffered at Lanark,'—that is to say, was hanged there. A genealogical fact, Forster said, which made me at last intelligible for him; 'a cross between John Knox and a gipsy—how that explained all!' By the way, my uncle has told me, since I came here, that the wife of that Matthew Baillie, Margaret Euston by name, was the original of Sir W. Scott's 'Meg Merrilies.' Matthew himself was the last of gipsies; could steal a horse from under the owner

if he liked, but left always the saddle and bridle; a thorough gentleman in his way, and six feet four in stature!"

Mrs. Oliphant (review date May 1883)

SOURCE: Oliphant, Mrs. "Mrs. Carlyle," review of *Letters and Memorials of Jane Welsh Carlyle*, edited by James Anthony Froude. *Littell's Living Age* 42 (5th series), no. 2034 (16 June 1883): 673-84.

[*In the following excerpts, originally published in the* Contemporary Review *in May 1883, Mrs. Oliphant describes Carlyle's letters in admiring terms, while at the same time criticizing Froude, the editor of the collection, for allowing her more intimate writings to be revealed to the public.*]

Mrs. Carlyle, the writer of the letters now given to the world in three large volumes, following in the wake of four other large volumes—all given to the elucidation of a portion of the life of a great writer, to whom very few things ever happened—has had a cruel fate since the death of her husband deprived her of her last bulwark against that Nemesis known amongst men by the name of Froude. Her fate is all the harder that she has done nothing to deserve it. She narrated freely all the events of her life as they occurred, according to the humor of the moment, and the gift that was in her: which was a very rare and fine gift, but one that naturally led to an instinctive seizing of all possible dramatic effects, and much humorous heightening of color and deepening of interest. Her power of story telling was extraordinary, as well as the whimsical humor that took hold of every ludicrous incident, and made out of a walk in the streets a whole amusing Odyssey of adventure; and it was one of the chief amusements of her house and her friends. What she thus did in speech she did also in her letters, with a vivacity and humor which lend something interesting even to the hundredth headache, domestic squabble, or house-cleaning recorded. But all this was for her friends; there is not the slightest evidence that she, at least, ever intended these narratives for the world. She was the proudest woman—as proud and tenacious of her dignity as a savage chief. And of all things in the world, to be placed on a pedestal before men as a domestic martyr, an unhappy wife, the victim of a harsh husband, is the last which she would have tolerated. As a matter of fact, her whole existence has been violated, every scrap of decent drapery torn from her, and herself exhibited as perhaps never modest and proud matron was before to the comments of the world. Carlyle himself rushed upon his fate by his will and choice, by foolish belief in the flattering suggestion that everything that concerned him must be interesting to the world, and by a misplaced and too boundless trust in the friends of his later life. But Mrs. Carlyle did nothing to lay herself open to this fate. She did not confide her reputation to Mr. Froude, or give him leave to unveil her inmost life according to his own interpretation of it: and it is thus doubly hard upon her that she should have been made to play the part of heroine in the tragedy which his pictorial and artistic instincts have made out of his master's life. . . .

The volumes before us begin with the life of the Carlyles in London, when the pair settled down there in the same small house, trim and neat and not unlovely, in which they spent all the rest of their lives. Mrs. Carlyle was at this time thirty-three, at the very height and prime of life, fully developed in mind, with no diminution of beauty or high spirits, notwithstanding the loneliness of Craigenputtock and the early struggles of poverty: a woman of genius scarcely inferior to that of her husband, of observation far more lively and keen, of whimsical humor, and a gift of self-revelation as rare as it is delightful. Her account of what she saw and heard and did, if it were only an encounter with a washerwoman, or a tramp, would keep half-a-dozen men of letters—the best of their time, Mill, Darwin, Forster, many more—in delighted attention. She saw nothing that she did not extract some interest out of, some gleam of reflection or sparkle of discovery. Charitable she was not, at least in words, but tender, sympathetic, pitiful to the bottom of her heart. To see her coax and subdue a semi-madman out of his misery, making him in the very jaws of hell "pass an agreeable evening," and cultivate the small gifts of the little "peasweep" of a plaintive child-servant, and at the same time pronounce sharp judgment on the bores that troubled her, and keenly characterize in a few contemptuous, amusing words even the old friends for whom she had at bottom a kind of regard, places at once before us the paradox of the woman, full of intolerance and patience, of kindness, irritability, quick anger, love, enthusiasm, cynicism—all the most opposed and antagonistic qualities. It was this that made her so full of interest, so amusing and delightful, if sometimes also a puzzle and pain to her hearers, who could not see in this infinite variety of moods the very essence of her being, and concluded her to be permanently possessed by the last variation of feeling in which she had written and spoken. Here we have her in all the variety of these changing dispositions, making everything brilliant, lifelike, interesting that her hand touches, feeling intensely whatever that mood dictated, yet changing in the twinkling of an eye from one to another. Haddington is hateful to her—a place to be abandoned at all hazards: yet with what exquisite pathos and tenderness does she tell the story of her return *incognita* to visit the old home of her youth! Her heart melts altogether when she is taken into the kind arms of her old friends there: yet even with the tear in her eyes, she is caught by a sudden sense of the ludicrous and shoots forth her sharp-pointed arrow of

laughter in the midst of her weeping. She describes it as a mark of her heavenly temper on one occasion that her mother and she had been a few days together without quarrelling, then deifies that mother, and weeps her loss with almost tragic passion. Thus she goes on through all her life at Cheyne Row; by times the tenderest mother-mistress to her servants; by times an indignant fury, sweeping them forth before her. Monotony, one would say, was the sole thing she could not endure. Her house-cleanings, even, are a drama; her nervous illnesses run through every note of the gamut, from keen self-ridicule to lyrical strains of despair. And to come to the central interest of her life—that one in which she has been most severely judged, and, we think, most cruelly belied—she is at one moment never so happy as when her husband is out of the house, at the next overwhelmed with anguish because the post has not brought her the longed-for letter, and filled with all the exasperation of a disappointed lover, when a newspaper arrives as a sign of his welfare, instead of the communication for which she thirsts; at one moment making us the most amusing semi-bitter, (if not altogether bitter) sketch of him, the restless and never satisfied, stalking about the house all night long because the cocks will crow and the dogs bark, always in the valley of the shadow of some piece of terrible work or other. But when we turn the page we find her chattering to her Good (masculine of Goody, her pet name, one of the love-titles of that little language which we all in our foolish days resort to) of everything in heaven and earth, with a hundred little phrases which he has to explain, and of which he and she alone knew the meaning—idioms of Italian, Mazzini, fussy speeches of brother John, the proverbs of the house—supplying what he evidently desires before all things, her own intimate brilliant comment upon all that happened, with now and then a word of love, reticent, delicate, worth volumes of endearments. We confess for our own part that the manner of mind which can deduce from this long autobiography an idea injurious to the perfect union of these two kindred souls is to us incomprehensible. They tormented each other, but not half so much as each tormented him and herself; they were too like each other, suffering in the same way from nerves disordered and digestion impaired, and excessive self-consciousness, and the absence of all other objects in their life. They were, in the fullest sense of the word, everything to each other—both good and evil, sole comforters, chief tormenters. "Ill to hae but waur to want," says the proverb, which must have been framed in view of some such exaggerated pair; perhaps since the proverb is Scotch the condition of mind may be a national one. Sometimes Carlyle was "ill to have," but it is abundantly evident that he was "waur to want,"—*i.e.*, to be without—to his wife. To him, though he wounded her in a hundred small matters, there is no evidence that she was ever anything else than the most desirable of women, understood and acknowledged as the setter-right of all things, the providence and first authority of life.

If these two remarkable people had been, like others, allowed without any theory to tell their own story, and express their own sentiments, what we should now do would be to give our readers a glimpse, tranquilly, of the domestic economy of that little house, of which its mistress was justly proud, as a triumph of her own exertions, and its master somewhat grandiloquent upon, as something in itself more beautiful and remarkable than any house in Cheyne Row could ever be. We would tell them of her tea-parties, her evening visitors, of the little peasweep of a maid who insisted upon bringing up four teacups every evening, while Mrs. Carlyle and her mother were alone in the house, with a conviction, never disappointed, that "the gentlemen" would drop in to use them; of how she bought her sofa, and adapted an old mattress to it, and made a cover for it, and so procured this comfort, at the small cost of one pound, out of her own private pocket; of how the cocks and hens next door, and the dog that would bark, and even the piano on the other side of the party-wall, were "written down" by appeals to the magnanimity of the owners, on behalf of the unfortunate man of genius who could not get his books written, or even by bribes cleverly administered when persuasion and reason both failed. The pages teem with domestic incidents in every kind of ornamental setting, all told with such an unfailing life and grace, that, had the facts themselves been of the first importance, they could not have charmed us more; and we do not grudge the three big volumes so filled, in which there is not from beginning to end an event more important than new painting and papering, new maid-servants, an illness, or an expedition. But as circumstances stand, the reader is not sufficiently easy in his mind to be content with these, but has been so fretted and troubled by Mr. Froude and his theories, and the determination which molds all that gentleman's thoughts to make out that Carlyle was a sort of plowman-despot, and his wife an unwilling and resentful slave, that we must proceed first to find foundations for the house, of which we know more in all its details than perhaps of any house that has been built and furnished in this century. Was it founded on the rock of love and true union, or was it a mere four walls, no home at all, in which the rude master made his thrall labor for him, and crushed her delicate nature in return?

The only way to come to any conclusion on this point is to see what she herself says. "God keep you, my own dear husband," she says (the first absence we find recorded), "and bring you safe back to me. The house looks very empty without you, and my mind feels empty too." "I expect with impatience the letter that is to fix your return." "Your letter has just come," she says an-

other time; "I thank you for never neglecting me. Dearest, the postman presented me with your letter to-night in Cheyne Walk, with a bow extraordinary. He is a jewel of a postman; whenever he has put a letter from you into the box, he both knocks and rings, that not a moment may be lost in taking possession of it." "Thanks for your constant little letters: when you come back I do not know how I shall learn to do without them; they have come to be as necessary as any part of my daily bread." On her part she is distressed beyond measure when by accident of posts or importunity of visitors there is any breach in the constant succession of her letters to him, fearing he will be "vaixed" (Scoticè, distressed, not angered), and will write him a scrap, to "keep your mind easy by telling you that I have a headache," lest he should think there was something worse that she did not tell. How provoked is she when brother John (untidy, fussy person, turning her orderly rooms into chaos, "born in creaking boots") announces his arrival before her husband's return. "I had set my heart on your hanselling the clean house yourself, and that there would have been a few days in peace to inspect its curiosities and niceties before he came plunging in. . . . Howsomdever! only when you come I shall insist on going into some room with you, and locking the door till we have had a quiet, comfortable talk about 'Time and Space,' untormented by his blether." Then there is a little matter of a birthday recollection, which runs lightly through many pages, and culminates in such a letter as is in itself enough for our purpose. Carlyle had known nothing about birthdays, the large rustic family to which he belonged being altogether out of the way of such delicacies; which, indeed, were little enough thought of in the somewhat sternly mannered Scotland of his time. But with the instinct of the heart he had divined (the ill-tempered tyrant!) that the first birthday after her mother's death his Jane would miss one tender, habitual greeting. He "who dislikes nothing in the world so much as going into a shop to buy anything," "actually risked himself" on this occasion in uncouth tenderness. "I cannot tell how *wae* his little gift made me as well as glad," she writes to another correspondent; "it was the first thing of the kind he ever gave me in his life. In great matters he is always kind and considerate, but these little attentions, which we women attach so much importance to, he was never in the habit of rendering to any one. And now the desire he has to replace the irreplaceable makes him as good in little things as he used to be in great." There is a great deal more about this, which throws much light upon their relations. On one occasion, she being absent on a succession of visits, he asks where she is to be on this anniversary. "My dear, in what view do you ask," she says; "to send me something? Now, I positively forbid you to send me anything but a letter, with your blessing. It is a positive worry for you, the buying of things. And what is the chief pleasure of a birthday present? Simply that it is evidence of one's birthday being remembered; and now I know, without any birthday present, that you have been thinking of it, my poor Good, for ever so long before. So write me a longer letter than usual, and leave presents to those whose affection stands more in need of vulgar demonstration than yours." But this harsh husband, this thoughtless and gloomy despot, paid no attention to the tender prohibition. "Oh, my darling," she writes a few days after, "I want to give you an emphatic kiss rather than to write. But you are at Chelsea, and I at Seaforth, so the thing is clearly impossible for the moment. But I will keep it for you till I come, for it is not with words that I can thank you adequately for that kindest of birthday letters and its small inclosure. I cried over it, and I laughed over it, and could not sufficiently admire the graceful idea—an idea which might come under the category of what Cavaignac used to call *idées de femme,* supposed to be unattainable by the coarser sex." The climax of all is in the following letter, which in the point of view of an unhappy marriage—love worn out on one side, never existent on the other—is as unaccountable, we should imagine, as any undiscovered hieroglyphic ever was:

Seaforth, *Tuesday, July* 14, 1846.

> Oh, my dear husband, fortune has played me such a cruel trick this day! and I do not even feel any resentment against fortune for the suffocating misery of the last two hours. But you shall know how it was.
>
> Not a line from you on my birthday, the postmistress averred! I did not burst out crying, did not faint, did not do anything absurd so far as I know; but I walked back again without speaking a word, and with such a tumult of wretchedness in my heart as you, who know me, can conceive; and then I shut myself in my own room to fancy everything that was most tormenting. Were you finally so out of patience with me that you had resolved to write to me no more at all? Had you gone to Addiscombe, and found no leisure there to remember my existence? Were you taken ill, so that you could not write? That last idea made me mad to get off to the railway and back to London. Oh mercy, what a two hours I had of it!
>
> And just when I was at my wits' end I heard Julia crying through the house: "Mrs. Carlyle, Mrs. Carlyle! are you there? Here is a letter for you!"
>
> And so there was after all! The postmistress had overlooked it, and had given it to Robert when he went afterward, not knowing we had been. I wonder what love-letter was ever received with such thankfulness. Oh, my dear! I am not fit for living in the world with this organization. I am as much broken to pieces by this little accident as if I had come through an attack of cholera or typhus fever; I cannot even steady my hand to write decently. But I felt an irresistible need of thanking you by return of post. Yes, I have kissed the dear little card-case; and now I will lie down awhile and try to get some sleep, at least to quiet myself. I will try to believe—oh, why cannot I believe it once for all—that

with all my faults and follies I am "dearer to you than any earthly creature."

Your own, J. C.

Many a sober matron of forty-five, who has never doubted of her husband's love or her own, will read this letter with a smile and a sigh. How to preserve this love passion, this absorption in one object, and lover-like dependence on his love, through all the calming influences of serious years! Most of us have been trained (*pace* Mr. Froude) in a harder school, taught to believe it a very simple matter that our birthday might be forgotten, nothing to faint or weep or be miserable about; a small piece of neglect, perhaps, to be remedied by next post, and no harm done; perhaps to be thought of weeks after with a calm "I am sorry I forgot," perhaps not even so much as that. How many women in the world, more than twenty years married and long past the period of passion, would think of it at all? The misery, the transport, are all out of the common lines of life. So was she, it may be said; but who shall tell us, after this, either that she was a loveless wife, or that her husband was a selfish tyrant to her? She was not a happy woman, and never could have been so in any circumstances, unless, indeed, we may believe (which is a perfectly tenable argument) that the rapture of the reassurance was enough to counterbalance the anguish that preceded it. With persons of excessively keen susceptibilities this is often so, but in such a case they have no just claim upon our pity, since they have compensation for what they suffer. And we doubt whether any individual gifted with this organization would be content to exchange it for the more placid temperament which, if it suffers less, enjoys less also.

Before we leave this branch of the subject we may quote one letter of this terribly ill-used wife to her husband's mother, showing with what feelings she regarded her own fate. It was written as a postscript to his letter announcing his return home after a visit to his family:—

> My dear Mother,—You know the saying "It is not lost that a friend gets," and in the present case it must comfort you for losing him. Moreover, you have others behind, and I have only him, only him in the whole wide world to love me and take care of me, poor little wretch that I am. Not but that numbers of people love me after their fashion far more than I deserve, but then his fashion is so different from all these, and seems alone to suit the crotchety creature that I am. Thank you then for having in the first place been kind enough to produce him into this world, and for having in the second place made him scholar enough to recognize my various excellences; and for having in the last place sent him back to me again to stand by me in this cruel east wind.

Carlyle himself did not suffer from any doubts of his wife's love for him (being unenlightened by Mr. Froude on this subject) and did not suffer as she did from those horrible clouds of unbelief. It is not, perhaps, the way in which a man is apt to torment himself, since we can remember no instance on record except De Musset's "*Enfant du Siècle,*" in whom the frenzy of doubt becomes somewhat contemptible from reiteration. But though he did not suffer with her in this respect, they had an abundance of other miseries in common. Both of them were driven frantic at night by those external sounds which most of us are hardened to endure. When she was at home, her susceptibility was diverted from herself into the horror of hearing her husband's sudden stamp overhead, and wild rampage through the sleeping house, or declaration (if it was the daytime) that he could neither "think nor live" while the noise went on, both things so necessary to be done. But when she was alone she was herself every whit as susceptible, found *that dog* something unendurable, and was afflicted, while on a visit, almost to madness, by the voice of an ass, more portentous even than Peter Bell's, which she describes with a vehemence half mocking yet wholly real, and the most whimsical exaggerations; which, however, were not exaggerations to either of them, so much were they at the mercy of their sensations. The curious household it was! the one maidservant downstairs—too often changed, yet, whenever it was possible, made into an affectionate friend, kissing her mistress vehemently after a separation, humored and quoted when she happened to have anything original in her, scorned and vituperated when there was no human response: the mistress, whether up on a ladder arranging her curtains, or down on her knees nailing the carpet, or lying on a sofa with one of the many nervous ills that flesh is heir to, in all but the most desperate circumstances, and even sometimes in these, carrying on her bright life-narrative, brilliant, caustic, never to be calculated upon what next she might do or say: the husband laboring heavily through his work, trying every room in succession, finding everything unsatisfactory. A wonderful northern-Gothic couple, blazing off into thunder and lightning of fierce sudden wrangle, with volleys of rolling words, far too mighty for the occasion, fire and flame and the smoke of battle, and laughter ringing through. No wonder that people misunderstood them. It is so easy to misunderstand; and perhaps difficult for a gentleman of chastened politeness and the habits of the best society, to make out, even with the help of genius, what was the meaning of it all.

Amid all the carpet-laying, paper-hanging, and so forth, there was an abundant supply of fine company in the little Chelsea house. "I had some private misgivings that your men would not mind (Anglicè, remember) me when you were not here, and I should have been mortified in that case, though I could not have blamed them. But it is quite the reverse," she writes. At one terrible height of domestic misfortune, after she had gaily "swept the parlor, brushed the grate," etc., her mother cheerfully aiding, the two ladies received John Mill,

Sterling, Count Pepoli, and various other notables to tea, Mrs. Welsh, the country lady, thinking not much of any of them, except the Italian, who pleased her. Mazzini and Darwin, two of the closest circle of intimates, sometimes even bored the object of their friendship and admiration. She found them one evening "mortally stupid." Then there is a bishop discreetly (for once in a way, with a prudence to which we begin to be unaccustomed in biography) disguised in a——and who is profanely called by the Carlyles "Cuittikins," a Scotch adaptation of Gaiters, who is an infliction almost beyond bearing. One night, suddenly, Alfred Tennyson appears, and that is an honor! but alas! there was Dr. John already there, and excellent Professor Craik, both of them it may easily be supposed too happy to meet the poet. "Craik prosed and John babbled for his entertainment, and I, whom he had come to see, got scarcely any speech of him." "The exertion, however," she adds, "of having to provide him with tea, through my own unassisted ingenuity (Helen being gone for the evening), drove away my headache, also perhaps a little feminine vanity at having inspired such a man with the energy to take a cab on his own responsibility and to throw himself on Providence for getting away again." The Sterlings, as a family, both sons and the father, the old Jupiter of the *Times,* were devoted friends and servants, the elder man making a sort of fatherly claim upon her services. And if, perhaps, she was invited to some great houses, naturally enough, not for herself but as her husband's wife, there were scarcely any of his most prized associates who did not very soon distinguish and identify the second member of that co-partnership, bringing to her often their secrets and troubles, and always their cordial brotherhood. Certainly anything less like effacement or absorption in a greater could not be. She had to talk so much, she declares, on some of these evenings, that she was good for nothing next morning. And she had no respect for anybody, she who found Darwin "mortally dull" on occasion. When she went to see those theatricals which opened a kind of new career to Dickens, revealing, as every one has said, his wonderful gift for dramatic representations, her opinion was different from the judgment of the world.

> "How did the creatures get through it?" Too well and not well enough. The public theatre, the scenes painted by Stansfield, costumes "rather exquisite," together with a certain amount of proficiency in the amateurs, overlaid all idea of private theatricals; and considering it as public theatricals, the acting was most insipid, not one performer among them that could be called good, and none that could be called absolutely bad. Douglas Jerrold seemed to me the best, the oddity of his appearance greatly helping him. Forster as Kitely, and Dickens as Captain Bobadil, were much on a par; but Forster preserved his identity even through the loftiest flights of Macreadyism, while poor little Dickens all painted in black and red, and affecting the voice of a man of six feet, would have been unrecognizable by the mother that bore him. On the whole, to get up the

smallest interest in the thing one needed to be always reminding one's self "all these actors were once men," and will be men again to-morrow morning.

There are times, however, when this keen-sighted critic, so independent and outspoken in her judgment, is touched by an enthusiasm which overmasters her. And of all persons in the world to have this effect upon her, Father Matthew was the man. She makes a long pilgrimage in an omnibus "to Mile End," wherever that may be, and penetrates with beating heart through the audience, "thousands of people all hushed into awful silence." until she reaches with her companion the neighborhood of the priest and apostle.

> He made me sit down on the only chair a moment: then took me by the hand as if I had been a little girl, and led me to the front of the scaffold to see him administer the pledge. From a hundred to two hundred took it, and all the tragedies and theatrical representations I ever saw melted into one, could not have given me such emotions as that scene did. There were faces both of men and women that will haunt me while I live, faces exhibiting such concentrated wretchedness, making, you would have said, its last deadly struggle with the powers of darkness. . . . And in the face of Father Matthew, when one looked from them to him, the mercy of heaven seemed to be laid bare. . . . . I was turning sick and needed to get out of the thing, but in the act of leaving him—never to see him again through all time, most probably—feeling him to be the very best man of modern times (you excepted), I had another moment of youthful enthusiasm which you will hold up your hands and eyes at. Did I take the pledge then? No; but I would have though, if I had not feared it would be put in the newspapers. No, not that: but I drew him aside, having considered if I had any ring on, any handkerchief, anything that I could leave with him in remembrance of me; and having bethought myself of a pretty memorandum-book in my reticule, put it into his hand and bade him keep it for my sake, and asked him to give me one of his medals to keep for his! And all this in tears and in the utmost agitation. Had you any idea that your wife was still such a fool? I am sure I had not. The Father got through the thing admirably. He seemed to understand what it all meant quite well, inarticulate though I was. He would not give me a common medal, but took a little silver one from the neck of a young man who had just taken the pledge for example's sake, telling him he would get him another presently, and laid the medal in my hand with a solemn blessing. I could not speak for excitement all the way home. When I went to bed I could not sleep, the pale faces I had seen haunted me, and Father Matthew's smile; and even next morning I could not anyhow subside into my normal state until I had sat down and written Father Matthew a long letter, accompanying it with your "Past and Present." Now, dear, if you are ready to beat me for a distracted gomeril, I cannot help it. All that it was put into my heart to do. *Ich konnte nicht anders.*

This capacity for generous enthusiasm had seldom such large utterance in her. With her constant caustic, sharp-biting criticism, her indisposition to run in the rut of ordinary opinions, her jibes and satirical vein, it is strange indeed to see her so entirely mastered by her emotion. But upon this point of high philanthropy she was always approachable. She was the confidante in general of people in trouble, and when there was somebody to be helped out of the fearful pit and miry clay, whether a poor maidservant tempted by drink, or friend on the brink of despair, would spare no pains upon the work, though making little pretence to charity in deed, and still less to charity in speech. As we are about it we may add another instance of this little appreciated side of Mrs. Carlyle's character, the fervid-sympathetic—in which her enthusiasm finds a vent in so characteristic, so delightful and womanly a way (though sadly against Mr. Froude's theory), that we cannot refuse ourselves the pleasure of quoting it. She had been taken by Mr. W. E. Forster to a meeting at Bradford "for Roman liberty," whatever that may mean: and found the Bradford gentlemen, "like Ben Stodart's legs, no great things," but "the Bradford men, who filled the hall to suffocation, a sight to see!"

> And I must tell you "I aye thought mickle o' you," but that night "I thought mair o' you than ever." A man of the people mounted the platform and spoke: a youngish intelligent-looking man, who alone of all the speakers seemed to understand the question, and to have feelings as well as notions about it. He spoke with a heart eloquence that "left me warm." I never was more affected by public speaking. When he ceased I did not throw myself on his neck and swear everlasting friendship; but I assure you it was in putting constraint on myself that I merely started to my feet and shook hands with him. Then "a sudden thought" struck me. This man would like to know you; I would give him my address in London. I borrowed a pencil and piece of paper and handed him my address. When he looked at it he started as if I had sent a bullet into him, caught my hand again, almost squeezed it into "immortal squash," and said: "Oh, it is your husband! Mr. Carlyle has been my teacher and master, I have owed everything to him for years and years." I felt it a credit to you to have had a hand in turning out this man: was prouder of that heart-tribute to your genius than any amount of reviewer-praises or aristocratic invitations to dinner.

That the wife, and such a wife, should think of this supreme reward for the speaker who pleased her, "This man would like to know you," is pretty, as Carlyle himself would have said; so pretty that it makes the heart swell with sympathetic emotion.

Space fails us, however, for all the extracts which we are tempted to make. If Carlyle, in the remorseful misery that seized upon him (in some great measure unnecessarily, in our opinion), had not felt every scrap from her hands to be precious, his judgment, no doubt, would have curtailed a great deal that we find here of the domestic economy of Cheyne Row. We need not have had all the vicissitudes attending all the maids, nor all the house-cleanings, nor in such full detail those nervous sufferings which laid her prostrate and the remedies she took to ameliorate her state—all quite natural and befitting as addressed to correspondents, all of whom had the interest of kindred or the most intimate friendship in everything that concerned her, but unnecessary here. Notwithstanding these repetitions, there is not a dull page in the book: but it would have been more perfect without them. And it is, perhaps, the polemics that have arisen about the history of this pair that make us seek the passages that concern their mutual relations rather than the many independent pictures of the most vivid kind in which these home scenes are set, and which are better adapted for the public eye. There would not be, for example, a more effective picture than that of the rural rectory at which she visited one memorable August, the home of the youngest of the Bullers, an "utterly stupid, somnolent reverend incumbent," according to Carlyle's usual mode of description. The household seems to have been a strange enough one. The father and mother accomplished people of the world, of little, or any religious belief; the son one of those parsons, of a school that is happily almost extinct, to whom the routine of their office suffices. Here is the Sleepy Hollow of a place, in the haze of the August heat and sunshine:—

> It stands in the midst of green fields and fine tall trees; with the church (if such a dilapidated old building can be called a church) within a bowshot of it. Around the church is a little quiet-looking churchyard, which, when the sun is shining on it, does not look sad. A footpath, about half a yard wide and overgrown with grass and strewn with fallen apples, cuts across the bit of green field between the church and the rectory, and being the only road to the church, one may infer from it several things: I went into the church last night with Reginald while Mrs. Buller was having her dinner; and when I looked at *him* and at *it,* and thought of the four hundred and fifty living souls who were to be saved by such means, I could almost have burst into tears. Anything so like the burial-place of revealed religion you have never seen, nor a rector more fit to read its burial service. The church bell rings night and morning with a plaintive clang. I asked was it for prayers. "No; it was to warn the gleaners that it was their time to go out and come in." . . . I feel already quite at home and almost wishing you were rector of Troston; what a blessed exchange would it be for those poor people whom I hear at this moment singing feckless psalms! I could almost find it in my heart to run over to the old tower and give them a word of admonition myself. . . . The service went off quite respectably; it is wonderful how little faculty is needed for saying prayers perfectly well! But when we came to the sermon! greater nonsense I have often enough listened to,—for, in fact, the sermon, Mrs. Buller with her usual sincerity informed me before I went, "was none of his; he had scraped together as many by other people as would serve him for years, which was much better for the congregation;" but he delivered it as daft Mr. Hamilton used to read the newspaper, with a noble disdain of anything in the nature of a stop, pausing just when he needed breath at the end of a sentence or in the middle of a word, as it hap-

pened. . . . And this was the Gospel of Jesus Christ I was hearing—made into something worse than the cawing of rooks.

The woman who speaks thus, evidently had enough of Scotch feeling about her to object to the game of chess which concluded the Sunday evening; "decidedly improper, but I could not refuse," she says.

Among these, and many more sketches, the description of her first going to Haddington *incognita,* is the one perhaps which will most touch the heart of the reader. Twenty-three years after she had left the home of her youth, her mother being dead in the mean time, and all her early life disappeared like the mists, although still some dear friends remained, and many inhabitants of the place cast wistful looks at her, divining a personality they knew, she arrived suddenly in a July afternoon at the George Inn, "alone amid the silence of death," coming apparently to see whether she could bear it before she made herself known to her old friends.

> I sat down quite composedly at a window, and looked up the street toward our old house. It was the same street, the same houses, but so silent, dead, petrified. It looked the old place just as I had seen it at Chelsea in my dreams, only more dream-like. Having exhausted that outlook, I rang my bell, and told the silent landlord to bring tea and take orders about my bedroom. The tea swallowed down, I notified my wish to view "the old church there," and the keeper of the keys was immediately fetched in. In my part of stranger in search of picturesque, I let myself be shown the way which I knew every inch of; shown the schoolhouse, where myself had been bred; the playground, the "boolin' green," and so on to the churchyard, which, as soon as my guide had unlocked for me, I told him he might wait there, I needed him no further. The churchyard had become very full of graves: within the ruins were two smartly got-up tombs. His (her father's) looked old, old, was surrounded by nettles, the inscription all over moss, except two lines which had been quite recently cleared—by whom? Who had been there before me, caring for his tomb after twenty-nine years? The old ruin knew, and would not tell me. That place felt the very centre of eternal silence—silence and sadness world without end! When I returned, the sexton, or whatever he was, asked, "Would I not walk through the church?" I said yes, and he led the way, but without playing the cicerone any more; he had become pretty sure there was no need. Our pew looked to have never been new lined since we occupied it; the green cloth was become all but white from age. I looked at it in the dim twilight, till I almost fancied that I saw my beautiful mother in her old corner, and myself a bright-looking girl in the other. It was time to "come out of that!" Meaning to return to the churchyard in the morning to clear the moss from the inscription, I asked my conductor where he lived—with his key. "Next door to the house that was Dr. Welsh's," he answered, with a sharp glance at my face; then added gently, "Excuse me, me'm, for mentioning that, but the minute I set eyes on you at the George, I jaloused it was her we all looked after whenever she went up or down."

She went then in the lingering Scotch twilight to the front of the house in which her old friends lived, and wondered what they would think did they know of her presence there, and longed but feared to enter: then kissing the familiar gate, went back to her inn in silence, "the silentest inn on the planet, nothing stirring." In this stillness she wrote to her husband, then in Ireland, but as her letter was "all about feelings," she tore it up in the morning when, before the world was awake, she was up and out again, looking wistfully at the closed and sleeping house which had been her home: then took her way to the churchyard, where, impatient of waiting, the slim, light creature, a girl still, though she was approaching fifty, climbed the wall rather than wait for the key, feeling herself to breathe freer there "with the bright morning sunshine streaming down upon it, then near that so-called habitation of the living," the doctor's old house: where "it was difficult to me to realize to myself that the people inside were only asleep, and not dead—dead since many years." In the churchyard she found the names which, it had struck her painfully, had disappeared from the signboards.

> It was strange the feeling of almost glad recognition that came over me in finding so many familiar figures out of my childhood and youth all gathered together in one place; but still more interesting for me than these later graves were two that I remember to have wept little innocent tears over before I had a conception what real weeping meant—the grave of the little girl who was burnt to death while drying her white muslin frock at the fire; and that of the young officer (Rutherford) who was shot in a duel. The oval tablet of white marble over the little girl's grave was as bright and spotless as on the first day—as emblematic of the child's existence it commemorated; it seemed to my somewhat excited imagination that the youthfulness and innocence there buried had impregnated the marble to keep it snow-white forever.

There she now lies in her turn, by her father's side, restored to him in death, though one grudges to think so far apart and separated from him who was the companion of her life.

How she ventured at last to the house of the old ladies whom she loved, and was recognized by them; how the town woke up to recognize her, and the old servant Jamie knew her before he saw her. "Then you were told it was me?" "No; they told us just we was to speak to a lady at the George, and I knew it was Mrs. Carlyle." "But how could you tell, dear Jamie?" "Hoots, who else could it be?" There could not be a more pathetic story, though all so simple. The little town so still, the schoolroom door open in the early brightness of the newborn day, showing her the place where "at seven in the morning James Brown found me asleep after two hours' hard study, asleep between the leaves of the great Atlas;" the houses all shut up, but gradually awakening to life and knowledge. She went back frequently afterward, visit-ing her old friends, and recognized by everybody, and gradually the pathos and the wonder died away.

In Edinburgh, there were aunts, loved, but gently caricatured, and Betty—Betty, the beloved servant-woman of old, to whom she was always the "dear bairn," whom she sent the writer once to see in a little roadside hamlet out of Edinburgh, an old woman with a still, wise face that had seen many a sorrow, in the still, little room, with its spark of fire, and the house door which admitted straight into it open to the summer air. Is she there still, one wonders, in her close cap and gray gown, and patient gravity and love? There seems no reason why such an example of the antique world should ever die. She outlived her mistress, her "bairn," at least, so far as our recollection goes.

This sweet and tender picture it would be well to end upon: but in the painful circumstances of the case it will not be for such touching episodes as this that reviewers or critics will look, but for something that will throw light upon the canker of this woman's life, so full of impassioned feeling as she was. And such passages will not be far to seek. The canker was chiefly in herself—in the self-tormenting faculty which never existed in greater perfection in any woman, though that is saying much. Those keen and passionate souls each with the sharp two-edged sword of speech, cutting this way and that, each so intolerant, so impatient, so incapable of endurance, all nerves and sensation, and nothing but themselves to try their spirits—would they have been better apart, each perhaps sheathed in the silky tissues of a milder and softer nature? We doubt it much. The milder partner would have bored them both, whereas in swift change of mood, in infinite variety, in passions of misery and recovered happiness, there was no weariness. "I am always wondering," she says, after one of her bad moments, "how I can, even in my angriest mood, talk about leaving you for good and all; for to be sure were I to leave you to-day on that principle, I should need absolutely to go back to-morrow to see how you were taking it!" Most true and certain! There were times when they could with difficulty live together; and yet there was never a time when they could have done without each other. It was always "Ill to hae, but waur to want."

We must, however, before leaving this publication, do what is odious to us if it were not necessary, and that is, call the attention of our reader to what we cannot call less than a deliberate outrage upon a helpless dead woman, with neither son nor champion to stand up for her. These volumes were announced as prepared for publication by Carlyle himself, and so they were in great part, with many interjected notes which we can scarcely call less than foolish, besides some valuable explanatory details. But in the midst of this mass of letters, thus prepared (enough of them, Heaven knows! to have been by good judgment, one would have said, pared and weeded a little, rather than increased), Mr. Carlyle's executor found certain brief extracts whch he did not quite understand. This set his curiosity to work, and he once morc examined the mass of papers left to him by the fond old man who trusted him, and found therein a diary of Mrs. Carlyle which explained the matter. The matter was that there had once crossed that self-tormented spirit a cloud of bitter but visionary jealousy: the word is too strong—of hot intolerance rather, impatience, bitter irritation, called forth by the pleasure her husband took in the company of a certain great lady, a brilliant woman of society, whom she did not herself love, but whose charm and influence fascinated him. There were none of the features of ordinary jealousy in this dark fit, no possibility of unfaithfulness, unless it might be intellectual—a preference for the talk, the dazzle of a witty circle in which worship was paid to him, and the still more flattering devotions of its presiding spirit. This fascination drew him night after night away from home, depriving his wife of his society, and suggesting to her over and over again by that whisper of the devil at her ear, which she was always too ready to listen to, that she had ceased to be the first and only woman in the world to him. Such a breath of hell has crossed and withered many a blooming life; in this case the fit was temporary, lasting but a short time, and buried in the tender *rapprochement* of the later chapter of life. The discovery of this bit of writing was a godsend to the biographer, who must have felt by this time that the mass of letters were by no means so conformable to his theory as might have been desired. He sent it off at once to Miss Jewsbury to have her elucidations, the only person living who could speak with authority on the subject. Neither the one nor the other seem to have asked themselves what right they had to spy into a secret which the husband had respected. Geraldine, good and kind as woman ever was, but romantic and officious, and pleased too in a regretful way at the discovery, did her part, as may be imagined. "The reading has been like the calling up of ghosts. It was a very bad time with her then, no one but herself, or one constantly with her, knows what she suffered, physically as well as morally," Miss Jewsbury says. And here is produced triumphantly between them this little basket of fragments, with a preface from the male friend, historical and philosophical, "married him against the advice of friends," "worked for him like a servant," all over again: and a postscript from the female friend, sentimental and descriptive: "She was bright and beautiful, with a certain star-like radiance and grace. She had gone off into the desert with him. The offering was accepted, but like the precious things flung by Benvenuto into the furnace when his statue was molten, they were all consumed in the flames: he gave her no human help and tenderness." So Geraldine, in a piece of fine writing—words as untrue as ever words were, as every un-

prejudiced reader of this book will see for himself, and entirely contrary to that kind soul's ordinary testimony. Not a critic, so far as we are aware, has ever suggested that this proceeding was unjustifiable, or outside of the limits of honor. Is it then permissible to outrage the memory of a wife, and betray her secrets because one has received as a gift her husband's papers? She gave no permission, left no authority for such a proceeding. Does the disability of women go so far as this? or is there no need for honor in respect for the dead? "There ought to be no mystery about Carlyle," says Mr. Froude. No, poor, foolish, fond old man! there is no mystery about him henceforward, thanks to his own distracted babble of genius, first of all. But how about his wife? Did she authorize Mr. Froude to unveil her most secret thoughts, her darkest hours of weakness, which even her husband passed reverently over? No woman of this generation, or of any other we are acquainted with, has had such desperate occasion to be saved from her friends: and public feeling and sense of honor must be at a low ebb indeed when no one ventures to stand up and stigmatize as it deserves this betrayal and exposure of the secret of a woman's weakness, a secret which throws no light upon anything, which does not add to our knowledge either of her character or her husband's, and with which the public had nothing whatever to do.

Atlantic Monthly (review date June 1883)

SOURCE: "Jane Welsh Carlyle," review of *Letters and Memorials of Jane Welsh Carlyle,* edited by James Anthony Froude. *Atlantic Monthly* 51, no. 308 (June 1883): 837-40.

[*In the following review, the author discusses the underlying pathos that characterizes Carlyle's descriptions of marriage and domestic life.*]

Unconscious autobiography is interesting, but it is seldom fair and adequate. In this last instance, **The Letters and Memorials of Jane Welsh Carlyle,** one reads plainly the petty and mean details of a thirty years' housekeeping; but it is only inferentially that one gains an impression of the charm that, before Mrs. Carlyle's marriage, surrounded her with lovers, and, after it, made her the prized friend of men of intellect, and the refuge of all mad and miserable people, and won for her, when she grew old, the enthusiastic affection of her associates of all ages and all degrees of talent or stupidity. She has fared ill in having her familiar letters given to the world just as they were written, in the raw, with all their feminine confidences, which an editor with a touch of the old-fashioned chivalrous feeling for women would have suppressed, with their hasty account of her domestic vexations of body and mind, their revelation of her little necessary social hypocrisies, and even the heartburnings that she entrusted only to her diary. Her husband, it is true, prepared the letters for publication; he was led to do so by a wish to honor her, and also by a feeling of remorse and a desire to do penance for his ill-treatment; but he left the decision in the matter to Froude, on whom the responsibility lies. It is useless to lament the indiscretion and obtuseness of this editor; the hero has found his valet, and the preacher of silence is to have as many words made about him and his as possible; it is only left to the public to be thankful that the house, which is now lighted up and thrown open from kitchen to bedroom, had no worse secrets for disclosure.

The letters, being written by an unsuspecting woman who was unusually genuine, frank, original, audacious in word and act, and unconventional to a fault, and being, moreover, seasoned with entertaining literary and social gossip, are, of course, full of interest. Vivacity is the marked trait of the writer; but the continual reference to her happy girlhood and its scenes, growing more pathetic year after year, and the continual lament of Carlyle in his notes,—like a Greek chorus, giving a kind of artistic unity to the series,—lend an effect of sadness to the whole. The life of the heroine—she deserves the name—was impressive; amid the ignoble trivialities that fell to her daily lot, she kept to the high purposes involved in them with great courage and self-control, and with unremitting devotion. An only child, reared in a wealthy and refined home, the favorite of all who knew her, with many rich and intelligent suitors about her, she had chosen to wed the poor and obscure man in whose genius she alone believed, and, against the advice of her friends, had married him, and gone to the lonely Scotch farm to be practically his household servant; there she had spent six toilsome years, and now they had come to London, to the house that was to be her home until death. These letters cover this latter period, of the household affairs of which they contain a complete account. Her work was less menial, since they kept a servant, so that she no longer had to mop up her own floors; but the tasks set her were difficult and exhausting. To provide meals that Carlyle could eat without too violent storming,—for, as she said in Mazzini's phrase, Carlyle "loved silence somewhat platonically;" to shield him from the annoyances of visitors and bad servants; to rid the neighborhood, by ingenious diplomacy, of the nuisances of ever-reappearing parrots, dogs, cocks, and the like enemies of sleep and meditation, her own as well as his; to buy his clothes, see lawyers and agents, even to protest against his high taxes before the commissioners, and, in all possible ways, to save his money at the expense of her own tastes and even of her health; to attend to refittings of the house by carpenters, painters, and masons, while he was away on his summer vacations; in brief, to spare him all the ills of the outer world, to make the conditions of his work favorable, and himself as comfortable as it was possible for a morose dyspeptic to be, and at the same time to prevent his seeing how much trouble and anxiety it cost her,—such was the duty prescribed to herself and done faithfully for years without complaint, amid illnesses not light nor few, which were "not without their good uses," she wrote, because she arose from them "with new heart for the battle of existence,—what a woman means by new heart, not new brute force, as you men understand it, but new power of loving and enduring." In this effective practical life she tried to repress some portion of her womanly nature, for she agreed, verbally at least, with Carlyle's disapproval of "moods," "feelings," "sentiments," and similar phases of emotion not resulting in work done; but her nature, being pathetically susceptible to these forbidden experiences, often overruled her philosophy, and brought the knowledge of her solitude home to her; for she had no direct share in her husband's work, no marks of tenderness from him, and few words or deeds in recognition of her sacrifices for him. She succeeded only too well in blinding him to her own pain, which was, indeed, the easiest of her tasks. Her words on Carlyle's sending her a birthday present just after her mother's death are significant of much that is unsaid, and contain the explanation she gave to herself of his earlier neglect. "I cannot tell you," she writes, "how *was* his little gift made me, as well as glad; it was the first thing of the kind he ever gave to me in his life. In great matters he is always kind and considerate; but these little attentions, which we women attach so much importance to, he was never in the habit of rendering to any one; his up-bringing and the severe turn of mind he has from nature had alike indisposed him toward them. And now the desire to replace to me the irreplaceable makes him as good in little things as he used to be in great." This was in the sixteenth year after marriage.

There was a limit, however, to Mrs. Carlyle's power of self-sacrifice. Her proud, spirited, sensitive nature was ever reasserting itself, persistently refusing to be lost in her husband's individuality. She thirsted both for expressed recognition and for expressed affection. In an early letter to Sterling she writes thus: "In spite of the honestest efforts to annihilate my *I-ety* or merge it in what the world doubtless considers my better half, I still find myself a self-subsisting and, alas! self-seeking *me*. Little Felix in the Wanderjahre, when, in the midst of an animated scene between Wilhelm and Theresa, he pulls Theresa's gown and calls out, 'Mama Theresa, I, too, am here!' only speaks out with the charming trustfulness of a little child what I am perpetually feeling, though too sophisticated to pull people's skirts, or exclaim, in so many words, 'Mr. Sterling, I, too, am here!'" The recognition which she desired was abundantly given by the men who gathered about Carlyle, many of whom were more attached to her than to him; and the despised "feelings" found an outlet in brightening various miserable lives, poor exiles of all nations, unfortunate maidens, lost children, and, in general, all people in affliction, who were attracted to her, she said, as straw to amber. Notwithstanding the affection and devotion of her many friends, she seems to have remained lonely at heart; but she kept on with the old routine, while the French Revolution and Cromwell were being written, and she found comfort, if not contentment, in the sense of fulfilled duty and the knowledge that she had materially helped her husband in her silent way. The whisper of fame grew loud, the doors of the great flew open; but when her faith in Carlyle's genius was at last justified and her hopes for him realized, something happened that had not entered into her calculations. Carlyle was finding the sweetest reward in the society of another woman. This was the first Lady Ashburton, who was "the cleverest woman out of sight" that Mrs. Carlyle ever saw, and at whose home, a centre of intellectual society, both she and her husband often visited; but it seems that in London the wives of men of genius, like the wives of bishops, do not take the social rank of their husbands; so Froude assures us, and Lady Ashburton made the fact plain to Mrs. Carlyle. The result was, that, toward the close of a ten years' acquaintance, the latter grew so jealous of the former's fascination as to make herself very wretched. Miss Geraldine Jewsbury, her most intimate friend, explains the affair in a very sensible note. She says that any other wife would have laughed at Carlyle's bewitchment, but this one, seeing Lady Ashburton admired for sayings and doings for which she was snubbed, and contrasting the former's *grand-dame* manners with her own homely endeavors to help her husband and serve him through years of hardship, became more abidingly and intensely miserable than words can utter; her inmost life was solitary, without tenderness, caresses, or loving words from him, and she felt that her love and life were laid waste. All this she willingly endured while he neglected her for his work; but when this excuse could no longer be made for him, the strain told on her, and, without faltering from her purpose of helping and shielding him, she became warped. Such is Miss Jewsbury's account, nearly in her own words. There is no need to apportion the blame between the pair. The fact is that Mrs. Carlyle suffered, and that, for some time after she became aware of her own real feeling, her letters are less confidingly affectionate in regard to her husband, and contain more or less open discontent of a very justifiable kind. After Lady Ashburton's death, she writes to him as follows: "I have neither the strength and spirits to bear up against your discontent, nor the obtuseness to be indifferent to it. You have not the least notion what a killing thought it is to have put into one's heart, gnawing there day and night, that one ought to be dead, since one can no longer make the same exertions as formerly;" and there is more to the same effect, to which Carlyle affixes his note, "Alas! alas! sinner that I am!" Notwithstanding such plain words, which are indeed in-

frequent, Mrs. Carlyle still guarded her husband, standing between him and the objects of his wrath, "imitating, in a small, humble way, the Roman soldier who gathered his arms full of the enemy's spears, and received them all into his own breast," on which sentence Carlyle again comments, "Oh heavens, the comparison! it was too true." As time went on they drew together more closely. The second Lady Ashburton appeared, who became very dear to Mrs. Carlyle, and was even advised by her to "send a kiss" to the now aging philosopher. Carlyle himself understood better his wife's moods and needs, though still imperfectly, and he was more kind in word and more thoughtful in act than of old. Thus, at last, the letters conclude as pleasantly as they began, with Mrs. Carlyle's elation over the Edinburgh triumph, from which her husband returned to find her dead.

On the whole, we think that, in spite of appearances, the married life here laid bare was not an exceptionally unhappy one; nor does it seem to us that Carlyle's neglect of his wife sprang from any moral fault, but merely from his native insensibility, his absorption in his work, and that unconscious selfishness which is ordinarily induced in even the best men by persistent silent sacrifice on their behalf. He simply did not see, did not know, did not understand his wife's trials and nature; but that he had deep tenderness in his heart is plain, both from his works, where it is shown imaginatively, and from many things recorded of his own acts in these volumes and elsewhere. That his love was single and his loyalty entire these pitiful notes amply and painfully prove. But independently of him altogether, Mrs. Carlyle deserves remembrance for her own sake, not merely for the work done by her as a true wife, nor for the heroic spirit shown in the doing it, but for an intrinsically refined and gentle nature, the history of which leaves the impression that, although it always remained noble and attractive, it was injured by the circumstances amid which she was placed. The total effect of her letters, so far as they relate to herself, goes to confirm Miss Jewsbury's summary, that "the lines in which her character was laid down were very grand, but the result was blurred and distorted and confused."

Gail Hamilton (essay date January 1884)

SOURCE: Hamilton, Gail. "The Day of Judgment, Part 2." *North American Review* 138, no. 326 (January 1884): 60-77.

[*In the following excerpts, Hamilton analyzes Carlyle's letters as a record of her tumultuous domestic life. Hamilton asserts that Jane Carlyle's talents were unjustly overshadowed by her husband's fame during her lifetime.*]

In reading Mrs. Carlyle's letters, it should always be remembered that we gather into a day the petty perplexities, the domestic torments, of forty years. The impression produced upon the reader is entirely different from the actual repression of her life. So far from proclaiming her trials, it was her unwisdom to conceal them too much. Her habit—which Carlyle uses, and has a color of right to use, in self-defense, and which Froude freely presents in his favor—was so studiously to hide from him the anguish which he cost her that he did not suspect its existence. This is no valid plea, because he wrested this very silence to his own destruction by charging it to her want of care about household matters. "Alas! can that need to be said? Insane that I was!" he moans in the stern awakening of death. But the letter in which she wrote it was addressed to him; and he read it in life, in her life as well as his, without remorse, without feeling, without notice. Guilty as he was for not knowing her sadness, it seems certain that he did not know it.

In reviewing the notes containing her planning and counterplanning to meet his caprices, and to take advantage even of his roughnesses, "Alas!" he cries, "how little did I ever know of these secret wishes and necessities—now or ever!"

"She flickered round me like perpetual radiance." "Her intellect was clear as starlight, and continued so; the clearest intellect among us all." "She shone round me like a bright aureola when all else was black and chaos." "At lowest," he bears witness, "nothing unpleasant was ever heard from her. All that was gloomy she was silent upon, and had strictly hidden away." "She was weak, weak,—far weaker than I understood. But to me she was bright always as stars and diamonds. Nay, I should say a kind of cheery sunshine in those otherwise Egyptian days."

In fact, household and petty cares did not disturb her. She was a natural housekeeper. She made no clamor herself about work. It was his clamor that destroyed her peace. "Now that I do not see you driven desperate with the chaos, I can take a quiet view of it. . . . I clean beautifully when you do not dishearten me with hypercriticism. Try all that ever you can to be patient and good-natured with your Goody, and then she loves you and is ready to do anything on earth that you wish. But when the *signor della casa* has neither kind look nor word for me, what can I do but grow desperate and fret myself to fiddle-strings?"

"With no husband to study, housekeeping is mere play." It was his violent, unreasonable, unending exactions that broke her down; his heartless, reckless, personal indifference to herself that wrecked her life. He must be alone by day, because otherwise he could not write. He must be alone by night, because otherwise he could not sleep. When he worked, he could bear no one in the room; when he walked or rode, he could bear no one at his side. She was loth to see it. When she found he did not care for her singing and playing, she merrily consoled herself with imputing the blame to his want of taste rather than her want of skill. So far from being quick to take offense, she was slow, reluctant,—eager to forgive. Her letters are playful, tender, caressing, long after terrible misgivings are revealed. She wore away in solitude because Carlyle plunged away from her. . . .

Intellectually she could and practically she sometimes did give as sharp cut and thrust as Carlyle himself. One seldom gets from one's dearest foe a cleaner, keener satire than she dealt to her husband at Dingwall.

> For the rest, in spite of all objections, 'for the occasion got up,' I dare say you are pretty comfortable. Why not? When you go to any house, one knows it is because you choose to go; and when you stay, it is because you choose to stay. You don't, as weakly amiable people do, sacrifice yourself, for the pleasure of 'others.' So, pray, do not think it necessary to be wishing yourself at home, and 'all that sort of thing' on paper. 'I don't believe thee.' If I were inclined to, I should only have to call to mind the beautiful letters you wrote to me during your former visit to the Ashburtons in the Highlands, and which you afterward disavowed and trampled into the fire!
>
> Lady Ashburton is very kind to offer to take me back. Pray, make her my thanks. . . . If you go back with the Ashburtons it would be different, as then I should be going merely as part of your luggage, without self-responsibility. Settle it as you like, it will be all one to me, meeting you at Scotsbrig, or in Edinburgh, or going by myself from Thornhill.

On a journey home, her husband had insisted on her sitting in a violent draught all the way—the same husband who so properly counseled his Brother James to "Do nothing that is selfish"; in consequence of which he had to record "a sad, sick winter awaited my dear one," which sad, sick winter made such an impression on his dear one that, two years afterward, she refused to join him because she might need to have a window shut when he preferred it open!

A woman who could remember so long and write so keenly could not have been altogether and at all times a comfortable woman for an intensely selfish man to live with. If, instead of suffering at the time and satirizing afterward, she had at the beginning quietly, resolutely, immovably resisted his will, gently instructed him in the rudiments of manly behavior to woman, and so developed the germ of love which unquestionably lay sleeping in his bosom, it would have been as much better for his character as for her happiness. . . .

The publication of these tell-tale letters, with all their remorseful confessions and annotations, are not the atonement for life-long sin which some would fain believe. They speak as strongly of Carlyle's lack of delicacy as of his love of truth. Death was indeed to him a great and terrible revealer. He saw as he had never seen before; but even then his long blindness made him see men only as trees walking. He repented as far as he saw, but he only saw through a glass darkly.

Significant is the difference between the accounts given by husband and wife of the same event. Unquestionably Carlyle meant to tell the truth. Rent with remorse, in his desolated home, he even meant to tell the truth against himself, and doubtless the penance ministered to him a bitter consolation. Yet human nature was strong in him and often he gave unconsciously a softer touch to his own portrait than the life permitted. He describes a visit to Lady Sandwich. "We staid some twelve or more days, which, except for my own continual state of worn-out nerves, were altogether graceful, touching, and even pleasant. . . ." Needless to say, his nerves were not worn out. They were in good preservation and stood him in good stead a score of years longer. But what says Mrs. Carlyle?

> For the rest I should have enjoyed this beautiful place excessively if Eve hadn't eaten that unfortunate apple,—in result of which there has ever since been always a something to prevent one's feeling one's self in paradise. The something of the present occasion came in the form of lumbago! not into my own back but into Mr. C.'s, which made the difference so far as the whole comfort of my life was concerned. For it was the very first day of being here that Mr. C. saw fit to spread his pocket-handkerchief on the grass just after a heavy shower, and sit down on it for an hour and more in spite of all my remonstrances!! The lumbago following in the course of nature, there hasn't been a day that I felt sure of staying over the next, and of not being snatched away like Proserpine, as I was from the Grange last winter. For what avail the 'beauties of nature,' the 'ease with dignity' of a great house, even the hero worship accorded one, against the lumbago. . . . Lumbago, my dear, it is good that you should know in time, admits of but one consolation,—of but one happiness! viz., 'perfect liberty to be as ugly and stupid and disagreeable as ever one likes!' And that consolation, that happiness, that liberty reserves itself for the domestic hearth! And so all the ten days we have been here, it has been a straining on Mr. C.'s part to tear his way, through the social amenities, back to Chelsea,—while I have spent all the time I might have been enjoying myself in expecting to be snatched away.

This is somewhat less "graceful, touching, and even pleasant" to Mrs. Carlyle in the experience than to Mr. Carlyle in the retrospect. But "the lumbago, indeed, I have entirely forgotten," says this philosopher of the easiest minor morals. He is not without a certain jaunty repentance. "It seems, by this letter,"—he has no personal conscience of sin, but he gives in to documentary evidence!—"I was at times a very bad boy; and alas! my repentant memory answers too clearly, 'Yes.'"

When the "demon fowls" made the "sound-proof room" too noisy to be borne, Carlyle remembers only some thirteen years after that she came to him and proposed go to Ronca and rent the cottage outright, and "turn Ronca with his vermin out of it." "I looked at her with admiration, with grateful assent, 'Yes, if you can,' which I could only half believe." But in her letter contemporary, Carlyle's grace and gratitude find no record. She was nearly recovered from an accident, "when Mr. Carlyle came to me one morning, all of a sudden, and told me I must go up to London myself and take charge of some business—nothing less than trying to take the adjoining house ourselves. . . . I thought it a most wild-goose enterprise. I was sent on; and when Lady Ashburton and the others asked him why he sent poor me instead of going himself," he coolly answered, "Oh, I should only spoil the thing. She is sure to manage it." The contemporary document is more credible than the subsequent verbal report. Carlyle did not mean to give a false report, but he instinctively shrank before the revealing light of his newly awakened conscience. . . .

Carlyle's tardy but enthusiastic appreciation of his wife's intellect was not the partial and worthless judgment of a too late aroused and morbid affection. It is founded on the indisputable facts of her history, which only a colossal self-absorption and self-conceit hid so long from his eyes; on indubitable gifts of her nature, crushed so heavily under his hand.

It is not simply that her slight, fragmentary writings show discrimination, originality, the vision and the faculty divine. It is not simply that she read, criticised, and appreciated Carlyle. Her life was lofty. Her moral plane was immeasurably above Carlyle's. Her intellectual forces were far more accurately poised. Her human insight was keener and clearer. While Carlyle clamored through the amazed earth for his right relations with the universe, Mrs. Carlyle calmly and silently adjusted her visible relations with time and with Carlyle. While Carlyle was clattering in all ears the stern command to be rigidly virtuous, Mrs. Carlyle was quietly, in the devil's name, being virtuous, and no more about it. Carlyle spent a long life of the deepest fancied woe in explaining, enforcing, inculcating himself, under the mistaken idea, indeed, that himself was the universe. Mrs. Carlyle effaced herself, considering truly that her theory of the infinite was unimportant; while her discharge of the finite duty imported all. Carlyle was not content to become the best kind of man; but he made the poorest kind of god. Mrs. Carlyle, looking upward in her enforced low estate, discerned a truth of which Carlyle never dreamed—that it is not the victory, but the struggle which signifies. To man belongs the struggle. The victory is to the Power outside of ourselves which established the universe. . . .

It is a misuse of words to say that Jane Carlyle has her revenge. It is not a misuse of words to say that she has her vindication. Forty years long was this temple in building—forty long years without sound of hammer or axe, with no visible sign of architecture; and suddenly it rears its gracious majesty and purity forever to the skies. "Gone in her car of victory in that beautiful death" was the sad shadow of the radiant girl, and knew not that of her name and fame would be left even a shadow; and wheresoever the gospel of Carlyle shall be preached in the whole world, there shall also what this woman hath done be told for a memorial of her. What she had said in youthful gayety is the fulfilled prophecy of her warped and somber life: "Were you to look through a microscope, you might be puzzled to discover a trace of what I do. Nevertheless, depend upon it, my doings are not lost; but, invisible to human eyes, they 'sail down the stream of time into the ocean of eternity,' and who knows but I may find them after many days?" They are found after many days, for God is the only public opinion. The dreams of her aspiring girlhood in practical fulfillment, the gratification of every taste, the congenial occupation of every faculty could have built her no fairer monument than did her baffled, broken life. Like all mortals, she would have failed in accomplishment; now the imagination credits her with all it creates.

Alice Hyneman Rhine (essay date March 1884)

SOURCE: Rhine, Alice Hyneman. "Neither Genius nor Martyr." *North American Review* 138, no. 328 (March 1884): 246-62.

[*In the following excerpts, Rhine attempts to debunk the perception held by a number of critics that Jane Carlyle's career was thwarted by the selfishness and egotism of her husband. Describing Carlyle's letters as trivial and "puerile," Rhine contends that her posthumous literary fame rests heavily on her husband's stature.*]

There are women, like men, of whom "Some are born great, some achieve greatness, and some have greatness thrust upon them." Among these last must be reckoned Jane Welsh Carlyle, a woman who, without strength of her own to rise above the common level, has been lifted into prominence through the greatness of her husband. It has been claimed for her, by Froude, that she was both genius and martyr; that splendid talents were repressed by constant exactions of her husband; that she was "a human sacrifice" slain upon the altar of his ambition. He has compared her to an "Iphigenia in Aulis." Gail Hamilton and other writers have followed his conception and comparisons.

Taken away from the nimbus of Carlyle's fame and the overpraise of critics, the history of Jane Welsh Carlyle's life does not show her to have been a great or even a

remarkable woman, if steadfastness of purpose or heroic endurance of ills common to humanity typifies that which is worthy of admiration. Of herself, she accomplished nothing beyond writing two volumes of mediocre letters. Yet, few women of genius ever had better preparation than she for a career of intellectual labor. She was the only child of well educated parents, possessed of wealth, and having liberal ideas respecting the education of women. Through them she received an amount of instruction not common for girls at that period to obtain, as Latin and some knowledge of the sciences supplemented for her the ordinary branches of a girls' school. In addition to this, from early childhood until her twentieth year, she had the assistance and encouragement of the brilliant Edward Irving. The beloved friend as well as pupil of this renowned orator, it had been Irving's pleasure to expand her powers to the utmost, to cultivate her taste to a level with his own. With him she studied "Virgil"; he was her adviser in literary matters, and her attempts at composition in poetry and prose were submitted to him for approval and correction. Upon Irving's departure from Haddington, Carlyle was requested to supply his place as Miss Welsh's literary adviser. This position Carlyle filled with great assiduity for the five years which preceded their marriage. He studied German with her; introduced her to the works of Goethe and Schiller; supervised, as Irving had done, her verses and tales, and with the same result. The children of her brain died with their birth.

Enough women have written, and will continue to write, for this individual failure to be unworthy of mention, were it not that Mrs. Carlyle's claim to genius has been asserted by numerous English and American critics. One of these asserts that Mrs. Carlyle was not her husband's "inferior in intelligence." Another, reviewing the letters edited by Froude after Carlyle's death, compares her abilities to George Eliot's. "So unmistakeable," [sic] says this writer, "are the signs of uncommon literary talent in these letters, that one cannot help thinking with a twinge of regret and indignation that with a little loving appreciation and generous encouragement from him whose commendation she would have accounted priceless, the world might have gained in Mrs. Carlyle a great novelist. . . . Had he done for her a tithe of what George Henry Lewes did for Mary Ann Evans, . . . English literature might have had a double reason to be grateful to the name of Carlyle."

As if every reader was not aware that Marion Evans had achieved a position in literature for herself long before she made the acquaintance of Lewes. Assistant editor of the *Westminster Review,* an able writer of essays and translator of abstruse German philosophical works before she met Lewes, she required no fostering care from him to make her genius blossom. Between herself and Lewes, the connection was in one phase a literary partnership, contracted when both were in the prime of life, and where the woman furnished an equal amount of capital with the man in the form of brain vitality. Between the two women not a shadow of intellectual similarity existed. George Eliot shunned the world to have leisure for thinking and working. Never less alone than when alone, her days and nights were devoted to study. She had mastered many sciences. "Probably," says Justin McCarthy, "no other novel writer since novel writing became a business, possessed one tithe of her scientific knowledge." Mrs. Carlyle, on the contrary, was a superficial woman, lost without society. Her learning was little beyond that of the average school-girl of today. According to her husband, she did not know enough of grammar to correct proof-sheets of her friend Caroline Jewsbury's novels,—an assertion that she did not contradict, and which is borne out by passages in her letters which remained untouched by their editors.

Partly exiled from society during the first seven years of her married life, Mrs. Carlyle was in a constant state of *ennui*. Unlike a woman of genius, she found no solace in books which could ripen into fruition talents she might have possessed. Her reading was that which exacted no attention. The literature which her husband enjoyed was to her positively distasteful. Old folios, and almost illegible manuscripts which he ransacked for materials to write a *French Revolution* or a *Cromwell* [*Oliver Cromwell's Letters and Speeches*], were in her eyes "rubbish which she wished at the bottom of something where she might hear less about it." "She read the first two volumes of *Friedrich* [*History of Friedrich II of Prussia*]," says Carlyle, "most of it in the printer's sheets. . . . The other volumes (hardly even the third, I think,) she never read." The circulating libraries supplied her with novels, which she read lying on a sofa, after the manner of fashionable women, who utilize the thoughts of others for the purpose of stifling their own. It is against Carlyle and in favor of a woman of this caliber that Froude complains. "Carlyle consulted her judgment about his writings, for he knew the value of it; but in his conceptions and elaborations he chose to be always by himself. He said truly he was a Bedouin." This is amusing, since all men and women, when writing, desire to be alone. Did Froude wish the wife to conceive *Sartor Resartus* and Carlyle to elaborate it, or should she have elaborated her husband's conceptions? Either way, it would have been a strange medley.

That great men admired Mrs. Carlyle does not prove her possessed of sufficient ability to assist in the elaboration and conception of her husband's works. Intellectual men take as much delight as others in listening to airy nothings spoken by pretty women who come within the radius of their social circle, and shine there either by their own or, as in Mrs. Carlyle's case, by reflected light. Some kind of brilliancy, however, they must have. It is without the bounds of possibility that Jane Carlyle, as plain Jane Welsh, would have provoked Tennyson, as is said, into throwing himself into a cab for the express purpose of going to the other end of London to visit her; that Leigh Hunt would have embalmed her name in verse; that Darwin would have attended her; or that the great Jeffrey, like the old flirt he was proud of being considered, would have courted her with sufficient *impressement* "to cause considerable jealousy of the reigning queen among the non-reigning." . . .

A loving, self-sacrificing son and brother, it was impossible that Carlyle could have been the monster of ferocious selfishness that his wife with her caustic pen has pictured him, not only in letters to her friends, but in the note-book kept for her own private use. In her diary, written in 1855, the records are of one resentful, who has brooded over small things until they have assumed large proportions.

This diary of Mrs. Carlyle's tallies with her character. Coming into contact with the greatest men and women of her day, she found no higher use for this journal than to record in it her jealousies and domestic services. The very commencement of this note-book is an outrage against womanly dignity. Its entire contents almost justify Charles Buller's defense of the Duchess de Praslin's murderer: "What could a poor fellow do with a wife who kept a journal, but murder her." An absurd jealousy of Lady Ashburton, her husband's friend, is one plea for writing this book; and yet she confesses, "What good is to result from writing it in a paper book is more than I can tell."

Some of the entries are, to say the least, exceedingly puerile. A *miserere* is made out of so small a thing as this: "The evening devoted to mending Mr. C.'s trowsers, among other things: 'Being an only child,' I never wished to sew men's trowsers, no never!" . . . "Mended Mr. C.'s dressing-gown."

> When I think of what I is, and what I used to was,
> I gin to think I've sold myself for very little cas.

This entry is on a par with a long letter addressed to a physician, which is filled by her with a description of how she took two days to mend a pair of her husband's old boots. This service a cobbler would have done much better, and in half the time, for the compensation of a few shillings,—money that she was well able to pay, as Carlyle was then (1863) in the zenith of his fame, and in excellent circumstances. Over the funds she had unlimited control. Carlyle, always liberal with his means, was at that very time urging her to purchase a carriage for her own use,—a luxury which, in the autumn of that same year, he presented her with himself. For allowing his wife to put a flannel lining in his boots, Carlyle has been called "a brute" and "a cad." The probability is that, immersed in *Friedrich* as he was, until the thing was done he did not know how it was being accomplished. Through doing just such unnecessary things, and crying about them afterward, Mrs. Carlyle has gained the reputation of having been a martyr to the whims of an exacting husband, when she was only a thrifty Scotch woman, trying "to make a crown a pound" by saving on the household economies,—a habit which had grown upon her, perhaps, in the poverty of those early years when Carlyle haunted the libraries and roamed the streets of London with worn boots "and hat well nigh rimless."

Still, even when begirt with this, which Emerson called "the most honorable poverty he ever knew," Mrs. Carlyle was no martyr. A linnet carried on the eagle's back to the sun, she was always bathed in a glory. . . .

[T]he world will know her neither as genius nor martyr, but simply as the wife of the great man whose name she bore. Her highest praise will be that in an age of *gig-women,* as well as gig-men, she chose to encounter poverty with love and Carlyle rather than a life of ease and luxury without him.

Sir James Crichton-Browne (essay date 1903)

SOURCE: Crichton-Browne, Sir James. Introduction to *New Letters and Memorials of Jane Welsh Carlyle,* edited by Alexander Carlyle, pp. v-lxxxvii. London: John Lane, The Bodley Head, 1903.

[*In the following excerpts, Crichton-Browne evaluates the literary merit of Carlyle's letters, focusing in particular on Carlyle's discussions of her numerous physical and emotional ailments. Crichton-Browne remarks that, while her candid descriptions offer valuable insight into her character, they also lend her writings a distinctly "sick-room flavour."*]

The New Letters and Memorials of Jane Welsh Carlyle, which Mr. Alexander Carlyle has with pious care arranged and annotated, will give pleasure to those who are capable of appreciating the brilliant epistolary powers of that remarkable woman, and satisfaction to those who have made acquaintance with the works of her husband, and who desire to revere the man as well as admire the writer. They sparkle with wit; they afford delightful glimpses of the meagre fireside in Cheyne Row, around which the great ones of the greatest epoch of a great age were glad to gather; they throw illuminative side-lights on memorable events, and above all smooth out the dints and brush away the stains and blurs with which negligent usage and venomous breathings have blemished and tarnished the most massive and shining literary reputation of the last century. The letters are residual in character, for they are those which Mr. James Anthony Froude mutilated or put aside, and

he of course selected from Mrs. Carlyle's writings whatever was of most literary merit or popular interest; but they are still intrinsically worthy of publication, for even her "notekins," as her husband called them, contain pungent particles and happy turns of expression, while adscititiously they deserve attention, because they clear up some obscure points in a complicated controversy and help towards a just judgment of two prominent figures in our English Pantheon. Like the letters published in 1883 they are open to the objection that they are overloaded with domestic details about spring-cleanings and other housewiferies, trivial incidents of travel, intricate itinerary arrangements and complaints of postal irregularities; but as Froude who had a free hand with Mrs. Carlyle's correspondence introduced such superfluities while he omitted much that was essential to the understanding of her story, it is undesirable that there should be any avoidable elisions in the letters that are intended to refute his errors. Had Mrs. Carlyle's correspondence as a whole to be edited *de novo* a very different method of dealing with it from that adopted would have been followed, but Froude's indiscretions have made complete candour necessary, and it has been felt that the text of Mrs. Carlyle's letters which have been preserved, set forth with all practicable fulness would best serve to dissipate the cloud of disparagement which Froude has succeeded in gathering around her husband's memory. The letters are not studied compositions, but free-flowing unpremeditated missives, written mainly to bring letters in return. . . .

The drawback to her writings, it must be allowed, is the sick-room flavour that pervades them and the frequent invocations of castor-oil. They are of scientific interest as presenting an instructive series of studies in neurotics, but they are perhaps a little too bulletinish for the general taste.

As early as 1841, Mrs. Carlyle complains of low spirits, due, as she then correctly surmised, to some sort of nervous ailment, and after that there were from time to time periods of gloom, which, as nervous people are apt to do, she attributed to the pressure of some passing event; but it was not until 1846, when she was forty-five years of age, that her despondency assumed a morbid complexion. Then, however, there enveloped her a cloud of wretchedness, an emanation of her own vapour-breeding brain, which deepened and darkened until 1855, when that excruciating 'Journal' was written. It was all but completely dispelled in 1857, leaving behind it, however, impaired bodily health and the seeds of serious evils in the nervous system, which afterwards sprouted and brought renewed depression of a very different nature from that previously experienced.

Mrs. Carlyle's mental malady was emotional throughout, and did not in any appreciable degree involve her intellectual powers. Her letters written during its continuance are, I think, less sprightly and discursive than those written before its invasion; but advancing years might account for that, and at their feeblest they are of more intellectual value than are most other women's letters at their strongest and best. Her marvellous will-power enabled her to a great degree to suppress the outward manifestation of the gnawing mind-cancer within, but not altogether, for some of her friends condoled with her on her haggard and careworn look; the dressmaker remarked how emaciated she had become, and she herself refers more than once to her withered appearance. But what she could conceal when abroad flowed forth freely in the privacy of her own room, and her Journal bears unmistakably the stigmata of mental disorder—not insanity in the crude sense of the word, but a derangement of the feelings, with consequent delusional beliefs, having no rational foundation, and irremovable by demonstrative proof of their untenability, all due to a disease of the brain and nervous system which it is customary to call functional, because of the invisibility of the changes that accompany it and their remediable character. "My constant and pressing anxiety," she wrote, "is to keep out of Bedlam." "That eternal Bath House!" she exclaims. "I wonder how many thousand miles Mr. C. has walked between there and here, setting up always another milestone and another between him and me." "Alone this evening," she complains, "Lady A. in town again, and Mr. C. of course at Bath House." "Dear, dear!" she goes on, "what a sick day this has been! Oh, my mother, nobody sees what I am suffering now!" "Much movement under the free sky is needful for me to keep my heart from throbbing up into my head and maddening it." "It was with a feeling like the ghost of a dead dog that I rose and dressed and took my coffee." "Weak as water. To-day I walked with effort one little mile, and thought it a great feat." "How I keep on my legs and in my senses with such little snatches of sleep is a wonder to myself." "*O me miseram*, not one wink of sleep the whole night through." "My heart is very sore to-night, but I have promised not to make this Journal a *miserere*, and so I will take a dose of morphia and do the impossible to sleep."

In these, and many other passages that might be quoted, the alienist will readily recognise the cerebral neurasthenia that is so often accompanied by profound dejection and mad fancies. And many collateral proofs of the existence of that condition might be quoted. While borne down by her own sorrows, Mrs. Carlyle developed some of that hunger for the horrible, which is morbid when it appears in a woman on her mental level. She searched the evening papers for thrilling incidents, and noted in her private journal the cases of a workman suffocated in a sewer by the falling in of earth, of a boy who was killed by a great waggon crashing over his head, and, with great minuteness, that of a woman who threw her three children into the Thames, drowning one

of them—from jealousy of a pretty apple woman, as Mrs. Carlyle was fain to believe, although she was judicially found insane. She actually at this time procured photographs of a number of noted murderers and placed them in her album, where they remain to this day. Mrs. Carlyle came herself rightly to understand her own frame of mind at the time of the anguish that burst forth in the Journal. The plaintive and tortured expressions cited were written in 1855 and 1856; but in 1857, she had largely recovered her equanimity and adopted a very different strain. Writing to her husband from Haddington in July that year, she said: "I never saw the country about here look so lovely, but I viewed it all with a calm about as morbid as my excitement was last year." A little later she tells him: "And so I have made up my mind to turn over a new leaf, and no more give words to the impatient or desponding thoughts that rise in my mind about myself. It is not a natural vice of mine, that sort of egotistic babblement, that has been fastened in me by the patience and sympathy shown me in my late long illness." Again: "So long as I had a noisy bedroom or miscooked food, even I had something to attribute my sleeplessness to; now I can only attribute it to my diseased nerves."

Had the symptoms at the time left any doubt as to the real meaning of the terrible despondency from which Mrs. Carlyle suffered, her subsequent history must have removed it. In 1863 she suffered from violent neuralgia which deprived her of the use of her left hand and arm, and two years later the same malady, after internal complications, rendered her right hand and arm powerless, at the same time partially paralysing the muscles of the jaw and causing difficulty in speech. Along with the neuralgia, as it was then labelled—the more advanced neuro-pathology of to-day would probably give it another name—phrenalgia or mind pain returned, very acutely, but this time it did not become delusional, but was connected with her bodily sufferings. So far was there from being any jealousy of her husband at this time, that her affections went forth towards him with bounteous confidence. From St. Leonards, she writes to him, "Oh! my darling, God have pity on us." "Oh, my husband I am suffering torments; each day I suffer more horribly. Oh I would like you beside me! But I wish to live for you if only I could live out of torment." But with all her gushing love for her husband there were strong suicidal promptings. Direct admissions and allusions show this. In September, 1864, she wrote: "After all those nights that I lay meditating on self-destruction as my only escape from insanity." "White lace and red roses," she remarks in another letter, "don't become a woman who has been looking both death and insanity in the face for a year." With her great load of misery there came to her—who shall say whence or how?—a revival of religious sentiment. She who had so long stood at the Centre of Indifference, became profuse in ejaculatory prayer and echoes of the creed of her childhood. "God knows if we shall ever meet again," she wrote to her Aunt Miss Welsh, "and His will be done. I commit you to the Lord's keeping, whether I live or die." "Oh, if God would only lift my trouble from off me," she cried, "so far that I could bear it all in silence and not add to the trouble of others." "God can raise me up, but will He? Oh, I am weary, weary." "Nobody can help me! Only God, and can I wonder if God take no heed of me when I have all my life taken no heed of Him?" Mrs. Carlyle died in 1866 from failure of the heart's action caused by the shock of seeing her little dog run over and injured by a carriage in Hyde Park.

Up till the date I have fixed for the incursion of her illness, Mrs. Carlyle's letters to her husband are like those of one still in love's young dream, ardent and playful. "God keep you, my own dear husband, and bring you safe back. The house looks very empty without you, and I feel empty too." "She (your wife) loves you and is ready to do anything on earth that you wish, to fly over the moon if you bade her." And so on until 1844, when we read, "Oh, my darling, I want to give you an emphatic kiss rather than to write. But you are at Chelsea and I am at Seaforth, so the thing is clearly impossible for the moment. But I must keep it for you till I come, for it is not with words that I can thank you for that kindest of birthday letters and its small enclosure—the little key." And so on indeed, until 1846, when the glimmerings of distrust appear. "Yes," she then writes, "I have kissed the dear little card case (another birthday gift) and now I will lie down awhile and try to sleep. At least to quiet myself I will try to believe, Oh! why cannot I believe once for all? that with all my faults and follies I am still dearer to you than any other earthly creature." But after this the correspondence cools. The letters have no amatory introduction, are subscribed "faithfully yours" or "yours ever," and contain sometimes sharp taunts and querulous reproaches, sometimes acknowledgments of her own infirmity. "God knows," she tells him in 1850, "how gladly I would be sweet-tempered and cheerful-hearted and all that sort of thing for your single sake, if my temper were not soured and my heart saddened beyond my power to amend them." It was not until the lapse of years had brought healing, and convinced her that his strange humours had never arisen from any real indifference towards her that the old tenderness returned: but it is pleasant to know that it did return, for in 1864 we find her beginning her letters with all a girl's effusive fondness: "Oh, my own Darling Husband." . . .

The letters written in her girlhood to Eliza Stodart display a somewhat headstrong disposition and biting sarcasm, remarkable in one still in the bright and genial morning of youth, who had suffered no hardships or disappointments, and are couched in language so frank and strong as to make it certain she did not derive from her husband the expletives she used in later life. "Do

you know, Mrs. Carlyle," the elder Stirling once said to her, "you would be a vast deal more amiable if you were not so damnably clever." "It must be admitted," says even her champion, Froude, "Mrs. Carlyle knew how to administer a shrewing"; but much of his blundering arose out of his inability to distinguish between her shrewing and croaking and cooing covertly. Preconceived idea again uppermost, he took literally many of her sallies and allusions to her husband, which were purposely Brobdingnagian in their dimensions. He failed to realise that hyperbole was her favourite figure. Had he taken her jocose descriptions of her negotiations with her domestic servants as seriously as he does some of her denunciations of her husband, he must have written her down the veriest termagant. Had he listened gravely to her anathemas on bugs, he must have regarded her as an Entomological mono-maniac. . . .

To many of Carlyle's readers in all parts of the world these ***New Letters and Memorials*** will be acceptable by removing misconceptions about him and his wife, and affording good proof that they really lived if not an ideal married life, a nearer approach to that than has been believed since Froude besmirched the record of it. And beyond this the ***Letters*** have a distinctive relish of their own. "Jane," Mrs. Montague once said to Mrs. Carlyle, "everybody is born with a vocation, and yours is to write little notes."

The Nation (review date 28 May 1903)

SOURCE: "The Carlyles," review of *New Letters and Memorials of Jane Welsh Carlyle*, edited by Alexander Carlyle. *The Nation* 76 (28 May 1903): 439-40.

[*In the following brief excerpt, the reviewer remarks on the distinctly feminine quality of Carlyle's letters.*]

Mrs. Carlyle was a born letter-writer, and no one can take up these volumes [***New Letters and Memorials of Jane Welsh Carlyle***] without finding in them something amusing, witty, gay and original. With all their strength, they are thoroughly feminine. In her notebook she jots down among her memorabilia that "letters are of the neuter gender," but she spent her life in disproving it. A great number of them possess no particular interest; but this, as the introduction explains, was to be expected.

Lord Ernle (review date July 1924)

SOURCE: Ernle, Lord. "Mrs Carlyle and English Letter-Writing," review of *Jane Welsh Carlyle: Letters to Her Family, 1839-1863*, edited by Leonard Huxley. *Quarterly Review* 242, no. 480 (July 1924): 193-210.

[*In the following excerpt, Ernle evaluates the content and style of Carlyle's letters, appraising her writing both for its high literary quality and for what it reveals about her personality.*]

It is the personal interest which makes the posthumous publication of any new collections of modern letters irresistibly attractive. A private correspondence, especially if it is unreserved in its intimacy, strongly appeals to the wide circle of readers who despise avowed fiction or prefer real life to literature. Genuine letters bring us into actual intercourse with other human beings on terms of peculiar intimacy. They may contain for us true comedies and tragedies, which are as dramatic as any of the creations of the imagination of the novelist. If they are written by eminent persons, or deal with remarkable events, the attractions are doubtless enhanced. It is agreeable to know how great people deal with domesticities or to have sketches of historical scenes from the pens of eye-witnesses and actors. But letters of the highest class are independent of such supports. The writer may be obscure, the life uneventful, the subject-matter commonplace. If the self-portraiture is unconscious, and is aided by the natural charm of presentation, the letters will live on their own merits.

It is often difficult to distinguish how far the interest of a collection of letters is derived from the subject-matter, from the writer's personality, or from the literary form. Yet, in considering critically whether the letters are in themselves of first-rate value, the distinction may become necessary. Some correspondences, for instance, which, from the literary point of view, are of very second-rate importance, are widely read because of the autobiographical, biographical, or historical matter that they contain. The writers are not, for that reason, among the great masters. But, in the case of Jane Welsh Carlyle it is unnecessary to attempt to draw the distinction, because all three sources of interest contribute to the attraction. Her own character is singularly arresting; she is the wife of Thomas Carlyle; she is the friend of many well-known contemporaries; she is a mistress of literary form. Her letters are in the modern rather than in the classic style. They chronicle her own personal feelings and the impressions that events or people produce upon her. Her own life-history is laid bare without reserve yet not without restraint. Her daily life, domestic, social, personal, is recorded with an amazing facility of expression and frequent felicity of phrase, with a keen eye for the ludicrous, and with a humour which masks the earnestness, and sometimes the bitterness, of the thought and feeling.

Mrs Carlyle's story has in it the elements of tragedy. In her romantic youth she had, with the help of Rousseau, pictured an imaginary husband.

> No lover [she wrote to her cousin, Miss Stodart, in 1821], will Jane Welsh ever find like St Preux, no husband like Wolmar (I don't mean to insinuate that *I should like both*); and to no man will she ever give her heart and pretty hand who bears to these no resemblance. . . . O Lord, O Lord! Where is the St Preux? Where is the Wolmar? Bess, I am in earnest—I shall never marry.

Later, in the same letter, she says that she has heard from Thomas Carlyle.

> He is something liker to St Preux than George Craik is to Wolmar. He has *his* talents, *his* vast and cultivated mind, *his* vivid imagination, *his* independence of soul, and *his* high-souled principles of honour. But then—Ah, these *buts*—St Preux never kicked the fire-irons, nor made puddings in his tea-cup. Want of Elegance! Want of Elegance, Rousseau says, is a defect which no woman can overlook.

Above all things, she wanted a man of genius for her husband. It was her youthful ambition, and it was gratified. If happiness always lay where Gibbon so complacently found it—in the mature fulfilment of an aspiration of youth—she should have been abundantly happy. Unfortunately, her life rather illustrated the cruel maxim that to those whom the gods curse they grant the desire of their hearts. She could not always take Carlyle humorously, or habitually practise the cheerful Horatian philosophy of her rival among women letter-writers, Lady Mary Wortley Montagu. In the course of years, the 'buts' of life, aided by ill-health, became too strong for her happiness.

In her correspondence, as well as in her social intercourse with friends, acquaintances, and strangers, she made a gallant fight, with fine courage. To her came for sympathy and help all the 'maimed and halt' in life, and to none did she refuse her best. She was worshipped with foreign fervour by the political refugees who flocked to Cheyne Row, and in her presence even the craziest recovered their sanity. She was adored by a succession of servants. Socially, she was much more than the Lion's Wife; she made her own position, and won her own triumphs. She was asked out to make parties 'go.' However ill she might feel, 'even when in a humour that a person under sentence of death might have envied,' her vivacity and wit did not fail. At the Macreadys, she had not had, she says:

> one cheerful feeling in my mind for days and weeks; but of course one does not make calls to make oneself a *spectacle of woe*. I talked—talked about the feats of Carlyle's horse &c.—and they laughed till their tears ran down. *I* could not *laugh*—but no matter—perhaps my own gravity made the things I was saying only more amusing by contrast.

No wonder that Mrs Macready should have believed that Mrs Carlyle did not know what it 'is to be ever sad for a minute!!! One never sees you that you do not keep one in fits of laughter!' Even an 'outrageous pimple' on her nose, which distressed her sorely, did not alienate her admirers. 'Damn your nose,' said Anthony Sterling, to whom she complained of the annoyance, 'for a sensible woman you have really the *oddest* ideas! As if anybody really attached to you could love you an atom less if you were all covered over with smallpox!'

Yet the letters of the last twenty-five years of her life are not those of a happy woman. If this new collection [*Jane Welsh Carlyle: Letters to Her Family, 1839-1863*], which belongs to the period 1839-63, stood alone, or were taken with absolute literalness, it might be thought that things were worse with her than, in all probability, they really were. Allowances must be made. Some of the letters were written in the morbid mood of ill-health. In others, as Mr Huxley reminds us, she uses the language of humorous exaggeration in writing to a niece who had been an inmate of Carlyle's household and an eye-witness of his wife's domestic troubles. Yet, in spite of discounting much that appears on the surface of the letters, they do, as we turn the pages, strengthen the impression that we are the spectators of the tragedy of a woman's heart. It was not that she seriously doubted Carlyle's deep affection for her. But, as penurious of praise as he was of pence, he was too self-centred to be considerate or to pay those small tributes of recognition which mean much to a wife. Toiling for him from morning to night, mending his clothes, cooking, cleaning, upholstering, and papering and painting with her own hands, her Cinderella-like labours were grudgingly accepted as something less than his due. She was starved for the expression of affection or approval from the man whom she admired and loved.

Great books are not written without blood and tears, nor is it always only the writer who weeps and bleeds. Habit and custom had done something for Mrs Carlyle, though they never subdued the 'fatal romance' of her character. She had passed beyond the 'dreary helpless' stage of 'first unlearning to be a much-made-of Only Child.' But her 'fur mantle of imperturbability' was not always proof against 'the winter of our discontent' which set in when a book was being written. These were indeed times of tribulation. Carlyle, never easy to live with, must have been almost intolerable to the inmates of his household. He ought to have had, says Mrs Carlyle,

> a strong-minded woman for wife, with a perfectly sound liver, plenty of *solid fat,* and mirth and good humour world without end—men do best with their opposites. *I* am too like himself in some things—especially as to the state of our lives, and so we aggravate one another's tendencies to despair!

The fattest and strongest-minded of women might have endured the 'sulphury and brimstoneish' atmosphere of one of the periods of composition with more philosophic calm; she could not have described these occasions with more vivacity.

> Carlyle [says his wife] is now got about as deep in the *Hell* of his Cromwell as he is likely to get—there is a certain point of irritability and gloom, which, when attained, I say to myself "now soul take thy ease—such ease as thou canst get—for nothing worse can well be!" Desperation in that case induces a sort of content.

Or again:

> The Cromwell-turmoil is again subsiding. . . . *Thanks God!* and now I hope we shall really be done with that man! if he had been my husband's own Father he could not have gone thro' more hardship for him! We have lived in the valley of the shadow of Cromwell now, as of Death, for some three years. But everything comes to an end if one have patience. What is to come next Heaven knows.

At times like these, Carlyle was 'a man of sorrows *not* acquainted with *silence*—tho' he does love it platonically.' Even when some 'Reign of Terror,' established by the writing of a book, was not raging at its full height, there were other permanent troubles. Carlyle belonged, said his wife, to the 'perplexed and perplexing section of humanity,' to whom 'the difficulty of realising their desires is small, compared with the difficulty of ascertaining for themselves what their real desires are.' Incessant changes of plans exercised Mrs Carlyle's patience sorely. She found it impossible to live 'a rational, never to say a contented life' in a state of always 'hanging in the wind.' Nor, if she had really been the kind of woman who could never overlook 'Want of Elegance,' would she have always been satisfied with her husband's appearance. Carlyle was in the habit of stuffing his ears with cotton wool to shut out the sound.

> C's hair [writes his wife] is creeping slowly over the tops of his ears, but that is all the way it has got. Meanwhile the *cotton* is still used for *one* ear—in which, however, it never stays long, but is generally to be seen (not without astonishment by the uninitiated) sticking, a small white pellet, at the end of some stray hair—for all the world like a snow berry.

On the other hand, there are abundant signs of mutual affection and good understanding between husband and wife. She knew that he could always be relied on to be 'good on great occasions'; she wrote to him every second day when he was absent, defended him against his critics, treasured his sayings, took pride in his growing fame, noted with satisfaction the signs of the 'Millennium—attentions from Booksellers are more infallible proof of *rise in the world* for people in our line than a whole string of coroneted carriages at the door.' She helped him to choose his pipes. He even trusted her to order his coats and trousers, till, one day, she ordered a coat of '*Sky blue* and *yellow buttons* which made him an ornament to Society in every direction'—and quite shook his 'faith in my judgement (he told me) "so far as the dressing of him was concerned."' He, on his side, was proud of her social gifts, of her popularity with his men friends, nicknamed her 'Destroyer of the peace of families' from the number of wives whom she made jealous, or suddenly exclaimed, as she was sitting half-awake over her coffee, 'just to look at you there, looking as if butter would not melt in your mouth, and think of the profligate life you lead!' Readers of the ***Letters and Memorials of Jane Welsh Carlyle*** will remember her touching letter (No. 87, July 14, 1846) expressing her delight at a birthday present of a card-case, and her remorse at having, for a moment, thought herself forgotten. In the new collection of letters two similar presents are recorded, and the explanation given illustrates the thoughtful kindness of Carlyle. It shows him in a pleasant light. So 'sacred' was his 'horror of shopping,' that he was 'puzzled to buy his own indispensables.' It needed no ordinary effort for such a man, not only to buy but to devise a gift. Yet, after the death of Mrs Welsh, in order that his wife might feel less desolate on such anniversaries as her birthdays and New Year's Day, Carlyle made a practice of giving her presents on these occasions. For Christmas, 1847, he had

> in a fit of audacity almost incredible chosen to buy a cloak! a woman's cloak . . . he was much consoled by my assurance that *it could be worn.* He had bought it by gaslight, he said, and "felt quite desperate about it when he saw it in the morning." But it is a wonderful cloak for *him* to have bought—warm and not *very* ugly—and a good shape.

The letters contain many details about Carlyle's friendship with Lady Ashburton. Mrs Carlyle was by no means always blind to the comedy of the situation. She notes with amused satisfaction that Lady Ashburton has set up

> a green parrot to which she pays the most marked attention even in spite of his calling it a *green chimera.* And the Parrot does not mind interrupting *him* when he is speaking—does not fear to *speak thro' him* (as the phrase is) and her Ladyship *listens to the parrot*—even when C is saying the most sensible things! By Heaven she is *the very cleverest* woman I ever saw or heard of.

Nor, whatever Mrs Carlyle might write in private letters to her cousin, did she wear her heart on her sleeve. Waiting for dinner at a party given by Dickens,

> old Rogers, who ought to have been buried long ago, so old and ill-natured is he grown, said to me, pointing to a chair beside him, "Sit down, my dear,—I want to ask you; is your husband as much infatuated as ever with Lady Ashburton?" "Oh, of course," I said *laughing,* "why shouldn't he?" "Now—do you *like* her—tell me honestly is she kind to *you*—as kind as she is to your husband?" "Why you know it is impossible for *me* to know *how* kind she is to my husband; but I *can* say she is extremely kind to *me* and I should be stupid and ungrateful if I did *not* like her." "Humph! (disappointedly) Well! it is very good of you to like her when she takes away all your husband's company from you—he is always there isn't he?" "Oh gracious no! (still laughing *admirably*) he writes and reads a great deal in his own study." "But he spends all his evenings with her I am told?" "No—not all—for example you see he is *here* this evening." "Yes," he said in a tone of vexation, "I *see* he is here *this* evening—and hear him

too—for he has done nothing but talk across the room since he came in." Very devilish old man! but he got no satisfaction to his devilishness out of *me.*

Whatever may have been the trials of Mrs Carlyle's life, there were compensations. As 'the Man of Genius's Wife'—it is her own phrase—she lived among some of the most interesting men of the day. If they came to Cheyne Row, in the first instance, to see Carlyle, not a few returned to see his wife. Alfred Tennyson was one of those who did so. On the first occasion, he had come to see Carlyle who was dining out.

> Alfred is dreadfully embarrassed with women alone—for he entertains at one and the same moment a feeling of almost adoration for them and an ineffable contempt! adoration I suppose for what they *might* be—contempt for what they *are!* The only chance of my getting any right good of him was to make him forget my womanness—so I did just what Carlyle would have done, had he been there; got out *pipes* and *tobacco*—and *brandy* and *water*—with a deluge of *tea* over and above. The effect of these accessories was miraculous—he *professed* to be *ashamed* of polluting my room, felt, he said, "as if he were stealing cups and sacred vessels in the Temple"—but he smoked all the same—for *three* mortal hours!—talking like an angel—only exactly as if he were talking with a clever *man.*

The humility of the attitude of a clever woman towards a man, and, perhaps, even the adoration for Tennyson, may strike some people as early Victorian. Anyhow, it was not long before Tennyson came again—this time to see Mrs Carlyle and not her husband. At an 'Amateur Play,' in which Dickens and Forster acted, she

> met Alfred Tennyson in the lobby—and that was the best of it! And better still he came to take tea and talk and smoke with me—me—by myself me—the following evening—such at least was his *intention,* not a little flattering to my vanity considering his normal state of indolence—but the result was that he found *Creek* (Craik) and *John* (Carlyle) and *they* made a mess of it. "The Devil fly away with them both."

Interesting figures, vivaciously described, appear in the letters, or take part in improvised dinner-parties at Cheyne Row. Mazzini and other political refugees, especially Godefroi Cavaignac, drop in at all hours of the day or night. Many ludicrous episodes are recorded of the Italian artist, Gambardella, who painted her portrait for nothing, or, as Carlyle suggested, because 'he must be very much in love with the *subject*—that is all.' One of the most absurd arose out of his unfortunate wording of an advertisement for a servant which he had inserted in the press: 'Wanted a very genteel girl to do very genteel work—not under fifteen nor exceeding eighteen years of age,' etc. But the whole story, told with admirable spirit, is too long to quote.

In December 1843, at past the age of forty-two, Mrs Carlyle danced. The occasion was that of a party at Mrs Macready's house. It was the *very* most agreeable party that ever I was at in London—everybody there seemed animated with one purpose to make up to Mrs Macready and her children for the absence of "The Tragic Actor" and so amiable a purpose produced the most joyous results. Dickens and Forster above all exerted themselves till the perspiration was pouring down and they seemed *drunk* with their efforts! Only think of that excellent Dickens playing the *conjuror* for one whole hour—the *best* conjuror I ever saw—(and I have paid money to see several) . . . Then the dancing—old Major Burns with his one eye—old Jerdan of the Literary Gazette (escaped out of the Rules of the Queen's Bench for the great occasion!)—the gigantic Thackeray &c &c all capering like Mænades!! Dickens did all but go down on his knees to make *me*—waltz with him! But I thought I did my part well enough in talking the maddest nonsense with *him*, Forster, Thackeray and Maclise—without attempting the Impossible—however *after supper* when we were all madder than ever . . . a universal country dance was proposed, and Forster *seizing me round the waist* whirled me into the thick of it and *made* me dance!! like a person in the tread-mill who must move forward or be crushed to death. Once I cried out "Oh for the love of Heaven let me go! you are going to dash my brains out against the folding doors!" to which he answered (you can fancy his tone)—"your brains? who cares about their brains *here?* let them go!" . . . After all! the pleasantest company, as Burns thought, *are* the *blackguards!*—that is: those who have just a sufficient dash of blackguardism in them to make them snap their fingers at *ceremony* and "all that sort of thing." I question if there was as much witty speech uttered in all the aristocratic, conventional drawing rooms thro'out London that night as among us little knot of blackguardist literary people who felt ourselves above all rules, and independent of the universe!

Another ball at which Mrs Carlyle was present was at Bath House in July 1850. Carlyle insisted on her going. He was 'quite determined for once in his life to see an aristocratic Ball.' Her objections were overruled. He would buy the dress. Of course, it must be cut low.

> True propriety consisted in conforming to other people's fashions!!! and Eve he supposed had as much sense of decency as I had and *she* wore no clothes at all!!! So I got a white silk dress . . . cut down to the due pitch of indecency! I could have gone into fits of crying when I began to put it on—but I looked so astonishingly well in it by *candle light,* and when I got into the fine rooms amongst the universally *bare* people I felt so much in *keeping,* that I forgot my neck and arms almost immediately. I was glad *after* that I went—not for any pleasure I had at the time, being past dancing, and knowing but few people—but it is an additional idea for life, to have seen such a party—all the Duchesses one ever heard tell of blazing in diamonds, all the young beauties of the season, all the distinguished statesmen &c &c were to be seen among the six or seven hundred people present—and the rooms all hung with artificial roses looked like an Arabian Nights entertainment—what pleased me best was the good look I got *into the eyes* of the old Duke of Wellington—one has no notion, seeing him in the streets, what a dear kind face he has.

The times at which Mrs Carlyle wrote were less passionate and exciting than those of Byron and Shelley. The temperature had cooled. The tone of feeling had dropped to a lower pitch. But whatever was left of fervour and unconventionality was to be found in Mrs Carlyle's intimate circle, and she lived in daily communion with the man who was the potent influence in new movements, social, political, and intellectual. There is, therefore, in the material of the correspondence abundance of vitality and interest. The letters touch life at many varied points. There is little literary criticism. But the writers of many books pass across the pages—not only Dickens, Thackeray, and Tennyson, but lesser lights like Harriet Martineau, Helps, Monckton, Milnes, Mrs Gaskell, Lady Eastlake, FitzGerald, George Lewes, Aubrey de Vere. Nor do literary celebrities occupy the whole of the picture. Life in Cheyne Row is mixed with that of great houses both in London and in the country. Musicians like Chopin, painters like Maclise, rising politicians like Charles Buller, social leaders like Lady Ashburton, mingle in the scene.

The wish is often expressed for the opportunity of talking with those who lived a century or more ago. The desire is gratified by Mrs Carlyle's correspondence. Her letters afford the privilege of listening to the vivacious sparkling conversation of one of the most gifted women of last century. They preserve much of the animation and charm of her spoken talk. They are genuine improvisations, frank outpourings of what was uppermost in her mind. Nothing is studied—least of all the punctuation. Mrs Carlyle is, as all good letter-writers must be, sensitive to external impressions, and she sets them down with an extraordinary facility of expression, and with all the naturalness of unpremeditated art. It is these characteristics, sustained throughout her copious correspondence, that give her one of the highest places among English letter-writers. Possibly, many readers will agree that, while the new collection confirms her position, it does not enhance her reputation. The letters do not belong to the best period of her life. In nearly every case, people write their finest letters in the freshness, buoyancy, and fearlessness of youth. It is true of Mrs Carlyle. First-rate letter-writers need a dash of egotism. In youth, it is swallowed up in the triumphant joy of life. In middle age, it tends to become more self-concentrated, and with some, as with Mrs Carlyle, to be absorbed in personal ailments. Her letters in the new collection suffer from an excess of headaches and blue pill.

H. L. Creek (essay date April 1926)

SOURCE: Creek, H. L. "The Opinions of Jane Welsh Carlyle." *Sewanee Review* 34 (April 1926): 156-68.

[*In the following essay, Creek examines the influence of romantic literature on Carlyle's letters.*]

Jane Welsh was married to Thomas Carlyle on October 17, 1826, and lived with him during thirty-nine and one-half years. In a massive and brilliant biography of the husband, Froude made of her a tragic heroine, sacrificed to her husband's greatness and selfishness, and described those four decades as if they had been, for the wife, forty years of torture. Indignant friends and relatives of Carlyle at once denied Froude's allegations bitterly, beginning a controversy that has already lasted longer than four decades. Now Mr. D. A. Wilson, hoping to supersede Froude, writes another and what promises to be an even more massive biography of that husband in which he says that their life together was one long honeymoon.

This dispute, involving as it does an interpretation of the character of the greatest writer of English prose of the nineteenth century, has created an interest in Mrs. Carlyle that shows no signs of diminishing. That interest is sustained by the brilliancy of her letters, which, according to Lord Ernle, editor of Byron's letters and a competent judge, are those of the last of the great English letter-writers. In an attempt to understand her and the tragedy of her life, I have collected from these letters, so frankly written to her intimate friends and relatives and so copiously and even brutally given to the world, some of the opinions that show as well as anything can what manner of woman she was.

In reading these opinions one should have in mind the main facts in the life, particularly the early life, of Jane Welsh Carlyle. She was an only child, perhaps a spoiled one, belonging to a family of some means as well as of superior social standing. Her youth was protected and happy, and as she grew up she did not lack admirers among the young men who knew her. She was not inexperienced in affairs of the heart when she met Carlyle. Although she recognized his superior powers, she did not find him—not quickly, and perhaps not ever—the ideal lover for whom her heart longed. Nevertheless, Jane became Mrs. Thomas Carlyle in time, attached to her husband, if not deeply in love, admiring his genius, and having faith in his future greatness. And after ten or twelve years of sacrifice and hardship, six of them spent at Craigenputtock and, later, three or four in London, Mrs. Carlyle began to see her faith justified. Her husband was acclaimed one of the greatest of English men of letters. This success brought rewards to Mrs. Carlyle in a vivid and interesting social life which she evidently enjoyed so far as her uncertain health made enjoyment possible. She had many masculine admirers, who visited her constantly, keeping her in touch with the world. Among these were several distinguished persons, both English and foreign—Mazzini, the Italian patriot; Godefroi Cavaignac, a French republican and brother of a man who later was President of France; Anthony Sterling, brother of the John made famous by Carlyle's *Life of John Sterling*; Erasmus Darwin, brother of Charles, and John Forster. These were her friends rather than her husband's. It seems that she was even suspected—by persons who did not know the facts—of being too fond of one or two of them, particularly Cavaignac. The wife of Anthony Sterling was insanely jealous of her. Mrs. Carlyle mentions humorously in one of her letters written in middle life a declaration of love by one of her admirers. Her husband was pleased, it seems, by the attentions she received, and was amused by the jealousy she excited among women. Unfortunately, ill health pursued her during many years, making continued happiness difficult if not impossible.

In reading the letters, one is never unconscious of this ill health for long, and yet one is more conscious of an intense life. It is intensity of life that make the letters so good. At their best, they are superb—extraordinarily vivid and witty, with satirical sketches of people, humorous accounts of the trifling events that make up life, and scattered bits of philosophy, often decidedly cynical. Even the quotations I shall make will reveal the literary power of this strange and interesting woman at the same time that they explain her character and her unhappiness.

First of all I shall try to show some of Mrs. Carlyle's opinions of books and their writers. She was a copious but capricious reader, entirely without her husband's ability to plough through twenty solid volumes at the rate of a volume a day. As a girl she selected extremely romantic books. Byron was her particular idol, as numerous references show. After reading Irving's *Bracebridge Hall*, she wrote to Carlyle, then a warm friend, in 1822: "He is a witty, amiable sort of person, Mr. Irving; but oh, he wants fire and he is *far too happy* for me. Dear Byron, sinner as he is, there is nobody like him. I have got his likeness; better done than the one I had. I can scarcely help crying when I look at it and think I may chance to go out of the world without seeing its original. What nonsense!"

Even before this she had referred to Byron's "Fare Thee Well" as her favorite song. After reading Byron's volume containing *Sardanapalus* she wrote to her admirer: "I have read the Tragedies. I thank you for them. They are Byron's: need *I* praise them?" Again, she exalts Byron's *Werner*: "Is it not a masterly performance? He is my own matchless Byron after all!" And her receiving the news of Byron's death is told thus: "And Byron is dead! I was told it all at once in a roomful of people. My God, if they had said that the sun or moon had gone out of the heavens, it could not have struck me with the idea of a more dreary blank in the creation than the words, 'Byron is dead!' I have felt quite cold and dejected ever since: all my thoughts have been fearful and dismal."

The same devotion to Byron appears in a letter written in January, 1825, several months after Byron's death.

Carlyle had sent her some autographs, among which was a scrap of writing by Byron. Jane wrote: "The autographs you have sent me have all of them a value in my curiosity-loving eyes; but Byron's handwriting—my own Byron—I esteem not as a *curiosity,* but rather as a relic of an honoured and beloved friend."

The twin god of Jane Welsh's idolatry was Rousseau. Irving, her former lover, who continued for some years to take a Platonic interest in her welfare, wrote to Thomas Carlyle: "I could wish to see her surrounded by a more sober set of companions than Rousseau (your friend) and Byron, and such like." A quotation from a letter to a girl friend, Miss Stodart, which is devoted mainly to Rousseau's *Héloise,* will show how great her enthusiasm was: "Alas! I told you I should die a virgin, if I reached twenty *in vain.* Even so will it prove. This book, this fatal book, has given me an idea of a love so *pure* (yes, you may laugh! but I repeat it), so pure, so constant, so disinterested, so exalted, that no love the men of this world can offer me will ever fill up the picture my imagination has drawn me with the help of Rousseau. No lover will Jane Welsh ever find like St. Preux, no husband like Wolmar (I don't mean to insinuate that *I should like both*); and to no man will she ever give her heart and pretty hand who bears to these no resemblance."

Carlyle was far from being the perfect lover. "He is something liker St. Preux than George Craig is to Wolmar. He has *his* talents, *his* vast and cultivated mind, *his* vivid imagination, *his* independence of soul, and *his* high-souled principles of honour. But then—Ah, these *buts*! St. Preux never kicked the fire-irons, nor made puddings in his teacup. Want of Elegance! Want of Elegance, Rousseau says, is a defect which no woman can overlook."

Another romantic writer who aroused Jane Welsh's enthusiasm was Ann Radcliffe. The allusions to Mrs. Radcliffe's sentimental romances of terror that I have found are in the letters of later years, but the time of Jane's enthusiasm was in her 'teens or earlier. A passage from a letter of 1848 will be sufficient to indicate the strength of that early enthrallment: "I had been reading Swift all day; but I found that now too prosaical for my romantic circumstances [she was then at Addiscombe, the home of the Barings, later Lord and Lady Ashburton]; and, seeking through the books, I came upon *The Romance of the Forest,* which I seized on with avidity, remembering the 'tremendous' emotions with which I read it in my night-shift, by the red light of our dying school-room fire, nearly half a century ago, when I was supposed to be sleeping the sleep of good children. And over that I actually spent the whole evening; it was so interesting to measure my progress—downwards, I must think—by comparing my present feelings at certain well-remembered passages with the past. After all, it

might have been worse with my imaginative past. I decidedly like the dear old book, even in this year of grace, better than *Rose Blanche, &c.*"

Other romantic writers who were read by Jane in her early twenties included Chateaubriand, Madame de Staël, and Alfieri. In connection with Madame de Staël's *Delphine,* she wrote: "I declare the idea of having Madame de Staël for an acquaintance in the world of spirits makes me half wish to die." A few months later she wrote to Carlyle: "My mother thanks you for *Delphine,* but declares she will never undertake six volumes of love again. I think such beautiful love is very endurable."

Carlyle introduced her to German writers, and she took strongly to Schiller, particularly *Die Jungfrau von Orleans,* but cared less for Goethe—at least at first. "He has fire enough, but it is not the celestial fire of Schiller." Under Carlyle's influence she also tried historical reading—Gibbon, Sismondi, Robertson; Hume she refused to try again, having formerly failed with him. This reading apparently progressed rather slowly. The chapter on Christianity in Gibbon she called "really capital"; her religious views were evidently none too orthodox. Latin studies, we are told, had made her into a sort of pagan.

That reading romantic literature left a marked impression on the mind of Miss Welsh appears in the following lines from a letter to Thomas Carlyle written in October, 1823, three years before the marriage: "Oh, be careful of yourself! for the world's sake and for mine. Were I again to lose the friend of my soul, again to be left alone in the midst of society,—loving no one yet possessing the faculty to love, perceiving nothing but the blackness of death in the universe around me; in the bustle and glitter and grandeur of the earth, nothing but the parade of a funeral,—Great God, how wretched, how ruined I should be! But you shall live to be my Guardian-Angel—it cannot be the will of a merciful God that I should return to the dreary existence which I endured before we met—it cannot be His will that a soul born to enlighten the earth, to be the Daystar of ages, should be obscured by the shadows of death ere a world has perceived its splendour. You shall live to love me while I live, and to mourn for me when I die; and the thought that I shall be mourned by a heart so warm and true will overcome the terrors of death."

Thus far I have been quoting from the correspondence of Jane Welsh, the romantic girl of twenty or so. Now I ask you to imagine that about twenty years had passed. The Carlyles were in London, associating freely with most distinguished people of the time. The comments that Mrs. Carlyle made in her letters were chiefly on the people she met, but books were included too, and since the people she met were often the authors of the books she read, I shall not separate sharply the comments upon the authors from the comments upon the books.

We find that we have passed from romantic youth to sharp-sighted, disillusioned middle age. I begin with a remark or two upon Dinah Mulock, later famous as the author of *John Halifax, Gentleman,* who had just published *The Ogilvies* (1849). They show the changed woman who wrote them. "The Ogilvies—curious as being written by a young Irish girl—twenty years old [eighteen in another letter of Mrs. Carlyle's; twenty-three actually]—with little knowledge of *anything,* Society included—but it is full of Love 'as an egg's full of meat'—the old high-flown romantic circulating library sort of love—which one looks at in these days of 'the new ideas' as one would look at a pair of peaked shoes or a ruff out of the reign of Elizabeth." Even more pointed are these sentences in another letter (to John Forster): "Meanwhile thanks for Mulock's book, which I read with immense interest. It is long since I fell in with a novel of this sort, all about love, and nothing else whatever. It quite reminds one of one's own love's young dream. I like it, and like the poor girl who can still believe, or even 'believe that she believes' all that. God help her! She will sing to another tune if she go on living and writing for twenty years."

Perhaps with this may be mentioned Mrs. Carlyle's opinion of the separation of the Ruskins. "I know nothing about it, except that I have always pitied Mrs. Ruskin, while people generally blame her,—for love of dress and company and flirtation. She was too young and pretty to be so left to her own devices as she was by her husband who seemed to wish nothing but the credit of having a pretty, well-dressed wife."

There is a long account of a Dickens dinner, in which she speaks of three famous literary persons. Of the dinner itself which was a very elaborate one, she wrote: "Such getting up of the steam is unbecoming to a literary man who *ought* to have his basis elsewhere than on what the old Annandale women called 'Ornament and grander'." Mrs. Gaskell, who was present, she called "a natural unassuming woman whom they have been doing their best to spoil by making a lioness of her." But on Samuel Rogers, who at the same dinner tried to quiz her about Carlyle's attentions to Lady Ashburton, she vented her spleen. "Old Rogers," she called him, "who ought to have been buried long ago, so old and ill-natured he is grown. . . . Very devilish old man!"

At another time we have a glimpse of Dickens at a party given by the family of Macready, the famous actor, who was then away from home. "Everybody there seemed animated with one purpose to make up to Mrs. Macready and her children for the absence of 'The Tragic Actor'. . . . Dickens and Forster, above all exerted themselves till the perspiration was pouring down

and they seemed drunk with their efforts. Only think of Dickens playing the *conjuror* for one whole hour!—the best conjuror I ever saw—. . . Dickens did all but go down on his knees to make *me* waltz with him . . . After all—the pleasantest company, as Burns thought, *are* the *blackguards!*—that is: those who have just a sufficient dash of blackguardism in them to make them snap their fingers at ceremony and 'all that sort of thing'."

Mrs. Carlyle's observation on *A Christmas Carol* will give a slight idea of her critical powers; friendly as it is, it yet contains a sting. "It is really a kind-hearted, almost poetical little thing well worth any lady or gentleman's perusal—somewhat too much imbued with the Cockney-admiration of *The Eatable,* but as Dickens wrote for 'the greatest happiness of the greatest number' (of Cockneys) he would not be expected to gainsay their taste in that particular."

Of Thackeray there is little of importance in the letters. Her comment on *Vanity Fair*—"very good, indeed, beats Dickens out of the world"—is well known.

Tennyson was a favorite with Mrs. Carlyle as well as with her husband, and asperity disappeared when she wrote of him. "A very handsome man," she commented, "and a noble-hearted one, with something of the gypsy in his appearance, which, for me, is perfectly charming." I find no real criticism of his poetry, but two remarks in regard to his attitude toward women are of interest, and one of them shows real penetration. Both date from 1845. The first was occasioned by a visit from Tennyson. "Alfred is dreadfully embarrassed with women alone—for he entertains at one and the same moment a feeling of almost adoration for them and ineffable contempt! Adoration for what they *might be*—contempt for what they *are!*" The second is: "Lady Harriet told me that he [Tennyson] wanted to marry; 'must have a woman to live beside; would *prefer a lady,* but—cannot afford one; and so must marry a maidservant'."

I find a single sentence on Macaulay that is worth repeating; it has the usual caustic note. "I used to think my husband the most copious talker, when he liked, that was anywhere to be fallen in with; but Macaulay beats him hollow! in quantity."

Mrs. Carlyle's remarks on the Brownings are surprising to Browning worshippers. Here are two from 1852: "Oh, such a fuss the Brownings made over Mazzini this day! My private opinion of Browning is, in spite of Mr. C's favour for him, that he is 'nothing', or very little more, but a fluff of feathers." About two months later: "I like Browning less and less; and even *she* does not grow on me."

There are many kind references to Mazzini, her intimate friend, but the following shows that she was not blind to his weaknesses: "Mazzini was here on Sunday morning, and made my hair stand on end with his projects. If he is not shot, or in an Austrian fortress within a month, it will be more by good luck than good guiding. I rely on the promise, 'God is kind to women, fools, and drunk people'." And again: "Surely between the highest virtue and the beginning of madness the line of separation is infinitesimally small."

Mrs. Carlyle's judgment of Kingsley's *Alton Locke* was on the whole unfavorable. Evidently she did not recognize her husband's portrait, if such it was, in Saunders Mackaye, for she wrote: "But the old Scotchman is capital,—only that there never was nor ever will be *such* an old Scotchman. I wonder what will come of Kingsley—go mad, perhaps."

I end this list of comments on contemporary men and women with the remark about the most influential book of the century: "But even when Darwin, in a book that all the scientific world is in ecstasy over, proved the other day that we all come from shell-fish, it didn't move me to the slightest curiosity whether we are or not. I did not feel that the slightest light would be thrown on my practical life for me, by having it ever so logically made out that my first ancestor, millions of millions of ages back, had been, or even had not been, an oyster. It remained a plain fact that I was no oyster, nor had any grandfather an oyster within my knowledge; and for the rest, there was nothing to be gained, for this world, or the next, by going into the oyster-question, till all more pressing questions were exhausted!"

In almost all these allusions to contemporaries, the cynicism of Mrs. Carlyle's mature years is plain enough. Cynicism appears also in her opinions of love, marriage, religion, and death. Her remarks on marriage and love will interest most those who are curious about her domestic troubles.

To Carlyle, after a quarrel, she wrote: "Husbands are so obtuse. They do not understand one's movements of impatience; want always 'to be treated with the respect due to genius'; exact common sense of their poor wives rather than 'finer sensibilities of the heart'; and so the marriage state 'by working late and early, has come to what ye see'—if not precisely to immortal smash as yet, at least to within a hair's-breadth of it." This was in 1845. From various letters the following are culled:

In 1846 (apropos of marriage): "Every mortal woman I fancy is born to be made miserable thro' one cause or other."

In 1847: "I do think there is much truth in the young German idea that marriage is a shockingly immoral institution, as well as what we have long known it for—an extremely disagreeable one."

In 1849, in connection with the conjugal troubles of Mr. and Mrs. Anthony Sterling: ". . . it is a great pity she will not separate from him—. . . . A little of 'the new ideas' might really be introduced into English married life with profit."

And ten years later, in 1859, Mrs. Carlyle wrote to a young lady who had just become engaged: "If ever one is to pray—if ever one is to feel grave and anxious—if ever one is to shrink from vain show and vain babble—surely it is just on the occasion of two human beings binding themselves to one another, for better and for worse, till death part them; just on that occasion when it is customary to celebrate only with rejoicings, and congratulations, and *trousseaux,* and white-ribbon! Good God!"

Not immediately connected with marriage but entitled to inclusion here are the following:

"People who are so dreadfully 'devoted' to their wives are so apt, from mere habit, to get devoted to other peoples' wives as well!"

"Sentiment, you see, is not well looked on by the present generation of women; there is a growing taste for fastness, or, still worse, for strong-mindedness!" That was in 1859.

There are also many comments on death and a possible future life. After the death of her mother in 1842 she wrote: "Nobody can bring me any news from her more, but only the Angel of Death—in that must be all my hope henceforward—hope full of terror too—for how unfit I am to die." But usually her attitude is more skeptical. "Death—either we shall have a trial at existence again under new conditions, or sleep soundly through all eternity. The last used to be a horrible thought for me, but it is not so any longer. I am weary, weary to such a point of moral exhaustion, that any anchorage were welcome, even the stillest, coldest, where the wicked should cease from troubling, and the weary be at rest, understanding both by the wicked and the weary myself." And on the occasion of the death of her dog she asked: "What is become of that little beautiful graceful *Life,* so full of love and loyalty and sense of duty, up to the last moment that it animated the body of that little dog? Is it to be extinguished, abolished, annihilated in an instant, while the brutalized, two-legged, so-called human creature who dies in a ditch, after having outraged all duties, and caused nothing but pain and disgust to all concerned with him,—is he to live forever? It is impossible for me to believe *that*."

Some rather subtle thinking is revealed in a letter of 1845: "Yesterday in the evening came Dr. James C—and young N—, all in black, this last being just returned from the funeral of his only sister, a promising girl of sixteen, the poor mother's chief comfort of late years. I recollected the time when Mrs. N—, then Agnes L—, consulted me whether she ought to marry J. N—. Where were all these young N—'s then—the lad who sat there looking so sadly, the girl who had just been laid under the earth? Had Agnes L— lived true to the memory of her first love, would these existences have been for ever suppressed by her act? If her act could have suppressed them, what pretension have they to call themselves immortal, eternal?"

And in her religious attitude there is the same scepticism, the same questioning. On the death of her father, the girl of eighteen had written to her grandmother: "The ways of the Almighty are mysterious; but in this instance, *though* He has left thousands in the world whose existence is a burden to themselves and to those around them, *though* He has cut off one who was the glory of his family, a most useful member of society, one who was respected and beloved by all who knew him, and *though* He has afflicted those who we thought deserved to be happy, yet His intention appears to me clear and intelligible. Could the annihilation of a thousand useless and contemptible beings have sent such terror and submission to the hearts of the survivors, as the sudden death of one whom their love would, if possible, have gifted with immortality? Oh, no! Hard it is, but we must acknowledge the wisdom of his sentence, even while we are suffering under it—we must kiss the rod even while we are writhing under the tortures which it inflicts."

This is conventional but apparently sincere. Contrast with it her remark in connection with the tragedy of the Indian mutiny in 1857: "Love? It isn't much like a world ruled by Love, this. My dear, I am tempted to write a good deal of blasphemy just at this moment." Before this we find her saying: "Either I am just what God intended me for, or God cannot 'carry out' His intentions, it would seem. And in that case I, for 'one solitary individual,' can't worship Him the least in the world." But toward the end of her life, she became a little more reverent: "Nobody can help me! Only God: and can I wonder if God take no heed of me when I have all my life taken so little heed of Him?" Perhaps as typical of her usual attitude as anything she said is the following, written when she was about forty: "Dear Susan, I am sorry to say this world looks always the more absurd to me the longer I live in it! But, thank heaven, I am not the shepherd set over them, so let them go their way: while we, who are a little higher than the sheep, go ours!"

But this scepticism was accompanied by a persistent sense of duty, which is revealed over and over again. Two quotations, one of 1843 and the other of 1856, will be sufficient to show this: "One can never be too much alive to the consideration that one's every slightest action does not end when it has acted itself, but propagates itself on and on, in one shape or other, through all time and away into eternity." "Look straight before you, then, Jane Carlyle, and, if possible, not over the heads of things either, away into the distant vague. Look, above all, at the duty nearest hand, and, what's more, do it."

Of Carlyle's books she always spoke with respect. Of *Past and Present* she wrote: "I consider it a *great* book—calculated to waken up the Soul of England, if it have any longer a living soul in it." And even of *Frederick,* which caused both so much suffering, she wrote to him: "Oh, my dear! What a magnificent book this is going to be!"

One is tempted to add quotation to quotation, for there are innumerable passages that catch the attention of the fascinated reader. But I hope my purpose has been accomplished. Sharp-tongued and bitter the later Mrs. Carlyle was. Many persons, and even her husband, at times, must have shrunk from the whip of her caustic wit. Life had disappointed her, and she poured out her scorn on life.

Mrs. Carlyle would be excellent grist for Professor Babbitt's mill. When she was an intellectual babe, she was nourished on the worst of romantic milk—Byron and Rousseau. From them she learned to believe that the exquisite emotions of youth—love, desire for fame, sentimental melancholy—are the essence of the life of great souls. Early a sceptic, she lost the comfort and the discipline of the Christian religion. While youth and adoring admirers supported her, all went reasonably well. But when the shock of reality came, as it had to come, she had nothing to support her but her sense of duty. She had much to make her unhappy, it is true: ill heath, loss of parents, and, sometimes, an irritable husband. But she had many things to make her happy: intelligence and wit, success, money enough for comfort, many sympathetic and interesting friends, a famous and ever admiring husband. But these were not enough. Her letters reveal the tragedy of the disillusioned romanticist. They reveal, clearly and poignantly, the tragedy that pursues the sentimental romanticist of every century.

V. S. Pritchett (review date 4 February 1950)

SOURCE: Pritchett, V. S. "Books in General," review of *The Letters of Jane Welsh Carlyle,* arranged by Trudy Bliss. *New Statesman and Nation* n.s. 39, no. 987 (4 February 1950): 134-35.

[*In the following review, Pritchett discusses Jane Carlyle's lively intellect, as well as her notoriously scathing wit.*]

What was it that bound the Carlyles, the most touching of unhappy and clinging couples? Sincere love and long affection, admiration, too; but that says all and nothing. Getting her blow in first, as usual, Jane Welsh said that habit was stronger in her husband than the passions. And she herself had, or came to have, short patience with them in other people. The pitiful side of her story is well known, but it has always been clear that she was not the down-trodden Victorian wife. The Carlyle marriage was a marriage between equals. On the negative side, difficulty must have been a bond between these arduous Scots; Scottishness, also, with its dry appreciation of the angers and humours of domestic recollection. The couple would be just a little tough about the miseries created by bad nerves, bad health, bad temper. On the positive side, the bond was surely their tongues; they had a common taste for satire, malice, exaggeration and everything that was singular, a zest for scorn and the damaging, picturesque images it could be expressed in. At their worst moments, in the absences brought about by their disagreements or their health, each could be tantalised by the thought that the other was seeing, saying, thinking or writing exaggerations of the most intimidating piquancy. Each would be feeling the hypnotic challenges of the other's wit.

There is a quality here that makes both of them arresting. Mrs. Carlyle is one of the best letter-writers of the nineteenth century. He writes large and she writes small, but she rules her page, as certainly as he does his, like a circus master. Her exaggeration is conscious, too; it is not the helpless, personal hyperbole of a bosom too full. She was always fashioner to the subtle, disguising whalebone of common sense. She picks her subject and electrifies her brain. It is all irony. Why did she not, with her Jane Austenish tongue, become a novelist? Here, it is instructive to compare her with that disturbing gusher, Geraldine Jewsbury, of whom she said, "her speech is so extremely insincere that I feel in our dialogues we are always acting in a play, and as we are not to get either money or praise for it, and not being an amateur of play-acting, I prefer good honest *silence* . . . she is as sharp as a meat axe—but as narrow." With all her quick, fantastic interest in people, Mrs. Carlyle did not become a novelist and the gusher did. Mrs. Carlyle was too interested in hitting people off, and in keeping on top herself, for the novelist's life; she totally lacked that Messiah-producing and soulful inner glumness of the pregnant artist; the inner silence which a Jane Austen had.

The good letter-writer has to be an egotist with a jumping mind. Even at 19 Jane Welsh was the born boss of the notepad:

> Allons ma chère!—let us talk of the "goosish" man, my quondam lover.

> He came; arrived at the George Inn at eleven o'clock at night, twelve hours after he received my answer to his letter; slept there "the more soundly" according to his statement "than was to have been expected, all the circumstances of the case being considered" and in the morning sent a few nonsensical lines to announce his nonsensical arrival . . . In a day or two after his return . . . there came a quantity of music from him. (Pour parenthese, I shall send you a sheet of it, having another copy of *Home Sweet Home* beside.)

If Carlyle howled like a dervish, and went lamenting about his house like the Wandering Jew, when the cocks crowed or the dogs barked in the Chelsea gardens or the piano played next door, Mrs. Carlyle had a tongue. It missed nothing. One evening, the impossible Mrs. Leigh Hunt "behaved smoothly, looked devilish and was drunkish." Plain drunk would have been more amiable. When Mr. Leigh Hunt, after the the same party, went downstairs and gave a lady a couple of handsome smacks as he left and whispered "God bless you, Miss Hunter," Mrs. Carlyle, with her "wonted glegness," heard! Poor Mr. Severn, so devoted to his wife, goes off to Italy alone with the sting that "people who are so devoted to their wives are apt from mere habit, to get devoted to other people's." What a power, "beside a fund of vitality" Mr. Sterling had of "getting up a sentiment about anything or nothing." And Geraldine, the never-spared, gets a letter with the immortal beginning: "Dearest Geraldine, I am sending you two men." The only way to get even with a lady as sharp as this was to use her own methods and make her laugh at herself; and this happily she could do. A young Charles Buller who had been snubbed by her on the sound Annandale ground that he was an expert philanderer and unkind to his parents, was not going to be put down. For two days she held out against him without a smile—and her face with its fine but sullen brow, its full-orbed eyes and hard mouth could look formidable—when a brilliantly silly idea occurred to him. They were all standing in the hall watching the rain fall on the Norfolk garden when the young man exclaimed, "I will shoot a hollyhock" and did so at once, bringing her the trophy with all the solemnity (the learned and topical lady writes) of Mr. Petrucci in the character of Heraclitus. She was obliged to laugh, "to the disgrace of her originality." The immoral Mr. Buller had subdued a fantastic satirist, by a fantastic touch.

Mrs. Carlyle was the most amusing woman in London. Everyone with any brains came to her house. She astonished Tennyson by allowing him to smoke; she gave Mazzini many a dressing down. D'Orsay called twice: "at first sight his beauty is that of the rather disgusting sort which seems to be like genius of no sex." But he had wit and sense on the first occasion; they had diminished by the second. No longer dressed like a humming bird, he had cleverly subdued his finery to the recognition that five years had made a difference to his figure. She was quite aware, in spite of a flutter of pretence, that people like seeing her as much as they like seeing her husband; and when Carlyle was beguiled to Bath House by Lady Ashburton, there was a lively salon in Cheyne Row to put against it. And put against it was. With the acid relish of inner loneliness, she was a great deal out and about observing the human comedy. The born letter-writer sees incident or absurdity in the smallest things and picks out what will divert the reader. This was written for the scornful preacher in Carlyle:

> A Mrs. Darbyshire, whom you saw once, came the night before last to stay while I stayed. She seems a sensible *gentlewoman* enough—a Unitarian *without the* Doctrines. But I could not comprehend at first why she had been brought, till at last Mrs. Paulet gave me to understand that she was there to use up Miss Newton. "Not," she said, "that my sister is an illiberal person, though she believes in Christ, and *all that sort of thing.* She is quite easy to live with; but it will be pleasanter for herself as well as for us that she should have somebody to talk to of her own sort—a Catholic or Unitarian, she doesn't mind which." After this initiation I could hardly look with gravity on these two shaking heads into one another's faces and bum-bumming away on *religious* topics, as they flatter themselves.

And she was capable of folly. There was the wonderful party when Dickens did his marvellous conjuring tricks, where the crackers went bang and the champagne flowed. She had been green, bilious and ill with her terrible nerves when she left Cheyne Row, but here in the uproar, she was suddenly cured. She talked mad nonsense to Thackeray; and at the climax Forster

> seized me *round the waist,* whirled me into the thick of it and *made* me dance!!! Like a person in the treadmill who must move forward or be crushed to death! Once I cried out, "For the love of heaven let me go; you are going to dash my brains out against the folding doors!" to which he answered, "Your brains! Who cares about their brains here? Let them go."

There were other lettings go of the brain. Obviously, taken in by Geraldine Jewsbury, she had let herself go too far for a moment or two. There was the Father Matthew episode, a pure case of hero worship, when she rushed to his meeting in the East End, and, climbing on to the platform, fell flat at the priest's feet. She gripped his hands, burst into tears and after a few choking words gave him a memento of herself, and went home sick and mad with exaltation. After her husband, the Father was "the best man of modern times." But here the ironist returned: "Had you any idea your wife was such a fool?" And there was the sobering reflection that the "Father got through the thing admirably."

There must have been a good deal of "getting through the thing" at Cheyne Row. It was, for all its striking sociability, a fort, with the old warrior upstairs, bloody and unbowed, and herself the sentinel below. They had, in this marriage, the belligerence and tenderness of soldiers. The attraction of this selection of **Letters** [**The**

Letters of Jane Welsh Carlyle] is that, with a bare minimum of necessary comment, we see her life, through Mrs. Carlyle's own eyes. We are spared the hysteria of a Countess Tolstoy, for Jane Welsh and her husband were stoics; when the woe comes through, the illness, the insomnia, the loneliness, the jealousy and the wary hardness that followed their insoluble differences, it comes through a mind capable of some self-criticism. Strangely, it is not the suffering that moves one—only by great effort can one sympathise with neurotic or imaginary suffering, one is always aware of how strong and relentless the neurotics are—it is the happiness, the devotion, the love and the deep deposit of friendship that accumulates in a marriage, and the whole exquisitely marked passage of time, that bring tears to the eyes. How quickly the early excitement goes; how warmly the devotion expands; how strong the ties between the contestants become. The Carlyle marriage becomes an archetype of the marriage of genius. We owe to Mrs. Carlyle an intimate picture of a remarkable man caught, as in the Laocoon, by his own gifts; not once is there any attempt at that reckless, destructive criticism of his work, which animal jealousy and mania aroused in a woman like the Countess Tolstoy, unless the journals Mrs. Carlyle destroyed contained such outbursts. We owe to her a brilliant domestic picture of her age, from its famous people down to its servants; and the decided impression of a vivacious intellect.

Elizabeth Drew (essay date 1964)

SOURCE: Drew, Elizabeth. "Jane Carlyle. 1801-1866." In *The Literature of Gossip: Nine English Letterwriters,* pp. 187-212. New York: W. W. Norton and Company, Inc., 1964.

[*In the following excerpts, Drew analyzes Carlyle's personality through a close reading of her letters. Drew praises the unflinching honesty of Carlyle's writings, asserting that they provide a glimpse into "the worst as well as the best of her."*]

We know Jane Carlyle better than any other English letter writer. We have an unbroken series of her letters from the age of eighteen to the very morning of her sudden death at sixty-five. The gaps are never for more than a few weeks, and the letters are a complete self-portrait and a continuing drama of married life. She was never one to be careful in the expression of her feelings; she was always spontaneous and impulsive. As she wrote to a young cousin, Jeanie Welsh: "I have got into the way of *splashing* off whatever is on my mind when I write to you, without forethought or backthought." She did the same with her husband, whether she was in good spirits or bad, full of affection or full of anger or full of self-pity. She was a volatile creature with extremes of all these; a complex personality of many moods: so loving and so cynical, so sympathetic and so harsh, so intolerant and so patient, so clear-sighted and so blind.

* * *

All these moods naturally affected her relations with her husband, but it is impossible to read her letters to him during their whole life together, even during the years of near estrangement, without recognizing the unbreakable bonds of deep understanding, trust and devotion between them. Take these passages from different decades. In 1837 she wrote to her mother-in-law:

> I have only him in the whole wide world to love me and take care of me, poor little wretch that I am. Not but what numbers of people love me after their fashion far better than I deserve; but then *his* fashion is so different from all these and seems alone to suit the sort of crotchetty creature that I am.

In 1844, she suspected that he is going to buy her a birthday present:

> Write me a longer letter than usual, and leave presents to those whose affection stands more in need of vulgar demonstration than yours does.

In 1863 she had a long and painful illness and had gone to the seaside to try and regain health:

> O my Dear! Shall I ever make fun for you again? . . . I want so much to *live*—and to be to you more than I have ever been. . . . I am terribly alone. But I don't want to interrupt your work.

Carlyle wrote to her continually in the same loving terms. But this is not to say that superficial storms were not frequent. Carlyle's life was centered in his writing, Jane's life was centered in him, and this in itself caused inevitable stresses and strains. She put her husband's work before any other consideration in her life, but that could not prevent her frequent bitter resentment of its claims. She once wrote grimly: "Harriet Martineau used to talk of writing being such a *pleasure* to her. In this house we should as soon dream of calling the bearing of children such a pleasure." Getting his books written meant to Carlyle untold—or rather very loudly told—struggle and travail. It threw him into "bewildered wrestlings"; a book, he said, was like a load of fire burning his heart, it roasted his life out until it was thrown out of him; his imagination was a black smithy of the Cyclops where his mind must work in continual darkness, broken only by lightnings. As Jane says on her side, the home atmosphere was full of sulphur and brimstone all the time. And these spells of creative activity would be interspersed with periods of the blackest depression, of what he himself called "sulky despair," full of egotistical lamentations and irritability, in which he had no

room to consider the needs of others. In one of these Jane writes that she is coming home from a visit in low spirits, and hopes to be cheered up. He replies:

> My poor Goody, depending on cheerful looks of *mine* for thy cheerfulness. How I love thee, it is not probable that thou or any mortal will know. But cheerful looks, when the heart feels slowly dying in floods of confusion and obstruction, are not the things I have to give.

When Jane is cheerful herself, she can make excellent comedy out of her trials as "a human partition" standing between a temperamental genius and an unsympathetic external world. She can work up brilliant extravaganzas of how she copes with landlords, tax assessors, demands for jury service, and more particularly with the eternal problem of distracting noises—girls playing the piano, howling dogs, crowing roosters and screaming parrots. Carlyle's personal nervous restlessness is vividly presented: moving around the house "like a sort of domestic Wandering Jew . . . lounging about from the mantelpiece to the table—from the table to the chairbacks—touching everything and contradicting everything"; or being so wild to get away and so incapable of making up his mind where he wants to go, "that living beside him has been like living the life of a weathercock in a high wind, blowing from all points at once." Or he returns home after she has had a tremendous housecleaning and rearranged everything for his comfort, only to be told after three days "he can neither think nor live with the rooms as they are" and so she finds herself "in the thick of a new mess":

> The carpets, which I had nailed down so well with my own hands, tumbled up again . . . and the prospects of new cleanings, new sewings, new arrangements, stretching away into eternity for anything I see.

No wonder that after this she declares defiantly: "I will lie on the sofa by heaven for two weeks and read French novels!"

For Jane could be as tempestuous as her husband, and if he was difficult to live with, so was she. She confesses herself "a brimstone of a creature," and one suspects that an entry in Carlyle's journal in 1840 tells of a common occurrence: "Work ruined for the day. Imprudently expressed complaints in the morning filled all the sky with clouds." Jane is excellent at giving good advice: "When one can only ray out darkness, best clap an extinguisher on yourself," but often she cannot follow it. Sometimes she is unforgivable in her own egotisms, and one wants to shake her! She will write a furiously angry letter one evening, "shrewing" her husband for changing plans and upsetting her own arrangements, find two letters from him next morning with full explanations and apologies, but conclude: "I must let the long letter I wrote yesterday go. . . . It is too much writing to throw away, after having given myself a headache over it." She can't resist wounding little jabs. When he writes a long letter about his doings and opinions, but not enough about *her,* she dismisses it: "It will read charmingly in your biography"; or she will describe a bad night: "Not what *you* call awake, that is, dozing, but broad wide awake." Moreover, not only did she write such jibes *to* him, she wrote them *of* him to others, a disloyalty of which he was never guilty. She will say she has a faceache, as the result of his insisting on her sitting in a draught on a train journey; or that no attention need be paid to any report he makes about her health, because as long as she can stand on her legs he never notices if anything is wrong with her. She jeers at his vanity: "With all his hatred of being made a lion of, he seems to tolerate those that make him so marvellously well"; and she suggests that it is for the same reason that he loves the attentions of their little dog:

> The infatuated little beast dances round him on its hind legs as I ought to do and can't; and he feels flattered and surprised by such unwonted capers to his honour and glory.

Much of this can no doubt be put down to ill-health. She wrote in 1846:

> Carlyle should have had a "strong-minded woman" for wife, with a perfectly sound liver, plenty of *solid fat,* and mirth and good humour without end.

They are too much alike, she thinks, especially as to their digestions and nervous systems, and so "we aggravate one another's tendency to despair." That many of Jane's physical symptoms were emotional in origin we cannot doubt, but they were none the less torturing for that. Even before her marriage we hear of her agonizing migraine headaches, which would last from twenty-four to sixty hours and leave her "all beaten into impalpable pulp." Her chronic digestive troubles, her sleeplessness and her depressions all sound as if they were the result of nervous stress, and the fact that they so often disappeared when she was happy and busy perhaps proves it. In spite of all her humorous or blistering accounts of the horrors of her household "earthquakes" during Carlyle's absences, she is never better than when she is having a "sack of Troy" in the home. She owns she finds it "rather inspiriting," and when the house is full of plasterers, plumbers, bricklayers, carpenters, painters, and paperhangers, she rigs up a gypsy tent in the garden with the "crumb-cloth" and the clothes props and sits there happily writing letters and making chair and sofa covers. The workmen arrive at six in the morning, but Jane, usually so full of complaints at being disturbed, comments only: "It makes a prodigious long day; but I do not weary, having so many mechanical things to do." Or again, she describes how one afternoon she is lying, a physical wreck, on the sofa, when an old beau of hers from Haddington days, walks in on her. They embrace and she is transformed:

> My bright, whole-hearted, impulsive youth seemed conjured back. . . . For certain my late deadly weakness was conjured away . . . dissolved in the unwonted feeling of gladness. I am a different woman this evening. I am well! I am in an atmosphere of *home* and *long ago.*

But a change of atmosphere in the immediate present has the same effect. Another day, in the same condition of lonely depression, Mrs. Macready (wife of the actor) persuades her to come to a party. It proved a very merry and wild affair, with Dickens performing conjuring tricks for the children, and "the gigantic Thackeray" capering like a Maenad, and much of Bohemian London playing the fool whole-heartedly far into the night. Jane describes it all with great gusto:

> And the result? Why, the result, my dear, was that I went to bed on my return and slept like a top!!! Plainly proving that excitement is my rest.

Perhaps that wasn't quite the right diagnosis, but that Jane lacked any regular pleasurable activity to absorb her nervous energies and take her mind off her many frustrations undoubtedly added much to her unhappiness and ill-health. The conventions of the day prevented women from pursuing many of the outlets we enjoy nowadays, but even so, Carlyle himself saw very clearly to the heart of her need. As early as 1842 he writes:

> My prayer is always and always has been that you would rouse up the fine faculties that *are* yours into some course of real true work, which you felt to be worthy of them and you! . . . I know well, none better, how difficult it all is,—how peculiar and original your lot looks to you, and in many ways *is.* . . . But I will never give up hope to see you adequately *busy* with your whole mind.

Jane too came to recognize the folly of centering her life on a husband whose engrossing interest was in his work. She writes bitterly in 1850:

> It is sad and wrong to be so dependent for the life of my life on any human being as I am on you; but I cannot by any force of logic cure myself at this date, when it has become second nature. If I have to lead another life in any of the planets, I shall take precious good care not to hang myself round any man's neck, either as a locket or a millstone. . . .

The climax of Jane's wretchedness came in 1855 when she kept the Journal which was to cause her husband such profound remorse when he found it after her death, and read of her agonies and repressions.

> Oct. 22. That eternal Bath House. I wonder how many thousand miles Mr. C. has walked between there and here . . . setting up always another milestone betwixt himself and me. Nov. 5. Alone this evening. Lady A. in town again; and Mr. C. of course at Bath House.

She is pathetic in her efforts to check her morbidity; trying to busy herself with practical things to give her mind no time to fester; mending Carlyle's dressing-gown to keep her heart from throbbing up into her head and maddening it; trying to tire herself with walking. When things seem more than she can bear, she tells herself to say over and over: "Look straight before you, Jane Carlyle. . . . Look above all at the duty nearest hand and what's more, do it."

Serving her husband's work, lovingly, humorously or grudgingly, certainly took first place in Jane's own existence, but it is time to see what made her "the light of his life" and gave her the reputation for the charm, warmth, vivacity, and wit described by so many of her circle, and which lives for us in the letters. Her correspondents were seldom people of any distinction—uncles, cousins, family friends, and in-laws form the bulk of them. To them all she recounts all the doings of her London life and the gossip about her London friends and acquaintances. She did the same to Carlyle at home in what she calls their Chelsean Nights Entertainments, when, after his working hours were over he would stretch himself on the hearthrug and smoke up the chimney ("if I were careful!" said Carlyle, describing such scenes), and she would lie on her sofa and give vivid accounts, grave or gay, of her own doings.

We come to know all her contradictory qualities. She had said when she was twenty-eight: "the only thing that makes one place more attractive to me than another is the quantity of *heart* I find in it," and that she had the warmest affections and most generous sympathies is clear enough. One friend called her "the most *concrete* woman" she knows, and her many practical kindnesses bear it out. In the early days in Edinburgh, when de Quincey fell ill—from a diet of seven wineglasses of laudanum a day, and all the game that went bad on the poulterer's hands, says Jane—she took him into their house and nursed him back to health. She declares that she has the same attraction for miserable people and mad people that amber has for straws. When a young German friend disappears, it is Jane who tracks him to the asylum where he has been taken, rescues him and cares for him until his friends can come from Germany. Again, when she finds a lost child in the street, she does not take her to the police station lest she should be frightened, but brings her home, leaving her address with the police, and keeps her fed and amused for five hours. If she catches some boys torturing "a little ugly brown bird," she immediately buys it from them for twopence and tries to save its life. She cannot understand how Lady Ashburton, who spends seven hundred pounds on a ball at Bath House, can be so stingy about her village children's party at The Grange. She spends only two pounds on forty-eight rubbishy presents: "I should have liked every child to have got at least a *frock* given it," Jane says indignantly.

She has indeed plenty of what she calls caustically "that damned thing, the milk of human kindness"; yet very close behind it is that disillusioned wry humor which causes her to comment on it in that way. She is often limited by her "concreteness." She is incapable of understanding any beliefs outside her own sturdy agnosticism, and like Carlyle himself, she has very little in the way of esthetic taste. She can appreciate George Eliot's deep humanity, and feels as a woman an affinity with Charlotte Brontë: "I perceive in her book so many things I have said myself." She can enjoy the social satire of *Vanity Fair,* but finds *David Copperfield* "arrant nonsense," Jane Austen "water-gruel for the mind," Browning "nothing but a fluff of feathers," and sees Taglione, the greatest ballet-dancer of the day, simply as "a woman, not even pretty, balancing herself on the extremity of one great toe, and stretching the other foot high into the air—much higher than decency ever dreamt of." But in spite of her rationalistic prejudices she has a refreshing intolerance of humbug. The barbarism of a fashionable wedding brings the comment: "All that senseless singing of *Te Deum* before the battle has begun!" and she disposes acidly of the cant that happiness is found in the happiness of others: "To eat a beefsteak when one is hungry yields a satisfaction of a much more positive character than seeing one's neighbour eat it."

She was by no means one of those who see only the best in others; but then those people are not often the best company, and Jane is very good company. She rings a bell in many memories when she describes a dinner with some very dull acquaintances:

> It's like seasickness: one thinks at the time one will never risk it again, and then the impression wears off and one thinks perhaps one's constitution has changed and that this time it will be more bearable.

Or the account of a visit to the country rectory where Regy Buller, the dullest of the two brothers whom Carlyle had tutored during their courtship, now holds the living. It is all so vividly deadly: the daily drive with old Mrs. Buller, the nightly game of chess with old Mr. Buller, the mouldering church—"anything so like the burial place of revealed religion you have never seen—nor a rector more fit to read the burial service." When Sunday comes, she has to listen to the "imbecilities" of Regy's sermon, which goes on "like the cawing of rooks," and to his giving out the psalm "in a loud, sonorous, perfectly Church of England tone." And since it is a day of rest, the carriage horses are only *walked* "on principle."

* * *

Yet all this satirical exaggeration was part of the vivacity which was one of her great attractions. She never lost her zest for life in spite of all her miseries. When at the age of fifty-two she finds "Scotch-looking snow" in the street on coming home from the theatre, she reports that she was so "drunk" with the sensation that she ran along the street with her bonnet hanging down her back, one minute taking a slide and the next lifting a handful of snow to eat it! Or she is glad she was persuaded to get an evening dress, "cut down to the due pitch of indecency" to go to a ball at Bath House, "not for any pleasure I had at the time, being past dancing and knowing but few people—but it is an additional idea for life to have seen such a party."

She never had conventional beauty, but was always "that very elegant creature" that Anne Thackeray found her in her sixties; always slim and alert, with a fragile body and colorless face, abundant black hair never touched with gray and expressive dark eyes which could be either tender or mischievous: "a face full of intellect and kindness blended gracefully and lovingly together" as one of her men friends described it. "Shall I ever make fun for you again" she said pathetically to her husband in a letter already quoted, and jokes flew about at Cheyne Row. Indeed Tennyson made a very shrewd remark when he said that no couple who chaffed one another as heartily as the Carlyles could possibly be unhappily married. Jane is full of good-natured mischief. In a gay mood she fetches a supply of light French novels from the London Library, but "having still however some sense of decency remaining" she reports that she signed in the ledger for them "Erasmus Darwin"; or she creates a ridiculous picture of herself riding up the Malvern Hills with Old Sterling, leader writer to *The Times*: "each on a live donkey! Just figure it! With a Welsh lad whipping us from behind; for they were the slowest of donkeys, though named, in defiance of all probability, *Fly* and *Lively*." She confesses to nervousness lest Carlyle will address his lecture audience: "Fool creatures come here for diversion," instead of "Ladies and Gentlemen," and wonders if the best way to stop him at the end will be to have a lighted cigar laid on the desk as the clock strikes four. Carlyle of course is in the letters as vividly as herself—with pellets of cotton, with which he has hopefully plugged his ears, sticking at the end of some stray hairs; or in uncongenial company looking like a chained tiger; or setting out with three maps of Great Britain and two of the world in his pocket, to find a house within twenty miles of London; or with clumsy tenderness, presenting her with a cloak he has chosen himself: "not *very* ugly, only entirely unsuitable to the rest of my habiliments, being a brownish colour with orange spots."

* * *

We meet many of the great names of the age in what she describes as "our long, dimly-lighted, perfectly neat and quaint room." Tennyson, embarrassed to find Carlyle is out, but wooed out of his shyness by Jane getting out pipes and tobacco, brandy and water, with the triumphant result that he stayed "for three mortal hours—talking like an angel—only exactly as if he were talking with a clever *man,* which strained me to a terrible pitch of intellectuality"; Browning, asked to put the kettle back on the hob and depositing it on the hearth-rug while he went on with his conversation; George Eliot, "with her look of Propriety personified, and oh, so *slow!*" Harriet Martineau holding up her ear-trumpet to Carlyle "with a pretty, blushing air of coquetry"; Carlyle expounding the Schleswig-Holstein question "from a few hundred years before the beginning of it" to poor Mrs. Oliphant, who had to sit like a passive bucket being pumped into; or Macaulay, beating even Carlyle himself as a talker—"in quantity," adds Jane loyally.

Or we catch cosy intimate glimpses of Jane with her particular friends. She and Mazzini, their feet on the fender, regaling themselves with wine, figs, and gingerbread; or Erasmus Darwin (elder brother of Charles), having heard Mazzini say that Jane should wear a shawl, returning next day with "an immense gauze-looking shawl of white lambswool"; or gossiping with Mrs. Macready over Harriet Martineau's novel *Deerbrook*:

> She asked me how I liked Harriet's book. I answered "How do *you* like it?" She made wide eyes at me and drew her little mouth together into a button. We both burst out laughing and that is the way to get fast friends.

Some readers claim that the letters are too full of health, servants and domestic difficulties, that they are as a friend of Jane Austen said of *Emma,* "too natural to be interesting." But Jane's talent was, in its small way, like that of her greater namesake, to transform the commonplace. Even her complaining is vivid: lying sleepless in misery "pitted against chaos" and coming off second best; or listening to a barking dog until the universe seems one great dog-kennel; or, more cheerfully, on the way to convalescence, "not quite well yet—at least, I am still wearing signals of distress, a nightcap and shawl—partly, I confess, from a secret persuasion that these equipments render my appearance more interesting." Or who can find it dull to visualize a housecleaning with the tables and chairs "all with their legs in the air, as if in convulsions"; or to hear of the applicant for a job who recommended herself by declaring: "When people die, I can lay 'em out perfect."

* * *

When the first edition of the **Letters and Memorials** was published in 1883, Jane's unconventionality was deplored. Her jokes about blue pills and bedbugs upset the reviewers, and as one American critic remarked: "Whatever else she was, she was manifestly no lady."

Not only did she make unseemly jokes, but her standards of ladylike refinement and language were low. She refused to wear a crinoline, she lunched alone in restaurants and rode on the top of omnibuses, and on being accosted in the street, merely said "Idiot," and passed on with no shrinking panic. She starts a letter to a neglectful friend: "Why the devil don't you write?" and on a dull visit to the country heads her letter, in place of address: "Hell." But it is all this which makes her the most unaffected of letter-writers; so gusty and vivid, "splashing off" whatever she has to say, with such natural vitality and phrasing—whether she is sending Carlyle a howl from the midst of a household "earthquake" to stop his brother from coming to stay: "For God's sake don't let John plump in upon me in my present puddlement," or describing one of her own moods of angry misery: "the mind of me all churned into froth," or picturing herself coming home from a few days at an Inn in the Isle of Wight: "I looked (and felt) as if just returned from the Thirty Years War. Sleepless, bug-bitten, bedusted and bedevilled." Letters, she said, were a poor substitute for a warm, breathing personality: "One cannot, in writing, eke out one's words with tones of the voice—looks, gestures, an occasional *groan*, an occasional kiss!" Yet she can make her charm glow through her words; in a greeting: "I kiss you from ear to ear"; in a bantering signature: "Your adorable wife"; in an opening reminder: "Now stop! Have you eaten your breakfast? If not, eat it: the letter will not cool by keeping—the tea and toast will!"

* * *

Jane Carlyle's letters are so spontaneous and uninhibited that inevitably we know the worst as well as the best of her. But there is no doubt which tips the balance. She can be jealous, neurotic, self-complacent and malicious. At times we can think of her in the words of Charlotte Cushman, the American actress, who found her "that plain, keen, unattractive and yet inescapable woman." But how much more often she is generous, witty, entertaining and lovable. To Carlyle she may have been all that her epitaph said, as wife and helpmate to a man of genius; to her friends, and to her sympathetic readers, more of her essential impulsive warmth was caught by Leigh Hunt in his well-known little poem. He had been sick for some time and came to call on his recovery. Jane welcomed him with a heartfelt embrace.

> Jenny kissed me when we met,
>   Jumping from the chair she sat in;
> Time, you thief, who love to get
>   Sweets into your list, put that in!
> Say I'm weary, say I'm sad,
>   Say that health and wealth have missed me,
> Say I'm growing old, but add
>   Jenny kissed me.

Jean Wasko (essay date fall and winter 1997)

SOURCE: Wasko, Jean. "The Angel in the Envelope: The Letters of Jane Welsh Carlyle." *Modern Language Studies* 27, nos. 3 and 4 (fall and winter 1997): 3-18.

[*In the following essay, Wasko argues that Carlyle's writings, far from relegating her to the margins of Victorian literary history, in fact represent a radical new form of autobiography. Wasko interprets Carlyle's letters as a subtle subversion of traditionally masculine expressions of identity and self.*]

Mrs. Montagu, an ardent admirer of the great Victorian sage, Thomas Carlyle, commented as well on the epistolary talents of his wife, Jane Welsh Carlyle: "'Jane,'" she is reported to have said, "'everybody is born with a vocation, and yours is to write little notes'" (Crichton-Browne lxxxv). While Jane Carlyle received accolades from her circle, and even from her husband, for her epistolary genius, Mrs. Montagu's comment helps characterize the prevailing view of epistolary art, as feminine, agreeable, and diminutive. Similarly, when Henry Tilney, in Jane Austen's *Northanger Abbey,* notes that "'the talent for writing agreeable letters is peculiarly female,'" he is putting women in their place. Describing their style as "'faultless, except in three particulars,'" he articulates a masculine view of women's texts, which are distinguished by "'a general deficiency of subject, a total inattention to stops, and a very frequent ignorance of grammar'" (13). That is to say, they deal with trivial issues and demonstrate the inferior minds of their authors. Moreover, these comments appear in the context of a discussion of that other "peculiarly female" genre, the journal, which, it is clear, Tilney views as a "delightful" vehicle for recording the dresses, curls, and curtesies [*sic*] that adorn the lives of young ladies. The materiality and triviality that Tilney criticizes in the prose of women is, as Jane Austen would have us know, a product of the cultural context that defined the "feminine," and, in doing so, limited or, at best, determined the nature of female authorship, both stylistically and generically. To limit one's literary production to what was "peculiarly female," it would seem, was to surrender to the strictures of the social construction of femininity. Thus, one might argue, in becoming the greatest female letter writer of the nineteenth century, Jane Carlyle, the wife of a literary giant, configured herself in the diminutive and, thereby, consigned herself to the literary margins.

For the familiar letter, which focuses on what is daily, material, and trivial, in a style characterized as spontaneous, sincere, and conversational, fits a social construction of femininity which Teresa de Lauretis describes as fraught with "irreducible contradictions" that "at once excluded" women "from discourse" and "imprisoned [them] within it" (7). In *Outside the Pale:*

Cultural Exclusion, Gender Difference and the Victorian Writer, Elsie B. Michie posits four culturally determined characteristics of "femininity" that worked to exclude nineteenth-century women writers and to underscore their differences from their male counterparts. First, the perceived materiality of a woman's nature rendered her unable "to exercise the abstract powers of the imagination" associated with the Romantic poet. Secondly, women, confined to the sphere of the home, were excluded from the "realm of the marketplace" where literary fortunes were made. Thirdly, participation in the highly public activities associated with professional authorship might leave a woman open to charges of impropriety, and, finally, women confronted "a definition of femininity as fragmented, as opposed to masculinity, which was defined as whole" (4-5). Thus, in summary, the social construction which worked to marginalize literary women associated the feminine with materiality, domesticity, privacy, and fragmentation, characteristics that describe, quite precisely, the epistolary genre in the hands of Jane Carlyle. This well-educated woman, a gifted writer who once entertained literary aspirations, allowed her culture, it would seem, to define her authorship and became the angel in the envelope, the literary equivalent of the Victorian domestic goddess, immortalized by Coventry Patmore.

Yet it is also possible to look beyond the brilliant and apparently satisfying conformity to the role of epistolary angel and argue that Jane Welsh Carlyle, in adopting the letter as her literary mode, permitted herself a subtle subversion of literary lionizing and, more specifically, of the spiritual autobiography, so central in Victorian literature.[1] Regarded as a feminine mode of autobiography, the letters become subversive rather than conformist, denying as they do the masculine authority of autobiography that Sidonie Smith describes as "an assertion of arrival and embeddedness in the phallic order" (40). As wife to the author of *Sartor Resartus* and the biographies of Frederick of Prussia and Cromwell, Jane Carlyle surely recognized the authority and the grandeur represented by these works that construct the self and, with it, the life of the age, imposing a single human form on historical experience. Perhaps her life-long dedication to the letter represents a woman's attempt to undermine the self-assertive egocentricity of masculine autobiography. For letters, it seems, represent the kind of autobiography that Bonnie TuSmith finds in the writings of Maxine Hong Kingston, a "new form of autobiography," apparently not so new after all, which "replaces the notion of self as already constituted with the notion of self as continuity through change" (Singley and Sweeney xxiii). According to Carol J. Singley and Susan Sweeney, contemporary writers like Kingston and Sandra Cisneros "transform . . . the Bildungsroman" into a vehicle for the discovery of self in relationship to others, a transformation which may involve "multiple narrative voices" (xxiii). Sweeney, discussing

these multiple voices, attributes this tendency to "a peculiarly feminine ambivalence toward narrative authority" (23), grounded in "women's encounter with the social construction of femininity" (28n. 2). In light of these theories of female autobiography, Jane Carlyle's letters, it may be argued, show her ambivalence as she simultaneously accepts the socially constructed role of the angel in the envelope and creates a subversive mode of autobiography, embracing, in the private sphere, a female narratology characterized by a fragmented and a fluid idea of the self.

Lacking the revolutionary courage of Virginia Woolf, who overcame ambivalence and murdered the angel for the sake of her literary career, Jane Carlyle seems, on the one hand, to embrace this cultural construction, creating, in her voluminous correspondence, a persona who "was immensely charming" and "utterly unselfish," who "preferred to sympathize always with the minds and wishes of others" at the expense of self-expression (Woolf 278). For the letter, equated by Henry Tilney with the diary, is, in fact, a uniquely social medium, quite unlike that other peculiarly female genre, which allowed a woman to construct herself in private. Virginia Walcott Beauchamp describes the significant difference between the two forms of female discourse, emphasizing the social demands of the epistolary genre:

> The diary, a record of pain and endurance, affirms an inner reality of the writer. The letter, a social contract of sorts, represents in its seemingly happy messages the acceptance of responsibility and obligation between two beings and with a larger society. It depends on reticence. Through what it withholds it creates an idealized image of a woman's life. It is a fiction.
>
> (40)

Overtly signing on to the social contract, Jane Carlyle created a fiction of self in conformity with the eighteenth-century standards for epistolary art and the nineteenth-century definition of femininity, both of which preclude genuine self-expression.

"Letters," Ruth Perry suggests, "were the perfect vehicle for women's highly developed art of pleasing, for in writing letters it is possible to tailor a self on paper to suit the expectations and desires of the audience" (69). And Jane Carlyle, it is clear, aimed to delight her audience. Critical of herself, for example, for producing "just such a letter as a raven might write," Carlyle notes that "when one can only ray out darkness, one had best clap an extinguisher on oneself" (***Letters*** [*Letters and Memorials of Jane Welsh Carlyle*] 2: 143). A letter to John Sterling, written in 1837, makes her epistolary standards even more clear:

> since I became so sick and dispirited, I have contracted a horror of letter-writing almost equal to the hydrophobea . . . horror of cold water. I would write anything

under Heaven fairy tales, or advertisements for Warren's blacking even rather than a letter! A letter behooves to tell about oneself, and when oneself is disagreeable to oneself; one would rather tell about anything else.

> (*Collected Letters* [*The Collected Letters of Thomas and Jane Welsh Carlyle*] 9: 133)

Carlyle, it is clear, understood the challenge that defines the epistolary genre, a challenge that Elizabeth L. Barnes describes as paradoxical since "the goal became to express oneself sincerely, but with good taste; to write within the boundaries of prescribed epistolary etiquette, and yet to be completely genuine" (165). When the paradox overwhelmed, when being genuine meant violating epistolary decorum and failing to delight her audience, Jane Carlyle opted out of the conversation.

Thus, prevented by feelings of self from creating a socially acceptable fiction of self, Carlyle adopted, from time to time, another highly acceptable female mode—silence. Writing about the social pressures that worked to silence women writers, Singley describes the "anxiety, or fear," which is "at the root of ambivalence" toward authorship. "In the best case," this anxiety, she notes, is "about being considered inadequate or trivial; in the worst, of being reviled, persecuted, or even extinguished. In its extreme, anxiety silences, blocks, or kills creativity" (8-9). The alternative to such silence, Singley suggests, is insincerity, for anxiety "may express itself indirectly in forms of politeness, circumlocution, deference or denial" (9). Carlyle's sense of these limiting alternatives—silence or insincerity—is articulated in a letter to Helen Welsh where she describes a difficult social situation and comments as well on a woman's relationship to authorship. Writing about a visit to her husband from "'his Royal Highness Reigning Duke of Saxe Weimer,'" Carlyle focuses on her decorous and wifely efforts to prepare her home and her servants for the reception of this honored dignitary (*Collected Letters* 22: 8). Then she characterizes her own role in this drama of manners:

> . . . and then—I walked off into space!
>
> Had I staid at home I was going to have felt myself "in a "false position" [sic]—either I must have been put *au secret* . . . in my own house—or invited down to my sitting room, as an ineffable condescension—and I did not feel any *besoin* . . . of *condescension* of anybody."

> (*Collected Letters* 22: 9)

In this letter, Jane Carlyle expresses anxiety regarding her position, while for her husband, "it was all right—the Prince had to do with *him*." Thus Thomas Carlyle's authorship earned him the right to visits from princes, but this same authorship put his wife in a "false position," requiring that she acquiesce to the Prince's condescension or disappear. Perhaps a similar sense of fal-

sity, of disjunction between an acceptable epistolary persona and the pressure of self-consciousness, produced what Jane Carlyle describes as "periods of devil-possessedness" characterized by "a horror at letter-writing similar to the horror mad-dogs conceive at water" (*Collected Letters* 24: 8).

There is no question that Jane Carlyle, like many of her female contemporaries, was uncomfortable with authorship—both her husband's and her own. As companion to the great sage of Chelsea and witness to his unremitting agony of creation, it is small wonder that she suffered an "'anxiety of authorship'" characterized by ambivalence (Gilbert and Gubar 48). While, on the one hand, Carlyle described "writing to people who like to hear from me" as "the only real business I have, '*here down*,'" on the other hand she was often kept from correspondence with those she loved by the daily epistolary demands created by Thomas Carlyle's celebrity (*Collected Letters* 23: 205):

> the great business of life for a woman like me, in this place, is an eternal writing of little unavoidable notes—It falls upon me to answer all the invitations, and make lying excuses world without end, so that I sometimes look back with the tear in my eye to the time when we were not celebrated, and were left to provide our own dinners as we could!

> (*Collected Letters* 24: 43)

Although Jane Carlyle uses the plural pronoun *we* in reference to celebrity, it is clear that Thomas Carlyle's fame compromised the authorship of this great letter writer by placing her, once again, in a "false position," this time as social secretary.

Jane Carlyle's "anxiety of authorship," which takes the form of simultaneous attraction and repulsion, seems to extend beyond problems associated with her husband's celebrity to an ambivalence more deeply rooted in the cultural construction of the female. A number of letters written in November of 1849, for example, reveal Carlyle's fascination with the rumors that she might be the author of Charlotte Brontë's novels. Writing to her sister-in-law, Jean Carlyle Aitken, Carlyle explains that she has just read a three-volume novel by "an authoress who goes by *my* name so I wanted to see whether the present work came up to *my reputation!*" Not particularly impressed by Brontë's *Shirley*, Carlyle notes, nevertheless, that "it is quite curious how this woman says things that I have said exactly in my own words—which are often absurd and wild enough" (*Collected Letters* 24: 281). While, on the one hand, Carlyle seems to enjoy contemplating herself as author, the idea of her words on the printed page ultimately strikes her as absurd, and she undercuts with self-deprecation. Other letters show a similar ambivalence. Writing to the child of a friend, for example, Carlyle encloses a poem, which she describes as "Goethe's mermaid, whom I merely did into English, when long ago, a young lady about your own age, I aspired to the reputation of a Poetess Heaven forgive me!" (*Collected Letters* 23: 246). Thus, again, she tentatively figures herself as an author and then quickly issues a disclaimer.

This authorship, which she had eluded, however, lived and suffered beside her in the gigantic figure of Thomas Carlyle, with his sense of the sacred nature of the written word and of the heroism of the "Man of Letters." Jane Carlyle's letters document the difficulty involved in living in "'the Valley of the shadow'" of a celebrated author, a fate she had courted as a young woman (*Letters* 2: 74). In both content and form these texts seem to exist as a reaction against the figure of the literary lion and against the theory of writing embodied in the work and the life of Thomas Carlyle, which are, ultimately, inseparable. For the essence of Thomas Carlyle can be captured in his favorite phrase—"I as one solitary individual"—which his wife echoes often and always with a note of irony. What it implies is the great man's sense of the integrity and coherence of self, apparent in all his works. It describes the autobiographical impulse as defined by George Gusdorf and cited by Shari Benstock: "'Autobiography . . . requires a man to take a distance with regard to himself in order to reconstitute himself in the focus of his special unity and identity across time'" (14-15). Thomas Carlyle's "special identity," embodied in his singular style, unites every utterance in a consistent form and creates, as a result, just such an integrity of self. The sage's own remarks on style prove telling: "'The poor people seem to think style can be put off or put on, not like a skin but like a coat. Is not skin verily a product and close kinfellow of all that lies under it, exact type of the nature of the beast, not to be plucked off without flaying and death?'" (T. Carlyle cited in Waring 62-63). For Thomas Carlyle, then, "the style is the man," and the man projects himself uniquely and coherently in volume upon volume, year after year. Without regard for the genre, the author stands as an "'Immortal one!'"— the "*colossal Carlyle*" (*Collected Letters* 22: 105).

Jane Carlyle, however, consistently refused to validate her husband as a literary lion, calling attention, instead, to the gap between the sage, projected so vividly and consistently in the voice of Thomas Carlyle, and the man in his dressing gown, "looking remarkably bilious" (*Letters* 2: 72). While the husband may have engaged in "hero-worship," the wife maintained a sense of proportion, separating the man from the Man-of-Letters in a way that Thomas Carlyle never could. Her irony, for example, is directed at Carlyle's application of his great mind to a practical problem as he arrives late in meeting his wife's train: "—in hurrying along the Strand pretty sure of being too late—amidst all imaginable and unimaginable phenomena which that immense thorough

fare of a street presents; his eyes (heaven bless the mark!) had lighted *on my trunk* perched on top of the omnibus and . . . recognized it! This seems to me one of the most indubitable proofs of *genius* which he ever manifested" (*Collected Letters* 9: 48). In a similar vein, just weeks before her death, writing to Thomas Carlyle regarding his triumphant address at Edinburgh, Jane Carlyle undercuts the grandeur of the moment with a reminder of mortality: "What pleases me most in this business—I mean the business of your success—is the hearty personal affection towards you that comes out on all hands . . . one general, loving, heartfelt throwing up of caps with young and old, male and female! If we could only sleep, dear, and what you call *digest*, wouldn't it be nice?" (*Letters* 2: 377). In treating her husband's celebrity with irony, Carlyle insists upon a separation that undermines autobiographical posturing. When such objectivity is lost in the ideal union of the hero and the hero-worshipper, Carlyle finds a target for her wit. For example, forwarding a book of essays on poets and divines, sent to Thomas Carlyle by an admirer, Jane Carlyle mocks the ecstatic author and her husband in the process:

> "Immortal one!" the note I send is accompanied by a blood-red volume entitled *Criticisms*. I have looked at *the gratitude* in the preface—A very grand paragraph indeed about "the magnificent—*Trench*! and the *colossal Carlyle*; one of whom reminds us of some gigantic river, now winding &c &c; the other of some tremendous being struggling with mighty power &c &c." A very tremendous blockhead does this writer *remind* us of!

> (*Collected Letters* 22: 105)

Jane Carlyle, here and elsewhere, shows little reverence for the sage and for those who lionize him.

Carlyle's many comments on her husband's unique style, which is, of course, "the exact nature of the beast" himself, also serve to undercut the "Hero as Man of Letters." In a letter to her husband's mother, for example, she turns a fan letter from a "prim Quakeress" into an opportunity to debunk. With feigned magnanimity, Jane Carlyle forgives the woman's "Transcendental flatteries," expressing a willingness to "pardon her any absurdity almost, in consideration of that beautiful peculiar[i]ty [s]he possesses, of admiring his very *style*, which has hitherto exceeded the capacity of admiration in all men women and children that have made the attempt" (*Collected Letters* 9: 331-32). Her own parody proves even more telling. Costuming her diminutive figure in "the skin" that is his style, Carlyle undermines the authorial colossus:

> "Bow-wow-wow," roared the Dog, and "dashed the cup of fame from my brow"!—"Bow-wow-wow" again and again, till the whole Universe seemed turned into one great Dog-kennel! I hid my face in my hands and

groaned inwardly, "O Destiny accursed! what use of scrubbing and sorting?—all this availeth me nothing so long as *The Dog* sitteth at the Washerman's gate!" I could have burst into tears; but I did not! "I was a republican before the Revolution, and I never wanted energy"! I ran for ink and paper, and wrote.

(*Collected Letters* 20: 6)

Adopting the rhetoric that her husband used to oppose the steam engine of the mechanistic universe, Jane Carlyle deflates and feminizes. Most significantly, the weapon she chooses to win the day is the familiar letter, her own subversive approach to autobiography.

This weapon, wielded in ways more subtle than broad parody, works to undermine the authority of the Carlylean hero, an authority gained through self-construction. For Thomas Carlyle is the epitome of the Gusdorfian autobiographical subject who, according to Benstock, presumes "to *know* (himself)," and for whom, "the process of knowing is a process of differentiating himself from others" (16). Such a process, ultimately, dissolves the boundaries between the writing "Subject" and the "Object of investigation" and creates a self that is seamless, organic, and whole, much like the Thomas Carlyle of the collected works (19). His wife's autobiographical texts, on the other hand, insist, by their very nature, on the impossibility of such authority. In such texts, according to Benstock, "'self' and 'self image' might not coincide" because the writers "have no investment in creating a cohesive self over time. Indeed, they seem to exploit difference and change over sameness and identity" (15). Rather than erecting walls around the self and creating a singular, authoritative, immortal self, letters dissolve boundaries between self and other and emphasize fluidity and fragmentation; they are, in short, a subversion of autobiographical posturing.

A reaction against the idea of "I" as "one solitary individual," the letters of Jane Carlyle show her fear of self-exposure, an anxiety in relation to "I," and, ultimately, an effort to overcome that anxiety through the development of a communal sense of "me." Some of Carlyle's reticence, as I have said, can be attributed both to the decorum associated with the genre and to the social construction of the angel, whose mission to please requires "politeness, circumlocution, deference or denial" (Singley 9). But a more significant source of this autobiographical anxiety is, perhaps, her inability to see and feel an integrated and significant self and a complementary fear of exposing personal failure. Clearly, the contrast between herself and her husband is, in part, responsible for her anxiety. Masking her pain with characteristic wit, Carlyle recognizes that her own identity has been swallowed up by her husband's celebrity:

But the greatest testimony to your fame seems to me to be the fact of my photograph—the whole three, two of them very ugly . . . stuck up in Macmichael's shop-

window. Did you ever hear anything so preposterous in your life? . . . But it proves the interest or curiosity you excite; for being neither a 'distinguished authoress,' nor 'a celebrated murderess,' nor an actress, nor a 'Skittles' (the four classes of women promoted to shop-windows), it can only be as Mrs. Carlyle that they offer me for sale.

(*Letters* 2: 345-46)

Her sense that her status depends upon her role as wife gains poignancy as she recognizes the possibility of female authorial celebrity. In a letter to John Stodard, acknowledging her vanity as a girl, Carlyle comments even more overtly on the way in which her husband's stature has diminished her: "I should like to see *the individual vanity* that could hold its own in the position of worser half to a 'celebrated author'!" (*Collected Letters* 24: 258). Similarly, in a letter to Margaret Carlyle, her mother-in-law, Carlyle speaks of a woman's struggle to see herself clearly and to validate her efforts:

For my part I am always busy as possible—on that side at least I hold out no encouragement to the Devil—and yet, suppose you were to look thro' a microscope—you might be puzzled to discover a trace of what I do—nevertheless depend on [it—] my doings are not lost—but invisible to human eyes they "sail down the stream of time onto the ocean of eternity" and who knows but I may find them after many days?

(*Collected Letters* 12: 301)

Carlyle, fearing her invisibility, can only express herself through a quoted phrase, and she ends this brave assertion of her own significance with a question mark.

Ambivalence permeates Carlyle's correspondence even as she seeks personal affirmation in spite of herself. In a letter to John Sterling, for example, she speaks of her inability "to annihilate my *I-ity* or merge it in what the world doubtless considers my better half." In spite of angelic efforts at self-denial, Carlyle finds herself "a self-subsisting and alas! self-seeking *Me,*" asserting like "Little Felix, in Wanderjahre, . . . '*I too am here*'" (*Collected Letters* 8: 138). Yet, elsewhere, she questions overtly the coherence and the worth of the "self-seeking *Me*" that she imposes upon her epistolary audience. In a letter to Joseph Neuberg, who was her husband's secretary, an assistant to his process of self-creation, Jane Carlyle proffers a journal describing her return, after many years, to Haddington, her childhood home. Rather significantly, the journal is entitled ***Much Ado About Nothing,*** her self-effacing assessment of an emotionally wrenching experience. She describes the journal to Neuberg as "made for *my own* edification—thereby proving to you my immense faith in your sympathy—as from all but the most sympathetic friend one would naturally withhold such outpourings of human egotism as is here written down" (*Collected Letters* 24: 214). The journal itself suggests that this fear of "egotism" goes beyond feminine decorum and epistolary etiquette to something more personal. For, in concluding her nostalgic description of her childhood home, Carlyle denies the possibility of achieving coherence between the belle of Haddington and the lonely and unhappy woman who seeks to rediscover her history:

> And now having brought myself to Edinr and under the little protecting wing of Jeanie, I bid myself adieu and "wave my lily white hand"—I was back into the Present! and it is only in connection with the Past that I can get up a sentiment for myself—The Present M*rs* Carlyle is what shall I say?—*detestable*—upon *my* honour!

> (*Collected Letters* 24: 171)

In speaking of her present self, Carlyle becomes ironic, using an expression that her husband glosses in editing her letters as a "Mazzini Invent*n.*" Thus as she gets close to her present emotion, Carlyle beats a characteristic retreat from self-disclosure and self-assertion, both unable and unwilling, perhaps, to construct and confront an "I" that is coherent, eternal, and essentially masculine.

Joan Didion's comments on the impact of "I," which she savors in her title, "Why I Write," help put the meaning of this first person pronoun in perspective: "I I I . . . writing is the act of saying *I,* of imposing yourself on other people. . . . It's an aggressive, even a hostile act" (Didion 17). But the epistolary genre, particularly as practiced by Jane Carlyle, is something else entirely. Rather than the assertion of "I," it is the achievement of "me," of self in relation to other. And, in fact, it can be viewed as a subversion of self-assertion and the imposition that it involves. Thus Carlyle clarifies the reason behind her prolific letter writing in a letter to her cousin, Helen Welsh:

> You write very nice letters and you are a very nice cousin, and I have no fault to find with you but that you are not sufficiently sensible of your importance to me.

> For *me*; I am incorrigible as to "the welfare of others"—at least in the matter of letter writing the idea of *giving pleasure* cannot prevail with me to write and I write always from one of two motives, from a *need to receive* a letter, only to be extracted by *giving* one, or from gratitude for what is vouchsafed me "on the voluntary principle. [sic]

> (*Collected Letters* 23: 140-41)

Writing for a response, with her eye on the other, Carlyle produces a female mode of autobiography which subverts the masculine genre, characterized by the tendency to impose boundaries, to build walls, in the process of self definition. In letter after letter she reveals her acute sense of audience and its fundamental significance in determining the shape of her utterance. Writing to Jeannie Welsh, for example, Carlyle describes her inability to produce a "*merry* letter such as would beseem the season" to convey her Christmas greetings: "And therefore do I write to *you* instead of to my Uncle to whom my heart most devotedly wishes all the good wishes that one is in the habit of giving voice or ink to on the approach of a new year" (*Collected Letters* 23: 184). Thus, the self she is able to project is fit only for the eyes of her loving cousin, Jeannie, who will play a role in reconstructing it for yet another audience. A letter to Jean Carlyle Aitken shows even more clearly the close connection between the writer and the reader. "Please burn this letter," she writes, "I mean dont hand it to the rest—there is a circulation of letters in families that frightens me from writing often—it is so difficult to write a circular to *one*" (*Collected Letters* 24: 272). In yet another instance, this fear of circulation, which would undermine her persona, keeps her from corresponding with her cousin, Jeannie Welsh:

> Babbie I *could* not write to you while my husband was there, because I could and would and needed to write *thee* more confidentially than to *him* even, and I felt that it were placing you in an embarrassing predicament to send you letters which he naturally would wish to see and which you would not feel at liberty to show him—better—easier and more prudent, to write always straight to himself than to write as it were *for* him *thro* you, or else *for* you to the exclusion of him . . . when I tried to *compose* a letter to you a letter for the public—Ach Gott I found it not possible—I have got so in the way of *splashing* off whatever is on my mind when I write to you. . . .

> (*Collected Letters* 17: 16)

Because of the contingent nature of the self that she constructs, the prospect of her letter's being read by someone other than the intended audience places her, once again, in a false position. Finally, in a letter to Thomas Carlyle, her most appreciative audience, she describes, once again, the significance of relationship in the process of self-definition:

> It is certainly a questionable privilege one's best friend enjoys, that of having all one's darkness rayed out on him. If I were writing to—who shall I say?—Mr. Barlow, now, I should fill my paper with 'wits,' and elegant quotations, and anecdotes; should write a letter that would procure me laudations sky-high, on my 'charming unflagging spirits,' and my 'extraordinary freshness of mind and feeling;' but to you I cannot for my life be anything but a bore.

> (*Letters* 2: 81)

To suggest that Carlyle has mastered the art of the literary persona does not obviate the equally persuasive notion that her concept of self is fluid rather than fixed, and that autobiography for her has more to do with a sense of self as object than as subject. Ultimately, to overcome the anxiety of authorship, Carlyle needed to construct herself in the particular eyes of a trusted reader.

Another way of mastering this anxiety, Leslie S. Gutiérrez-Jones argues, is through the use of "multiple narrative voices to balance the needs for connection and separation" (Singley and Sweeney xxiii). The polyvocal nature of female narratology represents an effort to overcome the discomfort associated with the voice of authority. In yet another way it serves to construct a communal and fluid self. The editions of Jane Carlyle's letters are full of glosses that identify various passages as "coterie speech," Thomas Carlyle's term for phrases his wife appropriated from members of her circle. Sometimes these echoes mock their original sources. For example, she turns the evangelical language of Edward Irving against him, writing to her future husband about Irving's courtship: "'*Is it not a shame, yea a black and a burning shame*' to enslave his gigantic powers to such paltry worse than womanish affectations?" (*Collected Letters* 2: 264). At other times, the sounds of many voices seem merely to expand the conversation in order to delight the audience. Thus a letter written to her mother-in-law soon after Carlyle settled with her husband in Chelsea contained a pompous phrase picked up from Basil Montagu, the Scottish verb *traiked* meaning collapsed, and an Annandalism which echoes Carlyle's father, "bankrape and go out o sight" (*Collected Letters* 7: 287-88), all calculated to draw Margaret Carlyle into the conversation. More often than not, however, the voices of others seem to deflect attention from the subject, especially when the writer risks the charge of egotism. Thus addressing a young friend, asking her to pay a visit, Carlyle writes: "Pray come to tea with me to-morrow evening at seven, if my husband's particular friends 'the destinies,' *alias* 'the Upper Powers,' *alias* 'the Immortal Gods' (your father says you read Mr. C., so you will understand me), don't interfere to keep you away" (*Letters* 2: 138). While the invitation is offered in her own voice, she adopts the voice of another to deflect from this act of self-assertion. More poignantly, in her old age, Carlyle writes, "I have too 'fertile an imagination,' like 'oor David,'" recalling a phrase which her husband annotates as a reference to "a lying boy at Haddington, whom his mother excused in that way" and skirting the need to talk about herself (*Letters* 2: 374). If her recollection of language that is nearly fifty years old creates a sense of coherence over time, that coherence is grounded in communal conversation and not self-construction.

Using the voices of others allows Jane Carlyle to avoid writing that comes from the "interior," a word that she almost always puts in quotes. Writing to Jeannie Welsh, for example, she says, "But I should tell you of my interior—not what Mr C means by that, but interior in the French sense—" and then she proceeds to tell the story of her household, her kitten, and her maid (*Collected Letters* 23: 185). Similarly, and more significantly, Carlyle rejects overtly the sort of writing that involves introspection:

> I remember Charles Buller saying of the Duchess de Praslin's murder, 'What could a poor fellow do with a wife who kept a journal but murder her?' There was a certain truth hidden in this light remark. Your journal all about feelings aggravates whatever is factitious and morbid in you; that I have made experience of. And now the only sort of journal I would keep should have to do with what Mr. Carlyle calls 'the fact of things.'
>
> (*Letters* 2: 37)

Thus her autobiographical writings, the letters that contain Carlyle's personal history, deflect attention from the self as subject.

Eschewing introspection, Carlyle shows a penchant for drama, a mode that places the personal at a distance and allows her to exercise her talent for irony. Lyn Lloyd Irvine, who finds this technique typical of the female writer, describes a kind of dissociation that is similar to what Carlyle achieves: "She [the female letter writer] undergoes a temporary metamorphosis; the self divides in two, one person observes and records, the other acts and feels and is observed, and both escape—for the moment—from the vexations and tedium of existence" (Irvine 23). Thus the observer Jane, author of the letters, distances herself as she dramatizes a scene at the breakfast table where the character Jane confronts a domestic vexation:

> Figure this: (Scene—a room where everything is enveloped in dark-yellow London fog! For air to breathe, a sort of liquid soot! Breakfast on the table—'adulterated coffee,' 'adulterated bread,' 'adulterated cream,' and 'adulterated water'!) Mr. C. at one end of the table, looking remarkably bilious; Mrs. C. at the other, looking half dead! Mr. C.: 'My dear, I have to inform you that my bed is full of bugs, or fleas, or some sort of animals that crawl over me all night.'
>
> (*Letters* 2: 71-72)

Through dramatization, Carlyle makes the personal public and avoids, as a good letter writer must, "Lamentations of Jeremiah, for which transient human breath is only too good" (*Collected Letters* 24: 50). To dignify personal pain with the permanence of writing represents an imposition of the "self-seeking *Me*," which Carlyle struggled to avoid in her epistolary autobiography.

In fact, in rejecting the idea of a separation between self and world, between interior and exterior, between self and other, in projecting the self as object rather than subject, and in adopting a multitude of voices to avoid the assertion of ego, Carlyle calls into question the whole idea of autobiography. Because Thomas Carlyle believed that biography is history, that the figure of a great man embodies the spirit of an age, he wrote the lives of Cromwell, of Frederick the Great and, over and over again, of Thomas Carlyle. Jane Carlyle, no mean historian herself, took pen in hand to create the lives of women. On the one hand, her epistolary authorship conforms to the feminine ideal of the Victorian era, constructing the figure that I have called "the angel in the envelope." But in embracing materiality, domesticity, privacy, and fragmentation, the traits that define the angel, Carlyle seizes upon the perfect form, a "peculiarly female" genre, for subverting the idea of history as autobiography and, in fact, of autobiography itself. In a text written over a period of fifty years, Jane Carlyle wages a subtle war against the figure of the literary lion and denies, over and over again, the centrality of self, the coherence of form, and the authoritative, masculine view of the unity of the autobiographical subject as "one solitary individual."

Note

1. In his discussion of the "pattern of conversion," which characterizes Victorian autobiography in works as diverse as *David Copperfield* and "In Memoriam," Jerome Buckley points out that in *Sartor Resartus,* Thomas Carlyle "was able to objectify in terms of allegory relevant details from his personal experience, and thereby to suggest what seemed to him the requisite pattern for all conversions." While John Henry Newman and John Stuart Mill, "the Major Victorian autobiographers," recorded similar conversions, they were "limited to specific facts." It was for Carlyle to extract the essential form of the experience and to supply the "categories" that characterize the "common regenerative process," thereby making of his own life the pattern of the age (95).

Works Cited

Austen, Jane. *Northanger Abbey, Lady Susan, The Waltons, and Sanditon.* Oxford: Oxford UP, 1990.

Barnes, Elizabeth L. "Mirroring the Mother Text: Histories of Seduction in the American Domestic Novel." Singley and Sweeney 157-72.

Beauchamp, Virginia Walcott. "Letters and Diaries: The Persona and the Real Woman—A Case Study." *Women's Personal Narratives: Essays in Criticism and Pedagogy.* Ed. Leonore Hoffman and Margo Culley. New York: MLA, 1985. 40-47.

Benstock, Shari. "Authorizing the Autobiographical." *The Private Self: Theory and Practice of Women's Autobiographical Writing.* Ed. Shari Benstock. Chapel Hill: U of North Carolina P, 1988. 10-33.

Buckley, Jerome Hamilton. *The Victorian Temper: A Study of Literary Culture.* New York: Vintage, 1951.

Carlyle, Jane Welsh. *Letters and Memorials of Jane Welsh Carlyle Prepared for Publication by Thomas Carlyle.* Ed. James Anthony Froude. 2 vols. New York: Scribner's, 1883.

Carlyle, Jane Welsh and Thomas Carlyle. *The Collected Letters of Thomas and Jane Welsh Carlyle.* Duke-Edinburgh Edition. Ed. Charles Richard Sanders, Clyde de L. Ryals, Kenneth Fielding. 24 vols. Durham: Duke UP, 1970-1995.

Crichton-Browne, Sir James. Introduction. *New Letters and Memorials of Jane Welsh Carlyle: Annotated by Thomas Carlyle.* Ed. Alexander Carlyle. 2 vols. London: Lane, 1903.

de Lauretis, Teresa. *Alice Doesn't: Feminism, Semiotics, Cinema.* London: MacMillan, 1984.

Didion, Joan. "Why I Write." *The Writer and Her Work.* Ed. Janet Sternburg. New York: Norton, 1980. 17-25.

Gilbert, Sandra M. and Susan Gubar. *The Madwoman in the Attic: The Woman Writer and the Nineteenth-Century Literary Imagination.* New Haven: Yale UP, 1979.

Irvine, Lyn Lloyd. *Ten Letter Writers.* 1932. Freeport, New York: Books for Libraries, 1968.

Michie, Elsie B. *Outside the Pale: Cultural Exclusion, Gender Differences, and The Victorian Woman Writer.* Ithaca: Cornell UP, 1993.

Perry, Ruth. *Women, Letters, and the Novel.* New York: AMS, 1980.

Singley, Carol J. "Female Language, Body, and Self." Singley and Sweeney 3-15.

Singley, Carol J. and Susan Elizabeth Sweeney. Introduction. *Anxious Power: Reading, Writing and Ambivalence in Narrative by Women.* Ed. Carol J. Singley and Susan Elizabeth Sweeney. Albany: State U of New York P, 1993. xiii-xxvi.

Smith, Sidonie. *A Poetics of Women's Autobiography: Marginality and the Fictions of Self-Representation.* Bloomington: Indiana UP, 1987.

Sweeney, Susan Elizabeth. "Formal Strategies in a Female Narrative Tradition: The Case of *Swann: A Mystery.*" Singley and Sweeney 19-32.

Waring, Walter. *Thomas Carlyle.* Twayne Author Series. Boston: Twayne, 1978.

Woolf, Virginia. "Professions for Women." *The Virginia Woolf Reader.* Ed. Mitchell A. Leaska. New York: Harcourt, 1984. 276-82.

Rodger L. Tarr (essay date 2004)

SOURCE: Tarr, Rodger L. "'The Victorian Lady'—Jane Welsh Carlyle and the Psycho-Feminist Myth: A Retrospective." In *The Carlyles at Home and Abroad,* edited by David R. Sorenson and Rodger L. Tarr, pp. 196-208. Aldershot, England: Ashgate Publishing Limited, 2004.

[*In the following essay, Tarr explores critical misconceptions concerning Jane Carlyle's private life.*]

The alleged tragedy of Jane Welsh Carlyle's life is one built upon ignorance and founded upon falsehood. For over one hundred years, she has been damned and defamed. In spite of her nobility of character and wit, and her talents as a writer and thinker, Jane Carlyle has been consistently condemned because she dared to marry the irascible Thomas Carlyle. Many psychoanalytic critics and feminist scholars feel, in varying degrees, betrayed by her—she has become the symbol of the presumed oppression in Victorian marriage. She is at once the martyr and the scapegoat for unbridled indignation. How dare she marry someone not suitable for marriage; how dare she betray the growing conviction that women (and men) are destined for higher goals than slavish devotion to legalised cohabitation?

The Prufrockian challenge—'How dare?'—is not exclusively a modern or post-modern perspective—in fact, the seeming pathological violations of Jane Carlyle's life have been going on—largely unchecked until the recent and welcome appearance of Rosemary Ashton's *Thomas & Jane Carlyle: Portrait of a Marriage* (2002), and Kenneth Fielding and David Sorensen's **Jane Carlyle: Newly Selected Letters** (2004)—since her death in 1866. The maltreatment of her character has even wider implications, for she has become a symbol of what happens when so-called scholars and intellectuals choose to live outside the realm of accepted taste, common decency and historical perspective. The question that emerges is crucial: do we as scholars have an obligation to the truth, or do we have free licence to any opinion regardless of the consequences? Over one hundred years ago John Stuart Mill set an ethical standard when he argued that we do not have a right to any opinion; rather we have only the right to responsible opinion. If Mill is correct, then what has happened to Jane Carlyle should serve as a demonstration of what can and still does happen when patent falsehood is presented as scholarly truth.

The known facts of Jane Carlyle's life can be repeated. She was christened Jane Baillie Welsh, the daughter of a distinguished medical doctor from Haddington, a tiny village of classical character to the east of Edinburgh. Documents indicate that Jane was a precocious child who spurned the habits of her domestic mother and instead persisted in being close to her professional father. As she told the Anglo-Indian journalist William Knighton in 1857, 'My father was very anxious for a boy. He was disappointed that I was born a girl. However, he brought me up as much as possible as a boy. I was taught as a boy. When my mother remonstrated he would say, at eighteen I will hand her over to you, and you can teach her all a girl ought to know' (915). Her father, who had already witnessed his daughter finishing a five-act tragedy at fourteen, never stood in her way. As the fates would have it, at the age of twenty Jane met Thomas Carlyle, a young man of Calvinist peasant

stock from Ecclefechan, a village in the southwest of Scotland, a land immortalised in the poetry of Robert Burns. Under the tutelage of Carlyle, she read voraciously and eclectically, but the passion that drove her was her love of Byron.

The unsettled state of the Regency period in Britain had spawned the Byronic misanthrope, and Jane identified immediately with this Byronic solitary. With some reluctance she also followed Carlyle's urging to learn German and to read particularly the pronouncements of Goethe, Schiller, and Kant. But in the end Byron's 'Manfred' spoke to her of other ideals—and at one point she proclaimed the intention of physical celibacy with the view of achieving intellectual chastity. On the other hand, the letters exchanged between Jane and Thomas during this period demonstrate that Carlyle's attraction to her was almost instantly transformed to love. He persisted, and she resisted, writing to him some of the most comic rejections ever penned. After all, what future would the Belle of Haddington have with a crude peasant from Ecclefechan? She was wealthy, he poor; she was sophisticated, he bumbling; she was the epitome of grace, he rude beyond words. Still, they did have Byron in common; and, yes, she was coming to appreciate the Germanic longing of Carlyle. Indeed, in the prophetic words of Byron from *Don Juan,*

> But who, alas! can love, and then be wise?
>   Not that remorse did not oppose temptation;
> A little still she strove, and much repented, And whis-
>   pering 'I will
> ne'er consent'—consented.

In 1826, two Romantics became Victorian, a marriage that was to become the most famous in nineteenth-century Britain.

During the early years of their marriage, the Carlyles were nourished by their idealism. Thomas made a sufficient but not extravagant living. He was already well-known in critical circles for his translation of *Wilhelm Meister* (1824), his biography of *The Life of Friedrich Schiller* (1825), and his four-volume translation of German fiction, *German Romance* (1827). The novelist Sir Walter Scott was an acquaintance, the classical critic Francis Jeffrey a mentor, and the immortal Goethe an epistolary friend. However, the Carlyles did suffer early failure. He was turned down for the chair of Moral Philosophy at Saint Andrews University, in spite of letters of recommendation from Professor John Wilson, Jeffrey and Goethe; he had failed at writing a novel; and the remoteness of their farm Craigenputtoch—one hour by horseback from the nearest village—put a strain upon his young wife, who was accustomed to refinement. Thomas composed *Sartor Resartus* and tended the livestock; Jane wrote poetry and worked in her beloved flower garden. Isolation had its impact, but as their letters of the period indicate, it seldom caused domestic acerbity.

In 1834, the Carlyles removed to London and for the next three decades their home in Chelsea became a centre of Victorian intellectual life; the liberals John Stuart Mill and Harriet Taylor were constant visitors during the 1830s; Dickens knew them; Thackeray came by for walks by the river; Emerson visited and revisited, taking home to America a renewed transcendental faith; the Brownings, Robert and Elizabeth, became friends and admirers; Tennyson was a constant companion, who on occasion came specifically to visit Jane; Leigh Hunt was so overcome by the aura that he penned the famous poem 'Jenny Kissed Me', after an impulsive greeting from Jane; and then there was the confused but brilliant John Ruskin, who was to address Carlyle as 'Papa'. Chopin was there, as well as the young German intellectuals of the day. The list of prominent visitors is endless. By 1854, George Eliot was to declare without equivocation that Carlyle was an 'oak' among 'acorns'.

The Carlyles shared an incredible life. If Jane suffered neglect when Thomas was at work, it was all but made up for by their associations. True, she complained when she felt ignored; she once wrote him a lengthy letter, entitled '**Budget** *of a Femme* incomprise' (7 Feb. 1855), addressing him as a government minister after Carlyle complained of her extravagances. She was also upset, even bitter, over what she perceived as Carlyle's increasingly intimate relationship with Lady Harriet Ashburton. They endured periods of great emotional pain, but in the end the strength of their union was preserved, a strength confirmed in the passions of their letters. Carlyle called her 'Goody', 'My Necessary Evil', and in return, she called him bluntly 'Carlyle'.

Jane was Thomas's host, but never his ring bearer. She was a host in the medieval sense, one who was responsible for the moral as well as the physical well-being of the guests, most of them friends of hers. And, she knew cleverly how to irritate Carlyle: she pressed the French feminist George Sand upon him, and he responded by denouncing her novels as 'Phallus-Worship'; and she brought her feminist friends before him. The Americans, Margaret Fuller and Lydia Maria Child, and their English counterparts, Harriet Martineau and Geraldine Jewsbury, were welcomed, if somewhat reluctantly, by Thomas. George Eliot pestered Jane to get Thomas to read *Adam Bede*; Jane pestered Thomas to read the Brontës; each pestered the other with their literary tastes. In all this, Jane was always at the front, never did she trail, never did she cower. Certainly she suffered—so many visitors, so much bombast, became an intrusion. Thomas would retire cursing in broad Scots, while Jane was left to increasing migraines and the opiate laudanum. Colds, influenza, and unidentified ailments became her constant companions. Yet her wit never abandoned her; she persevered, defending Carlyle to the end. In 1866 she died, without a struggle or sound, during a ride in her brougham in Hyde Park;

Carlyle, almost at the very moment, was at Edinburgh University accepting the Lord Rectorship. Jane Carlyle was born a Romantic and died a Romantic, even though she suffered the tragedies and triumphs of being what Virginia Woolf called 'The Victorian Lady' (150).

Without doubt, the Carlyles lived a tumultuous life. As intellectuals, both held fervently to the past; both lived uneasily in the present; and each had an apocalyptic vision of the future. Their marriage was not perfect. Carlyle was demanding, punctual and certainly stern. Jane was acerbic, witty and equally stern. They clashed frequently. There was thunder, but always it was followed by periods of redemptive rain. Yet they seemed to have a single flaw—a flaw whose magnitude has been exacerbated in the minds of those whose passion it was and is to examine the passions of the Carlyles. Quite simply, they were childless. Childless couples are childless because one or both suffer from sexual dysfunction. One is impotent, or the other is frigid. It cannot be any other way. Choice and/or ill-fortune were hardly possibilities. To the psychoanalytic mind that believes this, to the feminist who finds sustenance in it, there can be no other answer. The Carlyles were flawed—they must be exposed.

The primary architect of this exposure forces another irony upon the situation. One of Jane's best friends, the celebrated feminist and novelist Geraldine Jewsbury, in 1873, upon her deathbed and thus presumably in candour, imparted the news to Carlyle's official biographer James Anthony Froude: 'Carlyle was one of those persons who ought never to have married' (*My Relations* [*My Relations with Carlyle*] 21). Froude translates this confession by Jewsbury into a portrait of pain. Throughout his biography he implies, suggests, cajoles; and, when the reader is finished, the portrait is sharp: Thomas was a cruel, insensitive and uncaring husband. Froude, however, avoids direct discussion of the Jewsbury allegation, that Carlyle suffered from either impotence or sexual dysfunction. Instead he paints a long-suffering Jane whose life was mercifully cut short in 1866. The Carlyle descendants were stunned by Froude's conclusions. Mary Aitken, Carlyle's niece and amanuensis, demanded an apology and return of the papers that Carlyle had entrusted to Froude. Froude declined, and the whole affair was taken to the pages of the London *Times*.

Charges and countercharges were filed. Friends and acquaintances were appalled. Froude subsequently appealed to Jane's first biographer, Mrs Alexander Ireland, to tell the truth, and to discuss openly Carlyle's impotence and its impact on Jane. Mrs Ireland declined, although her work is decidedly sympathetic to Jane. The furor continued. By the turn of the century, some corrections were attempted. Carlyle's nephew Alexander published *New Letters and Memorials of Jane*

Welsh Carlyle (1903), and in his preface he challenged Froude's pronouncements. Froude, now dead, was defended by his family, and the rejoinder *My Relations with Carlyle* (1903), a short book of 80 pages founded upon a manuscript Froude left behind, was hurried to press. In it we are told explicitly that the only source for Froude's assertions was in fact Geraldine Jewsbury, who claimed a special intimacy with Jane. The 'mystery', as Froude calls it, was finally exposed: Carlyle had been impotent; the proof: 'The morning after his wedding-day he tore to pieces the flower-garden at Comeley Bank' (*My Relations* 23), the Carlyles' residence in Edinburgh. Just who saw Carlyle do this is unclear, and it did not seem to matter that there was no flower garden at Comely Bank.

The implication is clear: men who despoil flower-gardens after their wedding-night are confirming their sexual impotence. To this Froude adds, '[Jane] had longed for children, and children were denied her' (*My Relations* 21). In response to these new allegations, the prestigious *British Medical Journal* in 1903 offered a lead article by Sir James Crichton-Browne on the impossibilities of this all being medically provable, much less true. The noted writer Andrew Lang wrote a summary of the sordid situation, entitled 'The Carlyle Scandal' (1903). Crichton-Browne and Alexander Carlyle next devoted a book to the subject, *The Nemesis of Froude* (1903), in which they denounced such insufferable innuendo. Still, this now barebones psychoanalytic controversy would not go away. The crowning achievement to psychoanalysis was yet to come, however.

In 1911 the already infamous Bloomsbury addict Frank Harris reported with his usual sincerity that in 1878 Carlyle in a state of remorse had confided to him that he 'had never consummated the marriage or lived with his wife as a wife' ('Talks' ['Talks with Carlyle'] 432). Carlyle was eighty-three when this alleged discussion took place; Harris was twenty-two. Harris insists that his knowledge was later corroborated at the Garrick Club in London by the distinguished physician Sir Richard Quain. Harris then reports at length Dr Quain's alleged club-room confessional. As the story goes, Quain was visiting the Carlyles when Jane suffered abdominal pains and retired to her room. Quain followed to offer assistance. The following excerpt from Harris's *My Life and Loves* (1925) suggests the extent of his retreat from the truth:

> Mrs. Carlyle was lying on the bed with a wooly-shawl round her head and face. I thought it an absurd affection in an old married woman, so I resolved on drastic measures: I turned the light full on, then I put my hand under her dress and with one toss threw it right over her head. I pulled her legs apart, dragged her to the edge of the bed and began inserting the speculum in her vulva: I met an obstacle—I looked—and immediately sprang up. 'Why, you're a virgo intacta!'
>
> (209)

Harris's vulgar, demeaning, and insulting description marked the birth of the central myth of the Carlyles' supposedly disastrous marriage: Jane died a virgin.

It is discouraging to think that such psychoanalytic twaddle would be taken seriously by intellectuals, especially one as distinguished as Virginia Woolf. Yet in 1929 in her article 'Geraldine and Jane', she accepts and contributes to the myth. In general her account of the friendship of Geraldine Jewsbury and Jane Carlyle is remarkable for its depth of passionate understanding. She recounts deftly how Geraldine gave tea parties with Jane, where Geraldine 'discussed literature rather boldly, with a cigar in her mouth' (149). She points out how Geraldine 'dressed herself in a low-neck dress to receive visitors on Sunday' (149). And she observes how Geraldine revised the manuscripts of her first novel *Zoe* (1845) because Jane thought it too 'indecent' (150). To Woolf, both women are feminists. Jane was quiet, usually observing, whereas Geraldine was outspoken, always pugnacious: her 'blood boiled in her at the power men had over women'. Woolf's own blood boils at the thought of Jane's marriage to Carlyle, who 'hated . . . strong-minded women of the George Sand species' (150).

Woolf's anger leads her to extreme conclusions. She argues that Geraldine was unnaturally jealous of Jane, and quotes the latter's remark that Geraldine had 'some sort of strange, passionate . . . incomprehensible *attraction* towards me . . . such mad, lover-like jealousy' (150). Decorously but firmly Woolf raises the issue of lesbianism. She seems convinced, in the absence of any concrete evidence, that there was a passion between the two—a bodily attraction, at least on Geraldine's part. As if sorry for intruding upon the friendship, Woolf offers an apologia: 'It is difficult to persuade ourselves that we can judge Geraldine Jewsbury and the true nature of her feeling for Jane Carlyle' (150). Woolf almost seems to be appealing on her own behalf. In the end, however, she had left her impression for the future to consider: Geraldine Jewsbury and Jane Carlyle, Woolf concludes, 'discussed everything' (150). Unwittingly and without malice, she added a new chapter in the life of Jane Carlyle, who was linked on an intimate level with the 'Feminist from Manchester'. Woolf understood lesbian yearnings in the context of volatile marriage, and intuitively, she read her own life into Jane's. She could not possibly have anticipated how her impressions would become facts in the eyes of future (and lesser) psycho-feminist critics, and serve as a springboard for ludicrous charges and false innuendo.

To a certain extent, post World War II criticism attempted to salvage Jane Carlyle's reputation. In 1949, Trudy Bliss edited a selection of her letters in a noble and partially successful attempt to present the real Jane Carlyle. In 1952, Lawrence and Elisabeth Hanson wrote a sympathetic biography that relegates the whole controversy to an appendix. For a moment Jane Carlyle was restored, her dignity returned. However, it was only a brief respite. As psychoanalytic study and feminist perspective increased in the 60s and 70s, Jane Carlyle again became fair game. The myths created by the Victorians and Edwardians were once again translated into facts. The Victorians, seemingly notorious for chauvinistic behaviour, became the staples to feed the myth. In her book, with the leading (and misleading) title of *Seduction and Betrayal* (1975), Elizabeth Hardwick concedes from the outset that the Carlyles' marriage was '*the* Victorian marriage' (165), and then proceeds to dismantle it. Hardwick sees the marriage as a 'domestic comedy' because Jane had to subvert her 'genius' to Thomas's 'gigantism' (165). Hardwick insists that while Thomas chased the bitch-goddess success, Jane was 'cleaning, dusting, chasing bedbugs, sewing, [and] supervising redecorations' (168). In the midst of these unsupported observations, Hardwick repeats Frank Harris's mythical assertion that Jane was a lifelong virgin as a result of Carlyle's fumbling (174). With no more understanding than taste, Hardwick concludes that Jane Carlyle was no different from other Victorian women who had no 'bulwark against sufferings of neglect and the humiliations of lovelessness' (181). Perhaps such nonsense needs no refutation, but we can only regret that it comes from a woman who identifies herself as a feminist.

What Hardwick lacks in judgement is more than compensated for by the ebullient Phyllis Rose, who stretches decency to its nadir. In *Parallel Lives* (1984)—another best seller—Rose devotes upwards of four chapters to the Carlyles' marriage. She recounts as facts all previous myths, and concludes confidently that Carlyle 'is a great man, a great thinker, but a pathetic human being . . . a terrible, a cruel, husband. The idol has feet of clay' (257). To prove her point, Rose retreats to the well-known story of Carlyle and his neighbour's rooster, sometimes called cock, which much to Carlyle's consternation awoke him at all hours of the night and early morning. The story is true enough. Thomas was so put out with the noise that he implored Jane, among others, to do something about it. They planned all sorts of intrigues, including buying the cock and killing it. Victorian intellectuals sat around and ruminated on what the Carlyles should do. Thomas fumed, Jane sympathised, they all laughed, and in the end a sound-proof study was built at Cheyne Row.

Rose subjects this comic interlude to humourless psychoanalysis. Jane was always 'her husband's protector, slaying the serpents without so that he could concentrate on slaying the serpents within' (246). For Rose it follows that 'no one who has been awakened in darkness by cock crows will be tempted to put down [Carlyle's] resentment of cocks as wholly symbolic' (246).

Thomas's resentment of the rooster has taken a Freudian turn. Of course, Jane herself is implicated. Referring to a letter in which Jane mentions a dream about a cock, Rose triumphantly declares, 'Even in her dreams, [Jane Carlyle] fended off cocks' (247). Rose's prurient implication is clear—Jane had phallic dreams because of her sexless marriage. Fred Kaplan embraced similar conclusions in his Freudian biography of Carlyle, written in the same period. Without a shred of evidence, he asserts that Carlyle suffered from an Oedipal complex so deep-seated that as a child he was afraid to masturbate (35). With equal certainty (and with no evidence) he states that Jane Welsh was 'frightened of sex' (72).

Perhaps inevitably, post-modern criticism has perpetuated the myth of Jane Carlyle, to the point where the windmill of illusion spins to a blur. Sandra Gilbert and Susan Gubar emerged as the chief spokespersons of psycho-feminist theory, and they comfortably and without hesitation asserted that the Victorian pen and the Victorian penis were indistinguishable, at least metaphorically. *Madwoman in the Attic* (1979)—an immediate best seller—was devoted to the proposition that the 'poet's pen is in some sense . . . a penis' (93-4). This link supposedly explained why women such as Jane Carlyle were intellectually unfulfilled. Males were the controlling force in literature and publishing, and of course, Carlyle was one of the central figures at the helm. In a rather dense syllogism Gilbert and Gubar hold him responsible for promoting the maleness of Victorian society. They argue that Carlyle was responsible for canonising Goethe, and that Goethe was the progenitor of 'the eternal feminine, the angel women' (23). In his climactic injunction in *Sartor Resartus*—'Close thy *Byron*; open thy *Goethe*'—Carlyle encouraged the oppression of women. The suggestion that *Sartor Resartus,* with its emphatic transcendentalism, is a specific articulation of Victorian chauvinism is absurd. Typically, Gilbert and Gubar overlook the fact that Carlyle's bildungsroman was especially admired by feminists such as Lydia Maria Child, Margaret Fuller, Harriet Martineau, and Geraldine Jewsbury. It was also a favourite of Virginia Woolf's. Are we to believe that these distinguished women and others—Elizabeth Barrett Browning, Louisa May Alcott, Elizabeth Gaskell, and Emily Dickinson, among others, missed the antifeminist thrust seen by Gilbert and Gubar? Their claim is embarrassing as well as inaccurate.

Feminists since Gubar and Gilbert have used increasingly sophisticated arguments to reinforce the myth of the Carlyle marriage. In *Ambitious Heights* (1990), Norma Clarke argues that Geraldine Jewsbury's testimony was discredited because she was a female novelist working in a patriarchal world: 'Geraldine had provided a convenient scapegoat. She had furnished Froude with some of the anecdotes which placed Thomas Carlyle in a particularly bad light . . . and her capacity to tell the simple truth was easily called into question by referring to her occupation: she was a novelist; her brain teemed with "romance"' (148). Clarke simply refuses to accept the possibility that Jewsbury may have exaggerated, and curiously defends her decision to destroy Jane Carlyle's letters to her as 'honourable' (149) without questioning her motives. Jane's own complaints about Geraldine's misdirected sentiment and excessive emotion are dismissed and turned against her. They are the consequence of her envy at Geraldine's 'capacity to go out and live her life in a way that suited her' (152). Of course Carlyle himself is finally to blame for this state of affairs, since he is the one who shapes Jane to be, in Jewsbury's language, 'the beautiful reflex of him' (190). The psycho-feminist argument here takes a new turn, transforming the victim into the aggressor.

Adopting a different tactic, Aileen Christianson in 1997 drew welcome attention to the literary qualities of Jane Carlyle's letters. But the attention, it should be noted, came at a heavy price where Thomas Carlyle himself is concerned. In her essay, Christianson subordinates the discussion of the letters to the question of 'Welsh Carlyle's' status as a writer. By referring to her as a 'life-writer', Christianson intends to raise Jane's literary reputation to that of a Victorian novelist, which according to Christianson, 'Welsh Carlyle' chose not to be: 'In the end her choice was not to seek fame, to publish, or to challenge social constraints. It was to accept the dictates of a conventional "wifely" life of duty, of repression; and, in sarcastic and humorous counterpoint to that life, to weave her continuous web of commentary on her life and the lives surrounding her' (243). What begins as an appreciation of Jane's epistolary skills ends with a claim for her as a novelist manqué. In her conclusion, Christianson implies that Jane Carlyle fails to become a Dickens because of her 'repressed' existence as Thomas's wife—it follows that her achievement as a 'life-writer' is all the more significant, given her life of 'duty' and 'repression'. In a recent review of Rosemary Ashton's *Portrait of a Marriage,* Kathryn Hughes has trenchantly exposed the dubious psycho-feminist assumptions underlying these claims: 'While other commentators have rushed to see Jane as a thwarted artist, whose prolific and entertaining letters are a sad token of all the brilliant novels that marriage to Carlyle stopped her from writing, Ashton is far cooler in her analysis. Other women in difficult situations managed to write novels—the Brontës, George Eliot, and even Mrs Gaskell all succeeded in domestic circumstances that were far from ideal. If Jane Carlyle never managed to make it into print, then something more complicated than patriarchy must have been to blame'.

In *Men of Letters, Writing Lives* (1999), Trev Lyn Broughton sought to explain the Froude controversy in the context of late nineteenth-century shifting attitudes towards the ideal of the 'man of letters'. Barely con-

cealing her delight in the triumph of 'psycho-history' over history proper, Broughton blithely disregards the moral implications of the charges made against Carlyle: 'With the publication of the impotence allegation, the Froude-Carlyle embroilment ceased to be a recognisably political struggle for justice . . . and devolved into an unsavoury struggle for the right to guarantee the meaning of sex: struggle, finally, for the phallus' (171). Truth here becomes a casualty of a larger and more important movement against the hegemony of 'autocratic' husbands and literary men. In her typically inflated idiom, Broughton observes that Froude's *My Relations* 'precipitated a crisis of legitimation for Victorian biography, and marks a faultline in biographical epistemology . . . [which] . . . calls a habitually psychoanalytic reader into being' (171). The arrival of psychoanalysis coincides with the disposal of old and tired complaints about accuracy and fairness: 'The fuss [the allegation of impotence] caused, and went on causing, was as much about this fracturing and redrawing of disciplinary and professional boundaries as about the truth, or otherwise, of Froude's revelations on ticklish topics' (172). For Broughton, the 'fuss' is incidental to these larger psycho-feminist concerns.

The myth of the Carlyle marriage has been resurrected in less obscure ways by Julia Markus in *Across an Untried Sea* (2000). She straightforwardly repeats Frank Harris's tale and declares that 'All the evidence points to the fact that both Quain and Harris were telling the truth' (300). As Brent Kinser has discovered, Markus's belief in Harris and Quain is the result of somewhat baffling logic. While she admits that Harris's memoir was 'ignored through the twentieth century, the message bearer in this case being long considered a liar' (167), she nevertheless maintains his truthfulness. Unfortunately, Markus has only Harris's version of Quain's testimony to offer as a defence of Harris's honesty. She undermines her position further by committing basic errors of fact and chronology. According to the *Dictionary of National Biography,* the Dr Richard Quain (1800-87) to whom Harris, Hardwick, Rose, and Markus herself refer is not the Dr Richard Quain (1816-98) who attended the Carlyles. As Kinser has further discovered, there were two Sir Richard Quains in London at this time, cousins, both of whom were physicians, and both of whom attended Queen Victoria. Markus claims that her Dr Quain 'was a literary man and a raconteur' (167), which is true: he published *The Diseases of the Rectum* in 1854. The Richard Quain who treated Jane Carlyle had a fashionable London practice and was an expert in diseases of the chest. Markus's mistake is no doubt an honest one. John Gallagher, who edited the 1963 Grove Press edition of *My Life and Loves,* identifies the wrong Dr Quain in Harris's account as well. It may be, however, that Harris was responsible for the error. If so, then his tale can be confirmed as an outright lie.

Markus further weakens her argument in her summary of Harris's report. She concludes her account of the examination after Dr Quain's pronouncement of 'virgo intacta', when Jane asks, '"What did you expect?"' (168). Harris, however, continues with Quain's response to Jane: '"Anything but that"', I cried, '"in a woman married these five and twenty years"' (210). It is surprising that Markus would leave out Quain's response, for it seems to date his examination to 1851 (the Carlyles married in 1826). However, in a letter to Betty Braid, dated 25 December 1862, Jane writes of Quain: 'My first words to him (he had never been in the house before) were "Oh Dr. Quain what has brought you here"' (Froude, *LM* [*Letters and Memorials of Jane Welsh Carlyle*] 3:144). Thus, according to Jane, Quain's first visit to Cheyne Row is 1862, not 1851. Perhaps an aging Harris has confused his dates—if so, it is a peculiar testimony to what Markus calls his 'unusually retentive memory' (300). If Markus is correct about Harris's memory, then it seems reasonable to conclude that in constructing his lie, he chose the wrong Quain and the wrong date.

It is remarkable, given the weight of misunderstanding that surrounds Jane Carlyle and her marriage to Thomas Carlyle, that so few psycho-feminists have bothered to ask the relevant questions: what was Geraldine Jewsbury's motive in giving Froude such malicious gossip about the Carlyles? And armed with the gossip of Carlyle's alleged impotence, why did not Froude bother to check with other intimates of the Carlyles? Why, indeed, was he content to rely on the testimony of a woman whose propensity for exaggeration was well documented, especially by Jane Carlyle herself? The example of Jane Carlyle—an extraordinary woman in every respect—suggests how fragile the reputations of literary figures can be. Yet surely John Stuart Mill's injunction on responsible opinion still deserves to be respected. The foundation of any empirical truth should be fact rather than fiction. Psycho-feminists and their followers have, either wittingly or unwittingly, participated in the creation and the perpetuation of the myth of Jane Carlyle that undercuts the integrity of both feminism and psychoanalysis. Perhaps it is time for them to heed Carlyle's words in his essay 'Biography' (1832): '[I]t is good that every reader and every writer understand, with all intensity of conviction, what quite infinite worth lies in *Truth*' (*Works* 28:53).

Works Cited

Ashton, Rosemary. *Thomas and Jane Carlyle: Portrait of a Marriage*. London: Chatto & Windus, 2002.

Broughton, Trev Lynn. *Men of Letters, Writing Lives. Masculinity and Literary Auto/Biography in the Late Victorian Period*. London and New York: Routledge, 1999.

[Carlyle, Thomas. *Works*. Ed. H. D. Traill. Centenary Edition. 30 vols. London: Chapman and Hall, 1896-99.]

Christianson, Aileen. 'Jane Welsh Carlyle's Private Writing Career'. In *A History of Scottish Women's Writing*. Ed. Douglas Gifford and Dorothy McMillan. Edinburgh: Edinburgh UP, 1997. 232-45.

Clarke, Norma. *Ambitious Heights. Writing, Friendship, Love—The Jewsbury Sisters, Felicia Hemans, and Jane Welsh Carlyle*. London and NY: Routledge, 1990.

Crichton-Browne, James. 'Froude and Carlyle: The Imputation Considered Medically'. *British Medical Journal* (27 June 1903): 1498-1502.

———, and Alexander Carlyle. *The Nemesis of Froude. A Rejoinder to J. A. Froude's 'My Relations with Carlyle'*. London and New York: Lane, 1903.

Fielding, Kenneth J. and David R. Sorensen, eds. *Jane Carlyle: Newly Selected Letters*. Aldershot, UK: Ashgate, 2004.

[Froude, James Anthony, ed. *Letters and Memorials of Jane Welsh Carlyle*. London: Longman and Green, 1883.

———. *My Relations with Carlyle*. London: Longman and Green, 1903.]

Gilbert, Sandra, and Susan Gubar. *The Madwoman in the Attic*. New York: Yale UP, 1984.

Hardwick, Elizabeth. *Seduction and Betrayal*. New York: Vintage, 1975.

Harris, Frank. 'Talks with Carlyle'. *English Review* 7 (1911): 419-34.

———. *My Life and Loves*. New York: Grove Press, 1963.

Hughes, Kathryn. 'Marriage of Opposites'. Rev. of *Thomas and Jane Carlyle: Portrait of a Marriage*. By Rosemary Ashton. *The Guardian* (9 Feb. 2002): B3.

Kaplan, Fred. *Thomas Carlyle: A Biography*. Ithaca, New York: Cornell UP, 1983.

Kinser, Brent. 'Jane and Shirley'. Unpublished research. Used with the permission of the author.

Knighton, William. 'Conversations With Carlyle'. *Contemporary Review* 30 (June 1881): 904-20.

Lang, Andrew. 'The Froude-Carlyle Dispute'. *Independent* (Bombay, 1903): 1565-7.

Markus, Julia. *Across an Untried Sea: Discovering Lives Hidden in the Shadow of Convention and Time*. New York: Knopf, 2000.

Rose, Phyllis. *Parallel Lives: Five Victorian Marriages*. New York: Knopf, 1984.

[Woolf, Virginia]. 'Geraldine and Jane'. *Times Literary Supplement* (28 Feb. 1929): 149-50.

Aileen Christianson (essay date 2004)

SOURCE: Christianson, Aileen. "Jane Welsh Carlyle's Travel Narratives: 'Portable Perspectives.'" In *The Carlyles at Home and Abroad,* edited by David R. Sorenson and Rodger L. Tarr, pp. 209-18. Aldershot, England: Ashgate Publishing Limited, 2004.

[*In the following essay, Christianson examines the satirical elements in Carlyle's travel writings, describing her as a "skeptical anti-tourist."*]

That Jane Welsh Carlyle controls her material and the presentation of her life in her writing through her literary skills is now generally accepted. Townsend Scudder, editor of her letters to Joseph Neuberg, wrote in 1931 that 'her literary effects . . . will be found to have something of a method in it' (Scudder [*Letters of Jane Welsh Carlyle to Joseph Neuberg 1848-1862*] xiii). Yet her skill as a writer contains much more than 'something of a method'. Her travels narratives in particular reveal the full range of her talents, conveying a subtle grasp of the ironies implicit in tourist narratives. In July 1858, she satirically headed two letters written from Cheyne Row with **'Notes of a Sitter-still'** and **'Notes of a Still-sitter'** (Froude *LM* [*Letters and Memorials of Jane Welsh Carlyle*] 2:355; MS NLS [National Library of Scotland] 606.486). But her 'annals of visiting' that could 'fill a volume' (*CL* [*The Collected Letters of Thomas and Jane Welsh Carlyle*] 21: 22), as she referred to a trip to Manchester in 1846, give evidence of a woman who was less sedentary—neither a 'Sitter-still' nor a 'Still-sitter'—than is sometimes assumed.

They provide examples of a self-conscious narrator travelling beyond that 'home' and contain different kinds of travel narratives: explorations of the return to the familiar, voyages into the new (which are then contained by literary metaphors), and awareness and a critique of the picturesque. In *Penelope Voyages: Women and Travel in the British Literary Tradition* (1994), Karen Lawrence refers usefully to the 'various plots of wandering (in romance, adventure, exploration, and travel narratives)' (17). The material explored here covers Lawrence's 'various plots', and includes Jane's trip to the Highlands in 1822, Manchester in 1846, Matlock (with Thomas) in 1847, as well as her notebook sketch of 'Tiger Wull', journey to Scotland in 1849, **'Letter of Travel and Romance'** in 1852, and visit to Moffat in 1853.

In her youth, Jane Welsh was part of the world of romantic sensibilities that idolised both Byron and Napoleon as romantic icons. It was the revolutionary and

Napoleonic wars, following earlier eighteenth century wars, which had contributed to the development of 'internal tourism' (Colley 186) in Britain. With the European tour no longer seen as safe, the upper classes travelled to 'the more isolated regions' of North Wales, the Lake Districts, and the Highlands. They carried with them, in Linda Colley's words, their fashionable 'aesthetic education: a knowledge of Edmund Burke's theory of the sublime, a properly developed understanding of the picturesque and the ability to read key texts like William Gilpin's *Observations on the River Wye* (1782), which was littered with untranslated Latin quotations and allusions to Old Masters such as Claude Lorraine and Salvator Rosa' (Colley 186-7). By 1822, when Jane was to make her journey to Fort Augustus, new elements had been added to the potent mix of Burke and Gilpin: Wordsworth's poetry and his cult of the sublime in the Lake District, *Ossian,* and Goethe's travel narratives.

There was also the satire of William Combe and Thomas Rowlandson's *Tour of Dr Syntax in Search of the Picturesque* (1809), with their conflicting tourist and anti-tourist tendencies. As Ian Ousby has pertinently remarked, 'almost as soon as the vocabulary of tourism emerged it was invaded by self-doubt and self-criticism' (19). Ousby points out that whereas the cult of the sublime 'concentrated on the masses of rock, hill and lake to solicit from their wildness and immensity an answering violence . . . of feeling in the spectator', the cult of the picturesquè focused on 'the variegation and harmony expressed by the maundering curve of the river or lake shore, the grouping of the rocks and trees which flank it . . . and the subtle gradations of colour which blend the scene together' (152). Nonetheless, disagreement persisted as to whether the categories of the sublime and the picturesque really were 'distinct from each other or from the traditional concept of Beauty', with writers in the late eighteenth century using the terms 'almost interchangeably' (Ousby 153-4).

Jane's letter to Thomas recounting her trip to Fort Augustus provides a fine example of the young tourist in action, who is full of romantic sensibility and adolescent aspirations and appreciates the wild landscape in the frame of the best romantic, historical, and literary reference points. In the central paragraph she demonstrates her range of descriptive powers:

> I am delighted with this country. My cousin's house stands near the top of Loch Ness, in the midst of a bright green lawn as smooth as velvet. The Tarffe flows down from Corryarrick through a deep wooded glen behind the house—and forms the boundary of this verdant spot. Steep wooded braes rise on the opposite side of the river. and behind these the vast range of heathy mountains that form the northern boundary of the Great Valley—a few yards from the house there is a bridge across Glen Tarffe the most romantic thing I ever saw.

I sit there whole hours admiring Loch Ness with its gigantic ramparts of bold mountains—and the beautiful little Fort Augustus and the green braes where Cumberland encamped with his ten thousand men after the battle of Culloden . . . I have seen Ben Nevis, the king of Mountains, and various other Bens, and Craigs, and Corrys; that I am neither learned enough to spell—nor poet enough to paint . . . in short (to use my highland cousin's words) 'I have been at all the knows [knolls] and *dubs* [puddles] in the country'—Of all I have seen what I admire most is Foyers—It is worth travelling a thousand miles to see the magnificent scenery around the fall—no description can convey an idea of its rude bold grandeur—while I stood on a projecting pocket between the stupendous rocks that seemed to have been torn asunder by some horrible convulsion I shuddered as if I looked upon an earthquake—and had not one of our party drawn me from the brink of rock I verily believe I should have thrown myself into the gulph beneath from absolute terror.

(24 Sept. 1822; *CL* 2:166-7)

Jane responds to landscape in terms of both the picturesque and the sublime, climaxing in her proper response of fear and terror at the 'stupendous rocks', yet she adroitly resists their formal requirements in her description. In her opening paragraph she satirises both the plight of the tourist in face of Highland weather and her own romantic tendencies, and invokes the names of Byron and de Staël to add weight to her predicament:

I was looking to the south and wondering if any living creature thought on me when your letter was put into my hand. Never did letter meet a warmer welcome. It was so unexpected and so different from anything I have read or heard these many weeks!—not a word of hogs, cheviots, Falkirk-fair or the Caledonian-canal! . . . I anticipated much enjoyment from our journey hither but, Alas! the wind blew, and the rain fell, and I was cold wet and woefully sick—From Glasgow to Fort-William I lay on the deck of the Steamboat praying to be again on terra firma and heedless of the magnificent scenery through which we passed—Everything is ordered for the best—had I been at all comfortable I should assuredly have fallen in love—deeply hopelessly in love with a handsome fascinating Colonel of the Guards who held an umbrella over me for four and twenty hours—You will wonder I escaped when I tell you this charming stranger is intimately acquainted with Lord Byron and enjoyed the friendship of our own de Stael—I never saw his like. He is all heart and soul—with the look of a Prince and the manners of a courtier—I could have wept at parting with him—but I could not get at my handkerchief without unbuttoning my boat-cloke and that was inconvenient—

(*CL* 2:165-6)

The portrait of the 'fascinating' Alexander Mair, deputy governor of Fort Augustus, serves to remind Thomas that he can make no assumptions about his possible status as a suitor. In the final paragraph she completes the frame for her picturesque and sublime tendencies by specifying the further 'sights' she has seen, including George IV's infamous orchestrated 'Scottish' parading in Edinburgh (although she does not refer to his appearance in an invented 'Highland' dress), and her failure in Glasgow to meet the Baron de Staël, the son of her heroine Madame de Staël. She also tells Thomas '*by the bye* I have got a new friend. I intend filling a sheet with his merits so shall say nothing of him at present' (*CL* 2:167-8). A month later in her next letter to Haddington, she satirises her 'new friend' Benjamin Bell, who has pretensions to being an artist but has 'no *genius*' (*CL* 2:280). In the same letter she offers a returned traveller's effusion on the superiority of the Highlands:

[W]ere it not for the magic in that word *home* which rivets the heart to the spot where it first beat, I verily believe I should emigrate to the North—Oh the 'Land of hills, glens and warriors!' Its wild romantic grandeur forms such a contrast with our flat, wearisome cornfield and the people there so frank, natural, and true-hearted! so different from the cold selfish well-bred beings lives among!

(24? Oct. 1822; *CL* 2:179)

Here Jane conforms to the necessity for the traveller to find authenticity amongst the more 'natural' surroundings of the picturesque landscape, whether of the Highlands, the Lakes, or Switzerland.

Elsewhere in her travel narratives, she participates in the tourist currencies of her time, and follows a pattern that Ousby discusses in relation to the Peak District, conveniently near Derby and Sheffield: '[I]ts growing industries appealed to the early generation of travellers whose eclectic interests always made them ready to break the journey with a visit to a porcelain factory, a lead mine, a cotton mill or a cutlery workshop' (Ousby 132). In 1846, she identifies herself with the practical traveller rather than the more frivolous tourist, by announcing that 'I am afraid I should not take half as much interest in the *Lakes* as in the Manchester Mills! My tastes being decidedly *Utilitarian* for the moment!' (*CL* 21:30). In a practical mood, she invests the 'mechanical' world with sublime features:

[D]ay after day has passed for me in going up and down in '*hoists*' and thro forest of machinery for every conceivable purpose—I have seen more of the condition of my fellow-creatures in these two weeks than in any dozen years of my previous existence . . . there is no lack of interesting people here—and they have a great superiority over the London people . . . Whitworth the inventor . . . has a face not unlike a baboon . . . to my taste worth any number of the Wits 'that go about'.

(27 Aug.; *CL* 21:22)

Disdainful of the picturesque, she captures the natural beauty of this 'forest of machinery'. But this passage is not just an example of Jane doing the utilitarian, as opposed to the picturesque. Earlier in the summer she had left Thomas and London in a state of depression and anger over his friendship with Lady Harriet Ashburton. As a result, the 'natives' in the North of England are shown as more useful and more truly interesting than the 'Wits' of London who, like Thomas, dance attendance on Lady Harriet.

Jane's practical outlook in this period is apparent too in her treatment of exotic subjects. In an April 1845 excerpt from her Notebook, she refers to her cousin William Dunlop, known as 'Tiger Wull', because of his zeal for stalking game in India:

> 'Tiger Wull' and some friends of his sailed once to Ailsey Craig in search of the picturesque and went on shore there. Was there ever such 'beautiful Nature'? So sublime a scene? Their Lyrical recognition of it had just reached the highest point of ecstacy when turning a corner they found themselves face to face with *a Paisley Weaver,* wearing his unmistakable green apron—They did not strangle him—tho his apparition there had been death to their picturesque enthusiasm they merely expressed a courteous surprise that he should be 'so far from home'. It *was* a wonder he owned; he had 'never been to that *spot* before'; but could they tell him how he might lay his hands on a young Solan goose? He had 'come for *two Goose* to eat the snails in Provost Dagleish's garden—' The Gentlemen made themselves very merry over his *wild goose Chase*—might he not have done the same over theirs.
>
> (13 April; *CL* 30:163)

Welsh Carlyle here responds satirically to the idea of the picturesque in 'beautiful Nature'. She also opposes the legendary hunter and author of *Sketches of Upper Canada by the Backwoodsman* (1832) to the simple 'native' of Paisley, who has made a journey 'so far from home' (about 50 miles) in search of the common gannet to eat the snails in the Provost's garden. Their obligatory lyrical expression of Ailsa Craig's picturesqueness is cut short and challenged by this intrusion into their 'beautiful Nature' of the Scottish industrial world in the person of the weaver. With her closing suggestion that the search for the picturesque itself might be the 'wild goose chase', Jane turns the table on her cousin's and his friends' witticism of the 'wild goose chase' and identifies herself firmly with the weaver.

In August 1847 she and Thomas, imitating the example of Ousby's early travellers, took a trip to Matlock in Derbyshire and the surrounding Peak District. She writes to Anna Jameson of their new situation:

> It is three weeks to-day since we started on *The Pursuit of the Picturesque under Difficulties,*—the first time in our married lives that we ever figured as declared Tourists. And I fancy we should have broken down in the first blush of the business, but for a special interposi-

tion of Providence in the shape of a spirited young Quaker who came to the rescue at Matlock, and guided us triumphantly thro' all the sights of Derbyshire, northwards to his own habitation, where we have remained stationary for ten days.

> (27 Aug.; *CL* 22:43-4)

Notable as the author of *Winter Studies and Summer Rambles in Canada* (1838) and recently returned from Italy where she had been preparing *Sacred and Legendary Art* (1848), Jameson was both travelled and 'cultured'. Jane's echo of Rolandson's satirical *Tour of Dr Syntax in Search of the Picturesque* and her characterisation of she and Thomas as 'declared Tourists' serves to establish them as anti-tourists. She is alert to the pretensions of nature-worship, and when she writes to Thomas during a visit to Barnsley in 1847, she juxtaposes 'nature' and 'industry', both of which provide tourists with entertainment. She reports that she and her hosts are 'going off now in a fourwheeled gig to see some *beautiful nature* somewhere and what is more to the purpose the largest shawl factory in Yorkshire' (7 Sept.; *CL* 22:55-6). The phrase '*beautiful nature*' seems to demand a source but remains untraced. It is apparently part of her coterie speech, used mainly as a satirical phrase to imply a composite critique of romantic attitudes to landscape.

In her 1849 piece **'Much ado about Nothing',** Welsh Carlyle frames her memories of her childhood and education in Haddington within a rail journey from the North of England to Haddington, and then from Haddington to Edinburgh. Her journey takes her from her present into her past and then back again to the present. It ends with the foregrounding of her present self waving goodbye to her past self: 'And now having brought myself to Edin*r* and under the little protecting wing of Jeanie, I bid my self adieu and "wave my lilly hand"—I was back into the Present! and it is only in connection with the Past that I can get up a sentiment for myself— The Present M*rs* Carlyle is what shall I say?— *detestable*' (*CL* 24:171). The journey begins in Morpeth in July when William Forster sees her into the train: 'I was shot off towards Scotland' and in effect also 'shot off' into her past as 'The first locality I recognised was *the Peas Bridge*: I had been there *once* before, a little child, in a postchaise with my Father; he had held his arm around me while I looked down at the ravine; it was my first sight of the Picturesque, *that,* I recognised the place even passing it at railway speed, after all these long years' (*CL* 24:160). The Pease Bridge was built over a large ravine near Cockburnspath, Berwickshire; Welsh Carlyle's memory of her introduction to this example of the picturesque from the safety of her father's arms remains uninflected by irony *because* it took place in the arms of her father. She then returns to a more familiar ironic stance with the adoption of the personae in Haddington of the 'stranger-in-search-of-the

Picturesque' and 'the character of the travelling Englishwoman' (*CL* 24:162,164). Stared at 'as a stranger, or even a *foreigner*' (*CL* 24:161) by a woman she recognises, Welsh Carlyle enacts the role of a travelling foreigner (that is an Englishwoman) in her progress round her childhood haunts in Haddington. These hints of the traveller-tourist become an element in the 'underlying narrative structure' and 'storyline' that constitute this most complicated of her 'travel performances' (Adler 1375; quoted Buzard 16). She plays in the piece as a whole with the ghosts of her former self and of her parents, and the idea of a lost and unattainable past and 'home'.

In other travel letters, Jane uses 'home' to establish a sense of her own 'discursive space' (Lawrence 18) with Thomas. In these instances she is always underpinned by a sense of dialogue with him, of communication (or refusal of communication), and of preserving a sense of her own authority. Burdened by renovations at Cheyne Row in 1852, she denies him his wish for a **'Letter of Travel and Romance'** (6 Aug.; *CL* 27:211):

> Oh my Dear! If I had but a pen that would *mark* freely—never to say *spell*—and if I *might* be dispensed from news of *the house*; I could write you such a *Lettre d'Une Voyageuse* as you have not read 'these seven years'. For it was not a commonplace journey this at all! It was more like that journey of a *Belinda* or *Evelina* or *Cecelea*. Your friends 'The Destinies', 'Immortal Gods', or whatever one should call them, transported me into the Regions of mild romance for that one day. But with this cursed house to be told about, and so little leisure for telling anything, my Miss Burney faculty cannot spread its wings—so I will leave my journey to Sherbourne for a more favourable moment, telling you only that I am no worse for it—rather better—. . . . Except that I sleep less than ordinary mortals do, I have nothing earthly to complain of nor have had since you left me—Nor will I even tell you of the Macreadys in this letter—I cannot mix up the image of that dear dying woman with details of bricklayers and carpenters—.

> (3 Aug.; *CL* 27:200)

The postponed letter is one of Welsh Carlyle's consciously shaped pieces that refers to her journey to Sherborne in Dorset to visit the dying Catherine Macready. The pain of the visit itself is only briefly referred to, contained between the adventures of her journey there and back: 'I was wonderfully little tired and able to make them all (*her* too) laugh with my adventures . . . My two days at Sherborne House were as happy as could possibly be with that fearfully emaciated dying woman before my eyes . . . I am so glad I went it pleased her and all of them so much!' (5 Aug.; *CL* 27:209). The first and largest part of the letter exemplifies Lawrence's idea that 'much travel writing self-consciously places itself in a tradition with aesthetic forbears, a tradition of mixed parentage of travel

narrative and fiction' (Lawrence 25). Jane herself presage this tradition in her reference to other female fictional journeys: George Sand's *Lettres d'un Voyageur* (1834-6), Maria Edgeworth's *Belinda* (1801), and Fanny Burney's *Evelina* (1788) and *Cecilia* (1782).

She describes the visit to Sherborne House as if it were a chapter in a novel. She travels to Frome on the railway and there finds that there are no coaches to Sherborne. She then leaves her parasol on the coach she takes to Sparkford Inn, eight miles from destination. An 'old gentleman' reminiscent of Richardson's Sir Charles Grandison offers to retrieve it the next day. Jane instructs the landlady, overheard by a gentleman in a barouchette with two horses, and her journey continues:

> I started myself, in a little gig, with a brisk little horse, and silent driver. Nothing could be more pleasant—than so *pirring* thro' quiet roads in the dusk—with the moon coming out—I felt as if I were *reading about myself in a Miss Austen novel*! But it got beyond *Miss Austen* when at the end of some three miles before a sort of Carrier's Inn, the gentleman of the barouchette stept into the middle of the road, making a sort of military signal to my driver . . . I sat confounded—expecting what he would do next. We had halted; the gentleman came to my side, and said exactly as in a book 'Madam! I have the happiness of informing you that I have reclaimed your parasol . . . I judged that it *would* be more pleasing for you to take the parasol along with yourself, than to trust to its being brought by the other gentleman—So I just galloped my horses, overtook the coach as it was leaving this court, reclaimed the parasol, and have waited here—knowing you could take no other road to Sherborne—for the happiness of presenting it to you!' . . . and then I found myself making a speech in the same style, caught by the infection of the thing. I said; 'Sir! this day has been full of mischances for me, but I regard this recovery of my parasol so unexpectedly as a good omen . . .'! I never certainly made so long and formal a speech in my life! And how I came to make anything like it I cant imagine unless it were under mesmerism! We bowed to each other like first cousins of Sir Charles Grandison—and I *pirred* on.

> (*CL* 27:208-9)

In 1851, Geraldine Jewsbury, talking of a dinner party, remembered it as 'like being translated into a novel . . . we all seemed like people and things out of a novel, and one wondered where the real life and human nature of the people had been stowed away, and whether any of them knew anything of the practical and economical difficulties of life' (Ireland 408-9). Using Jewsbury's conceit, Welsh Carlyle's allusions to novels by Richardson, Austen, Edgeworth, and Burney, provide a fine illustration of the intersection between fiction and non-fiction in her writing, with fiction impinging on her actual travel in a literal sense. Lawrence writes in *Penelope Voyages* of the 'female traveller's particular baggage' including 'the historical link between female wandering and promiscuity', citing a review of Frances

Trollope's travel books that 'link women's travel to promiscuity through a play on her name' (Lawrence 16). As if explicitly invoking this connection, Welsh Carlyle concludes the journey section of her August 1852 letter with 'My only *adventure* on the road back was falling in with a young *Unfortunate Female* on the Chelsea boat' (*CL* 27:209). The building works that had been used to postpone Thomas's pleasure in the earlier letter are confined in this letter to the postscript.

In Jane's later travel narratives, the sceptical anti-tourist who is resistant to the picturesque tends to dominate. For example, in her account of her visit to her brother-in-law and his new wife in Moffat in 1853, she provides an extended example of the interplay of the picturesque and the sublime, as well as a satire on the desirable pursuit of the exotic for the traveller:

> The most important thing I have to tell you is that you could not know me here as I sit from a red Indian! that I was kept awake the first night after my arrival by a——*Hyaena*! (yes upon my honour! and *you* complain of a simple *cock*!) and that yesterday I was as near as possible for giving occasion for the most romantic paragraph of the 'melancholy accident' nature that has appeared in any newspaper for some years! But first of the Hyaena. on my arrival I found an immense caravan of Wild Beasts pitched exactly in front of this House and they went on their way during the night and the animal in question made a devil of a row—I thought it was the Lion roaring but John said 'no—it was ONLY the Hyeana'! I rather enjoyed the oddness of having fled into the country for 'quiet' and being kept awake by *Wild Beasts*!

> (8 July 1853; *CL* 28:188)

Taken together, these narratives illustrate the way in which Welsh Carlyle absorbs the genre of travel writing into other modes of life writing. She uses the 'dual "theoretical position" of traveler and signatory of the discourse' (Lawrence 26), accommodating her journeys in her letters, and ensuring that the travel is satirised and controlled within the frame of her writer's eye. Her travel narratives belong to the same satirical tradition of Combe and Rowlandson, who 'mocked the sheep-like pilgrimages of tourists who, tinted Claude glasses in hand, trekked in their droves to the approved stations for a glimpse of the "correct" view' (Manning xvi). Unlike these touring spectators or her friend Benjamin Bell who wore 'a steel chain with a very ingenious, portable perspective (to denote he is an artist)' (24? Oct. 1822; *CL* 2:180), Jane's 'portable perspective' is internalised, allowing her to record, organise, and satirise her material. She shapes her journey narratives so that they become both 'Travel as Performed Art' (Adler 1366) and her own 'portable perspectives' on travel.

Works Cited

Adler, Judith. 'Travel as Performed Art'. *American Journal of Sociology* 94 (1989):1366-91.

Buzard, James. *The Beaten Track: European Tourism, Literature, and the Ways to Culture, 1800-1918*. Oxford: Clarendon Press, 1993.

Colley, Linda. *Britons: Forging the Nation 1707-1837*. London: Vintage, 1992.

[Fielding, K. J., et al., eds. *The Collected Letters of Thomas and Jane Welsh Carlyle*. 31 vols. Durham, NC: Duke UP, 1970-2004-.]

Froude, J. A., ed. *Letters and Memorials of Jane Welsh Carlyle*. 3 vols. London: Longmans, Green, 1883.

Ireland, Mrs. Alexander, ed. *Selections from the Letters of Geraldine Endsor Jewsbury to Jane Welsh Carlyle*. London: Longmans, Green, 1892.

Lawrence, Karen R. *Penelope Voyages: Women and Travel in the British Literary Tradition*. Ithaca and London: Cornell UP, 1994.

Manning, Susan, intro. *The Sketch-Book of Geoffrey Cannon, Gent*. By Washington Irving. Oxford: Oxford UP, 1996.

Ousby, Ian. *The Englishman's England: Taste, Travel, and the Rise of Tourism*. Cambridge: Cambridge UP, 1990.

Scudder, Townsend, ed. *Letters of Jane Welsh Carlyle to Joseph Neuberg 1848-1862*. London and New York: Oxford UP, 1931.

Kathy Chamberlain (essay date 2004)

SOURCE: Chamberlain, Kathy. "A 'Creative Adventure': Jane Welsh Carlyle's 'Simple Story.'" In *The Carlyles at Home and Abroad*, edited by David R. Sorenson and Rodger L. Tarr, pp. 230-39. Aldershot, England: Ashgate Publishing Limited, 2004.

[*In the following essay, Chamberlain analyzes Carlyle's rare attempts at writing fiction.*]

Jane Welsh Carlyle's principal contribution to English literature lies in her letters, but she occasionally experimented with becoming a public author. Three pieces in particular, not published in her lifetime, read as if they were intended for a larger audience: her 1849 autobiographical essay **'Much ado about Nothing'**, prompted by a visit to her Scottish birthplace, Haddington; her 1852 story of her first love; and her 1855 report on household expenses, **'BUDGET of a *Femme* incomprise'** (in which the 'unappreciated woman' addresses a formal request for funds to her husband, 'the Noble Lord'). Of the three, it is the second—**'*The simple Story* of my own first Love'**—in which Jane Carlyle, however unconsciously, makes her most ambitious attempt to transform an incident from her life into a clearly shaped piece of fiction.

Throughout her life, Jane toyed with the notion of being an author. In his *Reminiscences* Thomas Carlyle alludes to her efforts to write autobiography. She 'had written at one time something of her own early life; but she gave up, and burnt it' (72). Some pages later, he is moved to refer to the incident again, saying she was engaged 'at one time, upon a kind of Autobiography (had not *Craik* [Professor George Lillie Craik] . . . stept into it with swine's foot, most intrusively, though without ill intention,—finding it *unlocked*, one day;—and produced thereby an instantaneous *burning* of it, and of all like it which existed at that time)' (157).

As a letter writer Jane Carlyle had what amounted to 'a private writing career' (Hardwick 174; Christianson 232), but she often expressed a desire to find more ambitious and fulfilling creative work. This yearning seems to have been strongest in middle age, when her major transitional pieces were written. At the age of forty-four, she informed her cousin Jeannie Welsh that 'the natural sadness of the latter part of ones life may be cruelly *embittered* by the reflection, that ones best years, which might perhaps have produced something good have been suffered to run to waste, fertile only of tares and nettles!' And she added, 'I wish I *could* find some hard work I could do—and saw any sense in doing—If I do not soon it will be the worse for me—' (*CL* [*The Collected Letters of Thomas and Jane Welsh Carlyle*] 20:193, 194). A remarkable number of the Carlyles' friends believed that she was capable of writing for the public, and her husband was no exception. During their courtship, they had contemplated the idea of writing a novel together, and as late as 1842 he told her that 'My prayer is and has always been that you would rouse up the fine faculties that *are* yours into some course of real true work' (*CL* 14:134). Yet Thomas delivered mixed messages on the subject, and at times tried to discourage her. 'Do you know', he wrote in January 1825, 'I heartily rejoice that you *cannot* write a book at present! . . . as a woman it would have proved your ruin' (*CL* 3:270).

When Jane was fifty, her novelist friend Geraldine Jewsbury wrote a letter pleading with her to consider writing 'as an occupation': '[I]t not only blunts one's *amour propre*—or, as we politely term it, our sensibilities—so that we not only feel less acutely things that would otherwise irritate beyond endurance, but these things are transformed for us into artistic studies, instructions, experiences, and this goes a long way towards softening their intensely personal application to ourselves. Besides which, one's work is an "ark of refuge", into which one flings oneself on all occasions of provocation'. Geraldine even volunteered to help: 'Now, do set to work resolutely. I am just now open to any sort of arrangement you like to make. I will give the staple of my time to this mutual tale if you will begin' (Jewsbury 425-6).

There had been other offers to collaborate. In the 1840s Jane contemplated writing a novel with Jewsbury and Elizabeth Paulet, and later told her cousin Jeannie: '[L]ong ago—Geraldine and Mrs. P. and I were to write *a book* among us in the form of letters. I told them to start it and I would take it up when I saw their scheme—they *did* send me a screed of MS. which I augured no good of, it was so *stormy*—and so I backed out of my engagement' (*CL* 25:37). Jane later believed that pages resulting from Elizabeth and Geraldine's early collaborative efforts had found their way into Jewsbury's *Marian Withers* (1851): 'I remember much of *this* tale that seems bare-faced painting of Seaforth [where the Paulets lived] was in these pages *they* wrote between them!!' (*CL* 25:37; 15:246). The epistolary form was right, but the 'stormy' approach was incompatible with Jane's ironic and satirical novel-of-manners style.

In her correspondence, Jane frequently mentioned novels and novelists. In turn, literary London occasionally attributed anonymous works to Mrs Carlyle, such as Charlotte Brontë's *Shirley* (1848). Half-imagining herself as a collaborator, Jane asked her friend John Forster if he could tell her who had written the novel, stating that if the writer 'have not *kept company* with *me* in this life, we must have been much together in some previous state of existence—I perceive in her book so many things I have said myself printed without alteration of a word' (*CL* 24:280). Though initially offended by Jewsbury's *The Half Sisters* (1849), perhaps because she feared that it was based on the story of her own marriage, she later admitted to Mary Russell that it was 'the one of all her novels which I like the best. And it has *bonafide* arguments in it, betwixt her and me, written down almost word for word as we spoke them in our walks together' (28 November 1856; MS NLS [National Library of Scotland] 605.429).

In 1866, at a dinner given by John Forster, Jane discussed the plot of a novel with Charles Dickens. She began by describing a house down the street, which provided her with imaginative inspiration. As Forster recalled in his biography of Dickens, she constructed a narrative based on 'the condition of its blinds and curtains, the costumes visible at its windows, the cabs at its door, its visitors admitted or rejected'. He went on to describe how 'the subtle serious humour of it all, the truth in trifling bits of character, and the gradual progress into a half-romantic interest, had enchanted the skilled novelist' (2:252). Humour, character, and half-romance—these were elements that may have been missing from the 'stormy' plot of the Jewsbury-Paulet novel.

One other 'novel' by Jane Carlyle suggests the frustrations she experienced in trying to write fiction. In the Strouse collection at the University of California, Santa Cruz, there is a leather-bound volume entitled ***The***

School for Husbands, by Jane Carlyle, 1852. The title suggests a novel, or possibly a humourous advice book for men to balance comportment manuals for women, such as Sarah Stickney Ellis's *The Wives of England, Their Relative Duties, Domestic Influence, and Social Obligations* (1843), which she and Geraldine frequently ridiculed in their letters. But inside this beautifully made volume, all the pages are blank. Though she could not articulate her own public voice, Jane Carlyle formed friendships with women who did, including Harriet Martineau, Geraldine Jewsbury, Elizabeth Paulet, and Margaret Oliphant. Yet unlike them, she was unable to negotiate between her private world and the larger world around her. In the blank pages of her 'novel', she left a record of her inability to transcend the conventions that had frustrated her throughout her life.

From the early stages of her life, Jane Carlyle's inclination to take creative risks were checked by her deference to custom and authority. When she announced in childhood, 'I want to learn Latin—please let me be a boy', her parents had what Geraldine Jewsbury later called, in a narrative included in Thomas's *Reminiscences,* 'a division of opinion on the subject' (42). According to her first biographer Annie E. Ireland, Jane's mother 'considered Latin and mathematics sadly out of place in the little girl's education. Herself an accomplished and somewhat intellectual woman, she had kept to the old traditions, and desired nothing further for Jeannie. But the father divined his child's unusual capacity, and determined that it should have scope' (12). Dr John Welsh thought so well of his daughter's abilities that he overrode his wife's objections. Jane pleased him by being a precocious pupil, but she was only 18 when he died. The next year she lamented in a letter, 'I have lost my dearest and my best friend, whose love was my most valuable blessing' (*CL* 1:280). During her courtship with Thomas, she frequently reminded him about the efforts her father had taken to cultivate her mind and encouraged her ambitions and talents (*CL* 2:196). Her new 'genius' was fated to live in the shadow of Dr John Welsh.

Jane valued her mostly idyllic Haddington childhood and the years she spent there as a playful, cosseted, and spoiled only child. These experiences contributed to the antic and cavorting style of her letters. But clinging to an identification as a child can keep a woman in the position of an eternal daughter, and in Jane's case this may have been made more difficult by the ambivalent, unresolved feelings she had about her mother. Even after Grace Welsh died in 1842, Jane tried to be dutiful, and took up her needle to mend old clothes when she might have turned her mind to more ambitious pursuits. Yet she always sensed that duty was a poor substitute for more serious occupations. Writing in her *Journal,* 31 October 1856, she remarks bitterly: 'The evening devoted to mending; M*r* C's trousers among other

things! "Being an only child", I never "*wished*" to sew men's trowsers—no, never!' (*CL* 30:209). Guilt mixed with grief in her character. These two emotions can be seen at their most dramatic and extreme in 1847, five years after her mother's death, in an opium-induced dream she described to her young friend Caroline Fox. Jane told Caroline she had had 'a miserable feeling of turning to marble herself and lying on marble, her hair, her arms, and her whole person petrifying and adhering to the marble slab on which she lay. One night it was a tombstone—one in Scotland which she well knew. She lay along it with a graver in her hand, carving her own epitaph under another, which she read and knew by heart. It was her mother's' (Froude, *Life* 2:80).

This strong identification as a daughter placed Jane beyond reach of one of the more socially acceptable roles for women writers at the time, that of motherly advisor. In the same letter in which Geraldine urged Jane to take the idea of being a writer seriously, she also implored her to speak as a mother: 'It is not, however, altogether for your own sake that I am anxious you should set to work upon a story or a book of any kind that you are moved to do. You have more sense and stronger judgment than any other woman I ever knew . . . also, you have had such singular life-experiences that it is in your power to say both strengthening and comforting things to other women . . . If you had had daughters, they would have been educated as few women have the luck to be, and I think you might have enough maternal feeling, sisterly affection . . . to wish to help other women in their very complicated duties and difficulties. Do not go to Mr. Carlyle for sympathy, do not let him dash you with cold water. You must respect your own work and your own motives . . . So begin, begin! . . . You ought to have had a dozen daughters . . . So let your work be dedicated to your "unknown daughters". I am one of your children, after a fashion' (426-7). But Jane Carlyle was inhibited by the nagging sense that she had been undutiful. She was also someone who loved laughter, satire, and wit, and found the role of delivering 'strengthening' messages to a female public peculiarly tiresome. She could not imitate a woman such as Harriet Martineau, who confidently served as a counselor to the great, and a promoter of patriarchal ideas. As Deirdre David has remarked, Martineau's 'relatively untroubled acceptance of popularizing work in the service of male political ideas liberated her for a confident presentation of herself to the world' (227). Jane made friends with younger women and offered sisterly advice, but when she was obliged to dispense maternal wisdom, she tended to undercut her efforts with self-mockery.

In the fall of 1852, however, when she was 51, events in her life coalesced in such a way as to make her more creatively adventurous. In September of that year while Thomas was travelling in Germany, Jane was home in

Chelsea supervising renovations. Her health and spirits were better than usual, and she was involved in literary matters, having read and critiqued chapters of Geraldine's next book, *The History of An Adopted Child* (Jewsbury 440-1). On 10 September, she answered a letter from an old suitor, John Riddle Stodart, who had been infatuated with her when she was a young girl. She informs him that she has been trying to get a 'female M S' published—perhaps the religious novel written by the mother of her artist friend Penelope Sketchley—and wryly remarks 'if it were [*my own*] I would give more for its chances of getting published' (*CL* 27:280). Two days later she mentions to Thomas that on an errand to his publisher she had been offered '"very advantageous terms" for a novel of my own!' (*CL* 27:281).

The exchange of letters with a former lover seems to have inspired her. She lets Thomas know that Stodart 'thought himself sufficiently master of his emotions, to dare to tell me that for nearly *40* years (!) he had loved me with the same worship-ful love' (*CL* 27:272). Replying to Stodart, she mixes serious reflection with humour. His letter, she tells him, 'has produced considerable bewilderment of my matronly wits—so that I could almost fall to doubting for the moment, Whether I be the present flesh-and-blood M*rs* Carlyle or the Ghost of little Miss Welsh! a perpetually recurring form of doubt with me, to say the truth' (*CL* 27:278). He has awakened her sense of the past: 'Oh dear! a little old love, bringing with it airs from *long ago* (God bless it!) is worth a vast deal of new love—at least to my retrospective turn of thought' (*CL* 27:279).

In this letter, as well as in the **'simple Story'** [**'The simple Story of my own first Love'**] she was about to compose, Jane hovered between the impulse to express herself in a risky context and the need to observe propriety. She informs Stodart that it is 'in the highest degree unconventional to tell another man other than one's lawful husband, that one cares about his love and is grateful to him for it', yet she insists that she 'may speak with freedom' because their love is so old and they are so widely separated (*CL* 27:279). It was later said of John Stodart that while courting Jane Baillie Welsh, he had 'reached the point of trying to slip a ring over one of [her] fingers, only to see his ring sail through the air while Jane stamped with annoyance' (Chalmers 739). However ambivalent her feelings, Jane Carlyle expresses excitement at being back in touch with a man with whom she had once danced quadrilles.

In November or December 1852 she was confident enough to take up her pen and write a story in a notebook. Her aim was to contradict a remark that Thomas had made in his judgement of Thackeray's recently published novel, *The History of Henry Esmond* (1852): 'What "the greatest Philosopher of our day" execrates loudest in Thacke[r]ay's new novel—finds, indeed, "altogether false and damnable" in it, is, that "Love is represented as spreading itself over one's whole existence, and constituting the one grand interest of existence"; whereas Love,—*the thing people call Love,* is confined to a very few years of man's Life,—to, in fact, a quite insignificant fraction of it; and even then is but one thing to be attended to, among many infinitely more important things'. Indeed, 'so far as he (Mr C) has seen into it; the whole concern of Love is such a beggarly futility; that, in a Heroic Age of the World, nobody would be at the pains to think of it particularly; much less to open his jaw on it' (14).

In contrast to Mr C's 'infinitely more important things', Mrs C concentrates on a **'simple Story'**. Her straightforward, understated title is intended to distance herself ironically from her husband's 'genius' and to ease expectations of her own. Like **'Much ado about Nothing'** and **'BUDGET of a *Femme* incomprise'**, the title also disguises the importance of this piece to Jane. As Kenneth J. Fielding rightly observes, Jane's story 'can be read as an attempt to define herself' (*simple Story* [**'The simple Story of my own first Love'**] 3). Looked at from this perspective, it is anything but 'simple'. In a letter to her young friend Kate Sterling in December 1852, she refers to her new endeavour casually, though dignifying it with the word 'occupation': 'One of my occupations is teaching the little Countess [Reichenbach] English—with what *success* you may partly figure Another (not an *imperative* one you will say) has been writing the narrative of my *First Love*; good Heavens! you shall have it to read someday—it is short' (*CL* 27:383).

In the story she describes an engaging childhood incident that allows her to reflect on the vagaries of love and memory, and at the same time to challenge the statement Thomas had made. Is love merely an insignificant fraction of a life? Declares Jane, '[M]y whole inner woman revolts against such position, which I find to be neither true nor well imagined. and regard, moreover, as a personal affront' (14). She then tells how she fell in love for the first time at the age of nine: 'One night, at a Dancing-school-Ball, a Stranger-Boy put a slight on me which I resented to my very finger-ends, and out of that tumult of hurt vanity sprang my first love to life, like Venus out of the froth of the Sea!!—So my first love resembled my last in this at least, that it began in *quasi* hatred' (15). Jane overhears the Boy's mother telling him 'to ask little Miss W—h for a quadrille'. Like Darcy in *Pride and Prejudice,* he refuses. He leads up instead 'a fair, fat, sheep-looking Thing, with next to no sense' (16). The Boy, the son of an Artillery Officer at the Barracks, is named Scholey (Jane cannot recall his first name), and while a real Scholey may have been stationed at Haddington in her childhood—there were barracks in the Artillery Park, on the NE edge of the town—his name also suggests another early love: her scholarly ambitions at the important age of nine. According to Geraldine, this was the period in which Jane 'made great progress in Latin and was in Virgil' (*Reminiscences* 44).

Jane loves the Boy but he prefers the fat sheep girl. She then forms a friendship with his mother, believing Mrs Scholey would like to see them united. Later, when the Regiment is about to move on, Jane takes the mother a gold filigree needle case hoping to get a little portrait of the Boy in return. The mother, however, grabs the needle case, and gives nothing back. The next morning, the Regiment marches away 'with band playing gaily *"The Girl I've left behind me"'* (19). The Boy, Jane says as she winds up the tale, 'had slipt thro' my fingers like a knotless thread' and 'in no great length of time' he had 'passed for me into a sort of Myth; nor for a quarter of a century had I thought as much of him, put it altogether, as I have done in writing these few sheets' (20).

Her story lends itself to being interpreted mythically, as a kind of dream. Dreamlike elements dominate the story: a tale-telling cadence, simple figures with archetypal potency, and stock expressions and motifs. The mythical frame of mind matches her view of the world as a child. As she recalls in a footnote: 'Thus was my inner world at that period three fourths *Old Roman,* and one fourth Old Fairy' (24). The unnamed Boy may represent a masculine aspect of her creativity, an animus figure about whom she feels ambivalent. Like Jane, he is an only child. The picture she paints of him is vivid: he is twelve or thirteen, tall 'and very slight,—with sunshiny hair, and dark blue eyes,—a dark blue ribbon about his neck, and grey jacket with silver buttons', an 'Image', she says, 'stamped itself on my soul forever!' (16) The Boy's mother is also described in mythical terms as 'a sort of military *Holy Mother* for me', 'her Barrack . . . a sacred shrine!' (17)

But the Boy fails to unite with Jane, his true partner—the best dancer in her 'little white kid shoes'—choosing instead bland conventionality in the person of the fat sheep girl whose 'wax-doll face took the fancy of Boys at that period, as afterwards, it was *the rage* with men' (16). In an aside, Jane mentions that this archetype of conventionality came to a ghastly end in a Madhouse. The Boy has allowed himself to be captivated by a girl who, judging from her physical features, might have grown up to resemble Lady Harriet Baring, the woman Thomas Carlyle so admired. In the process Jane is abandoned, 'slighted, superfluous, *incomprise*'—that word again (17).

Jane Carlyle takes pains to portray her child self as not stepping *too* far beyond the bounds of the appropriate, as she explores the tension between prudent conven-

tionality and potentially daring actions. At one point she even assures the reader that she would never have gone so far as to tell the Boy directly that she loved him. Ironically, she reinforces this impression of propriety by swearing: 'This project then; could it be the confession of my love to its object, you may be thinking? Christ Almighty! No!—not *that*!' (18). In a further irony, Thomas's nephew Alexander Carlyle, the first editor of her story, changed this outburst to 'Almighty Gracious!' (*New Letters and Memorials* [*New Letters and Memorials of Jane Welsh Carlyle*] 2:54) in 1903.

Unable to have the Boy himself, the nine-year old Jane fixes her attention on the portrait of him, which belongs to his mother: '[A] dear little oval miniature of the Boy, in *petticoats*; done for him in his second or third year; and *so* like, I thought; making allowance for the greater chubbiness of Babyhood, and the little pink frock, of *no sex*. At each visit I drank in this "*Portrait charmant*" with my eyes, and wished myself artist enough to copy it. Indeed had one of the Fairies, I delighted to read of, stept *out of the Book,* in a moment of enthusiasm, to grant any one thing I asked; I would have said—I am sure I would—"the *Portrait charmant,* then, since you *are* so good, all to myself, for altogether!"' (18) She wants to possess an image of the little boy in pink petticoats of '*no sex*', a sign perhaps of her unconscious desire for what Virginia Woolf later called the 'androgynous mind', the union of opposite sets of qualities that are needed for creativity to flourish (98).

In the story Jane attempts to obtain the portrait by praying to the Roman goddess of art—'Minerva was my chosen goddess' (19). After Minerva fails her, she tries another tactic, presenting the Boy's mother with 'the only really valuable thing I possessed' (18), the gold filigree needle case from India. The object is possibly sexual, suggesting her ownership of instruments necessary for invention and synthesis. Jane even has a vague plan that when she is a wealthy adult, she will return a more dazzling version of the portrait: 'I would return it to her *set with diamonds*' (18). When Mrs Scholey snatches the needle case without any awareness of what Jane wants, the dream lesson seems to be that the greedy, self-absorbed mother is the wrong figure to appeal to for the gift of the boy baby in the pink frock.

The Boy and the image of the Boy are both lost. Traditional male qualities such as aggression, daring, and bravery of heart—the virtues of a soldier's son—will not characterise Jane's imaginative powers. The inner realignment she seems to be searching for has eluded her. She begins and ends the story with an image of her hand, suggestive of the writing process itself. In the beginning of the tale, she says she felt to her 'very fingerends' the potent mix of resentment and love that burst out for the Boy. At the conclusion, the needle case is gone and the Boy has slipped through her fingers 'like a knotless thread' (a conventional phrase for her). The mystery of love, as she says, 'passeth all understanding' (20). It is as if an opportunity for Jane Carlyle to dream herself into being a more adventurous writer has briefly appeared, then vanished.

With the spell broken, the dream ends. She declares the loss of the needle case to be of no consequence. The thread did not get knotted so the story unravels. The ring sailing through the air did not land on her finger and her pen will not dance in this particular way again, largely because there was too great a risk involved. Had she been able to continue, she half-jokingly speculates, 'such reflections . . . might lead me too far,—to the length namely, of my whole pamphlet, *in petto* [in my breast] on *the Marriage-question,* which I fear is too much in advance of the Century for being committed to writing' (20). She concludes the story humorously with a quotation from a preacher who, not knowing how to wind up a worship service, addresses the Almighty with a stock phrase for ending a letter: 'So—So "I add no more, but remain, my dear Sir, your obedient servant",' and she signs herself: 'J——' (20).

In her **'simple Story'**, she has extended the boundaries of convention—both personal and social—and found a small but fruitful space to engage her imaginative energies. Through the alchemy of fiction, she has transformed a childhood scene and returned it to her audience '*set with diamonds*'.

Works Cited

Carlyle, Alexander, ed. *New Letters and Memorials of Jane Welsh Carlyle.* 2 vols. London: Lane, 1903.

Carlyle, Jane Welsh. '*The simple Story* of my own first Love'. Ed. Kenneth J. Fielding and Ian Campbell, with Aileen Christianson. Introduction Kenneth J. Fielding. Edinburgh: University of Edinburgh, The Carlyle Letters, Department of English Literature, 2001.

Chalmers, E. B. 'Mrs Carlyle's Letters to John Stodart'. *Times Literary Supplement.* 25 June 1971: 739-41.

Christianson, Aileen. 'Jane Welsh Carlyle's Private Writing Career'. In *A History of Scottish Women's Writing.* Ed. Douglas Gifford and Dorothy MacMillan. Edinburgh: Edinburgh UP, 1997.

David, Deirdre. *Intellectual Women and Victorian Patriarchy: Harriet Martineau, Elizabeth Barrett Browning, George Eliot.* Ithaca, New York: Cornell UP, 1987.

[Fielding, K. J., et al, eds. *The Collected Letters of Thomas and Jane Welsh Carlyle.* 31 vols. Durham, NC: Duke UP, 1970-2004.

Fielding, K. J., and Ian Campbell, eds. *Reminiscences.* By Thomas Carlyle. London: Oxford UP, 1997.]

Forster, John. *The Life of Charles Dickens.* 2 vols. New York: Dutton, 1966.

Fox, Caroline. *Memories of Old Friends, Being Extracts from the Journals and Letters of Caroline Fox of Penjerrick, Cornwall from 1835 to 1871.* Ed. Horace N. Pym. 2 vols. London: Smith, Elder, 1882.

[Froude, J. A. *Thomas Carlyle. A History of the First Forty Years of His Life, 1795-1835.* 2 vols. London: Longman and Green, 1882.]

Hardwick, Elizabeth. *Seduction and Betrayal: Women and Literature.* New York: Random House, 1973.

Ireland, Mrs Alexander [Annie E.]. *Life of Jane Welsh Carlyle.* London: Chatto & Windus, 1891.

Jewsbury, Geraldine. *Selections from the Letters of Geraldine Endsor Jewsbury to Jane Welsh Carlyle.* Ed. Mrs Alexander Ireland. London: Longmans, Green, 1892.

Woolf, Virginia. *A Room of One's Own.* New York: Harcourt Brace, 1989.

FURTHER READING

Biographies

Ashton, Rosemary. *Thomas and Jane Carlyle: Portrait of a Marriage.* London: Chatto & Windus, 2002, 548 p.

> Examines Jane Carlyle's critical role in the emergence of her husband's literary reputation, while arguing that her own letters and journal writings represent an important contribution to English literature.

Drew, Elizabeth. *Jane Welsh and Jane Carlyle.* New York: Harcourt, Brace & Company, 1928, 282 p.

> Offers a largely sympathetic portrait of Carlyle, examining her intellectual and literary talents, her complicated personal relationships, and her marriage.

Hanson, Lawrence, and Elizabeth M. Hanson. *Necessary Evil: The Life of Jane Welsh Carlyle.* London: Constable, 1952, 618 p.

> Provides a comprehensive overview of Carlyle's life through an in-depth analysis of her letters.

Scudder, Townsend. *Jane Welsh Carlyle.* New York: The Macmillan Company, 1939, 406 p.

> Evaluates Jane Carlyle's role in the promotion of her husband's career, as well as her central place in the literary culture of her times.

Criticism

Bloom, Abigail Burnham. "Jane Welsh Carlyle: A Review of Recent Research, 1988-2003." *Carlyle Studies Annual* 21 (2003): 100-15.

Offers a general overview of criticism relating to Carlyle's writings.

Campbell, Ian. "Geraldine Jewsbury: Jane Welsh Carlyle's 'Best Friend'?" In *The Carlyles at Home and Abroad,* edited by David R. Sorenson and Rodger L. Tarr, pp. 185-95. Aldershot, England: Ashgate Publishers Limited, 2004.

Discusses the tumultuous relationship between Carlyle and her friend Geraldine Jewsbury, examining correspondence discovered only recently by scholars.

Chamberlain, Kathy. "Illness as Speech in the Life of Jane Welsh Carlyle." *Carlyle Studies Annual* 19 (1999): 63-75.

Examines the relationship between illness and expression in Carlyle's letters.

Christianson, Aileen. "Constructing Reality: Jane Welsh Carlyle's Epistolary Narratives." *Carlyle Studies Annual* 16 (1996): 15-24.

Examines the ironic qualities of Carlyle's letters.

————. "Jane Welsh Carlyle's Private Writing Career." In *A History of Scottish Women's Writing,* edited by Douglas Gifford and Dorothy McMillan, pp. 232-45. Edinburgh: Edinburgh University Press, 1997.

Discusses the private nature of Carlyle's body of work, analyzing the relationship between her public and literary personae.

Clarke, Norma. "Jane Welsh Carlyle: Letters, the Self, and the Literary." *Carlyle Studies Annual* 16 (1996): 7-14.

Explores questions of personal identity as they relate to Carlyle's letters, focusing in particular on her reflections on childhood and death.

Davidson, Mabel. "The Religion of Mrs. Carlyle." *Sewanee Review* 35 (October-December 1927): 448-59.

Analyzes the tension between skepticism and religious longing in Carlyle's letters.

Kinser, Brent E. "A Not So 'Simple Story': Jane Welsh Carlyle and Charlotte Brontë's *Shirley.*" *Midwest Quarterly: A Journal of Contemporary Thought* 46, no. 2 (winter 2005): 152-68.

Challenges traditional depictions of Jane Carlyle as a fragile, victimized woman, arguing that her strength of character lay in her prodigious intellect and literary talent.

Woolf, Virginia. "Geraldine and Jane." In *The Common Reader: Second Series,* pp. 186-201. London: Hogarth, 1965.

Examines the intimate, often troubled relationship between Geraldine Jewsbury and Jane Carlyle.

Moby-Dick

Herman Melville

American novelist, short story writer, and poet.

The following entry presents criticism of Herman Melville's 1851 novel *Moby-Dick*. For additional discussion of the novel, see *NCLC*, Volume 12. For information on Melville's complete career, see *NCLC*, Volume 3; for discussion of the novel *Billy Budd* (1924), see *NCLC*, Volume 29; for discussion of the novel *Typee* (1846), see *NCLC*, Volume 45; for discussion of the short story "Bartleby, the Scrivener" (1853), see *NCLC*, Volume 49; for discussion of the novel *Pierre* (1852), see *NCLC*, Volume 91; for discussion of the short story "Benito Cereno" (1855), see *NCLC*, Volume 93; for discussion of the novel *Redburn* (1849), see *NCLC*, Volume 123; for discussion of the novel *The Confidence-Man* (1857), see *NCLC*, Volume 157.

INTRODUCTION

Herman Melville's *Moby-Dick* (1851) maintains an unrivalled position in the history of the American novel. Scholars have debated the work's meaning since its publication; indeed, no other work of American fiction has elicited such a spectrum of diverse, ambivalent, and contradictory interpretations as Melville's magnum opus. The novel is remarkable for its multifaceted approach to its subject. At once a traditional adventure novel, an essay on the whaling industry, and a somber meditation on the nature of existence, *Moby-Dick* demands to be considered from more than one perspective. In addition, Melville's use of multiple literary styles, among them first-person narration, satire, expository analysis, and blank verse, was unprecedented in nineteenth-century American literature and lends the novel its distinctly modern quality. Melville originally conceived of the work as a straightforward whaling novel set in the South Pacific and based on legends surrounding a white whale named Mocha Dick. His approach to the novel's composition changed dramatically in the summer of 1850, however, after he read Nathaniel Hawthorne's story collection *Mosses from an Old Manse*. The dark poetry and metaphysical complexity of Hawthorne's writing exerted a profound effect on Melville, compelling him to undertake an exhaustive overhaul of his novel, a process that lasted more than a year and nearly left him bankrupt.

In developing the metaphysical underpinnings of his novel, Melville drew from a range of religious traditions, both mainstream and esoteric, including Hinduism, Gnostic Christianity, and Zoroastrianism. He also derived inspiration from a wealth of literary influences, and the novel bears the imprint of Homer, Emerson, Mary Shelley, Thomas De Quincy, and especially Shakespeare. The book was finally published in England in October 1851 under the title *The Whale*; the first American edition, *Moby-Dick; or, The Whale*, appeared a month later. Although the work elicited some positive reactions among contemporary critics, most early reviews expressed scorn, bewilderment, or indifference, and the book was largely neglected for decades after its publication. By the early twentieth century, however, scholars had rediscovered *Moby-Dick*, and the novel has held a central role in American literary studies ever since. By almost all modern accounts, *Moby-Dick* is the great inscrutable masterpiece of American literature, a tour-de-force unmatched in its scope, profundity, and ambition.

PLOT AND MAJOR CHARACTERS

Moby-Dick is a sprawling, digressive work, comprised of one hundred thirty-five chapters, two prologues, and an epilogue. While primarily a work of prose fiction, the novel employs a range of other literary genres, including poetry, songs, dramatic monologues, a brief play, quotations, and expository discussions of scientific and historical aspects of whaling. The novel also utilizes multiple points of view, ranging from the up-close first-person perspective of the main narrator, Ishmael, to a third-person omniscient viewpoint to the voice of the author himself, whose philosophical musings sound regularly throughout the work. In spite of its expansive, seemingly unruly quality, however, the book's numerous tangents are unified around a relatively simple plot line, and the main story, concerning Captain Ahab's pursuit of the white whale, Moby-Dick, unfolds in a straightforward chronological manner.

With the novel's first line, "Call me Ishmael," Melville introduces one of the most enigmatic and protean narrators in American literature. Ishmael is a representative nineteenth-century American man, a restless, ungrounded individual who, with "nothing particular" to compel him to remain on the mainland, decides to go to sea. He travels to Nantucket in the hopes of joining the crew of a whaling vessel. At a boarding house he shares a room with Queequeg, a harpooner from the South Pacific, whose enormous size and strange bathing rituals unnerve him. Ishmael soon recognizes that Queequeg is a generous, benevolent spirit, however, and the two become friends. Determined to sail together, they set out the next morning to find work on a ship. After searching the harbor they come across the *Pequod,* a vessel bound for the South Seas. Although the owners of the *Pequod* offer a meager salary and the ship is ominously adorned with whale bones, Ishmael and Queequeg agree to join the crew. As they prepare to embark, they hear rumors of the ship's captain, a mysterious figure with an ivory leg, but they see no sign of him in the days leading up to the vessel's departure.

The *Pequod* launches on Christmas Day. As the ship pushes further away from the cold waters of New England, Ishmael comments on various members of the crew. The principal characters include Starbuck, the conscientious, pensive first mate; the affable and easygoing second mate, Stubb; and the quick-tempered third mate, Flask, who demonstrates a singular drive to hunt and kill whales. While the crew awaits the first appearance of their captain, Ishmael also introduces the harpooners: Tashtego, a Native American hunter; and the enormous African, Daggoo, whom Ishmael describes as "imperial" in bearing. Finally, several days into the voyage, Ahab emerges from his cabin for the first time, although he says nothing to the crew.

Once the ship reaches equatorial waters, Ahab addresses the men. Calling the crew to the quarter deck, he unveils the true purpose of the voyage: to hunt and kill the infamous white whale, Moby-Dick. He nails a gold doubloon to the mast, announcing that it will go to the first man who spots the white whale. Starbuck expresses misgivings about Ahab's intent, declaring that it seems "blasphemous" to seek vengeance against a "dumb thing," while at the same time arguing that the mission is contrary to the vessel's commercial aims. Ahab delivers a fiery speech, and Starbuck falls silent, although he remains troubled about Ahab's maniacal demeanor. The *Pequod* continues its journey around the Cape of Good Hope and into the Indian Ocean, on its way toward the South Pacific.

Upon reaching the Indian Ocean, the ship comes across a pod of whales. As the men lower the boats for the first time, Ishmael remarks on a group of sailors, previously unnoticed men of "vivid, tiger-yellow complexion," who make up Ahab's personal hunting crew. At the head of this secretive band is Ahab's personal harpooner, a menacing figure named Fedallah. The hunting crews embark on a series of successful kills, and for several chapters the ship engages in typical whaling

business, harvesting the animals for oil, blubber, and bone. As the ship continues on its course, it passes a number of other whaling vessels. With each encounter Ahab interrogates the ship's captain for information about the white whale. The captain of one ship, the *Jeroboam,* issues an ominous warning concerning the danger of the white whale, but Ahab dismisses his concerns.

As the *Pequod* nears its fateful engagement with Moby-Dick, a series of foreboding incidents befall the crew. The most portentous scene comes when the ship's African-American cabin boy, Pip, falls out of a whaling boat and nearly drowns. Although Pip survives, he becomes insane and issues apocalyptic utterances throughout the remainder of the voyage. A short time later, Queequeg falls seriously ill. Anticipating death, he orders the ship's carpenter to construct a coffin, though he eventually recovers. As the ship approaches the equator, Ahab continues to gather intelligence concerning Moby-Dick's whereabouts through his discussions with the captains of other vessels. Although each captain describes the destruction and death wreaked by the white whale, Ahab remains undeterred.

Finally the crew of the *Pequod* sights Moby-Dick. A three-day hunt ensues, in the course of which Moby-Dick attacks the whaling boats, killing Fedallah. On the third day of the hunt, the whale rams the *Pequod,* sinking the vessel. Ahab becomes entangled in a harpoon line and is dragged out of his boat and drowned. The entire crew gets caught in the vortex of the *Pequod*'s sinking except Ishmael, who saves himself by clutching Queequeg's coffin. The novel concludes with a brief epilogue in which Ishmael describes his rescue by another whaling vessel.

Interwoven into the narrative of the *Pequod*'s journey are several chapters devoted to various technical aspects of whaling, including an overview of the various species of whales, analyses of whale physiology, descriptions of the commercial processes involved with the whaling industry, and discussions of geography. Although the style and content of these sections are not fictional, many scholars regard them as an essential counterpoint—"ballast," in the words of more than one commentator—to the poetry and symbolism of the central narrative.

MAJOR THEMES

In the broadest sense, *Moby-Dick* explores questions of humanity's relationship to nature, God, and the universe. At the core of the novel's thematic layers is the *Pequod*'s captain, Ahab. Some scholars have seen Ahab's pursuit of the whale as an allegory for humanity's pursuit of truth, whether religious, philosophical, or psychological. A war takes place within the character of Ahab that pits the reasoning power of the intellect against the irrational, emotion-driven force of the will. Even while Ahab comprehends that his quest is futile, he remains driven by his lust for revenge, that "cruel, remorseless emperor" that rules his passions. The power of his dark will insinuates itself into the entire crew; even Starbuck, whose reasonable objections to the hunt for Moby-Dick go unheeded, confesses that Ahab "drilled deep down, and blasted all my reason out of me!" Indeed, the figure of Ahab, teeming with violent contradictions, is emblematic of the novel's numerous ambiguities.

In contrast to the *Pequod*'s violent, monomaniacal captain stands the narrator, Ishmael, whose meditative, detached persona provides a perspective well-suited to the novel's multilayered storytelling technique. Ishmael, no less than Ahab, fulfills a vital symbolic role in the novel. Like his biblical antecedent, the outcast son of Abraham, Ishmael has no home and therefore makes no claim to a single interpretative model for the world around him. Through Ishmael's relentless investigations into the purpose of the voyage, as well as into the meaning of his own life, Melville gives voice to his far-reaching ruminations on the nature of humanity's place in the universe.

Ahab's antagonist, the whale, embodies an entirely separate system of symbols with many levels of meaning. In one sense, Moby-Dick represents nature, at the same time a provider of valuable resources such as food, oil, and whalebone and a source of harsher realities in the form of unpredictable, destructive behaviors. In a more profound manner, the white whale embodies the mystical, transcendent power of the universe itself. The whale exists below the surface of the ocean, invisible to human eyes; in this way he remains unknowable, "unaccountable to his pursuers." Ishmael describes him as "not only ubiquitous, but immortal."

Paradoxically, with every new avenue of inquiry into *Moby-Dick*, coherence and underlying meaning become more elusive. A number of scholars have contended that indefiniteness is, in fact, the novel's central meaning. Ishmael reflects on this condition of uncertainty late in the novel when he posits that "a careful disorderliness is the true method." Although Ishmael is referring specifically to the whaling industry, his sentiment can be interpreted to represent the structure and movement of the novel, as well as Melville's broader ideas concerning the nature of existence.

CRITICAL RECEPTION

Early reviews of *Moby-Dick* were mixed. A few contemporary critics praised the work's intelligence and poetic language, with one writer lauding Melville's ambition and power of perception, asserting that the work was far superior to the "crowd of successful mediocrities" that constituted the bulk of popular fiction. Other reviewers were nonplussed by the novel's unorthodox structure and rambling narrative technique. A reviewer for the London *Athenaeum* described the book as "an ill-compounded mixture of romance and matter-of-fact," while a writer for the *Spectator* dubbed it a "rhapsody gone mad."

After an initial wave of reviews, the novel fell into obscurity, remaining relatively neglected until the 1920s, when scholars like Raymond Weaver, Van Wyck Brooks, and Lewis Mumford began to explore the novel's stylistic and thematic complexities. The efforts of these critics ushered in a new era of scholarly interest in the work, one that would witness the emergence of an entire branch of literary criticism devoted to Melville's epic. In the 1920s and 1930s, writers as diverse as E. M. Forster, William Faulkner, and Hart Crane wrote admiringly of the novel. In his landmark *American Renaissance: Art and Expression in the Age of Emerson and Whitman* (1941), F. O. Matthiessen examined the influence of Shakespeare on Melville's prose, while at the same time asserting that the novel is decidedly American in style and ambition. Howard P. Vincent's *The Trying-Out of Moby-Dick* (1948) offers a comprehensive analysis of Melville's use of whaling sources in the novel's composition. Richard Chase, in *Herman Melville: A Critical Study* (1949), interprets the novel within the context of the emerging capitalist society of nineteenth-century America. A number of critics, notably Mumford, Alfred Kazin, and the poet Charles Olson, have written in-depth analyses of Ahab's character, describing him as a heroic figure struggling to assert humanity's supremacy in an indifferent universe.

In the 1960s, such scholars as Beongcheon Yu argued that Ishmael, rather than Ahab, serves as the symbolic focus of the novel. In his 1969 article "The Anti-Transcendentalism of *Moby-Dick*," Michael J. Hoffman asserted that the novel's complex web of symbols is intended to be read ironically and that the book represents Melville's statement on the inherent meaningless of existence. Other commentators, notably Paul Lukacs and E. L. Doctorow, have examined the novel's stylistic innovations. A number of scholars have offered historical readings of *Moby-Dick,* analyzing the novel within the framework of the formation of America's democratic society, its territorial expansion in the early nineteenth century, and the institution of slavery; others have read the work as a broad statement on the relationship between humanity and the environment. Some critics, such as William V. Spanos and Donald Pease, have written critiques of Melville criticism in general, arguing that interpretations of *Moby-Dick* are invariably shaped by dominant social, political, and cultural factors.

PRINCIPAL WORKS

Typee: A Peep at Polynesian Life. During a Four Months' Residence in a Valley of the Marquesas (novel) 1846

Omoo: A Narrative of Adventures in the South Seas (novel) 1847

Mardi: And a Voyage Thither (novel) 1849

Redburn: His First Voyage (novel) 1849

White-Jacket: or, The World in a Man-of-War (novel) 1850

Moby-Dick; or, The Whale (novel) 1851; also published as *The Whale,* 1851

Pierre; or, The Ambiguities (novel) 1852

Israel Potter: His Fifty Years of Exile (novel) 1855

The Piazza Tales (short stories) 1856

The Confidence-Man: His Masquerade (novel) 1857

Battle-Pieces and Aspects of the War (poetry) 1866

Clarel: A Poem and Pilgrimage in the Holy Land (poetry) 1876

John Marr and Other Sailors (poetry) 1888

Timoleon (poetry) 1891

Billy Budd and Other Prose Pieces (novel and short stories) 1924

CRITICISM

John Halverson (essay date fall 1963)

SOURCE: Halverson, John. "The Shadow in *Moby-Dick.*" *American Quarterly* 15, no. 3 (fall 1963): 436-46.

[*In the following essay, Halverson examines Melville's use of psychological archetypes in* Moby-Dick, *paying particular attention to his explorations into the "shadow" side of human nature.*]

Psychological penetration and archetypal power are plainly manifest in *Moby-Dick.* Melville, as an observer of mankind, often seems a forerunner of depth psychology. Often his probings into personality are in the imagery of a descent to a hidden inner being. One may think, for example, of the passage in *White-Jacket:* "It is no pleasing task, nor a thankful one, to dive into the souls of some men; but there are occasions when, to bring up the mud from the bottom, reveals to us on what soundings we are, on what course we adjoin." Or, again, that remarkable "Winding far down from within the very heart of this spiked Hotel de Cluny where we here stand" in Chapter XLI of *Moby-Dick.* The presen-

tation and analysis of Captain Ahab's madness might, barring the great poetry, have come from a Freud or a Jung or a Binswanger. It is Jung, of course, who has provided the only thorough investigation and formulization of psychological archetypes, and it is reasonable, therefore, to turn to analytical psychology to see what aid can be found there for the elucidation of Melville's masterpiece. It is particularly the archetype of the "shadow" which seems strikingly applicable and vital to this novel.

Jung did not discover the shadow side of man. Among countless earlier instances, let Plato's black horse of the *Phaedrus* parable suffice as an example; nearly all religious and philosophical men, including Melville, have known of it. It is that darker half of the human soul, its lower, primitive, instinctual, sensual half. It is mysterious, inarticulate, capricious demonic, even diabolical. All depth psychologists agree on this major part of the psyche, that it does not belong to ordinary consciousness, that it is essentially maternal. Jung was, however, the first to articulate the shadow figure as a concept and to explain its psychological function. It is, above all, a phenomenon of the preconscious mind, embodying those repressions of natural behavior which Freud acutely and gloomily demonstrated as the neurotic basis of civilization, and therefore, at least initially, sinister. In dreams and in the "forgotten language" of fairy tales and myths, the shadow side of the psyche may be constellated, embodied, into a single figure; in dreams it is a dark figure of the same sex as the dreamer. For obvious reasons, it is an alter ego, a "dark brother." It may also be projected in waking life onto other persons. Indeed an entire group may project its collective shadow onto another group, a possibility that Laurens van der Post has explored in *The Dark Eye in Africa* to help explain white prejudice there, particularly in his native South Africa. Nor is such a notion foreign to Melville, who has his Spanish Sailor say to the black giant Daggoo: "Aye, harpooner, thy race is the undeniable dark side of mankind—devilish dark at that."

Rather less pessimistic than his teacher, Jung believed mankind to be salvable. The way out of the Freudian dilemma is the process of "individuation," a way based on self-knowledge, acceptance of the shadow, and the raising into consciousness of whatever in the unconscious *can* be raised. Jung's way is a psychological elaboration of many a timeless precept from "Know thyself" to "The kingdom of God is within you." It assumes a *conatus* of the self toward integration. The development of the individual into wholeness requires as its first step the recognition and assimilation of the shadow, including, of course, the withdrawal of its projections. The next major step is the acceptance of the contrasexual element of the psyche, the "anima" for men—and for male-dominated civilization in general. This female component Jung designates broadly as Eros in opposition to the ego as Logos. It comprises those qualities of character which are traditionally associated with women: kindness, tenderness, mercy, the "pitee" that "renneth soone in gentil herte." It is the capacity to accept others and love them, a motherly quality and a non-rational one. One of Melville's contemporaries, Dickens, too often illustrates the ease with which the traditional association of such qualities with women becomes sentimentality. But another, a closer neighbor, reveals a truer understanding of the phenomenon; Thoreau, with the characteristic acumen of his genius, gives a precise account of the matter while writing of Chaucer: "A simple pathos and feminine gentleness . . . are peculiar to him. We are tempted to say that his genius was feminine, not masculine. It was such a feminineness, however, as is rarest to find in woman, though not the appreciation of it; perhaps it is not to be found at all in woman, but is only the feminine in man." Jung holds, as any rational humanist does, that the ideal personality maintains the feminine and masculine components in complementary balance. Justice should be tempered with mercy—and mercy should be tempered with justice.

The process of individuation reaches beyond the individual in its effects, for it raises and strengthens the sense of common humanity, the sense of human brotherhood. "If men can be educated to see the shadow-side of their nature clearly, it may be hoped that they will also learn to understand and love their fellow men better. A little less hypocrisy and a little more self-knowledge can only have good results in respect for our neighbor; for we are all too prone to transfer to our fellows the injustice and violence we inflict upon our own natures." (Jung, *Coll*[*ected*] *Works* [New York, 1953-], VII, 25)

The "meeting with the shadow," then, is crucial to the development of the self. As a preconscious phenomenon, the shadow figure is conceived by the analytical psychologists as an intermediary between the conscious mind (the ego) and the deep unconscious. The conscious ego may be symbolized by whatever is aerial or high, mountain peaks and particularly birds; the deep unconscious by whatever is deep and dark and formless, caves, for instance, but particularly the sea. The shadow is the "guardian of the threshold" who can lead the way to selfhood, symbolized by the mandala: the circle, the wheel with the vital center. To the ego the shadow may appear at first as frightening or evil, since it represents what the ego has repressed. But with its acceptance, the shadow reveals itself as the helpful friend, helping bring up to consciousness those elements of the unconscious, especially Eros, necessary to the wholeness and health of the self. Unassimilated, the

shadow figure becomes evil, a constellation of all that is demonic in the dark side of the psyche, which in itself is ethically neutral.

* * *

Seen in the light of Jung's theory of the shadow, some rather perplexing events and personal relationships in **Moby-Dick** become clear and significant, for they embody archetypal figures and dynamics. The two principal characters, Ishmael and Ahab, both setting out on journeys of the soul, encounter their "shadows" and are saved and damned by the results of these encounters. Their journey is on the sea of the unconscious, "the ungraspable phantom of life," "the mystic ocean," which for the "sunken-eyed young Platonist" is "the visible image of that deep, blue, bottomless soul, pervading mankind and nature; and every strange, half-seen, gliding, beautiful thing that eludes him; every dimly-discovered, uprising fin of some undiscernible form, seems to him the embodiment of those elusive thoughts that only people the soul by continually flitting through it." For Ishmael, the ocean is "the dark side of this earth," but "in landlessness alone resides the highest truth, shoreless, indefinite as God." He recognizes the necessity, the value, of confronting the unconscious.

It is a spiritual sickness that impels Ishmael to the sea: "a damp, drizzly November in my soul," as he says. On the ocean in pursuit of the leviathan whale, he hopes for a cure. Thus it is a spiritual journey he embarks on, and his first important encounter is with Queequeg. Though treated comically in retrospect, Ishmael's first meeting with Queequeg in the Spouter Inn is, at the time, an alarming and frightening event. In the middle of the night he is confronted by a purplish, yellow apparition covered with "blackish looking squares" of tattooing, a growling cannibal flourishing a tomahawk. No wonder he sings out, "Landlord! Watch! Coffin! Angels! save me!" But Peter Coffin assures him of Queequeg's harmlessness, and Ishmael takes a second look and realizes that "For all his tattooings he was on the whole a clean, comely looking cannibal." There quickly develops between them a profound rapport and friendship described in terms of marriage (language that causes some readers some uneasiness): "Thus, then, in our hearts' honeymoon, lay I and Queequeg—a cosy, loving pair." It is Queequeg's primitiveness that attracts Ishmael; he recognizes the validity of the primitive, which civilization represses: "There he sat, his very indifference speaking a nature in which there lurked no civilized hypocrisies and bland deceits. Wild he was; a very sight of sights to see; yet I began to feel myself mysteriously drawn towards him. And those same things that would have repelled most others, they were the very magnets that thus drew me." Almost at once Ishmael feels the beneficent influence of this "marriage": "No more my splintered heart and maddened hand were turned against the wolfish world. This soothing savage had redeemed it."

Where is an objective correlative for these strong emotions and extravagant language? Less than a day's acquaintance with an unprepossessing and nearly incoherent savage does not seem an adequate basis for Ishmael's feeling of redemption. Yet we do not doubt him; his words convince. We do not doubt, because the experience is archetypal.

Queequeg is twice dramatically presented as a rescuer; both times he dives into the sea to save a drowning man. In the first rescue (Chapter XIII), the "bumpkin" seems to be lost; Ishmael can see Queequeg, "the grand and glorious fellow," but "no one to be saved." But Queequeg dives down and disappears into the sea and rises again with the "lifeless form." This act confirms all of Ishmael's feelings for his friend: "From that hour I clove to Queequeg like a barnacle; yea, till poor Queequeg took his last long dive." The second rescue is the famous obstetric delivery of Tashtego from the sinking whale's head (Chapter LXXVIII), where once again Queequeg must dive deep into the sea to perform his heroic task. Even after his "last long dive," it is Queequeg's coffin that saves Ishmael. In all these things we can see the function of the helpful shadow.

The symbolic relationship between Ishmael and Queequeg is represented most vividly in Chapter LXXII. Queequeg, "cutting in" the dead whale, is on the surface of the sea, kicking sharks away with his bare feet. Ishmael is up above him on deck and attached to him by a "monkey-rope."

> It was a humorously perilous business for both of us. For, before we proceed further, it must be said that the monkey-rope was fast at both ends; fast to Queequeg's broad canvas belt, and fast to my narrow leather one. So that for better or for worse, we two, for the time, were wedded; and should poor Queequeg sink to rise no more, then both usage and honor demanded, that instead of cutting the cord, it should drag me down in his wake. So then, an elongated Siamese ligature united us. Queequeg was my own inseparable twin brother; nor could I any way get rid of the dangerous liabilities which the hempen bond entailed.

The dark twin brother, between Ishmael and the unconscious sea, attached to him by an indissoluble bond—this Queequeg is Ishmael's shadow.

By his acceptance and assimilation of his shadow, Ishmael discovers Eros, expressed as the sense of brotherhood and love. "I saw that this situation of mine was the precise situation of every mortal that breathes." Moving within himself closer to the human collectivity, he changes radically from the man who feels the urge to go about "methodically knocking people's hats off" to the celebrant of brotherly love who squeezes his neighbors' hands along with the spermaceti:

> Oh! my dear fellow beings, why should we longer cherish any social acerbities, or know the slightest ill-humor or envy! Come; let us squeeze hands all round; nay, let us all squeeze ourselves into each other; let us squeeze ourselves universally into the very milk and sperm of kindness.

And the celebrant of man and democracy:

> But this august dignity I treat of, is not the dignity of kings and robes, but that abounding dignity which has no robed investiture. Thou shalt see it shining in the arm that wields a pick or drives a spike; that democratic dignity which, on all hands, radiates without end from God; Himself! The great God absolute! The centre and circumference of all democracy! His omnipresence, our divine equality!

And the celebrant of the "First Congregational Church":

> I mean, sir, the same ancient Catholic Church to which you and I, and Captain Peleg there, and Queequeg here, and all of us, and every mother's son and soul of us belong; the great and everlasting First Congregation of this whole worshipping world; we all belong to that; . . . in *that* we all join hands.

The "process of individuation," says Jung, "does not lead to isolation, but to an intenser and more universal collective solidarity."

For Ahab, as for Ishmael, the ocean is the "dark Hindoo half of nature" and an infidel queen as well; he begins his spiritual journey on the unconscious sea with a profound sickness of soul. Whereas Ishmael's sickness is a vague, indefinite gloominess and dissatisfaction, Ahab's is sharply defined demonic possession. He is ego ridden, all Logos and no Eros. That his conscious ego is disproportionately swollen is clearly seen when he interprets the "equatorial coin": "There's something ever egotistical in mountain-tops and towers, and all other grand and lofty things; look here,—three peaks as proud as Lucifer. The firm tower, that is Ahab; the volcano, that is Ahab; the courageous, the undaunted, and victorious fowl, that, too, is Ahab; all are Ahab; and this round gold is but the image of the rounder globe, which, like a magician's glass, to each and every man in turn but mirrors back his own mysterious self." Correspondingly, he hates the unconscious and is maddened by it. "That inscrutable thing is chiefly what I hate." Whatever is not accessible to consciousness he violently rejects. The sea and the white whale are for him inarticulate evil. His own terrible eloquence demands Logos where there is only "speechless, placeless power"; the sea remains silent, the whale has "not one syllable." Projecting his own unconscious self onto the whale, he would assault and destroy it—and therewith destroy himself. The projection is elaborately explicit in the book: Ahab "at last came to identify with him [Moby-Dick] not only all his bodily woes, but all his intellectual and spiritual exasperations. The white whale swam before him as the monomaniac incarnation of all those malicious agencies which some deep men feel eating in them . . . all the subtle demonisms of life and thought; all evil, to crazy Ahab, were visibly personified, and made practically assailable in Moby Dick." Thus for Ahab the whiteness of the whale is like an empty canvas which he fills with the "subtle demonisms" from his own unconscious. Ahab's ego domination—in exact opposition to Ishmael's experience—breeds an arrogant solitude rejecting all sense of human brotherhood. "Cursed be that mortal inter-indebtedness," he cries, "which will not do away with ledgers. I would be free as air; and I'm down in the whole world's books:" There is Ahab, and there is the rest of the world: "Ahab stands alone among the millions of the peopled earth, nor gods nor men his neighbors!" Such a man must be, as Aristotle said, either a beast or a god, and Ahab is something of both, superhuman and subhuman at once. A consequence of his egocentricity is that he has no sense of responsibility. He is ready to destroy not only himself but all with him; it is not *his* doing—the "whole act's immutably decreed," Ahab is "the Fates' lieutenant."

> The effect of projection is to isolate the subject from his environment, since instead of a real relation to it there is now only an illusory one. Projections change the world into the replica of one's own unknown face. In the last analysis, therefore, they lead to an autoerotic or autistic condition in which one dreams a world whose reality remains forever unattainable. The resultant *sentiment d'incomplétude* and the still worse feeling of sterility are in their turn explained by projection as the malevolence of the environment, and by means of this vicious circle the isolation is intensified.
>
> (Jung, *Coll. Works*, IX.1, 9)

Ahab lives in his shadow: he is "darkness leaping out of light." Or, rather, his shadow side possesses him: "his special lunacy stormed his general sanity, and carried it." The "special lunacy" is the revenge of the unconscious on the ego.

Nevertheless, Ahab has had "his humanities," and his consuming obsession is intermitted by moments of awareness and regret. The possibility of redemption is agonizingly raised when the journey is nearly over, when Ahab, too, encounters a helpful shadow: the Negro boy Pip, whose diminutive size and timidity are in universe proportion to his master's ego. (Ishmael and Queequeg seem, appropriately, to be about the same size; at the other end of the scale, there is the amusing and suggestive picture of little, mindless Flask riding the shoulders of the majestic black giant Daggoo.) Pip's first appearance is with the promising circle of his tambourine in hand, but it is not until, leaping from Stubb's boat, he becomes a deep diver into the sea that the promise is renewed. There in the "wondrous depths, where strange shapes of the unwarped primal world

glided to and fro," there Wisdom "revealed his hoarded heaps." There Pip "saw God's foot upon the treadle of the loom, and spoke it; and therefore his shipmates called him mad."

With the same unexplained suddenness that Ishmael took to Queequeg, Ahab brings Pip under his protection: "Thou touchest my inmost centre, boy; thou art tied to me by cords woven of my heart-strings. Come, let's down." The imagery of the cords is picked up by Pip, gazing at Ahab's hand in his: "This seems to me, sir, as a man-rope; something that weak souls may hold by." Irresistibly the rope joining Ishmael and Queequeg is recalled, but the beauty and hope in that reminiscence are immediately tempered by the old Manxman pulling in the broken log-line: "But here's the end of the rotten line—all dripping, too. Mend it, eh? I think we had best have a new line altogether."

Ahab recognizes his potential salvation through Pip, who touches his "inmost centre," and it costs him much psychological effort to resist it. "There is that in thee, poor lad, which I feel too curing to my malady. Like cures like; and for this hunt, my malady becomes my most desired health. Do thou abide below. . . ." And Pip, too, knows Ahab's need for him: "No, no, no! ye have not a whole body, sir; do ye but use poor me for your one lost leg; only tread upon me, sir; I ask no more, so I remain a part of ye." As M. O. Percival has shown (*A Reading of* Moby-Dick [Chicago, 1950], pp. 97 ff.), Pip offers Ahab the way to love. Ahab knows his "fiery father," but "my sweet mother, I know not. Oh cruel! what hast thou done with her?" As if in answer to Ahab's plea to the "clear spirit" to "come in thy lowest form of love," Pip appears to show the way to the "compassionate feminine." But Ahab repeatedly admonishes Pip to stay below; he will not raise him up to the deck level as Ishmael did Queequeg. Ahab remains master to the end, and Pip laments, "Oh, master! master! I am indeed downhearted when you walk over me."

For Ahab has another shadow, an "evil shadow," as Starbuck explicitly calls him. It is not Pip he will tread upon; he has already "put his foot upon the Parsee" to defy the corpusants. Fedallah first appears "tall and swart," wearing a "Chinese jacket of black cotton" and "black trousers of the same dark stuff." His presence and identity are continually matters of wonder. Stubb takes him for the devil. It is even uncertain "whether indeed he were a mortal substance, or else a tremulous shadow cast upon the deck by some unseen being's body." But he is most particularly Ahab's "lean shade"; Fedallah and Ahab are seen gazing at each other "as if in the Parsee Ahab saw his forethrown shadow. . . ." Few question that Fedallah is evil, yet he does nothing remotely wicked. He is recognized as little more than Ahab's own demonic dark side embodied and externalized. He is sensed to have some strange control over

Ahab: "even as Ahab's eyes so awed the crew's, the inscrutable Parsee's glance awed his. . . ." Fedallah symbolizes Ahab's possession. It seems no accident that the touching rejection of Pip, quoted above (from Chapter CXXIX), is immediately followed in the next chapter by the picture of Ahab bound to Fedallah (bound as irrevocably to his evil shadow as Ishmael is to his helpful shadow). It is this iron hold that prevents the acceptance of Pip.

Yet twice after first taking Pip to him, Ahab shows signs of relenting; twice we see the welling up of humanity in him. "Close! stand close to me, Starbuck; let me look into a human eye; it is better than to gaze into sea or sky; better than to gaze upon God." And again, after the second day of the chase has ended disastrously and Ahab's ivory leg is shattered: "Aye, aye, Starbuck, 'tis sweet to lean sometimes, be the leaner who he will; and would old Ahab had leaned oftener than he has." But Starbuck is a bending reed; his simple-minded piety is hardly adequate to the old man's need. It has been said that Starbuck is not weak, but merely betrayed by the habit of obedience. Obedient he is, but his spiritual weakness is made quite clear, for he will not face the dark side of the world. More perceptive and intelligent than the other mates, he knows it exists but refuses to cope with it, taking refuge in piety, as Stubb takes refuge in his eternal jolliness. He shies away from that "highest truth" in the sea which Ishmael seeks there: "Tell me not of thy teeth-tiered sharks, and thy kidnapping cannibal ways. Let faith oust fact. . . ." As for the doubloon that "but mirrors back" the viewer's "mysterious self"—"I will quit it, lest Truth shake me falsely." He foolishly denies his own dark side: "Oh, life! 'tis now that I do feel the latent horror in thee! but 'tis not me! that horror's out of me!" No, it is not Starbuck who can help his captain. "Ahab is forever Ahab" and will keep to his fixed purpose still, even "against all natural lovings and longings." Yet in his relationship to Pip and his subsequent near rediscovery of his human soul, he reaches a tragic stature well beyond the merely demoniac.

Having just implied that the book *is* in some way a tragedy, I should like to digress for a paragraph to comment on what seems a frequent problem in the criticism of Melville's masterpiece, that is the problem of whether to treat the book as a novel or as tragic drama. Both modes are present obviously, sometimes interwoven, sometimes sharply separated. The dramatic element is in some ways more impressive: the sudden appearance of "scenes" complete with stage directions, and the deliberate Shakespearianism with its echoes of *Lear* and *Macbeth.* And here it is that Ahab takes the central position. But is Ahab then the "hero" of *Moby-Dick*? To answer with an unqualified affirmative is to neglect just half of the book. For if it is the tragedy of Captain Ahab, it is also the novel of Ishmael, whose

story follows, in essence, a rather traditional *Erziehungsroman* pattern of development of maturity, and occupies a good deal of space in the book. How successfully Melville pulled together all the diverse formal and substantial elements of the book is another question, but *Moby-Dick* without Ishmael, if not the same as *Hamlet* without the Prince, is nevertheless not *Moby-Dick.* Thus Professor Murray's fascinating essay "In Nomine Diaboli" (*New England Quarterly,* December 1951) seems finally very peculiar because it makes no room for Ishmael.

The story of Ishmael and Queequeg and Ishmael's salvation is essentially novelistic; Ahab's relationship to Pip (especially with its echoes of Lear and his fool) and Ahab's ultimate destruction belong to a dramatic mode. One story, moreover, is conducted predominantly in narrative, the other predominantly in dialogue.

* * *

Ahab fails because his hope for salvation arrives too late. The encounter with the helpful shadow is late and weak, and the sea must swallow him up at last. His evil shadow and true "pilot" has led the way to destruction. But even as his "soul's ship" starts on the third and final chase, Pip's voice cries out from the low cabin-window, "The sharks! the sharks! . . . O master, my master, come back!" "But Ahab heard nothing; for his own voice was high-lifted then; and the boat leaped on." And Ahab, for whom Logos is all, is ironically strangled: "voicelessly . . . he was shot out of the boat, ere the crew knew he was gone." At the same time, the *Pequod* is sinking, pulling down with her the sky-hawk ("the courageous, the undaunted, and victorious fowl, that, too, is Ahab") pinned to the mast by Tashtego: "and so the bird of heaven, with archangelic shrieks, and his imperial beak thrust upwards, and his whole captive form folded in the flag of Ahab, went down with his ship. . . ." The symbolism is fitting for the end of that great aspiring ego, obliterated at last by a greater power.

> Ishmael alone survives.
>
> Round and round, then, and ever contracting towards the button-like black bubble at the axis of that slowly wheeling circle, like another Ixion I did revolve. Till, gaining that vital centre, the black bubble upward burst; and now, liberated by reason of its cunning spring, and, owing to its great buoyancy, rising with great force, the coffin life-buoy shot lengthwise from the sea, fell over, and floated by my side. Buoyed up by that coffin, for almost one whole day and night, I floated on a soft and dirge-like main. The unharming sharks, they glided by as if with padlocks on their mouths; the savage sea-hawks sailed with sheathed beaks.

The symbolism is dense, compact and powerful. The circle image suggests the mandala, the symbol of the selfhood which Ishmael has attained. Queequeg's coffin is, as it were, the memory of the shadows, now assimilated. It appears at the "vital centre" of the self. Having achieved the wholeness of self, Ishmael is safe alike from the savage sea-hawks of the ego which ravaged Promethean Ahab and from the voracious sharks of the unconscious. Ishmael is saved because only he has fully accepted his own humanity. He is like, to invoke again that sanest of men, Thoreau, who could say: "I found in myself, and still find, an instinct toward a higher, or, as it is named, spiritual life, as do most men, and another toward a primitive rank and savage one, and I reverence them both." The center of Ishmael's being is serene: "But even so, amid the tornadoed Atlantic of my being, do I myself still for ever centrally disport in mute calm; and while ponderous planets of unwaning woe revolve round me, deep down and deep inland there I still bathe me in eternal mildness of joy." But "Ahab, in his hidden self, raved on."

To say that Queequeg and Pip are shadow figures is not, of course, to deny them status as living characters (to Fedallah, however, it might well be denied). Indeed, the term "shadow" may be discarded altogether and the same pattern is there. Queequeg and Pip are much alike (though their physical resemblance ends with their dark color), especially in their relationship with the two leading characters of the novel. Both are unconscious: Queequeg's unconsciousness is natural, he is always at ease, unaffected by the neuroses of civilized consciousness; Pip's unconsciousness is accidental, the withdrawal of consciousness from unbearable reality. Queequeg and Pip are the deep divers. But Pip's dive is metaphorical; there is no indication in the story that he actually gets very far under water: we see him treading water in an appalling expanse of sea, physically nowhere near any "wondrous depths" at any time. Rather his dive is into the unconscious mind as shock induces psychotic withdrawal. "The sea had jeeringly kept his finite body up, but drowned the infinite of his soul." It is there that he sees "God's foot on the treadle of the loom." And it is because Ahab is so alienated from the unconscious that he can "suck most wondrous philosophies" from Pip.

The two relationships (Queequeg-Ishmael, Pip-Ahab) are both formed almost instantly without any adequate overt explanation, as if both were encounters of recognition. Both Queequeg and Pip are obviously and explicitly instruments of salvation to their respective friends, whatever the reason may be. Both induce feelings of natural love of fellow men. Queequeg is accepted wholeheartedly by Ishmael, who thereupon grows as a human being and survives. Pip is finally rejected by Ahab, who is destroyed physically and spiritually. Ahab is made human only fleetingly. Usually he is as godlike and demoniac as he regards himself, but Pip, who knows his master is not a whole man, touches the center of Ahab's humanity. His influence is not enough to save Ahab; it is enough to transform de-

monic obsession into tragic agony. Ishmael is a whole man, and Queequeg is the accredited agent of his humanity and salvation. Ishmael's is a beautiful and free soul "that can alike dive down into the blackest gorges, and soar out of them again and become invisible in the sunny spaces."

Beongcheon Yu (essay date March 1965)

SOURCE: Yu, Beongcheon. "Ishmael's Equal Eye: The Source of Balance in *Moby-Dick*." *ELH* 32, no. 1 (March 1965): 110-25.

[*In the following essay, Yu interprets* Moby-Dick *as a chronicle of Ishmael's moral, intellectual, and spiritual education. Yu asserts that Ishmael, rather than Ahab, embodies the metaphysical core of the novel.*]

> . . . for all have doubts; many deny; but doubts or denials, few along with them, have intuitions. Doubts of all things earthly, and intuitions of some things heavenly; this combination makes neither believer nor infidel, but makes a man who regards them both with equal eye.
>
> Chapter LXXXV, "The Fountain"

Few readers of *Moby-Dick* would dismiss Ishmael as merely a narrative device, yet few credit his role as character, as flesh-and-blood entity. Olson, for instance, compares him to the chorus in Greek tragedy; Auden thinks that Ishmael becomes "simply the recording consciousness, the senses and the mind through which we experience everything"; Feidelson points out that Ishmael "increasingly becomes a presence, a visionary activity, rather than a man"; and Chase announces that Ishmael "all but disappears as a character," becoming "hardly more than the voice of the omniscient author."[1] These views reveal Ishmael's remarkable protean capacity for transformation; by overstressing it, however, they fail to grasp the full complexity of his personality.

Bezanson, by contrast, contends that Ishmael is "the real center of meaning and defining force of the novel," but concludes, rather disappointingly, that "narrator Ishmael is merely young Ishmael grown old," and that both are Melville.[2] The first to suggest Ishmael as hero, apparently, is Smith, who designates alienation as the central theme: "This view makes Ishmael rather than Ahab the 'hero,' and relegates the quest of the White Whale to a subordinate position in the basic structure of the narrative."[3] It is more likely, however, that the quest of *Moby-Dick* is still central and that even in this structure the hero is Ishmael rather than Ahab. Only by accepting Ishmael as narrator-hero can we dispose of such thorny issues as the cetological chapters, the relationship of Ishmael to Ahab, and that of these characters to Melville.

I

Moby-Dick has often been called a work *sui generis,* but no great work is composed in a vacuum; each synthesizes various traditions. Modern readers are more sophisticated than the librarians who catalogued *Moby-Dick* with books on the Sperm Whale Fisheries, although the book is still variously categorized as epic, tragedy, romance, or picaresque novel. But I would like to suggest that *Moby-Dick* is, first of all, Ishmael's cultural autobiography, and the Ahab tragedy was added onto this matrix, perhaps consciously at first, and in time grew organically into it.[4]

Scholars have often noted that Melville, critical of Emerson's brand of Transcendentalism, reacted against the Romantic spirit in general. But the truth is that Melville was basically Romantic as much as he was counter-Romantic. And precisely because of this he was more acutely aware of inner conflicts in Romanticism and more than other Romantic dived deeply in quest of survival and *almost* succeeded. Ishmael, with greater stamina and "an everlasting itch for things remote," fares even better. So dynamic an "I" as narrator is peculiarly Romantic, unlike the classical mode which limits any "I" to a technical convenience. The first person point of view was common in autobiographies, adventures, and travel stories, but Romantic writers elevated and elaborated this essentially lyrical technique into a more consciously symbolic vehicle.[5]

To locate Ishmael's cultural autobiography in a Romantic genre is not to question Melville's originality, but to place his masterpiece in perspective. Melville's originality lies in his ability to intensify Ishmael's cultural quest by the drama of Ahab, or more properly by the tragedy of the *Pequod* which serves him as one grand lesson. Ishmael's training ground, his Yale and Harvard, is the vast unbounded seas. Just as *Moby-Dick* is the culmination of Melville's earlier romances, so does Ishmael stand out in sharper relief than any of his earlier heroes. Although physically less active than Tom, Paul, Taji, Redburn, or White-Jacket, Ishmael is far more subtle, engaging, eager, and complex. Indeed, he alone has a more or less definite purpose; he alone can objectify himself to his searching consciousness and endow his experiences with symbolic significance.

Moby-Dick was first conceived as a continuation of those earlier romances. In the summer of 1850 Melville wrote to Richard Bentley: "The book is a romance of adventure, founded upon certain wild legends in the Southern Sperm Whale Fisheries, and illustrated by the author's own personal experience, of two years & more, as a harpooner."[6] Although we cannot know just how this "romance of adventure" was transformed into *Moby-Dick,*[7] Melville at this stage must have seen Ishmael emerging into clear focus and various legends

concentrating into one White Whale. This view suggests that Ahab was later introduced as the whale's antagonist rather than *vice versa,* especially since the novel was entitled first *The Whale* and then *Moby-Dick.* As the Ahab drama began to overshadow the wild legends (some of which may have also crept into the nine gams of the *Pequod*), Ishmael was turned into its "veritable witness" and the sole survivor who learns its "mighty" lesson. Nonetheless, the book remains a "Whaling Voyage by One Ishmael."

The difference between *Moby-Dick* and Melville's early romances, between Ishmael and his predecessors, is implied in "Call me Ishmael," an invitation so poetic and haunting that we are disappointed by Ishmael's later "disappearance," even though it is only a transformation through immersion. We know Ishmael better than his predecessors, the crew of the *Pequod,* or, surprisingly, even Ahab. A son of a decayed patrician family, Ishmael had gone to sea four times as a merchant sailor and finally, leaving his position as school master, returns to this familiar training ground. As Bezanson points out, Ishmael is an imaginative youth of complex temperament, a hearty lover of laughter and incongruities, who burns to "sail forbidden seas," ever alert for action as well as for scientific lore, indulging an instinct for the morally and psychologically intricate, and striving to satisfy an inexhaustible sense of wonder.[8] One might find developed in Ishmael every human trait (ranging from disillusion to exuberance, from bleakest doubt to mystic ecstasy) but one: he lacks Ahab's fanatic egotism; hence our illusion that Ahab is forcefully alive while Ishmael is not.

Yet "Call me Ishmael" is more vital than these personal qualities for understanding *Moby-Dick.* First, it echoes Emerson's "the first person singular" who finds that in nature "all mean egotism vanishes"; second, self-objectification or self-detachment (Ishmael speaks to himself as if to someone else: "Ishmael," "my dear Ishmael," etc.) sustains his inner monologue with humor and irony; third, a courageous acceptance of self as a man of wilderness, owing allegiance only to "the king of cannibals"; and last, his ceaseless quest of life's lost grandeur. Ishmael seeks something original and authentic: the life of man in its "ultimatum" and "unconditional skeleton." Therefore he embarks in search of "the ungraspable phantom of life." In returning to the sea he chooses whaling because, better than anything else, it can expose him to the most primitive dimensions of nature; and in finding passage he prefers "poor old Nantucket" to nouveau-riche New Bedford because Nantucket is "the Tyre of this Carthage," her "great original." His repeated emphasis on going to sea "as a simple sailor" (remember Melville's letter claiming experience *as a harpooner*),[9] suggests Ishmael's determination to experience life at its very source and drink it to the lees. "I love all men who *dive*" is Melville's axiom, and "Call me Ishmael" echoes the romantic cult of experience, the emphasis on subjectivity as defining the quality and range of reality. The transition from "Etymology" and "Extracts" to the voyage proper is the transition (which Ishmael calls "a keen one") from school teaching to seamanship. Ishmael is fully aware that he must survive or perish in the uncharted sea of life. His determination thus echoes Emerson's query: "Why should not we also enjoy an original relation to the universe?" as well as Thoreau's determination to "live deep and suck out all the marrow of life," or "drive life into a corner, and reduce it to its lowest terms."[10]

Once aboard the *Pequod* Ishmael seems almost to cease breathing. Rather than regret his "disappearance," many critics admire his new role as an epic poet or dramatist or choric embodiment of the consciousness of the crew. But Ishmael does not disappear as suddenly as Bulkington, washed overboard in the "Lee Shore" chapter. (Some critics even suggest that as an ideal norm Bulkington never really disappears!) As a common sailor, he becomes as anonymous as any crew member aboard the *Pequod,* where a rigid hierarchy reigns supreme. In fact, Ishmael call his part of the whaling voyage "shabby." The range of his action is limited to the routine operations of the crew—unless he is meant to be another Steelkilt, which he is not. Thus forced by circumstances and temperament, Ishmael becomes a quiet but all-seeing observer of the *Pequod* tragedy. If his action within this framework is characteristically devoid of outwardness, it is because his participation as a deck hand is taken for granted, and because his mental activity overshadows his physical involvement.

If Ishmael seems only a spectator, it is mainly because we falsely regard **Moby-Dick** as Ahab's story. Like any sailor, Ishmael stands mastheads, even though he often lapses into private reveries (XXXV); while weaving a sword-mat with Queequeg, he ponders the interaction of chance, free will, and necessity (XLVII); while holding Queequeg's monkey-rope (note Melville's qualification that *only in the Pequod* are the monkey and his holder tied together), Ishmael, recognizing the savage as his "inseparable twin brother," experiences fraternity (LXXII). Such experiences culminate in the hand-squeezing scene, in which Ishmael now celebrates universal fraternity: "Come; let us squeeze hands all round; nay, let us all squeeze ourselves into each other; let us squeeze ourselves universally into the very milk and sperm of kindness" (XCIV). This "Siamese connexion with a plurality of other mortals" Ishmael once again learns at great pains while standing by an inverted tiller, just in time to prevent the *Pequod* from flying into the wind and capsizing (XCVI). Ahab ignores what Ishmael learns both repeatedly and rapidly since leaving his inland home as a fretful, lonely youth. What "action"

could be more significant than such learning? And this is the kind of education available only to a common sailor like Ishmael.

But this does not exhaust Ishmael's education at his Yale and Harvard. (It is well to remember that one whaling voyage encircling the watery parts of the globe lasts three years or so) Besides his initiation into brotherhood, Ishmael as a whaler conscientiously subjects himself to a more formal discipline in cetology, without which his education would necessarily be incomplete. His enthusiastic plunge into whaling, exploring every possibility however limited in scope, marks him as a man who takes his part seriously. He scorns the dryness of the "Extracts," for life in its dynamism defies abstraction and fragmentation, always demanding one's total commitment. Critics have now begun to see these cetological chapters (which occupy more than half the novel) as integral to the artistic wholeness of **Moby-Dick.**[11] Similar in function to Homer's epic catalogue, they serve as effective means of the author's circumstantial realism providing necessary exposition as well as ballast of fact for the central drama; growing organically out of appropriate circumstances, they together constitute the bone and heart of a Gargantuan thesis.

To skip these cetological chapters is fatal to an appreciation of the novel, for in Ishmael's education, as he himself seems aware, they are vital, to judge by his patient thoroughness in these lessons, which begin with classifying the species and proceed through a history of whaling, whales in pictures, whales in a dish, the honor and glory of whaling, a modern interpretation of the Jonah story, and the biological, sociological, phrenological, paleontological, anatomical economical, and psychological studies of the whale. As he interweaves fact and fancy, history and legend, science and poetry, observation and speculation, Ishmael changes topics, tone, and level until he finally launches into meditation on dead whales, rising to the ultimate question of immortality: "Does the Whale's Magnitude Diminish?—Will He Perish?"

Exploring whales in every conceivable way, Ishmael moves from exterior to interior, from subjective to objective, and from whale to human, enlarging his vision to the breadth of life and the height of metaphysics. In scaling the heights where physical fact and spiritual truth fuse, Ishmael ignores nothing, for in pursuing total knowledge nothing is too small or too large, too insignificant or too obvious. He is determined to capture the whale not dead but alive, the mystery of life, with his net of science and metaphysics. His zealous persistence reminds us of Emerson's maxim that every truth properly understood implies all other truths. But Ishmael doesn't succeed as he himself already sensed in his preview, "The Whiteness of the White Whale." The mystery of life, remaining elusive, must be accepted rather than dissected. Still, such formal inquiry furthers his education.

Fraternity and cetology might be learned on any whaler, but on the *Pequod* Ishmael shares the fate of that particular floating community. Within its time-honored hierarchy his position, even as a common sailor, is public. In the sense that no man is an island, no sailor is allowed utter privacy. In this capacity Ishmael becomes a quiet witness to Ahab's tragedy, viewing it from start to finish and knowing that his own fate depends on the outcome. The tragedy of the *Pequod* is that she is forced to play a false role. Although her public mission is to fetch oil home to light millions of lamps, she follows her captain's private vengeance. Starbuck, who represents the norm of the crew's concern and ineffectuality, is stunned by Ahab's monomania. Within his domain Ahab exercises absolute dictatorship (XXVI & XXVII), bidding farewell to his pipe, symbol of inner serenity (XXX), mesmerizing the crew with oaths of revenge (XXXVI), spell-binding them to the Doubloon (XCIX), destroying the quadrant, sign of human rationality (CXVIII), and losing his hat to a sea-hawk (CXXX). The doom approaches nearer each time Ahab abandons his peace, reason, and judgment—becoming less human, turning from a whaling captain into a demonic agent, creating from his brain a creature that feeds on his soul, steering farther from the course of those nine ships, the waterway of humanity,[12] and by every known dictatorial means driving the *Pequod* to destruction. In his increasing confusion between official duties and private motives Ahab thus contrasts with Ishmael. As much as Ishmael experiences love and reverence, Ahab insists on alienation and destruction.

Yet there is mysterious kinship between them, although they never exchange a word. At first Ishmael, like the others, is swept away by Ahab's magnetism: "A wild, mystical, sympathetical feeling was in me; Ahab's quenchless feud seemed mine," says Ishmael (XLI). Through such affinity Ishmael sees more deeply into Ahab than anyone else and can even view the whale through his eyes; his cetological study is an unconscious attempt to exorcise Ahab's magic.[13] Despite his success in freeing himself from Ahab's potent spell, Ishmael's initial sympathy remains. He admires Ahab's godlikeness while pitying his ungodliness; after all, they alone embarked in search of the great whale. But their similarity ends here. Ahab pursues while Ishmael quests; one is obsessed, the other fascinated: pursuit and quest, obsession and fascination—they make the difference.

Ishmael, whose characteristic gesture is suspended judgment, accepts the merits of science together with its limits in his cetological explorations; but Ahab, smashing the quadrant, cries out: "Science! Curse thee, thou vain toy!" Whereas Ishmael's monkey-rope connects him to Queequeg for the latter's benefit, Ahab trusts his hoisting rope to Starbuck for his own (CXXX); and later, losing his ivory leg, he leans on Starbuck and exclaims nostalgically: "Aye, aye, Starbuck, 'tis sweet to learn sometimes, be the leaner who he will; and would old Ahab had leaned oftener than he has" (CXXXIV). At the inverted tiller Ishmael wakes in time to decry: "Look not too long in the face of the fire, O man! Never dream with thy hand on the helm! Turn not thy back to the compass" (XCVI), an expression of the crew's inarticulate wish to turn the doomed vessel homeward and also a sign of his awareness of the magnitude of his job on which the crew's welfare depends.

But the ultimate difference lies in their personal visions, especially in their views of the great whale. Ishmael accepts all the contrary associations its hue creates ("not so much a color as the visible absence of color, and at the same time the concrete of all colors"); Ahab, on the other hand, reduces all ambiguity to univocal evil. In the White Whale Ahab sees malice incarnate, assailable by man; however, no such Puritan obsession, no such dualistic distinction of man and nature beguiles Ishmael; to him the White Whale appears as a symbol of life itself which marries man and nature in mystery. Ahab's single-eyed vision lacks depth; Ishmael's sense of perspective and proportion combines irony and seriousness, enthusiasm and detachment. Theirs is the difference between an allegorical and a symbolic vision.

Ahab is an activist, driven to act, be it on the animate or the inanimate; by contrast Ishmael prefers to let himself be acted upon, apparently too passive to qualify for the title role. But his passivity is resilient unlike Pip's (his "passive eyes"), which grants divine wisdom but withholds the practicality needed for survival. In Ishmael's education the advantage of such resilient passivity is obvious: in acting one chooses only one direction, one objective, one possibility over others, but in alert passivity one makes no choices but remains poised in an awareness of life's complexities. Ahab never surmounts the barrier between "thou" and "I" save through drastic acting which only separates subject and object. But Ishmael's unique mode enables him to achieve metamorphosis: in weaving a sword-mat he exclaims, "I say so strange a dreaminess did there then reign all over the ship and all over the sea, only broken by the intermitting dull sound of the sword, that it seemed as if this were the Loom of Time, and I myself were a shuttle mechanically weaving away at the Fates"; attached to the monkey-rope he remarks, "So strongly and metaphysically did I conceive of my situation then, that while earnestly watching his motions, I seemed distinctly to perceive that my own individuality was now merged in a joint stock company of two"; and in the hand-squeezing scene, "I squeezed that sperm till I myself almost melted into it."

Ishmael's mode is undoubtedly a mode of union into oneness, a way of experiencing life to the fullest in all its dimensions. It suggests the essentially feminine nature of mysticism or mystic intuition.[14] Ishmael characterizes his friendship with Queequeg in terms of marriage: in their "hearts' honeymoon" Ishmael's role is that of a bride, not of a bridegroom. (Ishmael says, "You had almost thought that I had been his wife.") This relationship remains basically unchanged: in the mat-making scene Ishmael calls himself "the attendant" or "page" of Queequeg; in the monkey-role scene he is Queequeg's "bowsman." And their symbolic relationship culminates in Queequeg's "coffin," which he transforms into a sea-chest, carving the lid with grotesque figures copied from the tattooing on his body:

> And this tattooing had been the work of a departed prophet and seer of his island, who, by these hieroglyphic marks, had written out on his body a complete theory of the heavens and the earth, and a mystical treatise on the art of attaining truth; so that Queequeg in his own proper person was a riddle to unfold; a wonderous work in one volume; but whose mysteries not even himself could read, though his own live heart beat against them; and these mysteries were therefore destined in the end to moulder away with the living parchment whereon they were inscribed, so be unsolved to the last.
>
> (CX)

In copying his own tattooing Queequeg transfers his body and soul to the wood. No wonder then that his coffin-become-life-buoy rescues Ishmael from the vortex. (It is Queequeg's third and last diving-rescue, the first two being those of a "bumpkin" sailor and Tashtego.) Queequeg says in his early pledge of friendship with Ishmael that "he would gladly die for me, if need should be" (X). Surviving, however, does Ishmael learn that "complete theory of the heavens and the earth" (one may recall the famous design on Achilles' shield) and "the art of attaining truth"? In a word, does he master the riddle that Queequeg embodied in his own person? That is something Melville rather than Ishmael must try to unfold. In any case, Ishmael, in his quest of the great whale, learns universal fraternity from Queequeg's supreme example, a verity more human and immediate. That is the beginning and end of *Moby-Dick.*

II

In concluding with Ahab's death and Ishmael's survival, *Moby-Dick* provides a sense of balance as well as finality, a hint of inevitability in the scheme of things. Within the framework of the novel this double ending is justified psychologically, morally, and symbolically. But we appreciate this ending not for a resolution it offers but for the complexity of Ishmael's vision which keeps the Ahab drama in equilibrium. The solution, which, because of its suspended balance, is essentially provisional if not illusory, is possible only in fiction where imagination exercises its own logic. (All fiction, no matter how great or profound, stops short of the metaphysical ultimate; that is its strength as well as its limitation.) Neither death nor survival can replace a genuine resolution, especially in a book which contains great chunks of life itself. This is what made various critics express dissatisfaction with the ending of *Moby-Dick.* Matthiessen, for instance, referring to this point, observes that Ahab's fatalism "admits no adequate moral recognition," resulting in a tragedy of "an unregenerate will, which stifles his soul and drives his brain with an inescapable fierceness."[15] Smith also notes Melville's failure to provide "a fully specified resolution of his problem."[16] *Moby-Dick,* we must then admit, has not yet ended, because the White Whale, exuding mysteries, still swims on, beckoning to whoever may dare. If Ishmael sought "the overwhelming idea of the great whale himself," the question remains unresolved, challenging him even after his survival.

Moby-Dick is incomplete as life itself is. But we cannot indulge in such justification merely by way of dismissal. Only by probing this question further can we conclude our reading and begin to understand Melville's later career, a baffling problem in Melville criticism. It is through a revived Ahab rather than a surviving Ishmael that Melville resumes the search. Or because *Moby-Dick* merges into life, this problem becomes Melville's rather than Ishmael's, a problem which Queequeg embodied without understanding and Ishmael left without unfolding, "a complete theory of the heavens and the earth" and "the art of attaining truth." It is Ishmael's legacy to his own creator.

Both Ahab and Ishmael have been called the real Melville, but Melville, more properly, embodied both at the time of *Moby-Dick*—and this precariously delicate balance between these opposites sustains its inner structure. But then, why did he kill Ahab, while saving Ishmael? Suggestive in this regard is Melville's letter to Hawthorne, of June 1 (?), 1851, at the last stage of the composition of *Moby-Dick,* in which we read:

> With no son of man do I stand upon any etiquette or ceremony, except the Christian ones of charity and honesty. I am told, my fellow-man, that there is an aristocracy of the brain. Some men have boldly advocated and asserted it. Schiller seems to have done so, though I don't know much about him. At any rate, it is true that there have been those who, while earnest in behalf of political equality, still accept the intellectual estates. And I can well perceive, I think, how a man of superior mind can, by its intense cultivation, bring him-

self, as it were, into a certain spontaneous aristocracy of feeling,—exceedingly nice and fastidious,—similar to that which, in an English Howard, conveys a torpedo-fish thrill at the slightest contact with a social plebeian. So, when you see or hear of my ruthless democracy on all sides, you may possibly feel a touch of a shrink, or something of that sort. It is but nature to be shy of a mortal who boldly declares that a thief in jail is as honorable a personage as Gen. George Washington.[17]

Speaking here of his "ruthless democracy on all sides" is no doubt Melville the man who accepted Hawthorne's celebration of the human heart over the intellect, and made Ishmael exalt "democratic dignity" and "divine equality" (comparable to Whitman's "divine average"), and the saving virtue of universal fraternity (comparable to Hawthorne's "magnetic chain of humanity"). But equally significant is Melville's admission that he can well imagine a man of superior mind harboring "a certain spontaneous aristocracy of feeling." By juxtaposing these views we detect the peculiar polarity in which Melville's mind works,[18] duplicating a related conflict in Romanticism: intellectual individualism or aristocracy culminating in the cult of genius and hero, and political democracy leading to the historic upsurge of the common man. In *Moby-Dick* this clash defines the difference between Ahab's sultanism and Ishmael's "divine equality," and translated in moral terms, between Ahab's death and Ishmael's survival. Had Melville been Hawthorne he would have shown less hesitancy, less ambivalence. Compare Ahab with Hawthorne's Hollingsworth, for instance: one is basically a Prometheus, a Faustian hero; the other, a blacksmith, is a vile murderer.[19] Or had Melville been Whitman, who also noted this problem, he would not have found it irreconcilable; but he had neither Hawthorne's deep-rooted moral conviction nor Whitman's all-inclusive transcendental habit of mind.

Later in the same letter Melville, speaking of Hawthorne's Ethan Brand, declares: "I stand for the heart. To the dogs with the head! I had rather be a fool with a heart, than Jupiter Olympus with his head."[20] It is this Melville who killed Ahab. But his pity and admiration scarcely allowed him to deal Ahab a mortal blow. Thus, although in the novel Ahab is killed and Ishmael survives, in Melville's later career it is not Ishmael but rather Ahab who endures. (In this sense we may say that Ishmael disappears not at the midpoint of the novel, but rather at the zenith of Melville's career—in 1851 he was only 32 years old—not unlike Bulkington.) We may ask: Where now is the Melville who was so convinced of his own "ruthless democracy on all sides," the Melville who had Ishmael declare at the outset of the novel: "Not ignoring what is good, I am quick to perceive a horror, and could still be social with it" (I); at the beginning of the Ahab drama: ". . . that democratic dignity which, in all hands, radiates without end

from God; Himself! The great God absolute! The centre and circumference of all democracy! His omnipresence, our divine equality!" (XXVI); and at the height of his cetological speculation: "Doubts of all things earthly, and intuitions of some things heavenly; this combination makes neither believer nor infidel, but makes a man who regards them both with equal eye"? Why, in speaking of *Pierre*, which followed *Moby-Dick* immediately, do critics identify Pierre as Ahab's heir? And why did Melville on his visit to Hawthorne in 1856 confides without his habitual gusto that he had "pretty much made up his mind to be annihilated"?[21] In his post-*Moby-Dick* period, a long one of anti-climax (what could be otherwise after *Moby-Dick*?), especially in *Pierre, The Confidence Man,* and other writings, one sees, instead, the Melville, so much like Ahab trying to "strike through the mask" and "strike the sun" if it insulted him,—a man frustrated with the ultimate futility of pursuing his Great White Whale,—an artist vainly trying to penetrate the inscrutable masks of the metaphysical absolute. Indeed, one sees little of Ishmael, who, in his zest for life, never abandoned a boundless delight in appearances, with all his urge for ultimate questions; instead, much of Ahab, who, contemptuous towards pasteboard masks, recklessly confronts the Sphinx. This is hardly the attitude of one who has mastered "the art of attaining truth."

Better than anyone, Hawthorne could miss the "spirit of adventure" in his old friend and diagnose his Faustian malady:

> . . . and [Melville], I think, will never rest until he gets hold of a definite belief. It is strange how he persists—and has persisted ever since I knew him, and probably long before—in wandering to-and-from over these deserts, as dismal and monotonous as the sand hills amid which we were sitting. He can neither believe, nor be comfortable in his unbelief; and he is too honest and courageous not to try to do one or the other.[22]

This anguished Melville, incapable of either belief or unbelief, is no longer the same Melville who created Ishmael, but rather the Melville who has somehow lost Ishmael's "equal eye."[23] Probably for this reason Melville, in his post-*Moby-Dick* writings, is unable to use Ishmael again. Their heroes, who are, significantly, no longer narrator-heroes, strive for Ishmael's sense of balance, but to no avail. The fact that the creator's experience here seems mechanically separated from his media may explain why biographers have attempted to read Melville's later career into these writings. Ishmael disappears because Melville, by foregoing Ishmael, attacks headon the wall of metaphysics, which fiction can assault only obliquely, if at all.[24]

Glancing at Melville's entire career, we realize the importance of *Moby-Dick*. Both as artist and as thinker Melville is, as Chase says, an inspired amateur.[25] He began his career as fictional autobiographer, creating **Typee, Omoo, Mardi, Redburn,** and **White-Jacket** in a half-dozen years, learning his craft, with Melville the artist usually (except in **Mardi**) capable of controlling Melville the potential philosopher. Ishmael represents that artist in Melville who delights in surfaces, whereas Ahab is Melville the philosopher, who, forsaking his "low enjoying power," knows no content with this side of the "little lower layer." **Moby-Dick** becomes a masterpiece through its precarious balance, achieved by Melville's sure artistic instinct to subordinate Ahab to Ishmael. But this balance breaks down when Melville the metaphysician asserts his supremacy over Melville the poet, and Ahab's single eye (his allegorical vision) replaces Ishmael's "equal eye" (his symbolic vision). Melville's greatness is that an amateur who never degenerates into a professional artist playing his game safely and superbly without attempting the impossible, but his tragedy is that he did not fully realize his own limitations, or realizing them, was not content to stay within those limitations; it is in a word his failure to beware of Melville.

Notes

1. Charles Olson, *Call Me Ishmael* (New York, 1947), p. 58; W. H. Auden, *The Enchafed Flood* (New York, 1950), p. 115; Charles Feidelson, *Symbolism and American Literature* (Chicago, 1953), p. 31; Richard Chase, *The American Novel and Its Tradition* (New York, 1957), p. 94.

2. Walter Bezanson, "*Moby-Dick*: Work of Art," Moby-Dick *Centennial Essays,* eds. Tyrus Hillway and Luther S. Mansfield (Dallas, 1953), pp. 36-37.

3. Henry Nash Smith, "The Image of Society in *Moby-Dick*," *ibid.,* p. 75. Cf. Robert Shulman: "Ishmael's voice, to me, is fundamental to *Moby-Dick*. That voice, like any deeply human one, has many tones and accents; and, although not everyone agrees, I think that it is the ground chord of *Moby-Dick*. But Ishmael, who develops into a good storyteller, often loses himself in his tale" ("Melville's Thomas Fuller: An Outline for Starbuck and an Instance of the Creator as Critic," *Modern Language Quarterly* XXIII [1962], 351).

4. Melville jotted "Goethe's Autobiography" and "Eschylus Tragedies" on the flyleaf of his Shakespeare volume: see Luther S. Mansfield and Howard P. Vincent's centennial edition of *Moby-Dick or, The Whale* (New York, 1952), p. 644. For some reason Matthiessen fails to co-relate these two items which were apparently inseparable in Melville's mind. "It is significant that Melville wrote on the back inner cover of the last volume of his Shakespeare, 'Eschylus *Tragedies,*' as though intending to read them. Prometheus, whose desire to help humanity was also misdirected and led him into crime, makes a not unfitting counterpart for Ahab, for the stark grandeur of Melville's creation is comparable even to that of Aeschylus" (*American Renaissance* [New York, 1941], p. 448). It is more than probable that in *Moby-Dick* Melville attempted a concoction of Goethe's Autobiography (Ishmael's whaling voyage) and Aeschylus' Prometheus (the Ahab tragedy).

5. Rousseau's *Confessions* (1781-88), for instance, claims: "I have resolved on an enterprise which has no precedent, and which, once complete, will have no imitator. . . . Simply myself. I know my own heart and understand my fellow man. But I am made unlike any one I have met; I will even venture to say that I am like no one in the whole world. I may be no better, but at least I am different" (J. M. Cohen's translation [The Penguin Classics] [New York, 1953], p. 17). Goethe's autobiography, *Poetry and Truth: From My Own Life* (1811-33), opens by viewing his birth under the favorable conjunction of planets, under the aspect of eternity, in a way akin to Ishmael's penchant toward symbolism. Dana's *Two Years Before the Mast* (1840), Thoreau's *Walden* (1854), and Whitman's *Leaves of Grass* (1855) are contemporary American examples of this tradition.

6. Letter of 27 June, 1850 (*The Letters of Herman Melville,* eds. Merrell R. Davis and William H. Gilman [New Haven, 1960], p. 109).

7. For a thorough treatment of this problem, see George R. Stewart, "The Two Moby-Dicks," *American Literature,* XXV (1954), 417-448.

8. Bezanson, pp. 35-42.

9. Cf. *The Letters,* p. 109n: "At best Melville's claim to two years' experience as a harpooner is an exaggeration. There is no evidence that he ever hurled a harpoon in the eighteen months he spent on the *Acushnet* or the six or seven weeks on the *Lucy Ann.* On his third and last whaling voyage aboard the *Charles & Henry* he may possibly have been a boat-steerer and harpooner, but the trip lasted only six months."

10. For Ishmael's primitivistic trend in Melville's writings, see James Baird, *Ishmael* (Baltimore, 1956).

11. See J. A. Ward, "The Function of the Cetological Chapters in *Moby-Dick*," *American Literature,* XXVIII (1956), 164-183.

12. In his study of the nine gams James Dean Young concludes: "Through these meetings at sea, the *Pequod* experiences difficult relations to the world: communication is uncertain, and alternatives are inadequate" ("The Nine Gams of the *Pequod*," *American Literature,* XXV [1954], 463).

13. Mansfield and Vincent suggest that Melville's Ahab seems to owe much to Goethe's concept of the Demonic (*Poetry and Truth*, Bk. XX). See their Explanatory Notes pp. 678-679.

14. The same quality is found in Melville himself, for instance, in his essay, "Hawthorne and His *Mosses*," where he writes with unguarded enthusiasm: "To what infinite height of loving wonder and admiration I may yet be borne, when by repeatedly banqueting on these *Mosses* I shall have thoroughly incorporated their whole stuff into my being—that, I cannot tell. But already I feel that this Hawthorne has dropped germinous seeds into my soul. He expands and deepens down, the more I contemplate him; and further and further, shoots his strong New England roots into the hot soil in my Southern soul." Again in his letter to Hawthorne, of June 1 (?), 1851: "Until I was twenty-five, I had no development at all. From my twenty-fifth year I date my life. Three weeks have scarcely passed, at any time between then and now, that I have not unfolded within myself. But I feel that I am now come to the inmost leaf of the bulb, and that shortly the flower must fall to the mould" (*The Letters*, p. 130).

15. Matthiessen continues to point out: "He [Ahab] suffers, but unlike Hawthorne's Hester or Miriam, he is not purified by his suffering. He remains, like Ethan Brand, damned" (p. 457). Cf. Chase, p. 114: "The imagination that created *Moby-Dick*, and other American works from *The Scarlet Letter* to *Light in August* is, then, not specifically tragic and Christian, but melodramatic. It does not settle ultimate questions; it leaves them open."

16. Smith, p. 75.

17. *The Letters*, pp. 126-127. Melville echoes Ishmael's "Queequeg was George Washington cannibalistically developed" (X). For the Melville who cannot resist expressing to note that Schiller is also Dostoevsky's favorite scapegoat when he criticizes "Oh, my captain, my captain!—noble heart—go not—go not!—see, it's a brave man that weeps; how great the agony of the persuasion then!" (CXXXV). It is interesting to note that Schiller is also Dostoevsky's favorite scapegoat when he criticizes the rampant intellectualism of the age.

18. In the next paragraph Melville admits of his ambivalence: "It seems an inconsistency to assert unconditional democracy in all things, and yet confess a dislike to all mankind—in the mass" (*ibid.,* p. 125). Again in the same letter Melville, ridiculing Goethe's alleged maxim, "*Live in all,*" still admits: "As with all great genius, there is an immense deal of flummery in Goethe, and in propor-

tion to my own contact with him, a monstrous deal of it in me" (*ibid.,* p. 131). To Emerson too, he reacts similarly, as evident in his series of epithets: "a great man," "more than a brilliant fellow," "an uncommon man," "a humbug," "no common humbug," *etc.*

19. Much has been said of the Promethean, the Faustian aspect of Ahab. Goethe is reported to have said that in his "discontent" Faust is "not unlike Ahab, King of Israel, who fancied he possessed nothing, unless he could also make the vineyard of Naboth his own" (Eckermann's entry of June 6, 1831, *Conversations with Goethe* [Everyman's Library edition] [New York, 1930], p. 413). Mansfield and Vincent also cite this but erroneously date 29 May 1831 (p. 637-638).

Incidentally, there is much in common between *Moby-Dick* and *The Blithedale Romance*: Besides the contrast in their respective attitudes towards Ahab and Hollingsworth, there are a few points worth noting, especially in narrative methods and semi-autobiographical techniques. (Both works are based on the authors' new experiences of almost the same time, 1841.) Coverdale, a minor poet, as narrator of the *Romance* is unique in the Hawthorne canon. No one, of course, knows why so conscious and impersonal an artist as Hawthorne decided to use not only his own personal experience and this particular narrative method, both apparently alien to his usual manner, to his peculiar genius. It would seem not improbable that Hawthorne here, aware or not, was under the influence of his friend's recent book. Especially suggestive is Coverdale's choric role ("It resembled that of the Chorus in a classical play . . ."). Was Coverdale suggested by Ishmael? His irritating quality may be ascribed to Hawthorne's lukewarm attitude towards the utopian experiment, but could it not arise from his failure to emulate Melville's technique effectively? At the end of the novel Hawthorne has Coverdale apolize: "I have made but a poor and dim figure in my own narrative, establishing no separate interest, and suffering my colorless life to take its hue from other lives."

20. *The Letters*, p. 129.

21. From Hawthorne's *English Notebooks* as quoted by Randall Stewart, "Melville and Hawthorne," *Moby Dick Centennial Essays*, p. 153.

22. *Loc. cit.*

23. Ishmael's "equal eye" reminds us of Keats' "Negative Capability," to which should also be related the same poet's designation of "Impersonality" as the epitome of Poetical Character, Shakes-

peare being its supreme example. Compare also a neglected passage from "Solitude," *Walden:* "However intense my experience, I am conscious of the presence and criticism of a part of me, which is not a part of me, but a spectator, sharing no experience, but taking note of it, and that is no more I than it is you. When the play, it may be the tragedy, of life is over, the spectator goes his way. It was a kind of fiction, a work of the imagination only, so far as he was concerned. This doubleness may easily make us poor neighbors and friends sometimes."

24. In *Billy Budd* Melville solves this problem simply by accepting the conflict between the law of heaven and the law of man as it is, and here he seems closer to Ishmael than in any of his post-*Moby-Dick* writings.

25. Chase, pp. 90-92. While calling Melville's native gifts "perhaps the greatest ever given to an American," Chase nevertheless notes Melville's "dilemma" here and thereby tries to explain the failure of his later works.

Herbert G. Eldridge (essay date May 1967)

SOURCE: Eldridge, Herbert G. "'Careful Disorder': The Structure of *Moby-Dick.*" *American Literature: A Journal of Literary History, Criticism, and Bibliography* 39, no. 2 (May 1967): 145-62.

[*In the following essay, Eldridge explores questions of structure and pacing in* Moby-Dick. *Eldridge argues that Melville's depiction of the epic sea voyage creates an essential narrative framework for the novel.*]

Anyone interested in a structural approach to *Moby-Dick* is likely to be puzzled when he turns to the established theories concerning how the novel is blocked out and how various units and sequences of units are related to a larger framework. We are told either that no overall structure is discernible in a work whose growth was "organic" and spontaneous or that analogies with plays and epic poems can answer our questions about fundamental structure.[1] Somehow, with what we know about the professional novelist working with the familiar problems of length, proportion, emphasis, unity, all this rings false. We want the methods of fiction to explain the structure of fiction, and we search the novel for signs that they are there.

I

Suppose we start with the simple point that *Moby-Dick* represents a fictional voyage around the world, with the *Pequod* crossing oceans and sailing along coasts which

Melville himself knew as a seaman or as a reader of sea travels. Seeking a basic arrangement for this kind of narrative, Melville might well have used his artistic common sense, settled upon the obvious principle of spatial progress, and developed the sequence of chapters—however loosely and "organically" individual chapters were added—on the basis of phases in the journey from New Bedford and Nantucket to the equatorial Pacific. One need hardly insist that division of *Moby-Dick* on a spatial principle would free us from structural analogy. Melville was not writing a play or symphony, but he was a-voyaging, and his organic expression might be expected to derive its natural form from the movement of ship and crew over the watery world of the novel—just as the form of *A Week on the Concord and Merrimack Rivers* is based on the days of the week and that of *Walden* on the seasonal changes of the year.[2]

A justification of this approach is that both *Redburn* and *White-Jacket,* the novels immediately preceding *Moby-Dick,* are blocked out on this simple spatial pattern. The basic structure of the former reflects Wellingborough Redburn's journey to Liverpool and back: specifically, from his home to the New York docks, outbound sea voyage to England, shore leave in Liverpool, homebound voyage to New York, and epilogue. The same kind of arrangement gives order to White Jacket's experiences on board the homebound *Neversink:* Callao to Rio de Janeiro, anchor duty at Rio, and Rio to Norfolk. But Ishmael's voyage on the *Pequod* involves a circumnavigation without the ports of call which helped structure the earlier books. Hence, if Melville had in mind a spatial outline for *Moby-Dick* similar to those he had used for *Redburn* and *White-Jacket,* the most obvious potential units would be the successive oceans through which the *Pequod* was to pass.

What are the simple phases of a fictional non-stop ocean voyage from Nantucket around the Cape of Good Hope to the central Pacific? Various routes would be possible, but Melville takes the *Pequod* irregularly across and down the Atlantic to Good Hope, across the Indian Ocean to Sumatra and through the Sunda Strait, through the Java and China seas, into the Pacific to the Japanese whaling grounds, and east-southeast to the equatorial grounds for the fatal confrontation with Moby Dick. As Ishmael remarks in "The Chart," it is a "devious zig-zag world circle"—much different from the beeline voyages in *Redburn* and *White-Jacket;* but the major segments are clear enough: the Atlantic Ocean, Indian Ocean, Eastern seas, Pacific Ocean, and the central Pacific whaling grounds known as "On-the-Line."

But exactly where in the novel are we given the facts necessary to plot the interocean travels of the *Pequod?* Chapter XLIV, "The Chart," merely notes that Ahab has chosen the Cape of Good Hope route and intends to visit sundry whaling grounds before arriving the next season "on the line." Geographical phrases occasionally appear at the beginnings of chapters: "Some days elapsed, and ice and icebergs all astern, the Pequod now went rolling through the bright Quito spring" (Chapter XXIX),[3] "Steering northeastward from the Crozetts, we fell in with vast meadows of brit" (LVIII), "Now, from the South and West the Pequod was drawing nigh to Formosa and the Bashee Isles" (CIX). These squibs keep the *Pequod* moving, but they are cryptic and sometimes ambiguous, and so contribute little to what might be called the experiential quality of our presence on the fictional voyage.

On the other hand, certain distinctive chapters—four in all—provide the information necessary for charting the ship's course. In fact, they do more: they not only give geographical details related to the ship's itinerary and progress but use specific maritime settings for reaffirmation of Ahab's "fixed and fearless, forward dedication" to the quest, which is the primary unifying force in the novel. From these chapters—LI, "The Spirit-Spout"; LXXXVII, "The Grand Armada"; CXI, "The Pacific"; and CXXX, "The Hat"—we get the feel of movement around the world and, as well, the allegorical undertones of the voyage—however differently the meaning of the allegory might appear to each of us. Remembering the voyage-blocks in **Redburn** and **White-Jacket,** we should not be surprised to find that all four appear at points where the *Pequod* moves from one important stage of circumnavigation to another.

"The Spirit-Spout" moves the ship around the Cape of Good Hope from the Atlantic to the Indian Ocean, developing at some length the distinctive elements noted above. The chapter opens with a summary of progress: "Days, weeks passed, and under easy sail, the ivory Pequod had slowly swept across four several cruising-grounds; that off the Azores; off the Cape de Verdes; on the Plate (so called), being off the mouth of the Rio de la Plata; and the Carrol Ground, an unstaked, watery locality, southerly from St. Helena." Then the unit emphasizes with lively detail the specific geographical setting—the Cape of Good Hope, where the winds howl over "long troubled seas." Even more important, Melville focuses on Ahab and his quest within the setting. Sighting a mysterious whale spout on the Carrol Ground, the *Pequod* follows it around the stormy cape. Here, in the face of the wildest blasts, Ahab stands sleepless on his quarterdeck facing the plunging bow, the crew stationed day and night in bowlines along the bulwarks. By developing the figurative parallel between the ship's undeviating course amidst the cape storms and Ahab's monomania amidst the torment of his emotions—both tempted onward by the mysterious jet—Melville underlines the progress toward catastrophe.

In "The Grand Armada," Melville offers the account of the ship's experiences at Sunda Strait as it moves from the Indian Ocean into the Java and China seas. First, he locates the strait and discusses its strategic importance to mariners and whales heading into oriental waters; then he carefully reviews the itinerary, which will take the *Pequod* past the Philippines to the Japanese grounds, thence to the Line, where Ahab is sure he will encounter Moby Dick.

As in the Good Hope chapter at the beginning of the third stage of the voyage, the situation of the *Pequod* is made explicitly suggestive of Ahab's state of mind. The ship, beset by Malayan pirates behind, hurries through the "green walls of the watery defile" in hot pursuit of a pod of whales. With violence howling in the rear and the mysterious leviathan ahead, Ahab himself begins to perceive his insanity, and his brow is left "gaunt and ribbed." When the *Pequod* at last clears Cockatoo Point and emerges into the Java Sea, Melville uses the peaceful scene beyond to remind the reader of Ishmael's mental responses, which are often in contrast to those of his monomaniacal captain.

In "The Pacific," which takes the *Pequod* into "the midmost waters of the world," the specific geographical locale, the facts of spatial progress, and the restatement of Ahab's quest are all present, though in condensed form. The chapter opens with Ishmael's tribute to the Pacific as the *Pequod* passes to the north of the Batan Islands between the Philippines and Taiwan. But, as in the other transitional chapters, the reader's attention is directed to Ahab's relationship with Moby Dick:

> Launched at length upon these almost final waters, and gliding towards the Japanese cruising-ground, the old man's purpose intensified itself. His firm lips met like the lips of a vice; the Delta of his forehead's veins swelled like overladen brooks; in his very sleep, his ringing cry ran through the vaulted hull, "Stern all! the White Whale spouts thick blood!"

These are the last lines of a brief chapter, for the dramatic action has now quickened and there are to be no long units until the final narrative of conflict with Moby Dick.

The geographical comment of the opening paragraph of "The Hat," signaling the arrival of the *Pequod* at the central Pacific whaling grounds, is concise but emphatic; and its explicit comments on the past itinerary of the whaling voyage, the significance of the successive gams, and Ahab's ever-increasing tension announce clearly that the final stage of the narrative is at hand:

> And now that the proper time and place, after so long and wide a preliminary cruise, Ahab,—all other whaling waters swept—seemed to have chased his foe into an ocean-fold, to slay him the more securely there; now, that he found himself hard by the very latitude

and longitude where his tormenting wound had been inflicted; now that a vessel had been spoken which on the very day preceding had actually encountered Moby Dick;—and now that all his successive meetings with various ships contrastingly concurred to show the demoniac indifference with which the white whale tore his hunters, whether sinning or sinned against; now it was that there lurked a something in the old man's eyes, which it was hardly sufferable for feeble souls to see.

After a long exposition of Ahab's ferocious determination, Melville, as in the other three transitional chapters, dramatizes the situation in the context of the locale. Distrusting the skill of the lookouts, the impatient Ahab orders the crew to hoist him into the rigging, whereupon a Pacific sea fowl wheels down, snatches his hat, and, flying on ahead of the *Pequod,* drops the headpiece on the fatal equatorial waters, the haunt of Moby Dick.

If these four chapters mark the oceanic stages of the voyage, a unit equally crucial to spatial progress is "Merry Christmas," which launches the *Pequod* onto the wintry sea. No transition in the novel is clearer than that when Bildad and Peleg reluctantly leave in the Nantucket pilot boat, the crew offers its "heavy-hearted cheers," and the ship plunges into "the lone Atlantic." But "Merry Christmas" is in substance different from the other transitional chapters, for at this point the *Pequod* is just beginning its cruise, and Ahab has not yet come on deck. In his stead Melville presents Bulkington in "The Lee Shore" as the silent partner of the Ishmael of "Loomings," the epitome of the landlessness to which both Ahab and Ishmael aspire and which will bring death to one and homeless survival to the other.

Melville offers conspicuous transitional units, then, as the *Pequod* moves from segment to segment of the oceanic trip. Their geographical emphasis is strengthened by their development of the captain's strange and central business. If these chapters are genuine structural artifacts, they indicate a division of the book based on the spatial progress of the voyage.

But, in itself, identification of certain unique chapters at the sea corners of the novel, dividing the whole into six parts, proves little about Melville's craft. The real question is whether Melville used the geographical divisions thus defined in controlling and ordering the novel. The evidence is that he did.

On the basis of what has been said so far, the novel might be tentatively outlined as follows: I. New Bedford and Nantucket—twenty-two chapters, I, "Loomings," to XXII, "Merry Christmas"; II. Nantucket to Cape of Good Hope—twenty-eight chapters, XXIII, "The Lee Shore," to L, "Ahab's Boat and Crew. Fedallah"; III. Good Hope to Sunda Strait—thirty-six chapters, LI, "The Spirit-Spout," to LXXXVI, "The Tail"; IV. Sunda Strait to Pacific—twenty-four chapters, LXXXVII, "The Grand Armada," to CX, "Queequeg in his Coffin"; V. Pacific to Equator—nineteen chapters, CXI, "The Pacific," to CXXIX, "The Cabin. Ahab and Pip"; VI. Equator—six chapters, CXXX, "The Hat," to CXXXV, "The Chase. Third Day"; Epilogue. Obviously, this outline reflects a reasonably proportionate allocation of chapters, suggesting some management on Melville's part both before and during the process of composition. But, more important, a close look within the voyage blocks of this outline brings to light what seems to be repeated and regular structural activity—in this case on a numerical rather than geographical principle—so well defined that one is tempted to insist that we are following an authentic trail. For, at the numerical center of all six divisions are traces of craft clearly identifiable through peculiarities of style, technique, episode, and theme and suggesting a measured subdivision of the voyage outline.

Let us consider the evidence. Dividing the first segment, somewhat beyond midpoint, is the chapter entitled "Wheelbarrow," which depicts Ishmael's trip from New Bedford to Nantucket, that is, from continent to island—allegorically, from the land "all over dented with marks of slavish heels and hoofs" toward the intellectual and spiritual freedom of the sea. In this central chapter Ishmael also symbolically moves away from terrestrial conventions by explicitly identifying himself with the heathen Queequeg when, during the short voyage, the latter saves the life of a jeering Christian, foreshadowing, as any reader of **Moby-Dick** knows, the salvation of Ishmael at the end of the novel. In other words, there is a transitional quality to the center of the division, supported, one might add, by a spine-tingling change of narrative style when the Nantucket schooner dashes down the Acushnet River and into Buzzards Bay.

At the center of the next major segment of the novel, the Nantucket-to-Good Hope unit, there is even stronger evidence of juncture—in this case out-and-out "mechanical" structuring. The exact numerical center of this segment falls between the important chapter "The Quarter-Deck" and "Sunset," in which Melville shifts into stage directions, soliloquy, and dialogue.[4] A set of four chapters—"Sunset," "Dusk," "First Night-Watch," and "Midnight, Forecastle" (XXXVII to XL)—are presented as scenes in a play, each taking up the current states of mind of main participants in the tragedy: Ahab, Starbuck, Stubb, and the crew. Moreover, the eight central chapters of the Atlantic section are arranged in an "envelope" pattern. "The Mast-Head" (Ishmael's unsteadiness of mind aloft) and "The Quarter-Deck" (Ahab's monomaniacal quest) immediately precede the four stage-scene chapters; and "Moby-Dick" (what the Whale means to Ahab) and "The Whiteness of the Whale" (what the Whale means to Ishmael) immediately follow them.[5] The effect of this device, as well as the grouping of thematically and dramatically important chapters, is a decided structural emphasis, implying subdivision of the Nantucket-to-Good Hope unit.

When the *Pequod* leaves the environs of the Cape of Good Hope and moves into the heart of the Indian Ocean, Melville commences his long cetological discussion with "The Line" and "Stubb Kills a Whale." During the chases and oil extraction, the *Pequod,* her canvas taken in and helm "lashed a'lee," makes almost no headway on the journey. Time moves slowly, the action for some twenty chapters covering little more than twenty-four hours—from Saturday to Sunday afternoon. Midway through the Sabbath, in "The Funeral" (LXIX), the carcass is cast loose. This is midpoint in the third division of the book. With the white cadaver of the stripped whale slowly floating away surrounded by the "sea vultures" and "air sharks," an important phase of the cutting and baling process has been completed, and all the crewmen on deck go below to their midday meal.[6]

The second half of the segment commences with "The Sphinx" (LXX), in which Ahab comes up from his cabin in the noon hush to soliloquize on the huge head of the sperm whale, still hanging in the main chains at the ship's waist. Here, subdivision occurs not only from a shift into dramatic technique as in the Atlantic segment but from the termination of a major stage in the whaling process.

The captain's ruminations have been interrupted by the cry of "Sail Ho!" from aloft, and the *Jeroboam* bears down on the *Pequod* for a gam—still another episode in this Sabbath sequence of events. In this chapter Ahab, fresh from questioning the meaning of the sperm whale's head in "The Sphinx," confronts the demented Shaker prophet, Gabriel, who has already found the answer and warns Ahab of impending death. With two vivid chapters in the center of the division Melville has brought back the Ahab-Moby Dick theme, a device that he will use again at midpoint in the next phase of the journey.

The numerical center of the Java-China seas phase falls at the end of Chapter XCVIII, "Stowing Down and Clearing Up," which begins with a formal summary, unmistakably marking the end of the technical account of whaling and oil extraction:

> Already has it been related how the great leviathan is afar off descried from the mast-head; how he is chased over the watery moors, and slaughtered in the valleys of the deep; how he is then towed alongside and beheaded; and how . . . his great padded surtout becomes the property of his executioner; how, in due time, he is condemned to the pots, and . . . his spermaceti, oil, and bone pass unscathed through the fire;— but now it remains to conclude the last chapter of this part of the description by rehearsing . . . the romantic proceeding of decanting off his oil into the casks and striking them down into the hold. . . .[7]

Ishmael goes on to describe the decanting procedure and then the energetic scrubbing, swabbing, and stowing that bring the whaler back to order after the untidy "affair of oil." Like "The Funeral" at the center of the last division, this chapter produces a natural pause in the business at hand.

And the structural parallel with "The Sphinx" of the Indian Ocean division is "The Doubloon," which introduces the second part of this segment by shifting from exposition of the whaling process to dramatic soliloquy involving several main characters in solitary contemplation of the "strange figures and inscriptions" stamped on the gold coin.

Finally, to complete the pattern, the gam with the *Samuel Enderby* follows "The Doubloon"—balancing the meeting with the *Jeroboam* in the Indian Ocean and portraying a captain who is as firm in mind as Gabriel and Ahab are infirm.

At the center of the Pacific segment of the novel comes the great typhoon, which, with its aftermath, is developed in six chapters ("The Candles" to "The Needle"). Like "The Quarter-Deck," at the same place in the Atlantic segment, "The Candles" portrays Ahab in histrionic violence before the whole crew. And, as in the earlier division, the numerical midpoint here (CXX) is marked by a shift into stage directions, bare dialogue, and soliloquy, which are carried into additional chapters (CXXI and CXXII)—all three being involved in the typhoon episode. These chapters are developed as a dramatic series showing the crew's response to Ahab's defiance of the corposants: Ahab-Starbuck (CXX), Stubb-Flask (CXXI), and Tashtego in soliloquy (CXXII). They parallel the Atlantic series, which is arranged to show reactions to the oath-taking.

Actually the time sequence including the six typhoon chapters commences with "The Quadrant" (CXVIII), in which Ahab smashes his "vain toy" and orders the ship east-southeast toward the Equator and into the path of the storm, and ends with the loss of the log and line (CXXV) the morning after the typhoon. Thus the whole central section of this division—eight chapters in all— covers a period of about twenty-four hours, from noon of the day of the storm to about noon the next day, the three stage chapters being "enveloped" in this time sequence by two chapters of straight narrative on the one side and three on the other—somewhat like the pattern at the center of the Atlantic segment. All in all, the central portions of the Atlantic and Pacific divisions show resemblances that are too close to be coincidental.

The final segment, covering the catastrophe "on the line," is constructed very simply: three chapters of ominous developments—"The Hat," "The Pequod Meets the Delight," and "The Symphony,"—and the three chapters of "The Chase." In "The Symphony," which closes the first half of the segment, Melville manages a dramatic pause before the final action as Starbuck and the landlike beauties of the central Pacific bring Ahab to the verge of relinquishing the quest. As in the other five segments, the flow of the narrative alters at midpoint—here, an exciting shift into action, like that in the first division, with Ahab's unforgettable cry near the beginning of "The Chase. First Day," "'There she blows!—there she blows! A hump like a snow-hill! It is Moby Dick!'"

In short, if the novel is blocked out on the basis of the six segments of spatial progress, there is clear evidence of further division at all six centerpoints in the numerical sequence of chapters, indicated by singularly parallel devices. The presence of these skeletal manifestations tempts one to speculate that Melville was working with an outline, maintaining a general symmetry despite the "organic" addition of chapters or groups of chapters as the novel grew in size and complexity.[8]

As for the suspicion that the theory depends too heavily on numbers and mechanics whereas the artist himself described his structural methods in the organic terms of "branches and twigs,"[9] one need only point out that Melville certainly did use mechanical patterning in other respects. The gams are spaced with an eye to numbers, producing, as Walter Bezanson puts it, "a stiffening element in the structure of the book, a kind of counterforce, structurally, to the organic relationship of parts."[10] In fact, the seaman Jackson material in *Redburn* and the "jacket" chapters in *White-Jacket* are used in exactly the same way and with the same structural effect.[11] Moreover, Melville's architectural arrangement of the Grand Banks and Cape Clear episodes in the second and fourth segments of Redburn's travels and the Cape Horn and Equator sequences in the first and third divisions of *White-Jacket* suggests even more strongly that Melville was working mechanically within a basic spatial framework before *Moby-Dick.*[12]

In this context, one is reminded of the fact that the American romantics, in their attempt to produce in art the harmony of nature, made much not only of "those forms into which all matter is inclined to run, as foliage and fruit," as Thoreau phrased it in *A Week on the Concord and Merrimack Rivers,* but also of the regularities of natural form—circles, spirals, ripples, the units of time and space, the numbers common in nature such as fives, threes, and particularly twos. "The world looks like a multiplication table, or a mathematical equation," said Emerson in "Compensation," "which, turn it how you will, balances itself." Although one hesitates to speak of *Moby-Dick* in mathematical terms, such notions as the above do suggest that writers like Emerson, Thoreau, and Melville himself could find room in their artistic world for the "geometry" of composition—rep-

etition, proportion, balance, spacing, and the like—especially when these provided some plain answers as to what to do with a burgeoning essay or novel that had eventually to be put between covers.

As a matter of fact, the romantic attachment to numbers—especially the mystical harmony of pairs—suggests a further order within the spatial-numerical framework of which we have found evidence in *Moby-Dick.* For, if the evidence indicates that the voyage of the *Pequod* supplied Melville with the basic skeleton for the novel and that his "lower level" depended on numerical division, the same kind of analysis suggests that he arranged the six divisions of the voyage as balanced pairs. The most obvious signs of this arrangement are the structural parallels noted above, apparent at midpoint of the six sections: the sudden narrative change of pace as Ishmael sails from continent to island and the *Pequod* from "mild blue days" into tornadic battle with Moby Dick in the first and sixth divisions, the carefully wrought "envelopes" in the second and fifth, and the soliloquy-gam sets in the third and fourth. These patterns in themselves are interesting enough, but they are only part of the story. In theme as well as form there are important correspondences between the divisions.

As for the first and sixth sections, the gam with the *Delight* and the disaster that follows are an obvious comment on Father Mapple's sermon on the "delights" of Christian faith,[13] the sermon and the gam coming in approximately the same place in their respective segments of the novel. The love-marriage imagery of "The Counterpane," "A Bosom Friend," and "Nightgown," which appear immediately before the dash to Nantucket, is echoed and even at times duplicated in "The Symphony," placed just before the sighting of Moby Dick, as Ahab and Starbuck contemplate the seductive Pacific seascape and the mate is rejected in his final attempt to turn his old friend from the quest. Ishmael's survival by means of Queequeg's coffin in the Epilogue is Melville's logical conclusion to the friendly shenanigans in the Spouter Inn, as Ishmael's near loss of life (and the *Pequod*'s disaster) is the final comment on man's "itch for things remote" voiced in "Loomings."

The second and fifth divisions also contain some additional parallels. Admittedly, the narrative pace in the Pacific segment is less leisurely than in the Atlantic unit, in which Melville has the problem of introducing not only the major dramatic figures and their motivations but cetological themes as well. But in both, the main business is the movement of Ahab into the center of the stage—in the Atlantic out of the dark hints of Peleg and Elijah back at Nantucket, in the Pacific out of the cetological foliage at the center of the novel. The pair of histrionic chapters—"The Quarter-Deck" and "The Candles,"[14] appearing at the same architectural point in the two divisions—represent climaxes in

Ahab's two emergences, after similar series of chapters have prepared the way. On the other hand, the dramatic tension created at midpoint of the Atlantic segment dies down in the expository reaches of "Moby Dick," "The Whiteness of the Whale," and "The Chart"—chapters which set a slower pace for the third and fourth sections, whereas in the final half of the Pacific division, the cyclonic excitement generated in "The Candles" is maintained in preparation for the final chase, now only a few chapters away.

The correspondences and balances between the third and fourth segments are pronounced. As we have seen, at the center of both the Indian Ocean and Java-China seas divisions are pairs of chapters remarkably alike, involving Ahab and the crew in soliloquy and in confrontation with other maritime travelers. These appearances of Ahab at the centerpoints are particularly important to the ongoing of the drama, for in neither segment has the pursuit of the White Whale been in sight since the opening chapters, and in both segments Melville returns to cetological matters immediately after these interludes. The two sections, of course, also correspond in substance, being Melville's disquisition on whales and whaling.[15] These great themes have been introduced in the Atlantic division, as the *Pequod* cruises southward from Nantucket; but not until the long, tedious voyage across the Indian Ocean, with all introductory material taken care of, is there occasion for amplification of the "honor and glory of whaling."

Actually, there are two basic subjects involved here— the "natural philosophy" of whales and the technology of whaling on the *Pequod* and through the ages. Both receive close attention in each of the interior divisions— and through the same loose organizational devices. One of these is a simple association of ideas. For example, parallel associational sequences are appended to the transitional Good Hope and Sunda Strait units. While still in the busy Good Hope area ("much like some noted four corners of a great highway," says Ishmael in Chapter LIV), the *Pequod* meets first the *Albatross* and then the *Town-Ho*. The latter gam leads to Ishmael's famous tale of Steelkilt, Radney, and Moby Dick, told to an audience of Peruvian friends who doubt the verity of Ishmael's portrait of the White Whale. On this slender twig Melville leafs out three more chapters dealing with representations of leviathan: "Of the Monstrous Pictures of Whales" (LV), "Of the Less Erroneous Pictures of Whales, and the True Pictures of Whaling Scenes" (LVI), and "Of Whales in Paint; in Teeth; in Wood; in Sheet-Iron; in Stone; in Mountains; in Stars" (LVII). Similarly, the "grand armada" in the Sunda Strait episode leads to "Schools and Schoolmasters" (LXXXVIII), involving comment on waifs and waif-poles, which suggests "Fast-Fish and Loose-Fish" (LXXXIX), certain of whose details in turn bud into "Heads or Tails" (XC). This concentration of related chapters provides a kind of structural

emphasis to both the Good Hope and Sunda Strait corners of the novel.

The most important organizational device in the exposition of cetology and whaling is the use of whale-killings as, in the words of Bezanson, "structural occasions for ordering . . . essays and sermons."[16] For example, in the first half of the third segment Stubb kills the first whale of the voyage, in preparation for which Melville discusses whale food (LVIII, LIX) and the whale-line (LX) and following which he offers "The Dart," "The Crotch," "The Shark Massacre," "Cutting In," and "The Funeral"—all developing, in general chronological order, stages of the whaling process. Likewise, when in the first part of the Java-China seas division Stubb kills another whale (XCIII, "The Castaway"), the event leads to "A Squeeze of the Hand," "The Cassock," "The Try-Works," "The Lamp," and "Stowing Down and Clearing Up"—various steps in the trying-out phase of whaling. The latter halves offer parallel sequences dealing with the natural history of whales. In the third division, the chapters on the head of leviathan grow out of the dubious affair of killing a right whale (LXXIII) and suspending his head across-decks from that of the sperm whale. In the same location of the fourth, Melville strings out a sequence on leviathan's skeleton, the final cetological discourse of the novel. Skeletons can not be studied amidst the hectic oil extraction, as Ishmael points out at the beginning of Chapter CII, but Melville produces a dead whale for scientific consideration here by having Ishmael recall the whitened remains of a sperm whale, accidentally beached on one of the Solomon Islands. The parallel with the other whale-killings is close enough.

All this is not to say, of course, that the third and fourth, or the other paired divisions, have precisely the same design. The former is more densely packed with cetological and technical chapters and sequences, and it ends, appropriately enough, with a discourse on the tail of leviathan. On the other hand, with the *Pequod* approaching the fatal Pacific, the latter terminates with Ahab back on deck and Queequeg in and out of his coffin as cetology and technology recede. But, granted the voyage framework of six segments, the structure of one division generally balances that of its opposite as the story moves from point to point around a structural hexagon, with "Loomings" and the Epilogue closing the figure.

A final argument in support of the six-part structure is that it partitions the novel clearly and logically in respect to Melville's major artistic problems. Each of the spatial segments is well defined by the larger fictional issues it settles. In the New Bedford-Nantucket phase Melville establishes his point of view through Ishmael, who moves step by step from life on land to the landlessness of the voyage. As a part of this momentous transition, Melville involves Ishmael in a profound human attachment, a friendship from which he has carefully removed all impurities of sex and common cultural ties and by which he intends the young seaman, in contrast to the protagonist Ahab, to be saved. As the ship crisscrosses down the Atlantic, Melville's problem is introduction—of the heterogeneous crew, the world in microcosm; of the principal "Isolato," the monomaniacal captain, who rejects all human relationships for his terrible attachment to Moby Dick; of the universe of work and action and the senses, the "lords of life," which, if Emerson was right, spoke of things final and real; of the cetology that poses the ultimate questions of the book.

All preliminaries attended to, the everyday business of whale-slaying begins, and the Indian Ocean segment takes us through the whaling procedure from the sighting of the spout to the baling of the tun, presenting, in addition, the whale from spout to tail as a subject of scientific and philosophical disquisition. Chapter LXXXVI, "The Tail," the final unit of the division, offers an unsettling conclusion to what has gone before, for, despite this ocean-long analysis, Ishmael cannot penetrate leviathan's ambiguities: "Dissect him how I may, then, I but go skin deep; I know him not, and never will."

The Java-China seas sequence of chapters ends on the same theme, though with a dramatic statement of the idea, as Ahab, now returning to the fore, turns despairingly from the mysterious treatise on truth, tattooed on Queequeg's body. This conclusion takes on contextual significance from the fact that the division as a whole continues and finally completes the cetological discourse of the preceding segment. One phase of the discourse, whaling technology, is taken up at the point it was set aside in the third division, is developed through the trying-out and decanting processes, and ends at the halfway mark in "Stowing Down and Clearing Up." The other phase, the natural philosophy of whales, extends almost through the second half of the segment, asserting at the last not only the ultimate mystery of leviathan but, as in the final sentence of Chapter CV, the endurance of his challenge: "the eternal whale will . . . survive, and rearing upon the topmost crest of the equatorial flood, spout his frothed defiance to the skies."

In each of the two interior divisions of the novel Melville brings Ahab forward only at the beginning, midpoint, and end; but in the Pacific segment his problem is to refocus the story on the captain. This is done in a series of chapters that present Ahab in dramatic conflict: with the crew as a whole—in "The Forge," "The Candles," "The Needle," "The Life-Buoy"; with individual members of the crew—Perth, Starbuck, the Parsee, the Manxman, Pip, the carpenter; and with his own ideals and aims—in "The Dying Whale," "The Quadrant," "The Deck." In order to pace the narrative,

Melville varies the mood through scenes alternating between serenity and violence, but he keeps tension mounting steadily as the *Pequod* moves toward the equator.

In the last segment of the voyage, Melville manages one final omen in "The Hat," one final dramatic pause in "The Symphony," and one last ironic gam before he sends the *Pequod* into combat with Moby Dick. To the sailors the White Whale's jet seems "the same silent spout they had long ago beheld in the moonlit Atlantic and Indian Oceans." The three chase units complete the ever-narrowing circle of fate, and Ishmael alone is left to contemplate the vortex, clinging to his lost friend's coffin.

While a radical summary like this oversimplifies a complex set of artistic problems, its six-part structure does seem to identify the main stratagems of composition.

II

If one looks back at the novel's profile, with the various chapter sequences creating a kind of foliar contour, it is understandable that some critics stress Melville's "trunk, branches, twigs" metaphor as a comprehensive statement of method and imply, in the end, that the novel evolved without much premeditated order. For other critics an alternative has been to turn to analogies with other forms of art to identify some formal arrangement. Both approaches lead to interesting and sometimes useful suggestions concerning Melville's craft in *Moby-Dick.* But they do not answer our questions about fundamental order. Perhaps Melville had no overall strategy of composition and needed none as chapter after chapter branched out from that which had come before. But it is more probable that he did. On Emerson's assertion that his own verse was an attempt to imitate bird songs and bee flights, F. O. Matthiessen comments that, whatever the poet says about deriving artistic form from natural sounds and patterns, "the fact is not the form," and the poem is not a part of nature.[17] To Melville's assertion of organic methods of composition one is inclined to make a similar return. *Moby-Dick* is no more a tree than it is an epic poem or a five-act tragedy.

The argument here has been that Melville developed *Moby-Dick* through more artistically practical methods than analogies or mere association of ideas. Behind the chapter-clusters that define the novel's leafy configuration are solid trunk and branches: the interocean voyage divided on the basis of the ship's progress from watery world to watery world and subdivided on a simple numerical principle. The artifacts of this overall framework are regularly spaced transitional chapters with uniquely geographical emphasis, sets of chapters at midpoint of each division with unmistakable signs of juncture, a scheme employing parallels and balances between pairs of the six-part structure, and a logical apportioning of the substance of the novel on the basis of spatial units.

Once these structural principles and facts are identified, one understands the real meaning of another much-quoted remark, offered at the beginning of Chapter LXXXII: "There are some enterprises in which a careful disorderliness is the true method." Melville's disorder was simply that of the great organic artist who is careful to provide his work of art with the architecture necessary for orderly growth.

Notes

1. F. O. Matthiessen, *American Renaissance* (New York, 1964), pp. 417-421, and Charles Olson, *Call Me Ishmael* (New York, 1947), pp. 66-67, both offer a five-act structure, though their divisions are somewhat different. Newton Arvin, *Herman Melville* (New York, 1950), pp. 156-158, suggests an epic "wave" pattern similar to that underlying the *Iliad,* the *Odyssey,* the *Aeneid,* and the *Lusiads.* He finds four general wave movements, each with its climactic crest, as well as a series of billows within his ninety-five-chapter third wave. James E. Miller, Jr., *A Reader's Guide to Herman Melville* (New York, 1962), pp. 80-86, sees analogies to both the play and the symphony and ends with a structure of five parts each with a "single insistent theme." In contrast is Walter Bezanson's conclusion that *Moby-Dick* has no "over-reaching formal pattern": the "controlling structure . . . is an organic complex of rhetoric, symbols, and interfused units" ("*Moby-Dick*: Work of Art," Moby-Dick *Centennial Essays,* ed. Tyrus Hillway and Luther S. Mansfield, Dallas, 1961, p. 56).

2. Bezanson (p. 56) supplies an important suggestion in his rejection of plays and epics as models for the novel. "In the last analysis," he remarks, "if one must have a prototype, here is an intensively heightened rendition of the logs, journals, and histories of the Anglo-American whaling tradition."

3. All quotations are from *Moby-Dick,* ed. L. S. Mansfield and H. P. Vincent (Chicago, 1952).

4. There is some suggestion of dramatic technique in chaps. XXIX, XXX, and XXXI at the quarter-mark of this division, but the development of material is basically in the usual narrative style.

5. Leon Howard notes the possible "tinkering" involved here, pointing out that, at the beginning of chap. XLI, "Moby Dick," appears comment from Ishmael connecting himself with the great oath taken by the crew in chap. XXXVI, "The Quarter-Deck," a transition suggesting that originally the former immediately followed the latter in sequence (*Herman Melville,* Berkeley, 1951, p. 167).

6. Numerically, the central point comes one chapter earlier—i.e., between "The Blanket" and "The Funeral." However, the division of material is clearly as indicated.

7. Howard P. Vincent in *The Trying-Out of* Moby-Dick (Cambridge, Mass., 1949) unaccountably omits reference to this summary, and in fact to the chapter as a whole.

8. The much-discussed revision of the novel after Melville's meeting with Hawthorne need not concern us here, for we are tracing a blueprint of the final version, whatever revisions might have been made along the way within or without this hypothetical plan.

9. "Out of the trunk, the branches grow; out of them, the twigs. So, in productive subjects, grow the chapters" (beginning of chap. LXIII, "The Crotch").

10. Bezanson, p. 54.

11. The misanthropic Jackson is characterized in five regularly spaced chapters in *Redburn*—two during the outbound voyage (chaps. XII and XXII) and three during the homebound trip (XLVIII, LV, and LIX). In *White-Jacket* the chapters focused on the narrator's distinctive jacket are arranged at measured intervals throughout the three segments of the voyage, most being concentrated in the Callao-to-Rio division (chaps. I, IX, XV, XIX, XXV, and XXIX). It is interesting that not only are these chapters spaced like the gams of *Moby-Dick,* but also that there are nine jacket chapters and nine gams. In the arrangement I am suggesting for *Moby-Dick* the gams appear in the last four segments of the voyage, distributed 4, 2, 2, 1.

12. In *Redburn* the Grand Banks fog and storm cover exactly the third quarter of the *Highlander*'s outbound trip (chaps. XVII-XXII), and the ship's troubles off Cape Clear extend through the exact central portion of the homebound stage (chaps. LI-LVIII). Halfway through the Callao-to-Rio division of *White-Jacket* the *Neversink* reaches stormy Cape Horn waters, there to remain for eight crucial chapters (chaps. XXI-XXVIII: almost exactly the third quarter of the division) while Melville opens his first heavy attack on naval tyranny in the context of cape weather conditions. The central six chapters of the Rio-to-Norfolk segment (chaps. LXXVII-LXXXII) take the *Neversink* over the Equator, a setting used for further castigation of the navy when White Jacket's messmate dies in the stifling sick bay.

13. See Mansfield and Vincent, eds., *Moby-Dick,* p. 825.

14. Bezanson (p. 52) notes the similarity of these two units, offering them as examples of Melville's use of "balancing chapters."

15. The two divisions fall within the seventy-four-chapter "cetological center" described in Vincent, *The Trying-Out of* Moby-Dick.

16. Bezanson, p. 53.

17. Matthiessen, p. 137.

Charles Child Walcutt (essay date summer 1968)

SOURCE: Walcutt, Charles Child. "The Soundings of *Moby-Dick*." *Arizona Quarterly* 24, no. 2 (summer 1968): 101-16.

[*In the following essay, Walcutt discusses elements of ambiguity and metaphysical complexity in* Moby-Dick. *Citing Melville's radical use of symbolism, as well as his audacious prose style, Walcutt argues that the work represents a watershed moment in the history of the novel.*]

What Coleridge's ancient mariner said about his ill-fated voyage—

> We were the first that ever burst
> Into that silent sea—

might well have been said of Melville's **Moby-Dick.** It opened so strange a world to its readers and so shocked and startled their expectations that it did not get a fair hearing. Melville was famous already for his fresh and exciting adventure stories of the South Seas, **Typee** and **Omoo.** Then came his obscure allegory, **Mardi,** which people either read without expecting to understand—or read a few pages of and then set permanently aside waiting for a more serious frame of mind—or skipped as a respectable genre that was simply not their dish of tea. Two sea stories that followed, **Redburn** and **White Jacket,** were taken in stride by a reading public that welcomed their former Melville back and were not disturbed by bits of soul-searching and hints of allegory that added to the suspense even if they were not found particularly interesting in themselves. **Moby-Dick,** however, was not to be classified, and its treatment by the English and American reviewers revealed their impatience and bewilderment, as well as their respect. More than half the leading periodicals ignored it. The rest ranged from glowing praise of its lively and vigorous style to severe censures of its bombast and its failure to achieve a form proper to the novel. It seemed a wild mixture of philosophy, blasphemy, fancy, wit, exuberance, and adventure. It was the book that followed a year later, **Pierre,** that gave **Moby-Dick** the kiss of death; for the new book was met with a storm of angry abuse by the critics, and in the next few years they generalized this reaction to the whole "philosophical" Melville and thenceforth either denounced **Moby-Dick**

or ignored it. Only about 4,000 copies were sold in America up to 1921; since then over four million copies of more than sixty editions have been sold, and the number increases rapidly from year to year.[1]

The composition of **Moby-Dick** foreshadows the confusions attending its appearance. Melville began in February or March 1850 to write a book which he reported was half finished on May 1. On June 27 he wrote to an English publisher offering the manuscript, to be completed "in the latter part of the coming autumn." He said, "The book is a romance of adventure, founded upon certain wild legends in the Southern Sperm Whale Fisheries, and illustrated by the author's own personal experience, of two years and more, as a harpooner." Now came a turn in events: Melville was making a modest success with **Redburn** and **White Jacket.** In mid-July he read Nathaniel Hawthorne's *Mosses from an Old Manse* and was electrified by it. He reviewed it for the *Literary World* under the pseudonym of "A Virginian," and Mrs. Hawthorne wrote to the editor, "I cannot speak or think of anything now but the extraordinary review of Mr. Hawthorne in the *Literary World.* The Virginian is the first person who has ever in *print* apprehended Mr. Hawthorne. I keep constantly reading over and over the inspired utterances, and marvel more and more that the word has at last been said which I have so long hoped to hear, and so well said. . . . Who can he be, so fearless, so rich in heart, of such fine intuitions?" The irony of this letter is that in the next sentence Mrs. Hawthorne writes of being much "interested in Mr. Melville's books"!—for Melville had decided to move from the heat of New York to Pittsfield, in the Berkshires. There in August he had already met Hawthorne—and the deep minds of two geniuses joined in kinship over problems which they profoundly and almost uniquely shared, and yet Melville had not yet told Hawthorne of his review of the *Mosses.* Hawthorne, at forty-six, had perhaps come to terms with his gravest doubts. Melville, at thirty, invited to spend several days with the Hawthornes at Lenox, engaged in long sympathetic exchanges that moved him to set about a complete rewriting of his half-finished book. He had found a person who understood his most deeply suppressed intimations, a person who had, indeed, been deep into those ideas and written about them already but in a manner so restrained and evasive that no reviewer before "the Virginian" had apprehended him.

The book that was promised for autumn of 1850 did not appear until October 1851. During the extra year Melville produced a new and different book from the one he had started. We know that he visited Hawthorne frequently, that he poured out his heart in letters to him, that he dedicated **Moby-Dick** to him "In Token of my Appreciation for his Genius," and that he went into ecstasies of gratitude and enthusiasm in response to Hawthorne's letter written immediately after he had finished reading the book. He wrote to a friend, in 1851, that "I regard Hawthorne (in his books) as evincing a quality of genius, immensely loftier, & more profound, too, than any other American has shown hitherto in the printed form. Irving is a grasshopper to him." [To Evart Duyckinck, February 12, 1851.] He told Hawthorne what he may not have dared tell any other man: "The reason the mass of men fear God, and *at bottom dislike* Him, is because they rather distrust His heart, and fancy him all brain like a watch." In the same letter he said that he dated his life from his twenty-fifth year. "Three weeks have scarcely passed, at any time between then and now, that I have not unfolded within myself. But I feel that I am now come to the inmost leaf of the bulb, and that shortly the flower must fall to the mould. It seems to me now that Solomon was the truest man who ever spoke." Hawthorne's letter about *Moby-Dick* is lost. Melville received it about November 15, 1851, and replied, "A sense of unspeakable security is in me this moment, on account of your having understood the book. I have written a wicked book, and feel spotless as the lamb." And there is much more, of astonishment at Hawthorne's so exactly sharing his deepest thoughts—even to sensing completely what Melville despaired at having imperfectly communicated.

A good deal of interesting criticism has sought to deduce just how and where *Moby-Dick* was rewritten. It is known that he began rereading Shakespeare while he was working on the book, and the influence of *King Lear* seems to appear and grow some time after Chapter 30. He received books on whaling during the summer of 1850, notably Thomas Beale's *Natural History of the Sperm Whale,* and the materials on cetology begin in Chapter 24 and then roll forth in a flood in 32, 41, 45, 55, and solidly through the following chapters. One-fourth of the book—the so-called "cetological center"—consists of transformed information taken from Beale. It now seems probable that the first fifteen chapters were written for the original version and remained unchanged. Chapters 16-22 were also in the original version but were revised to lead into the new theme. From Chapter 23 to the end we have mostly new materials but also many chapters that were revised or augmented to fit the changing character of the book. Chapters 26, 34, and 35, for example, seem to have begun as Ishmael's early reactions to whaling, but they are enriched with speculations and hints of evil that make them contribute to the new theme, and they foreshadow some later events. Chapters 41 and 42 were surely written entirely in the onrush of his new conception.

It was to become a much larger book, too, for what Melville described as half of it in June 1850 must have become a small quarter of the finished work. The size and complexity of the final book can be attributed to a number of causes. In the first place, there is the fact, already noted, that Melville's symbols generated mean-ings and further meanings faster than they could be recorded. What began perhaps as a symbol of nature became a symbol of God and then of Man. What began with Calvinism reached out into Zoroastrianism and then traveled on East to somber imaginings about "the unchanging Asiatic communities [which] still preserve much of the ghostly aboriginalness of earth's primal generations, when the memory of the first man was a distinct recollection, and all men his descendants, unknowing whence he came, eyed each other as real phantoms, and asked of the sun and the moon why they were created and to what end; when though, according to Genesis, the angels indeed consorted with the daughters of men, the devils also, add the uncanonical Rabbins, indulged in mundane amours."

The dying fall of the last cadence of this sentence recalls no writer so richly as Sir Thomas Browne, the seventeenth-century stylist whose prose interested American authors of the nineteenth century. If anything, the sentence above improves on Browne, but listen to Browne in "Urn Burial":

> What song the Syrens sang, or what name Achilles assumed when he hid himself among women, though puzzling questions are not beyond all conjecture. What time the persons of these ossuaries entered the famous nations of the dead, and slept with princes and counsellors, might admit a wide solution. But who were the proprietaries of these bones, or what bodies these ashes made up, were a question above antiquarism; not to be resolved by man, nor easily perhaps by spirits, except we consult the provincial guardians, or tutelary observators.

or

> Now since these dead bones have already out-lasted the living ones of Methuselah, and in a yard under ground, and thin walls of clay, out-worn all the strong and spacious buildings above it; and quietly rested under the drums and tramplings of three conquests: what prince can promise such diuturnity unto his relicks, or might not gladly say, *Sic ego componi versus in osse velim*? Time, which antiquates antiquities, and hath an art to make dust of all things, hath yet spared these minor monuments.

Melville also drew on Shakespeare. Pip seems to be modeled after the Fool in *King Lear;* Ahab defying the dire in Chapter 119 recalls Lear out in the storm on the heath, challenging the ultimate gods in their injustice; and in the great chapter where Ahab declares his purpose (Ch. 36) to the crew, he speaks a creditable Shakespearean blank verse (although it is printed as prose):

> Take off thine eye! More intolerable
> Than fiends' glarings is a doltish stare!
> So, so, thou reddenest and palest;
> My heat has melted thee to anger-glow,

But look ye, Starbuck, what is said in heat,
That thing unsays itself. These are men
From whom warm words are small indignity.
I meant not to incense thee. Let it go.
Look! see yonder Turkish cheeks of spotted tawn—
Living, breathing pictures painted by the sun.
The Pagan leopards—the unrecking and
Unworshipping things, that live; and seek, and give
No reasons for the torrid life they feel!
The crew, man, the crew! Are they not one and all
With Ahab, in this matter of the whale?

The more one rereads this passage, the more strikingly he will find that it reproduces the movement of the verse in Shakespeare's great tragedies, and especially in *King Lear.* Even the slight irregularities that appear in the first three lines above are characteristic. The book grew in size with the vitality of style that its growing theme evoked. In the fervor and jubilation of his discoveries, Melville wrote to Duyckinck, "Can you send me about fifty fast-writing youths, with an easy style & not averse to polishing their labors?" With such a staff he might have been able to stay abreast of his inspiration. Without it, he was bound to feel that his creature grew faster than he could limn it: "God keep me from ever completing anything," he wrote when he came to understand that this condition was inevitable to a conception like his. "This whole book is but a draught— nay, but a draught of a draught. Oh, Time, Strength, Cash, and Patience!"

A second reason is that the thesis of **Moby-Dick** cannot be simply or even clearly stated. It has to be "rendered," to use Henry James's famous word, and the rendering involves indirections and ambiguities that carry the reader more and more deeply into the maze of Truth. At the same time, what Melville had to say was in some aspects so blasphemous, so utterly shocking to the religious sensibilities of his contemporaries that he dared not come out with it directly. On top of the proliferating symbols, then, he imposed a style of jocular evasion, of double and triple-talk, of sly hints and impudent ironies, which makes it possible to believe that many of his most audacious statements mean to deny or mock the impieties they express. In Chapter 35, "The Mast-Head," he achieves a mystical union with divinity—and then warns the reader of the imminent danger, in this trance, of falling "with one half-throttled shriek . . . through that transparent air into the summer sea, no more to rise for ever. Heed it well, ye Pantheists!" Discussing the whale's mighty tail, he slips in a quotation from the Bible into an irreverent, not to say impious context. In Exodus 33:23 God says to Moses, "And I will take away mine hand, and thou shalt see my back parts; but my face shall not be seen." Melville uses the passage to hint that his whale is like God—or does he mean that God is like the whale: "Thou shall see my back parts, my tail, he seems to say, but my face shall not be seen. But I cannot completely make out his back

parts; and hint what he will about his face, I say again he has no face" (Ch. 86). It would take several pages to disentangle the ironies that come at the end of Chapter 96, "The Try-Works"; here Ishmael has a vision of evil, which he proceeds to deny, then reaffirm, then deny, and then finally reaffirm with his famous image of the Catskill eagle swooping down into the dark gorges, in "a wisdom that is woe," where he is nevertheless "higher than other birds upon the plain, even though they soar." In the darkness of woe he is higher—that is, nearer to truth—than faithful souls upon the sunny plain who look up toward the light.

Most frightful in its mixed implications is the little chapter about young Pip, who jumps from a whaling boat fastened to a whale and in the dreadful emptiness of his ringed horizon goes out of his mind. Melville says that the sea kept his body up but drowned the infinite of his soul. "Not drowned entirely, though. Rather carried down alive to wondrous depths . . . where he saw God's foot upon the treadle of the loom, and spoke it; and therefore his shipmates called him mad. So man's insanity is heaven's sense; and wandering from all mortal reason, man comes at last to that celestial thought, which, to reason, is absurd and frantic; and weal or woe, feels then uncompromised, indifferent as his God" (Ch. 93). What that celestial thought is, Melville leaves us to ponder, if we are mariners, or skip laughingly over, if we are landsmen, for its implications are truly appalling.

Let us see how these appalling implications are managed, for a close examination of a bit of Melville's style will show how he was *working out,* in the very act of writing, the ambiguities he was discovering in his subject. On the first level, reading with the typical humble assumption that the ways of Providence are beyond man's feeble comprehension, one accepts the notion that divine truth is beyond mere "reason." The idea is familiar, and one tends to accept it more or less automatically, but various items in the passage disturb this simple acceptance. Poor little Pip was driven mad when, "among the joyous, heartless, ever-juvenile eternities . . . he saw God's foot upon the treadle of the loom, and spoke it." The triad of modifiers, "joyous, heartless, ever-juvenile" is disturbing, for these may suggest qualities of utter purity—until the word "heartless" strikes its false note upon the reader. The deities are traditionally gay; the Homeric "laughter of the gods" expresses their divine superiority to human folly (whom they nevertheless loved and consorted with!); the Christian God dwells in perfection far removed from human affairs too; but the word "heartless" put this notion so baldly, so coldly, that it plants a seed of doubt which may be nourished by the "ever-juvenile" that follows. Again, the gods are gay, hearty, deathless—yes, but the phrase "ever-juvenile" expresses this notion in a way to bring out an element of irresponsibility; the qualities of spirit suggested by, for example, "young" take on an unfavorable tinge when they are expressed by "juvenile." We speak of "juvenile" conduct pejoratively, whereas we admire what we describe with the words "youth" and "young." In the following clause, the ambiguous word "spoke" suggests that he "acknowledged" or "knew" or "realized" what the inner secret of the creation was, and the insight into this mystery drove him out of his mind with a vision of a truth that was not sublime but "absurd and frantic." Thus there intrudes the suggestion that what Pip saw of the very process of Creation was somehow horrible. It is possible to suggest a sublimity that goes beyond reason, but when it is described as "absurd and frantic" we are moved in another direction.

Another item, closely related, is that Pip, driven out of his mind and therefore moving in the celestial domains beyond reason, feels "uncompromised" and "indifferent." Now, these are strange terms. We feel compromised when we are somehow involved in a wrong, when we are "embarrassed" at the situation in which we find ourselves. To say that we feel "uncompromised" suggests that a wrong has occurred but that *for some reason* we do not share in the guilt it involves. For what reason might Pip's God feel uncompromised? If there is an answer suggested in the passage, it can be contained only in the word *indifferent:* this word does not concern the existence or the nature of the wrong but the attitude of Pip and his God. We are told, precisely, not that he *is* uncompromised but that he *feels* uncompromised because he is indifferent. The terms "heartless" and "ever-juvenile" are thus given a sharper sting.

These hints that, as Ishmael says elsewhere, "Though in many of its aspects this visible world seems formed in love, the invisible spheres were formed in fright," accumulate through the book to build an impression of cosmic horror that is the stronger because the reader cannot put his finger on its exact source and attempt to refute it once and for all. What eager reader, hurrying on toward the climax, would notice the sinister difference between "*seems* formed in love," and "*were* formed in fright"? Close study of the passage on Pip shows how the seeds are secretly planted even if the reader does not stop to notice what Melville is doing to him. If such seeds make their way into the reader's mind without his conscious realization, he is doubtless going below the first level in his reading; but no thinking person can drop *Moby-Dick* at this point. He must go back and search more and more deeply into the passages where these dark hints germinate; he must try to get the exact feel of the elusive style, which always conceals and obscures just when it touches on the profoundest doubts about the human condition and the Forces that may or may not preside over it. In his letters to Hawthorne and others, Melville complained that the public would not tolerate it if it were said plainly and fully. He did not dare to speak his mind.

Not only was Melville uneasy about speaking out directly; he was also oppressed by the realization that no artistic communication is more than a fraction of what the artist intends. Yet in his great "draught of a draught" he went further into the mystery of man's deathbound plight than any other American writer has done, before or since. On top of all this, he was not consistently sure of his beliefs, which certainly grew, and vacillated. his grimmest vision of a mad or an insensate cosmos was just a step from the perspective in which it all looked like a colossal joke, a joke so huge that it would require the laughter of a Paul Bunyan to do it justice. But we all know that laughter is only superficially an expression of healthy delight; more often it is a means of concealment or a release of tension. We hide ourselves behind the jokes, and we explode in laughter when we are baffled. So Melville.

There is, in connection with this question of complexity and ambiguity, a very widespread and dangerous misapprehension that all great works of art are "obscure," that they do not mean what they say, and that the best reader is the most imaginative one, which is to say the one who can work out the richest and most original "reading" of a great work. This position would seem—or might seem—to be supported by the case of *Moby-Dick* in which the greatness seems to be organically related to the obscurity. But the position is the dealiest error. It is deadly because it strikes at the very heart of art, which is *communication*. There is an ultimate difference between heroin or LSD, which stimulate, and art, which communicates. When art is complex it may be difficult, and therefore obscure; but this is because it is trying to communicate profundities and complexities. Great art does not try to reduce the mysteries of the world and of life to childish simplicities. It must be complex when it is dealing with profound and mysterious things. If *Moby-Dick* is finally obscure, no matter how hard the best critics work on it, this may be a defect, a defect suggested by Melville's repeated lament that he could not express all he meant—and his hints that he dared not bare some of his deepest thoughts; but it may be that we still have not read the work faithfully, carefully, objectively enough. The modern reader, however, begins with tremendous advantages. He has access to a body of criticism that has been drawing together toward a consensus. Even the small quantity of it assembled here will serve as a starting point from which the interested reader can be guided into further commentary on whatever aspect of the book he chooses to explore.

As a guide for reading as well as for making one's way among the great number of commentaries that have been written about *Moby-Dick,* one may keep in mind six possible views as to the nature of the universe. That they are not all equally probable or equally attractive goes without saying, but it is worth having the several possibilities:

(a) That the universe and God are all-good, essentially spiritual. This is the transcendental view that unites God, man, and nature in mutual perfection.

(b) That the universe is controlled by an omnipotent and benevolent God who permits evil in man and nature. This is Christian dualism, which carries an enormous range in dogma, interpretation, and philosophy.

(c) That good and evil are independent, equally powerful principles perpetually at war for control of the universe. This is Zoroastrian or Manichaean.

(d) That the universe or God is essentially evil.

(e) That the universe is chaotic.

(f) That the universe is orderly but godless, therefore indifferent.

These possibilities imply different responses in man, ranging from wonder and devout humility, through laughter, indifference, rage, and hate. Melville has dramatized his exploration of his great problem by presenting a range of characters whose attitudes are interestingly keyed to their views of reality. Stubb is jolly; Flask is cruel; Pip is mad; Starbuck is worried yet reverent; Fedallah is malicious and sinister; both Ishmael and Ahab change their attitudes, and there is disagreement among the critics as to whether Ishmael does not disappear into the author's voice after Ahab becomes the central figure in the story.

This mooted question of whether Ishmael is the real hero, whether he is the author's voice, whether he speaks the true philosophy of the book, whether he embodies the answer to the great riddle because he learns to accept the whale as Unknowable, or whether he lives while Ahab dies because he discovers Brotherhood with the crew—these are questions that may be resolved if we go back to a premise of Aristotle that is rarely invoked by critics today. This premise is that the action (by which he meant the plot plus everything in the way of idea and theme that went with it) is more basic than character. Aristotle was talking about tragedy, which he defined as the "imitation of action," but everything he said applies to the novel. The action is the base of the novel. Character is the product of the action. Character takes form from the choices the hero and others make when confronted with significant problems. These problems are the essence and the product of the *conflict* in a novel, and their significance determines the depth of the characterization. That is, when the character has to decide about a problem that is central to his society, he will take form in such terms; when, on the other hand, he decides on some trivial issue, he will take form as a trivial character. *Moby-Dick* is not simply a dramatic narrative; rather, it is a story contrived to explore and exemplify an idea. The journey in quest of Moby Dick is an intellectual journey in quest of a truth. The novel therefore does not take the traditional dramatic form of problem-conflict-choice (climax)- and denouement. Ahab is pitted against an antagonist that he does not understand. The action of the book is, physically, the pursuit of the white whale, but spiritually it is the story of Ahab's developing idea of what his antagonist represents and what he plans to *do* as his notion of his antagonist develops. By the end of the story Ahab has knowledge, warnings, and portents, the loving appeals of Pip, the noble eloquence of Starbuck, and the warmth of home to draw him away from a final engagement that he knows to be hopeless, yet he has to go on. Why he goes on is not a clear choice by Ahab, then, but rather a fatal compulsion, an irresistible drive. So rich was his problem that Melville used two symbolic patterns to express it. One is the whale; the other is fire. If the whale represents the physical issue, the fire symbolizes the more intellectual aspects of the quest. Fire as light, light as knowledge is a symbol cluster established since earliest times. The meaning of the quest is first realized by Ahab in a context of the fire symbolism and then enacted by him in the great chase of the closing chapters. But he does not know why he goes on. "What is it, what nameless, inscrutable, unearthly thing is it; what cozening hidden lord and master, and cruel, remorseless emperor commands me; that against all natural lovings and longings, I so keep pushing, and crowding, and jamming myself on all the time" (Ch. 132), he asks, and he has no answer. In fact, the Idea is in command, and the character of Ahab is dragged under and sacrificed to its surging force; for a great deal of the thought in *Moby-Dick* comes from Ishmael and from the author's voice, not really through the mind of Ahab. The great quest evokes a variety of genres: expository in the "cetological center," dramatic in for example Chapters 37 to 40, narrative elsewhere.

Turning now to Ishmael, who has been more variously described by the critics than any other character in our literature, we can see why he is a puzzle. Ishmael has no function in the plot. He begins as the central character, but when Ahab takes over, with Chapter 27, Ishmael fades into the author's voice. He serves to observe Ahab; he acts in an illustrative capacity, making a mat with Queequeg, tied to the monkey rope, up on the masthead, or squeezing the lumps out of the spermaceti oil; and he delivers many of the author's philosophical hints. He begins writing an autobiography. In the dramatic passages he becomes a Greek chorus. In the cetology he is a speculative expositor. But he has no function in the plot and so he does not take clear shape as a character. Talking and speculating are not enough to make a character; he must make a significant choice—indeed he must make a series of significant decisions in order to define himself—and Ishmael has no opportunity to do so. All this is not by way of reducing the stature of *Moby-Dick.* It is rather to suggest that the "problem" of Ishmael's character should not detain us from following the great intellectual quest of the book.[2]

All, or almost all critics have agreed on the special importance of the whale as a symbol. Indeed, when the discussion comes around to the question of symbolism, Moby Dick is recognized to have unique virtues. The whale stands for such a range of concepts and possibilities that it opens up grand vistas of exploration; the more meanings are identified in the whale, the more possible new meanings are suggested, and as these meanings are discovered, the argument of the book becomes richer and richer. At first, the whale is Nature, a source of oil, meat, whalebone, and the valuable spermaceti oil. It is also the largest and the most powerful of all creatures, capable of sudden and incredible feats of destruction. It is impossible, Ishmael discovers, to picture or describe the whale because it does not keep its shape unless it is in the water, and it is impossible to get close enough to it without being in the direst danger. Legends have grown around the White Whale among mariners, until he has come to be thought both immortal and ubiquitous. Ubiquity, Ishmael explains, is merely immortality in space.

Thus whalers grow under Melville's pen to be seekers of ultimate truth, which retreats farther and farther into the forbidden depths of the remotest seas. They discover "that mortally intolerable truth, that all deep, earnest thinking is but the intrepid effort of the soul to keep the open independence of her sea; while the wildest winds of heaven and earth conspire to cast her on the treacherous, slavish shore" (Ch. 23). From such tropes, generated by his exploration of his great symbol, Melville can go on to some of the most extraordinary sentences in American literature, sentences that derive their concreteness and vitality, their wonderful poetic qualities, directly from the powers that he releases in his symbol: Trying to get close enough to know Moby Dick, his pursuers come to the ultimate inseparable and incomprehensible juxtaposition of Good and Evil. But see how these abstractions are expressed through the concreteness of the symbol: "Judge, then, to what pitches of inflamed, distracted fury the minds of his more desperate hunters were impelled, when amid the chips of chewed boats, and the sinking limbs of torn comrades, they swam out of the white curds of the whale's direful wrath into the serene, exasperating sunlight, that smiled on, as if at a birth or a bridal" (Ch. 41). From this graphic image of horror and frustration, Melville can go on to more terrifyingly mysterious suggestions: "But not yet have we solved the incantation of this whiteness, and learned why it appeals with such power to the soul; and more strange and far more portentous—why, as we have seen, it is at once the most meaning symbol of spiritual things, nay, the very veil of the Christian's Deity; and yet should be as it is, the intensifying agent in things the most appalling to mankind" (Ch. 42). In abstracting and exploring a quality of the whale—its whiteness—he shows how his symbol generates meanings under his pen. The literary art

makes, indeed, worlds of suggestion and meaning that did not exist apart from its activity.

And there is still much more: beyond Christianity, beyond the various religions of the East, which are invoked to search into the unknown, beyond good and evil, almost beyond the possibility of meaning this whiteness takes us: "Is it that by its indefiniteness it shadows forth the heartless voids and immensities of the universe, and thus stabs us from behind with the thought of annihilation, when beholding the white depths of the milky way? Or is it, that as in essence whiteness is not so much a color as the visible absence of color; and at the same time the concrete of all colors; is it for these reasons that there is such a dumb blankness, full of meaning, in a wide landscape of snows—colorless, all-color of atheism from which we shrink?" This thought leads him to consider Aristotle's mistaken theory that it requires the medium of air to bring out the various colors in white light, and that without air there would be no color, till he touches a climax of ghastliness: ". . . and when we proceed further, and consider that the mystical cosmetic which produces every one of her hues, the great principle of light, for ever remains white or colorless in itself, and if operating without medium [i.e., air] upon matter, would touch all objects, even tulips and roses, with its own blank tinge—pondering all this, the palsied universe lies before us a leper; and like wilful travellers in Lapland, who refuse to wear colored and coloring glasses upon their eyes, so the wretched infidel gazes himself blind at the monumental white shroud that wraps all the prospect around him. And of all these things the Albino whale was the symbol. Wonder ye then at the fiery hunt?"

Passages like these, which become richer as the story moves along nourishing its marvelous growing canopy of meaning, suggestion, and mystery, reward (as they demand) the closest study. Only by skipping over them can one presume to say that *Moby-Dick* is no allegory but only a sea story; and to do this is to miss the essential character of this most deep, daring, and exciting book. It is precisely for its intellectual quest that the book is read—and celebrated. In such chapters as "The Castaway," "The Try-Works," "The Candles," and many others, the symbolism rises to insights that have been surpassed by no other American writer. Heed it well, ye readers all!

Notes

1. The authority on the reception of *Moby-Dick* is Hugh W. Hetherington, whose "Early Reviews of *Moby-Dick*," in Moby-Dick *Centennial Essays,* edd. Tyrus Hillway and Luther S. Mansfield (Dallas, Texas, 1953), contains the following summation: "The existence of the 'immediate reaction'

of reviews that were adulatory, even ecstatic, even reverently perceptive of the main themes, makes the complete contemptuousness or thorough obliviousness of the 'delayed reaction' [in the following six years] not less, but *more* dramatic, and perhaps inexplicable except on the basis of such denunciations of nineteenth-century timidity and blindness as flared out in the 'Melville Revival' of the twenties. True, a few watchers joyously announced in 1851 the new planet which so many were to believe was not discovered until seventy years later. But in the nineteenth century it was not the praise . . . that lingered in the mind. It was always the snide phrases ('trash belonging to the worst school of bedlam literature,' 'rhetorical artifice clumsy as it is ineffectual,' 'morbid self-esteem,' 'insinuating licentiousness,' . . .) that stung the memory and soon induced amnesia."

2. The question of characterization has been explored in detail by the present writer in *Man's Changing Mask: Modes and Methods of Characterization in Fiction* (Minneapolis: University of Minnesota Press, 1966), where there is a full discussion of *Moby-Dick.*

Michael J. Hoffman (essay date spring 1969)

SOURCE: Hoffman, Michael J. "The Anti-Transcendentalism of *Moby-Dick.*" *Georgia Review* 23, no. 1 (spring 1969): 3-16.

[*In the following essay, Hoffman interprets* Moby-Dick *as a parody of Transcendental philosophy. According to Hoffman, Melville's use of symbolism in the novel is essentially ironic and undermines any possibility of deriving coherent meaning from the work. Hoffman further argues that this subversion of narrative sense acts as a metaphor for the essential meaninglessness of human existence.*]

Let me suggest that *Moby-Dick* is an almost totally ironic novel, perhaps a parody. Bear with me. Though anti-Transcendental, it is written in the Transcendental style. A symbolic novel, its major 'symbol' symbolizes absolutely nothing. Its heroic central figure is a character on the epic scale, whose strength overwhelms all the men who surround him; but he is blinded by his own vision, mouths the ideas of an author whom Melville thought "a humbug," and is ultimately a parody of the Transcendentalist "great man." The white whale whose image Captain Ahab pursues around the world is nothing but a whale—an occasion for the projection of symbolism but not a symbol. In any larger context the *Pequod*'s quest means nothing and the fate of its crew little. Whatever meaning the novel has lies in the para-

digm presented to us by Ahab's quest and failure—that all attempts to force meaning upon the world are futile, are indeed more than futile: they are destructive. The world exists. Physical reality is nothing more nor less than what it is. Nature has no value; it wills nothing; its relation to man is one of coexistence.

By 1850, Transcendentalism was a long-established Romantic orientation and Emerson its American spokesman. As with all nineteenth-century cultural stages Transcendentalism attempted to solve the difficulties inherent in earlier Romantic 'solutions.' So, too, does Melville try to expose the problems he felt Emerson had failed not only to solve, but even to take into account—particularly the limitations of individual freedom. For Emerson the universe is a book that can be read by any individual: "Undoubtedly we have no questions to ask which are unanswerable" (*Nature* [1836]). A spiritual reality underlies the world and unites both man and the vegetable in an occult relationship. "Nature always wears the colors of the spirit" (*Ibid.*). Since the individual's origins are spiritual he may feel free to extend his spirituality outward, limited, for Emerson, only by the size of the spirituality of the universe. "Build therefore your own world. As fast as you conform your life to the pure idea in your mind, that will unfold its great proportions" (*Ibid.*). "The great man makes the great thing" ("The American Scholar" [1837]). He knows no master but his own will.

If the "great man" has no ordinary limitations, then he must bring with him a new morality. Emerson tells us in *Self-Reliance* ([1841]) that "nothing is at last sacred but the integrity of your own mind." And further:

> No law can be sacred to me but that of my nature. Good and bad are but names readily transferable to that or this; the only right is what is after my constitution; the only wrong what is against it.

It is just a short jump to "What I must do is all that concerns me, not what the people think"; and from Emerson to Ahab shaking his fist at the sun, and asking, "Who's over me?"

For Melville the problems of freedom and of good and evil resolve themselves into one. Suppose, he seems to ask in *Moby-Dick,* the great man is not a good man? What then? Melville creates within his own context the greatest of all possible "great men," Captain Ahab. That such a magnificent figure—symbolic of a whole Romantic orientation—can indeed fail is Melville's judgment of the inadequacies of Transcendentalism.

Ironically, when he wrote *Moby-Dick* Melville had not read Emerson. He had merely attended one of his lectures (5 February 1849), though he was of course familiar with his ideas. That Melville was impressed by Emerson's presentation is made clear in his correspondence with Evert Duyckinck. On 24 February he wrote, "I have heard Emerson since I have been here. Say what they will, he's a great man." A week later (3 March) he responded at more length:

> Nay, I do not oscillate in Emerson's rainbow, but prefer rather to hang myself in mine own halter than swing in any other man's swing. Yet I think Emerson is more than a brilliant fellow. Be his stuff begged, borrowed, or stolen, or of his own domestic manufacture he is an uncommon man. Swear he is a humbug—then is he no common humbug. . . . I had only glanced at a book of his once in Putnam's store—that was all I knew of him, till I heard him lecture. . . . Now, there is a something about every man elevated above mediocrity, which is, for the most part, instinctually perceptible. This I see in Mr. Emerson. And, frankly, for the sake of the argument, let us call him a fool;—then had I rather be a fool than a wise man.—I love all men who *dive*. Any fish can swim near the surface, but it takes a great whale to go down stairs five miles or more; & if he dont attain the bottom, why, all the lead in Galena can't fashion the plumet that will. I'm not talking of Mr. Emerson now—but of the whole corps of thought-divers, that have been diving & coming up again with bloodshot eyes since the world began.
>
> I could readily see in Emerson, notwithstanding his merit, a gaping flaw. It was, the insinuation, that had he lived in those days when the world was made, he might have offered some valuable suggestions. These men are all cracked right across the brow. And never will the pullers-down be able to cope with the builders-up.

In the opening sentence of the letter Melville rejects the notion that he might be a follower of the Transcendentalist camp. And yet, though he does not approve of what Emerson has to say, he nonetheless finds him "an uncommon man." Melville admires the figure Emerson cuts, not the words he utters. Emerson will take a chance; he is not just another pallid member of the intellectual elite. If there is something of the "fool" in Emerson, he is also "more than a brilliant fellow." Melville's feelings about the Concord lecturer are as ambivalent as those of Ishmael for his captain.

But it is Melville's imagery that is really striking. If Emerson is one of those men who dive, then he must be like "a great whale," for it takes an overwhelming creature to plumb the mysterious depths. Was he anticipating Moby Dick? But there is also "a gaping flaw" in Emerson that Melville will not let his other qualities obscure. Emerson gave Melville an impression of high presumptuousness, a feeling that had he been around when the world was created he could have given God some good advice—perhaps even taken His place. Nothing in this impression is inconsistent with the ideas in Emerson, who always felt that each man contained divinity because all physical and animal reality emanated from divine spirit. Men like Emerson "are all cracked right across the brow." And who in *Moby-Dick* is cracked across the brow but Captain Ahab, with a

jagged scar running from the side of his forehead down the side of his body? Once again, a prefiguring image. Obviously much of Melville's response to Emerson is in Ahab.

Melville identifies with the "pullers-down," for "builders-up" like Emerson always try to project—the dangerous results—their own values onto the universe. The skeptical irony of the "pullers-down" is the only possible stance for Melville. The tension in *Moby-Dick* is between such a "puller-down," Ishmael, and Ahab, the "builder-up." Ishmael is a "puller-down" because he is a skeptic, because he attempts to see the universe as clearly as possible without projecting his own values upon it. Ahab is a "builder-up," like Emerson, in that he comes to his perception of the world with his mind already made up, and so he "builds up" the real world into something that reflects his own preconceived ideas as to what it means and contains. He is, of course, Emerson carried to the extreme—and the irony of his building-up is that it leads to another kind of pulling down: the pulling down of the *Pequod* to the bottom of the sea.

Before he put *Moby-Dick* through its American publication Melville wrote two famous letters to Hawthorne. He does not mention Emerson by name, but he discusses the problems of Transcendentalism at some length. In the first letter (16 April 1851) he describes how, by turning words into symbols, we impose categories on the world.

> We incline to think that the Problem of the Universe is like the Freemason's mighty secret, so terrible to all children. It turns out, at last, to consist in a triangle, a mallet, and an apron,—nothing more! We incline to think that God cannot explain His own secrets, and that He would like a little more information upon certain points Himself. We mortals astonish Him as much as He us. But it is this *Being* of the matter; there lies the knot with which we choke ourselves. As soon as you say *Me*, a *God*, a *Nature*, so soon you jump off from your stool and hang from the beam. Yes, that word is the hangman. Take God out of the dictionary, and you would have Him in the street.

Intellectuality, the imposition of mental constructs upon the universe, is a form of suicide. The "word is the hangman"; by categorizing any area of the world we limit our ability to see—and this is self-destruction. As Ishmael tells us of Queequeg's native island: "It is not down in any map; true places never are." The only important measure of value is the accuracy with which the individual sees the world. Value lies in the confrontation, not in either the perceiver or the object, and the attempt to find value in the world or to see physical entities as symbols or retainers of meaning is a great mistake, a deadly mistake. When Melville tells Hawthorne that the Masonic mallet, triangle, and apron are nothing more than what they are, he is exhorting him to resist the temptation to develop a new category of symbols. Avoid giving things names at all, if possible, and if not, then avoid letting names bestow finality or 'significance' on the object. For names have nothing to do with "Being"; categories are antithetic to process, and the life process is ultimately the only reality.

Moby-Dick is a paradigm of the above point of view. While it is certainly about the search for an albino whale, it is more certainly about the incredible dangers of mythmaking. The whale symbolizes nothing. He is there, an occasion for others to create myths. Melville tells us as much in the chapter entitled "Moby Dick." Two generations of critics have busied themselves with worrying about what the whale symbolizes. They should have been concerned with the creator of meanings, Captain Ahab, for it is he (not Melville) who has created the 'meaning' of the white whale. He fashions the myth of Moby Dick to give substance, form, and value to his own unhappy life, and he is aided in his efforts by other mariners who in turn project their own meanings on to the animal. His entire crew begins to share his vision, until they are nothing more than instruments of their captain. When they agree to impose Ahab's arbitrary categories on the world they give up their own free will—whatever that may be—and join him in a massive suicide. Narcissus sees his reflection in the pool and drowns trying to merge with it. In the first chapter Ishmael tells us that the meaning of Narcissus is "the key to it all." And he further admits that going out to sea and committing himself to the watery world is his "substitute for pistol and ball."

Moby-Dick, then, may be a study of the mortido or death wish, the human will to suicide. Ahab convinces his crew of his delusion and they follow him, like lemmings, to the bottom of the ocean. To give their lives and deaths meaning they make Moby Dick their Great White Executioner, allowing him transcendent significance and epic power. Who, after all, would want to die in quest of an albino mouse?

But what, then, is the Great White Whale? A huge creature, no more, no less. All else is *chimera* and self-delusion—the inability of Ahab and his crew to see things as they are. Is Moby Dick the incarnation of Remorseless Providence or Evil; is he Ahab's soul, an alter ego that must be found and destroyed? All such questions are likewise *chimera,* borne in the minds of critics who have refused continuously to see Melville and his book as they really are. In the chapter "Moby Dick" Melville warns us at length that the whale of that name is a manufactured symbol, manufactured by ignorant sailors and a mad captain. The chapter begins soon in time after Ahab on the quarter deck has enlisted the aid of the crew in his search. Ishmael admits that "a wild, mystical, sympathetical feeling was in me; Ahab's

quenchless feud seemed mine." He admits to sharing his captain's vision. Then he begins to recount the growth of the Moby Dick legend.

Moby Dick has been widely known among whalemen, although mainly through rumor; few sailors have actually seen him in the flesh. There have, however, been a number of recent incidents in the sperm whale fishery "marked by various and not unfrequent instances of great ferocity, cunning, and malice in the monster attacked." Ishmael emphasizes the superstitiousness of sailors and stresses that in their work whalemen come across "whatever is appallingly astonishing in the sea."

> No wonder, then, that ever gathering volume from the mere transit over the widest watery spaces, the outblown rumors of the White Whale did in the end incorporate with themselves all manner of morbid hints, and half-formed foetal suggestions of supernatural agencies, which eventually invested Moby Dick with new terrors unborrowed from anything that visibly appears.

Coupled with Moby Dick's "supernatural" aspect is the general range of myths surrounding sperm whales. Ishmael tells us that even great naturalists like Cuvier have believed these fantastic legends. Sailors who fish for right whales feel that "to chase and point lance at such an apparition as the Sperm Whale was not for mortal man." When these myths are married to the prodigiousness of Moby Dick the following is the result:

> One of the wild suggestions referred to, as at last coming to be linked with the White Whale in the minds of the superstitiously inclined, was the unearthly conceit that Moby Dick was ubiquitous; that he had actually been encountered in opposite latitudes at one and the same instant of time.

And if this sense of ubiquity is coupled with the seeming indestructibility that Moby Dick has displayed in his many encounters with whaling vessels

> it cannot be much matter of surprise that some whalemen should go still further in their superstitions; declaring Moby Dick not only ubiquitous, but immortal (for immortality is but ubiquity in time) . . .

In the eyes of superstitious sailors Moby Dick has become a god, capable of ubiquity and immortality. Ishmael gives us a lesson in how myths and gods are created; the other half of the lesson shows us how an individual can respond to such a myth and use it as a projection of his disturbed mind.

Captain Ahab had on his previous voyage lost a limb to Moby Dick, who "reaped away Ahab's leg, as a mower a blade of grass in the field. No turbaned Turk, no hired Venetian or Malay, could have smote him with more *seeming* malice." I have italicized "seeming" as the key word in the quotation. To Ahab the whale 'seems' malicious. But Moby Dick is no more malicious than he is god-like. His reaping of Ahab's leg is an animal's dumb, instinctive response to danger. In order to give himself significance Ahab must imagine malice on the part of the whale. He feels chosen as the victim of fate, and his only response to this—given his nature—is to rebel outwardly and strike back at the universe, which he sees incarnate in Moby Dick.

> The White Whale swam before him as the monomaniac incarnation of all those malicious agencies which some deep men feel eating in them, till they are left living on with half a heart and half a lung.
>
> * * *
>
> . . . all evil, to crazy Ahab, were visibly personified, and made practically assailable in Moby Dick.

Ahab's monomania demands that Moby Dick be more than a whale. He is "intent on an audacious, immitigable, and supernatural revenge." For him the White Whale "might have seemed the gliding great demon of the seas of life." And the success with which Ahab is able to get the crew to share his projections of value onto a mute albino whale is stated by Ishmael in the last lines of the chapter:

> For one, I gave myself up to the abandonment of the time and the place; but while yet all a-rush to encounter the whale, could see naught in that brute but the deadliest ill.

Ishmael, like the rest of the crew, comes to see the whale as Ahab wishes.

In the most famous lines of his 16 April letter to Hawthorne Melville says:

> There is the grand truth about Nathaniel Hawthorne. He says NO! in thunder; but the Devil himself cannot make him say *yes.* For all men who say *yes,* lie; and all men who say *no,*—why they are in the happy condition of judicious, unencumbered travellers in Europe; they cross the frontiers into Eternity with nothing but a carpet-bag—that is to say, the Ego. Whereas those *yes*-gentry, they travel with heaps of baggage, and, damn them! they will never get through the Custom House. What's the reason, Mr. Hawthorne, that in the last stages of metaphysics a fellow always falls to *swearing* so? I could rip an hour.

Here he once again expresses his feelings about the "pullers-down" and the "builders-up," calling them now the "*yes*-gentry" and those "who say *no.*" Melville still stands not on the side of those who would project value onto the world or would tell how things are or should be made, but with the skeptic who takes an ironic stance and carries nothing with him but his ego or sense of self. For he has now taken an even stronger post-Transcendental position. The individual must bring nothing to confront the world but his unfettered self. In order to "get through" the Custom House, or the universe, one must travel light, as Ishmael does. But if you come, as does Ahab, to impose a vision, the customs inspector will never let you through.

Melville says it more gently here than in his novel. There the *yes*-sayer or projector of value, Ahab, not only fails to make it past the metaphorical customs house, but he leads an entire crew into the doors of eternity. Ahab expresses figuratively the ideas stated in Melville's letters, and it is through his example that Melville most effectively discredits Transcendentalism and Emerson.

Emerson postulated a universe whose ultimate reality was a spirit—divine spirit, oversoul—from which all of nature—animal and vegetable—derives. Therefore, all natural creations are equally endowed with divinity. If each person is potentially divine, then the godlike in the individual man can be explored, exploited, and developed with no limitation other than the size of the universe, which is infinite. There is no definable limitation or sanction on the will of an individual who develops his potential divinity. Now one thing the "great man" has is charisma. This quality was not only recognized by Emerson and Whitman, it was positively encouraged. Other men follow the "great man" because he is the model for their own quest for greatness or, at least, meaning. They are potentially he. This is fine if he is a good man as well as a great one. But with no sanctions, the man of infinite will can do whatever he wants.

Ahab is almost the embodiment of Emerson's "great man," feeling limited by nothing, privileged to do anything. His boundless hatred for the whale and his sense of emancipation from conventional morality cause him to stand apart in the manner of the Transcendental hero.

> That inscrutable thing is chiefly what I hate; and be the white whale agent, or be the white whale principal, I will wreak that hate upon him. Talk not to me of blasphemy, man; I'd strike the sun if it insulted me. . . . Who's over me? Truth hath no confines.

Ahab's charisma is apparent in the very way the crew follows him many times in dangerous situations with a veneration bordering on worship and cosmic fear. A single word or gesture from their captain turns them away from any thought of dissatisfaction or glimmer of mutiny.

But Ahab is not a "good" man. He has shut himself off from the most basic Romantic virtue—empathy. Even when his instincts lead him toward affection for and identification with another character—as in several confrontations with Starbuck and Pip near the end—he deliberately stiffens himself against his feelings. He tries to be all mind, all calculation. On 1 June Melville wrote to Hawthorne, "I stand for the heart. To the dogs with the head!" Melville is on the side of heart and emotion, and this statement to Hawthorne underlines the same attitude in the book. All of Ahab's *passion* is connected to his monomania; it is utterly dimensional and it has nothing to do with *compassion.* He orders from the carpenter an ideal man with "no heart at all, brass forehead, and about a quarter of an acre of fine brains . . ."

Ahab is a figure of genuine magnificence, but in his delusions as to how a malign universe embodied in Moby Dick has done him in, he uses his unchecked will to lead an entire crew to its death. In the nature of human relationships lesser men will follow a greater if he can supply their unconscious with the proper image. Emerson was right here. But Melville sees beyond Emerson, who did not take with sufficient seriousness the possibility that spirit could be anything other than "good." Evil, to Emerson, though it existed, was more than counter-balanced cosmically by a prevailing tendency to goodness in the collective actions of the world. He thus gave the impression to his contemporaries and to following generations that evil was of no great consequence in human events. By making Ahab the symbol of Transcendental magnificence, but by giving him the one flaw he felt that Emerson had not foreseen, Melville dramatizes this fallacy of the Transcendental position. Ironically, he accepts Emerson's prime image, but he rejects the value Emerson placed upon it.

Melville's *nay*-sayer is Ishmael, who comes to the whaling ports in a deep state of depression, on the verge of suicide, with no sense of value to project upon the world. Indeed, his sense of identity is so stunted at this point that he must gain it from contacts with stronger men like Queequeg and Ahab. Ishmael's stance is a peculiar blend of alienation and empathy. Because he lacks a strong sense of self (the prime sin for Emerson) Ishmael can understand the positions of all the characters in **Moby-Dick** but become permanently infected by none. To realize intuitively that man's greatest weakness is his need for illusion and to realize as well that any projection of meaning onto the world will result in illusion must finally mean a withdrawal from the traditional affairs of men to a kind of personal confrontation between one's individual naked self and the world as naked object. Ishmael is the new post-Transcendental man, whose ultimate ironic detachment will become a commonplace pose for the new "hero" of the "realist" novel.

Even the concepts of fate and free will that Ishmael proposes are consistent with Melville's total position. These notions, stated in "The Matmaker" chapter, are an attempt to avoid a fixed abstract stance. Neither fate nor free will as philosophical poles govern human events. Nor can one compromise a position by blending the two according to some formula and coming up with a set of regulations for running a life. The warp of necessity and the woof of free will still need "Queequeg's

impulsive, indifferent sword" of chance to complete the pattern. Chance "has the last featuring blow at events." An unknown factor in the play of reality makes it impossible ever to describe or control it. This is Melville's attempt to take a position that is really *not* a position. No metaphysic is sufficient to account for the way things are; to this stage of Romanticism all metaphysical systems are ultimately illusory. This is why Ishmael adds the final irony of chance, and Melville then exemplifies this position by having Ishmael's survival depend on an incredible series of coincidences. Witness:

Queequeg decides he is going to die and he requests that a coffin be built for him—it is; he then decides to live; a sailor falls from the mast and the original life buoy is thrown in after him—both sink to the bottom; Queequeg's coffin is then caulked and used as a replacement for the life buoy; on the second day of the chase Fedallah is dragged from Ahab's boat and killed; Ahab becomes harpooneer; the lead oarsman is put into Fedallah's place and everyone moves up a notch; because Ishmael is in Starbuck's crew he is on the *Pequod* rather than another boat on the sea; on the final day of the chase he is picked to replace the oarsman on Ahab's boat; because he has the seat near the block he is knocked overboard; since the chase goes away from him he can float free of the battle; when the *Pequod* sinks he is just far enough away not to be sucked down by the whirlpool; and to help [. . .] because it has been caulked for a life buoy has not sunk to the bottom along with everything else. There is nothing inevitable about any of these incidents. They are all a matter of the most intricate and yet random kind of coincidence. Chance certainly "has the last featuring blow" at Ishmael. And this is of course the point. There is no figuring out why things happen. They just do.

But the most seductive danger of the Transcendental point of view is described best in Melville's 1 June letter to Hawthorne. It is the feeling that we are at one with the world.

> In reading some of Goethe's sayings, so worshipped by his votaries, I came across this, *"Live in the all."* That is to say, your separate identity is but a wretched one,— good; but get out of yourself, spread and expand yourself, and bring to yourself the tinglings of life that are felt in the flowers and the woods, that are felt in the planets Saturn and Venus, and the Fixed Stars. What nonsense! Here is a fellow with a raging toothache. "My dear boy," Goethe says to him, "you are sorely afflicted with that tooth; but you must *live in the all,* and then you will be happy!" As with all great genius, there is an immense deal of flummery in Goethe, and in proportion to my own contact with him, a monstrous deal of it in me.

The "all" feeling corresponds to the Freudian "oceanic" feeling. The danger Melville felt in it apart from its sentimentality was that it deluded one into thinking life was comfortable and without any dangers. Throughout the book we are warned that to feel too comfortable and unwary brings with it the danger of death. At the end of "The Mast-Head":

> There is no life in thee, now, except that rocking life imparted by a gently rolling ship; by her, borrowed from the sea; by the sea, from the inscrutable tides of God. But while this sleep, this dream is on ye, move your foot or hand an inch; slip your hold at all; and your identity comes back in horror. Over Descartian vortices you hover. And perhaps, at midday, in the fairest weather, with one half-throttled shriek you drop through that transparent air into the summer sea, no more to rise for ever. Heed it well, ye Pantheists!

We can, with no distortion, translate "pantheist" to mean Transcendentalist. Later on, in "The Try-Works," Ishmael is lulled into dropping his guard by the speeding motion of the ship and by the brightness of the fire that melts the blubber. He almost turns the ship over, while he stands at the tiller immobilized. After finally recovering, he gives us this warning:

> Look not too long in the face of the fire, O man! Never dream with thy hand on the helm! Turn not thy back to the compass; accept the first hint of the hitching tiller; believe not the artificial fire, when its redness makes all things look ghastly.

Feelings of calm should alert men to the dangers of living that lie around the corner. But instead, for the early Romantic visionaries these "all" experiences were meaningful "mystical" moments, meaningful in themselves and leading to no positive action other than sitting back and feeling "the tinglings of life that are felt in the flowers and the woods." Melville is quite aware of the attractiveness of the "all" feeling, for he writes in his second postscript to the 1 June letter:

> N.B. This "all" feeling, though, there is some truth in. You must often have felt it, lying on the grass on a warm summer's day. Your legs seem to send out shoots into the earth. Your hair feels like leaves upon your head. This is the *all* feeling. But what plays the mischief with the truth is that men will insist upon the universal application of a temporary feeling or opinion.

And yet, characteristically, Melville is quick to counter the attractiveness with a caution.

Calmness is always a mask in *Moby-Dick* for dark and mysterious terrors. Melville emphasizes the contrasts at the heart of existence, the calms at the heart of storms. On the day before Moby Dick's arrival the sea and air seem quieter than ever before. Now Melville is not saying that this is in the design of things, that there is a plan that makes these contrasts a part of the essential fabric of the world's structure. To the contrary, there is no design at all. The problem is that this mystical sense of oneness makes you relax just a bit too much. For

Melville the prime virtue is the ability to perceive the world as object and to survive in it on the basis of one's clear perceptions. If one feels so comfortable that he ignores the possibilities of danger inherent in just living in the world, then he is in trouble. "Pantheists" beware!

After realizing that there is no profit in imposing value on a world without value one must accept things as they are and retreat from the field of battle. In the ecstasy of sperm squeezing Ishmael realizes his transcendent emotion is only a passing thing.

> Would that I could keep squeezing that sperm for ever! For now, since by many prolonged, repeated experiences, I have perceived that in all cases man must eventually lower, or at least, his conceit of attainable felicity; not placing it anywhere in the intellect or the fancy; but in the wife, the heart, the bed, the table, the saddle, the fire-side, the country . . .

This hope has at least some possibility of attainment, for it is tied to the physically tangible. The kind of quest undertaken by Ahab has none. Yet, Ahab's quest is magnificent nonetheless.

Ahab's grandeur derives from his imagination. He creates Moby Dick, himself, and the fate of an entire crew. The supreme Wordsworthian and Emersonian imagination that unites itself in visionary union with the object is his:

> O Nature, and O Soul of man! how far beyond all utterance are your linked analogies! not the smallest atom stirs or lives on matter, but has its cunning duplicate in mind.

But Melville must reject this, though through Ishmael he is ambivalent toward Ahab throughout the book.

Perhaps it is the imagination that must ultimately be condemned. Imagination *must* lead to illusion, as it does with Ahab. For that matter, so must art. And yet, it is the use of imagination and will that led the earliest Romantics out of their sloughs of despond to seek value in the world. This is the unalterable paradox of the Romantic dilemma. Imagination redeems, but it also destroys. For someone like Melville there is no choice left but lowering his gaze. That is why he has Ishmael conclude years after his experiences in the book that retreat is the only possibility left for him; and that is why Melville retreated in the latter half of his own life. Retreat and acceptance, but not struggle. In Melville's final and most awful irony, Billy Budd goes to the yardarm blessing the name of his executioner.

For Melville the universe is vast and indifferent. The little microcosm he creates and whose king and whose inhabitants we take with such seriousness for so many pages is swallowed up quietly and quickly at the end, and nothing is left of the drama we saw enacted.

> Now small fowls flew screaming over the yet yawning
> gulf; a sullen white surf beat against its steep sides;
> then all collapsed, and the great shroud of the sea rolled
> on as it rolled five thousand years ago.

To claim indifference for the universe is not to say that
it is hostile. It is just to say that we should expect nothing from it one way or the other and that we should not
conduct our battles against it. For they have no business
being fought; they can never be won, since we are the
only ones fighting. And yet, if pushed hard enough the
universe may, in recoil, destroy, or at least swallow. But
if we wait long enough, it will swallow us anyway.

Moby-Dick is almost totally ironic. For what it shows
us is that the most elaborate of "symbolic" tales has no
real "meaning," except to tell us that things in general
have no meaning; that our quests have no function except as the most dangerous forms of diversion; that life
is at its worst a struggle and at its best a surrender; and
that the magnificence of great men and of works of art
are only illusions that cannot capture reality because
each creates a false one of its own.

Warwick Wadlington (essay date June 1972)

SOURCE: Wadlington, Warwick. "Ishmael's Godly
Gamesomeness: Selftaste and Rhetoric in *Moby-Dick*."
ELH 39, no. 2 (June 1972): 309-31.

[*In the following essay, Wadlington examines aspects of
narrative playfulness in* Moby-Dick. *Wadlington describes the act of reading the novel as an "aesthetic
game," one in which both reader and narrator gain the
freedom to explore a range of interpretative possibilities.*]

The power of *Moby-Dick*—what D. H. Lawrence
praised as "the sheer naked slidings of the elements"—
has long been a subject of critical attention over and
above the usual interpretive interest in such notoriously
"difficult" novels. While one may assume that the final
secret of that power will always be safe, hermeneutic
probings at the mystery over the last several years have
shown clearly that Melville's masterpiece is not just
about the world. To an unusual degree the book is an
attempt at sharing in the life of the world: the fiction
exists not so much to mirror Life as to be in itself vital-
izing. I believe that one principal source of this animating energy is the peculiar sense of self dramatized both
thematically and rhetorically—that is, by the issues on
which the novel focuses and by an enactment of those
issues that intimately involves the reader and the narrator Ishmael in a creative act of "godly gamesomeness."

The phrase originates in Ishmael's own gamesome as-
signment of a family of porpoises—"Huzza" is the name
he invents for the breed—as a subcategory of the whale

species. The name is appropriate, Ishmael says in the
audience-oriented voice typical of his playful rhetoric,
because if the reader can resist three cheers at the sight
of the fishes' vivacity, "the spirit of godly gamesomeness is not in ye."[1] Gamesomeness can be taken as the
generic term for a significant constellation of ludic motifs in the novel. The trait helps to establish the porpoises's kinship with their larger cousins, the Hump-Back
whales, who are "the most gamesome and light-hearted
of all the whales" (p. 189), and with the entire "sporty,
gamy, jesty, joky" (p. 636) cetalogical catalogue. If the
whale is a joker, as Stubb sings out, he is also by grace
of Ishmael's whimsy a book in himself (the Hump-
Back is Book I, Folio, Chapter IV in Ishmael's bibliographical system; *The Whale* is the subtitle of Ishmael's
novel). The Whale is, moreover, the chief masquerader
obsessing a captain who rails that the masked gods are
"cricket-players . . . pugilists" (p. 227), who mutters
"'Here some one thrusts these cards into these old hands
of mine; swears that I must play them, and no others,'"
and of whom Stubb says admiringly, "And damn me,
Ahab, but thou actest right; live in the game, and die in
it!" (p. 635).[2] Ishmael comes to a comparable conclusion when he "takes this whole universe for a vast practical joke" at his own expense and consequently regards
the whaling quest and its object with a "free and easy
sort of genial, desperado philosophy" (pp. 302-03). This
is Ishmael's central and saving mood, a characteristic
ludic combination of his psychic extremes—on the one
hand the black despair of alienation and on the other a
genial expansive delight in fellowship with humankind
and with the All. Ishmael can "take" the vast practical
joke; Ahab refuses to.

All this is godly gamesomeness indeed, and prefigures
the jests of the player-deity of *The Confidence-Man*.
But the argument runs ahead of itself. First, as Ishmael
would say, a few preliminaries are required.

I

The power of *Moby-Dick* is ascribable not alone to its
mythopoeic creative force, although that of course is
considerable. Congruent and complementary with this
power is that arising from an unrelenting rhetorical exercise that establishes as an almost tactile presence the
tormenting, mild images of personal identity and vitality. This is "the ungraspable phantom of life" itself, and
it is, as Ishmael plainly says, "the key to it all" (p. 26).
The operative words in the preceding sentences are *almost* and *ungraspable:* the Narcissus image of the self
may be apprehended at an overwhelming pitch of concrete force or at a low, nearly imperceptible level; yet
in either case it is tormenting in its elusiveness from
cognitive processes and mild hint at the formless, unspeakable terror of essential being.

Perhaps the closest one can come to naming the sense
of oneself that is meant here is Gerard Manley Hop-

kins' coinage, "selftaste": "my selfbeing, my consciousness and feeling of myself, that taste of myself, of *I* and *me* above and in all things, which is more distinctive than the taste of ale or alum, more distinctive than the smell of walnutleaf or camphor, and is incommunicable by any means to another man. . . ."[3] Intimately precious and ineffable, beyond the reach of the descriptive words of public reality, the taste of self paradoxically combines the feeling of electric connectedness with everything and yet isolation from all others. Although it cannot be directly communicated, this reflexive sense is capable of stimulation both in oneself and others. Indeed, for Melville—and it is here, perhaps, that he is most centrally in the Romantic tradition—the savor of one's private being is a primary register of reality, and the heightening of selftaste a necessity for existence.

For Melville the matter is even more urgent than for most writers in the tradition: selftaste is unformulable not only because it is purely private feeling but because the self seems to be inherently without form, without properties, purely "white." Floating quietly before man the water-gazer, the self's mild reflection is the image of full life; but it is also, for Narcissistic man, potentially as fatal as the white *Requin* shark with its "ghostliness of repose" and "mild deadliness" (p. 255). The attempt to grasp the self directly means a destructive plunge to the primal fluid level of complete formlessness, where boundaries are confused, and gentleness and ferocity flow inseparably into one another, as they do in the White Whale. As the description of Ahab's "eternal, living principle" indicates, the self is "formless . . . being, a ray of living light, to be sure, but . . . a blankness in itself" (p. 272). It is the basis for all the "linked analogies" (p. 406) between Nature and man: the amorphous, blank lifestuff within resonates in a sympathy of fascination and horror with the universal whiteness which "by its indefiniteness . . . shadows forth the heartless voids and immensities of the universe" (p. 263). *Shadows forth* these voids, it should be noted, but is not *equivalent* to nothingness, non-being. On the contrary, in regard to both the individual and the visible world, whiteness and indefiniteness in general are the most important metaphors for the pure life principle, like the tingeless "great principle of light" (p. 264) and the shapeless white squid: "an unearthly, formless, chance-like apparition of life" (p. 366).

Though totally without qualities in itself, this life principle furnishes the necessary *stoff* for the individuating process of earthly existence. As Ishmael says, "Nothing exists in itself"; distinctive qualities exist merely "by contrast" (p. 86). In order to beget the experiential world, the principle of being combines with the nonbeing, the total void, that it horrifyingly adumbrates, just as in the Bower in the Arsacides the grim old god Death "wived with youthful Life" (p. 574) to beget the diverse colors and shapes of the beautiful scene. The crucial, nearly unthinkable paradox of the metaphysical marriage of opposites is that the union of an amorphous entity and nothingness produces the individual forms of life.

In short, at the profoundest level of his being, a man is not indelibly marked by the fixed, unique stamp of individuality. If the world is a kind of ludic construct in which all counters of reality are merely virtual, relational, dialectically contingent, the cultivation of selftaste is not a decadent Paterian exercise; it is of literally vital importance because it means the taking on of properties, the definition of an indefiniteness, and thus the creation of one's individual life. Self-being results from an endless cycle of activity pitting one's sense of separateness against its opposite—the obliteration of personal separateness either by a "pantheistic" merging with others or by death, real or metaphysical. Another way of putting this is to say that one's will to distinctive form is, and must be, recurrently hedged about by the antagonistic but tempting absences of form in both life and death—the undifferentiated, pure white lifestuff that all beings share and the dark void of nonbeing. Though perilous, these antithetical conditions are seductive because they are essential to intensifying selftaste. The Ishmael who takes to sea as a substitute for pistol and ball and never quite falls out of love with death is the obverse image of the Ishmael who is fond of pantheistic reveries at sea. Symbolically, whiteness and blackness are equally horrors and equally necessities, and one must, like Ishmael, learn to be sociable with "a horror" (p. 30).

Individuality is a willful fiction in perilous balance between cosmic nothingness and undifferentiated plenitude. Repeated confrontations with these opposed principles conjures up "by contrast" a selfhood that consists of a heightened sense of one's differentiation and individuality, sharply defined yet as elusively visceral as a physical taste, and accompanied by a wide range of emotions. Ishmael in the wintery darkness sharing bed and covers with Queequeg yields completely to the cozy, delicious feeling of oneself hugged close: "no one can ever feel his own identity aright except his eyes are closed; as if darkness were indeed the proper element of our essences, though light be more congenial to our clayey part" (p. 87). But when Ishmael opens his eyes to emerge from "my own pleasant and self-created darkness into the imposed and coarse outer gloom" and feels a sharp revulsion, we see the master pattern of his experience, a design that is carried out in the masthead and try-works scenes and in the other halcyon or tortured moments when Ishmael awakes from a visionary state with a shock. At one extreme of feeling is the reassuring selftaste of the "one insular Tahiti" deep down within where he can "disport in mute calm . . . [and] mildness of joy" amid an "appalling ocean" of storms (pp. 364, 499). But the self-image is transmogrified when seen in the perspective of isolated inadequacy that is presented to the castaway Pip: "The intense concentration of self in the middle of such a heartless immensity, my God! who can tell it?" (p. 529). Each captivating mood, each "enchanted" apprehension of self, has its truth (but "who can tell it?"); and each succeeds the other in an endless sequence.

One of the basic structural and rhetorical patternings of **Moby-Dick** is the repetition of these enchantment-like captivations or commitments and the subsequent releases from them, a cycle that generates Ishmael's self-being as both character and narrative consciousness. If one looks at the structure of action in the novel from Ishmael's standpoint, the pattern emerges clearly. Insofar as a cycle may be said to begin anywhere, the pattern of Ishmael's experience first entails a psychic state (for example, the famous "November of the soul") plus an external event or phenomenon that corresponds to it. Ishmael becomes *entranced* by the *spell*—to use two of his favorite words—of this state or, equivalently, indulges in a self-forgetting commitment to a vision of life embodied in the mood-phenomenon. In this phase of commitment there is a vibrant feeling of being electrically alive: "you only exist in a delirious throb" (p. 494), like Ishmael being towed furiously toward the "enchanted calm" (p. 496) of the encircling Grand Armada of whales, or Ishmael with the rest of the crew raising delirious shouts of vengeance while mesmerized by Ahab's quarterdeck rituals. But as personal autonomy is dissolved into the intensely immediate global experience and Ishmael descends to the level of undifferentiated existence or approaches self-destruction and void, a recoiling movement is initiated. This second phase, whether triggered by a fortuitous shock or a saving epiphany, usually involves a sudden terror or feeling of estrangement from the experience. This is followed by the third phase of reflection and conscious awareness of separate identity, often accompanied by a comic dismay or an ironic tone that helps to complete Ishmael's liberation from the bondage of his visionary commitment.

But this phase is no more stable or permanent than any other, for although there may be a feeling of relief in the emancipation from threatened loss of separate identity, there is also a residual stark, "drizzly November," a sort of post-partum mood of the soul, after one has ceased to live at the highly-charged level of unself-conscious psychic impulses. Self-aware, but also with a lurking sense of being empty, meaningless, and abandoned, one is again vulnerable to the next "spell" which seems brimming with full life, which seems an absolute condition and not a momentary one, and the cycle is repeated.

For Ishmael, a man's whole life shows this circular pattern: "infancy's unconscious spell, boyhood's thoughtless faith, adolescence' doubt (the common doom), then

skepticism, then disbelief, resting at last in manhood's pondering repose of If. But once gone through, we trace the round again; and are infants, boys, and men, and Ifs eternally" (p. 624). *Ifs*—the word communicates the almost unbearably contingent nature of identity that is the dynamic force in the cycle, moving one away from and then back toward the "unconscious spell" of an illusionistic world.

Time and again Ishmael comes to himself in a dangerous, enchanted circle where he is given a heightened self-savoring which in effect makes him Ishmael. Conceived in the broadest terms, the novel shows Ishmael gradually coming under the influence of Ahab's quest; identifying himself completely with it in the enchantment weaved on the quarterdeck; recoiling in horror from the hypnotic vision of the try-works and, symbolically, from Ahab's spell; and finally circling down to and being "liberated" from the "vital centre" (p. 724) of the destructive vortex that engulfs the *Pequod*. Every destructive vortex in the novel has a vital center. The story may be envisioned as a great spiral of repeating cycles leading to the final paradigmatic image of Ishmael captured and released, along with the coffin that symbolizes the potentially life-giving confrontation with the Formless or Void. It is of course possible to see Ishmael's sole survival at the end as replete with moral implications, as many commentators have; but, to repeat, the final action is fundamentally a paradigm of his recurrently generated individual existence that is at stake at every turn of the book.

Just as knowledge of the living whale can be attained "Only in the heart of quickest perils" (p. 578), Truth itself is inherently perilous; only "salamander giants" can glimpse it and survive. Endless voyaging is necessary not because Final Truth is attainable short of self-destruction—repeatedly the book tells us it is not—but because the quest entails the seductive and dreadful confrontations that engender identity. On the one hand one must be able to escape the emptiness of the soul by enthusiastic commitment to an experience through a warmhearted capacity for wonder and sympathy; on the other, one must be able to disengage oneself from the exclusive demands of the moment's mood and its partial vision of truth. The ideal combination of resources requires the unique double-consciousness, the "equal eye," of a master player. For him the ludic reality is for the time being universal, utterly absorbing, all-in-all, an "undoubted deed," a "living act" expressing his innermost needs; and yet it is an ultimately limited structuring of total reality, with a term, a boundary at which the experience must come to an end, the illusion of completeness abandoned.

So man's identity is to be conceived as diachronic, a process in time consisting of psychic phases and corresponding partial visions of truth that necessarily contradict earlier and later stages. Even within a brief space of time, as the mercurial Ishmael demonstrates most dramatically (see especially chapters like "The Chapel," fashioned out of Ishmael's quick turns and counterturns from confidence to doubt, somberness to jocularity), a man is a sequence of quick changes that seem, from a synchronous view of selfhood, mere inconsistencies. Later, in **The Confidence-Man,** Melville covertly and overtly makes sport of those who attempt to act in life as if identity were static in time and who thus balk at a fictional "inconsistent" character which is "to common view incongruous in its parts, as the flying-squirrel, and, *at different periods, as much at variance with itself as the butterfly is with the caterpillar into which it changes.* . . ."⁴ In **Moby-Dick,** Ishmael along with the diddling game-player Stubb can admire the unrelenting passional commitment that attempts to extend a moment's visionary rage into a whole life: "live in the game and die in it!" But Ishmael's goal is to live *through* the game by daring and then escaping the deadly tyranny of the moment's view. Like the mate who, amid "gamesome talk" in the unsteady boat, balances his lance like a "juggler" before casting it (p. 474), and like the whale who reveals "his power in his play" and hurls whaleboats in the air "as an Indian juggler tosses his balls" (pp. 484, 486), Ishmael endeavors to play the cycle of his being with balance, vivacity, and suppleness on the very edge of destruction.

If we turn now towards the book's heroic figures—heroic in the sense that they each in some way reach beyond the ordinary human, temporal state—we see that they embody alternative modes of being that are unavailable or unacceptable to Ishmael, however intriguing they may be. To be Ishmael means in part to be intrigued by these particular alternatives but not to choose them.

There is Bulkington, whose self-reliant and nearly uninterrupted commitment to "shoreless, indefinite" landlessness, to the fluid principle itself, entails an inevitable "ocean-perishing" but also an apotheosis beyond the endless circularity of personal existence (p. 149). That is, the apotheosis that Ishmael confers on Bulkington is a tribute to the massive strength of Bulkington's identity achieved by confrontation with the Formless as well as an admiring and tragic acknowledgment that not to recoil finally from this confrontation, not to return to the solid, circumscribed land-state, is to cease to exist within the cyclic pattern of ordinary life. Bulkington with his coffer-dam chest is, like the whale, a lode-star of Ishmael's search for a profound interior life secure against the threats that it must face: "the rare virtue of a strong individual vitality, and the rare virtue of interior spaciousness. Oh, man! admire and model thyself after the whale!" (p. 401). But at once Ishmael adds to this outburst of desire the punning, skeptical qualification that ironically disengages him, and us, from the enthu-

siastic vision and so completes one of the many cyclic sketches of his own being: "But how easy and how hopeless to teach these fine things! Of erections, how few are domed like St. Peter's! of creatures, how few vast as the whale!" (p. 402).

There is also, at the opposite extreme, the religious hero praised by Father Mapple as one who "stands forth his own inexorable self" precisely because he has abjured Bulkington's kind of autonomously directed effort in favor of complete commitment to God's will. If Bulkington's heroic identity is created by his purely private commitment to the sea which is "indefinite as God," the religious hero, who has submitted wholly to the ultimate indefinite Other, can perhaps even more strongly taste his vital "inexorable self" with "delight and deliciousness," as Father Mapple says (pp. 80-81). Ishmael's notable failure to comment directly after reporting Father Mapple's sermon and the immediate juxtaposition of the worship-scene involving Queequeg's idol bespeak eloquently the narrator's final skeptical unwillingness to commit himself to Father Mapple's Presbyterian Deity or in fact to any such religious self-definition through literal self-denial—"this disobeying ourselves," in the minister's words (p. 72).

To be Ishmael means to be neither the rare Bulkington nor the equally rare religious hero; but to be Ahab means to be a tragic combination of both: utterly dominated by a commitment that is ambiguously located somewhere between Bulkington's purely private drive toward apotheosis and the religious hero's achievement of identity by a willed abnegation of self. Ahab desires to set himself alone against gods and men, divested of all "mortal interdebtedness" (p. 601). And at some moments his thinking is a solipsistic parody of Ishmael's pantheistic reveries: "all are Ahab" (p. 551); other men are merely mechanical extensions, "my arms and my legs" (p. 716). Yet Ahab also clearly conceives of himself as "under orders" (p. 707) by a higher will and pledges his worship-by-defiance to the Spirit he glimpses behind the flames burning in the ship's rigging. Ahab is both defined and torn apart by the destructive split between his two visions of himself—as the autonomous hero who shouts "in the midst of the personified impersonal, a personality stands here" (p. 641); and also as the divinely-obsessed self-doubter who wonders, "Is Ahab, Ahab? Is it I, God, or who that lifts this arm?" (p. 685). Whereas Bulkington's end is recorded as an apotheosis leaping up from his sea-death, Ahab's fitting close is rendered in his epitaphic words, "let me then tow to pieces" (p. 721).

Two other characters complete the book's pantheon of heroic being. When Ishmael turns away without comment from Father Mapple's description of the religious hero, the subsequent chapter significantly focuses on the "calm self-collectedness" (p. 83) of Queequeg. The pagan savage, not the God-driven man, elicits the narrator's approving commentary on the serene integrity of one who is "always equal to himself." Perhaps, Ishmael says, "to be true philosophers, we mortals should not be conscious of so living or so striving" (p. 83). Queequeg represents the life of primitive, unreflective self-possession; but again, although Ishmael admires this form of being, it is beyond the grasp of the ordinary man, or ordinary Westerner at least. Queequeg is capable of intense, full commitment, as witness his youthful inauguration of wandering by clinging to a visiting whaling ship despite threats of being hacked to pieces, and his two life-saving exploits involving the greenhorn and Tashtego. The single-minded life-or-death resolve of Queequeg might be seen as roughly paralleling Ishmael's commitment to the sea at the novel's beginning; even though the pagan's mode of engagement is intense, however, it is not tortured by the self-consciousness of the Westerner such as Ishmael, Ahab, or even the brooding Bulkington. Similarly, Queequeg's abandonment of a resolve, as in his sudden, apparently superhuman decision not to die of fever, is made on the same flat, calm plane of self-collectedness—at no time does he threaten, Ishmael-fashion, to "lose" himself or return to himself with horror. Queequeg the exotic pagan hero is also outside the pale of those ordinary souls who are infants, boys, men, and Ifs eternally.

Similarly outside the pale and helping to delimit its boundaries is the "fool" Pip, whose "insanity is heaven's sense" (p. 530). The price of Pip's immersion in the depths of the indefinite sea, the locus of this wisdom, is the loss of a sane identity. Neither split asunder like tragic Ahab nor apotheosized like willful Bulkington, Pip is left to mourn his former possession of identity—"Where's Pip?" he cries—with plentiful insight to see its inadequacy: "'Pip, he died a coward!'" (p. 611). Willy-nilly, he has been brought to a condition comparable in one important respect to that of Father Mapple's religious hero: a "heaven's sense" that embodies ontological reality, a lack of definition congruent with the basic nature of things. The equation pointed to by Pip's fate—loss of autonomous self-definition equals heaven's wisdom—is seen benignly in the religious view and agonizedly in Ahab's. Pip is accidentally victimized by, and Ahab tragically acts out, the human original sin: the acute consciousness of a tenuous personal identity surrounded by an infinite, amorphous "heartless immensity."

However, for the vast majority of men, even as they water-gaze, the troubled awareness of this disparity only exists at the edges of consciousness, if at all. Men hungrily seek in the world the image of themselves, and it is this heightened subliminal sense of their own being that Ahab symbolically offers his crew when he holds out to them the promised doubloon. The round coin is not only a talisman of the Whale, it is a talisman of the self, of the self's perfected wholeness, and of the never-ending circle of experience that generates identity. As Ahab knows, like the ocean the silent crowds stare into, and like "the round globe itself," the doubloon "to each and every man in turn but mirrors back his own mysterious self" (p. 551). But Ahab's offer of selfhood to the crew is in the most important sense false because he pledges them to an unremitting "linear" food, a prolongation of one delirious moment on the quarterdeck of communally shared anger, fear, and hatred (and these directed at the very symbol of the elusiveness of self). There is to be no disengagement from this spell that merges them into one over-riding mood, a sinister version of Ishmael's visionary "melting" with his mates as they squeeze case together.

The quarter-deck scene follows immediately upon Ishmael's masthead reverie dramatizing Nature's inherent potential for swallowing up individual identity; in the ritual event, as elsewhere, Ahab mimics the same natural fact that outrages him. Instead of genuinely offering the crew members a viable selfhood, Ahab attempts to swallow up their separate personalities into his own to the degree that Starbuck eventually fears that "all of us are Ahabs" (p. 651). Even before they plunge into the indefinite sea, they have become an undifferentiated entity—"one man, not thirty . . . all varieties were welded into oneness, and were all directed to that fatal goal which Ahab their one lord and keel did point to" (pp. 700-01).

II

My next point has perhaps already been anticipated: that Ishmael in truth offers his readers, insofar as possible within the limits of an aesthetic experience, what Ahab purports to offer to his "audience"—selfhood; that is, that a primary effect of Ishmael's rhetoric is to stimulate what I, following Hopkins, have called self-taste. There is a sense in which this statement about the rhetorical effect of *Moby-Dick* might be though applicable to every successful book. We may cite Henry James, as Wayne Booth does in *The Rhetoric of Fiction:* "The author makes his readers, just as he makes his characters."[5] However, the preceding discussion has been intended to show that the making of individual identity is of primary thematic importance in *Moby-Dick.* Does a universe whose manifestations of individuality seem to be only pasteboard masks, whose life principle seems as terrifyingly characterless as non-being itself, offer any sanction for the human desire for selfhood? Or does this universe indeed "stab us from behind with the thought of annihilation" (p. 263)? To borrow Melville's phrase, what "ontological heroics"[6] are required to achieve genuine individual being in such a cosmos? This is precisely the issue at stake for Ishmael's hero, Ahab; and it is above all crucial for the younger voyager Ishmael who embarked on the *Pequod* as well as for the older Ishmael whom we experience as the book's narrative consciousness. In *Moby-Dick* rhetorical effect is knit organically into structure and theme; it is peculiarly true of Ishmael that he "makes his readers as he makes his characters," including himself. What remains to be seen is the way the processes of making fit seamlessly into each other.

The famous first sentence of the narrative assigns an identity that is less a statement of individuality than it is a relationship initiated between author and reader. The narrator's first creative act begins to establish the dependency of identity and of the creative act upon just such a relationship. No one in the novel *calls* the narrator Ishmael; only the reader is told to do so for patently symbolic reasons, as a convention of storytelling. Nevertheless, the narrator is as firmly impressed on the reader's mind as a real presence as if his name had been Huck Finn or Jake Barnes instead of one with such starkly portentous Biblical overtones. The name tendered us is a synonym for alienation and animosity between the name-bearer and all other men. Yet despite these forbidding connotations and the impression that the reader has been ironically fended off by a convention behind which the "real" narrator has retreated, a counter effect is produced by the device of literary allusion, which in itself rests upon an appeal to shared experience, an implicit assumption that writer and audience possess a common knowledge. Thus, even where a narrator's tone may be chilly, the reader is permitted, if not invited, to align himself, however slightly, with the writer and the writer's irony. Other slight tonalities of Ishmael's first words reinforce this latter effect; we are presented a "first" name, not a last, and there is a sort of agreeable bluffness implied in the narrator's willingness to assign himself such an apparently forbidding identity.

The combination of cool distance and sophisticated willingness to allow the reader to approach up to a point is the dominant note of the voice we begin to learn how to hear in the book's opening sentences. If the narrator is capable of saying to us, "never mind how long [ago] precisely" (p. 23) the story is set, we are still reassured by the fact that he applies the same offhand deprecation to himself and to his own adventures (". . . I thought I would sail about a little and see the watery part of the world. It is a way I have of driving off the spleen, and regulating the circulation"). Having apparently given notice at the outset that a certain unspoken distance between audience and narrator is part of the aesthetic decorum to be observed in this story, Ishmael becomes more expansive and intimate. But the reader is still kept at a little distance from Ishmael's private feelings of grim depression by such devices as the air of ironically calculated exaggeration (Ishmael speaks of "involuntarily pausing before coffin warehouses," "bringing up the rear of every funeral,"

and wanting to knock people's hats off) and the sophisticated collocation of Ishmael's own commitment to sea as a "substitute for pistol and ball" with Cato's committing suicide "with a philosophical flourish" (p. 23). At the same time that we are being made privy to the dreary November of the narrator's soul and to his suicidal mood, the studiedly unruffled tone as well as the open exhortation urges on us a man-of-the-world response of *nil admirari*: "There is nothing surprising in this. If they but knew it, almost all men in their degree, some time or other, cherish very nearly the same feelings toward the ocean with me."

But now, having identified the personal feeling with mankind's common experience and thus held us off from the *narrator's* deepest privacy, the narrative voice uses this same association as a transition to direct attention away from itself and to begin directly implicating the reader in the dynamics of the mood: "There is now your insular city . . . the streets take you waterward. . . . Look at the crowds of water-gazers there. Circumambulate the city. . . . What do you see? . . . How then is this? . . . But look!" (p. 24). Ishmael is no longer talking merely about his experience, but about the reader's, and that of all men. In the powerful evocation of the enchanting effect of water that follows, this association is emphasized and re-emphasized until all human and natural barriers seem dissolved. At the ocean's edge "all unite" (p. 24) in reverie, drawn by the dreamy allurement of water. Ishmael's very assertions of fact are founded on the sort of common sharing of outlook that he is depicting: "Yes, as every one knows, meditation and water are wedded for ever" (p. 25).

The watery world at its most spell-binding is linked to aesthetic experience, and the beholder's share is not neglected: "[The artist] desires to paint you the dreamiest . . . most enchanting bit of romantic landscape." The picture that Ishmael describes underscores the same universal quiescence in a kind of communal subjectivity that the water-gazing crowds represent: "here sleeps his meadow, and there sleep his cattle . . . and though this pine-tree shakes down its sighs like leaves upon this shepherd's head, yet all were vain, unless the shepherd's eye were fixed upon the magic stream before him" (p. 25). The rhetorical questions Ishmael has employed since the third paragraph as a means of implicating the reader begin to come one after another, in a long, insistent sequence: "Why is almost every robust healthy boy . . . crazy to go to sea? Why upon your first voyage as a passenger, did you yourself feel such a mystical vibration . . . ? Why did the old Persians hold the sea holy?" (pp. 25-26). The insistent repetitions and rhythms of the prose—note for example the repeated "ol" sound in the third sentence—and the suggestive indefiniteness of the questions all reflect and reinforce Ishmael's depiction of the sea's influence; and so the reader too is drawn increasingly into something very much like the oceanic feeling and self-forgetting meditation of the water-gazers.

It is at this point, immediately after having surrounded the sea and the dreaminess it begets with attractive connotations—aesthetic pleasure, youthfulness, holiness—that Ishmael abruptly sums up the allurement of water and reminds us in the same breath of its horror by alluding to the story of Narcissus and his drowning. Though the reader, caught up in the intensity of the experience, has probably forgotten why he initially began to consider the phenomenon of the sea's allure, he has full warrant now to recall that the sea was first referred to as a desperate surrogate for self-destruction. We are brought up short as we come to the heart of the mystery with the image of Narcissus' doom. The spell is ended that Ishmael has persuaded us to participate in, merging ourselves in the moods that were not so much his as ours in common with all men in oceanic self-forgetfulness.

The moods have traced a curve from a somewhat reversed, death-like emptiness of the soul to an enchanted "fullness" of communal subjectivism combining both dreaminess and intensity, and from this to a sudden confrontation with the idea of self-destruction. This curve represents the centripetal movement of Ishmael's rhetoric, dissolving his sophisticated reserve and pulling us toward identification with him and a pooled "pantheistic" consciousness. Now there is a rapid shift in direction as Ishmael once more refers to himself *in propria persona*. The tone becomes whimsical and rambling, a humorous, pleasant blend of old salt and schoolmaster as it ranges easily from the subject of broiling fowl at sea to that of Egyptian writing on broiled ibis. The voice is jauntier and more companionable than the one that we first heard, but still similar in its occasional darkly ironic overtones and willingness to take breathless jumps from 'fore-the-mast to metaphysics. Thus begins the centrifugal movement of the rhetoric, the curving away from the moment when all distances between reader, narrator, and dominant mood threatened to disappear. Now we again are aware of the distinction between what one critic has called "the conjured objectivity" and Ishmael's "conjuring subjectivity"[7] as Ishmael's shift in pitch and focus re-establishes the distances, tactfully re-affirms his separate reality as narrator, and we recoil from our absorbed identification and return to a sharpened sense of ourselves.

In short, the opening of the book is an epitome of the way Ishmael's rhetoric engenders self-taste by manipulating the reader's distance from him and the world of his fiction. In the process of moving into and out of the vortex of the moods and subjects that obsess the narrator we are made to define him and our proper selves as intricately involved but finally distinct entities. We are made to value the absorbed passion that not only admits us, but draws us into, his obsessions and to relish also the ironic, elusive reserve that releases us from them. And the rhetorical cycle thus described is the formal counterpart of the younger Ishmael's cycle of self-generation.

Everywhere in the novel the combination of allurement and distancing, attraction and disengagement, is in operation. This affective sequence can be seen operating, for example, over the several chapters initiated by the first appearance of Ahab's boat-crew. The creatures that modern men "only see in their dreams" (p. 307) are allowed to captivate the narrator's imagination, which indulges its fascination with them, gives them credence and credibility. This impulse is alternated, however, with what might be called Stubb's view, which in itself combines a certain imaginative insightfulness with a commonsensical, comic skepticism. Ishmael's incantatory musings in "The Mat-Maker" introduces the apparition-like appearance of Fedallah and his crew, but the apparition is followed quickly by a description of Stubb's ambiguous fashion of commanding his crew "in a tone so strangely compounded of fun and fury" that "pulling for dear life" they still pulled "for the joke of the thing" (p. 293). This in turn is succeeded by a centripetal intensification of mood as the whale-men pull toward the "charmed, churned circle of the hunted whale" (p. 299) and are overwhelmed by a sudden storm that obliterates distinctions ("Squall, whale, and harpoon . . . all blended together"). Ishmael's boat is left abandoned as if "immortal in the jaws of death," alone in "the heart of that almighty forlornness" (p. 301). The centrifugal movement is carried out in the grim laughter of "The Hyena" and its reflections on the universe as a vast practical joke. The pattern begins again immediately in Ishmael's renewed fascination with Ahab's unearthly crew. This is followed in the plot by the enchantment-like appearance of the Spirit Spout and the spell cast over the entire ship going around the Cape of Good Hope in which the vessel is silent, "as if manned by painted sailors in wax" (p. 313); then by the foreboding interchange with "The Albatross" and another image of solitary, deathly abandonment while "in pursuit of those far mysteries we dream of, or in tormented chase of that demon phantom that, some time or other, swims before all human hearts . . ." (p. 316). But we move away from this vision too in "The Gam," with its urbane tone and "gamesome stuff" (p. 319), and are off on another swing of the curve.

Other major attributes of Ishmael's style accentuate the alternating centripetal and centrifugal pressures of the book. Some of the most powerful of the former may be subsumed under the heading of the cognitive impulse, the desire to obtain final answers from an alluring world that stimulates interpretation. We see this in Ishmael's discursiveness, in his fact-mongering, and especially in his generalizing sententiousness, which tempts the reader to commit himself exclusively to a highly quotable passage as a way out of the endless succession of qualifications and changing perspectives Ishmael also gives us. This centripetal pull is reinforced by the immediate impression of formlessness given by the book, which, coupled with Ishmael's several teasing hints at his awareness of both formal difficulties and a kind of order—"careful disorderliness" he names it (p. 465)—stimulates the reader's projection and his attempt at closure of the all-but-completed form.[8] On the other hand there is the centrifugal force supplied by Ishmael's tentativeness—"Still, we can hypothesize," he characteristically says, "even if we cannot prove and establish" (p. 479); by his rambling chattiness; and by his tendency to subvert fact by blending it with legend, fancy, and frontiersman's tall talk. By turns intimate, urgent, frank, rhapsodic, but also superior, dry, and crafty, Ishmael's voice establishes our distinctiveness from the inspired poet even as he sweeps us along with him.

Ishmael's creativity is made a function of his relationship with his autonomous but intimately connected opposite, the reader, just as in nature distinctive qualities are created "by contrast." There is a revealing train of associations when Ishmael speaks of Ahab's use of "arts and entrenchments," the usages of the sea behind which "he sometimes masked himself" in order to gain supremacy over his crew, and then implicitly links this use of stage tricks to the writer's own practice:

> Nor, will the tragic dramatist who would depict mortal indomitableness in its fullest sweep and direct sway, ever forget a hint, incidentally so important in his art, as the one alluded to.
>
> But Ahab, my Captain, still moves before me in all his Nantucket grimness and shagginess; and in this episode touching Emperors and Kings, I must not conceal that I have only to do with a poor old whale-hunter like him; and, therefore, all outward majestical trappings and housings are denied me. Oh, Ahab! what shall be grand in thee, it must needs be plucked at from the skies, and dived for in the deep, and featured in the unbodied air!

(p. 199)

Ishmael's problem of aesthetic form, imaged in the words "unbodied air," finds its partial solution in the habitual open speculation which reveals his art as he works out his problems of composition before his readers. This habit, like the language ("I must not conceal"), elicits our confidence as well as our sympathetic participation in helping the apparent fledgling to create. The "unbodied air" is precisely where the creation comes to life, in the joint instrumentality between artist and audience that is summoned up by Ishmael's apparent artlessness. But as should be expected from his interest in Ahab's masking devices, the relationship of creator and perceiver is more than a little disingenuous; despite Ishmael's protestations, we see within a few

pages that he takes considerable pains to provide his hero with "majestical trappings and housings" when Ahab appears in the quarterdeck scene.

As recent critics have emphasized, Ishmael repeatedly calls attention to the illusionistic, "staged" nature of his book. In the very first chapter, he completes our liberation from the spell of Narcissus by using a Barnum-like playbill to make the entire voyage a matter of literary genre: he imagines that on the "grand programme of providence" there must have appeared a brief interlude ("WHALING VOYAGE BY ONE ISHMAEL"), and wonders why "those stage managers, the Fates, put me down for this shabby part of a whaling voyage, when others were set down for magnificent parts in high tragedies, and short and easy parts in genteel comedies, and jolly parts in farces . . ." (p. 29). Stage directions ("*Enter Ahab: Then, all*"); essayistic character outlines ("Nor will it at all detract from him, dramatically regarded, if . . ."); bibliographical categorization of whales—these devices and many others throughout the book designedly remind us that Ishmael is staging an illusion. Nevertheless the power of the illusion compels us to participate in it, so that after Ishmael has called our attention to the leader's external arts, "in themselves, more or less paltry and base," we are still caught up in Ahab's mastery of the crew and in his grandeur as an artistic creation. Like his hero, Ishmael has an instinct for both spellbinding and spell-breaking—for unmasking as well as for its opposite.

Ishmael must "make" his reader able to see the book's "whiteness" and also to wear "colored and coloring glasses" (p. 264). We must be supple enough, that is, to participate in the book's reality by both putting our confidence in it and being able to see it as an illusion. We too must be gamesome, and godly as well in that we participate in our creation as readers by going through a cyclic succession of "contradictory" relationships with the book: the unconscious spell, thoughtless faith, doubt, skepticism, disbelief, and pondering repose of If.

As Ishmael periodically "disappears" and the enacting narrative consciousness seems to plunge self-forgetfully into the life of its story and become a nameless omniscience, we are submerged in the spell cast by the conflict of Ahab, crew, and Nature. But inevitably the narrator's voice intrudes to remind us of the artist-audience relationship and the roles we must play in the aesthetic game. The narrator not only addresses us, he often characterizes us in relation to his own roles in a way that contrasts sharply with the mesmeric communal subjectivism of a dramatically shared experience.

He sets himself up as the advocate of whalemen, and we become like the green bumpkins the younger Ishmael mocks—mere landsmen who are duped by the world because of a lack of imaginative appreciation of its wonders: "I am all anxiety to convince ye, ye landsmen, of the injustice done to us hunters of whales" (p. 150). As elsewhere, Ishmael the old salt is both condescending and anxious to initiate us so that we may begin to lose what he calls our "ignorant incredulity" (p. 437) and cease to be such "provincials" (p. 438) concerning the truth. Ishmael is the artist above all: "I shall ere long paint to you as well as one can without canvas, something like the true form of the whale . . ." (p. 346). But before we can appreciate correct artistry we must first be disembarrassed of false notions and, most importantly, of an apparently formidable provinciality that Ishmael takes exception to in quasi-comic truculence: "Who ain't a slave? Tell me that" (p. 28); "Cannibals? Who is not a cannibal? I tell you . . ." (p. 393); *"The whale no famous author, and whaling no famous chronicler?"* (p. 154). Ishmael must have an audience that will give a particular kind of credence to his marvelous illusions, an audience retrained in the difficult balance of wonder and skepticism.

In instructing us the former schoolmaster adopts a great number of pedagogically useful roles: in one chapter alone, "Cetology," he becomes in succession naturalist, herald, biographer, bibliographer, and architect. All his roles are obviously made playfully dependent upon whimsical élan, reflected in remarks like this: "Unconsciously my chirography expands into placard capitals. Give me a condor's quill! . . . Ere entering upon the subject of Fossil Whales, I present my credentials as a geologist, by stating that in my miscellaneous time I have been a stonemason, and also a great digger of ditches, canals and wells, wine-vaults, cellars, and cisterns of all sorts" (p. 580). Such statements express the abiding aesthetic will that picks up and drops whatever is needful for its continued free play, with the combined enthusiastic engagement and oblique smile of the true gamesman.

But the narrator's playfulness and irony does not merely celebrate his authorial freedom; it coaches the reader to secure his own liberty. Attacking our provinciality, it asks us to engage our imaginations in awe; then subverting our trust and willingness to grant belief uncritically, it asks us to "contradict" ourselves by entering into another phase of partial truth. So Ishmael assigns roles that encourage us to abandon our landsmen status and to share more completely in the teacher's pursuit of knowledge: "I would have you, as a sensible physiologist . . . investigate . . . now with the sole view of forming to yourself some unexaggerated, intelligent estimate . . ." (p. 435). We are invited, implicitly and explicitly, to assume a cosmopolitan frankness in response to the narrator's own tonality: "I freely assert, that the cosmopolite philosopher cannot, for his life, point out one single [more] peaceful influence . . . than . . . whaling" (p. 152). Similarly we are urged to be among

the finer souls—"take your way, ye nobler, sadder souls" (p. 249)—and to be everywhere on our best individual mettle even as we are reminded of a communal sharing of vision: "But in a matter like this, subtlety appeals to subtlety, and without imagination no man can follow another into these halls. And though, doubtless, some at least of the imaginative impressions about to be presented may have been shared by most men . . ." (p. 259). The ultimate aim of Ishmael's rhetoric is to return us to ourselves. "I but put that [whale's] brow before you," says Ishmael. "Read it if you can" (p. 449). We cannot simply forget ourselves, nor our responsibility in the aesthetic play: "But look at this matter in other lights: weigh it in all sorts of scales" (p. 151); "But as you come nearer to this . . . it begins to assume different aspects, according to your point of view" (p. 432).

Thus it is clearly much more than convention or carelessness that causes Ishmael to put the masthead reverie scene not in terms of his experience directly, but that of a mediating "absent-minded youth" who imperceptibly changes into the reader himself, in his own proper identity:

> lulled into such an opium-like listlessness of vacant, unconscious reverie is this absent-minded youth by the blending cadence of waves with thoughts, that at last he loses his identity; takes the mystic ocean at his feet for the visible image of that deep, blue bottomless soul, pervading mankind and nature. . . . In this enchanted mood, thy spirit ebbs away to whence it came; becomes diffused through time and space. . . .
>
> There is no life in thee, now. . . . But while this sleep, this dream is on ye . . . slip your hold at all; and your identity comes back in horror. Over Descartian vortices you hover. . . . Heed it well, ye Pantheists!
>
> (pp. 214-15)

If we heed Ishmael's warnings well, we are prepared to read the long last enthralling section of the book, in which we must do without his guiding presence, as our final exercise in self-definition; and to emerge from its illusion as Ishmael does in the end, in the momentary repose of If.

III

The audience-awareness that Ishmael evinces is a reflection of his creator's increasing ambivalence towards his reading public and his growing sense of the effect his readers had on his role as a serious writer. Shortly after he completed **Moby-Dick,** Melville was openly skeptical of his public's appreciation of his work: "Appreciation! Recognition! Is love appreciated? Why, ever since Adam, who has got to the meaning of this great allegory—the world? Then we pygmies must be content to have our paper allegories but ill comprehended."[9] It is as if Melville, through the medium of Ishmael, were giving his audience one last chance to create itself, to discover its role in reading the book. It is understandable that at times Ishmael's voice has an edge on it. After *Moby-Dick,* there is no figure comparable to Ishmael in Melville's works to encourage and cajole the reader directly and to set the example by responding to the world and to the problem of artistic creation as he would have the reader respond to the act of reading—as forms of self-definition. *Moby-Dick*'s metaphysics and its meditations on the phantoms that turn out to "be" oneself are inseparable from its rhetorical goal of helping an audience to create itself.

That Melville did succeed in part with some members of his contemporary audience is indicated in a review of *Moby-Dick* that responds to something like the double, or cyclic, effect that I have described:

> The author's radiant imagination enthralls us in a delicious bondage, and the tide of his animal spirits sweeps all doubts and misgivings triumphantly before it. . . . He has a clever knack of identifying his own cause with ours. . . . His manner is so winning, and his language so persuasive, that there is no resisting him. . . . We share with him the perils he so graphically pictures, and merge our own identity in his. . . . As the gull (no inapt emblem, the matter-of-fact philosopher will say, of him who allows another man's imagination so to influence his own)—folds up her wings . . . and is wildly rocked through the hills and hollows of the waves—so does the mind of the sympathetic reader yield an unconscious allegiance to the resistless sway of this powerful writer.

The reviewer's gull metaphor piquantly sums up the opposite impulses felt in the book's rhetoric, which the reviewer elsewhere expresses in the language of the "Hyena" chapter: "there are occasions when the reader is disposed to believe that the whole book is one vast practical joke. We are half inclined to believe that the author is humbugging us, and with that suspicion comes its invariable accompaniment, a sense of offended dignity; but the spell of genius is upon us, and we are powerless to resist."[10]

The successor of that radiant, humbugging narrator is Melville's Confidence Man, who represents a further working out of the implications of Ishmael's art in a thoroughgoing game of confidence. The Confidence Man is the self-maker extraordinary, the player-deity who masters roles and illusions. He not only recasts himself in a series of identities, but his essential blankness defines and shapes the identities of his audience, as the colorless "ray of living light" does the experiential world; he is "a revolving Drummond light, raying away from itself all round it—everything is lit by it, everything starts up to it."[11] For the Confidence Man is also the poet, the Ishmael of negative capability who, like Melville, finds himself an outcast. So Melville in the opening pages of *The Confidence-Man* seems to echo the famous banishment passage of *The Republic:*

Suppose then there were a man so clever that he could take all kinds of shapes and imitate anything and everything, and suppose he should come to our city with his poems to give a display, what then? We should prostrate ourselves before him as one sacred and wonderful and delightful, but we should say that we cannot admit such a man into our city; the law forbids, and there is no place for him. We should anoint his head and wreathe about it a chaplet of wool, and let him go in peace to another city. . . .[12]

Notes

1. *Moby-Dick,* ed. Charles Feidelson, Jr. (Indianapolis, 1964), p. 193. As the Northwestern-Newberry standard edition is unavailable at this time, I cite Feidelson's edition because of its helpful notes, which, even where the interpretation differs from mine, often parallel the tenor and interests of my essay. Subsequent references to *Moby-Dick* will appear in the text.

2. In the last quotation I have adopted as more sensible the emendation offered by Hershel Parker and Harrison Hayford, Norton Critical Edition (New York, 1967), p. 413, instead of the usual reading ("die it!") that Feidelson uses. By my count, the novel contains twenty-two references to play, games, etc., including the word "juggle" and its variations—"bejuggled and destroyed," e. g., p. 690. The terms cover a wide range of responses to the world, from "merry's the play" (p. 627) shouted out by the *Bachelor*'s captain to Ahab's cries for "fair play" (pp. 221, 639).

3. *The Sermons and Devotional Writings of Gerard Manley Hopkins,* ed. Christopher Devlin (London, 1959), p. 123. Cited in J. Hillis Miller, *The Disappearance of God* (New York, 1965), p. 271. By adopting Hopkins' term, I do not mean to imply any further similarity on his part with Ishmael or Melville; as Miller notes, "Hopkins does not want to melt into the totality, to expand into vagueness, or to lose the sharp taste of himself in possession of the 'all'" (p. 286).

4. *The Confidence-Man,* ed. Elizabeth S. Foster (New York, 1954), p. 77; my italics. Cf. Melville's well-known statement to Hawthorne: "This 'all' feeling . . . there is some truth in it. . . . But what plays the mischief with the truth is that men will insist upon the universal application of a temporary feeling or opinion." *The Letters of Herman Melville,* ed. Merrell R. Davis and William H. Gilman (New Haven, 1960), p. 131.

5. Chicago, 1961, epigraph to Part I.

6. *Letters,* p. 133.

7. Glauco Cambon, "Ishmael and the Problem of Formal Discontinuities in *Moby-Dick,*" *MLN*

[*Modern Language Notes*], 76 (1961), 523. Cf. also Paul Brodtkorb, Jr., *Ishmael's White World: A Phenomenological Reading of* Moby-Dick (New Haven, 1965), p. 148: "*Moby-Dick* tries to persuade us to become [Ishmael's] moods in order to discover their meanings within ourselves; it does so by submerging the initially amusing character Ishmael into the ambiguous voice of the narrator, whose feelings in relation to his strange world provide analogues for ours." I am indebted to the general argument of Brodtkorb's book, although Brodtkorb places a much greater emphasis on Ishmael's irony and its part in the narrator-reader relationship than I do.

  8. Cf. E. H. Gombrich, *Art and Illusion* (New York: 1961), especially Part III, "The Beholder's Share."

  9. *Letters,* pp. 141-42.

 10. London *Morning Post,* November 14, 1851, in *Moby-Dick As Doubloon: Essays and Extracts (1851-1970),* ed. Hershel Parker and Harrison Hayford (New York, 1970), pp. 28-31.

 11. *The Confidence-Man,* p. 271.

 12. W. H. D. Rouse, trans., *Great Dialogues of Plato* (New York, 1956), pp. 195-96.

Stephen C. Ausband (essay date May 1975)

SOURCE: Ausband, Stephen C. "The Whale and the Machine: An Approach to *Moby-Dick.*" *American Literature: A Journal of Literary History, Criticism, and Bibliography* 47, no. 2 (May 1975): 197-211.

[*In the following essay, Ausband discusses Melville's use of machine imagery to describe the character of Ahab, arguing that Ahab's mechanical aspects symbolize his alienation from both society and nature.*]

Several critics of *Moby-Dick* have suggested that Ahab's chief sin is his separation from humanity. His deliberate, continued, and complete estrangement from the rest of mankind nourishes his monomania, and he willfully dooms himself and his followers to destruction in his quest for revenge. F. O. Matthiessen sees in the captain's isolation "a fearful symbol of the self-enclosed individualism that, carried to its furthest extreme, brings disaster both upon itself and the group of which it is a part."[1] Two articles by R. E. Watters in 1945 point to what Melville regarded as the dangers of such excessive isolation. "In Melville's opinion," says Watters, "prolonged isolation either chills the heart or corrupts the mind—or both."[2] In his mad hunt for vengeance on the white whale, Ahab becomes so thoroughly separated from his fellowmen that he can refuse even to join in

the search for a missing whale-boat. By the end of the first day's chase after Moby Dick, he senses that his isolation from the warmth of human company is complete: "Ahab stands alone among the millions of the peopled earth, nor gods nor men his neighbors. Cold, cold—I shiver."[3]

In developing Ahab as the supreme isolato in his fiction, Melville draws heavily on the kind of mechanistic imagery he had used (perhaps unconsciously) in earlier novels. A mutilated savage who decorates himself with knives and nails and a silent sailor who "revolves upon his own . . . axis, like a wheel which forever goes round, whether you look at it or not" accompany Taji, the quester in **Mardi.** Wellingborough Redburn and White-Jacket, the youthful protagonists of the next two novels [**Redburn** and **White-Jacket**], find themselves surrounded by isolated characters who are disfigured or diseased (symbolic of a spiritual loss) and mechanical in their actions and attitudes, one of the characters, Surgeon Cadwallader Cuticle in **White-Jacket,** being almost literally a machine. It is not surprising, then, that Melville describes Ahab as a physically wounded and disfigured man and as a mechanism. Repeated references to machinery in descriptions of Ahab are striking. He has a "steel skull" (p. 147); he likens himself to a locomotive (p. 147); he stands like an iron statue overlooking the men (p. 438); and he has an electric or magnetic effect on the crew.

A few critics have noted the presence of mechanistic imagery in **Moby-Dick.** Newton Arvin mentions the "images that come from nineteenth-century industry or technology, the images of drilling and blasting, of mining, of cogged wheels and mechanical looms and magnetic wires, and even the 'Leyden jar' of Ahab's 'own magnetic life."[4] R. P. Adams, commenting on the mechanistic-organic patterns of imagery in **Moby-Dick,** *Walden,* and *Song of Myself,* points out some of the mechanistic imagery associated with Ahab.[5] The most thorough treatment of the industrial references in the novel is by Leo Marx, who concentrates on chapter ninety-six, "The Try Works." In a discussion of the use of industrial and mechanical imagery by Hawthorne and Melville, Marx emphasizes the power of the new machine age on the popular mind.[6]

Not only the mere appearance of machinery on the American landscape but also the well established traditions of Romanticism, including the use of organic-mechanistic terminology, influenced Melville in his choice of imagery. The novel itself, Melville insists, is an organic work, something with a life of its own, and not a completed and perfect structure. Ishmael describes this organic theory of art in several chapters. He introduces chapter 63 by saying, "Out of the trunk, the branches grow; out of them, the twigs. So, in productive subjects, grow the chapters"; and in chapter 82 he says, "There are some enterprises in which a careful disorderliness is the true method." The best essay on the organic structure of **Moby-Dick** is by Walter E. Bezanson, who sees the novel as the supreme example of the Romantic concept of art. As Bezanson and other critics have noted, Melville was, by the late 1840's, very much aware of trends and developments in nineteenth-century literature. Like Leon Howard and F. O. Matthiessen, Bezanson stresses the importance of the theories of Coleridge and Carlyle to the minds of American writers, including Melville.[7]

Melville's familiarity with the organic-mechanistic dichotomy in theories of art is obvious in the style of the novel, and it is probably safe to say that his familiarity with Romantic cosmology (as well as artistic theory) accounts in large part for the mechanistic imagery in **Moby-Dick**.[8] Ahab, isolated from normal humanity to the point where he begins to regard himself as existing outside the flow of life, takes on the characteristics of a gigantic and threatening machine—a locomotive, say, or perhaps a huge mechanical man. Furthermore, he thinks in mechanistic terms; even his relation to the crew is mechanical (they are his "wheels" or "gears" or "tools"). He deals in one-to-one relationships; if the sun could insult him, then he could smite the sun, since "there is ever a sort of fair play herein" (p. 144). He lives in an orderly, predictable microcosm (the world of the *Pequod*), and he rages madly at the disorder, the "inscrutable thing" (p. 144), in brief, the organic nature the white whale represents. **Moby-Dick** pits a man who has become a machine against a whale which becomes, to Ishmael and to Ahab, the symbol of the organic, dynamic force in the universe.

It is tempting (and misleading) to oversimplify, to say that the mechanistic imagery associated with Ahab sets him apart from the rest of the men on board the *Pequod*. But Melville not only describes various members of the crew (and sometimes the crew as a whole) in mechanistic terms, he sometimes associates Ahab with an organic image, as in the passages likening the captain to a giant tree. The mechanistic-organic image patterns are by no means haphazard, however, and they can be summarized as follows. In his monomaniacal quest for revenge, Ahab assumes the driving purposefulness of a machine. He loses much of his humanity, his identity with the other, merely human souls who sail with him. As Richard Chase observes, Ahab's more than human desire for revenge transforms him not into a Prometheus, "but into the very image of the Beast-Machine."[9] During the course of the novel Ahab succeeds in fashioning from the crew a subordinate machine to do his bidding.

Ishmael's first description of Ahab suggests more a giant statue than a human being. Peleg had said earlier that Ahab was "above the common," but to Ishmael he seemed above the human. He showed "no sign of common bodily illness about him, nor of the recovery from any" (p. 109). Something had burned away much of Ahab's humanity without destroying his strength: "He looked like a man cut away from the stake, when the fire has over-runningly wasted all the limbs without consuming them, or taking away one particle from their compacted aged robustness. His whole high, broad form, seemed made of solid bronze, and shaped into an unalterable mould, like Cellini's cast Perseus" (pp. 109-110). The scar on Ahab resembled "that perpendicular seam sometimes made in the straight, lofty trunk of a great tree, when the upper lightning tearingly darts down it, and without wrenching a single twig, peels and grooves out the bark from top to bottom, are running off into the soil, leaving the tree still greenly alive, but branded" (p. 110).

This opening description, likening Ahab to something made of metal and to a tree, sets the stage for most of the subsequent descriptions of the captain. Ahab was a man, a part of life like a tree. Some confrontation with an immense natural force—literally, the whale; analogically, lightning—burned away much that was alive and human in him, leaving him "branded" by the scar and by the missing leg. With the strength remaining to him, however, he tried to reconstruct himself—not as a vulnerable man or tree this time but as a metallic demigod, a bronze (in other places iron or steel) slayer of monsters.

The obsessive nature of Ahab's hunt first becomes apparent in chapter 36, "The Quarter-Deck." In this chapter and the one following it, the number of mechanistic images associated with Ahab and his quest is striking. Descriptions of him in terms of magnetism, electricity, machinery, and various kinds of metals abound. He works "magnetically" on the excitement of the crew, and his own excitement resembles the activity of a machine: "While the mate was getting the hammer, Ahab, without speaking, was slowly rubbing the gold piece against the skirts of his jacket, as if to heighten its luster, and, without using any words, was meanwhile lowly humming to himself, producing a sound so strangely muffled and inarticulate that it seemed the mechanical humming of the wheels of his vitality in him" (p. 142). He generates and transmits a kind of electrical energy from "the Leyden jar of his own magnetic life" (pp. 142-143), and he even hints that the "full-forced shock" of his "electric thing" might be enough to kill an ordinary man (p. 146).

Ahab's description of his relationship with the crew leaves no doubt about his mechanical nature. He cares only for his quest, wishes only to force the crew mechanically to do his will: "My one cogged circle fits into all their various wheels, and they revolve. Or, if you will, like so many ant hills of powder, they all stand before me; and I their match" (p. 147). The sunset, Ahab says, has no power to soothe him now as it used to, nor can the sunrise move him. He now has a "steel skull, . . . the sort that needs no helmet in the most brain-battering fight," and there is a "dry heat upon [his] brow" (p. 147). Neither the beauty of nature nor the power of the gods can swerve Ahab from his purpose. He is as forceful as a locomotive: "The path to my fixed purpose is laid with iron rails, whereon my soul is grooved to run. Over unsounded gorges, through the rifled hearts of mountains, under torrents' beds, unerringly I rush! Naught's an obstacle, naught's an angle to the iron way" (p. 147).

Starbuck's soliloquy in chapter 38 shows the power of Ahab's initial speech to the crew and the success of the attempt to make of the men a subordinate machine. The mate admits that his soul is "more than matched; she's overmanned," and he likens Ahab's subversion of his will to a mining operation: "He drilled deep down, and blasted all my reason out of me!" Starbuck describes himself in mechanistic terms: "My whole clock's run down; my heart the all-controlling weight, I have no key to lift again" (p. 148).

In the three chapters immediately concerned with Ahab's quest and Ahab's effect on the crew, organic imagery is rare. The two slight references to an organic force that occur in chapter 36 refer to Ahab as he was before he was "dismasted" by Moby Dick. One, reminiscent of the image of the lightning-struck tree in chapter 28, is the captain's own reference to "this dead stump" of a leg he stands on. The other is the "terrific, loud, animal sob" torn from him when he recalls the actual encounter with the whale. Ahab now seems almost beyond human frailties. Even Stubb, who certainly is not among the most profound members of the crew, recognizes that Ahab now has no heart: "He smites his chest. . . . What's that for? Methinks it rings most vast, but hollow" (p. 144).

Chapter 46, "Surmises," brings out again the mechanistic quality of Ahab's relation to the crew. Ahab needs tools to accomplish his purpose, and the tools he must use are men—"of all tools used under the shadow of the moon, . . . the most apt to get out of order." The captain must use his magnetic power constantly to keep these tools of his in the best possible order, to keep them working as efficient machines: "Starbuck's body and Starbuck's coerced will were Ahab's, so long as Ahab kept his magnet at Starbuck's brain" (p. 183). It is interesting that the man in charge of repairing the tools should they wear out or break down, the man who would correspond to a physician for ordinary men, is the ship's carpenter. The carpenter and the blacksmith minister to Ahab's bodily ills.

When Ahab's ivory leg gets out of order, he finds it necessary to have the carpenter and the blacksmith make

another limb. The attitude of the carpenter toward his work and the attitude of Ahab toward the carpenter reinforce other references to mechanism in the novel. If there is a single spark of humanity in the carpenter, he keeps it hidden. He paints oars and extracts teeth with the same lack of emotion. (He even uses the same vise for both operations.) He regards heads as topblocks, men as capstans. Ishmael calls him a "pure manipulator," a kind of tool for repairing tools, as useful as "one of those *multum in parvo* contrivances," a multi-bladed pocket-knife "containing, not only blades of various sizes, but also screw drivers, corkscrews, tweezers, awls, pens, rulers, nail-files, countersinkers" (p. 388). An "all-ramifying heartlessness," a total lack of feeling for his fellow men, characterizes the carpenter. Ishmael's descriptions of the carpenter suggest machinery, despite the comment that the man "was, after all, no mere machine of an automaton." If he did not possess a real soul, says Ishmael, he at least had "a subtle something that somehow anomalously did its duty. What that something was, whether essence of quicksilver, or a few drops of hartshorn, there is no telling. . . . And this it was . . . that kept him a great part of the time soliloquizing; but only like an unreasoning wheel, which also hummingly soliloquizes" (p. 389).

The carpenter and the blacksmith are partners in the business of man-making, and from them Ahab orders his steel-shouldered ideal man: "Imprimis, fifty feet high in his socks; then, chest modelled after the Thames tunnel, then, legs with roots to 'em, to stay in one place; then, arms three feet through the wrist; no heart at all, brass forehead, and about a quarter of an acre of fine brains; and let me see—shall I order eyes to see outwards? No, but put a sky-light on top of his head to illuminate inwards" (p. 390). With the exception of the phrase, "legs with roots to 'em, to stay in one place," Ahab's order is for a gigantic, living statue of metal. The one organic reference lets the ideal man take on qualities of both a giant tree and the Colossus at Rhodes, qualities shared by Ahab himself. But Ahab does not simply order a copy of himself; he orders an ideal. He knows that the organic life has been torn out of him and that he has been uprooted and can never stay in one place. Furthermore, Ahab has no "sky-light on top of his head to illuminate inwards." He is not content to study his own soul. He sees outwards to what must be evil in the world around him. Indeed, his ability to see beyond Moby Dick to the "inscrutable thing" that may be behind the malice of the whale is a cause of his wandering. Ahab's pain and his insanity are due partly to his ability to "see outwards" farther than ordinary men. His ideal man would be large and strong enough to absorb the shocks of a malignant universe, would be self-sufficient and immovable, and would have no heart to feel grief and no eyes to see evil.

Ahab's conversations with the carpenter and the blacksmith demonstrate his frustration at his own weakness, a weakness inherent in a merely human body. He would be rid of the softness and fallibility of flesh: "When I come to mount this leg thou makest, I shall nevertheless feel another leg in the same identical place with it; that is, carpenter, my old lost leg; the flesh and blood one, I mean. Canst thou not drive that old Adam away?" (p. 391). Ahab wishes that his skull (which he describes as made of iron or steel) were really made of metal and not bone, for then the blacksmith could smooth out the scar on his forehead: "If thou could'st, blacksmith, glad enough would I lay my head upon thy anvil, and feel thy heaviest hammer between my eyes" (p. 403). When the whalebone leg breaks during the second day's chase, Ahab denounces to his mate the infirmity that slows down his pursuit of Moby Dick: "But even with a broken bone, Old Ahab is untouched; and I account no living bone of mine one jot more me, than this dead one that's lost. . . . Oh, oh, oh! How this splinter gores me now! Accursed fate! that the unconquerable captain in the soul should have such a craven mate. . . . My body, man, not thee" (p. 458). Alan Lebowitz says the artificial leg is an "instance of [Ahab's] mortality,"[10] but there is a great difference between the wounded leg of Tommo in *Typee* and the whalebone leg of Captain Ahab. Ahab's leg is mechanical, artificial, a product of the "man-makers," the carpenter and the blacksmith. Its failure foreshadows the breakdown or doom of Ahab's machine.

It is helpful to examine briefly the use of fire imagery as it relates to mechanistic imagery in the novel. References to fire are numerous: Perth works in fire; Fedallah and Ahab are fire worshipers; Ahab defies fire; Ishmael warns against looking too long into the face of the fire; both Ahab and Perth are called Prometheus, who was the fire-bringer and who, according to Ahab, "made men from fire"; and Ahab at one point says that even whales worship fire, since they turn toward the sun to die. Obviously, Ahab associates fire—or at least natural fire, including lightning, the sun, and the corposants— with the malevolent forces in the universe that he defies. He even turns his back to the sun when he dies, in contrast to dying whales, which seem to pay homage to the sun. But Ahab also associates fire with himself, with the quest, with the Parsee, and with various members of the crew (whom he describes as "brave as fearless fire, . . . and as mechanical" (pp. 452, 459). There are, as Paul Brodtkorb points out, two different kinds of fire in the novel: "The sun is preeminently natural light, and is . . . contrasted with mechanical, artificial, and conjuring fires; with fires such as Ahab's in which he has his harpoons forged—artificial fires with which to fight natural fire."[11] The sun, natural fire, suggests the light (or the truth) in the natural world. The fire under the try pots, the fire in Perth's forge as he makes fasteners for Ahab's leg, and the fire that forges the harpoons

are the weapons of an industrial, mechanical world in its fight against nature. Ahab was burned by natural fire (lightning); he now defies natural fire, arms himself with artificial fire, industrial fire, and almost literally fights fire with fire.[12]

The most effective use of fire imagery to suggest not only machinery but also the mechanistic nature of Ahab's quest appears in chapter 96, "The Try Works." What begins as a rather matter-of-fact description of a hard and grimy aspect of the whaling industry becomes, before the end of the chapter, Ishmael's personal view of hell, and he associates the hellish scene with Ahab's pursuit of the white whale:

> As [the crew] narrated to each other their unholy adventures, their tales of terror told in words of mirth; as their uncivilized laughter forked upwards out of them, like the flames from the furnace; as to and fro, in their front, the harpooners wildly gesticulated with their huge forks and dippers; as the wind howled on, and the sea leaped, and the ship groaned and dived, and yet steadfastly shot her red hell further and further into the blackness of the sea and the night, and scornfully champed the white bone in her mouth and viciously spat round her on all sides; then the rushing *Pequod*, freighted with savages, and laden with fire, and burning a corpse, and plunging into the blackness of darkness, seemed the material counterpart of her monomaniac commander's soul.
>
> (p. 354)

Many critics regard "The Try Works" as the central, pivotal chapter in the novel. Milton R. Stern calls it "the thematic center" of the book.[13] William Ellery Sedgwick and W. H. Auden see the chapter as the end of Ishmael's trial by isolation and the beginning of his initiation into understanding.[14] Richard B. Sewall regards it as the last and most important of "Ishmael's moral revelations." Says Sewall, "Here except for the occasional reflections on the likeness of whaling to human life and except for the Epilogue, where he recounts only in the barest fashion the circumstances of his lone survival, we leave him. With 'The Try Works' his main function in the novel is done. He has cast off his green and dreamy youth and brought us to the edge of the vortex. The drama is now Ahab's (with Starbuck the main but ineffectual human antagonist) and Moby Dick's."[15]

Ishmael says plainly here, as he has said in previous chapters, that he was once "welded" to Ahab's purpose. But suddenly he could see the "redness, the madness, the ghastliness" of the scene before him, and he took the action that was to account for his salvation later. He saw two contrasting ways of dealing with the problem of evil: one could become obsessed by it, or one could turn his back on it and ignore it completely. Both ways were destructive. Ishmael realized both the danger of being hypnotized by the fiery chase and the danger of ignoring evil. He explored both extremes: at one point he gave himself entirely to the quest to destroy evil; at another he turned his back on the quest. When he turned back around to face the prow and the compass, he did so with a different and more profound understanding of the dangers of extremism. Recounting his trial and rejection of the extremes of naivete and obsession while a member of Ahab's crew, a mature Ishmael cautions his reader against both extremes: "Look not too long into the face of the fire, O man! Never dream with thy hand on the helm! Turn not thy back to the artificial fire, when its redness makes all things look ghastly. Tomorrow, in the natural sun, the skies will be bright" (p. 354). The man who ignores evil will be destroyed by his ignorance, and the man who is obsessed by evil will be deadened by his obsession: "Give not thyself up, then, to the fire, lest it invert thee, deaden thee; as for the time it did me. There is a wisdom that is woe; but there is a woe that is madness" (p. 355). The healthy man can dive, like the Catskill eagle, into the blackest gorges, but he can also "soar out of them again and become invisible in the sunny spaces."

From this point on, Ishmael's view was implicitly in direct opposition to Ahab's. In the red light of the artificial fire—by extension, in the glow of Ahab's "fiery hunt"—all things, including the white whale, look ghastly. In the light of the natural sun, however, the whale appears not simply ghastly but majestic, god-like, beautiful, creative (as well as destructive), and worthy of awe. Ishmael had earlier confessed his tendency to "see naught in that brute but the deadliest ill" (p. 163). His descriptions of Moby Dick in the last third of the novel, however, suggest a new understanding of the whale.

The distinctly mechanistic aspects of Ahab contrast sharply with the profusion of organic imagery applied to Moby Dick. A whale, as Ishmael reminds us again and again, is a mysterious creature that cannot be perfectly analyzed or understood. A whale's antiquity (predating man), its inscrutability (no one has ever seen a whole whale, says Ishmael, and he despairs of ever giving his readers a notion of what a whale looks like), its association with sexuality and phallicism (especially in such chapters as "The Grand Armada," "The Cassock," and "The Chase—First Day") demand that the reader regard whales in general and Moby Dick in particular as suggestive of the organic principle in the universe. As J. A. Ward has pointed out, the cetological chapters in *Moby-Dick* are "in essence metaphorical. . . . The whale, with its great size and power, its ambiguity that can be interpreted as malice or indifference, its malignity and beneficence, is the central force in the world and the symbol of all the power of nonhuman nature."[16] To describe this natural force and to contrast it with the power of Ahab's quest, Melville makes

frequent use of sexual imagery. Newton Arvin and Robert Schulman have pointed out much of this imagery. Arvin notes descriptions of the whale that suggest both male and female sexuality. The spermaceti, the power and strength of the whale, the "battering ram" of the whale's head, and especially the description of the whale's phallus in chapter 95, "The Cassock," suggest the phallic nature of the whale, while the "beautiful" mouth, the "Great Kentucky Mammoth Cave of a stomach," and the obstetric imagery in the description of Queequeg's deliverance of Tashtego suggest the feminine principle.[17] Schulman's article explores the sexual punning in *Moby-Dick,* both the gratuitous punning (such as the references to gentlemen harpooning ladies or the account of Leicester's present to Elizabeth of a "horn, pertaining to a land beast of the unicorn nature") and the sexual word-play that contributes to thematic advancement in the novel. Schulman sees a major purpose of the sexual joking as satiric; it is Melville's way of poking fun at the limitations placed on the artist and the thinker by society:

> Primal, sexual energy is intrinsically subversive of conventional order and of respectable systems. Such energy can be horribly destructive, but it is also essentially creative, since in the natural world it is the source of all life. Ishmael's gigantic sexual pun is thus a perfect vehicle for conveying his radical rejection of conventional systems and their makers. His enormous phallic imagery also embodies Melville's belief that the sources of artistic and sexual creation are closely related. Similarly the very irreverence of his language renders his view of the artist as an independent man in touch with some of the sources of his creativity and at odds with forces which would restrict it.[18]

One can scarcely doubt Melville's satiric purpose in using sexual jokes, but I believe that the sexual imagery serves a more important purpose as well. By describing the enormous white whale in sexual terms that suggest the creative energy in the cosmos, Ishmael contrasts the antagonist effectively and dramatically with Ahab. Ahab is set apart from other men not only by his lack of humanity but also by his lack of sexuality. The loss of a leg suggests castration, as Auden notes; and chapter 106, revealing that the ivory leg pierced Ahab's groin, reinforces that suggestion.[19] The idea of castration serves to emphasize Ahab's estrangement from the vital forces in the universe. Among the many mutilated heroes in Melville's fiction, Ahab and his mutilation are especially significant. He suffered symbolic castration in losing his leg to the whale. Fashioning a mechanical leg to enable him to seek revenge on the whale, he was then symbolically (perhaps actually) castrated again by his contrivance.

In the last six chapters of the novel, as Ahab drives close to the fulfillment of his quest, Ishmael repeatedly describes both the captain and the chase in mechanistic terms. The old man's power holds in check all the natural inclinations of the crew. They are his entirely. Metaphorically, his machinery has overcome their organic nature: "Ahab's purpose now fixedly gleamed down upon the constant midnight of the gloomy crew. It domineered above them so, that all their bodings, doubts, misgivings, fears, were fain to hide beneath their souls, and not to sprout forth a single spear or leaf. . . . Alike, joy and sorrow, hope and fear, seemed ground to finest dust, and powdered, for the time, in the clamped mortar of Ahab's iron soul. Like machines, they dumbly moved about the decks, ever conscious that the old man's despot eye was on them" (pp. 437-438). In the same chapter and again in chapter 132, the image of the blasted or branded tree occurs several times. Ahab neither eats supper nor shaves, and his beard grows "all gnarled, as unearthed roots of trees blown over, which still grow idly on at naked base, though perished in the upper verdure" (p. 438). Lamenting his own loss of humanity, Ahab describes his hair as growing "from out some ashes," and he shakes "like a blighted fruit tree . . . and cast his last, cindered apple to the soil" (p. 444).

Despite Ahab's mechanism and despite his stated desire to be rid of the weakness of humanity, he is human enough to be appalled by what he sees himself becoming. Enough trace of humanity remains to permit him to shed a tear during his conversation with Starbuck. And he apparently has enough feeling left to shudder at the completely mechanical nature of his second mate, Stubb. Stubb was the most easily led, most easily satisfied member of the crew, and he has become the most unfeeling. His levity before a smashed whaleboat startles even Ahab: "What soulless thing is this that laughs before a wreck? Man, man! did I not know thee brave as fearless fire (and as mechanical) I could swear thou wert a poltroon. Groan nor laugh should be heard near a wreck" (p. 452).

The magnetic attraction of Ahab's personality was sufficient to excite the crew about his quest early in the voyage. By the second day of the chase this attraction has transformed the individual men into one working machine which Ahab intends to use to kill the whale:

> They were one man, not thirty. For as the one ship that held them all; though it was put together of all contrasting things—oak, and maple, and pine wood; iron, and pitch, and hemp—yet all these ran into each other in the one concrete hull, which shot on its way, both balanced and directed by the long central keel; even so, all the individualities of the crew, this man's valor, that man's fear; guilt and guiltlessness, all varieties were welded into oneness, and were all directed to that fatal goal which Ahab their one lord and keel did point to.
>
> (pp. 454-455)

On the third and final day of the chase the crew members function like a single mechanical man, of which Ahab is the head. "You are not other men," he tells them, "but my arms and legs" (p. 465). Under his control they continue to drive stubbornly toward certain death. Ahab, says Starbuck, has a "heart of wrought steel" (p. 463) which enables him to ignore sharks and other omens and to enforce the carrying out of the quest. Tashtego's insistent nailing of Ahab's pennant to the masthead even as the ship is sinking illustrates the degree to which Ahab has succeeded in fashioning from thirty men and a ship one machine to do his bidding. Tashtego carries out Ahab's last command to him, "What ho, . . . let me hear thy hammer," in what must be regarded as much more than a case of devotion to duty:

> A red arm and a hammer hovered backwardly uplifted in the open air, in the act of nailing the flag faster and yet faster to the subsiding spar. A sky-hawk that tauntingly had followed the maintruck downwards from its natural home among the stars, pecking at the flag, and incommoding Tashtego there; this bird now chanced to intercept its broad fluttering wing between the hammer and the wood; and simultaneously feeling that ethereal thrill, the submerged savage beneath, in his death-grasp, kept his hammer frozen there; and so the bird of heaven, with archangelic shrieks, and his imperial beak thrust upwards, and his whole captive form folded in the flag of Ahab, went down with the ship, which, like Satan, would not sink to hell till she had dragged a living part of heaven along with her, and helmeted herself with it.
>
> (p. 469)

This is a purely mechanical act, one no mere man would perform. The red arm "nailing the flag faster and yet faster to the subsiding spar" and finally catching the wing of a bird under the hammer in the last second and sinking out of sight seems as non-human as Ahab's artificial leg. In this rich and complex allegorical scene, Melville for the last time portrays the destructive qualities of the machine even as the machine itself is destroyed. The doomed bird, described first as a sky-hawk, then as a "bird of heaven," and finally as a fallen angel, suggests the plight of any man whose "whole captive form" is "folded in the flag of Ahab." Tashtego, with no regard for his own death and no notice of his fellows, acts with the singular purposefulness of a machine. The crewman is so much a part of his commander's quest, so completely one of the "various wheels" fitting Ahab's cogged circle, that he functions like a well-oiled machine part even after the water covers his head.

I do not mean this reading of the mechanistic imagery in the novel as a refutation or a diminution of the importance of other, equally valid approaches to a very complex work. Ahab is a Timon and a Lear; he is a Faust, attended by the Mephisophelean Parsee; he is a Lucifer; he is a Titan. And he is, unquestionably, a machine. Melville associates him consistently and convincingly with mills, trains, generators, and the fires of industry. Ahab is like Timon in his isolation, but Ahab's isolation is due to something worse than mere misanthropy; it is due to misophusism (if I may coin a word that seems to me needed and appropriate): hatred of the natural. A machine is the perfect metaphor to describe Ahab's force, and only in the opposition of the mechanical to the natural could Melville have pictured so powerfully and so perfectly a man waging relentless, mindless war on the essence of life.

Notes

1. *American Renaissance: Art and Expression in the Age of Emerson and Whitman* (New York, 1941), p. 459.

2. "Melville's Isolatoes," *PMLA,* LX (Dec., 1945), 1138-1148. See also "Melville's Sociality," *American Literature,* XVII (March, 1945), 33-49.

3. *Moby-Dick,* ed. Harrison Hayford and Hershel Parker (New York, 1967), p. 452. All references to *Moby-Dick* are to the Norton edition and are hereafter incorporated into the text.

4. *Herman Melville* (New York, 1950), p. 161.

5. "Romanticism and the American Renaissance," *American Literature,* XXIII (Jan., 1951), 419-432.

6. "The Machine in the Garden," *New England Quarterly,* XXIX (March, 1956), 30-31. See also Marx's longer study, *The Machine in the Garden: Technology and the Pastoral Ideal in America* (New York, 1964); and Henry Nash Smith, "The Image of Society in *Moby-Dick,*" Moby-Dick *Centennial Essays,* ed. Tyrus Hillway and Luther S. Mansfield (Dallas, 1953), pp. 59-75.

7. "*Moby-Dick:* Work of Art," Moby-Dick *Centennial Essays,* reprinted in the Norton Critical Edition of *Moby-Dick,* pp. 651-671. Bezanson contrasts Hawthorne's method in *The Scarlet Letter* with Melville's in *Moby-Dick:* "For Hawthorne the structural frame of reference was neoclassical, for Melville it was romantic. . . . To go from *The Scarlet Letter* to *Moby-Dick* is to move from the Newtonian world-as-machine to the Darwinian world-as-organism" (p. 669). See also Matthiessen, p. 385, for the influence of Carlyle on Melville's style. Leon Howard, in *Herman Melville: A Biography* (Berkeley and Los Angeles, 1967), compares Ahab with the Teufelsdröckh of the "Everlasting No" section of *Sartor Resartus.* Howard calls Ahab "a transcendentalist who had not achieved the Everlasting Yea of optimism" (pp. 171, 172).

8. The importance of the organic-mechanistic contrast in defining and commenting on Romanticism has been explored frequently. Among the excellent discussions of Romanticism that deal with the organic concept are:

Howard Mumford Jones, "The Influence of European Ideas in Nineteenth-Century America," *American Literature,* VII (Nov., 1935), 241-273.

A. O. Lovejoy, *The Great Chain of Being* (Cambridge, Mass., 1936). See especially the chapter entitled "Romanticism and Plenitude," pp. 284-314.

René Wellek, "The Concept of Romanticism," *Comparative Literature,* I (Winter, 1949), 1-23, 147-174.

Morse Peckham, "Toward a Theory of Romanticism," *PMLA,* LXVI (March, 1951), 5-23. Reprinted in *The Triumph of Romanticism* (Columbia, S. C., 1970).

M. H. Abrams, *The Mirror and the Lamp: Romantic Theory and the Critical Tradition* (New York, 1958).

9. "An Approach to Melville," *Partisan Review,* XIV (May-June, 1947), 290.

10. *Progress Into Silence: A Study of Melville's Heroes* (Bloomington, Ind., 1970), p. 15.

11. *Ishmael's White World: A Phenomenological Reading of* Moby-Dick (New Haven. 1965), p. 32. See also Marx, "The Machine in the Garden," p. 31.

12. It is interesting that Fedallah, a fire worshiper like Ahab, is described in terms that suggest both the satanic and the mechanic. Stubb calls the Parsee a devil, and he adds, "He's always wanting oakum to stuff into the toes of his boots." According to the mate, Fedallah is trying to exchange Moby Dick for Ahab's "silver watch, or his soul, or something of that sort" (p. 274). The first description of the Parsee and the other stowaways is in mechanistic terms. Fedallah has "steel-like lips," and the strange crew of Ahab's boat operates like a machine: "Those tiger yellow creatures of his seemed all steel and whalebone; like five trip-hammers they rose and fell with regular strokes of strength, which periodically started the boat along the water like a horizontal burst boiler out of a Mississippi steamer" (p. 190).

13. *The Fine Hammered Steel of Herman Melville* (Urbana, Ill., 1957), pp. 241-242.

14. See Auden, *The Enchaféd Flood, or the Romantic Iconography of the Sea* (New York, 1967), p. 119, and Sedgwick, *Herman Melville: The Tragedy of Mind* (New York, 1944), pp. 124-126. R. W. B. Lewis, *The American Adam: Innocence, Tragedy, and Tradition in the Nineteenth Century* (Chicago, 1955), pp. 132-134, provides an interesting treatment of this chapter.

15. *The Vision of Tragedy* (New Haven, 1950), p. 104.

16. "The Function of the Cetological Chapters in *Moby-Dick*," *American Literature,* XXVIII (May, 1956), 170.

17. Arvin [see note 4], pp. 170-175.

18. Schulman, "The Serious Function of Melville's Phallic Jokes," *American Literature,* XXXIII (May, 1961), 187.

19. See Auden, pp. 135-136. See also Arvin, p. 172.

Michael T. Gilmore (essay date 3rd quarter 1975)

SOURCE: Gilmore, Michael T. "Melville's Apocalypse: American Millennialism and *Moby-Dick*." *ESQ: A Journal of the American Renaissance* 21, no. 3 (3rd quarter 1975): 154-61.

[*In the following essay, Gilmore analyzes Ahab's character within the context of nineteenth-century millennialism. Gilmore interprets the novel as Melville's protest against the hypocrisy and self-righteousness of America's "apocalyptic nationalism."*]

Americans have traditionally thought of themselves as a millennial people, the people appointed by God to establish the heavenly kingdom on earth. Apocalyptic expectations did much to shape the outlook of the emigrant Puritans, who firmly believed that they were latter-day Israelites on their way to the new Promised Land. Seeing themselves as God's elect people, they felt they had been called out of England to complete the Reformation and inaugurate the reign of the saints. Edward Johnson, in the first published history of Massachusetts Bay, hailed the colonists as the vanguard of Christendom and boldly proclaimed of New England that "this is the place where the Lord will create a new Heaven, and a new Earth." Jonathan Edwards, writing a century later at the height of the Great Awakening, added his voice to the chorus of native millennialism when he prophesied that the spiritual Sun of Righteousness "will rise in the west, till it shines through the world, like the sun in its meridian brightness." The glorious work begun in America, so Edwards hoped, would radiate across the Atlantic and regenerate the whole human race.[1]

Later commentators increasingly emphasized the political aspects of America's millennial role. On the eve of the Revolution, an obscure Connecticut clergyman named Samuel Sherwood delivered a sermon on the twelfth chapter of Revelation entitled *The Church's Flight into the Wilderness,* in which he identified the British ministry with the forces of darkness. "The time is coming and hastening on," according to Sherwood, "when Babylon the great shall fall to rise no more; when all wicked tyrants and oppressors shall be destroyed for ever." To Timothy Dwight, Sherwood's younger contemporary and the grandson of Edwards, the new Republic was the fifth kingdom predicted in Daniel, the kingdom described by the prophet as spreading throughout the earth:

> A world is thy realm: for a world be thy laws,
> Enlarg'd as thine empire, and just as thy cause;
> On Freedom's broad basis, that empire shall rise,
> Extend with the main, and dissolve with the skies.

For George Bancroft, who espoused an apocalyptic nationalism similar to Dwight's, Jacksonian democracy was the culmination of spiritual progress. Even the Puritans, he claimed, had emigrated in search of a democratic society: "Like the favored evangelist, the exiles, in their western Patmos, listened to the angel that dictated the new gospel of freedom." Chosen race, chosen nation: the United States had a divine calling to diffuse the blessings of liberty and remake the world.[2]

Such was the myth of national destiny which dominated American thought in the nineteenth century and which decisively influenced the work of Herman Melville. It was a myth that Melville both absorbed and radically revised. As his early novels suggest, he was deeply stirred by the hope that America could rid itself of injustice and lead mankind into a new era by fusing democracy with Christian ideals. By the time he wrote *Moby-Dick,* however, Melville's awareness of his country's wrongs had dimmed his faith in its potential as world redeemer. The aggressive millennialism of his compatriots, he now felt, blinded them to their own faults and betrayed the very goal they professed to seek. In his portrait of Ahab, he registered his protest against the imperious messianic pretensions which he saw as perverting the Republic's genuine mission.

Numerous critics have pointed out that the *Pequod* bears a striking resemblance to the American ship of state which plied the oratorical seas in Melville's day.[3] As captain of the *Pequod,* Ahab is entrusted with the fate of the national Israel, and he is himself representative of the chosen people, having wandered for "forty years on the pitiless sea."[4] Potentially, of course, he is also a type of the Savior, since it is from the seed of Israel that the Messiah is born. Melville's contemporaries believed in the messianic role of the American people, and they were persuaded, as he put it in *Mardi,* that history had entered "the last scene of the last act of her drama."[5] As recently as *Redburn,* Melville himself had said of his countrymen that "We are the heirs of all time, and with all nations we divide our inheritance. On this Western Hemisphere all tribes and people are forming into one federated whole; and there is a future which shall see the estranged children of Adam restored as to the old hearth-stone in Eden" (IV, 169). It is hardly surprising, in view of these sentiments, that in *Moby-Dick* Ishmael characterizes the polyglot crew of the *Pequod* as "an Anacharsis Clootz deputation" drawn from all the ends of the earth and "federated along one keel" under the command of an American skipper (p. 108).

It is revealing to recall in this connection the traditional iconography of Christ as a dragon slayer.[6] The Bible speaks of the sea-serpent or Leviathan that will be destroyed on the day of judgment and whose death will deliver the children of Adam from bondage to sin. An illustration is the verse from Isaiah 27 which Melville quotes in the "Extracts": "In that day, the Lord with his sore, and great, and strong sword, shall punish Leviathan the piercing serpent, even Leviathan that crooked serpent; and he shall slay the dragon that is in the sea" (p. 2). The victory over Satan, which restores mankind to Paradise, fulfills God's prophecy in Genesis that the seed of Adam shall bruise the serpent's head. It is a prophecy of special significance for the redeemer nation, and it is cited repeatedly in writings of the emigrant Puritans. Two hundred years before the sailing of the *Pequod,* for example, John Winthrop recorded in his journal that during the synod at Cambridge a snake appeared in the midst of a sermon and was promptly killed by one of the elders. Winthrop interpreted the incident as follows: "The serpent is the devil; the synod, the representative of the churches of Christ in New England. The devil had formerly and lately attempted their disturbance and dissolution; but their faith in the seed of the woman overcame him and crushed his head."[7] The step from Winthrop's confident assertion to Melville's novel is long historically but short in imaginative terms; they draw on a common conception of American destiny. Ahab begins his hunt on December 25th, the date of the Savior's birth, and he is said to have "piled upon the whale's white hump the sum of all the general rage and hate felt by his whole race from Adam down" (p. 160). The God of Genesis declares to the serpent that "thou shalt bruise his heel," and in fulfillment of the prophecy that he would be dismembered, Ahab lost his leg to Moby Dick. "I now prophesy," he vows, "that I will dismember my dismemberer" (p. 147). As he prepares to embark on his millennial quest, the hymn "There is a land of pure delight" rings "full of hope and fruition" through the cold New England air:

> Sweet fields beyond the swelling flood,
>   Stand dressed in living green.
> So to the Jews old Canaan stood,
>   While Jordan rolled between.
>
> (p. 95)

The Canaan of the hymn corresponds to the Promised Land that Christ will conquer for the spiritual Israel by crushing the head of Leviathan.

Melville introduces a number of details to emphasize the parallel between Ahab and Christ, and he takes pains to present his "ungodly, god-like" protagonist in a dramatic and imposing light. Ahab bears a crucifixion in his face, he metaphorically wears the Crown of Lombardy, supposed to contain the nails used in the Cross, and he "lay like dead for three days and nights" after his first encounter with the white whale (p. 87). Impressing upon the "unconscious understandings" of the crew his own vision of Moby Dick as "the gliding great demon of the seas of life," he makes his grievance as real to them as it is to himself (p. 162). He thinks of himself as venturing forth on a mission to destroy "that intangible malignity which has been from the beginning" and which he views as the cause of all bodily and spiritual suffering (p. 160). The reader is encouraged to feel that he acts on behalf of all mankind.

Melville fosters this impression, however, only in order to dramatize the gap between the promise of America and its actual achievement—to hold up the Republic embodied by Ahab as a counterfeit rather than a real Christ. For if Ahab is Christlike, he also resembles the Satan of *Paradise Lost.*[8] In Milton's epic, the Archfiend, who has suffered a mighty woe, is a virtual caricature or parody of the Savior. Intent, like Ahab, on supernatural vengeance, he scorns submission and inspires his followers with the hope of regaining their lost estate. He too undertakes a perilous journey to "seek / Deliverance for us all," and he is hailed by the fallen host as a god "equal to the Highest in Heaven" (II, 464-465, 479). There are also similarities between Ahab and the Beast of Revelation, similarities which are not surprising in view of the American obsession with the quest for the millennium. Even Ahab's apparently fatal injury, from which he revives after three days, can be explained in terms of this identification, for it is stated of the Beast that he "was wounded to death; and his deadly wound was healed" (Rev. 13:3). Again, the Beast opens "his mouth in blasphemy against God, to blaspheme his name" (13:6), while Ahab baptizes his harpoon not in the name of the Father, but in the name of the Devil. What is more striking still, the Beast is reported to do "great wonders, so that he maketh fire come down from heaven on the earth in the sight of men / And deceiveth them that dwell on the earth by *the means of* those miracles . . ." (13:13-14). In the scene with the corposants, Ahab grounds the current and overawes "the enchanted crew" by hurling defiance at the lightning.

One can place these parallels in the most telling perspective by contrasting *Moby-Dick* with the first book of *The Faerie Queene,* where Spenser presents the story of St. George and the dragon as an allegory of the imitation of Christ. The contrast is implicit in the novel, for Ishmael includes St. George in his roster of illustrious whalemen, insisting that the dragon was "no other than the great Leviathan himself" (p. 305). As depicted by Spenser, St. George is the representative hero of the

English people. Insofar as he conforms to the image of Christ, he achieves salvation, and through him the nation at large fulfills its destiny as the new Israel. This outcome is assured by his defeat of the monster in the ferocious three-day battle which clearly prefigures the Savior's ultimate conquest of Satan. In the case of *Moby-Dick,* where the result is exactly the opposite, Ahab is shown to resemble his enemy. He conforms to the image not of the Savior but rather of the thing that he hunts.[9]

If the redeemer nation, in the person of Ahab, accordingly imitates Satan, it is because Ahab himself fails to profit from the example of Adam—as it is found, once again, in *Paradise Lost.* The Adam of Milton's epic appeases God's anger by acknowledging his own complicity in the Fall. He repents and is spread the fate of Satan, who knows himself to be damned but blames only God for his misery. As for Ahab, he too is damned, and damned, as he expresses it, "most subtly and most malignantly! damned in the midst of Paradise" (p. 147). Charles Olson once remarked that "the conflict in Ahab's world is abrupt, more that between Satan and Jehovah, of the old dispensation than the new."[10] It is a world of hunter and hunted, bereft of forgiveness, where a wrathful Deity is chiefly known by his rod. What is important to realize, however, is that it is a world of Ahab's own making. His quest is doomed to disaster because its object is really himself: like an unrepentant Adam, he "is very much his own Satan and his own vengeful God."[11] In *Mardi* Melville cautioned his countrymen that "all evils can not be done away. For evil is the chronic malady of the universe; and checked in one place, breaks forth in another" (III, 529). It is well to remember this caveat when Ishmael states that "all evil, to crazy Ahab, were visibly personified, and made practically assailable in Moby Dick" (p. 160). What Ahab is unable to see is that the evil he externalizes in the whale also exists in himself. As his likeness to the "white fiend" confirms, he is thoroughly implicated in "that intangible malignity" he hopes to destroy. It is his blindness that ultimately damns him—unlike Oedipus, for instance, who is humbled in his blindness and learns to see. Interestingly enough, Ahab suffers a literal attack of blindness and learns to see. Interestingly enough, Ahab suffers a literal attack of blindness moments before his death, crying out as Moby Dick bears down on the ship: "I grow blind; hands! stretch out before me that I may yet grope my way. Is't night?" (p. 467). The parallel to Oedipus appears to have been quite deliberate on Melville's part. In 1849 he purchased an edition of Sophocles,[12] and he wrote into *Moby-Dick* a chapter entitled "The Sphinx." It was Oedipus, of course, who solved the riddle of the sphinx, the answer to which was man. Moreover, he is lame like Ahab, and it turns out that the murderer he seeks is himself.

But the world of Ahab does not exhaust the world of *Moby-Dick.* Ishmael's narrative encompasses other worlds as well: he himself, as his name indicates, is excluded from God's covenant with Israel. His story can be read as a form of spiritual autobiography, with the life of the individual recapitulating in miniature the drama of paradise lost and regained. The novel opens, accordingly, with a reference to the "thieves" in the garden, and it terminates in the unmistakable accents of Revelation. Accounting for his wish to go whaling, Ishmael confides that the "portentous and mysterious monster roused all my curiosity" (p. 16). He is clearly a type of postlapsarian man who voyages in search of the knowledge of good and evil, which is also the knowledge of the self. He first beholds Moby Dick, after all, in his innermost soul, "one grand hooded phantom, like a snow hill in the air" (p. 16).

It is no small part of Ishmael's search that he must come to terms with Ahab and the "power of blackness" that Ahab represents—that power which Melville admired in the stories of Hawthorne and which his contemporaries seemed determined to ignore.[13] As it happens, Ishmael does at first try to discount the dark side by suppressing his forebodings with respect to the voyage. What he learns at sea, however, is that the old Adam cannot be denied. "Ahab's quenchless feud seemed mine," he confesses, adding that he listened with avidity to "the history of that murderous monster against whom I and all the others had taken our oaths of violence and revenge" (p. 155). Seeing "naught in that brute but the deadliest ill" (p. 163), regarding Moby Dick as the symbol of all that appalls and torments the soul of man, he abandons himself to the fiery quest.

Ishmael differs from Ahab, however, in his understanding that the savagery of nature corresponds to the savagery of the self. Man's capacity for violence and butchery, he realizes, is fully the equal of that of his prey. He speaks, for example, of "the universal cannibalism of the sea" (p. 235), a cannibalism from which the whalemen are by no means exempt, and he characterizes the *Pequod,* manned by savages and freighted with a burning corpse, as "the material counterpart of her monomaniac commander's soul" (p. 354). He is a killer and savage himself, he says elsewhere, "owing no allegiance but to the King of Cannibals" (p. 232), and in the chapter called "Stubb's Supper," where the second mate dines on a whale-steak while the dead whale is devoured by hundreds of sharks, he spells out the fundamental equivalence between the sharkishness of nature and the voracity of man. Fleece, the black cook, speaking with Ishmael's (and Melville's) approval, draws the appropriate conclusion: do not disown complicity in evil, but rather "gobern dat wicked natur . . . for all angel is not'ing more dan de shark well goberned."[14]

Once made aware of his own involvement in a fallen world, Ishmael is reconciled to his fellow men. Whereas

Ahab, in his blindness and pride, can only regret all "mortal inter-indebtedness" as a curse, Ishmael abjures his vow of vengeance in favor of brotherly love. Equally important are the political implications of his growth in self-knowledge, since for Melville democracy, like brotherhood, is anchored in an acceptance of the fallible nature of man—is impossible, indeed, without a conviction of "that Calvinistic sense of Innate Depravity and Original Sin" of which he wrote in his famous review of the *Mosses* [Hawthorne's *Mosses from an Old Manse*]. Apropos of the "deeply thinking" Hawthorne, for whom truth is inseparable from the "blackness of darkness," Melville says that his fiction is informed by that democratic spirit which is America's boon to the world. The same spirit infuses Ishmael's apostrophe to "The Great God Absolute! The centre and circumference of all democracy! His omnipresence, our divine equality!" Ishmael mentions Bunyan, Cervantes, and Andrew Jackson as exemplifying the "high qualities" with which the God of democracy invests the common man, and he calls upon the "just Spirit of Equality" to vindicate his presentation of Ahab, a lowly whale-hunter, as a subject commensurate in dignity with royalty and kings (pp. 104-105, 130). But Ishmael's democratic creed is betrayed rather than realized by Ahab, who sets himself up as an actual emperor in the American Israel and who is variously described as a mogul, autocrat, czar, and sultan. This side of his character is closely related to his identification with the Beast of the Apocalypse. For in John's vision the Beast has the power to reign over the earth and to terrorize nations; and the number of the Beast "is the number of a man; and his number is Six hundred threescore *and* six" (Rev. 13:18)—the sum of the numerical values of the Hebrew letters for Nero Caesar. In *Mardi* Melville ascribed to the natives of Vivenza (the United States) the conceit that their country was destined to establish a permanent and universal republic. In *Moby-Dick,* however, the American ship of state is commanded by a tyrant rather than a democrat.

And so it is fitting that Ahab, the would-be Messiah turned Caesar, spurns the plea for assistance by the *Rachel.* For the ship's namesake is the scriptural mother of Israel, a type of the true church whose marriage to Christ traditionally follows the final defeat of Leviathan. It is with considerable irony, therefore, that Melville describes the subsequent three-day chase in terms more appropriate to rape than to marriage. He compares Moby Dick, for example, to "the white bull Jupiter swimming away with ravished Europa clinging to his graceful horns; his lovely leering eyes sideways intent upon the maid" (p. 447). The quest that was to have inaugurated the apocalyptic union of heaven and earth comes to its end in a violent sexual assault. This climactic encounter gains in significance from Ishmael's characterization of Ahab as an "ungodly old man, chasing with curses a Job's whale round the world" (p.

162). It is Christ in his second coming who will fulfill the prophecy in Job 41 which Ishmael paraphrases with reference to an ulcerous sperm whale:

> Is this the creature of whom it was once so triumphantly said—'Canst thou fill his skin with barbed irons? or his head with fish-spears? The sword of him that layeth at him cannot hold, the spear, the dart, nor the habergeon: he esteemeth iron as straw; the arrow cannot make him flee; darts are counted as stubble; he laugheth at the shaking of a spear!'

> (p. 300)

The relevance of this prophecy to Ahab is confirmed by the fact that the white whale he hunts is introduced in the forty-first chapter of the novel. But whereas Christ will triumph on the day of judgment by putting a hook in the nostrils of Satan, Ahab fails to slay Moby Dick. The last words he speaks before he is dragged to his death are *"Thus,* I give up the spear!" (p. 468).

Only Ishmael, the outcast son of Abraham, escapes with his life in the demonic apocalypse that engulfs the *Pequod.* Since the ship itself is said to resemble its prey, and since Ahab is accounted "a great lord of Leviathans" (p. 114), Ishmael's survival on the third day of the chase may be seen as a symbolic rebirth from the belly of the whale. In this respect he invites comparison to Jonah, and he may be regarded as a type of the Savior himself, a detail which imparts special meaning to his eventual rescue by the *Rachel.* For Melville's objective in *Moby-Dick* is nothing less than to rewrite the covenant that God was presumed to have made with the American people as the heirs of the biblical Hebrews. According to Genesis, Ishmael and his mother Hagar were banished to the wilderness, and they were pointedly left out of God's covenant with Israel. The twelfth chapter of Revelation deals with a woman and a male child who flee into the wilderness to avoid the dragon. They are interpreted in Reformed theology as Rachel and the promised seed. Melville's startling revision consists in the fact that Hagar and Ishmael, who according to orthodoxy exemplify the gentiles, are made into types of the spiritual Israel. Thus the covenant forsaken by the nation at large survives in the person of Melville's fictional hero. And it is fitting that the "Epilogue" to the novel shows the influence of millennial prophecy, since for Ishmael at least paradise is figuratively regained. It is regained, that is, only in vision— regained because Ishmael realizes, as Ahab never does, that evil is intrinsic to the human condition and that destiny, as Melville suggested in *Mardi,* "is best served, by waiting events" (III, 530). As he floats away from the wreck on Queequeg's coffin, whose hieroglyphic markings contain an apocalyptic "theory of the heavens and earth, and a mystical treatise on the art of attaining truth" (p. 399), Ishmael watches the "unharming sharks" glide by "as if with padlocks on their mouths; the savage sea-hawks sailed with sheathed beaks" (p. 470). It is a common theme in the Old Testament, as well as in the millennial writings of divines such as Edwards, that in the kingdom to come the beasts of prey will be transformed into peaceable creatures. By virtue of his redemption, in short, Ishmael figures as the saving remnant, a concept that the emigrant Puritans were wont to apply to themselves. There is this crucial difference, however: in *Moby-Dick* the dreaded judgment befalls America rather than England.

It befalls America, that is, because the redeemer nation has become indistinguishable from Babylon, the historical oppressor of the chosen people. There are innumerable hints to this effect, and they build inexorably as the *Pequod* plunges on to its doom. The biblical Ahab introduced the worship of Baal into Israel, and the scholarship of Melville's day equated the Tyrian Baal with the Babylonian Bel.[15] The Ahab of the novel is compared to King Belshazzar, and the fate of his ship is directly connected to the judgment on Babylon. It is said of Moby Dick, for example, that he is regularly sighted at a "set time and place," the Season-on-the-Line, much "as the sun, in its annual round, loiters for a predicted interval in any one sign of the Zodiac" (p. 173). The Line, of course, denotes the equator, and it may be inferred from the zodiac inscribed on the doubloon that the sign in question is Libra or the scales. Also pictured on the coin, which comes from Ecuador, the country named for the equator, are three summits or peaks which Ahab sees as himself and which suggest the three masts of the *Pequod*. Starbuck, who observes Ahab studying the coin, makes the portentous comment that "the old man seems to read Belshazzar's awful writing" (p. 360), an allusion to the prophecy in Daniel 5 foretelling the destruction of Babylon. Since the *Pequod* does in fact meet Moby Dick on the Line, as Ahab knows it will, and since Melville makes a point of quoting Daniel's warning verbatim in connection with the corposants, it seems clear that the scales of Libra signify the balances in which the Babylonian kingdom was weighed and found wanting. Ahab's dying speech is a forceful reminder of the coin with its fateful inscription, for he refers to the masts of his foundering ship as "ye three unsurrendered spires of mine" (p. 468).

The fact that the *Pequod* sinks "to hell" under "the great shroud of the sea" suggests still another scriptural authority for the judgment on Babylon (p. 469): the Book of Jeremiah. Ahab has flouted the God of democracy by instituting tyranny over the crew. He has callously rejected the appeal by the *Rachel,* whose biblical namesake is imagined by Jeremiah to weep for the children of Israel as they pass on their way toward Babylon. Thus Ahab is associated not only with King Belshazzar but also with Nebuchadnezzar, who destroyed the Temple and carried off the Jews into captivity and exile. The ship he commands suffers the identical fate

that Jeremiah prophesied for the conqueror of Israel: "The sea is come up upon Babylon: she is covered with the multitude of the waves thereof" (51:42).

But it is more than the Old Testament Babylon that concerns Melville in *Moby-Dick;* for there is a Babylon in the New Testament as well. It appears in Revelation, where it is the antithesis of the New Jerusalem, and it is ruled by the Beast or the Antichrist. The Beast, of course, is the dragon of Revelation 12, and he is in pursuit of the woman and child who figure for Melville as the *Rachel* and Ishmael. Not only, then, is the United States identified with the ancient empire that enslaved the Jews, but it is also linked to the mystical Babylon, the city which epitomizes wickedness in John's vision of the Apocalypse. Far from ushering in Christ's kingdom on earth, the redeemer nation, as symbolized by the *Pequod,* meets with the very disaster which is prophesied for Babylon by John: "And a mighty angel took up a stone like a great millstone, and *cast* it into the sea, saying, Thus with violence shall that great city Babylon be thrown down, and shall be found no more at all" (18:21). It can hardly have escaped Melville's notice that the judgment on the mystical Babylon corresponds exactly to the fall which Jeremiah foresaw for the Babylon of old.

The foremost student of Melville's use of the Bible has argued persuasively that the conception of the prophet which underlies Father Mapple's sermon derives more from Jeremiah than Jonah.[16] Jeremiah was called by the Lord to prophesy against Israel, and he was vilified and imprisoned by his countrymen for daring to denounce their transgressions. In the words of the minister, he preached "the Truth to the face of Falsehood!" (p. 50). As such, as a "pilot-prophet, or speaker of true things," he inevitably suggests Melville's view of the artist as it appears in his essay on the *Mosses.* He suggests as well Melville's narrator Ishmael, who escapes "alone to tell" (p. 470) the story of the *Pequod* and whose vision of inner-worldly sainthood closely approximates Hawthorne's. Melville dedicated *Moby-Dick* to his fellow author, and rather like the narrator of "The Custom-House," his own narrator dons a veil by inviting us to call him Ishmael. For there can be no full "revelation" in "this world of lies," Father Mapple's sermon to the contrary notwithstanding. Ishmael quotes the minister as saying that woe is "to him who, as the great Pilot Paul has it, while preaching to others is himself a castaway" (p. 50). It is Ishmael himself who preaches the truth as a castaway, and who consequently knows the "wisdom that is woe" (p. 355). Certainly there is little reason to believe that his words will be taken to heart by his unheeding countrymen—a likelihood confirmed by the novel's concluding sentence, which again recalls Jeremiah: "It was the devious-cruising Rachel, that in her retracing search after her missing children, only found another orphan." Ishmael, as the solitary heir to the covenant, can only be an orphan in an America which has deserted its principles and turned a deaf ear to its speakers of truth.

Notes

1. J. Franklin Jameson, ed., *Johnson's Wonder-Working Providence* (New York: Barnes & Noble, 1959), p. 25; Jonathan Edwards, *Thoughts on the Revival of Religion in New England,* in *The Great Awakening,* ed. C. C. Goen (New Haven: Yale Univ. Press, 1972), p. 357.

2. Samuel Sherwood, *The Church's Flight into the Wilderness* (New York, 1776), p. 49; Timothy Dwight, "Columbia," in Vernon Louis Parrington, ed., *The Connecticut Wits* (Hamden, Conn.: Archon Books, 1963), p. 273; George Bancroft, *History of the United States* (Boston: Little, Brown, 1841), II, 454. My understanding of American millennialism has been especially aided by the following studies: Loren Baritz, *City on a Hill: A History of Ideas and Myths in America* (New York: John Wiley & Sons, 1964); Sacvan Bercovitch, *Horologicals and Chronometricals: The Rhetoric of the Jeremiad,* in Eric Rothstein, ed., *Literary Monographs* (Madison: Univ. of Wisconsin Press, 1970), III, 3-124; Charles L. Sanford, *The Quest for Paradise: Europe and the American Moral Imagination* (Urbana: Univ. of Illinois Press, 1961); and Ernest Lee Tuveson, *Redeemer Nation: The Idea of America's Millennial Role* (Chicago: Univ. of Chicago Press, 1968).

3. See in particular Alan Heimert, "*Moby-Dick* and American Political Symbolism," *American Quarterly,* 15 (1963), 498-534.

4. Harrison Hayford and Hershel Parker, eds., *Moby-Dick* (New York: Norton, 1967), p. 443. All quotations are from this edition; page references are cited in the text.

5. *The Writings of Herman Melville* (Evanston and Chicago: Northwestern Univ. Press and the Newberry Library, 1970), III, 525. Further references to this edition will be cited by volume and page number in the text.

6. Here I am indebted to the discussion of *Paradise Regained* in Northrop Frye, *The Return of Eden: Five Essays on Milton's Epics* (Toronto: Univ. of Toronto Press, 1965), pp. 118-143.

7. James Kendall Hosmer, ed., *Winthrop's Journal: "History of New England"* (New York: Barnes & Noble, 1966), II, 347-348.

8. The most thorough treatment of Melville's knowledge of Milton is Henry F. Pommer, *Milton and Melville* (Pittsburgh: Univ. of Pittsburgh Press,

1950). See in particular pp. 92-104. R. W. B. Lewis briefly discusses Ahab as the Antichrist in his essay "Days of Wrath and Laughter" which appears in *Trials of the Word: Essays in American Literature and the Humanistic Tradition* (New Haven: Yale Univ. Press, 1965), p. 208.

9. The resemblance between Ahab and the whale has often been noted, most recently by Richard Slotkin, *Regeneration Through Violence: The Mythology of the American Frontier, 1600-1860* (Middletown, Conn.: Wesleyan Univ. Press, 1973), p. 545.

10. Charles Olson, *Call Me Ishmael* (San Francisco: City Lights Books, 1947), p. 53.

11. The phrase is used by Lowry Nelson, Jr., in speaking of the monster in *Frankenstein.* See "Night Thoughts on the Gothic Novel," *The Yale Review,* 52 (1963), 247.

12. Merton M. Sealts, Jr., *Melville's Reading: A Check-List of Books Owned and Borrowed* (Madison: Univ. of Wisconsin Press, 1966), entry no. 147.

13. See Melville's review of "Hawthorne and His Mosses," conveniently reprinted in the Norton edition of *Moby-Dick,* pp. 535-551.

14. P. 251. For a more extensive analysis of Fleece's sermon, see Robert Zoellner, *The Salt-Sea Mastodon: A Reading of* Moby-Dick (Berkeley: Univ. of California Press, 1973), pp. 219-225.

15. See the "Explanatory Notes" by Luther S. Mansfield and Howard P. Vincent to the Hendricks House edition of *Moby-Dick* (New York, 1952), pp. 637, 654.

16. Nathalia Wright, *Melville's Use of the Bible* (rev. ed., New York: Octagon Books, 1969), pp. 82 ff.

Bert Bender (essay date fall 1978)

SOURCE: Bender, Bert. "*Moby-Dick,* an American Lyrical Novel." *Studies in the Novel* 10, no. 3 (fall 1978): 346-56.

[*In the following essay, Bender examines the novel's lyric qualities. Bender argues that Melville's attitude toward his art is fundamentally religious in nature.*]

"Dissect him how I may, then, I but go skin deep; I know him not, and never will."

Ishmael

Among the countless critical efforts to "know" **Moby-Dick,** those that have lanced closest to "the innermost life of the fish" have praised its deep poetic nature.[1]

These tributes range from Alfred Kazin's description of the novel's "poetic power" and Richard Chase's praise of "Melville the unsurpassable poet" to F. O. Matthiessen's more technical analysis of the Shakespearean influence on *Moby-Dick*'s language.[2] There is no question that *Moby-Dick* contains some of America's most impressive poetry. Yet there is still plenty of sea room in which to pursue the book's elusive but truly poetic nature as a whole. My proposition is that the best way to catch sight of *Moby-Dick*'s poetic wholeness is to approach it as a kind of lyrical novel whose form and organization derive from the psychological attitude Melville assumed in struggling to compose it.

Moby-Dick's essential lyricism is not fully appreciable simply through analysis of the technically "poetic" qualities of its language—e.g., its richness of rhythm, sound, or imagery: "lyric" and "poetic" are slippery and scarcely synonymous terms. And while most of the qualities that are now frequently associated with the lyric genre are to be found in *Moby-Dick* ("brevity, metrical coherence, subjectivity, passion, sensuality, and particularity of image"[3]), its lyricism is most deeply related to the origins of the lyric mode in ancient religious practices and to contemporary definitions of genres that focus on the artist's attitude toward his creation. According to such definitions, James Joyce, for example, sees the lyric as a personal utterance; Northrop Frye, in defining genres according to "the radical of presentation," sees the lyric as a form in which the poet turns his back on his audience and pretends "to be talking to someone else: a spirit of nature, a Muse . . . , a personal friend, a lover, a god, a personified abstraction, or a natural object"; and, more precisely to my point here, André Gide defines "lyricism as a state in which man allows himself to surrender to God."[4] *Moby-Dick* is obviously so protean as to defy absolute classification, but in its wholeness it comes to us most deeply as a religious lyric in which Melville finds and surrenders to his "God."

A theory of *The Lyrical Novel* has been provided, of course, by Ralph Freedman, who briefly mentions *Moby-Dick* as an example of the genre.[5] But, while Freedman's theory provides a general basis for discerning the nature of lyrical fiction, it is concerned with European and British literary traditions (offering detailed studies of Hesse, Gide, and Woolf), and does not adequately (because it does not intend to) account for the peculiar lyrical quality of *Moby-Dick*. According to Freedman, the essence of lyrical narrative is "a mood, a type of literary sensibility, a way of approaching knowledge," all of which is manifested in a particular work when "the world is reduced to *a* lyrical point of view, the equivalent of the poet's 'I': the lyrical self" (pp. 3-4, 8). This much of *The Lyrical Novel* helps explain the dynamics of *Moby-Dick*; but, devoted as it is to studies of Hesse, Gide, and Woolf, Freedman's analysis emphasizes formal aesthetics and techniques which do not characterize Melville. The "techniques" and "poetic effects" of the lyrical writers discussed by Freedman result in the transformation of their perceptions into "networks of images" or "designs" or "patterns of imagery," in short, "portraiture, the halting of the flow of time within constellations of images or figures" (p. 273). But the lyrical techniques of Hesse, Gide, and Woolf (as described by Freedman) are as foreign to Melville as his sensibility is to theirs. Thus, while the authors of *Moby-Dick* and, for example, *The Waves* might share a mood or "way of approaching knowledge" that is generally lyrical, a good deal remains to be said about how *Moby-Dick*'s lyricism is uniquely Melvillean and American.

The critical debate that tends to see either Ahab or Ishmael as the book's dominating consciousness has obscured what Freedman would call the lyrical "I" or the poet's (Melville's) mask in *Moby-Dick.* First Ahab and then, more recently, Ishmael have been taken as the dominating force in *Moby-Dick*; and, partly because Ahab and Ishmael are so different, many have concluded that the book as a whole lacks resolution. C. Hugh Holman, for example, has written that the book's "major weakness" is that "Ahab's story was Shakespearean and Ishmael's Dantesque"; the "imperfect fusion" of these "two elements" results from "Melville's having written the book on two different levels at two different times" and from his "ignorance of the importance of precisely defining the relation of the narrator to the story he narrates."[6] A more helpful analysis of the Ishmael/Ahab struggle is provided by Charles Feidelson, who feels that Ishmael is more than a mere "surrogate for an absentee author" but Melville's *Doppelgänger,* as well. But Feidelson concludes that the "obvious dilemma" in *Moby-Dick* is not resolved because "Melville has not resolved it for himself": Melville "discovers that he is potentially an Ahab, the devil's partisan, the nihilist," as well as an Ishmael, "the voyaging mind, the capacity for vision."[7]

My own interpretation of this dilemma is that, both before and after the composition of *Moby-Dick,* Melville struggled with the conflicting moods that he dramatized in 1850-51 as Ishmael and Ahab. Melville was neither Ahab nor Ishmael, simply, as we see in his famous letters to Hawthorne during this period, where both moods are evident. In *Moby-Dick* he managed momentarily to resolve this conflict in the same way that John Donne could temporarily resolve his own inner conflict in the Holy Sonnets—by dramatizing a colloquy between his conflicting selves within a single piece. Obviously, *Moby-Dick* and Donne's Holy Sonnets are more than just centuries apart; my comparison is intended to show only that in each we see the projected inner drama of the author's struggle to subdue his doubt and maintain his faith. In each case, the doubting or diabolic self is fully admitted into the dramatized struggle in order that it can be subdued at least momentarily. Thus Melville brings to life and dramatizes the full force of Ahab in order to purge it from himself; and Donne, in "Death Be Not Proud," for example, addresses "Death" directly in order that it be defeated within the meditation, which ends, "Death thou shalt die"; or he can, within other sonnets, affirm that, "to vex me, contraryes meete in one," or that "black sinne hath betraid to endlesse night/My worlds both parts"—only to imagine a cessation: "To morrow I quake with true feare of his rod," or "burne me ô Lord, with a fiery zeale."[8]

The psychology of creation involved in *Moby-Dick* and the Holy Sonnets is certainly more complex than the description I offer here, which is meant to comprehend the creative process on only one level. Other related but deeper and more complex psychological forces at work in *Moby-Dick* have been described in many famous Freudian and Jungian interpretations.[9] But my purpose here is to argue that the dramatized resolution of conflicting selves is part of the religious attitude assumed by Melville in composing *Moby-Dick*, and that this attitude determines its genre—a kind of lyrical novel in which Melville "allows himself to surrender to God." It would be foolish to insist that *Moby-Dick* is nothing but a lyrical novel, but in this religious sense it is akin to the lyrical genre which, as Frye has suggested, "is to *epos*, rhetorically, as prayer is to sermon. The radical of presentation in the lyric is the hypothetical form of what in religion is called the 'I-Thou' relationship."[10] But the question is, how does this all work in *Moby-Dick*; what is the nature of Melville's "God"; and where can he be seen surrendering to this "God"?

That Melville was powerfully influenced by the Bible and that he believed in "God," there is no doubt; nor is there any doubt that his attitude toward Christianity and his concept of God fluctuated with his moods throughout his life. His religious meditations were far too restless, complex, and doubt-ridden to allow his fixed belief in anything (particularly in any institution or dogma), or our efforts to systematize them. As Hawthorne wrote of him (after their visit in Liverpool, where Melville had stopped on his way to the Holy Land in 1856), "He can neither believe, nor be comfortable in his unbelief; and he is too honest and courageous not to try to do one or the other."[11] But his struggle with belief and his fluctuating attitudes toward "God" are due largely to the options that his culture made available to him, i.e., to particular definitions of the nature of God. If he was an "Accuser of the Deity," as William Braswell has argued, it is in the sense that he denied the Christian concept of a "wholly benevolent Deity";[12] and if he can be said to have "hated" God, as Lawrence Thompson has argued, it was for similar reasons.[13] Melville's main quarrel was not with God but with particular definitions of God. Certainly, this is the sense of his remark to Hawthorne: "Yes, that world [God] is the

hangman. Take God out of the dictionary, and you would have Him in the street."[14] Indeed, the most compelling attribute of Melville's God is His ambiguousness, even more than His terrifying power. For, as Nathalia Wright has concluded in *Melville's Use of the Bible,* he may be considered to have shared "the great tragic tradition of the Hebrews, who regarded the creation, for all its mystery and terror, as the garment of Jehovah."[15] Like the Hebrews, for whom "this world was vague," Melville believed that "the primal truth" was represented not by "order, rhetoric, and logic," but by "elemental and undisciplined energy" (p. 184).

We are therefore allowed only glimpses of Melville's "God" as he is imagined in various guises throughout the book—e.g., the Old Testament God invoked by Father Mapple; the "great democratic God" (invoked in "Knights and Squires"); the tolerator of voracious sharkishness (as in "Stubb's Supper" and "The Whale as a Dish"); the pagan "Yojo" through whom Queequeg "gave up his life into the hands of his gods" (in "The Monkey-Rope"); the seductive god . . . Pan" (in "The Pacific"); or the ubiquitous Moby Dick himself. But these accumulated glimpses are subsumed in a Godhead who, as in Isaiah, could declare, "I form the light, and create darkness: I make peace, and create evil: I the LORD do all these *things*" (Isa. 45:7). In *Moby-Dick* the presence of this kind of vague and dreadful God is explicit in passages where Melville addresses "God." And such a presence is implied throughout the book in general by Melville's Biblical language; his countless direct and indirect references to the Old Testament; his cast of such Old Testament names as Ishmael, Jonah, Job, or Ahab; and by the almost complete omission of any mention of Christ, who had figured so strongly in *White Jacket* (1850) and in whose image Melville cast Hawthorne in **"Hawthorne and His Mosses"** (1850). Further, the pervasive presence of a vague and awesome Godhead—the creator of light *and* dark—is the source of one of *Moby-Dick*'s deepest aesthetic principles: its sense of balance. The contrasting but complementary personalities of Ishmael and Ahab; the imaged balance in "The Mast-head," "A Right Whale Killed" (the *Pequod* regaining "her even keel" by counterpoising the hoisted sperm whale's head with that of the right whale—Kant balancing out Locke), and "The Monkey-Rope" (the civilized Ishmael again wedded with the primitive Queequeg); and the image of the Catskill Eagle diving and soaring: these are the products of a mind that, in projecting a sublimely balanced creation, can balance within itself "doubts of all things earthly, and intuitions of some things heavenly" (p. 314). But finally, a vague, all-encompassing God is present in *Moby-Dick* as the cause of the book's innumerable lyric flights, its wondering meditations on the sea and the soul, life, and death. In such lyric passages, as Gide might have remarked, Melville surrenders to his God, at once resolving his own inner conflict and realizing the means of Ishmael's survival.

These lyric passages comprise a large part of **Moby-Dick,** and many have been quoted at length by critics like Richard Chase in his tribute to Melville's "incomparable discoveries of language."[16] Often, they exist as small chapters characterized by a "wavelike amplification and building-up, followed by the lyric subsidence at the end" (Ibid., p. 52). One recalls, for example, the chapter "Nantucket," which sings "in Bible language" of the heroic Nantucketers, conquerors of the "watery world," and builds toward its quotable end: "With the landless gull, that at sunset folds her wings and is rocked to sleep between billows; so at nightfall, the Nantucketer, out of sight of land, furls his sails, and lays him to his rest, while under his very pillow rush herds of walruses and whales." And—to recall just a few more—there are memorable lyric passages in such chapters as "The Lee Shore," a commemoration of Bulkington's "ocean-perishing" and a celebration of the sea, where "alone resides the highest truth, shoreless, indefinite as God"; or "Knights and Squires," with its memorable tribute to "that democratic dignity which, on all hands, radiates without end from God; Himself! The great God absolute!"; or "The Mast-head," which depicts the mast-head's dreamy, dangerous loss of identity as, swayed aloft by "the inscrutable tides of God," he "takes the mystic ocean at his feet for the visible image of that deep, blue, bottomless soul, pervading mankind and nature"; or in such other chapters as "The Whiteness of the Whale," "Brit," "The Fountain," "The Grand Armada," "The Castaway," "A Squeeze of the Hand," "The Pacific," "The Blacksmith," and "The Gilder."

In these passages Melville confronts some thought or natural phenomenon which he finds rationally impenetrable and which elicits his characteristic response of lyric wonder. Thus, while he may begin such a passage by bidding us to "consider" a particular phenomenon, he ends in a lyric, awe-struck expression of wonder or amazement, a surrender to an unfathomable God whose presence he affirms. Confronted with the blank fact of whiteness, for example, he knows that "to analyze it, would seem impossible," for, among other things, it is "the very veil of the Christian's Deity" (pp. 166, 169). His response to the first albatross he ever saw is a model of this kind of experience: "At intervals, it arched forth its vast archangel wings, as if to embrace some holy ark. Wondrous flutterings and throbbings shook it. . . . As Abraham before the angels, I bowed myself" (p. 165). Or, again, contemplating similarly amazing phenomena, his response is to exclaim, "what are the comprehensible terrors of man compared with the interlinked terrors and wonders of God!" (p. 99). **Moby-Dick**'s ultimate values are evident in these submissive

lyric responses: the wondrous creation that they acknowledge, and the very capacity to *have* such responses—to make such gestures of faith. Decidedly, these are not Ahab's values, of whom Stubb said, "'I never yet saw him kneel'" (p. 197); but they give **Moby-Dick** its orientation, its sense of balance.

This posture of reverence and submission implies a kind of faith that many readers of Melville will not accept. But, always a pressing subject for Melville, the question of faith or confidence exists at the very heart of **Moby-Dick** in a way that distinguishes Melville's mood of 1850-51 from that darker one of 1857, for example, when he published **The Confidence-Man.** It is appropriate in **Moby-Dick** that Ishmael raises the question of faith in "The Chapel," where, contemplating the marble tablets that honored lost whaling men, he is moved to one of his first extended lyric expressions:

> Oh! ye whose dead lie buried beneath the green grasses; who standing among flowers can say—here, *here* lies my beloved; ye know not the desolation that broods in bosoms like these. What bitter blanks in those black-bordered marbles which cover no ashes! What despair in those immovable inscriptions! What deadly voids and unbidden infidelities in the lines that seem to gnaw upon all Faith, and refuse resurrections to the beings who have placelessly perished without a grave. As well might those tablets stand in the cave of Elephanta as here.
>
> (p. 41)

But, midway through this meditation, Ishmael turns from seeing Faith as gnawed upon by the fact of death to assert that "Faith, like a jackal, feeds among the tombs, and even from these dead doubts she gathers her most vital hope." Then, admitting that "there is death in this business of whaling—a speechlessly quick chaotic bundling of a man into Eternity," he goes on to think that "we have hugely mistaken this matter of Life and Death. . . . [W]hat they call my shadow here on earth is my true substance." "Therefore," he concludes, "come a stove boat and stove body when they will, for stave my soul, Jove himself cannot."

Exuberant as such moments are, it should be clear that Ishmael's is scarcely a blind faith. He maintains it with a certain willfulness, as Starbuck does when gazing into the sea: "'Loveliness unfathomable, as ever lover saw in his young bride's eye!—Tell me not of thy teeth-tiered sharks, and thy kidnapping cannibal ways. Let faith oust fact; let fancy oust memory; I look deep down and do believe'" (p. 406). The key to Ishmael's faith is that, while he has his doubts along with his divine intuitions, he can sense the inadequacy of reason and willfully suspend his doubts. This spiritual sense of balance distinguishes him from Ahab, whose willfully inverted faith *is* blind. Ahab finds only "tarnished" treasure when he gazes into the same sea that inspired

Starbuck to affirm his faith; and, later, he mocks the carpenter (at work on Ishmael's means of salvation, the life-buoy coffin): "'Faith? What's that?'" (p. 432). Ishmael's opposite, Ahab willfully denies any "intuitions of things heavenly" and therefore has nothing to balance his own "prouder, if . . . darker faith" (p. 409).

The question of faith, then, deeply underlies this whole book, but the form it takes is best characterized by the term "wonder." Perhaps because of its inherent complexity, "wonder" became one of Melville's favorite words in *Moby-Dick.* While it indicates something not only marvellous or surprising, but perhaps supernatural or miraculous, it also carries the sense, as a verb, "to think" or "to doubt." In *Moby-Dick* Melville uses the word in its fullest sense, indicating a state or mood in which analytical thought or doubt are suspended even though they are present beneath the surface. Thus, his meditations lead him repeatedly to the threshold of wonder, where he suspends reason in surrendering to his unreasonable God. Indeed, the entrance to *Moby-Dick* is accomplished in this way: having decided to see the "watery part of the world," Ishmael begins to think of the magic in water and concludes that the key to it all is that rivers and oceans contain "the image of the ungraspable phantom of life." Thus, the prelude "Loomings" ends: "the great flood-gates of the wonder-world swung open, and in the wild conceits that swayed me to my purpose, two and two there floated into my inmost soul, endless processions of the whale, and midmost of them all, one grand hooded phantom, like a snow hill in the air."

The capacity for lyric wonder and faith resides mainly within Ishmael, and it is the essential criterion by which Melville establishes his values and distinguishes between wisdom and madness. Ahab is himself no mean poet, but for all his grand style, he lacks Ishmael's consoling sense of wonder. Melville makes this crucial distinction in "The Dying Whale," where we see Ishmael again moved to wonder and reverence:

> It was far down in the afternoon; and when all the spearings of the crimson fight were done: and floating in the lovely sunset sea and sky, sun and whale both stilly died together; then, such a sweetness and such plaintiveness, such inwreathing orisons curled up in that rosy air, that it almost seemed as if far over from the deep green convent valleys of the Manilla isles, the Spanish landbreeze, wantonly turned sailor, had gone to sea, freighted with these vesper hymns.
>
> (p. 409)

By contrast, the same scene "only soothed [Ahab] to deeper gloom"; somehow it conveyed to him "a wonderousness unknown before," but his ensuing meditation leads him not to consoling reverence, but to a characteristic "lesson": the affirmation of his own "prouder . . . darker faith." Similarly, in what is certainly one of

Ahab's most memorable moments, he is moved—in contemplating a sperm whale's head in "The Sphynx"—to a poetic meditation that begins, "'Speak, thou vast and venerable head.'" (It is the head, of course, that inevitably fascinates Ahab, who sees in it a reflection of himself: "'Of all divers, thou hast dived the deepest. That head upon which the upper sun now gleams, has moved amid this world's foundations.'") But what amazes Ahab most is that the head remains silent: "'O head! thou hast seen enough to split the planets and make an infidel of Abraham, and not one syllable is thine!'" Ahab is momentarily amazed by this capacity for silence, for his own power of speech is his black power of defiance, his pride in the grandeur of his own mind. Thus he ends this meditation characteristically, not in a surrender to some higher power, but in an affirmation of mind: "'O Nature, and O soul of man! how far beyond all utterance are your linked analogies! not the smallest atom stirs or lives in matter, but has its cunning duplicate in mind'" (p. 264).

Ahab is under the spell of mind. And his intellectual pride is most obvious when he defies the lightning: "'There is some unsuffusing thing beyond thee, thou clear spirit, to whom all thy eternity is but time, all thy creativeness mechanical'" (p. 417). Like the unrepentant Job, whose story bears an enormous influence on *Moby-Dick,* Ahab would "desire to reason with God."[17] And like the unrepentant Job who spoke "without knowledge, and his words were without wisdom," Ahab fails to see that "we cannot order our speech by reason of darkness" (Job 34: 35; 37: 19). Forever given to his dark reasoning, Ahab can never really "consider the wondrous works of God" and confess, as Job does, his ignorance of "things too wonderful for me" (Job 42: 3). Recalling Melville's remark to Hawthorne—"I have written a wicked book, and feel spotless as the lamb,"[18] one might conclude that *Moby-Dick*'s "wickedness" is Ahab's unyielding defiance. But the emphasis of Melville's remark is on his feeling of being cleansed; and corresponding to the confessional tone of this remark, there is an echo of the confessional mode heard throughout the book as Melville (through his selves of Ishmael and Ahab) presses to reveal his deepest religious feelings. Indeed, according to Freedman's historical sketch, the confessional novel is an antecedent to the lyrical novel. But if Melville could not imagine God's direct intervention in his own life—as God intervened from the whirlwind to chastise Job into saving repentance—he could confess his own obsessive power of blackness, personifying it in Ahab, and arrange for it to be consumed in the sea. The peacefulness of "Epilogue"—introduced as it is with its epigraph from Job, "And I only am escaped alone to tell thee"—results from a confessional purgation of Ahab's blackness and corresponds to the peaceful ending of Job, when, having repented "in dust and ashes," Job is silent: then "the Lord also accepted Job."

But the prevailing calm in "Epilogue" is also Melville's emphatic affirmation of his capacity for lyric wonder. *Moby-Dick* is founded in Ishmael's capacity for wonder—not in his "boredom, dread, and despair," as a recent widely credited study claims.[19] Through Ishmael's lyric surrenderings to an unfathomable God, *Moby-Dick* centers itself in a peacefulness—forever withheld from Ahab—that corresponds to that place "in the soul of man," wherein "lies one insular Tahiti, full of peace and joy, but encompassed by all the horrors of the half known life. God keep thee! Push not off from that isle, thou canst never return!" (p. 236). Obviously, a precarious peace prevails in what might be called this Tahiti of trust; the struggle within Melville and within the novel is directly reflected by the exclamation, "God keep thee!" And if *Moby-Dick* fully renders the blackness, sharkishness, and death of the natural world, it does so in awe of a Creator of light *and* dark, good *and* evil. Ultimately, the book is the expression of a consciousness that, in the face of madness and evil, can affirm: "amid the tornadoed Atlantic of my being, do I myself still for ever centrally disport in mute calm; and while ponderous planets of unwaning woe revolve round me, deep down and deep inland there I still bathe me in eternal mildness of joy" (p. 326).

Finally, *Moby-Dick* is a celebration of the "ungraspable phantom of *life*" (my emphasis); for, although Ishmael's survival on a life-buoy coffin acknowledges death, it spites death. And as a lyric surrender to the light and dark Creator of life, *Moby-Dick* endures as a wholly American lyrical novel, despite its enormous assimilation of British and Continental influences. It continues to comprehend our Puritan sense of evil as well as our urge for transcendence and innocence, even as it resounds with a more modern sense of ambiguity and emptiness. With all of its learned references, it is a song of wonder in the spirit of Emerson's anti-intellectualism and Whitman's sense that if "I contradict myself," then "Very well . . . I contradict myself."[20] Even more fully than Whitman's song, Melville's contains "multitudes." If Whitman's song celebrates a new American sense of physical and sexual innocence, Melville's has its own sense of erotic innocence to counterpoint its sense of original sin. And far more deeply than Whitman, Melville can sense and accept the darkly disturbing yet primitive innocence of Nature's voraciousness, as imaged, for example, in the "chaste" whiteness of the whale's mouth (p. 280). Wracked as it certainly is with its sense of evil and voraciousness, *Moby-Dick* remains with *Leaves of Grass* as an American soul song, a lyric launched confidently into the "measureless oceans of space."[21]

Notes

1. Herman Melville, *Moby-Dick*, eds., Harrison Hayford and Hershel Parker (New York: Norton, 1967), p. 245. Further references to *Moby-Dick* are from this edition and are cited in the text by page number or, when appropriate, by chapter.

2. Alfred Kazin, Introduction to Riverside edition of *Moby-Dick* (Boston: Houghton Mifflin, 1950), rpt. in *Melville: A Collection of Critical Essays*, ed. Richard Chase (Englewood Cliffs, N.J.: Prentice-Hall, 1962), p. 48; Richard Chase, "Melville and *Moby-Dick*," in *Melville: A Collection of Critical Essays*, p. 60; F. O. Matthiessen, *American Renaissance* (New York: Oxford Univ. Press, 1941), pp. 421-31.

3. James Wm. Johnson, "Lyric," *Princeton Encyclopedia of Poetry and Poetics* (Princeton: Princeton Univ. Press, 1965).

4. James Joyce, *A Portrait of the Artist as a Young Man*, ed. Chester G. Anderson (New York: Viking, 1968), p. 214; [Frye,] *Anatomy of Criticism* (Princeton: Princeton Univ. Press, 1957), pp. 246-49; Gide's definition is quoted in Ralph Freedman, *The Lyrical Novel* (Princeton: Princeton Univ. Press, 1963), p. 122.

5. *The Lyrical Novel*, pp. 236, 304, 313. Further references to this work are cited parenthetically by page.

6. "The Reconciliation of Ishmael: *Moby-Dick* and the Book of Job," *The South Atlantic Quarterly*, 57 (Autumn 1958), 482-83.

7. *Symbolism and American Literature* (Chicago: Univ. of Chicago Press, 1953), pp. 34-35.

8. *The Complete Poetry of John Donne*, ed. John T. Shawcross (Garden City, N. Y.: Anchor, 1967), pp. 342, 350, 347.

9. Among the most famous are D. H. Lawrence, "Herman Melville's *Moby-Dick*" in *Studies in Classic American Literature* (New York: Seltzer, 1923); Henry A. Murray, "'In Nomine Diaboli,'" *The New England Quarterly*, 24 (Dec. 1951), 434-52; and James Baird, *Ishmael: A Study of the Symbolic Mode in Primitivism* (Baltimore: Johns Hopkins Univ. Press, 1956).

10. Frye, p. 249.

11. Randall Stewart, ed., *The English Notebooks of Nathaniel Hawthorne* (New York: Oxford Univ. Press, 1941), pp. 432-33.

12. *Melville's Religious Thought* (Durham, N.C.: Duke Univ. Press, 1943), p. 73.

13. *Melville's Quarrel with God* (Princeton: Princeton Univ. Press, 1952), p. 423.

14. In *Moby-Dick* (Norton), p. 555.

15. *Melville's Use of the Bible* (Durham, N.C.: Duke Univ. Press, 1949), p. 185.

16. *Melville: A Collection of Critical Essays,* p. 61.

17. Job 13: 3. Among the best discussions of *Moby-Dick*'s relationship to Job are C. Hugh Holman, "The Reconciliation of Ishmael: *Moby-Dick* and the Book of Job," *South Atlantic Quarterly,* 57 (Autumn 1958), 477-90; Nathalia Wright, "*Moby-Dick*: Jonah's or Job's Whale?" *American Literature,* 37 (May 1965), 190-95; and Thornton Booth, "*Moby-Dick*: Standing up to God," *Nineteenth-Century Fiction,* 17 (June 1962), 33-43.

18. In *Moby-Dick* (Norton), p. 566.

19. Paul Brodtkorb, Jr., *Ishmael's White World: A Phenomenological Reading of* Moby-Dick (New Haven: Yale Univ. Press, 1965), p. 148.

20. Walt Whitman, *Leaves of Grass,* eds., Scully Bradley and Harold W. Blodgett (New York: Norton, 1973), p. 88.

21. Ibid., p. 450.

Gustaaf Van Cromphout (essay date March 1979)

SOURCE: Van Cromphout, Gustaaf. "*Moby-Dick*: The Transformation of the Faustian Ethos." *American Literature: A Journal of Literary History, Criticism, and Bibliography* 51, no. 1 (March 1979): 17-32.

[*In the following essay, Van Cromphout examines questions of self-realization in* Moby-Dick. *In Van Cromphout's reading, a Faustian striving for power pervades all aspects of the novel: its plot, its symbolism, and even its narrative form. Van Cromphout argues that this expansive "Faustian ethos" ultimately lends the novel its ambiguity, while denying it any possibility of a clear resolution.*]

One major difference between *Moby-Dick* and its five predecessors in the Melville canon [*Typee, Omoo, Mardi, Redburn,* and *White-Jacket*] consists in its being its author's first exploration of "landlessness." Like *Moby-Dick,* the earlier novels recount actual or allegorical voyages, three of them even involving, briefly or incidentally, whaling ships. Like *Moby-Dick* also, those novels express what Merlin Bowen has rightly called Melville's "principal concern" in all his works, "a concern with the problem of self-discovery, self-realization." But unlike *Moby-Dick,* those novels also involve an "otherness" both sufficiently real and sufficiently comprehensible to act as a foil in the process of self-definition. Tommo and Redburn, for instance, learn much about themselves from their confrontations with the "other," whether this be the valley of Typee, or Liv-

erpool, or the complexities of life aboard ship. The same is true, mutatis mutandis, of the remaining early protagonists. In *Moby-Dick,* by contrast, this "other" ceases to function as an aid to self-knowledge because it ceases either to be truly "other" or to be accessible to human understanding, in the former case becoming a mere reflection of the self and in the latter becoming a world emptied of meaning and hence emptied of reality. In *Moby-Dick* the voyage is, literally and metaphorically, one into "landlessness." The formal implication of this "landlessness" have been noted by Edgar A. Dryden: "Unlike its predecessors, *Moby-Dick* is almost completely self-contained and self-referring . . . it is always moving away from the objective or factual world and persistently calling attention to itself as fiction." Melville's masterpiece brings to full imaginative development a tendency in his thought only implied by such earlier statements as Redburn's "I began to see, that my prospects of seeing the world as a sailor were, after all, but very doubtful; for sailors only go *round* the world, without going *into* it."[1]

The *Pequod*'s voyage into landlessness is Melville's version of the Romantic transformation of the Faustian ethos. When characterizing *Moby-Dick* as Faustian, I am not just referring to Ahab's being "the Faust of the quarter-deck," as Evert Duyckinck put it upon the novel's appearance and as Melville criticism has recognized ever since. Nor am I concerned with *Moby-Dick* as a variation upon the traditional Faust story, complete with a Faust, a devil, a pact, and a damnation, as William W. Betts and Charles Dédéyan have interpreted the book. I consider *Moby-Dick* Faustian in a more pervasive way. Following the lead of such students of our culture as Thomas Mann, Oswald Spengler, and T. K. Seung, I regard "Faustian" as almost synonymous with "Western," in that Faust represents what is most characteristic of the Western psyche: its boundless aspirations, its expansionism, its identification of knowledge with power, its attempt to subdue nature, its yearning for control over its own destiny. Thomas Mann's claim that Faust symbolizes the West's deepest essence receives considerable support from our obsessive concern with the Faust figure through the centuries; and no century was more Faust-conscious than the nineteenth, as a result primarily of Goethe's masterpiece.[2]

In the sense just indicated there is as much Faustianism in an Ishmael or a Bulkington as in Ahab himself. And the *Pequod*—a highly elaborate instrument for subduing nature, as Richard Chase has reminded us—is on a Faustian voyage. Ishmael's experience, as I shall try to show, brings him to an important insight, an insight reflecting Melville's awareness of the profound change then transforming the Faustian ethos. *Moby-Dick,* itself a Faustian venture in its epic ambitiousness, thus represents Melville's endeavor to understand some of the deepest spiritual tendencies shaping Western experience. In fact, Taji's claim in **Mardi,** "This new world here sought . . . is the world of mind," would have made an apt motto for the greatest among Melville's quests on the frontiers of human thought.[3]

There was a time when "limitless space," which Spengler regarded as the "prime symbol" (*Ursymbol*) of the Faustian psyche, made ceaseless striving objectively worthwhile. "The world-embracing metaphysical cupola," as Leo Spitzer put it, gave meaning to man's quest.[4] Such an early manifestation of the Faustian spirit as the Gothic cathedral represented the soul's attempt to escape from the confining heaviness of matter in order to achieve union with a God who was a personal presence rather than an abstraction.[5] Similarly Marlowe's well-known lines about

> Our souls, whose faculties can comprehend
> The wondrous Architecture of the world,
> And measure every wand'ring planet's course

reveal a faith in the objective substantiality of the universe that is in striking contrast with, say, Emerson's "It is the uniform effect of culture on the human mind . . . to lead us to regard nature as a phenomenon, not a substance." A Columbus, a Bacon, a Newton strove to bring within human ken realities that, until their advances in perception, had lain beyond it. And the Enlightenment, having postulated a universally valid and humanly intelligible "order" in nature, then appealed to that "order" to justify its intellectual and artistic endeavors. The Faustian mind aimed at knowledge of and, through knowledge, at benefit from or mastery over the forces it perceived. Faustian space symbolized "einen Herrschaftsanspruch der Seele über das Fremde"—the soul's claim to dominance over what is "other."[6]

Occasionally, however, this "other" raised disturbing questions. Pascal's modernity, which consists in what Georg Lukács has called his "phenomenology of despair" rather than in his Jansenist solution, is suggested by statements like "the eternal silence of infinite space frightens me" and "engulfed in the infinite immensity of space, which I do not understand and which knows me not, I am frightened." Space, which Western man had so daringly extended, lost its meaningful content and became the realm of the void. It gradually became, as Alexandre Koyré says, "the infinite, uncreated nothingness, the frame of the absence of all being; consequently also of God's." One Romantic response to this anguish of the void was to turn more emphatically inward. The Faustian quest was interiorized, eventually to culminate in Rilke's claim that the only meaningful space left is the space of the inner world ("Durch alle Wesen reicht der *eine* Raum:/Weltinnenraum . . .").[7]

In **Moby-Dick** Melville confronts this collapse of Faustian space and its consequences. The experience of space, Charles Olson has said, is a central factor in

Moby-Dick, but "space was the paradise Melville was exile of."[8] At first Ishmael voices the traditional Faustian yearning for "limitless space": "I am tormented with an everlasting itch for things remote."[9] In order to satisfy this yearning, he has repeatedly shipped as a merchant sailor (p. 15). His now opting for a whaling voyage will lead to a very different experience, although his early remarks reveal a duality of purpose consonant with traditional Faustian aspirations: he wants to experience not only the sea, which in the symbolic world of **Moby-Dick** is the mirror of the self, but also the alien worlds beyond the sea, that is, the truly "other." As he puts it: "I love to sail forbidden seas, and land on barbarous coasts" (p. 16). Somewhat later, replying to Peleg's question why he wants to go whaling, Ishmael reveals the same dual impulse: "Well, sir, I want to see what whaling is. I want to see the world" (p. 69). Perceiving the duality, Peleg brings Ishmael to a sense of its inadequacy:

> "Now then, thou not only wantest to go a-whaling, to find out by experience what whaling is, but ye also want to go in order to see the world? Was not that what ye said? I thought so. Well then, just step forward there, and take a peep over the weather bow, and then back to me and tell me what ye see there." . . .
>
> Going forward and glancing over the weather bow, I perceived that the ship swinging to her anchor with the flood-tide, was now obliquely pointing towards the open ocean. The prospect was unlimited, but exceedingly monotonous and forbidding; not the slightest variety that I could see.
>
> "Well, what's the report?" said Peleg when I came back; "what did ye see?"
>
> "Not much," I replied—"nothing but water."
>
> (p. 70)

The voyage of the *Pequod* bears out this landlessness, this failure to encounter "otherness":

> But how now? in this zoned quest, does Ahab touch no land? does his crew drink air? Surely, he will stop for water. Nay. For a long time, now, the circus-running sun has raced within his fiery ring, and needs no sustenance but what's in himself. So Ahab. Mark this, too, in the whaler. While other hulls are loaded down with alien stuff, to be transferred to foreign wharves; the world-wandering whale-ship carries no cargo but herself and crew, their weapons and their wants. . . . Hence it is, that, while other ships may have gone to China from New York, and back again, touching at a score of ports, the whale-ship, in all that interval, may not have sighted one grain of soil; her crew having seen no man but floating seamen like themselves. So that did you carry them the news that another flood had come; they would only answer—"Well, boys, here's the ark!"
>
> (p. 319)

The phrase "no man but floating seamen like themselves" suggests that the gams or near-gams do not modify this "landlessness." The other ships, whalers like the *Pequod,* but mirror back to the *Pequod*'s crew their own hopes, fears, or fates.[10]

Bereft of its "otherness," the voyage becomes an experience of the void that leads to a heightened experience of the self. "Boundless solitude," Spengler said, was ultimately "the homeland of the Faustian soul." Ishmael is a cosmic outcast to whom John Seelye rightly attributes the suspicion that nature is but "a hollow sham, hiding absolutely nothing."[11] There is a Pascalian despair in Ishmael's cosmic loneliness, as when he questions "the heartless voids and immensities of the universe," or when he exclaims: "The intense concentration of self in the middle of such a heartless immensity, my God! who can tell it?" (pp. 169, 347).

And yet it is precisely the voyage of the self into this heartless immensity that holds out the promise of one's experiencing "truth." Pip's confrontation with the void has led to the kind of insanity that is "heaven's sense" (p. 347); and Bulkington symbolizes the realization that "in landlessness alone resides the highest truth" (p. 97). But truth has clearly ceased to be an objective structure, identifiable and graspable. Even conventionally honest, upright Starbuck no longer finds its source: "Great God, where art thou?" (p. 422). The abolition of "otherness" had emptied also God and truth of content. The God of Faustian man in his Romantic stage is no longer the personal God "climbed after" in the great cathedrals, but instead has become "an impersonal principle, unimaginable, ungraspable . . . an inconceivable abstraction,"[12] much like the "nameless, inscrutable, unearthly thing" (p. 444) that Ahab sometimes holds responsible for his fate. How utterly God has become a *deus absconditus* is suggested by Gordon V. Boudreau in his study of Melville's architectural symbology. When Melville compares the whale to a Gothic cathedral, he commonly omits the "copestone (or its equivalent stone symbol)," which symbolized "Christ as passage-way from earthly city to heavenly city"; and though this "persistent absence of copestone," just because it is so striking, draws the reader's attention to the symbolic significance of the copestone, it is itself, as absence, symbolic of "a God that is always missing."[13] Truth also is nowhere to be found. It has become "shoreless, indefinite as God" (p. 97); it "hath no confines" (p. 144); and it is as inscrutable as the "sphinx" that Ahab questions (p. 264). As Melville already suggested in *Mardi,* truth, like God, has become an unanswerable question. "Tell us what is truth?" asks Mohi; to which the philosopher Babbalanja replies: "The old interrogatory; did they not ask it when the world began? But ask it no more . . . that question is more final than any answer."[14]

Turning truth into an unanswerable question meant temporalizing and subjectivizing it. If man is, like Bulkington, responsive to the highest imperative of his being,

he attempts without cease to formulate the question, whether in thought or in action. And "the presupposition that each man is locked in the prison of his consciousness," which the Romantics, as J. Hillis Miller has noted, shared with many modern thinkers, led them to conceive of truth as a metaphor of self—as a ceaseless attempt "to utter our painful secret," as Emerson put it, in order to achieve self-knowledge. "Truth . . . ," we are told in Goethe and Schiller's *Xenien,* "My truth—for I don't know of any other." Georges Poulet is right in stressing that one important aspect of Romanticism was "a taking possession by consciousness of the fundamentally subjective character of the mind." The aesthetic implications of this inward turn of consciousness are obvious. It is not surprising that Hegel, whose *Aesthetik* has been called "the culmination of all romantic theories of art and aesthetics," considered "the true content" of Romantic art to be "absolute inwardness." As suggested above, the real object of the Faustian quest had become the self in all its mysterious complexity. And *Moby-Dick* is emphatically the product of a mind "which has turned away from the chaos and confusion of the world toward a contemplation of its own activity."[15]

The *Pequod*'s element, after all, is water—the unlimited watery prospect that Ishmael faces during his first encounter with Peleg, instead of "the world" he expected to see. And as meaningfully as in Baudelaire's "L'Homme et la mer," water is in *Moby-Dick* the mirror of the soul; hence its universal attraction (pp. 12-14). Ahab, who, as a whaler, has preeminently been a man going "*round* the world, without going *into* it," is but universalizing his experience when he attributes the soul-reflecting significance of the sea to the world as a whole. The globe, in his view, "like a magician's glass, to each and every man in turn but mirrors back his own mysterious self" (p. 359). The voyage of the *Pequod* is an endeavor to see more clearly into the mystery of the self, but the endeavor being in vain, the mystery looms for ever unresolved. "The image of the ungraspable phantom of life" (p. 14) fuses with "the overwhelming idea of the great whale," that "grand hooded phantom" (p. 16) whose mystery will for ever encompass our existence (pp. 380, 384-385). Interested as he was in etymology, Melville must have been aware of the historical contiguities in meaning among "idea," "image," and "phantom." Their combined effect is to create an atmosphere of objective unreality in which the thinking "I," standing forth as the only essence, reduces the "other" to merely phenomenal existence.[16]

The confrontation with the whale most clearly reveals the problems facing Faustian man. T. K. Seung has shown that the formative period of Faustian culture (roughly the twelfth to the fourteenth centuries) witnessed a transition from allegorical to literal sensibility and modes of expression, a transition reflecting a shift from a theocentric to an anthropocentric world view. Literalism is a mode of expression revealing man's confidence in the objective validity of his perceptions; it reflects man's assumption that he knows or is able to know that which he perceives. Not surprisingly literalism, as Norman O. Brown has said in reference to its Protestant variety (Luther's *Eindeutigkeit*), did much to foster the modern scientific spirit with its assertion of man's knowledge-based power over nature. This argument can be applied in reverse to the transformation of Faustianism in the Romantic age: if the emergence of the Faustian ethos involved a transition from allegorical to literal sensibility, the Romantic transformation of that ethos may be said to have involved a transition from literal to symbolic sensibility. From the end of the eighteenth century onward the inadequacy of the literalist-scientific view became obvious. "The letter killeth" acquired a new and poignant meaning for Blake or Wordsworth or Keats observing the human spirit atrophied by the scientific mentality. The creative and unifying power of the symbolic imagination appeared to be the road to a new spiritual integrity. From a Faustian point of view, however, symbolism involved limitation. In much the same way that the allegorical sensibility reflected man's ultimate powerlessness in a theocentric universe, symbolism confronted man with a universe that exploded his pretense of knowing and controlling it. In *Die romantische Schule* (1836) Heinrich Heine pointed to the conceptual and formal implications of the shift from a literalist to a symbolist sensibility: "Classical art had to represent only the finite, and its forms could be commensurate with the artist's idea; Romantic art had to represent, or rather to suggest, the infinite and the purely spiritual."[17]

Ishmael approaches the whale on both the literal and symbolic levels. As exemplified by him, the literalist sensibility has clearly lost confidence in its own validity. The cetological chapters are riddled with confessions of inadequate treatment. The collapse of meaningful space, the disappearance of identifiable "otherness" is evidenced by the literalist inability to establish any real links between the "me" and the "not-me," an inability illustrating "how impassable is the gulf between the mind and its object."[18] The mind has no "hold" upon the whale; it cannot force him into any graspable forms. "If the Sperm Whale be physiognomically a Sphinx, to the phrenologist his brain seems that geometrical circle which it is impossible to square" (p. 293). Moreover, "If I know not even the tail of this whale, how understand his head? much more, how comprehend his face, when face he has none?" (p. 318). The whale shows "his great genius" by "his doing nothing particular to prove it" and by "his pyramidical silence" (p. 292). He cannot even be properly *seen*: "there is no earthly way of finding out precisely what the whale really looks like" (p. 228). Clearly we have here an instance of that "solipsistic unease" which, as A. D. Nuttall has bril-

liantly demonstrated, has affected many minds from the eighteenth century onward.[19] Ishmael's whale does "exist," but his insusceptibility to the mind's efforts at analysis and understanding, to the mind's attempts at assimilation, makes his objective existence ultimately irrelevant to the self. All the dissecting and analysis in the cetological chapters merely demonstrate the failure of literalism to bring us any closer to the "truth" about the whale. "Dissect him how I may . . . I but go skin deep; I know him not, and never will" (p. 318).

But if there is "no earthly way" to get to the truth about the whale, there is perhaps a "landless" way, a seaway (pp. 228, 97). The whale as symbol certainly brings us closer to the Faustian quest in its Romantic stage than the whale as objective reality: what is sought after is no longer knowledge of the "other," but knowledge of the self. Furthermore, Moby Dick as symbol transcends the connotations associated with the whale in traditional symbology and has thus lost that protection against merely personal interpretation which a culture confers upon its symbols. Moby Dick, like his element water, has become a portrait of every individual contemplating him: he means what anyone reads into him. Ahab, who, in Charles Olson's words, "had all space concentrated into the form of [the] whale,"[20] has come "to identify with him, not only all his bodily woes, but all his intellectual and spiritual exasperations. The White Whale swam before him as the monomaniac incarnation of all those malicious agencies which some deep men feel eating in them" (p. 160). To Gabriel of the *Jeroboam* the white whale is "the Shaker God incarnated" (p. 267). To Captain Boomer of the *Samuel Enderby* he has become a noli me tangere. Honest, upright Starbuck sees in Moby Dick the indifference and basic innocence of nature. The sailors in general, regarding Moby Dick with superstitious awe, credit him with ubiquity and immortality (p. 158) and with being an instrument of God (p. 208). Ishmael's interpretation in "The Whiteness of the Whale" is the least definitional of all, and it is for that reason symbolically the truest: more than anyone else Ishmael hints at the insoluble ambiguities, the endless mysteries suggested by the whale, whose color serves to reinforce his role as "phantom" and "idea," since whiteness "in its profoundest idealized significance . . . calls up a peculiar *apparition* to the soul" (p. 166; my italics). The paradox inherent in such a view of reality is well conveyed by a statement of Paul Brodtkorb's: "The emotion that constitutes white makes vibrantly visible as a presence the nothingness with which all existence is secretly sickened."[21]

Having been reduced to a medley of interpretations, the whale can no longer provide a meaning transcending individual perception. Reality has been reduced to the content of one's perceptions, as is demonstrated in "The Doubloon" and as Pip in his divine madness realizes: "I look, you look, he looks; we look, ye look, they look"

(p. 362). Herein lies the ultimate loneliness of the Faustian soul and its inability to achieve self-definition. As long as the world was "real," the soul was "possible," Spengler suggests; what gave direction and meaning to the soul was its striving to comprehend reality and in the process to realize its possibilities and thus its idea of its self. But the "other" having been abandoned as unreal, there remained only the self and that hypersubjectivism which Werner Kohlschmidt has called "Fichte's Greek gift [i.e., Trojan horse] to Romanticism" ("das Danaergeschenk Fichtes an die Romantik"). While ostensibly exalting the self, subjectivism undermined it: Romanticism, in Wylie Sypher's words, "created the self and destroyed the self."[22] Without the context of the "other," the self became indefinable; alienation became the crisis of identity. Teufelsdröckh's "unanswerable question: Who am *I;* the thing that can say 'I?'" echoes through the nineteenth century.[23]

Moby-Dick demonstrates that when the "not-me" becomes a mystery inaccessible to the mind and thus, in effect, a void, the "me" becomes a mystery insusceptible to definition. Ahab, who does not know whether the whale is "agent" or "principal," inscrutable mask or inscrutable essence (p. 144), has the same questions concerning the whale's counterpart, himself: "Is Ahab, Ahab? Is it I, God, or who, that lifts this arm?" (p. 445). Thomas Woodson's comment is to the point: Ahab "is continually in doubt of his identity. . . . [He] is never sure whether he is everything or nothing. . . . The mystery of things and the mystery of self become the same problem to him."[24] Ahab's plight is prefigured in his fantasy of the artificial man that he wants the blacksmith to forge. He does not want him to have "eyes to see outwards," but instead "a skylight on top of his head to illuminate inwards"; within, however, there is only a void, since the artificial man, though endowed with a "chest modelled after the Thames tunnel," will have "no heart at all" (p. 390).

In reference to the lack of progress into knowledge characterizing his quest, Ahab claims that "we are turned round and round in this world" (p. 445). The loss of "otherness" entails a reduction of the Faustian quest to an endless solipsistic circle from which there is no escape into something even resembling an absolute. Whether or not the circular quest destroys the quester, it never provides him with an answer, as Ishmael recognizes:

> Round the world! There is much in that sound to inspire proud feelings; but whereto does all that circumnavigation conduct? Only through numberless perils to the very point whence we started. . . . Were this world an endless plain, and by sailing eastward we could for ever reach new distances, and discover sights more sweet and strange than any Cyclades or Islands of King Solomon, then there were promise in the voyage. But in pursuit of those far mysteries we dream of, or in tor-

mented chase of that demon phantom that, some time or other, swims before all human hearts; while chasing such over this round globe, they either lead us on in barren mazes or midway leave us whelmed.

(p. 204)

The anacoluthon in the last sentence but reinforces the message that the quest leads nowhere.

The passage just quoted is not, however, Ishmael's final word on the subject. His emancipation from traditional Faustianism is incomplete so long as he has not transcended what Kierkegaard considered man's self-defeating desire "to lay hold of something so really fixed that it can exclude all dialectics,"[25] so long, that is, as he even desires a "final" answer. As a participant in the action of *Moby-Dick,* Ishmael shares with Ahab, Bulkington, and the others the dilemma inherent in the pursuit of an aim fatally beyond human reach, a dilemma well expressed by Charles Feidelson: "The phantom is ungraspable as long as we stand on the bank; and the ocean is annihilative once we dive into it."[26] But Ishmael dives and is not annihilated. He survives to become the narrator of the action he participated in, and it is as narrator that he best exemplifies the essence of Romantic Faustianism, the recognition that "the goal of the journey of life [is] the experience of the journey itself."[27]

My argument involves a distinction between the "two Ishmaels" in *Moby-Dick.* In Walter E. Bezanson's words, "the first Ishmael is the enfolding sensibility of the novel, the hand that writes the tale, the imagination through which all matters of the book pass. He is the narrator. . . . The second Ishmael is not the narrator, not the informing presence, but is the young man of whom, among others, narrator Ishmael tells us in his story. . . . This is forecastle Ishmael or the younger Ishmael of 'some years ago.'"[28] Narrator Ishmael, moreover, is concerned with both narrative and narration. When focusing on narrative, he tries imaginatively to recapture the moods and hopes and perceptions of forecastle Ishmael and his companions; his narrative deals with the *then*, with an experience already completed. When focusing on narration, Ishmael's concern is with the *now*—with his ongoing endeavor to put into words what happened *then*. The *now*, representing an experience not yet completed, puts its stamp upon the book as emphatically as the *then*: *Moby-Dick* "is always in process and in all but the most literal sense remains unfinished. For the good reader the experience of *Moby-Dick* is a participation in the act of creation."[29] Authorial Ishmael's endeavor to give form and tentative meaning to his journey in the *Pequod* resulted in a book that is as much about the experience of writing a book as about the experience recalled in the book. And in a sense, the writing turned out to be as frustrating as the journey: both experiences fail to provide answers to the questions they evoke. The difference consists in Ishmael's responses to these failures; and his responses reveal different Faustian selves.

Forecastle Ishmael regards life as an Ixionic experience, as in the "Round the world!" passage quoted above, or as in this meditation on human destiny from "The Gilder":

> There is no steady unretracing progress in this life; we do not advance through fixed gradations, and at the last one pause:—through infancy's unconscious spell, boyhood's thoughtless faith, adolescence' doubt (the common doom), then scepticism, then disbelief, resting at last in manhood's pondering repose of If. But once gone through, we trace the round again; and are infants, boys, and men, and Ifs eternally.
>
> (p. 406)

Whether these words be Ishmael's or not,[30] the fact remains that as long as Ishmael is the Ishmael evoked in "Loomings," an Ishmael questing for answers and solutions, he identifies himself with the other seekers and is bound to be as cruelly frustrated as they. Their quest tends to become his quest ("Ahab's quenchless feud seemed mine"—p. 155), and the despair inherent in their quest tends to become his despair, as in "The Lee Shore" (pp. 97-98), because like them he seeks answers, and through them he realizes the fatal impossibility of finding answers. The quest, for Ishmael and his companions alike, is thus reduced to an Ixionic experience in which the Faustian dream of knowledge and mastery has become the nightmare of total contingency. In this sense Carl F. Strauch is right in claiming that "If" is "the most important word in *Moby-Dick.*"[31]

In the "Epilogue," however, Ishmael ceases to be "another Ixion" (p. 470). Though his final self-characterization as "orphan" sounds like a conceptual echo of the "Call me Ishmael" of the opening, and though we might thus be tempted to conclude that in his beginning was his end, such a conclusion seems unwarranted in view of the striking tonal difference between the "Epilogue" and the opening. "Orphan" and "Ishmael" both suggest, to be sure, a crisis in self-definition: metaphorically they both stress the absence of any meaningful relation to the "other" and hence of any real understanding of the self. This point also is made in the "Ifs" passage in "The Gilder": "Our souls are like those orphans whose unwedded mothers die in bearing them: the secret of our paternity lies in their grave, and we must there to learn it" (p. 406). But whereas Ishmaelism or spiritual orphanhood is associated with bitterness and anguish in "Loomings," in the "Epilogue" it is accepted with a casualness that in no way disturbs the preternatural peace pervading the scene. Ishmael, in other words, has ceased tormenting himself about the ever-elusive answers to his questions concerning his place in the scheme of things and hence concerning his identity.[32]

Ishmael's new attitude does not amount, however, to his turning his back upon Faustian striving. The soul's "last limit," we were told in *Mardi,* "is her everlasting beginning."[33] And at the end of his *Pequod* experience Ishmael, a true embodiment of undying Faustianism, faces indeed a new and equally arduous task: "AND I ONLY AM ESCAPED ALONE TO TELL THEE" (p. 470). In his end is his true beginning: as author he embarks on another endless journey, and as author he demonstrates the principal lesson to be learned from his experience with the *Pequod*—that the journey itself is the goal of the journey. When Ishmael is at his most authorial, he sees virtue rather than horror in the absence of finality: "God keep me from ever completing anything" (p. 128), or, in reference to his cetological "books" and "chapters": "I promise nothing complete; because any human thing supposed to be complete, must for that very reason infallibly be faulty" (p. 118). Like Emerson, he regards Cologne Cathedral, not finished until 1880, as an apt symbol of the highest intellectual or artistic achievement: its very incompleteness, its "ever leav[ing] the copestone to posterity," is a measure of its greatness (pp. 127-28). For authorial Ishmael, as for Hölderlin's Hyperion, man's want and incompleteness have become grounds for self-congratulation.[34]

In its demonstration of the failure of traditional Faustianism, *Moby-Dick* is a deeply pessimistic book: all the aspirations of the captain and crew (including Ishmael as actor in the drama), whether outer-directed or inner-directed, meet with frustration or disaster. But once "the drama's done" and a "dirge-like main" (p. 470) has mourned the death of an illusion, Ishmael is ready for his exercise in negative capability—the capability, in Keats's words, "of being in uncertainties, Mysteries, doubts, without any irritable reaching after fact & reason." The result is a highly inconclusive book and, through authorial Ishmael's recognition of the value of such inconclusiveness, ultimately a book that transforms man's epistemic limitations into a glorious challenge. Its very inconclusiveness also makes *Moby-Dick* a fit chapter in the totality of Melville's oeuvre, which, as Albert Camus maintained, but consists of "le même livre indéfiniment recommencé."[35] Perhaps Melville was afraid of finality. In an age that predicted the death of art,[36] there was great value indeed in an undying artistic effort, especially since, as Nietzsche was to say, "we have art so that we won't perish of truth," or, in Ishmael's version, "clear Truth is a thing for salamander giants only to encounter" (p. 286).[37]

Notes

1. Bowen, *The Long Encounter: Self and Experience in the Writings of Herman Melville* (Chicago, 1963), p. 2; Dryden, *Melville's Thematics of Form* (Baltimore, 1968), p. 83; *Redburn,* [in] *The Writings of Herman Melville,* ed. Harrison Hayford,

Hershel Parker, and G. Thomas Tanselle (Evanston, Ill., and Chicago, 1969), IV, 133.

2. Duyckinck is quoted in Hershel Parker, ed., *The Recognition of Herman Melville* (Ann Arbor, Mich., 1967), p. 40. Betts, "*Moby Dick:* Melville's *Faust,*" *Lock Haven Bulletin,* I (1959), 31-44; Dédéyan, *Le Thème de Faust dans la littérature européenne* (Paris, 1961), IV, pt. 1, 206-224; Mann, *Gesammelte Werke* (Frankfurt am Main, 1960), IX, 599; Spengler, *Der Untergang des Abendlandes,* 2 vols. (Munich, 1922-1923), the most brilliant and elaborate argument for the identification of the Western mind with Faust; Seung, *Cultural Thematics: The Formation of the Faustian Ethos* (New Haven, Conn., 1976). The Western obsession with Faust is amply documented. See, e.g., E. M. Butler, *The Fortunes of Faust* (Cambridge, Eng., 1952); Geneviève Bianquis, *Faust à travers quatre siècles* (Paris, 1935); it took Dédéyan six volumes to chronicle the theme of Faust in Western literature; André Dabezies discovered that he had to take into account hundreds of works in order to produce a reasonably complete survey of *Visages de Faust au XXe siècle* (Paris, 1967). From among the innumerable nineteenth-century reactions to Faust, I select one whose origin (a newspaper article of 1835) shows how widespread even then was the idea of Faust's sentativeness; referring to Goethe's conclusion of his masterpiece, the *Zeitung für die elegante Welt* says that "to have abandoned Faust would have meant abandoning the entire modern world, since Faust is all of us" (quoted in Hans Schwerte, *Faust und das Faustische,* Stuttgart, 1962, p. 82; all translations in this essay are mine, unless otherwise indicated). On more exalted levels, Hegel and Schopenhauer, Mme de Staël and Carlyle, Emerson and Margaret Fuller were saying much the same thing. For Melville's familiarity with Goethe's *Faust,* see Henry A. Pochmann, *German Culture in America* (Madison, Wisc., 1961), p. 759, n. 262.

3. Chase, *The American Novel and Its Tradition* (Garden City, N.Y., 1957), p. 101; *Mardi,* [in] *The Writings of Herman Melville,* ed. Harrison Hayford, Hershel Parker, and G. Thomas Tanselle (Evanston, Ill., and Chicago, 1970), III, 557.

4. Spengler, I, 229; Spitzer, *Essays in Historical Semantics* (New York, 1968), p. 300, n. 70.

5. Spengler, I, 264, 512. Cf. D. W. Robertson, Jr., *A Preface to Chaucer* (Princeton, 1962), p. 182: "The God of the Middle Ages . . . may have been ineffable . . . but He was a much more immediate Being than the romantic infinite."

6. Christopher Marlowe, *Tamburlaine the Great,* Part I, II, vii, 21-23; Ralph Waldo Emerson, *Nature* (1836; facsimile rpt. San Francisco, 1968), p. 61; Spengler, I, 400.

7. Lukács, *Die Zerstörung der Vernunft* (Neuwied am Rhein, 1962), p. 103; Blaise Pascal, *Pensées, Oeuvres complètes* (Paris, 1954), pp. 1112-1113; Koyré, *From the Closed World to the Infinite Universe* (Baltimore, 1957), p. 275. On the extension of space see also Marjorie Hope Nicolson, *The Breaking of the Circle* (rev. ed.; New York, 1960). Rainer Maria Rilke, *Sämtliche Werke* (Wiesbaden, 1956), II, 93; see also his seventh *Duineser Elegie:* "Nirgends, Geliebte, wird Welt sein, als innen . . . immer geringer/schwindet das Außen" (*Sämtliche Werke,* Wiesbaden, 1955, I, 711).

8. *Call me Ishmael* (New York, 1947), p. 82.

9. Herman Melville, *Moby-Dick,* ed. Harrison Hayford and Hershel Parker (New York, 1967). p. 16. All page references to *Moby-Dick* are to this edition and will be given in the text.

10. For the possible compositional implications of the inconsistency between the book's "landlessness" and Ishmael's earlier stated desire to "land on barbarous coasts" (p. 16), see James Barbour, "The *Town-Ho*'s Story: Melville's Original Whale," *ESQ: A Journal of the American Renaissance,* XXI (2nd Quarter, 1975), 111, and "The Composition of *Moby-Dick,*" *American Literature,* XLVII (Nov., 1975), 352 and n. 22.

11. Spengler, I, 241; Seelye, *Melville: The Ironic Diagram* (Evanston, Ill., 1970), p. 64. For a general perspective, see Robert Martin Adams, *Nil: Episodes in the Literary Conquest of Void during the Nineteenth Century* (New York, 1966); pp. 141-148 deal with *Moby-Dick.*

12. Spengler, I, 512.

13. "Of Pale Ushers and Gothic Piles: Melville's Architectural Symbology," *ESQ: A Journal of the American Renaissance,* XVIII (2nd Quarter, 1972), 76, 79, 78.

14. *Mardi,* p. 284.

15. Miller, *The Disappearance of God* (Cambridge, Mass., 1963), p. 8; *The Complete Works of Ralph Waldo Emerson,* ed. Edward Waldo Emerson (Boston, 1903-1904), III, 5; Johann Wolfgang Goethe, *Gedenkausgabe der Werke, Briefe und Gespräche,* ed. Ernst Beutler (Zurich, 1962), II, 471; Poulet, *The Metamorphoses of the Circle,* trans. Carley Dawson, Elliott Coleman, and the author (Baltimore, 1966), p. 93; Georg Wilhelm Friedrich

Hegel, *Vorlesungen über die Aesthetik,* [in] *Sämtliche Werke,* XIII (Stuttgart, 1964), 122-123; the tribute to Hegel's aesthetic theories is from Paul Frankl, *The Gothic* (Princeton, N.J., 1960), p. 473; Dryden, p. 84.

16. For a different interpretation, one emphasizing "things rather than ideas," see Robert Zoellner, *The Salt-Sea Mastodon* (Berkeley, 1973; the quotation is from p. 8). Zoellner's argument is best summarized on p. 150: "The true narrative line of *Moby-Dick* is not the pursuit of the White Whale, but rather the transmutation which Ishmael's sensibility undergoes as that pursuit is prosecuted—and the essence of this transmutation is the gradual displacement of the conceptual whale by the perceptual whale."

17. Seung, *Cultural Thematics;* Brown, *Love's Body* (New York, 1966), pp. 191-200; Heine, *Sämtliche Werke* (Munich, 1923), V, 351.

18. Bowen, p. 122.

19. *A Common Sky: Philosophy and the Literary Imagination* (London, 1974). See also William Ellery Sedgwick, *Herman Melville: The Tragedy of Mind* (New York, 1962), pp. 111-112: ". . . the solipsism of consciousness, a theme which Melville continually broaches in *Moby Dick*"; and Thomas Woodson, "Ahab's Greatness: Prometheus as Narcissus," *ELH: A Journal of English Literary History,* XXXIII (Sept., 1966), 362: "Ahab is haunted by the unknowability of 'things,' and turns desperately to solipsism."

20. *Call me Ishmael,* p. 12.

21. *Ishmael's White World: A Phenomenological Reading of* Moby Dick (New Haven, 1965), p. 119.

22. Spengler, I, 75, 107; Kohlschmidt, *Form und Innerlichkeit* (Bern, 1955), p. 162; Sypher, *Loss of the Self in Modern Literature and Art* (New York, 1962), p. 19.

23. Thomas Carlyle, *Sartor Resartus* (New York, 1937), p. 53; Ralph Harper, *The Seventh Solitude: Metaphysical Homelessness in Kierkegaard, Dostoevsky, and Nietzsche* (Baltimore, 1965), pp. 11-13.

24. "Ahab's Greatness: Prometheus as Narcissus," pp. 363-364.

25. Søren Kierkegaard, *Concluding Unscientific Postscript,* trans. David F. Swenson and Walter Lowrie (Princeton, N.J., 1941), p. 35, n.

26. *Symbolism and American Literature* (Chicago, 1953), p. 29.

27. M. H. Abrams, *Natural Supernaturalism: Tradition and Revolution in Romantic Literature* (New York, 1973), p. 216.

28. "*Moby-Dick*: Work of Art," in Moby-Dick: *Centennial Essays,* ed. Tyrus Hillway and Luther S. Mansfield (Dallas, 1953), pp. 36-37.

29. Ibid., p. 56.

30. The Hayford-Parker edition of *Moby-Dick* follows textual tradition in attributing this passage to Ishmael; however, the editors note the possibility of Ahab's being the speaker of the passage (see p. 494).

31. "Ishmael: Time and Personality in *Moby-Dick,*" *Studies in the Novel,* I (Winter, 1969), 471.

32. Cf. Warwick Wadlington's interesting discussion of the cycle of experience in *Moby-Dick* and its role in generating an ever-contingent identity: *The Confidence Game in American Literature* (Princeton, N.J., 1975), pp. 73-103.

33. *Mardi,* p. 230.

34. Emerson, *Complete Works,* XII, 70; Friedrich Hölderlin, *Hyperions Jugend,* [in] *Sämtliche Werke und Briefe* (Munich, 1970), I, 524: "Das ist die Herrlichkeit des Menschen, daß ihm ewig nichts genügt. In deiner Unmacht tut sie dir sich kund. Denke dieser Herrlichkeit!"

35. *The Letters of John Keats,* ed. Hyder Edward Rollins (Cambridge, Mass., 1958), I, 193; Camus, "Melville: Un Créateur de mythes," in Moby-Dick *as Doubloon: Essays and Extracts,* ed. Hershel Parker and Harrison Hayford (New York, 1970), p. 248.

36. Hegel's *Vorlesungen über die Aesthetik* have often been considered a "funeral oration on art." See, e.g., René Wellek, *A History of Modern Criticism* (New Haven, Conn., 1955), II, 321, 334; Benedetto Croce, *Aesthetic,* trans. Douglas Ainslie (New York, 1968), p. 302; Erich Heller, *The Artist's Journey into the Interior and Other Essays* (New York, 1968), p. 115. Cf. also Macaulay's claim, in his essay on Milton (1825), that "as civilisation advances, poetry almost necessarily declines" (*Critical and Historical Essays,* London, 1961, I, 153). See also the references to the "Extinction of poetry" in Wellek, II, 456.

37. Friedrich Nietzsche, *Gesammelte Werke* (Munich, 1926), XIX, 229.

Larry J. Reynolds (essay date summer 1980)

SOURCE: Reynolds, Larry J. "Kings and Commoners in *Moby-Dick.*" *Studies in the Novel* 12, no. 2 (summer 1980): 101-13.

[*In the following essay, Reynolds analyzes the tension between democratic and aristocratic ideas in* Moby-Dick. *Reynolds argues that this opposition of political ideals reflects Melville's own ambivalence toward the prospects of egalitarianism in American society.*]

If one examines Herman Melville's sociopolitical thought in detail and depth, he will discover that it consists of two opposing sets of attitudes—one democratic, the other antidemocratic and elitist—that were in irreconcilable conflict throughout Melville's life. His democratic attitudes, what he called his "unconditional democracy," centered upon a high regard for the idea of man and were broadly social, rather than narrowly political, in meaning. For him, democracy meant recognizing the innate dignity and equality of man, in the ideal, and treating all men, particularly the lowly and oppressed, with respect and sympathy. His elitism, on the other hand, which was both social and intellectual, centered upon a low regard for the mass of actual men and meant viewing and treating the mass with dislike and disdain, while according admiration and empathy to a worthy few.[1] Although he had little regard for the wealthy and limited sympathy for feudal hereditary aristocracies, he, nevertheless, applied standards of birth and class along with intelligence and depth of vision in his evaluations of others. Throughout his works, his democracy expresses itself explicitly in a humanitarian concern for Polynesian natives, Negro slaves, Irish immigrants, common sailors, and the poor and outcast in general, while his elitism implicitly informs the attributes, attitudes, and actions of his main characters, who are socially and intellectually superior to the mass of ordinary men.

Unlike James Fenimore Cooper, whose background and thought parallel his own in many ways, Melville did not try to resolve the conflict in his attitudes by professing political democracy while insisting upon social aristocracy; instead, he paraded one set of attitudes and disclaimed the other. In an 1851 letter to Hawthorne, he exhibits the sweeping egalitarianism he liked to assert at the height of his career, declaring that "with no son of man do I stand upon any etiquette or ceremony, except the Christian ones of charity and honesty" and warning his friend: "When you see or hear of my ruthless democracy on all sides, you may possibly feel a touch of a shrink, or something of that sort. It is but nature to be shy of a mortal who boldly declares that a thief in jail is as honorable a personage as Gen. George Washington." In an afterthought, however, he reveals the tension underlying his boldness as he concedes: "It seems an inconsistency to assert unconditional democracy in all things, and yet confess a dislike to all mankind—in the mass."[2]

Recognition of this tension in Melville's thought is not prevalent among his major biographers and critics,[3] and, over the years, only a handful of commentators have pointed it out.[4] Moreover, no one to date, with one exception, has explored its importance in his literary work.[5] This essay is an attempt to show the most important ways it shapes Melville's greatest work, *Moby-Dick.*

* * *

In Melville's first five novels, *Typee* (1846), *Omoo* (1847), *Mardi* (1849), *Redburn* (1849), and *White-Jacket* (1850), the democratic-elitist tension can be seen growing stronger as he presents its two sides with more seriousness and force and becomes more concerned with resolving the conflict within his own mind. In *Moby-Dick* (1851), the rich and dark masterpiece he scraped "off the whole brain to get at,"[6] the underlying tension creates a thematic complexity and depth that all readers sense. In a very self-conscious way, *Moby-Dick* is an American book, constructed out of American materials and exploring the plight of the superior individual in American society. Not surprisingly, of all the novel's ideological dimensions, including the philosophical, the psychological, and the religious, none has engaged modern critical attention more consistently than has the sociopolitical. At first, this particular dimension of the work appears dualistic and clear, with democratic attitudes informing Ishmael's conduct and character and elitist attitudes informing Ahab's. In fact, most critics interpret the novel in this manner, taking sides with what they see as Ishmael's democratic liberalism or Ahab's kingly nobility, with the former receiving the admiration of most critics since F. O. Matthiessen's 1941 condemnation of Ahab as a destructive and alienated individualist.

In one of the most influential evaluations of *Moby-Dick* yet made, Matthiessen declares: "Without deliberately intending it, but by virtue of his intense concern with the precariously maintained values of democratic Christianity, which he saw everywhere being threatened or broken down, Melville created in Ahab's tragedy a fearful symbol of the self-enclosed individualism that, carried to its furthest extreme, brings disaster both upon itself and upon the group of which it is part."[7] A multitude of critics have echoed Matthiessen; Milton R. Stern and Ray B. Browne, to cite just two examples, have done so rather clearly. Stern observes that "as forecastle-Ishmael is identified with the history of common humanity, quarterdeck-Ahab is totally isolated," and he finds that the bulk of the novel's materials "work together to suggest that men, in the inescapable democracy of mutual mortality, must give their primary attention to the world they live in."[8] Similarly, Browne finds that in *Moby-Dick* "Melville suggests the eventual tragic failure of the Promethean impulse in the individual but its eventual triumph in massed Prometheanism in humanity—in democracy—in the person of Ishmael." For Browne, Ishmael is "the commonest of the commoners," who at the novel's end "has been apotheosized as a symbol of the rise of the common man."[9]

While such analyses of the novel have a satisfying formal neatness and an appealing liberal emphasis, they unfortunately result in an oversimplification of the complex sociopolitical views represented by Ishmael and, to a lesser extent, those represented by Ahab. As I hope to show, the attributes and attitudes of both characters arise from the tension that characterizes Melville's own thought.

Walter E. Bezanson has pointed out a critically important, but often ignored, feature of *Moby-Dick*; that is, it contains two Ishmaels. "The first Ishmael is the enfolding sensibility of the novel, the hand that writes the tale, the imagination through which all matters of the book pass. He is the narrator. . . . The second Ishmael is not the narrator, not the informing presence, but is the young man of whom, among others, narrator Ishmael tell us in his story. . . . This is forecastle Ishmael or the younger Ishmael of 'some years ago.'"[10] With the younger Ishmael we have indeed a Melvillean main character whose behavior is not elitist or antidemocratic in any discernible way. He eats, sleeps, and works with the "people" without reservation and is willing to be sociable with anyone, regardless of his social or intellectual status; the opening scenes where he befriends a "head-peddling" cannibal serve to dramatize this point. "It is but well to be on friendly terms with all the inmates of the place one lodges in,"[11] narrator Ishmael declares, and this philosophy is not contradicted by the account of his past practice, as it is with all of Melville's other first-person narrators.

When we consider the older Ishmael, the reflecting, brooding, wondering, explaining consciousness, whose voice is often indistinguishable from Melville's own, he seems at first to share the pure democratic sensibilities of his younger self. In his memorable "Knights and Squires" speech, he sings the praises of the crew, the "kingly commons," and celebrates "that democratic dignity which, on all hands, radiates without end from God; Himself! The great God absolute! The centre and circumference of all democracy! His omnipresence, our divine equality!" (p. 104). Elsewhere, like the narrators that precede him in the earlier works, Ishmael reveals his democratic abhorrence of the failure of men and institutions to recognize and value the inherent dignity, equality, and brotherhood of all. In *Moby-Dick*, of course, the most noticeable failure is Ahab's, and in

"The Specksynder," Ishmael specifically condemns his captain's "irresistible dictatorship," explaining that "be a man's intellectual superiority what it will, it can never assume the practical, available supremacy over other men, without the aid of some sort of external arts and entrenchments, always, in themselves, more or less paltry and base" (p. 129).

Nevertheless, while many of narrator Ishmael's attitudes are thoroughly democratic, the matter and manner of his narrative itself contain an elitist and antidemocratic bias that ultimately places him closer in attitude and outlook to Ahab than to any member of the crew. Ishmael's high regard for the idea of man and his sympathy for the lowly and oppressed are opposed and balanced by a dislike for the mass of mankind and an admiration for the noble few, among whom he includes himself and his captain. Like Emerson who admitted, "I like man, but not men,"[12] Ishmael acknowledges the paradox in his own thinking when he says, "take high abstracted man alone; and he seems a wonder, a grandeur, and a woe. But . . . take mankind in mass, and for the most part, they seem a mob of unnecessary duplicates . . ." (p. 387).

In the opening pages of the novel, Ishmael specifically disowns aristocratic pretensions by declaring, "when I go to sea, I go as a simple sailor, right before the mast, plumb down into the forecastle, aloft there to the royal mast-head" (p. 14), yet he soon admits that being ordered about "touches one's sense of honor, particularly if you come of an old established family in the land, the Van Rensselaers, or Randolphs, or Hardicanutes" (p. 14). Later, through casual, pretentious references, he further emphasizes his high birth and fallen lot. For example, in "The Town-Ho's Story" he refers to socializing in Lima with the circle of his Spanish friends, and adds that "of those fine cavaliers, the young Dons, Pedro and Sebastian, were on the closer terms with me" (p. 208). Similarly, in "A Bower in the Arsacides" he refers nonchalantly to his "late royal friend Tranquo, king of Tranque" and mentions vacationing "at his retired palm villa at Pupella" (p. 373).

Ishmael's dissatisfaction with his status as a "common" sailor and his pride in past aristocratic associations are complemented by a subtle personal antipathy toward democratic leveling, an antipathy that surfaces in his note on "gally," an English word obsolete except for its use by American whalemen. He laments that "much the same is it with many other sinewy Saxonisms of this sort, which emigrated to the New-England rocks with the noble brawn of the old English emigrants in the time of the Commonwealth. Thus, some of the best and furthest-descended English words—the etymological Howards and Percys—are now democratised, nay, plebeianised—so to speak—in the New World" (p. 322). (This sentiment would be echoed in *Pierre* in Melville's autobiographical lament that "in our cities families rise and burst like bubbles in a vat. For indeed the democratic element operates as a subtle acid among us; forever producing new things by corroding the old. . . .")[13]

Any study of the allusions of *Moby-Dick* reveals that Ishmael not only likes to display his uncommon erudition, but also in his thoughts prefers, like Taji of *Mardi,* to circulate "freely, sociably, and frankly, among the gods, heroes, high-priests, kings, and gentlemen."[14] As his metaphors and similes repeatedly disclose, nobility, royalty, and greatness fascinate him. He compares his captain to King Ahab and King Belshazzar and calls him "a Khan of the plank, and a king of the sea, and a great lord of Leviathans" (p. 114); he compares Queequeg to Czar Peter; Daggoo, the "imperial negro," to King Ahasuerus; the *Pequod* to an Ethiopian emperor; Steelkilt to Mark Antony and Charlemagne; and Moby Dick to King Antiochus's elephants and to the white bull Jupiter. He associates the whiteness of the whale with royalty and preeminence and claims that "whaling is imperial," noting that by old English law the whale is "a royal fish" (p. 101). Finally, in his discussion of his own vocation, he humorously becomes carried away with the honor and nobility of it all, claiming that Perseus, St. George, Hercules, and Jonah should be considered whalemen, and adding, "Nor do heroes, saints, demigods, and prophets alone comprise the whole roll of our order. Our grand master [Vishnoo] is still to be named; for like royal kings of old times, we find the head-waters of our fraternity in nothing short of the great gods themselves" (pp. 304-6).

Traditionally, critics have tried to reconcile Ishmael's admiration for the noble few with his democratic attitudes in two ways: first, by arguing that he appreciates various heroes and kings not for their own sakes but as metaphors to represent and emphasize the natural excellence of even the common man; and second, by proposing that his regard is artistic, rather than personal, in origin, that is, that it arises from his, or Melville's, attempt to create Shakespearean tragedy out of American materials, an attempt that demands the magnification and aggrandizement of the crew, "the Whale, the Ship, and, OVER ALL, the Captain."[15] Both of these theses, however, are only partially valid.

Although many of Ishmael's "outward majestical trappings and housings" (p. 130) are certainly intended to impart a nobility and grandeur to ordinary men and their disdainfully-regarded profession, this intent should be seen as an effect rather than a cause of his elitism. Like all of Melville's narrators, Ishmael values actual as well as figurative nobility. His reflections on Queequeg effectively reveal this. The younger Ishmael initially admires Queequeg because of the man's frankness, generosity, kindheartedness, and courage. Narrator Ishmael, however, delightedly announces that this friend was no "common" cannibal for "his father was a High Chief, a King; his uncle a High Priest; and on the maternal side he boasted aunts who were the wives of unconquerable warriors" (p. 56). In other words, blood will tell; Queequeg's noble character is explained by his noble lineage. And, although Ishmael makes this point in a humorous manner, the humor should not mislead anyone about Melville's acceptance of its validity, for he had made precisely the same point about King Mehevi in *Typee* and Jack Chase in *White-Jacket,* and he would make it again about the noble foundling Billy in *Billy Budd.*

As for the demands of genre as an explanation for Ishmael's emphasis on nobility and greatness, we need only recall the fascination with and appreciation of birth, rank, and power present in the earlier works, particularly *Mardi,* to realize that part of Melville's enthusiasm for Shakespeare (which he acquired during the spring of 1849 and defined during August of 1850 while in the first stages of writing *Moby-Dick*)[16] followed rather than preceded the formulation of his, and thus Ishmael's, attitudes. Certainly, much of the texture of *Moby-Dick,* including the stage directions, the soliloquies, the prophecies, and the poeticized rantings of Ahab, derives from Melville's recent rereading of Shakespeare, particularly *Macbeth* and *King Lear,* and it establishes the novel's uniqueness among Melville's works; nevertheless, Ishmael's elitist regard for uncommon men, particularly heroes and kings, is shared by Tommo, Omoo, Taji, Redburn, and White-Jacket and thus is not part of this uniqueness. As Nathalia Wright has observed with regard to the whole of Melville's works, "for all his democracy, Melville's world has an aristocratic cast."[17]

Ultimately, I think, narrator Ishmael's democratic attitudes must be viewed as irreconcilably in conflict with his intellectual tendency to align himself with superior individuals and groups. This tendency, however, forms only half of his elitism; his dislike and disdain for the mass of actual men form the other. When Ishmael observes that "men may seem detestable as joint stock-companies and nations" but "man, in the ideal," is "a grand and glowing creature" (p. 104), the qualification "in the ideal" is all-important. Interpretations of the novel that stress its democratic, Democratic, humanistic, or humanitarian aspects tend to overlook or blur the distinction between Ishmael's view of ideal man and his view of the mass of men. Like Ahab, he perceives that the "people" of the *Pequod* measure up to no ideal, and his narrative continually dramatizes the baseness, savagery, and ignorance that lie beneath the surface character of the inhabitants of this shipboard society.

For example, in "Midnight, Forecastle" he presents an account of a drunken fight between Daggoo and a Spanish sailor that reveals the murderous impulses of the crew and suggests that these impulses are God's work. As the fight begins, the sailors cry for a ring and the Old Manx sailor observes, "Ready formed. There! the ringed horizon. In that ring Cain struck Abel. Sweet work, right work! No? Why then, God, mad'st thou the ring?" (p. 154). The wild and brutal action of the scene confirms Starbuck's estimate of the men as "a heathen crew that have small touch of human mothers in them! Whelped somewhere by the sharkish sea. The white whale is their demogorgon" (p. 148).

The three sailors shown to respond most willingly and enthusiastically to Ahab's incitements are the harpooners, Daggoo, Tashtego, and Queequeg. Although Queequeg is initially characterized as noble, independent, and kindhearted, he later joins Tashtego and Daggoo "in an eager sympathy with Ahab's murderous purpose," as Merlin Bowen has pointed out.[18] Ahab calls the harpooners "my three pagan kinsmen" (p. 146), and as the novel progresses Ishmael uses them to symbolize the dark, primitive, and savage side of man and nature—the side seen by him as dominant and the only side seen by Ahab. When Ahab baptizes his harpoon in the name of the devil, these three willingly supply the baptismal blood, and when he presides over the black mass in "The Candles," they become, in appearance at least, his fellow devil worshippers. Finally, in "The Try-Works," they again lose their individuality and become "Tartean shapes" revealing the dark and unholy side of mankind.

The three mates, Starbuck, Stubb, and Flask are presented by Ishmael as less noticeably unadmirable than the "people" under their command, yet they, too, fail to live up to any ideal conception of man. The righteous Starbuck is, on the whole, a weak and shallow individual, lacking the intellectual depth necessary to understand Ahab's motives and the courage necessary to resist his designs. He can only naively and pathetically exclaim, "Let faith oust fact" (p. 406). Stubb, good-natured and courageous in his way, shares Starbuck's pragmatic and limited vision. He also displays an occasional insensitivity, and after abandoning the helpless Pip on the ocean justifies his action by hinting that "though man loves his fellow, yet man is a money-making animal" (p. 346). As for the third mate Flask, he can act with an appalling cruelty, as we see in the description of the blind and crippled whale that he needlessly tortures. This conduct, as F. O. Matthiessen has conceded, "becomes a contributing factor to our sense that . . . this crew may deserve something of the retribution that overtakes it."[19] Viewed realistically, then, the men of the *Pequod* are, as narrator Ishmael declares, "mongrel renegades, and castaways, and cannibals—morally enfeebled . . . by the incompetence of mere unaided virtue or right-mindedness in Starbuck, the invulnerable jollity of indifference and recklessness in Stubb, and the pervading mediocrity in Flask" (p. 162).

As such they are viewed with dislike and disdain not only by Ahab, but by narrator Ishmael as well.

It has been customary to see in *Moby-Dick* the theme of democratic brotherhood presented as the affirmative alternative to the tragic individualism embodied by Ahab. The friendship that develops between the younger Ishmael and Queequeg, that is, their "marriage" and "hearts' honeymoon" in "A Bosom Friend," is usually accepted as the introduction of the theme; "The Monkey-Rope" and "A Squeeze of the Hand" as the development and extension of it; and "The Epilogue" as its conclusion, with Ishmael appropriately saved by the "coffin life-buoy" of his friend. This view of the novel has obvious merit, and I have no intention of denying its validity; however, I want to stress that the view is limited and often results in an incomplete understanding of Ishmael's attitudes toward himself and others, particularly through the failure to recognize his deep reservations about the goodness and worth of his former fellow sailors, including Queequeg. Furthermore, critics who cite "A Squeeze of the Hand" as evidence of an affirmation of brotherhood in the novel, usually disregard the outrageous sexual implications of the chapter. As Robert Shulman has pointed out, although the chapter "may contain one of Melville's few social affirmations—that brotherhood saves and love redeems—it should be stressed that what is recommended is a peculiarly anti-social sociality."[20]

Although Ishmael as common sailor participates in the democratic society of the forecastle, as narrator, he is more closely allied with the uncommon individual occupying the quarterdeck. While he perceives and abhors Ahab's ruthless manipulation and sacrifice of others, he also sees and admires his "globular brain" and "ponderous heart" (p. 71) and the heroic suffering and courage they inspire. Ishmael's admiration for Ahab's greatness, a greatness that ultimately lies in grief,[21] is often explicit as when he explains that "great hearts sometimes condense to one deep pang, the sum total of those shallow pains kindly diffused through feebler men's whole lives. And so, such hearts, though summary in each one suffering; still, if the gods decree it, in their life-time aggregate a whole age of woe, wholly made up of instantaneous intensities; for even in their pointless centres, those noble natures contain the entire circumferences of inferior souls" (p. 451). At other times, his admiration is implicit and informs his consistent presentation of Ahab as "a mighty pageant creature, formed for noble tragedies" (p. 71) and accounts for the figurative superiority given him in the drama he acts out. In other words, while Ahab in his own right possesses an intellectual superiority accorded him by his rare mind, and tragic vision and a social superiority accorded him by his rank, authority, and power, Ishmael figuratively enhances the latter in tribute to the former. In the process, however, he ironically undercuts his idealization of democracy by presenting the crew as the knights, squires, and commoners of a feudal hierarchy.

Looking at Ahab apart from Ishmael's magnification of him, one sees a man thoroughly convinced of his superiority to all other men and expressing attitudes that, with just one exception, are totally elitist. As Captain Peleg says, "Ahab's above the common; Ahab's been in colleges, as well as 'mong the cannibals" (p. 76), and Ahab is acutely aware of his uncommonness, using it to justify his actions. Convinced that "the permanent constitutional condition of the manufactured man . . . is sordidness" (p. 184) and believing that he "stands alone among the millions of the peopled earth" (p. 452), he disdainfully uses his men as tools in his quest and maintains an "irresistible dictatorship" over them by exploiting their ignorance and depravity. His quarterdeck speech, his nailing of the doubloon to the mast, his magnetizing the compass needle, and his maintenance of the whaling voyage are some of the "external arts and entrenchments" (p. 129) by which he maintains his supremacy. Although Peleg also tells Ishmael that "Ahab has his humanities" (p. 77), they rarely appear. Except in his relationship with Pip and in his conversation with Starbuck in "The Symphony," Ahab is ruthlessly autocratic and shows no respect or sympathy toward his fellow man. (Ironically, of course, he nevertheless sees himself as a representative of mankind, as a Promethean savior defying "all the subtle demonisms of life and thought" (p. 160), all "the omniscient gods" who are "oblivious of suffering man" (p. 428).

Ahab's attitudes are democratic in one small aspect, however, and it forms his main link with Ishmael and with Melville as well. Starbuck isolates this aspect when he says, "Horrible old man! Who's over him, he cries;—aye, he would be a democrat to all above; look, how he lords it over all below!" (p. 148). Although Ahab's self-serving egalitarianism does not, of course, make him democratic in the broad humanitarian sense of the word, the consistent sense of pride that informs his inconsistent attitudes toward "all above" and "all below" does underlie both sides of the democratic-elitist tension found in all of Melville's works. Let me explain this important point, if I can. When Melville's narrators affirm the noble and godlike nature of man, in the ideal, they are, in effect, proudly asserting their own worth, and when they protest against the indignity and injustice inflicted upon the common man, these protests are inspired by proud indignation. Likewise, when his narrators express dislike and disdain for the mass of ordinary men, and when they identify with the superior few, these attitudes too can be traced to pride.

Although Ishmael's deep involvement in Ahab's tragic quest results in part from his sense of exile and alienation as well as from his acute awareness of the "heart-less voids and immensities of the universe" (p. 169), it is his rebellious sense of pride that brings him closest in spirit to his captain. While Ishmael begins his narrative humbly by referring to the "universal thump" and asking, "Who aint a slave?" (p. 15), he later declares, "I believe that much of a man's character will be found betokened in his backbone. . . . A thin joist of a spine never yet upheld a full and noble soul. I rejoice in my spine, as in the firm audacious staff of that flag which I fling half out to the world" (p. 294). Elsewhere, in a similar proud and defiant tone, he boasts, "come a stove boat and stove body when they will, for stave my soul, Jove himself cannot" (p. 41). And, in his famous tribute to Bulkington, he argues for earnest thinking and "the intrepid effort of the soul to keep the open independence of her sea; while the wildest winds of heaven and earth conspire to cast her on the treacherous, slavish shore" (p. 97).[22]

In the climactic "Try-Works" chapter, Ishmael discovers the dangers of looking too long in the face of the hellish fire, of seeing only "the redness, the madness, the ghastliness" (p. 354) around him, and for the first time clearly understands the distinction between his view of the world (which is two-thirds dark) and Ahab's (which is totally dark), between the "wisdom that is woe" and the "woe that is madness" (p. 355); nevertheless, both before and after this discovery, he vicariously participates in Ahab's heroic defiance of the god or gods that have maimed him. He shares Ahab's sense of self-respect and independence that bodies forth in opposition to anyone or anything that threatens to demean the self, and his assertion of Ahab's superiority to the mass of base, shallow, and "inferior souls" is indirectly an assertion of his own.

Melville, like Ishmael, felt a proud sense of superiority that he never abandoned, even in his most democratic moments. He was, as he told Sophia Hawthorne, "of Scotch descent—of noble lineage—of the Lords of Melville & Leven."[23] And although he tried to adjust to his family's fallen state and to the emergence of mass society in America by becoming an ardent democrat, he could not give up his view of himself as a déclassé patrician whom birth and genius placed far above the mass of ordinary men, but whom fate placed in lowly circumstances.

After writing *Moby-Dick,* in which his democratic and elitist attitudes conflict more vigorously than in any of his other writings, Melville began to lose his enthusiasm for democratic ideals, and his contempt for the tastes of the reading public (who failed to appreciate either *Moby-Dick* or *Pierre*) developed into contempt for the public itself. *The Confidence-Man* (1856) presents his strongest condemnation of all men, and **"Benito Cereno," "The House Top,"** and parts of *Clarel* (1876) contain conservative views of man and society that could not be much darker. In **Clarel** Mortmain declares "Man's vicious: snaffle him with kings; / Or, if kings cease to curb, devise / Severer bit," while Ungar sees life in America as "Myriads playing pygmy parts—/ Debased into equality."[24]

These articulate monomaniacs express the side of Melville's thought that grew stronger in his later years as he bitterly examined American society and its treatment of him. His last work, **Billy Budd,** represents a slight renaissance of his democratic attitudes and can be read as a defense of the dignity and rights of the common man; however, it can also be read, with perhaps more accuracy, as a work that defends the aristocratic Vere and supports his belief that "with mankind . . . forms, measured forms, are everything."[25] In other words, here, as in **Moby-Dick,** the democratic-elitist tension in Melville's thought performs a creative function, endowing his art with engaging complexity, depth, and contradiction.

Notes

1. Regrettably the term "elitism" is often used as a shibboleth in contemporary political rhetoric; I use it here for it is the only word which connotes the social and intellectual dimensions of this side of Melville's thought.

2. *The Letters of Herman Melville,* ed. Merrell R. Davis and William H. Gilman (New Haven: Yale Univ. Press, 1960), pp. 126-27.

3. During the 1920s and 30s, when it was customary to identify Melville with Ahab, scholars such as Raymond Weaver, in *Herman Melville: Mariner and Mystic* (New York: Doran, 1921), and Stanley Geist, in *Herman Melville: The Tragic Vision and the Heroic Ideal* (Cambridge: Harvard Univ. Press, 1939), emphasized Melville's high regard for the superior individual and said little about his democratic sympathy for others. Willard Thorp's Introduction to his *Herman Melville: Representative Selections* (New York: American Book Co., 1938), followed by F. O. Matthiessen's highly influential *American Renaissance: Art and Expression in the Age of Emerson and Whitman* (New York: Oxford Univ. Press, 1941), reversed this trend and focused critical attention on Melville's democratic humanism and social sympathies while de-emphasizing his elitist disdain for the mass and admiration for the superior few. Significantly, the beginning of this trend coincided with the rise of totalitarianism in Europe and new concern for the preservation of American democratic ideals. Today, this concern remains in the consciousness of the post-World War II generation of Melvilleans, and books and articles continue to appear that review his works through Matthiessen's eyes, seeing

there—particularly in the early works, *Typee* (1846) through *Moby-Dick* (1851)—liberal democratic attitudes in rather pure form. The 1950s saw a boom in such studies, but the trend remains prominent in the 1970s, as works such as Ray B. Browne's, *Melville's Drive to Humanism* (Lafayette, Ind.: Purdue Univ. Studies, 1971), Edward S. Grejda's *Common Continent of Men: Racial Equality in the Writings of Herman Melville* (Port Washington, N.Y.: Kennikat Press, 1974), and H. Bruce Franklin's *Victim as Criminal and Artist: Literature from the American Prison* (New York: Oxford Univ. Press, 1978) amply demonstrate.

4. Lewis Mumford, in his classic biography, *Herman Melville: A Study of His Life and Vision* (1929; rev. New York: Harcourt, Brace, 1962), p. 204, observes that Melville's "own outlook was emotionally patrician and aristocratic; but his years in the forecastle had modified those feelings, and one needs some such compound word as aristodemocracy to describe his dominant political attitude." Eleanor Metcalf, in *Journal of a Visit to London and the Continent by Herman Melville, 1849-1850* (Cambridge: Harvard Univ. Press, 1948), p. 144, also notes the "characteristic conflict in him of aristocratic leanings and democratic urgings." William H. Gilman, in his *Melville's Early Life and "Redburn"* (1951; rpt. New York: Russell and Russell, 1972), p. 15, observes the mingling of patrician and democratic sentiments in Melville's father and sees this mingling as "further curious evidence of the subtle influence extending from father to son." Similarly, Harrison Hayford and Merton M. Sealts, Jr., in the "Notes & Commentary" in *Billy Budd, Sailor (An Inside Narrative)* (Chicago: Univ. of Chicago Press, 1962), p. 180, note that throughout Melville's later works "runs a marked antithesis between . . . his 'ruthless democracy on all sides' and his evident pride of family, respect for tradition, and regard for those men who stand out from the mass, as do his own principal characters."

5. See my "Antidemocratic Emphasis in *White-Jacket,*" *American Literature,* 48 (March 1976), 13-28. Hershel Parker, "Melville and Politics: A Scrutiny of the Political Milieux of Herman Melville's Life and Works," Diss. Northwestern Univ. 1963, does an admirable job of dispelling the notion that Melville was an original political thinker and a prophet of democracy; however, it unfortunately discounts, rather than explores, the tension in Melville's thought by linking him with his shallow and opportunistic brother Gansevoort and claiming that Melville "was capable of elaborating contradictory arguments to fit the rhetorical demands of the work at hand, and to be as un-

troubled as Gansevoort had been about the need to 'believe' what he was saying" (p. 186).

6. *Letters,* p. 117.

7. *American Renaissance,* p. 459.

8. "*Moby-Dick,* Millennial Attitudes, and Politics," *Emerson Society Quarterly,* 54 (1st Qt. 1969), 59, 54.

9. *Melville's Drive toward Humanism,* pp. 39, 56. See also Willie T. Weathers, "*Moby Dick* and the Nineteenth-Century Scene," *Texas Studies in Literature and Language,* 1 (Winter 1960), 477-501; Charles H. Foster, "Something in Emblems: A Reinterpretation of *Moby-Dick,*" *New England Quarterly,* 34 (March 1961), 3-35; and Alan Heimert, "*Moby-Dick* and American Political Symbolism," *American Quarterly,* 15 (Winter 1963), 498-534.

10. "*Moby-Dick*: Work of Art," in Moby-Dick: *Centennial Essays,* ed. Tyrus Hillway and Luther S. Mansfield (Dallas: Southern Methodist Univ. Press, 1953), pp. 36-37.

11. *Moby-Dick,* ed. Harrison Hayford and Hershel Parker (New York: Norton, 1967), p. 16. All subsequent references are cited parenthetically in the text.

12. *The Heart of Emerson's Journals,* ed. Bliss Perry (1938; rpt. New York: Dover, 1958), p. 217.

13. [*Pierre,*] ed. Harrison Hayford, Hershel Parker, and G. Thomas Tanselle (Evanston and Chicago: Northwestern-Newberry, 1971), p. 9.

14. *Mardi,* ed. Harrison Hayford, Hershel Parker, and G. Thomas Tanselle (Evanston and Chicago: Northwestern-Newberry, 1970). p. 117.

15. Charles Olson, *Call Me Ishmael: A Study of Melville* (1947; rpt. San Francisco: City Light Books, n.d.), p. 71.

16. See *Letters,* p. 77 and "Hawthorne and His Mosses" in Norton *Moby-Dick,* pp. 541-42. Melville's primary enthusiasm was for Shakespeare's dark insights, for "those deep faraway things in him; those occasional flashings-forth of the intuitive Truth in him; those short, quick probings at the very axis of reality" ("Hawthorne and His Mosses," p. 541); however, he certainly also saw and appreciated what Erich Auerbach points out in *Mimesis,* trans. Willard Trask (Garden City, N.Y.: Doubleday, 1957), p. 277, that is, that Shakespeare's "conception of the sublime and tragic is altogether aristocratic."

17. *Melville's Use of the Bible* (Durham: Duke Univ. Press, 1949), p. 23.

18. *The Long Encounter: Self and Experience in the Writings of Herman Melville* (Chicago: Univ. of Chicago Press, 1960), p. 34.

19. *American Renaissance,* p. 437.

20. "The Serious Functions of Melville's Phallic Jokes," *American Literature,* 33 (May 1961), 185.

21. Stanley Geist's *Herman Melville: The Tragic Vision and the Heroic Ideal* brilliantly demonstrates this.

22. These sentiments are echoed by Melville himself in a letter to Hawthorne which expresses an admiration for the "man who, like Russia or the British Empire, declares himself a sovereign nature (in himself) amid the powers of heaven, hell, and earth. He may perish; but so long as he exists he insists upon treating with all Powers upon an equal basis. If any of those other Powers choose to withhold certain secrets, let them; that does not impair my sovereignty in myself; that does not make me tributary" (*Letters,* pp. 124-25). The transition from the third to the first person here reveals Melville's emotional identification with the man he describes.

23. Jay Leyda, *The Melville Log: A Documentary Life of Herman Melville, 1819-1891,* 2 vols. (1951; rpt. with new supplement, New York: Gordian Press, 1969), II, 925.

24. *Clarel,* ed. Walter E. Bezanson (New York: Hendricks House, 1960), pp. 154, 483.

25. Hayford and Sealts, *Billy Budd,* p. 128.

Michael Vannoy Adams (essay date winter 1983)

SOURCE: Adams, Michael Vannoy. "Whaling and Difference: *Moby-Dick* Deconstructed." *New Orleans Review* 10, no. 4 (winter 1983): 59-64.

[*In the following essay, Adams offers a theoretical reading of* Moby-Dick, *focusing on elements of ambiguity and eroticism in the novel.*]

From the Transparent Eyeball to the Pasteboard Mask

For a transcendentalist like Emerson, there is nothing arbitrary, "nothing lucky or capricious," in the relation between signifier and signified. The relation is, as Emerson says, "constant."[1] It is invariant: necessary and not contingent. The relation between signifier and signified "is not fancied by some poet," Emerson says. It does not depend, subjectively, on the whimsy of man "but stands in the will of God, and so is free to be known by all men," that is, to be discovered by them, objectively.[2] To the transcendentalist, nature is an appearance, behind or beyond which is reality—God, or the Over-Soul. Because signification is motivated by

God, vision is, for Emerson, unmediated. As he says, "I become a transparent eyeball. I am nothing. I see all."[3] Thus the ground of meaning for the transcendentalist is the ground of being, the ultimate transcendental signified, which is to say, the Over-Soul, or God, who wills it to be so. If nature is a sign that means something, what it means is designed by God, not assigned, arbitrarily, by man. In short, Emerson valorizes what Jonathan Culler calls a "theocritical" position.[4]

There are not seven but two types, or definitions, of ambiguity. That is, ambiguity may mean to be susceptible of multiple interpretation, or it may mean to be unamenable to any conclusive interpretation whatsoever. In this respect, Emerson says that "the highest minds of the world have never ceased to explore the double meaning, or shall I say the quadruple or the centuple or much more manifold meaning, of every sensuous fact."[5] According to Emerson, signification is polysemous. Every signifier—or sensuous fact—has not just one but many signifieds. The signifier is related to numerous, it may be to innumerable, signifieds. But this multiplicity is, for Emerson, grounded in what he calls "that Unity, that Over-Soul."[6] Hence what seems to be plurivocal signification is, finally, univocal signification—inasmuch as it is motivated, or willed, by God. In contrast, Melville defines ambiguity not as multiplicity of meaning but as indeterminacy of meaning. For Melville, signification is radically equivocal.

It is by means of Ahab that Melville expresses what is, to say the least, an ambivalent attitude toward transcendentalism [in *Moby-Dick*]. Ahab entertains seriously the possibility that nature is merely an appearance, or persona. "'All visible objects, man'" he says, "'are but as pasteboard masks.'" He declares that "'some unknown but still reasoning thing puts forth the mouldings of its features from behind the unreasoning mask.'" Insofar as Ahab insists that there is something behind or beyond the mask, he seems to be a transcendentalist. But to the extent that he has doubts and expresses them, he tends to be a deconstructor. "'Sometimes,'" he confesses, "'I think there's naught beyond.'"[7] Whether there is anything or nothing at all behind the mask, whether nature—in this case, the white whale—is appearance or reality, effect or cause, agent or principal, is a moot point. Ultimately, it matters not to Ahab whether the signifier is motivated by a transcendental signified. For if the white whale is finally caught by Ahab, if the floating signifier is harpooned, killed, dismembered, nature will, in effect, be grounded in a signified—an arbitrary one, it is true, but a signified nonetheless.

The relation between signifier and signified will depend on the whimsy of man; it will stand in the will, not of God, but of Ahab. What is at issue, of course, is the arbitrariness—or the willfulness—of signification. When all is said and done, Melville implies that signification is imputation. If anything means anything, it means what it means only because man endows it with what Derrida calls "the ideality of the sense."[8] Thus Ahab exercises the will and arbitrarily relates signifier to signified—which is to say, he realizes that signification is entirely at the discretion of man. In the end, the difference between the transparent eyeball and the pasteboard mask tends to be the difference between the transcendentalist and the deconstructor.

THE DOUBLOON OR THE DOUBLE (LOON)

Consider the doubloon that is nailed to the mast. Is it not the very epitome of ambiguity as double meaning, an exemplary instance of it, for does not "doubloon" mean, quite literally, "double"? The doubloon is a gold coin with a value of eight escudos, or sixteen dollars. But as Saussure says, value—either monetary or linguistic—is not strictly synonymous with significance.[9] What, then, is the significance of the doubloon? Ahab is obsessed by "the strange figures and inscriptions stamped on it," and he is determined "to interpret for himself in some monomaniac way whatever significance might lurk in them." The doubloon is strangely figured and inscribed, and what is minted, or written, must be read. Ishmael assumes that meaning is lurking in the doubloon and that what is concealed will be revealed by a reading of the writing. He says that "some certain significance lurks in all things, else all things are little worth, and the round world but an empty cipher" (p. 358). If everything is worth little, or worthless, if everything has little or no value, then what purpose does it serve to try to interpret anything, to attempt to decipher what is, after all, only a cipher, a nothing, a zero, an absence?

The doubloon, Ahab says, "'to each and every man in turn but mirrors back his own mysterious self'" (p. 359). To Ahab, interpretation is simply a solipsistic exercise, or fixation. It matters not what may be stamped on the doubloon, for whatever happens to be written will be read one way by one man, another way by another man. In effect, there is no double meaning (or for that matter, single meaning) either presented or represented by the doubloon. What is *inscribed on* the doubloon is *writing; meaning* is *ascribed to* the doubloon by *reading*. As Ahab says, the doubloon is a mirror, and signification is a self-reflective (or self-reflexive) activity. Thus those who look at the doubloon see in it only themselves. It is not the text itself but the self itself that matters. Signification is decentered precisely because it is self-centered. The text itself, the doubloon itself, is simply a point of departure, a convenient excuse for an egotistical imputation. The result, as John T. Irwin says, is "a study in multiple perspectivism." The doubloon "is indefinite in itself, and in its indefiniteness it allows the individual subject to project onto it the structure of a self as undecipherable as the world."[10]

Thus one sailor who tries to read "'a meaning out of these queer curvicues'" (p. 360) and then observes the attempts of the other sailors to read the doubloon says, "'There's another rendering now; but still one text'" (p. 362)—another reading but still one writing. Finally, Pip, who also "'has been watching all of these interpreters,'" approaches the doubloon. Pip is a grammatologist who conjugates the verb "to look" and in so doing reduces the ideality of the sense to utter nonsense. "'I look, you look, he looks; we look, ye look, they look,'" he repeats derisively (p. 362). The doubloon, he says, is "'the ship's navel,'" and in looking at it, the interpreters are not only contemplating their own navels but also, in their own screwy ways, attempting to unscrew them. "'But,'" Pip riddles as he ridicules, "'unscrew your navel, and what's the consequence?'" The consequence is that your backside may fall off, which is to say, you may lose your ass. And that, of course, is exactly what happens to all the sailors with the sole exception of Ishmael, whose ass just happens to be saved.[11]

Pip says that "'when aught's nailed to the mast it's a sign that things grow desperate'" (p. 363). If the doubloon is the aught that is nailed to the mast, it may mean—as Ahab says in reference to the white whale—naught. It may be only a zero, an absence. It may mean nothing, or at least nothing more than Ahab and the other sailors arbitrarily attribute to it.[12] (In this regard, Theodore Thass-Thienemann remarks that aught, which derives from "Old English *ā-wiht,* 'ever-wight,'" is "the goblin of mathematics, the cipher zero." He notes that "*aught* means the same as *naught*" and that naught, which derives from "Old English *ne-ā-wiht,* 'not-ever-wight,'" means the same as "*nought,* 'a nothing,'" which results in "*not,* the grammatical function of which is to negate.")[13] If so, Pip is the real doubloon, a double(loon) or double lunatic who supplements writing degree zero with reading degree zero, practices the metaphysics of absence, and employs double talk in order to deconstruct the assumption that meaning lurks in the object and exists independently of the observer, who, look as he may, sees only what he will: a mirror image or double self, the mere reflection of a projection.[14]

THE EGYPTIAN CONNOTATION: HIEROGLYPHIC AND PYRAMID

Ahab is sure that the felicities of life have "a certain unsignifying pettiness lurking in them" (just as Ishmael is sure that all things have a certain significance lurking in them, else all things have little or no value), while the miseries of life have "a mystic significance" (p. 386). There is no felicity to Ahab, only misery, for he is not a demystifier, or deconstructor. He is a constructor of significance. He is a mystifier—and not the sort that Ishmael is when he says that the spoutings and sprinklings of the white whale are mere "mistifyings" (p. 310)—that is, "nothing but mist" (p. 313). Ahab is in search of the white whale, which is to say, in pursuit of signs. The chase is a quest after a quarry that is both allusive (suggestive of significance) and elusive. It is an attempt to construe a significance, a futile effort to catch the one—in other words, the truth—that got away and always will get away.

Ahab offers the doubloon as a reward to the first sailor to sight the white whale. To set a sight on the white whale as it breaches the surface of the sea is, for Ahab, to catch a glimpse of the sign as it broaches the truth. In this respect, Derrida says that those who practice the metaphysics of presence assume that "the sign is maintained only *in sight of* truth"—in this case, in sight of the white whale. Why is the sign thus related to truth? Why, indeed? "This 'why,'" Derrida contends, "can no longer be understood as a 'What does this mean?'" He asserts that the questions "'What does signification signify?'—'What does meaning mean?'" are impertinent, or irrelevant. "Hence," he says, "we must posit our questions both at the point and in the form in which signification no longer signifies, meaning means nothing." This is the point at which and the form in which deconstruction is not only possible but also necessary. "'Why?' then no longer marks, here," Derrida says, "a question about the 'sight-set-on-what' (for what reason?), about the *telos* or *eskhaton* of the movement of signification; nor a question about an origin, a 'why?' as a 'because of what?' 'on the basis of what?' etc."[15]

In other words, the "why?" no longer poses a question about the sight-set-on-the-white-whale (for what reason, or purpose, does Ahab pursue the white whale?). It does not pose a question about how the process of signification ends, teleologically or eschatologically. Nor does it pose a question about how the process of signification begins (because of what, or on the basis of what, etc., does Ahab pursue the white whale?). No longer does the "why?" mark the answer "Ahab pursues the white whale in order to exact revenge" or, for that matter, the answer "Ahab pursues the white whale because it dismembered him," for these answers merely impose an arbitrary closure on the movement of signification. According to Derrida, such answers "would place a reassuring end to the reference from sign to sign."[16] In the name of meaning—that is, in the name of the truth of the sign—such answers, he says, "would arrest the concatenation of writing."[17] They would terminate a process that is interminable, which is to say, indeterminable. To explain what the white whale is, or signifies, "would be to dive deeper than Ishmael can go" (p. 162). The significance of the white whale is, finally, unfathomable.

Like the doubloon, the white whale is a text. It, too, is inscribed with signs—or, more specifically, engraved with hieroglyphics. Ishmael says that "if you call those mysterious cyphers on the walls of pyramids hiero-glyphics, then that is the proper word to use in the present connexion." The white whale is a sign, a hiero-glyphic, or a cipher that "remains undecipherable" (p. 260). It is a text that resists or defies interpretation. There is no Rosetta Stone to translate the significance of the white whale. "Champollion deciphered the wrinkled granite hieroglyphics," Ishmael says. "But there is no Champollion to decipher the Egypt of every man's and every being's face." How, then, can Ishmael hope to interpret the white whale's face? "Read it if you can," he dares the reader of *Moby-Dick* (pp. 292-293).

As a sign, the white whale is a hieroglyphic; as a text, it is a pyramid. (In *Pierre* Melville employs the pyra-mid to signify absolute absence: "By vast pains we mine into the pyramid; by horrible gropings we come to the central room; with joy we espy the sacrophagus; but we lift the lid—and no body is there!—appallingly vacant as vast is the soul of a man!")[18] *Moby-Dick* is an Egyptian book of the dead, or cryptogram, and the white whale is a crypt that is cryptic indeed. The white whale is a necrological enigma that, as Derrida says, "*warns* the soul of possible death, warns (of) death of the soul, turns away (from) death." In this respect, Ishmael re-lates the signifiers coffin, hearse, and tomb to the signi-fied life-in-death, death-in-life. To be "coffined, hearsed, and tombed in the secret inner chamber and sanctum sanctorum of the whale" (p. 290) is for the body proper to be embalmed, for the soul to be, as Derrida says, "enclosed, preserved, maintained," that is, to be "signi-fied"—even if the body happens to be, as with Ahab, only a leg, enclosed, preserved, maintained in a white whale. "The sign—the monument-of-life-in-death, the monument-of-death-in-life, the sepulcher of a soul or of an embalmed proper body," is, according to Derrida, the pyramid. "The pyramid becomes," he says, "the semaphor of the sign, the signifier of signification." That the pyramid is the very sign of the sign "is not an indifferent fact," Derrida says, especially as regards "the Egyptian connotation," for which the hieroglyphic serves as the example. To situate the pyramid in such a way is to establish "several essential characteristics of the sign." Perhaps the most important of these is "the *arbitrariness* of the sign, the absence of any natural re-lation of resemblance, participation, or analogy between the signified and the signifier," Derrida says.[19] (In con-trast, Irwin observes that in the hieroglyphic "a neces-sary though obscure correspondence" obtains between signifier and signified to the extent that "the shape of the sign" coincides with "the physical shape of the ob-ject it represents.")[20] There is no necessary, only a con-tingent, relation between the signifier white whale and the signified life-in-death, death-in-life. It is only the willfulness, or arbitrariness, of Ahab that establishes a relation in which to construe a significance is to commit suicide. Thus the white whale—as coffin, hearse, and

tomb—warns Ahab of possible death, warns him of death of the soul, turns him away from death. But he obstinately refuses to heed the warning. He will kill the white whale even if it kills him.

From Hermeneutic Polysemy to Erotic Dissemination

Susan Sontag defines interpretation as "the revenge of the intellect upon the world," in this case, the revenge of the intellect upon nature—upon a whale, a white one. "In place of a hermeneutics," she says, "we need an erotics of art."[21] Or, as Derrida says, in place of in-terpretation (even, or especially, interpretation that pur-ports to be polysemous) we need dissemination:

> If there is thus no thematic unity or overall meaning to reappropriate beyond the textual instances, no total message located in some imaginary order, intentional-ity, or lived experience, then the text is no longer the expression or representation (felicitous or otherwise) of any *truth* that would come to diffract or assemble itself in the polysemy of literature. It is this hermeneutic concept of polysemy that must be replaced by dissemi-nation.[22]

That is, the hermeneutic concept of polysemy must be replaced by the erotic concept of dissemination.

Ahab, however, is utterly incapable of dissemination. He has been dismembered, deprived of a leg, emascu-lated, as it were. For Ahab, amputation is tantamount to castration. The leg that the white whale devoured and swallowed assumes—in the monomaniac imagination of Ahab—the significance of a phallus, or symbolic pe-nis. Ahab has replaced the natural leg with an artificial leg that is not only impotent but also perverse, for it is not simply a whalebone but specifically a jawbone—the very bone of the jaw of a whale like the one that ren-dered him incapable of dissemination in the first place. This prosthetic device has added insult to injury, for it, too, has inflicted a grievous injury to the "groin" of Ahab (p. 385).

For Ahab, interpretation is phallocentric penetration of appearances. The megalomaniac will to power is a monomaniac will to knowledge—not an erotic, a de-constructive, or even a semiotic, but a hermeneutic vo-lition. Ahab wants to know the white whale intimately well, to the extent that he dares to wield not only a har-poon but also a knife, "a six inch blade to reach the fathom-deep life of the whale" (p. 159); he wants des-perately to probe what Whitman calls "the real reality" that is "behind the mask," which is to say, the persona of nature, and to pierce, once and for all, "this entire show of appearance."[23] He wants to dismember the white whale, to kill nature. In short, Ahab wants to pen-etrate the form in order to interpret the content of the white whale, to discover the truth behind the sign, what-ever that may seem, be, or mean.

The white whale is a sperm whale, "the only creature from which that valuable substance, spermaceti, is obtained." Spermaceti, Ishmael says, was once believed to be the "quickening humor" that "the first syllable of the word literally expresses" (p. 120). What the white whale contains is, in the words of Derrida, "SPERM, the burning lava, milk, spume, froth, or dribble of the seminal liquor."[24] In dissemination, the *sēmeion,* or sign, is the *sēmen.* The white whale is a pun, a sperma(ce)tic signifier floating on the seminal (or semiotic) fluid of the sea.

In the end, it is Ishmael, not Ahab, who is finally capable of dissemination. After the sperm is extracted from a whale, it is collected in tubs, where it is "cooled and crystallized" and "strangely concreted into lumps, here and there rolling about in the liquid part." Ishmael is obliged "to squeeze these lumps back into fluid." It is such a "sweet and unctuous duty" that Ishmael forgets the vow of vengeance that he and the other sailors have sworn against the white whale: "I forgot all about our horrible oath; in that inexpressible sperm, I washed my hands and my heart of it." As he squeezes the sperm, he feels no "ill-will, or petulance, or malice, of any sort whatsoever," only an orgasmic insanity:

> Squeeze! squeeze! squeeze! all the morning long; I squeezed that sperm till I myself almost melted into it; I squeezed that sperm till a strange sort of insanity came over me; and I found myself unwittingly squeezing my co-laborers' hands in it, mistaking their hands for the gentle globules. Such an abounding, affectionate, friendly, loving feeling did this avocation beget; that at last I was continually squeezing their hands, and looking up into their eyes sentimentally; as much as to say,—Oh! my dear fellow beings, why should we longer cherish any social acerbities, or know the slightest ill-humor or envy! Come, let us squeeze hands all round; nay, let us all squeeze ourselves universally into the very milk and sperm of kindness.

(pp. 348-249)

If for Ahab interpretation is penetration, for Ishmael dissemination is masturbation: a squeeze of the hand, a squeeze of the sperm, in which he forgets the revenge of the intellect upon the world, upon nature, upon the white whale. Ishmael no longer cares what the white whale may, or may not, signify to Ahab. Ultimately, all that matters to Ishmael is the sperm of dissemination, the significance of which is inexpressibly erotic.[25]

Notes

1. *Nature, Collected Works,* ed. Robert E. Spiller and Alfred R. Ferguson (Cambridge, Mass.: Belknap Press of Harvard University Press, 1971), I, p. 19.

2. *Nature,* p. 22.

3. *Nature,* p. 10.

4. *The Pursuit of Signs: Semiotics, Literature, Deconstruction* (Ithaca: Cornell University Press, 1981), p. 161.

5. "The Poet," *Complete Works,* ed. Edward Waldo Emerson (Cambridge, Mass.: Riverside, 1903), III, p. 4.

6. "The Over-Soul," *Collected Works,* ed. Joseph Slater, Alfred R. Ferguson, and Jean Ferguson Carr (Cambridge, Mass.: Belknap Press of Harvard University Press, 1979), II, p. 160.

7. *Moby-Dick; or, The Whale,* ed. Harrison Hayford and Hershel Parker (New York: W. W. Norton, 1967), p. 144; hereafter cited parenthetically in the text.

8. *Of Grammatology,* trans. Gayatri Chakravorty Spivak (Baltimore and London: The Johns Hopkins University Press, 1976), p. 63.

9. *Course in General Linguistics,* trans. Wade Baskin (New York: McGraw-Hill, 1966), pp. 114-115.

10. *American Hieroglyphics: The Symbol of the Egyptian Hieroglyphics in the American Renaissance* (New Haven and London: Yale University Press, 1980), p. 288. I regret not having had the pleasure of reading *American Hieroglyphics* before writing this essay in deconstruction. I should like to thank Bruce Henricksen for finally alerting me to the relevance of the book, so that I might take into account what Irwin has to say about Melville and *Moby-Dick.* One passage that Irwin cites from *Pierre* is especially pertinent to the difference of opinion between Emerson and Melville in regard to the interpretation of signs. In what is surely a reference to Emerson, Melville says that "nature is not so much her own ever-sweet interpreter, as the mere supplier of that cunning alphabet, whereby selecting and combining as he pleases, each man reads his own peculiar lesson according to his own peculiar mind and mood."

11. For more on the joke, see John D. Seelye, "The Golden Navel: The Cabalism of Ahab's Doubloon," *Nineteenth Century Fiction,* 14 (1960), pp. 350-355, and Paul Brodtkorb, Jr., *Ishmael's White World: A Phenomenological Reading of* Moby-Dick (New Haven and London: Yale University Press, 1965), p. 164n. Brodtkorb says that a modern version of the joke "involves an extremely long, dead-pan build-up that stresses the sanctity and sincerity of a Hindu holy man on a high mountaintop who after years of contemplating his navel decides that it ought to be possible to unscrew it, and that if he were to do so he would at last have all the final answers. In some versions of the story a golden screwdriver descends from the sky to the mountaintop (the story is full of archetypes); the mystic grasps it and unscrews his navel, only to have his ass fall off."

12. Other things besides the doubloon are finally nailed to the mast. Tashtego is in the process of

nailing a new flag to the mast when the white whale staves the *Pequod*. As the ship sinks and all the sailors but Ishmael drown, Tashtego continues to nail, even after his head is under water and all that remains above is his arm and hammer, "backwardly uplifted in the open air, in the act of nailing the flag faster and yet faster." At that instant, a sea-hawk (presumably the very one that earlier snatched Ahab's hat off his head), happens to fly "between the hammer and the wood" and is also nailed, or at least hammered, to the mast (p. 469).

13. *The Symbolic Language* (New York: Washington Square, 1967), pp. 67-68.

14. I am not equating deconstruction and the metaphysics of absence. What I am suggesting is that the very possibility of an absent meaning, of a meaning that may well mean nothing, is the negation that makes Pip capable of the deconstructive reading that he performs on the doubloon. For more on the doubloon, see Michael Vannoy Adams, "Ahab's Jonah-and-the-Whale Complex: The Fish Archetype in *Moby-Dick*," *ESQ* [*Emerson Society Quarterly*], 28 (1982), pp. 167-182.

15. *Margins of Philosophy,* trans. Alan Bass (Chicago: University of Chicago Press, 1982), pp. 80-81.

16. *Of Grammatology,* p. 49.

17. *Dissemination,* trans. Barbara Johnson (Chicago: University of Chicago Press, 1981), p. 5.

18. *Pierre; or, The Ambiguities,* [vol. 7 of] *Writings* [*The Writings of Herman Melville*], ed. Harrison Hayford, Hershel Parker, and G. Thomas Tanselle (Evanston and Chicago: Northwestern University Press and Newberry Library, 1971), VII, p. 285. Melville visited Egypt in 1857. He described the pyramids as "something vast, undefiled, incomprehensible, and awful." See *Journal of a Visit to Europe and the Levant: October 11, 1856-May 6, 1857,* ed. Howard C. Horsford (Princeton: Princeton University Press, 1955), pp. 117-119.

19. *Margins of Philosophy,* pp. 82-84.

20. *American Hieroglyphics,* p. 61. Irwin does say, however, that for Melville "indeterminacy is the essential characteristic" of the hieroglyphic (p. 286).

21. *Against Interpretation* (New York: Farrar, Straus and Giroux, 1966), pp. 7 & 14.

22. *Dissemination,* p. 262.

23. *Leaves of Grass, Collected Writings,* ed. Harold W. Blodgett and Sculley Bradley (New York: New York University Press, 1965), IX, p. 115.

24. *Dissemination,* p. 266.

25. A version of this essay was presented at the Northeast Modern Language Association Convention at Erie, Pennsylvania, 16 April 1983. I should like to thank Joseph N. Riddel and William Sharpe for (de) constructive criticism of the manuscript.

Frank G. Novak, Jr. (essay date winter 1983)

SOURCE: Novak, Frank G., Jr. "'Warmest Climes but Nurse the Cruellest Fangs': The Metaphysics of Beauty and Terror in *Moby-Dick*." *Studies in the Novel* 15, no. 4 (winter 1983): 332-43.

[*In the following essay, Novak examines the various dualities that pervade* Moby-Dick, *asserting that these tensions reflect a broader opposition between themes of beauty and terror. Novak suggests that, because beauty and terror each inform and intensify the experience of the other, the conflict between them lends the novel its dramatic power.*]

As the *Pequod* enters the cruising grounds where she will eventually encounter Moby Dick, a typhoon suddenly disrupts the beauty and calm of "these resplendent Japanese seas." The typhoon, Ishmael says, "will sometimes burst from out that cloudless sky, like an exploding bomb upon a dazed and sleepy town." Yet this phenomenon of unexpected terror suddenly erupting amidst peaceful beauty is not unusual; indeed, as Ishmael observes, it commonly occurs in nature: "Warmest climes but nurse the cruellest fangs: the tiger of Bengal crouches in the spiced groves of ceaseless verdure. Skies the most effulgent but basket the deadliest thunders: gorgeous Cuba knows tornadoes that never swept tame northern lands."[1]

This passage exemplifies a motif, a symbolic and thematic pattern, which pervades **Moby-Dick.** This recurrent motif consists of a binary opposition between beauty and terror. In the basic form of the motif, the appearance of beauty deceptively conceals the terror which inevitably lurks beneath the surface. The binary opposition of beauty and terror comprises the basic symbolic structure and thematic intent of many descriptive passages and, in a broader sense, sustains a dialectical tension which informs the entire novel. The beauty-terror dichotomy appears in a variety of combinations; it is often a contrast between physical appearances such as cats and tigers, days and nights, the ocean's surfaces and depths, male and female. These physical opposites frequently possess a metaphysical significance by symbolizing the difference between such concepts as thought and emotion, inner realities and outward appearances, truth and illusion. The novel is, of course, replete with dual oppositions—good-evil, order-chaos, Christian-pagan, and so forth. Such symbolic and thematic tensions can be generally stated in terms of the opposition between beauty and terror; in other words, many of the forces or qualities which exist in binary opposition can be subsumed under the beauty-terror paradigm. Underlying many individual passages describing natural scenes as well as the overall symbolic structure, the beauty-terror opposition is the pervasive, the most consistently developed binary contrast in the novel. The contrast developed by this motif produces an effect, a tension which animates many of the novel's descriptive and symbolic passages: the more beautiful the scene or image, the more ominous and malevolent is the terror associated with it.

As a pervasive symbolic structure, the beauty-terror opposition is a fundamental form of what Charles Feidelson calls the novel's "primal patterns of conflict."[2] Starbuck's tendency to discern "inward presentiments" in "outward portents" (p. 103) generally describes the way the universe is perceived in the book. This view also suggests a method of interpreting the images of binary opposition. Describing the dangers of waging war against the whale, Ishmael speaks of "the interlinked terrors and wonders of God" (p. 99).[3] This association of terror with wonder, Starbuck's "inward presentiment" ironically signified by the "outward portent," resonates powerfully throughout the novel. In "A Bower in the Arsacides," for example, the pattern is developed in terms of the intimate juxtaposition of life and death; as the vines covered the skeleton of the whale, "Life folded Death; Death trellised Life; the grim god wived with youthful Life, and begat him curly-headed glories" (p. 375). Ishmael's description of the whale line contains the same sort of contrast: "the graceful repose of the line, as it silently serpentines about the oarsmen before being brought into actual play . . . carries more of true terror than any other aspect of this dangerous affair" (p. 241). Whalemen, he contends, routinely encounter "virgin wonders and terrors" (p. 100). And the fact that "the incorruption of this most fragrant ambergris should be found in the heart of such decay" (p. 343) is typical of the many connected opposites one encounters at sea. These contrasts are at the heart of a basic symbolic and thematic pattern: the dual motif, the binary opposition of beauty and terror. Not incidentally do the passages which describe this startling but natural association of beauty and terror rank among the most poetic and powerful in the novel, containing rich, highly suggestive imagery and a sense of dramatic tension evoked by the contrast. The tension produced by the contrast charges these passages with a high level of poetic energy.

The beauty-terror antithesis which appears so frequently in *Moby-Dick* is adumbrated in Melville's review **"Hawthorne and His Mosses."** Here Melville asserts that the mind which possesses greatness and genius not only perceives the delightful, beautiful surfaces of life but also grapples with the terrors of existence which lie beneath; a recognition of life's beauty and joy must be accompanied by an awareness of what he calls the "power of blackness" (p. 540). The writer of genius possesses a highly developed sense of "humor and love," yet these sunny qualities must be complemented by "a great, deep intellect, which drops down into the universe like a plummet" (p. 539). Melville describes what he sees as the characteristic juxtaposition of beauty and terror, happiness and despair, joy and suffering manifest in Hawthorne's stories. In terms of both image and idea, several passages in the review presage what becomes a recurrent pattern in *Moby-Dick*: Melville notes the familiar "Indian-summer sunlight on the hither side of Hawthorne's soul," yet he emphasizes the other side which "is shrouded in a blackness" (p. 540). One should not be deceived by superficial appearances in Hawthorne, he says, for though one "may be witched by his sunlight . . . there is the blackness of darkness beyond" (p. 541). This basic dichotomy of a dark, terrifying underside beneath the deceptive surface of beauty and mildness appears again and again in *Moby-Dick,* especially in descriptions of natural phenomena. It is part and parcel of the basic imagistic and symbolic pattern of the novel. Melville recognized this polarity in Hawthorne, a symbolic pattern reflecting a tragic sense of life, and incorporated a similar binary structure into *Moby-Dick*.

There are four basic patterns by which the binary opposition of beauty and terror is developed in various descriptive passages. The first pattern contrasts the superficial loveliness and calmness of a mild day at sea with the destructive forces concealed beneath the surface of the ocean. Passages of this pattern simply indicate or describe a startling contrast and depict what Ishmael apparently accepts as a fact of nature. In "The Gilder," for example, Ishmael describes floating upon the calm ocean in pleasant weather: "The soft waves themselves, that like hearth-stone cats they purr against the gunwale; these are the times of dreamy quietude, when beholding the tranquil beauty and brilliancy of the ocean's skin, one forgets the tiger heart that pants beneath it; and would not willingly remember, that this velvet paw but conceals a remorseless fang" (p. 405). "The Symphony" presents a similar scene which is developed in terms of male-female opposition: "Hither, and thither, on high, glided the snow-white wings of small, unspeckled birds; these were the gentle thoughts of the feminine air; but to and fro in the deeps, far down in the bottomless blue, rushed mighty leviathans, swordfish, and sharks; and these were the strong, troubled, murderous thinkings of the masculine sea" (p. 442). This polarity of surface beauty and submerged terror, a juxtaposition of gentle creatures with savage ones, is an inherent quality of nature. In the above passage, the sexual differentiation merely hints at the profound differences hidden within—as Ishmael continues: "But though thus contrasting within, the contrast was only in shades and shadows without; those two seemed one; it was only the sex, as it were, that distinguished them" (p. 442). In this pattern, surface beauty belies the terror and horror which exist beneath. While fast to the aged whale, "the three boats lay there on that gently rolling sea, gazing down into its eternal blue noon," yet "beneath all that silence and placidity, the utmost monster of the seas was writhing and wrenching in agony!" (p. 300). These passages, presenting the binary motif in its most literal form, contain a straightforward message: one should beware of the terrors which are deceptively interlinked with the beauties of the sea. The sea's beautiful surface but masks bloodthirsty sharks lurking in the depths; there is a "tiger heart" beneath a velvet exterior.

Another manifestation of the binary opposition juxtaposes a tangible phenomenon with its intangible opposite. A physical scene of natural beauty evokes an inward, metaphysical terror of the mind. In a variation of the motif in which a beautiful scene is accompanied by a reminder that terror constantly lurks nearby, here a recognition of physical beauty paradoxically leads to a confrontation with the terror latent within each person. In a passage lush with sensuous imagery, Ishmael describes the beautiful days and nights encountered as the *Pequod* enters tropical waters: "The warmly cool, clear, ringing, perfumed, overflowing, redundant days, were as crystal goblets of Persian sherbet, heaped up—flaked up, with rose-water snow. The starred and stately nights seemed haughty dames in jewelled velvets. . . . For sleeping man, 'twas hard to choose between such winsome days and such seducing nights" (pp. 111-12). But there is a hint of foreboding and terror even here. Far from producing a soporific or calming effect, such beauties work upon the soul engendering a disturbed brooding, a restless fear: "But all the witcheries of that unwaning weather did not merely lend new spells and potencies to the outward world. Inward they turned upon the soul, especially when the still mild hours of eve came on; then, memory shot her crystals as the clear ice most forms of noiseless twilights. And all these subtle agencies, more and more they wrought on Ahab's texture" (p. 112). While the passages cited earlier describe a beautiful facet of nature inevitably accompanied by a malign aspect, the lovely days and nights described in this passage have their terrible complement in the mind. As the *Pequod* leaves "ice and icebergs all astern" and enters tropical climes, the ship encounters another type of glacial threat: the nameless terrors whose frozen crystals are etched on the mind. In this instance, physical beauty poetically and paradoxically suggests its metaphysical opposite.[4] In context, of course, the beauties of nature trigger dark thoughts particularly in the mind of Ahab; yet the passage generally implies that Ishmael, and possibly other members of the crew as well, also know the chilling terrors of memory.

Ishmael does not explain exactly how or why this connection takes place. Perhaps one's sins and imperfections become more sharply defined when contrasted with the serene perfection of natural beauty; perhaps these blissful tropical scenes are undermined by the terrors of death, addressed elsewhere by Ahab as the "dark Hindoo half of nature, who of drowned bones hast builded thy separate throne somewhere in the heart of these unverdured seas" (p. 409). In any event, scenes of beauty, by means of "witcheries," can turn inward upon the soul where terror and evil lurk.

In a third pattern of binary opposition, a phenomenon of nature can assume either a beautiful or terrifying appearance depending upon one's perspective. The example here is Ishmael's metaphorical description of Pip's transformation occurring as a result of his hours at sea as a castaway. While drifting for hours on the ocean, the innocent, happy cabin boy confronts the terrifying realities of existence, goes insane—according to conventional notions of insanity—and becomes the intimate of the even madder Ahab. As a result of viewing the "hoarded heaps" of wisdom and the "joyous, heartless, ever-juvenile eternities" (p. 347), the simple servant boy acquires forbidden knowledge and becomes the king's philosopher. Melville explains this metamorphosis by comparing Pip to a beautiful diamond:

> So, though in the clear air of day, suspended against a blue-veined neck, the pure-watered diamond drop will healthful glow; yet, when the cunning jeweller would show you the diamond in its most impressive lustre, he lays it against a gloomy ground, and then lights it up, not by the sun, but by some unnatural gases. Then come out those fiery effulgences, infernally superb; then the evil-blazing diamond, once the divinest symbol of the crystal skies, looks like some crown-jewel stolen from the King of Hell.
>
> (p. 345)

Here a natural object ostensibly displays a benign, salubrious beauty from one point of view but when viewed in a different light reveals an "evil-blazing" terror, emanating from sinister, satanic forces. Without undergoing structural change, the diamond with a "healthful glow" becomes the "crown-jewel" of the "King of Hell." It is at once the symbol of both good and evil, beauty and terror: its meaning varies with the viewer's perspective. In this relativistic pattern, a tangible object—Pip, the diamond, whiteness, even the whale—may signify innocence or evil, beauty or terror.

In the final variation of the binary motif as it appears in descriptive passages, the inevitable juxtaposition of terror and beauty in the natural world has its metaphysical counterpart. In other words, terror accompanies beauty in abstract, metaphysical realms just as in the physical world. In "Brit" Ishmael describes the polarity which typically exists in nature: "Consider the subtleness of the sea; how its most dreaded creatures glide under water, unapparent for the most part, and treacherously hidden beneath the loveliest tints of azure. Consider also the devilish brilliance and beauty of many of its most remorseless tribes, as the dainty embellished shape of many species of sharks" (p. 235). This link between terror and beauty in the natural world suggests an analogy with the realms of the soul where a similar connection, another "subtleness," exists: "do you not find a strange analogy to something in yourself? For as this appalling ocean surrounds the verdant land, so in the soul of man there lies one insular Tahiti, full of peace and joy, but encompassed by all the horrors of the half known life" (p. 236). In the metaphysical universe, however, the general pattern is reversed: beauty, the "insular Tahiti," lies at the heart of or concealed beneath terror—the "horrors of the half known life." A similar idea and symbolic pattern are presented in "The Grand Armada" where Ishmael observes the contrast between the "consternations and affrights" of the whales at the perimeter of the great school and the peaceful serenity of those at the center. This external, physical juxtaposition has its inward, philosophical corollary: "amid the tornadoed Atlantic of my being, do I myself still forever centrally disport in mute calm; and while ponderous planets of unwaning woe revolve round me, deep down and deep inland there I still bathe me in eternal mildness of joy" (p. 326). There is a serene beauty residing beneath the savage, terrifying appearance of Queequeg. Possessing a "Sublime" serenity, a "calm self-collectedness of simplicity" (p. 52), Queequeg nourishes a philosophical repose similar to that "insular Tahiti" which Ishmael elsewhere describes. Though wild and terrifying in appearance, Queequeg is a "soothing savage" who "redeems" the "wolfish world" from Ishmael's "splintered heart and maddened hand" (p. 53). In the natural world, the terror and malevolence which insidiously lurk beneath the surface of beauty, according to Melville's general pattern, are ultimately triumphant or, at least, unopposed. However, as the above examples indicate, in the metaphysical realm an inward sense of peace, joy, and beauty—if carefully nourished—can resist whatever terrors might beset the individual. An "insular Tahiti" of serenity and beauty can be a safe haven from the terrors of "tornadoed Atlantics" and "ponderous planets of unwaning woe"—what Ishmael elsewhere calls "the universal thump" which everyone will receive "either in a physical or metaphysical point of view" (p. 15).

Melville not only uses the binary opposition motif in individual descriptive or philosophical passages; he also develops the same themes and symbolic patterns on a more comprehensive scale. The association of beauty with terror, of course, often appears in descriptions of the white whale himself. One effect of the cetological chapters is to impart a sense both of the whale's magnificent beauty and his terrible, destructive power. When

first sighted, Moby Dick, unprovoked, is a creature of serene beauty, but his beauty is accompanied by an awesome capacity for violence and terror:

> A gentle joyousness—a mighty mildness of repose in swiftness, invested the gliding whale. Not the white bull Jupiter swimming away with ravished Europa clinging to his graceful horns . . . did surpass the glorified White Whale as he so divinely swam. . . . No wonder there had been some among the hunters who namelessly transported and allured by all that serenity, had ventured to assail it; but had fatally found that quietude but the vesture of tornadoes. . . . And thus, through the serene tranquillities of the tropical sea, among waves whose hand-clappings were suspended by exceeding rapture, Moby Dick moved on, still withholding from sight the full terrors of his submerged trunk, entirely hiding the wrenched hideousness of his jaw.

> (pp. 447-48)[5]

Or when the whale breaches, the scene is one of stunning color and beauty:

> as in his immeasurable bravadoes the White Whale tossed himself salmon-like to Heaven. So suddenly seen in the blue plain of the sea, and relieved against the still bluer margin of the sky, the spray that he raised, for the moment, intolerably glittered and glared like a glacier; and stood there gradually fading and fading away from its first sparkling intensity, to the dim mistiness of an advancing shower in a vale.

> (p. 455)

Yet when attacked, Moby Dick becomes a creature of malevolent fury who ruthlessly destroys his pursuers; in his next appearance, the whale strikes a "quick terror" in the pursuing crew by "rushing among the boats with open jaws, and a lashing tail," offering "appalling battle on every side . . . intent on annihilating each separate plank of which those boats were made" (p. 456). The whale, therefore, embodies the principle that, in nature, beauty is closely accompanied by terror; like the diamond symbolizing Pip, the salient attribute of the whale depends on one's perspective. Recounting "The Town-Ho's Story," Ishmael describes "the appalling beauty of the vast milky mass, that lit up by a horizontal spangling sun, shifted and glistened like a living opal in the blue morning sea" (p. 221). The phrase "appalling beauty" is used again to describe the whale's tail "where infantileness of ease undulates through a Titanism of power" (p. 315). Moby Dick, as it were, conspires with nature to vanquish his frustrated pursuers in scenes which are at once both beautiful and terrifying: "amid the chips of chewed boats, and sinking limbs of torn comrades, they swam out of the white curds of the whale's direful wrath into the serene, exasperating sunlight, that smiled on, as if at a birth or a bridal" (p. 159).[6]

This paradoxical, dual symbolism of Moby Dick is explored in "The Whiteness of the Whale." Here Ishmael grants the familiar significance of the color which suggests beauty, goodness, and purity; but he argues that under close scrutiny white ultimately connotes a paralyzing terror of the unknown. "Though in many natural objects," he says, "whiteness refiningly enhances beauty . . . there yet lurks an elusive something in the innermost idea of this hue, which strikes more of panic to the soul than that redness which affrights in blood" (pp. 163-64). This paradox, he maintains, is the essential quality of whiteness: "it is at once the most meaning symbol of spiritual things, nay, the very veil of the Christian's Deity; and yet should be as it is, the intensifying agent in things the most appalling to mankind" (p. 169). Conforming to the general pattern of the binary motif, the discussion of whiteness contrasts outward beauty with inward terror. The dual symbolism of whiteness is grounded in the basic assumption that unseen terrors lurk beneath the surface of beauty: "Though in many of its aspects this visible world seems formed in love, the invisible spheres were formed in fright." As the "visible absence of color," whiteness represents the unseen, unknown world beneath or beyond the visible world of tangible, physical reality—which it also symbolizes by being "the concrete of all colors." Ultimately, therefore, white evokes the terror of nothingness; as Melville says: "it shadows forth the heartless voids and immensities of the universe, and thus stabs us from behind with the thought of annihilation" (p. 169). The ultimate significance of whiteness is essentially identical to the tragic emptiness, the "blackness of darkness," Melville discerned in Hawthorne. Like the typhoon suddenly bursting from cloudless skies, the terror of whiteness strikes without warning. As the essence of light, whiteness exemplifies the deceptive quality of all physical appearances, beautiful though they may be: "all deified Nature absolutely paints like the harlot, whose allurements cover nothing but the charnel-house within" (p. 170). While superficially benign, whiteness, then, deceptively evokes terrifying uncertainties—just as the azure surface of the sea barely conceals the bloodthirsty terrors lurking beneath, just as the beautiful days and nights of tropical climes engender frozen thoughts of dark terror in the mind, just as the white whale himself is at once a creature of intense beauty and annihilating terror. As the primary symbol of this dichotomy, Moby Dick embodies the inevitable juxtaposition of beauty with terror, in the physical world as well as in the metaphysical realm.

A recognition of the beauty-terror dualism is also fundamental to an understanding of Ahab, who dramatically reveals the tensions between the two poles. As part of the general pattern in which terror insidiously lurks beneath the surface of beauty, Ahab's maniacal quest taints the idyllic beauty of the ocean scenes which the *Pequod* and her crew encounter. The terror of Ahab's dark thoughts and suicidal quest opposes the benign beauties of the natural world. Ahab acknowledges the beauty of the sunset, for example, but he is incapable of enjoying its loveliness: "This lovely light, it lights not me; all loveliness is anguish to me, since I can ne'er enjoy. Gifted with the high perception, I lack the low, enjoying power; damned, most subtly and most malignantly! damned in the midst of Paradise!" (p. 147). Throughout the novel Ahab demonstrates an awareness of the binary opposition. According to his dualistic view, there is an "inscrutable malice" behind the "pasteboard masks" of "visible objects" (p. 144). While he temporarily responds to the beauty of the mild day described in "The Symphony," the "cankerous thing in his soul" (p. 443) abruptly dispels his pleasant reverie and fond thoughts of home. The inevitable terrors of his mad quest lurk behind the superficial beauties of that winsome day, which momentarily affects Ahab and causes him to drop a tear into the sea; seeing this, Ishmael observes that the "sweet childhood of air and sky" are "oblivious" to "old Ahab's close-coiled woe" (p. 442). Although the beauties of nature exert at least a temporary effect on Ahab, opening in him "secret golden treasures, yet did his breath upon them prove but tarnishing" (p. 406). While Ahab's terrible thoughts and ambition despoil the beauties of the natural world, he sees, paradoxically, a sort of beauty in the terrors he must confront. He believes that "all heart-woes" have "a mystic significance" and, occasionally, "an archangelic grandeur"; "mortal miseries," he thinks, have their origins in the "sourceless primogenitures of the gods" (p. 386).[7] Yet this "divine" beauty which evolves from terror leads inescapably to a species of ultimate terror which the gods themselves cannot overcome: "so that, in the face of all the glad, hay-making suns, and soft-cymballing, round harvest-moons, we must needs give into this: that the gods themselves are not for ever glad" (p. 386). Unlike Queequeg and Ishmael, who are apparently able to maintain a serene "insular Tahiti" within themselves, Ahab's soul nourishes a dark madness, "a cunning and most feline thing." Ishmael compares this "larger, darker, deeper part" lurking in Ahab to the "vast Roman halls of Thermes" underground beneath the apparently "grand and wonderful" Hotel de Cluny. In these subterranean halls, "far beneath the fantastic towers of man's upper earth . . . his whole awful essence sits in bearded state; an antique buried beneath antiquities, and throned on torsoes!" (p. 161). For Ahab beauty exists only externally, terror is the inner reality: "So far gone am I in the dark side of earth, that its other side, the theoretic bright one, seems but uncertain twilight to me" (p. 433).

Melville's pervasive use of the beauty-terror motif suggests at least two general observations. First of all, the novel argues that entities have reality or can be defined only by contrast with their opposites. As Ishmael observes: "truly to enjoy bodily warmth, some small part of you must be cold, for there is no quality in this world that is not what it is merely by contrast. Nothing exists in itself" (p. 55). In fact, contrasting opposites comprise the essential fabric of existence. As much as one might wish happiness to endure, "the mingled, mingling threads of life are woven by warp and woof; calms crossed by storms, a storm for every calm. There is no steady unretracing progress in this life; we do not advance through fixed gradations, and at the last one pause" (p. 406). Ishmael consistently establishes the pattern in which scenes that are calm and "monotonously mild" inevitably presage "some riotous and desperate scene" (p. 428). The "alluring" but dangerous "spirit-spout" is first descried on a "serene and moonlight night" (p. 199); this ghostly phenomenon "derived a wondrous potency from the contrasting serenity of the weather, in which, beneath all its blue blandness, some thought there lurked a devilish charm" (p. 201). The ominous, terrifying squid is sighted on a "transparent blue morning . . . when the long burnished sun-glade on the waters seemed a golden finger laid across them" (p. 236). Not surprisingly, each of the three days of the chase is one of supreme beauty—contrasting with the destructive terror of the white whale. The fundamental component of life itself, Ishmael argues, consists of contrasting forces set in binary opposition, each giving reality, identity, or significance to its counterpart. Beauty or terror, therefore, can be defined only in terms of its opposite. This antithesis occasionally evolves into a synthesis: just as "there is a wisdom that is woe" (p. 355), there is also a beauty which is terror. The white whale, of course, is the embodiment of this synthesis.

Second, the juxtaposition of beauty and terror as an inherent quality of nature holds significance in terms of Emersonian symbolism. Ahab clearly states the link which is assumed throughout the novel: "O Nature, and O soul of Man! how far beyond all utterance are your linked analogies! not the smallest atom stirs or lives in matter, but has its cunning duplicate in mind" (p. 264). One is reminded of Emerson's basic premise: "Every natural fact is a symbol of some spiritual fact." According to Ishmael, the juxtaposition of beauty and terror in the natural world has its counterpart in the metaphysical realm.[8] Beauty, goodness, and joy, on one side, are counterbalanced by terror, evil, and suffering on the other—in the world empirically perceived or in Emerson's "apocalypse of the mind." Starbuck, ever the pious optimist, relishes the beauty of the day described in "The Gilder," yet he knows that beneath the dazzlingly beautiful surface lie "teeth-tiered sharks" and "kidnapping cannibal ways." The reality, the supremacy of these terrors can be denied only by letting "faith oust fact" and "fancy oust memory" (p. 406). Depending on one's philosophical or theological perspective, however, the scales may be weighted toward either pole. As far as Ahab is concerned, "every revelation partook more of significant darkness than of explanatory light" (p. 386). Yet Father Mapple asserts that "on the starboard hand of every woe, there is a sure delight; and higher the top of that delight, than the bottom of the woe is deep" (p.

50). Whatever the case, the novel repeatedly demonstrates that for every softly purring "hearth-stone cat" there is a terrifying "panting tiger"—and that each creature conceals a "remorseless fang" within a "velvet claw."

A simple yet powerful symbolic structure, the binary opposition, structuralist theorists argue, serves "as a fundamental operation of the human mind basic to the production of meaning."[9] Bruno Bettelheim's interpretation of Freudian analysis underscores the significance of the binary opposition and suggests why it is such a pervasive structure in *Moby-Dick*. According to Bettelheim, the Eros-Thanatos antithesis is at the heart of Freud's thought and theory. These two forces "struggle for dominance in shaping our lives," and this struggle creates a tension which gives life intensity and meaning. Because a life emphasizing either extreme will be warped and empty, there must be constant mediation between the happy and the tragic, between optimism and pessimism. Poets, Bettelheim observes, have been particularly sensitive to the necessity of this conflict which both endows life with a tragic dimension and accounts for man's highest, most satisfying achievements.[10] Similarly, in *Moby-Dick* the threat of inevitable terror heightens the sense of beauty. This tension not only delineates and intensifies both beauty and terror but, as seen above, can also merge one with the other. Out of the continuous dialectic between the two, borrowing a line from Yeats, "a terrible beauty is born." Yet the novel does not advance a synthesis in which one emerges triumphant.[11] In nature and in the mind, beauty and terror exist, paradoxically, only in tandem. To understand fully the distinctions between the two and, consequently, the ultimate nature of each comprises a vexing riddle—which, like the meaning of Queequeg's tattoos, remains a "devilish tantalization of the gods" (p. 399).

Notes

1. *Moby-Dick,* ed. Harrison Hayford and Hershel Parker (New York: W. W. Norton, 1967), p. 413. All subsequent references to the novel as well as to "Hawthorne and His Mosses" are from this edition and are noted by page in the text.

2. "Introduction," *Moby-Dick* (Indianapolis: Bobbs, Merrill, 1964), p. xxi.

3. Following the lead of Robert Zoellner, I, too, am cutting the "Gordian Knot"—the interpretive problem of point of view—by assuming that it is Ishmael, not Melville, who speaks throughout the novel—*The Salt-Sea Mastodon: A Reading of Moby Dick* (Berkeley: Univ. of California Press, 1973), p. xi. While Zoellner's reading is essentially an epistemological one and mine is an imagistic-thematic one, our discussions merge and diverge at critical points.

4. Although the pleasant tropical weather would cause even a "thunder-cloven old oak" like Ahab to "send forth some few green sprouts" (p. 111), the ultimate effect appears to be a negative one. After Stubb respectfully requests that the captain do something to muffle the reverberations of his ivory limb against the wooden planks during his nightly vigils, Ahab, unassuaged by the nocturnal beauty he apparently enjoys, turns on him viciously and insultingly—"Down, dog, and kennel!" (p. 113).

5. H. Bruce Franklin calls this passage "one of the great moments of revelation in literature. It is a revelation of horror, the revelation of fearfully potent malice masked by graceful beauty" (*The Wake of the Gods* [Stanford: Stanford Univ. Press, 1963], p. 64).

6. Zoellner emphasizes the "dualistic cluster of meanings" (p. 153) the whale carries; he says that "again and again, Ishmael cites that inner fragility and delicacy lying beneath the gross ponderosity of outer Leviathan" (p. 156). He sees the dualism of the whale as one of beauty and power—essentially identical, I believe, to the beauty-terror opposition.

7. Ishmael sees a similar glory or beauty in the terror of the sea when, in discussing Bulkington, he argues that it is better "to perish in that howling infinite" than cravenly to seek land. Because he courageously confronts the "terrors of the terrible," Bulkington's "apotheosis" leaps from the spray of his "ocean-perishing" (pp. 97-98).

8. Yet, as Milton R. Stern points out, "Melville's insistence that significance lurks in the thing as well as the viewer" separates him from Emersonian transcendentalism. His perception of "the external independence of the matter of experience" is "closer to naturalism than to romantic, cosmic idealism" ("Some Techniques of Melville's Perception," *PMLA*, 73 [1958], 251, 255).

9. Jonathan Culler, *Structuralist Poetics: Structuralism, Linguistics and the Study of Literature* (Ithaca: Cornell Univ. Press, 1975), p. 15.

10. *Freud and Man's Soul* (New York: Knopf, 1983), pp. 109-12.

11. Robert Zoellner sees the passage from "The Symphony," quoted above, "as reflecting a final synthesis in Ishmael's mind and heart" (p. 238). His contention that "the brutal, the ensanguined, the predatory in natural process" intermingle with the benign and beautiful to produce "an on-going, immanent, virtually immortal act of creation and renewal" is certainly consistent with the novel. However, I am not prepared to grant his thesis that

"the demonic and malign" are merely "appearances" and that "the cosmos, though frightful, is [ultimately] benign" (p. 238). In spite of the beauty which Ahab observes in "The Symphony," he is not deterred from his "quenchless feud" (p. 155); and the fact that the chapter ends with Ahab's seeing the haunting, evil eyes of Fedallah reflected in the water certainly bodes ill rather than good. Similarly, in his discussion of the whale, Zoellner maintains that "there is a sweetness, a vitality, a purity, an inherent preciousness which affirms the fundamental goodness of existence and the preponderant salubrity of cosmic activity" (p. 162), that, in short, "power is redeemed by beauty" (p. 164). Yet the fact is that in the mind of Ishmael neither good nor evil, beauty nor terror is ultimately triumphant. Both forces exist in the noumenal realm as well as the natural world, both work to create the tension which informs existence, and whatever synthesis that may emerge from their continuous dialectical interchange is at best a provisional, insubstantial one. Whether the cosmos is ultimately benign or malign perhaps depends on one's perspective—whether one nurtures in his heart, like Ishmael, an "insular Tahiti" or, like Ahab, a "close-coiled woe."

Mark R. Patterson (essay date fall 1984)

SOURCE: Patterson, Mark R. "Democratic Leadership and Narrative Authority in *Moby-Dick*." *Studies in the Novel* 16, no. 3 (fall 1984): 288-303.

[*In the following essay, Patterson discusses the contrasting functions of language in the mouths of the characters Ahab and Ishmael. Patterson contends that, while Ahab's diction is forceful and exhortative, Ishmael's is ambiguous and subtle, refusing to embrace a particular attitude or belief. In Patterson's view, Ishmael's noncommittal communication style represents a subversion of authority, one intended to liberate the reader from preconceived notions of culture and power.*]

Beginning a novel is like an introduction into polite society. Attendant are the proprieties of social position—the "buzz and hum" of meaning—that direct our response. The first line of *Moby-Dick,* "Call me Ishmael," unsettles us because its familiarity carries with it the force of command.[1] Uncertain of our true relation to the speaker, we hesitate momentarily in order to determine whether we are addressed as peers or subordinates. In addition to questioning the speaker's ambiguous intentions, we are doubly mystified by his assumption of a fictive name.[2] With this self-assured gesture, Ishmael almost capriciously teases those readers who, like Melville's upright publisher, John Murray, wish to be convinced that his "Books are not fictions."[3] Unlike many of Melville's narrators who insist on the truth of their travelogues, Ishmael purposely blurs the borders between fact and fiction as he tests the boundaries of credibility without irrevocably crossing them. He continues to guide us by controlling our access to the facts of his narrative in the next line: "Some years ago—never mind how long precisely—having little or no money in my purse, and nothing particular to interest me on shore, I thought I would sail about a little and see the watery part of the world." Ishmael's elusiveness, combined with his insistence that he set the limits of the narrative, makes us dependent on his disembodied voice.

Like Herman Melville's earlier novels, *Moby-Dick* opens as a first-person account of a sea adventure. This opening, however, initiates us into a world different from that of *Typee, Omoo, White-Jacket,* or even *Mardi.* Here, the use of the first-person narrator orients the reader to Ishmael in a special way.[4] Besides warranting Ishmael's recounting of his past life from the perspective of this assumed persona, the autobiographical narration permits him to speak openly to us, drawing us into the story through the urgency of his words. For our purposes, this first-person narration is most significant in its ability to create, in Dorrit Cohn's words, an "existential relationship" with the reader.[5] First-person narration is grounded in the present; we experience the narration, "hear" the narrating voice, at the moment of locution.[6] We are arrested by the first sentence of *Moby-Dick,* not only because the narrator assumes a fictional identity, but, more importantly, because he *commands* us to give him that identity. We are immediately implicated in Ishmael's story, almost against our will. His pressing directive subordinates the question of fiction while establishing a bond of intimacy between himself and the reader. It matters less that Ishmael is a persona than that he has the power to command our cooperation. In short, the issue that confronts us first in *Moby-Dick* is not the narrator's fictiveness, but his authority.

In linguistic terms, Ishmael's first command is an illocutionary, or speech, act. We can distinguish between a normal locutionary act, which produces a recognizable grammatical utterance, and an illocutionary act, which attempts to accomplish some communicative purpose.[7] In other words, illocutionary acts include those forms of language—warnings, greetings, promises, commands, etc.—which have a definite intention and goal. Frequently, as with wedding vows, the purpose is accomplished by the illocutionary act itself. Each illocutionary act is constituted by the rules and conventions which permit that act to have meaning. The efficacy of saying "I do" in a marriage ceremony arises from the couple's agreement on the cultural conventions, laws, and religious beliefs underlying those words. A successful illocutionary act reinforces the conditions, the rules of society, institutions, and culture, through which we communicate in the world. In a command, there must be a commander who utters the speech act and a subordinate who literally "understands" the rules legitimizing the act, thus guaranteeing the command's success.

Returning to Ishmael's first sentence, we can see that the circumstances of the command, its position as the initiating sentence in a work of fiction, calls attention to the nature of our relationship with the speaker. Ishmael's request relies on our necessary trust in the conventions of fiction, conventions to which he is equally bound. We must call him Ishmael for the simple reason that we know him by no other name. But our dependence reveals the arbitrariness of the rules by which we acknowledge his authority. Like Ishmael and Queequeg tied by the monkey-rope, we are joined to the narrator as in "a joint stock company of two" (*MD* [*Moby-Dick*], p. 271), and the loss of autonomy is the cost of admission to the novel. Ishmael's insistent control over the narrative continually emphasizes the contingencies of the relationship: bound to our narrator, we are always reminded of the precariousness of our position.

The problem of authority in *Moby-Dick,* therefore, begins before Ahab steps on deck. However, Ahab's mastery over his crew and his usurpation of their wills in the quest for Moby Dick increasingly attract our attention during the voyage. Ishmael's initial, equivocal command precipitates the action and prefigures Ahab's ability to impose his supreme authority on the quarter deck. Ishmael purposely presents an analogous, but alternative version of Ahab's authority. This doubling of roles—Ahab's leadership over his crew and the relationship of authority in which we participate as readers—reveals the remarkably similar rhetorical premises of Ahab and Ishmael. Ahab's end, however, marks the danger of democratic leadership. In order to understand Ishmael's position, it is important first of all to establish the basis of Ahab's authority and his resemblance to Melville's other authority figures. Then, Ishmael's contrasting narrative authority, which leads us in search of "the Whale," can be seen as a keen analysis of the psychological and linguistic sources of authority in a democracy, those bonds that tie individuals together in the *Pequod*'s doomed enterprise.

II

Melville's preoccupation with authority is not surprising for an ex-sailor who observed firsthand its most artificial and extreme forms aboard whalers and U.S. Navy ships. In Melville's early novels, resistance to the confining, ordered life of the ship becomes the impetus for escape into the romance of South Sea society.[8] In *Typee,* for example, Tommo defends his desertion from the *Dolly* by calling the captain's actions "unmitigated tyranny."[9] Under similar circumstances, Omoo and Taji escape the structure and routine of ship life only to find themselves in subtler, self-created forms of enslavement to the very quest for freedom.

In the succeeding novels, *Redburn* and *White-Jacket,* Melville shifts his attention from resistance to obedience as he dramatizes the hidden psychological springs of compliance and command from which authority arises. In *White-Jacket,* stressing the degeneration of legitimate authority into coercive tyranny, he exposes the despotic means used to maintain the highly structured order on a man-of-war. The ship "is no limited monarchy, where the sturdy commons have a right to petition, and to snarl if they please; but almost a despotism, like the Grand Turk's."[10] The source of this hierarchical order is the captain: "The captain's word is law; he never speaks but in the imperative mood" (*WJ* [*White-Jacket*], p. 23).

Supported by powerful traditional and legal codes, the captain—as later Ishmael—expresses his authority through his imperative language. Compliance, however, involves more complex psychological bases of motivation. Fear, insecurity, even anger compel Melville's characters to tolerate the most tyrannical rule.[11] In *Redburn* and *White-Jacket,* Melville looks forward to the complex interrelationships of Ahab and his crew by establishing two distinct centers of authority: the aristocratic and the democratic. On one hand, the captain stands aloof as the delegated, but absolute, dictator. Captain Claret of *White-Jacket* and Captain Riga of *Redburn* are despotic representatives of maritime law who manipulate the forms of their office to maintain their superior positions. In contrast stand the democratic leaders of the crew, Jack Chase of *White-Jacket* and, especially, Jackson in *Redburn.* Through admiration and fear, respectively, Chase and Jackson naturally assume positions of authority over their shipmates.

For Wellingborough Redburn, Captain Riga and Jackson present opposing figures of leadership. A fatherless, prematurely embittered youth, Redburn naturally gravitates to Riga, the image of paternal authority. Unable to rise into Riga's aristocratic society, however, Redburn recoils into the demonic power of Jackson, a relationship that resembles Ahab's domination aboard the *Pequod.* Without Riga's institutional authority, Jackson's sway arises out of his own malicious personality. Perhaps like his relative, Andrew Jackson, Jackson "seemed to be full of hatred and gall against every thing and every body in the world; as if all the world was one person, and had done him some dreadful harm, that was rankling and festering in his heart."[12] Prefiguring Ahab's rule, Jackson's power over his men arises from his very monomaniacal bitterness. Both Jackson and Ahab combine keen penetration into human drives with their own overwhelming and compelling sense of the world's ulti-

mate malevolence. "[H]is wickedness," Redburn comes to understand of Jackson, "seemed to spring from his woe" (*R* [*Redburn*], p. 105). Jackson's horror, like Ahab's, exhibits the "woe that is madness" (*MD,* p. 355), which exerts such seductive attraction for Ishmael. We glimpse the origin of Jackson's woe in the world Redburn encounters. Poverty, social injustice, and oppression reign; wealth presents the only means of escape and domination. Deformed by his hate, Jackson nevertheless comes to mirror the bitterness and impotent defiance felt by all. The sailors obey him because he represents their own frustrated lives. In Michael Davitt Bell's words, he "is a democratic leader, exerting power not through the channels of institutionalized authority, as does Captain Riga, but through his almost magnetic authority over the minds of the men."[13]

It is in Redburn himself that we see the source of Jackson's authority. Redburn's poverty and diffidence drive him into Jackson's control. Confessing his terror of Jackson, Redburn also admits his kinship with the monomaniacal leader: "I began to feel a hatred growing up in me against the whole crew—so much so, that I prayed against it, that it might not master my heart completely, and so make a fiend of me, something like Jackson" (*R,* p. 62).

The danger of Redburn's transformation into another Jackson reflects a continuing fear among American writers that democratic leadership too often arises from the psychological identification of leader and follower.[14] Without an artificially defined hierarchy of power, democracy relies on extra-institutional means of exacting obedience. Coercion, flattery, and social pressure replace dictatorial sovereignty; the authority relationship becomes highly volatile as it threatens either to produce anarchic distrust or complete psychological submission. If Jackson represents the dangers of democratic leadership, Redburn's simultaneous repulsion and fascination represent the contradictory American attitudes toward leadership. Melville's own deepening interest in the phenomena of authority, its source in the human psyche and its evocation through language, led him into the complex relationships between Ahab and his crew.

In *Moby-Dick,* the discussion and dramatization of Ahab's power and ascendency occur in a short span, from Chapter 33 ("The Specksynder") through Chapter 40 ("Midnight, Forecastle"). In these chapters we move from an abstract dissertation on the forms of authority aboard a whaling ship to the confrontation between Ahab and his men on the quarter deck in which he unites his obsession of hunting the white whale with their individual motivations. Briefly, the action involves the transformation of Ahab's authority from legitimate and institutional to charismatic, that is, from Captain Riga's to Jackson's. By blurring the distinction between the two, Ahab is able to alloy the routinized conformity of the men with the powerful primitive drives that originally compel them to hunt the sperm whale.

"The Specksynder" begins as a general discussion of the traditional hierarchy aboard whalers. The chapter explains that American whalers ignore the European custom of dividing the ship's authority between the chief whaling master (the specksynder) and the ship's commander. Unlike Captain Riga, Ahab ostensibly encompasses all authority aboard the *Pequod*.[15] The chapter evolves into a description of the ceremonies associated with the captain's authority. Like other sea captains, Ahab uses the traditional artifices of his office to distinguish his superiority: "though the only homage he ever exacted, was implicit, instantaneous obedience; . . . yet even Captain Ahab was by no means unobservant of the paramount forms and usages of the sea" (*MD*, p. 129). Disdainful of most conventions, especially those associated with genial society, Ahab nevertheless uses them to assert his power. Although these forms create the mask through which he would strike to clutch the inscrutable whale, he is tied to them as means to his end. Indeed, these rituals themselves provide the only means of expressing his authority, which by its very nature is conventional. As Erving Goffman has pointed out, such a position "is not a material thing, to be possessed and then displayed; it is a pattern of appropriate conduct, coherent, embellished, and well-articulated."[16] It is Ishmael who tells us, "be a man's intellectual superiority what it will, it can never assume the practical, available supremacy over other men, without the aid of some sort of external arts and entrenchments, always, in themselves, more or less paltry and base" (*MD*, p. 129). Using social forms to compel the men to hunt the whale, Ahab's success promises the destruction of these conventions when he meets his antagonist.

The following two chapters, "The Cabin-table" and "The Mast-head," are linked by the contrasting descriptions of elaborate social ceremony and the malevolent vortex that such ceremony conceals. In part, Ahab's complete control over his officers result from the ritual, "a witchery of social czarship which there is no withstanding" (*MD*, p. 131), of his meals.[17] Yet his authority does not reside in the ceremony so much as in his mates' willingness and desire to participate in the rite and grant it meaning. "They were as little children before Ahab," and, like children, their obedience is rewarded with security. We see the danger which threatens this security in the following chapter, "The Mast-head." Here, Ishmael challenges the image of order presented by the ritualized meals as he warns us of the "deep, blue, bottomless soul pervading mankind and nature" (*MD*, p. 140) that lies beneath the sailors' feet. These "Descartian vortices" of nature are antithetical to the routine of the sailors' daily lives. His warning appropriately introduces the next chapter, "The Quarter-

deck," in which Ahab makes his Mephistophelian pact with the crew to search for Moby Dick.

Ahab's strategy on the quarter deck is a masterful fusion of democratic demagoguery and religious ritual. Like Captain Claret, Ahab "never speaks but in the imperative mood." Even his initial questions on the quarter deck—recalling Ishmael's questions in "Loomings"—galvanize the men with a commanding directness while unifying their separate purposes with his. The ritual of question and response, heightened by his own animation, introduces the elaborate ceremony and invocation of nailing the doubloon on the masthead: "Whosoever of ye raises me a white-headed whale with a wrinkled brow and a crooked jaw; whosoever of ye raises me that white-headed whale, with three holes punctured in his starboard fluke—look ye, whosoever of ye raises me that same white whale, he shall have this gold ounce, my boys!" (*MD*, p. 142). His imperative, "look ye," like Ishmael's first commands to the reader, focuses the crew's attention on the symbol of his obsession and unites the sailors' individual motives with his own design. Randomness, chance, and individuality are replaced by Ahab's order and goal. The gold doubloon becomes the mirror for each man's reason to catch the whale.

Despite Ahab's theatricality, the mere act of nailing the doubloon on the mast would have no significance if the men did not invest it with a kind of magical power like that in a primitive hunting ceremony. It is the crew's intention, as it is Ahab's, "to chase that white whale on both sides of land, and over all sides of the earth, till he spouts black blood and rolls fin out" (*MD*, p. 143). For Ishmael and his fellow crew members, the whale comes to represent the forces of nature which threaten each of them. Meditating on the sources of Ahab's authority, Ishmael suggests the resemblance of their separate quests:

> How it was that they so aboundingly responded to the old man's ire—by what evil magic their souls were possessed, that at times his hate seemed almost theirs; the White Whale as much their insufferable foe as his; how all this came to be—what the White Whale was to them, or how to their unconscious understandings, also, in some dim, unsuspected way, he might have seemed the gliding great demon of the seas of life,—all this to explain would be to dive deeper than Ishmael can go.
>
> (*MD*, p. 162)

Melville implies here, as in *Redburn,* that Ahab's hate summons and focuses his men's resentment against "the universal cannibalism of the sea; all whose creatures prey upon each other, carrying on eternal war since the world began" (*MD*, pp. 235-36). This primeval warfare against the uncaring universe, unsparing even of "creatures which itself hath spawned" (*MD*, p. 235), drives the men onto the whaler and into battle with the whale.[18] An unconscious desire for revenge against a world intent on their destruction forces the men to accept Ahab's challenge. It is the "instinct of the knowledge of the demonism in the world" (*MD,* p. 169) that motivates them. Each man has his secret terror or hate which Ahab extracts and infuses with his own. In Ahab's words, his "one cogged circle fits into all their various wheels, and they revolve" (*MD,* p. 147).

Ahab's calculated effort to implicate the men in his personal revenge (as Ishmael enlists the reader's help in initiating the narrative) adopts the magistral invocation of Moby Dick and the demagogue's skill of arousing the listener's impassioned, sympathetic identification. Remembering the effects of Ahab's show on himself and the crew, Ishmael recounts: "my shouts had gone up with the rest; my oath had been welded with theirs; and stronger I shouted, and more did I hammer and clinch my oath, because of the dread in my soul. A wild, mystical, sympathetical feeling was in me; Ahab's quenchless feud seemed mine" (*MD,* p. 155). Horror and instinctive antipathy to a hostile universe draws the men to Ahab's own mad scheme. Thus Ahab effectively unites the artificial forms inherent in his station with the demagogue's knowledge of human nature. He is both Captain Riga and Jackson, aristocrat and democrat. Near the end of the novel, Starbuck meditates on his plan to murder Ahab, but his own will continues to belong to Ahab even as he implicates the reader in the hunt: "and say'st the men have vow'd thy vow; say'st all of us are Ahabs" (*MD,* p. 422).

Ishmael's ironic position as a retrospective narrator makes clearer the disjunction between legitimate ritual and a confidence game. Located in the forms and usages of Ahab's position, ceremony enhances the credibility of action and reforges the ties of the participants. The readiness of the men to believe in Ahab's power underscores their need to believe in the ship's masklike order that disguises the abyss over which they sail. Ahab can be a confidence man because the world threatens the sailors' confidence at every moment. Recoiling from the dangers inherent in their world, the sailors themselves warrant the corruption of institutional authority into tyranny and their obedience into servility.

Melville's insight into the springs of authority suggests that leader and follower, master and slave, are inextricably bound up with the desires and terrors of the world. Ahab adroitly uses both the verbal and dramatic forms of his position in conjunction with the motives of the men in order to bind them to his cause: "all the individualities of the crew, this man's valor, that man's fear; guilt and guiltlessness, all varieties were welded into oneness, and were directed to that fatal goal which Ahab their one lord and keel did point to" (*MD,* p. 455). Throughout the novel, the commonality of the cause erases the distinctions between individuals. Narcissus-like, each man is mirrored in his quest for the whale: "that same image, we ourselves see in all rivers and oceans. It is the image of the ungraspable phantom of life; and this is the key to it all" (*MD,* p. 14). The final spectacle of the undifferentiated, monomaniacal crew, mirroring the whale they seek to kill, suggests the suicidal nature of their hunt. The melting of thirty individuals into a single sympathetic identity, which is the human analogue to the creation of the whale's whiteness out of all colors, makes the *Pequod* as terrifying a vision as Moby Dick.

Part charismatic leader, part confidence man, Ahab uses the power of language and ritual simultaneously to evoke belief and obscure understanding. The ease with which he molds the crew to his purpose results from their own terror and desire for revenge; from this instinctive fear, he constructs belief. Ahab draws on this distrust, this lack of confidence in the world's benevolent order, to seek his own mad ends. His failure to achieve his goal, especially seen in the light of his success in persuading his men to fulfill his means, suggests the susceptibility of legitimate authority relationships to the tyrannical control of the subordinates' belief. With the *Pequod*'s destruction and Ishmael's salvation, we circle back to the novel's beginning and Ishmael's own attempt to establish his authority as he seeks out the whale through his cetological investigations.

III

We return to the beginning of *Moby-Dick* after the rescue of Ishmael more fully aware of the import of his first imperative words to us and the intent of his preliminary actions. Like many autobiographical narrators, Ishamel seeks to recover and narrate his story in order to understand the causal links between motivation and consequence. In part, he seeks to understand Ahab and Ahab's vision of the whale "as the monomaniac incarnation of all those malicious agencies which some deep men feel eating in them" (*MD,* p. 160). Thus, for Ishmael and the reader, the final battle with Moby Dick is also an uncovering of a beginning, because we see for the first time the impetus for the entire voyage in Ahab's antagonist. Yet despite its obvious importance, Ahab's story is subordinate to Ishmael's search for his own motives: "now that I recall all the circumstances, I think I can see a little into the springs and motives which being cunningly presented to me under various disguises, induced me to set about performing the part I did" (*MD,* p. 16). From his experiences, he realizes that "chief among these motives was the overwhelming idea of the great whale himself" (*MD,* p. 16). Ahab seeks revenge on Moby Dick; Ishmael is driven by the "idea" of the whale. Their stories are inextricably bound, but each must be understood to unfold independent of the other. The goal of Ishmael's narrative is not revenge, but revelation.

Reentering the novel, we find Ishmael confidently asserting his own authority as raconteur and tour guide. His authority is clearly of a different sort than Ahab's: Ishmael has a story to tell and information to present us, but he does not have the position of a ship's commander. His authority is didactic, that is, he is an authority in something—in this case whales and whaling. Like the Sub-Sub Librarian, Ishmael presents himself as an expert in whale lore and facts, one who has dived deeply into the literature. With his didactic authority, Ishmael seeks to instruct us from his experience, to shape our perception of the whale from his reading and life aboard whalers. Yet, as we participate in an interchange of information, the goal of the relationship is to achieve equilibrum in a shared vision of the whale. Resembling Ahab's power over the crew, Ishmael's authority depends on the coincidence of our belief with his. The effect of his cetology chapters, as Richard Brodhead notices, "is gradually to break down our sense of incredulity and to move us closer and closer to entertaining their beliefs ourselves."[19] However, unlike Ahab, Ishmael comes to break the spell holding the reader in order to preseve his saving skepticism.

Ishmael's authority is not merely different from Ahab's, it deliberately runs counter to the captain's. Because authority is purposive, we can distinguish between Ahab's authority and Ishmael's by their contrasting goals. Melville's initial decision to call his novel "The Whale" makes clear that Ishmael's quest for an ultimate understanding of the whale parallels Ahab's particular quest—his desire to wreak revenge on Moby Dick. Although Ahab continues to assert his magnetism on many critics, it is the whale which receives the bulk of Ishmael's attention. In fact, during the composition of the novel, Melville balanced Ahab's story of human will with the philosophical complexities of Ishmael's cetological search.[20] Even as Ahab's presence rules over the narrative of the *Pequod*'s voyage, the cetology chapters serve as the field of Ishmael's quest. Variously functioning as sermon, textbook, and philosophical tract, the cetology chapters, describing the capture and trying out of the whale, form a frequently comic analogue to Ahab's mad hunt for Moby Dick. Finally, however, these chapters serve as autobiography, for Ishmael too must confront the "dead, blind wall" of the whale in order to understand his own "springs and motives." "Loomings" thus establishes the alternative quest as Ishmael initiates his own story. In so doing he creates what Edward Said calls the authority of a beginning:

> The necessary creation of authority for a beginning is also reflected in the act of achieving discontinuity and transfer; while in this act a clear break with the past is discernible, it must also connect the new direction not so much with a wholly unique venture, but with the established authority of a parallel venture.[21]

In the first chapters of *Moby-Dick,* Ishmael maintains an ironic distance from his younger self as a means of breaking with the past, and so is able to chart his new course.

Even as the first sentence of "Loomings" raises the question of narrative authority and presents it as a *fait accompli,* the remainder of the first chapter sets the course we will follow. Ishmael's assertive presence in the first chapter is particularly remarkable because his voice later seems to disappear into the narrative itself, mimicking a variety of other voices as the novel progresses. Significantly, in this chapter Ishmael's voice is authoritative. His first command is repeated in a number of imperatives: "Look," "Go," "Circumambulate," "Take," etc. Most striking is his use of the imperative "Look," the same directive that Ahab continually speaks to his men. Ishmael's role as the reader's cicerone, revealed through this demanding language, is necessitated by our dependence on him. As he commands us to see the crowds of men "fixed in ocean reveries," we participate in the central perceptual act of the novel.

Characteristically, Ishmael never lets us rest secure in our reliance upon his vision. By alternating command with question, Ishmael throws us back on our own resources. Even the rhetorical quality of some of his questions—for example, "Who aint a slave? Tell me that"—momentarily disengages us from his voice and reveals the essential similarity between illocutionary act and question.[22] A speech act involves a series of implied questions about its appropriateness, questions to which the hearer must silently respond in order to complete the communicative act. In *Moby-Dick,* Ahab's questions function aggressively in decisive moments to capture his crew's attention. For example, his litany of questions to the sailors on the quarter deck subtly unite captain and crew in an awareness of their common purpose. In contrast, Ishmael's questions demand the sovereignty of our perceptions.

Moby-Dick thus offers a series of parallels between Ahab and Ishmael. There are two epic quests for the whale, the success of which ultimately depends on the possibility of knowing the whale's absolute significance. Leading these separate, yet related, quests are the different authorities of Ahab and Ishmael. Ahab's authority is, in part, institutional and coercive; it commands the men's actions. Ishmael's authority is verbal and didactic; in the cetology chapters it seeks to share knowledge and reveal hidden truth. However, as we have seen, much of Ahab's authority also depends on his use of language. Both share the common ground that language and authority are intimately related and rest finally in man's faith and belief. *Moby-Dick* declares that this authority can lead either to destruction or insight.

The effect of Ishmael's cetological dissertations is to expand the narrative of the *Pequod*'s voyage into a search for the ultimate significance of the whale. The weaving metaphor, which itself is woven throughout the novel, depicts the structural importance of Ishmael's cetology chapters. The "straight warp of necessity" is Ahab's story, "not to be swerved from its ultimate course" (*MD,* p. 185). Ishmael's chapters are "free to ply [their] shuttle between given threads" (*MD,* p. 185). Resisting Ahab's relentless, grim pursuit, these chapters present a mind's free play over a universe of objects and ideas. Parody, symbolism, and double entendres proliferate among the great chunks of facts lifted intact from whaling books. In turn, the bare facts accumulate, generate insights into the whale, and coalesce in the shape of a whale. Following the etymological meaning of "instruct"—to erect or build on—Ishmael literally uses the facts to construct a didactic model of a whale. These chapters serve to create a spatial form existing apart from the time-bound vision of Ahab.[23] As if commenting on the swelling size of **Moby-Dick,** Ishmael remarks, "Such, and so magnifying, is the virtue of a large and liberal theme! We expand to its bulk. To produce a mighty book, you must choose a mighty theme" (*MD,* p. 379).

Every intention presumes a goal. Unlike Ahab, whose purpose never varies, Ishmael circles his subject, first classifying and then presenting historical background before cutting in. Ishmael's intention is to capture the "grand hooded phantom" that drove him, Ahab-like, onto the *Pequod.* Roughly described, his method is to move from an external view—the description of whiteness and the whale's capture—through the various stages of cutting-in and trying-out, finally ending with a discussion of the whale's skeleton, fossils, and immortality. Motivating his discussions is a desire for possession of the whale's truth. As he says, "unless you own the whale, you are but a provincial and sentimentalist in Truth" (*MD,* pp. 285-86). To possess the whale is to speak with authority for it: "the only real owner of anything is its commander" (*MD,* p. 393). Language is Ishmael's only means to unite intention and goal; that is, to possess the whale's significance he must be able to express it. Like Ahab, he faces the twin specters of failure: his authority over the reader and his search for truth will fail if he does not successfully rarefy the whale's bulk into certitude.

The cetology chapters, then, are hermeneutic exercises with the whale as the text. However, each attempt to own the whale by interpretation is frustrated by the whale's indeterminacy. Safe in its mystery, the whale overwhelms man's limited perception. As a result, the cetological system is left unfinished, whiteness erases meaning because it incorporates all meaning, Moby Dick is found to be ubiquitous in both time and space. The whale is the indecipherable hieroglyphic: "how

may unlettered Ishmael hope to read the awful Chaldee of the Sperm Whale's brow?" (*MD,* p. 293).[24] After having described many of the whale's features, Ishmael finally admits, "Dissect him how I may, then, I but go skin deep, I know him not, and never will" (*MD,* p. 318).

As the expert in whaling and whale lore, Ishmael undermines his authority by admitting his limitations. In Chapter 83, "Jonah Historically Regarded," the biblical account is scrutinized by historical exegetes until it loses it paradigmatic authority and becomes just another story in a work comprised of competing narratives. If Ishmael's principal desire is to own the whale, then it is clear that his quest, like Ahab's, is doomed from the first. As Brodhead states, "Ishmael's scientific procedures are almost without exception extravagant failures."[25] The inability of both Ahab and Ishmael to realize their goals suggests the omnipotent inaccessibility of Moby Dick and "the Whale" and the epistemological gulf between human perception and the world. Yet, despite their similar failures, it is important to remember that Ishmael purposely mars his cetological chapters. Withstanding the temptation that destroys Ahab, Ishmael admits the limits of his knowledge and the danger present in the successful completion of his search.

As we have seen, Ishmael mimics Ahab to the point of beginning his narrative with Ahab's imperative voice. He continues to employ Ahab's oratorical constructions in order to call attention to the common linguistic basis of their authority. For example, Ahab's incantation as he nails the doubloon to the mast finds its counterpart in the periodic rhythms and force of Ishmael's Ciceronian sentences. Ishmael's epic invocation in "Knights and Squires" is typical of this particular style:

> If, then, to meanest mariners, and renegades and castaways, I shall hereafter ascribe high qualities, through dark; weave round them tragic graces; if even the most mournful, perchance the most abased among them all, shall at times lift himself to the exalted mounts; if I shall touch that workman's arm with some ethereal light; if I shall spread a rainbow over his disastrous set of sun; then against all mortal critics bear out in it, thou just Spirit of Equality, which has spread one royal mantle of humanity over all my kind!
>
> (*MD,* pp. 104-05)

Bearing echoes of Father Mapple and Ahab, Ishmael's homiletic style unfolds with the undercutting extravagance of parody. However, the building of the conditional, "if-then," Ciceronian period reflects the fundamentally contingent nature of belief and action in the novel. Variations of this construction, like Ahab's hortatory pronouncements, or Fedallah's conditional prophecy, are used to incite action by instilling belief in the propositions' absolute truth. As in many tragedies,

Ahab's destruction results from an ironic misapprehension of this very linguistic construction. He confidently attacks Moby Dick, in part, out of a mistaken trust in Fedallah's mysterious prophecy, but is tricked by the obscurity of its meaning. Having himself used language to mystify, Ahab cannot interpret this veiled warning and so becomes the victim as well as victimizer of language. By revealing the inherent artificiality of this prophetic style, Ishmael's parodic voice claims the primacy of language and at the same time counters its insidious power to coerce belief.

In such cases, Ishmael deliberately undermines his authority by calling into question its very source—language. As James Guetti has pointed out, Ishmael's variety of voices remind us that language remains removed from the reality of the whale.[26] Using the whale's spine as a model, Ishmael often begins his descriptions with universal matters and "tapers off at last into simple child's play" (*MD,* p. 378); verbal play once again detaches language from absolute significance by calling attention to itself and reaffirms the conventionality of all knowledge. It is Ahab's belief that he can break through this cardboard-mask reality to grasp the phantom of life. For him, and in contrast to Ishmael, "the world beyond the artifices of the visible—the supposed reality—is not unknowable but only unknown."[27] Finally, encountering this reality, Ahab and his crew sink into its inevitable silence. Saved by Queequeg's coffin covered with hieroglyphics, Ishmael floats above the mute vortex: "The unharming sharks, they glided by as if with padlocks on their mouths; the savage sea-hawks sailed with sheathed beaks" (*MD,* p. 470). Despite its inability to express absolutes, language protects Ishmael from the abyss over which he hovered and attaches him to the world of shared beliefs and values in which we first encounter him.

At those moments in the novel when Ishmael admits his own defeat by the whale, he will often turn the tables on us, making us question our belief in the whale. At the end of "The Whiteness of the Whale" the reader is asked why this color is "the very veil of the Christian's Diety; and yet should be as it is, the intensifying agent in things the most appalling to mankind" (*MD,* p. 169). Similarly, "Fast-Fish and Loose-Fish" ends with aggressive questioning: "And what are you, reader, but a Loose-Fish and a Fast-Fish, too?" (*MD,* p. 334). Questions, like commands, reestablish the link of intention between speaker and hearer; they seek fulfillment and completion from the hearer's own beliefs. Ahab's questions on the quarter deck capture the entire crew's attention because they are easily answered. Ishmael's questions, like his commands, unsettle the hearer and try to loosen the grip of the hearer's beliefs. In short, the basis of authority comes down to a matter of belief

and faith. Without faith (or confidence) in the voice of command and the unspoken rules supporting it, authority cannot exist.

If *Moby-Dick* questions the nature of authority (both Ahab's and Ishmael's), it does so because it subverts our bases for belief. Ahab's authority is based on his crew's faith; he federates these Isolatoes by inspiring a religious awe in them and leads them to destruction. Ishmael survives to tell his story, but he speaks not with the authority of absolute Truth, but through the perception of multiple truths. The doubling of Ahab's and Ishmael's language, their similar uses of commands, questions, and conditional clauses, serve to exploit their dissimilarities. While Ahab uses language to extort belief, Ishmael subverts both language and belief in order to preserve them. Ishmael's first command demands our trust in him as the autobiographical narrator of the story. His subsequent narration involves an intricate strategy calculated to undermine our confidence in all forms of authority. Our initial relationship with him, however, matures in the manner of one's life: "through infancy's unconscious spell, boyhood's thoughtless faith, adolescence' doubt (the common doom), then scepticism, then disbelief, resting at last in manhood's pondering repose of If" (*MD,* p. 406).[28] Significantly, Ishmael's (and the reader's) final stage of understanding is his own ubiquitous grammatical construction of contingency. "If" presents us finally with an awareness that has moved beyond disbelief into an acceptance of what we know through language. If "Silence is the only Voice of our God," Ishmael understands that language creates the potential for either destruction or salvation within human relationships.[29]

Notes

1. Herman Melville, *Moby-Dick; or, The Whale,* ed. Harrison Hayford and Hershel Parker (New York: W. W. Norton, 1967), p. 12. Hereafter cited as *MD* in text.

2. The first chapter has prompted a number of excellent discussions. Of particular interest are Howard P. Vincent, *The Trying Out of* Moby-Dick (1949; Kent, Ohio, Kent State Univ. Press, 1980), pp. 55-63; Warner Berthoff, *The Example of Melville* (Princeton: Princeton Univ. Press, 1962), pp. 115-32, et passim; Paul Brodtkorb, Jr., *Ishmael's White World* (New Haven: Yale Univ. Press, 1965), p. 51, et passim; Warwick Wadlington, *The Confidence Game in American Literature* (Princeton: Princeton Univ. Press, 1975), pp. 87-92.

3. Murray's letter to Melville is found in Merrell R. Davis, *Melville's "Mardi": A Chartless Voyage* (New Haven: Yale Univ. Press, 1952), p. 61.

4. For an additional discussion of Ishmael's first-person narrative, see Glauco Cambon, "Ishmael

and the Problem of Formal Discontinuities in *Moby Dick,*" *Modern Language Notes,* 76 (1961), 516-23.

5. Dorrit Cohn, *Transparent Minds* (Princeton: Princeton Univ. Press, 1978), p. 144.

6. See Cohn, p. 198, for her discussion of the "evocative present," the momentary illusion of the present tense among first-person narratives. See also Käte Hamburger's excellent study of narrative, *The Logic of Literature,* trans. Marilynn J. Rose (Bloomington: Indiana Univ. Press, 1973), esp. pp. 58-59, 313-18.

7. For background on speech-act theory see J. L. Austin, *How to Do Things With Words* (Cambridge: Harvard Univ. Press, 1962); John Searle, *Speech Acts* (Cambridge: Harvard Univ. Press, 1969); Mary Louise Pratt, *Toward a Speech Act Theory of Literary Discourse* (Bloomington: Indiana Univ. Press, 1977). For a useful word of warning, see also Stanley Fish, "How to Do Things with Austin and Searle: Speech Act Theory and Literary Criticism," *MLN,* 91 (1976), 983-1025.

8. For an overview of Melville's idea of authority, see Nicholas Canday, Jr., *Melville and Authority* (Gainesville: Univ. of Florida Press, 1968).

9. Herman Melville, *Typee,* ed. Harrison Hayford, Hershel Parker, G. Thomas Tanselle (Evanston: Northwestern Univ. Press and The Newberry Library, 1968), p. 21.

10. Herman Melville, *White-Jacket; or, the World in a Man-of-War,* ed. Harrison Hayford, Hershel Parker, G. Thomas Tanselle (Evanston: Northwestern Univ. Press and the Newberry Library, 1970), p. 23. Hereafter cited as *WJ* in text.

11. For different approaches to the relationship between personality and authority, see Richard Sennett, *Authority* (New York; Alfred A. Knopf, 1980), and Irvine Schiffer, *Charisma* (Toronto: Univ. of Toronto Press, 1973).

12. Herman Melville, *Redburn,* ed. Harrison Hayford, Hershel Parker, G. Thomas Tanselle (Evanston: Northwestern Univ. Press and the Newberry Library, 1969), p. 61. Hereafter cited as *R* in text.

13. Michael Davitt Bell, "Melville's Redburn: Initiation and Authority," *New England Quarterly,* 46 (1973), 568.

14. Michael Davitt Bell (*The Development of American Romance* [Chicago: The Univ. of Chicago Press, 1980], p. 119 et passim) suggests the importance of this same kind of identification between narrator and reader for American writers.

15. See Vincent, pp. 143-45, for a discussion of the technical background to this chapter.

16. Erving Goffman, *The Presentation of Self in Everyday Life* (Garden City, N.Y.: Doubleday, 1959), p. 75.

17. See Goffman, p. 67, for his discussion of awe in authority relationships.

18. See Merlin Bowen, *The Long Encounter* (Chicago: Univ. of Chicago Press, 1960), pp. 74-81, for his discussion of the theme of the world's hostility.

19. Richard Brodhead, *Hawthorne, Melville and the Novel* (Chicago: Univ. of Chicago Press, 1976), p. 139.

20. Despite the controversy over the novel's composition, most scholars would agree that the revisions were meant to provide balance between the two narratives. For discussions of the novel's composition, see Vincent, pp. 22-52; Leon Howard, *Herman Melville* (Berkeley: Univ. of California Press, 1951), pp. 163-79; James M. Barbour, "The Composition of *Moby-Dick,*" *American Literature,* 47 (1975), 343-60; and especially, Robert Milder, "The Composition of *Moby-Dick:* A Review and a Prospect," *ESQ* [*Emerson Society Quarterly*], 23 (1977), 203-16.

21. Edward Said, *Beginnings: Intention and Methods* (New York: Basic Books, 1975), p. 33.

22. For the relationship between illocutionary acts and questions, see Paul Ricoeur, *Interpretation Theory* (Fort Worth: Texas Christian Univ. Press, 1976), p. 14, and Pratt, pp. 132-33.

23. Brodhead, p. 158, appropriately cites Frank Kermode's distinction between *chronos* and *kairos.* Ishmael sees time as *chronos,* the perpetual present of unfolding time; Ahab sees it as *kairos,* in which "meaning is derived from its relation to the end."

24. See John T. Irwin, *American Hieroglyphics* (New Haven: Yale Univ. Press, 1980), pp. 285-93, for the use of the hieroglyphic motif as a description of indecipherability.

25. Brodhead, p. 152.

26. See James Guetti, *The Limits of Metaphor* (Ithaca: Cornell Univ. Press, 1967), p. 16, for a list of Ishmael's vocabularies.

27. Guetti, p. 35.

28. The editors of the Norton Edition of *Moby-Dick,* p. 494, suggest that this speech might belong to Ahab. However, it is clearly connected with Ishmael's final understanding and his own linguistic interests.

29. Herman Melville, *Pierre; or, the Ambiguities,* ed. Harrison Hayford, Hershel Parker, G. Thomas Tanselle (Evanston: Northwestern Univ. Press and The Newberry Library, 1971), p. 204.

Gayle L. Smith (essay date 4th quarter 1985)

SOURCE: Smith, Gayle L. "The Word and the Thing: *Moby-Dick* and the Limits of Language." *ESQ: A Journal of the American Renaissance* 31, no. 4 (4th quarter 1985): 260-71.

[*In the following essay, Smith explores Melville's use of verbal ambiguity in the novel.*]

"Oh, man! admire and model thyself after the whale! Do thou, too, remain warm among ice. Do thou, too, live in this world without being of it . . . retain, O man! in all seasons a temperature of thine own," Ishmael advises as he examines the whale's insulating blanket of skin [in *Moby-Dick*].[1] This, of course, is Ishmael's great challenge, to confront the complexity of the whale and all reality on his own terms, neither adopting uncritically any single, insufficient explanation nor lapsing into a desperate nihilism. At the heart of Ishmael's ability to maintain an epistemological "temperature of [his] own" is his deviation from ordinary language patterns in order to express perceptions otherwise inexpressible and perhaps even unable to be considered. Ishmael's language choices reflect Melville's awareness that the received language is not adequate to his perceptions of reality, that the normal strictures of language must be transcended if it is to begin to be fully expressive. The most significant, deviant, and unexplored of Ishmael's patterns involve negation, particularly the doubling up of negatives to create phrases such as "not seldom," "not unattended," and "not disincline" (pp. 260, 385, 77). Ahab too engages in a kind of semantic doubling that calls attention to itself, but his patterns reflect both a different consciousness and a different understanding of the role of language,

The linguistic patterns Melville has his protagonists use reflect his awareness of the contemporary controversies about the relationship between language and meaning, signifier and signified. Philip F. Gura argues cogently for the impact of the linguistic theories of nineteenth-century thinkers such as Alexander Bryan Johnson and Horace Bushnell on the writers of the American Renaissance.[2] Johnson and Bushnell were alike in rejecting the Transcendental notion of simple correspondence between words and things, but while Johnson despaired of the ambiguity of language and advocated a persistent return to the senses and contemplation lest one stray too far from meaning in mere words, Bushnell celebrated the ambiguity of language as a means of communicat-

ing complex, even spiritual, ideas. Specifically, Bushnell recommended a rhetoric of multiple perspectives, contradiction, and paradox, a position that leads Gura to observe that, although there is no direct evidence that Melville read Bushnell's works, he became "the novelist of Bushnell's imaginative universe" as he explored "the 'rupture' between language and meaning" that Bushnell had exposed ("Language ["Language and Meaning: An American Tradition,"]," pp. 19, 17). Gura documents some of the larger ways in which *Moby-Dick* demonstrates the need for pluralistic interpretations, for using different "grammars" to read the provoking "text" of the whale, referring specifically to the chapters "The Whiteness of the Whale" and "The Doubloon." I would like to show how, even more pointedly, Ishmael and Ahab act out in dramatic form the debate about the nature of language. Ishmael's strategies dynamically reflect Bushnell's theory, as he creates patterns that force readers into a realm of thought virtually beyond the reach of ordinary language. He uses language not merely to refer to things and ideas but to point beyond this sort of signification. In contrast, Ahab's linguistic choices reflect a rigid, correspondential notion of language, a faith that meaning and reality somehow inhere in language itself. Among Americans, Sampson Reed probably articulated this position most clearly: "There is a language, not of words but of things," he declared in his 1826 "Growth of the Mind." The inherently meaningful nature of language, especially of names for things, is clear as Reed continues his thought:

> Every thing which surrounds us, is full of the utterance of one word, completely expressive of its nature. This word is its name; for God, even now could we but see it, is creating all things, and giving a name to every work of his love, in its perfect adaptation to that for which it is designed.[3]

In *Moby-Dick* Melville displays the limitations of Ahab's view of language and reality; as he believes that each word has a given, unalterable meaning independent of the interpreter, so he maintains that phenomena, such as the whale, stand for some specific meaning to which he imagines himself privy. Ishmael, on the other hand, knows that no one word or combination of words can fully convey the reality either of things or of thoughts, but that, creatively used, language can engage the consciousness of the listener or reader as well as that of the speaker in a search for deeper understanding.

Speaking of *Moby-Dick,* Nina Baym maintains, "Truth is doubted, but not language," pointing out that Ishmael never questions his activity of verbalizing his experiences.[4] Maintaining as she does that an "Emersonian," correspondential theory of language infuses the entire book, she does not pay particular attention to the way Ishmael must constantly struggle to adapt the rigid language available to him to what he must say. Language as it is normally used, language as a transparent medium, is doubted here. James Nechas claims that "Melville discovered that language was quite capable of expressing all that man can with assurance know," but, according to his reading of *Moby-Dick,* the most man can know is that the universe is unknowable: "Melville found that his language, man's language, was completely able to express the failure of his imagination."[5] A closer look at Ishmael's linguistic choices, however, shows that his search for truth and his intensely creative use of language constitute instead a great victory of the imagination. Finally, this victory is Melville's, as he demonstrates his ability to transcend the limits of ordinary language.

As Newton Arvin observes, "One feels . . . that the limits of even the English vocabulary have suddenly begun to seem too strict, too penurious, and that the difficult things Melville has to say can be adequately said only by reaching beyond those limits." Arvin cites, for example, Melville's tendency to create nouns and modifiers out of participles and to pluralize abstract nouns.[6] These are important aspects of Ishmael's language and consciousness; Ishmael seems determined to infuse his language with the dynamism he feels, to mingle in his language the static and the active, the abstract and the concrete, theoretical opposites that seem mysteriously joined in the reality he alone among the crew perceives. Every time Melville has Ishmael derive a new word form such as "ponderings," "palpableness," "uninvitedly," or "sentinelled" (pp. 20, 424, 109, 112), he is arguing the insufficiencies not merely of our ordinary vocabulary but of the forms of ordinary language classification. As the lines between parts of speech begin to blur, so do the distinctions between what is real and what is fanciful, what is known, what is expressible, and what is not. Ishmael's language, in stark contrast to Ahab's, reflects the need to go beyond the common forms and structures of language to contemplate and express the complex reality he has experienced.

One index to Ishmael's sense that there is no exact correspondence between language and reality is his heavy use of the very word "nameless." Seventeen times he refers to things, people, or abstractions as "nameless"; once he uses "namelessly."[7] Most frequently he is referring to the whale, whaling, or to Ahab.[8] He opens Chapter 42, "The Whiteness of the Whale," tentatively, referring to "another thought, or rather vague, *nameless* horror concerning him, which at times by its intensity completely overpowered all the rest; and yet so mystical and well nigh ineffable was it, that I almost despair of putting it in a comprehensible form" (p. 163). Fully aware of the difficulties, however, he says, "explain myself I must" and launches into one of the more speculative and metaphysical chapters of the book (p. 163)— and the only chapter in which he must use the word "nameless" three times. "Nameless" is but one of many

negative words that begin to take on positive meaning, to be more than privative. Ahab asks what "*nameless,* inscrutable, unearthly thing" drives him on, but instead of following out all the possibilities as Ishmael might, he quickly decides that he has no separate power, that God "does that thinking" and "Fate is the handspike" (pp. 444, 445). Using a related form with very different implications, Ahab tells the dying whale, "All thy *unnamable* imminglings float beneath me here" (p. 409).

Nameless though Ishmael finds many aspects of reality to be, none seems really unnamable. In an effort to communicate qualities that have no proper names but nonetheless exist for him, he sometimes resorts to two-part noun phrases such as "a certain wild vagueness of painfulness" and "a weariness and faintness of pondering" (pp. 77, 174). Each of these constructions creates a noun phrase, normally an agreed upon "something," of ambiguous, difficult to verbalize or even isolate, yet very real impressions. If Ishmael cannot quite define his perceptions, he will at least suggest them. Elsewhere he gives us alternatives. In the passage cited above, the whale's whiteness is "another thought, or rather vague, nameless horror" (p. 163). Speaking of the feeling he had about Ahab before seeing him, he says, "But whatever it was of apprehensiveness or uneasiness—to call it so—" which he felt, it was allayed when he considered the three mates (p. 109). Similarly, he shows scrupulous attention to Ahab; he describes how Ahab reacts to Stubb's whale, how "some vague dissatisfaction, or impatience, or despair, seemed working in him" (p. 248). No single word is adequate, so he gives us the words that he uses to approximate his feelings and perceptions. Ishmael uses language not only to communicate specific ideas, but to formulate those ideas and communicate his own thinking process; Ahab makes speeches.

Words with negating affixes abound in *Moby-Dick,* hinting all the time at the power and the reality of the negative, which is, of course, dramatically manifested in the whiteness of the whale.[9] The presence and the terrific weight of Melville's negatives remind one of Shakespeare's examination in *King Lear* of the enormous meaning of "nothing" and of Donne's passionate analysis of nothing as absence or substance in "A Nocturnall upon St. Lucies Day." Many of the negative words in *Moby-Dick* are unusual if not deviant derivations, and the great majority of them are Ishmael's creations. I find at least seventy-two such formations, but after reading and rereading *Moby-Dick,* one's sense of what is and what is not deviant becomes somewhat undependable: "unceasingly," "incorruption," and "familyless" (pp. 170, 343, 402) seem rather less odd now than they might have earlier. Certainly they are not in the same category with "uneventfulness," "unnearable," and "uncatastrophied" (pp. 137, 201 and 304, 401). Some call attention to themselves because the root word in any of its derivations does not usually accept a negative affix, as with "unoutgrown," "unlimbed," "unloitering," "unnearable," and "unsupplied" (pp. 71, 160, 173, 201 and 304, 318). Others are peculiar because the negative affix is not generally found with that particular derived form of the root word, as with "undeliverable," "unsay," and "uninvitedly" (pp. 16, 26, 109). As these examples demonstrate, it is not necessarily the negative affix that makes the words unusual: "invitedly" would be just as aberrant as "uninvitedly" and "uninvited" is fully acceptable. But the negative words do constitute a special group among the larger set of words created by piling up unlikely affixes. When we entertain other ways of expressing these ideas, we appreciate more fully Melville's stylistic choices and the mentality he reveals in Ishmael. When Ishmael calls the spirit-spout and the Fin-Back's spout "unnearable," he asserts something about the spout itself, something that makes it all the more mysterious, a quality totally absent in a more conventional statement such as, "They were unable to come near the spouts" (pp. 201 and 304). Similarly, the Fin-Back is a "species of uncapturable whales" (p. 304). Ishmael's adjectives translate an inability in the agent into a positive, even magical quality in the object. Other negated words are significant for the way in which they simultaneously assert the negative and imply the positive, as when Ishmael speaks of the sailor's belief that no matter how often speared, the white whale's "unsullied jet" would again be seen in "unensanguined billows" (pp. 158-159). He suggests the doom that awaits the crew when he speaks of the blacksmith's "as yet uncatastrophied fifth act of the grief of this life's drama" (p. 401).

Negated verbs and nouns are the most curious of the negated forms. Ishmael is so disturbed by his landlord's stories about Queequeg that he begs him to "*unsay* that story about selling his head," as though it could be undone (p. 26). Ahab puts his typical reflexive twist on the same verb when he tells Starbuck that "what is said in heat, that thing *unsays* itself" (p. 144). Ishmael expresses a special appreciation of paradox when he asserts the substantive quality of negative concepts by creating negated nominals. Were Ishmael to say that the ship's carpenter was "unintelligent," he would not create the same impression he does when he says that "this strange *uncompromisedness* in him involved a sort of *unintelligence*" (p. 388). To be "unintelligent" is simply to be lacking mental power; "unintelligence" seems a radical quality in its own right, a sense amplified of course by Ishmael's indefinite modifiers and the other unusual abstract nominalization, "uncompromisedness." Ahab's "breezelessness" and Ishmael's "unbecomingness," "landlessness," "uneventfulness," "unfulfillments" and "passionlessness" can be seen as backformations, nouns formed from adjectives (pp. 264, 33, 97, 137, 300, 411). But the most striking thing about these negative forms is that they do not have clear positive counterparts; these negatives have an existence all their own while "incorruption," for example, though it is somewhat odd, does not (p. 343). Since comprehending a negative construction seems to require first conceptualizing the positive and then going back and mentally negating that concept, these words present special problems. When we encounter "uneventfulness," since there is no word "eventfulness" in most lexicons, we must imagine that there is, establish what it would mean, and then negate it. This kind of negative in a sense presupposes the existence of its opposite; the negative in fact contains its contrary as it undoes its meaning. The fact that Ishmael calls the "uneventfulness" of the whaler's days "sublime" stretches our appreciation of the negative further still (p. 137). Equally provoking is his exclamation about the leviathan, "Oh! that *unfulfillments* should follow the prophets" (p. 300). While "fulfillments" is deviant because of the plural affix which mass nouns do not accept, the negated form is doubly strange, suggesting that these abstract nonentities may have concrete, countable existences.[10] Taken together, these constructions reflect a consciousness that blurs some of the distinctions between singular and plural, concrete and abstract, and positive and negative. Melville's vocabulary suggests that these distinctions may be imposed by the structure of language rather than by the structure of reality.

Such distinctions are further compromised when Ishmael negates words that are already semantically negative as he does with "unceasingly," "undecreasing," "unwaning," and "unenervated" (pp. 170, 294, 326 and 359, 435). Elizabeth Closs Traugott notes that while we can negate semantically positive adjectives, creating words like "ungood" or "unhappy," when we negate semantically negative adjectives, we get deviant results like "unsad" and "unfalse."[11] Whether Ishmael's terms are technically deviant or not, they require a deliberate effort by the reader to negate an already negative concept. The "unceasingly advancing keel" seems to be working against greater forces than a "steadily advancing keel" would be (p. 170). More difficult to trace out is Ishmael's statement about the whalemen who are not "as a body *unexempt* from that ignorance and superstitiousness hereditary to all sailors" (p. 156). Ishmael's multilayered constructions that require such consideration suggest how much is not directly understandable, not neatly this or that. They suggest that there are indeed layers upon layers of meanings, each of which qualifies the others and all of which we must consider.

Melville adds to the layers of negation and required processing when he in turn negates such words. When Ishmael says that the Canaller in "The Town-Ho's Story" is "*not un*shunned in cities," he makes us wonder if he really means that he is shunned (p. 215). More baffling is Father Mapple's assertion that the sailors "*not un*reluctantly lay hold of Jonah," a phrase whose three layers of negatives make it very difficult to ascertain just what the sailors' attitude was, particularly since the term "unreluctantly" is new to us (p. 49). The difficulty the reader has is indicative of the difficulty Ishmael accepts as inherent in understanding reality and finding the words to express that understanding.

The most conspicuous and significant feature of Ishmael's language is his persistent negation of words that are already negative. When he negates words that are semantically negative, he creates phrases such as "not seldom," "not without," and "not a little" (pp. 260, 262, 110). Negating words that already contain the negative morpheme produces less familiar constructions such as "not unworthy," "not unpleasing," and, of course, "not unreluctantly" (pp. 71, 96, 49). Taken individually, some of those in the first group particularly seem to be simple examples of litotes: when Ishmael says the Malay pirates "*by no means renounce* their claim" to tribute, or when he says that "*no small* excitement was created among the sharks" by the dead whale, his negatives combine to emphasize the positive (pp. 318, 257). Other superficially similar expressions cannot be classified so easily, however. When Ishmael observes that the ladder to Father Mapples's pulpit "seemed by *no* means in *bad* taste," it is not entirely clear that he found it to be in good taste either (p. 42); there are extenuating circumstances, he seems to be saying, that prevent it from being in bad taste. The apparently simple dichotomy between "good" and "bad" is called into question; there must be a gray area, a middle ground, whether or not there is a name for it. At least forty-three times Ishmael combines a negating word with a semantically negative word; Ahab does this just once, as he reflects on the meaning to him of the dying whale: "*Nor* has this thy whale sunwards turned his dying head, and then gone round again, *without* a lesson to me" (p. 409). Some of these expressions allow Ishmael to approach certain mysteries, as when he says of apparently illogical practices concerning the dead, "All these things are *not without* their meanings" (p. 41). This structure allows Ishmael to assert their meaningfulness without having to specify exactly what their meanings may be. In a more complicated sentence about the "unearthly conceit" that Moby Dick was ubiquitous, he qualifies his statement, saying, "*Nor*, credulous as such minds must have been, was this conceit altogether *without* some faint show of superstitious probability" (p. 158). The rather oxymoronic phrase "superstitious probability" further attests to his willingness to consider this idea about the whale.

A key chapter, "The Whiteness of the Whale," is marked by a cluster of these negated forms. Having "almost despair[ed] of putting [this horror of whiteness] in a comprehensible form," Ishmael seems to find the doubly negated pattern necessary to his explanation of his deep misgivings (p. 163). He argues through form as well as substance the overwhelming presence of the negative, one of whose manifestations is whiteness:

> *Nor*, in quite other aspects, does Nature in her *least* palpable but *not* the *less* malicious agencies, *fail* to enlist among her forces the crowning attribute of the terrible.
>
> *Nor*, in some historic instances, has the art of human malice *omitted* so potent an auxiliary.
>
> *Nor*, in some things, does the common, hereditary experience of all mankind *fail* to bear witness to the supernaturalism of this hue.
>
> It can*not* well be *doubted*. . . .
>
> *Nor* even in our superstitions do we *fail* to throw the same snowy mantle round our phantoms. . . .
>
> (p. 166)

Ishmael concludes this discussion by saying "*no man can deny*" the peculiar signifying power of whiteness (p. 166). The first example above nests negatives within one another. To start inside, he speaks of Nature's "*least* palpable but *not* the *less* malicious agencies," packing in three negative words and a semantically negative word, "malicious." It is the "*not the less*" structure that requires special attention; if Ishmael were to say instead, "least palpable but just as malicious agencies," what would change? The use of "least" and "less" serves to connect the two ideas, or rather, to show that there is much more to be concerned about than the strictly "palpable." Ishmael's structure obliges the reader to start with the concept "less malicious," which he hints the reader probably assumes to be the case if something is not palpable, and then, quite self-consciously no doubt, go back and negate both that quantifier "less" and the first assumption. The reading process forces us to enact in miniature just the thought process Ishmael attributes to us. This structure occurs in the middle of another like it, the main clause, "*Nor* . . . does Nature . . . *fail* to enlist among her forces the crowning attribute of the terrible." A positive, far simpler version would read, "Nature . . . enlists among her forces. . . ." But what Ishmael is considering is not simple; it is not a matter of adducing unambiguous evidence. As the whiteness has an angelic as well as a demonic aspect and the distinctions between them are notoriously unclear, so the language of Ishmael's explanation, an explanation that is addressed as much to himself as to us, is filled with qualification upon qualification. To say that Nature does "not fail" to do something implies that perhaps we expect her to "fail," a curious word in this context, for to "fail" here would be positive from man's point of view.

Nechas sees the tremendous presence of the negative as a sign of man's inability to know the whale and of Ishmael's balanced acceptance of that fact; he never considers, however, the great number of negated negatives, the peculiar demands they make on the reader, and the sensibility they project. Besides focusing attention on negatives themselves and suggesting that the second one is something of a positive, this structure frequently reveals a mind unwilling to adopt either pole in a situation, opting instead to suggest that an infinite, if unnamed, continuum lies between the named poles. Nechas argues that the negative affixes suggest the unknowability of the world, but Ishmael's pattern of negated negatives enacts a successful strategy for transcending whatever limits there are, for discovering all that can be known about such a world. The epistemological strategy embodied in this pattern proves to be a positive one in that it yields much more than a bare, insistent elimination of possible explanations of the meaning of reality. While Nechas maintains that being "unsuccessful" in finding a definite truth is in fact the only intellectual success and freedom obtainable in Melville's world, Ishmael's strategy offers a more positive, active, if sometimes puzzling, way of grappling with reality. Furthermore, Ishmael's pattern, his survival, and his writing this book argue that the problem lies not so much with the root unknowability of the world as with the strictures of our dichotomous language.

At least sixty-five times in the novel a word with a negative prefix or with an accompanying *no* or *not* is itself negated; sixty-two of these constructions are Ishmael's. Of all the negative formations, these are the most unusual and provide the clearest indication of Ishmael's distinctive habit of mind.[12] We can read some of these as positive statements by simply allowing the negatives to cancel each other out, as with "*not un*accompanied" "*not un*common," or even "*not un*vexed" (pp. 429, 440 and 456, 259). Similarly, Ishmael says that Ahab's hasty leave-taking from the Samuel Enderby "had *not* been *un*attended with some small violence to his own person" (p. 385). Because an event is generally either attended with something or it is not, one wonders why Ishmael chooses this particular form instead of the more direct positive. On the very next page, however, when he says that Ahab's injury "invested itself with terrors, *not* entirely *un*derived from the land of spirits and of wails," the qualified "not . . . un-" structure allows for both caution and ambiguity (p. 386). Ishmael reveals a great deal about his own open-mindedness when he uses this pattern to describe his reaction to Queequeg: "Savage though he was, and hideously marred about the face—at least to my taste—his countenance yet had a something in it which was by *no* means *dis*agreeable" (pp. 51-52). Despite the fact that the inverse of "disagreeable" is normally "agreeable," Ishmael's careful expression suggests that a meaningful range of reactions exists between the two, that "not disagreeable" does not necessarily equal "agreeable," however our bipolar language would seem to indicate that logically it must. Ishmael's freedom to reject the exclusivity of these choices allows him to develop his own

appreciation of Queequeg, on his own terms. As he does elsewhere, Ishmael refers to "a something" in Queequeg's face, a something which he cannot name but also cannot ignore. Similarly, Ishmael expresses his understanding of Ahab in language both cautious and exploratory: "And yet I also felt a strange awe of him; but that sort of awe, which I cannot at all describe, was not exactly awe; I do not know what it was. But I felt it; and it did *not dis*incline me towards him" (p. 77). Just as he can find no more precise word than "awe" to approximate his complex feelings, his being "not disincline[d]" points toward a middle ground, perhaps without a name, between a term and its opposite. What Ishmael conveys is that his response to Ahab, however elusive, is important, important enough to make him go outside the bounds of conventional language in an effort to both understand and talk about it. The fact that Ishmael cannot always neatly articulate his perceptions never stifles his inquiry or even his attempt at communication. Moreover, the reader, becoming more and more aware of this pattern, increasingly sees it with a new openness, entertaining the possibility, for example, that a "*not un*vexed subject" may not be quite the same as a "vexed" one (p. 259).

The chapter "Moby Dick" contains an especially heavy concentration of negated negatives, structures open and suggestive enough to allow us to appreciate the mystery of the whale and Ishmael's dealings with it:

> It was *hardly* to be *doubted*. . . .
>
> (p. 155)

> to some minds it was *not* an *un*fair presumption, I say, that the whale in question must have been *no* other than Moby Dick.
>
> (p. 155)

> Yet as of late the Sperm Whale fishery has been marked by various and *not un*frequent instances. . . .
>
> (p. 155)

> *Nor* did wild rumors of all sorts *fail* to exaggerate. . . .
>
> (p. 156)

> For *not* only are whalemen as a body *unexempt*. . . .
>
> (p. 156)

> *Nor* . . . was this conceit altogether *without* some faint show of superstitious probability.
>
> (p. 158)

> *Nor* is it to be *gainsaid*. . . .
>
> (p. 158)

> But though similar disasters . . . were by *no* means *un*usual in the fishery; yet, in most instances, such seemed the White Whale's infernal aforethought of fe-

rocity, that every dismembering or death that he caused, was *not* wholly regarded as having been inflicted by an *un*intelligent agent.

(p. 159)

Nor is it so very *un*likely. . . .

(p. 162)

These structures demand that as readers we keep circling back over the same territory, negating concepts, sometimes only to do so again, much as Ishmael keeps returning to the great questions before him. The dynamics of this communicative process are analogous to those described by Horace Bushnell; the semantic poles Melville has Ishmael establish are like the dictions and contradictions advocated by Bushnell. "We never come so near to a truly well-rounded view of any truth," Bushnell observed, "as when it is offered paradoxically; that is, under contradictions; that is, under two or more dictions, which, taken as dictions, are contrary one to the other."[13] Ishmael's language demands a fluid, approximating relationship between speaker and audience. Words are used not as signs or counters pointing to specific entities but as suggestions. Ishmael is both cautious and open to an exceptional range of phenomena and interpretations of those phenomena. Unlike others on the *Pequod*, Ishmael resists the temptation to commit himself to one view of the whale or its opposite, to Moby Dick as supernatural or utterly natural, as cosmic symbol or dumb beast, to the tales about him as gospel or mere humbug. When Ishmael studies the whale's head, he remarks on the fact that his eyes are so placed that they must produce not one blended image such as man sees but two entirely separate images. This drives him to ask whether the whale's brain is "so much more comprehensive, combining, and subtle than man's, that he can at the same moment of time attentively examine two distinct prospects, one on one side of him, and the other in an exactly opposite direction" (p. 280). Ishmael's favorite doubly negated structures lend him this very power of poised consciousness, elevated above the whale's by his unique ability to mediate between the two ideas that he can simultaneously entertain. It is this "rare virtue of interior spaciousness" that he so admires in the whale (p. 261).

Ishmael and Ahab reveal the most profound differences in their ways of conceptualizing reality in the patterns of their linguistic choices. Mark R. Patterson examines constructions both use and shows how their "similar uses of commands, questions, and conditional clauses, serve to exploit their dissimilarities," how "Ahab uses language to extort belief" while "Ishmael subverts both language and belief in order to preserve them."[14] As Patterson points out, Ishmael's questions and commands comment on Ahab's by having the very different effect of stimulating the reader to weigh various possibilities. Equally important is the contrast in their patterns of du-

plication. Their different patterns of semantic repetition reveal radically different ways of relating to reality and different assumptions about the relationship between language and reality. Ahab very rarely uses the fluid pattern of double negation, but he does use the rhetorical doubling devices of polyptoton, in which different forms of the same root word occur in different grammatical slots, and ploce, in which the identical word is repeated. Ahab focuses this special attention exclusively on referential words, often dwelling on forms of a word as though the word could somehow be made to yield its mysterious reality, as though meaning inhered in the very words we use to describe it. When Ishmael manipulates negatives, he shows the importance of these words that organize and reflect our perceptions about things in the world rather than attempting to name them. While Ahab's patterns suggest a rigidly correspondential, even magical, view of language, Ishmael's suggest a position more like Bushnell's, capitalizing on the conceptual, ambiguous nature of language. When Ishmael does use two forms of the same word or two similar words in close proximity, he is likely to be intensifying his expression or punning.

Ahab's doubling often has a hysterical quality about it, enhanced no doubt by the fact that these instances tend to cluster together and to occur in conjunction with heavy alliteration. For instance, he commands the harpooners, "Drink, ye harpooners! drink and swear, ye *men* that *man* the *deathful* whaleboat's bow—*Death* to Moby Dick!" (p. 146). That same night, he says of the sunset that once soothed him, "This lovely *light*, it *lights* not me" (p. 147). Ahab's egotism, his tendency to read all things in terms of himself, emerges when Starbuck tells him they must deal with the oil leaking below (*no* *in*considerable oil," as Ishmael says). Instead of responding to the situation, Ahab raves, "Let it *leak*! I'm all *aleak* myself. Aye! *leaks* in *leaks*! not only full of *leaky* casks, but those *leaky* casks are in a *leaky* ship; and that's a far worse plight than the Pequod's, man" (p. 393). Obsessed with ideas of manhood and of being unmanned himself, he rants to the Manxman, "Here's a *man* from *Man*; a *man* born in once independent *Man*, and now *unmanned* of *Man*" (p. 427). Ahab turns the word *man* over obsessively, as though through the words themselves he can heal himself or at least understand his injury.

Ahab's patterns of repetition also underscore the reflexive, eventually reductive, nature of his world view. The pattern is clear in the following passage: "They think me mad—Starbuck does; but I'm demoniac, I am *madness maddened*! That wild madness that's only calm to comprehend itself! The prophecy was that I should be *dismembered;* and—Aye! I lost this leg. I now prophesy that I will *dismember* my *dismemberer*" (p. 147). The persistent coming together of subject and object into one undifferentiated entity is epitomized by Ahab's very next sentence: "Now, then, be the prophet and the ful-filler one" (p. 147). How Ahab deals with opposition is shown again when he confronts the lightning storm. "In the midst of the *personified impersonal, a personality* stands here," he proclaims and promises that, made of fire, "like a true child of fire, I breathe it back to thee" (p. 417). Challenging the forces of nature, he analyzes the dynamics of his situation in severely polarized terms: "Light though thou be, thou leapest out of darkness; but I am darkness leaping out of light, leaping out of thee!" (p. 417). He perceives himself and the lightning as simple inverses of one another; light coming of darkness and darkness coming of light share one dynamic. It is not a great surprise, then, when Ahab identifies with his foe: "I leap with thee; I burn with thee; would fain be welded with thee; defyingly I worship thee!" (p. 417). Ahab can interpret anything or anyone that is not one with him only as his adversary; there are no neutrals. And the only way he can conceive of dealing with that adversary is by becoming one with it. Again, when he observes, "Oh! how *immaterial* are all *materials*!" he expresses his keen awareness of opposites and the space between them, but for Ahab there are no points along that space as there are for Ishmael; there is only the thing and its inverse, and they have a way of exchanging places (p. 432). Ahab demonstrates this foreshortened view when he says to Starbuck and Stubb, "Ye two are the opposite poles of one thing; Starbuck is Stubb reversed, and Stubb is Starbuck; and ye two are all mankind; and Ahab stands alone . . ." (p. 452). This gross oversimplification is but a single manifestation of his bipolar, ultimately monistic, view.

Ishmael's repetitions often act as intensifiers, as when he says, "Queequeg *vowed* his *vow*," or when he speaks of calamities "*fatal* to the last degree of *fatality*," or when he exclaims, "*Terrors* of the *terrible*!" (pp. 56, 156, 98). In his discussion of the whiteness of the whale, he cautions that in such a matter "*subtlety* appeals to *subtlety*" (p. 167). Ishmael is most insistent when he reminds us, "This whole book is but a *draught*—nay, but the *draught* of a *draught*" (p. 128). Clearly, Ishmael's "draughts" and "subtleties" are different from one another; these expressions, like his negated negatives, suggest change and variety. He repeats himself only to say that for which he can find no one word: "terrible" is not terrible enough and even "draught" implies more finality and form than Ishmael wants to claim for his work.

Ishmael's puns display an attitude toward language that is very different from Ahab's. When Ahab remarks, "Oh! how immaterial are all materials," he reads in this a message as dark as that he perceives in the "life-buoy of a coffin" (pp. 432, 433). Ahab, expecting reality to inhere in language, expecting a one-to-one correspondence between the word and the thing it represents, sounds perplexed and even angry that reality is more

contrary than language. He perceives logical conflicts where Ishmael, more playful and accepting of ambiguity, puns in order to show the inconsistencies of language. Thus he speaks of the "clammy" reception a mere cod or clam would constitute at the Try Pots and observes how the whalers put an end to the Sperm Whale's "*peculiarities* by killing him, and boiling him down into a *peculiarly* valuable oil" (pp. 64, 176). Astonished at being offered but the seven hundred and seventy-seventh lay by the pious Quaker, he thinks to himself, "Well, old Bildad, you are determined that I, for one, shall not *lay* up many *lays* here below, where moth and rust do corrupt" (p. 74, emphasis Melville's). Later, Ishmael imagines Ahab's ruminations about the need to hold out hope of a cash reward to the crew: "this same quiescent cash all at once mutinying in them, this same *cash* would soon *cashier* Ahab" (p. 184). It is unlikely, however, that Ahab would in fact engage in this sort of darkly humorous word play. Even as he describes Tashtego's fall into the whale's head, Ishmael says that the head throbbed and heaved "as if that *moment* seized with some *momentous* idea; whereas it was only the poor Indian *unconsciously* revealing by those struggles the perilous depth to which he had sunk" (p. 288). Very conscious himself of the language he uses, he continues to describe how "through the courage and great skill in obstetrics of Queequeg, the *deliverance,* or rather, *delivery* of Tashtego, was successfully accomplished, in the *teeth,* too, of the most untoward and apparently hopeless impediments" (p. 290). Ishmael's delight in language carries him right along to the comment about the "teeth," here literally as well as metaphorically true. In fact Ishmael tends to engage in just this sort of verbal play when dealing with gruesome realities, as when he describes the amputee who begs on the London docks. His "*stump* [is] as unquestionable a *stump* as any you will find in the western clearings," he observes. "But, though for ever mounted on that *stump,* never a *stump*-speech does the poor whale man make" (p. 232). Ishmael's language choices underscore the accidental and ambiguous relationship that may obtain between our words and the things we have them represent.

A passage in "The Gilder" has been attributed to Ishmael by most editors but to Ahab by others.[15] The reasons for confusion are evident. The context of the passage strongly suggests that Ahab is speaking, but the passage itself contains instances of semantic doubling that could suggest both characters' language. It is as though the "soothing scenes" which Ishmael observes had at least a temporary effect on Ahab, had moved him to adopt some of Ishmael's doubling patterns. "There is *no* steady *un*retracing progress in this life," he says, recalling Ishmael's negated negatives, and asks "Where lies the final harbor whence we *unmoor no* more?" (p. 406). While the punning on *moor* and *more* sounds like Ishmael, the emphasis here and in the rest of the passage on hopelessness and death reflects Ahab's thoughts. The next question, "In what rapt ether sails the world, of which the *weariest* will never *weary*?" certainly seems to continue Ahab's pattern of doubling. If Ahab sounds more and more like himself as the passage progresses, it is in keeping with Ishmael's observation that if the "golden keys" of the tranquil surroundings "did seem to open in him his own secret golden treasuries, yet did his breath upon them prove but tarnishing" (p. 406).

Ishmael uses a pattern of repetition that makes him sound like Ahab just once, and that is when he expresses his understanding of Ahab's self-destructive impulses. Having depicted Ahab's driven pursuit of the whale, he says, "God help thee, old man, thy thoughts have *created* a *creature* in thee; and he whose intense thinking thus makes him a Prometheus; a vulture feeds upon that heart for ever; that vulture the very *creature* he *creates*" (p. 175). This pattern of polyptoton is strikingly appropriate as it both echoes Ahab's pattern and imitates the kind of action it describes, the violence that can only relentlessly produce more of itself. Ishmael's repetition of the words in reverse order at the end of the passage forms an all-enclosing chiasmic pattern that further symbolizes Ahab's dilemma. Starbuck's language too reveals an awareness of the dynamics of Ahab's monomania; he says, "I ask thee not to beware of Starbuck; thou wouldst but laugh; but let *Ahab* beware of *Ahab*; beware of thyself, old man" (p. 394).

The contrast between Ishmael's and Ahab's views of reality surfaces again at the conclusion. On the third day of the chase, believing that he has oversailed Moby Dick, Ahab observes, "Aye, he's chasing *me* now; not I, *him*" (p. 461, emphases Melville's). These are the only alternatives Ahab can imagine, but later that day the whale seems "swimming with his utmost velocity, and now only intent upon pursuing his own straight path in the sea." As Starbuck says, "See! Moby Dick seeks thee not. It is thou, thou, that madly seekest him!" (p. 465). Whether the whale would have continued to swim away, we cannot say, because his actions are described by Ishmael in terms of "seems" and "as if," the only terms sufficient for our interpretation of nature.

While Ahab's speeches collapse toward the final, hopeless tautology, "Ahab is for ever Ahab," Ishmael's language is always searching, always fluid, coming to few sure conclusions, but surviving to tell us not only of Ahab and the White Whale, but of Ishmael and "the unharming sharks" that "glided by as if with padlocks on their mouths" (pp. 459, 470).

Notes

1. Herman Melville, *Moby-Dick,* ed. Harrison Hayford and Hershel Parker (New York: Norton, 1967), p. 261; hereafter cited by page number. Italics are mine unless otherwise noted.

2. Gura, "Language and Meaning: An American Tradition," *American Literature,* 53 (1981), 1-21; see also his *Wisdom of Words: Language, Theology, and Literature in the New England Renaissance* (Middletown, Conn.: Wesleyan Univ. Press, 1981).

3. Kenneth W. Cameron, *Emerson the Essayist* (Raleigh, N.C.: Thistle Press, 1945), II, 22.

4. Baym, "Melville's Quarrel with Fiction," *PMLA,* 94 (1979), 915.

5. Nechas, *Synonymy, Repetition, and Restatement in the Vocabulary of Herman Melville's* Moby-Dick (Norwood, Pa: Norwood Editions, 1979), pp. 20, 19.

6. Arvin, *Herman Melville* (New York: Viking, 1957), p. 163.

7. Where possible, I have checked such occurrences in *A Concordance to Melville's* Moby-Dick, ed. Hennig Cohen and James Cahalan (Ann Arbor, Mich.: University Microfilms International, 1978).

8. Seven of the instances refer to whales or whaling (pp. 16, 20, 163, 166, 169, 350, 447); four refer to Ahab (pp. 111, 133, 145, 451).

9. Nechas counts approximately 1,500 words with negative affixes in *Moby-Dick,* or one for every 170 words. While Nechas explores the effect of these words on the reader and the extent to which they imply the unknowable nature of the whale and the universe itself, he does not explore the more interesting, deviant, and dynamic aspects of negation in *Moby-Dick.*

10. I owe thanks to my colleagues John Bryant and John Dolis for reading an earlier draft and indicating, among other things, where more explicit grammatical explanation was in order.

11. Traugott, *A History of English Syntax* (New York: Holt, Rinehart & Winston, 1972), p. 7.

12. As Ian Watt remarks in "The First Paragraph of *The Ambassadors:* An Explication," *Contemporary Essays in Style,* ed. Glen A. Love and Michael Payne (Glenview, Ill.: Scott, Foresman, 1967), p. 274, "There are no negatives in nature but only in the human consciousness."

13. Bushnell, *Horace Bushnell,* ed. H. Shelton Smith (New York: Oxford Univ. Press, 1965), pp. 93-94.

14. Patterson, "Democratic Leadership and Narrative Authority in *Moby-Dick,*" *Studies in the Novel,* 16 (1984), 300-301.

15. The passage is the paragraph beginning "Oh, grassy glades . . . ," p. 406. Despite the fact that

no quotation marks appear in either the American or English edition, thus suggesting the passage is Ishmael's, Harrison Hayford and Hershel Parker suspect that Melville intended the passage to be Ahab's (pp. 493-494). I owe the information that this passage will in fact be attributed to Ahab in the forthcoming Northwestern-Newberry edition of *Moby-Dick* to a reader for *ESQ* [*Emerson Society Quarterly*].

Manfred Pütz (essay date summer 1987)

SOURCE: Pütz, Manfred. "The Narrator as Audience: Ishmael as Reader and Critic in *Moby-Dick*." *Studies in the Novel* 19, no. 2 (summer 1987): 160-74.

[*In the following essay, Pütz examines the various roles assumed by Ishmael, arguing that in addition to functioning as the narrator, Ishmael also identifies with the novel's audience, acts as the work's primary critic, and is at times a reflection of the author himself. Through the continual exploration of these shifting identities, Pütz suggests, Melville provides the reader with an interpretative model for the novel. In spite of this critical framework, however, the ambivalence and ambiguity of Ishmael's character undermines the possibility of a single, coherent reading of the work.*]

We are all aware of the fact that Ishmael, for the most part, is the narrator of *Moby-Dick.* Much less do we seem to be aware that he is also the most prominent reader and critic of the novel. Yet, throughout the book there are numerous scenes in which Ishmael the narrator demonstratively takes on these audience roles. For instance, in quite a number of memorable situations he deals with books and written documents of all sorts which trigger responses from him as a reader, a researcher, and a critical reviewer. In several other episodes of the novel, he plays the role of viewer and outspoken critic of non-verbal presentations of art such as paintings, illustrations, and drawings.

Melville criticism has dealt extensively with Ishmael the narrator and with the related problem of perspectivism and point-of-view in *Moby-Dick.* But little attention has so far been paid to Ishmael as an audience figure and to the related problem of reader response as it is worked into the novel.[1] In a way, this has something to do with the restrictions certain schools of criticism have placed on the subjects of their research. Thus, the bulk of reader-response criticism predominantly deals with the problems either of actual readers or of such tacitly assumed or openly addressed figures as the "implied," the "fictive," the "abstract," the "ideal," the "intended," and/or the "imagined" reader in their respective roles for the constitution and mediation of literary texts.[2] But decidedly less attention has been directed towards another type of reader figure who brings joined aspects of reader response and art criticism into play. I mean a reader figure who is not merely structurally implied in the text, or assumed, or explicitly addressed as a recipient of certain messages, but who is a character among other characters of a given story, and is himself, in the course of this story, shown in the act of reading books and responding to them.[3] Obviously, such a character, whom I would like to call a personified audience figure, may serve a variety of functions which are often similar but not necessarily identical to the functions of implied readers of texts: authors may cast protagonists as personified audience figures in order to deal with the complex dimension of intertextuality; in order to project reactions upon them which, in turn, may describe the assumed influence of literature on people; in order to delineate traditional stances of readers vis-a-vis texts; in order to discuss, in relation to specific characters of the fictional world, poetological concepts of literature and art as such. As will be shown below, personified audience figures may also serve as a means of introducing self-referential commentary into a given text in that they not only figure as objects of narrative communication but also reflect upon the process of narrative communication by making it the implicit topic of their own dealings with texts other than the one that brings them into existence.

I

The Ishmael of *Moby-Dick,* I would like to argue, is presented in the role of such a personified audience figure in many situations of the novel, and the stance of the critical spectator, which has so often been ascribed to him, meshes well with this role.[4] The recurrence of, and the emphasis on, situations in which he appears as a reader of books or a viewer of pictures, raises our suspicion that Melville might have certain functions and effects in mind when he casts his narrator as audience. But before we can proceed to a discussion of these functions, a general differentiation among Ishmael's various audience roles must be noted. Characteristic of Ishmael's diversified reactions as an audience figure is a basic division of orientation in his recurrent approaches towards literature and art. The division hinges on the fact that in some cases his responses are reader/viewer-oriented, whereas in others they are object-oriented, which is to say that in the one case they tell us something about the perceiver, while in the other they tell us something about the perceived.

A case in point for the differentiation between reader/viewer-oriented and object-oriented forms of audience response are Ishmael's varying attitudes as an art critic in certain passages of the novel. I would like to compare his approach towards two paintings he discusses in the earlier parts of the narrative with the way he describes and evaluates an assortment of graphic representations of the whale and the adventure of whaling later in the novel.

In the third chapter of **Moby-Dick,** Ishmael encounters a curious painting at the Spouter-Inn which obviously puzzles him and consequently puts his interpretive faculties to work. Since this encounter involves a highly compact description of *one* of Ishmael's typical attitudes, I would like to quote the passage in full:

> On one side hung a very large oil-painting so thoroughly be-smoked and every way defaced, that in the unequal cross-lights by which you viewed it, it was only by diligent study and a series of systematic visits to it, and careful inquiry of the neighbors, that you could any way arrive at an understanding of its purpose. Such unaccountable masses of shades and shadows, that at first you almost thought some ambitious young artist, in the time of the New England hags, had endeavored to delineate chaos bewitched. But by dint of much and earnest contemplation, and oft repeated ponderings, and especially by throwing open the little window towards the back of the entry, you at last came to the conclusion that such an idea, however wild, might not be altogether unwarranted.
>
> But what most puzzled and confounded you was a long, limber, portentous, black mass of something hovering in the centre of the picture over three blue, dim, perpendicular lines floating in a nameless yeast. A boggy, soggy, squitchy picture truly, enough to drive a nervous man distracted. Yet was there a sort of indefinite, half-attained, unimaginable sublimity about it that fairly froze you to it, till you involuntarily took an oath with yourself to find out what that marvellous painting meant. Ever and anon a bright, but, alas deceptive idea would dart you through.—It's the Black Sea in a midnight gale.—It's the unnatural combat of the four primal elements.—It's a blasted heath.—It's a Hyperborean winter scene.—It's the breaking-up of the icebound stream of Time. But at last all these fancies yielded to that one portentous something in the picture's midst. *That* once found out, and all the rest were plain. But stop; does it not bear a faint resemblance to a gigantic fish? even the great leviathan himself?
>
> In fact, the artist's design seemed this: a final theory of my own, partly based upon the aggregated opinions of many aged persons with whom I conversed upon the subject. The picture represents a Cape-Horner in a great hurricane; the half-foundered ship weltering there with its three dismantled masts alone visible; and an exasperated whale, purposing to spring clean over the craft, is in the enormous act of impaling himself upon the three mast-heads.[5]

Though the passage initially seems to present itself as the description of an object of art, it quickly shifts its main focus of orientation and emerges as a description of a viewer's *reaction* towards a specific work of art.[6] As such, it centers upon the viewer's ruminations and responses which run the whole gamut from confusion, irritation, and challenge to spontaneous interpretation,

speculation, doubt, and opinion mongering. The focus of the passage is so intensely fixed upon the viewer's state of mind that we cannot even develop a clear idea of what the picture really presents. Notwithstanding the attempted sketch of its content and design, confusion remains because this sketch is only offered as the result of a "final theory of my own," and is based upon "aggregated opinions" which a puzzled Ishmael must have collected considerably later than the evening he first encountered the painting at the Spouter-Inn.[7]

Prevalent throughout the passage is a tone of irony which occasionally borders on satire and parody. What eventually emerges from the ironies is that the joke is rather on the viewer than on the picture and that the ironic commentary is not primarily concerned with Ishmael as an individual person but rather as an audience figure generally representative of a certain type of reader/viewer. The bridge between Ishmael the character and the representative audience figure is grammatically enforced. For the narrator chooses to tell the passage not in the first person singular, but instead uses throughout the indefinite pronoun *you,* thus providing a grammatical link between Ishmael and the reader of the novel who may or may not take up the offer of identifying with the *you* at once addressed and characterized in the text.[8] In other words, what the passage offers is more than just a sketch of Ishmael's approach towards a work of art. It transcribes a role model for an imagined viewer/reader which can be taken over or rejected by the actual audience of the novel. Members of the audience may not be willing to slip into this role model. However, they will have been made aware of the dangers and the inadequacies, of the complexities and the blessings, of the foolishness and the wisdom of certain approaches to art, and hence of the role they themselves play as interpreters.

The intricacies of the passage are not exhausted by these observations. Though Melville criticism has been somewhat reticent on this point, the passage fairly obviously fulfills another important function within the context of the novel. If we run through Ishmael's concrete responses to the painting at the Inn, we get a model that anticipates responses of certain readers to **Moby-Dick** itself.[9] What better summary is there of the confusions and irritations, of the speculations, doubts, ambitions, and critical infights, of the ironies and pitfalls, of the rejections and allegorical searchings **Moby-Dick** itself has triggered off among its readers and critics? What better ironic formulas are there for the whole book itself than "Chaos bewitched" and "A boggy, soggy, squitchy picture truly, enough to drive a nervous man distracted?" In other words, the painting at the Spouter-Inn is also **Moby-Dick** in effigy, and the commentaries on the painting are an ironic form of Melvillean self-criticism, perhaps coupled with anticipations of future responses towards the novel.

In other episodes of the novel Ishmael's encounters with works of art are also rendered as a form of audience response which is essentially viewer-oriented. There is the episode in which Ishmael scans the interior of the chapel which will soon be the setting of Father Mapple's sermon. Behind the pulpit he observes "a large painting representing a gallant ship beating against a terrible storm off a lee coast of black rocks and snowy breakers" (p. 43). He notices the face of an angel hovering over the scene and he attributes the following words to the angel: "'Ah, noble ship,' the angel seemed to say, 'beat on, beat on, thou noble ship, and bear a hardy helm; for lo! the sun is breaking through; the clouds are rolling off—serenest azure is at hand'" (p. 43). Again the focus of attention is not so much on the painting as on Ishmael's reaction to it. Again the main response consists of an imaginative search for deeper meanings, a search which is intensified by Ishmael's momentary readiness to invest anything he encounters in the chapel with encompassing and profound significance. Moreover, the irony of Ishmael's response to the picture again lies in the intense concentration on his own state of mind which makes him misread signs. What Ishmael as a personified audience figure believes he has grasped—lost in himself though seemingly reaching out beyond himself to a world of signs and significances—is that the angel's message spells hope and blessing for the ventures he is soon to embark upon. What happens later, we all know.[10]

II

In marked contrast to Ishmael's viewer-oriented responses as an observer of art stands a type of object-oriented reaction in episodes which again cast Ishmael in the role of audience figure and critic. This reaction can perhaps best be studied in chapters 55 to 57 of the novel where Ishmael deals with the representation of whales in the graphic arts: "Of the Monstrous Pictures of Whales," "Of the Less Erroneous Pictures of Whales," and "Of Whales in Paint; in Teeth, in Wood." What is presented in these chapters is a gallery of whale pictures in the media of various graphic and plastic arts ranging from prints, painting, and engravings to vignettes, carvings, sign boards, and skrimshander articles.[11] In a way, Ishmael's exhaustive catalogue seems to be the pictorial counterpart of the "Extracts" preceding the novel where almost all extant verbal references to the whale are collected at random. In his catalogue of pictorial representations Ishmael intermixes the description of images with the notation of his own response to what he sees before him. In other words, he remains an audience figure of distinct personal contour, and the process and effects of perceiving are as much his topic as the substance of the perceived. Yet something in the balance and the emphasis between the two focal points of reference has drastically changed. We can see this, among other things, in the uses of irony

and satire prevalent in these chapters, which have undergone a change in function in that they are now addressed to a different target. Consider the following passages:

> Look at that popular work "Goldsmith's Animated Nature." In the abridged London edition of 1807, there are plates of an alleged "whale" and a "narwhale." I do not wish to seem inelegant, but this unsightly whale looks much like an amputated sow; and, as for the narwhale, one glimpse at it is enough to amaze one, that in this nineteenth century such a hippogriff could be palmed for genuine upon any intelligent public of schoolboys.
>
> (pp. 226-27)

> In 1836, he [Frederick Cuvier] published a Natural History of Whales, in which he gives what he calls a picture of the Sperm Whale. Before showing that picture to any Nantucketer, you had best provide for your summary retreat from Nantucket. In a word, Frederick Cuvier's Sperm Whale is not a Sperm Whale, but a squash. Of course, he never had the benefit of a whaling voyage (such men seldom have), but whence he derived that picture, who can tell?
>
> (p. 227)

Criticism, irony, and a satirical touch are still obvious, but the targets at which they are aimed have changed. In the Spouter-Inn scene the description of the design and the subject matter of the painting was subordinated to the description of the viewer's reaction. The former served as a springboard for the latter. Hence the irony and the satirical shots of the passage were directed predominantly against the viewer, his ineptitude in interpretation, and his dubious responses towards a work of art. In the two passages given above, things are quite the other way round. They deal with the responses of the viewer in order to launch from there into a criticism of the object presented, and hence the irony is now directed against the artists, their ineptitude, and finally against the sorry products of their blundering attempts. What has changed, then, is that these passages still circumscribe a form of audience response personified in Ishmael, yet the response is now predominantly object-oriented and tells us more about the perceived than about the perceiver.

It is unlikely that this change of orientation is due to a random decision of the narrator or to an unreflected change of narrative technique. Rather it seems to go back to a deeper change of orientation toward questions of the meaning and the function of the visual arts. Ishmael himself suggests as much at the beginning of chapter 55: "I shall ere long," he writes,

> paint to you as well as one can without canvas, something like the true form of the whale as he actually appears to the eye of the whaleman when in his own absolute body the whale is moored alongside the whaleship so that he can be fairly stepped upon there. It may

be worth while, therefore, previously to advert to those curious imaginary portraits of him which even down to the present day confidently challenge the faith of the landsman. It is time to set the world right in this matter, by proving such pictures of the whale all wrong.

(pp. 224-25)

Truthfulness to its full extent ("absolute body") is claimed as the criterion to which the graphic arts as arts of documentation have to be subjected, and any failure to meet this criterion will result in the ruthless criticism Ishmael directs against the products and the producers involved. This is not to say, of course, that either Ishmael's or Melville's idea of the visual arts exhausts itself in the demand for documentary and accurate representation.[12] Quite the contrary: Ishmael frequently seems to propose his own version of the protean nature and the inherent multi-functionality of art with, however, the further stipulation that any artistic enterprise once firmly committed to this or that possible function would necessarily have to stand by this commitment. Obviously, the pictures at the Spouter-Inn and at the chapel are not there in order merely to represent something truthfully. Hence they cannot be criticized for failing in this department. These pictures transmit other forms of meaning, perhaps of a symbolic nature. And if any viewer such as Ishmael misses this point or takes the wrong departure from the premises they encompass, this is more a comment upon his own inadequacies than upon a failure of art. But if, on the other hand, a form of art commits itself to true representation—as may be assumed with the documentary pictures of whales[13]— then it can surely be taken to task for its shortcomings in this department.[14] And this is the basis and meaning of Ishmael's object-oriented responses as a critic, responses which will repeat themselves, as we shall see, when he presents himself as a reader of books and a critic of texts.

Another crucial difference, however, between the viewer-oriented and the object-oriented responses of Ishmael as an audience figure has yet to be noted. Ishmael's viewer-oriented reactions are models of audience response predominantly concerning addressees. His object-oriented responses, on the other hand, concern objects of art, but also the creators of such objects. Consequently, the latter form of response delineates models for artists in the form of implicit maxims about how Ishmael expects them to go about their tasks. The audience model of Ishmael's viewer-oriented criticism is thus supplemented by an implicit author model behind his object-oriented criticism.

III

It is the latter model we will have to bear in mind when we observe Ishmael in his second important audience role, namely as a reader and critic of books. The middle sections of *Moby-Dick* contain extended passages in which Ishmael first reads and then responds to a welter of written documents relating to the whale and the business of whaling as literary and/or scientific topics. Melville criticism has diligently followed the tracks of Ishmael's paranomatic tour through the world of whaling literature and has identified numerous sources, references, and allusions.[15] Yet, this is not the point in the context of our investigation. What is important here is the way in which Ishmael responds to these texts. This response, taken as an evolving process, is almost uniform in its structure. As evidenced by the chapter on "Cetology," Ishmael usually starts by announcing his intention of achieving a thorough understanding of a given subject by systematically sorting through the information available on it. He then addresses the problem that writers before him must have tangled with the same task and that he must deal with their endeavors before proceeding to his own. It is here that he presents himself as an experienced researcher and a voracious reader of books who must have gathered his book knowledge in extensive studies long after the events young Ishmael was involved in aboard the Pequod.[16] And it is here that he shows many of the books he has consulted fail in their tasks. The motto for the state of affairs seems to be adequately transcribed by his famous line: "Nevertheless, though of real knowledge there be little, yet of books there are plenty" (p. 117). Ishmael then presents his own hard won credentials as a writer and researcher, emphasizing, among other things, his dual qualification as a mature man of books and, formerly, a youth of first-hand experience: "But I have swam through libraries and sailed through oceans; I have had to do with whales with these visible hands; I am in earnest; and I will try" (p. 118). The upshot of this technique of self-presentation is that Ishmael, while posing as an audience figure, lays open the orientation and the intentions of his own endeavors as a writer. What he seeks is books on the whale and on whaling is what he sought in the documentary pictures of whales, namely the closest possible approach to the truth of the matter which he himself wants to bring out in his writings.[17] Hence, he presents himself as a serious, questioning, meticulous reader whose critical responses, while distributing praise and rebuke, predominantly center upon the informational dimensions of the texts in hand and not so much on the implications of his own role and constitution as a reader vis-a-vis such texts. Consequently, if ironic commentary occurs in the passages dealing with his reading experiences, the irony functions as a critical weapon against *what* he reads and not against his own (often dubious) machinations and shortcomings as a reader. For instance, Captain Sleet's (alias William Scoresby, Jr.) description of the crow's-nest in the book *A Voyage among the Icebergs* as well as other passages from Scoresby are dealt with ironically.[18] However, the irony is almost entirely leveled against the contents and the author of the books under scrutiny.

We may say, then, that in *Moby-Dick* the self-presentation of Ishmael as a reader and critic of books is object-oriented in so far as it centers upon texts and their achievements, and only in a secondary sense upon readers and their reactions. But where does this leave Ishmael the writer, who would necessarily have to be seen as a party to the interplay between the two? In the given context, the answer is fairly obvious. Ishmael's object-oriented responses as a reader are at the same time an important comment upon his role as a writer. What he draws our attention to in his extensive dealings with books is, among other things, the complex dimension of intertextuality as a constitutive element in the process of generating texts.[19] Far beyond the aspect of source hunting, Ishmael the reader-turned-writer makes us aware of the phenomenon that texts derive from, and point to, other texts as constituents of a verbal universe which in its entirety of elements and intricate connections serves as the point of reference for further verbal artifacts which come into existence in constant interplay with them. In dealing with a vast array of pre-texts, Ishmael the reader in a way draws our attention to intertextuality as a precondition for his work as a writer. But his discussion of prior texts is not simply the playful approach of a writer who toys with the works of his predecessors in order to generate new works. It is rather that Ishmael the reader develops a whole panorama of texts and pre-texts in order to embed his own attempts into a body of works which as a writer he hopes to absorb, to modify, and to transcend. Ishmael's responses as a critic are thus a running commentary upon his own intentions and orientations as author, and they implicitly deal with such aspects as intertextuality, the treatment of sources, the reception of related works, and the whole problem of how a writer can achieved a secure stance in regard to his chosen subject. Although demonstratively written from a reader's perspective, his comments are really addressed to the writer's chores, and thus set a model for authors dealing with their materials.[20] In this respect, Ishmael's discussion of books reflects the preconditions, and clears the ground, for his own creation of a book which will partly be shaped out of his own experiences as reader. That the alleged project of presenting the truth about the whale and about whaling finally proves to be an immensely difficult, if at all feasible, task is a different problem.[21] And so is the fact that the central chapter Ishmael writes in pursuit of his project eventually turns out to be a highly ironic treatise and a parody of scientific and scholarly writings of all sorts. Regardless of such problematical twists, we have to bear in mind that

when Ishmael emphatically poses as a reader in the course of the novel, we are frequently meant to perceive behind this role the image of the narrator/writer of the book.

Audience response as an explicit topic is, of course, not only associated with the figure of Ishmael in *Moby-Dick.* It is also prevalent in other contexts and variations; but on the whole its forms and functions remain the same as outlined above. For instance, the "late consumptive usher" of "Etymology" and the "sub-sub-librarian" of the "Extracts" can be understood as personified audience figures. Regardless of the question of their identity[22] (are they independent figures in contrast to the narrator, or perhaps this narrator or even the author of the novel under the guise of a mask?), they are presented as mock ideals of what a reader and a scholar should be. They serve, as it were, as comic models of attitudes, activities, and orientations prevalent among readers and researchers of a certain twist. In a way, they even transcribe ironic role models for both the reader and the writer of the novel. Since what the late usher and the Sub-Sub do with and to their materials is precisely what Ishmael wants to avoid as a writer (it is a different question, however, whether he is successful in this respect). Nor do these models define attitudes and predilections Melville presumably hoped to find in his readers.

Similarly, "The Town-Ho's Story," various other stories within the story, and the episode of "Jonah Historically Regarded" function as sketches and ironic commentaries on forms of audience response. In the course of "The Town-Ho's Story" as told by Ishmael, his audience of Spanish gentlemen at the Golden Inn in Lima is pictured as a victim of its own comic inadequacies. The participation of the Spanish Dons in the form of questions, distracting comments, and interjections materializes as a body of responses which in essence mirror the reactions Melville had endured earlier to certain of his works, and which he anticipated again in response to *Moby-Dick.*[23]

In "Jonah Historically Regarded" the old Nantucketer "Sag-Harbor" develops an array of arguments against the accuracy of the story of Jonah in the Bible, and the defenders of the story give their counter-arguments. As it evolves, both parties are inadequate readers of the text, and their foolish bickerings over points beside the point constitute a graphic example for the charge that readers and exegetists all too often revert to trivialities, and reveal themselves as uncongenial partners in the reader-author covenant.[24] The double irony of the episode is further emphasized by the fact that the skeptic Sag-Harbor might have a point after all, except that he bases his critical readings on reason alone which, as an arbiter, seems the least acceptable faculty in such matters for other readers of the same texts.[25]

IV

What, then, happens in *Moby-Dick* when Melville turns Ishmael, his central narrator, into an audience figure and enforces the emphasis on viewer and reader models in various other situations of the novel? Moreover, what aims are being pursued by Melville's technique of presenting reader and writer models in interrelation with implied comments on critics, authors, and actual readers? Stanley Fish has persuasively argued, along with a whole line of reader-response critics, that readers, in a sense, are actually writers of texts, or, as Jane Tompkins would have it, that "Texts are written by readers, not read."[26] "That is to say," Stanley Fish argues,

> interpretive strategies are not put into execution after reading (the pure act of perception in which I do not believe); they are the shape of reading, and because they are the shape of reading, they give texts their shape, making them rather than, as it is usually assumed, arising from them.[27]

The proposition that readers are in a sense writers entails the intriguing possibility that we can see the relation under scrutiny from the opposite angle: writers (or narrators, for that matter) may be seen as readers of their texts. Generally, the following statement by Fish would seem to hold true of the process of literary mediation as such:

> In my model, however, meanings are not extracted but made and made not by encoding forms but by interpretive strategies that call forms into being. It follows then that what utterers do is give hearers and readers the opportunity to make meanings (and texts) by inviting them to put into execution a set of strategies. It is presumed that the invitation will be recognized, and that presumption rests on a projection on the part of a speaker or author of the moves *he* would make if confronted by the sounds or marks he is uttering or setting down.[28]

But if authors actually project themselves into the role of readers by first anticipating and then suggesting certain interpretive strategies to be applied to their works, they may also go one step further and introduce a personified audience figure who explicitly pursues these strategies and who presents the actual reader there and then with a model for interpreting the text. In a way, this procedure makes the phenomenon of the inherently dialectical reader-writer relationship visible by incorporating it into the responses and activities of a fictional figure who is described in the act of applying interpretive strategies to texts. And this is how things stand, in a sense, with Ishmael in Moby-Dick. Of course, the Ishmael of Moby-Dick reads, interprets, and criticizes texts (and pictures) other than the novel he appears in. But how he approaches them and deals with their intricacies can easily be generalized into a model of reader response as such, and be transferred from there to a model of what the reader of *Moby-Dick* is likely to do with this book.

Ishmael as a personified audience figure, then, functions as an interpretative model for the reading of the story he himself narrates. However, as we have seen earlier, this is only one of the functions he serves as an audience figure. It will be remembered that the other function rests in his role as a writer model contained in his predominantly object-oriented criticism of literature and art. By introducing Ishmael in these capacities, the novel foregrounds decisive elements of narrative literature in the course of a tricky form of self-referential commentary which concerns readers, writers, critics, and the literary work between them at the same time.[29] Casting Ishmael as an audience figure, the novel makes an interrelation transparent which is usually not at all transparent in a work of fiction. Narrators are supposed to narrate, writers to write, readers to read, and critics, perhaps, to serve as mediators between them. In *Moby-Dick,* however, we find an intriguing dialectical relationship between narrator, writer, reader, and critic which, in a sense, dissolves the fixed structure of their predefined objectives and responsibilities. Yet, structural relationships are not dissolved into nothing in this novel but rather transformed into a scheme which makes the relation of narrator, writer, reader, and critic visible in its potential complexities, and finally brings the elements of this relation to reflect upon themselves and the functions of each other. If *Moby-Dick* thus becomes a richer and more complex work of fiction, it does so at a price. It is the price of frequently confusing its audience by confronting it with images of itself in the figure of a narrator and writer who is also a reader and a critic.

Notes

1. Studies on the reader in Melville's fiction are usually addressed to the problem of actual readers and/or the function of implied readers in the context of his work. Compare, for instance, William Charvat, "Melville and the Common Reader," in *The Professions of Authorship in America, 1800-1870,* ed. Matthew J. Bruccoli (Columbus: Ohio State Univ. Press, 1968), pp. 262-82; Morton L. Ross, "*Moby-Dick* as an Education," *Studies in the Novel,* 6 (1974), 62-75; David L. Coss, "The Reader in 'Bartleby the Scrivener'," *Publications of the Missouri Philological Association,* 5 (1980), 39-43; Steven Mailloux, *Interpretive Conventions: The Reader in the Study of American Fiction* (Ithaca, NY: Cornell Univ. Press, 1982), pp. 170-78.

2. For a cross-section of the prevailing orientations of reader-response criticism, see Jane P. Tompkins, ed., *Reader-Response Criticism: From Formalism to Post-Structuralism* (Baltimore, MD: Johns Hopkins Univ. Press, 1980); Susan R. Suleiman and Inge Crosman, eds., *The Reader in the Text: Essays on Audience and Interpretation* (Princeton: Princeton Univ. Press, 1980); Harry R.

Garvin, ed., *Theories of Reading, Looking, and Listening* (Lewisburg, PA: Bucknell Univ. Press, 1981). A systematization and a taxonomy of the different concepts of reader figures is attempted by W. Daniel Wilson, "Readers in Texts," *PMLA,* 96 (1981), 848-63.

3. A comprehensive investigation of the role and function of this type of reader figure and its relation to other reader figures is offered in: Paul Goetsch, "Leserfiguren in der Erzählkunst," *Germanisch-Romanische Monatsschrift,* 33 (1983), 199-215. Personified audience figures of the type here described can also be defined in relation to a variety of other theoretical concepts of reader figures. For instance, in some respects the personified audience figure can be seen as a specific variation of Wilson's "characterized fictive reader" ("Readers in Texts," p. 855). Like the characterized fictive reader of Wilson's taxonomy the personified audience figure is described and dealt with explicitly *as* a reader of texts. However, it is also different from Wilson's concept in at least two respects: first, the personified audience figure must be a protagonist on the level of other protagonists of a given text; second, his reader responses are described in relation to a text or texts other than the one he appears in as a fictional character.

4. Audience figures of the type here investigated are prevalent in Melville's fiction. However, Melville criticism does not deal with them extensively. As exceptions to the rule, compare Edgar A. Dryden, "The Entangled Text: Melville's *Pierre* and the Problem of Reading," *Boundary* 2, 7, No. 3 (1979), 145-73; and Wai-Chee Sung Dimock, "Herman Melville: Authorship and Audience" (Diss., Yale University, 1982). Dryden deals with the central character of *Pierre* in his dialectical unity of writer and reader. He also observes in his introductory remarks that the Ishmael of *Moby-Dick* essentially functions as a reader of texts. However, Dryden's methodological orientation is different from the one proposed here; furthermore, he does not follow up on his observations concerning Ishmael as an audience figure. Dimock emphasizes in her chapter "*Moby-Dick:* Author and Audience Reconsidered" that Melville's attitude towards audiences changed in this novel. She observes that, at the beginning of the book, the narrator himself is pictured as audience. However, after some general remarks on Ishmael (pp. 118 ff.) Dimock leaves the subject without analyzing the implications of her initial observation. For a more general discussion of Ishmael as an "observer" and as a figure who responds to things, see Harrison Hayford, "'Loomings': Yarns and Figures in the Fabric," in *Artful Thunder: Versions of the Romantic Tradition in American Literature,* eds. Robert J. DeMott and Sanford E. Marowitz (Kent, OH: Kent State Univ. Press, 1975), pp. 119-37.

5. Herman Melville, *Moby-Dick,* eds. Harrison Hayford and Hershel Parker (New York: W. W. Norton, 1967), pp. 20-21. All subsequent quotations from the novel refer to the Norton Critical Edition. Page references are given in parentheses.

6. Describing a work of art in the medium of literature is, of course, a time-honored device of poetry and fiction. However, such descriptions of paintings, pictures, sculptures etc. in a literary text were traditionally object-oriented in that they tended to expose works of art rather than reactions of viewers vis-a-vis such works. For the relationship between poetry and art as reflected in literature, see Jean H. Hagstrum, *The Sister Arts: Tradition of Literary Pictorialism and English Poetry from Dryden to Gray* (Chicago: Univ. of Chicago Press, 1958);Eugene L. Huddleston and Douglas A. Noverr, *The Relationship of Painting and Literature: A Guide to Information Sources* (Detroit: Gale, 1978). For a discussion of the theoretical implications regarding common and comparable elements of looking and reading, see: Erdmann Waniek, "Looking and Reading: In Search of a *Tertium Comparationis,*" in *Theories of Reading, Looking, and Listening,* ed. Harry R. Garvin (Lewisburg, PA: Bucknell Univ. Press, 1981), pp. 131-38.

7. The time scheme of the chapter excludes the possibility that Ishmael's alleged lengthy conversations upon the subject with "many aged persons" can have taken place then and there.

8. For a linguistic analysis of the uses of the second personal pronoun and its literary function in *Moby-Dick,* see Merrel D. Clubb, Jr., "The Second Personal Pronoun in *Moby-Dick,*" *American Speech,* 35 (1960), 252-60.

9. Among the few critics mentioning this point are: Howard P. Vincent, "Ishmael, Writer and Art Critic," in *Themes and Directions in American Literature: Essays in Honor of Leon Howard,* eds. Ray B. Browne and Donald Pizer (Lafayette, IN: Purdue Univ. Studies, 1969), pp. 69-79; Thomas C. Carlson, "Ishmael as Art Critic: A Double Metrical Irony in *Moby-Dick,*" *Interpretations,* 11 (1979), 52-55; Edward H. Rosenberry, *Melville and the Comic Spirit* (New York: Octagon-Farrar, Straus and Giroux, 1979), p. 135; A. Robert Lee, "*Moby-Dick*: The Tale and the Telling," in *New Perspectives on Melville,* ed. Faith Pullin (Edinburgh: Edinburgh Univ. Press, 1978), pp. 99-100. Rosenberry, Carlson, and Lee offer passing

remarks in different contexts. Vincent gives a comprehensive reading of the passage. For a similar interpretation of the measuring episode in "A Bower in the Arsacides" as "an analogue to a good reader's attempt to read *Moby-Dick,*" compare Harrison Hayford in *Dimensions of* Moby-Dick, (New York: Library of America, n.d.), pp. 7-15.

10. Thomas C. Carlson deals with this point in his already quoted article, "Ishmael as Art Critic: A Double Metrical Irony in *Moby-Dick.*" However, Carlson is mainly interested in the ironic implications relating to Ishmael's use of a certain ballad meter when rendering the angel's words.

11. For a discussion of the range, the accuracy, and the evaluation of these pictures, see Sumner W. D. Scott, "The Whale in *Moby-Dick.*" (Diss., University of Chicago, 1950), pp. 28-88.

12. For Melville's somewhat complicated attitude towards the visual arts, see Morris Star, "Melville's Use of the Visual Arts" (Diss., Northwestern University, 1964). Cf. also the earlier contribution by Merton M. Sealts, Jr., in *Melville as Lecturer* (Cambridge, MA: Harvard Univ. Press, 1957). Sealt's discussion, however, is restricted to Melville's lecture on "Statues in Rome."

13. As Sumner W. D. Scott has convincingly argued, this assumption is predominantly valid for the first two of the three chapters here discussed, whereas the third chapter proposes different criteria of judgment. Cf. Scott, "The Whale in *Moby-Dick,*" pp. 29 ff.

14. Ishmael seems to be generally skeptical about the possibilities of the graphic arts representing a subject such as the whale in any adequate way. Compare, for instance, his statement: "the great Leviathan is that one creature in the world which must remain unpainted to the last. True, one portrait may hit the mark much nearer than another, but none can hit it with any very considerable degree of exactness" (p. 228). Perhaps his criticism of the graphic arts is meant to clear the ground for an attempt of literature as a verbal art to do the job other arts are incapable of doing.

15. Compare, for instance, Wilbur S. Scott, Jr., "Melville's Originality: A Study of Some of the Sources of *Moby-Dick*" (Diss., Princeton University, 1943). See also: Charles Roberts Anderson, *Melville in the South Seas* (New York: Columbia Univ. Press, 1939); Sumner W. D. Scott, "The Whale in *Moby-Dick*" (Diss., University of Chicago, 1950); Howard P. Vincent, *The Trying-Out of* Moby-Dick (1949; rpt. Kent, OH: Kent State Univ. Press, 1980), pp. 126 ff.

16. Repeatedly it is suggested that Ishmael must have spent a considerable time researching his subject before he sat down to write his book as a mature person. Compare, for instance, his remark: "Nor have I been at all sparing of historical whale research, when it has seemed needed" (p. 371), and his subsequent emphasis on his work as an amateur scholar: "During my researches in the Leviathanic histories, I stumbled upon an ancient Dutch volume" (p. 371).

17. This statement should not be confused with a statement of Melville's own poetics of the novel. For various reasons one should resist the temptation to associate Ishmael's attitude as a truth-seeker with Melville's famous poetological dictum in "Hawthorne and His Mosses" that literature equals "the Great Art of Telling the Truth." First, we should remember that the attitude in question is attributed to Ishmael, the narrator, and not to Melville, the author. For a sketch of the ongoing discussion whether the whole novel and its view has to be related exclusively to Ishmael's perspective, see Harrison Hayford, "'Loomings': Yarns and Figures in the Fabric," pp. 120-21. Second, Ishmael's demand for truth concerns, in the given context, writings of a documentary and expository nature rather than works of fictional literature. Finally, Melville's poetological concept of literature as the "Art of Telling the Truth" is primarily valid for the earlier stages of his development as a writer, and even there goes beyond a simple equation of truth with empirical truth. For extensive investigations of Melville's changing and debatable concepts of narrative literature and the art of the novel in relation to truth, see among others: Edgar A. Dryden, *Melville's Thematics of Form: The Great Art of Telling the Truth* (Baltimore, MD: The Johns Hopkins Univ. Press, 1968); Allen Hayman, "Herman Melville's Theory of Prose Fiction: In Contrast with Contemporary Theories" (Diss., University of Illinois, 1961); Nina Baym, "Melville's Quarrel with Fiction," *PMLA,* 94 (1979), 909-23; Thomas Edward Lucas, "Herman Melville as Literary Theorist" (Diss., University of Denver, 1963).

18. The ironization of Sleet occurs in the chapter "The Mast-Head." Satirical shots at Scoresby—to whom Melville owes a considerable amount of information on whaling and whom he usually pays a grudging respect—occur throughout but in particular in the chapters "Cetology" and "The Decanter." Cf. also Howard P. Vincent, *The Trying-Out of* Moby-Dick, pp. 132 ff., 142.

19. Intertextuality is, of course, a comprehensive and debatable concept that reaches further than can be discussed here. For the implications of the concept compare in particular: Julia Kristeva, *Semiotikè: Recherches pour une sémanalyse* (Paris:

Seuil, 1969); Kristeva, *La révolution du language poétique* (Paris: Seuil, 1974); Roland Barthes, *S/Z* (Paris: Seuil, 1970); and, as an elucidating short treatment, Jonathan Culler's chapter "Presupposition and Intertextuality," in *The Pursuit of Signs: Semiotics, Literature, Deconstruction* (London: Routledge & Kegan Paul, 1981), pp. 100-18.

20. In the given context, Ishmael's implicit writer model should not be associated with Wayne C. Booth's concept of the "implied author." It has been argued that in *Moby-Dick* the implied author of the novel "has taken shape in the fictional character Ishmael" (see Brian Way, *Herman Melville*: Moby-Dick [London: Edward Arnold, 1978], p. 56). However, though this may be true for extensive parts of the novel, the passages under scrutiny do not bear out this observation. It is rather that in these passages Ishmael as the fictive narrator of the novel displays attitudes and pursues implications which are not to be equated with the attitudes of either the implied or the actual author of the book.

21. Frequently enough, Ishmael himself seems to be skeptical about the success of his ventures as a writer and scholar. Compare, for instance, his closing remark of "Cetology": "God keep me from ever completing anything. The whole book is but a draught—nay, but the draught of a draught. Oh, Time, Strength, Cash, and Patience!" (p. 128).

22. Melville criticism has pursued the problem of who these two figures are and how they are to be understood through a welter of alternatives. Edward Stone, for instance, suggests the obscure figure of Eugene Aram in Thomas Hood's poem "The Dream of Eugene Aram" as a model for the late consumptive usher (cf. Stone "Melville's Late Pale Usher," *English Language Notes,* 9 [1971], 51-53). Other critics see Melville himself assuming the role of the two odd figures. Then again, some critics emphasize the similarities between the Sub-Sub's approach towards his materials and Ishmael's near encyclopedic treatment of the materials on whales and whaling. For a discussion of facts and functions in relation to the two figures, see A. Robert Lee, *"Moby-Dick*: The Tale and the Telling," pp. 105-10; Luther S. Mansfield and Howard P. Vincent, "Explanatory Notes," in *Moby-Dick or, The Whale,* eds. Luther S. Mansfield and Howard P. Vincent (New York: Hendricks House, 1952), pp. 578 ff.

23. Among the many critical contributions dealing with "The Town-Ho's Story," this point is perhaps most convincingly worked out in Heinz Kosok, "Ishmael's Audience in 'The *Town Ho*'s Story,'" *Notes and Queries,* 14 (1967), 54-56.

24. Compare Inge Leimberg, "*Moby-Dick*. Der weiße Wal historisch betrachtet," *Literatur in Wissenschaft und Unterricht,* 5 (1972), 7-21.

25. One might also point to the famous "Doubloon"-chapter where the reactions and readings of the principal actors of the novel vis-a-vis such a seemingly unambiguous "text" as the Ecuadorian gold coin underscore, perhaps most graphically, the point of inherent multi-perspectivism and subjective relativism in all matters of reading and interpretation. Needless to say, the "Doubloon"-chapter as an example of audience response also functions as an implicit comment of the novel upon its own anticipated reception by a crowd of significance-hunting critics to come. The connection made here between the doubloon and the novel itself is also strikingly presented in the title of Hershel Parker's and Harrison Hayford's anthology of reviews, essays, and extracts from critical works on the book: *Moby-Dick as Doubloon* (New York: W. W. Norton, 1970).

26. Jane P. Tompkins, "An Introduction to Reader-Response Criticism," in *Reader-Response Criticism* (Baltimore: The Johns Hopkins Univ. Press, 1980), p. xxii.

27. Stanley E. Fish, "Interpreting the *Variorum*," in *Reader-Response Criticism,* p. 180. Fish's contribution first appeared in *Critical Inquiry,* 2 (1976), 465-85.

28. Fish, "Interpreting the *Variorum*," p. 183.

29. Recently critics have begun to emphasize the self-referential, the meta-fictional, and the meta-narrative aspects of the novel in various contexts, elaborating on the somewhat homelier observation of earlier criticism that *Moby-Dick* is, among many other things, a brilliant novel on reading and writing. For some of the more recent examples cf. A. Robert Lee, *"Moby-Dick*: The Tale and the Telling," pp. 91, 103, 115 ff., 120-21; Charles Caramello, *Silverless Mirrors: Book, Self & Postmodern American Fiction* (Tallahassee: Univ. Press of Florida, 1983), pp. 64-71; and Steven Csaba Scheer, "Fiction as the Theme of Fiction: Aspects of Self-Reference in Hawthorne, Melville, and Twain" (Diss., The Johns Hopkins University, 1974). Critics should be aware that overemphasizing such aspects in Melville's fiction entails the danger of unjustifiably turning him into a proponent of postmodernism. Cf. Caramello who balances the statement that *Moby-Dick* is "the great American precursor of postmodern American fiction" with the observation: "But, then, contemporary American criticism has also invented *Moby-Dick* as such a precursor" (p. 54). For a discussion of other postmodern aspects in Melville, see also

Régis Durand, *Melville: signes et métaphores* (Lausanne: l'Age d'Homme, 1980), and, from a deconstructionist perspective, Rodolphe Gasché, "The Scene of Writing: A Deferred Outset," *Glyph: The Johns Hopkins Textual Studies,* 1 (1977), pp. 150-71.

Samuel Kimball (essay date December 1987)

SOURCE: Kimball, Samuel. "Uncanny Narration in *Moby-Dick." American Literature: A Journal of Literary History, Criticism, and Bibliography* 59, no. 4 (December 1987): 528-47.

[*In the following essay, Kimball analyzes Ishmael's sense of his own identity within the framework of Freud's theories of the uncanny.*]

The word "strange" appears in nearly every chapter of *Moby-Dick.* Why? To what effects? Is the repetition of "strange" itself strange?

Three arguments developed from Freud's essay, "The Uncanny," will orient the following discussion. (1) The structure of the uncanny is the structure of repression. Phenomenologically, the uncanny is experienced as a certain frightful feeling: it "belongs to all that is terrible," Freud says, "to all that arouses dread and . . . creeping horror."[1] This uncanny emotionality, however, functions within an economy of knowledge. On the one hand, "the 'uncanny' is that class of the terrifying which leads back to something long known to us, once very familiar" but now forgotten. On the other hand, "everything is uncanny that ought to have remained hidden and secret, and yet comes to light."[2] The uncanny signals a return of something repressed. This is Freud's interest: not the affective topography of the uncanny but its signifying character, the something that *was known* and *will be known* again.

(2) Freud identifies this "something" as "the dread of castration" and, in his analysis of Hoffman's "The Sand Man," locates it in the child's castration complex. However, if one were to understand the cutting off of a part of the body in castration as a particular instance of a larger category of severings, and if one were to understand certain of the infant's early experiences of separations from the mother as experiences of being cut off, then one would be able to conceptualize the uncanny in preoedipal as well as oedipal terms.

(3) In either case, the consequent psychic wounding is familial and of the home. Thus, it is overdetermined—and "uncanny"?—that Freud should designate the uncanny by the German *unheimlich,* the "unhomely," and that he should determine the unheimlich as "in some way or other a sub-species of *heimlich*."[3] The question of the uncanny, then, is the question of the home, of the unhomeness of the home.

Throughout *Moby-Dick,* Ishmael tries to economize the strange home, that is, to domesticate the strange so as to make a narrative home of homelessness.

I

Ishmael introduces the theme of the uncanny early in the novel when he recalls his boyhood counterpane dream. "My sensations were strange," Ishmael says. "Let me try to explain them" (p. 32).[4] Thereupon he tells how his stepmother, "who, somehow or other, was all the time whipping me, or sending me to bed supperless," had caught him "trying to crawl up the chimney" (p. 32). She punishes him by sending him to bed in mid-afternoon. Eventually he falls into "a troubled nightmare of a doze." When he awakens, "half steeped in dreams,"

> the before sunlit room was now wrapped in outer darkness. Instantly I felt a shock running through all my frame; nothing was to be seen, and nothing was to be heard; but a supernatural hand seemed placed in mine. My arm hung over the counterpane, and the nameless, unimaginable, silent form or phantom, to which the hand belonged, seemed closely seated by my bed-side. For what seemed ages piled on ages, I lay there frozen with the most awful fears, not daring to drag away my hand; yet ever thinking that if I could but stir it one single inch, the horrid spell would be broken. I knew not how this consciousness at last glided away from me. . . .
>
> (p. 33)

From his sense of fright (the nightmare sleep, the shock, the fears, the immobility) to his sense of the supernatural (the hand, the "nameless form or phantom," the spell), Ishmael recalls his confounding experience in terms of the uncanny. Of the terrifying sequence Ishmael remarks that "whether it was reality or dream, I could never entirely settle" (p. 32). This ambiguity itself doubles the ambiguity of the hand which is at once both at hand, literally, and yet, because he cannot recognize it, out of imaginative reach. The hand is too familiar, too intimate; and yet it belongs to a "phantom." Ishmael strains to give name and form to the specter, but it remains for him nameless, silent, and unimaginable.

What is this uncanny hand and Ishmael's dread of it? Perhaps it is the ambivalent hand of a stepmother who, having raised a hand against her stepson, now seeks to hold hands with him? Perhaps the uncanny hand is a canny one after all.

Perhaps, too, it is a masturbatory hand. Leslie Fiedler all but declares Ishmael's attempt "to crawl up his mother's chimney" a metaphorical enactment of oedipal desire.[5] Thus, the counterpane episode might work by reaction-formation to transform a masturbatory act or wish with respect to the stepmother—he is frozen (stiff?)—into a punishing sense of shock, vulnerability, and dread. Later, of course, Ishmael will be able to stir his hand—and no longer with petrifying horror but with dreamy, masturbatory delight as he squeezes whale sperm and expostulates: "Come; let us squeeze hands all around; nay, let us squeeze ourselves into each other" (p. 349). He seems to have returned from the uncanny, from the unhomely, to a realm of "attainable felicity" which he will seemingly cannily locate "in the wife, the heart, the bed, the table, the saddle, the fire-side, the country" (p. 349)—in the home.

Except that the home, the heimlich, is precisely the site of the unheimlich, so that to return home may not be to return from the uncanny but to return to it and yet another encounter with terror and dread.

Immediately after recalling the counterpane experience, Ishmael returns to his present feelings of strangeness upon awakening to the counterpaned arm of Queequeg: "Now, take away the awful fear, and my sensations at feeling the supernatural hand in mine were very similar, *in their strangeness,* to those which I experienced on waking up and seeing Queequeg's pagan arm thrown round me" (p. 33). But take away that awful fear and what is the strangeness? Isn't it a familiarity, an intimacy without threat? And yet isn't such intimacy strange in so far as the powerful hand and arm of this cannibal harpooner do not punish but are recognized by Ishmael to hold him "in the most loving and affectionate manner" (p. 32)? For the little boy who was all the time being whipped (p. 32), the supernatural hand might very well terrify, and terrify all the more in withholding its punishment, for the deferral of that punishment might itself be punishing by prolonging the time of threat and the child's anticipation of being hurt. Such a bind holds the child in a circuit of punishment effects even in the absence of punishment and is itself evocative of the feeling of the uncanny. Indeed, the very doubleness of the bind, of the double bind, reconstitutes one of the archaic features of the uncanny. Whereas the double usually appears as a separate figure, in the circuit of punishment-punishment withheld the double appears within the same person. Here, the non-punishing figure *prefigures* itself as a punishing one. This is Ishmael's dilemma with respect to Queequeg's embrace "as though naught but death should part us twain" (p. 33), for the embrace holds within itself just that possibility of death that would part the two. His embrace is, therefore, both a figure of love and life and also an uncanny prefigure of death. Such is the doubleness of the unheimlich that Ishmael approaches and avoids the uncanny by means of the uncanny itself, or at least by one of its affective effects.

Ishmael protects himself from the strange by rhetorically identifying with it, by reducing it to a familiar category. Such a strategy of address defers what would otherwise evoke fear and trembling by deferring to it. Any number of examples could be adduced of how Ishmael marks as strange just those moments of "attainable felicity," of intimacy, of homeness. When he and Queequeg become "bosom buddies," he relates that "I began to be sensible of *strange* feelings. I felt a melting in me. No more my splintered heart and maddened hand were turned against the wolfish world. This soothing savage had redeemed it" (p. 53). No doubt Ishmael here undercuts certain hypocritical pieties. In addition, he writes himself into the strange as into a fraternal communion. The terrifying nature of homelessness melts away; the strange becomes something which he can turn toward and merge with rather than something which petrifies and cuts through him. To put the matter differently, in so far as "the wolfish world" threatens to terrify or otherwise unman Ishmael, or to splinter his heart and madden his hand again, Ishmael appropriates the terror by signing it, by affixing it to himself—here, to his feelings—as a sign of his wonder that he could feel something other than fright or its splintering, maddening derivatives. Of course, he can only do so by acknowledging the wolfish world as an ever imminent possibility of what he would domesticate. Here, Ishmael displaces the relation between the uncanny and the canny in Freud's scheme. For Freud, the uncanny is a subset of the canny; here, the canny is the subset.

To take another example, "stricken, blasted, if he be, Ahab has his humanities," Peleg says, in summing up his description of that "moody—desperate moody, and savage sometimes" captain (p. 77). Peleg's words fill Ishmael "with a certain wild vagueness of painfulness concerning him. And somehow, at the time, I felt a sympathy and a sorrow for him, but for I don't know what, unless it was the cruel loss of his leg. And yet I also felt a *strange* awe of him; but that sort of awe, which I cannot at all describe, was not exactly awe; I do not know what it was" (p. 77). Again, Ishmael domesticates the strange in the very act of invoking the strange and its emotional context of desperation, savagery, strickenness, and pain. If such a rhetorical maneuver keeps at a distance the prospect of being blasted, it also keeps that prospect alive. It imaginatively vivifies the potential of the threat. Thus, again, Ishmael displaces the priority Freud assigns to the canny in his equivocation about the strange which is familiar only because the familiar is strange.

Yet another time Ishmael assimilates the strange and potentially uncanny to the familiar and safe. The occasion is Queequeg's death-bed fever and progressive emaciation. Ishmael understands full well why Queequeg takes sick—he is overworked in the best of the voyage's circumstances and must, among his worst labors, "finally descend into the gloom of the hold, and bitterly sweating all day in that subterraneous confinement, resolutely manhandle the clumsiest casks and see to their stowage" (p. 395). Nevertheless Ishmael remarks about Queequeg that, "*strange to say,* for all the heat of his sweatings, he caught a terrible chill which lapsed into a fever" (p. 395). "Strange to say"—Ishmael's formulaic invocation of the strange mystifies Queequeg's illness and suffering, cuts it off from its all too familiar material causes. Ishmael goes on to write of Queequeg's tabescent body, but what he sees of his wasting friend quickly becomes a sign of comfort: "How he wasted and wasted away . . . till there seemed but little left of him but his frame and tattooing. But as all else in him thinned, and his cheekbones grew sharper, his eyes, nevertheless, seemed growing fuller and fuller; they became of a *strange* softness of lustre; and mildly but deeply looked out at you there from his sickness, a wondrous testimony to that immortal health in him which could not die, or be weakened" (p. 395). Queequeg does recover, but he is not immortal; he is annihilated at the novel's end. Ishmael, then, evades any possible or actual horror at the sight of his dying friend by idealizing him, by attributing to the signs of his wasting an exactly contrary meaning, and a "strange" meaning for that very reason. The series of negative conjunctions—"but" repeats four times—sets up and frames the reversal by which Ishmael's use of the word "strange" can denote not a horror but a sceptical fullness and wonder, a softness, a luster, a mildness and profoundness. Ishmael envisions not death but death defeated, not an inexorable cutting off of life but the promise of a godly being now finally about to return home to, now at home in, his immortality.

The rest of Ishmael's paean to Queequeg continues in this strain and enables Ishmael to associate the strange with what he imagines to be Queequeg's apotheosizing ascension "higher and higher toward his destined heaven" (p. 396)—his home of homes. Ishmael idealizes the strange—he renders the strange familiar, safe, secure, comforting, and testamentary—and thus he severs the strange from itself. He forestalls the uncanny by trying to be at home with it.

The most uncanny example of this narrative strategy occurs in a sequence of self-inverting reflections on the "gallied" armada. After pursuing the magnificent school of whales for several hours, the chase boats are ready to give up "when a general pausing commotion among the whales gave animating token that they were now at last under the influence of that *strange* perplexity of inert irresolution" (p. 322). They are "gallied." And in that "strange" condition they unaccountably "seemed going mad with consternation" (p. 322). The panic of the herd of whales "was still *more strangely* evinced by those of

their number, who, completely paralysed as it were, helplessly floated" (p. 322). Having alluded to a sense of distress among the whales, Ishmael immediately familiarizes this scene and yet underscores its violence by comparing the whales to those alike gallied humans who, "when herded together in the sheep-fold of a theatre's pit . . . will, at the slightest alarm of fire, rush helter-skelter for the outlets, crowding, trampling, jamming, and remorselessly dashing each other to death" (p. 322). Ishmael then concludes: "Best, therefore, withhold any amazement at the *strangely* gallied whales before us, for there is no folly of the beasts of the earth which is not *infinitely* outdone by the madness of men." For Ishmael, the trebly remarked strangeness of the whales apparently disappears in relation to the infinite madness of men; and yet the strangeness of the whales remains visible, finite, bounded, limited, finally not strange compared to the unlimited strangeness of humans in their mad self-estrangement. The strangeness of the whales constitutes a specular image, for Ishmael, of human strangeness.

The image of the "strangely gallied" beasts, of their "strange perplexity," will shortly give way to an astonishing image of birth, maternal succor, and enchantment—a vision, for want of another word, of at-homeness. This strange sight comforts and solaces. At the center of the herd the "young, unsophisticated, and every way innocent and inexperienced" whales "evinced a wondrous fearlessness and confidence, or else a still, becharmed panic which it was impossible not to marvel at" (p. 325). Ishmael continues: "But far beneath this wondrous world upon the surface, another and *still stranger* world met our eyes as we gazed over the side. For, suspended in those watery vaults, floated the forms of the nursing mothers of the whales, and those that by their enormous girth seemed shortly to become mothers" (p. 325). What begins as the life-threatening strangeness, the commotions of the whales, becomes the contrary, life-affirming strangeness of "the innermost heart of the shoal" (p. 324) where fright has given way to an "enchanted calm" and where, "surrounded by circle upon circle of consternations and affrights," the whales "revelled in dalliance and delight" (p. 326). Ishmael, too, imaginatively revels in the "enchanted pond": "amid the tornadoed Atlantic of my being, do I still for ever centrally disport in mute calm . . . deep down and deep inland there I still bathe me in eternal mildness of joy" (p. 326). According to Fiedler, "Ishmael interprets his glimpse into the world of natural immortality, where life is endlessly renewed by physical generation, as a guarantee that there is a renewal of the spirit, too, in human 'dalliance and delight,' which is all the immortality man can ever achieve."[6] For Fiedler, "the heart of living mysteries" discloses "birth and copulation but *no* death."[7]

Not so, not so. In the midst of this living mystery there is not only death but the specter of terrible, uncanny death: a murderous violence riddles the scene of "natural immortality."

Just before he envisions "all peaceful concernments" (p. 326), and just after he evokes the "stranger world" of the "nursing mothers of the whale" and their cubs and the "maternal reticule" of the still pregnant dams "where, tail to head, and all ready for the final spring, the unborn whale lies bent like a Tartar's bow" (p. 325)—just after this evocation of birth, Ishmael returns to the business at hand, the killing of whales. The harpooned whale (victim of a different "Tartar's bow") that has pulled Ishmael's boat into "the innermost heart of the shoal," has back-tracked, and the now slack whale line has become entangled with the umbilical cord of a newly born cub. However, Ishmael does not note the impending infanticide. "Starbuck saw long coils of the umbilical cord of Madame Leviathan, by which the young cub seemed still tethered to its dam. Not seldom in the rapid vicissitudes of the chase, this natural line, with the maternal end loose, becomes entangled with the hempen one, so that the cub is thereby trapped. Some of the subtlest secrets of the seas seemed divulged to us in this enchanted pond. We saw young Leviathan amours in the deep" (pp. 325-26). "Birth and copulation but *no* death," Fiedler says? Of a whaler's meditation on a strange but not uncommon scene in the midst of the slaughter of nursing and still pregnant whales and newborn cubs? How has he passed over the image of the fatally snared cub, surely one of the most emotionally taxing images of the novel, and surely one that interprets Ahab's death? At the innermost heart of the shoal there is not just birth but birth in jeopardy. A parturition has become the impending destruction of a Leviathan mother and child. Fiedler's interpretation represses the matricidal and infanticidal moment just as Ishmael's does when he turns away from the endangered mother and cub to the amorous adult whales. So Fiedler is correct after all: "Birth and copulation and *no* death" in Ishmael's account. But no death only because Ishmael averts his eyes in an astonishing—an uncanny?—evasion. One of "the subtlest secrets" of the novel is divulged, I believe, in the "enchanted pond" of Ishmael's rhetoric—the way Ishmael protects himself, estranges himself, from the uncanny violence, the unheimlich violence, the unhoming or orphaning or killing violence amidst the "still stranger world" of maternal succoring and primal amours.

The pattern repeats. At the end of the just-cited passage, Melville includes a footnote in which he, too, enacts the repression of infanticide and matricide: "When by chance these precious parts [the teats] in a nursing whale are cut by the hunter's lance, the mother's pouring milk and blood rivallingly discolor the sea for rods. The milk is very sweet and rich . . . it might do well

with strawberries. When overflowing with mutual esteem, the whales salute *more hominum*" (p. 326n). Melville can note the mutilation of the mother whale, but he cannot—in any case he does not—bring himself to name the matricidal and infanticidal consequences: the whale may bleed to death and the cub will starve. One might, of course, interpret Melville's footnote as a canny framing of Ishmael's repression. In either case the two passages point to a breach in the rhetoric of maternity: the primal scenes of "Leviathan amours" in Ishmael's passage and of whales saluting "*more hominum*" in Melville's note replace the infanticidal and matricidal scenes of the trapped cub and the mutilated mother unable to nurse her young. The second passage, moreover, appended to the first as its explanatory subtext, elucidates the first by reconstituting its pattern in an uncanny doubling.

The pattern repeats yet again. Ishmael turns from the center of the shoal, from the copulating whales and the vision of dalliance and delight, to the circumference of the shoal where the *Pequod*'s other two boat crews are lancing whales. There, one whale in particular has been maimed: "in the extraordinary agony of the wound, he was now dashing among the revolving circles . . . carrying disarray wherever he went" (p. 326). The spectacle is, for Ishmael, "appalling," one of "peculiar horror":

> by one of the *unimaginable accidents* of the fishery, this whale had become entangled in the harpoon line that he towed; he had also run away with the cutting-spade in him; and while the free end of the rope attached to that weapon, had permanently caught in the coils of the harpoon-line round his tail, the cutting-spade itself had worked loose from his flesh. So that *tormented to madness,* he was now churning through the water, violently flailing with his flexible tail, and tossing the keen spade about him, *wounding and murdering his own comrades.*
>
> (p. 327)

Ishmael again represses the matricidal and infanticidal consequences of the appalling violence: some of the maimed and killed whales are mothers and cubs. Within a short while the violence that Ishmael has from the beginning associated with the boat's (phallic) penetration of the center returns from the circumference to the center. The whales "began to crowd a little, and tumble against each other." Then "the submarine bridal-chambers and nurseries vanished." Soon "the entire host of whales came tumbling upon their inner centre, as if to pile themselves up in one common mountain" (p. 327). Eventually Ishmael's boat "at last swiftly glided into what had just been one of the outer circles, but now crossed by random whales, all violently making for one centre" (p. 327). Just as for Freud the boundary between the "unhomely" and the "homely" collapses in upon itself as he formulates his notion of a certain aesthetic of horror, so too for Ishmael does the boundary between center and circumference disappear as he describes his experience of uncanny beauty and horror. No matter how much he tries to place the "appalling spectacle" and its terrifying violence on the horizon, he is haunted by their return to the center of his narration. And if the center designates a metaphorical home or homeness, it comes to designate an uncanny homelessness as well, and not just a homelessness but a homelessness at the very center of life, a homelessness of the home, with matricidal and especially infanticidal violence its most direful sign.

For Freud, the source of the uncanny is the dread of castration. In commenting upon Hoffman's tale, Freud resolutely traces all acts of violence against parts of the body (the mutilation of eyes, for example) or against the body as a whole to fears of violence against the genitals. Freud alludes to his interpretation of Oedipus to validate this reduction. Nevertheless, Oedipus himself is the intended victim of his father's infanticidal attempts on his life. Freud notes that "in blinding himself, Oedipus . . . was simply carrying out a mitigated form of the punishment of castration—the only punishment that according to the *lex talionis* was fitted for him."[8] To be sure, the slashing of his eyes makes sense as a displacement of a genital slashing, especially insofar as Oedipus has committed a genital crime. But the slashing of eyes also makes sense as a displacement of the father's efforts to kill Oedipus by piercing his ankles and letting him die of exposure. The Greek word *arthron* signifies both socket and the piece that moves within the socket and thus was used to designate both eye and joint. Oedipus was pierced through the ankles or joints (*arthra*) of his feet, and he sticks Jocasta's pins into his eyeballs (*arthra*).[9] In blinding himself, Oedipus may have acted out a version of the violence directed against him by his father. So, too, Nathaniel in "The Sand Man": in flinging himself off the roof he may have acted out his father's infanticidal wish or the similar wish of the Sand Man. Such possibilities provide a way of understanding the *unheimlich*, the homelessness of the home, as a preoedipal experience of infanticidal jeopardy as well as an oedipal one. Allusions to such uncanny jeopardy recur throughout **Moby-Dick.**

Ishmael adopts his narrative name, perhaps as he wishes himself to be adopted, and in any case thereby anticipates how he, as an orphan, will be rescued by his *Rachel*. Ishmael's name, of course, alludes to the Biblical Ishmael, disinherited son of Abraham, a disinheriting evocative of Abraham's willingness to sacrifice—to make an infanticide of—his other son, Isaac. The Biblical Ishmael is fated to be "a wild man: his hand will be against every man, and every man's hand against him" (Genesis 16:12). Melville's Ishmael shares his counterpart's rage: "whenever my hypos get such an upper hand of me, that it requires a strong moral principle to

prevent me from . . . knocking people's hats off—then, I account it high time to get to sea as soon as I can." This, he says, "is my substitute for pistol and ball" (p. 12).

Going to sea is also his substitute for infanticidal jeopardy. A kind of internal compass points Ishmael to the "great original" of the whaling business, Nantucket (p. 17), for he has determined to ship out from this spot of land only. Why? Ishmael explains the "wondrous" "legend" of this island:

> In olden times an eagle swooped down upon the New England coast, and carried off an infant Indian in his talons. With loud lament the parents saw their child borne out of sight over the wide waters. They resolved to follow in the same direction. Setting out in their canoes, after a perilous passage they discovered the island, and there they found an empty ivory casket,—the poor little Indian's skeleton.

> What wonder, then, that these Nantucketers, born on a beach, should take to the sea for a livelihood!

> (p. 62)

The founding event—an infanticide—makes explicit the foundling event—the orphaning threat of infanticide. In relation to this legend, which doubles as a "legend" for his psychic geography, Ishmael signs aboard the *Pequod*. For Ishmael as for the aboriginal Nantucketers, the sea—not the land, above all not the land of infanticide, but the sea—is *home*: "*There* is his home. . . . For years he knows not the land; so that when he comes to it at last, it smells like another world, *more strangely* than the moon would to an Earthsman. With the landless gull, that at sunset folds her wings and is rocked to sleep between billows; so at nightfall, the Nantucketer, out of sight of land, furls his sails, and lays him to rest, while under his very pillow rush herds of walruses and whales" (p. 63; first emphasis in the original). And yet, if the Nantucketer is at home only when at sea, he is never simply at home, never simply at sea, since he always carries the designation of the land, of Nantucket, with him. The designation is inscribed in the categorical name—Nantucketer—Ishmael gives to this person. It is a proper name that is "improper," a canny or *heimlich* name that contains the trace of the *unheimlich*. The strange smell of the land reminds the Nantucketer—or Ishmael—that his birthplace was a place of estrangement, nonidentity, and death. Ishmael, then, will ship out from the island of infanticide aboard a ship named after a "now extinct" tribe of Indians (p. 67). Of course extinct: because the threat of infanticidal extinction, whether individual or tribal, defines and has defined from the dead end of the beginning the course of uncanny wandering, of the homelessness, inscribed in the name "Ishmael."

If infanticide can denote the extremest danger and the uncanniest of human relations, then Queequeg's "Congo idol" (p. 30) comically represents the nature of Queequeg's ironically pagan solution—a form of religious observance that specifies in its iconography the fact of infant jeopardy. Thus, Queequeg worships "a curious little deformed image with a hunch on its back, and exactly the color of a three days' old Congo baby" (p. 30). Ishmael, hidden in Queequeg's bed, is quick to wonder whether "this black manikan was a real baby"—an infanticide—embalmed like the heads Queequeg peddles. Ishmael watches Queequeg honor his "wooden idol" and notes that "all these *strange* antics" of Queequeg "were accompanied by *still stranger* guttural noises from the devotee" (p. 30). When he is done, Queequeg "bags" his idol, his "Congo baby," "as carelessly as if he were a sportsman bagging a dead woodcock" (p. 30). A parodic inversion of the primal father, Queequeg's totem is the image of a child, one that recalls an insistent fear of childhood injury. Thus, Ishmael witnesses Queequeg's rites from the wedding bed of Mr. and Mrs. Coffin. It is in this bed, shared with his young children and his wife, that Peter Coffin "somehow" kicked one of his sons onto the floor, "near breaking his arm" (p. 27). In this bed, Ishmael finally falls blissfully asleep only to awaken in a "strange house" to the memory of the counterpane nightmare, Queequeg's "horse collar" grip, and a "slight scratch" from the pagan's tomahawk which Ishmael calls, in terms evocative of infanticide—or parricide—a "hatchet-faced baby" (p. 33). Congo idol, marriage bed, nightmare, and tomahawk: four times over Ishmael invokes an image of infant or childhood danger. Four times over he experiences a return of anxiety, comically framed, over the strange possibility of primal harm.

This sense of harm pervades Ishmael's sense of the world and recurs throughout the novel in the many allusions to being abandoned or castaway and to child abuse. These allusions insistently reconstitute the danger of a time long past that haunts time present in Ishmael's narrative. They weave the uncanny, the homelessness of the home, in its preoedipal expressions into the very texture of the text.

One sequence of allusions occurs shortly before the *Pequod* meets the *Rachel*. The log line has just broken and the log been lost. Ahab declares he "can mend all" and shortly thereafter addresses Pip, who answers with an uncanny evocation of his own dismembered and castaway condition: "Pip's missing. . . . Ho! there's his arm just breaking water. A hatchet! a hatchet! cut it off—we haul in no cowards here" (p. 427). Pip's language underscores the threat of mutilation contained in Queequeg's Congo idol; and Pip's deference to the threat of dismemberment doubles but reverses Queequeg's rite of worship. Pip's gesture of submission also doubles but reverses Ahab's postures of domination. In any case, Ahab is moved; he reaches out to this orphan and makes explicit the context of infant abandonment as he discovers in Pip a living log and in himself a liv-

ing line: "Oh, ye frozen heavens!" Ahab expostulates: "Ye did beget this luckless child, and have abandoned him. . . . Here, boy; Ahab's cabin shall be Pip's home henceforth, while Ahab lives. Thou touchest my inmost centre, boy; thou art tied to me by cords woven of my heart-strings" (p. 428). Ahab then repudiates "the omniscient gods oblivious of suffering man." He presumes to speak in the name of man who, "though idiotic, and knowing not what he does," is "yet full of sweet things of love and gratitude" (p. 428), as if he himself were the exemplary Comforter, maternal paraclete to castaway humankind. Ahab will reject this self-image and its obligations just as he will refuse the *Rachel*'s search for her homeless ones.

In the meantime, guided by Ahab's instruments of homelessness, his "level log and line," the *Pequod* sails through "strange" "monotonously mild" waters "preluding some riotous and desperate scene" (p. 428). It is a scene of infanticidal haunting, and it repeats the archetypal circumstances of Christ's birth. Thus, as the *Pequod* and crew near the "Equatorial fishing-ground" during the night, "the watch . . . was startled by a cry so plaintively wild and unearthly—like half-articulated wailings of the ghosts of all Herod's murdered Innocents—that one and all, they started from their reveries" (pp. 428-29). Ahab sleeps through the ghastly sounds. In the morning he "hollowly laughs" as he scorns the crews' fears. But even Ahab, in explaining away the cries as merely those of seals, invokes the specter of (matricidal and infanticidal) homelessness. "Some young seals that had lost their dams, or some dams that had lost their cubs, must have risen nigh the ship . . . crying and sobbing with their human sort of wail" (p. 429). Shortly thereafter the crew hears another homeless, haunting cry: "a cry and a rushing—and looking up they saw a falling *phantom* in the air; and looking down, a little tossed heap of white bubbles in the blue of the sea" (p. 429). A sea of death—of the mother, of the infant.

If we are "whelped somewhere by the sharkish sea," as Starbuck says (p. 148); if the sea is "a foe to man who is an alien to it" (p. 235); if the sea is "fiend to its own offspring" and will "insult and murder" "baby man" (p. 235); if "all men live enveloped in whale lines" and "are born with halters around their necks" (p. 241); if we are "born in throes" and if "'tis fit that man should live in pains and die in pangs" (p. 360)—then, in the "step-mother world" (p. 443) of **Moby-Dick,** death must bear the uncanny mark of infanticide in particular and parricide in general.[10]

How, then, to survive the orphaning threat of parricide, where parricide denotes the murder of parent or child? Perhaps by somehow incorporating within life the imminence of such death. Such is the dynamism of the castaway fantasy which would defer the possibility of parricide by deferring to it. Thus, through a certain language of self-splitting, Ahab begets and destroys himself as his own castaway and casting away double, living and yet dead, dead and yet hauntingly alive.

Ishmael attempts to describe Ahab's doubleness in Christian terms. "Ah, God! what trances of torments does that man endure who is consumed with one unachieved revengeful desire. He sleeps with clenched hands; and wakes with his own bloody nails in his palms" (p. 174), a living but self-consuming double (for whom "the very throbbing of his life-spot became insufferable anguish" [p. 174]) of the dead but resurrected Christ. Ahab's satanic mimesis entails an apocalyptic self-division: the "spiritual throes in him heaved his being up from its base, and a chasm seemed opening in him, from which forked flames and lightnings shot up, and accursed fiends beckoned him to leap down among them" (p. 174). At once internal and external to him, the chasm delimits the extremity of Ahab's self-fissuring and self-displacement. The psychic space thus constituted is in general the space of incorporation[11] and in particular the space of nightmarish self-conception and hysterical self-gestation.[12] From "this hell" something will "burst" forth in "horror" (pp. 174, 175)—Ahab himself. His parturition will be monstrous: "one supreme purpose . . . by its own sheer inveteracy of will, forced itself against gods and devils into a kind of self-assumed, independent being of its own. Nay, could grimly live and burn, while the common vitality to which it was conjoined, fled horror-stricken from the unbidden and unfathered birth" (p. 175). He is incubus to his own spectral being: "the tormented spirit that glared out of bodily eyes, when what seemed Ahab rushed from his room, was for the time but a vacated thing; a formless somnambulistic being, a ray of living light, to be sure, but without an object to color, and therefore a blankness in itself" (p. 175). Possessing himself, dispossessing himself, Ahab conceives himself in his own haunted image. "God help thee, old man," Ishmael says, "thy thoughts have created a creature in thee; and he whose intense thinking thus makes him a Prometheus; a vulture feeds upon that heart for ever; that vulture the very creature he creates" (p. 175). Near the end of the novel, the vulture becomes a hawk which pecks at Ahab's brain (p. 495). Here, carrion to his own raptorial self, Ahab is always already dead to himself, a being and the ghost of a being, a "living light" and a "blankness in itself," vulture and carcass: a living parricide. At the end, when the vulture has become the heavenly sky-hawk nailed to the (phallic) mast (p. 469), patricide becomes infanticide as the satanic energies of Ahab manifest themselves in a final apocalyptic violence of uncreation or decreation.

The living parricide, the self-begetting self-murdering revenant—if such a nonperson dies again and again in every vulturous attack, he or she also seeks it out, even

to the extent of becoming the uncanny agent of self-destruction, as Ahab's suicidal throw of the harpoon at Moby Dick indicates. He is not just a wounded man but the wound and wounding themselves, exile of himself, the casting away castaway who experiences self and world as places of radical, uncanny homelessness.[13]

II

If in deriving the uncanny from the canny Freud introduces the possibility of reading the homelessness of the home, then the meaning of "narration" introduces the antithetical possibility. For "narration" and "canny" share the same Indo-European root, *gno-*, meaning to know. Thus narration is in some sense a trope of the canny, a knowing how to tell, a telling knowledge; and to narrate includes the other side of the uncanny, the homeness of homelessness.

Homelessness is not simply a condition of loss and wound, of isolation and fright, of craving, of estrangement, of self-division, of outrage or loathing hatred of abandoned self or casting away other. It is not only a negative ontology, the "un" of what would otherwise be the canny moment of origin, safety, and at-homeness. Homelessness also harbors within itself a condition of possibility, gain, contact, and homeness. The divisions that produce homelessness are at work within the condition of homelessness itself, so that the experience of homelessness can never be absolute, can never be an absolute lostness, for example. One can represent homelessness only partially, if for no other reason than that representation to some extent overcomes whatever one means by homelessness by bringing it into the register of language where homelessness's absence is made present, where the condition of being cast away is not itself cast away but retrieved. This retrieval reconstitutes the foundling event as the event of narration: the moment Ishmael is found, he once again finds his identity as "Ishmael," the homeless one, the narrator. But his finding also brings him out of his homeless condition. At the same moment that his rescue confirms him as yet "another orphan," it also cuts him off—orphans him—from his orphan status.

Ishmael has said as much throughout his narration. To take but one example, insofar as the Nantucketer shoves off from infanticidal shores to find his home at sea, homelessness becomes the condition of his homecoming vocation. Ishmael repeats this pattern of identity: by telling the story of the orphan he is and yet is not, he finds his narrative vocation in the homelessness around which his narrative circles. He establishes a self-relation, an identity, out of or with his homelessness.

The emotional consequences of this strategy coincide with its textual effects. Both converge in Ishmael's self-doubling efforts to *relate:* to tell his story, but also to connect with self and other.

The question of emotionality in *Moby-Dick* has been explored in relation to various psychologies, especially psychoanalytic, but not in relation to the novel's textuality. Psychoanalytic readings generally attempt to fathom Ahab's and Ishmael's affective responses: what is the deepest level of feeling, they ask, and how does such feeling underwrite the language of the characters? According to these perspectives, the novel means in relation to what characters (or author or readers) feel. Such perspectives tend to operate deterministically: meanings code feelings the vicissitudes of which produce the meanings. Ultimately, feelings reveal the existential condition of the self. But what is a self?

In *Moby-Dick* selfhood is defined relationally in terms of homelessness, that is, in terms of jeopardy, of the specter of abandonment or annihilation—of nonrelation. Selfhood, in short, always contains the threat of the loss of self. Selfhood, then, is not a solution to the problem of being—to the problem of self-relation or relation to others—it is the problem of being. The problem—the homelessness of being, of the would-be home of the self and self-relation—underwrites Ishmael's efforts to "relate" in the double meaning of the term. If parricide haunts the home, if it turns the home into a site of homelessness, homelessness in turn evokes the need, want, lack, loss, desire—call it what you choose—that makes relating both possible and urgent. Such is the ontological ground, so to speak, of the watery world of *Moby-Dick*. And such is the textual ground, too, of this novel, for the structural possibility of emotion, canny or uncanny, and the structural possibility of narration are the same.

The term "relation" provides a fortuitous indication of how each of the two grounds—the ontological and the textual—is a double of the other. The root meanings of *-lation* or *-lating*, "re-" or otherwise, include the major motifs Freud implicitly assigns to the unheimlich: "the family side," "the carrying of children," "to bear children," "birth"; and "the hidden," "the furtive," "the carried past," "to suffer," "to retaliate," "to defer." A "relation," a "relating" of one to another, then, bears two moments—the family side, the carrying of the child to term; and the secret, the retaliation, the deferential deferral, and a spectrum of (parricidal) possibilities of non-relation or unrelation. "Relation," thus, like the "heimlich," includes its opposite. It designates the ontological structure of *Moby-Dick:* the canny or uncanny simultaneity of emotional connection and disconnection. The term also designates the textual conditions of the novel: the canny or uncanny simultaneity of a telling that arises from the threat of Ishmael's death. Here, the *problem* of feeling or relating, which is also the *possibility* of feeling, repeats the problematic possibility of telling; *mutatis mutandis,* the problematic possibility of telling repeats the emotional problem of a homelessness or nonrelation which is also the possibility of relation.[14]

At the end, the coffin-life-buoy arises from the "cunning spring" (= the "canny spring"—"cunning" and "canny" are cognates) of "the closing vortex" set in motion by the sinking *Pequod* (p. 470). This strange machine bears Ishmael to term, it carries him to his terms, gives birth to him as a narrative function. Only at the end of the novel does he become the voice at the beginning—and thus the voice of the beginning ending—of the novel. This two-fold moment determines the "I" of *Moby-Dick,* for at the double terminal, Ishmael adopts the identity of the orphaned and wandering son who is never adopted: "Call me Ishmael," says the voice of "another orphan." Thus, in *Moby-Dick* the identity event, the narration event, the moment "Ishmael" relates himself, is also the uncanny event, the foundling event, the event of homelessness.

Notes

1. Sigmund Freud, "The Uncanny," trans. Alix Strachey. In *Studies in Parapsychology,* ed. Philip Reiff (New York: Collier, 1963), p. 19.

2. Freud, "The Uncanny," pp. 20 and 28.

3. Freud, "The Uncanny," p. 30.

4. Subsequent references to *Moby-Dick,* ed. Harrison Hayford and Hershel Parker (New York: Norton, 1967) will appear in parentheses in the text. Unless otherwise noted, all emphases are mine.

5. Leslie A. Fiedler, *Love and Death in the American Novel,* rev. ed. (New York: Norton, 1967), p. 375.

6. Fiedler, pp. 383-84.

7. Fiedler, pp. 384 and 383.

8. Freud, "The Uncanny," p. 36.

9. Seth Bernardete has noted the implications of this etymological coincidence in "Sophocles' *Oedipus Tyrannus.*" In *Sophocles: A Collection of Critical Essays,* ed. Thomas Woodward (Englewood Cliffs, N. J.: Prentice-Hall, 1966), pp. 105-22.

10. The relation between infanticide and the uncanny is inscribed in the German, *unheimlich,* as the unhomely; it is also inscribed in the English term "uncanny." According to the O. E. D. [*Oxford English Dictionary*], "canny wife" is a "wise woman" or midwife and the canny moment the moment of childbirth. To which I would add that the canny moment is also the uncanny moment, the moment of childbirth compromised, either by the death of

the child or the death of the mother. "There is a wisdom that is woe," Ishmael says, "but there is a woe that is madness" (p. 355). And there is Ahab who is "madness maddened" (p. 147) in that egregiously compromised and self-compromising figure of the living parricide.

11. For a discussion of this peculiar psychic space, see Nicolas Abraham and Maria Torok, *The Wolf Man's Magic Word: A Cryptonymy,* trans. Nicholas Rand (Minneapolis: Univ. of Minnesota Press, 1986).

12. Freud, in "A Special Type of Object-Choice Made by Men," *Standard Edition,* trans. and ed. James Strachey (London: Hogarth, 1953-74), XI, 164-65, discusses the "rescue phantasy" as a variation on the "wish *to be his own father.*" Freud interprets this wish in terms of his oedipal hypothesis. David Bakan interprets the wish in relation to the fantasy of outliving one's death. See his *Disease, Pain, and Sacrifice: Toward a Psychology of Suffering* (Boston: Beacon, 1968), pp. 95-128.

13. An entire *matrix* of images of mutilation, dismemberment, castration, and more generally of reversal underscores Ahab's uncanny self-transmogrification. These images are too numerous and detailed to analyze here, but I would note that they extend the metaphorical reach of homelessness in this novel.

14. I would like to acknowledge Eric J. Sundquist's work, *Home as Found: Authority and Genealogy in Nineteenth-Century American Literature* (Baltimore: Johns Hopkins Univ. Press, 1979). My question about the meaning of home is, I think, different from his. I would indicate this difference by pointing out that, at least in *Moby-Dick,* the home cannot be found without being lost, and that the genealogical moment is also the moment of orphanhood. I would argue that this doubleness of the home (and the doubleness of the attendant notions of the uncanny, infanticide, authority in general, and so on) is not the result of desire (it is not the consequence of an ambivalence, for example) but is the circumstance of it.

John W. Rathbun (essay date June 1989)

SOURCE: Rathbun, John W. "*Moby-Dick*: Ishmael's Fiction of Ahab's Romantic Insurgency." *Modern Language Studies* 21, no. 3 (summer 1991): 3-9.

[*In the following essay, originally presented at the 1989 Cal State Symposium on American Literature, Rathbun explores layers of fictional narration in* Moby-Dick.]

In Melville's first five novels [*Typee, Omoo, Mardi, Redburn,* and *White-Jacket*] his narrators seem more or less to play dual roles that are different and even contrary to one another. As chroniclers they give us descriptive accounts of events and data designed to add to readers' education and experience, the effect of which is to validate the "truth" of what they are saying. As writers of books, on the other hand, they allow themselves an imaginative leeway which compromises the aims of the plain language of journalistic discourse even as it intensifies the "meaning" of what they are telling us.[1] With *Moby-Dick* Melville carries this strategy about as far as it can go when he develops two separate kinds of fictions, one embedded in the other. The larger of the two is Ishmael's chronicle of the whaling voyage of the Pequod, and in his recounting of what happened we are asked to follow the standard convention of accepting the fictive historicity of his account.[2] The shorter narrative makes no claim to have really "happened," but is instead Ishmael's deliberate authorial intrusion into his chronicle in order to present an interpolated, wholly imagined, self-contained "story" that intersects so inconspicuously with the chronicle that readers are hard put to figure out just when one or the other is in the ascendancy. It is with this shorter narrative that I wish to deal.

Two references in Father Mapple's sermon—Jonah's slouched hat and the self-correcting cabin lamp—provide Ishmael the means to imaginatively control his tale by demarcating the limits within which Ahab is made to act. The hat allows Ishmael to vest in Ahab an authoritative prophetic voice, while the cabin lamp suggests that the fanaticism reflected in that voice must necessarily fail. The "mission" that Ishmael assigns Ahab is to confront the world-as-is in order to transform it into something more closely corresponding to the human hopes and aspirations of Melville's contemporary radical humanists: say, a real-life Feuerbach or a fictional Ivan Karamazov. Ishmael simultaneously sees this mission in two quite different ways. It is dramatically compelling, but it is also a delusive wholly unrealistic act of resistance to a world that itself resists all human attempts to make it over. Because Ahab's quest is momentous, it is only fitting that he should pursue it in prophetic guise, but the imperturbable silence of the world as exemplified in the cabin lamp renders the enterprise ineffectual. Ishmael's tale thus reveals that he is more in tune with the philosophical uncertainties of twentieth-century thought than with the romantic posturing of nineteenth-century metaphysical insurgency. There is a problem, however, with the cabin lamp. Its relevance to the tale is so stubbornly opposed to interpretation that we must ultimately decide that Ishmael is uncertain as to what the lamp might mean, and this in turn erodes his confidence in the ability of imagination to translate sign into symbol. Consequently language dwindles into silence, and Ishmael leaves us unenlightened, as if imagination entices but does not reveal.

In Father Mapple's sermon Jonah is converted from the petulant somewhat comical prophet of the Old Testament who has trouble coping with God's apparently capricious sense of justice into a frenzied, troubled man who mirrors Mapple's own anguished spirit. He skulks about the wharves of Joppa with "slouched hat and guilty eye," so distressed that the sailors and ship's captain know he is a fugitive (839). What they do not know is that the hat is intended to hide him from the eyes of God, an exercise which Jonah himself understands is futile.

On four occasions—in "The Pipe," "The Quarter-Deck," and twice in "The Hat"—Jonah's slouched hat reappears on the head of Ahab, too often, I think, to be coincidence. Ahab's wearing of the hat obviously links him to Jonah in terms of their troubled spirits and isolation from human comfort. But with Ishmael, as with Melville generally, inversions and variations can transform the simplest references. As the crazy ship's captain of Ishmael's chronicle, Ahab cuts no heroic figure. He is gripped by personal hysteria, is singularly possessed by his own phantoms, and is indifferent to the larger imperatives of human beings. This Ahab has the same fictive historicity we conventionally ascribe to Ishmael, Starbuck and other members of the crew. The Jonah-Ahab link illustrates the myth-making propensities of Ishmael by imagining a "larger" Ahab who is put through a series of episodes—for example, the ritualistic drinking from the harpoon sockets and the demonic blessing of the javelings—that are patently fictional. In a little-noted passage which amounts almost to an apostrophe to his skill, Ishmael explicitly reminds us that he has the resources to endow Ahab with a stature bigger than life. "Oh, Ahab! what shall be grand in thee, it must needs be plucked from the skies, and dived for in the deep, and featured in the unbodied air!" (949).[3]

In linking Ahab to Jonah, Ishmael goes beyond the matter of their respective emotional pain to concentrate on the attributes Ahab gains in being associated with an Old Testament prophet in particular and a prophetic tradition in general: social distance, moral fervor, a sense of justice, extraordinary and passionate commitment, a profound belief that the world is out of kilter and must be redeemed.[4] He would also seem to ascribe to Ahab the twin objectives of the biblical voice as Reinhold Niebuhr has described them: that is, to protest the present order of things; and to castigate the indifferent, indolent complacency of others in order to recall them to righteousness. The nature of that protest, however, is scarcely biblical, for Ishmael assigns to Ahab a stubborn prophetic/satanic role which echoes (and questions) the views of nineteenth-century radical intellectuals.

The prophetic tradition inveighed against unrighteousness and spoke for a justice that transcended the earth, but Ishmael's prophetic Ahab sees transcendent justice as emblematic of all that troubles human beings. That justice is not only inimical to the larger interests of human beings, but it has been conceived and administered by a non-human whose position is privileged and whose authority is perverse. Ahab is made to engage in a contest which if successful can result in a new hypostatic humanity. Not only must humans break with God, there is as well the added provocative thought that God himself might subscribe to this effort to rid the earth of Him. If the world and the human beings in it are unconditionally submissive to the compulsory divine will, then "Fate is the handspike" to which all men dance. God, having established the conditions of Fate, may well be working through a human agent such as Ahab in order to effect His own death. In any case, "Who's to doom," Ahab asks rhetorically, "when the judge himself is dragged to the bar?" (1375). Whether through direct defiance or in league with God's own plan for His demise, the purpose is to alter the teleological course of history and bring about the final conclusion: God's death, the defeat of evil, and the installation of man as the world's authority. All this is certainly in line with Feuerbach's position that man defrauds himself in ascribing to a god such virtues as wisdom, will and justice which more properly belong to himself. Even Ahab's very real sense of alienation may have less to do with Jonah's anguish than with Feuerbach's intuitive perception that the Hebraic/Christian tradition has so degraded human beings that they no longer have the "true" vision of the fellowship that follows upon allegiance to our generic humanity and have retreated to the disorder of individualistic self-reliance a la Emerson. "*Homo homini Deus!*" as Feuerbach put it.

However dramatic all this might be, in "The Hat" Ishmael abruptly terminates this story of Ahab-as-prophet and returns him to his real-life role as a mad old sea-captain who leads his crew in a futile three days' fight with a whale. As Ahab is hoisted to the mizzen-masthead a hawk appears and circles, rises a thousand feet into the air, then plummets towards him and with a scream snatches the hat from off Ahab's head. Ishmael breaks into the account to tell us of how an eagle thrice removed and thrice replaced the hat of Tarquin, whereupon in response to the omen he was named king of Rome. Ahab's hat, however, is not replaced. As the bird recedes into the distance "a minute black spot was dimly discerned, falling from that vast height into the sea" (1369).

This clear deflation of Ahab's role suggests that Ishmael's thought may have had a progress of its own: from initial caution to fiery if reluctant support to ultimate disenchantment with Ahab's quest, and partly Ishmael's story supports that view.[5] Yet from the beginning Ishmael makes it clear that he regards belligerencies such as Ahab's foolhardy, forlorn, and ineffectual, however mesmerizing the intent. If Ahab's quest is cancelled short of conclusion, so to speak, then the reader has to ask just why Ishmael chooses this point to remove the prophetic mantle from Ahab's shoulders and to return him to his role as the demented captain of a whaler. After all, the sea-fight with the whale would have become an epic confrontation if the opponents were a rebellious prophet on the one hand and God on the other.[6] The second reference in Father Mapple's sermon would seem to provide the answer.

Like the slouched hat, Ishmael's references to the cabin lamp hold the promise of blossoming into symbol, thereby suggesting dimensions of reality hidden to our otherwise conventional wisdom. At one point in his sermon, Father Mapple draws an elaborate analogy between the verticality of truth and the way that a cabin lamp maintains its upright position despite the heeling of the ship. This "permanent obliquity" with reference to Jonah's room allows the minister to point his moral: "though, in truth, infallibly straight itself, it but made obvious the false, lying levels among which it hung." Jonah comes to the same conclusion. Ostensibly successful in his evasion of the divine mission enjoined by God, he sights the lamp and realizes that he cannot evade his own conscience: "Oh!, so my conscience hangs in me! straight upward, so it burns; but the chambers of my soul are all in crookedness!" (841).

Ishmael appropriates this image of the lamp with its symbolic overtones and uses it several times in the tale he tucks into his chronicle, always in reference to Ahab. The connection that can be drawn between Jonah and Ahab as a result is the anguish, near despair, wretchedness and pain the two men experience in their rebellions against divine ordination. These psychological dislocations, however, while important, are not the sum of the connection to be drawn between Ahab and the cabin lamp.

Equally important is the distinction between what the lamp would seem to represent in the separate cases of the two men. In Jonah's case the lamp clearly calls attention to the complementarity that should exist between conscience and action. Its function in Ahab's case is more ambiguous for never being directly stated. Those passages in which the cabin lamp figures are tonally ominous, while the lamp itself is passive and mute. Never openly threatening, it is nevertheless peculiarly unsettling to those who mark its presence, as if its very inconceivability establishes it as a fixed reminder of a resistant, voiceless infra-structure within the macrocosm, and so emblematic of a cosmic omnipotence past all understanding.

In the chapter titled "The Chart," for example, Ahab is pictured leaning over his maps to trace the route of Moby Dick. Above him the pewter lamp adjusts itself to the surge of the ship. To Ishmael's imagination the lines drawn by Ahab have their complement in the gleams and shadows which trace "lines and courses upon the deeply marked chart of his forehead" (1003). This sense of a menacing almost sinister presence occurs again in the remarkable scene in "The Spirit-Spout." Starbuck observes Ahab asleep in his chair, his hand-held lantern adjusting to the roll of the ship even as his closed eyes point towards the cabin-compass on the ceiling. The lantern adjusts to an intrinsic principle in the order of nature. But Ahab is mindful only of the compass, which, in telling him the course of the ship, serves his steadfast purpose of seeking out and destroying the white whale. The tableau causes Starbuck to unaccountably shudder.

This distinction between the lantern as mutely testifying to a higher if inscrutable purpose and the compass as Ahab's tool for pursuing and killing his adversary is clarified in "The Quadrant." Ishmael compares the "nakedness of unrelieved radiance" of the "unblinkingly vivid Japanese sun" to the "insufferable splendors of God's throne" (1326). Almost immediately he has Ahab do likewise. Contemplating the quadrant with its "numerous cabalistical contrivances," Ahab realizes that it is the means for looking into God's eye. But the eye discloses only Ahab's position in the larger world. It remains silent in predicting the success of Ahab's quest or even whether he is on the right track. Cursing "all the things that cast man's eyes aloft to that heaven, whose live vividness but scorches him," Ahab destroys the quadrant, and resolves to rely on the "earthly way" of computing direction and destination: that is, "the level ship's compass, and the level dead-reckoning" (1327).

This desperately rebellious gesture resolves nothing. Five chapters later Starbuck descends to Ahab's cabin, like Jonah's an isolated subterranean room serving almost as a cell, and pauses in the dim gleam of the cabin lamp. Swinging on its axle in response to the roll of the ship, the lamp casts ominous "fitful shadows" upon Ahab's door (1341). Unlike the reassuring monolith in Kubrick's *2001,* the cabin lamp communicates nothing, reveals nothing. It is just *there,* an unannounced, seemingly baleful presence that unaccountably stirs Ishmael and Starbuck to a sense of dread. To their imaginations the cabin lamp undoubtedly suggests power, but the nature of that power remains concealed.

The two images of hat and lamp underscore the fact that Ishmael uses his imagination to control his fiction of Ahab's mission. But one must ask, what precise insights does his imagination come to? Imagination to the romantic mind, after all, can encode meanings which become operative when objective events and personal responses coincide.[7] Just as Hawthorne's narrators often suggest without confirming relations between signs and what are signified, so Ishmael seems continually on the verge of giving us "meanings," only to continually shy away. When topped by his slouched hat, for example, Ahab is raised to a potentially symbolic level where he becomes a sort of extension of Ishmael's own personal frustrations. But in withholding his "response" to what the symbolic Ahab might mean, Ishmael refuses to grant Ahab a final revelatory role, and instead aborts an analogy which he has taken many pages to establish. In today's jargon, Ahab's quest has no meaningful "closure" on the symbolic level. As a consequence the reader has two options: to see Ahab's quest as little more than an amplification of Ishmael's self-indulgent disposition to oppose what he cannot understand or as a cunning criticism of nineteenth-century radical intellectualism.

The abrupt cancellation of Ahab's role does serve to suggest that romantic insurgency is not part of Ishmael's theory of how human beings should cope with the world within which they live, and so one is virtually required to turn to the cabin lamp to see what it discloses. Most notably, it has an existential thereness, and it is silent. For Jonah, the lamp has a rational meaning which can serve as a guide for action, but no such meaning is drawn from the lamp in Ahab's case. Blocked off from any rational understanding of what the lamp might represent, Starbuck and Ishmael react on the subjectively intuitive level. Tonally, their reactions chiefly reveal dread, anxiety, psychological discomfort, and a sense of estrangement between their selves and what Robert Midler calls a "cosmic nothingness."[8] In an otherwise uncertain world, such painful feelings appear to be the only certitudes available.[9] Ishmael thus anticipates the observation of Ionescu: "The absurd thing is to be conscious of the fact that human existence is unbearable, that the human condition is unbearable—intolerable—and nevertheless cling to it." More might be said. In an otherwise uncertain world, one's subjective reponses, when translated into art, can take on an order which validates that art as more real than the confusion it presumably documents. Such a view suggests that Ishmael is much more relevant to twentieth-century perceptions than if he were somehow associated with super-charged forms of romantic rebellion.[10]

It is perhaps possible to update him even more. When Jonah and Ahab are linked together a conflation occurs that is wholly compelling, so that when Ahab's hat is removed, and thereby his prophetic role, the reader can see in that action a final dismissal of the prophetic tradition as a guide to human conduct. A number of problems occur when dealing with the image of the lamp, however. For one thing, when the reader establishes the analogy between the lamp and some noumenal reality, the latter term never really appears in the text. Perhaps no analogy is being drawn? One way to affirm the analogy is to adopt the ploy necessary in reading much

symbolist power. The reader makes an intuitive "leap" to identification of the second leg of the analogy and proceeds from there. That is certainly defensible, so long as we acknowledge what we are doing.

Another way is to deal with the probable. Despite their disparate personalities, both Starbuck and Ishmael have similar subjective reactions to the lamp. They see it as an unpropitious reflection on Ahab's quest, hostile to his purpose, and as something fearful, inimical to their well-being. These interpretations stir dim subjective responses on a number of occasions spanning a considerable amount of time. Probabilities do not make for demonstrable conclusions, however, just as finally we must admit that analogies do not make for certitude. Analogies always seem to have an element of improvisation about them. In this sense, Ishmael may well realize that he is in a dilemma. On the one hand, both the romantic and Modernist faiths esteem analogy as a revelatory act that transcends the normal resources of language. On the other hand, language itself can seem ephemeral as it dissolves and re-forms human experience while the reality it seeks to describe remains remote and ultimately unattainable and all the time evasive. Reality itself, in fact, may be a metafiction, so that the discontinuities and fragmentations of language actually reveal more than we are prepared to accept. Ishmael may hide behind Ahab as Melville hides behind Ishmael, but it is Ishmael as both chronicler and author who observes that the "tormenting, mild image" thrown back by refractive water is "the image of the ungraspable phantom of life, and this is the key to all" (797).[11] In the two images of the hat and the cabin lamp, Ishmael clearly establishes the bounds for his cautionary tale within the larger chronicle, but a kind of sober probity prompts him to continually waver on what may be gained from them.

Notes

This paper was originally presented in the Melville session of the Cal State Symposium on American Literature (June 1-3, 1989), organized to explore the feasibility of establishing a national coalition of the societies devoted to the study of American authors. Page references in the body of the text are to the Literary Classics of the United States edition of *Moby-Dick* (New York, 1983).

1. Carolyn Porter develops this point at some length in "Call Me Ishmael, or How to Make Double-Talk Speak," in Richard H. Brodhead, ed., *New Essays on* Moby-Dick (Cambridge, 1986), pp. 73-108. Similar views can be found in Nina Baym, "Melville's Quarrel with Fiction," *PMLA,* 94 (Oct. 1979), 909-23; William B. Dillingham, "The Narrator of *Moby-Dick*," *English Studies,* 49 (Feb. 1968), 20-29; and A. Robert Lee, "*Moby-Dick* as

Anatomy," in Lee, ed., *Herman Melville: Reassessments* (Totowa, N.J., 1984), especially p. 78.

2. Edgar A. Dryden for his part sees Ishmael's entire account as deliberately "fictional," and in the larger sense that may be true. It is nevertheless worthwhile to distinguish between that fiction which validates itself as a faithful account of what "really" happened and the kind of fiction which makes no pretense to being anything other than what it is—an extravagant tall tale, a fairy tale, or what have you. Dryden, *Melville's Thematics of Form: The Great Art of Telling the Truth* (Baltimore, 1968).

3. See John W. Young, "Ishmael's Development as Narrator: Melville's Synthesizing Process," *College Literature,* 9 (Spring, 1982), 105.

4. As Bainard Cowan says, the belief of both Jonah and Ahab in their roles is so profound that they are intolerant of the ambiguities of interpretation that accompany speculation on the allegorical or symbolic levels. *Exiled Waters*: Moby-Dick *and the Crisis of Allegory* (Baton Rouge, 1982), p. 85.

5. The view of John Rothfork, "The Sailing of the *Pequod:* an Existential Voyage," *Arizona Quarterly,* 28 (Spring, 1972), 55-60.

6. Lawrence Buell notes that "the inevitability of thematic nonresolution makes Ishmael's desire to keep his work unfinished a completely honest and proper stance," but then goes on to assert that Ishmael's "mythicized images and the climactic position of the sea fight underscore the continuing apocalyptic and substantive relevance of the whale." "*Moby-Dick* as Sacred Text," in Brodhead, ed., *New Essays on* Moby-Dick, p. 64.

7. To David Hirsch, for example, Melville's "belief in the ultimate potency and generative capacity of language" leads to language itself becoming part of the "reality" of the novel. See "Verbal Reverberations and the Problem of Reality in *Moby-Dick,*" *Books at Brown,* 24 (1971), 45-67.

8. Robert Midler, "The Composition of *Moby-Dick*: A Review and a Prospect," *ESQ* [*Emerson Society Quarterly*], 23 (4th quarter, 1977), 210.

9. Cf. Paul Brodtkorb, Jr., who says that for Ishmael "the only truth is in subjectivity." *Ishmael's White World: A Phenomenological Reading of* Moby-Dick (New Haven, 1965), p. 125.

10. Along this line, it is certainly feasible to think that Ishmael's impatience with the prophetic tradition is due to its arrogance in assuming that the world has a univocal meaning to which it has the key. Cf., to[o], Emerson's observation in "Nature": "Each prophet comes presently to identify himself with his thought, and to esteem his hat and shoes sacred."

11. A number of scholars cite this passage as central to an understanding of the novel. See e.g., William B. Dillingham, *Melville's Later Novels* (Athens, GA, 1986), p. 165.

Mark Bauerlein (essay date autumn 1990)

SOURCE: Bauerlein, Mark. "Grammar and Etymology in *Moby-Dick.*" *Arizona Quarterly* 46, no. 3 (autumn 1990): 17-32.

[*In the following essay, Bauerlein analyzes the novel's linguistic complexity. In one sense, Bauerlein asserts,* Moby-Dick *represents humanity's struggle to name, and thereby define and control, inscrutable and unwieldy natural forces.*]

> To philosophize is to inquire into the *extraordinary*. But because . . . this questioning recoils upon itself, not only what is asked after is extraordinary but also the asking itself.
>
> —Heidegger

The words "call me Ishmael" are not the first words of **Moby-Dick.** Before introducing his narrator and starting the narrative proper (a questionable category in this novel), Melville opens with the science of first words: "Etymology." The novel begins with an outline of the history of the word "whale," its derivation, definition, spelling, and, in the succeeding "Extracts" section, a chronicle of its usage from Genesis to Darwin, from the mythic to the mundane. Melville sets the term in the context of a dictionary entry, regarding the name first and foremost philologically, much as would the "late consumptive usher" and the "sub-sub-librarian" whose portraits precede, respectively, the etymology of and allusions to the word "whale." The latter chronology does not, Melville notes, propose to set forth a "veritable gospel cetology," a series of authoritative statements intended to render the essential or symbolic nature of whales, but rather it offers an "entertaining" glimpse into "what has been promiscuously said, thought, fancied, and sung of Leviathan." That is, the list of quotations has less to do with the whale itself than with the way the whale has been variously and plurivocally represented. Similarly, the etymological citations confine themselves strictly to the term, not the real thing: the Hakluyt reference emphasizes the importance of the "letter H" in the word: the Webster note specifies the word's original denotation—"rolling"; and the Richardson quotation traces the word's close relation to Dutch and German.[1]

In other words, instead of framing the prospect of the story to follow and foregrounding the novel's concerns, these prefatory sections unveil a philological background, a lexical history, a retrospective index of meaning and usage from which the ensuing whaling narrative will draw (and which it will parody, critique, and outright attack). In one sense, these time-bound and seemingly inessential definitions, etymologies, classifications, and citation lists, concerned more with language and categories than with nature, are but the first of many verbal representations of the whale which more or less fail to comprehend it adequately and accurately within a cultural understanding. Along with the "Etymology" and "Extracts," the novel contains a "Sermon," an "Affadavit," an incomplete "Cetology," a eulogy to "The Honor and Glory of Whaling," and, in reference to the White Whale, rumors, legends, and stories, as well as reports from passing ships about their own direct encounters with Moby-Dick. As Charles Feidelson, Paul Brodtkorb, Robert Zoellner, and many others have rightly concluded, these testimonies are sometimes parodic, sometimes pathetic human constructions designed to implement the production of "meaning" and the commodification of "nature." Whether contrasted with Ishmael's "visionary activity" (a transcendental "seeing" valorized by Emerson and questioned by Melville) or parallelled with the technology of whaling (best illustrated by Stubb's various "consumptions" of whales), Melville's opening indicates language's origin in the desire for ground and certainty *and* its inability to satisfy entirely and permanently that desire. That is, while inevitably accompanying the epistemological or corporeal assimilation of nature (as in Ishmael's "final theory" of the Spouter Inn's painting's referent, the cook's "sermon" over Stubb's supper, or Ahab's final defiant speech—all Melvillean "Fort!-Da!" announcements structuring a self-perpetuating game of mastery or death), but never equalling the mystical moment in "The Masthead" or in "The Gilder," language remains a seemingly necessary but ultimately ineffective strategy of resolution, a transitory appeasement giving way to "manhood's pondering repose of If" (Ch. 114). Ever lapsing back into the conditional "If" (the condition of hope and frustration), these linguistic pursuits of natural force proceed from Ishmael's endless need to alleviate his ontological insecurity by humanizing the inhuman, "colorless" "Albino whale" (Ch. 42), to resolve "the problem of the universe revolving in [him]" (Ch. 35) by drawing nature's sublimity into man-made representations (an epistemological impossibility).

Just how effective these strategies of conventionalizing natural and supernatural forces are in **Moby-Dick** may be measured by the dissatisfaction persistently felt by the book's central character (Ahab) and its presiding narrator (Ishmael-"Melville"). The captain's rage and the storyteller's frustration are the outcome of their recognition that all ways of seeing and knowing and telling are factitious, that social constructions, be they stories, pictures, religious rites, principles of philosophy, or systems of classification, fail to penetrate the "pasteboard mask" of appearances. Being themselves "masks,"

these anxiety-ridden representations do not manifest the essential living power of nature, but instead inevitably recoil upon their own representational mode. They illustrate the universal law of narcissism Ishmael proclaims in "Loomings" (Ch. 1): "And still deeper the meaning of that story of Narcissus, who because he could not grasp the tormenting, mild image he saw in the fountain, plunged into it and was drowned. But that same image, we ourselves see in all rivers and oceans. It is the image of the ungraspable phantom of life; and this is the key to it all." Not even Starbuck's unexamined faith—"Let faith oust fact; let fancy oust memory; I look deep down and do believe" (Ch. 114)—can escape the specular medium and its tantalizing promise of depth. Starbuck's will to believe only underscores the dubiousness of representation and raises the question of whether, at any time, surface can yield to depth, image to idea, word to object. If not, then all human applications of technique, schema, language, even faith, remain as misguided, all-too-human attempts to render the essence of nature to consciousness, to negate it in the service of desire. Not only do they arbitrarily impose a technical or linguistic structure upon nature, but, more radically, they constitute nature as a "thing" to be imposed upon, to be processed, to be incorporated.

Much of the satire in the novel is directed at these presumptions, especially the confident way in which orthodox religion and specialized science arrogate to themselves the locus of truth and presume that their discourses and taxonomies refer to the actual center and circumference of the universe. The antidote to man's intellectual pride is the enigmatic White Whale, always beyond signification, exceeding rational study or moral contemplation, and bedeviling those who would seek to master it physically or through an interpretation that passes itself off as truth. Recall that Ishmael is captivated by and Ahab obsessed with Moby-Dick most of all because of his appalling white inscrutability, his refusal, like an unwritten page, to be read (Latin *in-* + *scrutari* "to search"). He is a "dumb blankness, full of meaning" (Ch. 42), a divine symbol and an empty sign, and as such marks the threshold between man and God, convention and nature, language and reality, the very limit Ahab must cross or die, and die to cross. Ahab's ultimate fate is a profound lesson in *hubris,* in trying to surpass one's own fabrications, to transcend those anxiety-relieving representations with "the living act, the undoubted deed" (Ch. 36).

But what has this to do with etymology, and what has Captain Ahab brooding over the mystic, measureless ocean to do with the dusty usher and the cloistered librarian? As Ishmael says, ". . . the only mode in which you can derive even a tolerable idea of [the whale's] living contour, is by going a whaling yourself . . ." (Ch. 55), so what can the bookish, vicarious ways of philologists tell us about the Pequod's and its captain's adventures on the high seas? In Ahab's obsession lies the answer, the parallel motive, for he himself indicates the relation between whaler and scholar by interpreting the Pequod's purpose as metaphysical—that is, to "strike through the unreasoning mask" of nature—and thus analogous to the philologist's logocentric purpose (though they choose different means to reach their common end). Though the etymologist surrounds himself with the dry-as-dust records of civilized cultures and Ahab must flee from civilization and all its instruments in order to meet his fate, they still share the same onto-theological dream. Ahab yearns to stand face to face with the elemental forces impelling but withdrawing from the show of nature and the etymologist searches to uncover the elemental ground of words which has become obscured by centuries of abstraction and uninspired talk. Whereas Ahab proceeds by attempting to eradicate violently the intermediary representative, the etymologist works "textually" by pursuing representations back to their inception. Etymology does not simply chart the history of a referent's transmission from one language and time to another; it attempts to trace a referent back to its original name, the initial representation, when Adamic man first abstracted a sign from a thing. Though a contrived strategy, etymology is not simply one linguistic representation amongst many others, just another verbal schema in *Moby-Dick* which reflects back upon its own artifice. A historian of signs, the etymologist recovers the source of representation, the primordial moment whereby a namer first supplemented the order of things with a label. This originary displacement, while allowing "man" to "think" the world and himself and thus to become *homo sapiens* (or *homo fabricans,* as Roland Barthes describes "him"), also disturbed his unconscious participation in and affinity with the world, objectified the world and subjectified the self, with language mediating and dividing them. Herein we have the philologist's version of the Romantic's Fall, the irruption of language and self-consciousness and the premonition of death into the innocent simplicity of ignorant natural bliss. No wonder the "old grammars . . . somehow mildly reminded [the usher] of his mortality."

It is fitting, therefore, that Melville should begin a book exploring myths of origin and destiny, a book whose characters battle their metaphysical discomfort by trying to neutralize and master the sign's inscrutability, by foregrounding the origin of signmaking and narrating the genesis and history of a sign's semiosis. This is why the most famous "original" naming in *Moby-Dick*—"Call me Ishmael"—actually follows the attempt to reenact the original naming of "whale" and its successive translations and reinscriptions. By opening his novel with a series of citations and calling himself a "commentator" upon the "sub-sub-librarian's" activities, Melville places his book on the margins of a philology, makes his own "extract" both a "backward

glance" upon that history and the latest stage in it. Etymology produces this history, offering Melville a convenient model of interpretation that posits an origin (the "etymon," grounded in a "real" object), constructs a temporal scheme (conceived by many 18th- and 19th-century etymologists as a progressive decline of concrete referentiality), and a final closure of history (through a corrective reappropriation of the term's founding inspiration, a pre-historical experience). As Melville's citation makes clear, the reigning etymologist in post-Revolutionary America, Noah Webster, aimed to do just that in his landmark masterwork, *An American Dictionary of the English Language* (completed in England in 1825, published in New York in 1828).[2] The *Dictionary*'s title page indicates that Webster "intend[s] to exhibit" not only "II. The genuine orthography and pronounciation of words . . . [and] III. Accurate and discriminating definitions . . . ," but first "I. The origin, affinities, and primary signification of English words, as far as they have been ascertained." Webster then proceeds, in an extensive 46-page, double-columned, small-typed "Introductory Dissertation," to outline his eccentric (and thoroughly American) assumptions regarding and methods for determining those "primary significations," the "radical" meaning of a word. That root, it turns out, has a divine origin, for, in a literal reading of Genesis, Webster faithfully concludes that language "was the *immediate gift of God,*" an originally candid, organic idiom regulated by God's Word and not yet corrupted and clouded by Fallen usage, the most cataclysmic example being "the confusion of languages at Babel . . ." ("Origin of Language" section, pages unnumbered).

Webster proposes to redress this divergence and dissemination of tongues by uncovering the radical "affinities" underlying seemingly unrelated languages, and therefore to reveal the theological unity of all speech. In less messianic terms, he practices "to obtain a more correct knowledge of the primary sense of original words, . . . and thus to enable [him]self to trace words to their source" ("Preface," *Dictionary,* pages unnumbered)[3] and in that history recover man's providential truth. The "source," the founding event in this history, Webster says, is a "visible or physical action," the concrete "motion" and "drive" from which all abstract ideas and moral principles descend. Hence, in the beginning was the verb, "the radix or stock from which have sprung most of the nouns, adjectives, and other parts of speech belonging to each family" ("Introduction," *Lego* section). Articles, modifiers, prepositions, even the unique name of the thing, the noun, to Webster are posterior accessories to the inaugural action and its participial term. Instead of designating things in a straightforward, deictic manner, they mark relations "between" things (and constitute them as "things") and between words, thus diffusing the discrete "contents" of natural reality across a synthetic field of factitious associations and infrastructures. Etymology, so the argument goes, peels away all such later (and belated) additions to the essential action, purifies the natural, fundamental verb (Webster claims there are 30 to 40 of them) of its linguistic attributes. These later complications, the by-products of situating the verb in an intricate grammatical network, undermine the organic bond of verb and thing or action, cause the verb's position in a linguistic structure to prevail over its proper one-to-one referential function.

Webster intends to arrest this progressive entangling of stable organic denotation in ever more complex arrangements, in compound tenses, qualifications, subordinations, prolixity, and so on. (The *Dictionary* also contains an introductory treatise on grammar.) He aims to curb "the mischievous influence of scoliasts and that dabbling spirit of innovation which is perpetually disturbing [the language's] settled usages and filling it with anomalies . . ." ("Introduction"). The American etymologist guards his language against unnatural excesses, false derivations, deviations, and "anomalies," as it evolves in the New World. Though Webster is a revolutionary patriot, his effort is a conservative one: to emend current usage by revivifying the idiom's radical substratum, its natural roots.[4] While the "scoliast" (whom Webster defines as "A commentator or annotator") merely proliferates verbiage, piles texts upon texts and thereby fosters the linguistic departure from nature, the etymologist deciphers the text back into its primitive elements. An archaeologist of utterances, the etymologist historicizes the text and excavates its point of origin, the inaugural concourse of reality and signs, the proper standard or context of all later translations.

As conceived by Webster, the etymologist interprets signs by tracing them to their source, at which point interpretation may cease, for the first sign is itself an intuitive response to physical stimuli and hence needs no analysis to be apprehended. The original verb, issuing directly from matter and motion, belongs to the natural course of events and precedes artificial impositions of human will. Only after being placed in an articulate discourse does the verb come to acquire abstract grammatical properties, linguistic superventions which an etymological interpretation must retract in order to regain the word's radical content. A "painstaking burrower and grubworm," the etymologist exposes and discards the linguistic accretions surrounding the essential meaning and circulating it across a temporal sequence of signifiers. He restores the positive identity of a word, its concrete referent, and rescues that identity from implication in a play of negative differences.

In other words, Webster's etymologist is a linguist against language. He devotes his life to words, but he interprets words retrospectively until he gets *before* them. He studies word origins and then, having determined the word's founding referent, he prescribes its proper historically and naturally sanctioned usage (Webster's cardinal ambition). By resurrecting the word's authoritative "real" origin, Webster ensures that the development of English in America will remain within valid organic limits. That is, he steps outside of language to arbitrate language's rightful functioning, to forestall its abuse, mistranslation, and misinterpretation. He interprets backward to a fixed reference that stabilizes future representations, an extra-linguistic presence that measures truth and accuracy and is immune to linguistic distortion. With the concrete referent faithfully adhered to, unnatural fraudulent practices made possible by language (lies, misrepresentations, sophistry, rhetoric) are curtailed and a living vernacular bound by its natural wellspring unites the people with themselves and their locale. This is the goal of etymological investigation (as Webster views it): to ground language in a natural event outside the text, an unambiguous, pre-interpretive action universally understood, despite its heterogeneous verbal representations.

Webster's etymology, then, proposes to circumscribe languages and limit their dispersal, to center representation on an unmistakable objective certainty that pacifies man's metaphysical anxiety, his need to discover design and intention in the universe, a yearning profoundly illustrated by Ahab, Ishmael, *et al.* However, Melville's "Etymology" does not finalize representation and interpretation—in **Moby-Dick,** etymology serves mainly as an introduction to a diversity of representations which are never reduced to a master code, as the first in a miscellaneous succession of verbal, pictorial, and taxonomic descriptions of nature which Ishmael and the other characters are called upon to interpret and evaluate. Instead of revealing the true essence of whales and whaling, the "Etymology" and "Extracts" sections open up the narrative that follows to a hermeneutical perspective and set the stage for numerous scenes of reading that emphasize the particular act of interpretation more than any meaning produced. Indeed, the character's interpretive strategies consistently fail to yield a permanent satisfactory resolution, leaving each character to cope with "inscrutability" in his own peculiar manner (Ahab madly chasing the White Whale, Queequeg rehearsing his primitive rituals, Starbuck falling back upon Christian truisms, and so on).

Nowhere are these interpretive projects more explicitly dramatized and contrasted than in the well-known, amply-scrutinized "Doubloon" chapter.[5] Prominently nailed to the mainmast, the gold doubloon goes to whoever sights Moby-Dick first, and as a token of this first vision of their sublime antagonist, the coin consolidates all the desires and fears of Ahab and his crew. A "tropic token-piece" stamped with "strange figures and inscriptions," the doubloon is the semiotic opposite of Moby-

Dick—while the "Albino whale" forestalls any reading of its "visible absence" (Ch. 42), the "equatorial coin" solicits a hermeneutical interpretation of its occult "letters" and "likeness[es]." In Chapter 99, the coin's cabalistic "signs and wonders" compel Ahab, Starbuck, Flask, the Manxman, Queequeg, and Fedallah each to "interpret for himself . . . whatever significance might lurk in them," to, in Stubb's words, "try [his] hand at raising a meaning out of these queer curvicues."[6] Trusting that "some certain significance lurks in all things, else all things are little worth, and the round world itself but an empty cipher . . . ," each character offers an idiosyncratic exegesis of the coin. Ahab, in his "monomaniac way," reads it as a reflection of Ahab, Starbuck as an "earthly symbol" of the "Trinity," Stubb as a Zodiacal narrative of a man's life, Flask as the equivalent of "nine hundred and sixty cigars," while Fedallah "only makes a sign to the sign" (to the observing Stubb, a secret communique of "fire worship"). Appearing successively as an image of self, a Christian icon, a pagan biography, an exchange value, and a demonic emblem, the doubloon receives momentarily definitive interpretations that relate its curious imprint to a ruling ground.

Like the etymologist, these interpreters reach behind the sign to extract its authentic meaning, and at that point they end, having achieved their purpose. But this is not where the chapter ends. Melville introduces one more commentator into his complex scene of reading, this time not a hermeneuticist or etymologist but a grammarian—Pip. After watching each interpreter take his turn, Pip, in Stubb's words,

> "comes to read, with that unearthly idiot face. Stand away again and hear him. Hark!"
>
> "I look, you look, he looks; we look, ye look, they look."
>
> "Upon my soul, he's been studying Murray's Grammar! Improving his mind, poor fellow! But what's that he says now—hist!"
>
> "I look, you look, he looks; we look, ye look, they look."
>
> "Why he's getting it by heart—hist! again."
>
> "I look, you look, he looks; we look, ye look, they look."

That is, they "look," but they do not "see." However, Pip's gloss does more than just affirm the relativism and inadequacy of interpretation, the proposition that readers "look" from their own partial, eccentric perspectives. His conjugation situates readings together in a grammatical order, uniting them in a formal structure that underscores the inalterably linguistic basis of interpretation. Instead of interpreting the coin, he positions interpretations of the coin. Like a good grammarian, he articulates the systematic rules and arrangements that make meaning possible, leaving etymologists and other genetic interpreters to determine what that meaning is.

The reference to Lindley Murray's *English Grammar*, the most popular textbook in 19th-century American classrooms, is appropriate, for Murray makes explicit what is implicit in Pip's critique of hermeneutics at the end of his chapter on "Etymology."[7] There he confines his study to a synchronic classification of parts of speech, to outlining "the different sorts of words, their derivation, and the various modifications by which the sense of a primitive word is diversified" (19). To Murray, etymology is the study of how a "primitive word," the root or base phoneme (not a historical origin), is "diversified" into other parts of speech—for example, how a noun is made a verb or how a verb is made an adverb, and so on. Derivation is a matter of grammatical, not historical, transformation. Stating in the chapter's final sentences that the analysis of origins and derivations can be found in the "best English dictionaries . . . [by] those who are desirous of obtaining it" (85), Murray simply dismisses the importance of a historical understanding of language. His relegation of philology to the study of ancient languages—"There are many English words which are derived from the Greek, Latin, French, and several other languages; but as the English scholar is not supposed to be acquainted with these languages, this part of derivation must be omitted" (85)—implies that knowing a word's history and "primitive sense" (in Webster's definition of the term) are not requisite to using it correctly. Philology is the scholar's province, and has no place in American mass education (as Murray envisions it). With ordinary language—which *is* American language—propriety is a matter of formal compliance with grammatical prescriptions, not of direct descendence from a semantic lineage, and interpretation rests upon an utterance's compatibility with contemporary usage, not its fidelity to an authenticated history.

On Murray's example, Pip recasts the premises and purposes of interpretation, brackets etymology and its critical equivalent (trying to ground the text in the extratextual: history, biography, psyche, nature) within an inescapable textual structure. His inflectional summary of seven readers reading circumscribes their collected "meanings" within a linguistic frame, foreclosing their attempted leaps out of language into a reassuring "truth" or "reality." He disdains giving merely another reading of the coin, opting instead to transcend the interpreters' limited perspectives by enumerating the entire manifold of perspectives permitted by language. Restricting his commentary to formal categories and therefore avoiding the charge of relativism or bias, committing his annotation to a universality which effaces the narcissistic self, Pip speaks with more logical and disinterested authority than Ahab and the others. He has the final word and he asserts the finality of words.

But that authority comes at the cost of insight, for Pip tells us nothing about the coin other than calling it in a later paragraph the ship's "navel" upon which the seamen gaze. Reductive and indiscriminate, Pip's conjugation suspends all questions of content and preserves the coin's inscrutability. Previously abandoned by Stubb to the "sweet mysteries about this sea, whose gently awful stirrings seem to speak of some hidden soul beneath," but encountering there not a "soul" but rather "millions of mixed shades and shadows, drowned dreams, somnambulisms, reveries" (Ch. 111), Pip has left the boat and broken the "surface" only to find yet more representations, more appearances in the unconscious deeps. Despairing of "depth" (Melville's synonym for meaning), Pip recognizes the peremptory rule of language, of a grammar that proposes only the possibility of a content (there would be no grammar without this possibility, just as Pip could not perform his conjugation without witnessing others' "looks"—this is why grammar can never be reduced to purely formal categories and why Pip's scholia is "meaningless" apart from the seamen's search for meaning). His grammatical method, the method of his madness, treats all worldly objects, even divine symbols, as "empty ciphers," mere algebraic variables which apprehensive selves suffuse with meaning and value. Determining whether those surmises are valid or accurate is less important to him than organizing them in a linguistic formula.

So where does this leave metaphysical inquiry? And on what basis is one to resolve a conflict of interpretations? Pip levels all interpretations to an equal grammatical footing, invalidating any non-linguistic yardstick by which to evaluate competing readings and cancelling the possibility of reaching an unmediated truth. But the desire for truth, for certainty and immediacy and resolution continues, for Pip's formal conclusions do not relieve the others' anxiety over the grounds and destiny of existence—their nostalgia demands a real content, a knowledge universal and fixed, not an abstract, empty structure. But, as Pip points out, not only here but in the fact that he must lose himself—when addressed, Pip responds, "Pip? whom call ye Pip? Pip jumped from the whaleboat. Pip's missing" (Ch. 123)—before he can acknowledge the linguistic underpinnings of desire and reason, that structure is inescapable: the interpreters do not read the coin so much as they expose themselves and their presuppositions. This is the fundamental dilemma Melville poses for his characters: to waver back and forth between antithetical interpretive poles, between etymology and grammar, genesis and structure, meaning and form. The former satisfies momentarily the desire for origin and explanation, but eventually collapses upon its own representational medium; the latter retains its validity, but fails to satisfy any metaphysical longing. Therein lies the characters' tragedy. Caught up in a transitive game of signs and interpretations, their desires and fears at stake in its provisional outcomes, Melville's *personae* succumb to their own peculiar, interminable obsessions, the con-

sumptive usher fetishizing his "old lexicons and grammars," the "poor devil of a Sub-Sub" browsing through the world's libraries and bookshops gathering whale allusions, Ishmael periodically lapsing into grim "unseasonable meditativeness" and shipping out, and Ahab relentlessly chasing Moby-Dick and his own death. Theirs is a riddling despair, a vexing linguistic predicament. Compelled by human desire to "delineate chaos" (Ch. 3) and rationalize the unknown, yet suspecting their results (and the materials of investigations: themselves and their inventions), they alternate between confidence and skepticism, the gratification that comes with a commensurate image or statement and the dismay that follows their recognition of a representation's insurmountable *in*commensurability.

However, Ishmael is not simply another character myopically pursuing the truth and consuming nature to satisfy a self-absorbed desire. Although he occasionally foists his own interpretations and actions upon his listeners, after the first few chapters he devotes himself almost solely to telling the tale of his shipmates' quest for knowledge and belief, to interpreting their interpretations. Ishmael may withdraw from the foreground of his narrative in the latter two-thirds of the book, but his storytelling presence remains to narrate and adjudicate the others' etymological desires and grammatical frustrations. Not that Ishmael escapes the interpretive problematics plaguing Ahab, Starbuck, and the rest; but in detaching himself from his descriptions of the Pequod's adventures and thereby achieving the reflective distance necessary for a critical understanding of interpretation, Ishmael does occupy a partially disengaged position from which he can wield not only an expository rendering of events but also a discursive critique of those events (using analytic terms such as "etymology" and "grammar"). Ever "floating on the margin of the ensuing scene" ("Epilogue") and dramatically recreating it, Ishmael is, above all, the historian of interpretation, the wandering "orphan" bard assuming various identities to narrate the course of human knowledge and human striving. As such, he is the etymologist of grammar, surviving on the coffin remains of others' writings, living by translation while knowing its pitfalls. Ishmael facilitates a juncture of languages (Christian sermons on Jonah and offerings to Yojo, cetological treatises and superstitious White Whale rumors, the Old Testament lament of the Rachel and the Shakespearean rage of the Pequod, and so on) and guarantees their semiotic continuity (upon which history depends). In a supremely fictional mode, he recounts his comrades' search for fact, recording (like Melville, with anguish) for an inimical posterity what happened when to whom. He is the ideal poet-historian.

While Ishmael may elude the etymology-grammar dilemma by writing a poetical history of its *aporias*, the modern prosaic literary critic remains thoroughly implicated in this troublesome questioning of interpretation, a questioning pathetically illustrated by the sailors' plight and teasingly begged by Ishmael's ultimate fate. Melville's cast of readers intensely exemplify the critical activity and more than one study of *Moby-Dick* has taken the "Doubloon" chapter as an analogue of the entire book and its reception. In staging this and numerous other scenes of reading throughout his novel, Melville anticipates future interpretations and, instead of enabling a single reading, he incorporates a variety of historical, theological, and formalist critical approaches into the body of Ishmael's narrative. This doubly complicates the critic's task. If the critic attempts to penetrate the surface of *Moby-Dick* and uncover its essential meaning, he risks the same kind of self-reflexive snares undermining the interpreters' reading of the doubloon. If the critic withholds his hermeneutical impulse and undertakes only an exhaustive structural analysis of its repetitions, contradictions, and tropes, he leaves the secret of its creation a tantalizing mystery. And finally, how is the critic to relate his activities, his observations and judgments and narrations, to Ishmael's? From the opening "Etymology" to the closing "Epilogue," Melville re-examines these questions, forcing the aspiring critic to re-think his methods. In the passages analyzed above and the outside texts to which they refer, Melville uses contrasting philological procedures to frame his critique of interpretation. Etymology and grammar are not simply pedantic scholarly endeavors hostile to creative expression, disciplines appropriate to arid, tedious academicians but not to inspired artists. They are crucial to the general interpretive project carried out in *Moby-Dick*—they set the parameters by which the author's, the characters', and the critic's quest for truth must navigate.

Notes

1. The only critics who have devoted serious attention to the "Etymology" and "Extracts" sections are Edgar Dryden and William Dillingham. Dryden contrasts the Sub-Sub, whom he regards as a naive collector of "pure facts" (84), with Ishmael, who "destroys the reassuring but naive assumption that the world can be explained and controlled by the collection of its facts and the description of its objects" (83). Dillingham interestingly contrasts the Sub-Sub, who "is always in danger of burrowing too long without returning to the surface," with the usher, who is "not a burrower but a duster, lightly sweeping over life. (23).

2. For discussions of Webster and his *Dictionary,* see Krapp I: 362-70; Rollins 123-38; Baron 41-67; Simpson 52-90; and Lawson-Peebles 73-83. Although Webster is an established figure in social, political, and literary histories of America, the texts cited are virtually the only ones to treat him as more than simply a historical personage and to

probe his understanding of language in the New World. My comments differ from these critics' analyses in that their intention generally is to extract Webster's political ideas from his philological practice, to focus upon the programmatic thrust of the *Dictionary,* but my intention is to examine the philosophical and linguistic assumptions of his methods.

3. In his research and composition of the *Dictionary,* Webster traced etymologies by mounting on a large semicircular desk every dictionary he could find. He then took an English word and followed it from text to text, usually marking relations through similarities in the sound or spelling of consonants (he believed vowel changes were too volatile to reconstruct). In each search he hoped to track a word back to the language he believed to be the most "Adamic": Chaldean.

4. Given American Renaissance writers' well-known fascination with language and philology—recall that Section IV of Emerson's *Nature* speculates upon the material origins of "Language"; sometime in 1856, Whitman began to compile his observations on "Words," on their pronunciation, spelling, grammar, and etymology, all in an attempt to create a new dictionary in the American grain; and in *Walden,* a book whose "senses" are adumbrated through an etymological punning, Thoreau casts himself as an archaeologist of nature "burrowing" not only into the grounds of Being but also through the layers of languages blanketing Being—it is surprising that Webster should have received so little attention in studies in classic American literature. One reads of the Main Currents in American Thought, of American Adams, American Hieroglyphics, Worlds Elsewhere, Literary Democracies, Visionary Compacts, Puritan Origins, Symbolisms, Continuities, Femininizations, Regenerations, and so on, in vain for any reference to Webster, despite the fact that the philologist's corpus exemplifies many such themes and that the canonized writers raising those concerns all had some familiarity with Webster. (Whitman quotes Webster several times in his notebook and Leyda reports that Melville ordered Webster's *Dictionary* twice.)

5. For readings of the "Doubloon" chapter, see Feidelson, *passim;* Chase 109-10; Brodtkorb, *passim;* Zoellner 9-11; McIntosh 27-28; and Wolf 174-75. Wolf is the only critic here who underscores the "grammar of seeing" implied in Pip's conjugation.

6. Significantly, Ishmael is absent from this list—he does not try to interpret the coin. His restraint suggests that he accepts inscrutability in the coin and in nature, that he is content with the play of

surfaces. Indeed, in *Moby-Dick* (Ch. 41), Ishmael says of himself (in contradistinction to Ahab), "—all this to explain, would be to dive deeper than Ishmael can go."

7. Upon its publication in England in 1795 and in America a few years later, Murray's *Grammar* competed with Webster's until it squeezed the latter out of the market and Webster had to content himself with the popularity of his spelling book alone. Webster did nurse a resentment that ultimately took the form of an accusation of plagiarism: in the "Advertisement" to the *Dictionary*, Webster claims (two years after Murray's death), "On carefully comparing [Murray's *Grammar*, 1808 edition] with my own Grammar, I found most of his *improvements* were selected from my book. In the first edition of this work, the compiler gave me credit for one passage only, (being nearly three pages of my Grammar,) which he acknowledges to be *chiefly* taken from my work. In later editions, he says, this is *in part* taken from my book, and he further acknowledges that a *few positions* and *illustrations,* among the syntactical notes and observations, were selected from my Grammar. Now the fact is, these passages borrowed amount to *thirty* or more, and they are so incorporated into his work, that no person except myself would detect the plagiarisms, without a particular view to this object" (pages unnumbered). Webster proceeds to offer a corrective "Philosophical and Practical Grammar, & c." to "arrest the progress of error" both in daily usage and in such like fraudulent textbooks. Given Webster's many shameless self-promotions and contentious polemics (he even wrote censorious letters to Jefferson and Madison while they were in office), it need not be said how often Webster himself borrowed examples and definitions from Johnson, Lowth, and other philologists.

Works Cited

Baron, Dennis. *Grammar and Good Taste.* New Haven: Yale University Press, 1982.

Brodtkorb, Paul. *Ishmael's White World: A Phenomenological Reading of* Moby Dick. New Haven: Yale University Press, 1965.

Chase, Richard. *The American Novel and Its Tradition.* Baltimore: Johns Hopkins University Press, 1957.

Dillingham, William. *Melville's Later Novels.* Athens, Ga.: University of Georgia Press, 1986.

Dryden, Edgar. *Melville's Thematics of Form: The Great Art of Telling the Truth.* Baltimore: Johns Hopkins University Press, 1968.

Feidelson, Charles. *Symbolism and American Literature.* Chicago: University of Chicago Press, 1953.

Krapp, George Philip. *The English Language in America.* 2 vols. New York: Frederick Ungar, 1925, 1960.

Lawson-Peebles, Robert. *Landscape and Written Expression in Revolutionary America: The World Turned Upside Down.* Cambridge: Cambridge University Press, 1988.

Leyda, Jay. *The Melville Log.* 2 vols. New York: Harcourt, Brace, 1953.

McIntosh, James. "The Mariner's Multiple Quest." In *New Essays on* Moby-Dick. Edited by Richard H. Brodhead. Cambridge: Cambridge University Press, 1986. 23-52.

Melville, Herman. *Moby-Dick.* Norton Critical Edition. Edited by Harrison Hayford and Hershel Parker. New York: Norton, 1967.

Murray, Lindley. *English Grammar.* Menston, England: The Scolar Press Limited, 1968 (a facsimile reprint of the 1795 edition).

Rollins, Richard. *The Long Journey of Noah Webster.* Philadelphia: University of Pennsylvania Press, 1980.

Simpson, David. *The Politics of American English, 1776-1850.* New York: Oxford University Press, 1986.

Webster, Noah. *An American Dictionary of the English Language.* New York: S. Converse, 1828.

Wolf, Bryan. "When Is a Painting Most Like A Whale?: Ishmael, *Moby-Dick,* and the Sublime." In *New Essays on* Moby-Dick. Edited by Richard H. Brodhead. Cambridge: Cambridge University Press, 1986. 141-79.

Zoellner, Robert. *The Salt-Sea Mastodon: A Reading of* Moby-Dick. Berkeley: University of California Press, 1973.

Paul Lukacs (essay date winter 1991)

SOURCE: Lukacs, Paul. "The Abandonment of Time and Place: History and Narrative, Metaphysics and Exposition in Melville's *Moby-Dick.*" *CLIO: A Journal of Literature, History, and the Philosophy of History* 20, no. 2 (winter 1991): 139-55.

[*In the following essay, Lukacs examines questions of narrative structure in* Moby-Dick. *According to Lukacs, Ishmael assumes three distinct narrative attitudes over the course of the novel: in the first, he reveals his own story; in the second, he abandons conventional novelistic technique in order to launch into a prolonged exposition on whaling; and in the third, he unfolds the tale of Ahab. This continually shifting approach to the novel's subject, Lukacs argues, represents Ishmael's determined, yet ultimately futile, attempt to discover "timeless, unconfined truth."*]

Reviewing his friend Herman Melville's new book for the New York *Literary World* in November of 1851, Evert Duyckinck offered praise tempered by an awareness of what he called "critical difficulty." He had discovered "two if not three books" in the one volume, and he found considerable "difficulty in [their] estimate" because he did not understand how they fit together. This was as much a question of interpretation as of categorization. While he recognized that *Moby-Dick* had a "double character," being simultaneously a romantic fiction and a statement of fact, he at the same time identified *three* very separate books "rolled into one"—the "moralizing" of "the narrator . . . one Ishmael," an "exhaustive account" of whales and whaling, and finally "the romance of Captain Ahab, Queequeg, Tashtego, Pip & Co." More than most subsequent commentators, Duyckinck had gleaned Melville's recipe for what he pronounced "a most remarkable sea-dish."[1] As "an intellectual chowder" (or in Melville's own words, a "hash"[2]), *Moby-Dick* does have three main ingredients. Yet because it also contains spicy bits of different genres and subgenres (travelogues, sermons, instruction manuals, etc.), many readers contend that its form is loose or free. Others, however, insist on tasting only two dominant flavors, and conclude that the form is double. Yet the book's sustained narratives, which are divided from each other by the plotless "cetological center," contain different protagonists, different settings, and indeed different themes. Hence it is more accurate to attend to the recipe's call for roughly equal parts story, then exposition, and then another, quite new story. And the interpretive difficulty remains the one Duyckinck identified—trying to figure out not only what the exposition has to do with the narratives, but also what the narratves have to do with each other.

Nina Baym argues that the complex form of *Moby-Dick* reflects Melville's "quarrel with fiction," a quarrel that he began in *Mardi* and then continued in *Pierre* and *The Confidence-Man.*[3] She may well be right, but Melville dramatized his concerns through the voice he called "Ishmael;" and *that* voice is the one that expresses itself through story, exposition, and then story again.[4] Indeed, Ishmael's struggle as the narrator to make sense of what he experienced as a character is what leads to the radical changes in the book's form. Those changes do not signal a quarrel with fiction. Instead, they signal a quarrel with narrative history—the chronological form supporting factual as well as fictional story-telling.[5] The expository middle third of the book, in which for chapter after chapter Ishmael dissects both a whale and the business of whaling, exists in the present of his composition, not in the past of the *Pequod*'s sailing. It not only divides his narratives, but also calls into question the assumption underlying them—namely, that a history that tells "what happened" can truly represent reality.

Throughout *Moby-Dick,* Ishmael as author faces what 20th-century literary theory considers "the necessity of having to choose a language,"[6] a form of discourse with which to represent experience. When he first turns away from narrative, he gives "[him]self up to the abandonment of the time and the place" (163). And he only returns to narrative once he recognizes that his decision to leave it was indeed *of* time and place—that is, that his motivation for attempting to transcend the confines of history was itself confined by history. For Ishmael, the issue is never fiction as opposed to fact—in Edgar Dryden's terms, art rather than life; in Paul Brodtkorb's, subjective rather than objective truth.[7] Instead, the issue is history, the necessity of choosing a discourse that grounds the representation of truth or life in the changing verities of time and place. His expository cetological center attempts to represent a reality greater (because unconfined by time and place) than history allows. Yet *before* Ishmael chooses the encyclopedic form of exposition, he tries history and narrative; and *after* he abandons exposition, he chooses narrative again. As author, then, he makes three very separate choices of language or form in *Moby-Dick*—first, when he tells his story, second when he abandons story-telling, and third when he chooses to tell someone else's story rather than continue with his own.

Ishmael's first narrative, lasting for approximately forty chapters, tells the story of his going whaling. Its theme grows out of a contrast between land and sea, a contrast that comes to incorporate other, related contrasts—e.g., civilization and savagery, democracy and dictatorship, freedom and slavery. As the author of these chapters, Ishmael is constantly crossing boundaries, inverting terms, and speculating (in Duyckinck's words, "moralizing") on the meaning of both his experience and his language. Rather than write exclusively from within any established category, he moves between categories, speaking simultaneously as an eccentric exile and as a representative of all mankind, as a free agent and as a puppet in the "grand programme of Providence" (16). Not only does what seems savage come to seem civilized (and vice versa), but the very meaning of such terms becomes called into question. This rhetorical strategy reaches a climax in "The Lee Shore" (chap. 23). There the land, which seemed initially to hold "all that's kind to our mortalities," is viewed as "pitiful," "treacherous," and "slavish;" and the sea, which seemed deceptive and forbidding, is held to be a realm of "open independence" and infinite glory. The thematic contrast, then, involves two visions of reality and two attendant forms of discourse—one which locates truth in time and space, confined and indeed defined by history ashore, the other which locates a greater truth beyond history, in the shoreless, infinite deep. Ishmael here so inverts his terms that the ahistorical sea replaces hearth and home as the true locus of his nature and identity. Concluding that it is better "to perish in that howling infinite, than be ingloriously dashed upon the lee," he summarizes his theme as the realization that "in landlessness alone resides the highest truth, shoreless, indefinite as God" (97).

Throughout his narrative, Ishmael contends that man's quest for "highest truth" is itself a condition of human nature. Beginning in the very first paragraph, when he suggests that "almost all men in their degree" share his feelings towards the sea (12), he proposes its universality. He claims that the highest, or alternately "deepest," truth is timeless and permanent, not subject to change in history, and that all men, regardless of their histories, pursue it, "bound for a dive" (13). Precisely because such truth bespeaks "what is" and not "what was," Ishmael writes the initial story of his quest in what Carolyn Porter calls a "double-voiced discourse," expressing himself through and at the same time against the landed language of history and shore.[8] Just as the *Pequod*'s crew incorporates men of different nationalities into its "Anacharsis Clootz deputation" (108), he incorporates different voices into his story. He uses the rhetoric of politics, science, law, and philosophy, in language that is sometimes serious, sometimes humorous, and sometimes parodic; and while he speaks for no one other than himself, the self he speaks for is always representative. Yet while he moralizes, digresses, and speculates incessantly, his writing in the first forty chapters of *Moby-Dick* remains essentially narrative. That is, within those chapters he never stops telling his story—the story that begins with his decision to go to sea, takes him to New Bedford, Nantucket, and out into the Atlantic, and then reaches its climax when he joins with the rest of the crew and takes Ahab's oath to pursue Moby Dick.

As a character, Ishmael takes that oath because Ahab gives powerful voice to his own desires. When in "The Quarter-deck" (chap. 36) Ahab declares that his hunt for the white whale is motivated by something greater than revenge, he echoes Ishmael's initial motivation for going whaling—"the wild conceits that swayed me to my purpose" (16). Ahab is pursuing the "unknown but still reasoning thing" hidden "behind [or beneath] the unreasoning mask" of the whale's body. "That inscrutable thing is chiefly what I hate," he tells the crew; "and be the white whale agent, or be the white whale principal, I will wreck that hate upon him." In his eyes, the whale embodies a deep and infinite truth. And because that truth is a product of nature rather than history, he does not care if his whaling makes him a profit ashore. Striking his chest, he declares that it is designed to fetch "a great premium *here,*" and he justifies his quest with the deceptively simple credo, "Truth hath no confines" (144).

Ahab woos Ishmael and the rest of the *Pequod*'s crew to his purpose through the fire of his passion, convincing them that despite their different histories, they share a common nature and a common goal. Only Starbuck resists, and his resistance fails in part because "the long howl" of the crew's passion "thrills [even him] through" (148). Starbuck is tied to history. But Ahab and Ishmael are engaged in an attempt to transcend history. While Starbuck goes whaling because he needs to earn a living, they insist on a greater cause than past circumstance and a greater necessity than commercial profit. Their shared quest is for a truth unconfined by circumstance or even ideology. Yet as mid-19th-century Americans, their faith in the existence of "unconfined Truth" is itself part and parcel of an ideology. That ideology found expression in Jeffersonian and Jacksonian democracy; so that the *Pequod*'s voyage, which in being transformed from a capitalistic venture into a metaphysical one may appear to undermine American cultural values, actually reaffirms those values.[9] The unconfined, or to echo Jefferson, "self-evident"[10] truth that all save Starbuck hunt exists in an eternal present. Because it belongs to nature and not history, it transcends the changing surface of what was and will be. The vision that seeks to find it looks beneath that surface, to what Ahab calls "the little lower layer" (144), and the attempt to realize it is a deep dive indeed. A "subterranean miner . . . works in us all," says Ishmael, as he explains why he "so aboundingly responded" to Ahab's appeal: "Who does not feel the irresistible arm drag?" (162-63).

As Ishmael's first narrative nears its close, he makes explicit the connection between his and Ahab's quests. "A wild, mystical, sympathetical feeling was in me," he writes; "Ahab's quenchless feud seemed mine" (155). Ahab thinks of himself as chosen or elect, but aboard the *Pequod,* sailing under an American flag, with a global citizenry for a crew, *all* are chosen. Ishmael sails as a common sailor, but he only considers that rank to be "beneath" any other when he views it from a "physical" or historical perspective. From a "metaphysical point of view," he contends, all are equal (15). In turn, the contrast between these two points of view is what divides his authorship. He writes his two narratives historically, and no matter how much he digresses from their plots, he concentrates on recounting "what happened"—first to himself, and then to Ahab. When he writes his exposition, however, he pays no attention at all to plot or story-line. Instead, he tries to look beneath the surface of history and circumstance to the unchanging nature of his subject, the whale's internal, self-evident composition. In short, as a character he chooses to follow Ahab because Ahab's quest echoes his own. And as an author, he chooses not only to tell the story of those quests but also to reenact them. His book's extended cetological center functions, then, as an extension of his whaling. Using pen rather than harpoon, he penetrates and dissects a whale, all because he still wants to realize the deepest truth of its lower layer.

The essential connection between Ishmael's whaling and writing is first suggested in chapter 32, "Cetology," which interrupts his narrative and serves as a sort of premonition or warning of what is to come. There he divides all the whales in all the seas into "primary BOOKS (subdivisible into CHAPTERS)," thinking that "these shall comprehend them all" (120). This association of whale and book suggests the radical shift in authorial strategy to come. By treating whales as a text, Ishmael will attempt to "read" and "comprehend" them, and his representation of this attempt will give his text expository rather than narrative form. At the same time, the desire to "comprehend them all" is what unites character and author. On board the *Pequod,* Ishmael willingly transforms his sailing from an ordinary commercial venture into an extraordinary metaphysical quest. So too, when sitting at his writing desk, he turns a relatively conventional story into an extremely unconventional analysis. His motivation in both instances is his desire to comprehend deepest truth, a desire rooted in his insistence that "some certain significance lurks in all things" (358). At issue is *how* to comprehend that significance. Ishmael knows what whales do, but he does not know what they *are,* the secrets that lie within their nature. "Unless you own the whale," he writes, speaking as much to himself as to anyone else, "you are but a provincial and sentimentalist in Truth" (285). Both of his enterprises, the character's whaling and the author's writing, are attempts at unsentimental comprehension, efforts to realize or "own" total and unconfined truth.

Ishmael spends a series of chapters shifting from narrative to exposition. He presages the transition with "Cetology," and he begins it in earnest with the five-act drama (chaps. 36-40) of Ahab's wooing the crew. In those five chapters he appears as neither character nor narrator. Instead, he separates his present consciousness from past event, and represents the action through dialogue and soliloquy, ending with the crew's drunken revelry in "Midnight, Forecastle." Although the dramatic form clearly marks a shift in authorial strategy, Ishmael continues in these chapters to advance his story. And that the story still is *his* becomes clear at the start of chapter 41, itself titled "Moby-Dick," when he writes: "I, Ishmael, was one of that crew; my shouts had gone up with the rest; my oath had been welded with theirs" (155). Yet when Ishmael returns to his role as first-person narrator here, he no longer advances the plot. Instead he looks backwards in order to explain how Ahab's desires mirrored his own. And two chapters later, having completed that explanation, he effectively takes himself as a character out of his book. Then he makes the first of his two extreme shifts in form, abandoning narrative for exposition, a story of what happened for an analysis of what is.

Chapters 41 and 42, "Moby-Dick" and "The Whiteness of the Whale," mark the end of Ishmael's first narrative.

Here he explains why he took Ahab's oath, joined Ahab's quest, and gave himself up to the abandonment of time and place. From this point on, whatever plot his book advances will center upon Ahab rather than himself. Yet since *Moby-Dick* contains virtually no plot at all for the next forty-odd chapters, Ishmael here explains not only his past action as a character but also his present action as an author—why he is about to abandon the time and place of narrative for the timeless exposition of cetology. He begins by trying to recount "the history of that murderous monster against whom I and all the others had taken our oaths of violence and revenge" (155). He soon admits, however, that he does not know the whale's history, and he starts repeating wild rumors that have no basis in fact. This absence of history is significant. Like Ahab, Ishmael is able to conceive of the whale as an "incarnation" of otherwise unconfined truth only because he does not know it in terms of space and time (160). Back in the first chapter he had written that "the whaling voyage was welcome" because, "in the wild conceits that swayed me to my purpose, two and two there floated into my inmost soul, endless processions of the whale" (16). Here he struggles to explain those conceits. "In some dim, random way, explain myself I must," he writes, "else all these chapters might be naught" (163).

The specific chapters that might prove naught are those Ishmael is just about to write, his book's ahistorical cetological center. There he sometimes tells stories (as, for example, in his accounts of the *Pequod*'s gams), but he never links these together in a single narrative line. Instead, only his authorial strategy can hold the cetological chapters together. Step by step and layer by layer, he dismembers the whale, thus creating a textual alternative to the *Pequod*'s sailing. As a character aboard ship, Ishmael was "appalled" by "the thought of [the whale's] whiteness," an "innermost idea" that intimated the presence of mysteries within (164). He followed Ahab, and thus when the story of the hunt for Moby Dick resumes, Ahab becomes its protagonist. As author, however, Ishmael first turns his back on storytelling and, for chapter after chapter, he dissects and analyzes his subject, all in an effort to realize and then express the self-evidence that lies beneath its surface. His exposition takes him deep into the whale, and with each stage, he comes closer and closer to the apparent object of his metaphysical quest.

Although as an author Ishmael again seeks to realize unconfined truth, his method is far different than Ahab's or even his own as a character. On board the *Pequod* he was "all arush to encounter the whale" (163). His quest burned with passion because, like Ahab, he was convinced that only when the whale lay dead would he be freed from "the dread in [his] soul" (155). Yet when sitting at his desk some years later, Ishmael is anything but "arush." In his book's expository middle third, he becomes dispassionate and analytic, methodical and deliberate, in this sense almost the antithesis of both Ahab and his earlier self. This difference accounts for the sudden change in tempo that has perplexed so many readers.[11] It also accounts for his decision to distance and eventually separate himself from the story he still has to tell. Ishmael is writing *after* having witnessed the failure of his and his captain's quest, and his writing is at least in part an attempt to find out *why* that quest failed. There are only two possible explanations. Perhaps something was wrong with their shared end, or perhaps something was wrong with their means. That is, either their goal was unobtainable, or their method in trying to reach it was wrong-headed. Ishmael, through writing, will find out. Hence he adopts new means to the same end, his quest now being slow and deliberate instead of fiery and furious. His goal, however, remains constant—to understand more than the superficial evidence of history, to realize shoreless, unconfined truth.

In the cetology chapters, Ishmael tries to confront the whale on its own terms, not his captain's. Yet he by no means ignores its lower layer. He dissects his subject and analyzes its physical composition, all in an effort to comprehend what that composition *means.* This is not an exercise in objective science, for he is never content with simply identifying and categorizing physical facts. Instead, he insists on interpreting those facts, making them yield something other than themselves, and his enterprise continually transcends its scientific foundation. Ishmael's interpretations are not designed, however, to be subjective hypotheses. Like Emerson's transcendental poet, he writes of "the manifold meaning of [a] sensuous fact,"[12] hoping always that his analysis of the whale's anatomy will allow him to realize the truth he pursues. That truth is of nature, *the* nature or essence of physical nature, no matter whether it be embodied in a whale or a man. Ishmael, like Ahab, does not know whether nature is agent or principal—that is, whether it is its own author or whether some greater force has authored it and decreed its meaning. He insists, however, that it is meanin*ful.* Its meaning is not beyond or outside, but is literally within; and his exposition becomes a dissection because he is after the lowest layer of the whale, the locus of its self-evidence. "Some certain significance lurks *in* all things," he declares, "else all things are little worth, and the round world itself but an empty cipher" (358, my italics).

This metaphor of "reading" runs through the cetology chapters, and Ishmael reads whatever is set before him. He does so in an orderly manner—first the blubber, then the head, then the brain, going deeper into the whale with each move. At the same time, he constantly interrupts his dissection with descriptions of the ship's business in order to explain how he knows what he does. In turn, he reads and interprets that business as something more than a commercial enterprise (which

aboard the *Pequod* it indeed is). So too with his forays into philosophy, art history, geology, physiognomy, etc., all of which are efforts to explain how to read the whale. For simply considered as a physical thing, a whale, being little more than sperm-filled flesh, is easy enough to comprehend. The difficulty comes when it is read as the embodiment of some greater truth. And the difficulty is compounded because, being composed almost entirely of blubber, the whale has no true inner or outer layer. Its surface *is* its essence, and its essence its surface, which renders it "full of strangeness, and unaccountable" to a mind intent on penetrating its deepest mysteries. "Dissect him how I may," Ishmael laments in "The Tail" (chap. 86), "I but go skin deep" (318).

Ishmael's strategy is to begin his chapters on the whale's anatomy with physical facts and end them with speculations on what those facts mean. In "The Nut" (chap. 80), for example, he starts by literally measuring the whale's skull, but concludes by observing that "the whale, like all things that are mighty, wears a false brow to the common world" (293). And in "The Blanket" (chap. 68) he carefully explains that the whale's thick blubber "is all over obliquely crossed and recrossed with numberless straight mark[ings]," signs carrying what he believes to be an "undecipherable" hidden meaning (260). Robert Greenberg argues that this meaning is itself discordant, and that "the aesthetic and philosophic goal of the cetological material is to convey a sense of epistemological fragmentation and disarray."[13] But Greenberg confuses the aim of the cetology chapters with the effect they produce. Ishmael's goal is comprehension, and only his failure to reach that goal produces fragmentation and discord. His writing provides him with a wealth of empirical data, but this data does not yield the comprehension he wants. Indeed, his encyclopedic exposition keeps raising the very problem it seeks to resolve; for as it becomes more comprehensive, the truth he seeks becomes ever more elusive. He speculates repeatedly about the whale's meaning, but he laments that his speculations are just that—guesses and hypotheses, "only . . . opinion" (259).

By the close of the cetology section, it becomes clear that Ishmael's dissection fails to provide him with the truth he seeks. It fails on the level of physical facts because, no matter that the whale is right before him, its body does not provide the evidence he needs. And it fails on the level of nature or essence, that which the whale is said to embody, because the mind that set out to read truth turns back on itself to admit that its readings are hypotheses. Ishmael considers the whale from nearly every conceivable angle of inquiry, bringing to bear on the investigation what Greenberg calls, "a farcical mass of pseudo-erudition and specialization" (2). Yet his readings become increasingly desperate and indeed satiric. He simply does not comprehend what he most wants to comprehend. And the more he considers his mighty subject, all "the more [does he] deplore [his] inability to express it" (317).

Ishmael does have one moment of transcendent glory before he admits the failure of his exposition. That euphoric moment comes in "A Squeeze of the Hand" (chap. 94), when he declares that "in visions of the night, [he] saw long rows of angels in paradise" (349). By this point the whale has been totally dismembered, the cutting and hoisting operations completed, and character and narrator come back together one last time.[14] As he describes how sperm is prepared for refining in the try-pots, Ishmael recalls a day when, "under a blue tranquil sky," he sat with his crew-mates and squeezed lumps of partially crystallized sperm back into fluid. "I declare to you," he writes, "that for the time I lived as in a musky meadow; I forgot all about our horrible oath; in that inexpressible sperm, I washed my hands and my heart of it" (348). Shifting into the present tense of his composition, he tries to explain the "abounding, affectionate, friendly, loving feeling" that replaced the memory of his vow to hunt the white whale, exclaiming euphorically: "Oh! my dear fellow beings, why should we longer cherish any social acerbeties, or know the slightest ill-humor or envy! Come . . . let us squeeze ourselves universally into the very milk and sperm of kindness" (348-49).

Ishmael's vision in "A Squeeze of the Hand" is, he thinks, a vision of shoreless, unconfined truth. He holds in his hands the sperm of the sperm whale, the evidence of its deepest self. And he momentarily believes that he comprehends the true nature of man as well as beast, the very essence of being. Hence he feels "for the time . . . divinely free" (348). Yet precisely because it exists only "for the time," this "conceit of attainable felicity" cannot be the comprehension Ishmael seeks (349). The evidence that inspires it may come from the whale's lowest layer, but it slides right through his fingers; and his vision of transcendent reverie only begins when he grasps the wrong evidence—his coworkers' hands. Those hands are not part of the whale. Instead, they are what destroy the whale, and in two chapters they will be busy tending the try-pots, transforming the sperm into the stuff of profit. When Ishmael describes them doing that, he admits his failure—not only as character, but as author as well. Then he also admits the conceit that is its cause, the same conceit that swayed him to his purpose in going whaling. "All is vanity," he says, woefully quoting Ecclesiastes. "ALL" (355).

Ishmael as author also destroys the whale, dissecting it and turning it into something that will bring him profit—his book. Since his exposition reflects his continuing desire to realize unconfined truth, his motivation is more ideological than financial. Yet his exposition is itself a form of confinement. For chapter after chapter, the whale is penned in and by Ishmael's writing; and

no matter how he textualizes it, he is unable to compel it to yield pure significance or certain meaning. Moreover, Ishmael's writing is not his alone. It has a history, as indeed does his desire (shared by both character and author) to transcend history and realize timeless truth. From the very beginning Ishmael contends that the quest for such truth is rooted in human nature itself. He declares that "almost all men" share his feelings towards the ocean, that "every robust healthy boy with a robust healthy soul" is "crazy to go to sea," and that all men and women feel "a mystical vibration" upon leaving shore for the first time. (13) But of course most people never think of the ocean in such metaphysical terms. Many healthy boys do not want to go to sea, and many people feel ill (not mystical) if they have to leave shore. Despite his claims to the contrary, Ishmael's quest clearly is not universal. His abandonment of time and place, first as character and then as author, is itself rooted in time and place—both in the specific history of the *Pequod*'s sailing and in the broader history of American ideology. Because the failure of his quest is accompanied by a realization of such, the Ishmael who writes **Moby-Dick** becomes exiled from both landed society and the company of all those who are seduced into believing that they are "divinely free." He becomes but "another orphan," someone "floating on the margin of the ensuing scene" (470).

Ishmael admits his failure in "The Try-Works" (chap. 96), which along with "A Squeeze of the Hand" marks the effective end of the expository cetological center just as "Moby Dick" and "The Whiteness of the Whale" mark its start. Afterward he returns to narrative, content to tell the story of Ahab's quest rather than his own. As with his earlier movement away from narrative, he spends some time shifting roles, gradually working his way back toward story-telling by doing what the title of one chapter calls "Stowing Down and Clearing Up" (chap. 98). But his vision of his enterprise in "The Try-Works" is what proves to him that he needs to change course. Here he sees his co-workers not as "dear fellow beings" but as "fiend shapes," and the Pequod itself as "a red hell . . . the material counterpart of her monomaniac commander's soul." As the direct opposite of transcendent reverie, this hellish vision shows him that all his previous readings, far from being avenues to timeless truth, were only personal interpretations. Consequently it begets "kindred visions in [his] soul," visions which make him suddenly "conscious of something fatally wrong." Here Ishmael moves beyond his reading of a whale to a reading of himself, both the part he plays aboard the ship and the part he plays in the book. Instead of continuing to look at the whale, he looks at *how* he has been looking up to now. "Nothing seemed before me but a jet gloom," he confesses: "Uppermost was the impression, that whatever swift, rushing thing I stood on was not so much bound to any haven ahead as rushing from all havens astern" (354).

Uppermost in Ishmael's mind two-thirds of the way through *Moby-Dick* is the realization that his authorial quest for truth has paradoxically taken him away from truth. He clearly hoped that his exposition could provide him with a comprehension that narrative could not, an awareness of "what is" as opposed to merely "what happened." Yet although the cetology chapters end up telling him a great deal about whales, they do not provide him with the truth he seeks. Indeed, in one respect they take him away from truth because away from what he already knows—the story he tells in the past tense, what exists in his metaphor as a "haven astern." Ishmael himself recognizes as much when he sees that the hell of the *Pequod*'s try-works was mirrored by a kindred hell within himself. He then admits that his exposition has not exposed his subject with certainty, just as what he found when he squeezed the whale's sperm through his fingers was not comprehensive, shoreless truth. Hence he reluctantly but quite clearly changes course and heads back—to history and narrative rather than metaphysics and exposition. As he does, he warns the reader: "Give not thyself up, then, to the fire, lest it invert thee, deaden thee; as for the time it did me. There is a wisdom that is woe; but there is a woe that is madness" (355).

The idea of the whale as spiritual essence as well as physical fact, the identification of it with pure nature, the desire to dive within and reach the lower layer—these are Ishmael's motives in the cetology chapters. So too, they are Ahab's as he drives the Pequod and its crew toward destruction. In "The Try-Works" Ishmael concludes that they are all vanity, the ideological vanity of the self-proclaimed elect. He does so because he has taken the whale apart piece by piece, only to discover that everything he found (besides sperm and blubber) was of his own making. Of course Ahab refuses to admit anything of the sort. Thus the story becomes his when Ishmael reassumes a narrative stance. And one of the first things that Ishmael details then is how "the old man's purpose intensified" over and over again: "His firm lips met like the lips of a vice; the Delta of his forehead's veins swelled like overladen brooks; in his sleep, his ringing cry ran through the vaulted hull, 'Stern all! the White Whale spouts thick blood'" (400).

"The key to it all," Ishmael writes in the very first chapter, is "the image of the ungraspable phantom of life," the same image "we ourselves see in all rivers and oceans," the same image Narcissus saw when he gazed into the fountain (14). Ahab may not care that Narcissus drowned, but Ishmael does; and because he does there are important differences between the story he tells in the final third of the novel and the story he tells in the first third. For one, his style is less playful. For another, he hardly digresses to moralize anymore, the intervals between the separate stages of Ahab's hunt becoming smaller and smaller until finally "Chase" is followed by "Chase" and then "Chase" again. But the most important difference is that whereas Ishmael is the protagonist in the first third of the novel, here he is barely even a character. Now Ahab becomes the protagonist, and *Moby-Dick* becomes the story of *his* choice. Yet that it once again is a story at all points back to Ishmael's choice, his decision to accept the realities of time and space and return to story-telling.

The narrative that Ishmael resumes in the final third of *Moby-Dick* is not only the expected story of Ahab's hunt, but also the somewhat unexpected story of Ahab's decision to make that hunt. Beginning when the carpenter makes him a new leg, moving through his defiance in "The Candles" (chap. 119), and reaching a climax when he opens his soul to Starbuck in "The Symphony" (chap. 132), Ahab dives deeper and deeper into himself. He again and again asks why—why this hunt and why this hate, why the whale and why me. He knows what alternatives are open to him, and while the choice he makes echoes the choice he made before the novel even began, he here explains why he makes it. Put simply, he regards incomprehensibility and inscrutability as personal insults, and he craves comprehension. In "The Symphony" he almost chooses to abandon his quest and return to the safe "haven astern" of his Nantucket home. But he cannot. The one thing he craves to comprehend is the one thing he does not comprehend—himself. Hence with glance averted from Starbuck to self he asks: "What is it, what nameless, inscrutable, unearthly thing is it . . . [that keeps] pushing, and crowding, and jamming [me] on all the time; recklessly making me ready to do what in my own proper, natural heart, I durst not so much as dare? Is Ahab, Ahab? Is it I, God, or who, that lifts this arm?" (445)

Ahab's choice to continue with his fiery hunt is born of precisely this uncertainty. Am I God's agent or am I my own principal? he asks, his questions echoing his earlier cry on the quarterdeck. He believes that he must kill the whale in order to solve its mystery. He believes too that once the mystery is solved and the inscrutable thing made known, he at last will comprehend himself. Thus almost immediately after he averts his gaze from Starbuck's eye, he sights Moby Dick for the first time. And when, on the second day of the chase, Starbuck implores him to "but for one single instant show [him]self," his reply is firm. "Ahab," he declares, "is forever Ahab, man" (459).

Although forever man, Ahab's "special fate" is, in Richard Brodhead's words, "to become inhuman in his assertion of humanity."[15] The truth he seeks has nothing to do with human history. "Cursed be all the things that cast man's eyes aloft to that heaven, whose live vividness but scorches him," he declares (412). Of course Moby Dick is the most prominent such thing in the book. Yet the whale itself does not cause him to cast his eyes aloft. Instead, as with Ishmael, the innermost *idea* of the whale impels him to question who he is and to search after an omniscient certainty that transcends time and place. "Towards thee I roll, thou all-destroying but unconquering whale," says Ahab at the very end; "to the last I grapple with thee; from hell's heart I stab at thee; for hate's sake I spit my last breath at thee" (468). But the white whale only responds by sounding and diving, sounding and diving, unharmed and still unknown. And Ahab, forever man, dies forever unsure.

At the close of **Moby-Dick,** the whale, when considered from a metaphysical point of view, remains inscrutable. Yet it is not at all inscrutable when considered in terms of the sea rather than whatever ideas the sea might inspire. Because Ishmael's return to narrative promotes a physical or historical point of view, it implicitly indicts his and Ahab's shared attempt to locate "what is" in a more certain lower layer. While he concludes the book without realizing (or being able to express) unconfined truth, he offers instead the history of his captain and himself, the story of how the one perished and the other survived.

Ishmael's achievement as an author is not, then, a victory of art over life—what Edgar Dryden calls a movement away "from both nature and society" to "a fanciful world of his own creation" (112). The world he presents in the final third of his book is not at all a product of his imagination. Instead, it is part of history, and in presenting it he writes from a point of view that is confined by the changing verities of time and place. The only question that remains unanswered is whether this point of view will suffice. On the one hand, the simple fact that Ishmael survived the Pequod's wreck suggests that it must. He contends in his epilogue that he survived "only . . . to tell thee" (470), and although his "telling" is divided, he concludes by choosing narrative and history over exposition and metaphysics. On the other hand, the story he tells depicts failed means, not a failed end. Ishmael may consider Ahab's quest the epitome of vanity, but he can neither change nor escape the fact that he too desires to transcend history's uncertainty. In this view, the story that culminates with the three-day chase for Moby Dick is only a superficial record, the more essential truth of the matter remaining concealed in the "howling infinite" and "open independence" of the ocean depths (97).

Such of course would be Ahab's view. More importantly, such indeed *was* Ishmael's view—not only when he sailed aboard the *Pequod,* but also when he returned home. Ishmael claims that he survived in order to write; but this suggestion of an unbroken connection between experience and authorship is misleading because, before he sat down to write, he went to sea again.[16] He speaks of one such voyage as he makes his transition away from exposition and back to narrative, in a chapter titled

"A Bower in the Arsacides" (chap. 102). There he remembers sailing to a South Sea island and "reading all the contents" of a whale's skeleton, one which the natives used as both a chapel and a god (373). This "reading" echoes Ahab's failure and prefigures his own, since when he "dived within" he "saw no living thing." He marvelled at the vanity of the priests who lit fires on their altars, and swore that the smoke ascending from the whale's spout was genuine, for he saw that "naught was there but bones" (375). Nonetheless, when he finally did sit down to write, some years afterwards, Ishmael tried one last time to see more than bone or blubber. Using new means, he read and interpreted his subject, only to reach the same end that he did on the *Pequod,* in the Arsacides, and countless times before. His final view, then, is not at all what it was when he escaped the *Pequod*'s wreck. When he returns to narrative as an author, he is forced to choose, albeit reluctantly, history and shore, the safety of that known "haven astern." And implicit in his choice is his theme, the theme that holds all three of **Moby-Dick**'s "books" together. Mad or sane, fiery or dispassionate, the search for timeless, unconfined truth is not a condition of human nature but a conceit of ideology. It is itself a product of history, and it is all vanity, ALL.

Notes

1. Evert A. Duyckinck, "Melville's *Moby-Dick; or, The Whale,*" in *Moby-Dick,* ed. Harrison Hayford and Hershel Parker (New York: Norton, 1967), 613-14. Hereafter, "Hayford and Parker." All subsequent quotations from *Moby-Dick* are taken from this edition.

2. Feeling "rather sore," Melville admitted in a letter to Hawthorne: "What I feel most moved to write, that is banned,—it will not pay. Yet, altogether, write the *other* way I cannot. So the product is a final hash . . .": in Hayford and Parker, 557-58. The "other way," it is safe to assume, would be the undivided form of narrative romance, a form that, then as now, can pay quite well.

3. Nina Baym, "Melville's Quarrel With Fiction," *PMLA* 94 (1979):909-23.

4. As William Dillingham observes, one can avoid becoming ensnared in the critical debate over *Moby-Dick*'s point of view by thinking of Ishmael as the fictional author while at the same time recognizing that his concerns are Melville's own: *Melville's Later Novels* (Athens, GA: U of Georgia P, 1986), 1-2.

5. Whether narrative is necessary for historical understanding is today an open theoretical question. Of course, it was not so in Melville's day.

6. The phrase is M. M. Bakhtin's from "Discourse in the Novel," in *The Dialogic Imagination,* trans.

M. Holquist and C. Emerson (Austin: U of Texas P, 1981), 295.

7. Edgar Dryden, *Melville's Thematics of Form* (Baltimore: Johns Hopkins UP, 1968), chap. 3; Paul Brodtkorb, *Ishmael's White World* (New Haven: Yale UP, 1965), chap. 6.

8. Carolyn Porter, "Call Me Ishmael, or How to Make Double-Talk Speak," in *New Essays on Moby-Dick*, ed. Richard Brodhead (Cambridge: Cambridge UP, 1986), 94.

9. For a more detailed examination of American ideology and values in these terms, see Sacvan Bercovitch, *The American Jeremiad* (Madison: U of Wisconsin P, 1978), esp. chap. 8.

10. When Jefferson declared "these truths" to be "self-evident," he employed a long-standing philosophical distinction between propositions whose truth-value depends upon empirical evidence (e.g., "this apple is red") and propositions whose truth-value depends upon the logic of their own terms (e.g., "all men are created equal"). He did not simply mean "obvious."

11. These readers often have been distinguished authors in their own right. Van Wyck Brooks, for instance, complained that "no book could be more exasperating" than *Moby-Dick* since the author "loses himself in the details of cetology" and the characters disappear "for hundreds of pages in the middle." And George Santayana admitted that he gave up trying to read it when, "in spite of much skipping, [he] got stuck in the middle": see *Moby-Dick as Doubloon,* ed. Hershel Parker and Harrison Hayford (New York: Norton, 1970), 145, 173.

12. Ralph Waldo Emerson, "The Poet," in *Essays and Lectures* (New York: Library of America, 1983), 447.

13. Robert Greenberg, "Cetology: Center of Multiplicity and Discord in *Moby-Dick*," *ESQ* [*Emerson Society Quarterly*] 27 (1981):1.

14. Although character and narrator come back together for the next few chapters, Ishmael cannot be said to have returned to his narrative. He does not advance a plot or extend a story-line, but instead uses isolated experiences to illustrate his theme.

15. Richard Brodhead, *Hawthorne, Melville, and the Novel* (Chicago: U of Chicago P, 1976), 145.

16. In this, Ishmael resembles no one more than Bulkington, who comes ashore only to leave again. Bulkington, however, is silent, and Ishmael stops being silent when he comes ashore permanently to write his book.

John J. Staud (essay date December 1992)

SOURCE: Staud, John J. "*Moby-Dick* and Melville's Vexed Romanticism." *American Transcendental Quarterly* n.s. 6, no. 4 (December 1992): 279-93.

[*In the following essay, Staud discusses Melville's attitudes toward Romanticism in* Moby-Dick, *paying particular attention to his ambivalence toward Romantic conceptions of nature and the self. Staud contends that the absolute destruction that occurs at the novel's conclusion represents Melville's repudiation of Romantic ideals.*]

"Give not thyself up, then, to fire, lest it invert thee, deaden thee; as for the time it did me."

At first, it may appear that Herman Melville's critique of romanticism obeys the conventional division of romantic writers into a party of nature and a party of consciousness. Melville, of course, condemns both the acolytes of nature and of self. In his well-known jibes at Goethe's "All feeling" he mocks, in a letter to Nathaniel Hawthorne of June 1851, the inapplicability of an ideal melding of the human and the natural to the inescapable details of ordinary life:

> In reading some of Goethe's sayings, so worshipped by his votaries, I came across this, "Live in the all." That is to say, your separate identity is but a wretched one,—good; but get out of yourself, spread and expand yourself, and bring to yourself the tinglings of life that are felt in the flowers and the woods, that are felt in the planets Saturn and Venus, and the Fixed Stars. What nonsense! Here is a fellow with a raging toothache. "My dear boy," Goethe says to him, "you are sorely afflicted with that tooth; but you must *live in the all,* and then you will be happy!" As with all great genius, there is an immense deal of flummery in Goethe, and in proportion to my own contact with him, a monstrous deal of it in me.

(*Letters* [*The Letters of Herman Melville*] 130-131)

Then too, he acknowledges in a postscript the thrillingly real moments when the self at once melts and is absorbed into nature: "That 'all' feeling, though, there is some truth in. You must have often felt it lying on the grass on a warm summer's day. Your legs seem to send out shoots onto the earth. Your hair feels like leaves upon your head. This is the *all* feeling" (*Letters* 131). Though he admits its occurrence, Melville decries a philosophy built out of such evanescent experiences: "[W]hat plays mischief with the truth is that men will insist upon a universal application of a temporary feeling or opinion" (*Letters* 131). The party of consciousness, of a self-assertive heroism in which the highest deity is seen to be a possible attainment for the human personality, fares no better with Melville. He saw Emerson, the American prophet of romantic self-reliance, as problematic indeed.[1] "Alas! the fool again!" writes

Melville in his copy "Heroism," in the margin next to an underlined passage of Emerson, "heroism feels and never reasons, and therefore is always right" (Cowen 18). In his fiction, Ahab stands as Melville's most complex and complete rebuttal to the party of consciousness. The allure of Ahab's energy as he thrusts his being into defiance of Nature, as I will argue in greater detail, fades in light of the political consequences of his single-minded quest. Like the "all" feeling, the self-absorbed consciousness has an appeal both transitory and dangerous.[2]

In *Moby-Dick* Melville confounds the opposition of the two Romantic strains in a critique of both as equally seductive prescriptions for self-fulfillment that delude and threaten individual identity and, finally, the larger community. Viewed together as a sequence of chapters whose choreographed ordering reveals the stages of Ishmael's inner development—an inner development marked by narrow escape from the pitfalls which destory Ahab and the crew—"The Mast-Head," "The Quarter-Deck," "The Castaway," "A Squeeze of the Hand," and "The Try-Works" can be seen to dramatize the moral and political disaster looming behind the enactment in the world of experience of these seemingly disparate, but frightfully similar, elements of Romanticism. These pitfalls are carefully designed to show that both elements emphasize the relationship of the self with the natural world, that is, all phenomena external to individual consciousness, in such a way that other human beings are objectified as phenomena.[3] In *Moby-Dick* Melville has Ishmael come to discern a paradoxical solipsism bound up with this abandonment of the self: "living in the all" and radical self-assertion are two sides of the same coin. Both entail debilitating isolation from the human community, as Melville criticizes Romantic self-fashioning in fundamentally moral and social terms. In these orchestrated chapters, Ishmael's growing insight frames Ahab as a self-reliant tyrant who welds the *Pequod*'s crew, and even the ship itself, into union with his fiery will, exposing the perils confronting both individuals and cultures in the embrace of Romantic conceptions of the self.

Melville announces his specific quarrel with Romanticism in "The Mast-Head," a chapter where Melville criticizes the extension of self into "the all" in a transparent caricature of Transcendental philosophy. In *Mardi* and *White-Jacket,* Melville uses the spatial separation between the mast-head and the deck below to dramatize escape from social duties and cares. As early as *Mardi* he even connects the space above the deck to Romantic subjectivity by alluding to Byron: "Manfred-like, you talk to the clouds; you have a fellow feeling for the sun" (27). Yet even in earlier works, Melville takes care not to idealize the world aloft, illustrating its danger through White-Jacket's near-fatal plunge and, in *Redburn,* Jackson's death-dive. In "The Mast-Head,"

Melville yokes these opposed visions within the same chapter, using sequence as a means to strip away the blissful mask of Transcendentalism and reveal its face of terror. Perched high above the sea on a balmy, blue day, Ishmael loses himself in transcendental daydreams: "In this enchanted mood, thy spirit ebbs away to whence it came; becomes diffused through time and space. . . . lulled into such an opium-like listlessness of vacant, unconscious reverie is this absent minded youth by the blending of cadence of waves with thoughts, that at last he loses his identity" (140). The connection to Romantic figures like Coleridge and DeQuincey is strengthened by the phrase "opium-like listlessness," which also evokes a sense of the moral lassitude associated with such yielding of one's powers of discernment and judgment.[4] Enchanting as the Sirens, and as ominous, this precarious self-dissolution jars Ishmael into awareness that allowing the self to be subsumed by the natural world is fraught with danger. Nature is not permanently benevolent. Ishmael's insight prompts a sermon-like admonition against transcendent immersion in nature, in which he equates his experience with self-forgetful sleep to suggest the problem of utter loss of identity in the rarified "all": "But while this sleep is on ye, move your foot or hand an inch; slip your hold at all; and your identity comes back in horror" (140). The "Descartian vortices" over which Ishmael hovers point ironically to the danger of splitting the mind from the body by recalling the philosopher who proposed their distinction. As in his ridicule for Goethe, Melville locates physical pain—in this case, death—as the inescapable reminder that real identity remains bounded by corporeal limits.

To augment the unforeseen danger in yielding to the "all," Melville is careful to dress nature in all its seeming benevolence. All images describe a fair setting—it is "summer . . . at mid-day, in the fairest weather." Airy flight belies the solid reality of the ship's deck and liquid, sharkish ocean; even the most pleasant transcendental reverie has the potential for self-destruction. Melville need not invoke the "toothache" side of nature in this case; doom can occur even when nature appears most innocuous, precisely because the "all" feeling results from an interpretation of nature that excludes its darker sides. By admonishing "ye Pantheists" at chapter's end, Melville classifies the error in the language of religious heresy. For the moment at least, Melville finds it convenient to ally himself in tone with orthodox Christianity, seeing nature, and the natural self ennobled in Romantic thought, as vexed. That Christian tradition holds noon to be the time of the Fall is not lost on Melville, as an orthodox moral fall into sin echoes within Ishmael's imminent fall from the mast-head due to self-dissolution in nature. In a sense Ishmael's noontime interpretation resembles a natural theology in which nature evinces God's goodness, a theology that draws its tenets from dancing daffodils and ignores tempests. Melville's insight recalls his insistence to

Hawthorne that "a universal application of a temporary feeling or opinion . . . plays mischief with the truth." For it is not so much the vision itself which Ishmael comes to denounce, but the very act of relinquishing one's reason and will in escapist fantasy. As Ishmael comes to realize, the material world he wanted to dissolve into can return with frightful immediacy and dire consequences if one takes a part for the whole, a glimpse for a gaze.

This unmasking sequence within "The Mast-Head" opens on a larger sequential paradigm in which chapters are ordered to show that the parties of nature and consciousness are, at root, synonymous and deadly. With "the Mast-Head," Melville also calls attention to the importance of chapter sequence as a semantic structure. This chapter inaugurates a series of chapters linked by the presence of prefatory stage directions, which set the five chronologically organized scenes of one day aboard the *Pequod*. For after Ishmael's noontime reverie, the next five chapters follow the day like a clock: "The Quarter-Deck," "Sunset," "Dusk," "First Night Watch," "Forecastle,—Midnight." The dialogue of chapter sequence allows Melville to nuance, to qualify, previous ideological propositions. Far from being random or episodic, Melville's chapter ordering carries an idea from one realm to another and probes the consequences, in this case enabling him to extend his critique of Romantic notions of the self from metaphysical musings in the empyrean to the *Pequod*'s deck and the messy world of politics and ethics. Engaged as he is in "The Mast-Head" at exposing the threat to identity posed by Transcendental philosophy, Melville deepens his warning about the dangers of melding with the all by exemplifying the social hazards bound up with the forfeiture of consciousness, conscience, and will. This political lesson is borne out by Melville's strategic placement of "The Quarter-Deck" immediately after "The Mast-Head." Ahab's successful exhortation to the crew to take their bitter oath of vengeance upon Moby-Dick, in which he crushes Starbuck's vain opposition, highlights the political disaster that can result from self-abandonment.

Ahab's tyrannical will defines the political and social universe on the *Pequod*. Hence "living in the all" for the crew aboard the *Pequod* implies yielding to the coercion of its monomaniacal captain. High above the deck Ishmael has just experienced how "the all" feeling can not only delude but destroy one's identity. The lesson is valid on the deck as well. That the crew, a collection of "Isolatoes," embrace Ahab's tyranny only underscores Melville's belief that despotism often depends on the willingness of the people to yield their freedom to an alluring self-forgetfulness. Ishmael escapes physical death by regaining consciousness above the ship only to relinquish it to Ahab's version of nature aboard the *Pequod*. Near loss of identity in the empyreal "all"

softens Ishmael for easy acquiescence to a tyrant's will on the political deck. Social and political enslavement are likely to ensue from a blind devotion to a hero, suggesting Melville's deep skepticism of such a work as Carlyle's *On Heroes* [*On Heroes, Hero = Worship and the Heroic in History*], which urges whole societies to follow the Great Man. That the *Pequod* ultimately sinks in a great vortex recalls Ishmael's recognition of "Descartian vortices" atop the masthead, thereby connecting the ship's demise with the crew's capitulation to a tyranny defined by Ahab's obsessive will. Certainly Ahab's Faust-like drive is a critical commonplace, but Melville's juxtaposition of "The Mast-Head" and "The Quarter-Deck" underscores the role played by the crew which submits to a "great man's" vision of nature as adversary and identifies Ishmael's political submission as an outgrowth of his dabblings in pantheistic metaphysics.

"The Mast-Head" nonetheless represents an important stage in Ishmael's development because it initiates his resilience, his ability to recover from a potentially disastrous loss of identity and learn a valuable lesson. To be sure, Ishmael's "shouts had gone up with the rest" in concession to Ahab's will, but "the dread in [his] soul" indicates an awareness of what he had done (155). In fact, Ishmael's recovery from his isolated reverie informs the later chapter sequence of "The Castaway," "A Squeeze of the Hand," and "The Try-Works"—chapters that connect the need for human bonds with the necessity of duty toward others. In Ishmael's growing recognition of the psychological perils of isolation we see Melville's suspicion of a solitude so enthusiastically valued in Romantic literature.

In *Nature,* for example, Emerson affirms the self-fulfilling value of contemplating nature in solitude. So important is solitude in Emerson's philosophy that he makes it the first point in the essay's first chapter: "To go into solitude, a man needs to retire as much from his chamber as from society. . . . If a man would be alone, let him look at the stars" (188). For Emerson, contemplation of nature's most vast dimension, "the stars," prompts a salutary appreciation of the sublime. Melville portrays nature's immensity in wholly different terms in "The Castaway." Announcing its theme in its title, this chapter describes Pip's abandonment in the middle of the ocean. Like the setting that induced Ishmael's reverie on the masthead, "It was a beautiful, bounteous, blue day" exemplifying nature's most splendid aspect (346). Yet the solitude, the solitude of Emerson's *Nature* taken to its experiential extreme, overwhelms Pip and causes him to go mad. Emerson places the vastness of the stars at a respectful distance; Melville shows what can happen when that vast sublime engulfs the puny self: "In calm weather, to swim in the open ocean is as easy to the practiced swimmer as to ride in a spring-carriage ashore. But the loneliness is intolerable.

The intense concentration of self in the middle of such a heartless immensity, my God! who can tell it?" (347). The adjective "heartless" sums up nature's absolute indifference towards humanity, pointing to the problems of basing one's identity on a dialectic with a nature that ignores human contact. Emerson's stars reside at a safe distance; available through sight, not touch, they stimulate, not threaten, the mind. But when the sublime becomes immediate and tactile, as the ocean does for Pip, the touch of nature proves too much for the mind to process without the supporting comfort of human contact. Later in *Nature,* Emerson elaborates the benefits of experiencing nature in solitude: "So shall we come to look at the world with new eyes" (222). In this Melville concurs, for Pip attains "celestial thought" as his soul is "carried down alive to wondrous depths" (347). But this episode constitutes a gruesome critique of solitary plummets into nature, as Pip's deeper vision is attained at the cost of a fractured mind and tortured soul.

Emerson's emphasis on that solitude which verges on self-reliance lies at the root of Melville's discomfort with his Romanticism. Like his friend Hawthorne, Melville invariably sees absence of human contact as a horrible affliction.[5] Isolation threatens or destroys healthy identity as early as "The Counter-Pane," where Ishmael tells of the horror of being consigned to his room by his step-mother. This pattern becomes a paradigm in "The Mast-Head," "The Castaway," and "The Try-Works." In this sense Pip's abandonment comments on both Ishmael and Ahab. At the outset of the novel, Ishmael, like his biblical namesake, is himself a castaway bereft of human companionship. A fate like Pip's may well have been his had Queequeg not befriended him. Ishmael's "marriage" with Queequeg is the single most important factor in a maturation process whose extent is displayed by the symbolism of his survival. Friendship teaches Ishmael to achieve a proper attitude toward nature, as the salvific presence of Queequeg's coffin prevents him from drowning.

On the other hand, the neurosis resulting from isolation climaxes in Ahab, who has confronted the immensity of nature in Moby-Dick and maintains a self-willed exile from any human contact that threatens to soften his heart. The lone exception, and a partial one at that, Pip touches Ahab's "humanities" because he has as intensely encountered the vast mystery of nature and bears a madness to show for it: "Thou touchest my inmost center, boy; thou art tied to me by cords woven of my heart-strings" (428). Yet Pip's madness is distinguished from Ahab's, for Ahab refuses to accept the "indifferent . . . God" at the center of Pip's vision. His refusal to admit to an indifferent deity reflects a deep solipsism, a solipsism which causes him to strike at a malevolent god of his own construction. Hence his obsession with killing Moby-Dick. Ultimately this obsession overwhelms Ahab's bond with Pip, for he threatens to kill

the poor boy before allowing him to melt his forged will: "Like cures like; and for this hurt, my malady most becomes my most desired health. . . . Weep so and I will murder thee! have a care, for Ahab too is mad" (436). In this light, the final words of "the Castaway"—" . . . in the sequel of the narrative, it will then be seen what like abandonment befell myself"—do more than prefigure Ishmael's survival at the end (347). This specific foreshadowing demonstrates how Ishmael's inner development highlights Ahab's solitary, inverted self. Unlike Pip and Ahab, he endures his abandonment on Queequeg's coffin without succumbing to madness.

Representative of the way Melville plays chapters against one another, "A Squeeze of the Hand" follows "The Castaway" to underscore the need for human companionship. Overcome by "a strange sort of insanity" while squeezing sperm with his shipmates, Ishmael undergoes a baptism that cleanses his animosity towards others: "I washed by hands and my heart of it. . . . I felt divinely free from all ill-will, or petulance, or malice, of any sort whatsoever" (348). His mention of a "strange sort of insanity" recalls his reverie atop the masthead, but he melts with *others* rather than an ethereal other, a central distinction that indicates his insight into the value of human fellowship. In keeping with the chapter's title, Ishmael's vision is prompted by the sense of touch rather than sight, the sense most detached from direct physical contact, and the sense that triggered his purely intellectual contemplation atop the mast-head:

> Such an abounding, affectionate, friendly, loving feeling did this avocation beget; that at last I was continually squeezing their hands, and looking up into their eyes sentimentally; as much as to say,—Oh! my dear fellow beings, why should we longer cherish any social acerbities, or know the slightest ill-humor or envy! . . . Would that I could keep squeezing that sperm forever! For now, since by many prolonged, repeated experiences, I have perceived that in all cases man must eventually lower, or at least shift, his conceit of attainable felicity; not placing it anywhere in the intellect or the fancy; but in the wife, the heart, the bed, the table, the saddle, the fire-side, the country; now that I have perceived all this, I am ready to squeeze case eternally.
>
> (349)

"A Squeeze of the Hand" parallels "The Mast-Head" to the extent that both chapters revel in dreamy detachment from the mechanized slaughter and dissection aboard the *Pequod*. But the parallel ultimately diverges. Ishmael's domestic catalogue—"the wife, the heart, the bed, the table"—talks back with tactile persuasion to the abstract and solitary ruminations above the ship. "The Mast-Head" is explicitly directed at "Pantheists" such as Goethe and Emerson, for high above the deck where the crew walk, Ishmael finds "asylum . . . [from] the carking cares of earth" in a dreamy space devoid of human presence (139). While "A Squeeze of the Hand" does present an unattainable ideal, its spatial and social location—on the deck and bound up with human fellowship—is in the plane of daily experience unlike "The Mast-Head." Here the transcendence is prompted, literally and figuratively, by fellow feeling rather than philosophic or aesthetic contemplation of nature. It does not reside "in the intellect or the fancy"; it is not prompted by sight but by touch, the most intimate of all senses. It counters Emerson, in whose writings human "others" are conspicuously absent amid exhortations to merge with the "other." "Alms to sots," he cries in "Self-Reliance," where he displays only contempt for traditional notions of charity: "I tell thee, thou foolish philanthropist, that I grudge the dollar, the dime, the cent, I give to such men as do not belong to me and to whom I do not belong" (261). Though Melville also held suspicions about philanthropy as a substitute for genuine charity, the rhetorical intensity of Emerson's repudiation of generous impulses accompanies his narrow and divisive vision of community and communal obligations. Even when the mellowing Emerson urges charity in "Experience," his laconic "if" and "perhaps" contrast the hyperbolic certitude of "Self-Reliance": "Let us treat the men and women well: treat them as if they were real: perhaps they are" (335).

Melville finds problematic this Romanticism that emphasizes the intellect at the expense of human contact and love. He typically figures this potential conflict in physical terms, as a dichotomy between the head and the heart, in his fiction, marginalia, and letters. "The brains grow maggoty without a heart; but the heart's the preserving salt itself, and can keep sweet without the head," he writes in *Pierre* (361). Marginalia in Melville's copy of "The Poet" yields specific evidence of his disquiet with Emerson over his preoccupation with the head. He brackets with a vertical line Emerson's claim that the poet "comes one step nearer than any other" to reviving language that has become "fossil poetry," in which tropes no longer "remind us of their poetic origins." At the bottom of the page Melville contends: "This is admirable, as many other thoughts of Mr. Emerson's are. His gross and astonishing errors and illusions spring from a self-conceit so intensely intellectual and calm that at first one hesitates to call it by its right name. Another species of Mr. Emerson's errors, or rather, blindness, proceeds from a defect in the region of the heart" (Cowen 27-28). In the letter where he criticizes Goethe, Melville identifies, and in fact questions, the heartless intellectual as a commonplace: "It is a frightful poetical creed that the cultivation of the brain eats out the heart. But it's my *prose* opinion that in most cases, in those men who have fine brains and work them well, the heart extends down to the hams" (*Letters* 129). But Melville's discomfort is evident as

he recinds his claim with exuberance: "I stand for the heart. To the dogs with the head! I had rather be a fool with a heart than a Jupiter Olympus with his head" (*Letters* 129).

Aside from its placement immediately after Pip's separation from human contact and its consistency with Melville's emphasis on human intimacy, Ishmael's vision in "A Squeeze of the Hand" is further validated by its internal narrative sequence. Unlike the reveries in "The Mast-Head" and "The Try-Works," from which Ishmael awakens and immediately concludes with a sermon-like admonition to avoid his dangerous dreams, he never recants his ideal vision of squeezing sperm. Nor does he describe it as a drifting into sleep as he does in the earlier moments of self-forgetfulness. Instead, he plunges back into the description of the whale's production, expressing an awareness that his vision is only ideal by concluding the chapter with a reference to the dismembered toes of the blubber-men, a far cry indeed from the impression of his fingers elongating in the sperm, where they began "to serpentine and spiralize" (348). Sharon Cameron argues that this episode "punishes the wish behind the fantasy" out of "fury at its unfulfillment" (59). Certainly the dichotomy between Ishmael's imaginings and the sober realism of the blubber room implies that the world of hunting and manufacturing, and its dismemberment of nature, has its origin inside the human character. Once again the sharkish sea is mirrored on the *Pequod* and precludes any lasting fulfillment of Ishmael's ideal. But Cameron fails to note that "the wish behind the fantasy" provides an antidote to the mast-head and try-works ideals, *as* ideals. Melville debunks the possibility that universal squeezing of hands can heal the severed bodies and bonds in the world of experience, but vision remains valid as a vision. Here is one instance in the novel where a reverie is not derided for endangering its practitioner. Scarce toes among blubbermen remind Ishmael not to become intoxicated with hope, but he is not jolted from his trance by a personal brush with death as he is in "The Mast-Head" and "The Try-Works." A line of asterisks marks this break in the text, a silent spot that provides abrupt transition into a more matter-of-fact description of the manufacturing process. Ishmael's sudden departure from his musings and his quick resumption of the narrative line describing the whale's dissection can be seen as a strategy to maintain the beauty and promise of true fellowship while admitting that it could never be permanently achieved aboard the *Pequod*.[6]

While Ishmael's euphoria is indeed temporary, his vision of communal bliss presents a humanizing alternative to the radical individualism embodied in Ahab, and within the larger Romantic tradition, to the solitary pastorals of Emerson and Thoreau, the lonely wanderings of Byron's Manfred and Childe Harold, and the aloof heroism of Carlyle's Great Man. Self-imposed banishment is the problematic common denominator for both the parties of nature and consciousness. Signalling Ishmael's growing insight, "A Squeeze of the Hand" italicizes the resistance to human touch that characterizes Ahab's inverted moral world. Ahab has lost more than toes, and his torn body symbolizes his severance from other members of the larger body politic. But the symbolic conclusion of dismembering, though apt for Ahab, is not inevitable. Ivory-armed Captain Boomer enjoys a jovial friendship with Bunger, a counterexample that physical dismemberment need not produce a vengeful obsession that cuts human bonds, or apropos Ahab, tightens them into bonds of slavery, in order to strike back at the source of the suffering. The thought of Ahab squeezing sperm with his crew is absurd. His men are literally *his* men, real to him only as tools bent to his "fixed purpose . . . laid with iron rails" (147). In "Sunset," in the aftermath of his demogogic captivation of the crew in "The Quarter-Deck," Ahab delivers a soliloquy laden with technological imagery that conveys his mastery over men reduced to machines, his total control of their no-longer separate or free wills: "I thought to find one stubborn, at the least; but my cogged circle fits into all their various wheels, and they revolve" (147). Given the chance to restore separated humanity by helping the *Rachel* search for her missing children, Ahab opts for heartless refusal. When, for a brief moment in "The Symphony," "a mild, mild wind, and a mild looking sky" elicit Ahab's lament for his solitary life and the "poor girl" he "widowed . . . when [he] married her" (443), we recall as potentially salvific Ishmael's domestic ideal from "A Squeeze of the Hand," which stresses "the wife, the heart, the bed. . . ." Ahab bewails his self-willed isolation with metaphors of walls and enslavement, not only recalling his comparision in "The Quarter-Deck" of the white whale to a "wall" that impedes him, but describing the political reality of the *Pequod*: "When I think of this life I have led; the desolation of solitude it has been; the masoned, walled-town of a captain's exclusiveness, which admits but small entrance to any sympathy from the green country without—oh, weariness! heaviness! Guinea-coast slavery of solitary command! . . . Stand close to me, Starbuck; let me look into a human eye; it is better than to gaze into the sea or sky; better than to gaze upon God" (443-444). At this moment of choice Ahab's language contrasts nature's most mysterious and sublime aspects, "the sea or sky," with the "human eye." Contact with elemental nature, indeed, with its very creator, cannot compare with human intimacy. Ahab knows this well; too well, perhaps, for he flees this temptation to forego his quest and excuses his obsession as having been decreed by some "hidden lord and master . . . that against all natural lovings and longings, so I keep pushing" (445). Even Ahab realizes that the desire for human love is "natural." Yet his longing for "the humanities"

which Peleg attributes to him, like his contact with the clinging Pip, so threatens to soften his resolve to hunt down Moby-Dick that he hardens his heart even further and steels himself for the final confrontation, without mercy for the whale, his crew, and his wife and child at home.

If "The Symphony" contains Ahab's insight into the value of domestic love, expressed in a manner strongly akin to Ishmael's in "A Squeeze of the Hand," "The Try-Works" describes Ishmael's nearly disastrous apprehension of Ahab's dark vision of nature. Following "A Squeeze of the Hand," "The Try-Works" intensifies the contrast between Ishmael's moral growth and Ahab's tyranny. While both characters receive insight into the importance of "the milk and sperm of kindness," only Ishmael is able to recover from his foray into the dark side of nature (349). While "The Mast-Head" describes Ishmael's seductive midday vision, "The Try-Works" reveals his midnight peril, where his glimpse of the hellish world the *Pequod* has become under Ahab takes on a Poe-like surrealism:

> The burning ship drove on, as if remorselessly commissioned to some vengeful deed . . . the ship groaned and dived, and yet steadfastly shot her red hell further and further into the blackness of the sea and the night, and scornfully champed the white bone in her mouth, and viciously spat round her on all sides; then the rushing *Pequod,* freighted with savages, and laden with fire, and burning a corpse, and plunging into that blackness of darkness, seemed the material counterpart of her monomaniac commander's soul.
>
> (353-354)

More than a passive hell, the *Pequod* is personified as an active agent of evil "remorselessly commissioned to some vengeful deed," which is how Ahab perceives Moby-Dick. Indeed, it is arguable that here the *Pequod* represents Satan himself, particularly in light of the close connection between Ishmael's vision of the ship "scornfully champ[ing]" and "viciously [spitting]" and Dante's portrayal of Satan chewing Judas, Cassius, and Brutus in the *Inferno:* "With six eyes he was weeping and over three chins dripped tears and bloody foam. In each mouth he crushed a sinner with his teeth as with a heckle and thus he kept three of them in pain" (423). Cast in satanic terms, the *Pequod* both commits evil and suffers punishment. Melville's emphasis on the *Pequod* as an *active* extension of Ahab's soul rather than a mere site of oppression suggests the power of his will to co-opt those of his crew to his own. "The Try-Works" thus portrays a transcendental dissolution of self into a wholly diabolical nature, a nature blithely ignored in the Transcendental "pantheism" caricatured in "The Mast-Head." That the ship "seemed the material counterpart of her monomaniac commander's soul" gives a dark twist to Emerson's contention in "The Poet" that "the Universe is an externalization of the soul" (312).

Melville again literalizes Emersonian ideas to expose the political reality they imply, for Ahab turns the *Pequod* into the evil it believes it is chasing. Foreshadowing the crew's eventual demise, "The Try-Works" also harks back to "The Quarter-Deck," when they resigned their identities to the depraved universe of the *Pequod*. This results, as Mark Patterson persuasively argues, in a crew that comes to resemble Moby-Dick: "the undifferentiated monomaniacal crew, mirroring the whale they seek to kill . . . is the human analogue to the creation of the whale's whiteness out of all colors" (295). Actually the *Pequod* does not mirror Moby-Dick as much as Ahab's conception of his adversary; "The Try-Works" strongly intimates that Ahab's midnight vision of nature is the very thing that drives him to "strike through the mask" at Moby-Dick. Gene Bluestein underscores the disparity between this view of nature's malevolence and the benevolent universe of Emerson's early writings, implying a direct connection between identity and the way the self interprets the external world: "Ahab is clearly a Transcendentalist, but because he chooses a totally different set of natural facts to read for his spiritual truths, the resulting epiphanies are dark rather than ecstatically benign like Emerson's" (106). In Melville's vexed romanticism, however, Emersonian epiphanies are anything but benign, for they distort reality and threaten the integrity of the self. Ishmael testifies against such naivete in "The Mast-Head" and broadens its malignity in subsequent chapters.

Recalling "The Mast-Head," Ishmael in "The Try-Works" temporarily succumbs to a sleep that symbolizes his ebbing resistance to the urge to melt with nature in self-abandonment: "The continual sight of the fiend shapes before me, capering half in smoke and half in fire, these at last begat kindred visions in my soul, so soon as I began to yield to that unaccountable drowsiness which ever would come over me at a midnight helm" (354). Also like his reverie atop the mast, Ishmael awakens just in time. But his different assessment of these reveries reveals a marked development, one which displays the progress he has made in coming to understand the importance of the human "other." Unlike a plummet from the mast-head, which is fatal only to oneself, falling asleep at the tiller jeopardizes the entire crew: "Convulsively my hands grasped the tiller, but with the crazy conceit that the tiller was, somehow, in some enchanted way, inverted. My God! what is the matter with me? Lo! in my brief sleep I had turned myself about, and was fronting the ship's stern, with my back to the prow and the compass. In an instant I faced back, just in time to prevent the vessel from flying up into the wind, and very probably capsizing her" (354). Ishmael has come to see the danger of an identity so enamored of dissolving into the "all" that it neglects communal responsibility: "Look not too long in the face of fire, O man! never dream with thy hand on the helm! turn not thy back to the compass; accept the first hint of the hitching tiller; believe not the artificial fire, when its redness makes things looks ghastly" (354). This admonition comments directly on Ahab, whose lurid monomania is implicit in Ishmael's rejection of the "artificial fire" whose "redness makes all things look ghastly." Ishmael's images of "the compass" and "the hitching tiller" and his imprecation to steer correctly take on larger significance when Ahab restores the *Pequod*'s providentially "inverted" compass needle and resumes his course toward Moby-Dick: ". . . the thunder turned old Ahab's needles; but out of this bit of steel Ahab can make one of his own, that will point as true as any" (425). Viewed in concert with "The Try-Works," Ahab's confidence that his needle "will point as true as any" betrays his own hubris. But Ishmael recognizes its fatal consequences for the *Pequod*: "In his fiery eyes of scorn and triumph, you then saw Ahab in all his fatal pride" (425).

These images of inverted tiller and lurid fire become emblems of Ahab's maddened, "demoniac" self, emblems validated by Ishmael's maturely qualified sermon on his hellish nightmare: "give not thyself up, then, to fire, lest it invert thee, deaden thee; as for the time it did me" (355). Ishmael warns against yielding the self to an "all feeling" in which nature is wholly malevolent or, to return to Melville's critique of Goethe, against accepting light or darkness as universally descriptive of reality. Far from being a true surrender of the self, holding such a monolithic interpretation precludes the possibility that one's vision may be flawed, or only temporarily valid. On the surface, Ahab seems to conflict with Goethe's advice to "live in the all." His is a Promethean, not a passive identity. Yet Ishmael's escape from the deadening fire brings into relief the cause of Ahab's "inverted" self, providing a hermeneutic key for reading Ahab and linking two ostensibly opposed aspects of Romantic thought.

At the end of "The Try-Works," when Ishmael praises the natural light of "the glorious, golden, glad sun, the only true lamp" (354), he is careful to avoid returning like a pendulum to an Emersonian thrill that ignores the dark side of nature he has just experienced. The sun sheds true light, but remembering "the Mast-Head," Ishmael restrains easy reassurance, pausing to consider what it illuminates: "Nevertheless the sun hides not Virginia's Dismal Swamp, nor Rome's accursed Campagna, nor wide Sahara, nor all the missions of miles of desert and of griefs beneath the moon. The sun hides not the ocean, which is the dark side of this earth, and which is two thirds of this earth" (354-355). Neither a noon nor a midnight vision, neither the light of the sun nor the light of the fire, is sufficient to illumine a complex cosmos. "Nevertheless" is the key word in Ishmael's reflection, for it signals both his rejection of an insincere platitude on the revealing power of natural sunlight and his ability to confront the stern reality besetting "mortal man." Ishmael's sermon verbalizes the structural dialogue between "The Mast-Head" and "The Try-Works," whose theme Melville articulates even more plainly in his next work, **Pierre:** "Say what *some poets* will, Nature is not so much her own ever-sweet interpreter, as the mere supplier of that cunning alphabet, whereby selecting and combining as he pleases, each man reads his own peculiar lesson according to his own peculiar mind and mood" (383-384, my italics). Ishmael condemns the prideful temptation to presume one's "own peculiar lesson" to be Nature's. To authorize his insight, Melville has him quote Ecclesiastes, biblical repository of the wisdom that declares the futility of trying to explain an inscrutable universe: "The truest of all men was the Man of Sorrows, and the truest of all books is Solomon's, and Ecclesiastes is the fine hammered steel of woe. 'All is vanity.' ALL" (355). Especially "the all" so beloved of "some poets," romantics like Emerson and Goethe.

In contrast to Ishmael, who recovers at the helm before he capsizes the ship, Ahab dooms the *Pequod* by knowingly embracing his mad obsession with killing Moby-Dick just after "The Quarter-Deck": "They think me mad, Starbuck does; but I'm demoniac, I am madness maddened. . . . The path to my fixed purpose is laid with iron rails, whereon my soul is grooved to run" (147). In yielding or, more precisely, welcoming his tyrannical "fixed purpose," Ahab can be seen as a corrupt extension of the self-reliant man, particularly in his attempts to impose his will on the universe and define his own morality. "Power is in nature the essential measure of right," writes Emerson in "Self-Reliance" (270). In this light Ahab's invocation of the railroad to image his relentless will represents an artificial assertion of the will aimed at bypassing natural moral impediments. In drawing a tyrant like Ahab, Melville shows the outcome of Emersonian thought projected on a political level. Again, in "Self-Reliance": [I]f I am the Devil's child, I will live then from the Devil. No law can be sacred to me but that of my own nature. Good and bad are but names very readily transferable to that or this; the only right is what is after my constitution, the only wrong what is against it" (260). What Melville highlights through Ahab's tyranny and the *Pequod*'s resulting destruction is Emerson's neglect to account for the social impact of an individualism based on an inherently subjective view of nature. Becoming one with the "all" and narcissistic self-absorption are finally related and problematic.

Determined to strip through the "pasteboard masks" to seize the truth behind, Ahab describes himself in "The Quarter-Deck" as jailed by these "visible objects," specifically by Moby-Dick. "How can the prisoner reach outside except by thrusting through the wall?" he asks (144). Later he defines his quest in a final shout to *The Bachelor* that invites a figurative reading: "Thou art a full ship and homeward bound, thou sayst; well then, call me an empty ship, and outward bound" (408). Such boldness to venture past human limits calls to mind Ulysses in Dante's *Inferno,* a magnificent yet unscrupulous egotist whose "passion . . . to gain experience of the world" prompted him to sail beyond the boundaries of the known world only to arrive in hell (325). Like Ahab, Ulysses incites his companions to sail on an ill-fated quest. Like the *Pequod,* Ulysses' ship sinks beneath the waves. Dante may admire the "great man" of antiquity but condemns him nonetheless. Similarly, Ishmael bows before Ahab's majestic tyranny but never condones it. He suggests that the search for ultimate truth must never be founded on exploitation of others; Ahab embodies the moral blindness of a prescription for self-fulfillment that ignores those figuratively in front of his fist as he strives to "strike through the mask." Through Ahab, an avatar of Romantic consciousness who bears an uncanny resemblance to Thomas Carlyle's portrait of the political "Great Man," Melville characterizes the political extension of Romantic ideology. Claiming in *On Heroes* that kingship is the highest heroic category because it combines all other classifications, Carlyle holds up "the rugged outcast Cromwell, [who] grappled like a giant, face to face, heart to heart, with the naked truth of things!" (209). Carlyle's Cromwell is an analogue to Melville's Ahab, who acts as diabolical priest, prophet, and demogogue, swaying the crew to his will in order to grapple with the white whale in an attempt to apprehend "naked truth." Boasts Carlyle at the outset of *On Heroes:* "[A]ll things that we see standing accomplished in the world are properly the outer material result, the practical realization and embodiment, of thoughts that dwelt in the Great Men sent into the world" (1). Melville's criticism of Carlyle's Romantic hero culminates in the irony that Ahab's sole "practical realization" is the *Pequod* sinking beneath "the great shroud of the sea [that] rolled on as it had five thousand years ago" (465). The ocean swamps Ahab and the crew. Elemental nature drowns consciousness, climactic death dramatizing quite literally Melville's critique of the consequences of both strains of Romantic thought on the body and the body politic. Only Ishmael, "floating on the margin of the ensuing scene," resists self-dissolution into Ahab's tyrannical "all" and survives to tell the story (470).

Notes

1. Author of both *Nature* and "Self-Reliance," two essays whose titles embody Romanticism's party of nature and party of consciousness, Emerson wears the hats of both parties, thus serving as a useful foil to highlight Melville's critique. For Emerson to extol both procedures for self-fulfillment is to support the logic of Melville's insight; in a sense Melville observes a certain equivalence between the two strands, an equivalence of which Emerson has at least tentative

awareness. Though we know Melville began reading Emerson shortly before the composition of *Moby-Dick* and can point to particular essays marked by marginalia, we cannot prove that he read, for example, *Nature* or "Self-Reliance." Nor can we prove that he did not read them. Whether Melville read specific works by Emerson becomes a less urgent question in the face of plausible Melvillean responses to them in *Moby-Dick*. Emerson's nationality and fame, Romanticism's leading American voice, demonstrate his status as the mouthpiece and disseminator of ideas that came to have popular currency even among those who never read or heard his writings and finally warrants setting off representative ideas and passages from Emerson against *Moby-Dick*.

In "Melville and Emerson's Rainbow" (1980), an essay in *Pursuing Melville, 1940-1980,* Merton Sealts gives a detailed account of proofs and probabilities and dates of Melville's reading in Emerson. Sealts surveys debates over the extent and nature of Emerson's influence on Melville, pointing to the general consensus that the influence was major. For more on this subject, see Nina Baym. Sealts' catalogue of books owned or borrowed by Melville, *Melville's Reading,* reveals his marked interest in European Romanticism shortly before and during the composition of *Moby-Dick*. Goethe's *Autobiography* was among the books he purchased during his European travels in 1849. In 1850 Evert Duyckinck lent him *Sartor Resartus* and *On Heroes and Hero-Worship,* and Melville was to borrow later that same year Goethe's *Wilhelm Meister* and Carlyle's anthology, *German Romance*. Clearly the two strains of Romanticism which so enticed and maddened Melville come from more sources than Emerson, but his writings provide an apt focus for the purposes of analysis.

2. These claims may seem to depart from conventional critical and pedagogical groupings which classify Melville as a Romantic. He certainly writes out of that tradition, but I see him as using the Romantic idiom to contend with the moral and political consequences of its metaphysical assumptions. Of course, trying to assign labels rigidly, to determine whether Melville was or was not a Romantic, creates a false dilemma, further muddled by the endlessly debatable terms of the question.

3. Frequently initiated by flight from the social to the natural world, advocated by Wordsworth and later practiced by Thoreau, the internalized quest which Harold Bloom deems characteristic of Romantic literature establishes a dialectic between self and other in which interpersonal relations are of diminished importance.

4. Certainly the drug addiction of Coleridge and DeQuincey was common knowledge; in *Melville's Reading,* Sealts demonstrates that Melville purchased DeQuincey's *Confessions of an Opium-Eater* in London in December 1849 and read it with enthusiasm (172).

5. That Hawthorne and Melville are at pains to emphasize the importance of human contact was noted long ago by F. O. Matthiessen: "As Melville examined man's lot, he was impressed, no less than Hawthorne, by the terrifying consequences of an individual's separation from his fellow human beings" (443). More recently, Sharon Cameron declares that the central theme of *Moby-Dick,* often obscured amid the vast critical attention directed at issues of epistemology, concerns the way human identity is bound up with physical bodies. Her analysis of the threat and presence of dismemberment in *Moby-Dick* intensifies the "terrifying consequences" of being cut off from the social body, focusing on the more primal fear of literally being cut off from oneself.

6. It is arguable that Ishmael's deliberate overstatement and self-conscious exploitation of a subject conducive to ribald jokes and innuendos reveal a self-conscious narrator firmly in control of his material. He admits to the sentimental quality of his vision by brazenly using the word "sentimentally." Far from undercutting his vision as a noble ideal, the humor is essential to keep his musings legitimate on a deeper level by deflecting criticism to their heady, exuberant presentation rather than their content.

Works Cited

Baym, Nina. "Melville's Quarrel with Fiction," *PMLA* 94 (October 1979): 909-923.

Bloom, Harold, ed. *Romanticism and Consciousness: Essays in Criticism.* New York: Norton, 1970.

Bluestein, Gene. "Ahab's Sin." *Arizona Quarterly.* 41(2) (1985): 101-116.

Cameron, Sharon. *The Corporeal Self: Allegories of the Body in Melville and Hawthorne.* Baltimore: Johns Hopkins Press, 1981.

Carlyle, Thomas. *On Heroes, Hero-Worship and the Heroic in History.* Ed. Carl Niemeyer. Lincoln: University of Nebraska Press, 1966.

Cowen, Walker. "Melville's Marginalia," Diss. Harvard University, 1965, vol. 5.

Dante Alighieri, *Inferno.* Trans. John D. Sinclair. New York: Oxford University Press, 1939.

Davis, Merrill R. and William H. Gilman, eds. *The Letters of Herman Melville.* New Haven: Yale University Press, 1960.

Gilman, William H., ed. *Selected Writings of Ralph Waldo Emerson.* New York: New American Library, 1983.

Matthiessen, F. O. *American Renaissance: Art and Expression in the Age of Emerson and Whitman.* New York: Oxford University Press, 1941.

Melville, Herman. *Mardi: And a Voyage Hither.* New York: Signet, 1964.

———. *Moby-Dick.* New York: Norton, 1967.

———. *Pierre or, The Ambiguities.* New York: Signet, 1964.

Patterson, Mark. "Democratic Leadership and Narrative Authority in *Moby-Dick*," *Studies in the Novel* 16(3) (1984): 288-303.

Sealts, Merton. *Melville's Reading.* Columbia: University of South Carolina Press, 1988.

———. *Pursuing Melville, 1940-1980.* Madison: University of Wisconsin Press, 1982.

Michael C. Berthold (essay date spring 1994)

SOURCE: Berthold, Michael C. "*Moby-Dick* and American Slave Narrative." *Massachusetts Review* 35, no. 1 (spring 1994): 135-48.

[*In the following essay, Berthold examines the relationship between* Moby-Dick *and the nineteenth-century slave narrative, analyzing both the novel's literary techniques and its thematic concerns.*]

Ishmael's cry of "Who aint a slave?" (6) in **Moby-Dick**'s first chapter plaintively, playfully expresses the textual and human centrality of enslavement for Melville; but the "Tell me that" that immediately follows the question, Ishmael's direct address to the readers he constructs as brethren slaves, may be an even more crucial figuring for Melville of inevitable captives and captivities always being dialogically engaged. This essay will explore Ishmael's own dialogical engagement with the strategies and tropes of American slave narratives, particularly in "The Town-Ho's Story" and the "Epilogue." Generally, I wish to respond to Henry Louis Gates's notice of the lack of discussion of relationships between slave narratives and American Romanticism (*Figures* [*Figures in Black*], 50-51) and consider how **Moby-Dick** might be embedded in what Hortense Spillers has described as "a potential configuration of slavery's discursive field" (31). Although some Americanists—who will be cited in this essay—have speculated on **Moby-Dick**'s politics of slavery, little if any notice has been taken of the novel's affinities with the *genre* of the slave narrative, and this argument intends to establish how the intertextual relations at work here are both formalistic and thematic.

Before and during the Civil War, the whale itself was a popular symbol for slavery and its prophesied eradication. In *Running a Thousand Miles for Freedom,* for example, William Craft uses the whale to condemn various clergymen who supported the Fugitive Slave Bill and to signify slavery's larger threat to America's integrity:

> These reverend gentlemen pour a terrible cannonade upon "Jonah" for refusing to carry God's message against Nineveh, and tell us about the whale in which he was entombed; while they utterly overlook the existence of the whales which trouble their republican waters, and know not that they themselves are the "Jonahs" who threaten to sink the ship of state, by steering in an unrighteous direction.
>
> (324)[1]

Stephen Butterfield has also documented several instances of this iconography. Black New Bedford churches regularly associated whaling images with antislavery. An article in the *Abolitionist* proclaimed:

> We found the Leviathan weltering in the sea of popularity . . . We have fixed the harpoon, and the monster begins to blow and bellow. We are now pulling upon the line, and we shall soon, we trust, come to lancing.
>
> (Butterfield, 59)

Lincoln, in the Emancipation Proclamation, spoke similarly:

> we are like whalers who have been on a long chase. We have at last got the harpoon into the monster, but we must now look how we steer, or with one flop of his tail he will send us all into eternity.
>
> (Butterfield, 291)

Within **Moby-Dick** itself, Michael Rogin argues via Michael Gilmore, Ishmael's rescue foretells the emancipation of the slaves (Rogin, 140).[2] Ishmael, in fact, is a literal captive of a dense ring of whales in "The Grand Armada" chapter and is forced to "watch for a breach in the living wall that hemmed us in; the wall that had only admitted us in order to shut us up" (387).

Although, as Butterfield has pointed out, **Moby-Dick**'s language tends to be more symbolically freighted than that of the slave narratives (36-37), its narrative rhythms recall a fundamental rhythm of the slave narrative: a movement or swing between abstract speculations of freedom and palpable challenges to that freedom. For example, when William Wells Brown is escaping north with his mother, he comforts himself with "the thought that I should one day be free, and call my body my own" (206).[3] But as he continues to muse about the bountiful possibilities of a "Free Home," his sentence is suddenly fractured by a comma, a dash, and the jarring phrase "when three men came up on horseback, and ordered us to stop," a phrase which brings his whole paragraph to an abrupt halt (206). Textually, Brown reproduces the disruption he felt at that moment, and by the end of the chapter, he has been returned to captivity. Analogous to this disruption is the movement of "The Mat-Maker" chapter of **Moby-Dick**. Through his "Loom of Time" metaphor, Ishmael finds some solace imagining "free will still free to ply her shuttle between given threads" (215). But his meditations are interrupted by a cry of "'There she blows,'" his first lowering for a whale ensues, and, he says, "the ball of free will dropped from my hand" (215). Abstractions on freedom are abandoned for the lust of the hunt, and Ishmael learns quickly that he must "resign" his own life "into the hands of him who steered the boat" (227). Ishmael, of course, has a freedom of movement and a luxury of speculation that are unavailable to a William Wells Brown. But there are, at the very least, textual precedents and parallels for **Moby-Dick**'s bi-planing of free will and restriction in the slave narratives.

Such connections between Melville and black culture are even more pronounced in "The Town-Ho's Story," an interpolated captivity narrative in **Moby-Dick** that in many ways coincides with slave narratives. Carolyn Karcher has aptly noted that in "The Town-Ho's Story," Steelkilt, "Lakeman and desperado from Buffalo," is a frontier analogue for the African slave, and that his conflict with Radney, the ship's mate, is "a paradigm of master-slave conflict" and the mutiny in which it culminates "a paradigm of slave insurrection" (57, 58).[4] But it is also important to emphasize that the very textual shape of Melville's story is analogous to that of the slave narrative.

Melville's initial concern in "The Town-Ho's Story" has to do with the actual dissemination of the narrative. The essence of the story, "the secret part of the tragedy" as Ishmael calls it, "never reached the ears of Captain Ahab" (242) or the captain of the *Town-Ho* himself. Rather, the story belongs to the underclass, the "private property" of three "confederate" seaman of the ship who "communicated it to the Indian Tashtego with Romish injunctions of secrecy" (242). The notion that narrativized experience constitutes "private property" echoes, verbatim, James Pennington's internal declaration in *The Fugitive Blacksmith* (to the slavehunters who want to know who owns him and where he is from) that "the facts in this case are my private property" (22).[5] In both Pennington and Melville, as Andrews says of *The Fugitive Blacksmith,* the "declarative act of defining autobiographical truth as one's inalienable private possession" turns chattel logic to one's own advantage (164). This notion is complicated by Ishmael's own reception of the *Town-Ho*'s story, which he hears much of when Tashtego talks in his sleep; "when he was wakened," says Ishmael, "he could not well withhold the rest" (243). That Tashtego issues the story out of the depths of sleep perhaps attests both to the intrin-

sic fascination of the story and to an irresistible need to pass it on, or perhaps Ishmael coerces it from him. Ishmael, in turn, becomes the story's transmitter when he relates it to a circle of Spanish dons in Lima. On the one hand, he is the vehicle by which a private captivity narrative is made public, by which the narrative is made to cross class and race lines. But in that the story was not in fact intended for him, in that he overhears and appropriates it from Tashtego, his own role as recorder and editor is itself called into question, and his own relationship to "The Town-Ho's Story" is not unlike, say, that of William Lloyd Garrison's to Frederick Douglass's narrative.

It is also worth noting that at the end of "The Town-Ho's Story" Ishmael swears on his "honor" that the story is no fiction: "I know it to be true" (259). Such an avowal is uncharacteristic of Ishmael and points to another parallel between "The Town-Ho's Story" and slave narratives, which typically begin with declarations of and testimonies to their authenticity; for example, as Solomon Northup states at the outset of his narrative, "My object is, to give a candid and truthful statement of facts" (227). Ishmael further authenticates his own narrative by claiming to have actually spoken with Steelkilt; like the slave narrator, in his zeal to commit himself to his narrative's truth he proclaims the historical irrefutability of American captivity.

The staging of character and conflict in "The Town-Ho's Story" also parallels that of male slave narratives. Like the male slave's, Steelkilt's world is essentially one of work, obedience, and humiliation. Radney, for example, exploits Steelkilt's "corporeally exasperated state" by commanding him to clean up the "offensive matters" of one of the ship's pigs (246), demasculating Steelkilt by assigning him a task properly designated only to the ship's boys. But Steelkilt, like Douglass, for example, in his autobiography, incarnates a rugged individualism that spurns such tyranny and equates floggings with dishonor, and both men engage in isolated battles royal with their nemeses that function as ritualized acts of liberation. Douglass describes his thrashing of Mr. Covey, the "nigger-breaker," as "the turning point in my career as a slave" (298); Steelkilt nearly kills Radney after the mate starts to strike him with a hammer and then leads a mutiny.

The mutiny, as Karcher has pointed out, gives way to a "self-defeating form of rebellion" in which Steelkilt and his band agree to be locked in the forecastle "until guaranteed amnesty" (58). But Steelkilt's passivity is not entirely toothless, for in part it serves as a calculated labor strike—a refusal to "sing out for whales" (254) or do a "hand's turn" (251) of work—that challenges both the personal authority of the captain and the capitalist mission of the ship.

Steelkilt's own personal vendetta against Radney, moreover, is fulfilled by the timely intervention in the story of Moby Dick who, sighted and pursued by the *Town-Ho* crew (temporarily forsaking their strike), seizes Radney in his jaws and plunges to the ocean floor with him. The whale, in fact, seems to be a kind of swimming panopticon ever watchful of tyrants like Radney; the last we see of Radney, in a particularly chilling image, is the mate's "wildly seeking to remove himself from the eye of Moby Dick" (257). Moby Dick grants Steelkilt a script of perfect revenge—"complete revenge he had, and without being the avenger" (255)—that once again has its counterpart in slave literature. In *The Fugitive Blacksmith,* especially the second chapter, Pennington repeatedly wishes that his own escape from slavery had been morally unambiguous: *"See,"* he apostrophizes, "how human bloodhounds gratuitously chase, catch, and tempt" the runaway slave "to shed blood and lie; how when he would do good, evil is thrust upon him" (30). For Steelkilt, this desire for a purity of release, an escape from tyranny without recourse to violence or deceit, is actualized by the appearance of Moby Dick; as tyrant-killer, the whale seems to restore to Steelkilt his natural integrity and autonomy. Perhaps Ishmael himself needs to believe that Moby Dick sides with the good and the free; one defense against his own potential captor is to identify sympathetically with him. In this regard the story functions as captivity wish-fulfillment.

Still, to whatever degree "The Town-Ho's Story" might be read as an allegory of oppressor, victim, and savior, its events are finally resituated in the quotidian. The slave's freedom is hardly secured by escape from literal bondage and the arrival north—Douglass has to contend with the economic racism of New Bedford, Linda Brent "could not feel safe in New York" and reaches a point where she will not regard "Northern soil" as "free soil" (496, 505); similarly, even after Moby Dick's elimination of Radney, Steelkilt continues to fear "legal retribution" (258) from his captain. By the end of "The Town-Ho's Story," any sense of Moby Dick as a violent son of liberty is replaced by Radney's widow's dreams of "the awful white whale that destroyed him," and Steelkilt's freedom becomes a matter of indeterminacy and disappearance: "Where Steelkilt now is, gentlemen, none know" (258).

Moby-Dick's most interesting alignment with slave literature, however, occurs in the book's epilogue. Melville's scene of Ishmael, buoyed up by Queequeg's coffin, caps what Gates identifies as the "ur-trope of the Anglo-African tradition" (*Monkey* [*The Signifying Monkey*], 131), the trope of the talking book. This trope originates in the 1770 narrative of James Albert Ukawsaw Gronniosaw, an African price sold into slavery who

eventually finds freedom and Christianity in England. Abroad the slave ship, Gronniosaw observes his Dutch master reading from and apparently conversing with the Bible and wishes the book would talk to him as well. But when Gronniosaw opens the book and puts his ear to it, he is disappointed to find that it will not speak to him (because, he speculates, he is black). For Gronniosaw, argues Gates, the Bible "constituted a silent primary text, a text, however, in which the black man found no echo of his own voice" (*Monkey,* 136). Subsequently, it is this "desire for recognition of his self in the text of Western letters" (*Monkey,* 137) that motivates his own creation of a narrative. Later black writers (Marrant, Cugoano, Equiano, Jea) refigure Gronniosaw's talking book trope, questioning his conflation of voice and presence with blackness and absence.

In Melville's epilogue, Queequeg's coffin stands as the talking book and Ishmael as the Gronniosaw figure. The coffin is Queequeg's sacred text and co-extensive with his own body. He carves its lid, says Ishmael, with "all manner of grotesque figures and drawings" that are copies of the tattoos on his own body, tattoos that "had been the work of a departed prophet and seer of his island, who, by those hieroglyphic marks, had written out on his body a complete theory of the heavens and the earth, and a mystical treatise on the art of attaining truth" (480). This act of narrative inscription by Queequeg corrects and amplifies an earlier moment where Queequeg is also an author of sorts. His signing aboard the *Pequod* involves the making of a collaborative text with Captain Peleg; on this document, Peleg misrepresents Queequeg as "Quohog," beneath which "appelative" Queequeg makes his mark, a copy of one of the tattoos on his arm (89). This splitting of Queequeg between a white authoritarian's primary misrepresentation (and animalizing) of him and his own subordinated attempt at writing himself into the registers of Western letters is amended when Queequeg designs his coffin; as a solo work that allows him to reproduce his entire body, rather than one tattoo from his arm, the coffin for Queequeg is a means of reclaiming the wholeness that the official discourse of a Peleg denies him.

A prince in his homeland like Gronniosaw, Queequeg abjures Gronniosaw's need to see himself in and speak himself through the white man's sacred text. This resistance is in part adumbrated in the negro church in New Bedford where Ishmael witnesses a black preacher "beating a book in a pulpit" (10); the book is not even identified as the Bible, and the preacher, a "black Angel of Doom," seems less to take his text from it than to chastise and do violence to it. The very act of reading is also parodied by Queequeg at an early moment in the text when, in the Spouter Inn, he takes up a large book and placing it on his lap began counting the pages with de- liberate regularity; at every fiftieth page . . . stopping a moment, looking vacantly around him, and giving ut- terance to a longdrawn gurgling whistle of astonish- ment.

(49)

Sundering reading and meaning, reading and revelation, Queequeg objectifies the book—merely a quantifiable binding of pages—to carnivalize it. Denuding the text, he takes his own pleasure from it. One of the most memorable aspects of Melville's portrayal of Queequeg is in fact this consistent, unapologetic, playful evasion of the literacy that, claims Gates, is "Western culture's trope of dominance over the peoples of color it had 'discovered'" (*Monkey,* 165).

The trope of the talking book, Gates makes clear, is "more properly the trope of the un-Talking Book" (*Monkey,* 165). Like Gronniosaw, baffled and compelled by the Bible, Ishmael in the epilogue embraces the coffin-text of Queequeg that he avers is a "riddle to un- fold" (480). Like the Bible for Gronniosaw, the coffin is at once silent and redemptive. It withholds its secrets from Ishmael while literally saving him; it neither re- flects nor acknowledges the white presence before it. Admittedly, as Peter Bellis has pointed out, not even Queequeg can read his tattoos, but his hieroglyphics are something other than "a set of empty signs" (63). The problem here may be one of hermeneutics, but not of belief; the coffin's hieroglyphics may be incomprehen- sible, but they are not valueless. They may be a "riddle," but, adds Ishmael, they are a "wondrous work" as well; it is Ahab, not Ishmael, who regards them as "devilish tantalization" (481).

Ishmael, of course, is a more privileged interpreter of the alien than Gronniosaw. He does not conflate voice and face, as Gronniosaw does, and attribute the coffin's silence to his whiteness; he does not have to master the cunning alphabet of Queequeg to articulate himself. Melville's epilogue is remarkable nonetheless for its re- versal of the trope of the talking book and its bold pre- sentation of a white narrator dependent on some unin- terpretable but meaningful black text. Not only does Ishmael overcome his initial prejudice against Quee- queg—"I could not help it, but I began to feel suspi- cious of this 'dark complexioned' harpooner" (15)—he comes himself to take on attributes of non-whiteness by the book's "Epilogue." Allegorically, in the "Epilogue," Ishmael is in fact quite plainly redeemed from "white- ness" by "blackness;" it is a "black bubble" that bursts and releases the coffin that saves Ishmael from sinking into the "creamy pool" of the "closing vortex" (573). In these regards Ishmael offers something of an elabora- tion of Toni Morrison's recent argument that, explicitly or implicitly, some "dark, abiding" presence informs "in compelling and inescapable ways the texture of

American literature" and that the *fabrication* of this persona provides powerful, self-reflexive meditations on the white American self (5, 46, 17). That Ishmael sur- vives the demise of *The Pequod* rather than Queequeg (what would his version of life with Ahab say?) might suggest that Melville's instinctive pity in the novel is for the white figure most like himself; but to the degree that by the "Epilogue" Ishmael is made to incorporate that fabricated dark persona, Melville at least rearranges the "hierarchic difference" emblazoned in "racial differ- ence."[6]

As the reconstituted slave "reader," Ishmael confounds standard American binarisms of slavery and freedom ("Nothing," Morrison in fact claims, "highlighted free- dom—if it did not in fact create it—like slavery" (37)). The very passivity of Ishmael's escape repudiates ro- manticized captivities that posit escape, in Primo Levi's phrase, as "moral obligation" (57). Melville thus quar- rels with prevailing mythologies of the whaleman as the seamanly incarnation of American freedom and self- reliance. In J. N. Reynolds's "Mocha Dick" (an 1839 text that Melville probably knew (Parker, 636-37))[7], for example, a stalwart Nantucket mate conquers the levia- than to reap fame for himself and his homeland. Says Reynolds at the end of "Mocha Dick" of the "intrepid- ity, skill, and fortitude" of the whaleman:

> These characteristics are not the growth of forced exer- tion; they are incompatible with it. They are the natural result of the ardor of a free people; of a spirit of fear- less independence, generated by free institutions.

(590)

Early in ***Moby-Dick*** Melville may to some degree ad- here to Reynolds's formulations, especially in the nov- el's apostrophe to the "Nantucketer" who "owns" the sea as "Emperors own empires" and ploughs it "as his own special plantation" (64). By the final position of Ishmael, however, such metaphors of New England mastery, curiously evocative of the slave-holding south, give way to Melville's dismantling of Reynolds's as- sumptions about "free people" and "fearless indepen- dence;" the novel in fact with relentless variety—"the stage managers, the Fates" that mock Ishmael's "unbi- ased freewill" (7), the "loose fish" that are embryonic "fast fish" (chapter 89), the "wildest winds of heaven and earth" that conspire to cast the soul "on the treach- erous slavish shore" (107)—doubts the philosophical realizability of Reynolds's freedom, and, in breaking down the binarism of freedom and slavery, Melville grants captivity near normative status. Even Ahab, the book's ostensible "supreme lord and dictator" (122), can be understood as an epitome of Nietzschean slave morality, the reactive figure whose *ressentiment* in the face of a hostile external world generates compensatory fictions that say "No to what is 'outside,' what is 'different,'" what is not the self (Nietzsche, 36).[8]

One final parable in *Moby-Dick,* seldom discussed in criticism of the novel, conflates captivity, textualization, and whiteness. In a footnote to "The Whiteness of the Whale" chapter, Ishmael describes the first albatross he ever saw, an "inexpressible" and "glorious thing" (190) of "unspotted whiteness, and vast archangel wings" (190). Like the ships on the Chesapeake, "robed in purest white," that Frederick Douglass beseeches for deliverance (293), the albatross stands for a transcendent freedom that liberates Ishmael from the "exiled waters" he sails and from the "warping memories of traditions and of towns" (190). The bird, however, is the ship's captive, taken "with a treacherous hook and line, as the fowl floated on the sea" (190). The captain frees it, but its flight is contingent on its being made into a "postman," "a lettered, leathern tally round its neck, with the ship's time and place" (190). Like Ishmael, the albatross escapes alone to tell its news, its "tally," like Ishmael's story, connected with its deliverance. But the status of the albatross's text is problematic. It bears the captain's data, not its own, and its tally, "meant for man" (190), reaches instead the other white fowl of Heaven. Ishmael's own proprietorship of his text is similarly ambiguous: he cannot determine its reception; there is no guarantee whom, if anyone, the text will reach. Whiteness, thus (and its associations with muteness and misdelivery), finally underlines essential anxieties of authorship for Ishmael and anticipates Melville's "dead letter" metaphor in **"Bartleby"** (particularly in the image of the albatross as postman) and the writerly imprisonment of Pierre in Melville's next novel [*Pierre*].

Moby-Dick can be regarded as a palimpsest of American captivity writing generally, quoting and embellishing the tradition that begins with Mary Rowlandson's 1682 narrative and includes the slave narratives published in Melville's own lifetime.[9] But, more exactly, as reconstruction of the American literary canon proceeds, I think it is necessary to consider how "majority" texts such as *Moby-Dick* can resemble and revise "minority" texts such as the slave narratives in the interests of challenging presumptions about the contingency of the minority on the majority and of drawing more graceful matrices for the nation's disparate yet enmeshed stories. One way to conflate Ishmael and the male narrator/hero of the slave narrative might be to think of them both as belonging to the larger literary family of the picaro. But a curious synchronicity also exists between Ishmael and later black singers whose blues, theorizes Houston Baker, become the "robust matrix" of Afro-American culture:

> Even as they speak of paralyzing absence and ineradicable desire, their instrumental rhythms suggest change, movement, action, continuance, unlimited and unending possibility. Like signification itself, blues are always nomadically wandering . . . they are ever on the move, ceaselessly summing novel experience.
>
>   (7, 8)[10]

It is of course questionable to what degree a white boy like Ishmael is capable of singing the blues. But his own vocalization of "unlimited and unending possibility," nomadic wandering, and "novel experience" suggest a style and ethos perfected by the bluesman, and, in at least some of its inflections, *Moby-Dick* yearns toward this robust matrix.

Notes

1. Although the narrative was not published until 1860, the Crafts spoke publicly about their escape from 1849 on. See also Wright for the argument that "Moby Dick is indeed a 'Job's whale rather than Jonah's'" (194).

2. David S. Reynolds also notes of Ishmael's "Who aint a slave" rhetoric that it "would seem to owe much to the attitude of the fiery New York radical Mike Walsh, who in the 1840s famously universalized the notion of slavery by emphasizing that both Northern wage slaves and Southern chattel slaves were equally exploited" (156).

3. Originally published in 1847.

4. Karcher demonstrates throughout her study that Melville "generalized about slavery by analogy" (2). In pointing out affinities between Steelkilt and Christ, particularly when Steelkilt is "betrayed" in the forecastle by his fellow mutineers, Karcher also suggests how "The Town-Ho's Story" fuses Biblical narrative with frontier and slave narratives.

5. Originally published in 1849.

6. Morrison makes only two specific (but very helpful) comments on Melville in *Playing in the Dark*: "Consider the ways that Africanism in other American writers (Mark Twain, Melville, Hawthorne) serves as a vehicle for regulating love and the imagination as defenses against the psychic costs of guilt and despair" (51-52) and "Melville uses allegorical formations—the white whale, the racially mixed crew, the black-white pairings of male couples, the questing, questioning white male captain who confronts impenetrable whiteness—to investigate and analyze hierarchic difference. Poe deploys allegorical mechanisms in *Pym* not to confront and explore, as Melville does, but to evade and simultaneously register the cul de sac, the estrangement, the non-sequitur that is entailed in racial difference" (68-69); I quote from the latter. Somewhat more generally, I am not sure that critics of *Moby-Dick* have paid sufficient attention to what happens to Ishmael after the *Pequod* goes down. Do Queequeg's lessons in reciprocity have any felt meaning for Ishmael? He continues to live a nomadic life (narrating "The Town-Ho's Story" in Lima,

drinking flip with the crew of the *Samuel Enderby,* surveying a whale's skeleton in a bower in the Arsacides), but that life has the ring of anti-climax, of recurrence without intimacy. Brodtkorb's comments in *Ishmael's White World* are helpful: Ishmael's "survival is prior to all ethics; the existentially sufficient reason for his survival is that what transcends death in time is art" (138); "Ishmael is a mental traveler who accepts with minimal illusions and defenses his human condition in that world of experience to which, like the lone figure floating on a coffin at the end, humanity seems abandoned" (148). See also Egan and Cowan (179-80).

7. "Mocha Dick" was originally published in the May 1839 edition of *The Knickerbocker, New York Monthly Magazine.*

8. Ishmael, on the other hand, epitomizes Nietzschean "gay mistrust." There is a variety of critical opinion on Ahab's "servitude." See especially Matthiessen, who regards Ahab as "an embodiment of his author's most profound response to the problem of the free individual will *in extremis*" (447) and Zoellner, who argues that "Ahad *willed the fundamental destruction of his will,* placing himself permanently . . . beyond the possibility of further choice or retraction" (100).

9. Breitwieser suggests that Rowlandson comes to anticipate Ishmael's "vision of the circulation of pure anomaly and mutation . . . each item of experience being wholly singular and without the redemption of a stable and credible explanatory context" (79). Rowlandson in fact also uses the same line from Job that introduces *Moby-Dick*'s "Epilogue." Frontier captivity narratives, too, still enjoyed great popularity in Melville's lifetime. Samuel Drake, for example, issued reprints of Puritan and Colonial captivity narratives in the 1820s that continued to appear into the 1860s. The single most popular narrative was his edition of Benjamin Church's 1716 story of his 1676 pursuit of the Indian Annawon (Slotkin, 444). Melville indicates his familiarity with this text in *Moby-Dick* when he confuses Church's pursuit of Annawon with Butler's pursuit of the Indian Brant in 1778 after the siege of Fort Stanwix (Rogin, 438). See also Fussell, who catalogues the profusion of western metaphors in *Moby-Dick.*

10. See also Hedin on slave narratives and the picaro.

Works Cited

Andrews, William L. *To Tell a Free Story: The First Century of Afro-American Autobiography, 1760-1865.* Urbana and Chicago: U of Illinois P, 1986.

Baker, Houston A., Jr. *Blues, Ideology, and Afro-American Literature: A Vernacular Theory.* Chicago and London: U of Chicago P, 1984.

Bellis, Peter J. *No Mysteries Out of Ourselves: Identity and Textual Form in the Novels of Herman Melville.* Philadelphia: U of Pennsylvania P, 1990.

Breitwieser, Mitchell Robert. *American Puritanism and the Defense of Mourning: Religion, Grief, and Ethnology in Mary White Rowlandson's Captivity Narrative.* Madison: U of Wisconsin P, 1990.

Brent, Linda. *Incidents in the Life of a Slave Girl.* Gates, *Narratives,* 333-513.

Brodtkorb, Paul, Jr. *Ishmael's White World: A Phenomenological Reading of* Moby-Dick. New Haven: Yale UP, 1965.

Brown, William Wells. *Narrative of William Wells Brown, a Fugitive Slave. Puttin' on Ole Massa.* Ed. Gilbert Osofsky. New York: Harper & Row, 1969, 173-223.

Butterfield, Stephen. *Black Autobiography in America.* Amherst: U of Massachusetts P, 1974.

Cowan, Bainard. *Exiled Waters:* Moby-Dick *and the Crisis of Allegory.* Baton Rouge: Louisiana State UP, 1982.

Craft, William. *Running a Thousand Miles for Freedom. Great Slave Narratives.* Ed. Arna Bontemps. Boston: Beacon, 1969, 269-331.

Douglass, Frederick. *Narrative of the Life of Frederick Douglass, an American Slave.* Gates, *Narratives,* 243-331.

Egan, Philip J. "Time and Ishmael's Character in 'The Town-Ho's Story' of *Moby-Dick*." *Studies in the Novel* 14 (1982): 337-47.

Fussell, Edwin. *Frontier: American Literature and the American West.* Princeton: Princeton UP, 1965.

Gates, Henry Louis, Jr., ed. *The Classic Slave Narratives.* New York: Mentor, 1987.

————. *Figures in Black: Words, Signs, and the "Racial" Self.* New York: Oxford UP, 1987.

————. *The Signifying Monkey: A Theory of Afro-American Literary Criticism.* New York: Oxford UP, 1988.

Hedin, Raymond. "The American Slave Narrative: The Justification of the Picaro." *American Literature* 53 (1982): 630-45.

Karcher, Carolyn. *Shadow Over the Promised Land: Slavery, Race, and Violence in Melville's America.* Baton Rouge: Louisiana State UP, 1980.

Levi, Primo. *The Drowned and the Saved.* Trans. Raymond Rosenthal. New York: Summit, 1988.

Matthiessen, F. O. *American Renaissance: Art and Expression in the Age of Emerson and Whitman.* 1941. Reprint. New York: Oxford UP, 1974.

Melville, Herman. *Moby-Dick or The Whale.* Evanston and Chicago: Northwestern UP and the Newberry Library, 1988.

Morrison, Toni. *Playing in the Dark: Whiteness and the Literary Imagination.* Cambridge, Ma. and London: Harvard UP, 1992.

Nietzsche, Friedrich. *On the Genealogy of Morals.* Trans. Walter Kaufmann. New York: Vintage, 1969.

Northup, Solomon. *Twelve Years a Slave.* 1853. New York: Miller, Orton & Mulligan, 1855.

Parker, Herschel. "Historical Note IV." Melville, 635-47.

Pennington, James W. C. *The Fugitive Blacksmith.* Westport: Negro Universities P, 1971.

Reynolds, David S. *Beneath the American Renaissance: The Subversive Imagination in the Age of Emerson and Melville.* Cambridge: Harvard UP, 1989.

Reynolds, J. N. "Mocha Dick: or the White Whale of the Pacific." Herman Melville. *Moby-Dick: or, The Whale.* New York: Norton, 1967, 571-90.

Rogin, Michael Paul. *Subversive Genealogy: The Politics and Art of Herman Melville.* Berkeley: U of California P, 1983.

Slotkin, Richard. *Regeneration Through Violence: The Mythology of the American Frontier, 1600-1860.* Middletown: Wesleyan UP, 1973.

Spillers, Hortense J. "Changing the Letter: The Yokes, the Jokes of Discourse, or, Mrs. Stowe, Mr. Reed.: *Slavery and the Literary Imagination.* Ed. Deborah E. McDowell and Arnold Rampersad. Baltimore and London: Johns Hopkins UP, 1989, 25-61.

Wright, Nathalia. "Moby Dick: Jonah's or Job's Whale?" *American Literature* 37 (1965): 190-95.

Zoellner, Robert. *The Salt Sea Mastodon: A Reading of Moby-Dick.* Berkeley and Los Angeles: U of California P, 1973.

Etsuko Taketani (essay date June 1994)

SOURCE: Taketani, Etsuko. "*Moby-Dick*: Gnostic Re-Writing of History." *American Transcendental Quarterly* 8, no. 2 (June 1994): 119-35.

[*In the following essay, Taketani explores elements of Gnostic theology in* Moby-Dick. *Taketani contends that Melville's exploration of Gnostic themes represents his attempt to relativize the authority of the Bible, as well as of traditional interpretations of history.*]

Gnosticism is an ancient religious belief of the first through third centuries. Although the belief colored the creation of the New Testament, it was labeled as a heresy by early Christians whose faith would later be regarded as orthodox. The fact that Herman Melville had an acquaintance with Gnosticism is corroborated by several direct references to the subject in his works. In Chapter 38 of **White-Jacket** (1850), he mentions not only the Gnostics but also Tertullian, the first important Latin Father who tried to refute the claims of the Gnostic heretics, and Marcion, whose teachings about the two Gods, the "just" God of law in the Old Testament and the "good" God of salvation in the New Testament, are understood in the context of the Gnostic heresy (156). Melville also refers to the Ophites in Chapter 41 of **Moby-Dick** (1851), a Gnostic sect which worshipped the Serpent who had brought *gnosis* (knowledge) to Adam and Eve (184). In **Clarel** (1876), he explains the Gnostic belief that "Jehovah was construed to be / Author of evil, yea, its god; / And Christ divine his contrary: / A god was held against a god, / But Christ revered alone . . . / . . . If no more / Those Gnostic heretics prevail / Which shook the East from shore to shore, / Their strife forgotten now and pale; / Yet, with the sects, that old revolt / Now reappears" (277). **Timoleon** (1891) includes a poem whose title, "Fragments of a Lost Gnostic Poem of the 12th Century," refers to Gnosticism (40).

Though in much evidence, Melville's relationship with Gnosticism received very little notice from Melville scholars until 1986 when William B. Dillingham brought it into the center of attention as "Ahab's Heresy" (91-124). With his discovery of Ephraim Chambers' *Cyclopaedia; or, An Universal Dictionary of Arts and Sciences* (1728) as Melville's principal source of Gnosticism (before that, only Pierre Bayle's *An Historical and Critical Dictionary* and Andrews Norton's *The Evidences of the Genuineness of the Gospels* were thought to be his sources), and his impressively complete survey of early scholarship on Melville's relationship with Gnosticism, Dillingham's accomplishment was epochal in Melville studies.[1]

Dillingham, moreover, pointed out an interesting fact in one of his footnotes, which I wish to develop further. As Dillingham observes, "It is difficult not to assume . . . that [Melville] would have seen various other materials on the Gnostics, for the nineteenth century saw a great surge of interest in them" (93n). In October of 1835, the *Edinburgh Review,* for example, "severely criticized George Waddington's *History of the Church from the Earliest Ages to the Reformation* (London, 1835) for its neglect of the Gnostics" (qtd. in Dillingham 93n). According to the *Edinburgh Review,* Gnosticism was "one of the most interesting and important [subjects] that can attract the notice of the historian, the philosopher, or the divine" (qtd. in Dillingham 94n).

Not only this British periodical, but also an American periodical, *Ladies' Repository,* was interested in Gnosticism at about this time. Dillingham notes that the October, 1843, issue of this journal "warned its readers against the seduction of the Gnostic vision" (93n) which puts "the God of the Jews in supreme contempt—esteeming him as a malicious being, whom Jesus came to destroy" (qtd. in Dillingham 93n).

What interests me most is how Gnosticism could be regarded as a threat in a nation such as nineteenth-century America, where Protestantism dominated all levels of culture. What appeal did the ancient heresy of Gnosticism possibly have for Americans?[2]

The appearance of Gnosticism in the United States probably was not the result of popular interest. Rather, interest in Gnosticism seems to have revolved around the authority of Christianity as history. In reviewing Andrews Norton's *The Evidences of the Genuineness of the Gospels* (1844), the *North American Review* (hereafter *NAR*) (July 1844) remarked, "Looking only at the character of the events narrated, the history contained in the Gospels may be only a skilfully contrived romance" (["Norton on *the Genuineness of the Gospels*" 1844b,] 151). Indeed, when it comes to the relation of history to romance as narrative, real distinctions quickly faded from view. The journal observes, "If we . . . look only at the face of the narrative, Robinson Crusoe appears as true a story as Cook's Voyages, and Richardson, the novelist, is as faithful a historian as Hume" (150). The narrative itself, then, "has no weight whatever" (150) in determining the difference between history and romance.

The question of the relation between history and romance was probably as interesting an issue in the nineteenth century as it is today. "If the gospel narrative is merely a cunningly devised fable or *myth,*" the *NAR* said, "then we may give up history, and throw all such works as the one now before us in the fire" (151). Losing the gospel narrative was tantamount to losing the whole concept of "history" itself.[3]

It was the "genuineness" of the Scriptures that seemed to matter most to interested parties. As for the difference between authenticity and genuineness, the *NAR* (Jan. 1836) explains, "Writings are said to be *genuine,* when it can be satisfactorily established that they were written by the *persons,* and of course, at the *time* assigned, and that they have *not undergone any material change* in the course of transmission to us" (["Means of Ascertaining the Genuineness and Integrity of Ancient Writings"] 5). On the other hand, "[w]ritings . . . are said to be *authentic,* when they can be shown to be trust-worthy in regard to the facts they state" (5). Genuineness referred to a text that was "not *forged*"; authenticity to a text that included neither "*falsehoods or fic-*

tions" (6). By these criteria, the genuineness of the Scriptures might be examined, but their authenticity as history could never be known. According to the *NAR*'s logic, the Bible was a genuine text; however its authenticity was another question. Of course what this subtle distinction meant was that the constructedness of the Scriptures was now open to consideration.

Andrews Norton's *The Evidences of the Genuineness of the Gospels,* dealing with Gnosticism, was published in 1844 to verify the validity of the Gospels. Norton tried to demonstrate that "the Gospels were written by the authors to whom they are ascribed" (3: 309). This Unitarian minister had in 1839 attacked Ralph Waldo Emerson's "denial of the truth of the Gospel history" or "rejection of *historical* Christianity" (*Discourse* [*A Discourse on The Latest Form of Infidelity*] 30) as "the latest form of infidelity." And he himself devoted much of his time and labor to the history of Gnosticism, which "subject has occupied the author's mind for a quarter of a century" ("Norton" 1844b, 143).

Of course, Norton's purpose was not to investigate Gnosticism itself, but to substantiate the genuineness of the historical records of Christianity. He argued that the Gospels were not forged, because "Gnostics, having every reason to impeach the authority of the received accounts, if they were able, and to substitute others for them, did not attempt either course, but submitted to be judged by the books of their opponents" ("Norton" 1844b, 153). If the heretics acknowledged the authority of the Bible, the only conceivable reason why they did so was because the Gospels are genuine.

More importantly, Norton concluded that the Gospels were also authentic if they were genuine. "If the Gospels be genuine, there are but two conclusions which are possible": the narrative of Christ is "either essentially true, or it is essentially false" (*Evidences* [*The Evidences of the Genuineness of the Gospels*] 3: 317-18). If it is a "fiction," it is "an absurdity so repulsive, that it would be equally offensive and unprofitable to dwell on it longer" (*Evidences* 3: 318). Therefore, "[i]t follows . . . that the history of Jesus contained in the Gospels is true" (*Evidences* 3: 318). Norton's conclusion is that the Narrative authored by God should never be refuted, and it was out of question even to doubt it. The American Unitarian minister could not bear the slightest suspicion that Christianity might be no less a myth or a fable than Greek or Roman or any other religion. The revival of Gnosticism in the nineteenth century thus ran concurrent with a growing skepticism about the historical veracity of Christianity.

While interest in Gnosticism first arose in the United States in the nineteenth century, in Europe Gnosticism had captured the interest of thinkers much earlier, especially in Germany. Modern European inquiries into

Gnostic beliefs got under way in the eighteenth century and remained strong through the nineteenth. In 1699 Gottfried Arnold's *Unparteiische Kirchen- und Ketzer-historie* (*Impartial History of the Churches and Heresies*) was published. Isaac de Beausobre researched Manichaeism in *Histoire critique de Manichee et du manicheisme* (1734-9), and Johann Lorenz von Mosheim's *Institutiones historioe ecclesiasticoe anti-quoe et recentioris* (*Institutes of ecclesiastical history, ancient and modern*) came out in 1755. It was not until the nineteenth century, however, that an independent study of Gnosticism was started. In this sense, August Neander's *Genetische Entwicklung der vornehmsten gnostischen Systeme* (*Genetic Evolution of the Most Important Gnostic Systems*) (1818) was a breakthrough. Neander also dealt with Gnosticism in *Allgemeine geschichte der christlichen religion und kirche* (*General history of the Christian religion and church*) (1825-31). Jacques Matter's *Histoire critique du Gnosticisme* appeared in France in 1828. In 1835, Ferdinand Christian Baur, who is called the real founder of modern Gnostic research, published *Die christliche Gnosis* (*The Christian Gnosis*), a landmark in this field in that it is "even today still worth reading" (Rudolph 30-31). Thus, a revaluation of Gnosticism was vigorously pursued in the early nineteenth century.

Although it did not match Germany's production of original studies of Gnosticism, the United States in the early nineteenth century was much more active in learning about Gnosticism than we usually imagine. Norton's *The Evidences of the Genuineness of the Gospels* (1844) was the first scholarly book of Gnosticism ever produced by an American. Despite the fact that it was written to confirm the genuineness of the Gospels, this was an amazingly extensive book covering all imaginable topics on Gnosticism, including chapters "On the System of the Gnostics, as intended for a Solution of the Existence of Evil in the World," "On the Opinions of the Gnostics concerning the Evil as inherent in Matter," and "On the Opinions of the Gnostics concerning the Person of Christ."

Norton's book was not, however, the only means by which information about Gnosticism was diffused in the United States (in fact, the *NAR* said of Norton's book, "It is not in its nature a popular one; the multitude will not read and cannot appreciate it" ["Norton" 1844b, 143]). A more widespread source for learning about Gnosticism would have been through translations of the German scholars' books. Interestingly, it was Evert Duyckinck, Sr., the father of Melville's close friend, who initiated the translation enterprise in America. In 1821 Duyckinck published Mosheim's *Ecclesiastical History, ancient and modern* in New York. This book criticizes Gnosticism as the leading heretical sect that "troubled the tranquillity of the christian [sic] church" (1: 111). According to Mosheim, the Gnostics "boasted

of their being able to restore mankind to thc *knowledge, gnosis,* of the true and Supreme Being, which had been lost in the world," and abhorred "Moses and the religion he taught" because, "in imposing such a system of disagreeable and severe laws upon the Jews, he was only actuated by the malignant author of this world, who consulted his own glory and authority, and not the real advantage of men" (1: 111, 113). Another translation of Mosheim's book, "much corrected, enlarged and improved," appeared in 1832 (New Haven: A. H. Maltby) under the title of *Institutes of Ecclesiastical History, ancient and modern.* Its revised and enlarged second edition was published in New York in 1839 by Harper & Brothers, later Melville's chief American publishers.

The year 1843 saw the publication of the translation of August Neander's *The History of the Christian Religion and Church,* which examined Gnosticism and its various sects, "Cerinthus," "Basilides," "Valentinus," "Ophites," "Pseudo-basilidians," "Saturninus," "Tatian," and "Marcion," as well as Manichaeism. As Neander explained, the concept of divinity for the Gnostics was not only complicated but very irregular:

> The Demiurgos (according to this system) is a limited and limiting being, proud, envious, and revengeful. . . . These Gnostics believed that they recognised the form of that hateful Demiurgos in the Old Testament, and also in nature. . . . The Supreme God, the God of holiness and love, who stands in no connection with the world of sense, has not revealed himself in this earthly creation by any thing, except by some Divine seeds of life which are scattered abroad in human nature, and whose unfolding the Demiurgos endeavours to stop and to overwhelm.
>
> (249)

Another translation of Neander from the second and improved edition, *General History of the Christian Religion and Church,* came out in 1847 in Boston, Philadelphia, and New York through Wiley & Putnam whose distinguished "Library of Choice Reading" was edited by Evert Duyckinck, Jr.[4] Matter's *Histoire critique du Gnosticisme* and Baur's *Die christliche Gnosis* were not translated at this time, but Norton referred to them in the footnotes of *The Evidences of the Genuineness of the Gospels* (2: 40, 41). In 1848, the second edition of Norton's book appeared as well.

Periodicals were also instrumental in introducing Gnosticism to the general public in the United States. In 1837, the *NAR* had printed the Preface of volume 1 of Norton's *The Evidences of the Genuineness of the Gospels,* which proposed his next project on Gnosticism ("Norton" 1837a, 221). When volumes 2 and 3 finally came out, the *NAR* observed that Gnosticism was the product of "an insane imagination," which "rejectcd the Jewish Scriptures . . . and denied the perfections of the

Jewish God," and "contrived the most elaborate and fantastic theogony" in order to "fill up the vacuity" they themselves created by demoting Jehovah in Christianity ("Norton" 1844b, 158). The journal portrayed Gnostics as those who

> held, that the material universe was not made by the Supreme Being, but by an inferior agent, the Creator, who was also the God of the Jews. The true Deity presided over the spiritual world, or Pleroma, as they called it, which was widely separated from the material universe, being absolutely pure, while evil was inherent in matter. The visible world was full of imperfection and sin, and the Saviour descended to it from the Pleroma, to make a revelation of the Supreme God to men, and to deliver what was spiritual from the bondage of matter. Before his advent, the true Deity was hidden from the knowledge of men; for the God of the Old Testament was only the inferior agent, the God of the Jews.
>
> ("Norton" 1844b, 165-66)

The inferior Creator "was not self-existent, [and yet] he was even ignorant of the existence of the Supreme Being" ("Norton" 1844b, 171). The human body created by him was "the great source of moral evil, the prison in which the soul is confined and debased" ("Norton" 1844b, 175-76).

The Unitarian *Christian Examiner* seems to have been more liberally interested in Gnosticism and spoke positively about what the heresy offers rather than condemning it, unlike, for example, the *Ladies' Repository* which wondered, "How men calling themselves Christians could adopt such monstrous notions" ([Waterman] 293). In 1837, the *Christian Examiner* reviewed *Some Account of the Writings and Opinions of Clement of Alexandria* (London, 1835) and distinguished "the true or Christian Gnostic" from "the philosophical or heretical Gnostic" (Lamson 162). The journal situated the former even higher than the "ordinary Christian," because of his "likeness of God" (Lamson 163). Rev. Alvan Lamson, who wrote this review, attached a special importance to Gnosticism:

> Of all the heresies which sprung up in the bosom of the early church, Gnosticism, from the conspicuous part it long played, the loftiness of its pretensions, the learning and skill of several of its chiefs, and the traces it left behind, and which remained long visible, after the system itself had crumbled away and disappeared, furnishes most matter of curiosity and wonder, and presents the strongest claim to the attention of the philosophical inquirer.
>
> (169)

Other publications expressed a similar admiration toward Gnosticism. The following year, the *Christian Examiner* (Mar. 1838) called Gnosticism the "most beautiful system of ancient Theosophy" ([Parker] 116). In reviewing Matter's *Histoire critique du Gnosticisme*

(Paris, 1828), the journal presented a brief history of the books dealing with Gnosticism: Ittig's *De Haeresiarchis aevi apostolici et apostolico proximi* (1690), Mosheim's *Institutiones historiae christianae majores* (1739), *Versuch einer unpartheiischen und grundlichen Ketzer-geschichte* (1748), and *De rebus Christianorum ante Constantinum magnum* (1753), Arnold's *Unpartheiische Kirchen-und Ketzer-Historie* (1740), Buddaeus' *Introductio ad Historiam philosoph*, Wolf's *Manicheismus ante Manicheos* (1707), Beausobre's *Histoire critique de Manichee* (1734), Neander's *Genetische Entwickelung der vornehmesten gnostichen systeme* (1818), Ewald's *Commentatio ad hist. Rel. Vet. illustrandam pertinens de doctrina Gnostica* (1818), and Baur's *Die christliche Gnosis* (1835) (Parker 112-14).

Interestingly enough, this review, written by Theodore Parker, divined a potential germ of romanticism in the ancient religion. If the American Renaissance was, as F. O. Matthiessen suggests, a period of a shift in emphasis "from God-Man to Man-God" and "from Incarnation to Deification" (446), Parker was certainly perceiving man's divinity in Gnosticism:

> Gnosticism, or its Psychology, has told man that his soul is a ray of the essence of light which constitutes the Divinity; . . . that even its miseries in this transitory existence are a proof of its condition of exile; . . . that, if it remembers its celestial origin . . . it will recover the rank . . . and will re-enter the bosom of him who is All.
>
> (128)[5]

Although it is a matter of speculation to what degree the general public of the United States was really familiar with Gnosticism and how much the knowledge of it was disseminated by means of Norton's book, translations from the German, or from periodicals, one thing seems to be certain: Melville's Gnosticism in the text of *Moby-Dick* is not so much a product of personal curiosity as it is of American culture's mid-nineteenth-century anxieties about the status of the Biblical Scriptures. The text of *Moby-Dick* not only reflects the debate over the relation between history, narration and authority, but contributes its own 'two cents' to the question.

Moby-Dick, a romance, I will argue, can be seen as Melville's attempt at relativizing the presumed authority of the Bible as the ultimate narrative and true history. Melville creates another history of humanity, an alternative Gnostic version, and makes the two histories compete. While Christians had the Bible, the "Holy Guide-Book" (Melville, *Redburn* 157) as their narrative paradigm, the Gnostics had none. "None of the writings of the Gnostics are extant, except some short extracts preserved in the works of their opponents," said the *NAR* ("Norton" 1844b, 162). Theodore Parker also commented that "[n]o one can fail to lament the loss of the works of the Gnostics themselves, for their language is said to have had an inexpressible charm, stealing away men's hearts before they were aware, and worthy of this most beautiful system of ancient Theosophy" (116). The lost narrative of the ancient Gnostics was revived in the nineteenth-century United States, in Melville's imagination.

The Gnostic narrative discourse in **Moby-Dick** interrogates the concept of the only Father as the transcendental, as well as historical, origin of humanity. The characterization of Jehovah the Father was originally a focal issue of controversy between Gnostics and Christians. As the *NAR* says, the ancient Gnostics "thought it impossible to reconcile the character and actions of the Creator, as therein [in the Old Testament] represented, with the perfections of the God of Christianity" ("Norton" 1844b, 166). Both Gnostics and Christians acknowledged the existence of Jehovah, but they diverged on the status of the Father, the latter conceptualizing him as the only Father, the former as the inferior Father beyond whom there exists the true, but unknown, supreme being. When **Moby-Dick** presents a Gnostic possibility of two Gods, the text undermines the monotheism of the West, whereby Jehovah stood as the undisputed center of authority.

The Gnostic notion of plural Fathers is central to **Moby-Dick.** To Ahab, Moby Dick is not "a dumb brute" (163). The Leviathan is a "pasteboard mask" which may or may not conceal the existence of the true Father behind it (164). The Leviathan is a sign of Jehovah behind whom the unknown Father might or might not be hidden. Ahab tries to fill the gap between the signifier and the absent referent, as Redburn did in his search for his father. In a Chapter called "The Chart," Ahab "bring[s] out a large wrinkled roll of yellowish sea charts" and "stud[ies] the various lines and shadings" on it every night (198), just as young Redburn once traced dotted lines in the map of *The Picture of Liverpool,* from a signifier to its absent referent, the father. The attempt at uniting a signifier and its absent referent is an act of creation, since it rejects the standard codification of the language system. Creating a new correspondence, where none had before existed, Melville transforms the "Holy Guide-Book" into something else.

For Melville, the authority of Jehovah as the only Father had to be questioned, if only because of the problem of evil as it appeared in the ultimate narrative, the Bible. The question of evil was the focus of great controversy among the Gnostics and the Fathers of the Christian Church. The Fathers defined evil as "privatio boni" (the privation of good) in order to reconcile the two concepts that God was the supreme good (Summum bonum) and that the world was created out of thin air (creatio ex nihilo). The Gnostics, on the other hand, did not deny the existence of evil as the Fathers did, but acknowledged Jehovah (the Demiurge) as its Creator.

In the nineteenth century, Ralph Waldo Emerson, much like the Christian Fathers, tried to solve the question of evil by regarding it as the absence of good, not as positive "being." He had declared in "The Divinity School Address" (1838):

> Good is positive. Evil is merely privative, not absolute: it is like cold, which is the privation of heat.

> ([*Selected Writings*] 69)

Melville, unlike Emerson, could not look upon evil as the deprivation of good. His obsession with evil had existed from the beginning of his literary career and took the form of the riddle of theodicy in **Mardi** (1849):

> "Well, Oro [God] is every where. What now?"

> "Then, if that be absolutely so, Oro is not merely a universal on-looker, but occupies and fills all space; and no vacancy is left for any being, or any thing but Oro. Hence, Oro is *in* all things, and himself *is* all things—the time-old creed. But since evil abounds, and Oro is all things, then he can not be perfectly good; wherefore, Oro's omnipresence and moral perfection seem incompatible."

> (427)

As opposed to Emerson and the Fathers of the Church who defined evil as the lack of good,[6] Melville took up the Gnostic version of evil. In **Moby-Dick,** "evil" appears in the corporeal form of the whale.

In Captain Ahab, Melville created an "American" who aspired to eradicate the origin of all evil personified by Moby Dick, the great white whale. What made Ahab see the whale as the origin of evil involved an accident in which his leg was dismembered by Moby Dick. This loss drove Ahab to see Moby Dick as the root of all evil, from Adam on. Not everyone responded this way to mishaps with Moby Dick. Melville tells his readers of another sea captain—the captain of the Samuel Enderby of London—who gave up a limb (his arm) to Moby Dick, but who did not claim revenge. Ahab's monomania is obviously unique. His irrational pursuit of the great white whale is driven by an unorthodox interpretation of history, a point of view much closer to Gnosticism than to anything else.

Ahab's unusual approach to history was originally motivated by humiliation at being crippled. Had it not been for the amputation, he might well have been an Emersonian American who believed in the divine genealogy of man. As Captain Peleg, an old friend of Ahab, said, Ahab was after all "a grand, ungodly, god-like man" who could dart "his fiery lance . . . the keenest and the surest . . . out of all our isle" (79). When his amputation transformed the great Ahab into "an old man cut down to the stump" (561), Ahab felt cast out from the divine genealogy of humanity. Ahab, however, refuses to surrender his god-like will, saying in effect, "NO! in thunder; but the Devil himself cannot make [me] say *yes.*"[7]

Still in order to be a "god-like man," Ahab needs another kind of body. In Chapter 108, Ahab tells the ship carpenter to stop making the substitute ivory leg for him and instead to take to the blacksmith the order for "a complete man after a desirable pattern" (470):

> Imprimis, fifty feet high in his socks; then, chest modelled after the Thames Tunnel; then, legs with roots to 'em, to stay in one place; then, arms three feet through the wrist; no heart at all, brass forehead, and about a quarter of an acre of fine brains; and let me see—shall I order eyes to see outwards? No, but put a sky-light on top of his head to illuminate inwards. There, take the order, and away.
>
> (470)

Although this passage recalls Mary Shelley's *Frankenstein* (which Melville obtained from Richard Bentley in 1849 [Leyda 351; Sealts 214]), an important Gnostic idea is suggested here. Ahab sees his own flawed human body as an inferior product, because he can visualize "a complete man after a desirable pattern." The human body could have been created perfectly if the Creator desired and had the power to do so.

Since it is impossible to alter the history of the human race or improve an imperfect body, Ahab tries to revise it textually. He compensates for his personal humiliation by creating a world through discourse where his plight comes to epitomize the human condition. Ousted from the American myth of human divinity, Ahab produces an alternative myth of human genealogy. According to the Gnostic Genesis of humanity, the body is created inferior from the beginning by the evil Creator named the Demiurge or Jehovah, who put man in the darkness of ignorance.[8] In Gnostic mythology, Ahab's body is not inferior simply because he is crippled; his body is inherently inferior because it was willed so by a malevolent god.

Ahab tries to 'historicize' the Gnostic idea of creation, which was made a "myth" by Christianity, by actually living it out. He compels his crew to toe the line as well. Pious Christian Starbuck was virtually the only one on board who resisted Ahab's Gnostic re-writing of history, believing that Ahab was "blasphemous" (164). Only when he successfully manages to make the myth live for him is Ahab redeemed from the humiliation of being crippled, an indignity that was all the more unbearable because of his old pride in being a "god-like man."

Gnosticism postulates two origins, two Fathers, for the genealogy of the human race. Gnosticism argues that, although the inferior body was created by Jehovah (the Demiurge),[9] man's innermost Self is related to the Unknown God (Forefather) who exists beyond the visible world created by the inferior God. The spiritual core of man has a kinship with the highest, eternal and unbegotten God beyond. It is a divine seed deriving from the Forefather. The Gnostic belief in man's divine genealogy thus restores Ahab to his primordial status as a "god-like man" despite his detestable body.

All of this was undoubtably appealing to a man of Ahab's temperament. What makes Gnosticism still more captivating for Ahab is that the Gnostic vision posits man in a higher authority than Jehovah the Father, by linking the origin of man's spiritual genealogy with the Forefather.[10] In a way, Gnosticism is far more radical than Transcendentalism. Ahab says that if the sun insulted him, he would strike it back (164). But even fair play is not his guiding principle. "Who's over me?" (164), Ahab exclaims. Ahab's divine genealogy, formulated in accordance with the Gnostic paradigm, topples the old hierarchy of Christianity where the creator stood above humankind on the ladder of being.

In *Moby-Dick,* man's divine core, a gift from the Forefather, is compared to a "captive king" imprisoned in the inferior body and world (185). Far down within man's soul, Melville says, there exists "his root of grandeur, his whole awful essence" (185-86). The captive king refers to what the Gnostics call the divine Archetypal Man, whose existence nobody (except perhaps Ahab) knows, because by Jehovah man is reduced to servile ignorance. Ahab says, "Here's a man from Man; a man born in once independent Man, and now unmanned of Man" (521). Man is an "exiled royalt[y]" doubly cut off by the body and the world from the Forefather beyond (186). It is no wonder that Melville's writings abound in exile figures, particularly ones who are orphans. In *Moby-Dick,* the main characters (Ishmael, Queequeg, and Ahab) are all "exiled royalties" in a sense. For them, the question is: "Where is the foundling's father hidden?" (492).

It is only the existence of the Forefather which can justify Ahab's invention of an alternative self, by situating himself in a cosmology different from that plotted by Jehovah. The Forefather functions, in this sense, as the higher authority by which Ahab transcends the limitations of Christianity and the command of Jehovah as origin of all being. Ironically, however, the Forefather operates not only as the presence of authority, but also as the absence of it, since He is unknown.

The famous corposant scene, before Ahab's showdown with Moby Dick, exposes the precariousness of the presence and the absence of authority in Ahab's Gnostic philosophy. He addresses the corposants in darkness:

> Oh, thou clear spirit, of thy fire thou madest me, and like a true child of fire, I breathe it back to thee. . . . Oh, thou magnanimous! now I do glory in my geneal-

ogy. But thou art but my fiery father; my sweet mother, I know not. Oh, cruel! what hast thou done with her? There lies my puzzle; but thine is greater. Thou knowest not how came ye, hence callest thyself unbegotten; certainly knowest not thy beginning, hence callest thyself unbegun. I know that of me, which thou knowest not of thyself, oh, thou omnipotent. There is some unsuffusing thing beyond thee, thou clear spirit, to whom all thy eternity is but time, all thy creativeness mechanical. Through thee, thy flaming self, my scorched eyes do dimly see it.

(508)

Ahab's Gnostic genealogy should give him a double parentage, a "fiery father" and "some unsuffusing thing beyond," who are respectively his corporeal and his spiritual origins. The visible fire is the representation of Jehovah (the Demiurge) who made man." Beyond the fiery father, Ahab's Gnostic discourse invents the presence of another father, the Unknown God (absence) whose realm is called *Pleroma* (fullness), which in Ahab's version he calls "some unsuffusing thing" (absence).

According to Gnosticism, beyond Jehovah (or the Demiurge) exists the Unknown God. To this Forefather, the "creativeness" of the Biblical Creator is "mechanical." Derived from the Greek term *demiourgos,* which means "artisan," the word Demiurge contains the meaning of methodic invention—or craftsmanship. This mechanical creativity of the Demiurge is represented by the "carpenter" figure in **Moby-Dick.** Melville devotes one chapter to the carpenter (Chapter 107), describing how he works like "an automaton" (468). Ahab calls the carpenter a "manmaker" (470), suggesting a connection between this carpenter and Jehovah (the Demiurge), and asks the carpenter when making his ivory leg whether he would "rather work in clay"; he also asks the carpenter if he could not "drive that old Adam [i.e., Ahab's feeling of his lost leg] away" (471).

In fact, Melville had already speculated on Jehovah's ignorance of his own origin and his mechanical creativity in letters to Hawthorne while writing **Moby-Dick.** In a letter of April 16?, 1851, Melville said that "God cannot explain His own secrets, and . . . He would like a little information upon certain points Himself" (Davis and Gilman 125). In a letter of June 1?, 1851, he says, "The reason the mass of men fear God, and *at bottom dislike* Him, is because they rather distrust His heart, and fancy Him all brain like a watch" (Davis and Gilman 129).

However, the Christian God is not the only object of man's defiance in Gnosticism. All the tyrannical gods who function as the center of authority in other narrative paradigms of the West, including Zeus, become objects of distrust. As Melville says, "I had rather be a fool with a heart, than Jupiter Olympus with his head"

(Davis and Gilman 129). According to Hans Jonas, in Gnostic allegory Zeus is identified with the *heimarmene* (the kingdom of "fate") which controls man tyrannically. Zeus is the Demiurge of Greek mythology. Against him, Prometheus stands as "the type of the 'spiritual' man whose loyalty is not to the god of this world but to the transcendent one beyond" (Jonas 97). In **Moby-Dick,** as one chapter is given over to the carpenter, so another chapter is devoted to the blacksmith (Chapter 112) whom Ahab calls "Prometheus" (470). The two figures, carpenter and blacksmith, make a Gnostic pair analogous to the Demiurge and Prometheus. It is important to note why Ahab told the carpenter to take the order for "a complete man after a desirable pattern" to the blacksmith when the carpenter was mechanically making the ivory leg for Ahab. Ahab distrusts the carpenter (the Demiurge) as the Creator, but he trusts the blacksmith (Prometheus) to create "a complete man."

Ahab's Gnostic manipulation of discourse, however, seems impotent in altering the material history. For Ahab cannot change the fact that man is physically incomplete. He is irritated that he even "owe[s] for the flesh in the tongue [he] brag[s] with," and expresses his passionate wish to get rid of the inferior body, saying, "I'll get a crucible, and into it, and dissolve myself down to one small, compendious vertebra" (472). Indeed death may be the only way of freeing himself from the inferior body.

But in Ahab's climactic moment, the word "surrender" does not exist, despite his infuriation with the limitations of bodily existence. Rather, Ahab confronts his arch nemesis with the passionate fury of an epic warrior, as his personal desire for revenge against Moby Dick transforms itself from egotism to heroism. In order to restore the divine genealogy of "his whole race from Adam down" (184), Ahab chooses to fight against Jehovah (the Demiurge). He is a Gnostic Christ who seeks to redeem the old history of the human race, and to re-direct it into a new historical stage. Indeed Ahab is explicitly linked to Christ in **Moby-Dick**: "moody stricken Ahab stood before them [his officers] with a crucifixion in his face" (124). Ahab himself asks: "Is, then, the crown too heavy that I wear? this Iron Crown of Lombardy [a crown said to contain a nail from the Cross]" (167). As Melville implies, Ahab's opponent is Jehovah (the Demiurge), who is "visibly personified" in Moby Dick (184). In the Old Testament, the Leviathan is associated with Jehovah as the Supreme Good. But in **Moby-Dick,** the whale is associated with Jehovah in his capacity as Demiurge or evil creator. Ahab says that the corposants "light . . . the way to the White Whale" (507), "the grand god" (549). As Starbuck observes, "The white whale is their demogorgon" (169). Luther S. Mansfield and Howard P. Vincent adopted the spelling, "demigorgon," in editing **Moby-Dick** (New York:

Hendricks House, 1962) and guessed that "Melville's spelling possibly came from confusion with Demiurge, the Creator god according to the mythology of some of the early Gnostic sects—notably the Ophites" (690). In the cosmology of the Ophites, the Demiurge is identified with the Leviathan who shuts the earthly world off from the kingdom of light or the highest God. Ahab regards the Leviathan as the wall obstructing man's vision and tries to liberate man imprisoned in it:

> How can the prisoner reach outside except by thrusting through the wall?

> (164)

Ahab's personal revenge against Moby Dick assumes a cosmic role here, as the whale is transformed into the representation of the Demiurge in Ahab's Gnostic discourse.

Ahab fails in the end, of course. He cannot convert the Gnostic myth into history. Instead he perishes in the ocean. Nor does Melville say for Ahab as he did for Bulkington, "Up from the spray of thy ocean-perishing—straight up, leaps thy apotheosis!" (107). The Gnostic apotheosis is not fulfilled even when Ahab dies, despite the earlier promise in the chapter of "The Lee Shore."[12] Ahab, chasing after Moby Dick as a tricky signifier with an absent referent, is dragged deep into the ocean forever. Since he could not reach the referent, nothing in History seems to have changed. In fact, the romance ends with a phrase, "the great shroud of the sea rolled on as it rolled five thousand years ago" (572), suggesting the unchangeability of the Christian paradigm of the Narrative.

To be sure, this may seem strange. Why did Melville try to create a Gnostic history in **Moby-Dick** if he nullifies it at the end? Ahab had to die because he tried to re-write the Narrative according to his personal vision, as if he were the Author of the universe, and coerced his crew or even the whole human race to adopt it in *reality* as *the* History.

But the romance is not finished there. And that is because Ishmael, "another orphan" (573), was saved from the shroud of the ocean. The Gnostic history was not nullified with the death of Ahab. Instead it is turned into a textual narrative by Ishmael, the narrator who voyaged with Ahab. As the epigraph suggests—"And I only am escaped alone to tell thee" (*Job*)—the story stays alive in the voice of Ishmael (573). The two narrative discourses, **Moby-Dick** and the Scriptures, are thus to continue competing forever.

It is not Ahab, then, but Ishmael who finally relativizes the concept of History as a textual narrative discourse. At the outset of this romance, Ishmael situated the historical incident of himself going on a whaling voyage as a "shabby part" in "the grand programme of Providence" (7). According to the Narrative, the History of humanity emplotted by Providence, the event narrated in **Moby-Dick** should have been an insignificant one. Ishmael says ironically:

> And, doubtless, my going on this whaling voyage, formed part of the grand programme of Providence that was drawn up a long time ago. It came in as a sort of brief interlude and solo between more extensive performances. I take it that this part of the bill must have run something like this: "*Grand Contested Election for the Presidency of the United States.*"
>
> "WHALING VOYAGE BY ONE ISHMAEL."
>
> "BLOODY BATTLE IN AFFGHANISTAN [*sic*]."

> (7)

Ishmael, however, met Ahab on board the Pequod. Escaping from the catastrophe, Ishmael is liberated from the Christian paradigm into which he was compulsorily cast as a minor character. And with Ahab as a protagonist, Ishmael recasts the plot of the Providential History, the Narrative sanctioned by Jehovah the Author, and creates a grand romance of Gnosticism claiming his own authorship.

When Melville finished **Moby-Dick,** he wrote to Hawthorne: "I have written a wicked book, and feel spotless as the lamb" (Leyda 434). He felt purged after he challenged the Book of Books once and for all. The American romancer, with Ahab and Ishmael, tried to relativize the Book of Books as no less a literary artifact than his own "wicked book." When Melville pluralized History by juxtaposing rival cosmological concepts in **Moby-Dick,** the romance achieved a turning point in American literary history, and the "fictive" dimension of narrative gained discursive power over the presumed authenticity of non-fictional history.[13]

Notes

1. As for an earlier study of Melville's Gnosticism, see Thomas Vargish.

2. We can barely speculate on it through Lawrance Thompson's endnote which claims that Andrews Norton's book on Gnosticism, *The Evidences of the Genuineness of the Gospels,* was "a scholarly landmark of the period" and "[w]idely reviewed, widely read, widely quoted, much discussed" (430).

3. The question of the history in the Bible was not confined to the Gospels, but the *NAR* 26 (Jan. 1828) observed that "[m]uch criticism has been expended on the Book of Job . . . [concerning] whether the history be true or fabulous" (40).

4. It is worth recalling that Melville's *Typee* was published the previous year in another series of

Wiley & Putnam, the "Library of American Books," which was also edited by Duyckinck.

5. The extract of this article was reprinted in the *New Jerusalem Magazine* (11 [Apr. 1838]: 281-283).

6. Emerson, however, opposes *historical* Christianity, and also the "ecclesiastical history [where] we take so much pains to know what the Gnostics, what the Essenes, what the Manichees . . . believed" ("The Transcendentalist," *Selected Writings* 94).

7. Melville's letter of April 16?, 1851, to Hawthorne (Leyda 410).

8. That is why man needs, as Ahab says, "a sky-light on top of his head to illuminate inwards." According to Ahab, man is "a blind dome" (470). Resisting this benighted condition of human beings, Ahab exclaims, "No, no, no; I must have a lantern" (470).

9. Strictly speaking, in Gnosticism, the Demiurge created both the body and the inferior part of the soul which are in an ignorant, servile condition, against which the spirit, the superior part of the soul, stands as the divine seed of gnosis.

10. Yet, since the origin of the higher authority, i.e., the Forefather, is unknown, the Gnostic discourse is always on the verge of deconstructing itself.

11. The connection between fire and the Demiurge is clearly Gnostic; as Hans Jonas says, "in many gnostic systems the Demiurge is expressly called the god of the fire" (198).

12. In *Moby-Dick,* there is a strange early chapter, "The Lee Shore," which Melville calls "the stoneless grave of Bulkington" (106). Bulkington claims the independence of the soul against its servile situation, fighting against "the wildest winds of heaven and earth [which] conspire to cast her [i.e., the soul] on the treacherous, slavish shore" (107). Bulkington makes "the intrepid effort of the soul to keep the open independence of her sea" (107). When he dies, the divine spirit imprisoned in the body will be released and ascend. The narrator says:

> Take heart, take heart, O Bulkington! Bear thee grimly, demigod! Up from the spray of thy ocean-perishing—straight up, leaps thy apotheosis!
>
> (107)

13. This paper was written with the support of a research grant from Seikei University. I am grateful to Christopher Sten and Claire Sponsler for their comments on early drafts.

Works Cited

Davis, Merrell R., and William H. Gilman, eds. *The Letters of Herman Melville.* New Haven: Yale University Press, 1960.

Dillingham, William B. *Melville's Later Novels.* Athens: University of Georgia Press, 1986.

Emerson, Ralph Waldo. *The Selected Writings of Ralph Waldo Emerson.* Ed. Brooks Atkinson. New York: Modern Library, 1940.

"Gnosticism." *New Jerusalem Magazine* 11 (Apr. 1838): 281-83.

Jonas, Hans. *The Gnostic Religion.* Rev. ed. Boston: Beacon Press, 1963.

Lamson, A. Rev. of *Some Account of the Writings and Opinions of Clement of Alexandria,* by John, Bishop of Lincoln. *Christian Examiner* 23 (Nov. 1837): 159-70.

Leyda, Jay. *The Melville Log.* Vol. 1. New York: Gordian Press, 1969.

Mansfield, Luther S., and Howard P. Vincent, eds. *Moby-Dick.* New York: Hendricks House, 1962.

Matthiessen, F. O. *American Renaissance.* New York: Oxford University Press, 1941.

"Means of Ascertaining the Genuineness and Integrity of Ancient Writings." *North American Review* 42 (Jan. 1836): 1-51.

Melville, Herman. *Mardi.* Evanston: Northwestern University Press; Chicago: Newberry Library, 1970.

———. *Redburn.* Evanston: Northwestern University Press; Chicago: Newberry Library, 1969.

———. *White-Jacket.* Evanston: Northwestern University Press; Chicago: Newberry Library, 1970.

———. *Moby-Dick.* Evanston: Northwestern University Press; Chicago: Newberry Library, 1988.

———. *Clarel.* Evanston: Northwestern University Press; Chicago: Newberry Library, 1991.

———. *Timoleon.* 1891. Norwood: Norwood Editions, 1976.

Mosheim, John Lawrence. *Ecclesiastical History.* New York: Evert Duyckinck, 1821.

Norton, Andrews. *A Discourse on the Latest Form of Infidelity.* Cambridge: John Owen, 1839.

———. *The Evidences of the Genuineness of the Gospels.* Vols. 2-3. Cambridge: John Owen, 1844.

"Norton on *the Genuineness of the Gospels.*" *North American Review* 45 (July 1837a): 206-22.

"Norton on *the Genuineness of the Gospels.*" *North American Review* 59 (July 1844b): 142-189.

"Noyes's Translation of Job." *North American Review* 26 (Jan. 1828): 40-59.

Parker, T. Rev of *Histoire critique du Gnosticisme,* by Jacques Matter. *Christian Examiner* 24 (Mar. 1838): 112-130.

Rudolph, Kurt. *Gnosis: The Nature and History of Gnosticism.* San Francisco: Harper & Row, 1983.

Sealts, Merton M., Jr. *Melville's Reading.* Rev. ed. Columbia: University South Carolina Press, 1988.

Thompson, Lawrance. *Melville's Quarrel with God.* Princeton: Princeton University Press, 1952.

Vargish, Thomas. "Gnostic Mythos in *Moby-Dick*." *PMLA* 81 (1966): 272-277.

Waterman, George, Jr. "Gnosticism." *Ladies' Repository* 3 (Oct. 1843): 292-293.

John Alvis (essay date winter 1996)

SOURCE: Alvis, John. "*Moby-Dick* and Melville's Quarrel with America." *Interpretation: A Journal of Political Philosophy* 23, no. 2 (winter 1996): 223-47.

[*In the following essay, Alvis takes discusses the political undercurrents in* Moby-Dick. *Alvis interprets the novel as a metaphor for the struggle between individual sovereignty and popular will in American democracy.*]

I

Melville works out his thoughts on America's political character in his fifth novel, **White-Jacket** and in his sixth, **Moby-Dick.** The latter meditation is related to the former as antithesis to thesis; a hopeful confidence in his country's national purpose gives way to skeptical reflections on a dilemma inseparable from those founding principles that for Melville had once promised an enlightened and morally improved public life. In **Moby-Dick** Melville confronts a tension between the substantive and formal principles of the American regime, between a conception of the maintenance of human rights founded in nature, the nation's final cause, and the formal requirement of sovereignty, the democratic imperative of popular consent. The problem I suppose Melville to have puzzled over in the course of producing his nearest approach to a masterwork is this: How other than by appeal to Christian tradition does modern democracy produce needful restraints upon democratic will?

II

To see why one can speak of needful restraints on a popular sovereign it is pertinent to appreciate Melville's radicalizing of the political issue as he passed from **White-Jacket** to **Moby-Dick.** Both novels acquaint us with the mechanisms that sustain despotism aboard an American ship. Yet the specific difference points to an enlargement of subject. The military despotism Melville anatomizes in **White-Jacket** is circumscribed and remediable by act of Congress, possibly even by executive directives. Troubles on the *Neversink* amount to an excrescence upon an American body politic which, as such bodies go, Melville seems to consider essentially healthy. The earlier novel exposes bad military usages evidently on the assumption that an informed citizenry will not give their consent to unnecessarily harsh navy discipline once they know of these abuses. With **Moby-Dick,** however, we are presented with a despotism over the spirit that relies on the consent of the very men whose lives, liberty, and pursuit of happiness will be sacrificed to the will of their leader. By thus raising the stakes the later novel calls attention to a conflict of principle latent within that Lockian [*sic*]-Jeffersonian political creed to which the youthful narrator of **White-Jacket** had attached his hope of world redemption.[1]

Locke is mentioned by name in the chapter (79) that recounts Stubb and Flask killing a Right whale, then attaching its head to the *Pequod*'s hull so as to balance a Sperm whale's head already depending from the opposite side. The whaleman's practice inspires Ishmael with an academic plan to balance Kantian with Lockian philosophy. Ishmael evidently has in mind the Locke of the *Essay Concerning Human Understanding* with its materialist skepticism that might balance Kantian idealism. But Melville may have also been aware that Locke's skeptical epistemology subserves a revolutionary political teaching. His contractarian theory rejects the assumption of ancient and Christian political philosophy that government ought to aim at forming the moral character of citizens. Locke's explanation of the origins and nature of civil society rests solely upon self-interested material calculation. Lockian rights reduce at bottom to civil guarantees for freedoms conducive to self-preservation. Government no longer rests on a claim to divine favor or on the natural superiority of virtue but upon the consent of the governed. That consent depends in turn upon the individual's estimate of what he will need to preserve his life and property against a hostile nature and hostile men. Yet it is quite conceivable that to subdue stepdame nature one might think it necessary to animate men with a collective zeal that would make them indifferent to safeguarding the freedom of their neighbors. Locke's doctrine of consent promotes a tension within the secular, democratic regime, a conflict of purposes which Melville examines through his portrayal of Ahab's rule over the *Pequod*.

By depicting Ahab's successful subjugation of a crew among whom we find representatives of the nation's religious heritage as well as an Ishmael widely read in the philosophic tradition, Melville dramatizes a problem implicit in that founding creed which rests upon Jefferson's espousal of Locke's doctrine of consent. Whereas for the Melville of **White-Jacket** Lockian reasoning mediated through the Declaration of Independence provides adequate political guidance, the Melville of **Moby-Dick** discerns in Jefferson's two arch-principles of inalienable rights and consent an unresolved tension: legitimate government rests upon the consent of the governed, its formal principle, and secures rights, its substantive principle. Yet what if the formal and substantive principles should prove to be at odds? Cannot the majority consent to laws that infringe rights of the minority or of individuals? Jefferson certainly thought so in his first inaugural address when he warned that Americans should "bear in mind this sacred principle, that though the will of the majority is in all cases to prevail, that will to be rightful must be reasonable." The same difficulty beset Locke, who had grounded his doctrine of the contractual origin of civil society upon the necessity of protecting rights, but had subsequently stipulated sovereignty for the majority without indicating how democratic majorities could be relied upon to respect the rights of man. Melville perceived lying at the heart of American democracy this dilemma of reconciling evidently necessary democratic means to more evidently obligatory moral ends. Moreover, **Moby-Dick** throws another shadow over the sunny political messianism voiced in **White-Jacket.** By the time he completed his greater work, Melville seems to have become aware of the despotic potential implicit in the Lockian concept of society as an engine for overcoming nature's scarcity and violence.

To appreciate the scope of the Lockian issues implicit in the novel we should begin by noting how Melville works up emotions more proper to heroic epics than to modern prose fiction. In the chapter "The Advocate," Ishmael exhorts readers to agree with him that the commercial-manufacturing enterprise he details merits literary treatment traditionally reserved for loftier subjects. At times the claim is put forward facetiously, Perseus and Vishnoo as archetypal harpooners and so forth. Plot and incident, however, establish heroic credentials for the seamen. Resembling armies on campaign, whalemen leave home and family for lengthy intervals of hardship and strenuous action. If hunting ordinary whales exposes men to risks nearly comparable with hazards of warfare, an antagonist equipped with the white whale's cunning malignancy justifies the heroic terms Ishmael adopts when he refers to the ship's mates and their harpoon bearers as knights and squires. Furthermore, slaughtering whales requires virtues of leadership in addition to feats of individual courage and prowess. The whale killer needs to make sure of loyal subordinates, just as Beowulf had to secure the assistance of his comitatus following. Ahab, consequently, like the classical and Renaissance epic heroes Melville mentions in his novels and poems, must fulfill an administrative as well as a combatant's role.

Even so, the opportunities whaling affords for depicting quest, combat and leadership do not reassure the narrator he will accomplish heroic amplitude by incorporating these vivid activities. When Ishmael complains,

> Oh, Ahab! what shall be grand in thee, it must needs be plucked at from the skies, and dived for in the deep, and featured in the unbodied air[2]

we hear Melville's own exertion to elevate mundane material. The material seems more refractory than it need have been precisely because Melville has chosen to present a documentary on whaling as industry rather than focussing solely on its adventurous aspects. He makes Ishmael complain of a difficulty he appears in large part to have brought on himself by insisting on minute descriptions of provisioning the ship, rendering blubber, and cleaning up. If only artistic considerations impelled him, Melville could avail himself of a poet's liberty to ignore ship business and to confine his attention to exciting chases with their attendant psychological and metaphysical soundings. Who faults Homer for withholding details of Achaean sumptering and latrine? Yet probably Melville makes much of overcoming the inertia of his materials because his theme is the struggle of a commercial society to escape routine, illiberal drudgery wherein the terms of life are set by the balance sheet.

Putting aside Southern slaveholders, the nineteenth-century Americans toiled for their livelihood, and, if they cultivated aristocratic virtues relating to war, command, sanctity, literature or other liberal arts, they did so in the course of gainful employment. So in this novel set at midcentury, Bohemian Ishmael and Faustian Ahab have no choice but to earn their daily bread, whatever their eccentric aspirations. "Socratic" Queequeg (Ishmael's epithet) cannot indulge a Socratic leisure except during the few days he decides to spend awaiting death. Nineteenth-century authors had to write for cash, as the hard-pressed author of South Sea literary vendibles attests in his letters. We observe Melville turning an apparent literary liability into an asset by taking as his subject the effort his narrator shares with Ahab of sublimating an economic activity, transforming commercial necessities into spirit-challenging undertakings.

If one identifies this subject with capitalism, one construes it too narrowly. A more uncompromisingly capitalist management of the *Pequod* would have avoided its catastrophe. No capitalist at all attentive to his interests would pursue a particular Sperm whale. On such grounds Starbuck challenges Ahab's fidelity to his contract, "How many barrels will thy vengeance yield thee . . . ?" (36. 163). New England's whaling industry seems, moreover, to operate on the principle of employee profit-sharing (granted labor's share is as small as the market permits). Melville does brood over the absence of moral restraint in a society avid for new technologies to multiply securities and material gratification, but he seems indifferent to whether the means of production be in private hands or collectively owned. Instead, the issue for him is whether an understanding of political obligations resting upon no other basis than calculations of partnership in acquisition, self-preservation, and mutual security will suffice to secure political justice and freedom.

III

Melville may find himself balked before the task of inventing the American epic because he senses that assumptions apparently necessary for an audience's reception of the kind of heroism proper to epic poetry run counter to American beliefs. Such misgiving seems warranted if we consider the distance between traditional views of the grounds for civil society, on the one hand, and, on the other, the predominantly modern liberal democratic perspective adopted in the Declaration of Independence. The argument of the Declaration rests partly—some say it rests altogether—on a modern version of the contractarian theory of civil society elaborated by Locke in his *Second Treatise*. A brief reflection on Locke's thought will display its nonheroic tendency.

Locke hypothesized a state of nature existing prior to any civil order and characterized by such equality that no man was subject to the will of any other. Aboriginal men produced civil government with its laws in order to escape the inconveniences of their primal atomistic condition. They desired to make themselves more secure by protecting themselves against the depredations of stronger individuals, but they also needed to find means of cooperating in order to wrest a more certain and more abundant livelihood from natural resources. Free and equal individuals thus banded together surrendered to a commonly acknowledged authority some of their primordial liberty for the sake of enjoying greater security for themselves and their property. According to Locke's view, therefore, organized society exists because it offers a good bargain for otherwise vulnerable individuals. The bargain consists in their retaining as much of the original freedom and equality as they deem compatible with their safety and comfort.

Locke's balance sheet of revenue and costs looks to self-preservation through generating and protecting property. One's allegiance to the civil order is, and ought to be, utilitarian in outlook, provisional in temper. Tendering one's liberties to the community, one expects something in return, and, if returns are not forthcoming, one's contribution will not continue willingly to be made. The bond between individual person and state is calculated and selfish, or, at any rate, self-interested, rather than reverential or self-forgetful.

Thinkers who commend these arrangements call them enlightened and argue that government becomes more responsible once everyone has been brought to think rulers have no claim to divine authority and must earn respect by convincing the governed of their having provided safety and comfort.

Whether regarded as refreshingly enlightened or discouragingly low-minded, we may deduce that once Lockian teaching on the relatedness of the individual to society has come to prevail, prospects for heroic literature memorializing national founders turn doubtful. First, what should an epic poet find to celebrate in nations that think of themselves merely as markets dealing in personal security? Insurance brokers do not inspire songs. Should one expect men to expend themselves in serving a people, as Moses, Aeneas, and Milton's Messiah did, if that people proclaims itself animated by no common purpose more inspiriting than nursing comforts in safety? There is something contradictory about dying for security or about undertaking every sort of privation and inconvenience, as heroes of epic poems do, in order to arrange for someone else's future ease. The contractarian notion appears to disparage self-sacrifice. Why should one self-seeking party to a contract for protecting property give himself up for another? Locke's conception places at the origin of a political order not God's providence, the foundation of community for Moses, Virgil, or Milton, but human contrivance, thereby confining collective effort to human secular projects remote from divine interest. If men come to view their own will rather than the will of God as the source of law, they will hardly endorse the enabling premise of traditional heroic literature: the hero leads his people under the supervision of a divine sponsor who judges conduct while inspiring hero and community alike. Inasmuch as contractarian models require a suppression of religious enthusiasms, which would inject unnegotiables into the social calculus, it is not coincidental that Hobbes, Locke, and Rousseau all seek to moderate religious attachments, and that the Locke of *The Letter on Toleration* produces the definitive modern argument for compromising belief. Lockian man in Lockian society practices religion diffidently, conforming his conduct to nonheroic expectations. Once Lockian teaching informs manners and guides judgment, the modern writer who seeks heroic subjects finds himself dispossessed of suitable material, i.e., ideals of self-sacrifice, dispossessed of a people worth the efforts of a hero and appreciative of his deeds, and dispossessed of divine authority, of a providential scheme and a theodicy.

My supposition that Melville means to present his tale against the backdrop of such a society organized along lines prescribed by Lockian theory throws some light on a problem of the novel's construction. *Moby-Dick* contains 135 chapters plus prefatory "Extracts" and an

"Epilogue." Although the dramatic interest attaches to Ahab's pursuit of the white whale, Melville delays the first appearance of Ahab until the twenty-eighth chapter, after almost a fourth of the book has elapsed. Granted, important matter transpires in the exposition—Ishmael's meeting Queequeg, Elijah's warnings at the wharf, Father Mapple's Jonah sermon—still, the foreground seems of such inordinate length as to require justification. We are told Melville was well along in composition before he decided to throw his focus upon Ahab, but whatever the exigencies of composition, he chose to retain at publication all the detail of arranging transportation and lodging in two towns, plus a tavern scene, bargaining with shipowners, and elaborate ship descriptions, although all this delays introducing Ahab and launching the action proper. Justification for this undramatic foreground may lie in Melville's intent to make us feel the unleavened weight of a society given to getting and spending. Ahab will have to overcome this utilitarian preoccupation in pursuing his metaphysical vengeance, and Melville must overcome the same inertia if he means to convey a sense of epic momentousness.

The link with Lockian thought is commerce. A society organized for trade on the modern scale answers best to the project of enlarging and securing property, the goal of political association in Locke's contractarian theory. Commercial activity combined with the effects commerce works on manners and moral outlook occupy the reader's attention from the moment Ishmael hits upon the notion of going to sea until Ahab steps out of his cabin more than a hundred pages later. From initial musings on Manhattan clerks "tied to counters" to the moment of Ahab's entrance, commercial transactions absorb Ishmael, Queequeg, and several minor characters who make their brief entrances for no apparent reason other than that they serve to establish a busy commercial atmosphere. We see almost no occasion for man meeting man in New Bedford and Nantucket other than seller finding buyer or employee seeking employer. A tavern-keeper purveys doubtful liquor in cheating tumblers and lodges a cannibal since "He pays reg'lar." Even the non-Westerner, South-Sea-Islander Queequeg, first appears as a vendor (of shrunken skulls). The proprietress of the second inn Ishmael visits worries about the damage suicides inflict on her business—a harpooner killed himself with the tool of his profession in one of her rooms, provoking her to complain that he has ruined one of her counterpanes. Melville prepares us for the disappearance from the story of the most romantic figure among his characters, the shore-despising Bulkington, with the authorial remark that Bulkington remains a "sleeping-partner" (3.16), a term borrowed from nineteenth-century financial jargon signifying an investor whose role in a firm went unpublicized. The cenotaphs on the walls of a church emphasize the perils of the industry that dominates this region. On the deck

of the *Pequod,* we observe the painful husbandry of the ship's owners and are instructed in their practice of paying the seamen by assigning various fractions of the net profit. Then we discover that ledger calculations induce these Christian owners to several accommodations with Mammon. The long passage to the hunting zones permits no delays for religious observances, hence once outfitted the ship must set sail even though the day is Christmas (22.104). Bible-quoting Quaker shipmasters urge the mates not to work too much on Sundays, but not to miss a fair chance of a whale, Sunday or not (22.105). Ishmael will later characterize whalemen as "Ex officio professors of Sabbath breaking" (67.303). Bildad and Peleg are not going to allow pagan Queequeg aboard, but put their scruples aside once they see him dart a harpoon (18.89). The owners' anxiety for gain prevails over their trust in providence and thrift pinches their charity. Stubb warns Pip a whale will fetch much more in the market than a black boy. Not surprisingly, then, the only formal definition of man to occur in the novel is "money-making animal" (93.413). Strenuous belief does not appear once we read beyond Father Mapple's sermon, and his preaching makes something of a quaint impression since Melville suggests that commercial avidity has supplanted once-paramount religious concerns.

By this portrayal of New England manners, Melville means to establish at the outset the impression of a society engaged in exchanging Christian standards for Lockian. Older religious pieties are at the point of yielding to new passions generated by emancipated avarice. Commercial preoccupations follow naturally from Lockian ideas of atomistic individuals devising cooperative social arrangements to make themselves secure in their accumulation of property. A regime organized for commercial activity on a large scale answers to Locke's teaching that men seek, and ought to seek above all else, to preserve their lives, and then to preserve them in some comfort. Whale oil brings comfort to buyers by providing fuel for their lamps, while profits from whaling secure the estates of Nantucket men and their families. The constant press of business in port and aboard ship seems designed to suggest that for owners and mariners alike, light from whale oil takes precedence in their moment-by-moment consciousness over the light which ancestral piety had identified with God's son.

Melville devotes lengthy passages to explaining the whaling industry so as to keep in sight the image of the *Pequod* as an epitome of a society organized for the sake of commercial venturing. Excepting Ahab and Ishmael, who says he goes to sea for what we today would call psychic therapy, the men, diverse in race, regional ties, and religion, agree to be shipmates for no other reason than making their livelihood. If they have their further motivation, both Ahab and Ishmael nonetheless must get their living in their present circumstances by contributing to a commercial enterprise. Ishmael appreciates the cash motive, as we see from his trite meditation on original sin:

> The act of paying is perhaps the most uncomfortable infliction that the two orchard thieves entailed upon us. But *being paid,*—what will compare with it? The urbane activity with which a man receives money is really marvelous, considering that we so earnestly believe money to be the root of all earthly ills, and that on no account can a monied man enter heaven. Ah! how cheerfully we consign ourselves to perdition!
>
> (1.6)

Even Ahab must have a care for maintaining appearances of managing a profitable voyage (46.212-13). Not surprisingly, then, Ishmael characterizes as "sage and sensible" the latter-day Puritan's accommodation to the spirit of acquisition: "a man's religion is one thing, and this practical world quite another. This world pays dividends" (16.74). Similarly the Locke of the *Second Treatise* pays lip service to the Christian teaching that covetousness is "the Root of all Evil." Yet the invention of money is for Locke the key to man's transition from a simple, rude existence to civilization, since "a little piece of yellow Metal" makes possible the accumulation of property and with it that stimulation of acquisitiveness which for Locke is the engine of human advancement. Melville thus makes clear enough that he intends to portray a utilitarian society colliding with a man of spirit who despises comfort and cares nothing for preserving his body. In Ahab Melville imagines the sort of leader capable of making Americans shift their bearings from preoccupation with gainful toil to willing service in a project promising more risk than profit. Yet, as I will argue presently, for all its daring his project is more Lockian than traditionalist in its premises.

Ahab's nobility consists in his impatience with utility, pleasure, accommodation, compromise, and conventional attitudes of piety. Observing on his first view of his captain the physique of a man whose spiritual energy seems to have consumed his own flesh, Ishmael likens Ahab to a martyr suffering for some as yet undefined heterodoxy, "a man cut away from the stake, when the fire has overrunningly wasted all the limbs without consuming them" (28.123). Melville plays up without explaining a livid scar which one old tar maintains runs the entire length of Ahab's body. He alludes to a rumor of Ahab having been branded, presumably by lightning, in some elemental clash. Finally, Ahab himself hints at the scar's having been made by divine fiat to chastise him. Whatever its origins, the scar and the extraordinary vigorous spareness of Ahab's person combine with his whalebone leg to convey the sense of a spirit scornful of comforts in his preoccupation with mental struggle. We are not surprised to see such a man fling the pipe he has been smoking into the sea. Easy-living Stubb smokes continually, and companionable Quee-

queg shares a peacepipe with Ishmael, but Ahab looks upon bodily comforts as obstacles to the high intensity he maintains awake and, according to the steward's report, even in his dreams. During the final chase, like an Achilles become all spiritedness in his rampage, Ahab scarcely needs sleep or food. Melville contrives a certain dignity for his chief character by making him, as it were, so much compressed spiritedness in contempt of the compromising materialism now gaining authority over his New England compatriots.

Commercial manners favor the easy familiarity Flask enjoys and an originally misanthropic Ishmael learns to practice. Although not insensible to human affections, Ahab holds himself unselfconsciously aloof. He makes no show of his dignity; but because all his attention turns inward, he is oblivious of other men until he has some use for them, or until they happen to obstruct his quest or, like unthinking Stubb, belittle his affliction. Ahab doesn't smile, speak at table, nor, excepting fitful and quickly repented confidences half-opened to Starbuck and a despotic benevolence toward the cabin boy, does he enter into familiarity with anyone. Yet the distance he preserves between himself and his men results solely from self-torment. We are supposed to regard him not as snob but troubled visionary.

Lockian bargain-seekers doubtless experience the common run of vexations, but large sorrow is presumed to convey extraordinary spiritual capacity beyond a utilitarian's conception of human likelihoods. Ishmael says Ahab bears a "crucifixion" in his face. Without making extensive inventory of his injuries—a coming to cases that would certainly diminish our sense of his grievance—Ahab displays his continual consciousness of some unpardonable if unspecified affront. His language resounds with melancholy, resentful expressions evocative of Hamlet, outraged Lear, or the broodings of the author of Ecclesiastes. Melville depicts strength in grief, never plaintive or self-commiserating—a strength, moreover, which offers to champion the cause of all deep-grieving men. Ahab's sorrow appears magnificently in excess of the wound inflicted by the whale, since eventually we meet another ship captain who has had an arm taken in the same way Ahab had lost a leg (chap. 100), yet the tangy good spirits of the British whaleman remind us that physical impairment need not be taken as revelation of some altogether unacceptable malignity deep down in things.

In fact there is evidence suggesting that Ahab's rebellion against a cosmos he finds malevolent could not have had its origin in his physical loss. From close attention to Melville's chronology one concludes that the most shocking blasphemy charged to Ahab appears to have occurred *prior to* the voyage that brought his injury, since Elijah speaks of his having defiled a chalice in a church sometime previous to the voyage during which the whale took off his leg (19.92). Already before he encountered the whale Ahab thought he had sufficient cause thus to express his *non serviam*. Consequently, we are supposed to recognize in Ahab's grievance against Moby-Dick the culmination rather than the origin of a protracted period of spiritual rebellion.

What lies back of Ahab's defiance, then, is evidently some animus resembling the theological equivalent of unrequited love. We see this as the novel builds toward the final chase, when Melville discloses the origin of Ahab's mysterious scar in another act of defiance directed toward God-in-nature. The crucial chapter, "The Candles," depicts an Ahab who demonstrates his indifference to terrors of a typhoon as he stands up to lightning and ostentatiously extinguishes the corpusant fire with his breath. He stands with right arm uplifted to salute lightning which still shows on the mast, and while he keeps his foot in contact with devil-worshiping Fedallah, Ahab addresses the spirit of fire:

> Oh! thou clear spirit of clear fire whom on these seas I as Persian once did worship, till in the sacramental act so burned by thee, that to this hour I bear the scar; I now know thee, thou clear spirit, and I now know that thy right worship is defiance.
>
> (119.507)

Ahab was once prepared to worship the source of light and life, but the wound suffered in the act of devotion he interprets as a rebuff and an admonition to stand off in fear rather than approach in amity. We know Ahab feels thwarted in his love because he subsequently says, "Come in thy lowest form of love and I will kneel and kiss thee." Ahab would hold out an open hand to a God who showed himself disposed to love, yet he has convinced himself that no such loving God presides over nature, and he will not respond to a ministry of fear because to do so, he feels, would be to submit a higher agency to a lower. Ahab's greatness of soul will not permit him to worship except on his own terms and only if God meets a test Ahab will set him.

Ahab seems to have rejected altogether such proofs of love as his fathers once ascribed to Christ's redemptive generosity. In fact, Ahab never mentions Christ, insisting instead that natural phenomena be the sole test of divine beneficence. Ahab will not subscribe to the idea of a loving God from the evidences of created beauty and order that Ishmael observes at times because he thinks rapacity and ugliness ultimately prevail in physical nature. In the chapter immediately preceding the first day's chase, Ahab confides to Starbuck the lesson he has learned from forty years of whaling. He thinks of himself as having warred all that time against "horrors of the deep." Observing the oceanic phenomena from Ishmael's perspective, a reader will likely be as impressed with its tranquil, life-producing rhythms as with its death-dealing commotions. The "Grand Armada" chapter serves to focus this sense of order with its tender sea pastoral. Against Ishmael's testimony Ahab's career spent in chase and combat has so concentrated his imagination upon the rigors of his profession that he becomes indifferent to these benign aspects of the seascape. Habits of aggressiveness long reinforced make Ahab keen to perceive—and to exaggerate—nature's own destructiveness. Therefore when Starbuck attempts to dissuade Ahab from further pursuit by appealing to the serenity of a fine day, the old man considers he has refuted the mate when he points to an instance of nature's law of eat or be eaten:

> "Look! see you Albacore! Who put it into him to chase and fang that flying-fish? Where do murderers go, man! Who's to doom, when the judge himself is dragged to the bar?"
>
> (132.545)

Melville intends us to think of Shakespeare's Lear when we hear Ahab's indictment of the Creator. Like Lear on the heath and for much the same reasons of disillusionment, Ahab ascribes perversity to nature. All living beings are murderers. Whoever has made them and continues to govern them has made them to be killers. The supreme law of creation is self-preservation, life overbearing life with no assurance that the devourer can claim to be "higher" than the devoured in any other regard than in its capacity to exert superior force. Melville evidently would have it that Ahab's experience is shared by honest observers of carnage between the species. Queequeg moralizes on a shark feeding-frenzy: "Queequeg no care what god made him shark . . . wedder Fejee god or Nantucket god; but de god wat made shark must be one dam Ingin" (66.302). Ishmael can ask, "Who is not a cannibal?" (65.300), and he meditates upon "the universal cannibalism of the sea; all whose creatures prey upon each other, carrying on eternal war since the world began" (58.274). Stubb approves Fleece's sermon exhorting large-mouth sharks to share with those who "can't get into de scrouge to help demselves." Stubb's comment: "that's Christianity."

The narrative action suggests that nature's law of domination by bloodshed extends up to the human realm. Ahab's charge echoes the irreligion of the Manxman in "Forecastle-Midnight" who had commented on one mariner's drawing a knife against another:

> In that ring Cain struck Abel. Sweet work, right work! No? Why then, God, mad'st thou the ring?
>
> (40.178)

If God has created men with the disposition to kill their brothers, such a God ought to be defied, and the most practical way to defy is to war against God's death-dealing creatures while boasting consciousness of thereby expressing one's resentment against the Author of this botched creation. It appears there embitters Ahab's defiance something of the resentment associated with apostasy, disappointment that experience has denied him his fathers' trust in a benevolent Deity. Nature having shown itself to be what it is, however, he will dedicate himself to a religion of hate as fervently as, had the world borne out the hopes of believers, he would have devoted himself to practicing loving kindness. Melville seems to suggest that trust in the kindness of a personal providence once it collapses under adverse experience yields to immoderate resentment against a natural scheme now seen as cruel, hostile, and capriciously wasteful.

Christian explanations of evil which blame Satan run against the further question why God, having the power to overcome Satan, should apparently comply with his adversary. Responding to Flask, Stubb gives Melville's reply to the orthodox:

> do you suppose I'm afraid of the devil? Who's afraid of him, except the old governor who daresn't catch him and put him in double-darbies, as he deserves, but lets him go about kidnapping people; aye, and signed a bond with him, that all the people the devil kidnapped, he'd roast for him? There's a governor!
>
> (73.326-27)

By extending to several spokesmen freethinking doubts of a just governor for this cosmos, Melville means to suggest that Ahab's dispute with God proceeds from intellectually honest confrontation of evidence widely felt but rarely acted upon with the resoluteness Ahab embodies. Melville means also to indicate the grounds on which some of the crew will make common cause with their commander in a quest the impiety of which he inclines rather to emphasize than conceal. Ahab thinks he is more just than God, because if the world were his to govern, he would rule it with less tolerance for cruelty and waste than God, as he thinks, stands accountable for.

Ahab's quarrel rests on a wider basis of inference than that provoked by bloody spectacles in predatory nature. The chapter in which he meditates on the severed head of a whale recently taken has Ahab address the scheme of things with challenging questions. He imagines this "Sphinx" (so Melville refers to the head) has witnessed the full scope of human woe under a heartless or unobservant heaven. The head has seen in sunken navies the ruin of national hopes, children torn from their mothers, and lovers who "sank beneath the exulting wave; true to each other, when heaven seemed false to them." Ahab continues his indictment with Job's complaint of decent men slain and the wicked prospering and concludes with the fancy of a ship struck by lightning as it transported a "righteous husband to outstretched loving arms" (70.312). Since he draws the moral "thou hast seen enough to split the planets and make an infidel of Abraham," we realize Ahab has taken the very widest survey of man's lot and has ascribed its misfortunes to divine spitefulness. Moby-Dick simply incarnates the general malignity Ahab sees everywhere. As Ishmael convincingly speculates, "he piled upon the white whale's hump the sum of all the general rage felt by his whole race from Adam down" (41.184). At another place Ishmael compares Ahab's indignation with the anguish Prometheus suffered (44.202). Both the Titan and Christian rebel insist that human misery proceeds from a cruel supreme deity.

More disturbing than Ahab's obsession is his ability to induce other men to acquiesce in it or even willingly to serve it. Ahab practices Caesarism, despotism advancing by the politician's manipulation of popular passions rather than by reliance on mere terror. He succeeds partly by accommodating to the tendencies of a Lockian social system and partly by appealing to needs neglected by such a society. Despotic control on the warship in *White-Jacket* had depended on a legally authorized monopoly of force exercised by the officers backed by their praetorian guard, the detachment of marines included in the ship's ordinary complement. Ahab never employs force, relying instead on the arts of incitement, self-dramatization, flattery, bluff, and appeal to self-interest.

Ahab could not succeed in making himself despot over the souls of his crew did he not first take care to conceal his violation of the mercantile purpose of the voyage. By cruising the ordinary whaling grounds and taking some few whales en route to the site where he plans to seek Moby-Dick, he protects himself from a charge of usurpation for which he could be legally removed from command. The one custom he permits himself to violate is the unwritten law of helping the distressed, yet this abrogation of maritime *ius gentium* is less risky than misappropriating property. Ahab senses he can safely ignore the Christian commandment of neighborly charity as long as he makes show of observing the Lockian commandment to respect another's property. Moreover, Ahab undermines Starbuck's chances for leading a successful revolt by winning the approval of common sailors. Following the example of Caesar, he enlists the commoners against an "aristocratic" rival.

Caesarism requires a certain flexibility from the despot who must know how to work upon a variety of human materials. Ahab knows the variety of means at his disposal for fashioning his malleable populace. Some men will kindle merely in response to a show of energy. The publicist in Ahab enables him to know how to stage himself so as to provide the excitement that will stir the shallow sort, while he also contrives for the somewhat more intellectually able an appeal to more solid motives of avarice. Ishmael attributes to Ahab the axiom that "The permanent condition of the manufactured man . . . is sordidness" (46.212). A doubloon he nails to the mast combines appeals to passions of excitement, low ambition, and greed. The gold piece looks rich beyond its exchange value, comes bearing glory to the winner of a contest, is earned without sweat, and stirs the envy of everyone who loses out. Besides these ordinary mainstays of the demagogue, Ahab knows how to mystify. His sense of grand purpose will allow him to employ cheap tricks without embarrassing himself, as is evident from his astonishing some of the crew by making a lightning rod of his own arm when the corpusants descend, and from his effort to overawe ignorant seamen by making a compass of an ordinary sail needle. Somewhat more subtly, Ahab knows how to enlist a man's piety in a bad cause. When he must choose a watchman to guard the line that has hoisted him aloft in the rigging, he chooses God-fearing Starbuck. Ahab knows Starbuck's conscience will not permit him to kill even though Starbuck has said Ahab's mania will destroy ship and crew (130.538-39; 123.515).

In addition to these time-tested expedients of business administration, Ahab possesses two other holds upon his men, and these he enjoys precisely because both provide relief from the shortcomings characteristic of a Lockian, commercial society. The reason heroic tempers from Homer's time to our own have despised merchants and mechanical toil is from aversion to the unadventurous, meanly calculating transactions required for buying low and selling high. Upon the uncontestable observation that merchants must cut corners, seize little advantages, and minimize risks literary men have propagated the sizeable exaggeration that commercial manners are inconsistent with generosity and adventure. Several of Melville's poems suggest he endorsed this prejudice. In any event, the hunt for the white whale gives scope to emotions larger than those connected with the whalemen's routine, workaday world of mechanical labor. Ahab invites all hands to try out the exhilaration of expending themselves as warriors rather than laborers. Furthermore, he adds a common touch to this feeling of the sport. They will join with him as comrades-in-arms, their subjugation to his will obscured by their inebriation in enjoying a sense of a common will, a shared cause.

Beyond adventure-sharing, Ahab's quest promises a purpose that dignifies even the meanest auxiliaries, because the hunt for Moby-Dick fabricates a *telos* for otherwise aimless lives. It affords a pretense of purposefulness, of that which we today are accustomed to speak of as "meaning." The crewmen feel larger and more alive once they conceive their exertions count toward some end beyond their personal desires. Ahab knows that human beings respond to appeals to unite with something larger than themselves. Accordingly he calls for sacramental rum, delivers existentialist sermons, and exploits this yearning by offering his own conduct as a model for perseverance in sublimity. Ahab embodies a modern substitute for the sublimation once identified with either philosophy, patriotism, sanctity, or selfless love.

What is this meaning to which the men of the *Pequod* assent, however vague, partial, and inarticulate may be their grasp of it, when they raise their voices to consent to Ahab's quarterdeck oath? At bottom, they and Ishmael—or part of him—find Ahab a compelling leader rather than a negligible bedeviled crank, because some portion of their own soul takes his part. In his attack on the white whale, they acknowledge a poetically emphatic version of an impulse of resentment which most heirs of the Enlightenment can lay claim to, a resentment directed against limitations imposed by nature, by the sum of things not amenable, or not yet amenable, to human improvements. In their most telling form, these limits impose physical affliction, injury depriving us of that which is most intimately our own—our bodily limbs and faculties. The most vivid form of human defiance, therefore, is a war conducted against natural limits for the sake of relieving man's afflicted condition. My supposition is that Ahab's vengeance against Moby-Dick is one in principle with a program set by Machiavelli, Bacon, Hobbes, Descartes, Locke, Kant, and Marx, and eloquently endorsed this side of the Atlantic by Franklin, Jefferson, Hamilton, and Emerson (excepting Marx, Melville mentions all these authors in his writings). The project of the modern technological regime in either its free or collectivist versions has been to assault unimproved nature for the sake of enlarging man's estate, to liberate from limits imposed by a nature which opposes human effort but yields to our socially concerted technological efforts. Struggles against disease, against all defects of birth and circumstance, against natural scarcity of food or energy, efforts to prolong life or to make it more secure or more accommodating—all these strenuous and well-organized expeditions against nature's empire take their rise from the impulse which Melville symbolizes in Ahab's vengeance upon his whale. That malignant principle which Ahab would strike at, piercing through its masks, is the grudging, confining, unfair, and bullying aspect the cosmos displays to a modern man when he meets opposition to his will where he had required compliance.

A recurrent theme of modern teaching asserts that we properly define ourselves as human beings by opposing a world which appears blindly to frustrate or even capriciously to maim and destroy human beings, who on all accounts are supposed the noblest product and lords of earth, and who therefore ought to find in nature resources instead of obstacles. Holding it nobler to oppose than submit, Ahab will not patiently endure what he supposes to be either nature's despotism or its indifferent stupidity. If he cannot make it over, he will at least strike back at one of the malign agents of this despotism. He shows, thereby, that human will cannot be cowed, even if the body be subject to such humiliation as he has suffered in the loss of the leg. The men of the *Pequod* respond to a leader who represents in large and clear terms a resentment they each harbor, although inchoately. As Starbuck ultimately perceives, "all of us are Ahabs" (123.515). Ahab can be seen as having succeeded in supplanting a traditional with a modernist view of the etiology of evil. For the Christian doctrine of the fall and original sin, Ahab substitutes resentment against a coquette nature who provokes desire, then withholds the means to satisfaction. Man is innocent of any originary wrongdoing yet all the same suffers the straitened condition Christians impute to an aboriginal fall. Like Locke, Ahab transfers the onus from man to nature, or nature's God, yet Locke's remedy, the cultivation of productive arts, is too tame for Ahab. He will take more literally the project of making war on nature while he invests the struggle with poetic color and religious zeal.

Melville troubles us with the intimation that the project Ahab takes on deliriously might just as effectively be pursued in cold blood on a national scale and with the same baneful consequences for the citizens of the republic as is suffered by the crew of the *Pequod*. The number Melville sets for the crew on this "federated keel" (30) is the number of the states of the U.S.A. prior to the admission of California. Although to be sure it is elsewhere the standard complement of a whaler, Melville has made a symbolic use of the number *thirty* for the states of the union in *Mardi,* Chapter 158 (thirty stars) and Chapter 160 (thirty palms). Ahab's success in imposing his despotic will on a ship flying the flag of a republic points to a weakness in the foundations of the American republic. As indicated previously, Lockian teaching has men form civil society in the hope of overcoming two obstacles to their security, one human, the other nonhuman. The threat posed by the unrestrained wills of other men is allayed by the institution of a government which secures rights, but the same civil institution also promotes the overcoming of nature's scarcity by facilitating acquisition of property and division of labor. Peaceable association with other men makes feasible a more vigorous prosecution of that campaign against nature which arises from the same sovereign cause of self-preservation as does the contrivance of civil government. Nothing insures, however, that the first end will not be compromised for the sake of the second. Will men not agree to sacrifice liberties of their fellow citizens and risk losing some of their own if the inducement comes in the form of a strong leader who promises in exchange relief from nature's despotism? If the social contract reduces to a bargain negotiated on calculations of self-preservation, it seems not improbable that self-interest might consent to despotic power in the hope of maximizing power over nature's resources.

To bring home this threat Melville does not have to project some hypothetical situation remote from his contemporaries. The prolonged national temporizing with slavery would have seemed to him proof of his countrymen's liability to accept limits upon human rights in exchange for an institution considered by some Americans indispensable for subduing the land. He has Ishmael protest in his cynical reflections on "Fast Fish and Loose Fish":

> What are the sinews and souls of Russian serfs and Republican [United States] slaves but Fast-Fish, whereof possession is the whole of the law?
>
> (89.398)

Ishmael's disillusionment over the equivalence of Russian and American despotism in the matter of slaveholding extends to his country's foreign policy, "What was Poland to the Czar? What Greece to the Turk? What India to England? What at last will Mexico be to the United States? All Loose-fish." If the republic the narrator of *White-Jacket* praised as bearer of "the ark of man's liberties" can countenance slavery in its domestic policy and is no respecter of rights in its foreign policy, Melville, speaking through Ishmael, feels justified in now concluding, "What are the Rights of Man and the Liberties of the World but Loose-Fish?" (89.398).

Melville is no proto-environmentalist protesting species-centric depredations or sounding alarms for a putatively fragile ecosystem. He fears rather that the more radical impulse driving modern, particularly American, politics may overwhelm the more benign liberalism of Jeffersonian dedication to natural rights. The problem arises from the amoral character of the principle upon which the social contract rests. Self-preservation is, first and last, the engine that drives and the destination sought. To preserve himself the Lockian individual consents to creating a civil authority, agreeing thereby to regard other men as equals under law, yet to preserve his life and to preserve it more abundantly that individual may consent to a despotism which regards men as tools. Within the system founded in a calculus of self-preservation there appears no moral cause for self-restraint, and, moreover, the system undermines those religious sanctions supporting self-restraint that were once sustained in pre-Lockian polities.

When Ahab makes his display of defying the lightning in the scene previously discussed, he proclaims:

> In the midst of the personified impersonal, a personality stands here. Though but a point at best; whencesoe'er I came; wheresoe'er I go; yet while I earthly live, the queenly personality lives in me, and feels her royal rights.
>
> (119.507)

Ahab's "personality" has been affronted by the maiming dealt by the whale as well as by the attempted intimidation he presently reads in the storm. He affirms this personality by persisting in his quest and by communicating his animus to a body of men. *Personality* is modernity's substitute for soul. Its other name for personality is the *self*, which Locke defined as "that conscious thinking thing . . . which is sensible, or conscious of Pleasure and Pain, capable of Happiness or Misery, and so is concern'd for it *self*, as far as that consciousness extends." Without the immortal ordination held by Christians to ennoble the soul, the modern thinkers' "personality" or "self" is nonetheless sovereign, and without needing to establish its virtue against such generic standards as are upheld by classical moral philosophy it nonetheless is held to deserve a special dignity. This "queenly personality" is altogether individual because it is the result of individual will putting its stamp on human nature and producing thereby a unique version of human potential brought to specific act. The individual will, the personality, is what the all-compelling passion of self-preservation preserves. It is the beneficiary of "the pursuit of happiness," Locke's phrase before it was Jefferson's. One may suspect the notion reduces to a grandiloquent excuse for willfulness, but however that may be, Melville will not go so far in questioning Ahab's greatness. Yet he does indicate that although Ahab's character is heroically ample, his efforts are demonic in the degree that he promotes hatred rather than benevolence. Because he regards other men only as instruments to be employed in executing his wrath against nature and nature's God, Ahab neglects, and finally chooses deliberately to renounce, promptings of humanity. His obsessiveness precludes companionable feeling with the one crew member—Starbuck—with whom he might make a friendship, and he renounces the fellowship available in the faith of his fathers only to espouse the bleak Manichee worship practiced by the Parsee, Fedallah. Most tellingly, Ahab betrays the trust of subordinates pledged to unquestioning obedience. Just before the final chase, Starbuck reminds the older man of the wife and young son who await his return to Nantucket. But an Ahab almost past feeling, certainly past acting upon, family affections pushes down husbandly and fatherly emotions and turns away from Starbuck to cross the deck and gaze into the water where he sees reflected Fedallah's face (132.545). Melville here directs his irony toward an Ahab who himself now causes those sorrows he had charged to divine indifference in the Sphinx chapter. In the present instance, not an uncaring God but a preoccupied Ahab sends sailors to the deep and separates husbands (Starbuck and himself) from faithful wives (Starbuck's, his own).

A parallelism between Prometheus and Ahab reinforces the latter's violation of loving kindness. Melville has Ahab evoke the Prometheus myth when he makes himself a fire bearer ("The Candles"), when he braves a God he acknowledges to be his superior in power, and when he supplies substitutes for divine providence with his technical resourcefulness ("The Chart," "The Needle," "Log and Line"). After the manner of the Titan depicted in Aeschylus, Ahab practices a science altogether utilitarian. Ahab exhibits no interest in knowing for its own sake.

A chapter depicting the repair of Ahab's ivory leg conveys Melville's skeptical estimate of this new Prometheus. We overhear his requirements for reconstructing human nature to produce a machine all will and power:

> while Prometheus is about it, I'll order a complete man after a desirable pattern. Imprimis, fifty feet high in his socks; then chest modelled after the Thames Tunnel; then, legs with roots to 'em, to stay in one place; then, arms three feet through the wrist; no heart at all, brass forehead, and about a quarter of an acre of fine brains. . . .
>
> (108.470)

In Melville's romantic hierarchy of faculties, the heart stands for moral judgment, while the calculative technical agency is the brain. He declared in a letter to Hawthorne: "I stand for the heart. To the dogs with the head! I had rather be a fool with a heart than Jupiter Olympus with his head." Ahab would remove the heart because he realizes that feelings generated there—his residual attachments to wife, child, Starbuck, Pip—could soften his otherwise unbending resolve. Promethean revisionism serves the will, finds its instrument in brain power, and confronts its internal adversary in an opposed moral sense which prompts love rather than resentment. Early on we were told Ahab had "his humanities," yet this late soliloquy indicates he would suppress whatever remains of compunctions of fellow-feeling for the sake of giving free rein to power and will.

Although Ahab means to imitate Prometheus as benefactor, Melville suggests he is a specious friend to man. He states his case for revising nature in terms of philanthropy: contesting with God as mankind's advocate. Ahab boasts his love for oppressed human beings and seems to act upon pity for the outcast when he takes up with Pip, the black cabin boy who jumps from a whaleboat in mid-chase and, left for a time alone in the sea, emerges a demented, intermittently insightful visionary. Melville so constructs Ahab's scenes with Pip, however, that he exposes the shallowness of Ahab's pity, if not its perversity. Ahab has taken no notice of his subordinate until the boy's misfortune makes him suitable as an exhibit illustrating human providence stepping in to rectify God's unconcern. When Ahab takes Pip under protection, Melville intends we should recall Lear's meeting houseless Tom o'Bedlam. Yet an equally pathetic Pip elicits from Ahab nothing of the self-recognition Lear had been moved to. Instead, Ahab arraigns God and befriends the boy so that he may congratulate himself for his benevolence. Ahab taunts storming skies, not as Lear had his own "pomp," to "take medicine, take medicine" (120.509). Shakespeare's king had charged himself to learn sympathy, whereas Melville has Ahab boast he surpasses God in pity for suffering human beings. Three chapters later egoism decked out in ostentatious kindness becomes obvious when Ahab offers Pip as court evidence to prove "there can be no hearts above the snow-line" (125.522). Taking the boy to his cabin, Pip's new protector treats him to some Enlightenment sermonizing:

> Lo! ye believers in gods all goodness, and in man all ill, to you! See the omniscient gods oblivious of suffering man; and man, though idiotic, and knowing not what he does, yet full of the sweet things of love and gratitude. Come! I feel prouder leading thee by thy black hand, than though I grasped an Emperor's!

From Melville's vantage, what offends in Ahab's vaunt is less some affront to deity but rather the insult to human dignity. Ahab violates the secular humanist's moral code when he debases its supreme good of benevolence by turning kindnesses into expressions of hatred. Taking up Pip as a cat's-paw to strike at the gods shows his philanthropy is adjunct to his pride. His dream of revising human nature has so chilled his heart that, although he professes love of man, he neglects to be kind to the actual human beings whose lives are in his care. Obviously, Pip goes down with all the other mariners dependent on Ahab.

Melville introduces the three-day death chase of Moby-Dick with an episode designed to gauge the inhumanity of a philanthropy founded in resentment. The incident of the *Pequod*'s encountering the *Rachel*, previously alluded to, registers the irony of an Ahab who has voiced his pity for mankind in the abstract and has rebuked heaven and sea for their unkindness to the human race, now refusing to interrupt his hunt at the entreaty of a fellow sufferer. Ahab's last contact with human community beyond the decks of the *Pequod* shows his having become so entirely consumed by his obsession with his role as protesting champion of oppressed humanity that he chooses protest over such remedy as lies within his power, at this moment refusing help to another father, compatriot, and fellow captain. Self-pity, although it has expanded to pity for mankind at large, causes Ahab to be cruel to men one by one. Rights of man have become fast-fish hostages to this embodiment of despotic potentials inherent in the technocratic impulse, the gentler aspect of Locke mastered by the more compelling.

IV

Melville encloses Ahab's story within Ishmael's in order to juxtapose the former's career in resentment against the latter's education in self-preserving acceptance. The contrast has led some readers to suppose Melville offers in Ishmael a correction to Ahab. This hypothesis proves out well enough when applied to the novel's theme of discovering proper ways of knowing. Ishmael's character supplies no corrective to Ahab's, however, in the matter of locating better guidance for America's political destiny.

The very source of the mental flexibility which makes Ishmael the superior student of nature incapacitates him for effective political action. He cultivates intellectual independence by taking up and then discarding one after another a number of antithetical perspectives on every issue he inspects. Compounded with continual irony and self-deprecation, this strategy causes Ishmael to attach himself only provisionally to any intellectual position. He enjoys exploding conventional opinion, arguing the humanity of cannibals and the difficulty of accepting the biblical story of Jonah (chap. 83). A latter-day Montaigne whose mobility as seaborne intellectual permits his sampling a diversity of cultural tenets on questions metaphysical, religious, or ethical, Ishmael feels wise not to be bound by any creed. Both as character and as author, he makes the most of a freedom from sectarianism won for American intellectuals by Jefferson's and Madison's arguments for toleration drawn from Locke. Ishmael protects himself from narrowness by keeping a mind open even to the possibility of yet discovering a transcendent order, "Ah, mortal! then be heedful; for so, in all this din of the great world's loom, thy subtlest thinkings may be overheard afar" (102.450). He remains steadfast only in nonsubscription:

> Long exile from Christendom and civilization inevitably restores a man to that condition in which God placed him, i.e. what is called savagery. Your true whalehunter is as much a savage as an Iroquois. I myself am a savage, owning no allegiance but to the King of the Cannibals; and ready at any moment to rebel against him.
>
> (57.270)

Ishmael boasts himself a philosopher because he sees the merely conventional basis of opinions less-enlightened minds mistake for truths and because he maintains a stoic composure while loose harpoons dart about his head (60.281). His cetology attests to Melville's preference for Ishmael's intellectual method over Ahab's. Collecting and playing off multiple perspectives serves to correct Ahab's tense, humorless fixation, enabling Ishmael to grasp that the way to transcend Ahab's allegorizing lies not in rejecting analogies altogether (the opposed imperci009pience of soulless utilitarians like Flask and Stubb), but in imagining a range of analogies from various vantages not excluding those of scientific measurement and commercial utility. If we accept Melville's implication that study of whales stands as a synecdoche for study of anything, we acknowledge Ishmael's better way. To credit him with philosophy, however, seems a bit grand. We might suspect Ishmael enjoys less the rigors of pursuing wisdom than the pleasures of evasion and withdrawal. An alert, supple receptivity toward the spectacle of manners and opinion he achieves by learning to detach himself from practical concerns. Yet he also thereby insulates himself from pressures to settle into moral judgments which might implicate him in dangerous action.

The skepticism he carefully preserves permits Ishmael, as Ahab's monomania permits *him,* to elude obligations that might restrain his will. In one of his reveries, Ishmael thinks it prudent to lower aims of "attainable felicity" to the "hearth and home" (94.416), yet he does not seem to have married (see the "Town-Ho" digression). He professes admiration for Jacksonian democracy without, as far as we can see, intending to stump for candidates. On which side of the national division over slavery would Ishmael enlist: for Lincoln, because he despises people who consider a white man "anything more dignified than a white-washed negro" (13.60)? Or would he hold with the neutrals since in another mood he seems to trivialize the issue with characteristic flippancy, "Who aint a slave" (1.6)? Ishmael's fondness for discovering antinomies prevents his having any political view worth taking trouble for.

His independence from conventional opinion allows Ishmael to make a reliable friend of a cannibal, and that opening to affection, he says, generates kind feelings toward humankind at large. Queequeg has worked him to a mollification of temper in the glow of which no longer were "splintered heart and maddened hand turned against the wolfish world" (10.51). Not surprisingly for an Ishmael who likens all orthodoxy to submerged yet dangerous wreckage of ships (69.309), religion must give way to freethinking and sailors' camaraderie. Even friendship must yield nonetheless to concern for self-preservation. Ishmael draws a line beyond which he will not extend his tolerance even to have his new friend's approval. He refuses to imitate or to sympathize with self-severe devotions that require something of heroic discipline. Although a latitudinarian in most articles of religious observance, Ishmael reacts with disgust to Queequeg's keeping a lengthy fast. His friend's zeal provokes him to a lecture on minding one's comforts. He has determined that such rigors as "Lents and Ramadans" violate "obvious laws of Hygiene and common sense" and that "hell is an idea born on an undigested apple-dumpling." So that we do not take this scoffing to be a banalism that Ishmael grows beyond over the course of the novel, Melville has his narrator switch to the editorial present when he voices his creed of self-preservation in comfort:

> I have no objection to any person's religion, be it what it may, so long as that person does not kill or insult any other person, because that other person don't believe it also. But when a man's religion becomes really frantic, when it is a positive torment to him, and in fine, makes this earth of ours an uncomfortable inn to lodge in; then I think it high time to take that individual aside and argue the point with him.

(17.84-85)

Ishmael's is the liberal catechism of Locke, a resolve to tolerate diverse theologies for the sake of peace while encouraging unofficial uniformity of belief in the priority of pleasure. His aptness to accommodate sets Ishmael in contrast to Ahab and allows him to experience sentimental fellowship in the scene of "squeezing case," where he touches the hands of his shipmates and moist-eyed, forgets "[his] horrible oath" to pursue the white whale (94.416).

Since Melville appears to approve his narrator's progress in secular humanitarianism by arranging the ponderous symbolism of Ishmael's escape from death by means of Queequeg's coffin cum lifebuoy, it may seem the end of *Moby-Dick* leads us back to Lockianism by a road lower than Ahab's but more humane. Ishmael's softer version of modern individualism corrects the militant harshness of Ahab's stern version, allowing hope for the gradual pacification of man's estate through self-interested pursuit of comfort and opening the way to human compassion by suppressing anxiety concerning doctrinal questions over which Europe had bled during its two centuries of sectarian fervor. A dividend accrues in the freedom to muse, an approximation of philosophy sufficient to satisfy most writers and academics. A reader cannot be certain Melville means to convey reservations against Ishmael's corrective of Ahab, and yet consideration of the political theme will cause us to think there must be a further word than the antitheses posed by Melville's opposition of Ishmael's "desperado philosophy" to Ahab's promethean despotism.

We can see, for instance, that Ishmael escapes Ahab's inhumanity at the cost of dampening heroic spiritedness. One admires the generosity Queequeg displays, first when he dives into an icy sea to save a stranger and, subsequently, when he plunges into a whale's carcass to rescue a shipmate. Although Ishmael also admires this nobility in Queequeg, he does not recognize that his friend's selflessness may be owing to beliefs in a law higher than self-preservation, beliefs supported by those religious disciplines Ishmael finds offensive to hygiene and common sense. Clearly enough, Ishmael proves incapable of heroism for any reason, not even on behalf of friendship. When a bumpkin insults Queequeg, Ishmael evidently sits passively awaiting his friend's response (13.60). Despite his secret decision to dissociate from Ahab, a change of mood recorded in the "Try-works" scene and confirmed during the case-squeezing, Ishmael neither opposes Ahab publicly nor reproaches himself for inaction, although Melville inserts the "Town-Ho" digression with its account of a mutiny against a despot captain apparently to show that resistance to the *Pequod*'s despot was for all its risks not impossible. Against Ahab's tyranny by persuasion some counter-persuasion is called for. Since the first mate and the man of learning are the only spokesmen capable of opposing rhetoric to Ahab's rhetoric, the ship's company can be saved only by their alliance. During the quarterdeck crisis Ahab succeeds in dominating because at the moment Starbuck makes his gesture of opposition Ishmael not only fails to support him but adds his voice to the crew which is shouting its consent.

The well-known chapter on "The Whiteness of the Whale" gives Ishmael's reason for siding with Ahab at the one moment he might have been successfully opposed. A tortuous series of meditations on whiteness as symbol for cosmic meaninglessness builds up to Ishmael's concluding that he was moved to identify the white whale with nature's false promise of a final meaning, white being "a colorless all-color of atheism" (p. 195) underlying all natural hues and exposing them for "subtle deceits, not actually inherent in substances, but only laid on from without; so that all deified Nature absolutely paints like the harlot, whose allurements cover nothing but the charnel-house within" (p. 195). For all his care ordinarily to look on all sides, Ishmael here succumbs to Ahab's determination to perceive the whale under one aspect only. Ishmael makes a symbol of Moby-Dick as Ahab is doing, and their overlapping reductions are evident in Ahab's remark that he dreads to find the whale to be the symbol of meaninglessness: "Sometimes I think there's naught beyond" (36.164). Ishmael admires Ahab for striking back at deceitful Nature and thereby creating by an act of will a meaning for his life in despite of Nature's general meaninglessness. Creating meaning where there is none to discover is the post-Enlightenment intellectual's version of the common human impulse toward self-preservation. At a moment when political action is most requisite, Ishmael proves as vulnerable as the rest of the seamen to Ahab's proposal because a part of him admires Ahab's force, and the remainder which would resist cannot make alliance with pious Starbuck, since Ishmael believes he has liberated himself from the traditional religious belief Starbuck embodies. In Melville's allegory of the national character, a Christianity weakened by accommodation to commercial prosperity proves a feeble protector of the ark of man's liberties, while America's intellectual class, skeptical of a higher law it identifies with rejected Christian teaching, now holds no beliefs which might inspire dangerous political effort on behalf of freedom. The intellectual suffers a further debility in an ambivalence that has him partly admire despotic concentrations of the national prowess in an assault on deceitful or begrudging Nature. Although Ishmael may discover an intellectual vocation in the celebration of the whaling industry, his insistence on his doctrinal independence is such that he never becomes attached to the political life of an actual community. That is why in the editorial present he stipulates we are to call him Ishmael. He was at the time of the *Pequod*'s voyage and continues now to be a deracinated observer. Melville may be tracing likelihoods and suggesting that a liability of a Lockian society is the tendency of its intellectuals to purchase their freedom of inquiry at the cost of their countrymen's political liberties.

V

Moby-Dick leaves Melville with the problem of imagining a hero suitable to realize America's mission as "bearer of the ark of the liberties of the world" against a despotism grounded in the American doctrine of popular consent. The alliance Ishmael and Starbuck fail to arrange suggests the shape Melville judges heroic action might take in a more politically effective Christian endowed with learning or, alternatively, in a more spirited intellectual capable of appealing to Christians. Statesmanship founded in a political religion transforming passive piety into active devotion to the rights of man could suffice to meet Ahab's zeal with an equal but opposite republican temper. An appreciation of the timeliness of such a statesmanship so founded seems to have set the plan Lincoln adhered to throughout a career in which he tried to win assent to the proposition that the principle of natural rights has priority in the national purpose over the principle of consent. This was the issue Lincoln debated with Stephen A. Douglas in the Illinois Senate campaign of 1858. Lincoln thought America's conquest of nature—represented by expansion westward and industrialization through the railroad—could not be allowed to extend slavery, even if the people of the territories consented to importation of slaves.

Although Melville's literary career spanned Lincoln's political career, I find no evidence that Melville followed Lincoln's speeches in the forties and fifties. His volume of poetry, *Battle Pieces and Aspects of War,* deals directly with Lincoln in a single poem lamenting his assassination. Instead of focussing the series of Civil War poems on the man who presided over the Union at war, Melville throws his emphasis upon portraying a people, offering his own thoughts as a projection of the national temper Lincoln had forged between 1860 and 1865. The dedicatory notice announces this emphasis on a heroism of collective sacrifice: "To the Memory of The Three Hundred Thousand Who in the War for the Maintenance of the Union Fell Devotedly Under the Flag of Their Fathers." Lincoln's statesmanship is best shown, Melville may have decided, through his effect upon the people he led.

From the outset Melville invites his readers to perceive his particular stance toward the Civil War: the lavish expenditure of blood and resources for a cause not evidently profitable to the ordinary Union soldier attests human capacity to rise beyond calculations of self-interest. The sacrifice offered by the three hundred thousand implicitly rebukes both the cautious self-preservation practiced by Ishmael and the self-assertive individualism pursued by Ahab in his exaltation of "queenly personality."

Notes

1. White-Jacket's expectation for America as a redeemer nation is evident in the rhetoric of his tribute to "the Israel of our time" entrusted by providence "to bear the ark of the liberties of the world" (chap. 36).

2. *The Writings of Herman Melville,* ed. Harrison Hayford, Hershel Parker, and G. Thomas Tanselle (Evanston, IL: Northwestern University Press; Chicago: Newberry Library, 1988), vol. 6, chap. 33, p. 148. Subsequent citations within parentheses refer to chapter and page of this edition.

Jamey Hecht (essay date spring 1999)

SOURCE: Hecht, Jamey. "Scarcity and Compensation in *Moby-Dick.*" *Massachusetts Review* 40, no. 1 (spring 1999): 111-29.

[*In the following essay, Hecht examines the tension between intelligibility and the unknowable in* Moby-Dick.]

Moby-Dick is about the continual, tragic struggle between a finite human space of strictly local meanings and attachments, and an infinite, non-human universe wherein language and knowledge can never be at home. The whale is a metonym for that non-human universe, but it is also the test-object upon which consciousness attempts to work its conquering will. This essay contrasts the strong efforts made by Ishmael and by Ahab to definitively locate the meaning of the whale in general and of Moby-Dick in particular. Those efforts are articulated in terms of *compensation,* a broad, Emersonian term covering a range of hypotheses about the reciprocation of gain and loss.

Ishmael is an epistemological hero, a protagonist whose *agon* is always that of knowledge: the novel's famous first sentence defines him as a name-bearing name-giver. His delight in his own encyclopedic knowledge of the world of objects—his Homeric catalogues of terms and tools, his taxonomic zeal in the "Cetology" chapter—is not the innocent, Adamic happiness it often resembles. In its underlying seriousness, Ishmael's paratactic rummaging through the object-world constitutes a struggle for human space in a potentially absurd cosmos whose operative principle of intelligibility is *compensation*—a cybernetic idea which Emerson permanently inserted into American thought in his essay of that title in 1841.[1]

Melville read Emerson's *Essays* in the autumn of 1850 (during a visit to Hawthorne)[2]; he took from that book a capacity for world-governing abstractions that is nearly absent in the earlier novels. Consider Ishmael's lament about the balance of good and evil: "But it's too late to make any improvements now. The universe is finished . . ." (34). Here Melville inherits Descartes's concept of the conservation of motion (which was experimentally verified and extended by James Prescott Joule in the 1850's, in his work on the Conservation of Energy). For Descartes, God has already given the universe all the motion it will ever have; therefore, none can be lost.[3] For Emerson, Ishmael, and Descartes alike, it is the finished-ness of the universe which demands the conservation of its quantities and qualities.[4] *Compensation* is, then, the Emersonian, American equivalent of the Cartesian term *conservation.* Both terms denote a *static* economy in which nothing can be lost. Now, whaling was the normative regional industry of the Massachusetts coastline in the first half of the 19th Century, and its peak of productivity was, during the writing of *Moby-Dick,* about to give way to irreversible decline. It's ironic that, in the environmental movement that forms a later chapter in the history of American nature writing, the word "conservation" came to refer to the perilous *scarcity* of wildlife, a post-industrial scarcity which no natural principle of inherent balance could offset. That irony has its rhetorical birthplace in *Moby-Dick.*

The increasing scarcity of whales (which caused the gradual collapse of whaling as a commercial enterprise) is epitomized in the unique albino whom Ahab pursues. Moby-Dick's very existence, and the *Spermaceti*'s brush with extinction, each precipitate a crisis (experienced by Ahab and Ishmael respectively) in the intelligibility of the world altogether. At Melville's writing, Darwin had recently overturned the Biblical taxonomy of animals, deploying a new, dynamic understanding of animal species as temporally fluid, rather than eternally static, categories. But the Darwinian explanation of the origin of species was by no means a settled affair in the public mind; indeed the intellectual climate of this novel is one of fragmented and incompatible theories, all equally available to that roving intellectual opportunist, the narrator, all equally inadequate to his elusive object.

Ishmael gives a "proof" of the sustainability of whaling (CV: "The Shark Massacre") that includes a clear model of compensation:

For they are only being driven from promontory to cape; and if one coast is no longer enlivened with their jets, then, be sure, some other and remoter strand has been very recently startled by the unfamiliar spectacle.

(587)

The universe is finished; the universe includes whales; therefore, whales will always exist. The root of this logic is the Authorized Version of Genesis 1:21, which specifically mentions the creation of whales as prior to that of all other sea creatures. The pedagogical use of biblical materials in 19th Century America proffered Holy Scripture as the permanently reliable catalogue of the contents of the universe. For example, *The New England Primer,* of which Melville acquired a reprint in 1851, teaches the alphabet using rhymed mnemonic poems whose content is predominantly Biblical.[5] These poems socialize children by providing a shared expression of their culture's most important rules, processes and schemata: most of the mnemonics deal with the seasons, the necessity of social authority, the brevity of life, and theology. But the mnemonic for the letter W preserves the strikingly specific mention of whales found in Genesis:

Whales in the sea
God's voice obey.

(from the facsimile in Jay Leyda,
The Melville Log, p. 407)

The Biblical precedent, repeated in the *Primer,* of singling out the whale as a species apart, guarantees the integrity of "whale" as a taxonomic category inherent in the world. This already static, Biblical taxonomy had a neoPlatonic counterpart, with which it almost seamlessly merged during the medieval period. The result was an essentialist zoology, for which animal genera were divinely designed categories, constituted by the reflection, in each species, of its own Ideal Form.[6]

In the 18th Century, Goethe attempted to employ this neo-Platonic essentialism in botany.[7] And while 19th Century scientific biology had turned away from Goethe and neoPlatonic essentialism, toward positivism and the Aristotelian tradition of empirical observation, *the writing of* **Moby-Dick** *was contemporaneous with a plurality of biologies, no one of which had achieved hegemony.*[8] Whether or not Melville was aware of the possibility that Sperm Whales might soon become extinct, there was nothing unrealistic in his representation of Ishmael as a well-informed man completely convinced that the whale "will not perish." This is not a mistake about how many whales are left, but a circular argument that adduces compensation to support its taxonomic conclusions, and taxonomy to support its compensatory theory. "To be short, then, a whale is a spouting fish with a horizontal tail."

Ishmael recognizes the exceptional, multivalent complexity of the whale as a species, yet he boldly hyposta-

sizes it: "a spouting fish with a horizontal tail." Like the similar chapters, XXXII: "Cetology," CIV: "The Fossil Whale," and CV: "Does the Whale Diminish? Will He Perish?"—that remark occupies a historically transitional moment between an essentialist notion of the whale as an eternal and imperishable element of the creation, and a dynamic conception of the whale as a set of diverse species found within specific parameters of geological time and geographic habitat.[9] The transition between the two is observable in Ishmael's rhetoric in these chapters on his knowledge of the whale. It corresponds to the transition obtaining in mid-century between an economy to which whaling is vital and an economy to which it is vestigial.

From 1805 to 1875, the per capita demand for whale oil was increasing at an average of 15.76% per year.[10] "Whale products were displaced by mineral oils and gas as illuminants between 1850 and 1860," writes Michael Maran, in his econometric analysis of the whaling industry's decline:

However, this did not mean that the total demand for whale products decreased . . . *It was the scarcity of whales* that shifted the industry's relatively inelastic supply schedule toward the left . . . The industry's demand schedule shifted to the right as *the market for whale products grew,* but not by enough to offset the loss of revenues caused by the shift of the supply schedule to the left. [my emphasis][11]

The whaling industry was destroyed not by competition from alternative products like petroleum and kerosene (which were developed in quantity only as whale products became increasingly unavailable) but by the inability of the whale populations to recover from relentless hunting.[12] In 1852 (one year after the quite obscure publication of **Moby-Dick**), *Scientific American* reported at the conclusion of a market analysis that "the exports of the present year do not come up to half the demand."[13] In 1856 *Frank Leslie's Illustrated Newspaper* warned: "The whale, upon which we depend for oil, is rapidly being driven . . . into inaccessible seas, and will before many years . . . entirely disappear."[14] As Maran writes, "Each phase of whaling marked the exhaustion of one stock of whales and the exploitation of a new stock," beginning with the off-shore whaling of the colonial period, which sufficed until the 1760's, when deep sea whaling was begun of necessity.[15]

But Ishmael, who sees compensation everywhere, imagines that there will always be someplace for the prey to hide:

[Right whales] have two firm fortresses, which, in all human probability, will for ever remain impregnable. And as upon the invasion of their valleys, the frosty Swiss have retreated to their mountains; so, hunted from the savannas and glades to the middle seas, the whale-bone whales can at last resort to their Polar citadels, and diving under the ultimate glassy barriers and walls there, come up among icy fields and floes; and in a charmed circle of everlasting December, bid defiance to all pursuit from man.

(588)

In 1873 thirty-three out of forty whaling ships cruising in the Arctic were destroyed by ice[16]—indicating that no matter how hazardous the region was to the whalers, they drove into it until there was simply negligible quarry left to be hunted. Hence the whaleman's anxiety about the stock of whales, and hence his heavy reliance on the biblical ontology of species, whose essentialist logic promises Ishmael his livelihood. This double attitude is already operative in Ishmael's reverence for the sperm whale whom he commercially exterminates, and in his insistence on its being called a fish.

The Whalemen's Monument outside the New Bedford Public Library bears the motto: "A DEAD WHALE OR A STOVE BOAT." New England, and America in general, defined its relation to the whale this way until the last moment of whaling's profitability, after which it slowly became profitable to define the citizen as adoring steward and the whale as elusive paragon of natural beauty. Having made whales so scarce, it was for the first time reasonable to expect citizens to pay money just to see one; hence the commercial "whale-watch," aptly named for its parent institution, the hunter's lookout on the mast-head.[17]

Ishmael's occasional forgetting of his formidable knowledge of cetology allows him to fantasize that Right whales might eventually be "diving under the ultimate glassy barriers . . . and coming up . . . in a charmed circle of everlasting December. . . ." In fact, just as whales allow themselves to be fatally stranded on beaches, they occasionally swim under ice-covered waters and drown for lack of access to the surface. Indeed, whales would *only* be able to do what Ishmael expects in the above passage, *if they were actually the fish he supposes them to be*. But his criterion for fish-ness is not whether an animal breathes air with lungs, or water with gills, but whether it lives in the water, or not.

> First: The uncertain, unsettled condition of this science of Cetology is in the very vestibule attested by the fact, that in some quarters it still remains a moot point whether a whale be a fish. In his System of Nature, A.D. 1776, Linnaeus declares, 'I hereby separate the whales from the fish.' But of my own knowledge, I know that down to the year 1850, sharks and shad, alewives and herring, against Linnaeus' express edict, were still found dividing possession of the same seas with the Leviathan.

(182)

This is perhaps a Melvillean joke about that other Declaration of 1776, separating the dominion of the British Empire from what had been the American colonies, a moment at which classification was by all means a moot point in the old sense of that term, whereby the "mooted" issue is the one at the *top* of the agenda for debate. Ishmael sneers at Linnaeus's "declaration" in favor of his own hard-headed taxonomy—fish are animals that "divide possession of the sea"; a whale is a "spouting fish with a horizontal tail"—exactly the kind of mere *fiat* that Ishmael mocks in Linnaeus's rhetorical flourish, "I hereby separate." By separating the whales from the fish, Linnaeus obviously doesn't mean any physical lifting of the whales onto the land—only whalemen can do that, not biologists. Ishmael's Linnaeus is the whaleman's bad conscience:

> The grounds upon which Linnaeus would fain have banished the whales from the waters, he states as follows: 'On account of their warm bilocular heart, their lungs, their movable eyelids, their hollow ears, *penem intrantem feminam mammis lactantem*' [a penis which enters the female, whose breasts lactate], and finally, '*ex lege naturae jure meritoque*' [justly and deservedly because of the law of nature].

(182)

But all this data comes to nothing, because Ishmael's sole taxonomic criterion is the habitat of the animal, and not its physiology—except insofar as that physiology conforms to his needs. The first step of Ishmael's prolix execution of the "ponderous task" of cetology is to "waive all argument":

> Be it known that, waiving all argument, I take the good old fashioned ground that the whale is a fish, and call upon holy Jonah to back me. This fundamental thing settled, the next point is, in what internal respect does the whale differ from other fish. Above, Linnaeus has given you those items. But in brief, they are these: lungs and warm blood, whereas, all other fish are lungless and cold blooded.

> * * *

> Next: how shall we define the whale, by his obvious externals, so as conspicuously to label him for all time to come? To be short, then, a whale is *a spouting fish with a horizontal tail*. There you have him. [emphasis in original]

(183)

In this brusque pseudo-argument Melville shows his hand, indicating that Ishmael's "old fashioned ground" is not solid at all. The aim of Ishmael's cetology, it turns out, is "conspicuously to label [the whale] for all time to come," that is, to defend once-and-for-all against the charge that whaling is a nearly cannibalistic activity whose victim is hauntingly similar to its perpetrator. But in "The Whale As A Dish" Ishmael renders the word "cannibalism" nearly meaningless, with the same rhetoric of compensation he used in "Loomings" to empty-out the force of the word "slave."

"Loomings," the novel's first chapter, describes Ishmael's signing-on as a sailor: "True, they rather order me about some, and make me jump from spar to spar, like a grasshopper in a May meadow" (27). This is, of course, a rationalization, since a grasshopper in a meadow is subject to *no one's* authority. "What of it," he continues, "if some old hunks of a sea-captain orders me to get a broom and sweep down the decks? What does that indignity amount to, weighed, I mean, in the scales of the New Testament?" It is in just that cosmic scale that the grasshopper's natural action can be troped as labor, since his master is only God, just as Ishmael's labor can be troped as free activity, since "the archangel Gabriel thinks [no]thing less of me." By predicating the whole membership of the cosmos with the sweeping phrase "Who ain't a slave?" (28), Ishmael effaces the difference between labor and freedom—effectively rendering both terms meaningless. If we are all slaves, we must be all free, since slavery only has meaning if some people are exempt from it.

> Well, then, however the old sea-captains may thump and punch me about, I have the satisfaction of knowing that it is all right; that everybody else is one way or other served in the same way—either in a physical or metaphysical point of view. . . .
>
> (28)

Only if the physical and the metaphysical are interchangeable, as they are here, can either one serve to demonstrate that *everybody* is subject to getting "thumped and punched." In other words, it's by effacing the difference between physical and metaphysical that Ishmael effaces the difference between slave and free; the ontological obfuscation enables the ethical one. His next argument for shipping out as a sailor, that "there is all the difference in the world between paying and being payed" (28) is belied by his earlier phrase, "everybody else is one way or other served in the same way." Emerson's *Compensation* has the same problem:

> For every thing you have missed,
> you have gained something else.
>
> (*Essays,* 70)

> Men suffer all their life long under the foolish superstition
> that they can be cheated.
>
> (*Essays,* 86)

Contrary to Ishmael's remark, there is, for Emerson, little difference between paying and being payed, since each (eventually) incurs the other. Though appearances suggest that this world is unjust, unbalanced and out of kilter, we will discover its hidden balance if we intrepidly investigate—more of these same appearances. The power of Emerson's essay lies precisely in its vacillation between immanent and transcendent models of justice; in "Compensation" debts are repaid, either here or in the afterworld, and it isn't for us to know where, in any given case. Here again, ethics merges with ontology:

> But it is as impossible for a man to be cheated by any one but himself, as for a thing to be and not to be at the same time.
>
> (*Essays,* 86)

You can't be cheated because "for every thing you have missed, you have gained something else; and for every thing you gain, you lose something" (71). These sentences from Emerson, and Ishmael's rhetorical question—"Who ain't a slave?"—share the belief that every relationship (that of master to slave, hunter to victim, pursuer to pursued) finds its compensatory opposite in due course. But this belief impoverishes the meaning of those relations: "What does that indignity amount to, weighed, I mean, in the scales of the New Testament?" (28). The same process occurs in "The Whale As A Dish," when the narrator asks "Who is not a cannibal?"

> I tell you it will be more tolerable for the Fejee that salted down a lean missionary in his cellar against a coming famine; it will be more tolerable for that provident Fejee, I say, in the day of judgment, than for thee, civilized and enlightened gourmand, who nailest geese to the ground and feastest on their bloated livers in thy *pate-de-foie-gras.*
>
> (393)

Why should the day of judgment be more tolerable for the literal cannibal than the metaphoric one, if Ishmael's original point was that there is no difference? The sentiment "Who is not a cannibal?" declares that compensation obtains *within* this world—since every creature eats some other one—but it ignores the specificity on which the concept "cannibalism" depends (a cannibal is a creature that eats others *of its own species*). Ishmael invokes the day of judgment as a compensation *outside* this world, at the end of its history, as if he recognized the mendacity of the rhetorical question "Who ain't a cannibal?"

The prolixity and bounty of **Moby-Dick** is generated by Ishmael's hunger for the object-world, as much as by Ahab's hatred for it. In his lengthy stint as narrator, Ishmael's talent for equivocation serves both the ideological purposes of whaling and the narratological purposes of the open sea: no premature closure can be permitted. Equivocation, the effacing of divisive difference, generates the most striking rhetorical excesses. Consider this description from "The Shark Massacre":

> It was unsafe to meddle with the corpses and ghosts of these creatures. A sort of generic or Pantheistic vitality seemed to lurk in their very joints and bones, after what might be called the individual life had departed.
>
> (395)

Ishmael is profoundly ambivalent about the problem posed by the biting head of the dead shark. He cannot choose between "generic or pantheistic" vitality, nor between "corpses and ghosts," and by saying *both* alternatives (as Ishmael so often does), he shows the richesse of diverse and often contradictory knowledges put into play in Ishmael's discourse by Melville's range and erudition. Ishmael's equivocations of the problem in "The Shark Massacre," like his equivocations of the problem in "Does the Whale Diminish? Will He Perish?," seem to forestall a threatening closure that is both narrative and epistemic. To be the survivor, the Odysseus figure, is to keep talking, to prolong the journey and the narrative, and by equivocating, keep in play all the available knowledges that might afford some intellectual protection from the tragic closure that destroys an Achilles or an Ahab. Whereas Ahab pursues *consummation* in the experience of the ineffable sublimity of Moby-Dick, and in the revenge against life that Ahab might exact from him, Ishmael *does not want* epistemic closure any more than he wants narrative closure to end this novel.

This ambivalence about death and endings is common to both ***Moby-Dick,*** the many-chaptered book that won't end, and to Moby-Dick, the many-wounded whale that won't die. Closure is a threat to everyone (except Ahab, who is indifferent to his own extinction). The uniqueness of the *white* whale predicts the uniqueness of the *last* whale. Ishmael's reference to the last whale and the last man in the same sentence—"whether he must not at last be exterminated from the waters, and the last whale, like the last man, smoke his last pipe, and then himself evaporate in the final puff" (586)—suggests that he too, as the last man of the *Pequod,* prefigures the last man of humanity. D. H. Lawrence heard this apocalyptic tone in the novel: "It makes us feel that our day is only a day. That in the dark of the night ahead other days stir fecund, when we have lapsed from existence. Who knows how utterly we shall lapse."[18]

Hence the importance of the fantasy of the Right whale's escape to an impregnable Arctic fortress, "their Polar citadels." This haven guarantees the whales their future physical existence as a species; those "ultimate glassy barriers" are, in the Greek sense of the term, an *eschaton:* a "furthest place," which secures for Ishmael a kind of moral blackhole in which to dump all the taxonomically ambiguous carnage he has witnessed. Similarly, "I call upon holy Jonah to back me," that crucial testimonial in Ishmael's anti-Linnaeus argument, conducts the responsibility for meaning away from the speaker and onto the prophet.

In 1847 Melville bought a copy of Darwin's *Journal of Researches into the Natural History and Geology of the Countries Visited during the Voyage of H.M.S. Beagle round the World,* published in the previous year.[19] And as Ernst Mayr explains,

> [O]ne might assert that the age of evolutionism started even before Buffon [1707-1788], and that the publication of the *Origin of Species* in 1859 was merely the last straw that broke the camel's back.
>
> (987)

> Stirrings of evolutionary thinking preceded the *Origin* by more than 100 years, reaching an earlier peak in Lamarck's *Philosophie Zoologique* in 1809.
>
> (988)

So Melville knew something of the evolutionary account of speciation, which, after all, *rationalizes* the origin of species and dispenses with the *mythos* of divine artifice. But unlike that *mythos,* evolutionary theory requires vast aeons for the emergence of life from the early Earth. Free to pick and choose, Ishmael takes these vast aeons from Darwin but keeps the species-as-eternal-category that he had from Genesis:

> I am horror-struck at this antemosaic, unsourced existence of the unspeakable terrors of the whale, which, having been before all time, must needs exist after all humane ages are over.
>
> (582)

> Leviathan comes floundering down upon us from the headwaters of the Eternities . . .
>
> (584)

Here the vast length of time for which whales have been in existence is evoked by the vastness of the whales themselves.

One need not be so astute a reader of Kant as Herman Melville was, to grasp that the prodigious size of the whale evokes something uncanny, foreign, and quite alien from men and whales alike. Already in the Book of Job, the sublimity of Leviathan is about God, not the whale. It is always a metonym for its maker, *a fortiori:* so great as Leviathan is, so much greater must be the Lord who made Leviathan.

> Canst thou draw out Leviathan with an hook? or his tongue with a cord which thou lettest down? Canst thou put an hook into his nose? or bore his jaw through with a thorn? Will he make many supplications unto thee? will he speak soft words unto thee? Will he make a covenant with thee? wilt thou take him for a servant forever? Wilt thou play with him as with a bird? or wilt thou bind him for thy maidens? Shall the companions make a banquet of him? *shall they part him among the merchants? Canst thou fill his skin with barbed irons? or his head with fish spears? Lay thine hand upon him, remember the battle, do no more. Behold, the hope of him is in vain: shall not one be cast down even at the sight of him? None is so fierce that dare stir him up: who then is able to stand before me?* [my emphasis]
>
> (Job 41:1-10)

The subject of the Book of Job is knowledge; the sublimity of God's power ropes off the mystery of God's justice, and Job's newfound wisdom is precisely his awed willingness to remain ignorant of God's designs. However much we learn about the whale, we remain ignorant of this ultimate, religious knowledge, for which even Cetology is a metonymic substitute. Job 41:12, "I will not conceal his parts, nor his power, nor his comely proportion," introduces God's description of Leviathan—a list of terrifyingly prodigious characteristics which amounts to the warning of 41:8: "Lay thine hand upon him, remember the battle, do no more."

Sometimes Melville directly juxtaposes the martial and the epistemological uses of the whaling lexicon:

> —the conclusion aimed at will naturally follow of itself. First: I have personally known three instances where a whale, after receiving a harpoon . . .
>
> (273)

One *aims at* the knowledge of the whale just as one aims at the whale; indeed, one does the former only by doing the latter ("the only mode . . . is by going a-whaling yourself"). The phrase *hit the mark* evokes the harpoon, in chapter LV: "Of the Monstrous Pictures of Whales":

> True, one portrait may hit the mark much nearer than another, but none can hit it with any considerable degree of exactness. So there is no earthly way of finding out precisely what the whale really looks like. And the only mode in which you can derive even a tolerable idea of his living contour, is by going a-whaling yourself; but in so doing, you run no small risk of being eternally stove and sunk by him. Wherefore, it seems to me you had best not be too fastidious in your curiosity touching this Leviathan.
>
> (352)

Fine advice from the speaker of "Cetology."[20] Ishmael himself is plenty curious about the whale, but, as we have seen, he is none too fastidious. Just as Ishmael alone lives to tell of the wreck of the *Pequod,* so his ramblings about the whale are both contradictory and interminable. All the detailed research of Ishmael-the-naturalist in chapters like "Cetology" and "Measurement of The Whale's Skeleton" serves him as insulation against the deadly knowledge which the whale bears within it, a knowledge that remains inherently beyond human space. Ishmael is willing to employ any strategy available to abbreviate the depth (but not the breadth) of his intellectual transaction with the whale. Consider the waiver that prefaces "Cetology":

> I promise nothing complete; because any human thing supposed to be complete, must for that very reason infallibly be faulty . . . I am the architect, not the builder.
>
> (181)

Complete knowledge of the whale is death: Jonah, who achieved it, is outside of life, among holy things, and Ahab, who came close, "lay like dead for three days"

and lost a leg. If Ishmael momentarily affects an epistemological confidence about the whale, that gesture obliges him to reduce Leviathan to a mere tub of guts: it is only safe to claim knowledge of the whale if one trivializes either that knowledge or the animal which is its object:

> Since I have undertaken to manhandle this Leviathan, it behooves me to approve myself omnisciently exhaustive in the enterprise; not overlooking the minutest seminal germs of his blood, and spinning him out to the uttermost coil of his bowels.
>
> (579)

But a moment later the whale is, once again, majestic and inscrutable. Ishmael is less interested in consistency than in protecting himself from the perilous depth of a total confrontation with the sublime.

The opposite attitude is Ahab's Faustian thrust beyond the limits of experience, as in his demonically Kantian speech at the quarterdeck:

> Hark ye yet again,—the little lower layer. All visible objects, man, are but as pasteboard masks. But in each event—in the living act, the undoubted deed—there, some unknown but still reasoning thing puts forth the mouldings of its features from behind the reasoning mask. If man will strike, strike through the mask! How can the prisoner reach outside except by thrusting through the wall? To me, the white whale is that wall, shoved near to me. Sometimes I think there's naught beyond.
>
> (220)

When Starbuck questions the safety and the economic viability of hunting a single, notoriously vicious whale, Ahab announces openly that his mission is not a commercial but an epistemological one. Starbuck's failure to understand this mission is a specifically hermeneutic failure: "Hark ye yet again,—the little lower layer." This downward progress toward the hidden truth resembles the downward sinking of the Pequod at the novel's end, as well as the downward thrust of the harpoon that searches and destroys.

Critics have often indexed **Moby-Dick** as a novel of Calvinist introspection because its hero is a driven man, and since Max Weber's famous *Protestant Ethic* it has been difficult to ignore the role doctrinal commitments play in determining behavior. We ought not to ignore it, and Ahab's crisis can indeed be read as the response to a Calvinist God's icy silence. Alienated from moderate Europe, the radical Puritans crossed the Atlantic with a theology that so emphasized the transcendent aspect of God as to eclipse the mediating, gentle Christ to whom other Protestant sectarians could and did continually appeal. Their commitment to the doctrine of predestination left the Puritans mazed in a cosmos of reward and punishment whose schedule of outcomes remained forever illegible, like the hieroglyphics on Queequeg's coffin. But Ahab is not Theron Ware; he baptizes his spear in the name of the Devil, as if deliberately to end the wearisome game of faith by losing it once and for all.

In a temporary coma from a wound inflicted by his whalebone leg, Ahab "sought speechless refuge, as it were, among the marble senate of the dead" (591). Elsewhere in the novel, Elijah hints to Ishmael and Queequeg about the mysterious, laconic Ahab: "long ago, when he lay like dead for three days and nights" (133). "Speechless refuge" is what you get from being gored by whalebone, whereas Ishmael talks endlessly, and outlives everyone.[21]

The other loquacious character is the carpenter:

> And this it was, this same unaccountable life-principle in him; this it was, that kept him a great part of the time soliloquizing, but only like an unreasoning wheel, which also hummingly soliloquizes; or rather, his body was a sentry-box and this soliloquizer on guard there, and talking all the time to keep himself awake.
>
> (596)

Yet all this babbling amounts to a kind of silence, like that of the phenomenal world (or the Calvinist god) which, for all its activity, will not acknowledge us:

> For nothing was this man more remarkable, than for a certain impersonal stolidity as it were; impersonal, I say, for it so shaded off into the surrounding infinite of things, that it seemed one with the general stolidity discernible in the whole visible world; which while pauselessly active in uncounted modes, still eternally holds its peace, and ignores you, though you dig foundations for cathedrals.
>
> (595)

The carpenter's presence evokes no individual human psyche behind the face, but the facticity of the world as a whole, the "surrounding infinite of things." In a similar way, Queequeg's coffin and Moby-Dick's hide are each covered in symbols, but those symbols remain unintelligible to any interpreter and so are at least as mysterious as silence. If this idiot-carpenter resembles Ishmael in his garrulity, he also resembles God, since he "seemed one with" the failure of acknowledgment which persists "though you dig foundations for cathedrals."[22] For this reason Ahab calls him "manmaker" during his work on the prosthetic leg (598).

> The weaver-god, he weaves; and by that weaving is he deafened, that he hears no mortal voice; and by that humming, we, too, who look on the loom are deafened; and only *when we escape it* shall we hear the thousand voices that speak through it.
>
> [my emphasis] (573)

The noise of the god deafens our ears, as the "pasteboard masks" of "all visible objects" deceive our eyes. These abuses of the senses are not that special, surreal experience Rimbaud wrote about; they are, for Ahab, the chronic and ubiquitous condition of the will, marooned in a world it did not make. Here, object-relations are as inevitable as they are disappointing, because "all visible objects are but as pasteboard masks." For Ahab, Moby-Dick is the supreme such object, whose very particularity—his bizarre white skin, his intelligence, and, not least, Ahab's personal vendetta, the mutuality of which is never quite clear—makes him the representative of both this world's ontological stinginess and our epistemological poverty.

The chapter called "Brit" begins with a description of the Right Whale:

> Seen from the mast-heads, especially when they paused and were stationary for a while, their vast black forms looked more like lifeless masses of rock than anything else. And as in the great hunting countries of India, the stranger at a distance will sometimes pass on the plains recumbent elephants without knowing them to be such, taking them for bare, blackened elevations of the soil; even so, often, with him, who for the first time beholds this species of the leviathans of the sea. And even when recognized at last, their immense magnitude renders it very hard really to believe that such bulky masses of overgrowth can possibly be instinct with the same sort of life that lives in a dog or a horse.
>
> (362)

Ever since Kant declared that the thing-in-itself was altogether unknowable, there have been readers of Kant who urgently decry the intolerable alienation which this doctrine imposes upon them.[23] The spectacle of living islands, or whales and elephants which appear to be lifeless land, exemplifies the Ishmaelian fantasy of a beating, warm heart inside the relentlessly dead object-world in which man finds himself.[24] The passage recalls the moment in *King Lear* when the difference between the dead and the living is bitterly compared with the difference between people and animals:

> No, no, no life!
> Why should a dog, a horse, a rat, have life,
> And thou no breath at all?
>
> (V.iii.306-8)

In a description of the *Pequod*'s ropes and spars crowded with lookouts, Ishmael says, in "The Chase—Second Day," "The rigging lived" (701). Like the lines from Lear, or like the passage about the biting, undead shark, this phrase rages against the scarcity of spirit in the material world, and against the mystery of its distribution.

In "Compensation," Emerson describes the way human choices engage uncontrollable, non-human energies, with potentially disastrous results:

Every opinion reacts on him who utters it. It is a thread-ball thrown at a mark, but the other end remains in the thrower's bag. Or, rather, it is a harpoon thrown at the whale, unwinding, as it flies, a coil of cord in the boat, and, if the harpoon is not good, or not well thrown, it will go nigh to cut the steersman in twain or to sink the boat.

(80)

The pathos of Emerson's maxim is in the disproportion between the act and the result; in a contingent world, the casually held opinion, the loose remark, can bring death. Like his philosophical descendants Austin and Searle, Emerson is eager to show that speech is not a neutral description appended to the world of action, but a form of action itself, vital and often deadly. This is just what Ishmael wishes to avoid, and his ingenious narrative effusion is an effort to postpone the same decisive closure that Ahab suicidally desires.

Ishmael convinces himself that the whale cannot be driven to extinction, even as Ahab convinces himself that killing Moby-Dick will disclose metaphysical secrets. By attending to the ecological vicissitudes of the 19th Century whaling industry, along with contemporary evolutionary science, we discover that these ideological efforts are desperate struggles with real dangers. Emerson's essay "Compensation" is an indispensible key to understanding the articulation of those efforts, and their curious power over us. To Melville, the American psyche seemed split between a Faustian hero of self-destructive pride and an Odyssean, hypocritical charmer who lived to tell the tale. That is still what the mirror shows.

Notes

1. All citations of Emerson are from the Apollo Edition of *Essays: First Series* (New York, 1926).

2. Merton M. Sealts, Jr., *Melville's Reading* (Madison, 1966): pp. 19, 31.

3. Eugene Hecht, *Physics in Perspective* (Reading: Addison-Wesley, 1980): pp. 170, 191.

4. Compare Whitman (Library of America Edition, *Walt Whitman,* ed. Justin Kaplan [London: Fitzroy, Dearborn, 1997]: p. 28), in the 1855 "Song of Myself":

   There was never any more inception than there is now,
   Nor any more youth or age than there is now;
   And will never be any more perfection than there is
     now
   Nor any more heaven or hell than there is now [. . .]

5. Jay Leyda, *The Melville Log* (New York, 1951): p. 407.

6. Ernst Mayr, "The Nature of The Darwinian Revolution," *Science,* 2 June 1972, Vol. 176, No. 4083.

7. Monroe Strickberger, *Evolution* (Boston, 1990): pp. 5-6.

8. Ernst Mayr, *Animal Species and Evolution* (Cambridge, 1963): pp. 1-2.

9. "For Lyell [author of *Principles of Geology* (1835)], since species are fixed and unchangeable, everything about them, such as the area of distribution, the ecological context, adaptations to cope with competitors and enemies, and even the date of extinction, was previously 'appointed,' that is, predetermined." Mayr, "Darwinian Revolution," p. 983. The Biblical taxonomy, to which Ishmael appeals in refutation of Linnaeus, does not include the idea of species extinction.

   "Robert Chambers, the author of the *Vestiges of the Natural History of Creation* (1844), developed quite a consistent and logical argument for evolutionism, and was instrumental in converting A. R. Wallace, Ralph Waldo Emerson, and Arthur Schopenhauer to evolutionism." Ibid, p. 982.

10. Michael Maran, *The Decline of the American Whaling Industry,* Doctoral Dissertation in Economic History, University Microfilms (Ann Arbor, 1974): p. 40.

11. Maran, p. 3.

12. Ibid, pp. 3, 40-42.

13. Quoted in Maran, p. 40.

14. Quoted in Maran, p. 45.

15. Maran, pp. 9-10.

16. Ibid, p. 31.

17. For the monument see George Francis Dow, *Whale Ships and Whaling* (New York, 1967): p. 429.

18. *Studies in Classic American Literature,* 1923, p. 160.

19. Sealts, p. 55

20. Readers of Aristotle's treatise on tragedy, the *Poetics,* will recognize the pedigree of Ishmael's phrase "hit the mark." It is the literal sense of the Greek verb *tunchanein* (also, *kurein*), whose opposite is *hamartanein,* "to miss the mark"—Aristotle's word for what causes the fall of the tragic hero. Ishmael invokes the epistemological mark which pictures of whales cannot quite hit; Ahab urges Starbuck to strike "through the mask" at, and beyond, this same mark. The tragic "missing the mark" is, paradoxically, the outcome of the hero's insistence upon hitting it: as Oedipus says himself, "I hit the mark with my own mind" (*Oedipus Tyrranus,* line 398). This insistence is what Ishmael lacks, hence his survival.

21. This equation between silence and death is familiar from Whitman's "Song of the Answerer,"
which ends: "[T]o sweep through the ceaseless
rings and never be quiet again." Here the "ceaseless rings" of the soul's prospect are commensurate with the abundance of its verbal resources
("never be quiet again"). Both are protections
against the finality of the poem's closure. Incidentally, this scheme may appear to contradict the
Biblical injunction that "the letter killeth, but the
spirit giveth life." In fact, however, the "letter killeth" precisely because adherence to the literal
sense of scripture obviates all commentary, silenc-
ing the reader: whereas the non-literal reading, or
"spirit," of any passage is what gives us a chance
to speak new words of our own.

22. The carpenter is also like Hawthorne's Customs-
House Inspector: outwardly human, inwardly
blank.

23. For example, Rudolph Steiner, *The Gates of
Knowledge* (New York, 1912), especially pp. 149-
187; Owen Barfield, *Saving the Appearances*
[1957]; Morris Berman, *The Reenchantment of the
World* [1981].

24. Ishmael finds it "really hard to believe" that the
whales are not "lifeless masses," though his business is to help stab the living whale until it is just
that.

E. L. Doctorow (essay date 2001)

SOURCE: Doctorow, E. L. "Composing "*Moby-Dick*:
What Might Have Happened." *Kenyon Review* 26, no. 3
(summer 2004): 55-66.

[*In the following essay, originally presented at Moby-
Dick 2001, a conference hosted by the Melville Society,
and subsequently published in* Leviathan: A Journal of
Melville Studies *in 2003, Doctorow reflects on
Melville's literary technique in the novel.*]

I for one, appreciate my courage in speaking here this
evening. For what can I presume to say about Melville's
Moby-Dick to a congregation of literary harpooners
who have heaved their darts time and time again into
the textual hide of this Leviathan? I suspect that while I
seem to be standing in an academic setting facing a
company of scholars, I am actually in the fo'c'sle of the
Pequod with the oil lamp swinging from the headbeam
and throwing lights and shadows over the faces of a
crew of savage old salts who have lit their pipes and
downed their drams of literary theory and await the
words from me that will persuade them to throw me to
the sharks.

For we know from Melville that we are never in one
place alone at any given minute, but in two—in the
present that is the past, or on the land that is the sea, or
in the sea that is the soul, or in the novel that is God's
ineffable realm.

There is only one recourse for me, and that is to speak
of *Moby-Dick* as a working writer looking at another
writer's work. I will leave the profoundly ambiguous
art object to you. I will leave the thematics, the influences, the symbols, the historico-ideological contexts to
you. I will attempt to see what is being done in this
book and perhaps why it is being done. I think that is
the only way I can sensibly and truthfully go about this
talk, as a writer seeing the writerly things, making the
practical if awed, and envious observations in presump-
tive collegiality of one literary tradesman with another.

I can claim a personal relationship to Melville and his
works, having read *Moby-Dick* three and a half times.
The half time came at the age of ten when I found a
copy in my grandfather's library. It was one of a set of
great sea novels all bound in green cloth, and it was
fair sailing until the cetology stove me in. I first read
the book in its entirety, (and *Typee, Omoo, Billy Budd,*
and **"The Encantadas,"** and **"Benito Cereno,"** and
"Bartleby," for that matter) as an undergraduate at
Kenyon College. Later, as a young editor at the New
American Library, a mass-market paperback publisher. I
persuaded a Kenyon professor, Denham Sutcliffe, to
write an afterword to the Signet Classic edition of
Moby-Dick, and so read the book again by way of editorial preparation. In anticipation of this evening I have
after too many years read *Moby-Dick* for the third time.
And the surprise to me, at my age now, is how familiar
the voice of that book is, and not merely the voice, but
the technical effrontery, and not merely the technical effrontery, but the character and rhythm of the sentences.
And so with some surprise, I've realized, how much of
my own work, at its own level, hears Melville, responds
to his perverse romanticism, endorses his double dip-
ping into the accounts of realism and allegory, as well
as the large risk he takes speaking so frankly of the crisis of human consciousness, that great embarrassment
to us all that makes a tiresome prophet of anyone who
would speak of it.

Hawthorne I have always understood as a writer who
affected me deeply and I have realized my sometime inclination to write romances in the Hawthornian sense—
novels set in the past that would cure up real life into a
gamier essence. But whatever rule breaking I have done
in my work I probably owe to Melville, Hawthorne's
devoted admirer, but also his saboteur, in taking the elements of the well-constructed novel and making a cub-
ist composition of them.

Literary history finds among the great novelists a few
who achieved their greatness from an impatience with

the conventions of narrative. Virginia Woolf composed *Mrs. Dalloway* from the determination to write a novel without a plot or indeed a subject. And then Joyce, of course: Like Picasso who was an expert draftsman before he blew his art out of the water, James Joyce proved himself in the art of narrative writing before he committed his assaults upon it. The author of the sterling narratives **Typee** and **Omoo** precedes Joyce with his own blatant subversion of the narrative compact he calls **Moby-Dick.** Yet I suspect that, in this case, the subversion may have been if not inadvertent, then only worked out tactically given the problem of its conception. I would guess that what Melville does in **Moby-Dick** is not from a grand preconceived aesthetic (Joyce: I will pun my way into the brain's dreamwork; I will respect the protocols of grammar and syntax but otherwise blast the English language all to hell) but from the necessity of dealing with the problem inherent in constructing an entire nineteenth-century novel around a single life and death encounter with a whale. The encounter clearly having to come as the climax of his book, Melville's writing problem was how to pass the time until then—until he got the *Pequod* to the Southern Whale fisheries and brought the white whale from the depths. Ahab crying "There she blows—there she blows! A hump like a snow hill! It is Moby Dick!" She blows, I point out to you, not until page 537 of a 566-page book—in my old paperback Rhinehart edition.

A writer lacking Melville's genius might conceive of a shorter novel, its entry point being possibly closer in time to the deadly encounter. And with maybe a flashback or two thrown in. A novelist of today, certainly, would eschew exposition as far as possible, let the reader work out for herself what is going on, which is a contemporary way of maintaining narrative tension. Melville's entry point, I remind you, is not at sea aboard the *Pequod,* not even in Nantucket: he locates Ishmael in Manhattan, and staying in scene every step of the way, takes him to New Bedford, has him meet Queequeg at the Spouter Inn, listen to a sermon, contrive to get them both to Nantucket, meet the owners of the *Pequod,* endure the ancient hoary device of a mysterious prophecy; and it isn't until chapter 20 which begins "A day or two passed" that he elides time. Until that point, some ninety-four pages into the book, the writing has all been a succession of unbroken real time incidents. Another ten pages elapse before the *Pequod* "thrust[s] her vindictive bows into the cold malicious waves (chap. 23).

I wouldn't wonder if Melville at this point, the *Pequod* finally underway, stopped to read what he had written to see what his book was bidding him to do.

Now this is sheer guesswork, of course. I have not read the major biographies, and I don't know what Melville himself may have said about the writing of **Moby-Dick**

beyond characterizing it as a "wicked book." Besides, whatever any author says of his novel is of course another form of the fiction he practices and is never, never, to be trusted.

Perhaps Melville had everything comfortably worked out before he began, though I doubt it. Perhaps he had a draft completed of something quite conventional before his writer's sense of crisis set in. The point to remember is the same that Faulkner once reminded his critics of: that they see a finished work and do not dream of the chaos of trial and error and torment from which it has somehow emerged.

No matter what your plan for a novel—and we know Melville was inspired by the account of an actual whaling disaster (the destruction of the ship Essex in 1819) and we know whaling was a subject he could speak of with authority of personal experience, and we know he understood as well as the most commercial practitioner of the craft, that a writer begins with an advantage who can report on a kind of life or profession out of the ken of the ordinary reader—nevertheless, I say that no matter what your plan or inspiration, or trembling recognition for an idea that you know belongs to you, the strange endowment you set loose by the act of writing is never entirely under your control. It cannot be a matter solely of willed expression. Somewhere, from the depths of your being you find a voice: it is the first and most mysterious moment of the creative act. There is no book without it. If it takes off it appears to you to be self-governed. To some degree you will write to find out what you are writing. And you have no sense of possession for what comes onto the pages—what you have is a sense of discovery.

So let us propose that having done his first hundred or so pages of almost entirely land-based writing, Melville stopped to read what he had written. What have I got here?—The author's question.

"This Ishmael—he is logorrheic! He is entirely confident of holding my attention whatever he writes about, and whatever he writes about, *he takes his time*. With this Ishmael, I have a hundred or so land-based pages, so if I am to keep the proportion of the thing, I will need five hundred at sea. And if the encounter with the Whale is my climax it will need—what?—maybe four hundred and fifty pages of sailing before I find him? Migod."

And there was the problem. His sentences had a texture that could conceivably leave his book wallowing with limp sails in a becalmed narrative sea.

I will not speculate that there may have come to Melville one of those terrible writer's moments of despair that can be so useful in fusing as if with lightning the book so far with the book to come. In any event he would for his salvation have to discover that his pages manifested not one but two principles of composition. First, a conventional use of chronological time and a narrator, Ishmael, whose integrity was maintained. And that in this extended opening or land prelude there was dutiful attendance to the dramatic necessities of conventional fiction—e.g. the biblical Elijah figure who issues his cryptic prophecy, the suspenseful nonappearance above deck of Captain Ahab—and surely at this early stage, as we readers can see, the use of humor, good abiding humor of language, and loving character depiction, that suggests the shrewdness of a writer who knows his story will end in horror. (Perhaps the least of the things Shakespeare taught Melville was the value of tangential humor to the bloodiest stories: it establishes the hierarchy of human souls that brings the few at the top into tragic distinction.)

All well and good. Melville could project from these traditional storytelling observances a whole series of narrative tropes. Ahab would have to allow the crew the hunting of other whales. So there was that action. Bad weather and worse could reasonably be invoked. There might be the threat of piracy. As Ahab's maniacal single-mindedness became apparent to the crew, some of them, at least, might contest his authority. Other whalers were abroad around the world. They could be met and inquired of. As indeed there are what?—perhaps eight or nine such encounters—the *Albatross,* the *Town-Ho,* the *Virgin* and on to, the *Bachelor,* the *Rachel,* the *Delight*—each ship the occasion for a story, and depending on the usefulness to Ahab's passion, a matter for his approval or rejection. Given this pattern, a habitual recourse of the narrative, we readers today can make a case for **Moby-Dick** as a road novel. (This is not a misnomer when we constantly find through the text equivalences between sea and land, the representation of the one by means of the other. When Ishmael takes up the *Town Ho* story of Steelkilt and Radney, he steps out of the time of the book and takes us to Peru to tell it, at which point we know he has read *Don Quixote* and perhaps *Jacques the Fatalist.*)

But while in these first 105 pages, Ishmael's integrity as a narrator is maintained, and the setup for the voyage suggests an assiduous, and conventional narrative, there is something else, possibly less visible, a second principle of composition lurking there. It would come to Melville incipiently as a sense of dissatisfaction with his earlier books, and their gift for nautical adventure. While we may know that there is nobody, before or since, who has written better descriptions of the sea and its infinite natures and the wrathful occasions it can deliver, to Melville himself this talent would be of no consequence as he contemplated the requirements of his **Moby-Dick,** and felt the aching need to do this book, to bring it to fruition out of the depths of his consciousness—to resolve into a finished visionary work, everything he knew.

So he looks again at his Ishmael. And he finds in him the polymath of his dreams: "Yes, Ishmael tells a chronological story well enough. But look how he does it. He breaks time up into places, things, like someone planting the stones of a mosaic one by one. He has read his Shakespeare. He knows European history. He is conversant with biblical scholarship, philosophy, ancient history, classical myth, English poetry, lands and empires, geography. Why stop there? He can express the latest thinking in geology (he would know about the tectonic plates), the implications of Darwinism, and look, his enlightened cultural anthropology (that I have lifted from **Typee**) grants Queequeg a system of belief finally no more bizarre or less useful than Christendom's.

"I can make this fellow an egregious eavesdropper, so talented as to be able to hear men think, or repeat their privately muttered soliloquies verbatim. See when he finally gives me some action on the schooner from New Bedford to Nantucket—when Queequeg first roughs up a mocking passenger and then saves him from drowning—and this is nautical adventure despite all—see how when he finally allows a physical action, Ishmael hurries through it to get back to his contemplative ways. My Ishmael was born to be a tactless writer of footnotes—yes, I will make him the inexhaustible author of my water world."

And it is a fact that no sooner are we at sea, in chapter 24, "The Advocate," does Ishmael step out of time in a big way and give us the first of his lectures on whaling. Melville's big gamble has begun—to pass the time by destroying it, to make a new thing of the novel form by blasting its conventions.

I know this to be true: Herman Melville may have been theologically a skeptic, philosophically an Existentialist, personally an Isolato, with a desolation of spirit as deep as any sea dingle—but as a writer he is exuberant.

Even if my scenario is false, and Melville did not need to stop and read what he had written at the point the *Pequod* goes to sea, even so, at a hundred or so pages into a book that is working, it begins to give things back to you, it begins to generate itself from itself, a matter, say, of its stem cells differentiating into the total organism. Even with a completed draft of conventional storytelling before him, when the author reads to see what he has done, the lightning strikes early on, it is the book's beginnings that tell him what finally he must do by way of revision. Thus, from Father Mapple's pulpit like a ship's prow, a rope ladder its means of access, from the story of Jonah as a seaman's sermon, from the Try Pots chowder house, and the whalebone tiller of the

Pequod, we derive a landless realm; and by the time much later in the book, when the ship and its crew are four hundred and fifty pages at sea, Ishmael tells us we—*we*—are still in Noah's flood, that it is eternal, with only the whale able to "spout his frothed defiance to the skies" (chap. 105), we need no persuading—the story of Ahab is realized as the universal punishment.

It interests me that Ishmael, who is the source of Melville's inspired subversion of the narrative compact, must therefore be himself badly used by the author. Ishmael is treated with great love but scant respect—he is Ishmael all right in being so easily cast out, and if he is called back, it is only to be cast out again. I wonder if it was not a private irony of his author that the physically irresolute Ishmael, with roughly the same protoplasm of the Cheshire cat, is the *Pequod*'s sole survivor. I can't help feeling that he would not be so, if his continued life was not factually necessary to give voice to the tale—Melville's grudging deference to the simple Job-ic logic of storytelling.

In any event what Ishmael certainly knows about is whaling—despite his greenhorn status aboard the *Pequod.* He represents himself as having been new to the practice at the time, but by way of compensation, has become well-versed in the scientific literature. Like E. A. Poe, he has a habit of citing extraliterary sources. Now let me talk about Poe, for a moment. I don't know whether Melville read Poe, or what he thought of him, but among Poe's bad writing habits is his attempt to provide authority for the tale he is about to tell by citing factual precedents for it. He begins "The Premature Burial," for example, by citing three or four newspaper stories about people buried prematurely—just to establish that this sort of thing can happen. He would give his tale then the authority of borrowed fact. He argues from scientific authority in "Descent into the Maelstrom" that the Nordic waters are known to be susceptible to just such terrifying phenomena as he will describe. Poe likes to argue his way into his stories. It's the fiction writer's admission after all that he is not a factualist, that he stands outside the culture of empirical truth. And as such it is a fatally defensive move. On occasion, especially at the beginning of **Moby-Dick,** Melville might seem to be doing the same defensive thing: In the very first chapter, "Loomings," he cites men on Manhattan docks fixed in "ocean reveries" and argues the narcissistic attraction of rivers, lakes, and oceans to make Ishmael's decision to take to the sea more than just a personal matter. He cites authorities for the existence of albino whales. And in "The Advocate" chapter, of course, he argues for the social beneficence, the respectability, the grandeur, and so forth of the whaling profession. This sort of nonnarrative case-making to justify the telling of the tale would be as much of a mistake as it is in Poe—if that was as far as Melville took it. But of course, unlike Poe, Melville

doesn't stop there, he will load his entire book with time-stopping pedagogy—he will give us essays, trade lore, taxonomies, opinion surveys; he will review the pertinent literature—he will carry on to excess outside the narrative. It is indisputable in my mind that excess in literature is its own justification. It is a sign of genius, and in this case, turns the world on its head so that just what is a weakness when done in modest proportion is transformative as a consistent recourse and persuades the reader finally into the realm so nakedly proselytized.

And then of course the excess touches every corner, every nook and cranny below deck, every tool and technical fact of the life aboard the *Pequod,* and everything upon it from Ahab's prosthesis, to the gold doubloon he nails upon the mast, from Queequeg's tattoos, to the leaking oil barrels in the bowels of the ship. The narrative bounds forward from the discussion of things. So finally we look at the details and discover something else: whatever it is, Melville will provide us the meanings to be taken from it. The doubloon upon the mast will be described in such a way, its zodiac signs, its Andean symbols, a tower, a crowing cock, and so forth, as to affirm Ahab's rumination that it is emblematic of an Ahabian universe, the given horror of the half-known life. Queequeg's hieroglyphic tattoos are a "complete theory of the heavens and the earth, and a mystical treatise on the art of attaining truth; so that Queequeg in his own proper person was a riddle to unfold; a wondrous work in one volume" (chap. 110) though he himself could not hope to understand it. And of course Moby Dick's color is lifted from him to show "by its indefiniteness" (not a color so much as a visible absence of color) "the heartless voids and immensities of the universe," white being the "colorless, all-color of atheism from which we shrink," a "mystical cosmetic" colorless in itself that paints all Nature like a "harlot" (chap. 42).

Melville's irrepressible urge to make the most of everything suggests the mind of a poet. The significations, the meaningful enlargements he makes of tools, coins, colors, existent facts are the work of a lyric poet, a maker of metaphorical meanings, for whom unembellished linear narrative is but a pale joy. So I will say here Melville's solution is not a novelist's solution; it is a poet's solution. **Moby-Dick** can be read as a series of ideas for poems. It is a procession of ideational events. Melville's excesses are not mere pedagogical interruptions of the narrative; nor are they there to provide authority for the tale. They burst from the book as outward flarings or star births, as a kind of cosmology, finally, to imply a multiplicity of universes, one inside another, endlessly and each one of which could have its novel as the sea has this one.

At this point however I see that I am in danger of breaking the rules of this talk and am threatening to come up somewhat off the ground level observation of the writer at work. You will notice I have avoided the autonomy-of-literature argument, or the temptation to speak of the recurrent theme in Melville of the perversities of captainship, the rule of law, the law of men, in the universe of a ship, or of Ahab as an archetype, for example, and to find him today in such beings as Slobodan Milosevic, and so forth. I have not done any of that, but when I talk about the book as a procession, of ideational events, or a metaphoric cosmology, I begin to get nervous.

So let me veer off here to another claim I can make in my homage to Herman Melville. Many years ago I bought a home in Sag Harbor. Now you know Sag Harbor, at the east end of Long island, was a whaling town, and for some years in the nineteenth century with the whaling industry booming, its denizens had reason to believe that someday with its deep water harbor it would rival New York as a major port. Melville mentions Sag Harbor, gives Queequeg a funny anthropological moment there, and even today it has maintained its village character; a town that time has fortunately forgot: preserved are the larger Main Street homes with their widows' walks built by the whaling captains, as well as the smaller more modest cottages on the side streets where the ordinary seamen left their families when they went to sea. The village cemetery on Jermain Street provides gravestone records of the lost captains, the sunken ships, in this most dangerous of trades (so dangerous that it makes the age of Ahab the single most unlikely fact of the tale—most of the captains of the Sag Harbor whaling fleet were quite young, and if they were lucky enough to live to the age of forty or forty-five, they were likely to be burned-out and land-bound forever after—it was a young man's get-rich-quick game, whaling, in my understanding). But as I say, with Sag Harbor certainly a busy active whaling community, Melville chose to work his fleet out of Nantucket. Now, I know the Essex hailed from Nantucket, and he himself went whaling out of Fairhaven right next door and that he knew the area well enough. But I would like to believe he chose Nantucket because he brilliantly realized the Quaker speech that predominated there was his means of access, his bridge, to the Elizabethan diction he so exuberantly exercises in his Shakespearean riffs. I will make that my theory of why he chose Nantucket over Sag Harbor where the Quakers were very small in number, and there were no thees and thous and dosts to segue him into the soliloquies and dramatic dialogues that he cannot resist. And why would he? Perhaps you know—I don't—any other writer in history as uncannily able to iterate Shakespeare—at moments apt to be equal to him—with his monologues and scenes—but also to so successfully adopt the social structuring of his characters, their hierarchies of rank, comedy and tragedy, their parallel relationships to those in the master's plays all, of which I assume you have annotated in your scholarship—this is the exuberance in one of its manifestations, the irrepressible love of language that

causes Melville to be so eccentric, quirky, inconstant, toward the narrative demands of fiction as to render his book on publication unsaleable.

Certainly *Moby-Dick* is a very *written* book. If I may be crude for a moment, I'll distinguish those writers who make their language visible, who draw attention to it in the act of writing and don't let us forget it—Melville, Joyce, and Nabokov in our own time, the song and dance men, the strutting dandies of literature—from those magicians of the real who write to make their language invisible, like lit stage scrims that pass us through to the scene behind so that we see the life they are rendering as if no language is producing it. Tolstoy and Chekhov are in this class. Clearly, neither one nor the other method can be said to be *the way*. But the one is definitely more reader-friendly than the other. And Melville in his journey from *Typee* to *Moby-Dick* abandons the clear transparent pools of the one, for the opaque linguistic seas of the other.

In case you are curious: had I aspired to a scholarly position this evening, I would have invoked Northrop Frye's category of Menippean Satire. For after all, it can be argued that *Moby-Dick* is that—an Anatomy—a big kitchen sink sort of book into which the irrepressible author, a writing fool, throws everything he knows, happily changing voice, philosophizing, violating the consistent narrative, dropping in every arcane bit of information he can think of, reworking his research, indulging in parody, unleashing his pure powers of description—so that the real *Moby-Dick* is the voracious maw of the book swallowing the English language.

By way of conclusion, let me admit finally what you may by now have realized—that in interpreting Melville's writing process, perversely applying textual analysis of a sort to read from the finished book what it might have gone through to become itself, I am insisting not so much on the literal truth of my claims but on their validity as another kind of fiction.

I confess I have given you tonight not a speech so much as a story—a parable of the grubbiness and glory of the writer's mind.

We celebrate this evening the hundred and fiftieth anniversary of a revolutionary novel. Its importance is not negated by the fact that our culture has changed and we now no longer hunt the whale as much as we try to save it. In fact, according to newspaper reports, whale watching—not hunting—is now the greatest threat to their well being, or whalebeing. Going out in sightseeing boats to frolic with the whales is a bigger industry now, producing more income than fishing for them, and threatens to disrupt their migratory patterns and thus their organized means of survival. In fact, one can imagine *Moby-Dick* as possibly a prophetic document, if one day a Leviathan rises from the sea in total exasperation of being watched by these alien humans, humans who once at least in hunting them were marginally in the natural world, but now in only observing them are in that realm no longer, and so rightly destined for the huge open jaw, and the mighty crunch, and the triumphant slap of the horizontal flukes.

But whatever the case, I can assure you Ernest Hemingway was wrong when he said modern American literature begins with *Huckleberry Finn.* It begins with **Moby-Dick,** the book that swallowed European civilization whole. And we only are escaped alone on our own shore to tell our tales.

Homer B. Pettey (essay date spring 2003)

SOURCE: Pettey, Homer B. "Cannibalism, Slavery, and Self-Consumption in *Moby-Dick.*" *Arizona Quarterly* 59, no. 1 (spring 2003): 31-58.

[*In the following essay, Pettey examines the thematic relationship between cannibalism and capitalism in* Moby-Dick. *In Pettey's interpretation, Ishmael's service on the Pequod represents a period of enslavement, one during which he suffers under the hypocrisy, avarice, and cruelty of Ahab. Pettey argues that Ishmael's plight is a symbol of Melville's own disenchantment with the failures of American democracy.*]

> They were "slaves without masters," the little fish who were food for all the larger.
>
> George Fitzhugh, *Cannibals All! or, Slaves Without Masters*

In this vein, Maori cannibalism—well-documented from contemporary nineteenth-century accounts—was set in a context of ritual warfare; the consumption of human flesh paralleled that of birds and fish in hunting rituals. Men consumed at cannibalistic feasts were referred to as "fishes," and "first fish" being eaten by a chief who thus acquired control over the land of the vanquished.

> I. M. Lewis, *Religion in Context: Cults and Charisma*

> "Kill-e," cried Queequeg, twisting his tattooed face into an unearthly expression of disdain, "ah! him bery small-e fish-e; Queequeg no kill-e so small-e fish-e; Queequeg kill-e big whale!"
>
> Melville, "The Wheelbarrow," *Moby-Dick*

That Melville chose an unrepentant South Sea cannibal, Queequeg, to be his narrator's spiritual guide and savior in **Moby-Dick** (1851) certainly must have disturbed his nineteenth-century readers. Equally disconcerting, the novel's narrator assumes the allegorical guise of Ishmael, slave son of Abraham: symbol of alienated, social outcasts from the bosom of Abraham; progenitor

of enemies to Israel, whose tribe conspires with the nations of Edom, Moab, Ammon, and Assyria for Israel's destruction (Ps. [Psalms] 83); and in literature, wild man father (Gen. [Genesis] 16:12) of the enemies of Christianity, the "Africk" in Spenser's *Faerie Queene,* as well as father of Native Americans in Longfellow's *Evangeline* (1847).[1] By pairing Queequeg with Ishmael in **Moby-Dick,** Melville unites barbarous cannibal with outcast slave. Barbarity and slavery would also be recognizable in the ship's name, *Pequod:* these Amerindians, viewed by Puritan sages as "Bloody *Salvages*" (Mather, *Magnalia* [*Magnalia Christi Americana*] 166), were nearly decimated in a genocidal military campaign by New England settlers in 1637.[2] Pequot survivors were forced into the peculiar institution of Puritan slavery, sold to plantations in the Caribbean, given a status comparable to African slaves, and inhumanely branded for running away.[3] Historically, Pequots were faced with vicious New England slavers to the north and east and had nowhere to go westward, because beyond the Connecticut Valley lived hostile Mohawks, whose name also meant cannibals.[4] Puritans collected war trophies—severed heads and hands—of the Pequots as evidence to Bay Colony officials that their capital had been well invested in military protection; Thomas Hooker adopted a cannibalistic metaphor when preaching on these body parts, stating that "the Indians would be 'bread for us,'" a recognition of, if not praise for, New England's Christian brand of bloodthirsty aggression (Shuffelton 237-38). In the nineteenth century, numerous examples of Christians resorting to cannibalism at sea pre-dated **Moby-Dick,** among them, the *Medusa* in 1816, subject of Géricault's *Raft of the Medusa* (1819), and the *Essex* in 1820, subject of Chase's *Narrative* cited in his "Extracts."[5] Melville distrusted hypocritical condemnations of savages or cannibals by Christian culture, whose pieties he viewed as more gruesome than the rituals of so-called primitives.

In **Moby-Dick,** Melville uses cannibalism in order to attack the cruel institutions of slavery and capitalism which were eating away at American culture. Aware of the political rhetoric of slavery, particularly the denigration of African-Americans as savages by pro-slavery Southerners, Melville recognized the equally savage conditions imposed by Northern industrialism and American expansionism, not just upon indigenous and slave populations, but also upon Northern workers.[6] Cannibalism, then, served Melville as a socio-political metaphor by which he could attack America's hypocritical system of values. It also afforded Melville an allegorical and symbolic mode for representing acts of appropriation, subjugation, and consumption. For Melville, the whaling industry itself was a perfect symbol of American capitalism and expansion of his day; the enterprise of whaling also shared similarities with cannibalism—hunting, killing, possessing, dismembering, and consuming. Fish, sharks, and whales often function as metaphorical substitutes for mankind in *Moby-Dick;* as most readers recognize, the anatomy, dissection, and consumption of the whale thinly veil analogies to human beings.

Most certainly, Melville was fascinated with ethnography of primitive peoples, especially how these cultures were both set apart from American culture and paradoxically reflected it. Standard typology of cannibalism includes exocannibalism, the killing and eating of outsiders, usually in warfare; endocannibalism, kinship killing or kinship feeding that reinforces life process and regeneration; and autocannibalism, ingestion of one's own body.[7] Melville is keenly aware of just these sorts of cultural distinctions, as evidenced by Ishmael drawing literal and figurative distinctions between Queequeg and the other crew members of the *Pequod*. Melville populates the *Pequod* with cannibals, making the very vessel a symbol of cannibalistic urges. The voyage of the *Pequod* results in increasing stages of grotesque consumption, particularly evident from the cetological and cannibalistic centers of the novel. Structurally, the novel moves from ritualized exocannibalism to narcissistic autocannibalism. Rhetorically, cannibalism results in self-consuming fictions, by which political and economic structures based upon oppression lead inevitably to their own self-destruction.

Melville's approach to cannibalism in *Moby-Dick* and his characterization of Queequeg rely upon his reading of Montaigne's "Of Cannibals."[8] Montaigne provides a template for the novel's thematic dichotomy between savagery and civilization, as well as for Ishmael's *olla podrida* of allusions—biblical, classical, modern European and New World examples of barbarity. Like Montaigne, Melville recognized that civilized men had "changed artificially" and were "led astray from the common order" of Nature by their belief that others were inhuman, savage, and wild based on the paltry evidence that they practiced different customs ([Montaigne] 152). This sanctimonious bias by Christianity develops from its fervent belief that it will always have "the perfect religion, the perfect government, the perfect and accomplished manners in all things" (152). Montaigne uses as his counterexample the New World cannibal community whose way of life surpasses poetic visions of the classical golden age. Melville similarly uses Queequeg to underscore the hypocrisy of Christian morality. Michel de Certeau explains the structure of Montaigne's essay in terms that can be seen to parallel Ishmael's adventure in *Moby-Dick*. The essay lays out a narrative topography in the form of "a travel account" with three movements: the outbound journey that distances the narrator from his culture, intellectually and socially; the excursion among the savages in which "the discourse that sets off in search of the other with the impossible task of saying the truth returns from afar with the authority to speak in the name of the other"; and the return of the native, the now savage-minded narrator (69-70). Initially, Ishmael's tale maps out boundaries between cultures of land and sea; he adopts the pose of authority and often speaks for Queequeg, his cannibalistic alter ego; and the novel, as the reader discovers, is his retrospective account that is somewhat in sympathy with his cannibal's worldview. Distinctions occur in *Moby-Dick* among types of cannibalism; often Ishmael contrasts Queequeg's cannibalistic humanism to Ahab's Christian monomania. In *Moby-Dick,* however, socio-political topography demarcating civilized and savage worlds soon becomes less distinct as unchecked barbarism aboard the *Pequod* increases.

"Of Cannibals" sympathetically treats the practices of this New World savage community—symbolic warfare, enslavement, headhunting, communal killing, communal feasts on human flesh—that seem inimical to Western culture. Melville agreed with Montaigne's assertion that "treachery, disloyalty, tyranny, and cruelty" are "our ordinary vices" (156). By juxtaposing this civilized savagery with incidents of Christian barbarism such as the Inquisition, Montaigne renders these savage acts less barbarous than Western customs: "Truly here are real savages by our standards; for either they must be thoroughly so, or we must be; there is an amazing distance between their character and ours" (158). To add accuracy to his account, he informs his reader that he spoke with a New World warrior cannibal, "our sailors called him a king" (159), comparable to Queequeg's seafaring, royal heritage. Montaigne concludes his essay on a comical note concerning this distinguished spokesman of the cannibals, reminding his reader of culturally based prejudices: "All this is not too bad— but what's the use? They don't wear breeches" (159). Of course, Queequeg "staving about with little else but his hat and boots on" comes immediately to mind (35). For both Melville and Montaigne, those who denigrate the practice of cannibal cultures do so from the standpoint of blindness to their own culture's savage heritage. Montaigne demonstrates that contradictory images—utopian ideals and cannibalism, Christian pieties and savagery—are "interdependent mechanisms" (Klarer 395). In *Moby-Dick,* this interdependence first occurs in the marriage between Ishmael and Queequeg; Ishmael awakens in the Spouter-Inn in Queequeg's "bridegroom clasp," as though "I had been his wife" (33, 32). In Melville's comic marriage, Ishmael is wedded to paganism and divorces himself from the hypocrisies and barbarity of Western culture.

Queequeg's sign of exocannibalism, like that of Montaigne's New World primitives, is the New Zealand head he peddles about New Bedford, a town whose economy already has a surplus of shrunken heads, and where "actual cannibals stand at street corners; savages outright; many of whom yet carry on their bones unholy flesh" (37). Trophies of exocannibalism also present themselves in the patrician society of New Bedford, which "is a queer place" with a "bony" appearance placed upon a "scraggy scoria" of land; the skeletal and excremental puns are worth noting here in comparison with the cannibals in the streets (38). New Bedford, as Ishmael tells us, is no promised land, no land of milk and honey, "not like Canaan," but "a land of oil" (38), a symbol of nineteenth-century American capitalism. Natives of New Bedford, not unlike their pagan counterparts, engage in symbolic rituals, giving "whales for dowers to their daughters" (38). Like Queequeg's shrunken head, whales are trafficked in a kind of exocannibalism, serving as trophies of enemies to New Bedford warriors. Melville pointedly connects whale rituals with capitalism. Surplus profit and accumulation mark the conspicuous consumption of the New Bedford population, who "have reserves of oil in every house" and "recklessly burn" spermaceti candles (38). American consumption far outweighs that of the primitives. It is in New Bedford where Ishmael stands before gable-ended Spouter-Inn and recalls the New Testament parable of class division—Lazarus and Dives. Ishmael transforms Dives into a modern-day New England capitalist, who "lives like a Czar in an ice palace made of frozen sighs, and being a president of a temperance society, he only drinks the tepid tears of orphans" (19). By "temperance society" Melville probably means the Washingtonians, a charitable association devoted solely to moral suasion to rid society of the evils of drink, but not its more pressing needs, such as dismal poverty.[9] Melville's taste for liquor and his distaste for sanctimonious Christians explains his characterization for this Dives. The cannibalistic metaphor of living off the tears of orphans inverts the meaning of Luke's parable. In Luke 16, Dives ignores the suffering of the poor man Lazarus and his indifference results in his burning in Hades, while Lazarus ascends into the arms of father Abraham after death. Moreover, like Tantalus, Dives suffers from an unquenchable thirst in Hades, which Melville inverts by having him cannibalistically drink the sorrows of the poor. In New England's cruel system of amassing wealth and class division, Melville cynically sees no salvation for the poor and no punishment for callous, autocratic capitalists.

Queequeg's encounters with Christian culture are rarely harmonious as well. According to his biographical tale, he set out from Kokovoko in order "to learn among the Christians, the arts whereby to make his people still happier," but soon discovers "that even Christians could be both miserable and wicked; infinitely more so, than all his father's heathens" (57). Ishmael concurs. Without proselytizing, Queequeg converts Ishmael. In "A Bosom Friend," Ishmael works out a moral logic for transforming himself into Queequeg's pagan reflection:

> But what is worship?—to do the will of God—*that* is worship. And what is the will of God?—to do to my fellow man what I would have my fellow man to do to me—*that* is the will of God. Now, Queequeg is my fellow man. And what do I wish that this Queequeg would do to me? Why, unite with me in my particular Presbyterian form of worship. Consequently, I must then unite with him in his; ergo, I must turn idolator.
>
> (54)

Ishmael embraces Queequeg's customs, but he does so as an act of rebellion against American Christian prejudices, summed up in Ishmael's logic of inversion: "Better sleep with a sober cannibal than a drunken Christian" (31). Here, Ishmael's rejection of his culture echoes Satan's rebellion against God in Milton's *Paradise Lost:* "Better to reign in Hell, than serve in Heav'n" (1.263). Idolatry, however, does not mean becoming a religious fanatic. By explaining to Queequeg the history of religion from "the primitive religions, and coming down to the various religions of the present time," Ishmael hopes to dissuade his friend from fasting, since "all these Lents, Ramadans, and prolonged hamsquattings in cold, cheerless rooms were stark nonsense; bad for the health; useless for the soul; opposed, in short, to the obvious laws of Hygiene and common sense" (81). What eats at Ishmael is the emptiness of rituals. Religious self-punishment, as Ishmael sarcastically puts it, is based upon indigestion: "hell is an idea first born on an undigested apple-dumpling; and since then perpetuated through the hereditary dyspepsias nurtured by Ramadans" (82). This "apple-dumping," the forbidden fruit of Eden, recalls the action of the "two orchard thieves" (15) whose consumption brings sin and death into the world. Moreover, their desire to possess and to consume brings about their self-destruction. Religion, then, reminds us of our self-consuming impulses. In "Loomings," Ishmael has wryly warned his readers from the outset that myth of Narcissus "is the key to it all" (14).

Ishmael shows signs of transforming into a cannibal long before he sets sail aboard the *Pequod.* In "Chowder," Ishmael experiences a comic foreshadowing of the whale dissections and meals from the cannibalistic center of **Moby-Dick:** "Chowders for breakfast, and chowder for dinner, and chowder for supper, till you began to look for fish-bones coming through clothes" (65). From the first moment that Ishmael feasts his eyes upon the "ivory" *Pequod* (199), the narrative portends the cannibalism to come: "A cannibal of a craft, tricking herself forth in the chased bones of her enemies" (67). Captain Peleg warns Ishmael that Ahab has tasted the civilized and savage worlds: "Mark ye, be forewarned; Ahab's above the common; Ahab's been in colleges, as well as 'mong the cannibals" (76). Like the *Pequod* with its "jaw-bone tiller" (420), Ahab bears the symbols of his own cannibalistic urges, his "ivory leg had at sea been fashioned from the polished bone of a sperm whale's jaw" (110).

Dining experiences aboard the *Pequod* always include cannibalism. Even Ahab's "ivory-inlaid" cabin dining table is formed from the body of the whale (131). As opposed to the mealtime segregation of kingly Ahab and his knights, the "three savages"—Queequeg, Tashtego, and Daggoo—create an "almost frantic democracy," though they "dined like lords" (133). Melville's comic paradox of hierarchical stations reverses the presumed aristocracy of the "their masters, the mates," who are afraid of the "ungentlemanly" manners and hideous sounds of rapacious feeding coming from Queequeg, the Polynesian, and Tashtego, the Native American, and are perhaps surprised, as Ishmael's depictions suggest, by the "baronial," "dainty" manners of the "noble savage," the African Daggoo (133). Melville also provides comic scenes of the harpooners' "portentous appetites" that produce panic in the Dough-Boy, "the progeny of a bankrupt banker and a hospital nurse" (152), who represents American culture and its ridiculous ethnocentric dread of other cultures. Of course, this heir to a failed economic system and diseased morality cannot understand the ways of cannibal, slave, and savage. Tashtego, like Queequeg and Daggoo, is "unmixed," a pure specimen and "inheritor of the unvitiated blood" of his race of "proud warrior hunters" (107); and yet, his "snaky limbs" are reminders of the "superstitions of some of the earlier Puritans" who considered redmen to be sons of the "Prince of the Powers of the Air" (107). That satanic imagery will appear again when the *Pequod* sinks and Tashtego acts in a manner similar to the Devil himself. Daggoo, "a gigantic, coal-black negro-savage," is no slave, but freely volunteered to join a whaler's crew. Like Queequeg and Tashtego, he has "retained all his barbaric virtues," so much so that his very presence frightens American white men, who "standing before him seemed a white flag come to beg truce of a fortress" (107, 108).

From the outset of the *Pequod*'s voyage, Melville draws our attention to associations between types of cannibalism and slave labor in order to show the corrupt economic foundation of nineteenth-century American capitalism. Into his discussion of the lineage of the harpooners, Ishmael interjects an ironic anatomy of labor:

> Herein it is the same with the American whale fishery as with the American army and military and merchant navies, and as with the engineering forces employed in the construction of the American Canals and Railroads. The same, I say, because in all these cases the native American liberally provides the brains, the rest of the world as generously the muscles.
>
> (108)

America's Manifest Destiny and its military and commercial expansionist policies exploit the bodies of other cultures. As a scion of American superstition and racial prejudice, Dough-boy experiences the great American phobia—that the victims of rapacious American capitalism will turn the tables on him. He is consumed with fear of these savages: Queequeg's "barbaric smack" causes Dough-Boy "to see whether any marks of teeth lurked in his own lean arm"; Tashtego sings out for the frightened Steward "that his bones might be picked" (134). Reversing the roles of master and slave, capitalist and laborer, Ishmael wryly points out the dilemma awaiting America: "hard fares the white waiter who waits upon cannibals" (134).

Ishmael's theory of race in America is evident in "The Wheelbarrow." Here, he dismisses artificial racial distinctions "as though a white man were anything more dignified than a whitewashed negro" (60). By analogy, a Christian is hardly more virtuous than a cannibal. In this chapter, Ishmael speculates on the high moral character of Queequeg, a humane cannibal isolated among Christian heathens. Melville contextualizes racial issues with the description of the little *Moss* among the waves "as a slave before a Sultan" (60), metaphorically preparing the reader for the racial issues to come and prefiguring the crew before tyrannical Ahab. A greenhorn bumpkin aboard the little *Moss* mocks Queequeg on the sea journey from New Bedford to Nantucket; Queequeg responds with his own biting cannibalistic mockery, "Queequeg no kill-e so small-e fish-e" (60), but the Christians do not understand his joke. When the insolent man falls overboard and while good Christians gaze but do not stir to help him, the cannibal risks his life to save the very man who had offended him. Ishmael narrates Queequeg's thoughts after the rescue: "Was there ever such unconsciousness? He did not seem to think that he at all deserved a medal from the Humane and Magnanimous Societies . . . and mildly eyeing those around him, seemed to be saying to himself— 'It's a mutual, joint-stock world, in all meridians. We cannibals must help these Christians'" (61). Queequeg's cannibalism, then, is not a savage taking of life, but a reverence for life. His religion has nothing to do with Christian cannibalism, that oppressive obsession with death which Ishmael equates with faith: "But Faith, like a jackal, feeds among the tombs, and even from these dead doubts she gathers her most vital hope" (41). In contrast to the white, Christian world of suspicious xenophobes, Queequeg's indifference to race and his reverence for life attracts Ishmael. Critics often argue that Ishmael clings to Queequeg as an affirmation of a natural brand of humanism, Lockean ideals, and democratic gestures of racial and cultural inclusion.[10] We need to be wary of Ishmael's motives, since from the outset he simply seems fed up with his own culture.

Melville contrasts this scene of pagan altruism with Bulkington's death at sea in "The Lee Shore." One white Christian bigot is saved from the engulfing sea, while another white man is swallowed by it. In a howling gale, Bulkington stands at the *Pequod*'s helm, piloting its "vindictive bows in cold malicious waves" (97). Here, the *Pequod* attempts to master the sea, in sharp contrast to the little *Moss* which seems a slave before the Sultan sea in "The Wheelbarrow." But who is this Bulkington and why is he killed off so early in the novel? Scholars have made claims that Bulkington is an actual figure from Melville's own time, from the Missouri Senator Thomas Hart Benton to the British artist J. M. W. Turner.[11] William V. Spanos has politicized Bulkington as a symbol of Melville's "differential" and "disinherited" American (155). Most likely, though, this short epitaph of a chapter can be read as Melville's contempt for slave-abiding America. After all, Ishmael tells us in "The Spouter-Inn" that Bulkington's voice "at once announced that he was a Southerner" (23). Bulkington, even though he stands aloof from his mates, is among those "arrantest topers" in whose heads "liquor soon mounted" (23). Two enigmatic characters command Ishmael's attention and fascination at the Spouter-Inn—Bulkington and Queequeg. In that chapter, Ishmael's off-hand comic remark about preferring to sleep with a sober cannibal rather than a drunken Christian also can be read as his drawing distinctions between these two men—the humane cannibal and the white man from the enslaving South. Bulkington's demise is a misanthropic ritual sacrifice, the first of Melville's many death-wishes for America and its institutions.

Too often "The Lee Shore" is read as somehow lacking Ishmael's usual irony. Bulkington's apotheosis is no affirmation at all, but a bitterly sarcastic denunciation of what the man represents. Ishmael's topography betrays Melville's political context for this Southerner: even though it seems he will die in the infinite sea like a demi-god, the waves and winds, the conspiring forces of heaven and earth against which the *Pequod* sails, will toss his body toward "the treacherous, slavish shore" (97). Bulkington's death sets a pattern of cosmic political retributions in *Moby-Dick,* followed by the sea deaths of Radney in "The Town-Ho's Story" and of Ahab himself. In the final chapters of the novel, whenever Moby-Dick emerges from the sea and brings about death to whalers, it is worth recalling that he does so on the "leeward" side (433, 451, 465), an allegorical reprisal against those from that "slavish" shore. And, like Moby-Dick's warnings, the Bulkington chapter prophetically signals the inevitable self-destruction awaiting the unyielding "slavish" shores of America, in the South as well as in New England.

Melville concentrates his most explicit attacks upon Western slavery and cannibalism in those chapters often considered the cetological center of the novel. Ishmael's prolonged discussions of depictions of whales, whale anatomy, and whaling practices allegorize social and political problems in Melville's America. Western

culture's penchant for order—social, political, economic, and artistic structures—Ishmael playfully undercuts. Edgar A. Dryden's overview of *Moby-Dick* as self-consciously generating fictions is worth mentioning in this context: "The hierarchical social structure aboard a well-ordered ship, the constructs of science and pseudo-science, pagan and Christian religious systems, even the concepts of space and time—all of the forms which man uses to assure himself that everything which happens follow certain laws—are revealed, in *Moby-Dick,* as 'passing fables'" (83). It is not merely the constructs, but their interpretation and justification that Ishmael calls into question. For Ishmael, misinterpretation reveals the underlying presuppositions of America's attitudes toward race. In his observation of the obscured oil painting he tries to decipher at the Spouter-Inn, Ishmael initially misperceives its subject matter as figures of blackness: a portentous "black mass," "the Black Sea in a midnight gale" (20). His inability to see blackness occurs when he first enters New Bedford; Ishmael stops before a Negro church and at first perceives it to be "the great Black Parliament sitting in Tophet" (18). Ironically, Ishmael has difficulty at first recognizing the reality of blackness, but few problems distinguishing many variations of whiteness, as demonstrated in "The Whiteness of the Whale." Eventually, he arrives at an interpretation of the painting: "an exasperated whale, purposing to spring clean over the craft, is in the enormous act of impaling himself upon the three mastheads" (21). This final interpretation grandly portends self-destructive death, recalling Ishmael's suicidal impulses from "Loomings." After this episode of misconceptions, Ishmael sees "a heathenish array of monstrous clubs and spears," which make him shudder at the thought of "what monstrous cannibal and savage could ever have gone a death-harvesting with such a hacking, horrifying implement" (21). Ishmael's misinterpretation of the "monstrous cannibal and savage" Queequeg corresponds to his readers' and America's cultural misconceptions. In fact, the comedy of the bedroom scene at the Spouter-Inn would not work without the reader empathizing to some degree with Ishmael's fears.

In chapter 57, Ishmael addresses true portraits created by the barbaric whale hunters: "As with the Hawaiian savage, so with the white sailor-savage" (232). Ishmael concludes that the further one is removed from Christian, civilized depiction of whales, the closer one comes to their true representation. By the same token, the further one travels away from Christian culture, the closer one comes to exhibiting the inherent condition of man—savagery:

> Long exile from Christendom and civilization inevitably restores a man to that condition in which God placed him, *i.e.* what is called savagery. Your true

whale-hunter is as much a savage as an Iroquois. I myself am a savage, owning no allegiance but to the King
of the Cannibals; and ready at any moment to rebel
against him.

(232)

Here, two readings are suggested for the King of Cannibals: Ahab and the Christian God. Ishmael vows both
to serve and to rebel against the King of Cannibals, or
the King of Kings, since tyranny, especially the master
and slave relationship, is the primary form of political
cannibalism for Ishmael. Aboard the *Pequod,* Ahab
commands supreme authority over his crew. Ishmael regards Ahab's tyranny as "sultanism that became incarnate in an irresistible dictatorship" (129) and he likens
him to "Belshazzar, King of Babylon," ruler of the Old
Testament's most profligate enslaving state (131). His
allegorical name recalls the most tyrannical king of ancient Israel. As king over Israel, ruling from his "ivory"
house (1 Kings 22:39), Ahab conducted unspeakable
acts of violence and apostasy. Through treachery, usurpation, and murder, Ahab stole Naboth's vineyard, an
act which American politicians viewed as analogous to
the cupidity of the country's expansionist policies during the 1840s.[12] Ahab's hypnotic, antidemocratic command over the crew of the *Pequod* in "The Quarter-
Deck" includes Starbuck, who viewed the Deity as
"centre and circumference of all democracy! His omnipresence, our divine equality!" (104). Ahab's winning
over of Starbuck has replaced the democratic Lord of
equality with a sultan, czar, or king.

Even more evident, the relationship between Ahab and
Fedallah is characterized as master and slave: "And yet,
somehow, did Ahab—in his own proper self, as daily,
hourly, and every instant, commandingly revealed to his
subordinates,—Ahab seemed an independent lord; the
Parsee but his slave" (439). Fittingly, Fedallah's prophecy in "The Whale Watch" functions as the slave's retribution by means of irony, for he condemns Ahab to
see two hearses before he dies, "the first not made by
mortal hands; and the visible wood of the last one must
be grown in America" (410). Ahab's final vision must
be the product of that "slavish shore," America. The
madness of enslaving others, Ishmael views as a cannibalistic impulse of the darkest kind, which will invariably degenerate into self-destruction. Ishmael suggests
this connection when he observes that Ahab's soul, like
"the last of the Grisly Bears . . . fed upon the sullen
paws of its gloom!" (134). Ahab's unrelenting authority
and tyrannical mastery of the *Pequod,* thus, signals the
tragic movement from exocannibalism to self-
consumption in the novel.

Chapters 58-66 constitute the cannibalistic center of
Moby-Dick. Melville introduces his reader to more grotesque and disturbing scenes of cannibalism which eventually become graphic depictions of autocannibalism.

Like his earlier treatments of the subject in *Typee,*
Melville tries "to demystify the practice of cannibalism
and to defuse Western obsessions with cannibalism as
the crucial sign of savagery" (Otter 47). Melville's
method of demystification, though, is to infuse his cetology chapters with tropes of acquisition, feeding, and
power. In short, he universalizes cannibalism. Ishmael
concludes that the sea, like human world and God's
universe, is governed by one principle—cannibalism:
"Consider, once more, the universal cannibalism of the
sea; all whose creatures prey upon each other, carrying
on eternal war since the world began" (236). The sea
conceals its monstrous violence in its loveliest hues, not
unlike the way "all deified Nature absolutely paints like
the harlot, whose allurements cover nothing but the
charnel-house within" (170). That oceanic treachery
corresponds to that "treacherous, slavish shore," which
is Melville's not-too-subtle condemnation of tyrannical
governments and enslaving leaders. Like the cannibalistic cruelty of the creatures of the sea, so too does mankind live by the dictates of cannibalism.

Rituals of exocannibalism are observed aboard the *Pequod.* After all, it is a whaling ship, aboard which the
crew often dines cannibalistically on the brains of whale
calves. Brain-feeding, as Herbert N. Schneidau aptly
observes, is a prominent ritual among cannibals and
provides "the dead and the living an interpenetrating
identity" (83). Melville accentuates this point with a
political metaphor of betrayal: "And that is the reason
why a young buck with an intelligent looking calf's
head before him, is somehow one of the saddest sights
you can see. The head looks a sort of reproachfully at
him with an 'Et tu Brute!' expression" (255). Typical of
Ishmael's treatment of flesh-eating, exocannibalism
merges with endocannibalism; the enemy ingested by
the whalers reflects their very natures. Ishmael concludes "The Whale As A Dish" by asserting that man
has evolved into a cannibal, one who consumes that
creature which once was considered to be his equal:
"Go to the meat-market of a Saturday night and see the
crowds of live bipeds staring at the long rows of dead
quadrupeds. Does not that sight take a tooth out of the
cannibal's jaw? Cannibals? who is not a cannibal?"
(255). The marketplace and the economics of civilized
consumption are more ghastly than head-hunting and
cannibal feasts. For Ishmael, insatiable desires to consume transform man into a cannibal.

The extent of Ishmael's misanthropy and condemnations of his own culture are evident in his depictions of
sharks feeding. In Old Fleece's sermon, Stubb distinguishes Christianity at its essence. Oddly, Old Fleece's
comic sermon is to sharks not men, but Ishmael has already alluded to the shark's vicious behavior as being
analogous to men's aggressive consumption. Old Fleece
admonishes the sharks gathering over the side of the
Pequod to act with moral restraint and to correct their

greedy natures: "'Your woraciousness, fellow-critters, I don't blame ye so much for; dat is natur, and can't be helped; but to gobern dat wicked nature, dat is the pint. You is sharks, sartin; but if you gobern de shark in you, why den you be angel; for all angel is not'ing more dan de shark well goberned'" (251). The sharks tear blubber out of their "neighbor's mout," which Old Fleece condemns, asking for a communal sharing of the whale: "'but to bite off de blubber for de small fry ob sharks, dat can't get into de scrouge to help demselves'" (251). But his admonitions are of no matter, as Old Fleece tells Stubb: "'no use a-preachin' to such dam g'uttons'" (251). The *Pequod*'s crew members are little better than these savage sharks.

This universal law of blind consumption bears out most fascinatingly in "The Shark Massacre." In order to save the whale's body from the sharks surrounding the *Pequod,* Queequeg strikes the sharks in their skulls with the whale-spade, although missing at times and causing more frenzied feeding. Universal cannibalism of the sea ultimately results in horrible self-consumption. Here, we should recall again Ishmael's prophetic statement in "Loomings" that the story of Narcissus "is the key to it all" (14). Narcissism is the basis for the kinds of consumption that Ishmael views with disgust and horror aboard the *Pequod,* in the sea, and in the universe.[13] Cannibalism is an unnatural extension of Ahab's monomania, as is that of all tyrants blindly consuming the labor, liberty, and life of others. This is brought home when a dead shark hauled aboard the ship of sharks nearly takes off Queequeg's hand, an action ironically reversing the harpooners' comic cannibalistic attacks upon the Dough-Boy. Queequeg simply cannot conceive of a god who would create such a beast as the shark: "'wedder Fejee god or Nantucket god; but de god wat made shark must be one damn Ingin'" (257). Queequeg's comic irreverence and uncertainty about what power controls this aggressive universe is not shared by Ishmael, who already attributes this law of consumption to Western culture and its institutions.[14]

In "Loomings," Ishmael binds himself and his readers together as slaves: "Who aint a slave?" (15). Melville adopts a pose in this first chapter of the novel that is similar to the universal brotherhood of bondage that begins many slave narratives of the nineteenth century.[15] Quite cynically, he also forges a bond among all of mankind as cannibals. At this point, Ishmael's outrageous rhetorical questions—"Who aint a slave?" and "who is not a cannibal?"—have several affirmative responses, especially when the two concepts are conjoined—Who is not both a slave and a cannibal? Ishmael's association of slavery and cannibalism draws together two devastating social systems in nineteenth-century America: the institution of plantation slavery and its counterpart in industrial capitalism.

Idiosyncratic economic arguments against slavery were prevalent among Northern theorists in the nineteenth century. For example, Daniel Raymond's *The Elements of Political Economy* (1822) includes anticapitalist rhetoric but also upholds industrialization within limits, primarily to restrict its demoralizing power over laborers reduced to propertyless conditions (Kaufman 67-81). Southern endorsements of slavery saw the institution as more compatible with market capitalism than wage labor, as evidenced by the quirky works of Southerner Thomas Roderick Dew in the 1830s which viewed slavery, by means of racist logic, as epitomizing the evolution from barbarism to civilization.[16] As Laurence Shore points out in *Southern Capitalists,* William Gregg's *Essays on Domestic Industry* (1844) tried to shame Southern capitalists into developing their own manufacturing economy so that Southern states could maintain slavery at a profit, while Ellwood Fisher's famous lecture in 1849 claimed that statistically the Southern slave economy had attained a per capita wealth that "eclipsed the North" (32-33, 38). Shore also notes that Thomas Dew's very odd use of Adam Smith's capitalist theory revealed that "somehow, through market forces, slave labor and the black population would wither away" (27). In essence, for Dew, the marketplace will consume its own laborers.

George Fitzhugh's Virginia pamphlets of 1850 and 1851 propagandize the economic necessity of adopting Southern slavery and promulgated its social and moral advantages. His extended socialist rant against industrial capitalism favors the Southern slave system. As C. Vann Woodward explains, Fitzhugh's early Richmond pamphlets attack the failed concepts of liberty and equality, which he called "self-destructive and impracticable," and extolled the plantation system of slavery in the South against Northern capitalism: "To call free labor 'wage slavery' as the socialists did was 'a gross libel on slavery,' for the condition of free labor was 'worse than slavery.' The wage system was a contradiction of human needs" (xv). Fitzhugh maintains in *Cannibals All!, or Slaves Without Masters* (1856) that capitalistic exploitation results in "the White Slave Trade" which is far more cruel than its black counterpart, because "the master allows the slave to retain a larger share of the results of his own labor than do the employers of free labor" (15). Fitzhugh even compares his Northern capitalist reader to a cannibal: "You are a Cannibal! and if a successful one, pride yourself on the number of your victims quite as much as any Fiji chieftain, who breakfasts, dines, and sups on human flesh—and your conscience smites, you, if you have failed to succeed, quite as much as his, when he returns from an unsuccessful foray" (17). Such virulent racist rhetoric surfaced in the economic and political debates of Melville's day. In order to attack the hypocrisy of American sentiment for government by the consent of the governed, Fitzhugh proffers a number of examples in which the master and slave relationship must prevail, from fathers of families to military leaders and governmental officials who are little more than "self-elected despots," and, of interest for *Moby-Dick,* the dogmatic rule of sea captains (243). Fitzhugh's polemic somewhat fits Ahab's tyranny but not his cannibalistic urges, which contradict the illogical propaganda of *Cannibals All!* Of course, Melville uses cannibalism to attack exploitation; he does not limit it to capitalistic exploitation, but includes philosophical, legal, and religious exploitation. For Melville, the cannibal and the slave are aspects of the human condition, indeed shared by all alike.

To see Melville's enfolding of these two concepts, one needs to read carefully chapter 89, "Fast-Fish and Loose-Fish." Here, Melville uses the dislodging of a whale held fast to the ship, set adrift or made loose, then recovered by another ship as his metaphor for fugitive slave laws. Much mischief, Ishmael explains to the reader, has been played into this "masterly code" (331), an obvious reference to system of slavery. The specific loose-fish case that Ishmael cites reminds one of Fugitive Slave cases, for the whale was chased "in the northern seas" (332), but was lost when the chasers met peril and was captured by another vessel. In due course, the chasers, like Southern slavers, sue for recovery of their property. Melville's father-in-law, Chief Justice of the Supreme Judicial Court of Massachusetts Lemuel Shaw, had decided several points of law in the famous 1842 Latimer case in favor of the fugitive slave's captors; moreover, as Levy notes, "Shaw's opinion on the right of the states to provide machinery for the arrest of fugitives from justice became the law in every state in the country" (79, n. 19). In 1851, the year of *Moby-Dick*'s publication, Chief Justice Shaw decided another fugitive slave case involving a runaway slave, Thomas Sims; again, he decided against freedom, upholding the Fugitive Slave Law of 1850. His decision caused a furor in Boston, as can be evidenced by the outcries from William Lloyd Garrison, Ralph Waldo Emerson, Theodore Parker, and Frederick Douglass.

The Latimer case had incited rioters to attack the arresting officials and moved several African Americans to execute an escape for Latimer.[17] Massachusetts citizens, some 50,000 in number, protested Shaw's decision in the case and signed "a petition which former President John Quincy Adams had tried—unsuccessfully—to present to Congress" (Simpson 26). Ultimately, Latimer's freedom was not contingent upon any Constitutional application. As Louis Filler explains in *The Crusade Against Slavery: 1830-1860,* Latimer's owner, James B. Grey of Virginia (the same state that Ishmael assumes Bulkington hails from), faced with mounting court costs of more than Latimer's worth on the market, ironically sold his deed of emancipation to obliging

abolitionists (171). In November of 1842 Frederick Douglass sent an alarming letter to Garrison concerning the Latimer case and the appearance of slavery in Massachusetts:

> Slavery, our enemy, has landed in our very midst, and commenced its bloody work. Just look at it; here is George Latimer a man—a brother—a husband, a father, stamped with the likeness of the eternal God, and redeemed by the blood of Jesus Christ, out-lawed, hunted down like a wild beast, and ferociously dragged through the streets of Boston, and incarcerated within the walls of Leverett-st. jail. . . . Boston has become the hunting-ground of merciless men-hunters, and man-stealers.
>
> (*Liberator* 159)[18]

Douglass' depiction of "men-hunters, and man-stealers" certainly accords with Melville's cannibalistic depictions of the whaling industry, property rights of fast and loose fish, and the obsessive drive to possess. The "brutal overbearing" Radney of "The Town-Ho's Story" hypocritically slights Steelkilt without "common decency of human recognition which is the meanest slave's right" (210). Radney originates from Nantucket, which suggests Melville's allegorical condemnation of New England false piety. Radney's demise also recalls Bulkington's death at sea. This time, however, Moby-Dick consumes Radney in an act of cosmic justice and retribution. The scene foreshadows the political death of the tyrannical Ahab, the Massachusetts captain. Indeed, Starbuck, Stubb, and Flask all hail from Massachusetts: "every one of them Americans; a Nantucketer, a Vineyarder, and a Cape man" (109). Nineteenth-century Massachusetts never offered much in the way of tolerance: hence, Melville's revenge upon the Bay Colony crew of the *Pequod.*

Unlike the case before his father-in-law and the Massachusetts Supreme Court, in which a fugitive slave was ordered returned to Southern master, the loose whale of Ishmael's allegory was allowed to be kept by the northern vessel. A darker fugitive slave tale occurs in "The Castaway," when Pip, the Alabama cabin-boy, leaps out of Stubb's boat to become a loose-fish and only accidentally is recovered by the *Pequod.* Stubb ignores Pip in favor of hunting down whales, which are of greater economic value than the *Pequod*'s servant. Melville sternly allegorizes antebellum Massachusetts shipping and industrial interests outweighing African American and fugitive slaves' rights. Not content to end his analogy here, Melville expands upon the various conditions that exist for Fast-Fish and Loose-Fish throughout the world. Physically, Russian serfs and Republican slaves are caught fast to their masters; economically, the widow's last bit and the bankrupt man's interest on his loan are held by landlord and lender; religiously, the earnings of "broken-backed laborers" are seized in order to supplement the Church's already bloated income;

and politically, hamlets, Ireland, and Texas are held in bondage by their oppressors and enslavers (333). Serf, slave, and pauper define for Melville the vicissitudes of misery imposed by economic oppression. Dives as a "Czar" again comes to mind. "Republican slaves" can mean both chattel slavery in the South and wage slavery in the North. Melville is also relying upon conventional treatment of the other cultures as animals, a trope found in numerous seventeenth-century British discussions of neighboring countries and colonial inhabitants, as Margaret Hodgen reminds us: "Whether Irishmen or Pequots, Scots or Iroquois, they were enemies, they were ignorant, and they were animal-like. The only way to regard them was through the lenses of a quasi-philosophical, quasi-religious, and quasi-political 'anti-primitivism,' unembarrassed either by any recognition of brotherliness or by a more austere theological assumption of common humanity" (364-65). Melville has taken a similar approach in **Moby-Dick,** but for the purpose of uplifting the primitive and denouncing the civilized along lines that recall Montaigne's arguments in "Of Cannibals."

Yet, for Melville, history will always prove that what was once a Loose-Fish will in fact be made fast, as America was to Columbus, India to England, Poland to Russia, Greece to the Ottomans, and most recently for Melville, Mexico to the United States. Melville would have been aware of the historical oppression suffered by these cultures. During his day, the political rhetoric of anti-slavery in Massachusetts, as attested to by David Walker's *Appeal to the Coloured Citizens of the World,* often included references to these enslaved cultures.[19] Of interest, several of the countries Ishmael lists have also been treated as realms of cannibals. The Americas of Columbus were inhabited by the Caribs, from whose name the word cannibal derives. Ireland, according the geographer Strabo, was inhabited by a people, as Arens reminds us, "more savage than the Britons, since they are man-eaters" (14). Claude Rawson explains that this treatment of the Irish as savage or cannibalistic is all too evident among English writers, such as Spenser and Camden: "there are significant parallels between English descriptions of the Irish and European descriptions of Africans and Amerindians, a standard colonial discourse" (345). Nineteenth-century Massachusetts citizens would have been inclined to the same sentiments: after all, Nativism against Irish immigrants in the mid-1830s caused a Charlestown, Massachusetts mob to set an Ursuline convent ablaze and Nativists joined forces with Whigs to place their candidate in the office of mayor of Boston in 1845 (Anbinder 9, 12). Mexico, ancestral home of the Aztecs, was viewed by the Spanish, from accounts by Díaz and from Prescott's *History of the Conquest of Mexico* (1843), as populated by cannibals: "The most famous of the Amerindians cannibals, were, of course, the Mexica, whose spectacular bouts of human sacrifice were assumed to have been

followed by orgiastic feasts on the flesh of the victims" (Pagden 83). Melville, of course, is relying upon the mixing of metaphors in the rhetoric of Western political domination and conquest. Associating cannibalism with enslaved peoples belongs to an overriding master-slave dialectic that, as Hayden White observes, "permeates the psychosocial pathology of all oppressive systems" (188).[20]

Since the 1830s the abolitionist cause had met with some resistance from capitalists in Massachusetts, as Reinhard O. Johnson explains: "Textile manufacturers and shipping interests had formed a close relationship with southern planters, and these industrialists and merchants were reluctant to countenance any activity which was critical of a basic southern institution" (238). Melville would also have been aware of the connection between slavery and ghoulish consumption from the antislavery rhetoric in Massachusetts in the 1840s, as evidenced by Joshua Leavitt's "Financial Power of Slavery" (1841): "Slavery takes value out of the pockets of the free, as well as out of the sinews of the enslaved, without rendering an equivalent. It is a vampyre which is drinking up the life blood of free industry" (245). Once again, Dives drinking the tears of orphans comes to mind.

Ishmael's rhetoric cynically applies momentary freedom to inevitable enslavement on a universal scale:

> What are the Right of Man and the Liberties of the World but Loose-Fish? What all men's minds and opinions but Loose-fish? What is the principle of religious belief in them but a Loose-Fish? What to the ostentatious smuggling verbalists are the thoughts of thinkers but Loose-Fish? What is the great globe itself but a Loose-Fish?"
>
> (334)

Fitzhugh describes exploited labor in terms readily familiar to Melville: "To be exploitated ought to be more creditable than to exploitate. They were 'slaves without masters,' little fish who were food for all the larger" (38). While his major work postdates **Moby-Dick,** Fitzhugh took a number of expressions from Thomas Carlyle, among them the "slaves without masters" motif for alienated working class men reduced to a form of cannibalism; he also borrowed extensively from Carlyle's virulent attack in 1849 on British colonial policies supporting manumission in the West Indies.[21] Characteristically, Ishmael universally includes all humankind in this master and slave, cannibal and slave schema: "And what are you, reader, but a Loose-Fish and a Fast-Fish, too?" (334). Melville's answer to a Raymond, Dew, or Fitzhugh is not a choice between cannibal or slave, but the inevitability of suffering both fates at once.

In "Heads or Tails," Melville interjects a tale of English sailors losing the product of their labor—a whale and its market value—to the Duke of Wellington as a commentary on loose-fish capitalism. Antiquated laws of monarchical property extend privileges to those who "had nothing to do with taking this fish" (335). Ishmael condemns not just the exploitation of labor but the very appropriation of the product of that labor. Melville well understood the frenetic economy—bankruptcies, market downturns, depressions—facing Massachusetts workers during the 1840s and 1850s (Keyssar 31). Comparisons between the injustices of Southern slavery and the inhumane conditions of New England workers often resounded in the political battles of the period in attacks upon Lords of Lash and Loom (Laurie 47). In **"The Tartarus of Maids"** (1855), Melville denounced the factory system of New England capitalism: "Machinery—that vaunted slave of humanity—here stood menially served by humans, who served mutely and cringingly as the slave serves the Sultan" ([**"The Paradise of Bachelors and the Tartarus of Maids"**] 328). Melville employed the same metaphor—the slave before the Sultan—for the little *Moss* before the sea and for the *Pequod*'s crew before Ahab. For Melville, slavery, like cannibalism, is an inevitable consequence of capitalism and expansionism, nowhere more evident than in the whaling industry.[22] Just as the Duke of Wellington took possession of the labor of his whalers, so too does Stubb, although comically, exploit the labors of the whalers aboard the *Rose-Bud* by appropriating a fast whale. Melville's point is that human nature lends itself readily to be exploiter and exploited, cannibal and slave.

The complex dialectic of cannibalism and slavery also can be observed in the novel's polarizing of angels and devils, as seen in Old Fleece's sermon to the shark. "The Fossil Whale" provides an intriguing account of a pre-adamite whale discovered in Alabama in 1842 (coincidentally, the year of the Latimer case) on the slave plantation of one Judge Creagh. This fossilized fast-fish had two interpretations: by the slaves, it was seen as "a fallen angel"; by the Alabama doctors, "a huge reptile" (380). Given the name Basilosaurus, derived from the Greek for King, this monster was rechristened by Owen Zeuglodon, from the Greek for the slave yoke. Master-slave metaphors are conjoined in this "antemosaic" whale, so ancient that Ishmael claims "to shake hands with Shem" upon seeing it (380). Ishmael obviously refers to Genesis 9-10 and its curse upon the descendants of Ham and Canaan to be slaves in perpetuity to the descendants of Shem. Melville interjects angelic imagery to cast it in his familiar opposition, as Ishmael describes the tail of the whale:

> So in dreams, have I seen majestic Satan thrusting forth his tormented colossal claw from the flame Baltic of Hell. But in gazing at such scenes, it is all in all what mood you are in; if in the Dantean, the devils will occur to you; if in that of Isaiah, the archangels.
>
> (317)

The same opposition occurs at the conclusion of the final chase, when the sky-hawk enfolded in the flag, "with archangelic shrieks" disappears with the *Pequod* as Ahab "went down with his ship, which, like Satan, would not sink to hell till she had dragged a living part of heaven along with her" (469). Aboard the ship, the three harpooners remain aloft in the three masts, ready to be crucified. Although they were once princes in their domains, their contact with American commercial interests has reduced them to slaves. The Golgotha analogy has more cynical implications for Melville. Significantly, Queequeg is not on the main mast, the place of Christ, but along with Daggoo takes the position of one of the two malefactors.

Why does Melville not allow his noble cannibal the supreme sacrificial position in this final scene? No salvation of Queequeg's pagan variety is available to mankind. No humane cannibalism replaces the savagery of American economic, political, and social oppression. A lone survivor, Ishmael, the orphaned slave, returns quite the misanthrope. Reading the novel retrospectively, we discern the extent of Ishmael's cynicism. Ishmael sardonically recounts in allegorical terms his era of terrible slavery, bitter poverty, hypocritical Christian morality, cruel, monomaniacal expansionism, and of a Union on the verge of its own self-destruction. Melville, like Ishmael, simply could no longer stomach the corruption and hypocrisy of American culture. And who could blame him?

Notes

1. Westenbroek provides an extensive list of the use of this name Ishmael in English letters.

2. In addition to his characterization of the Pequots in the *Magnalia,* in 1718 Cotton Mather upbraided colonists for allowing native peoples to continue practicing "pagan impieties": "that in the very heart of a colony renowned for the profession of Christianity, there should for fourscore years together be a body of the aboriginals persisting in the darkest and most horrid paganism" (*Selected Letters* 265).

3. Fickes provides an extensive record of Pequot enslavement in early New England, especially the accounts of branding (75) and Captain Morris requesting from John Winthrop "compensation in 1647 so that he might replace his escaped Pequot captive with an African" (79). John Winthrop's diary entry of July 13, 1637 notes that Mr. Pierce sent fifteen Pequot boys and two women to Providence Isle (227). Thomas Hutchinson in his history admits that many Pequot "captives were sent to Bermuda and sold for slaves" (80).

4. For the Mohawk threat to Pequots, see Leach (21-22) and [Eric S.] Johnson who relates that "Pe-

quot sachems fled to the Mohawks seeking safety, but instead were executed" (34). For the etymological reference, see Sollers (27).

5. Crain provides detailed listings of incidents of cannibalism during nineteenth-century naval voyages (28).

6. Royster discusses Ishmael's pride in the whaling industry, his comic, ironic resignation toward labor, and Melville's supposedly tepid critique of capitalism in *Moby-Dick*. Dimock analyzes prophecy in the novel as imperialistic and adhering to the tenets Manifest Destiny.

7. For typologies of cannibalism, see Arens (17-18) and Goldman (1-26).

8. Melville owned a copy of Montaigne in 1848 (Howard 115). Beauchamp illustrates many similarities between Montaigne and Melville, as evidenced in Melville's early novels.

9. For an account of the Washingtonians and other temperance activities of this period, see Hampel.

10. For a detailed discussion of Queequeg as exemplifying Lockean ideals of life and liberty, see Markels. Fredricks' analysis of the politics of inclusion is typical of these uplifting readings of Melville's democratic tendencies: "They seal their bond by equally distributing Queequeg's money between them, pledging mutual devotion, and worshipping Queequeg's black idol together. Melville's subversion of the typology of covenant theology allows for a vision of democracy beyond the radical individualism of the Puritans: a vision of a democracy of multiculturalism and egalitarianism" (48-49).

11. Heimert proposes the Benton connection in his well-known and useful essay on *Moby-Dick*. Wallace draws some intriguing conclusions about Melville's appreciation for Turner; moreover, Wallace associates Melville's language in this short epitaph of a chapter to Turner's sea storm paintings, particularly *Fishermen upon a Lee-Shore* (1802) and *Waves Breaking on a Lee Shore* (1835). In this reading of "The Lee Shore," Wallace, however, neglects Turner's *The Slave Ship* (1840), which depicts horrible cruelty toward the slaves on the slavetrader *Zong,* as [John] Walker informs us: "When a epidemic broke out, the captain ordered the sick and dying to be thrown overboard so that he could say they were lost at sea and claim insurance" (110). In *The Slave Ship,* chattel slaves drown in a blood-red sea as large fish and sharks approach to devour the hapless victims.

12. Duban, who credits Heimert's scholarship on political rhetoric of the day, cites the remarks of Representative Kenneth Rayner of North Carolina in 1845: "Arguments . . . addressed to our national cupidity and pride . . . are the arguments with which Ahab reconciled to himself the seizing of Naboth's Vineyard" (88). Typical of typological readings from the text to the world, he incorporates phrases from political debates and sees them in the novel's symbolic and allegorical structure.

13. Bohrer presents Melville's doubling of sea and universe, man and shark, as consuming agents in *Moby-Dick;* in particular, Bohrer notes that the Narcissus passage of "Loomings" foreshadows the "pervasive system of linked 'consumptive' analogies" in the novel (84).

14. For a useful discussion on the types of cannibalism confronting Queequeg and of Ishmael's view of Western culture, see Sanborn (148-56).

15. Berthold provides a comparative analysis of the rhetorical correspondences between *Moby-Dick* and slave narratives.

16. Kaufman offers invaluable and exhaustive analyses of complex economic arguments of antebellum America, particularly his chapters "Daniel Raymond on Protecting the Republic from Slave Capital" and "Thomas Roderick Dew on Black Slavery as the Republic's Check on the Working Class."

17. For a full account of the Latimer case and the furor it caused among abolitionists in Massachusetts, see Quarles (193-95).

18. Douglass took Latimer on lecture tours immediately following his purchased freedom, and continued to lecture about this case for years, until 1854 when he learned that Latimer was arrested for pickpocketing and confessed to the crime (*The Frederick Douglass Papers* 230).

19. See the opening of Walker's *Appeal* which draws distinctions between subjugated men and animalized African Americans: "The Indians of North and South American—the Greeks—the Irish, subjected under the king of Great Britain—the Jews, that ancient people of the Lord—the inhabitants of the islands of the sea—in fine, all the inhabitants of the earth, (except however, the sons of Africa) are called *men,* and of course are, and ought to be free. But we, coloured people and our children, are *brutes!!*" (9). Of course, Walker's rhetoric relies upon conventional arguments of historical and contemporary enslavement, all too familiar to the abolitionist cause.

20. Of note, White provides an analysis of the caption for a 1505 engraving of natives of America that reveals five principal taboos to Europeans: "nakedness, community of property, lawlessness,

sexual promiscuity, and cannibalism" (187). Many of these traits can be observed among the crew aboard the *Pequod.*

21. Wish comments upon Fitzhugh's rhetorical appropriations from Carlyle's virulent racist polemics: "Especially valuable as propaganda material to Fitzhugh and the proslavery school were Carlyle's attacks on the West Indian experiment of emancipation. In December 1849, the Scot had published 'The Negro Question' in *Fraser's,* excoriating the results of freeing the blacks in the British Caribbean possessions" (74-75).

22. For a discussion of Melville holding the "minority position" in his indictment of the new economics of industrialism, see Thomas Bender (60).

Works Cited

Anbinder, Tyler. *Nativism & Slavery: The Northern Know Nothings & the Politics of the 1850s.* New York: Oxford University Press, 1992.

Arens, W. *The Man-Eating Myth: Anthropology & Anthropophagy.* New York: Oxford University Press, 1979.

Beauchamp, Gorman. "Montaigne, Melville, and the Cannibals." *Arizona Quarterly* 37 (1981): 293-309.

Bender, Thomas. *Toward An Urban Vision: Ideas and Institutions in Nineteenth Century America.* Baltimore: The Johns Hopkins University Press, 1975.

Berthold, Michael C. "*Moby-Dick* and American Slave Narrative." *Massachusetts Review* 35. 1 (1994): 135-48.

Bohrer, Randall. "Melville's New Witness: Cannibalism and the Microcosm-Macrocosm Cosmology of *Moby-Dick.*" *Studies in Romanticism* 22.1 (1983): 65-91.

Certeau, Michel de. "Montaigne's 'Of Cannibals': The Savage 'I.'" *Heterologies: Discourse on the Other.* Trans. Brain Massumi. Minneapolis: University of Minnesota Press, 1986. 67-79.

Crain, Caleb. "Lovers of Human Flesh: Homosexuality and Cannibalism in Melville's Novels." *American Literature* 66 (1994): 25-53.

Dimock, Wai-chee. *Empire of Liberty: Melville and the Poetics of Individualism.* Princeton: Princeton University Press, 1989.

Douglass, Frederick. *The Frederick Douglass Papers, Series One: Speeches, Debates, and Interviews,* Vol. 1, *1814-46.* Ed. John W. Blassingame. New Haven: Yale University Press, 1979.

———. *Liberator* (November 18, 1842). *Abolition and Social Justice in the Era of Reform.* Ed. Louis Filler. New York: Harper & Row, 1972. 156-60.

Dryden, Edgar A. *Melville's Thematics of Form: The Great Art of Telling the Truth.* Baltimore: The Johns Hopkins University Press, 1968.

Duban, James. *Melville's Major Fiction: Politics, Theology, and Imagination.* Dekalb: Northern Illinois University Press, 1983.

Fickes, Michael L. "'They Could Not Endure That Yoke': The Captivity of Pequot Women and Children after the War of 1637." *The New England Quarterly* 73.1 (2000): 58-81.

Filler, Louis. *The Crusade Against Slavery: 1830-1860.* New York: Harper & Brothers, 1960.

Fitzhugh, George. *Cannibals All! or, Slaves Without Masters.* Ed. C. Vann Woodward. Cambridge: Harvard University Press, 1982.

Fredricks, Nancy. *Melville's Art of Democracy.* Athens: University of Georgia Press, 1995.

Goldman, Laurence R. "From Pot to Polemic: Uses and Abuses of Cannibalism." *The Anthropology of Cannibalism.* Ed. Goldman. Westport, CT: Bergin & Garvey, 1999. 1-26.

Hampel, Robert L. *Temperance and Prohibition in Massachusetts, 1813-1852.* Ann Arbor: UMI Research Press, 1982.

Heimert, Alan. "*Moby-Dick* and American Political Symbolism." *American Quarterly* 15 (1963): 498-534.

Hodgen, Margaret T. *Early Anthropology in the Sixteenth and Seventeenth Centuries.* Philadelphia: University of Pennsylvania Press, 1964.

Howard, Leon. *Herman Melville, A Biography.* Berkeley: University of California Press, 1951.

Hutchinson, Thomas. *The History of the Colony of Massachusetts-Bay.* Vol. 1. New York: Arno Press, 1972.

Johnson, Eric S. "Uncas and the Politics of Contact." *Northeastern Indian Lives, 1632-1816.* Ed. Robert S. Grumet. Amherst: University of Massachusetts Press, 1996. 29-47.

Johnson, Reinhard O. "The Liberty Party in Massachusetts, 1840-1848: Antislavery Third Party Politics in the Bay State." *Civil War History* 28.3 (1982): 237-65.

Kaufman. Allen. *Capitalism, Slavery, and Republican Values: Antebellum Political Economists, 1819-1848.* Austin: University of Texas Press, 1982.

Keyssar, Alexander. *Out of Work: The First Century of Unemployment in Massachusetts.* Cambridge: Cambridge University Press, 1986.

Klarer, Mario. "Cannibalism and Carnivalesque: Incorporation as Utopia in the Early Image of America." *New Literary History* 30 (1999): 385-410.

Laurie, Bruce. "The 'Fair Field' of the 'Middle Ground': Abolitionism, Labor Reform, and the Making of an Antislavery Bloc in Antebellum Massachusetts." *Labor*

Histories: Class, Politics, and the Working-Class Experience. Ed. Eric Arnesen, Julie Greene, and Bruce Laurie. Urbana: University of Illinois Press, 1998. 45-70.

Leach, Douglas Edward. *Flintlock and Tomahawk: New England in King Philip's War.* New York: W. W. Norton, 1966.

Leavitt, Joshua. "Financial Power of Slavery." *Boston Free American* (August 19, 1841). Johnson, Reinhard [0. "The Liberty Party in Massachusetts, 1840-1848. *Civil War History* 28.3 (1982): 237-65.]

Levy, Leonard W. *The Law of the Commonwealth and Chief Justice Shaw.* Cambridge: Harvard University Press, 1957.

Lewis, I. M. *Religion in Context: Cults and Charisma.* Cambridge: Cambridge University Press, 1986.

Markels, Julian. *Melville and the Politics of Identity: From King Lear to Moby-Dick.* Urbana: University of Illinois Press, 1993.

Mather, Cotton. *Magnalia Christi Americana.* Books 1 and 2. Ed. Kenneth B. Murdock. Cambridge: Harvard University Press, 1977.

———. *Selected Letters of Cotton Mather.* Comp. Kenneth Silverman. Baton Rouge: Louisiana State University Press, 1971.

Melville, Herman. *Moby-Dick.* Ed. Harrison Hayford and Hershel Parker. New York: W. W. Norton, 1967.

———. "The Paradise of Bachelors and the Tartarus of Maids." *The Piazza Tales and Other Prose Pieces, 1839-1860.* Ed. Harrison Hayford, Alma A. MacDougall, and G. Thomas Tanselle. Evanston: Northwestern University Press, 1987. 316-35.

Milton, John. *The Poetical Works of John Milton.* Ed. H. C. Beeching. Oxford: Oxford University Press, 1925.

Montaigne. "Of Cannibals." *The Complete Essays of Montaigne.* Trans. Donald M. Frame. Stanford: Stanford University Press, 1958. 150-59.

Otter, Samuel. *Melville's Anatomies.* Berkeley: University of California Press, 1999.

Pagden, Anthony. *The Fall of Natural Man: The American Indian and the Origins of Comparative Ethnology.* Cambridge: Cambridge University Press, 1986.

Quarles, Benjamin. *Black Abolitionists.* New York: Oxford University Press, 1969.

Rawson, Claude. "'Indians' and Irish: Montaigne, Swift, and the Cannibal Question." *Modern Language Quarterly* 53 (1992): 299-363.

Royster, Paul. "Melville's Economy of Language." *Ideology and Classic American Literature.* Ed. Sacvan

Bercovitch and Myra Jehlen. Cambridge: Cambridge University Press, 1986. 313-36.

Sanborn, Geoffrey. *The Sign of the Cannibal: Melville and the Making of a Postcolonial Reader.* Durham: Duke University Press, 1998.

Schneidau, Herbert N. *Sacred Discontent: The Bible and Western Tradition.* Baton Rouge: Louisiana State University Press, 1976.

Shore, Laurence. *Southern Capitalists: The Ideological Leadership of an Elite, 1832-1855.* Chapel Hill: University of North Carolina Press, 1986.

Shuffelton, Frank. *Thomas Hooker, 1586-1647.* Princeton: Princeton University Press, 1977.

Simpson, Eleanor E. "Melville and the Negro: From *Typee* to 'Benito Cereno'." *American Literature* 41 (1969): 19-38.

Sollers, Werner. *Beyond Ethnicity: Consent and Descent in American Culture.* New York: Oxford University Press, 1986.

Spanos, William V. *The Errant Art of* Moby-Dick: *The Canon, the Cold War, and the Struggle of American Studies.* Durham: Duke University Press, 1995.

Walker, David. *Appeal to the Coloured Citizens of the World.* Ed. Peter P. Hinks. University Park: Pennsylvania State University Press, 2000.

Walker, John. *Joseph Mallord William Turner.* New York: Harry N. Abrams, 1983.

Wallace, Robert K. "Bulkington, J. M. W. Turner, and 'The Lee Shore.'" *Savage Eye: Melville and the Visual Arts.* Ed. Christopher Sten. Kent, OH: Kent State University Press, 1991. 55-76.

Westenbroek, Anthony. "Ishmael." *A Dictionary of Biblical Tradition in English Literature.* Ed. David Lyle Jeffrey. Grand Rapids, MI: William B. Eerdmans, 1992. 382-83.

White, Hayden. *Tropics of Discourse: Essays in Cultural Criticism.* Baltimore: The Johns Hopkins University Press, 1978.

Winthrop, John. *The Journal of John Winthrop, 1630-1649.* Ed. Richard S. Dunn, James Savage, and Laetitia Yeandle. Cambridge: Harvard University Press, 1996.

Wish, Harvey. *George Fitzhugh: Propagandist of the Old South.* Gloucester, MA: Peter Smith, 1962.

Woodward, C. Vann. "George Fitzhugh, *Sui Generis.*" *Cannibals All! or, Slaves Without Masters.* Ed. Woodward. Cambridge: Harvard University Press, 1982.

Philip Armstrong (essay date winter 2004)

SOURCE: Armstrong, Philip. "'Leviathan Is a Skein of Networks': Translations of Nature and Culture in *Moby-Dick*." *ELH* 71, no. 4 (winter 2004): 1039-63.

[*In the following essay, Armstrong analyzes the novel within the context of the tumultuous political climate of nineteenth-century America, focusing in particular on the process of territorial expansion and the rise of capitalism. In Armstrong's reading, the novel exposes the fragile balance between nature and culture in modern society while also portending this society's eventual destruction.*]

I.

Moby-Dick emerges at a point of crucial historical transition in several areas of American life. By the mid-nineteenth century, the growth and global expansion of the nation's economy following the War of 1812, and the pugnacious expansionism exemplified by the Mexican War and the ideology of manifest destiny, were giving way to signs of strain and impending civil discord: 1850 and 1851, the years during which Melville wrote his novel, were the years of the doomed compromise between opponents and proponents of slavery.

The oceans provided a space in which these contending currents met and mingled.[1] Echoing contemporary politicians and apologists, *Moby-Dick*'s narrator rhapsodizes about the contributions made to America's economy and the dissemination of its influence by the vast whaling fleet which, at the apogee of the industry, spanned the planet.[2] The tensions aboard the *Pequod*, condensed into the malignant figure of the White Whale, therefore embody contemporary strains and threats produced by industrialization, at both the natural and the cultural levels. Cesare Casarino has enumerated the vicissitudes of globalizing industry that were enacted on the "factory floor" of the whaleship: an epochal shift from mercantile to industrial capitalism, an ensuing redefinition of the relationship between labor and capital, and the unpredictable effects of intimate and extended interaction amongst a radically "international, multiethnic, multilingual and especially multiracial labor force."[3] Moreover, the catastrophic fate of the *Pequod*, suggesting the transience and fragility of these economic and social transactions, uncannily anticipated the collapse of the sperm whale fishery as well. For the middle of the century was also a turning point for whaling: during these years "Californian fever" began to take labor away from the centers of the industry, which were further undermined by the financial crisis of 1857 and the concurrent flight of investment capital; the obsolescence of spermaceti and whale oil was assured by a cleaner, cheaper and more easily accessible alternative once petroleum began to flow from Pennsylvanian oil wells in 1859; and the Civil War, during which whaling vessels proved easy targets, completed the decline. Meanwhile it became increasingly hard to deny, in the second half of the century, that overexploitation of cetacean species had made voyages longer, more expensive, and less remunerative—and thus, in the end, financially nonviable.[4]

That the animal, dead or alive, should figure at the center of these historical and economic shifts is no surprise. Over its two-hundred-year history, industrialization has produced, among its other effects—urbanization, degradation of the economic status of women, redefinition of labor structures, environmental depredation—a radically altered relationship between humans and other animals. Industrial techniques have absolved farmers from close proximity to their livestock; assembly-line specialization of tasks has alienated slaughterhouse workers from the living creature being processed; geographical and psychological gaps have widened between an increasingly urbanized human populace and other species.[5] Meanwhile, natural history and social science alike have dedicated themselves to modernity's long project of rewriting authoritative perceptions about relationships between human societies and nature; in the mid-nineteenth century this entailed a transition from Christian to evolutionary notions of the "chain of being," which simultaneously broke down received divisions between the human and the animal, and installed new ones.[6]

The whaleman stood with one foot on either side of these many faultlines. He was praised as a harbinger of American values and vilified for his immoral relationship with the "innocent savages" of the Pacific.[7] He was both a romantic adventurer into wild space and a prototype of the industrial laborer, farmer, and meat processor. His experience routinely alternated between dangerous encounters with the vast materiality of the living animal and its reduction to dead and partial resources, a commodity to be measured by the barrel, reified by the factory ship's technological procedures and its specialization of labor.[8] No wonder that *Moby-Dick,* like its sources, oscillates so vigorously between apparently opposed attitudes to the whale: wonder and contempt, mundane nonchalance and transcendent awe, humanized fellow feeling and the calculus of market value and profit.

In what follows, I will argue that "leviathan," as understood by Melville and his contemporaries, also crosses back and forth between the human and the nonhuman domains in ways that demonstrate the inextricable interimplication of these apparently discrete and opposed dimensions. In *We Have Never Been Modern*, Bruno Latour argues that such mediations between society and nature functioned as "the unthinkable, the unconscious" upon which depended the very establishment of "the modern constitution"—that is, the ideology of progressivist humanism that emerged in the European Enlightenment and was operating at full strength by the time Melville began his novel.[9] Latour suggests that seventeenth-century political and scientific theory inaugurated a false dichotomy between the realms of nature and society, assigning humans and nonhumans to separate ontological planes, upon which were predicated the most authoritative epistemologies of modernity: liberal democracy, capitalism, and scientific empiricism. To understand modernity, and in particular its insistent compartmentalization of knowledge, Latour invites analysis of what he calls "translation": the continuous process of exchange between nonhuman and human domains, recognition of which is foreclosed by the "modern constitution."[10]

Melville's whales, I will argue, evince precisely this kind of transgressive translation. At certain moments they act as screens for the projection of models for human society; at others they are called upon to shape that society, or are shaped by it. Hence, although Latour's comment that "leviathan is a skein of networks" actually refers to the famous Hobbesian allegory of civil collectivity, my title applies it to the whales represented in Melville's novel, because I think *Moby-Dick* represents the transfer point between modernity's constructions of human society and its perception of actual nineteenth-century cetaceans.[11] In what follows, I seek to pursue some of the networks—in particular those of racial and gender ideology—that entrap, or stitch together, the biological and cultural body of America's industrialized leviathan.[12]

II.

The modern constitution, as Latour puts it, "explained everything, but only by leaving out what was in the middle"—that is to say, "hybrids, monsters—what Donna Haraway calls 'cyborgs' and 'tricksters' . . . whose explanation it abandons."[13] Haraway's cyborg is a constructed entity that occupies more than one of the ontological realms into which modernity sought to divide the real. *Moby-Dick*'s Captain Ahab, for example, simultaneously inhabits the human, technological, and animal domains. He fuses his own body with the factory ship he commands, fitting his prosthetic leg into an auger hole in the deck, envisaging his relation to the crew in mechanical terms—"my one cogged circle fits into all their various wheels, and they revolve" (*M* [*Moby-Dick*], 143)—and fantasizing about the construction of a mechanical automaton completely obedient to his will (*M*, 359). In these ways, as critics have argued, Ahab embodies contemporary "American hopes that technology would empower free men," and his quest becomes an allegory of that attempt to master nature which characterized industrial capitalism in its new found confidence.[14]

At the same time, and more problematically, Ahab's body also relies upon its incorporation of the animal he hunts: his "ivory leg had at sea been fashioned from the polished bone of the sperm whale's jaw" (*M*, 109). In this way the captain's physical form again becomes interchangeable with that of his ship, insofar as the *Pequod* too is partly constructed from the bones of the animal it pursues and processes. Psychoanalytically inclined critics like David Mitchell argue that "disability . . . continually surfaces as an answer to Ahab's fathomless personality," citing as evidence the emergence of his madness during a stormy voyage around Cape Horn after the amputation of his leg during his first encounter with Moby Dick: "[T]hen it was, that his torn body and gashed soul bled into one another, and so interfusing made him mad" (*M*, 156).[15] But the rhetoric here suggests that Ahab's madness derives not from severance but from commingling, not from *lack* but from *augmentation*. Rather than the loss of a limb—as Ahab later tells the ship's carpenter, he still feels the phantom leg (*M*, 360)—the prosthetic represents its supplementation. The wound is a site of conjuncture—an "interfusing [that] made him mad"—wherein man and whale are grafted together, bone to bone, leg to jaw. Ahab's madness arises at the point of mediation between animal and human: the incommensurable contradiction produced by the human's material dependence on the body of the animal, combined with the simultaneous exclusion of the animal from the cultural definition of what it is to be a human. In all these ways, the two poles of the natural and social, or of the nonhuman and the human, are brought into communication.

If the human becomes a machinic and beastly cyborg in *Moby-Dick,* the animal also incorporates human and cultural dimensions. Melville's whales demonstrate other kinds of "translation" between the supposedly distinct domains of nature and society. Elizabeth Schultz has described a pattern of cyborg imagery in the novel that "simultaneously compares whales to natural forms and to human technological inventions. . . . Right whales, for example, are compared to great boulders and their eating to scything."[16] Such metaphorical transgressions of the dualism between the realms of human enterprise and animal activity were by no means uncommon in mid-nineteenth-century scientific writing, although they did not always serve the ideology of environmental care that twentieth-century ecocritics such as Schultz tend to project onto the novel. Just as *Moby-Dick* frequently uses mechanistic imagery to describe nature—for example, comparing the whale's regularity of locomotion with reference to "the mighty iron Leviathan of the modern railway" (*M*, 414)—Jeremiah Reynolds, one of the most energetic contemporary apologists for the whaling industry, whose account of "Mocha Dick, Or the White Whale of the Pacific" was a major influence on the novel, compares the breathing of his famous leviathan with the action of a steam engine.[17]

The comparison works in reverse when Reynolds describes a ship's tryworks in full operation. Melville's account of this process portrays it as the most infernal of industrial activities.[18] Reynolds, however, employs terms typical of the Romantic evocation of the natural sublime:

> [T]here are few objects in themselves more picturesque or beautiful, than a whaleship, seen from a distance of three or four miles, on a pleasant evening, in the midst of the great Pacific. As she moves gracefully over the water, rising and falling on the gentle undulations peculiar to this sea; her sails glowing in the quivering light of the fires that flash from below, and a thick volume of smoke ascending from her midst, and curling away in dark masses upon the wind; it requires little effort of the fancy, to imagine one's self gazing upon a floating volcano.[19]

Here, the Romantic association between natural sublimity and human sensibility is energetically read in reverse, since for Reynolds capitalist technology at work displays a beauty equal to the most awe-inspiring efforts of nature. Moreover this lyricism is evoked in the service of the very process, that of globalizing industry, against which literary Romanticism defined itself in the first place.

Clearly *Moby-Dick* emerges from a context in which, due to the volatility of contending economic and cultural ideologies, the boundary between human and nonhuman evinced greater permeability than would subsequently be admitted. Indeed, Melville's novel bears witness to forms of mediation—or, in Latour's term, translation—that prove considerably more radical than those identified so far, which remain at the level of rhetoric and representation. With greater or lesser degrees of consciousness, *Moby-Dick* registers, I think, several crucial ways in which the natural world and mid-nineteenth-century American social organization proved mutually constitutive. That is to say, the novel shows society making nature, and vice versa, both materially and representationally.

III.

At the time Melville was writing, a proliferation of stories about fighting whales betrayed the anxiety of globalizing industrial capitalism towards the animal nature upon which it depended, but which sometimes resisted or escaped its control.[20] The notorious sinking of the *Essex* in 1820 was the first documented case of a whale successfully attacking not a mere whaleboat but a full-sized ship.[21] Nathaniel Philbrick outlines other such well known incidents during the decades prior to *Moby-Dick*:

> In 1835 the crew of the English whaleship *Pusie Hall* were forced into full retreat by what they termed a "fighting whale." . . . In 1836, the *Lydia*, a Nantucket

whaleship, was struck and sunk by a sperm whale, as was the *Two Generals* a few years later. In 1850, the *Pocahontas,* out of Martha's Vineyard, was rammed by a whale but was able to reach port for repairs. Then, in 1851, the year that *Moby-Dick* was published, a whaleship was attacked by a sperm whale in the same waters where the *Essex* had been sunk thirty-one years before.[22]

The final reference here is to the sinking of the *Ann Alexander,* a New Bedford whaler commanded by Captain John DeBlois, who described the offending whale as an "artful beast" and a "crafty monster," attributing to it a high degree of intentional agency, expressed in humanized terms: "turning on his side, he looked at us, apparently filled with rage."[23]

To what should this profusion of effective attacks by animals upon human industry—or at least, this proliferation in *accounts* of such attacks—be attributed? Philbrick offers the following explanation by Charles Wilkes, commander of the United States Exploring Expedition of 1838-1842, which undertook a global survey of marine life, ocean currents, whale distribution, and the activities of the whaling industry:

> An opinion has indeed gained ground within a few years that the whales are diminishing in numbers; but this surmise, as far as I have learned from the numerous inquiries, does not appear to be well founded. They have indeed become wilder, or as some of the whalers express it, "more scary," and in consequence, not so easy to capture; but if we consider the numbers that continue to be yearly taken, there will, I think, be no reason to suppose that any great decrease has occurred.[24]

In nineteenth-century usage, "scary" usually meant shyer, more easily scared off—or in the whaleman's language, "gallied." But the same word could also be used, as it is more commonly today, as an adjective describing a *cause* of fear or alarm. The phrase Wilkes ascribes to the whalers thus occupies both of the poles between which accounts of recalcitrant whales tended to oscillate in contemporary explanations of their behavior: timid and bold, defensive and offensive, instinctually reactive and wilfully aggressive.[25]

Moreover, Wilkes hints that this increased "wildness"—a term encompassing the same pair of opposed denotations—might actually be a response produced by the whaling industry. If he is correct, the "scary" whale would have to be considered a human construction at the material, rather than just the rhetorical, level. Ecological historian Tim Flannery argues that human use of animals—especially the radical acceleration of extractive exploitation during the nineteenth century—created a wariness and antagonism on the part of certain species towards humans that they would not always have shown. As he puts it, "humans made the savage beast":

the "wild" animal, far from being pure nature, must be considered in this sense a product of human social, cultural, and economic forces.[26] Hence, even in the moment of their separation—the point at which industrial capitalism widened the division between an urban, technologized domesticity and an uncultivated natural wilderness—the social and natural domains are constructing and shaping each other.

Melville expands at length upon the inference by Wilkes that cetacean wildness arises from the co-construction of human and natural worlds.

> Nor, considered aright, does it seem any argument in favor of the gradual extinction of the Sperm Whale, for example that in former years (the latter part of the last century, say) these Leviathans, in small pods, were encountered much oftener than at present, and, in consequence, the voyages were not so prolonged, and were also much more remunerative. Because, as has been elsewhere noted, those whales, influenced by some views to safety, now swim the seas in immense caravans, so that to a large degree the scattered solitaries, yokes, and pods, and schools of other days are now aggregated into vast but widely separated, unfrequent armies.
>
> (*M*, 353)

Arguing against the perception that whale numbers have diminished overall, this passage repeats a striking hypothesis, first advanced in a chapter entitled "The Grand Armada" and reinforced here and elsewhere (*M*, 305), that the social structure of the sperm whale has fundamentally altered in response to the whaling industry:

> But here let it be premised, that owing to the unwearied activity with which of late they have been hunted over all four oceans, the Sperm Whales, instead of almost invariably sailing in small detached companies, as in former times, are now frequently met with in extensive herds, sometimes embracing so great a multitude, that it would almost seem as if numerous nations of them had sworn solemn league and covenant for mutual assistance and protection.
>
> (*M*, 298)

Howard Vincent plausibly attributes Melville's description of pods, schools and bodies of whales to Frederick Bennett, but he does not comment on Melville's addition of the above cited suggestion—which does not occur in the source text—that the social organization of whales had altered in response to human intervention.[27]

There is no clear origin for this idea anywhere in Melville's written sources, so it may derive from the collective first-hand observations and hypotheses of whalemen themselves, to which *Moby-Dick*'s author gained access during his own experience aboard whalers in the Pacific. The theory may also represent Melville's own extrapolation from the more general hints, common enough amongst whaling writers of the

time, regarding the increasing wariness or scarcity of whales. Thomas Beale, for example, writing about the Japan fishery after 1819, claimed that whales were no scarcer in number, but simply more "cautious" and full of "instinctive cunning" in avoiding boats.[28] And Francis Olmsted, another of Melville's favorites, commented that "[t]here are such numbers of whale ships scattered all over the ocean is not wonderful that whales have become shy."[29]

Nevertheless, Melville's description of "The Grand Armada" goes further than these writers, because it asserts a material influence that interfuses the supposedly separate domains of the natural and the cultural, in such a way that human economic and industrial enterprise shapes the animal's social formation. In this sense, *Moby-Dick* ascribes to sperm whales (and does so insistently, repeating the notion three times in different chapters) a capacity to learn and to pass on that learning which cannot be reduced to instinct, a form of "behavioral transmission that doesn't rest on genetics"—in other words, a culture.[30]

Furthermore, Latour's notion of "translation" would demand that this suggestion of a *material* co-construction be distinguished from a rather more familiar *representational* borrowing between the animal and human domains. This latter mode, discussed earlier in relation to the metaphorical comparisons by Melville and Reynolds between nature and technology, recurs when Ishmael describes various whale conglomerations in terms deriving from human society and politics, as in the title of the chapter "The Grand Armada," or in his comment that the new formations appear "as if numerous nations of them had sworn solemn league and covenant." Such conceits were actually typical of emergent modern natural history, which despite its inception as a crucial epistemological component of the separation between nature and human society, retained this symptom of an interimplication of the two domains.[31] Keith Thomas notes, for example, that the Linnaean system, "as propounded in late-eighteenth-century England," divided what it called the "Vegetable Kingdom" into "tribes" and "nations," allocating obviously sociological characteristics to its subdivisions within the latter class: grasses were described as "plebeians," lilies as "patricians," mosses as "servants," flags as "slaves" and so on.[32] Such rhetoric represented a vestige of the pre-Enlightenment analogical paradigm for understanding the relation between human beings and the natural world, whereby the macrocosm reflected the divinely ordained structure of human life, and vice versa. As Thomas goes on to note, however, the increasingly dominant scientific demarcation between nature and society meant that any comparison between the human and the nonhuman fell more and more into disrepute during the eighteenth and nineteenth centuries. He cites Hartley Coleridge, who wrote in 1835 that "The real habits of animals . . . should be carefully observed and they should not be described as performing human actions to which their natural actions have no imaginable analogy or resemblance."[33]

Nevertheless, the interfusion of humans and nature, although strictly foreclosed from consideration by the natural and social sciences alike, remained or returned in a variety of other forms. The ascription to animals of symbolic meanings significant to the human world remained "an article of faith for many Victorian country folk, [although] it no longer had the support of intellectuals"; moreover, "[e]ven as the older view was driven out by the scientists, it began to creep back in the form of pathetic fallacy of the Romantic poets and travelers, for whom nature served as a mirror to their own moods and emotions."[34] *Moby-Dick,* of course, gains much of its emotional power from its extensive and vivid deployment of precisely these popular and Romantic translations between nature and society.

One legacy of the modern constitution, therefore, is that the scientific disposition came to attribute all such forms of cultural "mediation" between the human and nonhuman domains, however different they might be from one another, to a singular, simple, primitive, and superseded anthropomorphism. More recently, such effects have been understood as signs of resistance to the gathering dominance of scientific epistemology itself.[35] Anthropomorphic rhetoric, interpreted in this way, can reveal forgotten dimensions of that historical separation between the domains of nature and culture which Latour attributes to modern sociological, political, and scientific thought alike. As I have begun to suggest, in *Moby-Dick* such metaphors, as well as projecting human social structures onto animals—mostly for satirical or comic effect—at times, repeatedly and seriously, demonstrate various kinds of material and practical interfusion between the human and nonhuman realms. The hypothesis regarding the change in whale distribution and social organization is only one instance. Others can be found in the novel's implied critique of capitalism.

As Marshall Sahlins has trenchantly argued, the development of natural history during the nineteenth and twentieth centuries should be considered inextricably influenced by the concurrent maturation of the values of bourgeois capitalism: "Conceived in the image of the market system, the nature thus culturally configured has been in turn used to explain the human social order, and vice versa, in an endless reciprocal interchange between social Darwinism and natural capitalism."[36] In *Moby-Dick*—and in its natural historical sources—this two-way traffic between constructions of "human nature" and "nature humanized" can be observed in the moment of its establishment. To choose one well known instance from a multitude, as the sharks gather in a

feeding frenzy around the corpse of a whale alongside the *Pequod*, Stubb goads Fleece into delivering a parodic sermon against the sin of greed (*M,* 237-40). Urging the sharks to share their food in a neighborly way, the ship's cook identifies in nature the very attributes of capitalism—competition and acquisitiveness—that Sahlins identifies at work in the occult exchange between nineteenth-century economic and evolutionary theory.[37] In the ensuing chapter the injured sharks are even seen greedily devouring their own entrails (*M,* 243). This image echoes Ishmael's suggestion that in its dependence upon consumption of other mammals like whales and oxen, insofar as the reader accepts their thoroughgoing humanization in the novel, the industrial economy itself must be considered inevitably and voraciously cannibalistic (*M,* 242).[38]

Moreover at such moments, which show the processes and products of the whaling industry substantially embedded in his fellow citizens' lives, Melville goes further than his sources, who merely emphasize their nation's economic dependence upon the income from whaling.[39] Contemplating American culture, the novel finds ubiquitous evidence of the material and constitutive presence of the nonhuman within the human. Arriving in New Bedford, Ishmael remarks that in spite of the barrenness of the local land,

> nowhere in all America will you find more patrician-like houses; parks and gardens more opulent, than in New Bedford. Whence came they? how planted upon this once scraggy scoria of a country?
>
> Go and gaze upon the iron emblematical harpoons round yonder lofty mansion, and your question will be answered. Yes; all these brave houses and flowery gardens came from the Atlantic, Pacific and Indian oceans. One and all, they were harpooned and dragged up hither from the bottom of the sea.
>
> (*M,* 42)

Moby-Dick simultaneously humanizes the whale and shows the whale voraciously consumed by humans, making visible the ways in which the lives of Melville's fellow Americans were reliant—for prosperous housing, for food and the implements with which it was consumed, for clothing and fashion, and even for the perfume of the body and the complexion of its skin—upon the consumption of the whale and other mammals.

Melville's satire therefore bears out another point made by Latour, who argues that the critique of anthropomorphism—which dismisses comparisons between humans and animals as poetic license, popular sentimental error, or scientific vice—attempts to maintain the strict separation of human and nonhuman ontologies upon which modernity relies. In this respect,

> the term "anthropomorphism" actually "underestimates our humanity," in that the "*anthropos*" and the "*morphos*" together mean both that which has human shape

and that which gives shape to humans. . . . People thus give form to non-humans, but are themselves acted upon and given form by non-humans.[40]

Alongside its anthropomorphic humanizing of the whale, Melville's novel invites the reader to recognize a zoomorphic animalizing of the human, radically locating the nonhuman, the inhuman, and the inhumane within Enlightenment humanism's own most crucial and privileged category. Taken together, these processes represent a mutual interchange between the social and the natural domains. This is nowhere more apparent than in the complex of transformations and translations by which *Moby-Dick* manages contemporary anxieties arising from the economics and politics of race and gender.

IV.

As Melville was aware, his nation's much vaunted ideal of democracy depended upon the exclusion of large sectors of the adult population. Many studies have shown how *Moby-Dick* satirically recognizes America's dependence upon the labor of Native Americans, African American slaves, and conscripted Pacific Islanders.[41] In 1953, C. L. R. James's classic study *Mariners and Renegades* described the novel as an allegory of the totalitarian tendencies within modern so-called democracies, particularly the management of racial difference in the service of capitalist endeavor: "The voyage of the Pequod is the voyage of modern civilization seeking its destiny."[42] Ten years later, Alan Heimert provided a more detailed allegorical reading according to which the harpooners represent the various ethnicities whose disenfranchisement financed mid-nineteenth-century American prosperity: Queequeg stands for Pacific enlistees in the whale fishery, a major contributor to the Northern economy; the Gay Head Indian Tashtego evokes the ongoing dispossession of Native Americans in the West; and the "coal-black negro-savage" Daggoo embodies the Southern economy's continued reliance on slavery.[43]

Thus *Moby-Dick* insistently parallels the commodification of the animal and that of nonwhite labor, for example in detailing the dangers endured by the three harpooners in processing the whale (*M*, 270-73), or in Ahab's demand for their blood to cool his newly forged harpoon (*M*, 371-72). The *Pequod* belongs to an industry that consumes some humans as it consumes animals—two processes that the text understands by interfusing them. Naming the ship after an indigenous people decimated and dispossessed by the settler forbears of its white crew, comparing the whalebone included in the vessel's construction to the wearing of ivory trophies by "any barbaric Ethiopian emperor," calling it a "cannibal of a craft, tricking herself forth in the chased bones of her enemies"—the novel uses the *Pequod*'s in-

gestion of Native American, African, and Pacific associations to characterize its devouring of the animal, and vice versa (*M*, 70).[44]

More recent critics who have built on the work of James and Heimert tend to emphasise the fragility and imminent crisis of mid-nineteenth-century American capitalism, and the ways in which Melville's text represents the potential for alternative modes of agency. Thus Casarino describes the novel's encapsulation of "the paradox beating at the very heart of capital . . . of having to continue to harness, exploit, and foment precisely that immanent power of production that . . . might at any given moment overflow beyond its confines, spin out of control, exceed itself, and bring about the catastrophe of a crisis beyond crisis."[45] Michael Paul Rogin identifies a key moment in this impending crisis when he relates the composition of *Moby-Dick* to a decision by Chief Justice Lemuel Shaw, who in April 1851 declared the Fugitive Slave Law constitutional, thereby returning Thomas Sims, an escaped slave, to servitude in Georgia. The verdict, which provoked public outrage, appeared to contradict Shaw's former opposition to slavery and his decision seven years earlier to free Robert Lucas, a slave brought to Massachusetts by his master aboard the ship *United States*. According to Rogin, the Sims judgment responded to growing fears about the threat to the Union posed by pro- and anti-slavery antagonism. But more particularly, it turned on the issue of nonwhite agency, because "Sims, unlike Lucas, had escaped from his master." The consistency between Shaw's decisions in Lucas and Sims therefore lies in a juridical determination to maintain the agency of white civility over that of black resistance: freedom could be granted only by the benevolence of white rule, whereas "Claims to freedom, by slaves against masters" would "cost them the paternal protection of the law."[46]

As Rogin also points out, in the same month that he delivered the Sims judgment, Shaw sent his son-in-law, Herman Melville, a copy of Owen Chase's account of the *Essex* sinking. In this moment of exchange, Shaw embodies simultaneously an interest in two kinds of agency—that of the animal, and that of the slave—both of which, in different but "translatable" ways, threatened the mid-nineteenth-century American economy. These coterminous assaults upon American confidence manifest themselves, in Melville's novel, in the intimacy of the relation between the threat represented by the agency of the animal, and that of those various human "others" upon whose labor, in 1851, American federal and economic stability remained tenuously poised. Given this mutual transference between anxieties about nonwhite and nonhuman agencies, the "Retribution, swift vengeance, eternal malice" ascribed to Moby Dick as he bears down upon the *Pequod* to bring about its destruction must be considered to derive simultaneously from industrial capitalism's anxiety about nonhuman agency, and from a more occult sense of those human debts which America in 1851 could scarcely admit, let alone address.

This element of the democratic unconscious is thrown into sharp relief when **Moby-Dick** is put alongside Melville's most important fictional source: Joseph Hart's Nantucket whaling story *Miriam Coffin*. Hart's narrative centers less upon the agency of the animal—a ship is indeed sunk by a whale, but only accidentally, as it thrashes about in its flurry—than upon its anxiety about human "savages," embodied initially by the murderous Native American Quibby, and later by the aggressive islanders who attack the ship in the Pacific.[47] Replacing these malign or bellicose primitives with the erotically primordial but acquiescent noble savages Queequeg, Tashtego, and Daggoo, and replacing an accidentally destructive whale with the intentionally vengeful Moby Dick, Melville transfers the threat posed to modern America by its economic dependence upon various disenfranchised human elements onto the White Whale—which "swam before [Ahab] as the monomaniac incarnation of all those malicious agencies which some deep men feel eating in them" (**M,** 156).

V.

The reliance of American mid-nineteenth-century democracy and economics upon the labor and lives of another disenfranchised population, however, remains rather less visible. Again this becomes apparent when **Moby-Dick** is compared with its precursor. Just as it displays overt paranoia about ethnic otherness, Hart's novel struggles explicitly with the role of women in the industrial economy. *Miriam Coffin* parallels the narrative about the voyages of two vessels, the *Grampus* and the *Leviathan,* with the activities of the eponymous character who, with her husband at sea, enters into the masculine sphere of entrepreneurial capitalism with considerable virtuosity. However, Miriam's business skills, which include speculation on credit rather than existing assets, the undercutting of competitors, and the fostering of business confidence through conspicuous consumption—tactics that might inspire admiration in today's money market—bring disaster in Hart's novel, and are roundly condemned by her husband on his return: "Get thee gone to thy kitchen, where it is fitting thou should'st preside . . . and do thou never meddle with men's affairs more!"[48]

Melville, however, represses the possibility of female economic and cultural agency altogether by utterly excluding women characters from his novel. But although *women* may be all but absent from the novel, *femininity* is not. On the contrary, **Moby-Dick** exemplifies a historically specific modification of gender codes, effected through complex transfers between nature and culture. Mid-nineteenth-century human masculinity and femi-

ninity, and the zoology of sexual difference, are used to define each other, and to naturalize the resulting gender ideology. Most obviously, Melville describes in "The Grand Armada"—the moment at which, in the middle of the novel, Ishmael gazes into the profound and mystical center of the sperm whale's social organization—precisely that gendered separation into supposedly complementary spheres of activity that was concurrently at work in American society, "as if the cows and calves had been purposely locked up in this innermost fold":

> But far beneath this wondrous world upon the surface, another and still stranger world met our eyes as we gazed over the side. For, suspended in those watery vaults, floated the forms of the nursing mothers of the whales, and those that by their enormous girth seemed shortly to become mothers. The lake, as I have hinted, was to a considerable depth exceedingly transparent; and as human infants while suckling will calmly and fixedly gaze away from the breast . . . even so did the young of these whales seem looking up towards us, but not at us, as if we were but a bit of Gulf-weed in their new-born sight. Floating on their sides, the mothers also seemed quietly eyeing us.

(M, 302-3)

The rhetoric of calm, transparency, and immediacy pervading this passage seems to guarantee its verisimilitude: here, of all the descriptions of whales offered by the novel, it appears to promise the reader a clear view of the intimate natural life of the animal, devoid of literary or symbolic coloration.

Of course this is far from being the case. As Vincent has argued, the passage draws closely upon descriptions of nursing whales in Melville's favored sources.[49] Furthermore, the comparison with human infants hints at a simultaneous co-construction of the natural history of the whale and the social life of nineteenth-century Americans. As Ann Douglas points out, the economic and cultural position of women in the American Northeast underwent a profound change during the first half of the nineteenth century. Industrial manufacture replaced female domestic labor, which had played a vital economic role during the so called "Age of Homespun" at the end of the eighteenth century, with a consequent loss in "self-reliance and social responsibility" for women. Education for young girls, instead of teaching them to be home workers, now trained them to spend their husbands' incomes, and their manual involvement in the material economy was substituted with an exorbitant cult of maternity: "Praise of motherhood could bolster and promote the middle-class woman's biological function as tantamount, if not superior, to her lost economic productivity."[50] The central nursery idyll of "The Grand Armada" evidently and vividly partakes of this apotheosis of human motherhood, while at the same time, typically, Melville implies that these whales, even the mothers and newborn offspring, are simply resources waiting to be harvested. Although critical attention has been paid to the footnote appended to this passage, which extends the comparison between cetacean and human reproductive and nursery habits, it has seldom been noticed that an economic imperative cuts violently through the idealized maternal imagery:[51]

> When by chance these precious parts in a nursing whale are cut by the hunter's lance, the mother's pouring milk and blood rivallingly discolor the sea for rods. The milk is very sweet and rich; it has been tasted by men; it might do well with strawberries.
>
> (*M,* 303 n. 7)

This characteristic juxtaposition of an emotional humanization of the whale and a brutal recognition of its consumption comes very close to an admission of the price paid by both the animal and the human female for their place within industrial capitalism.

All the same, I think Douglas overestimates the author's intentional commitment to the politics of gender equality when she concludes that "Melville consistently produced a literature of inclusiveness. What his society would not allow him to conceive—sexual equality, a non-oppressive economic system, an honest culture—he also included by making his work a recognition of the price of their loss."[52] But she does point out one important moment at which the novel does not ignore its own exclusion of women.[53] The last extended exchange between Ahab and Starbuck prior to the meeting with Moby Dick—the moment at which Ahab most nearly turns back from his destructive course—involves the Captain's recognition of the damage produced by the economic separation between the genders:

> Forty years of continual whaling! . . . for forty years has Ahab forsaken the peaceful land, for forty years to make war on the horrors of the deep! . . . away, whole oceans away, from that young girl-wife I wedded past fifty, and sailed for Cape Horn the next day, leaving but one dent in my marriage pillow—wife? wife?—rather a widow with her husband alive! . . . Starbuck; let me look into a human eye. . . . By the green land; by the bright hearth-stone! this is the magic glass, man; I see my wife and my child in thine eye.
>
> (*M,* 405-6)

But despite Starbuck's appeal to his affection for home and family, Ahab cannot turn back: "[W]hat cozening, hidden lord and master, and cruel, remorseless emperor commands me; that against all natural lovings and longings, I so keep pushing, and crowding, and jamming myself on all the time . . . ?" (*M,* 406). The novel implies a psychological or ontological answer to this question, but Ahab's monomaniac drive, frequently represented in reference to industrial technology—"The path to my fixed purpose is laid with iron rails, whereon my soul is grooved to run" (*M,* 143)—can equally be read as a metaphysical by-product of the industrial economy's impact upon the gender organization of mid-nineteenth-century America, a mythopoeic sublimation of an economically motivated separation of men and women into widely demarcated economic zones.

Such an interpretation is borne out by the case of John DeBlois, captain of the *Ann Alexander.* Although Melville could not have had access while writing his novel either to the letters of DeBlois or to his account of the sinking of his ship by a whale, these documents attest to the exaggerated bifurcation of masculine and feminine spheres of activity resulting from the peculiar demands of the whaling industry. DeBlois, according to Clement Cleveland Sawtell,

> was completely fearless and reckless of life, limb and equipment in the pursuit of whales, and expected others whom he lead [sic] to be the same. He was tireless, driving his ship, his crew and himself as long as there was a ray of light in the sky. . . . And finally, above all else, he resented long voyages that separated him from his wife, Henrietta, to whom he was deeply and undyingly devoted. For this reason and perhaps others he could not bear to miss a single whale, no matter how elusive, no matter how vicious, no matter how long the chase. Each fighting whale almost became, it seems, his personal antagonist, to be killed, no matter what the cost, and the final cost, as it turned out was his ship.[54]

The letters written by DeBlois to his wife, which Sawtell reproduces, testify to the adventurous, entrepreneurial mode of capitalism embodied by whaling captains, and to the impact of that habitus upon an increasingly exaggerated bifurcation between the genders.

Indeed, so harsh was this enforced separation that, years after the sinking of the *Ann Alexander,* Henrietta DeBlois actually took ship with her husband on board the *Merlin* on 25 June 1856. In fact, by the mid-century, a number of whaling wives were transgressing the gender roles implied by the industry. One of the first to do so, Mary Brewster, accompanied her husband aboard the *Tiger,* out of Stonington, Connecticut in 1845, and again in 1848. She recorded her delight at meeting Betsy Tower, wife of the captain of the New Bedford whaler *Moctezuma,* during a "gam" off Cape Horn in 1847. Other women taking ship at the time Melville was writing include Azubah Cash, who sailed from Nantucket aboard the *Columbia* in October 1850 and remained beside her husband on his voyages for the next several years, and Harriet Peirce, who stood by her man as the *Kutusoff* left New Bedford in the following year.[55] Although such cases represented only a small minority within the fishery, the determined infiltration of the factory ship by these women provides a sharp contrast to the exclusive masculinism of ***Moby-Dick***'s portrayal of contemporary whaling subculture. For Melville's novel determinedly banishes women beyond the perimeters of the whaling enterprise: they remain locked into an association with the "marriage pillow," "the green land," "the bright hearth-stone," permitted aboard the *Pequod* only in the idealized portrait that Ahab, in an atypical moment, imagines reflected in his first mate's eye.

Ahab's idyll, and his relentless pursuit of the whale, therefore represent the strictest imaginable adherence to the organization of gendered spheres of activity dictated by an industrializing economy, which required strengthened opposition between an aggressive, courageous, and active masculinity and a tender, nurturing, and passive femininity—complementary gender dispositions consonant with, respectively, the competitive and acquisitive arena of capitalist enterprise and the sanctum of the privatized nuclear family. Moreover, the novel illustrates how these attributes came to be located in nature. Just as a contemporary cult of American motherhood informs Ishmael's paean to the whale nursery in "The Grand Armada," the subsequent chapter discovers in bull whales the "naturally" opposing virtues of masculinity: "In cavalier attendance upon the school of females, you invariably see a male of full grown magnitude, but not old; who, upon any alarm, evinces his gallantry by falling in the rear and covering the flight of his ladies" (*M*, 305). The chapter then distinguishes between these "harem" schools, comprising females guarded by a single male, and the "schools composing none but young and vigorous males":

> while those female whales are characteristically timid, the young males, or forty-barrel-bulls, as they call them, are by far the most pugnacious of all the Leviathans, and proverbially the most dangerous to encounter; excepting those wondrous greyheaded, grizzled whales. . . . Like a mob of young collegians, [the young males] are full of fight, fun and wickedness, tumbling round the world at . . . a reckless, rollicking rate. . . . They soon relinquish this turbulence though, and when about three fourths grown, break up, and separately go about in quest of settlements, that is, harems.

> Another point of difference between the male and female schools is still more characteristic of the sexes. Say you strike a Forty-barrel bull—poor devil! all his comrades quit him. But strike a member of the harem school, and her companions swim around her with every token of concern, sometimes lingering so near her and so long, as themselves to fall a prey.

> (*M*, 307)

In this passage, a process that still characterizes wildlife documentaries today operates at full power, whereby human sociological "truth" and natural historical "fact" are engaged in a mutual authorization that irons out all contradictions. So, for instance, the inconsistency between the purported timidity of the females and their refusal to escape when their companions are struck is explained by an appeal to a femininity—animal and human—that finds its highest calling in maternity, which requires a deferential but intractable "concern" for the well-being of others at the expense of the self. And the incongruent combination of pugnacity and cowardice in the character of young males is processed into coherence by a notion of masculinity that manifests in youth as a reckless but selfish aggressivity, and in maturity by a courageous protection of the weaker members of the social order. In short, an entire sociology and psychology of gender, class, educational and social development—perfectly evolved to suit the economics of industrial capitalism—is being advanced by means of its interfusion with cetacean ethology.

Evidently, only a heroicization of the male leviathan could properly elevate his human antagonists to epic heights, thereby glorifying the whaling industry and the expansionist industrial capitalism that it represented. Hence, only the male rogue whales were ever made famous as individuals by being given names: New Zealand Tom, Mocha Dick, Timor Jack, Don Miguel. That captains saw the encounter with such animals as a contest of masculinities is again attested by DeBlois, who described a whale that had already destroyed several boats and would eventually sink his ship as a "Noble fellow," admitting that the increasing danger only strengthened his resolve "to secure this 'fighting whale.' . . . My blood was up, and I was fully determined to have that whale, cost what it might."[56] In the same manner, Reynolds immortalized Mocha Dick as a "renowned monster, who had come off victorious in a hundred fights with his pursuers," and his vanquisher as an embodiment of the free, unpretentious, everyday heroism of the worker under capitalism, "of a spirit of fearless independence, generated by free institutions."[57]

Nevertheless, the kinds of self contradiction that betray the work of gender construction emerge even in this apologia for virile capitalist endeavour, because in Reynolds's narrative, the fight with Mocha Dick actually occurs after, and in relation to, an attack upon the whaleboat initiated by a female sperm whale.[58] To be sure, this animal attacks only after her calf has been killed by the whalers, which helps to assimilate this evidence of feminine courage and aggression into the category of maternal care. On the other hand, Reynolds makes equally clear that Mocha Dick's attacks were always motivated by a desire to extract "vengeance" for the slaughter of his companion whales, so the only remaining trait that identifies the bull whale as a more willing, ferocious, and effective fighter than the cow is his greater size.

Similar contradictions appear in the natural historical accounts upon which Melville drew, where again they show the ideological complicity between natural history and human sociology. Most striking of all is the confusion, amongst *Moby-Dick*'s source texts, about whether the male or the female sperm whale was more liable to become "mischievous." Beale and Bennett, for example, agree that the nurturing tendencies of the females inclined them to remain with their wounded companions, while the young males would swiftly abandon their fellows.[59] Moreover, Bennett explicitly discounts the suggestion, advanced by Melville, that the most formidable opponents of the whalers were old solitary bulls, asserting instead that "[a]n old female, and a half-grown male, are considered the most troublesome to encounter, from their active and combative temper."[60] In fact, firsthand accounts by nineteenth century whaling writers of female fighting whales are not hard to find.[61] They are simply easy to overlook, for they were attributed with a far lower degree of significance than the epic battles with their larger male counterparts—precisely because, as I have suggested, the gender politics of nineteenth-century human family life and the complementary economics of industrial capitalism required that the true "fighting" or "mischievous" whale necessarily be perceived as masculine.

Such determined assertions of gender difference arise from the "crisis of gender re-organization" afflicting mid-nineteenth-century America, "a sharpening of the separation between the public and economically productive sphere of men and the private sphere of home, family, and culture reserved for women." The outrageous masculinism that pervades *Moby-Dick* thus comprises the necessary complement to the maternal idyll at its heart: "What is the hunt for the enormous sperm whale Moby Dick if not a quest for absolute potency, a quest in which the aggressive assertion of masculine strength calls up a fantastically enlarged version of that strength as its imagined nemesis?"[62] This exorbitant virility dictates the periphrases employed by Ishmael to refer to the whale's penis, "longer than a Kentuckian is tall, nigh a foot in diameter at the base, and jet-black as Yojo, the ebony idol of Queequeg" (*M,* 324), and permeates his account of the crew's manipulation of congealed lumps of spermaceti, in preparation for trying out:

> I squeezed that sperm till a strange sort of insanity came over me; and I found myself unwittingly squeezing my co-laborers' hands in it, mistaking their hands for the gentle globules. Such an abounding, affectionate, friendly, loving feeling did this avocation beget; that at last I was continually squeezing their hands, and looking up into their eyes sentimentally; as much as to say. . . . Come; let us squeeze hands all round; nay, let us all squeeze ourselves into each other; let us squeeze ourselves universally into the very milk and sperm of kindness.

(*M,* 322-33)

Here, as everywhere in the novel, the conceptual and commercial processing of the animal becomes inextricably associated with a shared masculinity, lovingly rendered as a sensuous homoeroticism that utterly excludes the feminine, or else replaces it—in this passage, even the proverbial "milk of human kindness" becomes transmuted into a more manly substance.

Such extravagant representations of difference vividly illustrate, I have argued, the ubiquitous mutual construction of nineteenth- and twentieth-century scientific and sociological epistemologies, and the concomitant naturalization of the racial and gendered economy required by capitalist modernity. At the same time *Moby-Dick* challenges these representations, by producing and juxtaposing them so prolifically, energetically, and exorbitantly that they are strained to the breaking point and beyond.[63] Hence, even as the novel documents America's consumption of the bodies and energies of women, people of color, and nonhumans, it ironically represents the fragility of the naturo-cultural network of modernity, and anticipates its imminent collapse and subsequent decay.

Notes

1. See Mark Niemeyer, "Manifest Destiny and Melville's *Moby-Dick;* or, Enlightenment Universalism and Aggressive Nineteenth-Century Expansionism in a National Text," *Q/W/E/R/T/Y* 9 (1999): 301-11.

2. Ishmael's panegyrics on the civilizing mission of American whaling draw on Edmund Burke's often cited speech in praise of the industry, cited in Thomas Beale's *Natural History of the Sperm Whale* (London: John Van Voorst, 1839), 142, and in Joseph Hart's *Miriam Coffin, or, the Whale Fishermen* (Nantucket: Mill Hill Press, 1995 [1834]), xxi, 4; on the "memorial" presented to Congress by representatives from Nantucket during the 1820s (Hart, xxvi-xix); on the conclusion to Charles Wilkes's *Narrative of the United States Exploring Expedition During the Years 1838, 1839, 1840, 1841, 1842,* 5 vols. (Philadelphia: Lea & Blanchard, 1845), 5:484-86; and on popular "true stories" about whaling life such as Jeremiah Reynolds's "Mocha Dick: Or, the White Whale of the Pacific," in Moby-Dick: *A Norton Critical Edition,* ed. Hershel Parker and Harrison Hayford, 2nd ed. (New York: W. W. Norton, 2002 [1839]), 549-65. Hereafter abbreviated *M* and cited parenthetically by page number. For Ishmael's panegyrics, see pages 65 and 99.

3. Cesare Casarino, *Modernity at Sea: Melville, Marx, Conrad in Crisis* (Minneapolis: Univ. of Minnesota Press, 2002), 5, 74-75.

4. The decline of the sperm whale fishery is described in Casarino, 82-83. For late-nineteenth-century accounts see Alexander Starbuck's 1882 *History of the American Whale Fishery* (Secaucus,

NJ: Castle, 1989), 110-13; and Thomas Macy's 1880 supplement to Obed Macy's 1835 *History of Nantucket* (Clifton: Augustus M. Kelley, 1972), 290 and following.

5. The impact of industrial modernity upon human-animal relations has been surveyed briefly by John Berger in "Vanishing Animals," *New Society* 39 (1977): 664-65. For more detailed accounts, see Barbara Noske, *Beyond Boundaries: Humans and Animals* (Montréal: Black Rose, 1997), and Adrian Franklin, *Animals and Modern Cultures: A Sociology of Human-Animal Relations in Modernity* (London: Sage, 1999).

6. See Eric Wilson, "Melville, Darwin, and the Great Chain of Being: Herman Melville's Influence on Charles Darwin's Theory of Evolution," *Studies in American Fiction* 28 (2000): 131-50.

7. The converse of Burke's vision of the civilizing influence of American whalers is best represented by Henry Cheever in his 1850 book *The Whale and His Captors* (Fairfield, WA: Ye Galleon Press, 1991); for Cheever, whaling proved morally debilitating because of the brutalizing nature of the trade, long absences from hearth and home, and exposure to the godless cultures of the Pacific and elsewhere.

8. For his detailed descriptions of the factory ship's processing of whales, Melville draws upon J. Ross Browne's 1846 *Etchings of a Whaling Cruise* (Cambridge: Belknap Press, Harvard Univ. Press, 1968).

9. Bruno Latour, *We Have Never Been Modern,* trans. Catherine Porter (Cambridge: Harvard Univ. Press, 1993), 37.

10. Latour, 32, 10-11.

11. Latour, 120.

12. For an excellent precursor to the reading I offer here, see T. Hugh Crawford's article "Networking the (Non)Human: *Moby-Dick,* Matthew Fontaine Maury, and Bruno Latour," *Configurations* 5 (1997): 1-21. Crawford focuses on mid-nineteenth-century oceanography as the domain within which Ahab represents the desire to standardize the unpredictable "networks that produce reality," while my own analysis concentrates on the politics and economics of race and gender as the contexts within which *Moby-Dick* maps out the complex of translations between nature and culture (Crawford, 9).

13. Latour, 47, citing Donna Haraway, *Simians, Cyborgs and Women: The Reinvention of Nature* (New York: Routledge, 1991).

14. Michael Paul Rogin, *Subversive Genealogy: The Politics and Art of Herman Melville* (Berkeley:

Univ. of California Press, 1985), 138. For readings of the novel that focus upon the idea of mastering nature through industrial technology, see Stephen Ausband, "The Whale and the Machine: An Approach to *Moby-Dick,*" *American Literature* 47 (1975): 197-211; Richard Wixon, "Herman Melville: Critic of America and Harbinger of Ecological Crisis," in *Literature and the Lore of the Sea,* ed. Patricia Ann Carlson (Amsterdam: Rodopi, 1986), 143-53; Elizabeth Schultz, "Melville's Environmental Vision in *Moby-Dick,*" *Interdisciplinary Studies in Literature and Environment* 7.1 (2000): 111.

15. David Mitchell, "'Too Much of a Cripple': Ahab, Dire Bodies, and the Language of Prosthesis in *Moby-Dick,*" *Leviathan* 1.1 (1999): 10.

16. Schultz, 111-12.

17. Reynolds, 551.

18. See *Moby-Dick,* 325-28.

19. Reynolds, 550.

20. Elsewhere I have discussed in detail how the agency demonstrated by the "fighting" whale is represented in *Moby-Dick* and its sources. See my "What Animals Mean, in *Moby-Dick* for Example" (forthcoming in *Textual Practice* 19.1 [February 2005]).

21. The most famous first-hand account of this incident is Owen Chase's *Wreck of the Whaleship Essex* (London: Review, 2000 [1821]).

22. Nathaniel Philbrick, *In the Heart of the Sea: The Epic True Story That Inspired* Moby-Dick (London: HarperCollins, 2000), 224.

23. John DeBlois, in Clement Cleveland Sawtell, *The Ship Ann Alexander of New Bedford, 1805-1851* (Mystic, Conn.: Marine Historical Association, 1962), 72-73.

24. Wilkes, 5:493.

25. See for example Beale, 9-10; or Frederick Bennett, *Narrative of a Whaling Voyage around the Globe from the Year 1833 to 1836,* 2 vols. (London: Richard Bentley, 1840), 2:176-77.

26. Tim Flannery, *The Future Eaters: An Ecological History of the Australasian Lands and People* (Chatswood, New South Wales: Reed, 1994), 188.

27. Howard Vincent, *The Trying-out of* Moby-Dick (Cambridge, MA: Riverside, 1949), 301-3; Bennett, 2:171-72.

28. Beale, 76-77.

29. Francis Olmsted, *Incidents of a Whaling Voyage* (Rutland, Vermont: C. E. Tuttle & Co., 1969 [1841]), 157.

30. The phrase cited here is Frans de Waal's gloss on a definition of culture proposed by Kinji Imanishi. As de Waal argues, the notion that animals possess the capacity for such nongenetic, noninstinctual learning, and furthermore for the transmission of this knowledge between individuals and generations, has only recently begun to be taken seriously (again?) by ethologists; see especially his brief comments on recent studies of cetacean cultural knowledge in *The Ape and the Sushi Master* (London: Penguin, 2001), 214, 270; this idea is also discussed in Noske (134-35, 155), and in Erica Fudge's *Animal* (London: Reaktion, 2002), 133.

31. For example Georges-Louis Leclerc de Buffon's voluminous and popular *Histoire Naturelle* "regularly draw[s] on anthropomorphic vocabulary . . . as a pedagogical and literary tool," as observed by Jeff Loveland in his book *Rhetoric and Natural History: Buffon in Polemical and Literary Context* (Oxford: Voltaire Foundation, 2001), 69.

32. Keith Thomas, *Man and the Natural World: Changing Attitudes in England 1500-1800* (Harmondsworth: Penguin, 1984), 66.

33. Thomas, 68.

34. Thomas, 91.

35. See Fudge; see also Chris Philo and Chris Wilbert's introduction to their collection *Animal Spaces, Beastly Places: New Geographies of Human-Animal Relations* (New York: Routledge, 2000), 1-36.

36. Marshall Sahlins, *The Use and Abuse of Biology: An Anthropological Critique of Sociobiology* (Ann Arbor: Univ. of Michigan Press, 1976), xv. See Noske (80-125) for an elaboration of Sahlins's thesis. Noske's emphasis on the co-construction of human and animal gender codes is particularly relevant to the remainder of my discussion.

37. See Sahlins, 93, 101.

38. For a detailed assessment of the assumption, shared by ecocritics, that *Moby-Dick*'s humanization of the whale functions to inspire compassion for animals, see my article "*Moby-Dick* and Compassion," *Society and Animals* 12.1 (2004): 19-38.

39. See Browne, 539-64; and Hart, xxi-xxix.

40. Philo and Wilbert, 19, citing Latour, 137.

41. As well as those discussed in detail in the remainder of this essay, persuasive accounts of the politics of race in *Moby-Dick* have been offered by Marius Bewley, "Melville and the Democratic Experience," in *Melville: A Collection of Critical Es-* says, ed. Richard Chase (Englewood Cliffs, NJ: Prentice-Hall, 1962), 91-115; John Bryant, "*Moby-Dick* as Revolution," in *The Cambridge Companion to Herman Melville,* ed. Robert Levine (Cambridge: Cambridge Univ. Press, 1998), 65-90; Niemeyer; Timothy Marr, "Melville's Ethnic Conscriptions," *Leviathan* 3.1 (2001): 5-29.

42. C. L. R. James, *Mariners and Renegades: The Story of Herman Melville and the World We Live In* (New York: C. L. R. James, 1953), 18.

43. Alan Heimert "*Moby-Dick* and American Political Symbolism," *American Quarterly* 15 (1963): 502.

44. See John Staud, "'What's in a Name?': The *Pequod* and Melville's Heretical Politics," *ESQ* [*Emerson Society Quarterly*] 48 (1992): 339-59.

45. Casarino, 141.

46. Rogin, 99-100, 107, 119, 143.

47. See Hart, 155-62, 282-88, 300.

48. Hart, 317.

49. See Vincent, 30-5; Beale, 65; Bennett, 2:179; and Olmsted, 139.

50. Ann Douglas, *The Feminization of American Culture* (New York: Noonday, 1998), 74.

51. See Robert Zoellner, *The Salt-Sea Mastodon: A Reading of* Moby-Dick (Berkeley: Univ. of California Press, 1973), 180-85; Schultz, 104-5.

52. Douglas, 329.

53. Douglas, 304-5.

54. Sawtell, 82.

55. See Joan Druett, *Petticoat Whalers: Whaling Wives at Sea, 1820-1920* (Auckland: Collins, 1991), 25-38.

56. DeBlois, quoted in Sawtell, 72.

57. Reynolds, 565.

58. Reynolds, 558.

59. Beale, 32; Bennett, 1:177-78.

60. Bennett, 1:206.

61. See Starbuck, 126-28; and Cheever, 185-88.

62. Richard Brodhead, intro. to *New Essays on* Moby-Dick, ed. Brodhead (Cambridge: Cambridge Univ. Press, 1983), 9-10.

63. See for example Geoffrey Sanborn's suggestion that the most vividly drawn nonwhite character in the novel, Queequeg, dissolves into a kind of phantom or simulacrum, a representation of the ultimate emptiness of capitalist modernity's desire

for (and, I would argue, anxiety about its economic dependence upon) "the ideality of savagery" (Sanborn, *The Sign of the Cannibal: Melville and the Making of a Postcolonial Reader* [Durham: Duke Univ. Press, 1998], 168).

FURTHER READING

Criticism

Bernard, Fred V. "The Question of Race in *Moby-Dick.*" *Massachusetts Review* 43, no. 3 (fall 2002): 383-404.

Examines issues of slavery and ethnic identity in the novel.

Bohrer, Randall. "Melville's New Witness: Cannibalism and the Microcosm-Macrocosm Cosmology of *Moby-Dick.*" *Studies in Romanticism* 22, no. 1 (spring 1983): 65-91.

Interprets the novel as an expression of a "microcosm-macrocosm world system" in which images of cannibalism and consumption are metaphors for Melville's dire vision of human existence.

Booth, Thornton Y. "*Moby-Dick*: Standing Up to God." *Nineteenth-Century Fiction* 17, no. 1 (June 1962): 33-43.

Argues that Ahab's pursuit of Moby-Dick represents a form of protest against a malevolent, unjust God.

Cowan, Bainard. *Exiled Waters:* Moby-Dick *and the Crisis of Allegory.* Baton Rouge: Louisiana State University Press, 1982, 194 p.

Evaluates the novel within the framework of nineteenth-century historical, social, and aesthetic contexts, focusing on the tension between temporal and timeless elements in the work.

Drurer, Christopher S. "Mocking the 'Grand Programme': Irony and After in *Moby-Dick.*" *Rocky Mountain Review of Language and Literature* 36, no. 4 (1982): 249-58.

Examines the character of Ishmael, arguing that he is both a mouthpiece for Melville's irony and a prototypical example of the existential hero.

Glenn, Barbara. "Melville and the Sublime in *Moby-Dick.*" *American Literature: A Journal of Literary History, Criticism, and Bibliography* 48, no. 2 (May 1976): 165-82.

Analyzes the novel as Melville's repudiation of mainstream nineteenth-century notions of the sublime.

Grove, James P. "Melville's Vision of Death in *Moby-Dick*: Stepping away from the 'Snug Sofa.'" *New England Quarterly* 52, no. 2 (June 1979): 177-96.

Contrasts Melville's uncompromising conception of death with depictions of mortality and the afterlife in nineteenth-century popular literature.

Hamilton, Carol Vanderveer. "The Evil of Banality: *Moby-Dick* vs. the Extreme Machine." *Iowa Journal of Cultural Studies* 4 (spring 2004): 7-18.

Interprets the novel as an expression of "narcissistic rage," comparing Melville's depiction of Ahab's monomaniacal quest and the modern American obsession with the sports utility vehicle.

Isani, Mukhtar Ali. "Zoroastrianism and the Fire Symbolism in *Moby-Dick.*" *American Literature: A Journal of Literary History, Criticism, and Bibliography* 44, no. 3 (November 1972): 385-97.

Analyzes the influence of Zoroastrian metaphysics and religious symbolism on Melville's development of the novel's central themes.

Kalter, Susan. "A Student of Savage Thought: The Ecological Ethic in *Moby-Dick* and Its Grounding in Native American Ideologies." *ESQ: A Journal of the American Renaissance* 48, nos. 1-2 (2002): 1-40.

Examines Melville's attitudes toward ecology and Native American culture within the framework of nineteenth-century notions of the "savage."

McGuire, Ian. "'Who Ain't a Slave?': *Moby-Dick* and the Ideology of Free Labor." *Journal of American Studies* 37, no. 2 (August 2003): 287-305.

Discusses the relationship between nineteenth-century political rhetoric and Melville's attitudes toward democracy, capitalism, and the institution of slavery.

Moynihan, Robert D. "Irony in *Moby-Dick.*" *Essays in Arts and Sciences* 6, no. 2 (1977): 55-67.

Examines the various forms of irony at play in the novel through a detailed analysis of several scenes.

Pease, Donald E. "*Moby-Dick* and the Cold War." In *The American Renaissance Reconsidered,* edited by Walter Benn Michaels and Donald E. Pease, pp. 113-55. Baltimore: Johns Hopkins University Press, 1985.

Offers a far-ranging critique of F. O. Matthiessen's reading of the novel, asserting that Matthiessen's interpretation of Ahab as an emblem of totalitarianism emerged from social and political pressures prevalent during the Cold War.

Post-Lauria, Sheila. "'Philosophy in Whales . . . Poetry in Blubber': Mixed Form in *Moby-Dick.*" *Nineteenth-Century Literature* 45, no. 3 (December 1990): 300-16.

Discusses the influence of contemporary literary conventions on Melville's approach to the novel's structure. Post-Lauria regards the work as part of a broader tradition of mixed-form narratives in the mid-nineteenth century.

Sanborn, Geoffrey. "The Name of the Devil: Melville's Other 'Extracts' for *Moby-Dick*." *Nineteenth-Century Literature* 47, no. 2 (September 1992): 212-35.

Explores the potential uses of Melville's notes for *Moby-Dick* in forming a critical interpretation of the novel.

Sattelmeyer, Robert. "'Shanties of Chapters and Essays': Rewriting *Moby-Dick*." *ESQ: A Journal of the American Renaissance* 49, no. 4 (2003): 213-47.

Examines the evolution of the novel's plot and major themes through an analysis of Melville's earlier drafts of the work.

Schultz, Elizabeth. "Melville's Environmental Vision in *Moby-Dick*." *ISLE: Interdisciplinary Studies in Literature and Environment* 7, no. 1 (winter 2000): 97-113.

Analyzes the novel within the framework of transcendentalist attitudes toward nature and progress.

Selby, Nick. *Herman Melville: Moby-Dick*. New York: Columbia University Press, 1998, 180 p.

Provides a range of critical approaches to *Moby-Dick,* including formalist, reconstructive, and postmodern readings of the novel.

Spanos, William V. *The Errant Art of* Moby-Dick: *The Canon, the Cold War, and the Struggle for American Studies.* Durham N.C.: Duke University Press, 1995, 374 p.

Examines *Moby-Dick* in the context of American cultural identity in the post-Cold War era, focusing in particular on the tension between theoretical and historical readings of the novel.

Trimpi, Helen P. "Conventions of Romance in *Moby-Dick*." *Southern Review* 7, no. 1 (winter 1971): 115-29.

Argues that a familiarity with the conventions of nineteenth-century literary romance is essential to understanding the novel's imaginative power and scope.

Vargish, Thomas. "Gnostic Mythos in *Moby-Dick*." *PMLA: Publications of the Modern Language Association of America* 81, no. 3 (June 1966): 272-77.

Discusses Melville's explorations of Gnostic doctrines of good and evil in the novel.

Werge, Thomas. "*Moby-Dick* and the Calvinist Tradition." *Studies in the Novel* 1, no. 4 (1969): 484-506.

Examines Melville's approach to questions of epistemology in the novel within the context of Calvinist theology.

How to Use This Index

The main references

Calvino, Italo
1923-1985 .... CLC **5, 8, 11, 22, 33, 39,**
73; SSC **3, 48**

list all author entries in the following Thomson Gale Literary Criticism series:

AAL = *Asian American Literature*
BG = *The Beat Generation: A Gale Critical Companion*
BLC = *Black Literature Criticism*
BLCS = *Black Literature Criticism Supplement*
CLC = *Contemporary Literary Criticism*
CLR = *Children's Literature Review*
CMLC = *Classical and Medieval Literature Criticism*
DC = *Drama Criticism*
FL = *Feminism in Literature: A Gale Critical Companion*
GL = *Gothic Literature: A Gale Critical Companion*
HLC = *Hispanic Literature Criticism*
HLCS = *Hispanic Literature Criticism Supplement*
HR = *Harlem Renaissance: A Gale Critical Companion*
LC = *Literature Criticism from 1400 to 1800*
NCLC = *Nineteenth-Century Literature Criticism*
NNAL = *Native North American Literature*
PC = *Poetry Criticism*
SSC = *Short Story Criticism*
TCLC = *Twentieth-Century Literary Criticism*
WLC = *World Literature Criticism, 1500 to the Present*
WLCS = *World Literature Criticism Supplement*

The cross-references

See also CA 85-88, 116; CANR 23, 61;
DAM NOV; DLB 196; EW 13; MTCW 1, 2;
RGSF 2; RGWL 2; SFW 4; SSFS 12

list all author entries in the following Thomson Gale biographical and literary sources:

AAYA = *Authors & Artists for Young Adults*
AFAW = *African American Writers*
AFW = *African Writers*
AITN = *Authors in the News*
AMW = *American Writers*
AMWR = *American Writers Retrospective Supplement*
AMWS = *American Writers Supplement*
ANW = *American Nature Writers*
AW = *Ancient Writers*
BEST = *Bestsellers*
BPFB = *Beacham's Encyclopedia of Popular Fiction: Biography and Resources*
BRW = *British Writers*
BRWS = *British Writers Supplement*
BW = *Black Writers*
BYA = *Beacham's Guide to Literature for Young Adults*
CA = *Contemporary Authors*
CAAS = *Contemporary Authors Autobiography Series*
CABS = *Contemporary Authors Bibliographical Series*
CAD = *Contemporary American Dramatists*
CANR = *Contemporary Authors New Revision Series*
CAP = *Contemporary Authors Permanent Series*
CBD = *Contemporary British Dramatists*
CCA = *Contemporary Canadian Authors*
CD = *Contemporary Dramatists*
CDALB = *Concise Dictionary of American Literary Biography*

CDALBS = *Concise Dictionary of American Literary Biography Supplement*

CDBLB = *Concise Dictionary of British Literary Biography*

CMW = *St. James Guide to Crime & Mystery Writers*

CN = *Contemporary Novelists*

CP = *Contemporary Poets*

CPW = *Contemporary Popular Writers*

CSW = *Contemporary Southern Writers*

CWD = *Contemporary Women Dramatists*

CWP = *Contemporary Women Poets*

CWRI = *St. James Guide to Children's Writers*

CWW = *Contemporary World Writers*

DA = *DISCovering Authors*

DA3 = *DISCovering Authors 3.0*

DAB = *DISCovering Authors: British Edition*

DAC = *DISCovering Authors: Canadian Edition*

DAM = *DISCovering Authors: Modules*

   DRAM: *Dramatists Module;* **MST:** *Most-studied Authors Module;*

   MULT: *Multicultural Authors Module;* **NOV:** *Novelists Module;*

   POET: *Poets Module;* **POP:** *Popular Fiction and Genre Authors Module*

DFS = *Drama for Students*

DLB = *Dictionary of Literary Biography*

DLBD = *Dictionary of Literary Biography Documentary Series*

DLBY = *Dictionary of Literary Biography Yearbook*

DNFS = *Literature of Developing Nations for Students*

EFS = *Epics for Students*

EXPN = *Exploring Novels*

EXPP = *Exploring Poetry*

EXPS = *Exploring Short Stories*

EW = *European Writers*

FANT = *St. James Guide to Fantasy Writers*

FW = *Feminist Writers*

GFL = *Guide to French Literature,* Beginnings to 1789, 1798 to the Present

GLL = *Gay and Lesbian Literature*

HGG = *St. James Guide to Horror, Ghost & Gothic Writers*

HW = *Hispanic Writers*

IDFW = *International Dictionary of Films and Filmmakers: Writers and Production Artists*

IDTP = *International Dictionary of Theatre: Playwrights*

LAIT = *Literature and Its Times*

LAW = *Latin American Writers*

JRDA = *Junior DISCovering Authors*

MAICYA = *Major Authors and Illustrators for Children and Young Adults*

MAICYAS = *Major Authors and Illustrators for Children and Young Adults Supplement*

MAWW = *Modern American Women Writers*

MJW = *Modern Japanese Writers*

MTCW = *Major 20th-Century Writers*

NCFS = *Nonfiction Classics for Students*

NFS = *Novels for Students*

PAB = *Poets: American and British*

PFS = *Poetry for Students*

RGAL = *Reference Guide to American Literature*

RGEL = *Reference Guide to English Literature*

RGSF = *Reference Guide to Short Fiction*

RGWL = *Reference Guide to World Literature*

RHW = *Twentieth-Century Romance and Historical Writers*

SAAS = *Something about the Author Autobiography Series*

SATA = *Something about the Author*

SFW = *St. James Guide to Science Fiction Writers*

SSFS = *Short Stories for Students*

TCWW = *Twentieth-Century Western Writers*

WLIT = *World Literature and Its Times*

WP = *World Poets*

YABC = *Yesterday's Authors of Books for Children*

YAW = *St. James Guide to Young Adult Writers*

Literary Criticism Series
Cumulative Author Index

Aleshkovsky, Yuz .... **CLC 44**
See Aleshkovsky, Joseph
See also DLB 317

Alexander, Lloyd (Chudley) 1924- ... **CLC 35**
See also AAYA 1, 27; BPFB 1; BYA 5, 6,
7, 9, 10, 11; CA 1-4R; CANR 1, 24, 38,
55, 113; CLR 1, 5, 48; CWRI 5; DLB 52;
FANT; JRDA; MAICYA 1, 2; MAICYAS
1; MTCW 1; SAAS 19; SATA 3, 49, 81,
129, 135; SUFW; TUS; WYA; YAW

Alexander, Meena 1951- .... **CLC 121**
See also CA 115; CANR 38, 70, 146; CP 5,
6, 7; CWP; DLB 323; FW

Alexander, Samuel 1859-1938 .... **TCLC 77**

Alexeiev, Konstantin
See Stanislavsky, Constantin

Alexeyev, Constantin Sergeivich
See Stanislavsky, Constantin

Alexeyev, Konstantin Sergeyevich
See Stanislavsky, Constantin

Alexie, Sherman 1966- .... **CLC 96, 154;
NNAL; PC 53**
See also AAYA 28; BYA 15; CA 138;
CANR 65, 95, 133; CN 7; DA3; DAM
MULT; DLB 175, 206, 278; LATS 1:2;
MTCW 2; MTFW 2005; NFS 17; SSFS
18

al-Farabi 870(?)-950 .... **CMLC 58**
See also DLB 115

Alfau, Felipe 1902-1999 .... **CLC 66**
See also CA 137

Alfieri, Vittorio 1749-1803 .... **NCLC 101**
See also EW 4; RGWL 2, 3; WLIT 7

Alfonso X 1221-1284 .... **CMLC 78**

Alfred, Jean Gaston
See Ponge, Francis

Alger, Horatio, Jr. 1832-1899 .... **NCLC 8, 83**
See also CLR 87; DLB 42; LAIT 2; RGAL
4; SATA 16; TUS

Al-Ghazali, Muhammad ibn Muhammad
1058-1111 .... **CMLC 50**
See also DLB 115

Algren, Nelson 1909-1981 ..... **CLC 4, 10, 33;
SSC 33**
See also AMWS 9; BPFB 1; CA 13-16R;
CAAS 103; CANR 20, 61; CDALB 1941-
1968; CN 1, 2; DLB 9; DLBY 1981,
1982, 2000; EWL 3; MAL 5; MTCW 1,
2; MTFW 2005; RGAL 4; RGSF 2

**al-Hariri, al-Qasim ibn 'Ali Abu
Muhammad al-Basri**
1054-1122 .... **CMLC 63**
See also RGWL 3

Ali, Ahmed 1908-1998 .... **CLC 69**
See also CA 25-28R; CANR 15, 34; CN 1,
2, 3, 4, 5; DLB 323; EWL 3

Ali, Tariq 1943- .... **CLC 173**
See also CA 25-28R; CANR 10, 99, 161

Alighieri, Dante
See Dante
See also WLIT 7

al-Kindi, Abu Yusuf Ya'qub ibn Ishaq c.
801-c. 873 .... **CMLC 80**

Allan, John B.
See Westlake, Donald E.

Allan, Sidney
See Hartmann, Sadakichi

Allan, Sydney
See Hartmann, Sadakichi

Allard, Janet .... **CLC 59**

Allen, Edward 1948- .... **CLC 59**

Allen, Fred 1894-1956 .... **TCLC 87**

Allen, Paula Gunn 1939- .... **CLC 84, 202;
NNAL**
See also AMWS 4; CA 143; CAAE 112;
CANR 63, 130; CWP; DA3; DAM
MULT; DLB 175; FW; MTCW 2; MTFW
2005; RGAL 4; TCWW 2

Allen, Roland
See Ayckbourn, Alan

Allen, Sarah A.
See Hopkins, Pauline Elizabeth

Allen, Sidney H.
See Hartmann, Sadakichi

Allen, Woody 1935- .... **CLC 16, 52, 195**
See also AAYA 10, 51; AMWS 15; CA 33-
36R; CANR 27, 38, 63, 128; DAM POP;
DLB 44; MTCW 1; SSFS 21

Allende, Isabel 1942- ... **CLC 39, 57, 97, 170;
HLC 1; SSC 65; WLCS**
See also AAYA 18, 70; CA 130; CAAE 125;
CANR 51, 74, 129; CDWLB 3; CLR 99;
CWW 2; DA3; DAM MULT, NOV; DLB
145; DNFS 1; EWL 3; FL 1:5; FW; HW
1, 2; INT CA-130; LAIT 5; LAWS 1;
LMFS 2; MTCW 1, 2; MTFW 2005;
NCFS 1; NFS 6, 18; RGSF 2; RGWL 3;
SATA 163; SSFS 11, 16; WLIT 1

Alleyn, Ellen
See Rossetti, Christina

Alleyne, Carla D. .... **CLC 65**

Allingham, Margery (Louise)
1904-1966 .... **CLC 19**
See also CA 5-8R; CAAS 25-28R; CANR
4, 58; CMW 4; DLB 77; MSW; MTCW
1, 2

Allingham, William 1824-1889 ...... **NCLC 25**
See also DLB 35; RGEL 2

Allison, Dorothy E. 1949- .... **CLC 78, 153**
See also AAYA 53; CA 140; CANR 66, 107;
CN 7; CSW; DA3; FW; MTCW 2; MTFW
2005; NFS 11; RGAL 4

Alloula, Malek .... **CLC 65**

Allston, Washington 1779-1843 .... **NCLC 2**
See also DLB 1, 235

Almedingen, E. M. .... **CLC 12**
See Almedingen, Martha Edith von
See also SATA 3

Almedingen, Martha Edith von 1898-1971
See Almedingen, E. M.
See also CA 1-4R; CANR 1

Almodovar, Pedro 1949(?)- .... **CLC 114, 229;
HLCS 1**
See also CA 133; CANR 72, 151; HW 2

Almqvist, Carl Jonas Love
1793-1866 .... **NCLC 42**

**al-Mutanabbi, Ahmad ibn al-Husayn Abu
al-Tayyib al-Jufi al-Kindi**
915-965 .... **CMLC 66**
See Mutanabbi, Al-
See also RGWL 3

Alonso, Damaso 1898-1990 .... **CLC 14**
See also CA 131; CAAE 110; CAAS 130;
CANR 72; DLB 108; EWL 3; HW 1, 2

Alov
See Gogol, Nikolai (Vasilyevich)

al'Sadaawi, Nawal
See El Saadawi, Nawal
See also FW

al-Shaykh, Hanan 1945- .... **CLC 218**
See Shaykh, al- Hanan
See also CA 135; CANR 111; WLIT 6

Al Siddik
See Rolfe, Frederick (William Serafino Austin Lewis Mary)
See also GLL 1; RGEL 2

Alta 1942- .... **CLC 19**
See also CA 57-60

Alter, Robert B. 1935- .... **CLC 34**
See also CA 49-52; CANR 1, 47, 100, 160

Alter, Robert Bernard
See Alter, Robert B.

Alther, Lisa 1944- .... **CLC 7, 41**
See also BPFB 1; CA 65-68; 30; CANR 12,
30, 51; CN 4, 5, 6, 7; CSW; GLL 2;
MTCW 1

Althusser, L.
See Althusser, Louis

Althusser, Louis 1918-1990 .... **CLC 106**
See also CA 131; CAAS 132; CANR 102;
DLB 242

Altman, Robert 1925-2006 .... **CLC 16, 116**
See also CA 73-76; CAAS 254; CANR 43

Alurista .... **HLCS 1; PC 34**
See Urista (Heredia), Alberto (Baltazar)
See also CA 45-48R; DLB 82; LLW

Alvarez, A. 1929- .... **CLC 5, 13**
See also CA 1-4R; CANR 3, 33, 63, 101,
134; CN 3, 4, 5, 6; CP 1, 2, 3, 4, 5, 6, 7;
DLB 14, 40; MTFW 2005

Alvarez, Alejandro Rodriguez 1903-1965
See Casona, Alejandro
See also CA 131; CAAS 93-96; HW 1

Alvarez, Julia 1950- .... **CLC 93; HLCS 1**
See also AAYA 25; AMWS 7; CA 147;
CANR 69, 101, 133; DA3; DLB 282;
LATS 1:2; LLW; MTCW 2; MTFW 2005;
NFS 5, 9; SATA 129; WLIT 1

Alvaro, Corrado 1896-1956 .... **TCLC 60**
See also CA 163; DLB 264; EWL 3

Amado, Jorge 1912-2001 ... **CLC 13, 40, 106,
232; HLC 1**
See also CA 77-80; CAAS 201; CANR 35,
74, 135; CWW 2; DAM MULT, NOV;
DLB 113, 307; EWL 3; HW 2; LAW;
LAWS 1; MTCW 1, 2; MTFW 2005;
RGWL 2, 3; TWA; WLIT 1

Ambler, Eric 1909-1998 .... **CLC 4, 6, 9**
See also BRWS 4; CA 9-12R; CAAS 171;
CANR 7, 38, 74; CMW 4; CN 1, 2, 3, 4,
5, 6; DLB 77; MSW; MTCW 1, 2; TEA

Ambrose, Stephen E. 1936-2002 .... **CLC 145**
See also AAYA 44; CA 1-4R; CAAS 209;
CANR 3, 43, 57, 83, 105; MTFW 2005;
NCFS 2; SATA 40, 138

Amichai, Yehuda 1924-2000 .. **CLC 9, 22, 57,
116; PC 38**
See also CA 85-88; CAAS 189; CANR 46,
60, 99, 132; CWW 2; EWL 3; MTCW 1,
2; MTFW 2005; PFS 24; RGHL; WLIT 6

Amichai, Yehudah
See Amichai, Yehuda

Amiel, Henri Frederic 1821-1881 .... **NCLC 4**
See also DLB 217

Amis, Kingsley 1922-1995 . **CLC 1, 2, 3, 5, 8,
13, 40, 44, 129**
See also AITN 2; BPFB 1; BRWS 2; CA
9-12R; CAAS 150; CANR 8, 28, 54; CD-
BLB 1945-1960; CN 1, 2, 3, 4, 5, 6; CP
1, 2, 3, 4; DA; DA3; DAB; DAC; DAM
MST, NOV; DLB 15, 27, 100, 139, 326;
DLBY 1996; EWL 3; HGG; INT
CANR-8; MTCW 1, 2; MTFW 2005;
RGEL 2; RGSF 2; SFW 4

Amis, Martin 1949- ... **CLC 4, 9, 38, 62, 101,
213**
See also BEST 90:3; BRWS 4; CA 65-68;
CANR 8, 27, 54, 73, 95, 132; CN 5, 6, 7;
DA3; DLB 14, 194; INT CANR-
27; MTCW 2; MTFW 2005

Ammianus Marcellinus c. 330-c.
395 .... **CMLC 60**
See also AW 2; DLB 211

Ammons, A.R. 1926-2001 .. **CLC 2, 3, 5, 8, 9,
25, 57, 108; PC 16**
See also AITN 1; AMWS 7; CA 9-12R;
CAAS 193; CANR 6, 36, 51, 73, 107,
156; CP 1, 2, 3, 4, 5, 6, 7; CSW; DAM
POET; DLB 5, 165; EWL 3; MAL 5;
MTCW 1, 2; PFS 19; RGAL 4; TCLE 1:1

Ammons, Archie Randolph
See Ammons, A.R.

Amo, Tauraatua i
See Adams, Henry (Brooks)

Amory, Thomas 1691(?)-1788 .... **LC 48**
See also DLB 39

Aragon, Louis 1897-1982 .... **CLC 3, 22; TCLC 123**
   See also CA 69-72; CAAS 108; CANR 28, 71; DAM NOV, POET; DLB 72, 258; EW 11; EWL 3; GFL 1789 to the Present; GLL 2; LMFS 2; MTCW 1, 2; RGWL 2, 3

Arany, Janos 1817-1882 .... **NCLC 34**

Aranyos, Kakay 1847-1910
   See Mikszath, Kalman

Aratus of Soli c. 315B.C.-c. 240B.C. .... **CMLC 64**
   See also DLB 176

Arbuthnot, John 1667-1735 .... **LC 1**
   See also DLB 101

Archer, Herbert Winslow
   See Mencken, H(enry) L(ouis)

Archer, Jeffrey 1940- .... **CLC 28**
   See also AAYA 16; BEST 89:3; BPFB 1; CA 77-80; CANR 22, 52, 95, 136; CPW; DA3; DAM POP; INT CANR-22; MTFW 2005

Archer, Jeffrey Howard
   See Archer, Jeffrey

Archer, Jules 1915- .... **CLC 12**
   See also CA 9-12R; CANR 6, 69; SAAS 5; SATA 4, 85

Archer, Lee
   See Ellison, Harlan

Archilochus c. 7th cent. B.C.- .... **CMLC 44**
   See also DLB 176

Arden, John 1930- .... **CLC 6, 13, 15**
   See also BRWS 2; CA 13-16R; 4; CANR 31, 65, 67, 124; CBD; CD 5, 6; DAM DRAM; DFS 9; DLB 13, 245; EWL 3; MTCW 1

Arenas, Reinaldo 1943-1990 .. **CLC 41; HLC 1**
   See also CA 128; CAAE 124; CAAS 133; CANR 73, 106; DAM MULT; DLB 145; EWL 3; GLL 2; HW 1; LAW; LAWS 1; MTCW 2; MTFW 2005; RGSF 2; RGWL 3; WLIT 1

Arendt, Hannah 1906-1975 .... **CLC 66, 98**
   See also CA 17-20R; CAAS 61-64; CANR 26, 60; DLB 242; MTCW 1, 2

Aretino, Pietro 1492-1556 .... **LC 12**
   See also RGWL 2, 3

Arghezi, Tudor .... **CLC 80**
   See Theodorescu, Ion N.
   See also CA 167; CDWLB 4; DLB 220; EWL 3

Arguedas, Jose Maria 1911-1969 .... **CLC 10, 18; HLCS 1; TCLC 147**
   See also CA 89-92; CANR 73; DLB 113; EWL 3; HW 1; LAW; RGWL 2, 3; WLIT 1

Argueta, Manlio 1936- .... **CLC 31**
   See also CA 131; CANR 73; CWW 2; DLB 145; EWL 3; HW 1; RGWL 3

Arias, Ron 1941- .... **HLC 1**
   See also CA 131; CANR 81, 136; DAM MULT; DLB 82; HW 1, 2; MTCW 2; MTFW 2005

Ariosto, Lodovico
   See Ariosto, Ludovico
   See also WLIT 7

Ariosto, Ludovico 1474-1533 ... **LC 6, 87; PC 42**
   See Ariosto, Lodovico
   See also EW 2; RGWL 2, 3

Aristides
   See Epstein, Joseph

Aristophanes 450B.C.-385B.C. .... **CMLC 4, 51; DC 2; WLCS**
   See also AW 1; CDWLB 1; DA; DA3; DAB; DAC; DAM DRAM, MST; DFS 10; DLB 176; LMFS 1; RGWL 2, 3; TWA; WLIT 8

Aristotle 384B.C.-322B.C. .... **CMLC 31; WLCS**
   See also AW 1; CDWLB 1; DA; DA3; DAB; DAC; DAM MST; DLB 176; RGWL 2, 3; TWA; WLIT 8

Arlt, Roberto (Godofredo Christophersen) 1900-1942 .... **HLC 1; TCLC 29**
   See also CA 131; CAAE 123; CANR 67; DAM MULT; DLB 305; EWL 3; HW 1, 2; IDTP; LAW

Armah, Ayi Kwei 1939- . **BLC 1; CLC 5, 33, 136**
   See also AFW; BRWS 10; BW 1; CA 61-64; CANR 21, 64; CDWLB 3; CN 1, 2, 3, 4, 5, 6, 7; DAM MULT, POET; DLB 117; EWL 3; MTCW 1; WLIT 2

Armatrading, Joan 1950- .... **CLC 17**
   See also CA 186; CAAE 114

Armin, Robert 1568(?)-1615(?) .... **LC 120**

Armitage, Frank
   See Carpenter, John (Howard)

Armstrong, Jeannette (C.) 1948- .... **NNAL**
   See also CA 149; CCA 1; CN 6, 7; DAC; SATA 102

Arnette, Robert
   See Silverberg, Robert

Arnim, Achim von (Ludwig Joachim von Arnim) 1781-1831 .. **NCLC 5, 159; SSC 29**
   See also DLB 90

Arnim, Bettina von 1785-1859 ...... **NCLC 38, 123**
   See also DLB 90; RGWL 2, 3

Arnold, Matthew 1822-1888 ..... **NCLC 6, 29, 89, 126; PC 5; WLC 1**
   See also BRW 5; CDBLB 1832-1890; DA; DAB; DAC; DAM MST, POET; DLB 32, 57; EXPP; PAB; PFS 2; TEA; WP

Arnold, Thomas 1795-1842 .... **NCLC 18**
   See also DLB 55

Arnow, Harriette (Louisa) Simpson 1908-1986 .... **CLC 2, 7, 18**
   See also BPFB 1; CA 9-12R; CAAS 118; CANR 14; CN 2, 3, 4; DLB 6; FW; MTCW 1, 2; RHW; SATA 42; SATA-Obit 47

Arouet, Francois-Marie
   See Voltaire

Arp, Hans
   See Arp, Jean

Arp, Jean 1887-1966 .... **CLC 5; TCLC 115**
   See also CA 81-84; CAAS 25-28R; CANR 42, 77; EW 10

Arrabal
   See Arrabal, Fernando

Arrabal (Teran), Fernando
   See Arrabal, Fernando
   See also CWW 2

Arrabal, Fernando 1932- ... **CLC 2, 9, 18, 58**
   See Arrabal (Teran), Fernando
   See also CA 9-12R; CANR 15; DLB 321; EWL 3; LMFS 2

Arreola, Juan Jose 1918-2001 .... **CLC 147; HLC 1; SSC 38**
   See also CA 131; CAAE 113; CAAS 200; CANR 81; CWW 2; DAM MULT; DLB 113; DNFS 2; EWL 3; HW 1, 2; LAW; RGSF 2

Arrian c. 89(?)-c. 155(?) .... **CMLC 43**
   See also DLB 176

Arrick, Fran .... **CLC 30**
   See Gaberman, Judie Angell
   See also BYA 6

Arrley, Richmond
   See Delany, Samuel R., Jr.

Artaud, Antonin (Marie Joseph) 1896-1948 .... **DC 14; TCLC 3, 36**
   See also CA 149; CAAE 104; DA3; DAM DRAM; DFS 22; DLB 258, 321; EW 11; EWL 3; GFL 1789 to the Present; MTCW 2; MTFW 2005; RGWL 2, 3

Arthur, Ruth M(abel) 1905-1979 ..... **CLC 12**
   See also CA 9-12R; CAAS 85-88; CANR 4; CWRI 5; SATA 7, 26

Artsybashev, Mikhail (Petrovich) 1878-1927 .... **TCLC 31**
   See also CA 170; DLB 295

Arundel, Honor (Morfydd) 1919-1973 .... **CLC 17**
   See also CA 21-22; CAAS 41-44R; CAP 2; CLR 35; CWRI 5; SATA 4; SATA-Obit 24

Arzner, Dorothy 1900-1979 .... **CLC 98**

Asch, Sholem 1880-1957 .... **TCLC 3**
   See also CAAE 105; DLB 333; EWL 3; GLL 2; RGHL

Ascham, Roger 1516(?)-1568 .... **LC 101**
   See also DLB 236

Ash, Shalom
   See Asch, Sholem

Ashbery, John 1927- ... **CLC 2, 3, 4, 6, 9, 13, 15, 25, 41, 77, 125, 221; PC 26**
   See Berry, Jonas
   See also AMWS 3; CA 5-8R; CANR 9, 37, 66, 102, 132; CP 1, 2, 3, 4, 5, 6, 7; DA3; DAM POET; DLB 5, 165; DLBY 1981; EWL 3; INT CANR-9; MAL 5; MTCW 1, 2; MTFW 2005; PAB; PFS 11; RGAL 4; TCLE 1:1; WP

Ashdown, Clifford
   See Freeman, R(ichard) Austin

Ashe, Gordon
   See Creasey, John

Ashton-Warner, Sylvia (Constance) 1908-1984 .... **CLC 19**
   See also CA 69-72; CAAS 112; CANR 29; CN 1, 2, 3; MTCW 1, 2

Asimov, Isaac 1920-1992 ..... **CLC 1, 3, 9, 19, 26, 76, 92**
   See also AAYA 13; BEST 90:2; BPFB 1; BYA 4, 6, 7, 9; CA 1-4R; CAAS 137; CANR 2, 19, 36, 60, 125; CLR 12, 79; CMW 4; CN 1, 2, 3, 4, 5; CPW; DA3; DAM POP; DLB 8; DLBY 1992; INT CANR-19; JRDA; LAIT 5; LMFS 2; MAICYA 1, 2; MAL 5; MTCW 1, 2; MTFW 2005; RGAL 4; SATA 1, 26, 74; SCFW 1, 2; SFW 4; SSFS 17; TUS; YAW

Askew, Anne 1521(?)-1546 .... **LC 81**
   See also DLB 136

Assis, Joaquim Maria Machado de
   See Machado de Assis, Joaquim Maria

Astell, Mary 1666-1731 .... **LC 68**
   See also DLB 252; FW

Astley, Thea (Beatrice May) 1925-2004 .... **CLC 41**
   See also CA 65-68; CAAS 229; CANR 11, 43, 78; CN 1, 2, 3, 4, 5, 6, 7; DLB 289; EWL 3

Astley, William 1855-1911
   See Warung, Price

Aston, James
   See White, T(erence) H(anbury)

Asturias, Miguel Angel 1899-1974 .... **CLC 3, 8, 13; HLC 1; TCLC 184**
   See also CA 25-28; CAAS 49-52; CANR 32; CAP 2; CDWLB 3; DA3; DAM MULT, NOV; DLB 113, 290, 329; EWL 3; HW 1; LAW; LMFS 2; MTCW 1, 2; RGWL 2, 3; WLIT 1

Atares, Carlos Saura
   See Saura (Atares), Carlos

Athanasius c. 295-c. 373 .... **CMLC 48**

Becker, Jurek 1937-1997 .... **CLC 7, 19**
See also CA 85-88; CAAS 157; CANR 60, 117; CWW 2; DLB 75, 299; EWL 3; RGHL

Becker, Walter 1950- .... **CLC 26**

Becket, Thomas a 1118(?)-1170 .... **CMLC 83**

Beckett, Samuel 1906-1989 ... **CLC 1, 2, 3, 4, 6, 9, 10, 11, 14, 18, 29, 57, 59, 83; DC 22; SSC 16, 74; TCLC 145; WLC 1**
See also BRWC 2; BRWR 1; BRWS 1; CA 5-8R; CAAS 130; CANR 33, 61; CBD; CDBLB 1945-1960; CN 1, 2, 3, 4; CP 1, 2, 3, 4; DA; DA3; DAB; DAC; DAM DRAM, MST, NOV; DFS 2, 7, 18; DLB 13, 15, 233, 319, 321, 329; DLBY 1990; EWL 3; GFL 1789 to the Present; LATS 1:2; LMFS 2; MTCW 1, 2; MTFW 2005; RGSF 2; RGWL 2, 3; SSFS 15; TEA; WLIT 4

Beckford, William 1760-1844 .... **NCLC 16**
See also BRW 3; DLB 39, 213; GL 2; HGG; LMFS 1; SUFW

Beckham, Barry (Earl) 1944- .... **BLC 1**
See also BW 1; CA 29-32R; CANR 26, 62; CN 1, 2, 3, 4, 5, 6; DAM MULT; DLB 33

Beckman, Gunnel 1910- .... **CLC 26**
See also CA 33-36R; CANR 15, 114; CLR 25; MAICYA 1, 2; SAAS 9; SATA 6

Becque, Henri 1837-1899 .... **DC 21; NCLC 3**
See also DLB 192; GFL 1789 to the Present

Becquer, Gustavo Adolfo
1836-1870 .... **HLCS 1; NCLC 106**
See also DAM MULT

Beddoes, Thomas Lovell 1803-1849 .. **DC 15; NCLC 3, 154**
See also BRWS 11; DLB 96

Bede c. 673-735 .... **CMLC 20**
See also DLB 146; TEA

Bedford, Denton R. 1907-(?) .... **NNAL**

Bedford, Donald F.
See Fearing, Kenneth (Flexner)

Beecher, Catharine Esther
1800-1878 .... **NCLC 30**
See also DLB 1, 243

Beecher, John 1904-1980 .... **CLC 6**
See also AITN 1; CA 5-8R; CAAS 105; CANR 8; CP 1, 2, 3

Beer, Johann 1655-1700 .... **LC 5**
See also DLB 168

Beer, Patricia 1924- .... **CLC 58**
See also CA 61-64; CAAS 183; CANR 13, 46; CP 1, 2, 3, 4, 5, 6; CWP; DLB 40; FW

Beerbohm, Max
See Beerbohm, (Henry) Max(imilian)

Beerbohm, (Henry) Max(imilian)
1872-1956 .... **TCLC 1, 24**
See also BRWS 2; CA 154; CAAE 104; CANR 79; DLB 34, 100; FANT; MTCW 2

Beer-Hofmann, Richard
1866-1945 .... **TCLC 60**
See also CA 160; DLB 81

Beg, Shemus
See Stephens, James

Begiebing, Robert J(ohn) 1946- .... **CLC 70**
See also CA 122; CANR 40, 88

Begley, Louis 1933- .... **CLC 197**
See also CA 140; CANR 98; DLB 299; RGHL; TCLE 1:1

Behan, Brendan (Francis)
1923-1964 .... **CLC 1, 8, 11, 15, 79**
See also BRWS 2; CA 73-76; CANR 33, 121; CBD; CDBLB 1945-1960; DAM DRAM; DFS 7; DLB 13, 233; EWL 3; MTCW 1, 2

Behn, Aphra 1640(?)-1689 .. **DC 4; LC 1, 30, 42, 135; PC 13; WLC 1**
See also BRWS 3; DA; DA3; DAB; DAC; DAM DRAM, MST, NOV, POET; DFS 16; DLB 39, 80, 131; FW; TEA; WLIT 3

Behrman, S(amuel) N(athaniel)
1893-1973 .... **CLC 40**
See also CA 13-16; CAAS 45-48; CAD; CAP 1; DLB 7, 44; IDFW 3; MAL 5; RGAL 4

Bekederemo, J. P. Clark
See Clark Bekederemo, J.P.
See also CD 6

Belasco, David 1853-1931 .... **TCLC 3**
See also CA 168; CAAE 104; DLB 7; MAL 5; RGAL 4

Belcheva, Elisaveta Lyubomirova
1893-1991 .... **CLC 10**
See Bagryana, Elisaveta

Beldone, Phil ''Cheech''
See Ellison, Harlan

Beleno
See Azuela, Mariano

Belinski, Vissarion Grigoryevich
1811-1848 .... **NCLC 5**
See also DLB 198

Belitt, Ben 1911- .... **CLC 22**
See also CA 13-16R; 4; CANR 7, 77; CP 1, 2, 3, 4, 5, 6; DLB 5

Belknap, Jeremy 1744-1798 .... **LC 115**
See also DLB 30, 37

Bell, Gertrude (Margaret Lowthian)
1868-1926 .... **TCLC 67**
See also CA 167; CANR 110; DLB 174

Bell, J. Freeman
See Zangwill, Israel

Bell, James Madison 1826-1902 .... **BLC 1; TCLC 43**
See also BW 1; CA 124; CAAE 122; DAM MULT; DLB 50

Bell, Madison Smartt 1957- ..... **CLC 41, 102, 223**
See also AMWS 10; BPFB 1; CA 183; 111, 183; CANR 28, 54, 73, 134; CN 5, 6, 7; CSW; DLB 218, 278; MTCW 2; MTFW 2005

Bell, Marvin (Hartley) 1937- .... **CLC 8, 31**
See also CA 21-24R; 14; CANR 59, 102; CP 1, 2, 3, 4, 5, 6, 7; DAM POET; DLB 5; MAL 5; MTCW 1; PFS 25

Bell, W. L. D.
See Mencken, H(enry) L(ouis)

Bellamy, Atwood C.
See Mencken, H(enry) L(ouis)

Bellamy, Edward 1850-1898 ..... **NCLC 4, 86, 147**
See also DLB 12; NFS 15; RGAL 4; SFW 4

Belli, Gioconda 1948- .... **HLCS 1**
See also CA 152; CANR 143; CWW 2; DLB 290; EWL 3; RGWL 3

Bellin, Edward J.
See Kuttner, Henry

Bello, Andres 1781-1865 .... **NCLC 131**
See also LAW

Belloc, (Joseph) Hilaire (Pierre Sebastien Rene Swanton) 1870-1953 .... **PC 24; TCLC 7, 18**
See also CA 152; CAAE 106; CLR 102; CWRI 5; DAM POET; DLB 19, 100, 141, 174; EWL 3; MTCW 2; MTFW 2005; SATA 112; WCH; YABC 1

Belloc, Joseph Peter Rene Hilaire
See Belloc, (Joseph) Hilaire (Pierre Sebastien Rene Swanton)

Belloc, Joseph Pierre Hilaire
See Belloc, (Joseph) Hilaire (Pierre Sebastien Rene Swanton)

Belloc, M. A.
See Lowndes, Marie Adelaide (Belloc)

Belloc-Lowndes, Mrs.
See Lowndes, Marie Adelaide (Belloc)

Bellow, Saul 1915-2005 ...... **CLC 1, 2, 3, 6, 8, 10, 13, 15, 25, 33, 34, 63, 79, 190, 200; SSC 14; WLC 1**
See also AITN 2; AMW; AMWC 2; AMWR 2; BEST 89:3; BPFB 1; CA 5-8R; CAAS 238; CABS 1; CANR 29, 53, 95, 132; CDALB 1941-1968; CN 1, 2, 3, 4, 5, 6, 7; DA; DA3; DAB; DAC; DAM MST, NOV, POP; DLB 2, 28, 299, 329; DLBD 3; DLBY 1982; EWL 3; MAL 5; MTCW 1, 2; MTFW 2005; NFS 4, 14; RGAL 4; RGHL; RGSF 2; SSFS 12, 22; TUS

Belser, Reimond Karel Maria de 1929-
See Ruyslinck, Ward
See also CA 152

Bely, Andrey .... **PC 11; TCLC 7**
See Bugayev, Boris Nikolayevich
See also DLB 295; EW 9; EWL 3

Belyi, Andrei
See Bugayev, Boris Nikolayevich
See also RGWL 2, 3

Bembo, Pietro 1470-1547 .... **LC 79**
See also RGWL 2, 3

Benary, Margot
See Benary-Isbert, Margot

Benary-Isbert, Margot 1889-1979 .... **CLC 12**
See also CA 5-8R; CAAS 89-92; CANR 4, 72; CLR 12; MAICYA 1, 2; SATA 2; SATA-Obit 21

Benavente (y Martinez), Jacinto
1866-1954 ... **DC 26; HLCS 1; TCLC 3**
See also CA 131; CAAE 106; CANR 81; DAM DRAM, MULT; DLB 329; EWL 3; GLL 2; HW 1, 2; MTCW 1, 2

Benchley, Peter 1940-2006 .... **CLC 4, 8**
See also AAYA 14; AITN 2; BPFB 1; CA 17-20R; CAAS 248; CANR 12, 35, 66, 115; CPW; DAM NOV, POP; HGG; MTCW 1, 2; MTFW 2005; SATA 3, 89, 164

Benchley, Peter Bradford
See Benchley, Peter

Benchley, Robert (Charles)
1889-1945 .... **TCLC 1, 55**
See also CA 153; CAAE 105; DLB 11; MAL 5; RGAL 4

Benda, Julien 1867-1956 .... **TCLC 60**
See also CA 154; CAAE 120; GFL 1789 to the Present

Benedict, Ruth 1887-1948 .... **TCLC 60**
See also CA 158; CANR 146; DLB 246

Benedict, Ruth Fulton
See Benedict, Ruth

Benedikt, Michael 1935- .... **CLC 4, 14**
See also CA 13-16R; CANR 7; CP 1, 2, 3, 4, 5, 6, 7; DLB 5

Benet, Juan 1927-1993 .... **CLC 28**
See also CA 143; EWL 3

Benet, Stephen Vincent 1898-1943 ..... **PC 64; SSC 10, 86; TCLC 7**
See also AMWS 11; CA 152; CAAE 104; DA3; DAM POET; DLB 4, 48, 102, 249, 284; DLBY 1997; EWL 3; HGG; MAL 5; MTCW 2; MTFW 2005; RGAL 4; RGSF 2; SSFS 22; SUFW; WP; YABC 1

Benet, William Rose 1886-1950 ..... **TCLC 28**
See also CA 152; CAAE 118; DAM POET; DLB 45; RGAL 4

Benford, Gregory (Albert) 1941- ..... **CLC 52**
See also BPFB 1; CA 175; 69-72, 175; 27; CANR 12, 24, 49, 95, 134; CN 7; CSW; DLBY 1982; MTFW 2005; SCFW 2; SFW 4

Betjeman, John 1906-1984 ...... **CLC 2, 6, 10, 34, 43; PC 75**
See also BRW 7; CA 9-12R; CAAS 112; CANR 33, 56; CDBLB 1945-1960; CP 1, 2, 3; DA3; DAB; DAM MST, POET; DLB 20; DLBY 1984; EWL 3; MTCW 1, 2

Bettelheim, Bruno 1903-1990 .... **CLC 79; TCLC 143**
See also CA 81-84; CAAS 131; CANR 23, 61; DA3; MTCW 1, 2; RGHL

Betti, Ugo 1892-1953 .... **TCLC 5**
See also CA 155; CAAE 104; EWL 3; RGWL 2, 3

Betts, Doris (Waugh) 1932- ..... **CLC 3, 6, 28; SSC 45**
See also CA 13-16R; CANR 9, 66, 77; CN 6, 7; CSW; DLB 218; DLBY 1982; INT CANR-9; RGAL 4

Bevan, Alistair
See Roberts, Keith (John Kingston)

Bey, Pilaff
See Douglas, (George) Norman

Bialik, Chaim Nachman
1873-1934 .... **TCLC 25**
See Bialik, Hayyim Nahman
See also CA 170; EWL 3

Bialik, Hayyim Nahman
See Bialik, Chaim Nachman
See also WLIT 6

Bickerstaff, Isaac
See Swift, Jonathan

Bidart, Frank 1939- .... **CLC 33**
See also AMWS 15; CA 140; CANR 106; CP 5, 6, 7

Bienek, Horst 1930- .... **CLC 7, 11**
See also CA 73-76; DLB 75

Bierce, Ambrose (Gwinett)
1842-1914(?) ..... **SSC 9, 72; TCLC 1, 7, 44; WLC 1**
See also AAYA 55; AMW; BYA 11; CA 139; CAAE 104; CANR 78; CDALB 1865-1917; DA; DA3; DAC; DAM MST; DLB 11, 12, 23, 71, 74, 186; EWL 3; EXPS; HGG; LAIT 2; MAL 5; RGAL 4; RGSF 2; SSFS 9; SUFW 1

Biggers, Earl Derr 1884-1933 .... **TCLC 65**
See also CA 153; CAAE 108; DLB 306

Billiken, Bud
See Motley, Willard (Francis)

Billings, Josh
See Shaw, Henry Wheeler

Billington, (Lady) Rachel (Mary)
1942- .... **CLC 43**
See also AITN 2; CA 33-36R; CANR 44; CN 4, 5, 6, 7

Binchy, Maeve 1940- .... **CLC 153**
See also BEST 90:1; BPFB 1; CA 134; CAAE 127; CANR 50, 96, 134; CN 5, 6, 7; CPW; DA3; DAM POP; DLB 319; INT CA-134; MTCW 2; MTFW 2005; RHW

Binyon, T(imothy) J(ohn)
1936-2004 .... **CLC 34**
See also CA 111; CAAS 232; CANR 28, 140

Bion 335B.C.-245B.C. .... **CMLC 39**

Bioy Casares, Adolfo 1914-1999 ... **CLC 4, 8, 13, 88; HLC 1; SSC 17**
See Casares, Adolfo Bioy; Miranda, Javier; Sacastru, Martin
See also CA 29-32R; CAAS 177; CANR 19, 43, 66; CWW 2; DAM MULT; DLB 113; EWL 3; HW 1, 2; LAW; MTCW 1, 2; MTFW 2005

Birch, Allison .... **CLC 65**

Bird, Cordwainer
See Ellison, Harlan

Bird, Robert Montgomery
1806-1854 .... **NCLC 1**
See also DLB 202; RGAL 4

Birkerts, Sven 1951- .... **CLC 116**
See also CA 176; 133, 176; 29; CAAE 128; CANR 151; INT CA-133

Birney, (Alfred) Earle 1904-1995 .. **CLC 1, 4, 6, 11; PC 52**
See also CA 1-4R; CANR 5, 20; CN 1, 2, 3, 4; CP 1, 2, 3, 4, 5, 6; DAC; DAM MST, POET; DLB 88; MTCW 1; PFS 8; RGEL 2

Biruni, al 973-1048(?) .... **CMLC 28**

Bishop, Elizabeth 1911-1979 ..... **CLC 1, 4, 9, 13, 15, 32; PC 3, 34; TCLC 121**
See also AMWR 2; AMWS 1; CA 5-8R; CAAS 89-92; CABS 2; CANR 26, 61, 108; CDALB 1968-1988; CP 1, 2, 3; DA; DA3; DAC; DAM MST, POET; DLB 5, 169; EWL 3; GLL 2; MAL 5; MBL; MTCW 1, 2; PAB; PFS 6, 12; RGAL 4; SATA-Obit 24; TUS; WP

Bishop, John 1935- .... **CLC 10**
See also CA 105

Bishop, John Peale 1892-1944 ..... **TCLC 103**
See also CA 155; CAAE 107; DLB 4, 9, 45; MAL 5; RGAL 4

Bissett, Bill 1939- .... **CLC 18; PC 14**
See also CA 69-72; 19; CANR 15; CCA 1; CP 1, 2, 3, 4, 5, 6, 7; DLB 53; MTCW 1

Bissoondath, Neil (Devindra)
1955- .... **CLC 120**
See also CA 136; CANR 123; CN 6, 7; DAC

Bitov, Andrei (Georgievich) 1937- ... **CLC 57**
See also CA 142; DLB 302

Biyidi, Alexandre 1932-
See Beti, Mongo
See also BW 1, 3; CA 124; CAAE 114; CANR 81; DA3; MTCW 1, 2

Bjarme, Brynjolf
See Ibsen, Henrik (Johan)

Bjoernson, Bjoernstjerne (Martinius)
1832-1910 .... **TCLC 7, 37**
See also CAAE 104

Black, Benjamin
See Banville, John

Black, Robert
See Holdstock, Robert

Blackburn, Paul 1926-1971 .... **CLC 9, 43**
See also BG 1:2; CA 81-84; CAAS 33-36R; CANR 34; CP 1; DLB 16; DLBY 1981

Black Elk 1863-1950 .... **NNAL; TCLC 33**
See also CA 144; DAM MULT; MTCW 2; MTFW 2005; WP

Black Hawk 1767-1838 .... **NNAL**

Black Hobart
See Sanders, (James) Ed(ward)

Blacklin, Malcolm
See Chambers, Aidan

Blackmore, R(ichard) D(oddridge)
1825-1900 .... **TCLC 27**
See also CAAE 120; DLB 18; RGEL 2

Blackmur, R(ichard) P(almer)
1904-1965 .... **CLC 2, 24**
See also AMWS 2; CA 11-12; CAAS 25-28R; CANR 71; CAP 1; DLB 63; EWL 3; MAL 5

Black Tarantula
See Acker, Kathy

Blackwood, Algernon (Henry)
1869-1951 .... **TCLC 5**
See also CA 150; CAAE 105; DLB 153, 156, 178; HGG; SUFW 1

Blackwood, Caroline (Maureen)
1931-1996 .... **CLC 6, 9, 100**
See also BRWS 9; CA 85-88; CAAS 151; CANR 32, 61, 65; CN 3, 4, 5, 6; DLB 14, 207; HGG; MTCW 1

Blade, Alexander
See Hamilton, Edmond; Silverberg, Robert

Blaga, Lucian 1895-1961 .... **CLC 75**
See also CA 157; DLB 220; EWL 3

Blair, Eric (Arthur) 1903-1950 .... **TCLC 123**
See Orwell, George
See also CA 132; CAAE 104; DA; DA3; DAB; DAC; DAM MST, NOV; MTCW 1, 2; MTFW 2005; SATA 29

Blair, Hugh 1718-1800 .... **NCLC 75**

Blais, Marie-Claire 1939- .... **CLC 2, 4, 6, 13, 22**
See also CA 21-24R; 4; CANR 38, 75, 93; CWW 2; DAC; DAM MST; DLB 53; EWL 3; FW; MTCW 1, 2; MTFW 2005; TWA

Blaise, Clark 1940- .... **CLC 29**
See also AITN 2; CA 231; 53-56, 231; 3; CANR 5, 66, 106; CN 4, 5, 6, 7; DLB 53; RGSF 2

Blake, Fairley
See De Voto, Bernard (Augustine)

Blake, Nicholas
See Day Lewis, C(ecil)
See also DLB 77; MSW

Blake, Sterling
See Benford, Gregory (Albert)

Blake, William 1757-1827 . **NCLC 13, 37, 57, 127, 173; PC 12, 63; WLC 1**
See also AAYA 47; BRW 3; BRWR 1; CD-BLB 1789-1832; CLR 52; DA; DA3; DAB; DAC; DAM MST, POET; DLB 93, 163; EXPP; LATS 1:1; LMFS 1; MAI-CYA 1, 2; PAB; PFS 2, 12, 24; SATA 30; TEA; WCH; WLIT 3; WP

Blanchot, Maurice 1907-2003 .... **CLC 135**
See also CA 144; CAAE 117; CAAS 213; CANR 138; DLB 72, 296; EWL 3

Blasco Ibanez, Vicente 1867-1928 . **TCLC 12**
See Ibanez, Vicente Blasco
See also BPFB 1; CA 131; CAAE 110; CANR 81; DA3; DAM NOV; EW 8; EWL 3; HW 1, 2; MTCW 1

Blatty, William Peter 1928- .... **CLC 2**
See also CA 5-8R; CANR 9, 124; DAM POP; HGG

Bleeck, Oliver
See Thomas, Ross (Elmore)

Blessing, Lee (Knowlton) 1949- .... **CLC 54**
See also CA 236; CAD; CD 5, 6; DFS 23

Blight, Rose
See Greer, Germaine

Blish, James (Benjamin) 1921-1975 . **CLC 14**
See also BPFB 1; CA 1-4R; CAAS 57-60; CANR 3; CN 2; DLB 8; MTCW 1; SATA 66; SCFW 1, 2; SFW 4

Bliss, Frederick
See Card, Orson Scott

Bliss, Gillian
See Paton Walsh, Jill

Bliss, Reginald
See Wells, H(erbert) G(eorge)

Blixen, Karen (Christentze Dinesen)
1885-1962
See Dinesen, Isak
See also CA 25-28; CANR 22, 50; CAP 2; DA3; DLB 214; LMFS 1; MTCW 1, 2; SATA 44; SSFS 20

Bloch, Robert (Albert) 1917-1994 .... **CLC 33**
See also AAYA 29; CA 179; 5-8R, 179; 20; CAAS 146; CANR 5, 78; DA3; DLB 44; HGG; INT CANR-5; MTCW 2; SATA 12; SATA-Obit 82; SFW 4; SUFW 1, 2

Blok, Alexander (Alexandrovich)
1880-1921 .... **PC 21; TCLC 5**
See also CA 183; CAAE 104; DLB 295; EW 9; EWL 3; LMFS 2; RGWL 2, 3

Blom, Jan
See Breytenbach, Breyten

Bloom, Harold 1930- .... **CLC 24, 103, 221**
See also CA 13-16R; CANR 39, 75, 92, 133; DLB 67; EWL 3; MTCW 2; MTFW 2005; RGAL 4

Bloomfield, Aurelius
See Bourne, Randolph S(illiman)

Bloomfield, Robert 1766-1823 ..... **NCLC 145**
See also DLB 93

Blount, Roy (Alton), Jr. 1941- .... **CLC 38**
See also CA 53-56; CANR 10, 28, 61, 125; CSW; INT CANR-28; MTCW 1, 2; MTFW 2005

Blowsnake, Sam 1875-(?) .... **NNAL**

Bloy, Leon 1846-1917 .... **TCLC 22**
See also CA 183; CAAE 121; DLB 123; GFL 1789 to the Present

Blue Cloud, Peter (Aroniawenrate)
1933- .... **NNAL**
See also CA 117; CANR 40; DAM MULT

Bluggage, Oranthy
See Alcott, Louisa May

Blume, Judy (Sussman) 1938- .... **CLC 12, 30**
See also AAYA 3, 26; BYA 1, 8, 12; CA 29-32R; CANR 13, 37, 66, 124; CLR 2, 15, 69; CPW; DA3; DAM NOV, POP; DLB 52; JRDA; MAICYA 1, 2; MAICYAS 1; MTCW 1, 2; MTFW 2005; NFS 24; SATA 2, 31, 79, 142; WYA; YAW

Blunden, Edmund (Charles)
1896-1974 .... **CLC 2, 56; PC 66**
See also BRW 6; BRWS 11; CA 17-18; CAAS 45-48; CANR 54; CAP 2; CP 1, 2; DLB 20, 100, 155; MTCW 1; PAB

Bly, Robert (Elwood) 1926- .... **CLC 1, 2, 5, 10, 15, 38, 128; PC 39**
See also AMWS 4; CA 5-8R; CANR 41, 73, 125; CP 1, 2, 3, 4, 5, 6, 7; DA3; DAM POET; DLB 5; EWL 5; MAL 5; MTCW 1, 2; MTFW 2005; PFS 6, 17; RGAL 4

Boas, Franz 1858-1942 .... **TCLC 56**
See also CA 181; CAAE 115

Bobette
See Simenon, Georges (Jacques Christian)

Boccaccio, Giovanni 1313-1375 ... **CMLC 13, 57; SSC 10, 87**
See also EW 2; RGSF 2; RGWL 2, 3; TWA; WLIT 7

Bochco, Steven 1943- .... **CLC 35**
See also AAYA 11, 71; CA 138; CAAE 124

Bode, Sigmund
See O'Doherty, Brian

Bodel, Jean 1167(?)-1210 .... **CMLC 28**

Bodenheim, Maxwell 1892-1954 .... **TCLC 44**
See also CA 187; CAAE 110; DLB 9, 45; MAL 5; RGAL 4

Bodenheimer, Maxwell
See Bodenheim, Maxwell

Bodker, Cecil 1927-
See Bodker, Cecil

Bodker, Cecil 1927- .... **CLC 21**
See also CA 73-76; CANR 13, 44, 111; CLR 23; MAICYA 1, 2; SATA 14, 133

Boell, Heinrich (Theodor)
1917-1985 ..... **CLC 2, 3, 6, 9, 11, 15, 27, 32, 72; SSC 23; WLC 1**
See Boll, Heinrich (Theodor)
See also CA 21-24R; CAAS 116; CANR 24; DA; DA3; DAB; DAC; DAM MST, NOV; DLB 69; DLBY 1985; MTCW 1, 2; MTFW 2005; SSFS 20; TWA

Boerne, Alfred
See Doeblin, Alfred

Boethius c. 480-c. 524 .... **CMLC 15**
See also DLB 115; RGWL 2, 3; WLIT 8

Boff, Leonardo (Genezio Darci)
1938- .... **CLC 70; HLC 1**
See also CA 150; DAM MULT; HW 2

Bogan, Louise 1897-1970 .... **CLC 4, 39, 46, 93; PC 12**
See also AMWS 3; CA 73-76; CAAS 25-28R; CANR 33, 82; CP 1; DAM POET; DLB 45, 169; EWL 3; MAL 5; MBL; MTCW 1, 2; PFS 21; RGAL 4

Bogarde, Dirk
See Van Den Bogarde, Derek Jules Gaspard Ulric Niven
See also DLB 14

Bogosian, Eric 1953- .... **CLC 45, 141**
See also CA 138; CAD; CANR 102, 148; CD 5, 6

Bograd, Larry 1953- .... **CLC 35**
See also CA 93-96; CANR 57; SAAS 21; SATA 33, 89; WYA

Boiardo, Matteo Maria 1441-1494 .... **LC 6**

Boileau-Despreaux, Nicolas 1636-1711 . **LC 3**
See also DLB 268; EW 3; GFL Beginnings to 1789; RGWL 2, 3

Boissard, Maurice
See Leautaud, Paul

Bojer, Johan 1872-1959 .... **TCLC 64**
See also CA 189; EWL 3

Bok, Edward W(illiam)
1863-1930 .... **TCLC 101**
See also CA 217; DLB 91; DLBD 16

Boker, George Henry 1823-1890 . **NCLC 125**
See also RGAL 4

Boland, Eavan 1944- ... **CLC 40, 67, 113; PC 58**
See also BRWS 5; CA 207; 143, 207; CANR 61; CP 1, 6, 7; CWP; DAM POET; DLB 40; FW; MTCW 2; MTFW 2005; PFS 12, 22

Boll, Heinrich (Theodor) .... **TCLC 185**
See Boell, Heinrich (Theodor)
See also BPFB 1; CDWLB 2; DLB 329; EW 13; EWL 3; RGHL; RGSF 2; RGWL 2, 3

Bolt, Lee
See Faust, Frederick (Schiller)

Bolt, Robert (Oxton) 1924-1995 ...... **CLC 14; TCLC 175**
See also CA 17-20R; CAAS 147; CANR 35, 67; CBD; DAM DRAM; DFS 2; DLB 13, 233; EWL 3; LAIT 1; MTCW 1

Bombal, Maria Luisa 1910-1980 .... **HLCS 1; SSC 37**
See also CA 127; CANR 72; EWL 3; HW 1; LAW; RGSF 2

Bombet, Louis-Alexandre-Cesar
See Stendhal

Bomkauf
See Kaufman, Bob (Garnell)

Bonaventura .... **NCLC 35**
See also DLB 90

Bonaventure 1217(?)-1274 .... **CMLC 79**
See also DLB 115; LMFS 1

Bond, Edward 1934- .... **CLC 4, 6, 13, 23**
See also AAYA 50; BRWS 1; CA 25-28R; CANR 38, 67, 106; CBD; CD 5, 6; DAM DRAM; DFS 3, 8; DLB 13, 310; EWL 3; MTCW 1

Bonham, Frank 1914-1989 .... **CLC 12**
See also AAYA 1, 70; BYA 1, 3; CA 9-12R; CANR 4, 36; JRDA; MAICYA 1, 2; SAAS 3; SATA 1, 49; SATA-Obit 62; TCWW 1, 2; YAW

Bonnefoy, Yves 1923- . **CLC 9, 15, 58; PC 58**
See also CA 85-88; CANR 33, 75, 97, 136; CWW 2; DAM MST, POET; DLB 258; EWL 3; GFL 1789 to the Present; MTCW 1, 2; MTFW 2005

Bonner, Marita . **HR 1:2; PC 72; TCLC 179**
See Occomy, Marita (Odette) Bonner

Bonnin, Gertrude 1876-1938 .... **NNAL**
See Zitkala-Sa
See also CA 150; DAM MULT

Bontemps, Arna(ud Wendell)
1902-1973 .. **BLC 1; CLC 1, 18; HR 1:2**
See also BW 1; CA 1-4R; CANR 4, 35; CANR 4, 35; CLR 6; CP 1; CWRI 5; DA3; DAM MULT, NOV, POET; DLB 48, 51; JRDA; MAICYA 1, 2; MAL 5; MTCW 1, 2; SATA 2, 44; SATA-Obit 24; WCH; WP

Boot, William
See Stoppard, Tom

Booth, Martin 1944-2004 .... **CLC 13**
See also CA 188; 93-96, 188; 2; CAAS 223; CANR 92; CP 1, 2, 3, 4

Booth, Philip 1925- .... **CLC 23**
See also CA 5-8R; CANR 5, 88; CP 1, 2, 3, 4, 5, 6, 7; DLBY 1982

Booth, Wayne C. 1921-2005 .... **CLC 24**
See also CA 1-4R; 5; CAAS 244; CANR 3, 43, 117; DLB 67

Booth, Wayne Clayson
See Booth, Wayne C.

Borchert, Wolfgang 1921-1947 .... **TCLC 5**
See also CA 188; CAAE 104; DLB 69, 124; EWL 3

Borel, Petrus 1809-1859 .... **NCLC 41**
See also DLB 119; GFL 1789 to the Present

Borges, Jorge Luis 1899-1986 ... **CLC 1, 2, 3, 4, 6, 8, 9, 10, 13, 19, 44, 48, 83; HLC 1; PC 22, 32; SSC 4, 41; TCLC 109; WLC 1**
See also AAYA 26; BPFB 1; CA 21-24R; CANR 19, 33, 75, 105, 133; CDWLB 3; DA; DA3; DAB; DAC; DAM MST, MULT; DLB 113, 283; DLBY 1986; DNFS 1, 2; EWL 3; HW 1, 2; LAW; LMFS 2; MSW; MTCW 1, 2; MTFW 2005; RGHL; RGSF 2; RGWL 2, 3; SFW 4; SSFS 17; TWA; WLIT 1

Borowski, Tadeusz 1922-1951 .... **SSC 48; TCLC 9**
See also CA 154; CAAE 106; CDWLB 4; DLB 215; EWL 3; RGHL; RGSF 2; RGWL 3; SSFS 13

Borrow, George (Henry)
1803-1881 .... **NCLC 9**
See also BRWS 12; DLB 21, 55, 166

Bosch (Gavino), Juan 1909-2001 ..... **HLCS 1**
See also CA 151; CAAS 204; DAM MST, MULT; DLB 145; HW 1, 2

Bosman, Herman Charles
1905-1951 .... **TCLC 49**
See Malan, Herman
See also CA 160; DLB 225; RGSF 2

Bosschere, Jean de 1878(?)-1953 ... **TCLC 19**
See also CA 186; CAAE 115

Boswell, James 1740-1795 ... **LC 4, 50; WLC 1**
See also BRW 3; CDBLB 1660-1789; DA; DAB; DAC; DAM MST; DLB 104, 142; TEA; WLIT 3

Bottomley, Gordon 1874-1948 ..... **TCLC 107**
See also CA 192; CAAE 120; DLB 10

Bottoms, David 1949- .... **CLC 53**
See also CA 105; CANR 22; CSW; DLB 120; DLBY 1983

Boucicault, Dion 1820-1890 .... **NCLC 41**

Boucolon, Maryse
See Conde, Maryse

Bourdieu, Pierre 1930-2002 .... **CLC 198**
See also CA 130; CAAS 204

Bourget, Paul (Charles Joseph)
1852-1935 .... **TCLC 12**
See also CA 196; CAAE 107; DLB 123; GFL 1789 to the Present

Bourjaily, Vance (Nye) 1922- .... **CLC 8, 62**
See also CA 1-4R; 1; CANR 2, 72; CN 1, 2, 3, 4, 5, 6, 7; DLB 2, 143; MAL 5

Brown, Alan 1950- .... **CLC 99**
See also CA 156
Brown, Charles Brockden
1771-1810 .... **NCLC 22, 74, 122**
See also AMWS 1; CDALB 1640-1865;
DLB 37, 59, 73; FW; GL 2; HGG; LMFS
1; RGAL 4; TUS
Brown, Christy 1932-1981 .... **CLC 63**
See also BYA 13; CA 105; CAAS 104;
CANR 72; DLB 14
Brown, Claude 1937-2002 ... **BLC 1; CLC 30**
See also AAYA 7; BW 1, 3; CA 73-76;
CAAS 205; CANR 81; DAM MULT
Brown, Dan 1964- .... **CLC 209**
See also AAYA 55; CA 217; MTFW 2005
Brown, Dee 1908-2002 .... **CLC 18, 47**
See also AAYA 30; CA 13-16R; 6; CAAS
212; CANR 11, 45, 60, 150; CPW; CSW;
DA3; DAM POP; DLBY 1980; LAIT 2;
MTCW 1, 2; MTFW 2005; NCFS 5;
SATA 5, 110; SATA-Obit 141; TCWW 1,
2
Brown, Dee Alexander
See Brown, Dee
Brown, George
See Wertmueller, Lina
Brown, George Douglas
1869-1902 .... **TCLC 28**
See Douglas, George
See also CA 162
Brown, George Mackay 1921-1996 ... **CLC 5,
48, 100**
See also BRWS 6; CA 21-24R; 6; CAAS
151; CANR 12, 37, 67; CN 1, 2, 3, 4, 5,
6; CP 1, 2, 3, 4, 5, 6; DLB 14, 27, 139,
271; MTCW 1; RGSF 2; SATA 35
Brown, Larry 1951-2004 .... **CLC 73**
See also CA 134; CAAE 130; CAAS 233;
CANR 117, 145; CSW; DLB 234; INT
CA-134
Brown, Moses
See Barrett, William (Christopher)
Brown, Rita Mae 1944- .... **CLC 18, 43, 79**
See also BPFB 1; CA 45-48; CANR 2, 11,
35, 62, 95, 138; CN 5, 6, 7; CPW; CSW;
DA3; DAM NOV, POP; FW; INT CANR-
11; MAL 5; MTCW 1, 2; MTFW 2005;
NFS 9; RGAL 4; TUS
Brown, Roderick (Langmere) Haig-
See Haig-Brown, Roderick (Langmere)
Brown, Rosellen 1939- .... **CLC 32, 170**
See also CA 77-80; 10; CANR 14, 44, 98;
CN 6, 7
Brown, Sterling Allen 1901-1989 ...... **BLC 1;
CLC 1, 23, 59; HR 1:2; PC 55**
See also AFAW 1, 2; BW 1, 3; CA 85-88;
CAAS 127; CANR 26; CP 3, 4; DA3;
DAM MULT, POET; DLB 48, 51, 63;
MAL 5; MTCW 1, 2; MTFW 2005;
RGAL 4; WP
Brown, Will
See Ainsworth, William Harrison
Brown, William Hill 1765-1793 .... **LC 93**
See also DLB 37
Brown, William Larry
See Brown, Larry
Brown, William Wells 1815-1884 ...... **BLC 1;
DC 1; NCLC 2, 89**
See also DAM MULT; DLB 3, 50, 183,
248; RGAL 4
Browne, (Clyde) Jackson 1948(?)- ... **CLC 21**
See also CA 120
Browne, Sir Thomas 1605-1682 .... **LC 111**
See also BRW 2; DLB 151
Browning, Robert 1812-1889 . **NCLC 19, 79;
PC 2, 61; WLCS**
See also BRW 4; BRWC 2; BRWR 2; CD-
BLB 1832-1890; CLR 97; DA; DA3;
DAB; DAC; DAM MST, POET; DLB 32,
163; EXPP; LATS 1:1; PAB; PFS 1, 15;
RGEL 2; TEA; WLIT 4; WP; YABC 1

Browning, Tod 1882-1962 .... **CLC 16**
See also CA 141; CAAS 117
Brownmiller, Susan 1935- .... **CLC 159**
See also CA 103; CANR 35, 75, 137; DAM
NOV; FW; MTCW 1, 2; MTFW 2005
Brownson, Orestes Augustus
1803-1876 .... **NCLC 50**
See also DLB 1, 59, 73, 243
Bruccoli, Matthew J(oseph) 1931- ... **CLC 34**
See also CA 9-12R; CANR 7, 87; DLB 103
Bruce, Lenny .... **CLC 21**
See Schneider, Leonard Alfred
Bruchac, Joseph 1942- .... **NNAL**
See also AAYA 19; CA 33-36R; CANR 13,
47, 75, 94, 137, 161; CLR 46; CWRI 5;
DAM MULT; JRDA; MAICYA 2; MAIC-
YAS 1; MTCW 2; MTFW 2005; SATA
42, 89, 131, 176; SATA-Essay 176
Bruin, John
See Brutus, Dennis
Brulard, Henri
See Stendhal
Brulls, Christian
See Simenon, Georges (Jacques Christian)
Brunetto Latini c. 1220-1294 .... **CMLC 73**
Brunner, John (Kilian Houston)
1934-1995 .... **CLC 8, 10**
See also CA 1-4R; 8; CAAS 149; CANR 2,
37; CPW; DAM POP; DLB 261; MTCW
1, 2; SCFW 1, 2; SFW 4
Bruno, Giordano 1548-1600 .... **LC 27**
See also RGWL 2, 3
Brutus, Dennis 1924- ... **BLC 1; CLC 43; PC
24**
See also AFW; BW 2, 3; CA 49-52; 14;
CANR 2, 27, 42, 81; CDWLB 3; CP 1, 2,
3, 4, 5, 6, 7; DAM MULT, POET; DLB
117, 225; EWL 3
Bryan, C(ourtlandt) D(ixon) B(arnes)
1936- .... **CLC 29**
See also CA 73-76; CANR 13, 68; DLB
185; INT CANR-13
Bryan, Michael
See Moore, Brian
See also CCA 1
Bryan, William Jennings
1860-1925 .... **TCLC 99**
See also DLB 303
Bryant, William Cullen 1794-1878 . **NCLC 6,
46; PC 20**
See also AMWS 1; CDALB 1640-1865;
DA; DAB; DAC; DAM MST, POET;
DLB 3, 43, 59, 189, 250; EXPP; PAB;
RGAL 4; TUS
Bryusov, Valery Yakovlevich
1873-1924 .... **TCLC 10**
See also CA 155; CAAE 107; EWL 3; SFW
4
Buchan, John 1875-1940 .... **TCLC 41**
See also CA 145; CAAE 108; CMW 4;
DAB; DAM POP; DLB 34, 70, 156;
HGG; MSW; MTCW 2; RGEL 2; RHW;
YABC 2
Buchanan, George 1506-1582 .... **LC 4**
See also DLB 132
Buchanan, Robert 1841-1901 .... **TCLC 107**
See also CA 179; DLB 18, 35
Buchheim, Lothar-Guenther
1918-2007 .... **CLC 6**
See also CA 85-88
Buchner, (Karl) Georg
1813-1837 .... **NCLC 26, 146**
See also CDWLB 2; DLB 133; EW 6;
RGSF 2; RGWL 2, 3; TWA
Buchwald, Art 1925-2007 .... **CLC 33**
See also AITN 1; CA 5-8R; CANR 21, 67,
107; MTCW 1, 2; SATA 10
Buchwald, Arthur
See Buchwald, Art

Buck, Pearl S(ydenstricker)
1892-1973 .... **CLC 7, 11, 18, 127**
See also AAYA 42; AITN 1; AMWS 2;
BPFB 1; CA 1-4R; CAAS 41-44R; CANR
1, 34; CDALBS; CN 1; DA; DA3; DAB;
DAC; DAM MST, NOV; DLB 9, 102,
329; EWL 3; LAIT 3; MAL 5; MTCW 1,
2; MTFW 2005; RGAL 4; RHW; SATA
1, 25; TUS
Buckler, Ernest 1908-1984 .... **CLC 13**
See also CA 11-12; CAAS 114; CAP 1;
CCA 1; CN 1, 2, 3; DAC; DAM MST;
DLB 68; SATA 47
Buckley, Christopher 1952- .... **CLC 165**
See also CA 139; CANR 119
Buckley, Christopher Taylor
See Buckley, Christopher
Buckley, Vincent (Thomas)
1925-1988 .... **CLC 57**
See also CA 101; CP 1, 2, 3, 4; DLB 289
Buckley, William F., Jr. 1925- ..... **CLC 7, 18,
37**
See also AITN 1; BPFB 1; CA 1-4R; CANR
1, 24, 53, 93, 133; CMW 4; CPW; DA3;
DAM POP; DLB 137; DLBY 1980; INT
CANR-24; MTCW 1, 2; MTFW 2005;
TUS
Buechner, Frederick 1926- ..... **CLC 2, 4, 6, 9**
See also AMWS 12; BPFB 1; CA 13-16R;
CANR 11, 39, 64, 114, 138; CN 1, 2, 3,
4, 5, 6, 7; DAM NOV; DLBY 1980; INT
CANR-11; MAL 5; MTCW 1, 2; MTFW
2005; TCLE 1:1
Buell, John (Edward) 1927- .... **CLC 10**
See also CA 1-4R; CANR 71; DLB 53
Buero Vallejo, Antonio 1916-2000 ... **CLC 15,
46, 139, 226; DC 18**
See also CA 106; CAAS 189; CANR 24,
49, 75; CWW 2; DFS 11; EWL 3; HW 1;
MTCW 1, 2
Bufalino, Gesualdo 1920-1996 .... **CLC 74**
See also CA 209; CWW 2; DLB 196
Bugayev, Boris Nikolayevich
1880-1934 .... **PC 11; TCLC 7**
See Bely, Andrey; Belyi, Andrei
See also CA 165; CAAE 104; MTCW 2;
MTFW 2005
Bukowski, Charles 1920-1994 ... **CLC 2, 5, 9,
41, 82, 108; PC 18; SSC 45**
See also CA 17-20R; CAAS 144; CANR
40, 62, 105; CN 4, 5; CP 1, 2, 3, 4, 5;
CPW; DA3; DAM NOV, POET; DLB 5,
130, 169; EWL 3; MAL 5; MTCW 1, 2;
MTFW 2005
Bulgakov, Mikhail 1891-1940 .... **SSC 18;
TCLC 2, 16, 159**
See also AAYA 74; BPFB 1; CA 152;
CAAE 105; DAM DRAM, NOV; DLB
272; EWL 3; MTCW 2; MTFW 2005;
NFS 8; RGSF 2; RGWL 2, 3; SFW 4;
TWA
Bulgakov, Mikhail Afanasevich
See Bulgakov, Mikhail
Bulgya, Alexander Alexandrovich
1901-1956 .... **TCLC 53**
See Fadeev, Aleksandr Aleksandrovich;
Fadeev, Alexandr Alexandrovich; Fadeyev,
Alexander
See also CA 181; CAAE 117
Bullins, Ed 1935- ... **BLC 1; CLC 1, 5, 7; DC
6**
See also BW 2, 3; CA 49-52; 16; CAD;
CANR 24, 46, 73, 134; CD 5, 6; DAM
DRAM, MULT; DLB 7, 38, 249; EWL 3;
MAL 5; MTCW 1, 2; MTFW 2005;
RGAL 4
Bulosan, Carlos 1911-1956 .... **AAL**
See also CA 216; DLB 312; RGAL 4

Cade, Toni
See Bambara, Toni Cade
Cadmus and Harmonia
See Buchan, John
Caedmon fl. 658-680 .... **CMLC 7**
See also DLB 146
Caeiro, Alberto
See Pessoa, Fernando (Antonio Nogueira)
Caesar, Julius .... **CMLC 47**
See Julius Caesar
See also AW 1; RGWL 2, 3; WLIT 8
Cage, John (Milton), (Jr.)
1912-1992 .... **CLC 41; PC 58**
See also CA 13-16R; CAAS 169; CANR 9,
78; DLB 193; INT CANR-9; TCLE 1:1
Cahan, Abraham 1860-1951 .... **TCLC 71**
See also CA 154; CAAE 108; DLB 9, 25,
28; MAL 5; RGAL 4
Cain, G.
See Cabrera Infante, G.
Cain, Guillermo
See Cabrera Infante, G.
Cain, James M(allahan) 1892-1977 .. **CLC 3,
11, 28**
See also AITN 1; BPFB 1; CA 17-20R;
CAAS 73-76; CANR 8, 34, 61; CMW 4;
CN 1, 2; DLB 226; EWL 3; MAL 5;
MSW; MTCW 1; RGAL 4
Caine, Hall 1853-1931 .... **TCLC 97**
See also RHW
Caine, Mark
See Raphael, Frederic (Michael)
Calasso, Roberto 1941- .... **CLC 81**
See also CA 143; CANR 89
Calderon de la Barca, Pedro
1600-1681 . **DC 3; HLCS 1; LC 23, 136**
See also DFS 23; EW 2; RGWL 2, 3; TWA
Caldwell, Erskine 1903-1987 ... **CLC 1, 8, 14,
50, 60; SSC 19; TCLC 117**
See also AITN 1; AMW; BPFB 1; CA 1-4R;
1; CAAS 121; CANR 2, 33; CN 1, 2, 3,
4; DA3; DAM NOV; DLB 9, 86; EWL 3;
MAL 5; MTCW 1, 2; MTFW 2005;
RGAL 4; RGSF 2; TUS
Caldwell, (Janet Miriam) Taylor (Holland)
1900-1985 .... **CLC 2, 28, 39**
See also BPFB 1; CA 5-8R; CAAS 116;
CANR 5; DA3; DAM NOV, POP; DLBD
17; MTCW 2; RHW
Calhoun, John Caldwell
1782-1850 .... **NCLC 15**
See also DLB 3, 248
Calisher, Hortense 1911- ..... **CLC 2, 4, 8, 38,
134; SSC 15**
See also CA 1-4R; CANR 1, 22, 117; CN
1, 2, 3, 4, 5, 6, 7; DA3; DAM NOV; DLB
2, 218; INT CANR-22; MAL 5; MTCW
1, 2; MTFW 2005; RGAL 4; RGSF 2
Callaghan, Morley Edward
1903-1990 ..... **CLC 3, 14, 41, 65; TCLC
145**
See also CA 9-12R; CAAS 132; CANR 33,
73; CN 1, 2, 3, 4; DAC; DAM MST; DLB
68; EWL 3; MTCW 1, 2; MTFW 2005;
RGEL 2; RGSF 2; SSFS 19
Callimachus c. 305B.C.-c.
240B.C. .... **CMLC 18**
See also AW 1; DLB 176; RGWL 2, 3
Calvin, Jean
See Calvin, John
See also DLB 327; GFL Beginnings to 1789
Calvin, John 1509-1564 .... **LC 37**
See Calvin, Jean
Calvino, Italo 1923-1985 .... **CLC 5, 8, 11, 22,
33, 39, 73; SSC 3, 48; TCLC 183**
See also AAYA 58; CA 85-88; CAAS 116;
CANR 23, 61, 132; DLB
196; EW 13; EWL 3; MTCW 1, 2; MTFW
2005; RGHL; RGSF 2; RGWL 2, 3; SFW
4; SSFS 12; WLIT 7

Camara Laye
See Laye, Camara
See also EWL 3
Camden, William 1551-1623 .... **LC 77**
See also DLB 172
Cameron, Carey 1952- .... **CLC 59**
See also CA 135
Cameron, Peter 1959- .... **CLC 44**
See also AMWS 12; CA 125; CANR 50,
117; DLB 234; GLL 2
Camoens, Luis Vaz de 1524(?)-1580
See Camoes, Luis de
See also EW 2
Camoes, Luis de 1524(?)-1580 . **HLCS 1; LC
62; PC 31**
See Camoens, Luis Vaz de
See also DLB 287; RGWL 2, 3
Campana, Dino 1885-1932 .... **TCLC 20**
See also CA 246; CAAE 117; DLB 114;
EWL 3
Campanella, Tommaso 1568-1639 .... **LC 32**
See also RGWL 2, 3
Campbell, John W(ood, Jr.)
1910-1971 .... **CLC 32**
See also CA 21-22; CAAS 29-32R; CANR
34; CAP 2; DLB 8; MTCW 1; SCFW 1,
2; SFW 4
Campbell, Joseph 1904-1987 .... **CLC 69;
TCLC 140**
See also AAYA 3, 66; BEST 89:2; CA 1-4R;
CAAS 124; CANR 3, 28, 61, 107; DA3;
MTCW 1, 2
Campbell, Maria 1940- .... **CLC 85; NNAL**
See also CA 102; CANR 54; CCA 1; DAC
Campbell, (John) Ramsey 1946- ..... **CLC 42;
SSC 19**
See also AAYA 51; CA 228; 57-60, 228;
CANR 7, 102; DLB 261; HGG; INT
CANR-7; SUFW 1, 2
Campbell, (Ignatius) Roy (Dunnachie)
1901-1957 .... **TCLC 5**
See also AFW; CA 155; CAAE 104; DLB
20, 225; EWL 3; MTCW 2; RGEL 2
Campbell, Thomas 1777-1844 .... **NCLC 19**
See also DLB 93, 144; RGEL 2
Campbell, Wilfred .... **TCLC 9**
See Campbell, William
Campbell, William 1858(?)-1918
See Campbell, Wilfred
See also CAAE 106; DLB 92
Campbell, William Edward March
1893-1954
See March, William
See also CAAE 108
Campion, Jane 1954- .... **CLC 95, 229**
See also AAYA 33; CA 138; CANR 87
Campion, Thomas 1567-1620 .... **LC 78**
See also CDBLB Before 1660; DAM POET;
DLB 58, 172; RGEL 2
Camus, Albert 1913-1960 ...... **CLC 1, 2, 4, 9,
11, 14, 32, 63, 69, 124; DC 2; SSC 9,
76; WLC 1**
See also AAYA 36; AFW; BPFB 1; CA 89-
92; CANR 131; DA; DA3; DAB; DAC;
DAM DRAM, MST, NOV; DLB 72, 321,
329; EW 13; EWL 3; EXPN; EXPS; GFL
1789 to the Present; LATS 1:2; LMFS 2;
MTCW 1, 2; MTFW 2005; NFS 6, 16;
RGHL; RGSF 2; RGWL 2, 3; SSFS 4;
TWA
Canby, Vincent 1924-2000 .... **CLC 13**
See also CA 81-84; CAAS 191
Cancale
See Desnos, Robert

Canetti, Elias 1905-1994 .. **CLC 3, 14, 25, 75,
86; TCLC 157**
See also CA 21-24R; CAAS 146; CANR
23, 61, 79; CDWLB 2; CWW 2; DA3;
DLB 85, 124, 329; EW 12; EWL 3;
MTCW 1, 2; MTFW 2005; RGWL 2, 3;
TWA
Canfield, Dorothea F.
See Fisher, Dorothy (Frances) Canfield
Canfield, Dorothea Frances
See Fisher, Dorothy (Frances) Canfield
Canfield, Dorothy
See Fisher, Dorothy (Frances) Canfield
Canin, Ethan 1960- .... **CLC 55; SSC 70**
See also CA 135; CAAE 131; MAL 5
Cankar, Ivan 1876-1918 .... **TCLC 105**
See also CDWLB 4; DLB 147; EWL 3
Cannon, Curt
See Hunter, Evan
Cao, Lan 1961- .... **CLC 109**
See also CA 165
Cape, Judith
See Page, P(atricia) K(athleen)
See also CCA 1
Capek, Karel 1890-1938 .... **DC 1; SSC 36;
TCLC 6, 37; WLC 1**
See also CA 140; CAAE 104; CDWLB 4;
DA; DA3; DAB; DAC; DAM DRAM,
MST, NOV; DFS 7, 11; DLB 215; EW
10; EWL 3; MTCW 2; MTFW 2005;
RGSF 2; RGWL 2, 3; SCFW 1, 2; SFW 4
Capella, Martianus fl. 4th cent. - .. **CMLC 84**
Capote, Truman 1924-1984 . **CLC 1, 3, 8, 13,
19, 34, 38, 58; SSC 2, 47, 93; TCLC
164; WLC 1**
See also AAYA 61; AMWS 3; BPFB 1; CA
5-8R; CAAS 113; CANR 18, 62; CDALB
1941-1968; CN 1, 2, 3; CPW; DA; DA3;
DAB; DAC; DAM MST, NOV, POP;
DLB 2, 185, 227; DLBY 1980, 1984;
EWL 3; EXPS; GLL 1; LAIT 3; MAL 5;
MTCW 1, 2; MTFW 2005; NCFS 2;
RGAL 4; RGSF 2; SATA 91; SSFS 2;
TUS
Capra, Frank 1897-1991 .... **CLC 16**
See also AAYA 52; CA 61-64; CAAS 135
Caputo, Philip 1941- .... **CLC 32**
See also AAYA 60; CA 73-76; CANR 40,
135; YAW
Caragiale, Ion Luca 1852-1912 ...... **TCLC 76**
See also CA 157
Card, Orson Scott 1951- .... **CLC 44, 47, 50**
See also AAYA 11, 42; BPFB 1; BYA 5, 8;
CA 102; CANR 27, 47, 73, 102, 106, 133;
CLR 116; CPW; DA3; DAM POP; FANT;
INT CANR-27; MTCW 1, 2; MTFW
2005; NFS 5; SATA 83, 127; SCFW 2;
SFW 4; SUFW 2; YAW
Cardenal, Ernesto 1925- .... **CLC 31, 161;
HLC 1; PC 22**
See also CA 49-52; CANR 2, 32, 66, 138;
CWW 2; DAM MULT, POET; DLB 290;
EWL 3; HW 1, 2; LAWS 1; MTCW 1, 2;
MTFW 2005; RGWL 2, 3
Cardinal, Marie 1929-2001 .... **CLC 189**
See also CA 177; CWW 2; DLB 83; FW
Cardozo, Benjamin N(athan)
1870-1938 .... **TCLC 65**
See also CA 164; CAAE 117
Carducci, Giosue (Alessandro Giuseppe)
1835-1907 .... **PC 46; TCLC 32**
See also CA 163; DLB 329; EW 7; RGWL
2, 3
Carew, Thomas 1595(?)-1640 . **LC 13; PC 29**
See also BRW 2; DLB 126; PAB; RGEL 2
Carey, Ernestine Gilbreth
1908-2006 .... **CLC 17**
See also CA 5-8R; CAAS 254; CANR 71;
SATA 2

Carey, Peter 1943- .... **CLC 40, 55, 96, 183**
See also BRWS 12; CA 127; CAAE 123;
CANR 53, 76, 117, 157; CN 4, 5, 6, 7;
DLB 289, 326; EWL 3; INT CA-127;
MTCW 1, 2; MTFW 2005; RGSF 2;
SATA 94

Carleton, William 1794-1869 .... **NCLC 3**
See also DLB 159; RGEL 2; RGSF 2

Carlisle, Henry (Coffin) 1926- .... **CLC 33**
See also CA 13-16R; CANR 15, 85

Carlsen, Chris
See Holdstock, Robert

Carlson, Ron 1947- .... **CLC 54**
See also CA 189; 105, 189; CANR 27, 155;
DLB 244

Carlson, Ronald F.
See Carlson, Ron

Carlyle, Jane Welsh 1801-1866 ... **NCLC 181**
See also DLB 55

Carlyle, Thomas 1795-1881 ..... **NCLC 22, 70**
See also BRW 4; CDBLB 1789-1832; DA;
DAB; DAC; DAM MST; DLB 55, 144,
254; RGEL 2; TEA

Carman, (William) Bliss 1861-1929 ... **PC 34;
TCLC 7**
See also CA 152; CAAE 104; DAC; DLB
92; RGEL 2

Carnegie, Dale 1888-1955 .... **TCLC 53**
See also CA 218

Carossa, Hans 1878-1956 .... **TCLC 48**
See also CA 170; DLB 66; EWL 3

Carpenter, Don(ald Richard)
1931-1995 .... **CLC 41**
See also CA 45-48; CAAS 149; CANR 1,
71

Carpenter, Edward 1844-1929 .... **TCLC 88**
See also CA 163; GLL 1

Carpenter, John (Howard) 1948- ... **CLC 161**
See also AAYA 2, 73; CA 134; SATA 58

Carpenter, Johnny
See Carpenter, John (Howard)

Carpentier (y Valmont), Alejo
1904-1980 . **CLC 8, 11, 38, 110; HLC 1;
SSC 35**
See also CA 65-68; CAAS 97-100; CANR
11, 70; CDWLB 3; DAM MULT; DLB
113; EWL 3; HW 1, 2; LAW; LMFS 2;
RGSF 2; RGWL 2, 3; WLIT 1

Carr, Caleb 1955- .... **CLC 86**
See also CA 147; CANR 73, 134; DA3

Carr, Emily 1871-1945 .... **TCLC 32**
See also CA 159; DLB 68; FW; GLL 2

Carr, John Dickson 1906-1977 .... **CLC 3**
See Fairbairn, Roger
See also CA 49-52; CAAS 69-72; CANR 3,
33, 60; CMW 4; DLB 306; MSW; MTCW
1, 2

Carr, Philippa
See Hibbert, Eleanor Alice Burford

Carr, Virginia Spencer 1929- .... **CLC 34**
See also CA 61-64; DLB 111

Carrere, Emmanuel 1957- .... **CLC 89**
See also CA 200

Carrier, Roch 1937- .... **CLC 13, 78**
See also CA 130; CANR 61, 152; CCA 1;
DAC; DAM MST; DLB 53; SATA 105,
166

Carroll, James Dennis
See Carroll, Jim

Carroll, James P. 1943(?)- .... **CLC 38**
See also CA 81-84; CANR 73, 139; MTCW
2; MTFW 2005

Carroll, Jim 1951- .... **CLC 35, 143**
See also AAYA 17; CA 45-48; CANR 42,
115; NCFS 5

Carroll, Lewis ...... **NCLC 2, 53, 139; PC 18,
74; WLC 1**
See Dodgson, Charles L(utwidge)
See also AAYA 39; BRW 5; BYA 5, 13; CD-
BLB 1832-1890; CLR 2, 18, 108; DLB
18, 163, 178; DLBY 1998; EXPN; EXPP;
FANT; JRDA; LAIT 1; NFS 7; PFS 11;
RGEL 2; SUFW 1; TEA; WCH

Carroll, Paul Vincent 1900-1968 ...... **CLC 10**
See also CA 9-12R; CAAS 25-28R; DLB
10; EWL 3; RGEL 2

Carruth, Hayden 1921- ..... **CLC 4, 7, 10, 18,
84; PC 10**
See also AMWS 16; CA 9-12R; CANR 4,
38, 59, 110; CP 1, 2, 3, 4, 5, 6, 7; DLB 5,
165; INT CANR-4; MTCW 1, 2; MTFW
2005; SATA 47

Carson, Anne 1950- .... **CLC 185; PC 64**
See also AMWS 12; CA 203; CP 7; DLB
193; PFS 18; TCLE 1:1

Carson, Ciaran 1948- .... **CLC 201**
See also CA 153; CAAE 112; CANR 113;
CP 6, 7

Carson, Rachel
See Carson, Rachel Louise
See also AAYA 49; DLB 275

Carson, Rachel Louise 1907-1964 .... **CLC 71**
See Carson, Rachel
See also AMWS 9; ANW; CA 77-80; CANR
35; DA3; DAM POP; FW; LAIT 4; MAL
5; MTCW 1, 2; MTFW 2005; NCFS 1;
SATA 23

Carter, Angela 1940-1992 ...... **CLC 5, 41, 76;
SSC 13, 85; TCLC 139**
See also BRWS 3; CA 53-56; CAAS 136;
CANR 12, 36, 61, 106; CN 3, 4, 5; DA3;
DLB 14, 207, 261, 319; EXPS; FANT;
FW; GL 2; MTCW 1, 2; MTFW 2005;
RGSF 2; SATA 66; SATA-Obit 70; SFW
4; SSFS 4, 12; SUFW 2; WLIT 4

Carter, Angela Olive
See Carter, Angela

Carter, Nick
See Smith, Martin Cruz

Carver, Raymond 1938-1988 ..... **CLC 22, 36,
53, 55, 126; PC 54; SSC 8, 51**
See also AAYA 44; AMWS 3; BPFB 1; CA
33-36R; CAAS 126; CANR 17, 34, 61,
103; CN 4; CPW; DA3; DAM NOV; DLB
130; DLBY 1984, 1988; EWL 3; MAL 5;
MTCW 1, 2; MTFW 2005; PFS 17;
RGAL 4; RGSF 2; SSFS 3, 6, 12, 13, 23;
TCLE 1:1; TCWW 2; TUS

Cary, Elizabeth, Lady Falkland
1585-1639 .... **LC 30**

Cary, (Arthur) Joyce (Lunel)
1888-1957 .... **TCLC 1, 29**
See also BRW 7; CA 164; CAAE 104; CD-
BLB 1914-1945; DLB 15, 100; EWL 3;
MTCW 2; RGEL 2; TEA

Casal, Julian del 1863-1893 .... **NCLC 131**
See also DLB 283; LAW

Casanova, Giacomo
See Casanova de Seingalt, Giovanni Jacopo
See also WLIT 7

Casanova de Seingalt, Giovanni Jacopo
1725-1798 .... **LC 13**
See Casanova, Giacomo

Casares, Adolfo Bioy
See Bioy Casares, Adolfo
See also RGSF 2

Casas, Bartolome de las 1474-1566
See Las Casas, Bartolome de
See also WLIT 1

Casely-Hayford, J(oseph) E(phraim)
1866-1903 .... **BLC 1; TCLC 24**
See also BW 2; CA 152; CAAE 123; DAM
MULT

Casey, John (Dudley) 1939- .... **CLC 59**
See also BEST 90:2; CA 69-72; CANR 23,
100

Casey, Michael 1947- .... **CLC 2**
See also CA 65-68; CANR 109; CP 2, 3;
DLB 5

Casey, Patrick
See Thurman, Wallace (Henry)

Casey, Warren (Peter) 1935-1988 .... **CLC 12**
See also CA 101; CAAS 127; INT CA-101

Casona, Alejandro .... **CLC 49**
See Alvarez, Alejandro Rodriguez
See also EWL 3

Cassavetes, John 1929-1989 .... **CLC 20**
See also CA 85-88; CAAS 127; CANR 82

Cassian, Nina 1924- .... **PC 17**
See also CWP; CWW 2

Cassill, R(onald) V(erlin)
1919-2002 .... **CLC 4, 23**
See also CA 9-12R; 1; CAAS 208; CANR
7, 45; CN 1, 2, 3, 4, 5, 6, 7; DLB 6, 218;
DLBY 2002

Cassiodorus, Flavius Magnus c. 490(?)-c.
583(?) .... **CMLC 43**

Cassirer, Ernst 1874-1945 .... **TCLC 61**
See also CA 157

Cassity, (Allen) Turner 1929- .... **CLC 6, 42**
See also CA 223; 17-20R, 223; 8; CANR
11; CSW; DLB 105

Castaneda, Carlos (Cesar Aranha)
1931(?)-1998 .... **CLC 12, 119**
See also CA 25-28R; CANR 32, 66, 105;
DNFS 1; HW 1; MTCW 1

Castedo, Elena 1937- .... **CLC 65**
See also CA 132

Castedo-Ellerman, Elena
See Castedo, Elena

Castellanos, Rosario 1925-1974 .... **CLC 66;
HLC 1; SSC 39, 68**
See also CA 131; CAAS 53-56; CANR 58;
CDWLB 3; DAM MULT; DLB 113, 290;
EWL 3; FW; HW 1; LAW; MTCW 2;
MTFW 2005; RGSF 2; RGWL 2, 3

Castelvetro, Lodovico 1505-1571 .... **LC 12**

Castiglione, Baldassare 1478-1529 ...... **LC 12**
See Castiglione, Baldesar
See also LMFS 1; RGWL 2, 3

Castiglione, Baldesar
See Castiglione, Baldassare
See also EW 2; WLIT 7

Castillo, Ana 1953- .... **CLC 151**
See also AAYA 42; CA 131; CANR 51, 86,
128; CWP; DLB 122, 227; DNFS 2; FW;
HW 1; LLW; PFS 21

Castle, Robert
See Hamilton, Edmond

Castro (Ruz), Fidel 1926(?)- .... **HLC 1**
See also CA 129; CAAE 110; CANR 81;
DAM MULT; HW 2

Castro, Guillen de 1569-1631 .... **LC 19**

Castro, Rosalia de 1837-1885 ... **NCLC 3, 78;
PC 41**
See also DAM MULT

Cather, Willa (Sibert) 1873-1947 . **SSC 2, 50;
TCLC 1, 11, 31, 99, 132, 152; WLC 1**
See also AAYA 24; AMW; AMWC 1;
AMWR 1; BPFB 1; CA 128; CAAE 104;
CDALB 1865-1917; CLR 98; DA; DA3;
DAB; DAC; DAM MST, NOV; DLB 9,
54, 78, 256; DLBD 1; EWL 3; EXPN;
EXPS; FL 1:5; LAIT 3; LATS 1:1; MAL
5; MBL; MTCW 1, 2; MTFW 2005; NFS
2, 19; RGAL 4; RGSF 2; RHW; SATA
30; SSFS 2, 7, 16; TCWW 1, 2; TUS

Catherine II
See Catherine the Great
See also DLB 150

Catherine the Great 1729-1796 .... **LC 69**
See Catherine II

The Coen Brothers
See Coen, Ethan; Coen, Joel

Coetzee, J.M. 1940- ...... **CLC 23, 33, 66, 117, 161, 162**
See also AAYA 37; AFW; BRWS 6; CA 77-80; CANR 41, 54, 74, 114, 133; CN 4, 5, 6, 7; DA3; DAM NOV; DLB 225, 326, 329; EWL 3; LMFS 2; MTCW 1, 2; MTFW 2005; NFS 21; WLIT 2; WWE 1

Coetzee, John Maxwell
See Coetzee, J.M.

Coffey, Brian
See Koontz, Dean R.

Coffin, Robert P(eter) Tristram
1892-1955 .... **TCLC 95**
See also CA 169; CAAE 123; DLB 45

Cohan, George M. 1878-1942 .... **TCLC 60**
See also CA 157; DLB 249; RGAL 4

Cohan, George Michael
See Cohan, George M.

Cohen, Arthur A(llen) 1928-1986 ...... **CLC 7, 31**
See also CA 1-4R; CAAS 120; CANR 1, 17, 42; DLB 28; RGHL

Cohen, Leonard 1934- .... **CLC 3, 38**
See also CA 21-24R; CANR 14, 69; CN 1, 2, 3, 4, 5, 6; CP 1, 2, 3, 4, 5, 6, 7; DAC; DAM MST; DLB 53; EWL 3; MTCW 1

Cohen, Leonard Norman
See Cohen, Leonard

Cohen, Matt(hew) 1942-1999 .... **CLC 19**
See also CA 61-64; 18; CAAS 187; CANR 40; CN 1, 2, 3, 4, 5, 6; DAC; DLB 53

Cohen-Solal, Annie 1948- .... **CLC 50**
See also CA 239

Colegate, Isabel 1931- .... **CLC 36**
See also CA 17-20R; CANR 8, 22, 74; CN 4, 5, 6, 7; DLB 14, 231; INT CANR-22; MTCW 1

Coleman, Emmett
See Reed, Ishmael

Coleridge, Hartley 1796-1849 .... **NCLC 90**
See also DLB 96

Coleridge, M. E.
See Coleridge, Mary E(lizabeth)

Coleridge, Mary E(lizabeth)
1861-1907 .... **TCLC 73**
See also CA 166; CAAE 116; DLB 19, 98

Coleridge, Samuel Taylor
1772-1834 .... **NCLC 9, 54, 99, 111, 177; PC 11, 39, 67; WLC 2**
See also AAYA 66; BRW 4; BRWR 2; BYA 4; CDBLB 1789-1832; DA; DA3; DAB; DAC; DAM MST, POET; DLB 93, 107; EXPP; LATS 1:1; LMFS 1; PAB; PFS 4, 5; RGEL 2; TEA; WLIT 3; WP

Coleridge, Sara 1802-1852 .... **NCLC 31**
See also DLB 199

Coles, Don 1928- .... **CLC 46**
See also CA 115; CANR 38; CP 5, 6, 7

Coles, Robert (Martin) 1929- .... **CLC 108**
See also CA 45-48; CANR 3, 32, 66, 70, 135; INT CANR-32; SATA 23

Colette, (Sidonie-Gabrielle)
1873-1954 .. **SSC 10, 93; TCLC 1, 5, 16**
See Willy, Colette
See also CA 131; CAAE 104; DA3; DAM NOV; DLB 65; EW 9; EWL 3; GFL 1789 to the Present; MTCW 1, 2; MTFW 2005; RGWL 2, 3; TWA

Collett, (Jacobine) Camilla (Wergeland)
1813-1895 .... **NCLC 22**

Collier, Christopher 1930- .... **CLC 30**
See also AAYA 13; BYA 2; CA 33-36R; CANR 13, 33, 102; JRDA; MAICYA 1, 2; SATA 16, 70; WYA; YAW 1

Collier, James Lincoln 1928- .... **CLC 30**
See also AAYA 13; BYA 2; CA 9-12R; CANR 4, 33, 60, 102; CLR 3; DAM POP; JRDA; MAICYA 1, 2; SAAS 21; SATA 8, 70, 166; WYA; YAW 1

Collier, Jeremy 1650-1726 .... **LC 6**

Collier, John 1901-1980 . **SSC 19; TCLC 127**
See also CA 65-68; CAAS 97-100; CANR 10; CN 1, 2; DLB 77, 255; FANT; SUFW 1

Collier, Mary 1690-1762 .... **LC 86**
See also DLB 95

Collingwood, R(obin) G(eorge)
1889(?)-1943 .... **TCLC 67**
See also CA 155; CAAE 117; DLB 262

Collins, Billy 1941- .... **PC 68**
See also CA 64; CA 151; CANR 92; CP 7; MTFW 2005; PFS 18

Collins, Hunt
See Hunter, Evan

Collins, Linda 1931- .... **CLC 44**
See also CA 125

Collins, Tom
See Furphy, Joseph
See also RGEL 2

Collins, (William) Wilkie
1824-1889 .... **NCLC 1, 18, 93; SSC 93**
See also BRWS 6; CDBLB 1832-1890; CMW 4; DLB 18, 70, 159; GL 2; MSW; RGEL 2; RGSF 2; SUFW 1; WLIT 4

Collins, William 1721-1759 ...... **LC 4, 40; PC 72**
See also BRW 3; DAM POET; DLB 109; RGEL 2

Collodi, Carlo .... **NCLC 54**
See Lorenzini, Carlo
See also CLR 5, 120; WCH; WLIT 7

Colman, George
See Glassco, John

Colman, George, the Elder
1732-1794 .... **LC 98**
See also RGEL 2

Colonna, Vittoria 1492-1547 .... **LC 71**
See also RGWL 2, 3

Colt, Winchester Remington
See Hubbard, L. Ron

Colter, Cyrus J. 1910-2002 .... **CLC 58**
See also BW 1; CA 65-68; CAAS 205; CANR 10, 66; CN 2, 3, 4, 5, 6; DLB 33

Colton, James
See Hansen, Joseph
See also GLL 1

Colum, Padraic 1881-1972 .... **CLC 28**
See also BYA 4; CA 73-76; CAAS 33-36R; CANR 35; CLR 36; CP 1; CWRI 5; DLB 19; MAICYA 1, 2; MTCW 1; RGEL 2; SATA 15; WCH

Colvin, James
See Moorcock, Michael

Colwin, Laurie (E.) 1944-1992 .... **CLC 5, 13, 23, 84**
See also CA 89-92; CAAS 139; CANR 20, 46; DLB 218; DLBY 1980; MTCW 1

Comfort, Alex(ander) 1920-2000 .... **CLC 7**
See also CA 1-4R; CAAS 190; CANR 1, 45; CN 1, 2, 3, 4; CP 1, 2, 3, 4, 5, 6, 7; DAM POP; MTCW 2

Comfort, Montgomery
See Campbell, (John) Ramsey

Compton-Burnett, I(vy)
1892(?)-1969 .... **CLC 1, 3, 10, 15, 34; TCLC 180**
See also BRW 7; CA 1-4R; CAAS 25-28R; CANR 4; DAM NOV; DLB 36; EWL 3; MTCW 1, 2; RGEL 2

Comstock, Anthony 1844-1915 ...... **TCLC 13**
See also CA 169; CAAE 110

Comte, Auguste 1798-1857 .... **NCLC 54**

Conan Doyle, Arthur
See Doyle, Sir Arthur Conan
See also BPFB 1; BYA 4, 5, 11

Conde (Abellan), Carmen
1901-1996 .... **HLCS 1**
See also CA 177; CWW 2; DLB 108; EWL 3; HW 2

Conde, Maryse 1937- ..... **BLCS; CLC 52, 92**
See also BW 2, 3; CA 190; 110, 190; CANR 30, 53, 76; CWW 2; DAM MULT; EWL 3; MTCW 2; MTFW 2005

Condillac, Etienne Bonnot de
1714-1780 .... **LC 26**
See also DLB 313

Condon, Richard (Thomas)
1915-1996 .... **CLC 4, 6, 8, 10, 45, 100**
See also BEST 90:3; BPFB 1; CA 1-4R; 1; CAAS 151; CANR 2, 23; CMW 4; CN 1, 2, 3, 4, 5, 6; DAM NOV; INT CANR-23; MAL 5; MTCW 1, 2

Condorcet .... **LC 104**
See Condorcet, marquis de Marie-Jean-Antoine-Nicolas Caritat
See also GFL Beginnings to 1789

Condorcet, marquis de
Marie-Jean-Antoine-Nicolas Caritat
1743-1794
See Condorcet
See also DLB 313

Confucius 551B.C.-479B.C. .... **CMLC 19, 65; WLCS**
See also DA; DA3; DAB; DAC; DAM MST

Congreve, William 1670-1729 ... **DC 2; LC 5, 21; WLC 2**
See also BRW 2; CDBLB 1660-1789; DA; DAB; DAC; DAM DRAM, MST, POET; DFS 15; DLB 39, 84; RGEL 2; WLIT 3

Conley, Robert J(ackson) 1940- .... **NNAL**
See also CA 41-44R; CANR 15, 34, 45, 96; DAM MULT; TCWW 2

Connell, Evan S., Jr. 1924- .... **CLC 4, 6, 45**
See also AAYA 7; AMWS 14; CA 1-4R; 2; CANR 2, 39, 76, 97, 140; CN 1, 2, 3, 4, 5, 6; DAM NOV; DLB 2; DLBY 1981; MAL 5; MTCW 1, 2; MTFW 2005

Connelly, Marc(us Cook) 1890-1980 . **CLC 7**
See also CA 85-88; CAAS 102; CAD; CANR 30; DFS 12; DLB 7; DLBY 1980; MAL 5; RGAL 4; SATA-Obit 25

Connor, Ralph .... **TCLC 31**
See Gordon, Charles William
See also DLB 92; TCWW 1, 2

Conrad, Joseph 1857-1924 ..... **SSC 9, 67, 69, 71; TCLC 1, 6, 13, 25, 43, 57; WLC 2**
See also AAYA 26; BPFB 1; BRW 6; BRWC 1; BRWR 2; BYA 2; CA 131; CAAE 104; CANR 60; CDBLB 1890-1914; DA; DA3; DAB; DAC; DAM MST, NOV; DLB 10, 34, 98, 156; EWL 3; EXPN; EXPS; LAIT 2; LATS 1:1; LMFS 1; MTCW 1, 2; MTFW 2005; NFS 2, 16; RGEL 2; RGSF 2; SATA 27; SSFS 1, 12; TEA; WLIT 4

Conrad, Robert Arnold
See Hart, Moss

Conroy, Pat 1945- .... **CLC 30, 74**
See also AAYA 8, 52; AITN 1; BPFB 1; CA 85-88; CANR 24, 53, 129; CN 7; CPW; CSW; DA3; DAM NOV, POP; DLB 6; LAIT 5; MAL 5; MTCW 1, 2; MTFW 2005

Constant (de Rebecque), (Henri) Benjamin
1767-1830 .... **NCLC 6, 182**
See also DLB 119; EW 4; GFL 1789 to the Present

Conway, Jill K(er) 1934- .... **CLC 152**
See also CA 130; CANR 94

Conybeare, Charles Augustus
See Eliot, T(homas) S(tearns)

Cook, Michael 1933-1994 .... **CLC 58**
　See also CA 93-96; CANR 68; DLB 53
Cook, Robin 1940- .... **CLC 14**
　See also AAYA 32; BEST 90:2; BPFB 1;
　CA 111; CAAE 108; CANR 41, 90, 109;
　CPW; DA3; DAM POP; HGG; INT CA-
　111
Cook, Roy
　See Silverberg, Robert
Cooke, Elizabeth 1948- .... **CLC 55**
　See also CA 129
Cooke, John Esten 1830-1886 .... **NCLC 5**
　See also DLB 3, 248; RGAL 4
Cooke, John Estes
　See Baum, L(yman) Frank
Cooke, M. E.
　See Creasey, John
Cooke, Margaret
　See Creasey, John
Cooke, Rose Terry 1827-1892 ...... **NCLC 110**
　See also DLB 12, 74
Cook-Lynn, Elizabeth 1930- .... **CLC 93;**
　NNAL
　See also CA 133; DAM MULT; DLB 175
Cooney, Ray .... **CLC 62**
　See also CBD
Cooper, Anthony Ashley 1671-1713 .. **LC 107**
　See also DLB 101
Cooper, Dennis 1953- .... **CLC 203**
　See also CA 133; CANR 72, 86; GLL 1;
　HGG
Cooper, Douglas 1960- .... **CLC 86**
Cooper, Henry St. John
　See Creasey, John
Cooper, J. California (?)- .... **CLC 56**
　See also AAYA 12; BW 1; CA 125; CANR
　55; DAM MULT; DLB 212
Cooper, James Fenimore
　1789-1851 .... **NCLC 1, 27, 54**
　See also AAYA 22; AMW; BPFB 1;
　CDALB 1640-1865; CLR 105; DA3;
　DLB 3, 183, 250, 254; LAIT 1; NFS 9;
　RGAL 4; SATA 19; TUS; WCH
Cooper, Susan Fenimore
　1813-1894 .... **NCLC 129**
　See also ANW; DLB 239, 254
Coover, Robert 1932- .. **CLC 3, 7, 15, 32, 46,**
　87, 161; SSC 15
　See also AMWS 5; BPFB 1; CA 45-48;
　CANR 3, 37, 58, 115; CN 1, 2, 3, 4, 5, 6,
　7; DAM NOV; DLB 2, 227; DLBY 1981;
　EWL 3; MAL 5; MTCW 1, 2; MTFW
　2005; RGAL 4; RGSF 2
Copeland, Stewart (Armstrong)
　1952- .... **CLC 26**
Copernicus, Nicolaus 1473-1543 .... **LC 45**
Coppard, A(lfred) E(dgar)
　1878-1957 .... **SSC 21; TCLC 5**
　See also BRWS 8; CA 167; CAAE 114;
　DLB 162; EWL 3; HGG; RGEL 2; RGSF
　2; SUFW 1; YABC 1
Coppee, Francois 1842-1908 .... **TCLC 25**
　See also CA 170; DLB 217
Coppola, Francis Ford 1939- ... **CLC 16, 126**
　See also AAYA 39; CA 77-80; CANR 40,
　78; DLB 44
Copway, George 1818-1869 .... **NNAL**
　See also DAM MULT; DLB 175, 183
Corbiere, Tristan 1845-1875 .... **NCLC 43**
　See also DLB 217; GFL 1789 to the Present
Corcoran, Barbara (Asenath)
　1911- .... **CLC 17**
　See also AAYA 14; CA 191; 21-24R, 191;
　2; CANR 11, 28, 48; CLR 50; DLB 52;
　JRDA; MAICYA 2; MAICYAS 1; RHW;
　SAAS 20; SATA 3, 77; SATA-Essay 125
Cordelier, Maurice
　See Giraudoux, Jean(-Hippolyte)

Corelli, Marie .... **TCLC 51**
　See Mackay, Mary
　See also DLB 34, 156; RGEL 2; SUFW 1
Corinna c. 225B.C.-c. 305B.C. ...... **CMLC 72**
Corman, Cid .... **CLC 9**
　See Corman, Sidney
　See also CA 2; CP 1, 2, 3, 4, 5, 6, 7; DLB
　5, 193
Corman, Sidney 1924-2004
　See Corman, Cid
　See also CA 85-88; CAAS 225; CANR 44;
　DAM POET
Cormier, Robert 1925-2000 .... **CLC 12, 30**
　See also AAYA 3, 19; BYA 1, 2, 6, 8, 9;
　CA 1-4R; CANR 5, 23, 76, 93; CDALB
　1968-1988; CLR 12, 55; DA; DAB; DAC;
　DAM MST, NOV; DLB 52; EXPN; INT
　CANR-23; JRDA; LAIT 5; MAICYA 1,
　2; MTCW 1, 2; MTFW 2005; NFS 2, 18;
　SATA 10, 45, 83; SATA-Obit 122; WYA;
　YAW
Corn, Alfred (DeWitt III) 1943- .... **CLC 33**
　See also CA 179; 179; 25; CANR 44; CP 3,
　4, 5, 6, 7; CSW; DLB 120, 282; DLBY
　1980
Corneille, Pierre 1606-1684 .. **DC 21; LC 28,**
　135
　See also DAB; DAM MST; DFS 21; DLB
　268; EW 3; GFL Beginnings to 1789;
　RGWL 2, 3; TWA
Cornwell, David
　See le Carre, John
Cornwell, Patricia 1956- .... **CLC 155**
　See also AAYA 16, 56; BPFB 1; CA 134;
　CANR 53, 131; CMW 4; CPW; CSW;
　DAM POP; DLB 306; MSW; MTCW 2;
　MTFW 2005
Cornwell, Patricia Daniels
　See Cornwell, Patricia
Corso, Gregory 1930-2001 .... **CLC 1, 11; PC**
　33
　See also AMWS 12; BG 1:2; CA 5-8R;
　CAAS 193; CANR 41, 76, 132; CP 1, 2,
　3, 4, 5, 6, 7; DA3; DLB 5, 16, 237; LMFS
　2; MAL 5; MTCW 1, 2; MTFW 2005; WP
Cortazar, Julio 1914-1984 ... **CLC 2, 3, 5, 10,**
　13, 15, 33, 34, 92; HLC 1; SSC 7, 76
　See also BPFB 1; CA 21-24R; CANR 12,
　32, 81; CDWLB 3; DA3; DAM MULT,
　NOV; DLB 113; EWL 3; EXPS; HW 1,
　2; LAW; MTCW 1, 2; MTFW 2005;
　RGSF 2; RGWL 2, 3; SSFS 3, 20; TWA;
　WLIT 1
Cortes, Hernan 1485-1547 .... **LC 31**
Corvinus, Jakob
　See Raabe, Wilhelm (Karl)
Corwin, Cecil
　See Kornbluth, C(yril) M.
Cosic, Dobrica 1921- .... **CLC 14**
　See also CA 138; CAAE 122; CDWLB 4;
　CWW 2; DLB 181; EWL 3
Costain, Thomas B(ertram)
　1885-1965 .... **CLC 30**
　See also BYA 3; CA 5-8R; CAAS 25-28R;
　DLB 9; RHW
Costantini, Humberto 1924(?)-1987 . **CLC 49**
　See also CA 131; CAAS 122; EWL 3; HW
　1
Costello, Elvis 1954- .... **CLC 21**
　See also CA 204
Costenoble, Philostene
　See Ghelderode, Michel de
Cotes, Cecil V.
　See Duncan, Sara Jeannette
Cotter, Joseph Seamon Sr.
　1861-1949 .... **BLC 1; TCLC 28**
　See also BW 1; CA 124; DAM MULT; DLB
　50

Couch, Arthur Thomas Quiller
　See Quiller-Couch, Sir Arthur (Thomas)
Coulton, James
　See Hansen, Joseph
Couperus, Louis (Marie Anne)
　1863-1923 .... **TCLC 15**
　See also CAAE 115; EWL 3; RGWL 2, 3
Coupland, Douglas 1961- .... **CLC 85, 133**
　See also AAYA 34; CA 142; CANR 57, 90,
　130; CCA 1; CN 7; CPW; DAC; DAM
　POP
Court, Wesli
　See Turco, Lewis (Putnam)
Courtenay, Bryce 1933- .... **CLC 59**
　See also CA 138; CPW
Courtney, Robert
　See Ellison, Harlan
Cousteau, Jacques-Yves 1910-1997 .. **CLC 30**
　See also CA 65-68; CAAS 159; CANR 15,
　67; MTCW 1; SATA 38, 98
Coventry, Francis 1725-1754 .... **LC 46**
Coverdale, Miles c. 1487-1569 .... **LC 77**
　See also DLB 167
Cowan, Peter (Walkinshaw)
　1914-2002 .... **SSC 28**
　See also CA 21-24R; CANR 9, 25, 50, 83;
　CN 1, 2, 3, 4, 5, 6, 7; DLB 260; RGSF 2
Coward, Noel (Peirce) 1899-1973 . **CLC 1, 9,**
　29, 51
　See also AITN 1; BRWS 2; CA 17-18;
　CAAS 41-44R; CANR 35, 132; CAP 2;
　CBD; CDBLB 1914-1945; DA3; DAM
　DRAM; DFS 3, 6; DLB 10, 245; EWL 3;
　IDFW 3, 4; MTCW 1, 2; MTFW 2005;
　RGEL 2; TEA
Cowley, Abraham 1618-1667 .... **LC 43**
　See also BRW 2; DLB 131, 151; PAB;
　RGEL 2
Cowley, Malcolm 1898-1989 .... **CLC 39**
　See also AMWS 2; CA 5-8R; CAAS 128;
　CANR 3, 55; CP 1, 2, 3, 4; DLB 4, 48;
　DLBY 1981, 1989; EWL 3; MAL 5;
　MTCW 1, 2; MTFW 2005
Cowper, William 1731-1800 ..... **NCLC 8, 94;**
　PC 40
　See also BRW 3; DA3; DAM POET; DLB
　104, 109; RGEL 2
Cox, William Trevor 1928-
　See Trevor, William
　See also CA 9-12R; CANR 4, 37, 55, 76,
　102, 139; DAM NOV; INT CANR-37;
　MTCW 1, 2; MTFW 2005; TEA
Coyne, P. J.
　See Masters, Hilary
Cozzens, James Gould 1903-1978 . **CLC 1, 4,**
　11, 92
　See also AMW; BPFB 1; CA 9-12R; CAAS
　81-84; CANR 19; CDALB 1941-1968;
　CN 1, 2; DLB 9, 294; DLBD 2; DLBY
　1984, 1997; EWL 3; MAL 5; MTCW 1,
　2; MTFW 2005; RGAL 4
Crabbe, George 1754-1832 .... **NCLC 26, 121**
　See also BRW 3; DLB 93; RGEL 2
Crace, Jim 1946- .... **CLC 157; SSC 61**
　See also CA 135; CAAE 128; CANR 55,
　70, 123; CN 5, 6, 7; DLB 231; INT CA-
　135
Craddock, Charles Egbert
　See Murfree, Mary Noailles
Craig, A. A.
　See Anderson, Poul
Craik, Mrs.
　See Craik, Dinah Maria (Mulock)
　See also RGEL 2
Craik, Dinah Maria (Mulock)
　1826-1887 .... **NCLC 38**
　See Craik, Mrs.; Mulock, Dinah Maria
　See also DLB 35, 163; MAICYA 1, 2;
　SATA 34

Cunninghame Graham, R. B.
See Cunninghame Graham, Robert (Gallnigad) Bontine
Cunninghame Graham, Robert (Gallnigad) Bontine 1852-1936 .... **TCLC 19**
See Graham, R(obert) B(ontine) Cunninghame
See also CA 184; CAAE 119
Curnow, (Thomas) Allen (Monro) 1911-2001 .... **PC 48**
See also CA 69-72; CAAS 202; CANR 48, 99; CP 1, 2, 3, 4, 5, 6, 7; EWL 3; RGEL 2
Currie, Ellen 19(?)- .... **CLC 44**
Curtin, Philip
See Lowndes, Marie Adelaide (Belloc)
Curtin, Phillip
See Lowndes, Marie Adelaide (Belloc)
Curtis, Price
See Ellison, Harlan
Cusanus, Nicolaus 1401-1464 .... **LC 80**
See Nicholas of Cusa
Cutrate, Joe
See Spiegelman, Art
Cynewulf c. 770- .... **CMLC 23**
See also DLB 146; RGEL 2
Cyrano de Bergerac, Savinien de 1619-1655 .... **LC 65**
See also DLB 268; GFL Beginnings to 1789; RGWL 2, 3
Cyril of Alexandria c. 375-c. 430 . **CMLC 59**
Czaczkes, Shmuel Yosef Halevi
See Agnon, S(hmuel) Y(osef Halevi)
Dabrowska, Maria (Szumska) 1889-1965 .... **CLC 15**
See also CA 106; CDWLB 4; DLB 215; EWL 3
Dabydeen, David 1955- .... **CLC 34**
See also BW 1; CA 125; CANR 56, 92; CN 6, 7; CP 5, 6, 7
Dacey, Philip 1939- .... **CLC 51**
See also CA 231; 37-40R, 231; 17; CANR 14, 32, 64; CP 4, 5, 6, 7; DLB 105
Dacre, Charlotte c. 1772-1825(?) . **NCLC 151**
Dafydd ap Gwilym c. 1320-c. 1380 ..... **PC 56**
Dagerman, Stig (Halvard) 1923-1954 .... **TCLC 17**
See also CA 155; CAAE 117; DLB 259; EWL 3
D'Aguiar, Fred 1960- .... **CLC 145**
See also CA 148; CANR 83, 101; CN 7; CP 5, 6, 7; DLB 157; EWL 3
Dahl, Roald 1916-1990 ...... **CLC 1, 6, 18, 79; TCLC 173**
See also AAYA 15; BPFB 1; BRWS 4; BYA 5; CA 1-4R; CAAS 133; CANR 6, 32, 37, 62; CLR 1, 7, 41, 111; CN 1, 2, 3, 4; CPW; DA3; DAB; DAC; DAM MST, NOV, POP; DLB 139, 255; HGG; JRDA; MAICYA 1, 2; MTCW 1, 2; MTFW 2005; RGSF 2; SATA 1, 26, 73; SATA-Obit 65; SSFS 4; TEA; YAW
Dahlberg, Edward 1900-1977 .. **CLC 1, 7, 14**
See also CA 9-12R; CAAS 69-72; CANR 31, 62; CN 1, 2; DLB 48; MAL 5; MTCW 1; RGAL 4
Daitch, Susan 1954- .... **CLC 103**
See also CA 161
Dale, Colin .... **TCLC 18**
See Lawrence, T(homas) E(dward)
Dale, George E.
See Asimov, Isaac
d'Alembert, Jean Le Rond 1717-1783 .... **LC 126**
Dalton, Roque 1935-1975(?) ..... **HLCS 1; PC 36**
See also CA 176; DLB 283; HW 2

Daly, Elizabeth 1878-1967 .... **CLC 52**
See also CA 23-24; CAAS 25-28R; CANR 60; CAP 2; CMW 4
Daly, Mary 1928- .... **CLC 173**
See also CA 25-28R; CANR 30, 62; FW; GLL 1; MTCW 1
Daly, Maureen 1921-2006 .... **CLC 17**
See also AAYA 5, 58; BYA 6; CAAS 253; CANR 37, 83, 108; CLR 96; JRDA; MAICYA 1, 2; SAAS 1; SATA 2, 129; SATA-Obit 176; WYA; YAW
Damas, Leon-Gontran 1912-1978 .... **CLC 84**
See also BW 1; CA 125; CAAS 73-76; EWL 3
Dana, Richard Henry Sr. 1787-1879 .... **NCLC 53**
Daniel, Samuel 1562(?)-1619 .... **LC 24**
See also DLB 62; RGEL 2
Daniels, Brett
See Adler, Renata
Dannay, Frederic 1905-1982 .... **CLC 11**
See Queen, Ellery
See also CA 1-4R; CAAS 107; CANR 1, 39; CMW 4; DAM POP; DLB 137; MTCW 1
D'Annunzio, Gabriele 1863-1938 ... **TCLC 6, 40**
See also CA 155; CAAE 104; EW 8; EWL 3; RGWL 2, 3; TWA; WLIT 7
Danois, N. le
See Gourmont, Remy(-Marie-Charles) de
Dante 1265-1321 .... **CMLC 3, 18, 39, 70; PC 21; WLCS**
See Alighieri, Dante
See also DA; DA3; DAB; DAC; DAM MST, POET; EFS 1; EW 1; LAIT 1; RGWL 2, 3; TWA; WP
d'Antibes, Germain
See Simenon, Georges (Jacques Christian)
Danticat, Edwidge 1969- ... **CLC 94, 139, 228**
See also AAYA 29; CA 192; 152, 192; CANR 73, 129; CN 7; DNFS 1; EXPS; LATS 1:2; MTCW 2; MTFW 2005; SSFS 1; YAW
Danvers, Dennis 1947- .... **CLC 70**
Danziger, Paula 1944-2004 .... **CLC 21**
See also AAYA 4, 36; BYA 6, 7, 14; CA 115; CAAE 112; CAAS 229; CANR 37, 132; CLR 20; JRDA; MAICYA 1, 2; MTFW 2005; SATA 36, 63, 102, 149; SATA-Brief 30; SATA-Obit 155; WYA; YAW
Da Ponte, Lorenzo 1749-1838 .... **NCLC 50**
d'Aragona, Tullia 1510(?)-1556 .... **LC 121**
Dario, Ruben 1867-1916 .... **HLC 1; PC 15; TCLC 4**
See also CA 131; CANR 81; DAM MULT; DLB 290; EWL 3; HW 1, 2; LAW; MTCW 1, 2; MTFW 2005; RGWL 2, 3
Darley, George 1795-1846 .... **NCLC 2**
See also DLB 96; RGEL 2
Darrow, Clarence (Seward) 1857-1938 .... **TCLC 81**
See also CA 164; DLB 303
Darwin, Charles 1809-1882 .... **NCLC 57**
See also BRWS 7; DLB 57, 166; LATS 1:1; RGEL 2; TEA; WLIT 4
Darwin, Erasmus 1731-1802 .... **NCLC 106**
See also DLB 93; RGEL 2
Daryush, Elizabeth 1887-1977 ...... **CLC 6, 19**
See also CA 49-52; CANR 3, 81; DLB 20
Das, Kamala 1934- .... **CLC 191; PC 43**
See also CA 101; CANR 27, 59; CP 1, 2, 3, 4, 5, 6, 7; CWP; DLB 323; FW
Dasgupta, Surendranath 1887-1952 .... **TCLC 81**
See also CA 157

Dashwood, Edmee Elizabeth Monica de la Pasture 1890-1943
See Delafield, E. M.
See also CA 154; CAAE 119
da Silva, Antonio Jose 1705-1739 .... **NCLC 114**
Daudet, (Louis Marie) Alphonse 1840-1897 .... **NCLC 1**
See also DLB 123; GFL 1789 to the Present; RGSF 2
Daudet, Alphonse Marie Leon 1867-1942 .... **SSC 94**
See also CA 217
d'Aulnoy, Marie-Catherine c. 1650-1705 .... **LC 100**
Daumal, Rene 1908-1944 .... **TCLC 14**
See also CA 247; CAAE 114; EWL 3
Davenant, William 1606-1668 .... **LC 13**
See also DLB 58, 126; RGEL 2
Davenport, Guy (Mattison, Jr.) 1927-2005 .... **CLC 6, 14, 38; SSC 16**
See also CA 33-36R; CAAS 235; CANR 23, 73; CN 3, 4, 5, 6; CSW; DLB 130
David, Robert
See Nezval, Vitezslav
Davidson, Avram (James) 1923-1993
See Queen, Ellery
See also CA 101; CAAS 171; CANR 26; DLB 8; FANT; SFW 4; SUFW 1, 2
Davidson, Donald (Grady) 1893-1968 .... **CLC 2, 13, 19**
See also CA 5-8R; CAAS 25-28R; CANR 4, 84; DLB 45
Davidson, Hugh
See Hamilton, Edmond
Davidson, John 1857-1909 .... **TCLC 24**
See also CA 217; CAAE 118; DLB 19; RGEL 2
Davidson, Sara 1943- .... **CLC 9**
See also CA 81-84; CANR 44, 68; DLB 185
Davie, Donald (Alfred) 1922-1995 .... **CLC 5, 8, 10, 31; PC 29**
See also BRWS 6; CA 1-4R; 3; CAAS 149; CANR 1, 44; CP 1, 2, 3, 4, 5, 6; DLB 27; MTCW 1; RGEL 2
Davie, Elspeth 1918-1995 .... **SSC 52**
See also CA 126; CAAE 120; CAAS 150; CANR 141; DLB 139
Davies, Ray(mond Douglas) 1944- ... **CLC 21**
See also CA 146; CAAE 116; CANR 92
Davies, Rhys 1901-1978 .... **CLC 23**
See also CA 9-12R; CAAS 81-84; CANR 4; CN 1, 2; DLB 139, 191
Davies, Robertson 1913-1995 .. **CLC 2, 7, 13, 25, 42, 75, 91; WLC 2**
See Marchbanks, Samuel
See also BEST 89:2; BPFB 1; CA 33-36R; CAAS 150; CANR 17, 42, 103; CN 1, 2, 3, 4, 5, 6; CPW; DA; DA3; DAB; DAC; DAM MST, NOV, POP; DLB 68; EWL 3; HGG; INT CANR-17; MTCW 1, 2; MTFW 2005; RGEL 2; TWA
Davies, Sir John 1569-1626 .... **LC 85**
See also DLB 172
Davies, Walter C.
See Kornbluth, C(yril) M.
Davies, William Henry 1871-1940 ... **TCLC 5**
See also BRWS 11; CA 179; CAAE 104; DLB 19, 174; EWL 3; RGEL 2
Davies, William Robertson
See Davies, Robertson
Da Vinci, Leonardo 1452-1519 ..... **LC 12, 57, 60**
See also AAYA 40
Davis, Angela (Yvonne) 1944- .... **CLC 77**
See also BW 2, 3; CA 57-60; CANR 10, 81; CSW; DA3; DAM MULT; FW

Diderot, Denis 1713-1784 .... **LC 26, 126**
See also DLB 313; EW 4; GFL Beginnings
to 1789; LMFS 1; RGWL 2, 3

Didion, Joan 1934- . **CLC 1, 3, 8, 14, 32, 129**
See also AITN 1; AMWS 4; CA 5-8R;
CANR 14, 52, 76, 125; CDALB 1968-
1988; CN 2, 3, 4, 5, 6, 7; DA3; DAM
NOV; DLB 2, 173, 185; DLBY 1981,
1986; EWL 3; MAL 5; MBL; MTCW 1,
2; MTFW 2005; NFS 3; RGAL 4; TCLE
1:1; TCWW 2; TUS

di Donato, Pietro 1911-1992 .... **TCLC 159**
See also CA 101; CAAS 136; DLB 9

Dietrich, Robert
See Hunt, E. Howard

Difusa, Pati
See Almodovar, Pedro

Dillard, Annie 1945- ...... **CLC 9, 60, 115, 216**
See also AAYA 6, 43; AMWS 6; ANW; CA
49-52; CANR 3, 43, 62, 90, 125; DA3;
DAM NOV; DLB 275, 278; DLBY 1980;
LAIT 4, 5; MAL 5; MTCW 1, 2; MTFW
2005; NCFS 1; RGAL 4; SATA 10, 140;
TCLE 1:1; TUS

Dillard, R(ichard) H(enry) W(ilde)
1937- .... **CLC 5**
See also CA 21-24R; 7; CANR 10; CP 2, 3,
4, 5, 6, 7; CSW; DLB 5, 244

Dillon, Eilis 1920-1994 .... **CLC 17**
See also CA 182; 9-12R, 182; 3; CAAS
147; CANR 4, 38, 78; CLR 26; MAICYA
1, 2; MAICYAS 1; SATA 2, 74; SATA-
Essay 105; SATA-Obit 83; YAW

Dimont, Penelope
See Mortimer, Penelope (Ruth)

Dinesen, Isak ..... **CLC 10, 29, 95; SSC 7, 75**
See Blixen, Karen (Christentze Dinesen)
See also EW 10; EWL 3; EXPS; FW; GL
2; HGG; LAIT 3; MTCW 1; NCFS 2;
NFS 9; RGSF 2; RGWL 2, 3; SSFS 3, 6,
13; WLIT 2

Ding Ling .... **CLC 68**
See Chiang, Pin-chin
See also DLB 328; RGWL 3

Diodorus Siculus c. 90B.C.-c.
31B.C. .... **CMLC 88**

Diphusa, Patty
See Almodovar, Pedro

Disch, Thomas M. 1940- .... **CLC 7, 36**
See Disch, Tom
See also AAYA 17; BPFB 1; CA 21-24R; 4;
CANR 17, 36, 54, 89; CLR 18; CP 5, 6,
7; DA3; DLB 8; HGG; MAICYA 1, 2;
MTCW 1, 2; MTFW 2005; SAAS 15;
SATA 92; SCFW 1, 2; SFW 4; SUFW 2

Disch, Tom
See Disch, Thomas M.
See also DLB 282

d'Isly, Georges
See Simenon, Georges (Jacques Christian)

Disraeli, Benjamin 1804-1881 ... **NCLC 2, 39, 79**
See also BRW 4; DLB 21, 55; RGEL 2

Ditcum, Steve
See Crumb, R.

Dixon, Paige
See Corcoran, Barbara (Asenath)

Dixon, Stephen 1936- .... **CLC 52; SSC 16**
See also AMWS 12; CA 89-92; CANR 17,
40, 54, 91; CN 4, 5, 6, 7; DLB 130; MAL
5

Dixon, Thomas, Jr. 1864-1946 ..... **TCLC 163**
See also RHW

Djebar, Assia 1936- .... **CLC 182**
See also CA 188; EWL 3; RGWL 3; WLIT
2

Doak, Annie
See Dillard, Annie

Dobell, Sydney Thompson
1824-1874 .... **NCLC 43**
See also DLB 32; RGEL 2

Doblin, Alfred .... **TCLC 13**
See Doeblin, Alfred
See also CDWLB 2; EWL 3; RGWL 2, 3

Dobroliubov, Nikolai Aleksandrovich
See Dobrolyubov, Nikolai Alexandrovich
See also DLB 277

Dobrolyubov, Nikolai Alexandrovich
1836-1861 .... **NCLC 5**
See Dobroliubov, Nikolai Aleksandrovich

Dobson, Austin 1840-1921 .... **TCLC 79**
See also DLB 35, 144

Dobyns, Stephen 1941- .... **CLC 37, 233**
See also AMWS 13; CA 45-48; CANR 2,
18, 99; CMW 4; CP 4, 5, 6, 7; PFS 23

Doctorow, Edgar Laurence
See Doctorow, E.L.

Doctorow, E.L. 1931- . **CLC 6, 11, 15, 18, 37, 44, 65, 113, 214**
See also AAYA 22; AITN 2; AMWS 4;
BEST 89:3; BPFB 1; CA 45-48; CANR
2, 33, 51, 76, 97, 133; CDALB 1968-
1988; CN 3, 4, 5, 6, 7; CPW; DA3; DAM
NOV, POP; DLB 2, 28, 173; DLBY 1980;
EWL 3; LAIT 3; MAL 5; MTCW 1, 2;
MTFW 2005; NFS 6; RGAL 4; RGHL;
RHW; TCLE 1:1; TCWW 1, 2; TUS

Dodgson, Charles L(utwidge) 1832-1898
See Carroll, Lewis
See also CLR 2; DA; DA3; DAB; DAC;
DAM MST, NOV, POET; MAICYA 1, 2;
SATA 100; YABC 2

Dodsley, Robert 1703-1764 .... **LC 97**
See also DLB 95; RGEL 2

Dodson, Owen (Vincent) 1914-1983 .. **BLC 1; CLC 79**
See also BW 1; CA 65-68; CAAS 110;
CANR 24; DAM MULT; DLB 76

Doeblin, Alfred 1878-1957 .... **TCLC 13**
See Doblin, Alfred
See also CA 141; CAAE 110; DLB 66

Doerr, Harriet 1910-2002 .... **CLC 34**
See also CA 122; CAAE 117; CAAS 213;
CANR 47; INT CA-122; LATS 1:2

Domecq, H(onorio Bustos)
See Bioy Casares, Adolfo

Domecq, H(onorio) Bustos
See Bioy Casares, Adolfo; Borges, Jorge
Luis

Domini, Rey
See Lorde, Audre
See also GLL 1

Dominique
See Proust, (Valentin-Louis-George-Eugene)
Marcel

Don, A
See Stephen, Sir Leslie

Donaldson, Stephen R(eeder)
1947- .... **CLC 46, 138**
See also AAYA 36; BPFB 1; CA 89-92;
CANR 13, 55, 99; CPW; DAM POP;
FANT; INT CANR-13; SATA 121; SFW
4; SUFW 1, 2

Donleavy, J(ames) P(atrick) 1926- .... **CLC 1, 4, 6, 10, 45**
See also AITN 2; BPFB 1; CA 9-12R;
CANR 24, 49, 62, 80, 124; CBD; CD 5,
6; CN 1, 2, 3, 4, 5, 6, 7; DLB 6, 173; INT
CANR-24; MAL 5; MTCW 1, 2; MTFW
2005; RGAL 4

Donnadieu, Marguerite
See Duras, Marguerite

Donne, John 1572-1631 ... **LC 10, 24, 91; PC 1, 43; WLC 2**
See also AAYA 67; BRW 1; BRWC 1;
BRWR 2; CDBLB Before 1660; DA;
DAB; DAC; DAM MST, POET; DLB
121, 151; EXPP; PAB; PFS 2, 11; RGEL
3; TEA; WLIT 3; WP

Donnell, David 1939(?)- .... **CLC 34**
See also CA 197

Donoghue, Denis 1928- .... **CLC 209**
See also CA 17-20R; CANR 16, 102

Donoghue, P. S.
See Hunt, E. Howard

Donoso (Yanez), Jose 1924-1996 ... **CLC 4, 8, 11, 32, 99; HLC 1; SSC 34; TCLC 133**
See also CA 81-84; CAAS 155; CANR 32,
73; CDWLB 3; CWW 2; DAM MULT;
DLB 113; EWL 3; HW 1, 2; LAW; LAWS
1; MTCW 1, 2; MTFW 2005; RGSF 2;
WLIT 1

Donovan, John 1928-1992 .... **CLC 35**
See also AAYA 20; CA 97-100; CAAS 137;
CLR 3; MAICYA 1, 2; SATA 72; SATA-
Brief 29; YAW

Don Roberto
See Cunninghame Graham, Robert
(Gallnigad) Bontine

Doolittle, Hilda 1886-1961 . **CLC 3, 8, 14, 31, 34, 73; PC 5; WLC 3**
See H. D.
See also AAYA 66; AMWS 1; CA 97-100;
CANR 35, 131; DA; DAC; DAM MST,
POET; DLB 4, 45; EWL 3; FW; GLL 1;
LMFS 2; MAL 5; MBL; MTCW 1, 2;
MTFW 2005; PFS 6; RGAL 4

Doppo, Kunikida .... **TCLC 99**
See Kunikida Doppo

Dorfman, Ariel 1942- .... **CLC 48, 77, 189; HLC 1**
See also CA 130; CAAE 124; CANR 67,
70, 135; CWW 2; DAM MULT; DFS 4;
EWL 3; HW 1, 2; INT CA-130; WLIT 1

Dorn, Edward (Merton)
1929-1999 .... **CLC 10, 18**
See also CA 93-96; CAAS 187; CANR 42,
79; CP 1, 2, 3, 4, 5, 6, 7; DLB 5; INT
CA-93-96; WP

Dor-Ner, Zvi .... **CLC 70**

Dorris, Michael 1945-1997 .... **CLC 109; NNAL**
See also AAYA 20; BEST 90:1; BYA 12;
CA 102; CAAS 157; CANR 19, 46, 75;
CLR 58; DA3; DAM MULT, NOV; DLB
175; LAIT 5; MTCW 2; MTFW 2005;
NFS 3; RGAL 4; SATA 75; SATA-Obit
94; TCWW 2; YAW

Dorris, Michael A.
See Dorris, Michael

Dorsan, Luc
See Simenon, Georges (Jacques Christian)

Dorsange, Jean
See Simenon, Georges (Jacques Christian)

Dorset
See Sackville, Thomas

Dos Passos, John (Roderigo)
1896-1970 ... **CLC 1, 4, 8, 11, 15, 25, 34, 82; WLC 2**
See also AMW; BPFB 1; CA 1-4R; CAAS
29-32R; CANR 3; CDALB 1929-1941;
DA; DA3; DAB; DAC; DAM MST, NOV;
DLB 4, 9, 274, 316; DLBD 1, 15; DLBY
1996; EWL 3; MAL 5; MTCW 1, 2;
MTFW 2005; NFS 14; RGAL 4; TUS

Dossage, Jean
See Simenon, Georges (Jacques Christian)

Dostoevsky, Fedor Mikhailovich
1821-1881 .. **NCLC 2, 7, 21, 33, 43, 119, 167; SSC 2, 33, 44; WLC 2**
See Dostoevsky, Fyodor
See also AAYA 40; DA; DA3; DAB; DAC;
DAM MST, NOV; EW 7; EXPN; NFS 3,
8; RGSF 2; RGWL 2, 3; SSFS 8; TWA

Dostoevsky, Fyodor
See Dostoevsky, Fedor Mikhailovich
See also DLB 238; LATS 1:1; LMFS 1, 2

Doty, M. R.
See Doty, Mark

Doty, Mark 1953(?)- .... **CLC 176; PC 53**
See also AMWS 11; CA 183; 161, 183;
CANR 110; CP 7

Doty, Mark A.
See Doty, Mark

Doty, Mark Alan
See Doty, Mark

Doughty, Charles M(ontagu)
1843-1926 .... **TCLC 27**
See also CA 178; CAAE 115; DLB 19, 57,
174

Douglas, Ellen .... **CLC 73**
See Haxton, Josephine Ayres; Williamson,
Ellen Douglas
See also CN 5, 6, 7; CSW; DLB 292

Douglas, Gavin 1475(?)-1522 .... **LC 20**
See also DLB 132; RGEL 2

Douglas, George
See Brown, George Douglas
See also RGEL 2

Douglas, Keith (Castellain)
1920-1944 .... **TCLC 40**
See also BRW 7; CA 160; DLB 27; EWL
3; PAB; RGEL 2

Douglas, Leonard
See Bradbury, Ray

Douglas, Michael
See Crichton, Michael

Douglas, (George) Norman
1868-1952 .... **TCLC 68**
See also BRW 6; CA 157; CAAE 119; DLB
34, 195; RGEL 2

Douglas, William
See Brown, George Douglas

Douglass, Frederick 1817(?)-1895 ..... **BLC 1;
NCLC 7, 55, 141; WLC 2**
See also AAYA 48; AFAW 1, 2; AMWC 1;
AMWS 3; CDALB 1640-1865; DA; DA3;
DAC; DAM MST, MULT; DLB 1, 43, 50,
79, 243; FW; LAIT 2; NCFS 2; RGAL 4;
SATA 29

Dourado, (Waldomiro Freitas) Autran
1926- .... **CLC 23, 60**
See also CA 25-28R, 179; CANR 34, 81;
DLB 145, 307; HW 2

Dourado, Waldomiro Freitas Autran
See Dourado, (Waldomiro Freitas) Autran

Dove, Rita 1952- .. **BLCS; CLC 50, 81; PC 6**
See also AAYA 46; AMWS 4; BW 2; CA
109; 19; CANR 27, 42, 68, 76, 97, 132;
CDALBS; CP 5, 6, 7; CSW; CWP; DA3;
DAM MULT, POET; DLB 120; EWL 3;
EXPP; MAL 5; MTCW 2; MTFW 2005;
PFS 1, 15; RGAL 4

Dove, Rita Frances
See Dove, Rita

Doveglion
See Villa, Jose Garcia

Dowell, Coleman 1925-1985 .... **CLC 60**
See also CA 25-28R; CAAS 117; CANR
10; DLB 130; GLL 2

Dowson, Ernest (Christopher)
1867-1900 .... **TCLC 4**
See also CA 150; CAAE 105; DLB 19, 135;
RGEL 2

Doyle, A. Conan
See Doyle, Sir Arthur Conan

Doyle, Sir Arthur Conan
1859-1930 ..... **SSC 12, 83, 95; TCLC 7;
WLC 2**
See Conan Doyle, Arthur
See also AAYA 14; BRWS 2; CA 122;
CAAE 104; CANR 131; CDBLB 1890-
1914; CLR 106; CMW 4; DA; DA3;
DAB; DAC; DAM MST, NOV; DLB 18,
70, 156, 178; EXPS; HGG; LAIT 2;

MSW; MTCW 1, 2; MTFW 2005; RGEL
2; RGSF 2; RHW; SATA 24; SCFW 1, 2;
SFW 4; SSFS 2; TEA; WCH; WLIT 4;
WYA; YAW

Doyle, Conan
See Doyle, Sir Arthur Conan

Doyle, John
See Graves, Robert

Doyle, Roddy 1958- .... **CLC 81, 178**
See also AAYA 14; BRWS 5; CA 143;
CANR 73, 128; CN 6, 7; DA3; DLB 194,
326; MTCW 2; MTFW 2005

Doyle, Sir A. Conan
See Doyle, Sir Arthur Conan

Dr. A
See Asimov, Isaac; Silverstein, Alvin; Silverstein, Virginia B(arbara Opshelor)

Drabble, Margaret 1939- ...... **CLC 2, 3, 5, 8,
10, 22, 53, 129**
See also BRWS 4; CA 13-16R; CANR 18,
35, 63, 112, 131; CDBLB 1960 to Present;
CN 1, 2, 3, 4, 5, 6, 7; CPW; DA3; DAB;
DAC; DAM MST, NOV, POP; DLB 14,
155, 231; EWL 3; FW; MTCW 1, 2;
MTFW 2005; RGEL 2; SATA 48; TEA

Drakulic, Slavenka 1949- .... **CLC 173**
See also CA 144; CANR 92

Drakulic-Ilic, Slavenka
See Drakulic, Slavenka

Drapier, M. B.
See Swift, Jonathan

Drayham, James
See Mencken, H(enry) L(ouis)

Drayton, Michael 1563-1631 .... **LC 8**
See also DAM POET; DLB 121; RGEL 2

Dreadstone, Carl
See Campbell, (John) Ramsey

Dreiser, Theodore 1871-1945 .... **SSC 30;
TCLC 10, 18, 35, 83; WLC 2**
See also AMW; AMWC 2; AMWR 2; BYA
15, 16; CA 132; CAAE 106; CDALB
1865-1917; DA; DA3; DAC; DAM MST,
NOV; DLB 9, 12, 102, 137; DLBD 1;
EWL 3; LAIT 2; LMFS 2; MAL 5;
MTCW 1, 2; MTFW 2005; NFS 8, 17;
RGAL 4; TUS

Dreiser, Theodore Herman Albert
See Dreiser, Theodore

Drexler, Rosalyn 1926- .... **CLC 2, 6**
See also CA 81-84; CAD; CANR 68, 124;
CD 5, 6; CWD; MAL 5

Dreyer, Carl Theodor 1889-1968 ...... **CLC 16**
See also CAAS 116

Drieu la Rochelle, Pierre
1893-1945 .... **TCLC 21**
See also CA 250; CAAE 117; DLB 72;
EWL 3; GFL 1789 to the Present

Drieu la Rochelle, Pierre-Eugene 1893-1945
See Drieu la Rochelle, Pierre

Drinkwater, John 1882-1937 .... **TCLC 57**
See also CA 149; CAAE 109; DLB 10, 19,
149; RGEL 2

Drop Shot
See Cable, George Washington

Droste-Hulshoff, Annette Freiin von
1797-1848 .... **NCLC 3, 133**
See also CDWLB 2; DLB 133; RGSF 2;
RGWL 2, 3

Drummond, Walter
See Silverberg, Robert

Drummond, William Henry
1854-1907 .... **TCLC 25**
See also CA 160; DLB 92

Drummond de Andrade, Carlos
1902-1987 .... **CLC 18; TCLC 139**
See Andrade, Carlos Drummond de
See also CA 132; CAAS 123; DLB 307;
LAW

Drummond of Hawthornden, William
1585-1649 .... **LC 83**
See also DLB 121, 213; RGEL 2

Drury, Allen (Stuart) 1918-1998 .... **CLC 37**
See also CA 57-60; CAAS 170; CANR 18,
52; CN 1, 2, 3, 4, 5, 6; INT CANR-18

Druse, Eleanor
See King, Stephen

Dryden, John 1631-1700 ..... **DC 3; LC 3, 21,
115; PC 25; WLC 2**
See also BRW 2; CDBLB 1660-1789; DA;
DAB; DAC; DAM DRAM, MST, POET;
DLB 80, 101, 131; EXPP; IDTP; LMFS
1; RGEL 2; TEA; WLIT 3

du Bellay, Joachim 1524-1560 .... **LC 92**
See also DLB 327; GFL Beginnings to
1789; RGWL 2, 3

Duberman, Martin (Bauml) 1930- ..... **CLC 8**
See also CA 1-4R; CAD; CANR 2, 63, 137;
CD 5, 6

Dubie, Norman (Evans) 1945- .... **CLC 36**
See also CA 69-72; CANR 12, 115; CP 3,
4, 5, 6, 7; DLB 120; PFS 12

Du Bois, W(illiam) E(dward) B(urghardt)
1868-1963 ..... **BLC 1; CLC 1, 2, 13, 64,
96; HR 1:2; TCLC 169; WLC 2**
See also AAYA 40; AFAW 1, 2; AMWC 1;
AMWS 2; BW 1, 3; CA 85-88; CANR
34, 82, 132; CDALB 1865-1917; DA;
DA3; DAC; DAM MST, MULT, NOV;
DLB 47, 50, 91, 246, 284; EWL 3; EXPP;
LAIT 2; LMFS 2; MAL 5; MTCW 1, 2;
MTFW 2005; NCFS 1; PFS 13; RGAL 4;
SATA 42

Dubus, Andre 1936-1999 ..... **CLC 13, 36, 97;
SSC 15**
See also AMWS 7; CA 21-24R; CAAS 177;
CANR 17; CN 5, 6; CSW; DLB 130; INT
CANR-17; RGAL 4; SSFS 10; TCLE 1:1

Duca Minimo
See D'Annunzio, Gabriele

Ducharme, Rejean 1941- .... **CLC 74**
See also CAAS 165; DLB 60

du Chatelet, Emilie 1706-1749 .... **LC 96**
See Chatelet, Gabrielle-Emilie Du

Duchen, Claire .... **CLC 65**

Duclos, Charles Pinot- 1704-1772 .... **LC 1**
See also GFL Beginnings to 1789

Ducornet, Erica 1943-
See Ducornet, Rikki
See also CA 37-40R; CANR 14, 34, 54, 82;
SATA 7

Ducornet, Rikki .... **CLC 232**
See Ducornet, Erica

Dudek, Louis 1918-2001 .... **CLC 11, 19**
See also CA 45-48; 14; CAAS 215; CANR
1; CP 1, 2, 3, 4, 5, 6, 7; DLB 88

Duerrenmatt, Friedrich 1921-1990 ... **CLC 1,
4, 8, 11, 15, 43, 102**
See Durrenmatt, Friedrich
See also CA 17-20R; CANR 33; CMW 4;
DAM DRAM; DLB 69, 124; MTCW 1, 2

Duffy, Bruce 1953(?)- .... **CLC 50**
See also CA 172

Duffy, Maureen (Patricia) 1933- ...... **CLC 37**
See also CA 25-28R; CANR 33, 68; CBD;
CN 1, 2, 3, 4, 5, 6, 7; CP 5, 6, 7; CWD;
CWP; DFS 15; DLB 14, 310; FW; MTCW
1

Du Fu
See Tu Fu
See also RGWL 2, 3

Dugan, Alan 1923-2003 .... **CLC 2, 6**
See also CA 81-84; CAAS 220; CANR 119;
CP 1, 2, 3, 4, 5, 6, 7; DLB 5; MAL 5;
PFS 10

du Gard, Roger Martin
See Martin du Gard, Roger

Ellison, Ralph 1914-1994 . **BLC 1; CLC 1, 3, 11, 54, 86, 114; SSC 26, 79; WLC 2**
See also AAYA 19; AFAW 1, 2; AMWC 2; AMWR 2; AMWS 2; BPFB 1; BW 1, 3; BYA 2; CA 9-12R; CAAS 145; CANR 24, 53; CDALB 1941-1968; CN 1, 2, 3, 4, 5; CSW; DA; DA3; DAB; DAC; DAM MST, MULT, NOV; DLB 2, 76, 227; DLBY 1994; EWL 3; EXPN; EXPS; LAIT 4; MAL 5; MTCW 1, 2; MTFW 2005; NCFS 3; NFS 2, 21; RGAL 4; RGSF 2; SSFS 1, 11; YAW

Ellmann, Lucy 1956- .... **CLC 61**
See also CA 128; CANR 154

Ellmann, Lucy Elizabeth
See Ellmann, Lucy

Ellmann, Richard (David)
1918-1987 .... **CLC 50**
See also BEST 89:2; CA 1-4R; CAAS 122; CANR 2, 28, 61; DLB 103; DLBY 1987; MTCW 1, 2; MTFW 2005

Elman, Richard (Martin)
1934-1997 .... **CLC 19**
See also CA 17-20R; 3; CAAS 163; CANR 47; TCLE 1:1

Elron
See Hubbard, L. Ron

El Saadawi, Nawal 1931- .... **CLC 196**
See also al'Sadaawi, Nawal; Sa'adawi, al-Nawal; Saadawi, Nawal El; Sa'dawi, Nawal al-
See also CA 118; 11; CANR 44, 92

Eluard, Paul .... **PC 38; TCLC 7, 41**
See Grindel, Eugene
See also EWL 3; GFL 1789 to the Present; RGWL 2, 3

Elyot, Thomas 1490(?)-1546 .... **LC 11**
See also DLB 136; RGEL 2

Elytis, Odysseus 1911-1996 .... **CLC 15, 49, 100; PC 21**
See Alepoudelis, Odysseus
See also CA 102; CAAS 151; CANR 94; CWW 2; DAM POET; DLB 329; EW 13; EWL 3; MTCW 1, 2; RGWL 2, 3

Emecheta, Buchi 1944- .... **BLC 2; CLC 14, 48, 128, 214**
See also AAYA 67; AFW; BW 2, 3; CA 81-84; CANR 27, 81, 126; CDWLB 3; CN 4, 5, 6, 7; CWRI 5; DA3; DAM MULT; DLB 117; EWL 3; FL 1:5; FW; MTCW 1, 2; MTFW 2005; NFS 12, 14; SATA 66; WLIT 2

Emerson, Mary Moody
1774-1863 .... **NCLC 66**

Emerson, Ralph Waldo 1803-1882 . **NCLC 1, 38, 98; PC 18; WLC 2**
See also AAYA 60; AMW; ANW; CDALB 1640-1865; DA; DA3; DAB; DAC; DAM MST, POET; DLB 1, 59, 73, 183, 223, 270; EXPP; LAIT 2; LMFS 1; NCFS 3; PFS 4, 17; RGAL 4; TUS; WP

Eminem 1972- .... **CLC 226**
See also CA 245

Eminescu, Mihail 1850-1889 .. **NCLC 33, 131**

Empedocles 5th cent. B.C.- .... **CMLC 50**
See also DLB 176

Empson, William 1906-1984 ... **CLC 3, 8, 19, 33, 34**
See also BRWS 2; CA 17-20R; CAAS 112; CANR 31, 61; CP 1, 2, 3; DLB 20; EWL 3; MTCW 1, 2; RGEL 2

Enchi, Fumiko (Ueda) 1905-1986 ..... **CLC 31**
See Enchi Fumiko
See also CA 129; CAAS 121; FW; MJW

Enchi Fumiko
See Enchi, Fumiko (Ueda)
See also DLB 182; EWL 3

Ende, Michael (Andreas Helmuth)
1929-1995 .... **CLC 31**
See also BYA 5; CA 124; CAAE 118; CAAS 149; CANR 36, 110; CLR 14; DLB 75; MAICYA 1, 2; MAICYAS 1; SATA 61, 130; SATA-Brief 42; SATA-Obit 86

Endo, Shusaku 1923-1996 ..... **CLC 7, 14, 19, 54, 99; SSC 48; TCLC 152**
See Endo Shusaku
See also CA 29-32R; CAAS 153; CANR 21, 54, 131; DA3; DAM NOV; MTCW 1, 2; MTFW 2005; RGSF 2; RGWL 2, 3

Endo Shusaku
See Endo, Shusaku
See also CWW 2; DLB 182; EWL 3

Engel, Marian 1933-1985 .... **CLC 36; TCLC 137**
See also CA 25-28R; CANR 12; CN 2, 3; DLB 53; FW; INT CANR-12

Engelhardt, Frederick
See Hubbard, L. Ron

Engels, Friedrich 1820-1895 .. **NCLC 85, 114**
See also DLB 129; LATS 1:1

Enright, D(ennis) J(oseph)
1920-2002 .... **CLC 4, 8, 31**
See also CA 1-4R; CAAS 211; CANR 1, 42, 83; CN 1, 2; CP 1, 2, 3, 4, 5, 6, 7; DLB 27; EWL 3; SATA 25; SATA-Obit 140

Ensler, Eve 1953- .... **CLC 212**
See also CA 172; CANR 126; DFS 23

Enzensberger, Hans Magnus
1929- .... **CLC 43; PC 28**
See also CA 119; CAAE 116; CANR 103; CWW 2; EWL 3

Ephron, Nora 1941- .... **CLC 17, 31**
See also AAYA 35; AITN 2; CA 65-68; CANR 12, 39, 83, 161; DFS 22

Epicurus 341B.C.-270B.C. .... **CMLC 21**
See also DLB 176

Epsilon
See Betjeman, John

Epstein, Daniel Mark 1948- .... **CLC 7**
See also CA 49-52; CANR 2, 53, 90

Epstein, Jacob 1956- .... **CLC 19**
See also CA 114

Epstein, Jean 1897-1953 .... **TCLC 92**

Epstein, Joseph 1937- .... **CLC 39, 204**
See also AMWS 14; CA 119; CAAE 112; CANR 50, 65, 117

Epstein, Leslie 1938- .... **CLC 27**
See also AMWS 12; CA 215; 73-76, 215; 12; CANR 23, 69; DLB 299; RGHL

Equiano, Olaudah 1745(?)-1797 . **BLC 2; LC 16**
See also AFAW 1, 2; CDWLB 3; DAM MULT; DLB 37, 50; WLIT 2

Erasmus, Desiderius 1469(?)-1536 ..... **LC 16, 93**
See also DLB 136; EW 2; LMFS 1; RGWL 2, 3; TWA

Erdman, Paul E(mil) 1932- .... **CLC 25**
See also AITN 1; CA 61-64; CANR 13, 43, 84

Erdrich, Karen Louise
See Erdrich, Louise

Erdrich, Louise 1954- .... **CLC 39, 54, 120, 176; NNAL; PC 52**
See also AAYA 10, 47; AMWS 4; BEST 89:1; BPFB 1; CA 114; CANR 41, 62, 118, 138; CDALBS; CN 5, 6, 7; CP 6, 7; CPW; CWP; DA3; DAM MULT, NOV, POP; DLB 152, 175, 206; EWL 3; EXPP; FL 1:5; LAIT 5; LATS 1:2; MAL 5; MTCW 1, 2; MTFW 2005; NFS 5; PFS 14; RGAL 4; SATA 94, 141; SSFS 14, 22; TCWW 2

Erenburg, Ilya (Grigoryevich)
See Ehrenburg, Ilya (Grigoryevich)

Erickson, Stephen Michael
See Erickson, Steve

Erickson, Steve 1950- .... **CLC 64**
See also CA 129; CANR 60, 68, 136; MTFW 2005; SFW 4; SUFW 2

Erickson, Walter
See Fast, Howard

Ericson, Walter
See Fast, Howard

Eriksson, Buntel
See Bergman, (Ernst) Ingmar

Eriugena, John Scottus c.
810-877 .... **CMLC 65**
See also DLB 115

Ernaux, Annie 1940- .... **CLC 88, 184**
See also CA 147; CANR 93; MTFW 2005; NCFS 3, 5

Erskine, John 1879-1951 .... **TCLC 84**
See also CA 159; CAAE 112; DLB 9, 102; FANT

Eschenbach, Wolfram von
See von Eschenbach, Wolfram
See also RGWL 3

Eseki, Bruno
See Mphahlele, Ezekiel

Esenin, S.A.
See Esenin, Sergei
See also EWL 3

Esenin, Sergei 1895-1925 .... **TCLC 4**
See Esenin, S.A.
See also CAAE 104; RGWL 2, 3

Esenin, Sergei Aleksandrovich
See Esenin, Sergei

Eshleman, Clayton 1935- .... **CLC 7**
See also CA 212; 33-36R, 212; 6; CANR 93; CP 1, 2, 3, 4, 5, 6, 7; DLB 5

Espada, Martin 1957- .... **PC 74**
See also CA 159; CANR 80; CP 7; EXPP; LLW; MAL 5; PFS 13, 16

Espriella, Don Manuel Alvarez
See Southey, Robert

Espriu, Salvador 1913-1985 .... **CLC 9**
See also CA 154; CAAS 115; DLB 134; EWL 3

Espronceda, Jose de 1808-1842 ..... **NCLC 39**

Esquivel, Laura 1950(?)- ... **CLC 141; HLCS 1**
See also AAYA 29; CA 143; CANR 68, 113, 161; DA3; DNFS 2; LAIT 3; LMFS 2; MTCW 2; MTFW 2005; NFS 5; WLIT 1

Esse, James
See Stephens, James

Esterbrook, Tom
See Hubbard, L. Ron

Estleman, Loren D. 1952- .... **CLC 48**
See also AAYA 27; CA 85-88; CANR 27, 74, 139; CMW 4; CPW; DA3; DAM NOV, POP; DLB 226; INT CANR-27; MTCW 1, 2; MTFW 2005; TCWW 1, 2

Etherege, Sir George 1636-1692 . **DC 23; LC 78**
See also BRW 2; DAM DRAM; DLB 80; PAB; RGEL 2

Euclid 306B.C.-283B.C. .... **CMLC 25**

Eugenides, Jeffrey 1960(?)- ...... **CLC 81, 212**
See also AAYA 51; CA 144; CANR 120; MTFW 2005; NFS 24

Euripides c. 484B.C.-406B.C. .... **CMLC 23, 51; DC 4; WLCS**
See also AW 1; CDWLB 1; DA; DA3; DAB; DAC; DAM DRAM, MST; DFS 1, 4, 6; DLB 176; LAIT 1; LMFS 1; RGWL 2, 3; WLIT 8

Evan, Evin
See Faust, Frederick (Schiller)

Fukuyama, Francis 1952- .... **CLC 131**
  See also CA 140; CANR 72, 125
Fuller, Charles (H.), (Jr.) 1939- .... **BLC 2; CLC 25; DC 1**
  See also BW 2; CA 112; CAAE 108; CAD; CANR 87; CD 5, 6; DAM DRAM, MULT; DFS 8; DLB 38, 266; EWL 3; INT CA-112; MAL 5; MTCW 1
Fuller, Henry Blake 1857-1929 .... **TCLC 103**
  See also CA 177; CAAE 108; DLB 12; RGAL 4
Fuller, John (Leopold) 1937- .... **CLC 62**
  See also CA 21-24R; CANR 9, 44; CP 1, 2, 3, 4, 5, 6, 7; DLB 40
Fuller, Margaret
  See Ossoli, Sarah Margaret (Fuller)
  See also AMWS 2; DLB 183, 223, 239; FL 1:3
Fuller, Roy (Broadbent) 1912-1991 ... **CLC 4, 28**
  See also BRWS 7; CA 5-8R; 10; CAAS 135; CANR 53, 83; CN 1, 2, 3, 4, 5; CP 1, 2, 3, 4, 5; CWRI 5; DLB 15, 20; EWL 3; RGEL 2; SATA 87
Fuller, Sarah Margaret
  See Ossoli, Sarah Margaret (Fuller)
Fuller, Sarah Margaret
  See Ossoli, Sarah Margaret (Fuller)
  See also DLB 1, 59, 73
Fuller, Thomas 1608-1661 .... **LC 111**
  See also DLB 151
Fulton, Alice 1952- .... **CLC 52**
  See also CA 116; CANR 57, 88; CP 5, 6, 7; CWP; DLB 193; PFS 25
Furphy, Joseph 1843-1912 .... **TCLC 25**
  See Collins, Tom
  See also CA 163; DLB 230; EWL 3; RGEL 2
Fuson, Robert H(enderson) 1927- .... **CLC 70**
  See also CA 89-92; CANR 103
Fussell, Paul 1924- .... **CLC 74**
  See also BEST 90:1; CA 17-20R; CANR 8, 21, 35, 69, 135; INT CANR-21; MTCW 1, 2; MTFW 2005
Futabatei, Shimei 1864-1909 .... **TCLC 44**
  See Futabatei Shimei
  See also CA 162; MJW
Futabatei Shimei
  See Futabatei, Shimei
  See also DLB 180; EWL 3
Futrelle, Jacques 1875-1912 .... **TCLC 19**
  See also CA 155; CAAE 113; CMW 4
Gaboriau, Emile 1835-1873 .... **NCLC 14**
  See also CMW 4; MSW
Gadda, Carlo Emilio 1893-1973 ...... **CLC 11; TCLC 144**
  See also CA 89-92; DLB 177; EWL 3; WLIT 7
Gaddis, William 1922-1998 ... **CLC 1, 3, 6, 8, 10, 19, 43, 86**
  See also AMWS 4; BPFB 1; CA 17-20R; CAAS 172; CANR 21, 48, 148; CN 1, 2, 3, 4, 5, 6; DLB 2, 278; EWL 3; MAL 5; MTCW 1, 2; MTFW 2005; RGAL 4
Gage, Walter
  See Inge, William (Motter)
Gaiman, Neil 1960- .... **CLC 195**
  See also AAYA 19, 42; CA 133; CANR 81, 129; CLR 109; DLB 261; HGG; MTFW 2005; SATA 85, 146; SFW 4; SUFW 2
Gaiman, Neil Richard
  See Gaiman, Neil
Gaines, Ernest J. 1933- .. **BLC 2; CLC 3, 11, 18, 86, 181; SSC 68**
  See also AAYA 18; AFAW 1, 2; AITN 1; BPFB 2; BW 2, 3; BYA 6; CA 9-12R; CANR 6, 24, 42, 75, 126; CDALB 1968-1988; CLR 62; CN 1, 2, 3, 4, 5, 6, 7; CSW; DA3; DAM MULT; DLB 2, 33,

152; DLBY 1980; EWL 3; EXPN; LAIT 5; LATS 1:2; MAL 5; MTCW 1, 2; MTFW 2005; NFS 5, 7, 16; RGAL 4; RGSF 2; RHW; SATA 86; SSFS 5; YAW
Gaitskill, Mary 1954- .... **CLC 69**
  See also CA 128; CANR 61, 152; DLB 244; TCLE 1:1
Gaitskill, Mary Lawrence
  See Gaitskill, Mary
Gaius Suetonius Tranquillus
  See Suetonius
Galdos, Benito Perez
  See Perez Galdos, Benito
  See also EW 7
Gale, Zona 1874-1938 .... **TCLC 7**
  See also CA 153; CAAE 105; CANR 84; DAM DRAM; DFS 17; DLB 9, 78, 228; RGAL 4
Galeano, Eduardo (Hughes) 1940- . **CLC 72; HLCS 1**
  See also CA 29-32R; CANR 13, 32, 100; HW 1
Galiano, Juan Valera y Alcala
  See Valera y Alcala-Galiano, Juan
Galilei, Galileo 1564-1642 .... **LC 45**
Gallagher, Tess 1943- .... **CLC 18, 63; PC 9**
  See also CA 106; CP 3, 4, 5, 6, 7; CWP; DAM POET; DLB 120, 212, 244; PFS 16
Gallant, Mavis 1922- ..... **CLC 7, 18, 38, 172; SSC 5, 78**
  See also CA 69-72; CANR 29, 69, 117; CCA 1; CN 1, 2, 3, 4, 5, 6, 7; DAC; DAM MST; DLB 53; EWL 3; MTCW 1, 2; MTFW 2005; RGEL 2; RGSF 2
Gallant, Roy A(rthur) 1924- .... **CLC 17**
  See also CA 5-8R; CANR 4, 29, 54, 117; CLR 30; MAICYA 1, 2; SATA 4, 68, 110
Gallico, Paul (William) 1897-1976 ..... **CLC 2**
  See also AITN 1; CA 5-8R; CAAS 69-72; CANR 23; CN 1, 2; DLB 9, 171; FANT; MAICYA 1, 2; SATA 13
Gallo, Max Louis 1932- .... **CLC 95**
  See also CA 85-88
Gallois, Lucien
  See Desnos, Robert
Gallup, Ralph
  See Whitemore, Hugh (John)
Galsworthy, John 1867-1933 .... **SSC 22; TCLC 1, 45; WLC 2**
  See also BRW 6; CA 141; CAAE 104; CANR 75; CDBLB 1890-1914; DA; DA3; DAB; DAC; DAM DRAM, MST, NOV; DLB 10, 34, 98, 162, 330; DLBD 16; EWL 3; MTCW 2; RGEL 2; SSFS 3; TEA
Galt, John 1779-1839 .... **NCLC 1, 110**
  See also DLB 99, 116, 159; RGEL 2; RGSF 2
Galvin, James 1951- .... **CLC 38**
  See also CA 108; CANR 26
Gamboa, Federico 1864-1939 .... **TCLC 36**
  See also CA 167; HW 2; LAW
Gandhi, M. K.
  See Gandhi, Mohandas Karamchand
Gandhi, Mahatma
  See Gandhi, Mohandas Karamchand
Gandhi, Mohandas Karamchand 1869-1948 .... **TCLC 59**
  See also CA 132; CAAE 121; DA3; DAM MULT; DLB 323; MTCW 1, 2
Gann, Ernest Kellogg 1910-1991 ..... **CLC 23**
  See also AITN 1; BPFB 2; CA 1-4R; CAAS 136; CANR 1, 83; RHW
Gao Xingjian 1940- .... **CLC 167**
  See Xingjian, Gao
  See also MTFW 2005
Garber, Eric 1943(?)-
  See Holleran, Andrew
  See also CANR 89

Garcia, Cristina 1958- .... **CLC 76**
  See also AMWS 11; CA 141; CANR 73, 130; CN 7; DLB 292; DNFS 1; EWL 3; HW 2; LLW; MTFW 2005
Garcia Lorca, Federico 1898-1936 ...... **DC 2; HLC 2; PC 3; TCLC 1, 7, 49, 181; WLC 2**
  See Lorca, Federico Garcia
  See also AAYA 46; CA 131; CAAE 104; CANR 81; DA; DA3; DAB; DAC; DAM DRAM, MST, MULT, POET; DFS 4, 10; DLB 108; EWL 3; HW 1, 2; LATS 1:2; MTCW 1, 2; MTFW 2005; TWA
Garcia Marquez, Gabriel 1928- ...... **CLC 2, 3, 8, 10, 15, 27, 47, 55, 68, 170; HLC 1; SSC 8, 83; WLC 3**
  See also AAYA 3, 33; BEST 89:1, 90:4; BPFB 2; BYA 12, 16; CA 33-36R; CANR 10, 28, 50, 75, 82, 128; CDWLB 3; CPW; CWW 2; DA; DA3; DAB; DAC; DAM MST, MULT, NOV, POP; DLB 113, 330; DNFS 1, 2; EWL 3; EXPN; EXPS; HW 1, 2; LAIT 2; LATS 1:2; LAW; LAWS 1; LMFS 2; MTCW 1, 2; MTFW 2005; NCFS 3; NFS 1, 5, 10; RGSF 2; RGWL 2, 3; SSFS 1, 6, 16, 21; TWA; WLIT 1
Garcia Marquez, Gabriel Jose
  See Garcia Marquez, Gabriel
Garcilaso de la Vega, El Inca 1539-1616 .... **HLCS 1; LC 127**
  See also DLB 318; LAW
Gard, Janice
  See Latham, Jean Lee
Gard, Roger Martin du
  See Martin du Gard, Roger
Gardam, Jane (Mary) 1928- .... **CLC 43**
  See also CA 49-52; CANR 2, 18, 33, 54, 106; CLR 12; DLB 14, 161, 231; MAICYA 1; SAAS 9; SATA 39, 76, 130; SATA-Brief 28; YAW
Gardner, Herb(ert George) 1934-2003 .... **CLC 44**
  See also CA 149; CAAS 220; CAD; CANR 119; CD 5, 6; DFS 18, 20
Gardner, John, Jr. 1933-1982 ... **CLC 2, 3, 5, 7, 8, 10, 18, 28, 34; SSC 7**
  See also AAYA 45; AITN 1; AMWS 6; BPFB 2; CA 65-68; CAAS 107; CANR 33, 73; CDALBS; CN 2, 3; CPW; DA3; DAM NOV, POP; DLB 2; DLBY 1982; EWL 3; FANT; LATS 1:2; MAL 5; MTCW 1, 2; MTFW 2005; NFS 3; RGAL 4; RGSF 2; SATA 40; SATA-Obit 31; SSFS 8
Gardner, John (Edmund) 1926- .... **CLC 30**
  See also CA 103; CANR 15, 69, 127; CMW 4; CPW; DAM POP; MTCW 1
Gardner, Miriam
  See Bradley, Marion Zimmer
  See also GLL 1
Gardner, Noel
  See Kuttner, Henry
Gardons, S. S.
  See Snodgrass, W.D.
Garfield, Leon 1921-1996 .... **CLC 12**
  See also AAYA 8, 69; BYA 1, 3; CA 17-20R; CAAS 152; CANR 38, 41, 78; CLR 21; DLB 161; JRDA; MAICYA 1, 2; MAICYAS 1; SATA 1, 32, 76; SATA-Obit 90; TEA; WYA; YAW
Garland, (Hannibal) Hamlin 1860-1940 .... **SSC 18; TCLC 3**
  See also CAAE 104; DLB 12, 71, 78, 186; MAL 5; RGAL 4; RGSF 2; TCWW 1, 2
Garneau, (Hector de) Saint-Denys 1912-1943 .... **TCLC 13**
  See also CAAE 111; DLB 88

Grade, Chaim 1910-1982 .... **CLC 10**
  See also CA 93-96; CAAS 107; DLB 333;
  EWL 3; RGHL
Grade, Khayim
  See Grade, Chaim
Graduate of Oxford, A
  See Ruskin, John
Grafton, Garth
  See Duncan, Sara Jeannette
Grafton, Sue 1940- .... **CLC 163**
  See also AAYA 11, 49; BEST 90:3; CA 108;
  CANR 31, 55, 111, 134; CMW 4; CPW;
  CSW; DA3; DAM POP; DLB 226; FW;
  MSW; MTFW 2005
Graham, John
  See Phillips, David Graham
Graham, Jorie 1950- .... **CLC 48, 118; PC 59**
  See also AAYA 67; CA 111; CANR 63, 118;
  CP 4, 5, 6, 7; CWP; DLB 120; EWL 3;
  MTFW 2005; PFS 10, 17; TCLE 1:1
Graham, R(obert) B(ontine) Cunninghame
  See Cunninghame Graham, Robert
  (Gallnigad) Bontine
  See also DLB 98, 135, 174; RGEL 2; RGSF
  2
Graham, Robert
  See Haldeman, Joe
Graham, Tom
  See Lewis, (Harry) Sinclair
Graham, W(illiam) S(ydney)
  1918-1986 .... **CLC 29**
  See also BRWS 7; CA 73-76; CAAS 118;
  CP 1, 2, 3, 4; DLB 20; RGEL 2
Graham, Winston (Mawdsley)
  1910-2003 .... **CLC 23**
  See also CA 49-52; CAAS 218; CANR 2,
  22, 45, 66; CMW 4; CN 1, 2, 3, 4, 5, 6,
  7; DLB 77; RHW
Grahame, Kenneth 1859-1932 ...... **TCLC 64,**
  136
  See also BYA 5; CA 136; CAAE 108;
  CANR 80; CLR 5; CWRI 5; DA3; DAB;
  DLB 34, 141, 178; FANT; MAICYA 1, 2;
  MTCW 2; NFS 20; RGEL 2; SATA 100;
  TEA; WCH; YABC 1
Granger, Darius John
  See Marlowe, Stephen
Granin, Daniil 1918- .... **CLC 59**
  See also DLB 302
Granovsky, Timofei Nikolaevich
  1813-1855 .... **NCLC 75**
  See also DLB 198
Grant, Skeeter
  See Spiegelman, Art
Granville-Barker, Harley
  1877-1946 .... **TCLC 2**
  See Barker, Harley Granville
  See also CA 204; CAAE 104; DAM
  DRAM; RGEL 2
Granzotto, Gianni
  See Granzotto, Giovanni Battista
Granzotto, Giovanni Battista
  1914-1985 .... **CLC 70**
  See also CA 166
Grass, Guenter
  See Grass, Gunter
  See also CWW 2; DLB 330; RGHL
Grass, Gunter 1927- .. **CLC 1, 2, 4, 6, 11, 15,**
  22, 32, 49, 88, 207; WLC 3
  See Grass, Guenter
  See also BPFB 2; CA 13-16R; CANR 20,
  75, 93, 133; CDWLB 2; DA; DA3; DAB;
  DAC; DAM MST, NOV; DLB 75, 124;
  EW 13; EWL 3; MTCW 1, 2; MTFW
  2005; RGWL 2, 3; TWA
Grass, Gunter Wilhelm
  See Grass, Gunter
Gratton, Thomas
  See Hulme, T(homas) E(rnest)

Grau, Shirley Ann 1929- .... **CLC 4, 9, 146;**
  SSC 15
  See also CA 89-92; CANR 22, 69; CN 1, 2,
  3, 4, 5, 6, 7; CSW; DLB 2, 218; INT CA-
  89-92; CANR-22; MTCW 1
Gravel, Fern
  See Hall, James Norman
Graver, Elizabeth 1964- .... **CLC 70**
  See also CA 135; CANR 71, 129
Graves, Richard Perceval
  1895-1985 .... **CLC 44**
  See also CA 65-68; CANR 9, 26, 51
Graves, Robert 1895-1985 ... **CLC 1, 2, 6, 11,**
  39, 44, 45; PC 6
  See also BPFB 2; BRW 7; BYA 4; CA 5-8R;
  CAAS 117; CANR 5, 36; CDBLB 1914-
  1945; CN 1, 2, 3; CP 1, 2, 3, 4; DA3;
  DAB; DAC; DAM MST, POET; DLB 20,
  100, 191; DLBD 18; DLBY 1985; EWL
  3; LATS 1:1; MTCW 1, 2; MTFW 2005;
  NCFS 2; NFS 21; RGEL 2; RHW; SATA
  45; TEA
Graves, Valerie
  See Bradley, Marion Zimmer
Gray, Alasdair 1934- .... **CLC 41**
  See also BRWS 9; CA 126; CANR 47, 69,
  106, 140; CN 4, 5, 6, 7; DLB 194, 261,
  319; HGG; INT CA-126; MTCW 1, 2;
  MTFW 2005; RGSF 2; SUFW 2
Gray, Amlin 1946- .... **CLC 29**
  See also CA 138
Gray, Francine du Plessix 1930- ..... **CLC 22,**
  153
  See also BEST 90:3; CA 61-64; 2; CANR
  11, 33, 75, 81; DAM NOV; INT CANR-
  11; MTCW 1, 2; MTFW 2005
Gray, John (Henry) 1866-1934 ...... **TCLC 19**
  See also CA 162; CAAE 119; RGEL 2
Gray, John Lee
  See Jakes, John
Gray, Simon (James Holliday)
  1936- .... **CLC 9, 14, 36**
  See also AITN 1; CA 21-24R; 3; CANR 32,
  69; CBD; CD 5, 6; CN 1, 2, 3; DLB 13;
  EWL 3; MTCW 1; RGEL 2
Gray, Spalding 1941-2004 .... **CLC 49, 112;**
  DC 7
  See also AAYA 62; CA 128; CAAS 225;
  CAD; CANR 74, 138; CD 5, 6; CPW;
  DAM POP; MTCW 2; MTFW 2005
Gray, Thomas 1716-1771 .... **LC 4, 40; PC 2;**
  WLC 3
  See also BRW 3; CDBLB 1660-1789; DA;
  DA3; DAB; DAC; DAM MST; DLB 109;
  EXPP; PAB; PFS 9; RGEL 2; TEA; WP
Grayson, David
  See Baker, Ray Stannard
Grayson, Richard (A.) 1951- .... **CLC 38**
  See also CA 210; 85-88, 210; CANR 14,
  31, 57; DLB 234
Greeley, Andrew M. 1928- .... **CLC 28**
  See also BPFB 2; CA 5-8R; 7; CANR 7,
  43, 69, 104, 136; CMW 4; CPW; DA3;
  DAM POP; MTCW 1, 2; MTFW 2005
Green, Anna Katharine
  1846-1935 .... **TCLC 63**
  See also CA 159; CAAE 112; CMW 4;
  DLB 202, 221; MSW
Green, Brian
  See Card, Orson Scott
Green, Hannah
  See Greenberg, Joanne (Goldenberg)
Green, Hannah 1927(?)-1996 .... **CLC 3**
  See also CA 73-76; CANR 59, 93; NFS 10
Green, Henry .... **CLC 2, 13, 97**
  See Yorke, Henry Vincent
  See also BRWS 2; CA 175; DLB 15; EWL
  3; RGEL 2

Green, Julian .... **CLC 3, 11, 77**
  See Green, Julien (Hartridge)
  See also EWL 3; GFL 1789 to the Present;
  MTCW 2
Green, Julien (Hartridge) 1900-1998
  See Green, Julian
  See also CA 21-24R; CAAS 169; CANR
  33, 87; CWW 2; DLB 4, 72; MTCW 1, 2;
  MTFW 2005
Green, Paul (Eliot) 1894-1981 .... **CLC 25**
  See also AITN 1; CA 5-8R; CAAS 103;
  CAD; CANR 3; DAM DRAM; DLB 7, 9,
  249; DLBY 1981; MAL 5; RGAL 4
Greenaway, Peter 1942- .... **CLC 159**
  See also CA 127
Greenberg, Ivan 1908-1973
  See Rahv, Philip
  See also CA 85-88
Greenberg, Joanne (Goldenberg)
  1932- .... **CLC 7, 30**
  See also AAYA 12, 67; CA 5-8R; CANR
  14, 32, 69; CN 6, 7; NFS 23; SATA 25;
  YAW
Greenberg, Richard 1959(?)- .... **CLC 57**
  See also CA 138; CAD; CD 5, 6
Greenblatt, Stephen J(ay) 1943- ...... **CLC 70**
  See also CA 49-52; CANR 115
Greene, Bette 1934- .... **CLC 30**
  See also AAYA 7, 69; BYA 3; CA 53-56;
  CANR 4, 146; CLR 2; CWRI 5; JRDA;
  LAIT 4; MAICYA 1, 2; NFS 10; SAAS
  16; SATA 8, 102, 161; WYA; YAW
Greene, Gael .... **CLC 8**
  See also CA 13-16R; CANR 10
Greene, Graham 1904-1991 .. **CLC 1, 3, 6, 9,**
  14, 18, 27, 37, 70, 72, 125; SSC 29;
  WLC 3
  See also AAYA 61; AITN 2; BPFB 2;
  BRWR 2; BRWS 1; BYA 3; CA 13-16R;
  CAAS 133; CANR 35, 61, 131; CBD;
  CDBLB 1945-1960; CMW 4; CN 1, 2, 3,
  4; DA; DA3; DAB; DAC; DAM MST,
  NOV; DLB 13, 15, 77, 100, 162, 201,
  204; DLBY 1991; EWL 3; MSW; MTCW
  1, 2; MTFW 2005; NFS 16; RGEL 2;
  SATA 20; SSFS 14; TEA; WLIT 4
Greene, Robert 1558-1592 .... **LC 41**
  See also BRWS 8; DLB 62, 167; IDTP;
  RGEL 2; TEA
Greer, Germaine 1939- .... **CLC 131**
  See also AITN 1; CA 81-84; CANR 33, 70,
  115, 133; FW; MTCW 1, 2; MTFW 2005
Greer, Richard
  See Silverberg, Robert
Gregor, Arthur 1923- .... **CLC 9**
  See also CA 25-28R; 10; CANR 11; CP 1,
  2, 3, 4, 5, 6, 7; SATA 36
Gregor, Lee
  See Pohl, Frederik
Gregory, Lady Isabella Augusta (Persse)
  1852-1932 .... **TCLC 1, 176**
  See also BRW 6; CA 184; CAAE 104; DLB
  10; IDTP; RGEL 2
Gregory, J. Dennis
  See Williams, John A(lfred)
Gregory of Nazianzus, St.
  329-389 .... **CMLC 82**
Grekova, I. .... **CLC 59**
  See Ventsel, Elena Sergeevna
  See also CWW 2
Grendon, Stephen
  See Derleth, August (William)
Grenville, Kate 1950- .... **CLC 61**
  See also CA 118; CANR 53, 93, 156; CN
  7; DLB 325
Grenville, Pelham
  See Wodehouse, P(elham) G(renville)

Hamilton, (Robert) Ian 1938-2001 . **CLC 191**
See also CA 106; CAAS 203; CANR 41, 67; CP 1, 2, 3, 4, 5, 6, 7; DLB 40, 155

Hamilton, Jane 1957- .... **CLC 179**
See also CA 147; CANR 85, 128; CN 7; MTFW 2005

Hamilton, Mollie
See Kaye, M.M.

Hamilton, (Anthony Walter) Patrick
1904-1962 .... **CLC 51**
See also CA 176; CAAS 113; DLB 10, 191

Hamilton, Virginia 1936-2002 .... **CLC 26**
See also AAYA 2, 21; BW 2, 3; BYA 1, 2, 8; CA 25-28R; CAAS 206; CANR 20, 37, 73, 126; CLR 1, 11, 40; DAM MULT; DLB 33, 52; DLBY 2001; INT CANR-20; JRDA; LAIT 5; MAICYA 1, 2; MAI-CYAS 1; MTCW 1, 2; MTFW 2005; SATA 4, 56, 79, 123; SATA-Obit 132; WYA; YAW

Hammett, (Samuel) Dashiell
1894-1961 .... **CLC 3, 5, 10, 19, 47; SSC 17; TCLC 187**
See also AAYA 59; AITN 1; AMWS 4; BPFB 2; CA 81-84; CANR 42; CDALB 1929-1941; CMW 4; DA3; DLB 226, 280; DLBD 6; DLBY 1996; EWL 3; LAIT 3; MAL 5; MSW; MTCW 1, 2; MTFW 2005; NFS 21; RGAL 4; RGSF 2; TUS

Hammon, Jupiter 1720(?)-1800(?) .... **BLC 2; NCLC 5; PC 16**
See also DAM MULT, POET; DLB 31, 50

Hammond, Keith
See Kuttner, Henry

Hamner, Earl (Henry), Jr. 1923- ...... **CLC 12**
See also AITN 2; CA 73-76; DLB 6

Hampton, Christopher 1946- .... **CLC 4**
See also CA 25-28R; CD 5, 6; DLB 13; MTCW 1

Hampton, Christopher James
See Hampton, Christopher

Hamsun, Knut .... **TCLC 2, 14, 49, 151**
See Pedersen, Knut
See also DLB 297, 330; EW 8; EWL 3; RGWL 2, 3

Handke, Peter 1942- .... **CLC 5, 8, 10, 15, 38, 134; DC 17**
See also CA 77-80; CANR 33, 75, 104, 133; CWW 2; DAM DRAM, NOV; DLB 85, 124; EWL 3; MTCW 1, 2; MTFW 2005; TWA

Handy, W(illiam) C(hristopher)
1873-1958 .... **TCLC 97**
See also BW 3; CA 167; CAAE 121

Hanley, James 1901-1985 ..... **CLC 3, 5, 8, 13**
See also CA 73-76; CAAS 117; CANR 36; CBD; CN 1, 2, 3; DLB 191; EWL 3; MTCW 1; RGEL 2

Hannah, Barry 1942- .. **CLC 23, 38, 90; SSC 94**
See also BPFB 2; CA 110; CAAE 108; CANR 43, 68, 113; CN 4, 5, 6, 7; CSW; DLB 6, 234; INT CA-110; MTCW 1; RGSF 2

Hannon, Ezra
See Hunter, Evan

Hansberry, Lorraine (Vivian)
1930-1965 ... **BLC 2; CLC 17, 62; DC 2**
See also AAYA 25; AFAW 1, 2; AMWS 4; BW 1, 3; CA 109; CAAS 25-28R; CABS 3; CAD; CANR 58; CDALB 1941-1968; CWD; DA; DA3; DAB; DAC; DAM DRAM, MST, MULT; DFS 2; DLB 7, 38; EWL 3; FL 1:6; FW; LAIT 4; MAL 5; MTCW 1, 2; MTFW 2005; RGAL 4; TUS

Hansen, Joseph 1923-2004 .... **CLC 38**
See Brock, Rose; Colton, James
See also BPFB 2; CA 29-32R; 17; CAAS 233; CANR 16, 44, 66, 125; CMW 4; DLB 226; GLL 1; INT CANR-16

Hansen, Karen V. 1955- .... **CLC 65**
See also CA 149; CANR 102

Hansen, Martin A(lfred)
1909-1955 .... **TCLC 32**
See also CA 167; DLB 214; EWL 3

Hanson, Kenneth O(stlin) 1922- .... **CLC 13**
See also CA 53-56; CANR 7; CP 1, 2, 3, 4, 5

Hardwick, Elizabeth 1916- .... **CLC 13**
See also AMWS 3; CA 5-8R; CANR 3, 32, 70, 100, 139; CN 4, 5, 6; CSW; DA3; DAM NOV; DLB 6; MBL; MTCW 1, 2; MTFW 2005; TCLE 1:1

Hardy, Thomas 1840-1928 .... **PC 8; SSC 2, 60; TCLC 4, 10, 18, 32, 48, 53, 72, 143, 153; WLC 3**
See also AAYA 69; BRW 6; BRWC 1, 2; BRWR 1; CA 123; CAAE 104; CDBLB 1890-1914; DA; DA3; DAB; DAC; DAM MST, NOV, POET; DLB 18, 19, 135, 284; EWL 3; EXPN; EXPP; LAIT 2; MTCW 1, 2; MTFW 2005; NFS 3, 11, 15, 19; PFS 3, 4, 18; RGEL 2; RGSF 2; TEA; WLIT 4

Hare, David 1947- . **CLC 29, 58, 136; DC 26**
See also BRWS 4; CA 97-100; CANR 39, 91; CBD; CD 5, 6; DFS 4, 7, 16; DLB 13, 310; MTCW 1; TEA

Harewood, John
See Van Druten, John (William)

Harford, Henry
See Hudson, W(illiam) H(enry)

Hargrave, Leonie
See Disch, Thomas M.

Hariri, Al- al-Qasim ibn 'Ali Abu
Muhammad al-Basri
See al-Hariri, al-Qasim ibn 'Ali Abu Mu-hammad al-Basri

Harjo, Joy 1951- ..... **CLC 83; NNAL; PC 27**
See also AMWS 12; CA 114; CANR 35, 67, 91, 129; CP 6, 7; CWP; DAM MULT; DLB 120, 175; EWL 3; MTCW 2; MTFW 2005; PFS 15; RGAL 4

Harlan, Louis R(udolph) 1922- .... **CLC 34**
See also CA 21-24R; CANR 25, 55, 80

Harling, Robert 1951(?)- .... **CLC 53**
See also CA 147

Harmon, William (Ruth) 1938- .... **CLC 38**
See also CA 33-36R; CANR 14, 32, 35; SATA 65

Harper, F. E. W.
See Harper, Frances Ellen Watkins

Harper, Frances E. W.
See Harper, Frances Ellen Watkins

Harper, Frances E. Watkins
See Harper, Frances Ellen Watkins

Harper, Frances Ellen
See Harper, Frances Ellen Watkins

Harper, Frances Ellen Watkins
1825-1911 ..... **BLC 2; PC 21; TCLC 14**
See also AFAW 1, 2; BW 1, 3; CA 125; CAAE 111; CANR 79; DAM MULT, POET; DLB 50, 221; MBL; RGAL 4

Harper, Michael S(teven) 1938- ... **CLC 7, 22**
See also AFAW 2; BW 1; CA 224; 33-36R, 224; CANR 24, 108; CP 2, 3, 4, 5, 6, 7; DLB 41; RGAL 4; TCLE 1:1

Harper, Mrs. F. E. W.
See Harper, Frances Ellen Watkins

Harpur, Charles 1813-1868 .... **NCLC 114**
See also DLB 230; RGEL 2

Harris, Christie
See Harris, Christie (Lucy) Irwin

Harris, Christie (Lucy) Irwin
1907-2002 .... **CLC 12**
See also CA 5-8R; CANR 6, 83; CLR 47; DLB 88; JRDA; MAICYA 1, 2; SAAS 10; SATA 6, 74; SATA-Essay 116

Harris, Frank 1856-1931 .... **TCLC 24**
See also CA 150; CAAE 109; CANR 80; DLB 156, 197; RGEL 2

Harris, George Washington
1814-1869 .... **NCLC 23, 165**
See also DLB 3, 11, 248; RGAL 4

Harris, Joel Chandler 1848-1908 ..... **SSC 19; TCLC 2**
See also CA 137; CAAE 104; CANR 80; CLR 49; DLB 11, 23, 42, 78, 91; LAIT 2; MAICYA 1, 2; RGSF 2; SATA 100; WCH; YABC 1

Harris, John (Wyndham Parkes Lucas)
Beynon 1903-1969
See Wyndham, John
See also CA 102; CAAS 89-92; CANR 84; SATA 118; SFW 4

Harris, MacDonald .... **CLC 9**
See Heiney, Donald (William)

Harris, Mark 1922- .... **CLC 19**
See also CA 5-8R; 3; CANR 2, 55, 83; CN 1, 2, 3, 4, 5, 6, 7; DLB 2; DLBY 1980

Harris, Norman .... **CLC 65**

Harris, (Theodore) Wilson 1921- .... **CLC 25, 159**
See also BRWS 5; BW 2, 3; CA 65-68; 16; CANR 11, 27, 69, 114; CDWLB 3; CN 1, 2, 3, 4, 5, 6, 7; CP 1, 2, 3, 4, 5, 6, 7; DLB 117; EWL 3; MTCW 1; RGEL 2

Harrison, Barbara Grizzuti
1934-2002 .... **CLC 144**
See also CA 77-80; CAAS 205; CANR 15, 48; INT CANR-15

Harrison, Elizabeth (Allen) Cavanna
1909-2001
See Cavanna, Betty
See also CA 9-12R; CAAS 200; CANR 6, 27, 85, 104, 121; MAICYA 2; SATA 142; YAW

Harrison, Harry (Max) 1925- .... **CLC 42**
See also CA 1-4R; CANR 5, 21, 84; DLB 8; SATA 4; SCFW 2; SFW 4

Harrison, James
See Harrison, Jim

Harrison, James Thomas
See Harrison, Jim

Harrison, Jim 1937- .... **CLC 6, 14, 33, 66, 143; SSC 19**
See also AMWS 8; CA 13-16R; CANR 8, 51, 79, 142; CN 5, 6; CP 1, 2, 3, 4, 5, 6; DLBY 1982; INT CANR-8; RGAL 4; TCWW 2; TUS

Harrison, Kathryn 1961- .... **CLC 70, 151**
See also CA 144; CANR 68, 122

Harrison, Tony 1937- .... **CLC 43, 129**
See also BRWS 5; CA 65-68; CANR 44, 98; CBD; CD 5, 6; CP 2, 3, 4, 5, 6, 7; DLB 40, 245; MTCW 1; RGEL 2

Harriss, Will(ard Irvin) 1922- .... **CLC 34**
See also CA 111

Hart, Ellis
See Ellison, Harlan

Hart, Josephine 1942(?)- .... **CLC 70**
See also CA 138; CANR 70, 149; CPW; DAM POP

Hart, Moss 1904-1961 .... **CLC 66**
See also CA 109; CAAS 89-92; CANR 84; DAM DRAM; DFS 1; DLB 7, 266; RGAL 4

Harte, (Francis) Bret(t)
1836(?)-1902 ... **SSC 8, 59; TCLC 1, 25; WLC 3**
See also AMWS 2; CA 140; CAAE 104; CANR 80; CDALB 1865-1917; DA; DA3; DAC; DAM MST; DLB 12, 64, 74, 79, 186; EXPS; LAIT 2; RGAL 4; RGSF 2; SATA 26; SSFS 3; TUS

LMFS 2; MAICYA 1, 2; MTCW 1, 2;
MTFW 2005; RGAL 4; SATA 9, 69;
SATA-Obit 56; SCFW 1, 2; SFW 4; SSFS
7; YAW

Helforth, John
See Doolittle, Hilda

Heliodorus fl. 3rd cent. - .... **CMLC 52**
See also WLIT 8

Hellenhofferu, Vojtech Kapristian z
See Hasek, Jaroslav (Matej Frantisek)

Heller, Joseph 1923-1999 . **CLC 1, 3, 5, 8, 11,
36, 63; TCLC 131, 151; WLC 3**
See also AAYA 24; AITN 1; AMWS 4;
BPFB 2; BYA 1; CA 5-8R; CAAS 187;
CABS 1; CANR 8, 42, 66, 126; CN 1, 2,
3, 4, 5, 6; CPW; DA; DA3; DAB; DAC;
DAM MST, NOV, POP; DLB 2, 28, 227;
DLBY 1980, 2002; EWL 3; EXPN; INT
CANR-8; LAIT 4; MAL 5; MTCW 1, 2;
MTFW 2005; NFS 1; RGAL 4; TUS;
YAW

Hellman, Lillian 1906-1984 . **CLC 2, 4, 8, 14,
18, 34, 44, 52; DC 1; TCLC 119**
See also AAYA 47; AITN 1, 2; AMWS 1;
CA 13-16R; CAAS 112; CAD; CANR 33;
CWD; DA3; DAM DRAM; DFS 1, 3, 14;
DLB 7, 228; DLBY 1984; EWL 3; FL 1:6;
FW; LAIT 3; MAL 5; MBL; MTCW 1, 2;
MTFW 2005; RGAL 4; TUS

Helprin, Mark 1947- .... **CLC 7, 10, 22, 32**
See also CA 81-84; CANR 47, 64, 124;
CDALBS; CN 7; CPW; DA3; DAM NOV,
POP; DLBY 1985; FANT; MAL 5;
MTCW 1, 2; MTFW 2005; SUFW 2

Helvetius, Claude-Adrien 1715-1771 .. **LC 26**
See also DLB 313

Helyar, Jane Penelope Josephine 1933-
See Poole, Josephine
See also CA 21-24R; CANR 10, 26; CWRI
5; SATA 82, 138; SATA-Essay 138

Hemans, Felicia 1793-1835 ...... **NCLC 29, 71**
See also DLB 96; RGEL 2

Hemingway, Ernest (Miller)
1899-1961 .... **CLC 1, 3, 6, 8, 10, 13, 19,
30, 34, 39, 41, 44, 50, 61, 80; SSC 1, 25,
36, 40, 63; TCLC 115; WLC 3**
See also AAYA 19; AMW; AMWC 1;
AMWR 1; BPFB 2; BYA 2, 3, 13, 15; CA
77-80; CANR 34; CDALB 1917-1929;
DA; DA3; DAB; DAC; DAM MST, NOV;
DLB 4, 9, 102, 210, 308, 316, 330; DLBD
1, 15, 16; DLBY 1981, 1987, 1996, 1998;
EWL 3; EXPN; EXPS; LAIT 3, 4; LATS
1:1; MAL 5; MTCW 1, 2; MTFW 2005;
NFS 1, 5, 6, 14; RGAL 4; RGSF 2; SSFS
17; TUS; WYA

Hempel, Amy 1951- .... **CLC 39**
See also CA 137; CAAE 118; CANR 70;
DA3; DLB 218; EXPS; MTCW 2; MTFW
2005; SSFS 2

Henderson, F. C.
See Mencken, H(enry) L(ouis)

Henderson, Sylvia
See Ashton-Warner, Sylvia (Constance)

Henderson, Zenna (Chlarson)
1917-1983 .... **SSC 29**
See also CA 1-4R; CAAS 133; CANR 1,
84; DLB 8; SATA 5; SFW 4

Henkin, Joshua .... **CLC 119**
See also CA 161

Henley, Beth .... **CLC 23; DC 6, 14**
See Henley, Elizabeth Becker
See also AAYA 70; CABS 3; CAD; CD 5,
6; CSW; CWD; DFS 2, 21; DLBY 1986;
FW

Henley, Elizabeth Becker 1952-
See Henley, Beth
See also CA 107; CANR 32, 73, 140; DA3;
DAM DRAM, MST; MTCW 1, 2; MTFW
2005

Henley, William Ernest 1849-1903 .. **TCLC 8**
See also CA 234; CAAE 105; DLB 19;
RGEL 2

Hennissart, Martha 1929-
See Lathen, Emma
See also CA 85-88; CANR 64

Henry VIII 1491-1547 .... **LC 10**
See also DLB 132

Henry, O. . **SSC 5, 49; TCLC 1, 19; WLC 3**
See Porter, William Sydney
See also AAYA 41; AMWS 2; EXPS; MAL
5; RGAL 4; RGSF 2; SSFS 2, 18; TCWW
1, 2

Henry, Patrick 1736-1799 .... **LC 25**
See also LAIT 1

Henryson, Robert 1430(?)-1506(?) ..... **LC 20,
110; PC 65**
See also BRWS 7; DLB 146; RGEL 2

Henschke, Alfred
See Klabund

Henson, Lance 1944- .... **NNAL**
See also CA 146; DLB 175

Hentoff, Nat(han Irving) 1925- .... **CLC 26**
See also AAYA 4, 42; BYA 6; CA 1-4R; 6;
CANR 5, 25, 77, 114; CLR 1, 52; INT
CANR-25; JRDA; MAICYA 1, 2; SATA
42, 69, 133; SATA-Brief 27; WYA; YAW

Heppenstall, (John) Rayner
1911-1981 .... **CLC 10**
See also CA 1-4R; CAAS 103; CANR 29;
CN 1, 2; CP 1, 2, 3; EWL 3

Heraclitus c. 540B.C.-c. 450B.C. ... **CMLC 22**
See also DLB 176

Herbert, Frank 1920-1986 ... **CLC 12, 23, 35,
44, 85**
See also AAYA 21; BPFB 2; BYA 4, 14;
CA 53-56; CAAS 118; CANR 5, 43;
CDALBS; CPW; DAM POP; DLB 8; INT
CANR-5; LAIT 5; MTCW 1, 2; MTFW
2005; NFS 17; SATA 9, 37; SATA-Obit
47; SCFW 1, 2; SFW 4; YAW

Herbert, George 1593-1633 . **LC 24, 121; PC
4**
See also BRW 2; BRWR 2; CDBLB Before
1660; DAB; DAM POET; DLB 126;
EXPP; PFS 25; RGEL 2; TEA; WP

Herbert, Zbigniew 1924-1998 ..... **CLC 9, 43;
PC 50; TCLC 168**
See also CA 89-92; CAAS 169; CANR 36,
74; CDWLB 4; CWW 2; DAM POET;
DLB 232; EWL 3; MTCW 1; PFS 22

Herbst, Josephine (Frey)
1897-1969 .... **CLC 34**
See also CA 5-8R; CAAS 25-28R; DLB 9

Herder, Johann Gottfried von
1744-1803 .... **NCLC 8**
See also DLB 97; EW 4; TWA

Heredia, Jose Maria 1803-1839 .... **HLCS 2**
See also LAW

Hergesheimer, Joseph 1880-1954 ... **TCLC 11**
See also CA 194; CAAE 109; DLB 102, 9;
RGAL 4

Herlihy, James Leo 1927-1993 .... **CLC 6**
See also CA 1-4R; CAAS 143; CAD;
CANR 2; CN 1, 2, 3, 4, 5

Herman, William
See Bierce, Ambrose (Gwinett)

Hermogenes fl. c. 175- .... **CMLC 6**

Hernandez, Jose 1834-1886 .... **NCLC 17**
See also LAW; RGWL 2, 3; WLIT 1

Herodotus c. 484B.C.-c. 420B.C. .. **CMLC 17**
See also AW 1; CDWLB 1; DLB 176;
RGWL 2, 3; TWA; WLIT 8

Herr, Michael 1940(?)- .... **CLC 231**
See also CA 89-92; CANR 68, 142; DLB
185; MTCW 1

Herrick, Robert 1591-1674 .... **LC 13; PC 9**
See also BRW 2; BRWC 2; DA; DAB;
DAC; DAM MST, POP; DLB 126; EXPP;
PFS 13; RGAL 4; RGEL 2; TEA; WP

Herring, Guilles
See Somerville, Edith Oenone

Herriot, James 1916-1995 .... **CLC 12**
See Wight, James Alfred
See also AAYA 1, 54; BPFB 2; CAAS 148;
CANR 40; CLR 80; CPW; DAM POP;
LAIT 3; MAICYA 2; MAICYAS 1;
MTCW 2; SATA 86, 135; TEA; YAW

Herris, Violet
See Hunt, Violet

Herrmann, Dorothy 1941- .... **CLC 44**
See also CA 107

Herrmann, Taffy
See Herrmann, Dorothy

Hersey, John 1914-1993 .. **CLC 1, 2, 7, 9, 40,
81, 97**
See also AAYA 29; BPFB 2; CA 17-20R;
CAAS 140; CANR 33; CDALBS; CN 1,
2, 3, 4, 5; CPW; DAM POP; DLB 6, 185,
278, 299; MAL 5; MTCW 1, 2; MTFW
2005; RGHL; SATA 25; SATA-Obit 76;
TUS

Herzen, Aleksandr Ivanovich
1812-1870 .... **NCLC 10, 61**
See Herzen, Alexander

Herzen, Alexander
See Herzen, Aleksandr Ivanovich
See also DLB 277

Herzl, Theodor 1860-1904 .... **TCLC 36**
See also CA 168

Herzog, Werner 1942- .... **CLC 16**
See also CA 89-92

Hesiod c. 8th cent. B.C.- .... **CMLC 5**
See also AW 1; DLB 176; RGWL 2, 3;
WLIT 8

Hesse, Hermann 1877-1962 ... **CLC 1, 2, 3, 6,
11, 17, 25, 69; SSC 9, 49; TCLC 148;
WLC 3**
See also AAYA 43; BPFB 2; CA 17-18;
CAP 2; CDWLB 2; DA; DA3; DAB;
DAC; DAM MST, NOV; DLB 66, 330;
EW 9; EWL 3; EXPN; LAIT 1; MTCW
1, 2; MTFW 2005; NFS 6, 15, 24; RGWL
2, 3; SATA 50; TWA

Hewes, Cady
See De Voto, Bernard (Augustine)

Heyen, William 1940- .... **CLC 13, 18**
See also CA 220; 33-36R, 220; 9; CANR
98; CP 3, 4, 5, 6, 7; DLB 5; RGHL

Heyerdahl, Thor 1914-2002 .... **CLC 26**
See also CA 5-8R; CAAS 207; CANR 5,
22, 66, 73; LAIT 4; MTCW 1, 2; MTFW
2005; SATA 2, 52

Heym, Georg (Theodor Franz Arthur)
1887-1912 .... **TCLC 9**
See also CA 181; CAAE 106

Heym, Stefan 1913-2001 .... **CLC 41**
See also CA 9-12R; CAAS 203; CANR 4;
CWW 2; DLB 69; EWL 3

Heyse, Paul (Johann Ludwig von)
1830-1914 .... **TCLC 8**
See also CA 209; CAAE 104; DLB 129,
330

Heyward, (Edwin) DuBose
1885-1940 .... **HR 1:2; TCLC 59**
See also CA 157; CAAE 108; DLB 7, 9,
45, 249; MAL 5; SATA 21

Heywood, John 1497(?)-1580(?) .... **LC 65**
See also DLB 136; RGEL 2

Heywood, Thomas 1573(?)-1641 .... **LC 111**
See also DAM DRAM; DLB 62; LMFS 1;
RGEL 2; TEA

Hibbert, Eleanor Alice Burford
　　1906-1993 .... **CLC 7**
　　See Holt, Victoria
　　See also BEST 90:4; CA 17-20R; CAAS
　　140; CANR 9, 28, 59; CMW 4; CPW;
　　DAM POP; MTCW 2; MTFW 2005;
　　RHW; SATA 2; SATA-Obit 74

Hichens, Robert (Smythe)
　　1864-1950 .... **TCLC 64**
　　See also CA 162; DLB 153; HGG; RHW;
　　SUFW

Higgins, Aidan 1927- .... **SSC 68**
　　See also CA 9-12R; CANR 70, 115, 148;
　　CN 1, 2, 3, 4, 5, 6, 7; DLB 14

Higgins, George V(incent)
　　1939-1999 .... **CLC 4, 7, 10, 18**
　　See also BPFB 2; CA 77-80; 5; CAAS 186;
　　CANR 17, 51, 89, 96; CMW 4; CN 2, 3,
　　4, 5, 6; DLB 2; DLBY 1981, 1998; INT
　　CANR-17; MSW; MTCW 1

Higginson, Thomas Wentworth
　　1823-1911 .... **TCLC 36**
　　See also CA 162; DLB 1, 64, 243

Higgonet, Margaret .... **CLC 65**

Highet, Helen
　　See MacInnes, Helen (Clark)

Highsmith, Patricia 1921-1995 ...... **CLC 2, 4,
　　14, 42, 102**
　　See Morgan, Claire
　　See also AAYA 48; BRWS 5; CA 1-4R;
　　CAAS 147; CANR 1, 20, 48, 62, 108;
　　CMW 4; CN 1, 2, 3, 4, 5; CPW; DA3;
　　DAM NOV, POP; DLB 306; MSW;
　　MTCW 1, 2; MTFW 2005

Highwater, Jamake (Mamake)
　　1942(?)-2001 .... **CLC 12**
　　See also AAYA 7, 69; BPFB 2; BYA 4; CA
　　65-68; 7; CAAS 199; CANR 10, 34, 84;
　　CLR 17; CWRI 5; DLB 52; DLBY 1985;
　　JRDA; MAICYA 1, 2; SATA 32, 69;
　　SATA-Brief 30

Highway, Tomson 1951- ...... **CLC 92; NNAL**
　　See also CA 151; CANR 75; CCA 1; CD 5,
　　6; CN 7; DAC; DAM MULT; DFS 2;
　　MTCW 2

Hijuelos, Oscar 1951- .... **CLC 65; HLC 1**
　　See also AAYA 25; AMWS 16; BEST 90:1;
　　CA 123; CANR 50, 75, 125; CPW; DA3;
　　DAM MULT, POP; DLB 145; HW 1, 2;
　　LLW; MAL 5; MTCW 2; MTFW 2005;
　　NFS 17; RGAL 4; WLIT 1

Hikmet, Nazim 1902-1963 .... **CLC 40**
　　See Nizami of Ganja
　　See also CA 141; CAAS 93-96; EWL 3;
　　WLIT 6

Hildegard von Bingen 1098-1179 . **CMLC 20**
　　See also DLB 148

Hildesheimer, Wolfgang 1916-1991 .. **CLC 49**
　　See also CA 101; CAAS 135; DLB 69, 124;
　　EWL 3; RGHL

Hill, Geoffrey (William) 1932- ...... **CLC 5, 8,
　　18, 45**
　　See also BRWS 5; CA 81-84; CANR 21,
　　89; CDBLB 1960 to Present; CP 1, 2, 3,
　　4, 5, 6, 7; DAM POET; DLB 40; EWL 3;
　　MTCW 1; RGEL 2; RGHL

Hill, George Roy 1921-2002 .... **CLC 26**
　　See also CA 122; CAAE 110; CAAS 213

Hill, John
　　See Koontz, Dean R.

Hill, Susan (Elizabeth) 1942- ...... **CLC 4, 113**
　　See also CA 33-36R; CANR 29, 69, 129;
　　CN 2, 3, 4, 5, 6, 7; DAB; DAM MST,
　　NOV; DLB 14, 139; HGG; MTCW 1;
　　RHW

Hillard, Asa G. III .... **CLC 70**

Hillerman, Tony 1925- .... **CLC 62, 170**
　　See also AAYA 40; BEST 89:1; BPFB 2;
　　CA 29-32R; CANR 21, 42, 65, 97, 134;
　　CMW 4; CPW; DA3; DAM POP; DLB
　　206, 306; MAL 5; MSW; MTCW 2;
　　MTFW 2005; RGAL 4; SATA 6; TCWW
　　2; YAW

Hillesum, Etty 1914-1943 .... **TCLC 49**
　　See also CA 137; RGHL

Hilliard, Noel (Harvey) 1929-1996 ... **CLC 15**
　　See also CA 9-12R; CANR 7, 69; CN 1, 2,
　　3, 4, 5, 6

Hillis, Rick 1956- .... **CLC 66**
　　See also CA 134

Hilton, James 1900-1954 .... **TCLC 21**
　　See also CA 169; CAAE 108; DLB 34, 77;
　　FANT; SATA 34

Hilton, Walter (?)-1396 .... **CMLC 58**
　　See also DLB 146; RGEL 2

Himes, Chester (Bomar) 1909-1984 .. **BLC 2;
　　CLC 2, 4, 7, 18, 58, 108; TCLC 139**
　　See also AFAW 2; AMWS 16; BPFB 2; BW
　　2; CA 25-28R; CAAS 114; CANR 22, 89;
　　CMW 4; CN 1, 2, 3; DAM MULT; DLB
　　2, 76, 143, 226; EWL 3; MAL 5; MSW;
　　MTCW 1, 2; MTFW 2005; RGAL 4

Himmelfarb, Gertrude 1922- .... **CLC 202**
　　See also CA 49-52; CANR 28, 66, 102

Hinde, Thomas .... **CLC 6, 11**
　　See Chitty, Thomas Willes
　　See also CN 1, 2, 3, 4, 5, 6; EWL 3

Hine, (William) Daryl 1936- .... **CLC 15**
　　See also CA 1-4R; 15; CANR 1, 20; CP 1,
　　2, 3, 4, 5, 6, 7; DLB 60

Hinkson, Katharine Tynan
　　See Tynan, Katharine

Hinojosa, Rolando 1929- .... **HLC 1**
　　See Hinojosa-Smith, Rolando
　　See also CA 131; 16; CANR 62; DAM
　　MULT; DLB 82; HW 1, 2; LLW; MTCW
　　2; MTFW 2005; RGAL 4

Hinton, S.E. 1950- .... **CLC 30, 111**
　　See also AAYA 2, 33; BPFB 2; BYA 2, 3;
　　CA 81-84; CANR 32, 62, 92, 133;
　　CDALBS; CLR 3, 23; CPW; DA; DA3;
　　DAB; DAC; DAM MST, NOV; JRDA;
　　LAIT 5; MAICYA 1, 2; MTCW 1, 2;
　　MTFW 2005; NFS 5, 9, 15, 16; SATA 19,
　　58, 115, 160; WYA; YAW

Hippius, Zinaida (Nikolaevna) .... **TCLC 9**
　　See Gippius, Zinaida (Nikolaevna)
　　See also DLB 295; EWL 3

Hiraoka, Kimitake 1925-1970
　　See Mishima, Yukio
　　See also CA 97-100; CAAS 29-32R; DA3;
　　DAM DRAM; GLL 1; MTCW 1, 2

Hirsch, E.D., Jr. 1928- .... **CLC 79**
　　See also CA 25-28R; CANR 27, 51, 146;
　　DLB 67; INT CANR-27; MTCW 1

Hirsch, Edward 1950- .... **CLC 31, 50**
　　See also CA 104; CANR 20, 42, 102; CP 6,
　　7; DLB 120; PFS 22

Hirsch, Eric Donald, Jr.
　　See Hirsch, E.D., Jr.

Hitchcock, Alfred (Joseph)
　　1899-1980 .... **CLC 16**
　　See also AAYA 22; CA 159; CAAS 97-100;
　　SATA 27; SATA-Obit 24

Hitchens, Christopher 1949- .... **CLC 157**
　　See also CA 152; CANR 89, 155

Hitchens, Christopher Eric
　　See Hitchens, Christopher

Hitler, Adolf 1889-1945 .... **TCLC 53**
　　See also CA 147; CAAE 117

Hoagland, Edward (Morley) 1932- .. **CLC 28**
　　See also ANW; CA 1-4R; CANR 2, 31, 57,
　　107; CN 1, 2, 3, 4, 5, 6, 7; DLB 6; SATA
　　51; TCWW 2

Hoban, Russell 1925- .... **CLC 7, 25**
　　See also BPFB 2; CA 5-8R; CANR 23, 37,
　　66, 114, 138; CLR 3, 69; CN 4, 5, 6, 7;
　　CWRI 5; DAM NOV; DLB 52; FANT;
　　MAICYA 1, 2; MTCW 1, 2; MTFW 2005;
　　SATA 1, 40, 78, 136; SFW 4; SUFW 2;
　　TCLE 1:1

Hobbes, Thomas 1588-1679 .... **LC 36**
　　See also DLB 151, 252, 281; RGEL 2

Hobbs, Perry
　　See Blackmur, R(ichard) P(almer)

Hobson, Laura Z(ametkin)
　　1900-1986 .... **CLC 7, 25**
　　See also BPFB 2; CA 17-20R; CAAS 118;
　　CANR 55; CN 1, 2, 3, 4; DLB 28; SATA
　　52

Hoccleve, Thomas c. 1368-c. 1437 ...... **LC 75**
　　See also DLB 146; RGEL 2

Hoch, Edward D(entinger) 1930-
　　See Queen, Ellery
　　See also CA 29-32R; CANR 11, 27, 51, 97;
　　CMW 4; DLB 306; SFW 4

Hochhuth, Rolf 1931- .... **CLC 4, 11, 18**
　　See also CA 5-8R; CANR 33, 75, 136;
　　CWW 2; DAM DRAM; DLB 124; EWL
　　3; MTCW 1, 2; MTFW 2005; RGHL

Hochman, Sandra 1936- .... **CLC 3, 8**
　　See also CA 5-8R; CP 1, 2, 3, 4, 5; DLB 5

Hochwaelder, Fritz 1911-1986 .... **CLC 36**
　　See Hochwalder, Fritz
　　See also CA 29-32R; CAAS 120; CANR
　　42; DAM DRAM; MTCW 1; RGWL 3

Hochwalder, Fritz
　　See Hochwaelder, Fritz
　　See also EWL 3; RGWL 2

Hocking, Mary (Eunice) 1921- .... **CLC 13**
　　See also CA 101; CANR 18, 40

Hodgins, Jack 1938- .... **CLC 23**
　　See also CA 93-96; CN 4, 5, 6, 7; DLB 60

Hodgson, William Hope
　　1877(?)-1918 .... **TCLC 13**
　　See also CA 164; CAAE 111; CMW 4; DLB
　　70, 153, 156, 178; HGG; MTCW 2; SFW
　　4; SUFW 1

Hoeg, Peter 1957- .... **CLC 95, 156**
　　See also CA 151; CANR 75; CMW 4; DA3;
　　DLB 214; EWL 3; MTCW 2; MTFW
　　2005; NFS 17; RGWL 3; SSFS 18

Hoffman, Alice 1952- .... **CLC 51**
　　See also AAYA 37; AMWS 10; CA 77-80;
　　CANR 34, 66, 100, 138; CN 4, 5, 6, 7;
　　CPW; DAM NOV; DLB 292; MAL 5;
　　MTCW 1, 2; MTFW 2005; TCLE 1:1

Hoffman, Daniel (Gerard) 1923- . **CLC 6, 13,
　　23**
　　See also CA 1-4R; CANR 4, 142; CP 1, 2,
　　3, 4, 5, 6, 7; DLB 5; TCLE 1:1

Hoffman, Eva 1945- .... **CLC 182**
　　See also AMWS 16; CA 132; CANR 146

Hoffman, Stanley 1944- .... **CLC 5**
　　See also CA 77-80

Hoffman, William 1925- .... **CLC 141**
　　See also CA 21-24R; CANR 9, 103; CSW;
　　DLB 234; TCLE 1:1

Hoffman, William M.
　　See Hoffman, William M(oses)
　　See also CAD; CD 5, 6

Hoffman, William M(oses) 1939- ..... **CLC 40**
　　See Hoffman, William M.
　　See also CA 57-60; CANR 11, 71

Hoffmann, E(rnst) T(heodor) A(madeus)
　　1776-1822 .... **NCLC 2; SSC 13, 92**
　　See also CDWLB 2; DLB 90; EW 5; GL 2;
　　RGSF 2; RGWL 2, 3; SATA 27; SUFW
　　1; WCH

Hofmann, Gert 1931-1993 .... **CLC 54**
　　See also CA 128; CANR 145; EWL 3;
　　RGHL

Hofmannsthal, Hugo von 1874-1929 ... **DC 4; TCLC 11**
See also CA 153; CAAE 106; CDWLB 2; DAM DRAM; DFS 17; DLB 81, 118; EW 9; EWL 3; RGWL 2, 3

Hogan, Linda 1947- ..... **CLC 73; NNAL; PC 35**
See also AMWS 4; ANW; BYA 12; CA 226; 120, 226; CANR 45, 73, 129; CWP; DAM MULT; DLB 175; SATA 132; TCWW 2

Hogarth, Charles
See Creasey, John

Hogarth, Emmett
See Polonsky, Abraham (Lincoln)

Hogarth, William 1697-1764 .... **LC 112**
See also AAYA 56

Hogg, James 1770-1835 .... **NCLC 4, 109**
See also BRWS 10; DLB 93, 116, 159; GL 2; HGG; RGEL 2; SUFW 1

Holbach, Paul-Henri Thiry
1723-1789 .... **LC 14**
See also DLB 313

Holberg, Ludvig 1684-1754 .... **LC 6**
See also DLB 300; RGWL 2, 3

Holcroft, Thomas 1745-1809 .... **NCLC 85**
See also DLB 39, 89, 158; RGEL 2

Holden, Ursula 1921- .... **CLC 18**
See also CA 101; 8; CANR 22

Holderlin, (Johann Christian) Friedrich
1770-1843 .... **NCLC 16; PC 4**
See also CDWLB 2; DLB 90; EW 5; RGWL 2, 3

Holdstock, Robert 1948- .... **CLC 39**
See also CA 131; CANR 81; DLB 261; FANT; HGG; SFW 4; SUFW 2

Holdstock, Robert P.
See Holdstock, Robert

Holinshed, Raphael fl. 1580- .... **LC 69**
See also DLB 167; RGEL 2

Holland, Isabelle (Christian)
1920-2002 .... **CLC 21**
See also AAYA 11, 64; CA 181; 21-24R; CAAS 205; CANR 10, 25, 47; CLR 57; CWRI 5; JRDA; LAIT 4; MAICYA 1, 2; SATA 8, 70; SATA-Essay 103; SATA-Obit 132; WYA

Holland, Marcus
See Caldwell, (Janet Miriam) Taylor (Holland)

Hollander, John 1929- .... **CLC 2, 5, 8, 14**
See also CA 1-4R; CANR 1, 52, 136; CP 1, 2, 3, 4, 5, 6, 7; DLB 5; MAL 5; SATA 13

Hollander, Paul
See Silverberg, Robert

Holleran, Andrew .... **CLC 38**
See Garber, Eric
See also CA 144; GLL 1

Holley, Marietta 1836(?)-1926 .... **TCLC 99**
See also CAAE 118; DLB 11; FL 1:3

Hollinghurst, Alan 1954- .... **CLC 55, 91**
See also BRWS 10; CA 114; CN 5, 6, 7; DLB 207, 326; GLL 1

Hollis, Jim
See Summers, Hollis (Spurgeon, Jr.)

Holly, Buddy 1936-1959 .... **TCLC 65**
See also CA 213

Holmes, Gordon
See Shiel, M(atthew) P(hipps)

Holmes, John
See Souster, (Holmes) Raymond

Holmes, John Clellon 1926-1988 ...... **CLC 56**
See also BG 1:2; CA 9-12R; CAAS 125; CANR 4; CN 1, 2, 3, 4; DLB 16, 237

Holmes, Oliver Wendell, Jr.
1841-1935 .... **TCLC 77**
See also CA 186; CAAE 114

Holmes, Oliver Wendell
1809-1894 .... **NCLC 14, 81; PC 71**
See also AMWS 1; CDALB 1640-1865; DLB 1, 189, 235; EXPP; PFS 24; RGAL 4; SATA 34

Holmes, Raymond
See Souster, (Holmes) Raymond

Holt, Victoria
See Hibbert, Eleanor Alice Burford
See also BPFB 2

Holub, Miroslav 1923-1998 .... **CLC 4**
See also CA 21-24R; CAAS 169; CANR 10; CDWLB 4; CWW 2; DLB 232; EWL 3; RGWL 3

Holz, Detlev
See Benjamin, Walter

Homer c. 8th cent. B.C.- .... **CMLC 1, 16, 61; PC 23; WLCS**
See also AW 1; CDWLB 1; DA; DA3; DAB; DAC; DAM MST, POET; DLB 176; EFS 1; LAIT 1; LMFS 1; RGWL 2, 3; TWA; WLIT 8; WP

Hongo, Garrett Kaoru 1951- .... **PC 23**
See also CA 133; 22; CP 5, 6, 7; DLB 120, 312; EWL 3; EXPP; PFS 25; RGAL 4

Honig, Edwin 1919- .... **CLC 33**
See also CA 5-8R; 8; CANR 4, 45, 144; CP 1, 2, 3, 4, 5, 6, 7; DLB 5

Hood, Hugh (John Blagdon) 1928- . **CLC 15, 28; SSC 42**
See also CA 49-52; 17; CANR 1, 33, 87; CN 1, 2, 3, 4, 5, 6, 7; DLB 53; RGSF 2

Hood, Thomas 1799-1845 .... **NCLC 16**
See also BRW 4; DLB 96; RGEL 2

Hooker, (Peter) Jeremy 1941- .... **CLC 43**
See also CA 77-80; CANR 22; CP 2, 3, 4, 5, 6, 7; DLB 40

Hooker, Richard 1554-1600 .... **LC 95**
See also BRW 1; DLB 132; RGEL 2

Hooker, Thomas 1586-1647 .... **LC 137**
See also DLB 24

hooks, bell 1952(?)- .... **CLC 94**
See also BW 2; CA 143; CANR 87, 126; DLB 246; MTCW 2; MTFW 2005; SATA 115, 170

Hooper, Johnson Jones
1815-1862 .... **NCLC 177**
See also DLB 3, 11, 248; RGAL 4

Hope, A(lec) D(erwent) 1907-2000 .... **CLC 3, 51; PC 56**
See also BRWS 7; CA 21-24R; CAAS 188; CANR 33, 74; CP 1, 2, 3, 4, 5; DLB 289; EWL 3; MTCW 1, 2; MTFW 2005; PFS 8; RGEL 2

Hope, Anthony 1863-1933 .... **TCLC 83**
See also CA 157; DLB 153, 156; RGEL 2; RHW

Hope, Brian
See Creasey, John

Hope, Christopher (David Tully)
1944- .... **CLC 52**
See also AFW; CA 106; CANR 47, 101; CN 4, 5, 6, 7; DLB 225; SATA 62

Hopkins, Gerard Manley
1844-1889 .... **NCLC 17; PC 15; WLC 3**
See also BRW 5; BRWR 2; CDBLB 1890-1914; DA; DA3; DAB; DAC; DAM MST, POET; DLB 35, 57; EXPP; PAB; RGEL 2; TEA; WP

Hopkins, John (Richard) 1931-1998 .. **CLC 4**
See also CA 85-88; CAAS 169; CBD; CD 5, 6

Hopkins, Pauline Elizabeth
1859-1930 .... **BLC 2; TCLC 28**
See also AFAW 2; BW 2, 3; CA 141; CANR 82; DAM MULT; DLB 50

Hopkinson, Francis 1737-1791 .... **LC 25**
See also DLB 31; RGAL 4

Hopley-Woolrich, Cornell George 1903-1968
See Woolrich, Cornell
See also CA 13-14; CANR 58, 156; CAP 1; CMW 4; DLB 226; MTCW 2

Horace 65B.C.-8B.C. .... **CMLC 39; PC 46**
See also AW 2; CDWLB 1; DLB 211; RGWL 2, 3; WLIT 8

Horatio
See Proust, (Valentin-Louis-George-Eugene) Marcel

Horgan, Paul (George Vincent O'Shaughnessy) 1903-1995 .. **CLC 9, 53**
See also BPFB 2; CA 13-16R; CAAS 147; CANR 9, 35; CN 1, 2, 3, 4, 5; DAM NOV; DLB 102, 212; DLBY 1985; INT CANR-9; MTCW 1, 2; MTFW 2005; SATA 13; SATA-Obit 84; TCWW 1, 2

Horkheimer, Max 1895-1973 .... **TCLC 132**
See also CA 216; CAAS 41-44R; DLB 296

Horn, Peter
See Kuttner, Henry

Horne, Frank (Smith) 1899-1974 ...... **HR 1:2**
See also BW 1; CA 125; CAAS 53-56; DLB 51; WP

Horne, Richard Henry Hengist
1802(?)-1884 .... **NCLC 127**
See also DLB 32; SATA 29

Hornem, Horace Esq.
See Byron, George Gordon (Noel)

Horney, Karen (Clementine Theodore Danielsen) 1885-1952 .... **TCLC 71**
See also CA 165; CAAE 114; DLB 246; FW

Hornung, E(rnest) W(illiam)
1866-1921 .... **TCLC 59**
See also CA 160; CAAE 108; CMW 4; DLB 70

Horovitz, Israel (Arthur) 1939- .... **CLC 56**
See also CA 33-36R; CAD; CANR 46, 59; CD 5, 6; DAM DRAM; DLB 7; MAL 5

Horton, George Moses
1797(?)-1883(?) .... **NCLC 87**
See also DLB 50

Horvath, odon von 1901-1938
See von Horvath, Odon
See also EWL 3

Horvath, Oedoen von -1938
See von Horvath, Odon

Horwitz, Julius 1920-1986 .... **CLC 14**
See also CA 9-12R; CAAS 119; CANR 12

Horwitz, Ronald
See Harwood, Ronald

Hospital, Janette Turner 1942- .... **CLC 42, 145**
See also CA 108; CANR 48; CN 5, 6, 7; DLB 325; DLBY 2002; RGSF 2

Hostos, E. M. de
See Hostos (y Bonilla), Eugenio Maria de

Hostos, Eugenio M. de
See Hostos (y Bonilla), Eugenio Maria de

Hostos, Eugenio Maria
See Hostos (y Bonilla), Eugenio Maria de

Hostos (y Bonilla), Eugenio Maria de
1839-1903 .... **TCLC 24**
See also CA 131; CAAE 123; HW 1

Houdini
See Lovecraft, H. P.

Houellebecq, Michel 1958- .... **CLC 179**
See also CA 185; CANR 140; MTFW 2005

Hougan, Carolyn 1943- .... **CLC 34**
See also CA 139

Household, Geoffrey (Edward West)
1900-1988 .... **CLC 11**
See also CA 77-80; CAAS 126; CANR 58; CMW 4; CN 1, 2, 3, 4; DLB 87; SATA 14; SATA-Obit 59

Housman, A(lfred) E(dward)
1859-1936 .... **PC 2, 43; TCLC 1, 10; WLCS**
See also AAYA 66; BRW 6; CA 125; CAAE 104; DA; DA3; DAB; DAC; DAM MST, POET; DLB 19, 284; EWL 3; EXPP; MTCW 1, 2; MTFW 2005; PAB; PFS 4, 7; RGEL 2; TEA; WP

Housman, Laurence 1865-1959 .... **TCLC 7**
See also CA 155; CAAE 106; DLB 10; FANT; RGEL 2; SATA 25

Houston, Jeanne Wakatsuki 1934- .... **AAL**
See also AAYA 49; CA 232; 103, 232; 16; CANR 29, 123; LAIT 4; SATA 78, 168; SATA-Essay 168

Howard, Elizabeth Jane 1923- ..... **CLC 7, 29**
See also BRWS 11; CA 5-8R; CANR 8, 62, 146; CN 1, 2, 3, 4, 5, 6, 7

Howard, Maureen 1930- .... **CLC 5, 14, 46, 151**
See also CA 53-56; CANR 31, 75, 140; CN 4, 5, 6, 7; DLBY 1983; INT CANR-31; MTCW 1, 2; MTFW 2005

Howard, Richard 1929- .... **CLC 7, 10, 47**
See also AITN 1; CA 85-88; CANR 25, 80, 154; CP 1, 2, 3, 4, 5, 6, 7; DLB 5; INT CANR-25; MAL 5

Howard, Robert E 1906-1936 .... **TCLC 8**
See also BPFB 2; BYA 5; CA 157; CAAE 105; CANR 155; FANT; SUFW 1; TCWW 1, 2

Howard, Robert Ervin
See Howard, Robert E

Howard, Warren F.
See Pohl, Frederik

Howe, Fanny (Quincy) 1940- .... **CLC 47**
See also CA 187; 117, 187; 27; CANR 70, 116; CP 6, 7; CWP; SATA-Brief 52

Howe, Irving 1920-1993 .... **CLC 85**
See also AMWS 6; CA 9-12R; CAAS 141; CANR 21, 50; DLB 67; EWL 3; MAL 5; MTCW 1, 2; MTFW 2005

Howe, Julia Ward 1819-1910 .... **TCLC 21**
See also CA 191; CAAE 117; DLB 1, 189, 235; FW

Howe, Susan 1937- .... **CLC 72, 152; PC 54**
See also AMWS 4; CA 160; CP 5, 6, 7; CWP; DLB 120; FW; RGAL 4

Howe, Tina 1937- .... **CLC 48**
See also CA 109; CAD; CANR 125; CD 5, 6; CWD

Howell, James 1594(?)-1666 .... **LC 13**
See also DLB 151

Howells, W. D.
See Howells, William Dean

Howells, William D.
See Howells, William Dean

Howells, William Dean 1837-1920 ... **SSC 36; TCLC 7, 17, 41**
See also AMW; CA 134; CAAE 104; CDALB 1865-1917; DLB 12, 64, 74, 79, 189; LMFS 1; MAL 5; MTCW 2; RGAL 4; TUS

Howes, Barbara 1914-1996 .... **CLC 15**
See also CA 9-12R; 3; CAAS 151; CANR 53; CP 1, 2, 3, 4, 5, 6; SATA 5; TCLE 1:1

Hrabal, Bohumil 1914-1997 ...... **CLC 13, 67; TCLC 155**
See also CA 106; 12; CAAS 156; CANR 57; CWW 2; DLB 232; EWL 3; RGSF 2

Hrabanus Maurus 776(?)-856 .... **CMLC 78**
See also DLB 148

Hrotsvit of Gandersheim c. 935-c. 1000 .... **CMLC 29**
See also DLB 148

Hsi, Chu 1130-1200 .... **CMLC 42**

Hsun, Lu
See Lu Hsun

Hubbard, L. Ron 1911-1986 .... **CLC 43**
See also AAYA 64; CA 77-80; CAAS 118; CANR 52; CPW; DA3; DAM POP; FANT; MTCW 2; MTFW 2005; SFW 4

Hubbard, Lafayette Ronald
See Hubbard, L. Ron

Huch, Ricarda (Octavia)
1864-1947 .... **TCLC 13**
See also CA 189; CAAE 111; DLB 66; EWL 3

Huddle, David 1942- .... **CLC 49**
See also CA 57-60; 20; CANR 89; DLB 130

Hudson, Jeffrey
See Crichton, Michael

Hudson, W(illiam) H(enry)
1841-1922 .... **TCLC 29**
See also CA 190; CAAE 115; DLB 98, 153, 174; RGEL 2; SATA 35

Hueffer, Ford Madox
See Ford, Ford Madox

Hughart, Barry 1934- .... **CLC 39**
See also CA 137; FANT; SFW 4; SUFW 2

Hughes, Colin
See Creasey, John

Hughes, David (John) 1930-2005 ..... **CLC 48**
See also CA 129; CAAE 116; CAAS 238; CN 4, 5, 6, 7; DLB 14

Hughes, Edward James
See Hughes, Ted
See also DA3; DAM MST, POET

Hughes, (James Mercer) Langston
1902-1967 ..... **BLC 2; CLC 1, 5, 10, 15, 35, 44, 108; DC 3; HR 1:2; PC 1, 53; SSC 6, 90; WLC 3**
See also AAYA 12; AFAW 1, 2; AMWR 1; AMWS 1; BW 1, 3; CA 1-4R; CAAS 25-28R; CANR 1, 34, 82; CDALB 1929-1941; CLR 17; DA; DA3; DAB; DAC; DAM DRAM, MST, MULT, POET; DFS 6, 18; DLB 4, 7, 48, 51, 86, 228, 315; EWL 3; EXPP; EXPS; JRDA; LAIT 3; LMFS 2; MAICYA 1, 2; MAL 5; MTCW 1, 2; MTFW 2005; NFS 21; PAB; PFS 1, 3, 6, 10, 15; RGAL 4; RGSF 2; SATA 4, 33; SSFS 4, 7; TUS; WCH; WP; YAW

Hughes, Richard (Arthur Warren)
1900-1976 .... **CLC 1, 11**
See also CA 5-8R; CAAS 65-68; CANR 4; CN 1, 2; DAM NOV; DLB 15, 161; EWL 3; MTCW 1; RGEL 2; SATA 8; SATA-Obit 25

Hughes, Ted 1930-1998 . **CLC 2, 4, 9, 14, 37, 119; PC 7**
See Hughes, Edward James
See also BRWC 2; BRWR 2; BRWS 1; CA 1-4R; CAAS 171; CANR 1, 33, 66, 108; CLR 3; CP 1, 2, 3, 4, 5, 6; DAB; DAC; DLB 40, 161; EWL 3; EXPP; MAICYA 1, 2; MTCW 1, 2; MTFW 2005; PAB; PFS 4, 19; RGEL 2; SATA 49; SATA-Brief 27; SATA-Obit 107; TEA; YAW

Hugo, Richard
See Huch, Ricarda (Octavia)

Hugo, Richard F(ranklin)
1923-1982 .... **CLC 6, 18, 32; PC 68**
See also AMWS 6; CA 49-52; CAAS 108; CANR 3; CP 1, 2, 3; DAM POET; DLB 5, 206; EWL 3; MAL 5; PFS 17; RGAL 4

Hugo, Victor (Marie) 1802-1885 .... **NCLC 3, 10, 21, 161; PC 17; WLC 3**
See also AAYA 28; DA; DA3; DAB; DAC; DAM DRAM, MST, NOV, POET; DLB 119, 192, 217; EFS 2; EW 6; EXPN; GFL 1789 to the Present; LAIT 1, 2; NFS 5, 20; RGWL 2, 3; SATA 47; TWA

Huidobro, Vicente
See Huidobro Fernandez, Vicente Garcia
See also DLB 283; EWL 3; LAW

Huidobro Fernandez, Vicente Garcia
1893-1948 .... **TCLC 31**
See Huidobro, Vicente
See also CA 131; HW 1

Hulme, Keri 1947- .... **CLC 39, 130**
See also CA 125; CANR 69; CN 4, 5, 6, 7; CP 6, 7; CWP; DLB 326; EWL 3; FW; INT CA-125; NFS 24

Hulme, T(homas) E(rnest)
1883-1917 .... **TCLC 21**
See also BRWS 6; CA 203; CAAE 117; DLB 19

Humboldt, Alexander von
1769-1859 .... **NCLC 170**
See also DLB 90

Humboldt, Wilhelm von
1767-1835 .... **NCLC 134**
See also DLB 90

Hume, David 1711-1776 .... **LC 7, 56**
See also BRWS 3; DLB 104, 252; LMFS 1; TEA

Humphrey, William 1924-1997 .... **CLC 45**
See also AMWS 9; CA 77-80; CAAS 160; CANR 68; CN 1, 2, 3, 4, 5, 6; CSW; DLB 6, 212, 234, 278; TCWW 1, 2

Humphreys, Emyr Owen 1919- .... **CLC 47**
See also CA 5-8R; CANR 3, 24; CN 1, 2, 3, 4, 5, 6, 7; DLB 15

Humphreys, Josephine 1945- ..... **CLC 34, 57**
See also CA 127; CAAE 121; CANR 97; CSW; DLB 292; INT CA-127

Huneker, James Gibbons
1860-1921 .... **TCLC 65**
See also CA 193; DLB 71; RGAL 4

Hungerford, Hesba Fay
See Brinsmead, H(esba) F(ay)

Hungerford, Pixie
See Brinsmead, H(esba) F(ay)

Hunt, E. Howard 1918-2007 .... **CLC 3**
See also AITN 1; CA 45-48; CANR 2, 47, 103, 160; CMW 4

Hunt, Everette Howard, Jr.
See Hunt, E. Howard

Hunt, Francesca
See Holland, Isabelle (Christian)

Hunt, Howard
See Hunt, E. Howard

Hunt, Kyle
See Creasey, John

Hunt, (James Henry) Leigh
1784-1859 .... **NCLC 1, 70; PC 73**
See also DAM POET; DLB 96, 110, 144; RGEL 2; TEA

Hunt, Marsha 1946- .... **CLC 70**
See also BW 2, 3; CA 143; CANR 79

Hunt, Violet 1866(?)-1942 .... **TCLC 53**
See also CA 184; DLB 162, 197

Hunter, E. Waldo
See Sturgeon, Theodore (Hamilton)

Hunter, Evan 1926-2005 .... **CLC 11, 31**
See McBain, Ed
See also AAYA 39; BPFB 2; CA 5-8R; CAAS 241; CANR 5, 38, 62, 97, 149; CMW 4; CN 1, 2, 3, 4, 5, 6, 7; CPW; DAM POP; DLB 306; DLBY 1982; INT CANR-5; MSW; MTCW 1; SATA 25; SATA-Obit 167; SFW 4

Hunter, Kristin
See Lattany, Kristin (Elaine Eggleston) Hunter
See also CN 1, 2, 3, 4, 5, 6

Hunter, Mary
See Austin, Mary (Hunter)

Hunter, Mollie 1922- .... **CLC 21**
See McIlwraith, Maureen Mollie Hunter
See also AAYA 13, 71; BYA 6; CANR 37, 78; CLR 25; DLB 161; JRDA; MAICYA 1, 2; SAAS 7; SATA 54, 106, 139; SATA-Essay 139; WYA; YAW

Iskander, Fazil' Abdulevich
　　See Iskander, Fazil (Abdulovich)
　　See also DLB 302
Isler, Alan (David) 1934- .... **CLC 91**
　　See also CA 156; CANR 105
Ivan IV 1530-1584 .... **LC 17**
Ivanov, V.I.
　　See Ivanov, Vyacheslav
Ivanov, Vyacheslav 1866-1949 .... **TCLC 33**
　　See also CAAE 122; EWL 3
Ivanov, Vyacheslav Ivanovich
　　See Ivanov, Vyacheslav
Ivask, Ivar Vidrik 1927-1992 .... **CLC 14**
　　See also CA 37-40R; CAAS 139; CANR 24
Ives, Morgan
　　See Bradley, Marion Zimmer
　　See also GLL 1
Izumi Shikibu c. 973-c. 1034 .... **CMLC 33**
J. R. S.
　　See Gogarty, Oliver St. John
Jabran, Kahlil
　　See Gibran, Kahlil
Jabran, Khalil
　　See Gibran, Kahlil
Jackson, Daniel
　　See Wingrove, David
Jackson, Helen Hunt 1830-1885 .... **NCLC 90**
　　See also DLB 42, 47, 186, 189; RGAL 4
Jackson, Jesse 1908-1983 .... **CLC 12**
　　See also BW 1; CA 25-28R; CAAS 109;
　　CANR 27; CLR 28; CWRI 5; MAICYA
　　1, 2; SATA 2, 29; SATA-Obit 48
Jackson, Laura (Riding) 1901-1991 .... **PC 44**
　　See Riding, Laura
　　See also CA 65-68; CAAS 135; CANR 28,
　　89; DLB 48
Jackson, Sam
　　See Trumbo, Dalton
Jackson, Sara
　　See Wingrove, David
Jackson, Shirley 1919-1965 . **CLC 11, 60, 87;**
　　SSC 9, 39; TCLC 187; WLC 3
　　See also AAYA 9; AMWS 9; BPFB 2; CA
　　1-4R; CAAS 25-28R; CANR 4, 52;
　　CDALB 1941-1968; DA; DA3; DAC;
　　DAM MST; DLB 6, 234; EXPS; HGG;
　　LAIT 4; MAL 5; MTCW 2; MTFW 2005;
　　RGAL 4; RGSF 2; SATA 2; SSFS 1;
　　SUFW 1, 2
Jacob, (Cyprien-)Max 1876-1944 .... **TCLC 6**
　　See also CA 193; CAAE 104; DLB 258;
　　EWL 3; GFL 1789 to the Present; GLL 2;
　　RGWL 2, 3
Jacobs, Harriet A(nn)
　　1813(?)-1897 .... **NCLC 67, 162**
　　See also AFAW 1, 2; DLB 239; FL 1:3; FW;
　　LAIT 2; RGAL 4
Jacobs, Jim 1942- .... **CLC 12**
　　See also CA 97-100; INT CA-97-100
Jacobs, W(illiam) W(ymark)
　　1863-1943 .... **SSC 73; TCLC 22**
　　See also CA 167; CAAE 121; DLB 135;
　　EXPS; HGG; RGEL 2; RGSF 2; SSFS 2;
　　SUFW 1
Jacobsen, Jens Peter 1847-1885 .... **NCLC 34**
Jacobsen, Josephine (Winder)
　　1908-2003 .... **CLC 48, 102; PC 62**
　　See also CA 33-36R; 18; CAAS 218; CANR
　　23, 48; CCA 1; CP 2, 3, 4, 5, 6, 7; DLB
　　244; PFS 23; TCLE 1:1
Jacobson, Dan 1929- ...... **CLC 4, 14; SSC 91**
　　See also AFW; CA 1-4R; CANR 2, 25, 66;
　　CN 1, 2, 3, 4, 5, 6, 7; DLB 14, 207, 225,
　　319; EWL 3; MTCW 1; RGSF 2
Jacqueline
　　See Carpentier (y Valmont), Alejo
Jacques de Vitry c. 1160-1240 ...... **CMLC 63**
　　See also DLB 208

Jagger, Michael Philip
　　See Jagger, Mick
Jagger, Mick 1943- .... **CLC 17**
　　See also CA 239
Jahiz, al- c. 780-c. 869 .... **CMLC 25**
　　See also DLB 311
Jakes, John 1932- .... **CLC 29**
　　See also AAYA 32; BEST 89:4; BPFB 2;
　　CA 214; 57-60, 214; CANR 10, 43, 66,
　　111, 142; CPW; CSW; DAM NOV,
　　POP; DLB 278; DLBY 1983; FANT; INT
　　CANR-10; MTCW 1, 2; MTFW 2005;
　　RHW; SATA 62; SFW 4; TCWW 1, 2
James I 1394-1437 .... **LC 20**
　　See also RGEL 2
James, Andrew
　　See Kirkup, James
James, C(yril) L(ionel) R(obert)
　　1901-1989 .... **BLCS; CLC 33**
　　See also BW 2; CA 125; CAAE 117; CAAS
　　128; CANR 62; CN 1, 2, 3, 4; DLB 125;
　　MTCW 1
James, Daniel (Lewis) 1911-1988
　　See Santiago, Danny
　　See also CA 174; CAAS 125
James, Dynely
　　See Mayne, William (James Carter)
James, Henry Sr. 1811-1882 .... **NCLC 53**
James, Henry 1843-1916 .... **SSC 8, 32, 47;**
　　TCLC 2, 11, 24, 40, 47, 64, 171; WLC
　　3
　　See also AMW; AMWC 1; AMWR 1; BPFB
　　2; BRW 6; CA 132; CAAE 104; CDALB
　　1865-1917; DA; DA3; DAB; DAC; DAM
　　MST, NOV; DLB 12, 71, 74, 189; DLBD
　　13; EWL 3; EXPS; GL 2; HGG; LAIT 2;
　　MAL 5; MTCW 1, 2; MTFW 2005; NFS
　　12, 16, 19; RGAL 4; RGEL 2; RGSF 2;
　　SSFS 9; SUFW 1; TUS
James, M. R. .... **SSC 93**
　　See James, Montague (Rhodes)
　　See also DLB 156, 201
James, Montague (Rhodes)
　　1862-1936 .... **SSC 16; TCLC 6**
　　See James, M. R.
　　See also CA 203; CAAE 104; HGG; RGEL
　　2; RGSF 2; SUFW 1
James, P. D. .... **CLC 18, 46, 122, 226**
　　See White, Phyllis Dorothy James
　　See also BEST 90:2; BPFB 2; BRWS 4;
　　CDBLB 1960 to Present; CN 4, 5, 6; DLB
　　87, 276; DLBD 17; MSW
James, Philip
　　See Moorcock, Michael
James, Samuel
　　See Stephens, James
James, Seumas
　　See Stephens, James
James, Stephen
　　See Stephens, James
James, William 1842-1910 .... **TCLC 15, 32**
　　See also AMW; CA 193; CAAE 109; DLB
　　270, 284; MAL 5; NCFS 5; RGAL 4
Jameson, Anna 1794-1860 .... **NCLC 43**
　　See also DLB 99, 166
Jameson, Fredric (R.) 1934- .... **CLC 142**
　　See also CA 196; DLB 67; LMFS 2
James VI of Scotland 1566-1625 .... **LC 109**
　　See also DLB 151, 172
Jami, Nur al-Din 'Abd al-Rahman
　　1414-1492 .... **LC 9**
Jammes, Francis 1868-1938 .... **TCLC 75**
　　See also CA 198; EWL 3; GFL 1789 to the
　　Present
Jandl, Ernst 1925-2000 .... **CLC 34**
　　See also CA 200; EWL 3

Janowitz, Tama 1957- .... **CLC 43, 145**
　　See also CA 106; CANR 52, 89, 129; CN
　　5, 6, 7; CPW; DAM POP; DLB 292;
　　MTFW 2005
Jansson, Tove (Marika) 1914-2001 ... **SSC 96**
　　See also CA 17-20R; CAAS 196; CANR
　　38, 118; CLR 2; CWW 2; DLB 257; EWL
　　3; MAICYA 1, 2; RGSF 2; SATA 3, 41
Japrisot, Sebastien 1931- .... **CLC 90**
　　See Rossi, Jean-Baptiste
　　See also CMW 4; NFS 18
Jarrell, Randall 1914-1965 .... **CLC 1, 2, 6, 9,**
　　13, 49; PC 41; TCLC 177
　　See also AMW; BYA 5; CA 5-8R; CAAS
　　25-28R; CABS 2; CANR 6, 34; CDALB
　　1941-1968; CLR 6, 111; CWRI 5; DAM
　　POET; DLB 48, 52; EWL 3; EXPP; MAI-
　　CYA 1, 2; MAL 5; MTCW 1, 2; PAB; PFS
　　2; RGAL 4; SATA 7
Jarry, Alfred 1873-1907 .... **SSC 20; TCLC 2,**
　　14, 147
　　See also CA 153; CAAE 104; DA3; DAM
　　DRAM; DFS 8; DLB 192, 258; EW 9;
　　EWL 3; GFL 1789 to the Present; RGWL
　　2, 3; TWA
Jarvis, E. K.
　　See Ellison, Harlan
Jawien, Andrzej
　　See John Paul II, Pope
Jaynes, Roderick
　　See Coen, Ethan
Jeake, Samuel, Jr.
　　See Aiken, Conrad (Potter)
Jean Paul 1763-1825 .... **NCLC 7**
Jefferies, (John) Richard
　　1848-1887 .... **NCLC 47**
　　See also DLB 98, 141; RGEL 2; SATA 16;
　　SFW 4
Jeffers, (John) Robinson 1887-1962 .. **CLC 2,**
　　3, 11, 15, 54; PC 17; WLC 3
　　See also AMWS 2; CA 85-88; CANR 35;
　　CDALB 1917-1929; DA; DAC; DAM
　　MST, POET; DLB 45, 212; EWL 3; MAL
　　5; MTCW 1, 2; MTFW 2005; PAB; PFS
　　3, 4; RGAL 4
Jefferson, Janet
　　See Mencken, H(enry) L(ouis)
Jefferson, Thomas 1743-1826 . **NCLC 11, 103**
　　See also AAYA 54; ANW; CDALB 1640-
　　1865; DA3; DLB 31, 183; LAIT 1; RGAL
　　4
Jeffrey, Francis 1773-1850 .... **NCLC 33**
　　See Francis, Lord Jeffrey
Jelakowitch, Ivan
　　See Heijermans, Herman
Jelinek, Elfriede 1946- .... **CLC 169**
　　See also AAYA 68; CA 154; DLB 85, 330;
　　FW
Jellicoe, (Patricia) Ann 1927- .... **CLC 27**
　　See also CA 85-88; CBD; CD 5, 6; CWD;
　　CWRI 5; DLB 13, 233; FW
Jelloun, Tahar ben 1944- .... **CLC 180**
　　See Ben Jelloun, Tahar
　　See also CA 162; CANR 100
Jemyma
　　See Holley, Marietta
Jen, Gish .... **AAL; CLC 70, 198**
　　See Jen, Lillian
　　See also AMWC 2; CN 7; DLB 312
Jen, Lillian 1955-
　　See Jen, Gish
　　See also CA 135; CANR 89, 130
Jenkins, (John) Robin 1912- .... **CLC 52**
　　See also CA 1-4R; CANR 1, 135; CN 1, 2,
　　3, 4, 5, 6, 7; DLB 14, 271

Krleza, Miroslav 1893-1981 .... **CLC 8, 114**
　　See also CA 97-100; CAAS 105; CANR 50; CDWLB 4; DLB 147; EW 11; RGWL 2, 3

Kroetsch, Robert (Paul) 1927- .... **CLC 5, 23, 57, 132**
　　See also CA 17-20R; CANR 8, 38; CCA 1; CN 2, 3, 4, 5, 6, 7; CP 6, 7; DAC; DAM POET; DLB 53; MTCW 1

Kroetz, Franz
　　See Kroetz, Franz Xaver

Kroetz, Franz Xaver 1946- .... **CLC 41**
　　See also CA 130; CANR 142; CWW 2; EWL 3

Kroker, Arthur (W.) 1945- .... **CLC 77**
　　See also CA 161

Kroniuk, Lisa
　　See Berton, Pierre (Francis de Marigny)

Kropotkin, Peter (Aleksieevich) 1842-1921 .... **TCLC 36**
　　See Kropotkin, Petr Alekseevich
　　See also CA 219; CAAE 119

Kropotkin, Petr Alekseevich
　　See Kropotkin, Peter (Aleksieevich)
　　See also DLB 277

Krotkov, Yuri 1917-1981 .... **CLC 19**
　　See also CA 102

Krumb
　　See Crumb, R.

Krumgold, Joseph (Quincy) 1908-1980 .... **CLC 12**
　　See also BYA 1, 2; CA 9-12R; CAAS 101; CANR 7; MAICYA 1, 2; SATA 1, 48; SATA-Obit 23; YAW

Krumwitz
　　See Crumb, R.

Krutch, Joseph Wood 1893-1970 ..... **CLC 24**
　　See also ANW; CA 1-4R; CAAS 25-28R; CANR 4; DLB 63, 206, 275

Krutzch, Gus
　　See Eliot, T(homas) S(tearns)

Krylov, Ivan Andreevich 1768(?)-1844 .... **NCLC 1**
　　See also DLB 150

Kubin, Alfred (Leopold Isidor) 1877-1959 .... **TCLC 23**
　　See also CA 149; CAAE 112; CANR 104; DLB 81

Kubrick, Stanley 1928-1999 .... **CLC 16; TCLC 112**
　　See also AAYA 30; CA 81-84; CAAS 177; CANR 33; DLB 26

Kumin, Maxine 1925- .... **CLC 5, 13, 28, 164; PC 15**
　　See also AITN 2; AMWS 4; ANW; CA 1-4R; 8; CANR 1, 21, 69, 115, 140; CP 2, 3, 4, 5, 6, 7; CWP; DA3; DAM POET; DLB 5; EWL 3; EXPP; MTCW 1, 2; MTFW 2005; PAB; PFS 18; SATA 12

Kundera, Milan 1929- . **CLC 4, 9, 19, 32, 68, 115, 135, 234; SSC 24**
　　See also AAYA 2, 62; BPFB 2; CA 85-88; CANR 19, 52, 74, 144; CDWLB 4; CWW 2; DA3; DAM NOV; DLB 232; EW 13; EWL 3; MTCW 1, 2; MTFW 2005; NFS 18; RGSF 2; RGWL 3; SSFS 10

Kunene, Mazisi 1930-2006 .... **CLC 85**
　　See also BW 1, 3; CA 125; CAAS 252; CANR 81; CP 1, 6, 7; DLB 117

Kunene, Mazisi Raymond
　　See Kunene, Mazisi

Kunene, Mazisi Raymond Fakazi Mngoni
　　See Kunene, Mazisi

Kung, Hans .... **CLC 130**
　　See Kung, Hans

Kung, Hans 1928-
　　See Kung, Hans
　　See also CA 53-56; CANR 66, 134; MTCW 1, 2; MTFW 2005

Kunikida Doppo 1869(?)-1908
　　See Doppo, Kunikida
　　See also DLB 180; EWL 3

Kunitz, Stanley 1905-2006 ..... **CLC 6, 11, 14, 148; PC 19**
　　See also AMWS 3; CA 41-44R; CAAS 250; CANR 26, 57, 98; CP 1, 2, 3, 4, 5, 6, 7; DA3; DLB 48; INT CANR-26; MAL 5; MTCW 1, 2; MTFW 2005; PFS 11; RGAL 4

Kunitz, Stanley Jasspon
　　See Kunitz, Stanley

Kunze, Reiner 1933- .... **CLC 10**
　　See also CA 93-96; CWW 2; DLB 75; EWL 3

Kuprin, Aleksander Ivanovich 1870-1938 .... **TCLC 5**
　　See Kuprin, Aleksandr Ivanovich; Kuprin, Alexandr Ivanovich
　　See also CA 182; CAAE 104

Kuprin, Aleksandr Ivanovich
　　See Kuprin, Aleksander Ivanovich
　　See also DLB 295

Kuprin, Alexandr Ivanovich
　　See Kuprin, Aleksander Ivanovich
　　See also EWL 3

Kureishi, Hanif 1954- .. **CLC 64, 135; DC 26**
　　See also BRWS 11; CA 139; CANR 113; CBD; CD 5, 6; CN 6, 7; DLB 194, 245; GLL 2; IDFW 4; WLIT 4; WWE 1

Kurosawa, Akira 1910-1998 ..... **CLC 16, 119**
　　See also AAYA 11, 64; CA 101; CAAS 170; CANR 46; DAM MULT

Kushner, Tony 1956- .... **CLC 81, 203; DC 10**
　　See also AAYA 61; AMWS 9; CA 144; CAD; CANR 74, 130; CD 5, 6; DA3; DAM DRAM; DFS 5; DLB 228; EWL 3; GLL 1; LAIT 5; MAL 5; MTCW 2; MTFW 2005; RGAL 4; RGHL; SATA 160

Kuttner, Henry 1915-1958 .... **TCLC 10**
　　See also CA 157; CAAE 107; DLB 8; FANT; SCFW 1, 2; SFW 4

Kutty, Madhavi
　　See Das, Kamala

Kuzma, Greg 1944- .... **CLC 7**
　　See also CA 33-36R; CANR 70

Kuzmin, Mikhail (Alekseevich) 1872(?)-1936 .... **TCLC 40**
　　See also CA 170; DLB 295; EWL 3

Kyd, Thomas 1558-1594 .. **DC 3; LC 22, 125**
　　See also BRW 1; DAM DRAM; DFS 21; DLB 62; IDTP; LMFS 1; RGEL 2; TEA; WLIT 3

Kyprianos, Iossif
　　See Samarakis, Antonis

L. S.
　　See Stephen, Sir Leslie

Labe, Louise 1521-1566 .... **LC 120**
　　See also DLB 327

Labrunie, Gerard
　　See Nerval, Gerard de

La Bruyere, Jean de 1645-1696 .... **LC 17**
　　See also DLB 268; EW 3; GFL Beginnings to 1789

LaBute, Neil 1963- .... **CLC 225**
　　See also CA 240

Lacan, Jacques (Marie Emile) 1901-1981 .... **CLC 75**
　　See also CA 121; CAAS 104; DLB 296; EWL 3; TWA

Laclos, Pierre-Ambroise Francois 1741-1803 .... **NCLC 4, 87**
　　See also DLB 313; EW 4; GFL Beginnings to 1789; RGWL 2, 3

Lacolere, Francois
　　See Aragon, Louis

La Colere, Francois
　　See Aragon, Louis

La Deshabilleuse
　　See Simenon, Georges (Jacques Christian)

Lady Gregory
　　See Gregory, Lady Isabella Augusta (Persse)

Lady of Quality, A
　　See Bagnold, Enid

La Fayette, Marie-(Madelaine Pioche de la Vergne) 1634-1693 .... **LC 2**
　　See Lafayette, Marie-Madeleine
　　See also GFL Beginnings to 1789; RGWL 2, 3

Lafayette, Marie-Madeleine
　　See La Fayette, Marie-(Madelaine Pioche de la Vergne)
　　See also DLB 268

Lafayette, Rene
　　See Hubbard, L. Ron

La Flesche, Francis 1857(?)-1932 ...... **NNAL**
　　See also CA 144; CANR 83; DLB 175

La Fontaine, Jean de 1621-1695 .... **LC 50**
　　See also DLB 268; EW 3; GFL Beginnings to 1789; MAICYA 1, 2; RGWL 2, 3; SATA 18

LaForet, Carmen 1921-2004 .... **CLC 219**
　　See also CA 246; CWW 2; DLB 322; EWL 3

LaForet Diaz, Carmen
　　See LaForet, Carmen

Laforgue, Jules 1860-1887 . **NCLC 5, 53; PC 14; SSC 20**
　　See also DLB 217; EW 7; GFL 1789 to the Present; RGWL 2, 3

Lagerkvist, Paer (Fabian) 1891-1974 ..... **CLC 7, 10, 13, 54; TCLC 144**
　　See Lagerkvist, Par
　　See also CA 85-88; CAAS 49-52; DA3; DAM DRAM, NOV; MTCW 1, 2; MTFW 2005; TWA

Lagerkvist, Par .... **SSC 12**
　　See Lagerkvist, Paer (Fabian)
　　See also DLB 259, 331; EW 10; EWL 3; RGSF 2; RGWL 2, 3

Lagerloef, Selma (Ottiliana Lovisa) .... **TCLC 4, 36**
　　See Lagerlof, Selma (Ottiliana Lovisa)
　　See also CAAE 108; MTCW 2

Lagerlof, Selma (Ottiliana Lovisa) 1858-1940
　　See Lagerloef, Selma (Ottiliana Lovisa)
　　See also CA 188; CLR 7; DLB 259, 331; RGWL 2, 3; SATA 15; SSFS 18

La Guma, Alex 1925-1985 .. **BLCS; CLC 19; TCLC 140**
　　See also AFW; BW 1, 3; CA 49-52; CAAS 118; CANR 25, 81; CDWLB 3; CN 1, 2, 3; CP 1; DAM NOV; DLB 117, 225; EWL 3; MTCW 1, 2; MTFW 2005; WLIT 2; WWE 1

Lahiri, Jhumpa 1967- .... **SSC 96**
　　See also AAYA 56; CA 193; CANR 134; DLB 323; MTFW 2005; SSFS 19

Laidlaw, A. K.
　　See Grieve, C(hristopher) M(urray)

Lainez, Manuel Mujica
　　See Mujica Lainez, Manuel
　　See also HW 1

Laing, R(onald) D(avid) 1927-1989 . **CLC 95**
　　See also CA 107; CAAS 129; CANR 34; MTCW 1

Laishley, Alex
　　See Booth, Martin

Lamartine, Alphonse (Marie Louis Prat) de 1790-1869 .... **NCLC 11; PC 16**
　　See also DAM POET; DLB 217; GFL 1789 to the Present; RGWL 2, 3

Lewis, Matthew Gregory
1775-1818 .... **NCLC 11, 62**
See also DLB 39, 158, 178; GL 3; HGG;
LMFS 1; RGEL 2; SUFW

Lewis, (Harry) Sinclair 1885-1951 . **TCLC 4,
13, 23, 39; WLC 4**
See also AMW; AMWC 1; BPFB 2; CA
133; CAAE 104; CANR 132; CDALB
1917-1929; DA; DA3; DAB; DAC; DAM
MST, NOV; DLB 9, 102, 284, 331; DLBD
1; EWL 3; LAIT 3; MAL 5; MTCW 1, 2;
MTFW 2005; NFS 15, 19, 22; RGAL 4;
TUS

Lewis, (Percy) Wyndham
1884(?)-1957 .. **SSC 34; TCLC 2, 9, 104**
See also BRW 7; CA 157; CAAE 104; DLB
15; EWL 3; FANT; MTCW 2; MTFW
2005; RGEL 2

Lewisohn, Ludwig 1883-1955 .... **TCLC 19**
See also CA 203; CAAE 107; DLB 4, 9,
28, 102; MAL 5

Lewton, Val 1904-1951 .... **TCLC 76**
See also CA 199; IDFW 3, 4

Leyner, Mark 1956- .... **CLC 92**
See also CA 110; CANR 28, 53; DA3; DLB
292; MTCW 2; MTFW 2005

Lezama Lima, Jose 1910-1976 .... **CLC 4, 10,
101; HLCS 2**
See also CA 77-80; CANR 71; DAM
MULT; DLB 113, 283; EWL 3; HW 1, 2;
LAW; RGWL 2, 3

L'Heureux, John (Clarke) 1934- ...... **CLC 52**
See also CA 13-16R; CANR 23, 45, 88; CP
1, 2, 3, 4; DLB 244

Li Ch'ing-chao 1081(?)-1141(?) .... **CMLC 71**

Liddell, C. H.
See Kuttner, Henry

Lie, Jonas (Lauritz Idemil)
1833-1908(?) .... **TCLC 5**
See also CAAE 115

Lieber, Joel 1937-1971 .... **CLC 6**
See also CA 73-76; CAAS 29-32R

Lieber, Stanley Martin
See Lee, Stan

Lieberman, Laurence (James)
1935- .... **CLC 4, 36**
See also CA 17-20R; CANR 8, 36, 89; CP
1, 2, 3, 4, 5, 6, 7

Lieh Tzu fl. 7th cent. B.C.-5th cent.
B.C. .... **CMLC 27**

Lieksman, Anders
See Haavikko, Paavo Juhani

Lifton, Robert Jay 1926- .... **CLC 67**
See also CA 17-20R; CANR 27, 78, 161;
INT CANR-27; SATA 66

Lightfoot, Gordon 1938- .... **CLC 26**
See also CA 242; CAAE 109

Lightfoot, Gordon Meredith
See Lightfoot, Gordon

Lightman, Alan P(aige) 1948- .... **CLC 81**
See also CA 141; CANR 63, 105, 138;
MTFW 2005

Ligotti, Thomas (Robert) 1953- ...... **CLC 44;
SSC 16**
See also CA 123; CANR 49, 135; HGG;
SUFW 2

Li Ho 791-817 .... **PC 13**

Li Ju-chen c. 1763-c. 1830 .... **NCLC 137**

Lilar, Francoise
See Mallet-Joris, Francoise

Liliencron, Detlev
See Liliencron, Detlev von

Liliencron, Detlev von 1844-1909 .. **TCLC 18**
See also CAAE 117

Liliencron, Friedrich Adolf Axel Detlev von
See Liliencron, Detlev von

Liliencron, Friedrich Detlev von
See Liliencron, Detlev von

Lille, Alain de
See Alain de Lille

Lillo, George 1691-1739 .... **LC 131**
See also DLB 84; RGEL 2

Lilly, William 1602-1681 .... **LC 27**

Lima, Jose Lezama
See Lezama Lima, Jose

Lima Barreto, Afonso Henrique de
1881-1922 .... **TCLC 23**
See Lima Barreto, Afonso Henriques de
See also CA 181; CAAE 117; LAW

Lima Barreto, Afonso Henriques de
See Lima Barreto, Afonso Henrique de
See also DLB 307

Limonov, Eduard
See Limonov, Edward
See also DLB 317

Limonov, Edward 1944- .... **CLC 67**
See Limonov, Eduard
See also CA 137

Lin, Frank
See Atherton, Gertrude (Franklin Horn)

Lin, Yutang 1895-1976 .... **TCLC 149**
See also CA 45-48; CAAS 65-68; CANR 2;
RGAL 4

Lincoln, Abraham 1809-1865 .... **NCLC 18**
See also LAIT 2

Lind, Jakov .... **CLC 1, 2, 4, 27, 82**
See Landwirth, Heinz
See also CA 4; DLB 299; EWL 3; RGHL

Lindbergh, Anne Morrow
1906-2001 .... **CLC 82**
See also BPFB 2; CA 17-20R; CAAS 193;
CANR 16, 73; DAM NOV; MTCW 1, 2;
MTFW 2005; SATA 33; SATA-Obit 125;
TUS

Lindsay, David 1878(?)-1945 .... **TCLC 15**
See also CA 187; CAAE 113; DLB 255;
FANT; SFW 4; SUFW 1

Lindsay, (Nicholas) Vachel
1879-1931 .... **PC 23; TCLC 17; WLC 4**
See also AMWS 1; CA 135; CAAE 114;
CANR 79; CDALB 1865-1917; DA;
DA3; DAC; DAM MST, POET; DLB 54;
EWL 3; EXPP; MAL 5; RGAL 4; SATA
40; WP

Linke-Poot
See Doeblin, Alfred

Linney, Romulus 1930- .... **CLC 51**
See also CA 1-4R; CAD; CANR 40, 44,
79; CD 5, 6; CSW; RGAL 4

Linton, Eliza Lynn 1822-1898 .... **NCLC 41**
See also DLB 18

Li Po 701-763 .... **CMLC 2, 86; PC 29**
See also PFS 20; WP

Lipsius, Justus 1547-1606 .... **LC 16**

Lipsyte, Robert 1938- .... **CLC 21**
See also AAYA 7, 45; CA 17-20R; CANR
8, 57, 146; CLR 23, 76; DA; DAC; DAM
MST, NOV; JRDA; LAIT 5; MAICYA 1,
2; SATA 5, 68, 113, 161; WYA; YAW

Lipsyte, Robert Michael
See Lipsyte, Robert

Lish, Gordon 1934- .... **CLC 45; SSC 18**
See also CA 117; CAAE 113; CANR 79,
151; DLB 130; INT CA-117

Lish, Gordon Jay
See Lish, Gordon

Lispector, Clarice 1925(?)-1977 .... **CLC 43;
HLCS 2; SSC 34, 96**
See also CA 139; CAAS 116; CANR 71;
CDWLB 3; DLB 113, 307; DNFS 1; EWL
3; FW; HW 2; LAW; RGSF 2; RGWL 2,
3; WLIT 1

Littell, Robert 1935(?)- .... **CLC 42**
See also CA 112; CAAE 109; CANR 64,
115; CMW 4

Little, Malcolm 1925-1965
See Malcolm X
See also BW 1, 3; CA 125; CAAS 111;
CANR 82; DA; DA3; DAB; DAC; DAM
MST, MULT; MTCW 1, 2; MTFW 2005

Littlewit, Humphrey Gent.
See Lovecraft, H. P.

Litwos
See Sienkiewicz, Henryk (Adam Alexander
Pius)

Liu, E. 1857-1909 .... **TCLC 15**
See also CA 190; CAAE 115; DLB 328

Lively, Penelope 1933- .... **CLC 32, 50**
See also BPFB 2; CA 41-44R; CANR 29,
67, 79, 131; CLR 7; CN 5, 6, 7; CWRI 5;
DAM NOV; DLB 14, 161, 207, 326;
FANT; JRDA; MAICYA 1, 2; MTCW 1,
2; MTFW 2005; SATA 7, 60, 101, 164;
TEA

Lively, Penelope Margaret
See Lively, Penelope

Livesay, Dorothy (Kathleen)
1909-1996 .... **CLC 4, 15, 79**
See also AITN 2; CA 25-28R; 8; CANR 36,
67; CP 1, 2, 3, 4, 5; DAC; DAM MST,
POET; DLB 68; FW; MTCW 1; RGEL 2;
TWA

Livy c. 59B.C.-c. 12 .... **CMLC 11**
See also AW 2; CDWLB 1; DLB 211;
RGWL 2, 3; WLIT 8

Lizardi, Jose Joaquin Fernandez de
1776-1827 .... **NCLC 30**
See also LAW

Llewellyn, Richard
See Llewellyn Lloyd, Richard Dafydd Viv-
ian
See also DLB 15

Llewellyn Lloyd, Richard Dafydd Vivian
1906-1983 .... **CLC 7, 80**
See Llewellyn, Richard
See also CA 53-56; CAAS 111; CANR 7,
71; SATA 11; SATA-Obit 37

Llosa, Jorge Mario Pedro Vargas
See Vargas Llosa, Mario
See also RGWL 3

Llosa, Mario Vargas
See Vargas Llosa, Mario

Lloyd, Manda
See Mander, (Mary) Jane

Lloyd Webber, Andrew 1948-
See Webber, Andrew Lloyd
See also AAYA 1, 38; CA 149; CAAE 116;
DAM DRAM; SATA 56

Llull, Ramon c. 1235-c. 1316 .... **CMLC 12**

Lobb, Ebenezer
See Upward, Allen

Locke, Alain (Le Roy)
1886-1954 .... **BLCS; HR 1:3; TCLC 43**
See also AMWS 14; BW 1, 3; CA 124;
CAAE 106; CANR 79; DLB 51; LMFS
2; MAL 5; RGAL 4

Locke, John 1632-1704 .... **LC 7, 35, 135**
See also DLB 31, 101, 213, 252; RGEL 2;
WLIT 3

Locke-Elliott, Sumner
See Elliott, Sumner Locke

Lockhart, John Gibson 1794-1854 .. **NCLC 6**
See also DLB 110, 116, 144

Lockridge, Ross (Franklin), Jr.
1914-1948 .... **TCLC 111**
See also CA 145; CAAE 108; CANR 79;
DLB 143; DLBY 1980; MAL 5; RGAL
4; RHW

Lockwood, Robert
See Johnson, Robert

McKay, Festus Claudius 1889-1948
See McKay, Claude
See also BW 1, 3; CA 124; CAAE 104;
CANR 73; DA; DAC; DAM MST, MULT,
NOV, POET; MTCW 1, 2; MTFW 2005;
TUS

McKuen, Rod 1933- .... CLC 1, 3
See also AITN 1; CA 41-44R; CANR 40;
CP 1

McLoughlin, R. B.
See Mencken, H(enry) L(ouis)

McLuhan, (Herbert) Marshall
1911-1980 .... CLC 37, 83
See also CA 9-12R; CAAS 102; CANR 12,
34, 61; DLB 88; INT CANR-12; MTCW
1, 2; MTFW 2005

McManus, Declan Patrick Aloysius
See Costello, Elvis

McMillan, Terry 1951- .. BLCS; CLC 50, 61,
112
See also AAYA 21; AMWS 13; BPFB 2;
BW 2, 3; CA 140; CANR 60, 104, 131;
CN 7; CPW; DA3; DAM MULT, NOV,
POP; MAL 5; MTCW 2; MTFW 2005;
RGAL 4; YAW

McMurtry, Larry 1936- .... CLC 2, 3, 7, 11,
27, 44, 127
See also AAYA 15; AITN 2; AMWS 5;
BEST 89:2; BPFB 2; CA 5-8R; CANR
19, 43, 64, 103; CDALB 1968-1988; CN
2, 3, 4, 5, 6, 7; CPW; CSW; DA3; DAM
NOV, POP; DLB 2, 143, 256; DLBY
1980, 1987; EWL 3; MAL 5; MTCW 1,
2; MTFW 2005; RGAL 4; TCWW 1, 2

McMurtry, Larry Jeff
See McMurtry, Larry

McNally, Terrence 1939- ... CLC 4, 7, 41, 91;
DC 27
See also AAYA 62; AMWS 13; CA 45-48;
CAD; CANR 2, 56, 116; CD 5, 6; DA3;
DAM DRAM; DFS 16, 19; DLB 7, 249;
EWL 3; GLL 1; MTCW 2; MTFW 2005

McNally, Thomas Michael
See McNally, T.M.

McNally, T.M. 1961- .... CLC 82
See also CA 246

McNamer, Deirdre 1950- .... CLC 70
See also CA 188

McNeal, Tom .... CLC 119
See also CA 252

McNeile, Herman Cyril 1888-1937
See Sapper
See also CA 184; CMW 4; DLB 77

McNickle, (William) D'Arcy
1904-1977 .... CLC 89; NNAL
See also CA 9-12R; CAAS 85-88; CANR
5, 45; DAM MULT; DLB 175, 212;
RGAL 4; SATA-Obit 22; TCWW 1, 2

McPhee, John 1931- .... CLC 36
See also AAYA 61; AMWS 3; ANW; BEST
90:1; CA 65-68; CANR 20, 46, 64, 69,
121; CPW; DLB 185, 275; MTCW 1, 2;
MTFW 2005; TUS

McPherson, James Alan 1943- . BLCS; CLC
19, 77; SSC 95
See also BW 1, 3; CA 25-28R; 17; CANR
24, 74, 140; CN 3, 4, 5, 6; CSW; DLB
38, 244; EWL 3; MTCW 1, 2; MTFW
2005; RGAL 4; RGSF 2; SSFS 23

McPherson, William (Alexander)
1933- .... CLC 34
See also CA 69-72; CANR 28; INT
CANR-28

McTaggart, J. McT. Ellis
See McTaggart, John McTaggart Ellis

McTaggart, John McTaggart Ellis
1866-1925 .... TCLC 105
See also CAAE 120; DLB 262

Mead, George Herbert 1863-1931 . TCLC 89
See also CA 212; DLB 270

Mead, Margaret 1901-1978 .... CLC 37
See also AITN 1; CA 1-4R; CAAS 81-84;
CANR 4; DA3; FW; MTCW 1, 2; SATA-
Obit 20

Meaker, Marijane 1927-
See Kerr, M. E.
See also CA 107; CANR 37, 63, 145; INT
CA-107; JRDA; MAICYA 1, 2; MAIC-
YAS 1; MTCW 1; SATA 20, 61, 99, 160;
SATA-Essay 111; YAW

Medoff, Mark (Howard) 1940- .... CLC 6, 23
See also AITN 1; CA 53-56; CAD; CANR
5; CD 5, 6; DAM DRAM; DFS 4; DLB
7; INT CANR-5

Medvedev, P. N.
See Bakhtin, Mikhail Mikhailovich

Meged, Aharon
See Megged, Aharon

Meged, Aron
See Megged, Aharon

Megged, Aharon 1920- .... CLC 9
See also CA 49-52; 13; CANR 1, 140; EWL
3; RGHL

Mehta, Deepa 1950- .... CLC 208

Mehta, Gita 1943- .... CLC 179
See also CA 225; CN 7; DNFS 2

Mehta, Ved 1934- .... CLC 37
See also CA 212; 1-4R, 212; CANR 2, 23,
69; DLB 323; MTCW 1; MTFW 2005

Melanchthon, Philipp 1497-1560 .... LC 90
See also DLB 179

Melanter
See Blackmore, R(ichard) D(oddridge)

Meleager c. 140B.C.-c. 70B.C. ...... CMLC 53

Melies, Georges 1861-1938 .... TCLC 81

Melikow, Loris
See Hofmannsthal, Hugo von

Melmoth, Sebastian
See Wilde, Oscar (Fingal O'Flahertie Wills)

Melo Neto, Joao Cabral de
See Cabral de Melo Neto, Joao
See also CWW 2; EWL 3

Meltzer, Milton 1915- .... CLC 26
See also AAYA 8, 45; BYA 2, 6; CA 13-
16R; CANR 38, 92, 107; CLR 13; DLB
61; JRDA; MAICYA 1, 2; SAAS 1; SATA
1, 50, 80, 128; SATA-Essay 124; WYA;
YAW

Melville, Herman 1819-1891 ..... NCLC 3, 12,
29, 45, 49, 91, 93, 123, 157, 181; SSC 1,
17, 46, 95; WLC 4
See also AAYA 25; AMW; AMWR 1;
CDALB 1640-1865; DA; DA3; DAB;
DAC; DAM MST, NOV; DLB 3, 74, 250,
254; EXPN; EXPS; GL 3; LAIT 1, 2; NFS
7, 9; RGAL 4; RGSF 2; SATA 59; SSFS
3; TUS

Members, Mark
See Powell, Anthony

Membreno, Alejandro .... CLC 59

Menand, Louis 1952- .... CLC 208
See also CA 200

Menander c. 342B.C.-c. 293B.C. .... CMLC 9,
51; DC 3
See also AW 1; CDWLB 1; DAM DRAM;
DLB 176; LMFS 1; RGWL 2, 3

Menchu, Rigoberta 1959- .. CLC 160; HLCS
2
See also CA 175; CANR 135; DNFS 1;
WLIT 1

Mencken, H(enry) L(ouis)
1880-1956 .... TCLC 13
See also AMW; CA 125; CAAE 105;
CDALB 1917-1929; DLB 11, 29, 63, 137,
222; EWL 3; MAL 5; MTCW 1, 2;
MTFW 2005; NCFS 4; RGAL 4; TUS

Mendelsohn, Jane 1965- .... CLC 99
See also CA 154; CANR 94

Mendoza, Inigo Lopez de
See Santillana, Inigo Lopez de Mendoza,
Marques de

Menton, Francisco de
See Chin, Frank (Chew, Jr.)

Mercer, David 1928-1980 .... CLC 5
See also CA 9-12R; CAAS 102; CANR 23;
CBD; DAM DRAM; DLB 13, 310;
MTCW 1; RGEL 2

Merchant, Paul
See Ellison, Harlan

Meredith, George 1828-1909 .. PC 60; TCLC
17, 43
See also CA 153; CAAE 117; CANR 80;
CDBLB 1832-1890; DAM POET; DLB
18, 35, 57, 159; RGEL 2; TEA

Meredith, William (Morris) 1919- .... CLC 4,
13, 22, 55; PC 28
See also CA 9-12R; 14; CANR 6, 40, 129;
CP 1, 2, 3, 4, 5, 6, 7; DAM POET; DLB
5; MAL 5

Merezhkovsky, Dmitrii Sergeevich
See Merezhkovsky, Dmitry Sergeyevich
See also DLB 295

Merezhkovsky, Dmitry Sergeevich
See Merezhkovsky, Dmitry Sergeyevich
See also EWL 3

Merezhkovsky, Dmitry Sergeyevich
1865-1941 .... TCLC 29
See Merezhkovsky, Dmitrii Sergeevich;
Merezhkovsky, Dmitry Sergeevich
See also CA 169

Merimee, Prosper 1803-1870 ... NCLC 6, 65;
SSC 7, 77
See also DLB 119, 192; EW 6; EXPS; GFL
1789 to the Present; RGSF 2; RGWL 2,
3; SSFS 8; SUFW

Merkin, Daphne 1954- .... CLC 44
See also CA 123

Merleau-Ponty, Maurice
1908-1961 .... TCLC 156
See also CA 114; CAAS 89-92; DLB 296;
GFL 1789 to the Present

Merlin, Arthur
See Blish, James (Benjamin)

Mernissi, Fatima 1940- .... CLC 171
See also CA 152; FW

Merrill, James 1926-1995 ...... CLC 2, 3, 6, 8,
13, 18, 34, 91; PC 28; TCLC 173
See also AMWS 3; CA 13-16R; CAAS 147;
CANR 10, 49, 63, 108; CP 1, 2, 3, 4;
DA3; DAM POET; DLB 5, 165; DLBY
1985; EWL 3; INT CANR-10; MAL 5;
MTCW 1, 2; MTFW 2005; PAB; PFS 23;
RGAL 4

Merrill, James Ingram
See Merrill, James

Merriman, Alex
See Silverberg, Robert

Merriman, Brian 1747-1805 .... NCLC 70

Merritt, E. B.
See Waddington, Miriam

Merton, Thomas (James)
1915-1968 . CLC 1, 3, 11, 34, 83; PC 10
See also AAYA 61; AMWS 8; CA 5-8R;
CAAS 25-28R; CANR 22, 53, 111, 131;
DA3; DLB 48; DLBY 1981; MAL 5;
MTCW 1, 2; MTFW 2005

Merwin, W.S. 1927- ..... CLC 1, 2, 3, 5, 8, 13,
18, 45, 88; PC 45
See also AMWS 3; CA 13-16R; CANR 15,
51, 112, 140; CP 1, 2, 3, 4, 5, 6, 7; DA3;
DAM POET; DLB 5, 169; EWL 3; INT
CANR-15; MAL 5; MTCW 1, 2; MTFW
2005; PAB; PFS 5, 15; RGAL 4

Metastasio, Pietro 1698-1782 .... LC 115
See also RGWL 2, 3

Metcalf, John 1938- .... **CLC 37; SSC 43**
See also CA 113; CN 4, 5, 6, 7; DLB 60;
RGSF 2; TWA

Metcalf, Suzanne
See Baum, L(yman) Frank

Mew, Charlotte (Mary) 1870-1928 .. **TCLC 8**
See also CA 189; CAAE 105; DLB 19, 135;
RGEL 2

Mewshaw, Michael 1943- .... **CLC 9**
See also CA 53-56; CANR 7, 47, 147;
DLBY 1980

Meyer, Conrad Ferdinand
1825-1898 .... **NCLC 81; SSC 30**
See also DLB 129; EW; RGWL 2, 3

Meyer, Gustav 1868-1932
See Meyrink, Gustav
See also CA 190; CAAE 117

Meyer, June
See Jordan, June

Meyer, Lynn
See Slavitt, David R(ytman)

Meyers, Jeffrey 1939- .... **CLC 39**
See also CA 186; 73-76, 186; CANR 54,
102, 159; DLB 111

**Meynell, Alice (Christina Gertrude
Thompson)** 1847-1922 .... **TCLC 6**
See also CA 177; CAAE 104; DLB 19, 98;
RGEL 2

Meyrink, Gustav .... **TCLC 21**
See Meyer, Gustav
See also DLB 81; EWL 3

Michaels, Leonard 1933-2003 ..... **CLC 6, 25;
SSC 16**
See also AMWS 16; CA 61-64; CAAS 216;
CANR 21, 62, 119; CN 3, 45, 6, 7; DLB
130; MTCW 1; TCLE 1:2

Michaux, Henri 1899-1984 .... **CLC 8, 19**
See also CA 85-88; CAAS 114; DLB 258;
EWL 3; GFL 1789 to the Present; RGWL
2, 3

Micheaux, Oscar (Devereaux)
1884-1951 .... **TCLC 76**
See also BW 3; CA 174; DLB 50; TCWW
2

Michelangelo 1475-1564 .... **LC 12**
See also AAYA 43

Michelet, Jules 1798-1874 .... **NCLC 31**
See also EW 5; GFL 1789 to the Present

Michels, Robert 1876-1936 .... **TCLC 88**
See also CA 212

Michener, James A. 1907(?)-1997 . **CLC 1, 5,
11, 29, 60, 109**
See also AAYA 27; AITN 1; BEST 90:1;
BPFB 2; CA 5-8R; CAAS 161; CANR
21, 45, 68; CN 1, 2, 3, 4, 5, 6; CPW; DA3;
DAM NOV, POP; DLB 6; MAL 5;
MTCW 1, 2; MTFW 2005; RHW; TCWW
1, 2

Mickiewicz, Adam 1798-1855 . **NCLC 3, 101;
PC 38**
See also EW 5; RGWL 2, 3

Middleton, (John) Christopher
1926- .... **CLC 13**
See also CA 13-16R; CANR 29, 54, 117;
CP 1, 2, 3, 4, 5, 6, 7; DLB 40

Middleton, Richard (Barham)
1882-1911 .... **TCLC 56**
See also CA 187; DLB 156; HGG

Middleton, Stanley 1919- .... **CLC 7, 38**
See also CA 25-28R; 23; CANR 21, 46, 81,
157; CN 1, 2, 3, 4, 5, 6, 7; DLB 14, 326

Middleton, Thomas 1580-1627 ...... **DC 5; LC
33, 123**
See also BRW 2; DAM DRAM, MST; DFS
18, 22; DLB 58; RGEL 2

Mieville, China 1972(?)- .... **CLC 235**
See also AAYA 52; CA 196; CANR 138;
MTFW 2005

Migueis, Jose Rodrigues 1901-1980 . **CLC 10**
See also DLB 287

Mikszath, Kalman 1847-1910 .... **TCLC 31**
See also CA 170

Miles, Jack .... **CLC 100**
See also CA 200

Miles, John Russiano
See Miles, Jack

Miles, Josephine (Louise)
1911-1985 .... **CLC 1, 2, 14, 34, 39**
See also CA 1-4R; CAAS 116; CANR 2,
55; CP 1, 2, 3, 4; DAM POET; DLB 48;
MAL 5; TCLE 1:2

Militant
See Sandburg, Carl (August)

Mill, Harriet (Hardy) Taylor
1807-1858 .... **NCLC 102**
See also FW

Mill, John Stuart 1806-1873 ... **NCLC 11, 58,
179**
See also CDBLB 1832-1890; DLB 55, 190,
262; FW 1; RGEL 2; TEA

Millar, Kenneth 1915-1983 .... **CLC 14**
See Macdonald, Ross
See also CA 9-12R; CAAS 110; CANR 16,
63, 107; CMW 4; CPW; DA3; DAM POP;
DLB 2, 226; DLBD 6; DLBY 1983;
MTCW 1, 2; MTFW 2005

Millay, E. Vincent
See Millay, Edna St. Vincent

Millay, Edna St. Vincent 1892-1950 ..... **PC 6,
61; TCLC 4, 49, 169; WLCS**
See Boyd, Nancy
See also AMW; CA 130; CAAE 104;
CDALB 1917-1929; DA; DA3; DAB;
DAC; DAM MST, POET; DLB 45, 249;
EWL 3; EXPP; FL 1:6; MAL 5; MBL;
MTCW 1, 2; MTFW 2005; PAB; PFS 3,
17; RGAL 4; TUS; WP

Miller, Arthur 1915-2005 ..... **CLC 1, 2, 6, 10,
15, 26, 47, 78, 179; DC 1; WLC 4**
See also AAYA 15; AITN 1; AMW; AMWC
1; CA 1-4R; CAAS 236; CABS 3; CAD;
CANR 2, 30, 54, 76, 132; CD 5, 6;
CDALB 1941-1968; DA; DA3; DAB;
DAC; DAM DRAM, MST; DFS 1, 3, 8;
DLB 7, 266; EWL 3; LAIT 1, 4; LATS
1:2; MAL 5; MTCW 1, 2; MTFW 2005;
RGAL 4; RGHL; TUS; WYAS 1

Miller, Henry (Valentine)
1891-1980 .... **CLC 1, 2, 4, 9, 14, 43, 84;
WLC 4**
See also AMW; BPFB 2; CA 9-12R; CAAS
97-100; CANR 33, 64; CDALB 1929-
1941; CN 1, 2; DA; DA3; DAB; DAC;
DAM MST, NOV; DLB 4, 9; DLBY
1980; EWL 3; MAL 5; MTCW 1, 2;
MTFW 2005; RGAL 4; TUS

Miller, Hugh 1802-1856 .... **NCLC 143**
See also DLB 190

Miller, Jason 1939(?)-2001 .... **CLC 2**
See also AITN 1; CA 73-76; CAAS 197;
CAD; CANR 130; DFS 12; DLB 7

Miller, Sue 1943- .... **CLC 44**
See also AMWS 12; BEST 90:3; CA 139;
CANR 59, 91, 128; DA3; DAM POP;
DLB 143

Miller, Walter M(ichael, Jr.)
1923-1996 .... **CLC 4, 30**
See also BPFB 2; CA 85-88; CANR 108;
DLB 8; SCFW 1, 2; SFW 4

Millett, Kate 1934- .... **CLC 67**
See also AITN 1; CA 73-76; CANR 32, 53,
76, 110; DA3; DLB 246; FW; GLL 1;
MTCW 1, 2; MTFW 2005

Millhauser, Steven 1943- ... **CLC 21, 54, 109;
SSC 57**
See also CA 111; CAAE 110; CANR 63,
114, 133; CN 6, 7; DA3; DLB 2; FANT;
INT CA-111; MAL 5; MTCW 2; MTFW
2005

Millhauser, Steven Lewis
See Millhauser, Steven

Millin, Sarah Gertrude 1889-1968 ... **CLC 49**
See also CA 102; CAAS 93-96; DLB 225;
EWL 3

Milne, A. A. 1882-1956 .... **TCLC 6, 88**
See also BRWS 5; CA 133; CAAE 104;
CLR 1, 26, 108; CMW 4; CWRI 5; DA3;
DAB; DAC; DAM MST; DLB 10, 77,
100, 160; FANT; MAICYA 1, 2; MTCW
1, 2; MTFW 2005; RGEL 2; SATA 100;
WCH; YABC 1

Milne, Alan Alexander
See Milne, A. A.

Milner, Ron(ald) 1938-2004 ..... **BLC 3; CLC
56**
See also AITN 1; BW 1; CA 73-76; CAAS
230; CAD; CANR 24, 81; CD 5, 6; DAM
MULT; DLB 38; MAL 5; MTCW 1

Milnes, Richard Monckton
1809-1885 .... **NCLC 61**
See also DLB 32, 184

Milosz, Czeslaw 1911-2004 .... **CLC 5, 11, 22,
31, 56, 82; PC 8; WLCS**
See also AAYA 62; CA 81-84; CAAS 230;
CANR 23, 51, 91, 126; CDWLB 4; CWW
2; DA3; DAM MST, POET; DLB 215,
331; EW 13; EWL 3; MTCW 1, 2; MTFW
2005; PFS 16; RGHL; RGWL 2, 3

Milton, John 1608-1674 ..... **LC 9, 43, 92; PC
19, 29; WLC 4**
See also AAYA 65; BRW 2; BRWR 2; CD-
BLB 1660-1789; DA; DA3; DAB; DAC;
DAM MST, POET; DLB 131, 151, 281;
EFS 1; EXPP; LAIT 1; PAB; PFS 3, 17;
RGEL 2; TEA; WLIT 3; WP

Min, Anchee 1957- .... **CLC 86**
See also CA 146; CANR 94, 137; MTFW
2005

Minehaha, Cornelius
See Wedekind, Frank

Miner, Valerie 1947- .... **CLC 40**
See also CA 97-100; CANR 59; FW; GLL
2

Minimo, Duca
See D'Annunzio, Gabriele

Minot, Susan (Anderson) 1956- ...... **CLC 44,
159**
See also AMWS 6; CA 134; CANR 118;
CN 6, 7

Minus, Ed 1938- .... **CLC 39**
See also CA 185

Mirabai 1498(?)-1550(?) .... **PC 48**
See also PFS 24

Miranda, Javier
See Bioy Casares, Adolfo
See also CWW 2

Mirbeau, Octave 1848-1917 .... **TCLC 55**
See also CA 216; DLB 123, 192; GFL 1789
to the Present

Mirikitani, Janice 1942- .... **AAL**
See also CA 211; DLB 312; RGAL 4

Mirk, John (?)-c. 1414 .... **LC 105**
See also DLB 146

Miro (Ferrer), Gabriel (Francisco Victor)
1879-1930 .... **TCLC 5**
See also CA 185; CAAE 104; DLB 322;
EWL 3

Misharin, Alexandr .... **CLC 59**

Mishima, Yukio ... **CLC 2, 4, 6, 9, 27; DC 1;
SSC 4; TCLC 161; WLC 4**
See Hiraoka, Kimitake
See also AAYA 50; BPFB 2; GLL 1; MJW;
RGSF 2; RGWL 2, 3; SSFS 5, 12

Mistral, Frederic 1830-1914 .... **TCLC 51**
See also CA 213; CAAE 122; DLB 331;
GFL 1789 to the Present

Mistral, Gabriela
See Godoy Alcayaga, Lucila
See also DLB 283, 331; DNFS 1; EWL 3;
LAW; RGWL 2, 3; WP

Mistry, Rohinton 1952- ... **CLC 71, 196; SSC 73**
See also BRWS 10; CA 141; CANR 86,
114; CCA 1; CN 6, 7; DAC; SSFS 6

Mitchell, Clyde
See Ellison, Harlan

Mitchell, Emerson Blackhorse Barney
1945- .... **NNAL**
See also CA 45-48

Mitchell, James Leslie 1901-1935
See Gibbon, Lewis Grassic
See also CA 188; CAAE 104; DLB 15

Mitchell, Joni 1943- .... **CLC 12**
See also CA 112; CCA 1

Mitchell, Joseph (Quincy)
1908-1996 .... **CLC 98**
See also CA 77-80; CAAS 152; CANR 69;
CN 1, 2, 3, 4, 5, 6; CSW; DLB 185;
DLBY 1996

Mitchell, Margaret (Munnerlyn)
1900-1949 .... **TCLC 11, 170**
See also AAYA 23; BPFB 2; BYA 1; CA
125; CAAE 109; CANR 55, 94;
CDALBS; DA3; DAM NOV, POP; DLB
9; LAIT 2; MAL 5; MTCW 1, 2; MTFW
2005; NFS 9; RGAL 4; RHW; TUS;
WYAS 1; YAW

Mitchell, Peggy
See Mitchell, Margaret (Munnerlyn)

Mitchell, S(ilas) Weir 1829-1914 .... **TCLC 36**
See also CA 165; DLB 202; RGAL 4

Mitchell, W(illiam) O(rmond)
1914-1998 .... **CLC 25**
See also CA 77-80; CAAS 165; CANR 15,
43; CN 1, 2, 3, 4, 5, 6; DAC; DAM MST;
DLB 88; TCLE 1:2

Mitchell, William (Lendrum)
1879-1936 .... **TCLC 81**
See also CA 213

Mitford, Mary Russell 1787-1855 ... **NCLC 4**
See also DLB 110, 116; RGEL 2

Mitford, Nancy 1904-1973 .... **CLC 44**
See also BRWS 10; CA 9-12R; CN 1; DLB
191; RGEL 2

Miyamoto, (Chujo) Yuriko
1899-1951 .... **TCLC 37**
See Miyamoto Yuriko
See also CA 170, 174

Miyamoto Yuriko
See Miyamoto, (Chujo) Yuriko
See also DLB 180

Miyazawa, Kenji 1896-1933 .... **TCLC 76**
See Miyazawa Kenji
See also CA 157; RGWL 3

Miyazawa Kenji
See Miyazawa, Kenji
See also EWL 3

Mizoguchi, Kenji 1898-1956 .... **TCLC 72**
See also CA 167

Mo, Timothy (Peter) 1950- .... **CLC 46, 134**
See also CA 117; CANR 128; CN 5, 6, 7;
DLB 194; MTCW 1; WLIT 4; WWE 1

Modarressi, Taghi (M.) 1931-1997 ... **CLC 44**
See also CA 134; CAAE 121; INT CA-134

Modiano, Patrick (Jean) 1945- .... **CLC 18, 218**
See also CA 85-88; CANR 17, 40, 115;
CWW 2; DLB 83, 299; EWL 3; RGHL

Mofolo, Thomas (Mokopu)
1875(?)-1948 .... **BLC 3; TCLC 22**
See also AFW; CA 153; CAAE 121; CANR
83; DAM MULT; DLB 225; EWL 3;
MTCW 2; MTFW 2005; WLIT 2

Mohr, Nicholasa 1938- .... **CLC 12; HLC 2**
See also AAYA 8, 46; CA 49-52; CANR 1,
32, 64; CLR 22; DAM MULT; DLB 145;
HW 1, 2; JRDA; LAIT 5; LLW; MAICYA
2; MAICYAS 1; RGAL 4; SAAS 8; SATA
8, 97; SATA-Essay 113; WYA; YAW

Moi, Toril 1953- .... **CLC 172**
See also CA 154; CANR 102; FW

Mojtabai, A(nn) G(race) 1938- ..... **CLC 5, 9, 15, 29**
See also CA 85-88; CANR 88

Moliere 1622-1673 ..... **DC 13; LC 10, 28, 64, 125, 127; WLC 4**
See also DA; DA3; DAB; DAC; DAM
DRAM, MST; DFS 13, 18, 20; DLB 268;
EW 3; GFL Beginnings to 1789; LATS
1:1; RGWL 2, 3; TWA

Molin, Charles
See Mayne, William (James Carter)

Molnar, Ferenc 1878-1952 .... **TCLC 20**
See also CA 153; CAAE 109; CANR 83;
CDWLB 4; DAM DRAM; DLB 215;
EWL 3; RGWL 2, 3

Momaday, N. Scott 1934- ...... **CLC 2, 19, 85, 95, 160; NNAL; PC 25; WLCS**
See also AAYA 11, 64; AMWS 4; ANW;
BPFB 2; BYA 12; CA 25-28R; CANR 14,
34, 68, 134; CDALBS; CN 2, 3, 4, 5, 6,
7; CPW; DA; DA3; DAB; DAC; DAM
MST, MULT, NOV, POP; DLB 143, 175,
256; EWL 3; EXPP; INT CANR-14;
LAIT 4; LATS 1:2; MAL 5; MTCW 1, 2;
MTFW 2005; NFS 10; PFS 2, 11; RGAL
4; SATA 48; SATA-Brief 30; TCWW 1,
2; WP; YAW

Monette, Paul 1945-1995 .... **CLC 82**
See also AMWS 10; CA 139; CAAS 147;
CN 6; GLL 1

Monroe, Harriet 1860-1936 .... **TCLC 12**
See also CA 204; CAAE 109; DLB 54, 91

Monroe, Lyle
See Heinlein, Robert A.

Montagu, Elizabeth 1720-1800 .... **NCLC 7, 117**
See also FW

Montagu, Mary (Pierrepont) Wortley
1689-1762 .... **LC 9, 57; PC 16**
See also DLB 95, 101; FL 1:1; RGEL 2

Montagu, W. H.
See Coleridge, Samuel Taylor

Montague, John (Patrick) 1929- ..... **CLC 13, 46**
See also CA 9-12R; CANR 9, 69, 121; CP
1, 2, 3, 4, 5, 6, 7; DLB 40; EWL 3;
MTCW 1; PFS 12; RGEL 2; TCLE 1:2

Montaigne, Michel (Eyquem) de
1533-1592 .... **LC 8, 105; WLC 4**
See also DA; DAB; DAC; DAM MST;
DLB 327; EW 2; GFL Beginnings to
1789; LMFS 1; RGWL 2, 3; TWA

Montale, Eugenio 1896-1981 ... **CLC 7, 9, 18; PC 13**
See also CA 17-20R; CAAS 104; CANR
30; DLB 114, 331; EW 11; EWL 3;
MTCW 1; PFS 22; RGWL 2, 3; TWA;
WLIT 7

Montesquieu, Charles-Louis de Secondat
1689-1755 .... **LC 7, 69**
See also DLB 314; EW 3; GFL Beginnings
to 1789; TWA

Montessori, Maria 1870-1952 ...... **TCLC 103**
See also CA 147; CAAE 115

Montgomery, (Robert) Bruce 1921(?)-1978
See Crispin, Edmund
See also CA 179; CAAS 104; CMW 4

Montgomery, L(ucy) M(aud)
1874-1942 .... **TCLC 51, 140**
See also AAYA 12; BYA 1; CA 137; CAAE
108; CLR 8, 91; DA3; DAC; DAM MST;
DLB 92; DLBD 14; JRDA; MAICYA 1,

2; MTCW 2; MTFW 2005; RGEL 2;
SATA 100; TWA; WCH; WYA; YABC 1

Montgomery, Marion H., Jr. 1925- .... **CLC 7**
See also AITN 1; CA 1-4R; CANR 3, 48;
CSW; DLB 6

Montgomery, Max
See Davenport, Guy (Mattison, Jr.)

Montherlant, Henry (Milon) de
1896-1972 .... **CLC 8, 19**
See also CA 85-88; CAAS 37-40R; DAM
DRAM; DLB 72, 321; EW 11; EWL 3;
GFL 1789 to the Present; MTCW 1

Monty Python
See Chapman, Graham; Cleese, John
(Marwood); Gilliam, Terry; Idle, Eric;
Jones, Terence Graham Parry; Palin,
Michael (Edward)
See also AAYA 7

Moodie, Susanna (Strickland)
1803-1885 .... **NCLC 14, 113**
See also DLB 99

Moody, Hiram 1961-
See Moody, Rick
See also CA 138; CANR 64, 112; MTFW
2005

Moody, Minerva
See Alcott, Louisa May

Moody, Rick .... **CLC 147**
See Moody, Hiram

Moody, William Vaughan
1869-1910 .... **TCLC 105**
See also CA 178; CAAE 110; DLB 7, 54;
MAL 5; RGAL 4

Mooney, Edward 1951-
See Mooney, Ted
See also CA 130

Mooney, Ted .... **CLC 25**
See Mooney, Edward

Moorcock, Michael 1939- .... **CLC 5, 27, 58**
See Bradbury, Edward P.
See also AAYA 26; CA 45-48; 5; CANR 2,
17, 38, 64, 122; CN 5, 6, 7; DLB 14, 231,
261, 319; FANT; MTCW 1, 2; MTFW
2005; SATA 93, 166; SCFW 1, 2; SFW 4;
SUFW 1, 2

Moorcock, Michael John
See Moorcock, Michael

Moore, Alan 1953- .... **CLC 230**
See also AAYA 51; CA 204; CANR 138;
DLB 261; MTFW 2005; SFW 4

Moore, Brian 1921-1999 ... **CLC 1, 3, 5, 7, 8, 19, 32, 90**
See Bryan, Michael
See also BRWS 9; CA 1-4R; CAAS 174;
CANR 1, 25, 42, 63; CCA 1; CN 1, 2, 3,
4, 5, 6; DAB; DAC; DAM MST; DLB
251; EWL 3; FANT; MTCW 1, 2; MTFW
2005; RGEL 2

Moore, Edward
See Muir, Edwin
See also RGEL 2

Moore, G. E. 1873-1958 .... **TCLC 89**
See also DLB 262

Moore, George Augustus
1852-1933 .... **SSC 19; TCLC 7**
See also BRW 6; CA 177; CAAE 104; DLB
10, 18, 57, 135; EWL 3; RGEL 2; RGSF
2

Moore, Lorrie .... **CLC 39, 45, 68**
See Moore, Marie Lorena
See also AMWS 10; CN 5, 6, 7; DLB 234;
SSFS 19

Moore, Marianne (Craig)
1887-1972 .... **CLC 1, 2, 4, 8, 10, 13, 19, 47; PC 4, 49; WLCS**
See also AMW; CA 1-4R; CAAS 33-36R;
CANR 3, 61; CDALB 1929-1941; CP 1;
DA; DA3; DAB; DAC; DAM MST,

Mqhayi, S(amuel) E(dward) K(rune Loliwe)
1875-1945 .... **BLC 3; TCLC 25**
See also CA 153; CANR 87; DAM MULT

Mrozek, Slawomir 1930- .... **CLC 3, 13**
See also CA 13-16R; 10; CANR 29; CD-WLB 4; CWW 2; DLB 232; EWL 3; MTCW 1

Mrs. Belloc-Lowndes
See Lowndes, Marie Adelaide (Belloc)

Mrs. Fairstar
See Horne, Richard Henry Hengist

M'Taggart, John M'Taggart Ellis
See McTaggart, John McTaggart Ellis

Mtwa, Percy (?)- .... **CLC 47**
See also CD 6

Mueller, Lisel 1924- .... **CLC 13, 51; PC 33**
See also CA 93-96; CP 6, 7; DLB 105; PFS 9, 13

Muggeridge, Malcolm (Thomas)
1903-1990 .... **TCLC 120**
See also AITN 1; CA 101; CANR 33, 63; MTCW 1, 2

Muhammad 570-632 .... **WLCS**
See also DA; DAB; DAC; DAM MST; DLB 311

Muir, Edwin 1887-1959 . **PC 49; TCLC 2, 87**
See Moore, Edward
See also BRWS 6; CA 193; CAAE 104; DLB 20, 100, 191; EWL 3; RGEL 2

Muir, John 1838-1914 .... **TCLC 28**
See also AMWS 9; ANW; CA 165; DLB 186, 275

Mujica Lainez, Manuel 1910-1984 ... **CLC 31**
See Lainez, Manuel Mujica
See also CA 81-84; CAAS 112; CANR 32; EWL 3; HW 1

Mukherjee, Bharati 1940- ..... **AAL; CLC 53, 115, 235; SSC 38**
See also AAYA 46; BEST 89:2; CA 232; 107, 232; CANR 45, 72, 128; CN 5, 6, 7; DAM NOV; DLB 60, 218, 323; DNFS 1, 2; EWL 3; FW; MAL 5; MTCW 1, 2; MTFW 2005; RGAL 4; RGSF 2; SSFS 7, 24; TUS; WWE 1

Muldoon, Paul 1951- .... **CLC 32, 72, 166**
See also BRWS 4; CA 129; CAAE 113; CANR 52, 91; CP 2, 3, 4, 5, 6, 7; DAM POET; DLB 40; INT CA-129; PFS 7, 22; TCLE 1:2

Mulisch, Harry (Kurt Victor)
1927- .... **CLC 42**
See also CA 9-12R; CANR 6, 26, 56, 110; CWW 2; DLB 299; EWL 3

Mull, Martin 1943- .... **CLC 17**
See also CA 105

Muller, Wilhelm .... **NCLC 73**

Mulock, Dinah Maria
See Craik, Dinah Maria (Mulock)
See also RGEL 2

Multatuli 1820-1881 .... **NCLC 165**
See also RGWL 2, 3

Munday, Anthony 1560-1633 .... **LC 87**
See also DLB 62, 172; RGEL 2

Munford, Robert 1737(?)-1783 .... **LC 5**
See also DLB 31

Mungo, Raymond 1946- .... **CLC 72**
See also CA 49-52; CANR 2

Munro, Alice 1931- .... **CLC 6, 10, 19, 50, 95, 222; SSC 3, 95; WLCS**
See also AITN 2; BPFB 2; CA 33-36R; CANR 33, 53, 75, 114; CCA 1; CN 1, 2, 3, 4, 5, 6, 7; DA3; DAC; DAM MST, NOV; DLB 53; EWL 3; MTCW 1, 2; MTFW 2005; RGEL 2; RGSF 2; SATA 29; SSFS 5, 13, 19; TCLE 1:2; WWE 1

Munro, H(ector) H(ugh) 1870-1916
See Saki
See also AAYA 56; CA 130; CAAE 104; CANR 104; CDBLB 1890-1914; DA; DA3; DAB; DAC; DAM MST, NOV; DLB 34, 162; EXPS; MTCW 1, 2; MTFW 2005; RGEL 2; SSFS 15

Murakami, Haruki 1949- .... **CLC 150**
See Murakami Haruki
See also CA 165; CANR 102, 146; MJW; RGWL 3; SFW 4; SSFS 23

Murakami Haruki
See Murakami, Haruki
See also CWW 2; DLB 182; EWL 3

Murasaki, Lady
See Murasaki Shikibu

Murasaki Shikibu 978(?)-1026(?) .. **CMLC 1, 79**
See also EFS 2; LATS 1:1; RGWL 2, 3

Murdoch, Iris 1919-1999 .. **CLC 1, 2, 3, 4, 6, 8, 11, 15, 22, 31, 51; TCLC 171**
See also BRWS 1; CA 13-16R; CAAS 179; CANR 8, 43, 68, 103, 142; CBD; CD-BLB 1960 to Present; CN 1, 2, 3, 4, 5, 6; CWD; DA3; DAB; DAC; DAM MST, NOV; DLB 14, 194, 233, 326; EWL 3; INT CANR-8; MTCW 1, 2; MTFW 2005; NFS 18; RGEL 2; TCLE 1:2; TEA; WLIT 4

Murfree, Mary Noailles 1850-1922 .. **SSC 22; TCLC 135**
See also CA 176; CAAE 122; DLB 12, 74; RGAL 4

Murglie
See Murnau, F.W.

Murnau, Friedrich Wilhelm
See Murnau, F.W.

Murnau, F.W. 1888-1931 .... **TCLC 53**
See also CAAE 112

Murphy, Richard 1927- .... **CLC 41**
See also BRWS 5; CA 29-32R; CP 1, 2, 3, 4, 5, 6, 7; DLB 40; EWL 3

Murphy, Sylvia 1937- .... **CLC 34**
See also CA 121

Murphy, Thomas (Bernard) 1935- ... **CLC 51**
See Murphy, Tom
See also CA 101

Murphy, Tom
See Murphy, Thomas (Bernard)
See also DLB 310

Murray, Albert 1916- .... **CLC 73**
See also BW 2; CA 49-52; CANR 26, 52, 78, 160; CN 7; CSW; DLB 38; MTFW 2005

Murray, Albert L.
See Murray, Albert

Murray, James Augustus Henry
1837-1915 .... **TCLC 117**

Murray, Judith Sargent
1751-1820 .... **NCLC 63**
See also DLB 37, 200

Murray, Les(lie Allan) 1938- .... **CLC 40**
See also BRWS 7; CA 21-24R; CANR 11, 27, 56, 103; CP 1, 2, 3, 4, 5, 6, 7; DAM POET; DLB 289; DLBY 2001; EWL 3; RGEL 2

Murry, J. Middleton
See Murry, John Middleton

Murry, John Middleton
1889-1957 .... **TCLC 16**
See also CA 217; CAAE 118; DLB 149

Musgrave, Susan 1951- .... **CLC 13, 54**
See also CA 69-72; CANR 45, 84; CCA 1; CP 2, 3, 4, 5, 6, 7; CWP

Musil, Robert (Edler von)
1880-1942 .... **SSC 18; TCLC 12, 68**
See also CAAE 109; CANR 55, 84; CD-WLB 2; DLB 81, 124; EW 9; EWL 3; MTCW 2; RGSF 2; RGWL 2, 3

Muske, Carol .... **CLC 90**
See Muske-Dukes, Carol (Anne)

Muske-Dukes, Carol (Anne) 1945-
See Muske, Carol
See also CA 203; 65-68, 203; CANR 32, 70; CWP; PFS 24

Musset, Alfred de 1810-1857 . **DC 27; NCLC 7, 150**
See also DLB 192, 217; EW 6; GFL 1789 to the Present; RGWL 2, 3; TWA

Musset, Louis Charles Alfred de
See Musset, Alfred de

Mussolini, Benito (Amilcare Andrea)
1883-1945 .... **TCLC 96**
See also CAAE 116

Mutanabbi, Al-
See al-Mutanabbi, Ahmad ibn al-Husayn Abu al-Tayyib al-Jufi al-Kindi
See also WLIT 6

My Brother's Brother
See Chekhov, Anton (Pavlovich)

Myers, L(eopold) H(amilton)
1881-1944 .... **TCLC 59**
See also CA 157; DLB 15; EWL 3; RGEL 2

Myers, Walter Dean 1937- .. **BLC 3; CLC 35**
See Myers, Walter M.
See also AAYA 4, 23; BW 2; BYA 6, 8, 11; CA 33-36R; CANR 20, 42, 67, 108; CLR 4, 16, 35, 110; DAM MULT, NOV; DLB 33; INT CANR-20; JRDA; LAIT 5; MAI-CYA 1, 2; MAICYAS 1; MTCW 2; MTFW 2005; SAAS 2; SATA 41, 71, 109, 157; SATA-Brief 27; WYA; YAW

Myers, Walter M.
See Myers, Walter Dean

Myles, Symon
See Follett, Ken

Nabokov, Vladimir (Vladimirovich)
1899-1977 .... **CLC 1, 2, 3, 6, 8, 11, 15, 23, 44, 46, 64; SSC 11, 86; TCLC 108, 189; WLC 4**
See also AAYA 45; AMW; AMWC 1; AMWR 1; BPFB 2; CA 5-8R; CAAS 69-72; CANR 20, 102; CDALB 1941-1968; CN 1, 2; CP 2; DA; DA3; DAB; DAC; DAM MST, NOV; DLB 2, 244, 278, 317; DLBD 3; DLBY 1980, 1991; EWL 3; EXPS; LATS 1:2; MAL 5; MTCW 1, 2; MTFW 2005; NCFS 4; NFS 9; RGAL 4; RGSF 2; SSFS 6, 15; TUS

Naevius c. 265B.C.-201B.C. .... **CMLC 37**
See also DLB 211

Nagai, Kafu .... **TCLC 51**
See Nagai, Sokichi
See also DLB 180

Nagai, Sokichi 1879-1959
See Nagai, Kafu
See also CAAE 117

Nagy, Laszlo 1925-1978 .... **CLC 7**
See also CA 129; CAAS 112

Naidu, Sarojini 1879-1949 .... **TCLC 80**
See also EWL 3; RGEL 2

Naipaul, Shiva 1945-1985 .... **CLC 32, 39; TCLC 153**
See also CA 112; CAAE 110; CAAS 116; CANR 33; CN 2, 3; DA3; DAM NOV; DLB 157; DLBY 1985; EWL 3; MTCW 1, 2; MTFW 2005

Naipaul, V.S. 1932- .. **CLC 4, 7, 9, 13, 18, 37, 105, 199; SSC 38**
See also BPFB 2; BRWS 1; CA 1-4R; CANR 1, 33, 51, 91, 126; CDBLB 1960 to Present; CDWLB 3; CN 1, 2, 3, 4, 5, 6, 7; DA3; DAB; DAC; DAM MST, NOV; DLB 125, 204, 207, 326, 331; DLBY 1985, 2001; EWL 3; LATS 1:2; MTCW 1, 2; MTFW 2005; RGEL 2; RGSF 2; TWA; WLIT 4; WWE 1

Nakos, Lilika 1903(?)-1989 .... **CLC 29**

O'Donovan, Michael Francis
　　1903-1966 .... **CLC 14**
　　See O'Connor, Frank
　　See also CA 93-96; CANR 84
Oe, Kenzaburo 1935- .. **CLC 10, 36, 86, 187;**
　　SSC 20
　　See Oe Kenzaburo
　　See also CA 97-100; CANR 36, 50, 74, 126;
　　DA3; DAM NOV; DLB 182, 331; DLBY
　　1994; LATS 1:2; MJW; MTCW 1, 2;
　　MTFW 2005; RGSF 2; RGWL 2, 3
Oe Kenzaburo
　　See Oe, Kenzaburo
　　See also CWW 2; EWL 3
O'Faolain, Julia 1932- .... **CLC 6, 19, 47, 108**
　　See also CA 81-84; 2; CANR 12, 61; CN 2,
　　3, 4, 5, 6, 7; DLB 14, 231, 319; FW;
　　MTCW 1; RHW
O'Faolain, Sean 1900-1991 ...... **CLC 1, 7, 14,**
　　32, 70; SSC 13; TCLC 143
　　See also CA 61-64; CAAS 134; CANR 12,
　　66; CN 1, 2, 3, 4; DLB 15, 162; MTCW
　　1, 2; MTFW 2005; RGEL 2; RGSF 2
O'Flaherty, Liam 1896-1984 .... **CLC 5, 34;**
　　SSC 6
　　See also CA 101; CAAS 113; CANR 35;
　　CN 1, 2, 3; DLB 36, 162; DLBY 1984;
　　MTCW 1, 2; MTFW 2005; RGEL 2;
　　RGSF 2; SSFS 5, 20
Ogai
　　See Mori Ogai
　　See also MJW
Ogilvy, Gavin
　　See Barrie, J(ames) M(atthew)
O'Grady, Standish (James)
　　　1846-1928 .... **TCLC 5**
　　See also CA 157; CAAE 104
O'Grady, Timothy 1951- .... **CLC 59**
　　See also CA 138
O'Hara, Frank 1926-1966 .... **CLC 2, 5, 13,**
　　78; PC 45
　　See also CA 9-12R; CAAS 25-28R; CANR
　　33; DA3; DAM POET; DLB 5, 16, 193;
　　EWL 3; MAL 5; MTCW 1, 2; MTFW
　　2005; PFS 8, 12; RGAL 4; WP
O'Hara, John (Henry) 1905-1970 . **CLC 1, 2,**
　　3, 6, 11, 42; SSC 15
　　See also AMW; BPFB 3; CA 5-8R; CAAS
　　25-28R; CANR 31, 60; CDALB 1929-
　　1941; DAM NOV; DLB 9, 86, 324; DLBD
　　2; EWL 3; MAL 5; MTCW 1, 2; MTFW
　　2005; NFS 11; RGAL 4; RGSF 2
O'Hehir, Diana 1929- .... **CLC 41**
　　See also CA 245
Ohiyesa
　　See Eastman, Charles A(lexander)
Okada, John 1923-1971 .... **AAL**
　　See also BYA 14; CA 212; DLB 312
Okigbo, Christopher 1930-1967 .... **BLC 3;**
　　CLC 25, 84; PC 7; TCLC 171
　　See also AFW; BW 1, 3; CA 77-80; CANR
　　74; CDWLB 3; DAM MULT, POET; DLB
　　125; EWL 3; MTCW 1, 2; MTFW 2005;
　　RGEL 2
Okigbo, Christopher Ifenayichukwu
　　See Okigbo, Christopher
Okri, Ben 1959- .... **CLC 87, 223**
　　See also AFW; BRWS 5; BW 2, 3; CA 138;
　　CAAE 130; CANR 65, 128; CN 5, 6, 7;
　　DLB 157, 231, 319, 326; EWL 3; INT
　　CA-138; MTCW 2; MTFW 2005; RGSF
　　2; SSFS 20; WLIT 2; WWE 1
Olds, Sharon 1942- .. **CLC 32, 39, 85; PC 22**
　　See also AMWS 10; CA 101; CANR 18,
　　41, 66, 98, 135; CP 5, 6, 7; CPW; CWP;
　　DAM POET; DLB 120; MAL 5; MTCW
　　2; MTFW 2005; PFS 17
Oldstyle, Jonathan
　　See Irving, Washington

Olesha, Iurii
　　See Olesha, Yuri (Karlovich)
　　See also RGWL 2
Olesha, Iurii Karlovich
　　See Olesha, Yuri (Karlovich)
　　See also DLB 272
Olesha, Yuri (Karlovich) 1899-1960 . **CLC 8;**
　　SSC 69; TCLC 136
　　See Olesha, Iurii; Olesha, Iurii Karlovich;
　　Olesha, Yury Karlovich
　　See also CA 85-88; EW 11; RGWL 3
Olesha, Yury Karlovich
　　See Olesha, Yuri (Karlovich)
　　See also EWL 3
Oliphant, Mrs.
　　See Oliphant, Margaret (Oliphant Wilson)
　　See also SUFW
Oliphant, Laurence 1829(?)-1888 .. **NCLC 47**
　　See also DLB 18, 166
Oliphant, Margaret (Oliphant Wilson)
　　　1828-1897 .... **NCLC 11, 61; SSC 25**
　　See Oliphant, Mrs.
　　See also BRWS 10; DLB 18, 159, 190;
　　HGG; RGEL 2; RGSF 2
Oliver, Mary 1935- ... **CLC 19, 34, 98; PC 75**
　　See also AMWS 7; CA 21-24R; CANR 9,
　　43, 84, 92, 138; CP 4, 5, 6, 7; CWP; DLB
　　5, 193; EWL 3; MTFW 2005; PFS 15
Olivier, Laurence (Kerr) 1907-1989 . **CLC 20**
　　See also CA 150; CAAE 111; CAAS 129
Olsen, Tillie 1912-2007 .... **CLC 4, 13, 114;**
　　SSC 11
　　See also AAYA 51; AMWS 13; BYA 11;
　　CA 1-4R; CANR 1, 43, 74, 132;
　　CDALBS; CN 2, 3, 4, 5, 6, 7; DA; DA3;
　　DAB; DAC; DAM MST; DLB 28, 206;
　　DLBY 1980; EWL 3; EXPS; FW; MAL
　　5; MTCW 1, 2; MTFW 2005; RGAL 4;
　　RGSF 2; SSFS 1; TCLE 1:2; TCWW 2;
　　TUS
Olson, Charles (John) 1910-1970 .. **CLC 1, 2,**
　　5, 6, 9, 11, 29; PC 19
　　See also AMWS 2; CA 13-16; CAAS 25-
　　28R; CABS 2; CANR 35, 61; CAP 1; CP
　　1; DAM POET; DLB 5, 16, 193; EWL 3;
　　MAL 5; MTCW 1, 2; RGAL 4; WP
Olson, Toby 1937- .... **CLC 28**
　　See also CA 65-68; 11; CANR 9, 31, 84;
　　CP 3, 4, 5, 6, 7
Olyesha, Yuri
　　See Olesha, Yuri (Karlovich)
Olympiodorus of Thebes c. 375-c.
　　　430 .... **CMLC 59**
Omar Khayyam
　　See Khayyam, Omar
　　See also RGWL 2, 3
Ondaatje, Michael 1943- ..... **CLC 14, 29, 51,**
　　76, 180; PC 28
　　See also AAYA 66; CA 77-80; CANR 42,
　　74, 109, 133; CN 5, 6, 7; CP 1, 2, 3, 4, 5,
　　6, 7; DA3; DAB; DAC; DAM MST; DLB
　　60, 323, 326; EWL 3; LATS 1:2; LMFS
　　2; MTCW 2; MTFW 2005; NFS 23; PFS
　　8, 19; TCLE 1:2; TWA; WWE 1
Ondaatje, Philip Michael
　　See Ondaatje, Michael
Oneal, Elizabeth 1934-
　　See Oneal, Zibby
　　See also CA 106; CANR 28, 84; MAICYA
　　1, 2; SATA 30, 82; YAW
Oneal, Zibby .... **CLC 30**
　　See Oneal, Elizabeth
　　See also AAYA 5, 41; BYA 13; CLR 13;
　　JRDA; WYA
O'Neill, Eugene (Gladstone)
　　　1888-1953 ... **DC 20; TCLC 1, 6, 27, 49;**
　　WLC 4
　　See also AAYA 54; AITN 1; AMW; AMWC
　　1; CA 132; CAAE 110; CAD; CANR 131;
　　CDALB 1929-1941; DA; DA3; DAB;

DAC; DAM DRAM, MST; DFS 2, 4, 5,
　　6, 9, 11, 12, 16, 20; DLB 7, 331; EWL 3;
　　LAIT 3; LMFS 2; MAL 5; MTCW 1, 2;
　　MTFW 2005; RGAL 4; TUS
Onetti, Juan Carlos 1909-1994 ... **CLC 7, 10;**
　　HLCS 2; SSC 23; TCLC 131
　　See also CA 85-88; CAAS 145; CANR 32,
　　63; CDWLB 3; CWW 2; DAM MULT,
　　NOV; DLB 113; EWL 3; HW 1, 2; LAW;
　　MTCW 1, 2; MTFW 2005; RGSF 2
O Nuallain, Brian 1911-1966
　　See O'Brien, Flann
　　See also CA 21-22; CAAS 25-28R; CAP 2;
　　DLB 231; FANT; TEA
Ophuls, Max
　　See Ophuls, Max
Ophuls, Max 1902-1957 .... **TCLC 79**
　　See also CAAE 113
Opie, Amelia 1769-1853 .... **NCLC 65**
　　See also DLB 116, 159; RGEL 2
Oppen, George 1908-1984 ..... **CLC 7, 13, 34;**
　　PC 35; TCLC 107
　　See also CA 13-16R; CAAS 113; CANR 8,
　　82; CP 1, 2, 3; DLB 5, 165
Oppenheim, E(dward) Phillips
　　　1866-1946 .... **TCLC 45**
　　See also CA 202; CAAE 111; CMW 4; DLB
　　70
Oppenheimer, Max
　　See Ophuls, Max
Opuls, Max
　　See Ophuls, Max
Orage, A(lfred) R(ichard)
　　　1873-1934 .... **TCLC 157**
　　See also CAAE 122
Origen c. 185-c. 254 .... **CMLC 19**
Orlovitz, Gil 1918-1973 .... **CLC 22**
　　See also CA 77-80; CAAS 45-48; CN 1;
　　CP 1, 2; DLB 2, 5
O'Rourke, Patrick Jake
　　See O'Rourke, P.J.
O'Rourke, P.J. 1947- .... **CLC 209**
　　See also CA 77-80; CANR 13, 41, 67, 111,
　　155; CPW; DAM POP; DLB 185
Orris
　　See Ingelow, Jean
Ortega y Gasset, Jose 1883-1955 ...... **HLC 2;**
　　TCLC 9
　　See also CA 130; CAAE 106; DAM MULT;
　　EW 9; EWL 3; HW 1, 2; MTCW 1, 2;
　　MTFW 2005
Ortese, Anna Maria 1914-1998 .... **CLC 89**
　　See also DLB 177; EWL 3
Ortiz, Simon J(oseph) 1941- ... **CLC 45, 208;**
　　NNAL; PC 17
　　See also AMWS 4; CA 134; CANR 69, 118;
　　CP 3, 4, 5, 6, 7; DAM MULT, POET;
　　DLB 120, 175, 256; EXPP; MAL 5; PFS
　　4, 16; RGAL 4; SSFS 22; TCWW 2
Orton, Joe ...... **CLC 4, 13, 43; DC 3; TCLC**
　　157
　　See Orton, John Kingsley
　　See also BRWS 5; CBD; CDBLB 1960 to
　　Present; DFS 3, 6; DLB 13, 310; GLL 1;
　　RGEL 2; TEA; WLIT 4
Orton, John Kingsley 1933-1967
　　See Orton, Joe
　　See also CA 85-88; CANR 35, 66; DAM
　　DRAM; MTCW 1, 2; MTFW 2005
Orwell, George ...... **SSC 68; TCLC 2, 6, 15,**
　　31, 51, 128, WLC 4
　　See Blair, Eric (Arthur)
　　See also BPFB 3; BRW 7; BYA 5; CDBLB
　　1945-1960; CLR 68; DAB; DLB 15, 98,
　　195, 255; EWL 3; EXPN; LAIT 4, 5;
　　LATS 1:1; NFS 3, 7; RGEL 2; SCFW 1,
　　2; SFW 4; SSFS 4; TEA; WLIT 4; YAW
Osborne, David
　　See Silverberg, Robert

Parker, Dorothy (Rothschild)
      1893-1967 . **CLC 15, 68; PC 28; SSC 2;**
      TCLC 143
      See also AMWS 9; CA 19-20; CAAS 25-
      28R; CAP 2; DA3; DAM POET; DLB 11,
      45, 86; EXPP; FW; MAL 5; MBL;
      MTCW 1, 2; MTFW 2005; PFS 18;
      RGAL 4; RGSF 2; TUS
Parker, Robert B. 1932- .... **CLC 27**
      See also AAYA 28; BEST 89:4; BPFB 3;
      CA 49-52; CANR 1, 26, 52, 89, 128;
      CMW 4; CPW; DAM NOV, POP; DLB
      306; INT CANR-26; MSW; MTCW 1;
      MTFW 2005
Parker, Robert Brown
      See Parker, Robert B.
Parkin, Frank 1940- .... **CLC 43**
      See also CA 147
Parkman, Francis, Jr. 1823-1893 .. **NCLC 12**
      See also AMWS 2; DLB 1, 30, 183, 186,
      235; RGAL 4
Parks, Gordon 1912-2006 .... **BLC 3; CLC 1,**
      16
      See also AAYA 36; AITN 2; BW 2, 3; CA
      41-44R; CAAS 249; CANR 26, 66, 145;
      DA3; DAM MULT; DLB 33; MTCW 2;
      MTFW 2005; SATA 8, 108; SATA-Obit
      175
Parks, Suzan-Lori 1964(?)- .... **DC 23**
      See also AAYA 55; CA 201; CAD; CD 5,
      6; CWD; DFS 22; RGAL 4
Parks, Tim(othy Harold) 1954- ...... **CLC 147**
      See also CA 131; CAAE 126; CANR 77,
      144; CN 7; DLB 231; INT CA-131
Parmenides c. 515B.C.-c.
      450B.C. .... **CMLC 22**
      See also DLB 176
Parnell, Thomas 1679-1718 .... **LC 3**
      See also DLB 95; RGEL 2
Parr, Catherine c. 1513(?)-1548 .... **LC 86**
      See also DLB 136
Parra, Nicanor 1914- ... **CLC 2, 102; HLC 2;**
      PC 39
      See also CA 85-88; CANR 32; CWW 2;
      DAM MULT; DLB 283; EWL 3; HW 1;
      LAW; MTCW 1
Parra Sanojo, Ana Teresa de la
      1890-1936 .... **HLCS 2**
      See de la Parra, (Ana) Teresa (Sonojo)
      See also LAW
Parrish, Mary Frances
      See Fisher, M(ary) F(rances) K(ennedy)
Parshchikov, Aleksei 1954- .... **CLC 59**
      See Parshchikov, Aleksei Maksimovich
Parshchikov, Aleksei Maksimovich
      See Parshchikov, Aleksei
      See also DLB 285
Parson, Professor
      See Coleridge, Samuel Taylor
Parson Lot
      See Kingsley, Charles
Parton, Sara Payson Willis
      1811-1872 .... **NCLC 86**
      See also DLB 43, 74, 239
Partridge, Anthony
      See Oppenheim, E(dward) Phillips
Pascal, Blaise 1623-1662 .... **LC 35**
      See also DLB 268; EW 3; GFL Beginnings
      to 1789; RGWL 2, 3; TWA
Pascoli, Giovanni 1855-1912 .... **TCLC 45**
      See also CA 170; EW 7; EWL 3
Pasolini, Pier Paolo 1922-1975 .. **CLC 20, 37,**
      106; PC 17
      See also CA 93-96; CAAS 61-64; CANR
      63; DLB 128, 177; EWL 3; MTCW 1;
      RGWL 2, 3
Pasquini
      See Silone, Ignazio

Pastan, Linda (Olenik) 1932- .... **CLC 27**
      See also CA 61-64; CANR 18, 40, 61, 113;
      CP 3, 4, 5, 6, 7; CSW; CWP; DAM
      POET; DLB 5; PFS 8, 25
Pasternak, Boris 1890-1960 ... **CLC 7, 10, 18,**
      63; PC 6; SSC 31; TCLC 188; WLC 4
      See also BPFB 3; CA 127; CAAS 116; DA;
      DA3; DAB; DAC; DAM MST, NOV,
      POET; DLB 302, 331; EW 10; MTCW 1,
      2; MTFW 2005; RGSF 2; RGWL 2, 3;
      TWA; WP
Patchen, Kenneth 1911-1972 .... **CLC 1, 2, 18**
      See also BG 1:3; CA 1-4R; CAAS 33-36R;
      CANR 3, 35; CN 1; CP 1; DAM POET;
      DLB 16, 48; EWL 3; MAL 5; MTCW 1;
      RGAL 4
Pater, Walter (Horatio) 1839-1894 . **NCLC 7,**
      90, 159
      See also BRW 5; CDBLB 1832-1890; DLB
      57, 156; RGEL 2; TEA
Paterson, A(ndrew) B(arton)
      1864-1941 .... **TCLC 32**
      See also CA 155; DLB 230; RGEL 2; SATA
      97
Paterson, Banjo
      See Paterson, A(ndrew) B(arton)
Paterson, Katherine 1932- .... **CLC 12, 30**
      See also AAYA 1, 31; BYA 1, 2, 7; CA 21-
      24R; CANR 28, 59, 111; CLR 7, 50;
      CWRI 5; DLB 52; JRDA; LAIT 4; MAI-
      CYA 1, 2; MAICYAS 1; MTCW 1; SATA
      13, 53, 92, 133; WYA; YAW
Paterson, Katherine Womeldorf
      See Paterson, Katherine
Patmore, Coventry Kersey Dighton
      1823-1896 .... **NCLC 9; PC 59**
      See also DLB 35, 98; RGEL 2; TEA
Paton, Alan 1903-1988 ..... **CLC 4, 10, 25, 55,**
      106; TCLC 165; WLC 4
      See also AAYA 26; AFW; BPFB 3; BRWS
      2; BYA 1; CA 13-16; CAAS 125; CANR
      22; CAP 1; CN 1, 2, 3, 4; DA; DA3;
      DAB; DAC; DAM MST, NOV; DLB 225;
      DLBD 17; EWL 3; EXPN; LAIT 4;
      MTCW 1, 2; MTFW 2005; NFS 3, 12;
      RGEL 2; SATA 11; SATA-Obit 56; TWA;
      WLIT 2; WWE 1
Paton Walsh, Gillian
      See Paton Walsh, Jill
      See also AAYA 47; BYA 1, 8
Paton Walsh, Jill 1937- .... **CLC 35**
      See Paton Walsh, Gillian; Walsh, Jill Paton
      See also AAYA 11; CANR 38, 83, 158; CLR
      2, 65; DLB 161; JRDA; MAICYA 1, 2;
      SAAS 3; SATA 4, 72, 109; YAW
Patsauq, Markoosie 1942- .... **NNAL**
      See also CA 101; CLR 23; CWRI 5; DAM
      MULT
Patterson, (Horace) Orlando (Lloyd)
      1940- .... **BLCS**
      See also BW 1; CA 65-68; CANR 27, 84;
      CN 1, 2, 3, 4, 5, 6
Patton, George S(mith), Jr.
      1885-1945 .... **TCLC 79**
      See also CA 189
Paulding, James Kirke 1778-1860 ... **NCLC 2**
      See also DLB 3, 59, 74, 250; RGAL 4
Paulin, Thomas Neilson
      See Paulin, Tom
Paulin, Tom 1949- .... **CLC 37, 177**
      See also CA 128; CAAE 123; CANR 98;
      CP 3, 4, 5, 6, 7; DLB 40
Pausanias c. 1st cent. - .... **CMLC 36**
Paustovsky, Konstantin (Georgievich)
      1892-1968 .... **CLC 40**
      See also CA 93-96; CAAS 25-28R; DLB
      272; EWL 3

Pavese, Cesare 1908-1950 .... **PC 13; SSC 19;**
      TCLC 3
      See also CA 169; CAAE 104; DLB 128,
      177; EW 12; EWL 3; PFS 20; RGSF 2;
      RGWL 2, 3; TWA; WLIT 7
Pavic, Milorad 1929- .... **CLC 60**
      See also CA 136; CDWLB 4; CWW 2; DLB
      181; EWL 3; RGWL 3
Pavlov, Ivan Petrovich 1849-1936 . **TCLC 91**
      See also CA 180; CAAE 118
Pavlova, Karolina Karlovna
      1807-1893 .... **NCLC 138**
      See also DLB 205
Payne, Alan
      See Jakes, John
Payne, Rachel Ann
      See Jakes, John
Paz, Gil
      See Lugones, Leopoldo
Paz, Octavio 1914-1998 . **CLC 3, 4, 6, 10, 19,**
      51, 65, 119; HLC 2; PC 1, 48; WLC 4
      See also AAYA 50; CA 73-76; CAAS 165;
      CANR 32, 65, 104; CWW 2; DA; DA3;
      DAB; DAC; DAM MST, MULT, POET;
      DLB 290, 331; DLBY 1990, 1998; DNFS
      1; EWL 3; HW 1, 2; LAW; LAWS 1;
      MTCW 1, 2; MTFW 2005; PFS 18;
      RGWL 2, 3; SSFS 13; TWA; WLIT 1
p'Bitek, Okot 1931-1982 .... **BLC 3; CLC 96;**
      TCLC 149
      See also AFW; BW 2, 3; CA 124; CAAS
      107; CANR 82; CP 1, 2, 3; DAM MULT;
      DLB 125; EWL 3; MTCW 1, 2; MTFW
      2005; RGEL 2; WLIT 2
Peabody, Elizabeth Palmer
      1804-1894 .... **NCLC 169**
      See also DLB 1, 223
Peacham, Henry 1578-1644(?) .... **LC 119**
      See also DLB 151
Peacock, Molly 1947- .... **CLC 60**
      See also CA 103; 21; CANR 52, 84; CP 5,
      6, 7; CWP; DLB 120, 282
Peacock, Thomas Love
      1785-1866 .... **NCLC 22**
      See also BRW 4; DLB 96, 116; RGEL 2;
      RGSF 2
Peake, Mervyn 1911-1968 .... **CLC 7, 54**
      See also CA 5-8R; CAAS 25-28R; CANR
      3; DLB 15, 160, 255; FANT; MTCW 1;
      RGEL 2; SATA 23; SFW 4
Pearce, Philippa 1920-2006
      See Christie, Philippa
      See also CA 5-8R; CANR 4, 109; CWRI 5;
      FANT; MAICYA 2
Pearl, Eric
      See Elman, Richard (Martin)
Pearson, T. R. 1956- .... **CLC 39**
      See also CA 130; CAAE 120; CANR 97,
      147; CSW; INT CA-130
Pearson, Thomas Reid
      See Pearson, T. R.
Peck, Dale 1967- .... **CLC 81**
      See also CA 146; CANR 72, 127; GLL 2
Peck, John (Frederick) 1941- .... **CLC 3**
      See also CA 49-52; CANR 3, 100; CP 4, 5,
      6, 7
Peck, Richard 1934- .... **CLC 21**
      See also AAYA 1, 24; BYA 1, 6, 8, 11; CA
      85-88; CANR 19, 38, 129; CLR 15; INT
      CANR-19; JRDA; MAICYA 1, 2; SAAS
      2; SATA 18, 55, 97, 110, 158; SATA-
      Essay 110; WYA; YAW
Peck, Richard Wayne
      See Peck, Richard
Peck, Robert Newton 1928- .... **CLC 17**
      See also AAYA 3, 43; BYA 1, 6; CA 182;
      81-84, 182; CANR 31, 63, 127; CLR 45;
      DA; DAC; DAM MST; JRDA; LAIT 3;
      MAICYA 1, 2; SAAS 1; SATA 21, 62,
      111, 156; SATA-Essay 108; WYA; YAW

Pincherle, Alberto 1907-1990 ...... **CLC 11, 18**
See Moravia, Alberto
See also CA 25-28R; CAAS 132; CANR
33, 63, 142; DAM NOV; MTCW 1;
MTFW 2005

Pinckney, Darryl 1953- .... **CLC 76**
See also BW 2, 3; CA 143; CANR 79

Pindar 518(?)B.C.-438(?)B.C. .... **CMLC 12;
PC 19**
See also AW 1; CDWLB 1; DLB 176;
RGWL 2

Pineda, Cecile 1942- .... **CLC 39**
See also CA 118; DLB 209

Pinero, Arthur Wing 1855-1934 .... **TCLC 32**
See also CA 153; CAAE 110; DAM DRAM;
DLB 10; RGEL 2

Pinero, Miguel (Antonio Gomez)
1946-1988 .... **CLC 4, 55**
See also CA 61-64; CAAS 125; CAD;
CANR 29, 90; DLB 266; HW 1; LLW

Pinget, Robert 1919-1997 .... **CLC 7, 13, 37**
See also CA 85-88; CAAS 160; CWW 2;
DLB 83; EWL 3; GFL 1789 to the Present

Pink Floyd
See Barrett, (Roger) Syd; Gilmour, David;
Mason, Nick; Waters, Roger; Wright, Rick

Pinkney, Edward 1802-1828 .... **NCLC 31**
See also DLB 248

Pinkwater, D. Manus
See Pinkwater, Daniel Manus

Pinkwater, Daniel
See Pinkwater, Daniel Manus

Pinkwater, Daniel M.
See Pinkwater, Daniel Manus

Pinkwater, Daniel Manus 1941- .... **CLC 35**
See also AAYA 1, 46; BYA 9; CA 29-32R;
CANR 12, 38, 89, 143; CLR 4; CSW;
FANT; JRDA; MAICYA 1, 2; SAAS 3;
SATA 8, 46, 76, 114, 158; SFW 4; YAW

Pinkwater, Manus
See Pinkwater, Daniel Manus

Pinsky, Robert 1940- .... **CLC 9, 19, 38, 94,
121, 216; PC 27**
See also AMWS 6; CA 29-32R; 4; CANR
58, 97, 138; CP 3, 4, 5, 6, 7; DA3; DAM
POET; DLBY 1982, 1998; MAL 5;
MTCW 2; MTFW 2005; PFS 18; RGAL
4; TCLE 1:2

Pinta, Harold
See Pinter, Harold

Pinter, Harold 1930- .. **CLC 1, 3, 6, 9, 11, 15,
27, 58, 73, 199; DC 15; WLC 4**
See also BRWR 1; BRWS 1; CA 5-8R;
CANR 33, 65, 112, 145; CBD; CD 5, 6;
CDBLB 1960 to Present; CP 1; DA; DA3;
DAB; DAC; DAM DRAM, MST; DFS 3,
5, 7, 14; DLB 13, 310, 331; EWL 3;
IDFW 3, 4; LMFS 2; MTCW 1, 2; MTFW
2005; RGEL 2; RGHL; TEA

Piozzi, Hester Lynch (Thrale)
1741-1821 .... **NCLC 57**
See also DLB 104, 142

Pirandello, Luigi 1867-1936 .. **DC 5; SSC 22;
TCLC 4, 29, 172; WLC 4**
See also CA 153; CAAE 104; CANR 103;
DA; DA3; DAB; DAC; DAM DRAM,
MST; DFS 4, 9; DLB 264, 331; EW 8;
EWL 3; MTCW 2; MTFW 2005; RGSF
2; RGWL 2, 3; WLIT 7

Pirsig, Robert M(aynard) 1928- ... **CLC 4, 6,
73**
See also CA 53-56; CANR 42, 74; CPW 1;
DA3; DAM POP; MTCW 1, 2; MTFW
2005; SATA 39

Pisan, Christine de
See Christine de Pizan

Pisarev, Dmitrii Ivanovich
See Pisarev, Dmitry Ivanovich
See also DLB 277

Pisarev, Dmitry Ivanovich
1840-1868 .... **NCLC 25**
See Pisarev, Dmitrii Ivanovich

Pix, Mary (Griffith) 1666-1709 .... **LC 8**
See also DLB 80

Pixerecourt, (Rene Charles) Guilbert de
1773-1844 .... **NCLC 39**
See also DLB 192; GFL 1789 to the Present

Plaatje, Sol(omon) T(shekisho)
1878-1932 .... **BLCS; TCLC 73**
See also BW 2, 3; CA 141; CANR 79; DLB
125, 225

Plaidy, Jean
See Hibbert, Eleanor Alice Burford

Planche, James Robinson
1796-1880 .... **NCLC 42**
See also RGEL 2

Plant, Robert 1948- .... **CLC 12**

Plante, David 1940- .... **CLC 7, 23, 38**
See also CA 37-40R; CANR 12, 36, 58, 82,
152; CN 2, 3, 4, 5, 6, 7; DAM NOV;
DLBY 1983; INT CANR-12; MTCW 1

Plante, David Robert
See Plante, David

Plath, Sylvia 1932-1963 ..... **CLC 1, 2, 3, 5, 9,
11, 14, 17, 50, 51, 62, 111; PC 1, 37;
WLC 4**
See also AAYA 13; AMWR 2; AMWS 1;
BPFB 3; CA 19-20; CANR 34, 101; CAP
2; CDALB 1941-1968; DA; DA3; DAB;
DAC; DAM MST, POET; DLB 5, 6, 152;
EWL 3; EXPN; EXPP; FL 1:6; FW; LAIT
4; MAL 5; MBL; MTCW 1, 2; MTFW
2005; NFS 1; PAB; PFS 1, 15; RGAL 4;
SATA 96; TUS; WP; YAW

Plato c. 428B.C.-347B.C. .... **CMLC 8, 75;
WLCS**
See also AW 1; CDWLB 1; DA; DA3;
DAB; DAC; DAM MST; DLB 176; LAIT
1; LATS 1:1; RGWL 2, 3; WLIT 8

Platonov, Andrei
See Klimentov, Andrei Platonovich

Platonov, Andrei Platonovich
See Klimentov, Andrei Platonovich
See also DLB 272

Platonov, Andrey Platonovich
See Klimentov, Andrei Platonovich
See also EWL 3

Platt, Kin 1911- .... **CLC 26**
See also AAYA 11; CA 17-20R; CANR 11;
JRDA; SAAS 17; SATA 21, 86; WYA

Plautus c. 254B.C.-c. 184B.C. ...... **CMLC 24;
DC 6**
See also AW 1; CDWLB 1; DLB 211;
RGWL 2, 3; WLIT 8

Plick et Plock
See Simenon, Georges (Jacques Christian)

Plieksans, Janis
See Rainis, Janis

Plimpton, George 1927-2003 .... **CLC 36**
See also AITN 1; AMWS 16; CA 21-24R;
CAAS 224; CANR 32, 70, 103, 133; DLB
185, 241; MTCW 1, 2; MTFW 2005;
SATA 10; SATA-Obit 150

Pliny the Elder c. 23-79 .... **CMLC 23**
See also DLB 211

Pliny the Younger c. 61-c. 112 ...... **CMLC 62**
See also AW 2; DLB 211

Plomer, William Charles Franklin
1903-1973 .... **CLC 4, 8**
See also AFW; BRWS 11; CA 21-22; CANR
34; CAP 2; CN 1; CP 1, 2; DLB 20, 162,
191, 225; EWL 3; MTCW 1; RGEL 2;
RGSF 2; SATA 24

Plotinus 204-270 .... **CMLC 46**
See also CDWLB 1; DLB 176

Plowman, Piers
See Kavanagh, Patrick (Joseph)

Plum, J.
See Wodehouse, P(elham) G(renville)

Plumly, Stanley (Ross) 1939- .... **CLC 33**
See also CA 110; CAAE 108; CANR 97;
CP 3, 4, 5, 6, 7; DLB 5, 193; INT CA-
110

Plumpe, Friedrich Wilhelm
See Murnau, F.W.

Plutarch c. 46-c. 120 .... **CMLC 60**
See also AW 2; CDWLB 1; DLB 176;
RGWL 2, 3; TWA; WLIT 8

Po Chu-i 772-846 .... **CMLC 24**

Podhoretz, Norman 1930- .... **CLC 189**
See also AMWS 8; CA 9-12R; CANR 7,
78, 135

Poe, Edgar Allan 1809-1849 ..... **NCLC 1, 16,
55, 78, 94, 97, 117; PC 1, 54; SSC 1,
22, 34, 35, 54, 88; WLC 4**
See also AAYA 14; AMW; AMWC 1;
AMWR 2; BPFB 3; BYA 5, 11; CDALB
1640-1865; CMW 4; DA; DA3; DAB;
DAC; DAM MST, POET; DLB 3, 59, 73,
74, 248, 254; EXPP; EXPS; GL 3; HGG;
LAIT 2; LATS 1:1; LMFS 1; MSW; PAB;
PFS 1, 3, 9; RGAL 4; RGSF 2; SATA 23;
SCFW 1, 2; SFW 4; SSFS 2, 4, 7, 8, 16;
SUFW; TUS; WP; WYA

Poet of Titchfield Street, The
See Pound, Ezra (Weston Loomis)

Poggio Bracciolini, Gian Francesco
1380-1459 .... **LC 125**

Pohl, Frederik 1919- .... **CLC 18; SSC 25**
See also AAYA 24; CA 188; 61-64; 188; 1;
CANR 11, 37, 81, 140; CN 1, 2, 3, 4, 5,
6; DLB 8; INT CANR-11; MTCW 1, 2;
MTFW 2005; SATA 24; SCFW 1, 2; SFW
4

Poirier, Louis 1910-
See Gracq, Julien
See also CA 126; CAAE 122; CANR 141

Poitier, Sidney 1927- .... **CLC 26**
See also AAYA 60; BW 1; CA 117; CANR
94

Pokagon, Simon 1830-1899 .... **NNAL**
See also DAM MULT

Polanski, Roman 1933- .... **CLC 16, 178**
See also CA 77-80

Poliakoff, Stephen 1952- .... **CLC 38**
See also CA 106; CANR 116; CBD; CD 5,
6; DLB 13

Police, The
See Copeland, Stewart (Armstrong); Summers, Andrew James

Polidori, John William
1795-1821 .... **NCLC 51; SSC 97**
See also DLB 116; HGG

Poliziano, Angelo 1454-1494 .... **LC 120**
See also WLIT 7

Pollitt, Katha 1949- .... **CLC 28, 122**
See also CA 122; CAAE 120; CANR 66,
108; MTCW 1, 2; MTFW 2005

Pollock, (Mary) Sharon 1936- .... **CLC 50**
See also CA 141; CANR 132; CD 5; CWD;
DAC; DAM DRAM, MST; DFS 3; DLB
60; FW

Pollock, Sharon 1936- .... **DC 20**
See also CD 6

Polo, Marco 1254-1324 .... **CMLC 15**
See also WLIT 7

Polonsky, Abraham (Lincoln)
1910-1999 .... **CLC 92**
See also CA 104; CAAS 187; DLB 26; INT
CA-104

Polybius c. 200B.C.-c. 118B.C. ...... **CMLC 17**
See also AW 1; DLB 176; RGWL 2, 3

Pomerance, Bernard 1940- .... **CLC 13**
See also CA 101; CAD; CANR 49, 134;
CD 5, 6; DAM DRAM; DFS 9; LAIT 2

Pritchard, William H(arrison)
1932- .... **CLC 34**
See also CA 65-68; CANR 23, 95; DLB
111

Pritchett, V(ictor) S(awdon)
1900-1997 ... **CLC 5, 13, 15, 41; SSC 14**
See also BPFB 3; BRWS 3; CA 61-64;
CAAS 157; CANR 31, 63; CN 1, 2, 3, 4,
5, 6; DA3; DAM NOV; DLB 15, 139;
EWL 3; MTCW 1, 2; MTFW 2005; RGEL
2; RGSF 2; TEA

Private 19022
See Manning, Frederic

Probst, Mark 1925- .... **CLC 59**
See also CA 130

Procaccino, Michael
See Cristofer, Michael

Proclus c. 412-c. 485 .... **CMLC 81**

Prokosch, Frederic 1908-1989 ...... **CLC 4, 48**
See also CA 73-76; CAAS 128; CANR 82;
CN 1, 2, 3, 4; CP 1, 2, 3, 4; DLB 48;
MTCW 2

Propertius, Sextus c. 50B.C.-c.
16B.C. .... **CMLC 32**
See also AW 2; CDWLB 1; DLB 211;
RGWL 2, 3; WLIT 8

Prophet, The
See Dreiser, Theodore

Prose, Francine 1947- .... **CLC 45, 231**
See also AMWS 16; CA 112; CAAE 109;
CANR 46, 95, 132; DLB 234; MTFW
2005; SATA 101, 149

Protagoras c. 490B.C.-420B.C. ...... **CMLC 85**
See also DLB 176

Proudhon
See Cunha, Euclides (Rodrigues Pimenta)
da

Proulx, Annie
See Proulx, E. Annie

Proulx, E. Annie 1935- .... **CLC 81, 158**
See also AMWS 7; BPFB 3; CA 145;
CANR 65, 110; CN 6, 7; CPW 1; DA3;
DAM POP; MAL 5; MTCW 2; MTFW
2005; SSFS 18, 23

Proulx, Edna Annie
See Proulx, E. Annie

Proust, (Valentin-Louis-George-Eugene)
Marcel 1871-1922 ..... **SSC 75; TCLC 7,**
13, 33; WLC 5
See also AAYA 58; BPFB 3; CA 120;
CAAE 104; CANR 110; DA; DA3; DAB;
DAC; DAM MST, NOV; DLB 65; EW 8;
EWL 3; GFL 1789 to the Present; MTCW
1, 2; MTFW 2005; RGWL 2, 3; TWA

Prowler, Harley
See Masters, Edgar Lee

Prudentius, Aurelius Clemens 348-c.
405 .... **CMLC 78**
See also EW 1; RGWL 2, 3

Prudhomme, Rene Francois Armand
1839-1907
See Sully Prudhomme, Rene-Francois-
Armand
See also CA 170

Prus, Boleslaw 1845-1912 .... **TCLC 48**
See also RGWL 2, 3

Pryor, Aaron Richard
See Pryor, Richard

Pryor, Richard 1940-2005 .... **CLC 26**
See also CA 152; CAAE 122; CAAS 246

Pryor, Richard Franklin Lenox Thomas
See Pryor, Richard

Przybyszewski, Stanislaw
1868-1927 .... **TCLC 36**
See also CA 160; DLB 66; EWL 3

Pseudo-Dionysius the Areopagite fl. c. 5th
cent. - .... **CMLC 89**
See also DLB 115

Pteleon
See Grieve, C(hristopher) M(urray)
See also DAM POET

Puckett, Lute
See Masters, Edgar Lee

Puig, Manuel 1932-1990 .... **CLC 3, 5, 10, 28,**
65, 133; HLC 2
See also BPFB 3; CA 45-48; CANR 2, 32,
63; CDWLB 3; DA3; DAM MULT; DLB
113; DNFS 1; EWL 3; GLL 1; HW 1, 2;
LAW; MTCW 1, 2; MTFW 2005; RGWL
2, 3; TWA; WLIT 1

Pulitzer, Joseph 1847-1911 .... **TCLC 76**
See also CAAE 114; DLB 23

Purchas, Samuel 1577(?)-1626 .... **LC 70**
See also DLB 151

Purdy, A(lfred) W(ellington)
1918-2000 .... **CLC 3, 6, 14, 50**
See also CA 81-84; 17; CAAS 189; CANR
42, 66; CP 1, 2, 3, 4, 5, 6, 7; DAC; DAM
MST, POET; DLB 88; PFS 5; RGEL 2

Purdy, James (Amos) 1923- .... **CLC 2, 4, 10,**
28, 52
See also AMWS 7; CA 33-36R; 1; CANR
19, 51, 132; CN 1, 2, 3, 4, 5, 6, 7; DLB
2, 218; EWL 3; INT CANR-19; MAL 5;
MTCW 1; RGAL 4

Pure, Simon
See Swinnerton, Frank Arthur

Pushkin, Aleksandr Sergeevich
See Pushkin, Alexander (Sergeyevich)
See also DLB 205

Pushkin, Alexander (Sergeyevich)
1799-1837 .... **NCLC 3, 27, 83; PC 10;**
SSC 27, 55, 99; WLC 5
See Pushkin, Aleksandr Sergeevich
See also DA; DA3; DAB; DAC; DAM
DRAM, MST, POET; EW 5; EXPS; RGSF
2; RGWL 2, 3; SATA 61; SSFS 9; TWA

P'u Sung-ling 1640-1715 .... **LC 49; SSC 31**

Putnam, Arthur Lee
See Alger, Horatio, Jr.

Puttenham, George 1529(?)-1590 ...... **LC 116**
See also DLB 281

Puzo, Mario 1920-1999 .... **CLC 1, 2, 6, 36,**
107
See also BPFB 3; CA 65-68; CAAS 185;
CANR 4, 42, 65, 99, 131; CN 1, 2, 3, 4,
5, 6; CPW; DA3; DAM NOV, POP; DLB
6; MTCW 1, 2; MTFW 2005; NFS 16;
RGAL 4

Pygge, Edward
See Barnes, Julian

Pyle, Ernest Taylor 1900-1945
See Pyle, Ernie
See also CA 160; CAAE 115

Pyle, Ernie .... **TCLC 75**
See Pyle, Ernest Taylor
See also DLB 29; MTCW 2

Pyle, Howard 1853-1911 .... **TCLC 81**
See also AAYA 57; BYA 2, 4; CA 137;
CAAE 109; CLR 22, 117; DLB 42, 188;
DLBD 13; LAIT 1; MAICYA 1, 2; SATA
16, 100; WCH; YAW

Pym, Barbara (Mary Crampton)
1913-1980 .... **CLC 13, 19, 37, 111**
See also BPFB 3; BRWS 2; CA 13-14;
CAAS 97-100; CANR 13, 34; CAP 1;
DLB 14, 207; DLBY 1987; EWL 3;
MTCW 1, 2; MTFW 2005; RGEL 2; TEA

Pynchon, Thomas 1937- .. **CLC 2, 3, 6, 9, 11,**
18, 33, 62, 72, 123, 192, 213; SSC 14,
84; WLC 5
See also AMWS 2; BEST 90:2; BPFB 3;
CA 17-20R; CANR 22, 46, 73, 142; CN
1, 2, 3, 4, 5, 6, 7; CPW 1; DA; DA3;
DAB; DAC; DAM MST, NOV; DLB 2,
173; EWL 3; MAL 5; MTCW 1,
2; MTFW 2005; NFS 23; RGAL 4; SFW
4; TCLE 1:2; TUS

Pythagoras c. 582B.C.-c. 507B.C. . **CMLC 22**
See also DLB 176

Q
See Quiller-Couch, Sir Arthur (Thomas)

Qian, Chongzhu
See Ch'ien, Chung-shu

Qian, Sima 145B.C.-c. 89B.C. .... **CMLC 72**

Qian Zhongshu
See Ch'ien, Chung-shu
See also CWW 2; DLB 328

Qroll
See Dagerman, Stig (Halvard)

Quarles, Francis 1592-1644 .... **LC 117**
See also DLB 126; RGEL 2

Quarrington, Paul (Lewis) 1953- ..... **CLC 65**
See also CA 129; CANR 62, 95

Quasimodo, Salvatore 1901-1968 .... **CLC 10;**
PC 47
See also CA 13-16; CAAS 25-28R; CAP 1;
DLB 114, 332; EW 12; EWL 3; MTCW
1; RGWL 2, 3

Quatermass, Martin
See Carpenter, John (Howard)

Quay, Stephen 1947- .... **CLC 95**
See also CA 189

Quay, Timothy 1947- .... **CLC 95**
See also CA 189

Queen, Ellery .... **CLC 3, 11**
See Dannay, Frederic; Davidson, Avram
(James); Deming, Richard; Fairman, Paul
W.; Flora, Fletcher; Hoch, Edward
D(entinger); Kane, Henry; Lee, Manfred
B.; Marlowe, Stephen; Powell, (Oval) Tal-
mage; Sheldon, Walter J(ames); Sturgeon,
Theodore (Hamilton); Tracy, Don(ald
Fiske); Vance, Jack
See also BPFB 3; CMW 4; MSW; RGAL 4

Queen, Ellery, Jr.
See Dannay, Frederic; Lee, Manfred B.

Queneau, Raymond 1903-1976 ..... **CLC 2, 5,**
10, 42
See also CA 77-80; CAAS 69-72; CANR
32; DLB 72, 258; EW 12; EWL 3; GFL
1789 to the Present; MTCW 1, 2; RGWL
2, 3

Quevedo, Francisco de 1580-1645 .... **LC 23**

Quiller-Couch, Sir Arthur (Thomas)
1863-1944 .... **TCLC 53**
See also CA 166; CAAE 118; DLB 135,
153, 190; HGG; RGEL 2; SUFW 1

Quin, Ann 1936-1973 .... **CLC 6**
See also CA 9-12R; CAAS 45-48; CANR
148; CN 1; DLB 14, 231

Quin, Ann Marie
See Quin, Ann

Quincey, Thomas de
See De Quincey, Thomas

Quindlen, Anna 1953- .... **CLC 191**
See also AAYA 35; CA 138; CANR 73, 126;
DA3; DLB 292; MTCW 2; MTFW 2005

Quinn, Martin
See Smith, Martin Cruz

Quinn, Peter 1947- .... **CLC 91**
See also CA 197; CANR 147

Quinn, Peter A.
See Quinn, Peter

Quinn, Simon
See Smith, Martin Cruz

Quintana, Leroy V. 1944- ...... **HLC 2; PC 36**
See also CA 131; CANR 65, 139; DAM
MULT; DLB 82; HW 1, 2

Quintilian c. 40-c. 100 .... **CMLC 77**
See also AW 2; DLB 211; RGWL 2, 3

Quintillian 0035-0100 .... **CMLC 77**

Quiroga, Horacio (Sylvestre)
1878-1937 ... **HLC 2; SSC 89; TCLC 20**
See also CA 131; CAAE 117; DAM MULT;
EWL 3; HW 1; LAW; MTCW 1; RGSF
2; WLIT 1

Reeve, Clara 1729-1807 .... **NCLC 19**
See also DLB 39; RGEL 2

Reich, Wilhelm 1897-1957 .... **TCLC 57**
See also CA 199

Reid, Christopher (John) 1949- .... **CLC 33**
See also CA 140; CANR 89; CP 4, 5, 6, 7;
DLB 40; EWL 3

Reid, Desmond
See Moorcock, Michael

Reid Banks, Lynne 1929-
See Banks, Lynne Reid
See also AAYA 49; CA 1-4R; CANR 6, 22,
38, 87; CLR 24; CN 1, 2, 3, 7; JRDA;
MAICYA 1, 2; SATA 22, 75, 111, 165;
YAW

Reilly, William K.
See Creasey, John

Reiner, Max
See Caldwell, (Janet Miriam) Taylor
(Holland)

Reis, Ricardo
See Pessoa, Fernando (Antonio Nogueira)

Reizenstein, Elmer Leopold
See Rice, Elmer (Leopold)
See also EWL 3

Remarque, Erich Maria 1898-1970 . **CLC 21**
See also AAYA 27; BPFB 3; CA 77-80;
CAAS 29-32R; CDWLB 2; DA; DA3;
DAB; DAC; DAM MST, NOV; DLB 56;
EWL 3; EXPN; LAIT 3; MTCW 1, 2;
MTFW 2005; NFS 4; RGHL; RGWL 2, 3

Remington, Frederic S(ackrider)
1861-1909 .... **TCLC 89**
See also CA 169; CAAE 108; DLB 12, 186,
188; SATA 41; TCWW 2

Remizov, A.
See Remizov, Aleksei (Mikhailovich)

Remizov, A. M.
See Remizov, Aleksei (Mikhailovich)

Remizov, Aleksei (Mikhailovich)
1877-1957 .... **TCLC 27**
See Remizov, Alexey Mikhaylovich
See also CA 133; CAAE 125; DLB 295

Remizov, Alexey Mikhaylovich
See Remizov, Aleksei (Mikhailovich)
See also EWL 3

Renan, Joseph Ernest 1823-1892 . **NCLC 26,
145**
See also GFL 1789 to the Present

Renard, Jules(-Pierre) 1864-1910 .. **TCLC 17**
See also CA 202; CAAE 117; GFL 1789 to
the Present

Renart, Jean fl. 13th cent. - .... **CMLC 83**

Renault, Mary .... **CLC 3, 11, 17**
See Challans, Mary
See also BPFB 3; BYA 2; CN 1, 2, 3;
DLBY 1983; EWL 3; GLL 1; LAIT 1;
RGEL 2; RHW

Rendell, Ruth 1930- .... **CLC 28, 48**
See Vine, Barbara
See also BPFB 3; BRWS 9; CA 109; CANR
32, 52, 74, 127; CN 5, 6, 7; CPW; DAM
POP; DLB 87, 276; INT CANR-32;
MSW; MTCW 1, 2; MTFW 2005

Rendell, Ruth Barbara
See Rendell, Ruth

Renoir, Jean 1894-1979 .... **CLC 20**
See also CA 129; CAAS 85-88

Resnais, Alain 1922- .... **CLC 16**

Revard, Carter 1931- .... **NNAL**
See also CA 144; CANR 81, 153; PFS 5

Reverdy, Pierre 1889-1960 .... **CLC 53**
See also CA 97-100; CAAS 89-92; DLB
258; EWL 3; GFL 1789 to the Present

Rexroth, Kenneth 1905-1982 .... **CLC 1, 2, 6,
11, 22, 49, 112; PC 20**
See also BG 1:3; CA 5-8R; CAAS 107;
CANR 14, 34, 63; CDALB 1941-1968;
CP 1, 2, 3; DAM POET; DLB 16, 48, 165,
212; DLBY 1982; EWL 3; INT CANR-
14; MAL 5; MTCW 1, 2; MTFW 2005;
RGAL 4

Reyes, Alfonso 1889-1959 .... **HLCS 2; TCLC
33**
See also CA 131; EWL 3; HW 1; LAW

Reyes y Basoalto, Ricardo Eliecer Neftali
See Neruda, Pablo

Reymont, Wladyslaw (Stanislaw)
1868(?)-1925 .... **TCLC 5**
See also CAAE 104; DLB 332; EWL 3

Reynolds, John Hamilton
1794-1852 .... **NCLC 146**
See also DLB 96

Reynolds, Jonathan 1942- .... **CLC 6, 38**
See also CA 65-68; CANR 28

Reynolds, Joshua 1723-1792 .... **LC 15**
See also DLB 104

Reynolds, Michael S(hane)
1937-2000 .... **CLC 44**
See also CA 65-68; CAAS 189; CANR 9,
89, 97

Reznikoff, Charles 1894-1976 .... **CLC 9**
See also AMWS 14; CA 33-36; CAAS 61-
64; CAP 2; CP 1, 2; DLB 28, 45; RGHL;
WP

Rezzori, Gregor von
See Rezzori d'Arezzo, Gregor von

Rezzori d'Arezzo, Gregor von
1914-1998 .... **CLC 25**
See also CA 136; CAAE 122; CAAS 167

Rhine, Richard
See Silverstein, Alvin; Silverstein, Virginia
B(arbara Opshelor)

Rhodes, Eugene Manlove
1869-1934 .... **TCLC 53**
See also CA 198; DLB 256; TCWW 1, 2

R'hoone, Lord
See Balzac, Honore de

Rhys, Jean 1890-1979 .... **CLC 2, 4, 6, 14, 19,
51, 124; SSC 21, 76**
See also BRWS 2; CA 25-28R; CAAS 85-
88; CANR 35, 62; CDBLB 1945-1960;
CDWLB 3; CN 1, 2; DA3; DAM NOV;
DLB 36, 117, 162; DNFS 2; EWL 3;
LATS 1:1; MTCW 1, 2; MTFW 2005;
NFS 19; RGEL 2; RGSF 2; RHW; TEA;
WWE 1

Ribeiro, Darcy 1922-1997 .... **CLC 34**
See also CA 33-36R; CAAS 156; EWL 3

Ribeiro, Joao Ubaldo (Osorio Pimentel)
1941- .... **CLC 10, 67**
See also CA 81-84; CWW 2; EWL 3

Ribman, Ronald (Burt) 1932- .... **CLC 7**
See also CA 21-24R; CAD; CANR 46, 80;
CD 5, 6

Ricci, Nino (Pio) 1959- .... **CLC 70**
See also CA 137; CANR 130; CCA 1

Rice, Anne 1941- .... **CLC 41, 128**
See Rampling, Anne
See also AAYA 9, 53; AMWS 7; BEST
89:2; BPFB 3; CA 65-68; CANR 12, 36,
53, 74, 100, 133; CN 6, 7; CPW; CSW;
DA3; DAM POP; DLB 292; GL 3; GLL
2; HGG; MTCW 2; MTFW 2005; SUFW
2; YAW

Rice, Elmer (Leopold) 1892-1967 ...... **CLC 7,
49**
See Reizenstein, Elmer Leopold
See also CA 21-22; CAAS 25-28R; CAP 2;
DAM DRAM; DFS 12; DLB 4, 7; IDTP;
MAL 5; MTCW 1, 2; RGAL 4

Rice, Tim(othy Miles Bindon)
1944- .... **CLC 21**
See also CA 103; CANR 46; DFS 7

Rich, Adrienne 1929- ..... **CLC 3, 6, 7, 11, 18,
36, 73, 76, 125; PC 5**
See also AAYA 69; AMWR 2; AMWS 1;
CA 9-12R; CANR 20, 53, 74, 128;
CDALBS; CP 1, 2, 3, 4, 5, 6, 7; CSW;
CWP; DA3; DAM POET; DLB 5, 67;
EWL 3; EXPP; FL 1:6; FW; MAL 5;
MBL; MTCW 1, 2; MTFW 2005; PAB;
PFS 15; RGAL 4; RGHL; WP

Rich, Barbara
See Graves, Robert

Rich, Robert
See Trumbo, Dalton

Richard, Keith .... **CLC 17**
See Richards, Keith

Richards, David Adams 1950- .... **CLC 59**
See also CA 93-96; CANR 60, 110, 156;
CN 7; DAC; DLB 53; TCLE 1:2

Richards, I(vor) A(rmstrong)
1893-1979 .... **CLC 14, 24**
See also BRWS 2; CA 41-44R; CAAS 89-
92; CANR 34, 74; CP 1, 2; DLB 27; EWL
3; MTCW 2; RGEL 2

Richards, Keith 1943-
See Richard, Keith
See also CA 107; CANR 77

Richardson, Anne
See Roiphe, Anne

Richardson, Dorothy Miller
1873-1957 .... **TCLC 3**
See also CA 192; CAAE 104; DLB 36;
EWL 3; FW; RGEL 2

**Richardson (Robertson), Ethel Florence
Lindesay** 1870-1946
See Richardson, Henry Handel
See also CA 190; CAAE 105; DLB 230;
RHW

Richardson, Henry Handel .... **TCLC 4**
See Richardson (Robertson), Ethel Florence
Lindesay
See also DLB 197; EWL 3; RGEL 2; RGSF
2

Richardson, John 1796-1852 .... **NCLC 55**
See also CCA 1; DAC; DLB 99

Richardson, Samuel 1689-1761 ...... **LC 1, 44;
WLC 5**
See also BRW 3; CDBLB 1660-1789; DA;
DAB; DAC; DAM MST, NOV; DLB 39;
RGEL 2; TEA; WLIT 3

Richardson, Willis 1889-1977 .... **HR 1:3**
See also BW 1; CA 124; DLB 51; SATA 60

Richler, Mordecai 1931-2001 .... **CLC 3, 5, 9,
13, 18, 46, 70, 185**
See also AITN 1; CA 65-68; CAAS 201;
CANR 31, 62, 111; CCA 1; CLR 17; CN
1, 2, 3, 4, 5, 7; CWRI 5; DAC; DAM
MST, NOV; DLB 53; EWL 3; MAICYA
1, 2; MTCW 1, 2; MTFW 2005; RGEL 2;
RGHL; SATA 44, 98; SATA-Brief 27;
TWA

Richter, Conrad (Michael)
1890-1968 .... **CLC 30**
See also AAYA 21; BYA 2; CA 5-8R;
CAAS 25-28R; CANR 23; DLB 9, 212;
LAIT 1; MAL 5; MTCW 1, 2; MTFW
2005; RGAL 4; SATA 3; TCWW 1, 2;
TUS; YAW

Ricostranza, Tom
See Ellis, Trey

Riddell, Charlotte 1832-1906 .... **TCLC 40**
See Riddell, Mrs. J. H.
See also CA 165; DLB 156

Riddell, Mrs. J. H.
See Riddell, Charlotte
See also HGG; SUFW

Saint-Exupery, Antoine Jean Baptiste Marie Roger de
See Saint-Exupery, Antoine de

St. John, David
See Hunt, E. Howard

St. John, J. Hector
See Crevecoeur, Michel Guillaume Jean de

Saint-John Perse
See Leger, (Marie-Rene Auguste) Alexis Saint-Leger
See also EW 10; EWL 3; GFL 1789 to the Present; RGWL 2

Saintsbury, George (Edward Bateman)
1845-1933 .... **TCLC 31**
See also CA 160; DLB 57, 149

Sait Faik .... **TCLC 23**
See Abasiyanik, Sait Faik

Saki .... **SSC 12; TCLC 3; WLC 5**
See Munro, H(ector) H(ugh)
See also BRWS 6; BYA 11; LAIT 2; RGEL 2; SSFS 1; SUFW

Sala, George Augustus 1828-1895 . **NCLC 46**

Saladin 1138-1193 .... **CMLC 38**

Salama, Hannu 1936- .... **CLC 18**
See also CA 244; EWL 3

Salamanca, J(ack) R(ichard) 1922- .. **CLC 4, 15**
See also CA 193; 25-28R, 193

Salas, Floyd 1931- .... **HLC 2**
See also CA 119; 27; CANR 44, 75, 93; DAM MULT; DLB 82; HW 1, 2; MTCW 2; MTFW 2005

Sale, J. Kirkpatrick
See Sale, Kirkpatrick

Sale, John Kirkpatrick
See Sale, Kirkpatrick

Sale, Kirkpatrick 1937- .... **CLC 68**
See also CA 13-16R; CANR 10, 147

Salinas, Luis Omar 1937- ... **CLC 90; HLC 2**
See also AMWS 13; CA 131; CANR 81, 153; DAM MULT; DLB 82; HW 1, 2

Salinas (y Serrano), Pedro
1891(?)-1951 .... **TCLC 17**
See also CAAE 117; DLB 134; EWL 3

Salinger, J.D. 1919- . **CLC 1, 3, 8, 12, 55, 56, 138; SSC 2, 28, 65; WLC 5**
See also AAYA 2, 36; AMW; AMWC 1; BPFB 3; CA 5-8R; CANR 39, 129; CDALB 1941-1968; CLR 18; CN 1, 2, 3, 4, 5, 6, 7; CPW 1; DA; DA3; DAB; DAC; DAM MST, NOV, POP; DLB 2, 102, 173; EWL 3; EXPN; LAIT 4; MAICYA 1, 2; MAL 5; MTCW 1, 2; MTFW 2005; NFS 1; RGAL 4; RGSF 2; SATA 67; SSFS 17; TUS; WYA; YAW

Salisbury, John
See Caute, (John) David

Sallust c. 86B.C.-35B.C. .... **CMLC 68**
See also AW 2; CDWLB 1; DLB 211; RGWL 2, 3

Salter, James 1925- .. **CLC 7, 52, 59; SSC 58**
See also AMWS 9; CA 73-76; CANR 107, 160; DLB 130

Saltus, Edgar (Everton) 1855-1921 . **TCLC 8**
See also CAAE 105; DLB 202; RGAL 4

Saltykov, Mikhail Evgrafovich
1826-1889 .... **NCLC 16**
See also DLB 238:

Saltykov-Shchedrin, N.
See Saltykov, Mikhail Evgrafovich

Samarakis, Andonis
See Samarakis, Antonis
See also EWL 3

Samarakis, Antonis 1919-2003 .... **CLC 5**
See Samarakis, Andonis
See also CA 25-28R; 16; CAAS 224; CANR 36

Sanchez, Florencio 1875-1910 .... **TCLC 37**
See also CA 153; DLB 305; EWL 3; HW 1; LAW

Sanchez, Luis Rafael 1936- .... **CLC 23**
See also CA 128; DLB 305; EWL 3; HW 1; WLIT 1

Sanchez, Sonia 1934- .. **BLC 3; CLC 5, 116, 215; PC 9**
See also BW 2, 3; CA 33-36R; CANR 24, 49, 74, 115; CLR 18; CP 2, 3, 4, 5, 6, 7; CSW; CWP; DA3; DAM MULT; DLB 41; DLBD 8; EWL 3; MAICYA 1, 2; MAL 5; MTCW 1, 2; MTFW 2005; SATA 22, 136; WP

Sancho, Ignatius 1729-1780 .... **LC 84**

Sand, George 1804-1876 ..... **NCLC 2, 42, 57, 174; WLC 5**
See also DA; DA3; DAB; DAC; DAM MST, NOV; DLB 119, 192; EW 6; FL 1:3; FW; GFL 1789 to the Present; RGWL 2, 3; TWA

Sandburg, Carl (August) 1878-1967 . **CLC 1, 4, 10, 15, 35; PC 2, 41; WLC 5**
See also AAYA 24; AMW; BYA 1, 3; CA 5-8R; CAAS 25-28R; CANR 35; CDALB 1865-1917; CLR 67; DA; DA3; DAB; DAC; DAM MST, POET; DLB 17, 54, 284; EWL 3; EXPP; LAIT 2; MAICYA 1, 2; MAL 5; MTCW 1, 2; MTFW 2005; PAB; PFS 3, 6, 12; RGAL 4; SATA 8; TUS; WCH; WP; WYA

Sandburg, Charles
See Sandburg, Carl (August)

Sandburg, Charles A.
See Sandburg, Carl (August)

Sanders, (James) Ed(ward) 1939- .... **CLC 53**
See Sanders, Edward
See also BG 1:3; CA 13-16R; 21; CANR 13, 44, 78; CP 1, 2, 3, 4, 5, 6, 7; DAM POET; DLB 16, 244

Sanders, Edward
See Sanders, (James) Ed(ward)
See also DLB 244

Sanders, Lawrence 1920-1998 .... **CLC 41**
See also BEST 89:4; BPFB 3; CA 81-84; CAAS 165; CANR 33, 62; CMW 4; CPW; DA3; DAM POP; MTCW 1

Sanders, Noah
See Blount, Roy (Alton), Jr.

Sanders, Winston P.
See Anderson, Poul

Sandoz, Mari(e Susette) 1900-1966 .. **CLC 28**
See also CA 1-4R; CAAS 25-28R; CANR 17, 64; DLB 9, 212; LAIT 2; MTCW 1, 2; SATA 5; TCWW 1, 2

Sandys, George 1578-1644 .... **LC 80**
See also DLB 24, 121

Saner, Reg(inald Anthony) 1931- .... **CLC 9**
See also CA 65-68; CP 3, 4, 5, 6, 7

Sankara 788-820 .... **CMLC 32**

Sannazaro, Jacopo 1456(?)-1530 .... **LC 8**
See also RGWL 2, 3; WLIT 7

Sansom, William 1912-1976 . **CLC 2, 6; SSC 21**
See also CA 5-8R; CAAS 65-68; CANR 42; CN 1, 2; DAM NOV; DLB 139; EWL 3; MTCW 1; RGEL 2; RGSF 2

Santayana, George 1863-1952 .... **TCLC 40**
See also AMW; CA 194; CAAE 115; DLB 54, 71, 246, 270; DLBD 13; EWL 3; MAL 5; RGAL 4; TUS

Santiago, Danny .... **CLC 33**
See James, Daniel (Lewis)
See also DLB 122

Santillana, Inigo Lopez de Mendoza, Marques de 1398-1458 .... **LC 111**
See also DLB 286

Santmyer, Helen Hooven
1895-1986 .... **CLC 33; TCLC 133**
See also CA 1-4R; CAAS 118; CANR 15, 33; DLBY 1984; MTCW 1; RHW

Santoka, Taneda 1882-1940 .... **TCLC 72**

Santos, Bienvenido N(uqui)
1911-1996 ... **AAL; CLC 22; TCLC 156**
See also CA 101; CAAS 151; CANR 19, 46; CP 1; DAM MULT; DLB 312; EWL; RGAL 4; SSFS 19

Sapir, Edward 1884-1939 .... **TCLC 108**
See also CA 211; DLB 92

Sapper .... **TCLC 44**
See McNeile, Herman Cyril

Sapphire
See Sapphire, Brenda

Sapphire, Brenda 1950- .... **CLC 99**

Sappho fl. 6th cent. B.C.- ... **CMLC 3, 67; PC 5**
See also CDWLB 1; DA3; DAM POET; DLB 176; FL 1:1; PFS 20; RGWL 2, 3; WLIT 8; WP

Saramago, Jose 1922- ..... **CLC 119; HLCS 1**
See also CA 153; CANR 96; CWW 2; DLB 287, 332; EWL 3; LATS 1:2; SSFS 23

Sarduy, Severo 1937-1993 .... **CLC 6, 97; HLCS 2; TCLC 167**
See also CA 89-92; CAAS 142; CANR 58, 81; CWW 2; DLB 113; EWL 3; HW 1, 2; LAW

Sargeson, Frank 1903-1982 ..... **CLC 31; SSC 99**
See also CA 25-28R; CAAS 106; CANR 38, 79; CN 1, 2, 3; EWL 3; GLL 2; RGEL 2; RGSF 2; SSFS 20

Sarmiento, Domingo Faustino
1811-1888 .... **HLCS 2; NCLC 123**
See also LAW; WLIT 1

Sarmiento, Felix Ruben Garcia
See Dario, Ruben

Saro-Wiwa, Ken(ule Beeson)
1941-1995 .... **CLC 114**
See also BW 2; CA 142; CAAS 150; CANR 60; DLB 157

Saroyan, William 1908-1981 ... **CLC 1, 8, 10, 29, 34, 56; SSC 21; TCLC 137; WLC 5**
See also AAYA 66; CA 5-8R; CAAS 103; CAD; CANR 30; CDALBS; CN 1, 2; DA; DA3; DAB; DAC; DAM DRAM, MST, NOV; DFS 17; DLB 7, 9, 86; DLBY 1981; EWL 3; LAIT 4; MAL 5; MTCW 1, 2; MTFW 2005; RGAL 4; RGSF 2; SATA 23; SATA-Obit 24; SSFS 14; TUS

Sarraute, Nathalie 1900-1999 .... **CLC 1, 2, 4, 8, 10, 31, 80; TCLC 145**
See also BPFB 3; CA 9-12R; CAAS 187; CANR 23, 66, 134; CWW 2; DLB 83, 321; EW 12; EWL 3; GFL 1789 to the Present; MTCW 1, 2; MTFW 2005; RGWL 2, 3

Sarton, May 1912-1995 ... **CLC 4, 14, 49, 91; PC 39; TCLC 120**
See also AMWS 8; CA 1-4R; CAAS 149; CANR 1, 34, 55, 116; CN 1, 2, 3, 4, 5, 6; CP 1, 2, 3, 4, 5, 6; DAM POET; DLB 48; DLBY 1981; EWL 3; FW; INT CANR-34; MAL 5; MTCW 1, 2; MTFW 2005; RGAL 4; SATA 36; SATA-Obit 86; TUS

Sartre, Jean-Paul 1905-1980 . **CLC 1, 4, 7, 9, 13, 18, 24, 44, 50, 52; DC 3; SSC 32; WLC 5**
See also AAYA 62; CA 9-12R; CAAS 97-100; CANR 21; DA; DA3; DAB; DAC; DAM DRAM, MST, NOV; DFS 5; DLB 72, 296, 321, 332; EW 12; EWL 3; GFL 1789 to the Present; LMFS 2; MTCW 1, 2; MTFW 2005; NFS 21; RGHL; RGSF 2; RGWL 2, 3; SSFS 9; TWA

Sassoon, Siegfried (Lorraine)
1886-1967 .... **CLC 36, 130; PC 12**
See also BRW 6; CA 104; CAAS 25-28R;
CANR 36; DAB; DAM MST, NOV,
POET; DLB 20, 191; DLBD 18; EWL 3;
MTCW 1, 2; MTFW 2005; PAB; RGEL
2; TEA
Satterfield, Charles
See Pohl, Frederik
Satyremont
See Peret, Benjamin
Saul, John (W. III) 1942- .... **CLC 46**
See also AAYA 10, 62; BEST 90:4; CA 81-
84; CANR 16, 40, 81; CPW; DAM NOV,
POP; HGG; SATA 98
Saunders, Caleb
See Heinlein, Robert A.
Saura (Atares), Carlos 1932-1998 .... **CLC 20**
See also CA 131; CAAE 114; CANR 79;
HW 1
Sauser, Frederic Louis
See Sauser-Hall, Frederic
Sauser-Hall, Frederic 1887-1961 ...... **CLC 18**
See Cendrars, Blaise
See also CA 102; CAAS 93-96; CANR 36,
62; MTCW 1
Saussure, Ferdinand de
1857-1913 .... **TCLC 49**
See also DLB 242
Savage, Catharine
See Brosman, Catharine Savage
Savage, Richard 1697(?)-1743 .... **LC 96**
See also DLB 95; RGEL 2
Savage, Thomas 1915-2003 .... **CLC 40**
See also CA 132; 15; CAAE 126; CAAS
218; CN 6, 7; INT CA-132; SATA-Obit
147; TCWW 2
Savan, Glenn 1953-2003 .... **CLC 50**
See also CA 225
Sax, Robert
See Johnson, Robert
Saxo Grammaticus c. 1150-c.
1222 .... **CMLC 58**
Saxton, Robert
See Johnson, Robert
Sayers, Dorothy L(eigh) 1893-1957 . **SSC 71;**
TCLC 2, 15
See also BPFB 3; BRWS 3; CA 119; CAAE
104; CANR 60; CDBLB 1914-1945;
CMW 4; DAM POP; DLB 10, 36, 77,
100; MSW; MTCW 1, 2; MTFW 2005;
RGEL 2; SSFS 12; TEA
Sayers, Valerie 1952- .... **CLC 50, 122**
See also CA 134; CANR 61; CSW
Sayles, John (Thomas) 1950- .... **CLC 7, 10,**
14, 198
See also CA 57-60; CANR 41, 84; DLB 44
Scamander, Newt
See Rowling, J.K.
Scammell, Michael 1935- .... **CLC 34**
See also CA 156
Scannell, Vernon 1922- .... **CLC 49**
See also CA 5-8R; CANR 8, 24, 57, 143;
CN 1, 2; CP 1, 2, 3, 4, 5, 6, 7; CWRI 5;
DLB 27; SATA 59
Scarlett, Susan
See Streatfeild, (Mary) Noel
Scarron 1847-1910
See Mikszath, Kalman
Scarron, Paul 1610-1660 .... **LC 116**
See also GFL Beginnings to 1789; RGWL
2, 3
Schaeffer, Susan Fromberg 1941- ..... **CLC 6,**
11, 22
See also CA 49-52; CANR 18, 65, 160; CN
4, 5, 6, 7; DLB 28, 299; MTCW 1, 2;
MTFW 2005; SATA 22

Schama, Simon 1945- .... **CLC 150**
See also BEST 89:4; CA 105; CANR 39,
91
Schama, Simon Michael
See Schama, Simon
Schary, Jill
See Robinson, Jill
Schell, Jonathan 1943- .... **CLC 35**
See also CA 73-76; CANR 12, 117
Schelling, Friedrich Wilhelm Joseph von
1775-1854 .... **NCLC 30**
See also DLB 90
Scherer, Jean-Marie Maurice 1920-
See Rohmer, Eric
See also CA 110
Schevill, James (Erwin) 1920- .... **CLC 7**
See also CA 5-8R; 12; CAD; CD 5, 6; CP
1, 2, 3, 4, 5
Schiller, Friedrich von 1759-1805 ...... **DC 12;**
NCLC 39, 69, 166
See also CDWLB 2; DAM DRAM; DLB
94; EW 5; RGWL 2, 3; TWA
Schisgal, Murray (Joseph) 1926- .... **CLC 6**
See also CA 21-24R; CAD; CANR 48, 86;
CD 5, 6; MAL 5
Schlee, Ann 1934- .... **CLC 35**
See also CA 101; CANR 29, 88; SATA 44;
SATA-Brief 36
Schlegel, August Wilhelm von
1767-1845 .... **NCLC 15, 142**
See also DLB 94; RGWL 2, 3
Schlegel, Friedrich 1772-1829 .... **NCLC 45**
See also DLB 90; EW 5; RGWL 2, 3; TWA
Schlegel, Johann Elias (von)
1719(?)-1749 .... **LC 5**
Schleiermacher, Friedrich
1768-1834 .... **NCLC 107**
See also DLB 90
Schlesinger, Arthur M., Jr.
1917-2007 .... **CLC 84**
See also AITN 1; CA 1-4R; CANR 1, 28,
58, 105; DLB 17; INT CANR-28; MTCW
1, 2; SATA 61
Schlesinger, Arthur Meier, Jr.
See Schlesinger, Arthur M., Jr.
Schlink, Bernhard 1944- .... **CLC 174**
See also CA 163; CANR 116; RGHL
Schmidt, Arno (Otto) 1914-1979 ...... **CLC 56**
See also CA 128; CAAS 109; DLB 69;
EWL 3
Schmitz, Aron Hector 1861-1928
See Svevo, Italo
See also CA 122; CAAE 104; MTCW 1
Schnackenberg, Gjertrud 1953- ...... **CLC 40;**
PC 45
See also AMWS 15; CAAE 116; CANR
100; CP 5, 6, 7; CWP; DLB 120, 282;
PFS 13, 25
Schnackenberg, Gjertrud Cecelia
See Schnackenberg, Gjertrud
Schneider, Leonard Alfred 1925-1966
See Bruce, Lenny
See also CA 89-92
Schnitzler, Arthur 1862-1931 ..... **DC 17; SSC**
15, 61; TCLC 4
See also CAAE 104; CDWLB 2; DLB 81,
118; EW 8; EWL 3; RGSF 2; RGWL 2, 3
Schoenberg, Arnold Franz Walter
1874-1951 .... **TCLC 75**
See also CA 188; CAAE 109
Schonberg, Arnold
See Schoenberg, Arnold Franz Walter
Schopenhauer, Arthur 1788-1860 . **NCLC 51,**
157
See also DLB 90; EW 5
Schor, Sandra (M.) 1932(?)-1990 ..... **CLC 65**
See also CAAS 132

Schorer, Mark 1908-1977 .... **CLC 9**
See also CA 5-8R; CAAS 73-76; CANR 7;
CN 1, 2; DLB 103
Schrader, Paul (Joseph) 1946- . **CLC 26, 212**
See also CA 37-40R; CANR 41; DLB 44
Schreber, Daniel 1842-1911 .... **TCLC 123**
Schreiner, Olive (Emilie Albertina)
1855-1920 .... **TCLC 9**
See also AFW; BRWS 2; CA 154; CAAE
105; DLB 18, 156, 190, 225; EWL 3; FW;
RGEL 2; TWA; WLIT 2; WWE 1
Schulberg, Budd (Wilson) 1914- .. **CLC 7, 48**
See also BPFB 3; CA 25-28R; CANR 19,
87; CN 1, 2, 3, 4, 5, 6, 7; DLB 6, 26, 28;
DLBY 1981, 2001; MAL 5
Schulman, Arnold
See Trumbo, Dalton
Schulz, Bruno 1892-1942 .. **SSC 13; TCLC 5,**
51
See also CA 123; CAAE 115; CANR 86;
CDWLB 4; DLB 215; EWL 3; MTCW 2;
MTFW 2005; RGSF 2; RGWL 2, 3
Schulz, Charles M. 1922-2000 .... **CLC 12**
See also AAYA 39; CA 9-12R; CAAS 187;
CANR 6, 132; INT CANR-6; MTFW
2005; SATA 10; SATA-Obit 118
Schulz, Charles Monroe
See Schulz, Charles M.
Schumacher, E(rnst) F(riedrich)
1911-1977 .... **CLC 80**
See also CA 81-84; CAAS 73-76; CANR
34, 85
Schumann, Robert 1810-1856 ...... **NCLC 143**
Schuyler, George Samuel 1895-1977 . **HR 1:3**
See also BW 2; CA 81-84; CAAS 73-76;
CANR 42; DLB 29, 51
Schuyler, James Marcus 1923-1991 .. **CLC 5,**
23
See also CA 101; CAAS 134; CP 1, 2, 3, 4,
5; DAM POET; DLB 5, 169; EWL 3; INT
CA-101; MAL 5; WP
Schwartz, Delmore (David)
1913-1966 ... **CLC 2, 4, 10, 45, 87; PC 8**
See also AMWS 2; CA 17-18; CAAS 25-
28R; CANR 35; CAP 2; DLB 28, 48;
EWL 3; MAL 5; MTCW 1, 2; MTFW
2005; PAB; RGAL 4; TUS
Schwartz, Ernst
See Ozu, Yasujiro
Schwartz, John Burnham 1965- .... **CLC 59**
See also CA 132; CANR 116
Schwartz, Lynne Sharon 1939- .... **CLC 31**
See also CA 103; CANR 44, 89, 160; DLB
218; MTCW 2; MTFW 2005
Schwartz, Muriel A.
See Eliot, T(homas) S(tearns)
Schwarz-Bart, Andre 1928-2006 .... **CLC 2, 4**
See also CA 89-92; CAAS 253; CANR 109;
DLB 299; RGHL
Schwarz-Bart, Simone 1938- . **BLCS; CLC 7**
See also BW 2; CA 97-100; CANR 117;
EWL 3
Schwerner, Armand 1927-1999 .... **PC 42**
See also CA 9-12R; CAAS 179; CANR 50,
85; CP 2, 3, 4, 5, 6; DLB 165
Schwitters, Kurt (Hermann Edward Karl
Julius) 1887-1948 .... **TCLC 95**
See also CA 158
Schwob, Marcel (Mayer Andre)
1867-1905 .... **TCLC 20**
See also CA 168; CAAE 117; DLB 123;
GFL 1789 to the Present
Sciascia, Leonardo 1921-1989 .. **CLC 8, 9, 41**
See also CA 85-88; CAAS 130; CANR 35;
DLB 177; EWL 3; MTCW 1; RGWL 2, 3

Shirley, James 1596-1666 .... **DC 25; LC 96**
See also DLB 58; RGEL 2
Sholokhov, Mikhail (Aleksandrovich)
1905-1984 .... **CLC 7, 15**
See also CA 101; CAAS 112; DLB 272,
332; EWL 3; MTCW 1, 2; MTFW 2005;
RGWL 2, 3; SATA-Obit 36
Sholom Aleichem 1859-1916 .... **SSC 33;**
TCLC 1, 35
See Rabinovitch, Sholem
See also DLB 333; TWA
Shone, Patric
See Hanley, James
Showalter, Elaine 1941- .... **CLC 169**
See also CA 57-60; CANR 58, 106; DLB
67; FW; GLL 2
Shreve, Susan
See Shreve, Susan Richards
Shreve, Susan Richards 1939- .... **CLC 23**
See also CA 49-52; 5; CANR 5, 38, 69, 100,
159; MAICYA 1, 2; SATA 46, 95, 152;
SATA-Brief 41
Shue, Larry 1946-1985 .... **CLC 52**
See also CA 145; CAAS 117; DAM DRAM;
DFS 7
Shu-Jen, Chou 1881-1936
See Lu Hsun
See also CAAE 104
Shulman, Alix Kates 1932- .... **CLC 2, 10**
See also CA 29-32R; CANR 43; FW; SATA
7
Shuster, Joe 1914-1992 .... **CLC 21**
See also AAYA 50
Shute, Nevil .... **CLC 30**
See Norway, Nevil Shute
See also BPFB 3; DLB 255; NFS 9; RHW;
SFW 4
Shuttle, Penelope (Diane) 1947- .... **CLC 7**
See also CA 93-96; CANR 39, 84, 92, 108;
CP 3, 4, 5, 6, 7; CWP; DLB 14, 40
Shvarts, Elena 1948- .... **PC 50**
See also CA 147
Sidhwa, Bapsi 1939-
See Sidhwa, Bapsy (N.)
See also CN 6, 7; DLB 323
Sidhwa, Bapsy (N.) 1938- .... **CLC 168**
See Sidhwa, Bapsi
See also CA 108; CANR 25, 57; FW
Sidney, Mary 1561-1621 .... **LC 19, 39**
See Sidney Herbert, Mary
Sidney, Sir Philip 1554-1586 .... **LC 19, 39,**
131; PC 32
See also BRW 1; BRWR 2; CDBLB Before
1660; DA; DA3; DAB; DAC; DAM MST,
POET; DLB 167; EXPP; PAB; RGEL 2;
TEA; WP
Sidney Herbert, Mary
See Sidney, Mary
See also DLB 167
Siegel, Jerome 1914-1996 .... **CLC 21**
See Siegel, Jerry
See also CA 169; CAAE 116; CAAS 151
Siegel, Jerry
See Siegel, Jerome
See also AAYA 50
Sienkiewicz, Henryk (Adam Alexander Pius)
1846-1916 .... **TCLC 3**
See also CA 134; CAAE 104; CANR 84;
DLB 332; EWL 3; RGSF 2; RGWL 2, 3
Sierra, Gregorio Martinez
See Martinez Sierra, Gregorio
Sierra, Maria de la O'LeJarraga Martinez
See Martinez Sierra, Maria
Sigal, Clancy 1926- .... **CLC 7**
See also CA 1-4R; CANR 85; CN 1, 2, 3,
4, 5, 6, 7
Siger of Brabant 1240(?)-1284(?) . **CMLC 69**
See also DLB 115

Sigourney, Lydia H.
See Sigourney, Lydia Howard (Huntley)
See also DLB 73, 183
Sigourney, Lydia Howard (Huntley)
1791-1865 .... **NCLC 21, 87**
See Sigourney, Lydia H.; Sigourney, Lydia
Huntley
See also DLB 1
Sigourney, Lydia Huntley
See Sigourney, Lydia Howard (Huntley)
See also DLB 42, 239, 243
Siguenza y Gongora, Carlos de
1645-1700 .... **HLCS 2; LC 8**
See also LAW
Sigurjonsson, Johann
See Sigurjonsson, Johann
Sigurjonsson, Johann 1880-1919 ... **TCLC 27**
See also CA 170; DLB 293; EWL 3
Sikelianos, Angelos 1884-1951 .... **PC 29;**
TCLC 39
See also EWL 3; RGWL 2, 3
Silkin, Jon 1930-1997 .... **CLC 2, 6, 43**
See also CA 5-8R; 5; CANR 89; CP 1, 2, 3,
4, 5, 6; DLB 27
Silko, Leslie 1948- ...... **CLC 23, 74, 114, 211;**
NNAL; SSC 37, 66; WLCS
See also AAYA 14; AMWS 4; ANW; BYA
12; CA 122; CAAE 115; CANR 45, 65,
118; CN 4, 5, 6, 7; CP 4, 5, 6, 7; CPW 1;
CWP; DA; DA3; DAC; DAM MST,
MULT, POP; DLB 143, 175, 256, 275;
EWL 3; EXPP; EXPS; LAIT 4; MAL 5;
MTCW 2; MTFW 2005; NFS 4; PFS 9,
16; RGAL 4; RGSF 2; SSFS 4, 8, 10, 11;
TCWW 1, 2
Sillanpaa, Frans Eemil 1888-1964 ... **CLC 19**
See also CA 129; CAAS 93-96; DLB 332;
EWL 3; MTCW 1
Sillitoe, Alan 1928- .. **CLC 1, 3, 6, 10, 19, 57,**
148
See also AITN 1; BRWS 5; CA 191; 9-12R,
191; 2; CANR 8, 26, 55, 139; CDBLB
1960 to Present; CN 1, 2, 3, 4, 5, 6; CP 1,
2, 3, 4, 5; DLB 14, 139; EWL 3; MTCW
1, 2; MTFW 2005; RGEL 2; RGSF 2;
SATA 61
Silone, Ignazio 1900-1978 .... **CLC 4**
See also CA 25-28; CAAS 81-84; CANR
34; CAP 2; DLB 264; EW 12; EWL 3;
MTCW 1; RGSF 2; RGWL 2, 3
Silone, Ignazione
See Silone, Ignazio
Silver, Joan Micklin 1935- .... **CLC 20**
See also CA 121; CAAE 114; INT CA-121
Silver, Nicholas
See Faust, Frederick (Schiller)
Silverberg, Robert 1935- .... **CLC 7, 140**
See also AAYA 24; BPFB 3; BYA 7, 9; CA
186; 1-4R, 186; 3; CANR 1, 20, 36, 85,
140; CLR 59; CN 6, 7; CPW; DAM POP;
DLB 8; INT CANR-20; MAICYA 1, 2;
MTCW 1, 2; MTFW 2005; SATA 13, 91;
SATA-Essay 104; SCFW 1, 2; SFW 4;
SUFW 2
Silverstein, Alvin 1933- .... **CLC 17**
See also CA 49-52; CANR 2; CLR 25;
JRDA; MAICYA 1, 2; SATA 8, 69, 124
Silverstein, Shel 1932-1999 .... **PC 49**
See also AAYA 40; BW 3; CA 107; CAAS
179; CANR 47, 74, 81; CLR 5, 96; CWRI
5; JRDA; MAICYA 1, 2; MTCW 2;
MTFW 2005; SATA 33, 92; SATA-Brief
27; SATA-Obit 116
Silverstein, Virginia B(arbara Opshelor)
1937- .... **CLC 17**
See also CA 49-52; CANR 2; CLR 25;
JRDA; MAICYA 1, 2; SATA 8, 69, 124
Sim, Georges
See Simenon, Georges (Jacques Christian)

Simak, Clifford D(onald) 1904-1988 . **CLC 1,**
55
See also CA 1-4R; CAAS 125; CANR 1,
35; DLB 8; MTCW 1; SATA-Obit 56;
SCFW 1, 2; SFW 4
Simenon, Georges (Jacques Christian)
1903-1989 .... **CLC 1, 2, 3, 8, 18, 47**
See also BPFB 3; CA 85-88; CAAS 129;
CANR 35; CMW 4; DA3; DAM POP;
DLB 72; DLBY 1989; EW 12; EWL 3;
GFL 1789 to the Present; MSW; MTCW
1, 2; MTFW 2005; RGWL 2, 3
Simic, Charles 1938- .... **CLC 6, 9, 22, 49, 68,**
130; PC 69
See also AMWS 8; CA 29-32R; 4; CANR
12, 33, 52, 61, 96, 140; CP 2, 3, 4, 5, 6,
7; DA3; DAM POET; DLB 105; MAL 5;
MTCW 2; MTFW 2005; PFS 7; RGAL 4;
WP
Simmel, Georg 1858-1918 .... **TCLC 64**
See also CA 157; DLB 296
Simmons, Charles (Paul) 1924- .... **CLC 57**
See also CA 89-92; INT CA-89-92
Simmons, Dan 1948- .... **CLC 44**
See also AAYA 16, 54; CA 138; CANR 53,
81, 126; CPW; DAM POP; HGG; SUFW
2
Simmons, James (Stewart Alexander)
1933- .... **CLC 43**
See also CA 105; 21; CP 1, 2, 3, 4, 5, 6, 7;
DLB 40
Simms, William Gilmore
1806-1870 .... **NCLC 3**
See also DLB 3, 30, 59, 73, 248, 254;
RGAL 4
Simon, Carly 1945- .... **CLC 26**
See also CA 105
Simon, Claude 1913-2005 ... **CLC 4, 9, 15, 39**
See also CA 89-92; CAAS 241; CANR 33,
117; CWW 2; DAM NOV; DLB 83, 332;
EW 13; EWL 3; GFL 1789 to the Present;
MTCW 1
Simon, Claude Eugene Henri
See Simon, Claude
Simon, Claude Henri Eugene
See Simon, Claude
Simon, Marvin Neil
See Simon, Neil
Simon, Myles
See Follett, Ken
Simon, Neil 1927- .... **CLC 6, 11, 31, 39, 70,**
233; DC 14
See also AAYA 32; AITN 1; AMWS 4; CA
21-24R; CAD; CANR 26, 54, 87, 126;
CD 5, 6; DA3; DAM DRAM; DFS 2, 6,
12, 18; DLB 7, 266; LAIT 4; MAL 5;
MTCW 1, 2; MTFW 2005; RGAL 4; TUS
Simon, Paul 1941(?)- .... **CLC 17**
See also CA 153; CAAE 116; CANR 152
Simon, Paul Frederick
See Simon, Paul
Simonon, Paul 1956(?)- .... **CLC 30**
Simonson, Rick .... **CLC 70**
Simpson, Harriette
See Arnow, Harriette (Louisa) Simpson
Simpson, Louis 1923- ... **CLC 4, 7, 9, 32, 149**
See also AMWS 9; CA 1-4R; 4; CANR 1,
61, 140; CP 1, 2, 3, 4, 5, 6, 7; DAM
POET; DLB 5; MAL 5; MTCW 1, 2;
MTFW 2005; PFS 7, 11, 14; RGAL 4
Simpson, Mona 1957- .... **CLC 44, 146**
See also CA 135; CAAE 122; CANR 68,
103; CN 6, 7; EWL 3
Simpson, Mona Elizabeth
See Simpson, Mona
Simpson, N(orman) F(rederick)
1919- .... **CLC 29**
See also CA 13-16R; CBD; DLB 13; RGEL
2

Snodgrass, W.D. 1926- .... **CLC 2, 6, 10, 18, 68; PC 74**
　See also AMWS 6; CA 1-4R; CANR 6, 36, 65, 85; CP 1, 2, 3, 4, 5, 6, 7; DAM POET; DLB 5; MAL 5; MTCW 1, 2; MTFW 2005; RGAL 4; TCLE 1:2

Snorri Sturluson 1179-1241 .... **CMLC 56**
　See also RGWL 2, 3

Snow, C(harles) P(ercy) 1905-1980 ... **CLC 1, 4, 6, 9, 13, 19**
　See also BRW 7; CA 5-8R; CAAS 101; CANR 28; CDBLB 1945-1960; CN 1, 2; DAM NOV; DLB 15, 77; DLBD 17; EWL 3; MTCW 1, 2; MTFW 2005; RGEL 2; TEA

Snow, Frances Compton
　See Adams, Henry (Brooks)

Snyder, Gary 1930- . **CLC 1, 2, 5, 9, 32, 120; PC 21**
　See also AAYA 72; AMWS 8; ANW; BG 1:3; CA 17-20R; CANR 30, 60, 125; CP 1, 2, 3, 4, 5, 6, 7; DA3; DAM POET; DLB 5, 16, 165, 212, 237, 275; EWL 3; MAL 5; MTCW 2; MTFW 2005; PFS 9, 19; RGAL 4; WP

Snyder, Zilpha Keatley 1927- .... **CLC 17**
　See also AAYA 15; BYA 1; CA 252; 9-12R, 252; CANR 38; CLR 31; JRDA; MAI-CYA 1, 2; SAAS 2; SATA 1, 28, 75, 110, 163; SATA-Essay 112, 163; YAW

Soares, Bernardo
　See Pessoa, Fernando (Antonio Nogueira)

Sobh, A.
　See Shamlu, Ahmad

Sobh, Alef
　See Shamlu, Ahmad

Sobol, Joshua 1939- .... **CLC 60**
　See Sobol, Yehoshua
　See also CA 200; RGHL

Sobol, Yehoshua 1939-
　See Sobol, Joshua
　See also CWW 2

Socrates 470B.C.-399B.C. .... **CMLC 27**

Soderberg, Hjalmar 1869-1941 ...... **TCLC 39**
　See also DLB 259; EWL 3; RGSF 2

Soderbergh, Steven 1963- .... **CLC 154**
　See also AAYA 43; CA 243

Soderbergh, Steven Andrew
　See Soderbergh, Steven

Sodergran, Edith (Irene) 1892-1923
　See Soedergran, Edith (Irene)
　See also CA 202; DLB 259; EW 11; EWL 3; RGWL 2, 3

Soedergran, Edith (Irene) 1892-1923 .... **TCLC 31**
　See Sodergran, Edith (Irene)

Softly, Edgar
　See Lovecraft, H. P.

Softly, Edward
　See Lovecraft, H. P.

Sokolov, Alexander V(sevolodovich) 1943-
　See Sokolov, Sasha
　See also CA 73-76

Sokolov, Raymond 1941- .... **CLC 7**
　See also CA 85-88

Sokolov, Sasha .... **CLC 59**
　See Sokolov, Alexander V(sevolodovich)
　See also CWW 2; DLB 285; EWL 3; RGWL 2, 3

Solo, Jay
　See Ellison, Harlan

Sologub, Fyodor .... **TCLC 9**
　See Teternikov, Fyodor Kuzmich
　See also EWL 3

Solomons, Ikey Esquir
　See Thackeray, William Makepeace

Solomos, Dionysios 1798-1857 .... **NCLC 15**

Solwoska, Mara
　See French, Marilyn

Solzhenitsyn, Aleksandr I. 1918- .. **CLC 1, 2, 4, 7, 9, 10, 18, 26, 34, 78, 134, 235; SSC 32; WLC 5**
　See Solzhenitsyn, Aleksandr Isayevich
　See also AAYA 49; AITN 1; BPFB 3; CA 69-72; CANR 40, 65, 116; DA; DA3; DAB; DAC; DAM MST, NOV; DLB 302, 332; EW 13; EXPS; LAIT 4; MTCW 1, 2; MTFW 2005; NFS 6; RGSF 2; RGWL 2, 3; SSFS 9; TWA

Solzhenitsyn, Aleksandr Isayevich
　See Solzhenitsyn, Aleksandr I.
　See also CWW 2; EWL 3

Somers, Jane
　See Lessing, Doris

Somerville, Edith Oenone 1858-1949 .... **SSC 56; TCLC 51**
　See also CA 196; DLB 135; RGEL 2; RGSF 2

Somerville & Ross
　See Martin, Violet Florence; Somerville, Edith Oenone

Sommer, Scott 1951- .... **CLC 25**
　See also CA 106

Sommers, Christina Hoff 1950- ...... **CLC 197**
　See also CA 153; CANR 95

Sondheim, Stephen (Joshua) 1930- . **CLC 30, 39, 147; DC 22**
　See also AAYA 11, 66; CA 103; CANR 47, 67, 125; DAM DRAM; LAIT 4

Sone, Monica 1919- .... **AAL**
　See also DLB 312

Song, Cathy 1955- .... **AAL; PC 21**
　See also CA 154; CANR 118; CWP; DLB 169, 312; EXPP; FW; PFS 5

Sontag, Susan 1933-2004 ... **CLC 1, 2, 10, 13, 31, 105, 195**
　See also AMWS 3; CA 17-20R; CAAS 234; CANR 25, 51, 74, 97; CN 1, 2, 3, 4, 5, 6, 7; CPW; DA3; DAM POP; DLB 2, 67; EWL 3; MAL 5; MBL; MTCW 1, 2; MTFW 2005; RGAL 4; RHW; SSFS 10

Sophocles 496(?)B.C.-406(?)B.C. .... **CMLC 2, 47, 51, 86; DC 1; WLCS**
　See also AW 1; CDWLB 1; DA; DA3; DAB; DAC; DAM DRAM, MST; DFS 1, 4, 8; DLB 176; LAIT 1; LATS 1:1; LMFS 1; RGWL 2, 3; TWA; WLIT 8

Sordello 1189-1269 .... **CMLC 15**

Sorel, Georges 1847-1922 .... **TCLC 91**
　See also CA 188; CAAE 118

Sorel, Julia
　See Drexler, Rosalyn

Sorokin, Vladimir .... **CLC 59**
　See Sorokin, Vladimir Georgievich

Sorokin, Vladimir Georgievich
　See Sorokin, Vladimir
　See also DLB 285

Sorrentino, Gilbert 1929-2006 .... **CLC 3, 7, 14, 22, 40**
　See also CA 77-80; CAAS 250; CANR 14, 33, 115, 157; CN 3, 4, 5, 6, 7; CP 1, 2, 3, 4, 5, 6, 7; DLB 5, 173; DLBY 1980; INT CANR-14

Soseki
　See Natsume, Soseki
　See also MJW

Soto, Gary 1952- ... **CLC 32, 80; HLC 2; PC 28**
　See also AAYA 10, 37; BYA 11; CA 125; CAAE 119; CANR 50, 74, 107, 157; CLR 38; CP 4, 5, 6, 7; DAM MULT; DLB 82; EWL 3; EXPP; HW 1, 2; INT CA-125; JRDA; LLW; MAICYA 2; MAICYAS 1; MAL 5; MTCW 2; MTFW 2005; PFS 7; RGAL 4; SATA 80, 120, 174; WYA; YAW

Soupault, Philippe 1897-1990 .... **CLC 68**
　See also CA 147; CAAE 116; CAAS 131; EWL 3; GFL 1789 to the Present; LMFS 2

Souster, (Holmes) Raymond 1921- .... **CLC 5, 14**
　See also CA 13-16R; 14; CANR 13, 29, 53; CP 1, 2, 3, 4, 5, 6, 7; DA3; DAC; DAM POET; DLB 88; RGEL 2; SATA 63

Southern, Terry 1924(?)-1995 .... **CLC 7**
　See also AMWS 11; BPFB 3; CA 1-4R; CAAS 150; CANR 1, 55, 107; CN 1, 2, 3, 4, 5, 6; DLB 2; IDFW 3, 4

Southerne, Thomas 1660-1746 .... **LC 99**
　See also DLB 80; RGEL 2

Southey, Robert 1774-1843 .... **NCLC 8, 97**
　See also BRW 4; DLB 93, 107, 142; RGEL 2; SATA 54

Southwell, Robert 1561(?)-1595 .... **LC 108**
　See also DLB 167; RGEL 2; TEA

Southworth, Emma Dorothy Eliza Nevitte 1819-1899 .... **NCLC 26**
　See also DLB 239

Souza, Ernest
　See Scott, Evelyn

Soyinka, Wole 1934- .. **BLC 3; CLC 3, 5, 14, 36, 44, 179; DC 2; WLC 5**
　See also AFW; BW 2, 3; CA 13-16R; CANR 27, 39, 82, 136; CD 5, 6; CDWLB 3; CN 6, 7; CP 1, 2, 3, 4, 5, 6 ,7; DA; DA3; DAB; DAC; DAM DRAM, MST, MULT; DFS 10; DLB 125, 332; EWL 3; MTCW 1, 2; MTFW 2005; RGEL 2; TWA; WLIT 2; WWE 1

Spackman, W(illiam) M(ode) 1905-1990 .... **CLC 46**
　See also CA 81-84; CAAS 132

Spacks, Barry (Bernard) 1931- .... **CLC 14**
　See also CA 154; CANR 33, 109; CP 3, 4, 5, 6, 7; DLB 105

Spanidou, Irini 1946- .... **CLC 44**
　See also CA 185

Spark, Muriel 1918-2006 .... **CLC 2, 3, 5, 8, 13, 18, 40, 94; PC 72; SSC 10**
　See also BRWS 1; CA 5-8R; CAAS 251; CANR 12, 36, 76, 89, 131; CDBLB 1945-1960; CN 1, 2, 3, 4, 5, 6, 7; CP 1, 2, 3, 4, 5, 6, 7; DA3; DAB; DAC; DAM MST, NOV; DLB 15, 139; EWL 3; FW; INT CANR-12; LAIT 4; MTCW 1, 2; MTFW 2005; NFS 22; RGEL 2; TEA; WLIT 4; YAW

Spark, Muriel Sarah
　See Spark, Muriel

Spaulding, Douglas
　See Bradbury, Ray

Spaulding, Leonard
　See Bradbury, Ray

Speght, Rachel 1597-c. 1630 .... **LC 97**
　See also DLB 126

Spence, J. A. D.
　See Eliot, T(homas) S(tearns)

Spencer, Anne 1882-1975 .... **HR 1:3; PC 77**
　See also BW 2; CA 161; DLB 51, 54

Spencer, Elizabeth 1921- .... **CLC 22; SSC 57**
　See also CA 13-16R; CANR 32, 65, 87; CN 1, 2, 3, 4, 5, 6, 7; CSW; DLB 6, 218; EWL 3; MTCW 1; RGAL 4; SATA 14

Spencer, Leonard G.
　See Silverberg, Robert

Spencer, Scott 1945- .... **CLC 30**
　See also CA 113; CANR 51, 148; DLBY 1986

Spender, Stephen 1909-1995 ..... **CLC 1, 2, 5, 10, 41, 91; PC 71**
　See also BRWS 2; CA 9-12R; CAAS 149; CANR 31, 54; CDBLB 1945-1960; CP 1, 2, 3, 4, 5, 6; DA3; DAM POET; DLB 20; EWL 3; MTCW 1, 2; MTFW 2005; PAB; PFS 23; RGEL 2; TEA

Spengler, Oswald (Arnold Gottfried) 1880-1936 .... **TCLC 25**
　See also CA 189; CAAE 118

T. O., Nik
See Annensky, Innokenty (Fyodorovich)

Tabori, George 1914- .... **CLC 19**
See also CA 49-52; CANR 4, 69; CBD; CD
5, 6; DLB 245; RGHL

Tacitus c. 55-c. 117 .... **CMLC 56**
See also AW 2; CDWLB 1; DLB 211;
RGWL 2, 3; WLIT 8

Tagore, Rabindranath 1861-1941 .... **PC 8;
SSC 48; TCLC 3, 53**
See also CA 120; CAAE 104; DA3; DAM
DRAM, POET; DLB 323, 332; EWL 3;
MTCW 1, 2; MTFW 2005; PFS 18; RGEL
2; RGSF 2; RGWL 2, 3; TWA

Taine, Hippolyte Adolphe
1828-1893 .... **NCLC 15**
See also EW 7; GFL 1789 to the Present

Talayesva, Don C. 1890-(?) .... **NNAL**

Talese, Gay 1932- .... **CLC 37, 232**
See also AITN 1; CA 1-4R; CANR 9, 58,
137; DLB 185; INT CANR-9; MTCW 1,
2; MTFW 2005

Tallent, Elizabeth 1954- .... **CLC 45**
See also CA 117; CANR 72; DLB 130

Tallmountain, Mary 1918-1997 .... **NNAL**
See also CA 146; CAAS 161; DLB 193

Tally, Ted 1952- .... **CLC 42**
See also CA 124; CAAE 120; CAD; CANR
125; CD 5, 6; INT CA-124

Talvik, Heiti 1904-1947 .... **TCLC 87**
See also EWL 3

Tamayo y Baus, Manuel
1829-1898 .... **NCLC 1**

Tammsaare, A(nton) H(ansen)
1878-1940 .... **TCLC 27**
See also CA 164; CDWLB 4; DLB 220;
EWL 3

Tam'si, Tchicaya U
See Tchicaya, Gerald Felix

Tan, Amy 1952- ...... **AAL; CLC 59, 120, 151**
See also AAYA 9, 48; AMWS 10; BEST
89:3; BPFB 3; CA 136; CANR 54, 105,
132; CDALBS; CN 6, 7; CPW 1; DA3;
DAM MULT, NOV, POP; DLB 173, 312;
EXPN; FL 1:6; FW; LAIT 3, 5; MAL 5;
MTCW 2; MTFW 2005; NFS 1, 13, 16;
RGAL 4; SATA 75; SSFS 9; YAW

Tandem, Carl Felix
See Spitteler, Carl

Tandem, Felix
See Spitteler, Carl

Tanizaki, Jun'ichiro 1886-1965 ... **CLC 8, 14,
28; SSC 21**
See Tanizaki Jun'ichiro
See also CA 93-96; CAAS 25-28R; MJW;
MTCW 2; MTFW 2005; RGSF 2; RGWL
2

Tanizaki Jun'ichiro
See Tanizaki, Jun'ichiro
See also DLB 180; EWL 3

Tannen, Deborah 1945- .... **CLC 206**
See also CA 118; CANR 95

Tannen, Deborah Frances
See Tannen, Deborah

Tanner, William
See Amis, Kingsley

Tante, Dilly
See Kunitz, Stanley

Tao Lao
See Storni, Alfonsina

Tapahonso, Luci 1953- .... **NNAL; PC 65**
See also CA 145; CANR 72, 127; DLB 175

Tarantino, Quentin (Jerome)
1963- .... **CLC 125, 230**
See also AAYA 58; CA 171; CANR 125

Tarassoff, Lev
See Troyat, Henri

Tarbell, Ida M(inerva) 1857-1944 . **TCLC 40**
See also CA 181; CAAE 122; DLB 47

Tarkington, (Newton) Booth
1869-1946 .... **TCLC 9**
See also BPFB 3; BYA 3; CA 143; CAAE
110; CWRI 5; DLB 9, 102; MAL 5;
MTCW 2; RGAL 4; SATA 17

Tarkovskii, Andrei Arsen'evich
See Tarkovsky, Andrei (Arsenyevich)

Tarkovsky, Andrei (Arsenyevich)
1932-1986 .... **CLC 75**
See also CA 127

Tartt, Donna 1964(?)- .... **CLC 76**
See also AAYA 56; CA 142; CANR 135;
MTFW 2005

Tasso, Torquato 1544-1595 .... **LC 5, 94**
See also EFS 2; EW 2; RGWL 2, 3; WLIT
7

Tate, (John Orley) Allen 1899-1979 .. **CLC 2,
4, 6, 9, 11, 14, 24; PC 50**
See also AMW; CA 5-8R; CAAS 85-88;
CANR 32, 108; CN 1, 2; CP 1, 2; DLB 4,
45, 63; DLBD 17; EWL 3; MAL 5;
MTCW 1, 2; MTFW 2005; RGAL 4;
RHW

Tate, Ellalice
See Hibbert, Eleanor Alice Burford

Tate, James (Vincent) 1943- ..... **CLC 2, 6, 25**
See also CA 21-24R; CANR 29, 57, 114;
CP 1, 2, 3, 4, 5, 6, 7; DLB 5, 169; EWL
3; PFS 10, 15; RGAL 4; WP

Tate, Nahum 1652(?)-1715 .... **LC 109**
See also DLB 80; RGEL 2

Tauler, Johannes c. 1300-1361 ...... **CMLC 37**
See also DLB 179; LMFS 1

Tavel, Ronald 1940- .... **CLC 6**
See also CA 21-24R; CAD; CANR 33; CD
5, 6

Taviani, Paolo 1931- .... **CLC 70**
See also CA 153

Taylor, Bayard 1825-1878 .... **NCLC 89**
See also DLB 3, 189, 250, 254; RGAL 4

Taylor, C(ecil) P(hilip) 1929-1981 .... **CLC 27**
See also CA 25-28R; CAAS 105; CANR
47; CBD

Taylor, Edward 1642(?)-1729 . **LC 11; PC 63**
See also AMW; DA; DAB; DAC; DAM
MST, POET; DLB 24; EXPP; RGAL 4;
TUS

Taylor, Eleanor Ross 1920- .... **CLC 5**
See also CA 81-84; CANR 70

Taylor, Elizabeth 1912-1975 ...... **CLC 2, 4, 29**
See also CA 13-16R; CANR 9, 70; CN 1,
2; DLB 139; MTCW 1; RGEL 2; SATA
13

Taylor, Frederick Winslow
1856-1915 .... **TCLC 76**
See also CA 188

Taylor, Henry (Splawn) 1942- .... **CLC 44**
See also CA 33-36R; 7; CANR 31; CP 6, 7;
DLB 5; PFS 10

Taylor, Kamala 1924-2004
See Markandaya, Kamala
See also CA 77-80; CAAS 227; MTFW
2005; NFS 13

Taylor, Mildred D. 1943- .... **CLC 21**
See also AAYA 10, 47; BW 1; BYA 3, 8;
CA 85-88; CANR 25, 115, 136; CLR 9,
59, 90; CSW; DLB 52; JRDA; LAIT 3;
MAICYA 1, 2; MTFW 2005; SAAS 5;
SATA 135; WYA; YAW

Taylor, Peter (Hillsman) 1917-1994 .. **CLC 1,
4, 18, 37, 44, 50, 71; SSC 10, 84**
See also AMWS 5; BPFB 3; CA 13-16R;
CAAS 147; CANR 9, 50; CN 1, 2, 3, 4,
5; CSW; DLB 218, 278; DLBY 1981,
1994; EWL 3; EXPS; INT CANR-9;
MAL 5; MTCW 1, 2; MTFW 2005; RGSF
2; SSFS 9; TUS

Taylor, Robert Lewis 1912-1998 .... **CLC 14**
See also CA 1-4R; CAAS 170; CANR 3,
64; CN 1, 2; SATA 10; TCWW 1, 2

Tchekhov, Anton
See Chekhov, Anton (Pavlovich)

Tchicaya, Gerald Felix 1931-1988 .. **CLC 101**
See Tchicaya U Tam'si
See also CA 129; CAAS 125; CANR 81

Tchicaya U Tam'si
See Tchicaya, Gerald Felix
See also EWL 3

Teasdale, Sara 1884-1933 .... **PC 31; TCLC 4**
See also CA 163; CAAE 104; DLB 45;
GLL 1; PFS 14; RGAL 4; SATA 32; TUS

Tecumseh 1768-1813 .... **NNAL**
See also DAM MULT

Tegner, Esaias 1782-1846 .... **NCLC 2**

Teilhard de Chardin, (Marie Joseph) Pierre
1881-1955 .... **TCLC 9**
See also CA 210; CAAE 105; GFL 1789 to
the Present

Temple, Ann
See Mortimer, Penelope (Ruth)

Tennant, Emma (Christina) 1937- .. **CLC 13,
52**
See also BRWS 9; CA 65-68; 9; CANR 10,
38, 59, 88; CN 3, 4, 5, 6, 7; DLB 14;
EWL 3; SFW 4

Tenneshaw, S. M.
See Silverberg, Robert

Tenney, Tabitha Gilman
1762-1837 .... **NCLC 122**
See also DLB 37, 200

Tennyson, Alfred 1809-1892 ... **NCLC 30, 65,
115; PC 6; WLC 6**
See also AAYA 50; BRW 4; CDBLB 1832-
1890; DA; DA3; DAB; DAC; DAM MST,
POET; DLB 32; EXPP; PAB; PFS 1, 2, 4,
11, 15, 19; RGEL 2; TEA; WLIT 4; WP

Teran, Lisa St. Aubin de .... **CLC 36**
See St. Aubin de Teran, Lisa

Terence c. 184B.C.-c. 159B.C. ...... **CMLC 14;
DC 7**
See also AW 1; CDWLB 1; DLB 211;
RGWL 2, 3; TWA; WLIT 8

Teresa de Jesus, St. 1515-1582 .... **LC 18**

Teresa of Avila, St.
See Teresa de Jesus, St.

Terkel, Louis .... **CLC 38**
See Terkel, Studs
See also AAYA 32; AITN 1; MTCW 2; TUS

Terkel, Studs 1912-
See Terkel, Louis
See also CA 57-60; CANR 18, 45, 67, 132;
DA3; MTCW 1, 2; MTFW 2005

Terry, C. V.
See Slaughter, Frank G(ill)

Terry, Megan 1932- .... **CLC 19; DC 13**
See also CA 77-80; CABS 3; CAD; CANR
43; CD 5, 6; CWD; DFS 18; DLB 7, 249;
GLL 2

Tertullian c. 155-c. 245 .... **CMLC 29**

Tertz, Abram
See Sinyavsky, Andrei (Donatevich)
See also RGSF 2

Tesich, Steve 1943(?)-1996 .... **CLC 40, 69**
See also CA 105; CAAS 152; CAD; DLBY
1983

Tesla, Nikola 1856-1943 .... **TCLC 88**

Teternikov, Fyodor Kuzmich 1863-1927
See Sologub, Fyodor
See also CAAE 104

Tevis, Walter 1928-1984 .... **CLC 42**
See also CA 113; SFW 4

Tey, Josephine .... **TCLC 14**
See Mackintosh, Elizabeth
See also DLB 77; MSW

Thackeray, William Makepeace
1811-1863 ...... **NCLC 5, 14, 22, 43, 169;**
WLC 6
See also BRW 5; BRWC 2; CDBLB 1832-
1890; DA; DA3; DAB; DAC; DAM MST,
NOV; DLB 21, 55, 159, 163; NFS 13;
RGEL 2; SATA 23; TEA; WLIT 3

Thakura, Ravindranatha
See Tagore, Rabindranath

Thames, C. H.
See Marlowe, Stephen

Tharoor, Shashi 1956- .... **CLC 70**
See also CA 141; CANR 91; CN 6, 7

Thelwall, John 1764-1834 .... **NCLC 162**
See also DLB 93, 158

Thelwell, Michael Miles 1939- .... **CLC 22**
See also BW 2; CA 101

Theobald, Lewis, Jr.
See Lovecraft, H. P.

Theocritus c. 310B.C.- .... **CMLC 45**
See also AW 1; DLB 176; RGWL 2, 3

Theodorescu, Ion N. 1880-1967
See Arghezi, Tudor
See also CAAS 116

Theriault, Yves 1915-1983 .... **CLC 79**
See also CA 102; CANR 150; CCA 1;
DAC; DAM MST; DLB 88; EWL 3

Theroux, Alexander (Louis) 1939- .... **CLC 2,**
25
See also CA 85-88; CANR 20, 63; CN 4, 5,
6, 7

Theroux, Paul 1941- .... **CLC 5, 8, 11, 15, 28,**
46, 159
See also AAYA 28; AMWS 8; BEST 89:4;
BPFB 3; CA 33-36R; CANR 20, 45, 74,
133; CDALBS; CN 1, 2, 3, 4, 5, 6, 7; CP
1; CPW 1; DA3; DAM POP; DLB 2, 218;
EWL 3; HGG; MAL 5; MTCW 1, 2;
MTFW 2005; RGAL 4; SATA 44, 109;
TUS

Thesen, Sharon 1946- .... **CLC 56**
See also CA 163; CANR 125; CP 5, 6, 7;
CWP

Thespis fl. 6th cent. B.C.- .... **CMLC 51**
See also LMFS 1

Thevenin, Denis
See Duhamel, Georges

Thibault, Jacques Anatole Francois
1844-1924
See France, Anatole
See also CA 127; CAAE 106; DA3; DAM
NOV; MTCW 1, 2; TWA

Thiele, Colin 1920-2006 .... **CLC 17**
See also CA 29-32R; CANR 12, 28, 53,
105; CLR 27; CP 1, 2; DLB 289; MAI-
CYA 1, 2; SAAS 2; SATA 14, 72, 125;
YAW

Thistlethwaite, Bel
See Wetherald, Agnes Ethelwyn

Thomas, Audrey (Callahan) 1935- .... **CLC 7,**
13, 37, 107; SSC 20
See also AITN 2; CA 237; 21-24R, 237; 19;
CANR 36, 58; CN 2, 3, 4, 5, 6, 7; DLB
60; MTCW 1; RGSF 2

Thomas, Augustus 1857-1934 .... **TCLC 97**
See also MAL 5

Thomas, D.M. 1935- ..... **CLC 13, 22, 31, 132**
See also BPFB 3; BRWS 4; CA 61-64; 11;
CANR 17, 45, 75; CDBLB 1960 to
Present; CN 4, 5, 6, 7; CP 1, 2, 3, 4, 5, 6,
7; DA3; DLB 40, 207, 299; HGG; INT
CANR-17; MTCW 1, 2; MTFW 2005;
RGHL; SFW 4

Thomas, Dylan (Marlais) 1914-1953 .... **PC 2,**
52; SSC 3, 44; TCLC 1, 8, 45, 105;
WLC 6
See also AAYA 45; BRWS 1; CA 120;
CAAE 104; CANR 65; CDBLB 1945-
1960; DA; DA3; DAB; DAC; DAM

DRAM, MST, POET; DLB 13, 20, 139;
EWL 3; EXPP; LAIT 3; MTCW 1, 2;
MTFW 2005; PAB; PFS 1, 3, 8; RGEL 2;
RGSF 2; SATA 60; TEA; WLIT 4; WP

Thomas, (Philip) Edward 1878-1917 . **PC 53;**
TCLC 10
See also BRW 6; BRWS 3; CA 153; CAAE
106; DAM POET; DLB 19, 98, 156, 216;
EWL 3; PAB; RGEL 2

Thomas, Joyce Carol 1938- .... **CLC 35**
See also AAYA 12, 54; BW 2, 3; CA 116;
CAAE 113; CANR 48, 114, 135; CLR 19;
DLB 33; INT CA-116; JRDA; MAICYA
1, 2; MTCW 1, 2; MTFW 2005; SAAS 7;
SATA 40, 78, 123, 137; SATA-Essay 137;
WYA; YAW

Thomas, Lewis 1913-1993 .... **CLC 35**
See also ANW; CA 85-88; CAAS 143;
CANR 38, 60; DLB 275; MTCW 1, 2

Thomas, M. Carey 1857-1935 .... **TCLC 89**
See also FW

Thomas, Paul
See Mann, (Paul) Thomas

Thomas, Piri 1928- .... **CLC 17; HLCS 2**
See also CA 73-76; HW 1; LLW

Thomas, R(onald) S(tuart)
1913-2000 .... **CLC 6, 13, 48**
See also CA 89-92; 4; CAAS 189; CANR
30; CDBLB 1960 to Present; CP 1, 2, 3,
4, 5, 6, 7; DAB; DAM POET; DLB 27;
EWL 3; MTCW 1; RGEL 2

Thomas, Ross (Elmore) 1926-1995 .. **CLC 39**
See also CA 33-36R; CAAS 150; CANR
22, 63; CMW 4

Thompson, Francis (Joseph)
1859-1907 .... **TCLC 4**
See also BRW 5; CA 189; CAAE 104; CD-
BLB 1890-1914; DLB 19; RGEL 2; TEA

Thompson, Francis Clegg
See Mencken, H(enry) L(ouis)

Thompson, Hunter S. 1937(?)-2005 .. **CLC 9,**
17, 40, 104, 229
See also AAYA 45; BEST 89:1; BPFB 3;
CA 17-20R; CAAS 236; CANR 23, 46,
74, 77, 111, 133; CPW; CSW; DA3; DAM
POP; DLB 185; MTCW 1, 2; MTFW
2005; TUS

Thompson, James Myers
See Thompson, Jim (Myers)

Thompson, Jim (Myers)
1906-1977(?) .... **CLC 69**
See also BPFB 3; CA 140; CMW 4; CPW;
DLB 226; MSW

Thompson, Judith (Clare Francesca)
1954- .... **CLC 39**
See also CA 143; CD 5, 6; CWD; DFS 22

Thomson, James 1700-1748 .... **LC 16, 29, 40**
See also BRWS 3; DAM POET; DLB 95;
RGEL 2

Thomson, James 1834-1882 .... **NCLC 18**
See also DAM POET; DLB 35; RGEL 2

Thoreau, Henry David 1817-1862 .. **NCLC 7,**
21, 61, 138; PC 30; WLC 6
See also AAYA 42; AMW; ANW; BYA 3;
CDALB 1640-1865; DA; DA3; DAB;
DAC; DAM MST; DLB 1, 183, 223, 270,
298; LAIT 2; LMFS 1; NCFS 3; RGAL
4; TUS

Thorndike, E. L.
See Thorndike, Edward L(ee)

Thorndike, Edward L(ee)
1874-1949 .... **TCLC 107**
See also CAAE 121

Thornton, Hall
See Silverberg, Robert

Thorpe, Adam 1956- .... **CLC 176**
See also CA 129; CANR 92, 160; DLB 231

Thubron, Colin 1939- .... **CLC 163**
See also CA 25-28R; CANR 12, 29, 59, 95;
CN 5, 6, 7; DLB 204, 231

Thubron, Colin Gerald Dryden
See Thubron, Colin

Thucydides c. 455B.C.-c. 395B.C. . **CMLC 17**
See also AW 1; DLB 176; RGWL 2, 3;
WLIT 8

Thumboo, Edwin Nadason 1933- .... **PC 30**
See also CA 194; CP 1

Thurber, James (Grover)
1894-1961 .. **CLC 5, 11, 25, 125; SSC 1,**
47
See also AAYA 56; AMWS 1; BPFB 3;
BYA 5; CA 73-76; CANR 17, 39; CDALB
1929-1941; CWRI 5; DA; DA3; DAB;
DAC; DAM DRAM, MST, NOV; DLB 4,
11, 22, 102; EWL 3; EXPS; FANT; LAIT
3; MAICYA 1, 2; MAL 5; MTCW 1, 2;
MTFW 2005; RGAL 4; RGSF 2; SATA
13; SSFS 1, 10, 19; SUFW; TUS

Thurman, Wallace (Henry)
1902-1934 ..... **BLC 3; HR 1:3; TCLC 6**
See also BW 1, 3; CA 124; CAAE 104;
CANR 81; DAM MULT; DLB 51

Tibullus c. 54B.C.-c. 18B.C. .... **CMLC 36**
See also AW 2; DLB 211; RGWL 2, 3;
WLIT 8

Ticheburn, Cheviot
See Ainsworth, William Harrison

Tieck, (Johann) Ludwig
1773-1853 .... **NCLC 5, 46; SSC 31**
See also CDWLB 2; DLB 90; EW 5; IDTP;
RGSF 2; RGWL 2, 3; SUFW

Tiger, Derry
See Ellison, Harlan

Tilghman, Christopher 1946- .... **CLC 65**
See also CA 159; CANR 135, 151; CSW;
DLB 244

Tillich, Paul (Johannes)
1886-1965 .... **CLC 131**
See also CA 5-8R; CAAS 25-28R; CANR
33; MTCW 1, 2

Tillinghast, Richard (Williford)
1940- .... **CLC 29**
See also CA 29-32R; 23; CANR 26, 51, 96;
CP 2, 3, 4, 5, 6, 7; CSW

Timrod, Henry 1828-1867 .... **NCLC 25**
See also DLB 3, 248; RGAL 4

Tindall, Gillian (Elizabeth) 1938- ...... **CLC 7**
See also CA 21-24R; CANR 11, 65, 107;
CN 1, 2, 3, 4, 5, 6, 7

Tiptree, James, Jr. .... **CLC 48, 50**
See Sheldon, Alice Hastings Bradley
See also DLB 8; SCFW 1, 2; SFW 4

Tirone Smith, Mary-Ann 1944- .... **CLC 39**
See also CA 136; CAAE 118; CANR 113;
SATA 143

Tirso de Molina 1580(?)-1648 .... **DC 13;**
HLCS 2; LC 73
See also RGWL 2, 3

Titmarsh, Michael Angelo
See Thackeray, William Makepeace

Tocqueville, Alexis (Charles Henri Maurice
Clerel Comte) de 1805-1859 .. **NCLC 7,**
63
See also EW 6; GFL 1789 to the Present;
TWA

Toer, Pramoedya Ananta
1925-2006 .... **CLC 186**
See also CA 197; CAAS 251; RGWL 3

Toffler, Alvin 1928- .... **CLC 168**
See also CA 13-16R; CANR 15, 46, 67;
CPW; DAM POP; MTCW 1, 2

Toibin, Colm 1955- .... **CLC 162**
See also CA 142; CANR 81, 149; CN 7;
DLB 271

Urista (Heredia), Alberto (Baltazar)
1947- .... **HLCS 1**
See Alurista
See also CA 182; CANR 2, 32; HW 1

Urmuz
See Codrescu, Andrei

Urquhart, Guy
See McAlmon, Robert (Menzies)

Urquhart, Jane 1949- .... **CLC 90**
See also CA 113; CANR 32, 68, 116, 157;
CCA 1; DAC

Usigli, Rodolfo 1905-1979 .... **HLCS 1**
See also CA 131; DLB 305; EWL 3; HW 1;
LAW

Usk, Thomas (?)-1388 .... **CMLC 76**
See also DLB 146

Ustinov, Peter (Alexander)
1921-2004 .... **CLC 1**
See also AITN 1; CA 13-16R; CAAS 225;
CANR 25, 51; CBD; CD 5, 6; DLB 13;
MTCW 2

U Tam'si, Gerald Felix Tchicaya
See Tchicaya, Gerald Felix

U Tam'si, Tchicaya
See Tchicaya, Gerald Felix

Vachss, Andrew 1942- .... **CLC 106**
See also CA 214; 118, 214; CANR 44, 95,
153; CMW 4

Vachss, Andrew H.
See Vachss, Andrew

Vachss, Andrew Henry
See Vachss, Andrew

Vaculik, Ludvik 1926- .... **CLC 7**
See also CA 53-56; CANR 72; CWW 2;
DLB 232; EWL 3

Vaihinger, Hans 1852-1933 .... **TCLC 71**
See also CA 166; CAAE 116

Valdez, Luis (Miguel) 1940- ..... **CLC 84; DC 10; HLC 2**
See also CA 101; CAD; CANR 32, 81; CD
5, 6; DAM MULT; DFS 5; DLB 122;
EWL 3; HW 1; LAIT 4; LLW

Valenzuela, Luisa 1938- .... **CLC 31, 104; HLCS 2; SSC 14, 82**
See also CA 101; CANR 32, 65, 123; CD-
WLB 3; CWW 2; DAM MULT; DLB 113;
EWL 3; FW; HW 1, 2; LAW; RGSF 2;
RGWL 3

Valera y Alcala-Galiano, Juan
1824-1905 .... **TCLC 10**
See also CAAE 106

Valerius Maximus fl. 20- .... **CMLC 64**
See also DLB 211

Valery, (Ambroise) Paul (Toussaint Jules)
1871-1945 .... **PC 9; TCLC 4, 15**
See also CA 122; CAAE 104; DA3; DAM
POET; DLB 258; EW 8; EWL 3; GFL
1789 to the Present; MTCW 1, 2; MTFW
2005; RGWL 2, 3; TWA

Valle-Inclan, Ramon (Maria) del
1866-1936 .... **HLC 2; TCLC 5**
See del Valle-Inclan, Ramon (Maria)
See also CA 153; CAAE 106; CANR 80;
DAM MULT; DLB 134; EW 8; EWL 3;
HW 2; RGSF 2; RGWL 2, 3

Vallejo, Antonio Buero
See Buero Vallejo, Antonio

Vallejo, Cesar (Abraham)
1892-1938 .... **HLC 2; TCLC 3, 56**
See also CA 153; CAAE 105; DAM MULT;
DLB 290; EWL 3; HW 1; LAW; RGWL
2, 3

Valles, Jules 1832-1885 .... **NCLC 71**
See also DLB 123; GFL 1789 to the Present

Vallette, Marguerite Eymery
1860-1953 .... **TCLC 67**
See Rachilde
See also CA 182; DLB 123, 192

Valle Y Pena, Ramon del
See Valle-Inclan, Ramon (Maria) del

Van Ash, Cay 1918-1994 .... **CLC 34**
See also CA 220

Vanbrugh, Sir John 1664-1726 .... **LC 21**
See also BRW 2; DAM DRAM; DLB 80;
IDTP; RGEL 2

Van Campen, Karl
See Campbell, John W(ood, Jr.)

Vance, Gerald
See Silverberg, Robert

Vance, Jack 1916-
See Queen, Ellery; Vance, John Holbrook
See also CA 29-32R; CANR 17, 65, 154;
CMW 4; MTCW 1

Vance, John Holbrook .... **CLC 35**
See Vance, Jack
See also DLB 8; FANT; SCFW 1, 2; SFW
4; SUFW 1, 2

Van Den Bogarde, Derek Jules Gaspard
Ulric Niven 1921-1999 .... **CLC 14**
See Bogarde, Dirk
See also CA 77-80; CAAS 179

Vandenburgh, Jane .... **CLC 59**
See also CA 168

Vanderhaeghe, Guy 1951- .... **CLC 41**
See also BPFB 3; CA 113; CANR 72, 145;
CN 7

van der Post, Laurens (Jan)
1906-1996 .... **CLC 5**
See also AFW; CA 5-8R; CAAS 155;
CANR 35; CN 1, 2, 3, 4, 5, 6; DLB 204;
RGEL 2

van de Wetering, Janwillem 1931- ... **CLC 47**
See also CA 49-52; CANR 4, 62, 90; CMW
4

Van Dine, S. S. .... **TCLC 23**
See Wright, Willard Huntington
See also DLB 306; MSW

Van Doren, Carl (Clinton)
1885-1950 .... **TCLC 18**
See also CA 168; CAAE 111

Van Doren, Mark 1894-1972 .... **CLC 6, 10**
See also CA 1-4R; CAAS 37-40R; CANR
3; CN 1; CP 1; DLB 45, 284; MAL 5;
MTCW 1, 2; RGAL 4

Van Druten, John (William)
1901-1957 .... **TCLC 2**
See also CA 161; CAAE 104; DLB 10;
MAL 5; RGAL 4

Van Duyn, Mona 1921-2004 .... **CLC 3, 7, 63, 116**
See also CA 9-12R; CAAS 234; CANR 7,
38, 60, 116; CP 1, 2, 3, 4, 5, 6, 7; CWP;
DAM POET; DLB 5; MAL 5; MTFW
2005; PFS 20

Van Dyne, Edith
See Baum, L(yman) Frank

van Itallie, Jean-Claude 1936- .... **CLC 3**
See also CA 45-48; 2; CAD; CANR 1, 48;
CD 5, 6; DLB 7

Van Loot, Cornelius Obenchain
See Roberts, Kenneth (Lewis)

van Ostaijen, Paul 1896-1928 .... **TCLC 33**
See also CA 163

Van Peebles, Melvin 1932- .... **CLC 2, 20**
See also BW 2, 3; CA 85-88; CANR 27,
67, 82; DAM MULT

van Schendel, Arthur(-Francois-Emile)
1874-1946 .... **TCLC 56**
See also EWL 3

Vansittart, Peter 1920- .... **CLC 42**
See also CA 1-4R; CANR 3, 49, 90; CN 4,
5, 6, 7; RHW

Van Vechten, Carl 1880-1964 ... **CLC 33; HR 1:3**
See also AMWS 2; CA 183; CAAS 89-92;
DLB 4, 9, 51; RGAL 4

van Vogt, A(lfred) E(lton) 1912-2000 . **CLC 1**
See also BPFB 3; BYA 13, 14; CA 21-24R;
CAAS 190; CANR 28; DLB 8, 251;
SATA 14; SATA-Obit 124; SCFW 1, 2;
SFW 4

Vara, Madeleine
See Jackson, Laura (Riding)

Varda, Agnes 1928- .... **CLC 16**
See also CA 122; CAAE 116

Vargas Llosa, Jorge Mario Pedro
See Vargas Llosa, Mario

Vargas Llosa, Mario 1936- .. **CLC 3, 6, 9, 10, 15, 31, 42, 85, 181; HLC 2**
See Llosa, Jorge Mario Pedro Vargas
See also BPFB 3; CA 73-76; CANR 18, 32,
42, 67, 116, 140; CDWLB 3; CWW 2;
DA; DA3; DAB; DAC; DAM MST,
MULT, NOV; DLB 145; DNFS 2; EWL
3; HW 1, 2; LAIT 5; LATS 1:2; LAW;
LAWS 1; MTCW 1, 2; MTFW 2005;
RGWL 2; SSFS 14; TWA; WLIT 1

Varnhagen von Ense, Rahel
1771-1833 .... **NCLC 130**
See also DLB 90

Vasari, Giorgio 1511-1574 .... **LC 114**

Vasilikos, Vasiles
See Vassilikos, Vassilis

Vasiliu, George
See Bacovia, George

Vasiliu, Gheorghe
See Bacovia, George
See also CA 189; CAAE 123

Vassa, Gustavus
See Equiano, Olaudah

Vassilikos, Vassilis 1933- .... **CLC 4, 8**
See also CA 81-84; CANR 75, 149; EWL 3

Vaughan, Henry 1621-1695 .... **LC 27**
See also BRW 2; DLB 131; PAB; RGEL 2

Vaughn, Stephanie .... **CLC 62**

Vazov, Ivan (Minchov) 1850-1921 . **TCLC 25**
See also CA 167; CAAE 121; CDWLB 4;
DLB 147

Veblen, Thorstein B(unde)
1857-1929 .... **TCLC 31**
See also AMWS 1; CA 165; CAAE 115;
DLB 246; MAL 5

Vega, Lope de 1562-1635 ... **HLCS 2; LC 23, 119**
See also EW 2; RGWL 2, 3

Veldeke, Heinrich von c. 1145-c.
1190 .... **CMLC 85**

Vendler, Helen (Hennessy) 1933- ... **CLC 138**
See also CA 41-44R; CANR 25, 72, 136;
MTCW 1, 2; MTFW 2005

Venison, Alfred
See Pound, Ezra (Weston Loomis)

Ventsel, Elena Sergeevna 1907-2002
See Grekova, I.
See also CA 154

Verdi, Marie de
See Mencken, H(enry) L(ouis)

Verdu, Matilde
See Cela, Camilo Jose

Verga, Giovanni (Carmelo)
1840-1922 .... **SSC 21, 87; TCLC 3**
See also CA 123; CAAE 104; CANR 101;
EW 7; EWL 3; RGSF 2; RGWL 2, 3;
WLIT 7

Vergil 70B.C.-19B.C. ... **CMLC 9, 40; PC 12; WLCS**
See Virgil
See also AW 2; DA; DA3; DAB; DAC;
DAM MST, POET; EFS 1; LMFS 1

Vergil, Polydore c. 1470-1555 .... **LC 108**
See also DLB 132

Verhaeren, Emile (Adolphe Gustave)
1855-1916 .... **TCLC 12**
See also CAAE 109; EWL 3; GFL 1789 to
the Present

Wagman, Fredrica 1937- .... **CLC 7**
    See also CA 97-100; INT CA-97-100
Wagner, Linda W.
    See Wagner-Martin, Linda (C.)
Wagner, Linda Welshimer
    See Wagner-Martin, Linda (C.)
Wagner, Richard 1813-1883 ..... **NCLC 9, 119**
    See also DLB 129; EW 6
Wagner-Martin, Linda (C.) 1936- .... **CLC 50**
    See also CA 159; CANR 135
Wagoner, David (Russell) 1926- .... **CLC 3, 5, 15; PC 33**
    See also AMWS 9; CA 1-4R; 3; CANR 2, 71; CN 1, 2, 3, 4, 5, 6, 7; CP 1, 2, 3, 4, 5, 6, 7; DLB 5, 256; SATA 14; TCWW 1, 2
Wah, Fred(erick James) 1939- .... **CLC 44**
    See also CA 141; CAAE 107; CP 1, 6, 7; DLB 60
Wahloo, Per 1926-1975 .... **CLC 7**
    See also BPFB 3; CA 61-64; CANR 73; CMW 4; MSW
Wahloo, Peter
    See Wahloo, Per
Wain, John (Barrington) 1925-1994 . **CLC 2, 11, 15, 46**
    See also CA 5-8R; 4; CAAS 145; CANR 23, 54; CDBLB 1960 to Present; CN 1, 2, 3, 4, 5; CP 1, 2, 3, 4, 5; DLB 15, 27, 139, 155; EWL 3; MTCW 1, 2; MTFW 2005
Wajda, Andrzej 1926- .... **CLC 16, 219**
    See also CA 102
Wakefield, Dan 1932- .... **CLC 7**
    See also CA 211; 21-24R, 211; 7; CN 4, 5, 6, 7
Wakefield, Herbert Russell
    1888-1965 .... **TCLC 120**
    See also CA 5-8R; CANR 77; HGG; SUFW
Wakoski, Diane 1937- ...... **CLC 2, 4, 7, 9, 11, 40; PC 15**
    See also CA 216; 13-16R, 216; 1; CANR 9, 60, 106; CP 1, 2, 3, 4, 5, 6, 7; CWP; DAM POET; DLB 5; INT CANR-9; MAL 5; MTCW 2; MTFW 2005
Wakoski-Sherbell, Diane
    See Wakoski, Diane
Walcott, Derek 1930- ... **BLC 3; CLC 2, 4, 9, 14, 25, 42, 67, 76, 160; DC 7; PC 46**
    See also BW 2; CA 89-92; CANR 26, 47, 75, 80, 130; CBD; CD 5, 6; CDWLB 3; CP 1, 2, 3, 4, 5, 6, 7; DA3; DAB; DAC; DAM MST, MULT, POET; DLB 117, 332; DLBY 1981; DNFS 1; EFS 1; EWL 3; LMFS 2; MTCW 1, 2; MTFW 2005; PFS 6; RGEL 2; TWA; WWE 1
Waldman, Anne (Lesley) 1945- .... **CLC 7**
    See also BG 1:3; CA 37-40R; 17; CANR 34, 69, 116; CP 1, 2, 3, 4, 5, 6, 7; CWP; DLB 16
Waldo, E. Hunter
    See Sturgeon, Theodore (Hamilton)
Waldo, Edward Hamilton
    See Sturgeon, Theodore (Hamilton)
Walker, Alice 1944- ...... **BLC 3; CLC 5, 6, 9, 19, 27, 46, 58, 103, 167; PC 30; SSC 5; WLCS**
    See also AAYA 3, 33; AFAW 1, 2; AMWS 3; BEST 89:4; BPFB 3; BW 2, 3; CA 37-40R; CANR 9, 27, 49, 66, 82, 131; CDALB 1968-1988; CN 4, 5, 6, 7; CPW; CSW; DA; DA3; DAB; DAC; DAM MST, MULT, NOV, POET, POP; DLB 6, 33, 143; EWL 3; EXPN; EXPS; FL 1:6; FW; INT CANR-27; LAIT 3; MAL 5; MBL; MTCW 1, 2; MTFW 2005; NFS 5; RGAL 4; RGSF 2; SATA 31; SSFS 2, 11; TUS; YAW
Walker, Alice Malsenior
    See Walker, Alice

Walker, David Harry 1911-1992 ...... **CLC 14**
    See also CA 1-4R; CAAS 137; CANR 1; CN 1, 2; CWRI 5; SATA 8; SATA-Obit 71
Walker, Edward Joseph 1934-2004
    See Walker, Ted
    See also CA 21-24R; CAAS 226; CANR 12, 28, 53
Walker, George F(rederick) 1947- .. **CLC 44, 61**
    See also CA 103; CANR 21, 43, 59; CD 5, 6; DAB; DAC; DAM MST; DLB 60
Walker, Joseph A. 1935-2003 .... **CLC 19**
    See also BW 1, 3; CA 89-92; CAD; CANR 26, 143; CD 5, 6; DAM DRAM, MST; DFS 12; DLB 38
Walker, Margaret 1915-1998 .. **BLC; CLC 1, 6; PC 20; TCLC 129**
    See also AFAW 1, 2; BW 2, 3; CA 73-76; CAAS 172; CANR 26, 54, 76, 136; CN 1, 2, 3, 4, 5, 6; CP 1, 2, 3, 4, 5, 6; CSW; DAM MULT; DLB 76, 152; EXPP; FW; MAL 5; MTCW 1, 2; MTFW 2005; RGAL 4; RHW
Walker, Ted .... **CLC 13**
    See Walker, Edward Joseph
    See also CP 1, 2, 3, 4, 5, 6, 7; DLB 40
Wallace, David Foster 1962- ... **CLC 50, 114; SSC 68**
    See also AAYA 50; AMWS 10; CA 132; CANR 59, 133; CN 7; DA3; MTCW 2; MTFW 2005
Wallace, Dexter
    See Masters, Edgar Lee
Wallace, (Richard Horatio) Edgar
    1875-1932 .... **TCLC 57**
    See also CA 218; CAAE 115; CMW 4; DLB 70; MSW; RGEL 2
Wallace, Irving 1916-1990 .... **CLC 7, 13**
    See also AITN 1; BPFB 3; CA 1-4R; 1; CAAS 132; CANR 1, 27; CPW; DAM NOV, POP; INT CANR-27; MTCW 1, 2
Wallant, Edward Lewis 1926-1962 ... **CLC 5, 10**
    See also CA 1-4R; CANR 22; DLB 2, 28, 143, 299; EWL 3; MAL 5; MTCW 1, 2; RGAL 4; RGHL
Wallas, Graham 1858-1932 .... **TCLC 91**
Waller, Edmund 1606-1687 .... **LC 86; PC 72**
    See also BRW 2; DAM POET; DLB 126; PAB; RGEL 2
Walley, Byron
    See Card, Orson Scott
Walpole, Horace 1717-1797 .... **LC 2, 49**
    See also BRW 3; DLB 39, 104, 213; GL 3; HGG; LMFS 1; RGEL 2; SUFW 1; TEA
Walpole, Hugh (Seymour)
    1884-1941 .... **TCLC 5**
    See also CA 165; CAAE 104; DLB 34; HGG; MTCW 2; RGEL 2; RHW
Walrond, Eric (Derwent) 1898-1966 . **HR 1:3**
    See also BW 1; CA 125; DLB 51
Walser, Martin 1927- .... **CLC 27, 183**
    See also CA 57-60; CANR 8, 46, 145; CWW 2; DLB 75, 124; EWL 3
Walser, Robert 1878-1956 ..... **SSC 20; TCLC 18**
    See also CA 165; CAAE 118; CANR 100; DLB 66; EWL 3
Walsh, Gillian Paton
    See Paton Walsh, Jill
Walsh, Jill Paton .... **CLC 35**
    See Paton Walsh, Jill
    See also CLR 2, 65; WYA
Walter, Villiam Christian
    See Andersen, Hans Christian
Walters, Anna L(ee) 1946- .... **NNAL**
    See also CA 73-76

Walther von der Vogelweide c.
    1170-1228 .... **CMLC 56**
Walton, Izaak 1593-1683 .... **LC 72**
    See also BRW 2; CDBLB Before 1660; DLB 151, 213; RGEL 2
Wambaugh, Joseph (Aloysius), Jr.
    1937- .... **CLC 3, 18**
    See also AITN 1; BEST 89:3; BPFB 3; CA 33-36R; CANR 42, 65, 115; CMW 4; CPW 1; DA3; DAM NOV, POP; DLB 6; DLBY 1983; MSW; MTCW 1, 2
Wang Wei 699(?)-761(?) .... **PC 18**
    See also TWA
Warburton, William 1698-1779 .... **LC 97**
    See also DLB 104
Ward, Arthur Henry Sarsfield 1883-1959
    See Rohmer, Sax
    See also CA 173; CAAE 108; CMW 4; HGG
Ward, Douglas Turner 1930- .... **CLC 19**
    See also BW 1; CA 81-84; CAD; CANR 27; CD 5, 6; DLB 7, 38
Ward, E. D.
    See Lucas, E(dward) V(errall)
Ward, Mrs. Humphry 1851-1920
    See Ward, Mary Augusta
    See also RGEL 2
Ward, Mary Augusta 1851-1920 ... **TCLC 55**
    See Ward, Mrs. Humphry
    See also DLB 18
Ward, Nathaniel 1578(?)-1652 .... **LC 114**
    See also DLB 24
Ward, Peter
    See Faust, Frederick (Schiller)
Warhol, Andy 1928(?)-1987 .... **CLC 20**
    See also AAYA 12; BEST 89:4; CA 89-92; CAAS 121; CANR 34
Warner, Francis (Robert Le Plastrier)
    1937- .... **CLC 14**
    See also CA 53-56; CANR 11; CP 1, 2, 3, 4
Warner, Marina 1946- .... **CLC 59, 231**
    See also CA 65-68; CANR 21, 55, 118; CN 5, 6, 7; DLB 194; MTFW 2005
Warner, Rex (Ernest) 1905-1986 ...... **CLC 45**
    See also CA 89-92; CAAS 119; CN 1, 2, 3, 4; CP 1, 2, 3, 4; DLB 15; RGEL 2; RHW
Warner, Susan (Bogert)
    1819-1885 .... **NCLC 31, 146**
    See also DLB 3, 42, 239, 250, 254
Warner, Sylvia (Constance) Ashton
    See Ashton-Warner, Sylvia (Constance)
Warner, Sylvia Townsend
    1893-1978 .. **CLC 7, 19; SSC 23; TCLC 131**
    See also BRWS 7; CA 61-64; CAAS 77-80; CANR 16, 60, 104; CN 1, 2; DLB 34, 139; EWL 3; FANT; FW; MTCW 1, 2; RGEL 2; RGSF 2; RHW
Warren, Mercy Otis 1728-1814 ..... **NCLC 13**
    See also DLB 31, 200; RGAL 4; TUS
Warren, Robert Penn 1905-1989 .. **CLC 1, 4, 6, 8, 10, 13, 18, 39, 53, 59; PC 37; SSC 4, 58; WLC 6**
    See also AITN 1; AMW; AMWC 2; BPFB 3; BYA 1; CA 13-16R; CAAS 129; CANR 10, 47; CDALB 1968-1988; CN 1, 2, 3, 4; CP 1, 2, 3, 4; DA; DA3; DAB; DAC; DAM MST, NOV, POET; DLB 2, 48, 152, 320; DLBY 1980, 1989; EWL 3; INT CANR-10; MAL 5; MTCW 1, 2; MTFW 2005; NFS 13; RGAL 4; RGSF 2; RHW; SATA 46; SATA-Obit 63; SSFS 8; TUS
Warrigal, Jack
    See Furphy, Joseph
Warshofsky, Isaac
    See Singer, Isaac Bashevis
Warton, Joseph 1722-1800 ... **LC 128; NCLC 118**
    See also DLB 104, 109; RGEL 2

3; EXPS; HGG; LAIT 3; MAL 5; MBL;
MTCW 1, 2; MTFW 2005; NFS 13, 15;
RGAL 4; RGSF 2; RHW; SSFS 2, 10;
TUS

Welty, Eudora Alice
See Welty, Eudora

Wen I-to 1899-1946 .... **TCLC 28**
See also EWL 3

Wentworth, Robert
See Hamilton, Edmond

Werfel, Franz (Viktor) 1890-1945 ... **TCLC 8**
See also CA 161; CAAE 104; DLB 81, 124;
EWL 3; RGWL 2, 3

Wergeland, Henrik Arnold
1808-1845 .... **NCLC 5**

Wersba, Barbara 1932- .... **CLC 30**
See also AAYA 2, 30; BYA 6, 12, 13; CA
182; 29-32R, 182; CANR 16, 38; CLR 3,
78; DLB 52; JRDA; MAICYA 1, 2; SAAS
2; SATA 1, 58; SATA-Essay 103; WYA;
YAW

Wertmueller, Lina 1928- .... **CLC 16**
See also CA 97-100; CANR 39, 78

Wescott, Glenway 1901-1987 .. **CLC 13; SSC
35**
See also CA 13-16R; CAAS 121; CANR
23, 70; CN 1, 2, 3, 4; DLB 4, 9, 102;
MAL 5; RGAL 4

Wesker, Arnold 1932- .... **CLC 3, 5, 42**
See also CA 1-4R; 7; CANR 1, 33; CBD;
CD 5, 6; CDBLB 1960 to Present; DAB;
DAM DRAM; DLB 13, 310, 319; EWL
3; MTCW 1; RGEL 2; TEA

Wesley, Charles 1707-1788 .... **LC 128**
See also DLB 95; RGEL 2

Wesley, John 1703-1791 .... **LC 88**
See also DLB 104

Wesley, Richard (Errol) 1945- .... **CLC 7**
See also BW 1; CA 57-60; CAD; CANR
27; CD 5, 6; DLB 38

Wessel, Johan Herman 1742-1785 .... **LC 7**
See also DLB 300

West, Anthony (Panther)
1914-1987 .... **CLC 50**
See also CA 45-48; CAAS 124; CANR 3,
19; CN 1, 2, 3, 4; DLB 15

West, C. P.
See Wodehouse, P(elham) G(renville)

West, Cornel 1953- .... **BLCS; CLC 134**
See also CA 144; CANR 91, 159; DLB 246

West, Cornel Ronald
See West, Cornel

West, Delno C(loyde), Jr. 1936- .... **CLC 70**
See also CA 57-60

West, Dorothy 1907-1998 ...... **HR 1:3; TCLC
108**
See also BW 2; CA 143; CAAS 169; DLB
76

West, (Mary) Jessamyn 1902-1984 ... **CLC 7,
17**
See also CA 9-12R; CAAS 112; CANR 27;
CN 1, 2, 3; DLB 6; DLBY 1984; MTCW
1, 2; RGAL 4; RHW; SATA-Obit 37;
TCWW 2; TUS; YAW

West, Morris L(anglo) 1916-1999 ..... **CLC 6,
33**
See also BPFB 3; CA 5-8R; CAAS 187;
CANR 24, 49, 64; CN 1, 2, 3, 4, 5, 6;
CPW; DLB 289; MTCW 1, 2; MTFW
2005

West, Nathanael 1903-1940 .. **SSC 16; TCLC
1, 14, 44**
See also AMW; AMWR 2; BPFB 3; CA
125; CAAE 104; CDALB 1929-1941;
DA3; DLB 4, 9, 28; EWL 3; MAL 5;
MTCW 1, 2; MTFW 2005; NFS 16;
RGAL 4; TUS

West, Owen
See Koontz, Dean R.

West, Paul 1930- .... **CLC 7, 14, 96, 226**
See also CA 13-16R; 7; CANR 22, 53, 76,
89, 136; CN 1, 2, 3, 4, 5, 6, 7; DLB 14;
INT CANR-22; MTCW 2; MTFW 2005

West, Rebecca 1892-1983 ... **CLC 7, 9, 31, 50**
See also BPFB 3; BRWS 3; CA 5-8R;
CAAS 109; CANR 19; CN 1, 2, 3; DLB
36; DLBY 1983; EWL 3; FW; MTCW 1,
2; MTFW 2005; NCFS 4; RGEL 2; TEA

Westall, Robert (Atkinson)
1929-1993 .... **CLC 17**
See also AAYA 12; BYA 2, 6, 7, 8, 9, 15;
CA 69-72; CAAS 141; CANR 18, 68;
CLR 13; FANT; JRDA; MAICYA 1, 2;
MAICYAS 1; SAAS 2; SATA 23, 69;
SATA-Obit 75; WYA; YAW

Westermarck, Edward 1862-1939 . **TCLC 87**

Westlake, Donald E. 1933- .... **CLC 7, 33**
See also BPFB 3; CA 17-20R; 13; CANR
16, 44, 65, 94, 137; CMW 4; CPW; DAM
POP; INT CANR-16; MSW; MTCW 2;
MTFW 2005

Westlake, Donald Edwin
See Westlake, Donald E.

Westmacott, Mary
See Christie, Agatha (Mary Clarissa)

Weston, Allen
See Norton, Andre

Wetcheek, J. L.
See Feuchtwanger, Lion

Wetering, Janwillem van de
See van de Wetering, Janwillem

Wetherald, Agnes Ethelwyn
1857-1940 .... **TCLC 81**
See also CA 202; DLB 99

Wetherell, Elizabeth
See Warner, Susan (Bogert)

Whale, James 1889-1957 .... **TCLC 63**
See also AAYA 75

Whalen, Philip (Glenn) 1923-2002 .... **CLC 6,
29**
See also BG 1:3; CA 9-12R; CAAS 209;
CANR 5, 39; CP 1, 2, 3, 4, 5, 6, 7; DLB
16; WP

Wharton, Edith (Newbold Jones)
1862-1937 ... **SSC 6, 84; TCLC 3, 9, 27,
53, 129, 149; WLC 6**
See also AAYA 25; AMW; AMWC 2;
AMWR 1; BPFB 3; CA 132; CAAE 104;
CDALB 1865-1917; DA; DA3; DAB;
DAC; DAM MST, NOV; DLB 4, 9, 12,
78, 189; DLBD 13; EWL 3; EXPS; FL
1:6; HGG; LAIT 2; LATS 1:1;
MAL 5; MBL; MTCW 1, 2; MTFW 2005;
NFS 5, 11, 15, 20; RGAL 4; RGSF 2;
RHW; SSFS 6, 7; SUFW; TUS

Wharton, James
See Mencken, H(enry) L(ouis)

Wharton, William (a pseudonym)
1925- .... **CLC 18, 37**
See also CA 93-96; CN 4, 5, 6, 7; DLBY
1980; INT CA-93-96

Wheatley (Peters), Phillis
1753(?)-1784 ... **BLC 3; LC 3, 50; PC 3;
WLC 6**
See also AFAW 1, 2; CDALB 1640-1865;
DA; DA3; DAC; DAM MST, MULT,
POET; DLB 31, 50; EXPP; FL 1:1; PFS
13; RGAL 4

Wheelock, John Hall 1886-1978 .... **CLC 14**
See also CA 13-16R; CAAS 77-80; CANR
14; CP 1, 2; DLB 45; MAL 5

Whim-Wham
See Curnow, (Thomas) Allen (Monro)

Whisp, Kennilworthy
See Rowling, J.K.

Whitaker, Rod 1931-2005
See Trevanian
See also CA 29-32R; CAAS 246; CANR
45, 153; CMW 4

White, Babington
See Braddon, Mary Elizabeth

White, E. B. 1899-1985 .... **CLC 10, 34, 39**
See also AAYA 62; AITN 2; AMWS 1; CA
13-16R; CAAS 116; CANR 16, 37;
CDALBS; CLR 1, 21, 107; CPW; DA3;
DAM POP; DLB 11, 22; EWL 3; FANT;
MAICYA 1, 2; MAL 5; MTCW 1, 2;
MTFW 2005; NCFS 5; RGAL 4; SATA 2,
29, 100; SATA-Obit 44; TUS

White, Edmund 1940- .... **CLC 27, 110**
See also AAYA 7; CA 45-48; CANR 3, 19,
36, 62, 107, 133; CN 5, 6, 7; DA3; DAM
POP; DLB 227; MTCW 1, 2; MTFW
2005

White, Elwyn Brooks
See White, E. B.

White, Hayden V. 1928- .... **CLC 148**
See also CA 128; CANR 135; DLB 246

White, Patrick (Victor Martindale)
1912-1990 ...... **CLC 3, 4, 5, 7, 9, 18, 65,
69; SSC 39; TCLC 176**
See also BRWS 1; CA 81-84; CAAS 132;
CANR 43; CN 1, 2, 3, 4; DLB 260, 332;
EWL 3; MTCW 1; RGEL 2; RGSF 2;
RHW; TWA; WWE 1

White, Phyllis Dorothy James 1920-
See James, P. D.
See also CA 21-24R; CANR 17, 43, 65,
112; CMW 4; CN 7; CPW; DA3; DAM
POP; MTCW 1, 2; MTFW 2005; TEA

White, T(erence) H(anbury)
1906-1964 .... **CLC 30**
See also AAYA 22; BPFB 3; BYA 4, 5; CA
73-76; CANR 37; DLB 160; FANT;
JRDA; LAIT 1; MAICYA 1, 2; RGEL 2;
SATA 12; SUFW 1; YAW

White, Terence de Vere 1912-1994 ... **CLC 49**
See also CA 49-52; CAAS 145; CANR 3

White, Walter
See White, Walter F(rancis)

White, Walter F(rancis) 1893-1955 ... **BLC 3;
HR 1:3; TCLC 15**
See also BW 1; CA 124; CAAE 115; DAM
MULT; DLB 51

White, William Hale 1831-1913
See Rutherford, Mark
See also CA 189; CAAE 121

Whitehead, Alfred North
1861-1947 .... **TCLC 97**
See also CA 165; CAAE 117; DLB 100,
262

Whitehead, Colson 1970- .... **CLC 232**
See also CA 202

Whitehead, E(dward) A(nthony)
1933- .... **CLC 5**
See Whitehead, Ted
See also CA 65-68; CANR 58, 118; CBD;
CD 5; DLB 310

Whitehead, Ted
See Whitehead, E(dward) A(nthony)
See also CD 6

Whiteman, Roberta J. Hill 1947- ...... **NNAL**
See also CA 146

Whitemore, Hugh (John) 1936- .... **CLC 37**
See also CA 132; CANR 77; CBD; CD 5,
6; INT CA-132

Whitman, Sarah Helen (Power)
1803-1878 .... **NCLC 19**
See also DLB 1, 243

Whitman, Walt(er) 1819-1892 .. **NCLC 4, 31,
81; PC 3; WLC 6**
See also AAYA 42; AMW; AMWR 1;
CDALB 1640-1865; DA; DA3; DAB;
DAC; DAM MST, POET; DLB 3, 64,

224, 250; EXPP; LAIT 2; LMFS 1; PAB;
PFS 2, 3, 13, 22; RGAL 4; SATA 20;
TUS; WP; WYAS 1

Whitney, Isabella fl. 1565-fl. 1575 ..... **LC 130**
See also DLB 136

Whitney, Phyllis A(yame) 1903- .... **CLC 42**
See also AAYA 36; AITN 2; BEST 90:3;
CA 1-4R; CANR 3, 25, 38, 60; CLR 59;
CMW 4; CPW; DA3; DAM POP; JRDA;
MAICYA 1, 2; MTCW 2; RHW; SATA 1,
30; YAW

Whittemore, (Edward) Reed, Jr.
1919- .... **CLC 4**
See also CA 219; 9-12R; 219; 8; CANR 4,
119; CP 1, 2, 3, 4, 5, 6, 7; DLB 5; MAL
5

Whittier, John Greenleaf
1807-1892 .... **NCLC 8, 59**
See also AMWS 1; DLB 1, 243; RGAL 4

Whittlebot, Hernia
See Coward, Noel (Peirce)

Wicker, Thomas Grey 1926-
See Wicker, Tom
See also CA 65-68; CANR 21, 46, 141

Wicker, Tom .... **CLC 7**
See Wicker, Thomas Grey

Wideman, John Edgar 1941- ... **BLC 3; CLC
5, 34, 36, 67, 122; SSC 62**
See also AFAW 1, 2; AMWS 10; BPFB 4;
BW 2, 3; CA 85-88; CANR 14, 42, 67,
109, 140; CN 4, 5, 6, 7; DAM MULT;
DLB 33, 143; MAL 5; MTCW 2; MTFW
2005; RGAL 4; RGSF 2; SSFS 6, 12, 24;
TCLE 1:2

Wiebe, Rudy 1934- .... **CLC 6, 11, 14, 138**
See also CA 37-40R; CANR 42, 67, 123;
CN 1, 2, 3, 4, 5, 6, 7; DAC; DAM MST;
DLB 60; RHW; SATA 156

Wiebe, Rudy Henry
See Wiebe, Rudy

Wieland, Christoph Martin
1733-1813 .... **NCLC 17, 177**
See also DLB 97; EW 4; LMFS 1; RGWL
2, 3

Wiene, Robert 1881-1938 .... **TCLC 56**

Wieners, John 1934- .... **CLC 7**
See also BG 1:3; CA 13-16R; CP 1, 2, 3, 4,
5, 6, 7; DLB 16; WP

Wiesel, Elie 1928- ...... **CLC 3, 5, 11, 37, 165;
WLCS**
See also AAYA 7, 54; AITN 1; CA 5-8R; 4;
CANR 8, 40, 65, 125; CDALBS; CWW
2; DA; DA3; DAB; DAC; DAM MST,
NOV; DLB 83, 299; DLBY 1987; EWL
3; INT CANR-8; LAIT 4; MTCW 1, 2;
MTFW 2005; NCFS 4; NFS 4; RGHL;
RGWL 3; SATA 56; YAW

Wiesel, Eliezer
See Wiesel, Elie

Wiggins, Marianne 1947- .... **CLC 57**
See also AAYA 70; BEST 89:3; CA 130;
CANR 60, 139; CN 7

Wigglesworth, Michael 1631-1705 .... **LC 106**
See also DLB 24; RGAL 4

Wiggs, Susan .... **CLC 70**
See also CA 201

Wight, James Alfred 1916-1995
See Herriot, James
See also CA 77-80; SATA 55; SATA-Brief
44

Wilbur, Richard 1921- .. **CLC 3, 6, 9, 14, 53,
110; PC 51**
See also AAYA 72; AMWS 3; CA 1-4R;
CABS 2; CANR 2, 29, 76, 93, 139;
CDALBS; CP 1, 2, 3, 4, 5, 6, 7; DA;
DAB; DAC; DAM MST, POET; DLB 5,
169; EWL 3; EXPP; INT CANR-29;
MAL 5; MTCW 1, 2; MTFW 2005; PAB;
PFS 11, 12, 16; RGAL 4; SATA 9, 108;
WP

Wilbur, Richard Purdy
See Wilbur, Richard

Wild, Peter 1940- .... **CLC 14**
See also CA 37-40R; CP 1, 2, 3, 4, 5, 6, 7;
DLB 5

Wilde, Oscar (Fingal O'Flahertie Wills)
1854(?)-1900 .... **DC 17; SSC 11, 77;
TCLC 1, 8, 23, 41, 175; WLC 6**
See also AAYA 49; BRW 5; BRWC 1, 2;
BRWR 2; BYA 15; CA 119; CAAE 104;
CANR 112; CDBLB 1890-1914; CLR
114; DA; DA3; DAB; DAC; DAM
DRAM, MST, NOV; DFS 4, 8, 9, 21;
DLB 10, 19, 34, 57, 141, 156, 190; EXPS;
FANT; GL 3; LATS 1:1; NFS 20; RGEL
2; RGSF 2; SATA 24; SSFS 7; SUFW;
TEA; WCH; WLIT 4

Wilder, Billy .... **CLC 20**
See Wilder, Samuel
See also AAYA 66; DLB 26

Wilder, Samuel 1906-2002
See Wilder, Billy
See also CA 89-92; CAAS 205

Wilder, Stephen
See Marlowe, Stephen

Wilder, Thornton (Niven)
1897-1975 .. **CLC 1, 5, 6, 10, 15, 35, 82;
DC 1, 24; WLC 6**
See also AAYA 29; AITN 2; AMW; CA 13-
16R; CAAS 61-68; CANR 40, 132;
CDALBS; CN 1, 2; DA; DA3; DAB;
DAC; DAM DRAM, MST, NOV; DFS 1,
4, 16; DLB 4, 7, 9, 228; DLBY 1997;
EWL 3; LAIT 3; MAL 5; MTCW 1, 2;
MTFW 2005; NFS 24; RGAL 4; RHW;
WYAS 1

Wilding, Michael 1942- ...... **CLC 73; SSC 50**
See also CA 104; CANR 24, 49, 106; CN
4, 5, 6, 7; DLB 325; RGSF 2

Wiley, Richard 1944- .... **CLC 44**
See also CA 129; CAAE 121; CANR 71

Wilhelm, Kate .... **CLC 7**
See Wilhelm, Katie
See also AAYA 20; BYA 16; CA 5; DLB 8;
INT CANR-17; SCFW 2

Wilhelm, Katie 1928-
See Wilhelm, Kate
See also CA 37-40R; CANR 17, 36, 60, 94;
MTCW 1; SFW 4

Wilkins, Mary
See Freeman, Mary E(leanor) Wilkins

Willard, Nancy 1936- .... **CLC 7, 37**
See also BYA 5; CA 89-92; CANR 10, 39,
68, 107, 152; CLR 5; CP 2, 3, 4, 5; CWP;
CWRI 5; DLB 5, 52; FANT; MAICYA 1,
2; MTCW 1; SATA 37, 71, 127; SATA-
Brief 30; SUFW 2; TCLE 1:2

William of Malmesbury c. 1090B.C.-c.
1140B.C. .... **CMLC 57**

William of Ockham 1290-1349 ..... **CMLC 32**

Williams, Ben Ames 1889-1953 ..... **TCLC 89**
See also CA 183; DLB 102

Williams, Charles
See Collier, James Lincoln

Williams, Charles (Walter Stansby)
1886-1945 .... **TCLC 1, 11**
See also BRWS 9; CA 163; CAAE 104;
DLB 100, 153, 255; FANT; RGEL 2;
SUFW 1

Williams, Ella Gwendolen Rees
See Rhys, Jean

Williams, (George) Emlyn
1905-1987 .... **CLC 15**
See also CA 104; CAAS 123; CANR 36;
DAM DRAM; DLB 10, 77; IDTP;
MTCW 1

Williams, Hank 1923-1953 .... **TCLC 81**
See Williams, Hiram King

Williams, Helen Maria
1761-1827 .... **NCLC 135**
See also DLB 158

Williams, Hiram Hank
See Williams, Hank

Williams, Hiram King
See Williams, Hank
See also CA 188

Williams, Hugo (Mordaunt) 1942- ... **CLC 42**
See also CA 17-20R; CANR 45, 119; CP 1,
2, 3, 4, 5, 6, 7; DLB 40

Williams, J. Walker
See Wodehouse, P(elham) G(renville)

Williams, John A(lfred) 1925- . **BLC 3; CLC
5, 13**
See also AFAW 2; BW 2, 3; CA 195; 53-
56, 195; 3; CANR 6, 26, 51, 118; CN 1,
2, 3, 4, 5, 6, 7; CSW; DAM MULT; DLB
2, 33; EWL 3; INT CANR-6; MAL 5;
RGAL 4; SFW 4

Williams, Jonathan (Chamberlain)
1929- .... **CLC 13**
See also CA 9-12R; 12; CANR 8, 108; CP
1, 2, 3, 4, 5, 6, 7; DLB 5

Williams, Joy 1944- .... **CLC 31**
See also CA 41-44R; CANR 22, 48, 97

Williams, Norman 1952- .... **CLC 39**
See also CA 118

Williams, Roger 1603(?)-1683 .... **LC 129**
See also DLB 24

Williams, Sherley Anne 1944-1999 ... **BLC 3;
CLC 89**
See also AFAW 2; BW 2, 3; CA 73-76;
CAAS 185; CANR 25, 82; DAM MULT;
POET; DLB 41; INT CANR-25; SATA
78; SATA-Obit 116

Williams, Shirley
See Williams, Sherley Anne

Williams, Tennessee 1911-1983 . **CLC 1, 2, 5,
7, 8, 11, 15, 19, 30, 39, 45, 71, 111; DC
4; SSC 81; WLC 6**
See also AAYA 31; AITN 1, 2; AMW;
AMWC 1; CA 5-8R; CAAS 108; CABS
3; CAD; CANR 31, 132; CDALB 1941-
1968; CN 1, 2, 3; DA; DA3; DAB; DAC;
DAM DRAM, MST; DFS 17; DLB 7;
DLBD 4; DLBY 1983; EWL 3; GLL 1;
LAIT 4; LATS 1:2; MAL 5; MTCW 1, 2;
MTFW 2005; RGAL 4; TUS

Williams, Thomas (Alonzo)
1926-1990 .... **CLC 14**
See also CA 1-4R; CAAS 132; CANR 2

Williams, William C.
See Williams, William Carlos

Williams, William Carlos
1883-1963 .... **CLC 1, 2, 5, 9, 13, 22, 42,
67; PC 7; SSC 31; WLC 6**
See also AAYA 46; AMW; AMWR 1; CA
89-92; CANR 34; CDALB 1917-1929;
DA; DA3; DAB; DAC; DAM MST,
POET; DLB 4, 16, 54, 86; EWL 3; EXPP;
MAL 5; MTCW 1, 2; MTFW 2005; NCFS
4; PAB; PFS 1, 6, 11; RGAL 4; RGSF 2;
TUS; WP

Williamson, David (Keith) 1942- ..... **CLC 56**
See also CA 103; CANR 41; CD 5, 6; DLB
289

Williamson, Ellen Douglas 1905-1984
See Douglas, Ellen
See also CA 17-20R; CAAS 114; CANR 39

Williamson, Jack .... **CLC 29**
See Williamson, John Stewart
See also CA 8; DLB 8; SCFW 1, 2

Williamson, John Stewart 1908-2006
See Williamson, Jack
See also CA 17-20R; CANR 23, 70, 153;
SFW 4

Willie, Frederick
See Lovecraft, H. P.
Willingham, Calder (Baynard, Jr.)
1922-1995 .... **CLC 5, 51**
See also CA 5-8R; CAAS 147; CANR 3;
CN 1, 2, 3, 4, 5; CSW; DLB 2, 44; IDFW
3, 4; MTCW 1
Willis, Charles
See Clarke, Arthur C.
Willy
See Colette, (Sidonie-Gabrielle)
Willy, Colette
See Colette, (Sidonie-Gabrielle)
See also GLL 1
Wilmot, John 1647-1680 .... **LC 75; PC 66**
See Rochester
See also BRW 2; DLB 131; PAB
Wilson, A.N. 1950- .... **CLC 33**
See also BRWS 6; CA 122; CAAE 112;
CANR 156; CN 4, 5, 6, 7; DLB 14, 155,
194; MTCW 2
Wilson, Andrew Norman
See Wilson, A.N.
Wilson, Angus (Frank Johnstone)
1913-1991 . **CLC 2, 3, 5, 25, 34; SSC 21**
See also BRWS 1; CA 5-8R; CAAS 134;
CANR 21; CN 1, 2, 3, 4; DLB 15, 139,
155; EWL 3; MTCW 1, 2; MTFW 2005;
RGEL 2; RGSF 2
Wilson, August 1945-2005 .. **BLC 3; CLC 39,**
50, 63, 118, 222; DC 2; WLCS
See also AAYA 16; AFAW 2; AMWS 8; BW
2, 3; CA 122; CAAE 115; CAAS 244;
CAD; CANR 42, 54, 76, 128; CD 5, 6;
DA; DA3; DAB; DAC; DAM DRAM,
MST, MULT; DFS 3, 7, 15, 17; DLB 228;
EWL 3; LAIT 4; LATS 1:2; MAL 5;
MTCW 1, 2; MTFW 2005; RGAL 4
Wilson, Brian 1942- .... **CLC 12**
Wilson, Colin (Henry) 1931- .... **CLC 3, 14**
See also CA 1-4R; 5; CANR 1, 22, 33, 77;
CMW 4; CN 1, 2, 3, 4, 5, 6; DLB 14, 194;
HGG; MTCW 1; SFW 4
Wilson, Dirk
See Pohl, Frederik
Wilson, Edmund 1895-1972 .. **CLC 1, 2, 3, 8,**
24
See also AMW; CA 1-4R; CAAS 37-40R;
CANR 1, 46, 110; CN 1; DLB 63; EWL
3; MAL 5; MTCW 1, 2; MTFW 2005;
RGAL 4; TUS
Wilson, Ethel Davis (Bryant)
1888(?)-1980 .... **CLC 13**
See also CA 102; CN 1, 2; DAC; DAM
POET; DLB 68; MTCW 1; RGEL 2
Wilson, Harriet
See Wilson, Harriet E. Adams
See also DLB 239
Wilson, Harriet E.
See Wilson, Harriet E. Adams
See also DLB 243
Wilson, Harriet E. Adams
1827(?)-1863(?) .... **BLC 3; NCLC 78**
See Wilson, Harriet; Wilson, Harriet E.
See also DAM MULT; DLB 50
Wilson, John 1785-1854 .... **NCLC 5**
Wilson, John (Anthony) Burgess 1917-1993
See Burgess, Anthony
See also CA 1-4R; CAAS 143; CANR 2,
46; DA3; DAC; DAM NOV; MTCW 1,
2; MTFW 2005; NFS 15; TEA
Wilson, Katharina .... **CLC 65**
Wilson, Lanford 1937- .. **CLC 7, 14, 36, 197;**
DC 19
See also CA 17-20R; CABS 3; CAD; CANR
45, 96; CD 5, 6; DAM DRAM; DFS 4, 9,
12, 16, 20; DLB 7; EWL 3; MAL 5; TUS

Wilson, Robert M. 1941- .... **CLC 7, 9**
See also CA 49-52; CAD; CANR 2, 41; CD
5, 6; MTCW 1
Wilson, Robert McLiam 1964- .... **CLC 59**
See also CA 132; DLB 267
Wilson, Sloan 1920-2003 .... **CLC 32**
See also CA 1-4R; CAAS 216; CANR 1,
44; CN 1, 2, 3, 4, 5, 6
Wilson, Snoo 1948- .... **CLC 33**
See also CA 69-72; CBD; CD 5, 6
Wilson, William S(mith) 1932- .... **CLC 49**
See also CA 81-84
Wilson, (Thomas) Woodrow
1856-1924 .... **TCLC 79**
See also CA 166; DLB 47
Winchilsea, Anne (Kingsmill) Finch
1661-1720
See Finch, Anne
See also RGEL 2
Winckelmann, Johann Joachim
1717-1768 .... **LC 129**
See also DLB 97
Windham, Basil
See Wodehouse, P(elham) G(renville)
Wingrove, David 1954- .... **CLC 68**
See also CA 133; SFW 4
Winnemucca, Sarah 1844-1891 .... **NCLC 79;**
NNAL
See also DAM MULT; DLB 175; RGAL 4
Winstanley, Gerrard 1609-1676 .... **LC 52**
Wintergreen, Jane
See Duncan, Sara Jeannette
Winters, Arthur Yvor
See Winters, Yvor
Winters, Janet Lewis .... **CLC 41**
See Lewis, Janet
See also DLBY 1987
Winters, Yvor 1900-1968 .... **CLC 4, 8, 32**
See also AMWS 2; CA 11-12; CAAS 25-
28R; CAP 1; DLB 48; EWL 3; MAL 5;
MTCW 1; RGAL 4
Winterson, Jeanette 1959- .... **CLC 64, 158**
See also BRWS 4; CA 136; CANR 58, 116;
CN 5, 6, 7; CPW; DA3; DAM POP; DLB
207, 261; FANT; FW; GLL 1; MTCW 2;
MTFW 2005; RHW
Winthrop, John 1588-1649 .... **LC 31, 107**
See also DLB 24, 30
Wirth, Louis 1897-1952 .... **TCLC 92**
See also CA 210
Wiseman, Frederick 1930- .... **CLC 20**
See also CA 159
Wister, Owen 1860-1938 .... **TCLC 21**
See also BPFB 3; CA 162; CAAE 108;
DLB 9, 78, 186; RGAL 4; SATA 62;
TCWW 1, 2
Wither, George 1588-1667 .... **LC 96**
See also DLB 121; RGEL 2
Witkacy
See Witkiewicz, Stanislaw Ignacy
Witkiewicz, Stanislaw Ignacy
1885-1939 .... **TCLC 8**
See also CA 162; CAAE 105; CDWLB 4;
DLB 215; EW 10; EWL 3; RGWL 2, 3;
SFW 4
Wittgenstein, Ludwig (Josef Johann)
1889-1951 .... **TCLC 59**
See also CA 164; CAAE 113; DLB 262;
MTCW 2
Wittig, Monique 1935-2003 .... **CLC 22**
See also CA 135; CAAE 116; CAAS 212;
CANR 143; CWW 2; DLB 83; EWL 3;
FW; GLL 1
Wittlin, Jozef 1896-1976 .... **CLC 25**
See also CA 49-52; CAAS 65-68; CANR 3;
EWL 3

Wodehouse, P(elham) G(renville)
1881-1975 . **CLC 1, 2, 5, 10, 22; SSC 2;**
TCLC 108
See also AAYA 65; AITN 2; BRWS 3; CA
45-48; CAAS 57-60; CANR 3, 33; CD-
BLB 1914-1945; CN 1, 2; CPW 1; DA3;
DAB; DAC; DAM NOV; DLB 34, 162;
EWL 3; MTCW 1, 2; MTFW 2005; RGEL
2; RGSF 2; SATA 22; SSFS 10
Woiwode, L.
See Woiwode, Larry (Alfred)
Woiwode, Larry (Alfred) 1941- ... **CLC 6, 10**
See also CA 73-76; CANR 16, 94; CN 3, 4,
5, 6, 7; DLB 6; INT CANR-16
Wojciechowska, Maia (Teresa)
1927-2002 .... **CLC 26**
See also AAYA 8, 46; BYA 3; CA 183;
9-12R, 183; CAAS 209; CANR 4, 41;
CLR 1; JRDA; MAICYA 1, 2; SAAS 1;
SATA 1, 28, 83; SATA-Essay 104; SATA-
Obit 134; YAW
Wojtyla, Karol (Jozef)
See John Paul II, Pope
Wojtyla, Karol (Josef)
See John Paul II, Pope
Wolf, Christa 1929- .... **CLC 14, 29, 58, 150**
See also CA 85-88; CANR 45, 123; CD-
WLB 2; CWW 2; DLB 75; EWL 3; FW;
MTCW 1; RGWL 2, 3; SSFS 14
Wolf, Naomi 1962- .... **CLC 157**
See also CA 141; CANR 110; FW; MTFW
2005
Wolfe, Gene 1931- .... **CLC 25**
See also AAYA 35; CA 57-60; 9; CANR 6,
32, 60, 152; CPW; DAM POP; DLB 8;
FANT; MTCW 2; MTFW 2005; SATA
118, 165; SCFW 2; SFW 4; SUFW 2
Wolfe, Gene Rodman
See Wolfe, Gene
Wolfe, George C. 1954- .... **BLCS; CLC 49**
See also CA 149; CAD; CD 5, 6
Wolfe, Thomas (Clayton)
1900-1938 ...... **SSC 33; TCLC 4, 13, 29,**
61; WLC 6
See also AMW; BPFB 3; CA 132; CAAE
104; CANR 102; CDALB 1929-1941;
DA; DA3; DAB; DAC; DAM MST, NOV;
DLB 9, 102, 229; DLBD 2, 16; DLBY
1985, 1997; EWL 3; MAL 5; MTCW 1,
2; NFS 18; RGAL 4; SSFS 18; TUS
Wolfe, Thomas Kennerly, Jr.
1931- .... **CLC 147**
See Wolfe, Tom
See also CA 13-16R; CANR 9, 33, 70, 104;
DA3; DAM POP; DLB 185; EWL 3; INT
CANR-9; MTCW 1, 2; MTFW 2005; TUS
Wolfe, Tom .... **CLC 1, 2, 9, 15, 35, 51**
See Wolfe, Thomas Kennerly, Jr.
See also AAYA 8, 67; AITN 2; AMWS 3;
BEST 89:1; BPFB 3; CN 5, 6, 7; CPW;
CSW; DLB 152; LAIT 5; RGAL 4
Wolff, Geoffrey 1937- .... **CLC 41**
See also CA 29-32R; CANR 29, 43, 78, 154
Wolff, Geoffrey Ansell
See Wolff, Geoffrey
Wolff, Sonia
See Levitin, Sonia (Wolff)
Wolff, Tobias 1945- .... **CLC 39, 64, 172; SSC**
63
See also AAYA 16; AMWS 7; BEST 90:2;
BYA 12; CA 117; 22; CAAE 114; CANR
54, 76, 96; CN 5, 6, 7; CSW; DA3; DLB
130; EWL 3; INT CA-117; MTCW 2;
MTFW 2005; RGAL 4; RGSF 2; SSFS 4,
11
Wolitzer, Hilma 1930- .... **CLC 17**
See also CA 65-68; CANR 18, 40; INT
CANR-18; SATA 31; YAW

Wollstonecraft, Mary 1759-1797 .... **LC 5, 50, 90**
See also BRWS 3; CDBLB 1789-1832; DLB 39, 104, 158, 252; FL 1:1; FW; LAIT 1; RGEL 2; TEA; WLIT 3

Wonder, Stevie 1950- .... **CLC 12**
See also CAAE 111

Wong, Jade Snow 1922-2006 .... **CLC 17**
See also CA 109; CAAS 249; CANR 91; SATA 112; SATA-Obit 175

Wood, Mrs. Henry 1814-1887 ...... **NCLC 178**
See also CMW 4; DLB 18; SUFW

Woodberry, George Edward
1855-1930 .... **TCLC 73**
See also CA 165; DLB 71, 103

Woodcott, Keith
See Brunner, John (Kilian Houston)

Woodruff, Robert W.
See Mencken, H(enry) L(ouis)

Woolf, (Adeline) Virginia 1882-1941 .. **SSC 7, 79; TCLC 1, 5, 20, 43, 56, 101, 123, 128; WLC 6**
See also AAYA 44; BPFB 3; BRW 7; BRWC 2; BRWR 1; CA 130; CAAE 104; CANR 64, 132; CDBLB 1914-1945; DA; DA3; DAB; DAC; DAM MST, NOV; DLB 36, 100, 162; DLBD 10; EWL 3; EXPS; FL 1:6; FW; LAIT 1; LATS 1:1; LMFS 2; MTCW 1, 2; MTFW 2005; NCFS 2; NFS 8, 12; RGEL 2; RGSF 2; SSFS 4, 12; TEA; WLIT 4

Woollcott, Alexander (Humphreys)
1887-1943 .... **TCLC 5**
See also CA 161; CAAE 105; DLB 29

Woolrich, Cornell .... **CLC 77**
See Hopley-Woolrich, Cornell George
See also MSW

Woolson, Constance Fenimore
1840-1894 .... **NCLC 82; SSC 90**
See also DLB 12, 74, 189, 221; RGAL 4

Wordsworth, Dorothy 1771-1855 . **NCLC 25, 138**
See also DLB 107

Wordsworth, William 1770-1850 .. **NCLC 12, 38, 111, 166; PC 4, 67; WLC 6**
See also AAYA 70; BRW 4; BRWR 1; CD-BLB 1789-1832; DA; DA3; DAB; DAC; DAM MST, POET; DLB 93, 107; EXPP; LATS 1:1; LMFS 1; PAB; PFS 2; RGEL 2; TEA; WLIT 3; WP

Wotton, Sir Henry 1568-1639 .... **LC 68**
See also DLB 121; RGEL 2

Wouk, Herman 1915- .... **CLC 1, 9, 38**
See also BPFB 2, 3; CA 5-8R; CANR 6, 33, 67, 146; CDALBS; CN 1, 2, 3, 4, 5, 6; CPW; DA3; DAM NOV, POP; DLBY 1982; INT CANR-6; LAIT 4; MAL 5; MTCW 1, 2; MTFW 2005; NFS 7; TUS

Wright, Charles 1935- ... **CLC 6, 13, 28, 119, 146**
See also AMWS 5; CA 29-32R; 7; CANR 23, 36, 62, 88, 135; CP 3, 4, 5, 6, 7; DLB 165; DLBY 1982; EWL 3; MTCW 1, 2; MTFW 2005; PFS 10

Wright, Charles Stevenson 1932- ..... **BLC 3; CLC 49**
See also BW 1; CA 9-12R; CANR 26; CN 1, 2, 3, 4, 5, 6, 7; DAM MULT, POET; DLB 33

Wright, Frances 1795-1852 .... **NCLC 74**
See also DLB 73

Wright, Frank Lloyd 1867-1959 .... **TCLC 95**
See also AAYA 33; CA 174

Wright, Harold Bell 1872-1944 .... **TCLC 183**
See also BPFB 3; CAAE 110; DLB 9; TCWW 2

Wright, Jack R.
See Harris, Mark

Wright, James (Arlington)
1927-1980 .... **CLC 3, 5, 10, 28; PC 36**
See also AITN 2; AMWS 3; CA 49-52; CAAS 97-100; CANR 4, 34, 64; CDALBS; CP 1, 2; DAM POET; DLB 5, 169; EWL 3; EXPP; MAL 5; MTCW 1, 2; MTFW 2005; PFS 7, 8; RGAL 4; TUS; WP

Wright, Judith 1915-2000 ... **CLC 11, 53; PC 14**
See also CA 13-16R; CAAS 188; CANR 31, 76, 93; CP 1, 2, 3, 4, 5, 6, 7; CWP; DLB 260; EWL 3; MTCW 1, 2; MTFW 2005; PFS 8; RGEL 2; SATA 14; SATA-Obit 121

Wright, L(auriali) R. 1939- .... **CLC 44**
See also CA 138; CMW 4

Wright, Richard (Nathaniel)
1908-1960 ... **BLC 3; CLC 1, 3, 4, 9, 14, 21, 48, 74; SSC 2; TCLC 136, 180; WLC 6**
See also AAYA 5, 42; AFAW 1, 2; AMW; BPFB 3; BW 1; BYA 2; CA 108; CANR 64; CDALB 1929-1941; DA; DA3; DAB; DAC; DAM MST, MULT, NOV; DLB 76, 102; DLBD 2; EWL 3; EXPN; LAIT 3, 4; MAL 5; MTCW 1, 2; MTFW 2005; NCFS 1; NFS 1, 7; RGAL 4; RGSF 2; SSFS 3, 9, 15, 20; TUS; YAW

Wright, Richard B(ruce) 1937- .... **CLC 6**
See also CA 85-88; CANR 120; DLB 53

Wright, Rick 1945- .... **CLC 35**

Wright, Rowland
See Wells, Carolyn

Wright, Stephen 1946- .... **CLC 33**
See also CA 237

Wright, Willard Huntington 1888-1939
See Van Dine, S. S.
See also CA 189; CAAE 115; CMW 4; DLBD 16

Wright, William 1930- .... **CLC 44**
See also CA 53-56; CANR 7, 23, 154

Wroth, Lady Mary 1587-1653(?) .... **LC 30; PC 38**
See also DLB 121

Wu Ch'eng-en 1500(?)-1582(?) .... **LC 7**

Wu Ching-tzu 1701-1754 .... **LC 2**

Wulfstan c. 10th cent. -1023 .... **CMLC 59**

Wurlitzer, Rudolph 1938(?)- .... **CLC 2, 4, 15**
See also CA 85-88; CN 4, 5, 6, 7; DLB 173

Wyatt, Sir Thomas c. 1503-1542 . **LC 70; PC 27**
See also BRW 1; DLB 132; EXPP; PFS 25; RGEL 2; TEA

Wycherley, William 1640-1716 .... **LC 8, 21, 102, 136**
See also BRW 2; CDBLB 1660-1789; DAM DRAM; DLB 80; RGEL 2

Wyclif, John c. 1330-1384 .... **CMLC 70**
See also DLB 146

Wylie, Elinor (Morton Hoyt)
1885-1928 .... **PC 23; TCLC 8**
See also AMWS 1; CA 162; CAAE 105; DLB 9, 45; EXPP; MAL 5; RGAL 4

Wylie, Philip (Gordon) 1902-1971 ... **CLC 43**
See also CA 21-22; CAAS 33-36R; CAP 2; CN 1; DLB 9; SFW 4

Wyndham, John .... **CLC 19**
See Harris, John (Wyndham Parkes Lucas) Beynon
See also DLB 255; SCFW 1, 2

Wyss, Johann David Von
1743-1818 .... **NCLC 10**
See also CLR 92; JRDA; MAICYA 1, 2; SATA 29; SATA-Brief 27

Xenophon c. 430B.C.-c. 354B.C. ... **CMLC 17**
See also AW 1; DLB 176; RGWL 2, 3; WLIT 8

Xingjian, Gao 1940-
See Gao Xingjian
See also CA 193; DFS 21; DLB 330; RGWL 3

Yakamochi 718-785 .... **CMLC 45; PC 48**

Yakumo Koizumi
See Hearn, (Patricio) Lafcadio (Tessima Carlos)

Yamada, Mitsuye (May) 1923- .... **PC 44**
See also CA 77-80

Yamamoto, Hisaye 1921- .... **AAL; SSC 34**
See also CA 214; DAM MULT; DLB 312; LAIT 4; SSFS 14

Yamauchi, Wakako 1924- .... **AAL**
See also CA 214; DLB 312

Yanez, Jose Donoso
See Donoso (Yanez), Jose

Yanovsky, Basile S.
See Yanovsky, V(assily) S(emenovich)

Yanovsky, V(assily) S(emenovich)
1906-1989 .... **CLC 2, 18**
See also CA 97-100; CAAS 129

Yates, Richard 1926-1992 .... **CLC 7, 8, 23**
See also AMWS 11; CA 5-8R; CAAS 139; CANR 10, 43; CN 1, 2, 3, 4, 5; DLB 2, 234; DLBY 1981, 1992; INT CANR-10; SSFS 24

Yau, John 1950- .... **PC 61**
See also CA 154; CANR 89; CP 4, 5, 6, 7; DLB 234, 312

Yearsley, Ann 1753-1806 .... **NCLC 174**
See also DLB 109

Yeats, W. B.
See Yeats, William Butler

Yeats, William Butler 1865-1939 . **PC 20, 51; TCLC 1, 11, 18, 31, 93, 116; WLC 6**
See also AAYA 48; BRW 6; BRWR 1; CA 127; CAAE 104; CANR 45; CDBLB 1890-1914; DA; DA3; DAB; DAC; DAM DRAM, MST, POET; DLB 10, 19, 98, 156, 332; EWL 3; EXPP; MTCW 1, 2; MTFW 2005; NCFS 3; PAB; PFS 1, 2, 5, 7, 13, 15; RGEL 2; TEA; WLIT 4; WP

Yehoshua, A(braham) B. 1936- .. **CLC 13, 31**
See also CA 33-36R; CANR 43, 90, 145; CWW 2; EWL 3; RGHL; RGSF 2; RGWL 3; WLIT 6

Yellow Bird
See Ridge, John Rollin

Yep, Laurence 1948- .... **CLC 35**
See also AAYA 5, 31; BYA 7; CA 49-52; CANR 1, 46, 92, 161; CLR 3, 17, 54; DLB 52, 312; FANT; JRDA; MAICYA 1, 2; MAICYAS 1; SATA 7, 69, 123, 176; WYA; YAW

Yep, Laurence Michael
See Yep, Laurence

Yerby, Frank G(arvin) 1916-1991 ..... **BLC 3; CLC 1, 7, 22**
See also BPFB 3; BW 1, 3; CA 9-12R; CAAS 136; CANR 16, 52; CN 1, 2, 3, 4, 5; DAM MULT; DLB 76; INT CANR-16; MTCW 1; RGAL 4; RHW

Yesenin, Sergei Aleksandrovich
See Esenin, Sergei

Yevtushenko, Yevgeny (Alexandrovich)
1933- ...... **CLC 1, 3, 13, 26, 51, 126; PC 40**
See Evtushenko, Evgenii Aleksandrovich
See also CA 81-84; CANR 33, 54; DAM POET; EWL 3; MTCW 1; RGHL

Yezierska, Anzia 1885(?)-1970 .... **CLC 46**
See also CA 126; CAAS 89-92; DLB 28, 221; FW; MTCW 1, 2; RGAL 4; SSFS 15

Yglesias, Helen 1915- .... **CLC 7, 22**
See also CA 37-40R; 20; CANR 15, 65, 95; CN 4, 5, 6, 7; INT CANR-15; MTCW 1

Yokomitsu, Riichi 1898-1947 .... **TCLC 47**
See also CA 170; EWL 3

Literary Criticism Series
Cumulative Topic Index

This index lists all topic entries in Thompson Gale's *Children's Literature Review* (CLR), *Classical and Medieval Literature Criticism* (CMLC), *Contemporary Literary Criticism* (CLC), *Drama Criticism* (DC), *Literature Criticism from 1400 to 1800* (LC), *Nineteenth-Century Literature Criticism* (NCLC), *Short Story Criticism* (SSC), and *Twentieth-Century Literary Criticism* (TCLC). The index also lists topic entries in the Gale Critical Companion Collection, which includes the following publications: *The Beat Generation* (BG), *Feminism in Literature* (FL), *Gothic Literature* (GL), and *Harlem Renaissance* (HR).

Topic Index

Topic Index

Topic Index

NCLC Cumulative Nationality Index

Goethe, Johann Wolfgang von **4, 22, 34, 90, 154**
Grabbe, Christian Dietrich **2**
Grimm, Jacob Ludwig Karl **3, 77**
Grimm, Wilhelm Karl **3, 77**
Hebbel, Friedrich **43**
Hegel, Georg Wilhelm Friedrich **46, 151**
Heine, Heinrich **4, 54, 147**
Herder, Johann Gottfried von **8**
Hoffmann, E(rnst) T(heodor) A(madeus) **2**
Hölderlin, (Johann Christian) Friedrich **16**
Humboldt, Alexander von **170**
Humboldt, Wilhelm von **134**
Immermann, Karl (Lebrecht) **4, 49**
Jean Paul **7**
Kant, Immanuel **27, 67**
Kleist, Heinrich von **2, 37**
Klinger, Friedrich Maximilian von **1**
Klopstock, Friedrich Gottlieb **11**
Kotzebue, August (Friedrich Ferdinand) von **25**
La Roche, Sophie von **121**
Ludwig, Otto **4**
Marx, Karl (Heinrich) **17, 114**
Mörike, Eduard (Friedrich) **10**
Novalis **13, 178**
Schelling, Friedrich Wilhelm Joseph von **30**
Schiller, Friedrich von **39, 69, 166**
Schlegel, August Wilhelm von **15, 142**
Schlegel, Friedrich **45**
Schleiermacher, Friedrich **107**
Schopenhauer, Arthur **51, 157**
Schumann, Robert **143**
Storm, (Hans) Theodor (Woldsen) **1**
Tieck, (Johann) Ludwig **5, 46**
Varnhagen, Rahel **130**
Wagner, Richard **9, 119**
Wieland, Christoph Martin **17, 177**

GREEK

Foscolo, Ugo **8, 97**
Solomos, Dionysios **15**

HUNGARIAN

Arany, Janos **34**
Madach, Imre **19**
Petofi, Sándor **21**

INDIAN

Chatterji, Bankim Chandra **19**
Dutt, Michael Madhusudan **118**
Dutt, Toru **29**

IRISH

Allingham, William **25**
Banim, John **13**
Banim, Michael **13**
Boucicault, Dion **41**
Carleton, William **3**
Croker, John Wilson **10**
Darley, George **2**
Edgeworth, Maria **1, 51, 158**
Ferguson, Samuel **33**
Griffin, Gerald **7**
Jameson, Anna **43**
Le Fanu, Joseph Sheridan **9, 58**
Lever, Charles (James) **23**
Maginn, William **8**
Mangan, James Clarence **27**
Maturin, Charles Robert **6, 169**

Merriman, Brian **70**
Moore, Thomas **6, 110**
Morgan, Lady **29**
O'Brien, Fitz-James **21**
Sheridan, Richard Brinsley **5, 91**

ITALIAN

Alfieri, Vittorio **101**
Collodi, Carlo **54**
Foscolo, Ugo **8, 97**
Gozzi, (Conte) Carlo **23**
Leopardi, Giacomo **22, 129**
Manzoni, Alessandro **29, 98**
Mazzini, Guiseppe **34**
Nievo, Ippolito **22**

JAMAICAN

Seacole, Mary Jane Grant **147**

JAPANESE

Akinari, Ueda **131**
Ichiyō, Higuchi **49**
Motoori, Norinaga **45**

LITHUANIAN

Mapu, Abraham (ben Jekutiel) **18**

MEXICAN

Lizardi, Jose Joaquin Fernandez de **30**
Najera, Manuel Gutierrez **133**

NORWEGIAN

Collett, (Jacobine) Camilla (Wergeland) **22**
Wergeland, Henrik Arnold **5**

POLISH

Fredro, Aleksander **8**
Krasicki, Ignacy **8**
Krasiński, Zygmunt **4**
Mickiewicz, Adam **3, 101**
Norwid, Cyprian Kamil **17**
Slowacki, Juliusz **15**

ROMANIAN

Eminescu, Mihail **33, 131**

RUSSIAN

Aksakov, Sergei Timofeevich **2, 181**
Bakunin, Mikhail (Alexandrovich) **25, 58**
Baratynsky, Evgenii Abramovich **103**
Bashkirtseff, Marie **27**
Belinski, Vissarion Grigoryevich **5**
Bestuzhev, Aleksandr Aleksandrovich **131**
Chernyshevsky, Nikolay Gavrilovich **1**
Dobrolyubov, Nikolai Alexandrovich **5**
Dostoevsky, Fedor Mikhailovich **2, 7, 21, 33, 43, 119, 167**
Gogol, Nikolai (Vasilyevich) **5, 15, 31, 162**
Goncharov, Ivan Alexandrovich **1, 63**
Granovsky, Timofei Nikolaevich **75**
Griboedov, Aleksandr Sergeevich **129**
Herzen, Aleksandr Ivanovich **10, 61**
Karamzin, Nikolai Mikhailovich **3, 173**
Krylov, Ivan Andreevich **1**
Lermontov, Mikhail Yuryevich **5, 47, 126**
Leskov, Nikolai (Semyonovich) **25, 174**
Nekrasov, Nikolai Alekseevich **11**
Ostrovsky, Alexander **30, 57**

Pavlova, Karolina Karlovna **138**
Pisarev, Dmitry Ivanovich **25**
Pushkin, Alexander (Sergeyevich) **3, 27, 83**
Saltykov, Mikhail Evgrafovich **16**
Smolenskin, Peretz **30**
Turgenev, Ivan **21, 37, 122**
Tyutchev, Fyodor **34**
Zhukovsky, Vasily (Andreevich) **35**

SCOTTISH

Baillie, Joanna **2, 151**
Beattie, James **25**
Blair, Hugh **75**
Campbell, Thomas **19**
Carlyle, Thomas **22, 70**
Ferrier, Susan (Edmonstone) **8**
Galt, John **1, 110**
Hogg, James **4, 109**
Jeffrey, Francis **33**
Lockhart, John Gibson **6**
Mackenzie, Henry **41**
Miller, Hugh **143**
Oliphant, Margaret (Oliphant Wilson) **11, 61**
Scott, Walter **15, 69, 110**
Stevenson, Robert Louis (Balfour) **5, 14, 63**
Thomson, James **18**
Wilson, John **5**
Wright, Frances **74**

SERBIAN

Karadžić, Vuk Stefanović **115**

SLOVENIAN

Kopitar, Jernej **117**
Prešeren, Francè **127**

SPANISH

Alarcon, Pedro Antonio de **1**
Bécquer, Gustavo Adolfo **106**
Caballero, Fernan **10**
Castro, Rosalia de **3, 78**
Espronceda, Jose de **39**
Larra (y Sanchez de Castro), Mariano Jose de **17, 130**
Martínez de la Rosa, Francisco de Paula **102**
Tamayo y Baus, Manuel **1**
Zorrilla y Moral, Jose **6**

SWEDISH

Almqvist, Carl Jonas Love **42**
Bremer, Fredrika **11**
Stagnelius, Eric Johan **61**
Tegner, Esaias **2**

SWISS

Amiel, Henri Frederic **4**
Burckhardt, Jacob (Christoph) **49**
Charriere, Isabelle de **66**
Gotthelf, Jeremias **117**
Keller, Gottfried **2**
Lavater, Johann Kaspar **142**
Meyer, Conrad Ferdinand **81**
Wyss, Johann David Von **10**

UKRAINIAN

Shevchenko, Taras **54**

VENEZUELAN

Bello, Andrés **131**

NCLC-181 Title Index

ISBN-13: 978-0-7876-9852-2
ISBN-10: 0-7876-9852-0

90000